Court of Protection Handbook

A user's guide

courtofprotectionhandbook.com

Court of Protection Handbook is supported by courtofprotectionhandbook.com

On the site, you will find links to relevant statutory materials and other guidance that space precluded us from including in the appendices, precedent orders covering most of the most common situations that arise before the Court, useful (free) web resources, and updates on practice and procedure before the Court of Protection. These updates take the form of posts on the site's blog, and also (where relevant) updates cross-referenced to the relevant paragraphs in the book.

Register to receive email updates at www.courtofprotectionhandbook.com

Follow us on Twitter @COPhandbook

The Legal Action Group is a national, independent charity which campaigns for equal access to justice for all members of society. Legal Action Group:

- provides support to the practice of lawyers and advisers
- inspires developments in that practice
- campaigns for improvements in the law and the administration of justice
- stimulates debate on how services should be delivered.

Court of Protection Handbook

A user's guide

FOURTH EDITION

Alex Ruck Keene QC (Hon), Kate Edwards,
Nicola Mackintosh QC (Hon) and
Sophy Miles

With Professor Anselm Eldergill

LAG the access to justice charity | 50 YEARS 1972–2022

This fourth edition published in Great Britain 2022
by LAG Education and Service Trust Limited
Gatehouse Chambers, 1 Lady Hale Gate, Gray's Inn, London WC1X 8BS
www.lag.org.uk

First edition published 2014
Revised first edition published 2016
Second edition published 2017
Revised second edition published 2018
Third edition published 2019

British Library Cataloguing in Publication Data
a CIP catalogue record for this book is available from the British Library.

Print ISBN 978 1 913648 40 4
eBook ISBN 978 1 913648 41 1
Bundle (print and ebook) ISBN 978 1 913648 42 8

Typeset by RefineCatch Ltd, Bungay, Suffolk
Printed in Great Britain by Hobbs the Printers, Totton, Hampshire

Preface

The Mental Capacity Act (MCA) 2005 is an extraordinarily wide-reaching piece of legislation: any of us at any time could find ourselves incapable of taking decisions about our health, our welfare, or our finances. The Court of Protection, the specialist court established by the MCA 2005 as the ultimate oversight body over the MCA 2005, is, in consequence a court with a very wide reach.

There are many books which deal with the MCA 2005, and there are also a number of books which deal with the Court of Protection. However, when the first edition was published in 2014, it was the first book to set out to address in detail the practice and processes of the court – across the whole range of its work – in terms aimed not solely at lawyers who are advising those bringing or responding to applications but also to the increasing numbers of people who either by choice or otherwise are involved in proceedings before the Court of Protection without the help of lawyers or specialist advisers.

The book has now firmly established itself as a fixture on the bookshelves of many practitioners, and was cited by the Vice-President of the Court of Protection, Hayden J, as establishing the principles to apply in the appointment of personal welfare deputies.[1]

We are now in its fourth edition, reflecting the many changes that have taken place since 2014. Some of them have already happened, most obviously the enactment of the Court of Protection Rules 2017, consolidating, updating, and entirely re-numbering all the procedural rules of the court. Some are working themselves out as we write, such as the consequences of the pandemic, which brought about radical changes to the court's practice (as well, as an unanticipated side-effect, easier public access to the court's workings as it went online[2]).

1 See *Re Lawson, Mottram and Hopton (appointment of personal welfare deputies)* [2019] EWCOP 22 at paras 52 and 53.

2 See, in particular, the work of the Open Justice Court of Protection Project: https://openjusticecourtofprotection.org/.

Some are still in the future at the time of writing, most obviously the implementation of the Mental Capacity (Amendment) Act 2019. In the third edition, we were anticipating implementation in October 2020; that date came and went, as did the second proposed date of April 2022, the message now being that the Government will provide a new date when (in effect) it has taken stock of the consultation upon the draft Code of Practice underway at the time of writing. That Act will replace the largely unlamented Deprivation of Liberty Safeguards with a new administrative scheme for authorising deprivation of liberty, and we set out in the book some preliminary thoughts as to how we think those concerned with the Court of Protection will want to approach that scheme so as to secure the rights of those subject to authorisations.

The book is accompanied by a website: www.courtofprotection-handbook, upon which will be found links to relevant statutory materials and other guidance that space precluded us from including in the appendices, together with updates on practice and procedure before the Court of Protection cross-referenced to the relevant paragraphs in the book.

It would not be right to go any further at this stage without paying tribute to Professor Anselm Eldergill, who formed a core part of the authorial team for the first three editions, and whose chapters (3-5) on the Act and the Court of Protection radiated the wisdom, pragmatism, and empathy which has been a hallmark of his judgments. We are very sad that he has decided to step back from the Handbook, but he has set his stamp on it, and we will do our best to maintain his standards.

In consequence of Anselm's departure, authorial responsibilities have been revised slightly, with Sophy Miles taking on responsibility for chapters 3-5. This is, in no small part, down to the fact that Sophy has added to her already lustrous portfolio an appointment as a Deputy District Judge nominated to sit in the Court of Protection, for which we congratulate her wholeheartedly.

We also say farewell to Mark Neary, who had in previous editions provided us with material that brought vividly to life his experiences navigating the sometimes surreal world of capacity with his son Steven. Mark's writings, on his Love, Belief and Balls blog,[3] remain just as relevant and challenging as ever, and we urge readers to follow him.

Special thanks must go to Inclusion London for their permission to reproduce in slightly different form an article Svetlana Kotlova coordinated and supported Andrew Lee and Christine Spooner (then

3 https://markneary1dotcom1.wordpress.com/.

Director and Chair respectively of People First) to write for the 39 Essex Chambers Mental Capacity Report.

We remain very fortunate that Dr Ian Hall was kind enough to contribute a concise account of how to get the best from an expert psychiatric witness, and Lynne Phair to give her perspective as an expert nursing witness.

We are very grateful to all those who have contributed their thoughts and expertise at various stages of the three editions of this book's life, and in particular the late Alastair Pitblado (the Official Solicitor to the Senior Courts), Neil Allen, Romana Canneti, Gordon Ashton OBE, Victoria Butler-Cole QC, Helen Clift, Penny Cooper, Joan Goulbourn, Janet Ilett, Lucy Series, Emma Stacey, Beverley Taylor, Susan Thompson and Aswini Weerawatne QC. We are grateful to Floyd Porter and the other partners at Miles and Partners LLP for allowing us to reproduce some of their precedents. We are, finally, very grateful to Hannah Nicholas (now the Mental Capacity Cat) for her hard work in updating precedent orders on the website to reflect the coming into force of the 2017 Rules, and Michelle Pratley for her work both in developing a sophisticated precedent order for case management and an equally sophisticated precedent letter of instruction to an expert to report upon capacity.

As ever, and against what appear to be ever increasing odds, Esther Pilger, our publisher at Legal Action Group, remains unflappable and a joy to work with; this book would not have existed without her, and a huge part of its continuing success is down to her skill, dedication, and ability to find humour in the strangest of places.

We would also like to thank those who have kept the authors going through the darker nights of the soul. Alex thanks, above all, his wife Pieta, for her unswerving support and tolerance for muttering about random capacity points. It is a mark of how long the Handbook has been in his life that a special thanks goes also this time to his daughter Zoë for her first design commission, choosing the colour of this edition's cover. Kate would like to thank her husband, Stephen Elliott, for his support and encouragement throughout the many hours spent shut away writing. Nicola would like to thank Gordon for being Gordon.

Sophy would like to thank Guy, Frank and Rebecca, as well as her mother Natalie, whose work as a social worker in the early years of the Mental Health Act 1983 sparked a long interest in mental health and mental capacity law.

We state the law as at June 2022

Alex Ruck Keene QC (Hon)
Kate Edwards
Nicola Mackintosh QC (Hon)
Sophy Miles
June 2022

Authors

Alex Ruck Keene QC (Hon) is a barrister at 39 Essex Chambers. Alex has been recommended as a leading expert in the field of mental capacity law for several years, appearing in cases involving the Mental Capacity Act 2005 at all levels up to and including the Supreme Court. He also writes extensively about mental capacity law and policy, works to which he has contributed including *Court of Protection Practice* (LexisNexis), *The International Protection of Adults* (2015, Oxford University Press) and *Assessment of Mental Capacity* (Law Society/BMA 2022, 5th edition). Alex is a Visiting Professor at King's College London, a Visiting Senior Lecturer at the Institute of Psychiatry, Psychology and Neuroscience, King's College London and a Research Affiliate at the Essex Autonomy Project, University of Essex. Alex is the creator of the website www.mentalcapacitylawand-policylaw.org.uk. He was made an Honorary QC in March 2022 in recognition of his services to mental capacity and mental health law outside the courtroom. In addition to editing this book, Alex wrote chapters 10, 11 (to which Sophy also contributed), 12, 14, 15, 17, 18, 19 and 22–28 (Sophy contributing to chapter 25).

Kate Edwards is a senior associate solicitor at Simpson Millar where she leads the property and affairs team. Kate is a personally appointed property and affairs deputy and a director of a trust corporation. In 2012 Kate founded the Court of Protection Practitioners Association (CoPPA) and she continues to serve on the national executive committee. She is also a member of STEP (Society of Trusts & Estates Practitioners). Kate wrote chapters 7 and 8 and co-wrote chapters 17 with Sophy and chapter 21 with Alex.

Nicola Mackintosh QC (Hon) is the founder and Director of Mackintosh Law, a specialist law firm providing expert legal advice and representation to disabled clients in the areas of mental capacity and community care. Nicola is co-chair of the Legal Aid Practitioners

Group and an Honorary Bencher of Middle Temple. She is a longstanding member of the Law Society's Mental Health and Disability Committee and previous member of the Law Society Council. Nicola is regularly instructed by the Official Solicitor in complex Court of Protection cases, including hybrid cases concerning health and welfare and finances, resulting in some of the leading judgments in the field. She continues to be a strong voice in support of improved access to justice for disabled and other vulnerable people and was made an Honorary QC in recognition of her contribution.

Sophy Miles is a barrister at Doughty Street Chambers. She qualified as a solicitor in 1989. She was a founding partner at Miles and Partners LLP where she led the mental health and capacity team for 16 years. She has been involved in significant cases under the inherent jurisdiction and in the Court of Protection, including *JE v DE and others* and *Hillingdon v Neary*. Sophy regularly appears in the Court of Protection. She sits as a Deputy District Judge in the Court of Protection and as a fee-paid judge of the First-tier Tribunal (Mental Health). Sophy writes and trains on mental health and mental capacity issues and writes the regular Court of Protection updates in *Legal Action*, is co-author of LAG's *Mental Heath Tribunal Handbook* and is on the editorial advisory board of the *Community Care Law Reports*. She is a member of the Court of Protection Bar Association committee and an accredited mediator (Regent's University London). Sophy wrote chapters 6, 9, 13 and 21, co-wrote (with Kate) chapters 17, and contributed to chapters 11 and 25.

Professor Anselm Eldergill is a district judge in the Court of Protection and a visiting professor at University College London. Before becoming a judge he was a practising legal aid solicitor specialising in mental health law for over 25 years, and then led the mental health team at Eversheds. He was President of the Mental Health Lawyers Association and of the Institute of Mental Health Act Practitioners, and ranked 1 in Chambers Directory. He is an Alexander Maxwell Scholar and the author of *Mental Health Review Tribunals: Law and Procedure* (Sweet & Maxwell 1997) and articles for journals such as the *Princeton University Law Journal*, *Journal of Forensic Psychiatry* and *The Guardian*. He was chairman of the Mental Health Act Commission's Law and Ethics Committee. Anselm wrote chapters 3–5.

Contents

Table of cases

Table of statutes

Table of statutory instruments

r20.11(4)	19.38
r20.11(5)–(6)	19.40
r20.13(1)	19.46
r20.14(1)(b)	19.47
r20.14(2)(a)	19.47
r20.14(2)(b)	19.47
r20.14(3)	19.49
r20.14(5)	19.36
PD 20A	19.2, 19.27, 19.30, 19.31
PD 20A para 5	19.19
PD 20A paras 8–9	19.20
PD 20A para 10	19.20
PD 20A para 11	19.27
PD 20A para 12	19.31
PD 20A para 14	19.27
PD 20A paras 16–17	19.27
PD 20A paras 18–21	19.32
PD 20A para 22	19.28
PD 20A para 23	19.28
PD 20A para 24	19.28
PD 20A para 25	19.29
PD 20A para 26	19.30
PD 20A paras 28–29	19.30
PD 20A para 31	19.21, 19.37
PD 20A para 32	19.35
PD 20A paras 33–34	19.36
PD 20A para 40	19.41
PD 20A para 41	19.41
PD 20A para 44	19.42
PD 20A paras 45–46	19.42
PD 20A para 47	19.42
PD 20A para 48	19.43
PD 20A para 49	19.42
PD 20B	19.2, 19.11, 19.14, 19.39
PD 20B paras 3.1–3.3	19.12
PD 20B para 3.4	19.13
Pt 21	18.5
r21.2	18.20
r21.2(3)	18.8
r21.9(1)	18.8
r21.10	18.13, 18.15
r21.15(1)	13.29, 18.15
r21.27(2)	18.18
r21.28(2)	18.19
PD 21A	13.29, 18.13, 18.15
PD 21A para 1	18.8
PD 21A para 8.5	18.13
PD 21A paras 31–31	18.24
r22.1	18.23, 18.24

Table of European and international legislation

Abbreviations

ABE	achieving best evidence
ACO	authorised court officer
ADR	alternative dispute resolution
ADRT	advance decision to refuse treatment
AJA 1960	Administration of Justice Act 1960
ALR	accredited legal representative
AMCP	approved mental capacity professional
Bailii	British and Irish Legal Information Institute
BC	borough council
BMA	British Medical Association
BSB	Bar Standards Board
CANH	clinically assisted nutrition and hydration
CC	county council
CCG	clinical commissioning group
CCMS	Client and Cost Management System
CEA	Civil Evidence Act
CFA	conditional fee agreement
CFO	Court Funds Office
ChA 1989	Children Act 1989
CHC	NHS continuing healthcare
CICA	Criminal Injuries Compensation Authority
CILEx	Chartered Institute of Legal Executives
CIW	Care Inspectorate Wales
CMC	Civil Mediation Council
COPR	Court of Protection Rules
CPR	Civil Procedure Rules
CRPD	UN Convention on the Rights of Persons with Disabilities)
CQC	Care Quality Commission
CTO	community treatment order
DHSC	Department of Health and Social Care
DOLS	deprivation of liberty safeguards

DPA 2018	Data Protection Act 2018
DRH	dispute resolution hearing
DWP	Department for Work and Pensions
ECF	exceptional case funding
ECHR	European Convention on Human Rights
ECtHR	European Court of Human Rights
ECT	electroconvulsive therapy
EPA	enduring power of attorney
EqA 2010	Equality Act 2010
FDIA	factitious disorder imposed on another
FDR	financial dispute resolution
FNC	NHS-funded nursing care
FPR	Family Procedure Rules
GDPR	General Data Protection Regulation
GP	general practitioner
GMC	General Medical Council
HCC	High Cost Case
HCPC	Health and Care Professions Council
HMCTS	Her Majesty's Courts and Tribunals Service
HMRC	Her Majesty's Revenue and Customs
HRA 1998	Human Rights Act 1998
ICPR	Institute for Crime and Justice Policy Research
IFA	independent financial adviser
IMCA	independent mental capacity advocate
IPSO	Independent Press Standards Organisation
JEB	Judicial Executive Board
LAA	Legal Aid Agency
LASPO	Legal Aid, Sentencing and Punishment of Offenders Act 2012
LBC	London Borough Council
LiP	litigant in person
LPA	lasting power of attorney
LPS	liberty protection safeguards
LSC	Legal Services Commission
MCA 2005	Mental Capacity Act 2005
MC(A)A 2019	Mental Capacity (Amendment) Act 2019
MHA 1983	Mental Health Act 1983
MHA 2007	Mental Health Act 2007
MoJ	Ministry of Justice
MP	Member of Parliament
NHS	National Health Service
NMC	Nursing and Midwifery Council

PACE	Police and Criminal Evidence Act 1984
PALS	patient advice and liaison service
PCT	primary care trust
PD	Practice Direction
PGO	Public Guardianship Office
PHA 1997	Protection from Harassment Act 1997
PHSO	Parliamentary and Health Service Ombudsman
PSU	Personal Support Unit
QBD	Queen's Bench Division
RGN	Registered General Nurse
RLDN	Registered Learning Disability Nurse
RMN	Registered Mental Nurse
RPR	relevant person's representative
RTM	round table meeting
SALT	speech and language therapist
SCCO	Senior Court Costs Office
SRA	Solicitors Regulation Authority
SSWWA 2014	Social Services and Well-being (Wales) Act 2014

CHAPTER 1

Introduction

The scheme of the book

1.1 The book is divided into four parts.

1.2 In the first section, we set out an overview of the Mental Capacity Act (MCA) 2005 and of the Court of Protection. In order to ensure that the book's focus is where it should be – on the people whose lives are affected by its decisions – we start with a version of a paper originally co-ordinated by Inclusion London for the 100th edition of the 39 Essex Chambers Mental Capacity Report, entitled *We are not Ps, we are people.*

1.3 In the second section, the book proceeds in chronological order through the life of an application (or, to be precise, from the point before an application is even prepared – by asking, first, the often overlooked question of whether it is actually appropriate to bring an application to the Court of Protection). We then trace the process through from the drafting of the application, pre-issue (where relevant), issue, response and then on to any directions hearings necessary before the final determination of the application, before dealing with the questions of costs, enforcement and appeals.

1.4 In a series of – mostly – shorter chapters in the third section, we address a number of specific issues that arise in connection with the Court of Protection's jurisdiction, such as applications in relation to deprivation of liberty and the interaction between the Court of Protection and the Administrative Court. In a new addition for this edition, and reflecting the considerable increase in case-law in this area, we cover the inherent jurisdiction in relation to so-called vulnerable adults.

1.5 The fourth section, the appendices, contain the key statutory materials and guidance, together with samples of important documents such as letters of instruction, as well as useful contact addresses and resources. Precedent orders can be found on the (free) website that accompanies the book: www.courtofprotectionhandbook.com. On the website can also be found links to relevant primary and secondary legislation, practice directions, and other useful resources, as well as blog posts and updates to the text of the work.

Approach

1.6 We need to make four important – linked – points at the outset of the book as to the approach that we have taken.

1.7 First, while it has deep historical roots, the Court of Protection in its new incarnation with jurisdiction to take decisions not solely in regard to the property and affairs of those without capacity but also in regard to their health and welfare has been in existence only since October 2007, and it is still therefore a comparative newcomer.[1] Its practices and processes are in significant measure still being worked out. This book is, in part, a contribution to the development of those practices and processes, although we have sought to make clear whenever we move beyond description into prescription.

1.8 Second, this book covers the span of the Court of Protection's work. However, only a very small number of applications relating to property and affairs received by the court are contentious; the vast majority are decided 'upon the papers' by either a judge or an authorised court officer. Those sections of the book which relate to the determination of contested applications, and, in particular, to hearings, are inevitably very much focused upon health and welfare applications.

1.9 Third, insofar as the book deals with the determination of health and welfare applications in particular, it does so from a starting point that there is a wealth of valuable guidance to be found from proceedings relating to children (and especially care proceedings). It is vital to emphasise, however, that we are *not* saying that incapacitated adults[2] are to be equated with 'big children'. Very far from it – the law that Court of Protection judges have to apply and the factors to take into account when considering what substantive decision to take upon an application relating to an incapacitated adult are – and should be – very different from the law and factors that apply in relation to a child. However, the forensic processes in both types of proceedings are – we suggest – very similar, and for very good reason: they are above all designed to ensure that, as best as possible, a judge is put in a position to take the decision that it right for a person who is not a protagonist in the proceedings but their subject[3]

1 Indeed, so new does it still appear to be to some that it was forgotten in the provisions of the Coronavirus Act 2020 relating to the operation of courts during the COVID-19 pandemic.

2 The Court of Protection can, of course, take decisions in relation to children of 16 and 17. This jurisdiction was not invoked often in the early years of the MCA 2005, but is increasingly invoked in relation to questions of deprivation of liberty. We touch on the position of those under 18 where relevant; see in particular chapters 12 and 22.

3 See, in this regard, The Honourable Mr Justice Baker, 'Reforming the Court of Protection: lessons to be learned from the Family Justice Reforms' [2014] 4 *Elder Law Journal* 1, 45–50.

1.10 Fourth and finally, hanging over the entirety of the book remains a very large question as to whether the MCA 2005 is compatible with the United Nations Convention on the Rights of Persons with Disabilities. The Committee on the Rights of Persons with Disabilities is clear that it is not.[4] Whether the MCA 2005 will be amended in due course remains a very open question, as is the extent to which the Committee's interpretation of the Convention goes beyond its obligations. And since the last edition, the Supreme Court has made it clear that it has only limited patience with the Convention as an unincorporated convention.[5] We nonetheless highlight ways that, even without statutory reform, practice can be changed to reflect the principles of the Convention in chapter 26.

1.11 It should be noted that the law relating to capacity issues is significantly different in both Northern Ireland and Scotland; this book should not be used as a guide to the principles and practices adopted in those jurisdictions.[6]

1.12 In this book we use 'P' to refer to the person – not the 'patient' (as some judges on occasion appear to suggest) – whom it is said lacks capacity to take the material decisions.

The Court of Protection and COVID-19

1.13 Much will no doubt be written in due course about the impact of the COVID-19 pandemic upon those with cognitive impairments.[7] The Court of Protection, along with wider society, went through a rapid transformation to address the consequences of the pandemic. We touch upon those aspects of its transformation which are likely to be of longer-term consequence in the relevant chapters, most obviously questions relating to remote hearings. A working group convened to advise the Vice-President on post-pandemic working practices repor-

4 Committee on the Rights of Persons with Disabilities, Concluding Observations on the Initial Report of the United Kingdom, CRPD/C/GBR/CO/1, 3 October 2017, available at: www.ohchr.org/en/treaty-bodies/crpd.

5 See, for instance, *A local authority v JB* [2021] UKSC 52, [2021] 3 WLR 1381.

6 Readers are directed, in particular, to chapter 12 of Baker et al, *Court of Protection Practice 2022*, Jordans; and also, for a fuller discussion, to Frimston et al, *The International Protection of Adults*, Oxford University Press, 2015.

7 A very early snapshot was given in April 2020 in Alex Ruck Keene, 'Capacity in the time of coronavirus,' *International Journal of Law and Psychiatry* 70 (2020) 101560. The report of the Joint Committee on Human Rights into the human rights implications of the government's response to COVID-19 makes sobering reading (HC 265, HL Paper 125, 21 September 2020).

ted in the autumn of 2021. At the time of writing, it is not yet clear what (if any) steps will be taken in response to the report.

1.14 A useful set of resources relating to the wider operation of courts (including legal aid) can be found on the Mental Health Law Online website[8]); the Judiciary website has also collated advice and guidance.[9] The Court of Protection Handbook website[10] also contains the current versions of guidance issued by the Vice-President.

8 See: https://www.mentalhealthlaw.co.uk/Coronavirus_resources.

9 See: www.judiciary.uk/coronavirus-covid-19-advice-and-guidance/.

10 See: https://courtofprotectionhandbook.com/.

CHAPTER 2

We are not Ps we are people

The content of this chapter has been co-ordinated by Svetlana Kotlova of Inclusion London (www.inclusionlondon.org.uk). It aims to highlight the experiences of those to whom the Mental Capacity Act (MCA) 2005 is applied day-in, day-out, inside and outside the Court of Protection. It first appeared in 39 Essex Chambers' Mental Capacity Report, December 2019, issue 100. We are grateful to Svetlana Kotlova, Inclusion London and 39 Essex Chambers for permission to reproduce it.

Introduction

2.1 There are too many problems with the law and how it doesn't uphold human rights of people with learning difficulties, autism and mental health support needs. It allows discrimination often in the name of protection and making sure people are safe. It often excludes people from making important decisions about their life and it does not address the power imbalance that so many individuals experience no matter where they live and what they do. Many problems are also to do with how the laws are implemented and enforced.

2.2 I asked Andrew Lee, director of People First, and Christine Spooner, chair of People First, to help me write this article. Below we discuss how the Mental Capacity Act (MCA) 2005 works for people who are on the receiving end. We also talk about fundamental problems that underpin our laws and the way people with learning difficulties are treated. We are very grateful for this opportunity to put across our point of view.

Why learning difficulties?

2.3 We use the term learning difficulties. We know in law these words have a different meaning. We use this term because we believe in the Social Model of Disability, which says disability is not about impairment, it is the barriers people with impairments face. Learning difficulties describes our impairment and we are disabled by the lack of accessible information, communication, prejudice and discrimination and the lack of support.

Compulsion in the name of caring

2.4 Christine told me:

> 'Too many people who come to my house somehow know what's best for me. They start telling me how to do things and what should happen before even talking to me and when I demand they get out of my house, I'm labelled as rude, unreasonable, ungrateful or angry. Yes, I get angry, and so I should be. Just imagine someone came to your house, started telling you what to do straight away, changed things how they wanted without talking to you. You would not be smiling and asking them to come again.
>
> Of course, most people want to help and do good, but somehow still deep down their mind they think they know better what is good for

> me. They almost treat me like a child. This attitude comes at every stage, from small decisions to big. Most of the time people do not even understand that what they are doing is wrong. I am used to fighting my corner. I don't care what they think. But it is not easy to live a life where you always have to fight with people who are close to you and are supposed to help you. Why do I have to remind people to recognise me as a person and respect my choices, no matter whether they agree or disagree? I feel the only people who can understand what I am going through are other people with learning difficulties. This is why self- advocacy and peer support are so important.'

2.5 Compulsion in the name of care is deeply rooted in discriminatory attitude towards disabled people and people with learning difficulties in particular. We have not been seen as 'normal' human beings. Society as a whole still doesn't know what to do with us. The support we need can cost a lot and the support that promotes our liberty and our autonomy costs even more.

Andrew says:

> 'Supporting us is a difficult and very skilled job. It is much easier to lock us away in institutions or our homes, make decisions for us and protect us from living a life. And although the laws have changed, discrimination is still there and real life does not resemble what should happen under the law. The choice we have are only the choices we are given, the often have nothing to do with our aspirations and we really want our life to be . . . the same as everybody else.'

Discriminatory nature of our laws

2.6 Only people with learning difficulties, autism and mental health support needs could be detained, preventatively because professionals think they are a danger to others. We as society would not agree with a proposition to detain all dangerous people, but we accept it when it comes to people with learning difficulties and mental health support needs. And it is often forgotten that there are many of us who experience abuse even in places that are supposed to protect us.

> 'There are many non-disabled people who would benefit from medical treatment, but it is only us who could be forced to undergo the treatment we do not want. On the other hand we often have to fight for the help and support that we really need and that would really help us.'

We need support and sometimes protection, that increase our choice and promotes our freedom, but we get protection and care that forces us to accept things we don't want.

2.7 People with learning difficulties are subjected to unbelievable levels of scrutiny. Take parents with learning difficulties, who have to prove they are good parents and battle for support, when non-disabled parents have to do something seriously wrong before anyone gets involved.

2.8 Many of us have to battle hard to have relationships or live where we want, while non-disabled people take it as normal part of life.

2.9 And the Human Rights Act 1998 allows all this.

2.10 And of course the MCA 2005 with all its protections and presumption of capacity still allows others to make decisions for us, override our wishes and decide what is good for us. In reality, people are not supported to make decisions, they are not given accessible information or real choices, what they get to choose from depends on what information they get given, time is not taken to see and understand what they want. Moreover, since many individuals need support their choices are often limited by decisions made by local authorities or CCGs about their support packages. Supporting people to make decisions requires time, commitment, skill and the right attitude. In a day-to-day life it is much easier and cheaper to just make decisions for them.

> 'There is a huge imbalance of power in our lives; we often depend on people who make decisions for us. And when we disagree, the onus is on us to dispute through the Court of Protection . . . the very system we cannot access.
>
> It feels like when the system was designed, no one really thought it through from our point of view. How is it supposed to work in practice for every person and every decision? How would it work for a friend of mine who was told by a care home manager they cannot have a relationship? Many of us need support to get support, not everyone has relatives who will fight for us, not everyone has an advocate. Most people would not know where to start and what to do. The process is so complex and inaccessible even for non-disabled people and it is just an illusion that we can challenge decisions about our capacity or best interests. We can only challenge when others around us are prepared to help us.
>
> Decision makers and legal systems don't have credibility with people with learning difficulties as the promises they have made, and make again, especially after scandals such as Winterbourne View and more recently Whorlton Hall, are never followed through.
>
> The Court of Protection feels more like a place where other people argue what is good for us, often without us. I was shocked that the law and the lawyers call us "P". I know it is legal language, but there is a life, a real person, Joe, Sarah, whose life is on the cards, not just a P. I

was also shocked to find out the lawyers who represent us will not always argue what we want. They will argue what they think is best for us. So who is there to represent our voice? It would be scandalous if something like this was happening to non-disabled people.

The advocacy that people with learning difficulties set up for themselves, and still use, needs to be accepted by the legal system – advocates recognised by the legal system such as barristers and lawyers are not always 'our' advocates.'

'The whole system is not fit for the XXI Century. It needs to be accessible, it needs to hear our voice and give us a real opportunity to exercise our rights.'

The change we need

2.11 There are international human rights standards like the UN Convention on the Rights of Persons with Disabilities (UNCRPD). Which talks about supported decision-making, it prohibits detention on the basis of disability and calls for respect for integrity of every disabled person. It requires support to be put in place in community to ensure we have choice and control in our lives. These standards challenge ways of thinking and working and this is why there is still a lot of scepticism among the professionals. It is worth remembering that UNCRPD is probably the only document which was developed with such extensive and meaningful input from disabled people. We therefore ask everyone to accept these standards, aspire to achieve them and focus on what to do to make it happen, rather than thinking and talking why it is impossible to achieve this.

2.12 We need support to make decisions ourselves. We need our wishes and views to be heard and respected in decision-making processes. We need supporters and allies who would help us advance our human rights and who would support and enable us to speak out for ourselves be it in court or when bigger policies are developed by the government.

2.13 In 2019, when the Mental Capacity Amendment Act was going through Parliament, we spoke to many people with learning difficulties about the Mental Capacity law and UNCRPD. We published a report which highlights some important issues for us.[1]

1 https://www.inclusionlondon.org.uk/wp-content/uploads/2018/09/Briefing-on-the-Mental-Capacity-Amendment-Bill-for-DDPOs.pdf/.

CHAPTER 3

An overview of the Mental Capacity Act 2005

continued

Introduction

3.1 The Mental Capacity Act (MCA) 2005 received royal assent on 7 April 2005. Most of its provisions came into effect on 1 October 2007. Prior to the MCA 2005:

- The Court of Protection only had jurisdiction over an incapacitated person's property and financial affairs. The relevant legal provisions were set out in Mental Health Act (MHA) 1983 Part VII and in rules made under that Act.
- Most treatment and care decisions were governed by the common law, in other words by laws and principles set down by judges rather than in legislation.
- The test which the judges formulated was beautifully simple: If the individual had capacity to make their own decision, treatment or care required their consent. If they lacked capacity, the clinician was under a duty to give any treatment or care necessary to preserve their life, health or well-being which was in their best interests.

3.2 The beauty of the scheme was its simplicity and the fact that it was non-prescriptive; it left much to the discretion of those providing the treatment or care. The weakness of the scheme was its simplicity and the fact that it was non-prescriptive; it left much to the discretion of those providing the treatment or care.

3.3 Because of the decision-making discretion given to professionals and family carers, few cases came to court. Only cases which involved especially significant or difficult decisions – such as life-sustaining treatment and sterilisation – tended to be referred.

3.4 As the years went by, many people became concerned by the lack of any structured process for deciding more commonplace personal welfare matters – issues such as where and with whom an incapacitated person should live, how much contact they should have with family members and friends, how to help them to develop their activities and skills, what medication they should receive, and so on.

3.5 Depending on the values, resources and time of family members and professionals, great to little or no care might be taken to establish which decisions the person could make for themselves. Similarly, if incapacitated, the individual might have considerable involvement in decisions about their welfare and future or, none at all.

The Law Commission's work

3.6 Much useful work was done by the Law Commission to address these difficult issues. The Commission's fourth programme published in September 1989 noted the view that existing legal mechanisms were 'complicated, inflexible and piecemeal' and stated that the recent House of Lords decision in *Re F*[1] could not provide a comprehensive solution.[2]

3.7 Lady Hale (then Brenda Hoggett) was an important driver of the reform programme, and the Law Commission's Report of 1995[3] which had a draft Bill appended to it was preceded by a number of consultation and discussion papers.

3.8 The Law Commission's proposals were debated and in some respects modified over the following years, eventually emerging as the MCA 2005.

3.9 Subsequently, a number of important insertions to the Act were made by the MHA 2007. In particular, a new scheme for authorising deprivation of liberty under the MCA 2005 was introduced, although this will be replaced in due course by a further scheme (see para 3.326 below).

Statutory principles (section 1)

3.10 The MCA 2005 starts with a number of fundamental statutory principles which apply, and must be applied, whenever a person does something under the Act.

THE STATUTORY PRINCIPLES	
MCA 2005 s1(1) provides that the following principles apply for the purposes of the Act:	
1	'A person must be assumed to have capacity unless it is established that he lacks capacity' (MCA 2005 s1(2)).
2	'A person is not to be treated as unable to make a decision unless all practicable steps to help him to do so have been taken without success' (MCA 2005 s1(3)).

1 Reported as *Re F (mental patient: sterilisation)* [1990] 2 AC 1, [1989] 2 WLR 1025, HL.

2 Fourth Programme of Law Reform (1989) Law Com NO 185, Item 9; Cm 800.

3 *Mental incapacity (report)* [1995] EWLC 231, 15 January 1995. Available at: https://www.lawcom.gov.uk/app/uploads/2015/04/lc231.pdf

3	'A person is not to be treated as unable to make a decision merely because he makes an unwise decision' (MCA 2005 s1(4)).
4	'An act done, or decision made, under this Act for or on behalf of a person who lacks capacity must be done, or made, in his best interests' (MCA 2005 s1(5)).
5	'Before the act is done, or the decision is made, regard must be had to whether the purpose for which it is needed can be as effectively achieved in a way that is less restrictive of the person's rights and freedom of action' (MCA 2005 s1(6)).

3.11 It is important to emphasise the importance of these principles at the outset, and useful to illustrate one or two of the situations in which they can be significant.

The presumption of capacity

3.12 The first principle is that the relevant person 'must be assumed to have capacity unless it is established that he lacks capacity'.

3.13 The starting point, therefore, is *always* that this person has capacity to make this particular decision for themselves. That remains the legal position before the courts until it is established that it is more likely than not that they lack this capacity.[4]

3.14 A fair number of cases brought to the Court of Protection are brought because the evidence is quite finely balanced and there is a dispute about the person's capacity. In such cases, the presumption of capacity may be decisive. In medical practice, for example in an A&E setting, it is not uncommon for a doctor when asked about a person's capacity to say that it is 'fifty-fifty'; evidently, the presumption of capacity has not been displaced. And, when it comes to depriving someone of their liberty under the Act, it follows that the presumption that they can make their own decision about whether to not to be in the particular hospital or care home must first be displaced.

4 MCA 2005 s2(4). In proceedings under the MCA 2005 'or any other enactment, any question whether a person lacks capacity within the meaning of this Act must be decided on the balance of probabilities'. The reference to proceedings under 'any other enactment' is likely to be relevant to certain proceedings taken under the MHA 1983. Strictly, the position where reliance is placed upon the defence in MCA 2005 s5 outside the courtroom is different: it is whether the person has a reasonable belief that the other lacks capacity to make the decision for themselves. See paras 3.147 and following.

Duty to help the person make their own decision where possible

3.15 The second principle is that a person is not to be treated as unable to make the particular decision for themselves unless all practicable steps to help them to do so have been taken without success.

3.16 What is practicable – that is, capable of being put into practice – depends on the circumstances at the time.

3.17 For example, if a person in need of immediate medical treatment is unconscious after a serious motorway accident, it will not be practicable before intervening to take any steps to help them make their own decision about the particular medical intervention.

3.18 At the other end of the scale is the situation where it is practicable to assist a person with a learning disability to make their own will. If there is no urgency, the fact that the person lacks capacity to make their own will today is not decisive if with assistance over weeks or months they can develop the necessary understanding. It may be possible to break the relevant information down into a more understandable form, to repeat key points over a number of weeks, to devise helpful visual aids and so on.

3.19 Likewise, an unwell person in hospital who is asked about a return home or a move into residential care may appear to lack capacity to make the decision at this moment. However, with more time to reflect, clearer explanations, and the benefit of discussing the options with family members, trusted friends or an advocate, they may well have capacity to make their own decision.

Unwise decision-making

3.20 The third principle is that 'A person is not to be treated as unable to make a decision merely because he makes an unwise decision'.

3.21 One can rephrase this by saying that a person is not to be treated as being unable to make their own decision merely because the decision they make *or propose making* is considered by some person or persons to be unwise.

3.22 Although a person cannot be found to lack capacity *merely* because their proposed decision is unwise, fairly obviously an unwise or irrational decision may raise significant doubts and so trigger an assessment of their capacity.

3.23 In practice this principle is often in play, particularly when it comes to decisions about whether to remove older people into residential care. There are many older people who prefer to 'take their chances' at home rather than live in a care home, notwithstanding the risk of falls and some physical suffering. Some of them, in common with all generations, will have a stubborn streak, 'unreasonably' refuse good or well-meant advice, or demonstrate a lifelong antipathy to being told what to do. The fact that others think they are being unwise is insufficient. They only lack capacity if their ability to understand, retain and weigh the information relevant to the decision, including the foreseeable benefits and risks of deciding one way or the other, is undermined in some significant way by an impairment or disturbance of their mind or brain. Otherwise, their decision is essentially no different to that of a person who goes mountaineering, hang-gliding or motor racing – risky and the doctor might not do it, arguably unwise, could end unhappily, but they are within their rights.

Duty to act in the person's best interests

3.24 The fourth principle is that, 'An act done, or decision made, under this Act for or on behalf of a person who lacks capacity must be done, or made, in his best interests'.

3.25 This was also part of the old common law test which, it may be recalled, required a clinician, social worker or other professional carer to give the incapacitated person any treatment or care necessary to preserve their life, health or well-being 'which was in their best interests'.

3.26 The final phrase drew attention to the fact that providing treatment or care is not always in a person's best interests. Obvious examples are where further prolonging a terminally ill patient's life would cause them considerable suffering for little benefit, and where a patient's fierce resistance to treatment means that it is not in their best interests to attempt to give it by restraint.

3.27 If a person lacks capacity to make a decision, so that someone else must make it for them, applying the best interests requirement does not mean that other people's interests are always irrelevant and must be given no weight. As an example, almost all parents want their children to be happy and free from worry. The Court of Protection may therefore authorise making a gift from the incapacitated person's funds to a child in need. If the incapacitated person still had capacity to make the gift they would wish to help in this way; and it is in their best interests to do on their behalf that which they themselves would obviously do if they could. Similarly, most people with capacity consider and take into account the wishes, feelings and needs of their spouse or partner when making decisions which affect them. It is in the incapacitated person's best interests to have regard to these historic genuine feelings and values if they can no longer hold or express them.

3.28 The critical error to avoid is an analysis of the person's best interests which disregards or downplays their wishes, feelings, values and beliefs in the perverted belief that critical objectivity is undermined by subjective considerations.

3.29 The law requires objective analysis of a subject not an object. The incapacitated person is the subject. Therefore, it is *their* welfare in the context of *their* wishes, feelings, beliefs and values that is important. This is the principle of beneficence which asserts an obligation to help others further *their* important and legitimate interests, not one's own.[5]

3.30 Why would anyone wish a person to receive care otherwise than in accordance with their wishes if they can be cared for adequately in accordance with their wishes?

Duty to consider less restrictive options

3.31 The fifth principle is that: 'Before the act is done, or the decision is made, regard must be had to whether the purpose for which it is needed can be as effectively achieved in a way that is less restrictive of the person's rights and freedom of action'.

3.32 This principle is sometimes paraphrased as 'one must choose the least restrictive option', which risks being misleading. The 'least restrictive option' of those available may be to do nothing and to neglect the person. That is not what the principle requires. The decision-maker must have regard to whether the necessary purpose or aim (eg treating a severe illness which is causing considerable suffering) can be as effectively achieved in a less restrictive way (eg in a way which is acceptable to the person or more acceptable to them). Why an act or decision is now needed, and the effectiveness of less restrictive approaches, must be considered.

5 From *Westminster City Council v Sykes* [2014] EWHC B9 (COP), (2014) 17 CCLR 139 at section 10.

Who lacks capacity (sections 2 and 3)

3.33 The purpose of the MCA 2005 is to provide a structure and appropriate mechanisms for making a decision on behalf of a fellow citizen who lacks capacity to make their own decision.

3.34 The first consideration therefore is, 'does this person lack capacity?' Does this person lack or now lack the capacity necessary to exercise a citizen's usual constitutional right to make their own decision? Does a decision now need to be made for them, in their best interests?

3.35 This is a matter of constitutional importance for a second reason. Those capable of acting are responsible for their actions and omissions and, being responsible for them, accountable to others. The counterpart of freedom and autonomy is accountability for acts freely and autonomously done.

3.36 The law takes what some people call an 'issue specific' or 'functional' approach to capacity. It assesses a person's ability to make a particular decision at a particular time, not their ability to make decisions generally.

3.37 As has been seen, everyone is assumed to have capacity to make the decision(s) in question unless and until it is established that they lack this capacity, which must be established on the balance of probabilities. Furthermore, a person is not to be treated as lacking capacity to make the decision in question unless all practicable steps to help them to do so have been taken without success.

3.38 A person does not lack capacity simply because they have a mental disorder or disability (sometimes described as a 'status approach' to capacity). Nor are they to be treated as lacking capacity to make the decision(s) in question merely because they propose making a decision which others consider to be unwise (sometimes called an 'outcome approach').

3.39 Furthermore, a lack of capacity cannot be established merely by reference to their age or appearance, a condition of theirs such as mental illness or a learning disability, or an aspect of their behaviour, which might lead others to make unjustified assumptions about their capacity.[6] One needs to be especially careful in the case of those who may merely be stubborn or eccentric. The correct test of capacity must be applied and lack of capacity be established.[7]

6 MCA 2005 s2(3).

7 See Baker LJ et al, *Court of Protection Practice* (annual) LexisNexis, chapter 2.

The incapacity test

3.40 For the purposes of the MCA 2005, a person lacks capacity in relation to a matter 'if at the material time he is unable to make a decision for himself in relation to the matter because of an impairment of, or a disturbance in the functioning of, the mind or brain' (MCA 2005 s2(1)).[8] The Supreme Court in *A Local Authority v JB*[9] made clear the correct ordering of the capacity test, ie that it is necessary to start with the question of whether the person is functionally capable or incapable of understanding, retaining, using and weighing the relevant information and communicating their decision. It is only if the person cannot make the decision that it is necessary to go on to consider why they cannot do so.

3.41 Accordingly, capacity is both:

- *time-specific*, focusing on the particular time when a decision has to be made – so the loss of capacity can be temporary, partial or fluctuating, and
- *decision- or issue-specific*, concentrating on the particular matter to which the decision relates, rather than the ability to make decisions generally – so, someone may lack capacity in relation to one particular matter but not another.

3.42 The fact that a temporary impairment or disturbance of the mind or brain suffices brings within the Act those who are unable to make a decision because of the effects of alcohol or drugs. This is particularly relevant for A&E staff.

What is meant by 'unable to make a decision'?

3.43 This is the 'section 3 test'. For these purposes, a person is unable to make a decision for themselves if they are unable:

- to understand the information relevant to the decision;
- to retain that information;
- to use or weigh that information as part of the process of making the decision; or
- to communicate their decision (whether by talking, using sign language or any other means).

8 It does not matter whether the impairment or disturbance is permanent or temporary.

9 [2021] UKSC 52, [2021] 3 WLR 1381.

3.44 It can be seen that being 'unable to decide' does not literally mean that. Demonstrating incapacity involves establishing that the person's capacity to make the decision in question is in some way fundamentally compromised by the fact that the functioning of their mind or brain is impaired or disturbed. In other words, because of an impairment or disturbance of their mind or brain they are unable to understand, retain or weigh the information relevant to the decision, or are unable to communicate their decision. A link must be demonstrated.

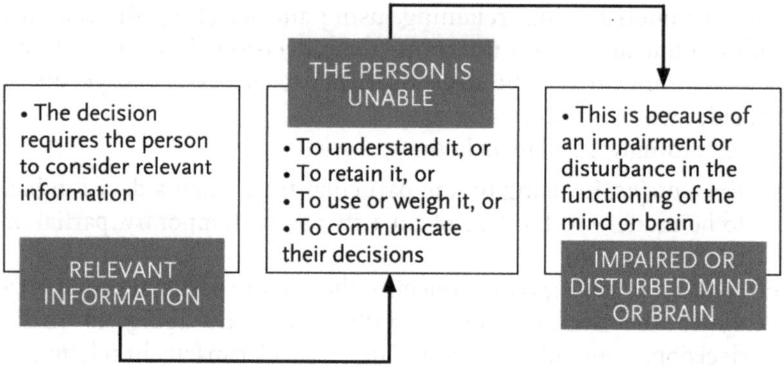

One of the reasons for it being necessary to demonstrate this link is that a person who cannot make the decision because they are under duress or coercion may well not be fall to be considered under the Act at all. Rather, their situation would have to be thought about under the High Court's inherent jurisdiction (see chapter 28).

3.45 The test is not purely about cognition or capacity to reason. A person may understand the relevant information, be able to retain it, and intellectually able to acknowledge its significance, but be unable to give it weight because of an overwhelming phobia, obsessive thoughts, compulsive behaviour, abnormally impulsive behaviour or some other impairment or disturbance. It is therefore going too far to say that the quality of the decision is irrelevant as long as the person 'understands' what they are deciding.[10]

10 For instance, in the pre-MCA 2005 case of *Mitchell v Alasia* [2005] EWHC 11 (QB), Cox J relied on qualities such as impulsiveness and volatility when deciding that the claimant was incapable of managing and administering his own affairs. Similarly, in *X NHS Trust v T* [2004] EWHC 1279 (Fam), (2005) 8 CCLR 38, although there was no problem in respect of Ms T's intellectual capacity, and she was able to acknowledge intellectually that her belief was delusional, her wishes were driven by a delusional belief that any transfusion would only add to the evil circulating within her system.

How much information is relevant information?

3.46 How much information is relevant – the level and amount of information which the person must be capable of understanding, retaining and weighing in order to have capacity to make the decision – turns on the significance and complexity of the decision in question. The Supreme Court has made clear that identifying the relevant information is a critical stage in thinking about someone's ability to make the decision.[11]

3.47 The MCA 2005 states that: 'The information relevant to a decision includes information about the reasonably foreseeable consequences of (a) deciding one way or another, or (b) failing to make the decision' (section 3(4)). This therefore is relevant information that needs to be understood, retained, used and weighed in order to have capacity to make the decision.

3.48 Some decisions are relatively insignificant and involve understanding and weighing very little information; other decisions are more complicated or have foreseeable consequences that are more significant. In some cases, the foreseeable consequences may not just be for the person, but could also be in relation to the impact of the person's actions on others.[12]

3.49 Regardless of whether a person has capacity, the aim of all explanations is to simplify matters as far as possible but no further. Once the information relevant to a decision has been communicated in as understandable a way as possible – by breaking it down and using plain language and aids, but without resorting to omitting information which is relevant if more difficult to understand and weigh – one is still left with a spectrum of decisions ranging from those which are simple and require understanding relatively little to those that require understanding and weighing more.

3.50 In the case of a simple and trivial gift, such as giving a small present to a friend, there is not much to it and very little to grasp in order to make a valid gift. By definition, more significant transactions – those where the reasonably foreseeable consequences are more significant for the person concerned – require the capacity to understand and weigh the more significant consequences. Thus, in the old case of *Re Beaney*,[13] where the person was giving her house and only main asset to one of three children at the end of her life

11 See *A Local Authority v JB* [2021] UKSC 52, [2021] 3 WLR 1381 at para 69.

12 See *A Local Authority v JB* [2021] UKSC 52, [2021] 3 WLR 1381 at para 73.

13 *Re Beaney* [1978] 1 WLR 770, [1978] 2 All ER 595, ChD.

instead of by will, and the significance was to disinherit the other two children, the degree of understanding required was as high as that required for a will: the donor had to understand the claims of all potential donees and the extent of the property being disposed of. Unless she understood that, she would be entirely failing to grasp the significance, the essence, of the transaction.

3.51 It follows from the fact that capacity is issue-specific, and partly depends on the nature or complexity of the decisions to be made, that a person may have capacity to make some decisions for themselves (eg capacity to marry) but lack capacity to do other things (eg to make a will). A person may have capacity to bring or defend a small, relatively trivial claim in court, where the nature of the dispute and the issues are simple to understand and weigh, but lack capacity to litigate a case where the nature of the dispute or the issues are more significant or complex. Likewise, they may have capacity to consent to a simple medical procedure but not something much more significant.

Capacity to understand the relevant information

3.52 The first of the four parts of the MCA 2005 s3 test concerns the person's capacity 'to understand' the relevant information.

3.53 The Act says that a person is not to be regarded as being unable to understand the information relevant to a decision if they are able to understand an explanation of it given to them in a way that is appropriate to their circumstances (using simple language, visual aids or any other means).[14] A relatively common example of a person being unable to understand the information relevant to a medical treatment decision would be an inability to understand the meaning of even common words, as a result of a very profound brain injury, learning disability or dementia.

Capacity to retain the relevant information

3.54 The fact that a person is able to retain the information relevant to a decision for a short period only does not prevent them from being regarded as able to make the decision.[15] However, by definition, before one can weigh relevant information one must be able to retain it long enough to do so. As an example, even a clear and simple explanation of the information relevant to a treatment decision involves communicat-

14 MCA 2005 s3(2).
15 MCA 2005 s3(3).

ing what is wrong (the diagnosis), what is proposed (the treatment), the likely outcome with and without treatment (the prognosis) and any significant treatment risks (adverse effects). If a person understands the diagnosis but has forgotten it by the time the proposed treatment is being explained, they are unable to retain all of the relevant information for long enough to enable them to weigh it and make a decision.

Capacity to use and weigh the relevant information

3.55 This is the ground which has proved to be the most difficult and controversial in practice.

3.56 Even though a person can understand and retain all of the information relevant to a decision, and can communicate their preferred decision, they will still be held to be unable to make the decision if they cannot 'use or weigh' the information as part of the process of making the decision.

3.57 A simple example is that of a person who because of mental illness believes that their consultant psychiatrist is an imposter. The individual can understand and retain the relevant information given to them by the psychiatrist about their diagnosis, the proposed treatment, and so forth. They can also communicate the decision they intend to make. However, because they do not believe the doctor is a doctor, and give no weight at all to what the person says, they cannot 'use or weigh' the information as part of the process of making the decision. Therefore, they will be held to lack capacity to make the decision, on the weighing ground.

3.58 In the old case of *Re MB (Caesarean section)*,[16] MB consented to a Caesarean operation but then refused to be given anaesthesia by injection because she had a phobia of needles. When MB went into labour, the hospital obtained a declaration that it would be lawful to perform any necessary Caesarean upon her because she was incapable of consenting to or refusing treatment.

3.59 In that kind of case, the individual can understand and retain the relevant information about the proposed treatment and the foreseeable consequences of deciding one way or the other, repeat it back word for word and communicate their decision to refuse. That is not the issue. However, as in *MB*, it may be held that she is unable to use or weigh this information as part of the process of making the decision because her mind is disturbed by a terror of needles. She is petrified. This is so overwhelming as to prevent her from being able

16 [1997] EWCA Civ 3093, [1997] 2 FLR 426.

to use or weigh the relevant information about the foreseeable consequences of declining the intervention.

3.60 All cases are, of course, fact-specific. The important point is that the weight a person gives to relevant information, and their ability to use it when making the decision, are legally important considerations.

3.61 Some say that as soon as you refuse or discontinue treatment against medical advice you risk being found to lack capacity because it will be said that you have not understood or used the medical information properly, or have given it insufficient weight. That may happen in practice to a degree but it is not a correct statement of the law. It has to be demonstrated that the person is *unable* to use or weigh the information given to them and that this inability is *because of* an impairment or disturbance of the mind or brain. A link must be established.[17]

3.62 What is true when it comes to serious medical treatment decisions is that the more autonomy the law sanctions the more deaths there will be. Freedom to make 'unwise' decisions comes at a price in terms of safety, and safety bears a price in terms of freedom. It is not possible to have it both ways.

3.63 It is important to be aware of any temptation to overcome this uncomfortable truth by a misuse of the intellect or evidence. One must not give in to 'the self-interested lie' and construct a contrived incapacity argument in order to release *oneself* from an almost unbearable burden.

Capacity to communicate one's decision

3.64 This applies to people who are unconscious or in a coma and those with the rare condition sometimes known as 'locked-in syndrome', who are conscious but cannot speak or move at all. If a person cannot communicate their decision in any way, the MCA 2005 says they should be treated as if they are unable to make that decision. However, before deciding that this is so, it is necessary to take all practicable steps to help them communicate; for example, one might involve speech and language therapists, specialists in non-verbal communication and other appropriate professionals. Communication by simple muscle movements can show that somebody may have capacity to make a decision.[18]

17 This point was emphasised strongly in *Kings College Hospital NHS Foundation Trust v C and V* [2015] EWCOP 80, [2016] COPLR 50, in which the judge also reviewed and summarised the case-law on the determination of capacity since the Act came into force.

18 See Mental Capacity Act Code of Practice, Office of the Public Guardian, published 22 July 2013, paras 4.23–4.25 (www.gov.uk/government/publications/mental-capacity-act-code-of-practice).

Best interests (section 4)

3.65 If it is the case that the relevant person is unable to make their own decision, then by definition unless the decision can be postponed someone else must make it for them.

3.66 The decision made for them must be made in their 'best interests'. The MCA 2005 provides that one must not determine what is in a person's best interests merely on the basis of their age or appearance, or a condition of theirs, or an aspect of their behaviour, which might lead others to make unjustified assumptions about what might be in their best interests.[19]

Matters to consider

3.67 The person making the determination must consider all of the relevant circumstances. Rather unhelpfully, the Act says that 'relevant circumstances' are those which the person determining best interests is aware of and which it would be reasonable to regard as relevant.[20] However, the person making the decision must in particular consider the matters set out in the table below.

BEST INTERESTS CONSIDERATIONS (MCA 2005 s4)	
The person determining what is in the person's best interests must in particular (MCA 2005 s4(2)):	
1	'[C]onsider– (a) whether it is likely that the person will at some time have capacity in relation to the matter in question and (b) if it appears likely that he will, when that is likely to be' (MCA 2005 s4(3)).
2	'[S]o far as reasonably practicable, permit and encourage the person to participate, or to improve his ability to participate, as fully as possible in any act done for him and any decision affecting him' (MCA 2005 s4(4)).
3	'[C]onsider, so far as is reasonably ascertainable– (a) the person's past and present wishes and feelings (and, in particular, any relevant written statement made by him when he had capacity), (b) the beliefs and values that would be likely to influence his decision if he had capacity, and (c) the other factors that he would be likely to consider if he were able to do so' (MCA 2005 s4(6)).

19 MCA 2005 s4(1).
20 MCA 2005 s4(11).

4	'[T]ake into account, if it is practicable and appropriate to consult them, the views of' the following people: '(a) anyone named by the person as someone to be consulted on the matter in question or on matters of that kind, (b) anyone engaged in caring for the person or interested in his welfare, (c) any donee of a lasting power of attorney granted by the person, and (d) any deputy appointed for the person by the court,' as to the matters mentioned in subsection 3 and what would be in the person's best interests (MCA 2005 s4(7)).
5	Not be motivated by a desire to bring about his death where the determination relates to life-sustaining treatment and considering whether the treatment is in the best interests of the person concerned (MCA 2005 s4(5)). ('Life-sustaining treatment' means treatment which in the view of a person providing healthcare for the person concerned is necessary to sustain life: s4(10).)

3.68 As to the five best interests considerations in the table:

1) The first of these considerations (MCA 2005 s4(3)) differs from the second guiding principle (MCA 2005 s1(3)), which stated that a person is not to be treated as unable to make a decision unless all practicable steps to help them to do so have been taken without success.

   Even if the person cannot *presently* make their own decision (for example, with the assistance of family members and simple, clear explanations) and so lacks capacity to decide the matter, one must consider if and when they are likely to have that capacity.

   It may be that with more time to reflect, further treatment, improved health, reduced medication levels, clearer explanations and the benefit of discussing the options with family members, trusted friends or an advocate, they are likely to develop or recover the capacity to decide.

   If so, this must be considered when deciding what is in their best interests. Depending on the urgency, it may be in their best interests to postpone the decision until they can make it for themselves.

2) The second best interests consideration (MCA 2005 s4(4)) makes a different point to that made by the second guiding principle (MCA 2005 s1(3)). The point here is that, if where the person cannot make their own decision because all practicable steps to help them to do so have failed, they must still be permitted and

encouraged to participate in the decision-making process and any act done on their behalf. This is, of course, provided that this is reasonably practicable.

3) The third best interest consideration (MCA 2005 s4(6)) draws attention to five matters:
   i) the person's present wishes and feelings;
   ii) the person's past wishes and feelings;
   iii) the beliefs and values that would be likely to influence their decision if they had capacity;
   iv) any relevant written statement made by the person when they had capacity (this could be a written statement about the treatment which the person wishes to receive rather than to reject);
   v) the other factors that they would be likely to consider if they were able to do so.
4) Provided that it is practicable and appropriate, the fourth best interests consideration (MCA 2005 s4(7)) imposes a requirement to consult carers, nominated persons and persons appointed under the MCA 2005 about the person's wishes, feelings, beliefs and values, and the factors which they would have been likely to take into account if they still had capacity to make their own decision.

   Clearly, family members and non-professional carers will often know much more than the professionals about the person's wishes, feelings, beliefs, values, life goals and views concerning care and treatment. Proper consultation and sharing of information is critical to building up a true picture of the person's best interests.
5) The final listed matter (MCA 2005 s4(5)) provides that any person determining whether life-sustaining treatment is in the best interests of the person concerned must not be motivated by a desire to bring about their death. This legal requirement ties in with section 62 which states that nothing in the Act constitutes a defence to a charge of manslaughter or murder or is to be read or taken as legalising or authorising assisted suicide.

3.69 None of the listed best interests considerations has automatic precedence.[21] This would be impossible, given that the person determining best interests must also consider any other (unlisted) relevant considerations of which they are aware.

21 See *ITW v Z* [2009] EWHC 2525 (Fam), (2009) 12 CCLR 635, per Munby J (as he then was) at para 32.

3.70 The weight to be attached to the various factors depends on the circumstances of the particular individual. A feature or factor which in one person's situation may carry great, possibly even preponderant, weight may in another, superficially similar, case carry much less, or even very little, weight. Sometimes one or more features or factors may be of 'magnetic importance' in influencing or even determining what is in the person's best interests.[22]

3.71 The person who determines best interests does not incur any legal liability for their determination simply because a court later comes to a different view. The MCA 2005 provides that there is sufficient compliance with section 4 if, having complied with the requirements of the section, the person 'reasonably believes' that what they do or decide is in the best interests of the person concerned.[23] Unless one takes a peculiarly authoritarian view, in many situations more than one belief can reasonably be held. It is quite possible that family members and/or members of the multi-disciplinary team may 'reasonably' believe something different.

Best interests and substituted judgment

3.72 To what extent must the aim of the person determining best interests be to identify and make the decision which they believe the person themselves would have made if they had, or still had, capacity to make it?

3.73 'Substituted judgment' is a principle which holds that surrogate decisions should be made by establishing as accurately as possible the decision which the incapacitated person would have made for themselves if they had capacity.

3.74 The Law Commission argued that 'best interests' on the one hand and 'substituted judgment' on the other were not in fact mutually exclusive. It favoured a 'best interests' criterion which contained a strong element of 'substituted judgment'.[24]

3.75 A main reason for rejecting a pure substituted judgment test was not that the views, beliefs and values of an incapacitated person were unimportant but that they are important:

> One of the failings of a pure 'substituted judgment' model is the unhelpful idea that a person who cannot make a decision should be

22 *ITW v Z* at para 32.

23 MCA 2005 s4(9).

24 Law Com No 231 para 3.25.

treated as if his or her capacity were perfect and unimpaired, and as if present emotions need not also be considered.[25]

3.76 One must take into account and give weight to the person's present wishes and feelings, and what they now view as important, and not just the values and beliefs which they held when they had capacity, even if more objective.

3.77 Furthermore, as the Commission noted when rejecting a pure substituted judgment approach, if a person has never had capacity then 'substituted judgment' is impossible and there is no viable alternative to a best interests approach.[26]

Safety, health, care, treatment and liberty

3.78 It must not be assumed that because the decision concerns care or medical treatment that therefore the person's care and medical treatment, and physical safety, are the most important considerations. There will usually be many other competing factors to consider, such as a person's attachment to their home, their privacy and sense of security at home, their attitude towards institutional life and the importance to them of their freedom.

3.79 The importance of individual liberty is of the same fundamental importance to incapacitated people who still have clear wishes and preferences about where and how they live as it is for those who remain able to make capacitous decisions. This desire to determine one's own interests is common to almost all human beings. Society is made up of individuals, and each individual wills certain ends for themselves and their loved ones, and not others, and has distinctive feelings, personal goals, traits, habits and experiences. Because this is so, most individuals wish to determine and develop their own interests and course in life, and their happiness often depends on this. The existence of a private sphere of action, free from public coercion or restraint, is indispensable to that independence which everyone needs to develop their individuality, even where their individuality is diminished, but not extinguished, by illness. It is for this reason that people place such weight on their liberty and right to choose.

25 Law Com No 231 para 3.29.

26 See further in this regard *Re Jones* [2014] EWCOP 59.

Wishes, feelings and objectivity

3.80 The fact that the individual's past and present wishes, feelings, beliefs and values must be considered[27] tells us that this is not a sterile objective test of best interests.

3.81 It is not a case of trying to determine what some hypothetical objective or rational person would decide in this situation when presented with these choices. Nor are aiming at nothing more sophisticated than to impose on the individual an objective and rational analysis based on professional expertise of what they ought sensibly to do in that situation.

3.82 The law requires objective analysis of a subject not an object. The incapacitated person is the subject. Therefore, it is *their* welfare in the context of *their* wishes, feelings, beliefs and values that is important. This is the principle of beneficence which asserts an obligation to help others further *their* important and legitimate interests, not one's own.

3.83 That this is so is emphasised by Lady Hale in the *Aintree* case:[28]

> Finally, insofar as Sir Alan Ward and Arden LJ were suggesting that the test of the patient's wishes and feelings was an objective one, what the reasonable patient would think, again I respectfully disagree. The purpose of the best interests test is to consider matters from the patient's point of view. That is not to say that his wishes must prevail, any more than those of a fully capable patient must prevail. We cannot always have what we want. Nor will it always be possible to ascertain what an incapable patient's wishes are. Even if it is possible to determine what his views were in the past, they might well have changed in the light of the stresses and strains of his current predicament. In this case, the highest it could be put was, as counsel had agreed, that 'It was likely that Mr James would want treatment up to the point where it became hopeless'. But insofar as it is possible to ascertain the patient's wishes and feelings, his beliefs and values or the things which were important to him, it is those which should be taken into account because they are a component in making the choice which is right for him as an individual human being.

3.84 It also emerges from various decisions of the former President of the Court of Protection, Sir James Munby. Naturally, precisely how much weight to give to a person's present wishes and feelings will depend on the particular context and the individual's circumstances. The

27 MCA 2005 s4(6).

28 *Aintree University Hospitals NHS Foundation Trust v James* [2013] UKSC 67, (2013) 16 CCLR 554 at para 45.

relevant circumstances will include the degree of their incapacity; the strength and consistency of their views; the possible impact on them of knowing that their wishes and feelings are not being given effect to; the extent to which their wishes and feelings are, or are not, rational, sensible, responsible and pragmatically capable of sensible implementation; and the extent to which their wishes and feelings, if given effect to, can properly be accommodated within the overall assessment of what is in her best interests. However, while the weight to be attached to the person's wishes and feelings will always be case-specific and fact-specific, their wishes and feelings will always be a significant factor to which the court must pay close regard.[29]

3.85 The drawing up of a 'balance sheet' in personal welfare cases, listing the actual and potential advantages and disadvantages of each alternative,[30] should not be a dry accountant's exercise which omits what is personal, but one that includes the 'personal' element of 'personal welfare'. It is also important that, if a balance sheet is to be used, it should only be used as a route to judgment and not a substitute for the judgment itself.[31]

3.86 Whatever weight is given to the person's wishes and feelings, it is imperative not to reformulate them and claim to know better than they do what they truly wish, feel or will; in other words, not to be an 'aesthetic bully'.[32]

Summary – waypoint

3.87 There is a lot here for a reader new to the subject to grapple with, so it is worth summarising where we have got.

29 *ITW v Z* [2009] EWHC 2525 (Fam), (2009) 12 CCLR 635, per Munby J at para 35.

30 *Re S (adult's lack of capacity: carer and residence)* [2003] EWHC 1909 (Fam), [2003] FLR 1235, (2004) 7 CCLR 132.

31 See *B v D* [2017] EWCOP 15, [2017] COPLR 347 at para 40. The current Vice-President of the Court of Protection, Hayden J, has made clear that he does not find balance sheets helpful in cases concerning medical treatment: see, for instance, *Cambridge University Hospitals NHS Foundation Trust v AH (by her litigation friend, the Official Solicitor)* [2021] EWCOP 51, at para 66.

32 Care must be taken not to treat humanity as the raw material upon which the professional imposes her or his creative will, for the last century exposed the dangers of this way of thinking. It is, Berlin suggested, a form of thinking to which the scientist may be especially prone; for if, as Comte believed, scientific method will in due course reveal all truths, then what case is there for freedom of opinion or action, at least as an end in itself, and why should any conduct be tolerated that is not authorised by appropriate experts? See Sir I Berlin, *Four essays on liberty*, OUP, 1969, pp150–151.

3.88 So far, in general terms, we have looked at three things:

1) the statutory principles to be applied to anything and everything done under the MCA 2005;
2) what we mean by lacking capacity to make a decision for oneself;
3) what we mean by best interests, and how to go about determining what is in a person's best interests.

We have also seen that the decisions which may be made for someone under the Act can relate to their personal welfare or to their property and financial affairs.

3.89 In diagrammatic form, this is where we have reached:

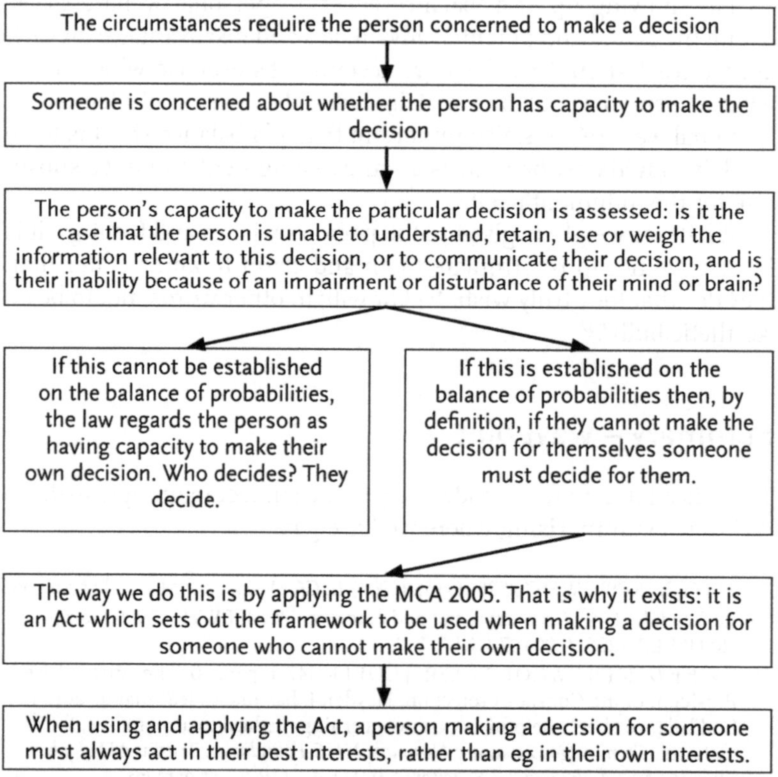
The circumstances require the person concerned to make a decision
Someone is concerned about whether the person has capacity to make the decision
The person's capacity to make the particular decision is assessed: is it the case that the person is unable to understand, retain, use or weigh the information relevant to this decision, or to communicate their decision, and is their inability because of an impairment or disturbance of their mind or brain?
If this cannot be established on the balance of probabilities, the law regards the person as having capacity to make their own decision. Who decides? They decide.
If this is established on the balance of probabilities then, by definition, if they cannot make the decision for themselves someone must decide for them.
The way we do this is by applying the MCA 2005. That is why it exists: it is an Act which sets out the framework to be used when making a decision for someone who cannot make their own decision.
When using and applying the Act, a person making a decision for someone must always act in their best interests, rather than eg in their own interests.

The statutory mechanisms

3.90 That helps but takes matters only so far.

3.91 What does the phrase, 'The way the person does that is by applying the MCA 2005', mean in practice? Are there forms or documents to complete, does an application need to be made to a court, does a decision-maker need to be formally appointed, and so on?

3.92 Put differently, we now know the principles, but what are the mechanisms – the mechanics of getting the job done?

Four main mechanisms

3.93 There are four main decision-making mechanisms, four ways of making decisions under the MCA 2005.

3.94 All of them are relevant to personal welfare decision-making. Only two of them – lasting powers of attorney (LPA) and the Court of Protection – are relevant to financial and property-related matters.

Arrangements made by the person themselves when they had capacity	
1) Advance decisions to refuse treatment	An adult with capacity to do so may make an advance decision to refuse a particular treatment at a later date should they lack capacity at that later time to decide whether or not to receive it. Because the decision was made when the person still had capacity, subject to certain exceptions it is binding on clinicians.
2) Lasting powers of attorney (LPA)	An adult with capacity to do so may make an LPA appointing one or more trusted persons to make decisions for them at a later date which they lack capacity to make for themselves. There are two types of LPA. One is used to authorise the person's chosen attorney(s) to make personal welfare decisions; the other is used to authorise making financial and property-related decisions on the individual's behalf. (LPAs replaced the old-style enduring powers of attorney (EPAs), which were limited to authorising financial and property-related decisions and could not provide for personal welfare matters. Previously made EPAs continue to have effect but no new ones may be created.)
Arrangements which can be made for them after capacity has been lost	
3) Court orders	The Court of Protection can make the particular decision(s) on the person's behalf or appoint a person called 'a deputy' to make personal welfare and/or financial and property-related decisions for the person as and when they arise.

4) Section 5	MCA 2005 s5 relates only to personal welfare matters and is an exemption from legal liability provision. In general terms, it states that a carer (paid or unpaid) will not be liable for non-negligent care and treatment given to an incapacitated person provided they comply with the conditions set out in section 5.

3.95 It is helpful to say a little more about this overall decision-making structure.

Above and below the line

3.96 The first two mechanisms – the 'above the line' mechanisms in the table above – are things which adults with capacity can do for themselves to plan for the day when they lose capacity:

- As regards personal welfare matters, they can make a decision in advance to refuse a particular treatment or treatments they dislike and/or appoint a person or persons they trust to make future personal welfare decisions for them which they lack the capacity to make.
- From this it can be seen that if a person lacks capacity to make the decision in question the first thing to do is to check whether they made their own arrangements to cater for this situation when they had capacity. If so then, unless their arrangement is invalid or inapplicable for some proper legal reason, apply this mechanism. If not 'go below the line' and – unless there are appropriate ways of dealing with the situation outside the MCA 2005 – make an application to the Court of Protection or rely on the protection afforded by section 5.
- As regards financial and property-related matters, the only mechanism 'above the line' is an LPA for property and financial matters.
- If the person has made an LPA (or previously an old-style EPA) then unless it requires registration, or is invalid or inapplicable for some proper legal reason, this is the appropriate mechanism to use.
- Because only adults (people aged 18 or over) can make these 'above the line' arrangements, necessarily it follows that if the incapacitated person is a child there cannot exist a valid LPA, EPA or advance decision to refuse treatment. In their case it will always be necessary either to go 'below the line' or to seek an alternative to the MCA 2005, such as parental authority or a provision of the Children Act 1989 or MHA 1983.

Going below the line

3.97 If the incapacitated person did not make their own 'above the line' arrangements in anticipation that subsequently they might lack capacity to make this decision, it will be necessary to resort to the two remaining mechanisms, 'below the line':

- As regards financial and property-related matters, the only mechanism 'below the line' is a court application. The usual application is to apply to the court for it to appoint a 'deputy for property and affairs' on the incapacitated person's behalf. The person appointed, who is often a close relative or a solicitor, is authorised by the court to deputise for the incapacitated person and to make financial and property-related decisions for them, subject to any restrictions in the court order. Because routine financial decisions – for example, paying bills – are needed on a day-to-day or week-to-week basis, this is more practical than going to court each time a financial decision is required.
- As regards personal welfare matters – for example, decisions about providing care or treatment to the individual – there are two options: making an application to court or applying section 5.

3.98 For reasons that may not always be valid, the Court of Protection has sometimes discouraged the appointment of personal welfare deputies (see also para 3.127 below).

3.99 An application for a court order should be made if it is in the person's best interests – for example, because the care or treatment is particularly intrusive, there is a significant dispute about what is in the person's best interests or appointing a personal welfare deputy is in the person's best interests.

3.100 In practice, almost all routine care and treatment is provided under the protection of section 5 without a court order or deputy in place. Many routine treatment and care decisions are not opposed by the incapacitated person, their family or paid carers. For example, decisions about bathing and treating an unconscious person or a decision to dress and help feed someone with severe dementia. Other decisions, where there is some difference of opinion, can be resolved by holding a best interests meeting at which the options are discussed and a resolution reached. In all of these cases, what is happening in legal terms is that the care and treatment is being provided in reliance on the last mechanism, section 5, and there will be no application to the Court of Protection for it to authorise the step in question.

3.101 MCA 2005 s5 does not as such authorise providing any care or treatment; rather, it exempts a person who does provide an incapacitated person with care or treatment from any legal liability, provided they reasonably believe it is in the individual's best interests and the other section 5 conditions are satisfied.

More about advance decisions

3.102 The purpose of this chapter is not to provide an exhaustive statement of the law, but to introduce the reader to the basic MCA 2005 principles and structures applicable to Court of Protection work. There are a few points concerning advance decisions which it is useful to know at the outset.

An advance decision 'to refuse treatment'

3.103 MCA 2005 s24(1) provides that an 'advance decision' means a decision made by an adult 'when he has capacity to do so' that if:

> (a) at a later time and in such circumstances as he may specify, a specified treatment is proposed to be carried out or continued by a person providing health care for him, and
> (b) at that time he lacks capacity to consent to the carrying out or continuation of the treatment,
>
> the specified treatment is not to be carried out or continued.

3.104 From this, it can be seen that:

- An advance decision can only relate to 'treatment' proposed by someone providing health care, not personal care. The term 'treatment' includes 'a diagnostic or other procedure'.[33] The intention presumably is that a person cannot refuse basic personal care which they may require upon becoming incapacitated such as shelter, feeding, drinking, clothing and washing. There is no right to die in squalor.
- Second, a person with capacity may decide in advance what treatment to refuse but not what treatment to receive. A clinician

33 See MCA 2005 s64(1).

cannot be required to give treatment which they consider is clinically inappropriate.[34]

- Third, on a literal reading, the right is to refuse a particular specified treatment, not to refuse treatment by a specified health care provider or treatment at a specified hospital or place.

Effect of advance decisions

3.105 The effect of a valid advance decision which it is accepted is applicable to the particular treatment is that the incapacitated person is treated as having made the decision with capacity on the future date when they would otherwise be given the treatment.[35] In other words, notwithstanding that the person now lacks capacity to consent or to refuse consent to the treatment, it operates as a valid and binding refusal of that treatment.

Formalities

3.106 In terms of the formalities, an advance decision can be expressed 'in layperson's terms',[36] provided of course it is sufficiently clear what treatment is being ruled out and the circumstances in which it is not to be given.

3.107 An advance decision to refuse treatment need not be in writing unless it relates to life-sustaining treatment. In this instance, to be applicable it must be in writing and include a statement 'to the effect that it is to apply to that treatment even if life is at risk'.[37] It must then be signed by the relevant person (or by someone in their presence and at their direction) in the presence of a witness who then signs as a witness.[38] These formalities exist because the individual may literally be signing their life away.

34 A person can of course set out in writing in advance what treatment they wish to receive if and when they lack capacity and this must be taken into account when deciding what treatment (if any) is in their best interests: see MCA 2005 s4(6)(a). However, such a statement is not binding in the way that an advance decision made under section 24 is. Since it is not binding, nothing has been decided in advance.

35 MCA 2005 s26(1).

36 MCA 2005 s24(2).

37 MCA 2005 s25(5)(a).

38 MCA 2005 s25(5).

3.108 The person concerned may withdraw or alter their advance decision at any time they have capacity to do so,[39] and a withdrawal (including a partial withdrawal) of an advance decision which relates to life-sustaining treatment need not be in writing.[40]

Validity and applicability of advance decisions

3.109 A person does not incur liability for the consequences of withholding or withdrawing a treatment if at the time the person reasonably believes that an advance decision refusing the treatment exists which is 'valid and applicable' to the treatment.[41]

3.110 Conversely, a person is liable in law to the incapacitated person if the person carries out or continues a particular treatment when at the time they are satisfied that an advance decision refusing the treatment exists which is 'valid and applicable' to it.[42]

3.111 The Court of Protection may make a declaration as to whether an advance decision exists, is valid or is applicable to a particular treatment.[43]

3.112 Nothing in an apparent advance decision stops a person providing life-sustaining treatment, or doing any act that the person reasonably believes to be necessary to prevent a serious deterioration in the person's condition, while a decision as respects any relevant issue is sought from the court.[44]

3.113 In any disputed case, it can be seen that the two key issues are validity and applicability.

Validity	• An advance decision is not binding if it is not valid. • An advance decision is not valid if the person lacked capacity to make it at the time. • An advance decision is not valid if the person withdrew it at any time when s/he had capacity to do so. • An advance decision is not valid if the person has done anything else clearly inconsistent with it remaining their fixed decision.[45]

39 MCA 2005 s24(3).
40 MCA 2005 s24(4).
41 MCA 2005 s26(3).
42 MCA 2005 s26(2).
43 MCA 2005 s26(4).
44 MCA 2005 s26(5).
45 This can include where the person has done something after having lost capacity: see *Re PW (Jehovah's Witness: validity of advance decision)* [2021] EWCOP 52, [2022] COPLR 201.

Applicability	• An advance decision is not binding if it is not applicable to the particular treatment. • An advance decision is not applicable if the person still has capacity to make this particular treatment decision (simply ask them for their decision). • An advance decision is not applicable if the treatment is not the treatment specified in the advance decision. • An advance decision is not applicable if any circumstances specified in the advance decision are absent. • An advance decision is not applicable if there are reasonable grounds for believing that circumstances exist which the person did not anticipate at the time of the advance decision which would have affected their decision. • An advance decision is not applicable to life-sustaining treatment unless it is verified by a statement to the effect that it is to apply to that treatment even if life is at risk, and the decision is in writing, signed and witnessed.

More about LPAs

3.114 Although not fully appreciated, the new personal welfare LPA was the 'game-changer' in the MCA 2005.

3.115 The previous common law position in relation to incapacitated persons was that the clinician, social worker or other professional carer was under a duty to give any treatment or care necessary to preserve their life, health or well-being which was in their best interests. In other words, the best interests care or treatment decision was taken by the relevant professional.

3.116 Where a registered LPA is in force, the position now is that there is in principle always someone from whom the relevant professional requires a consent. For as long as the receiver of the proposed care or treatment has capacity, treatment and care requires their consent. If they lack capacity to consent or refuse consent, the professional must go to the person nominated by them to make the decision. If the attorney feels *unable* to make the decision, for instance because they are overwhelmed by its consequences, they cannot be *forced* to and decision-making will revert to the process described elsewhere in this chapter.

3.117 This represents a considerable shift in the balance of power. Any adult with capacity can now nominate a trusted family member, friend, colleague or professional to make personal welfare decisions for them which they are unable to make in the future, in preference to leaving the best interests determination to the relevant professional.

3.118 The necessary detail is dealt with in the relevant chapters. However, it is probably helpful to emphasise the following points about LPAs at the outset:

- The person who makes the LPA is called the 'donor'. Strictly speaking, a person appointed is a 'donee'. However, in practice most people prefer 'attorney' because it is more natural and was the term used for many years in relation to the old-style EPAs.
- More than one attorney can be appointed but, if more than one, the document creating the LPA must state whether they are only authorised to make decisions jointly or can act alone or jointly ('jointly and severally').
- An LPA is not valid unless and until it has been registered (that is, stamped and entered on a register) by the Public Guardian.
- Completing an LPA is not difficult but involves using the prescribed form, and there are separate forms for the creation of a personal welfare LPA and for the creation of a property and financial affairs LPA.
- An attorney must act in accordance with the statutory principles and best interests requirements in MCA 2005 s4.
- What constitutes a 'personal welfare' decision is not exhaustively defined. However, the range of best interests decisions which may be made by a personal welfare attorney on behalf of an incapacitated person is likely to be extensive. The main Code of Practice suggests that they include decisions about:
  - where the incapacitated person should live and whom they should live with;
  - their day-to-day care, including diet and dress;
  - whom they may have contact with;
  - consenting to or refusing consent to medical examination and treatment;
  - necessary arrangements for medical, dental or optical treatment;
  - community care assessments and the provision of community care services;
  - participation in social activities, leisure activities, education or training;
  - personal correspondence and papers;
  - rights of access to personal information about the donor;
  - complaints about their care or treatment.[46]

46 See MCA Code of Practice para 7.21. The Code of Practice is under revision at time of writing.

- This decision-making authority is subject to the restriction that a donee may only make personal welfare decisions which they reasonably believe the donor lacks capacity to make for themselves.[47] Furthermore, a personal welfare donee has no authority to give or to refuse consent to life-sustaining treatment unless the LPA document expressly permits this.[48]
- A donor may revoke the power at any time they still have capacity to do so.[49]
- The Court of Protection can revoke an LPA in certain circumstances, for example where a donee has contravened their authority or has behaved in a way which is not in the person's best interests.[50]

3.119 Mencap, a charity supporting people with a learning disability and their families and carers, has published a suite of 'easy read' guides to the making and use of health and welfare LPAs.[51] They give easy-to-follow guidance on the setting up of such an LPA, and then separate guidance to the attorney as to how the attorney should operate the LPA.

Interplay between advance decisions and LPAs

3.120 An advance decision to refuse a particular treatment is not valid if the person later makes an LPA authorising an attorney to decide whether or not to consent to the particular treatment in the event they lack capacity to make the decision.[52]

3.121 That restriction aside, the existence of an LPA does not in itself prevent an advance decision from being valid and applicable.[53] Indeed, a valid and applicable advance decision made by a person with capacity after making an LPA prevents their donee from consenting to that treatment. This is because, other than the statutory exception just referred to, a donee's authority is subject to the person's advance decision 'rights' in MCA 2005 ss24–26.[54] Furthermore, a donee may only make those personal welfare

47 MCA 2005 s11(7)(a).
48 MCA 2005 s11(7)(c) and (8).
49 MCA 2005 s13(2).
50 MCA 2005 s22(3).
51 Available at: www.mencaptrust.org.uk/guides-lasting-power-attorney.
52 MCA 2005 s25(2)(b).
53 MCA 2005 s25(7).
54 MCA 2005 s11(7)(b).

decisions which they reasonably believe the donor lacks capacity to make[55] and the advance decision has effect as if the refusal of treatment was made with capacity at the time the treatment is proposed.[56]

More about court orders and deputies

3.122 Court orders and deputies are dealt with in greater detail later. However, in brief, MCA 2005 s15 provides that the Court of Protection may make declarations as to:

- whether a person has or lacks capacity to make a decision specified in the declaration;
- whether a person has or lacks capacity to make decisions on such matters as are described in the declaration;
- the lawfulness or otherwise of any act done, or yet to be done, in relation to that person.

3.123 MCA 2005 s16 applies if a person lacks capacity in relation to a matter or matters concerning their personal welfare or property and affairs.[57] It enables the court by order to make such decisions on their behalf or to appoint a deputy to make the decisions for the person.

3.124 Without prejudice to MCA 2005 s4, the court may make an order or appoint a deputy on such terms as it considers are in the incapacitated person's best interests – and may do so even though no application is before it 'on those terms'.

3.125 Naturally, if the judge can make the decision, it will generally be inappropriate for them to authorise someone else to make it.

3.126 Consequently, the Act provides that a decision by the court is to be preferred to the appointment of a deputy to make a decision; and that the powers conferred on the deputy should be as limited in scope and duration 'as is reasonably practicable in the circumstances': see MCA 2005 s16(4).

Personal welfare deputies

3.127 Personal welfare deputy orders are considerably less common than property and affairs deputyships for reasons which seem invalid or inconsistent to some incapacitated people and their families.

55 MCA 2005 s11(7)(a).
56 MCA 2005 s26(1).
57 MCA 2005 s16(1).

3.128 The circumstances in which it is appropriate to appoint a personal welfare deputy are explained in *Re P*,[58] *G v E, Manchester City Council and F*,[59] *SBC v PBA and others*,[60] *A Local Authority v TZ (No 2)*[61] and *Re Lawson, Mottram and Hopton (appointment of personal welfare deputies)*.[62]

3.129 Roderic Wood J observed in *SBC v PBA and others* that the test to be applied when determining whether to appoint a deputy (whether to manage a person's property and affairs or take decisions regarding their health and welfare) is to be derived from the unvarnished words of the MCA 2005. What is in the person's best interests is the governing criterion, as with all other decisions made under the Act.

3.130 As Roderic Wood J noted, nothing in the then two leading cases on the appointment of deputies compelled a different conclusion: *Re P (vulnerable adult: deputies)*[63] and *G v E (deputyship and litigation friend)*.[64]

3.131 Naturally, it will rarely be appropriate for a judge to effectively deputise someone to judge a dispute or make a decision brought before the court for a judicial decision. In *Re Lawson, Mottram and Hopton (appointment of personal welfare deputies)*,[65] Hayden J held that:

- The MCA Code of Practice was wrong insofar as it suggested[66] that the starting point is that personal welfare deputies should only be appointed in the most difficult cases.
- Each case fell to be decided on its merits, and by reference to whether an appointment is in the best interests of the person.
- The person's wishes and feelings will form an aspect of that decision (for instance if it is clear that P would wish a family member to be appointed to be their personal welfare deputy).
- The proper operation of MCA 2005 ss4 and 5 means that, in practice, personal welfare deputies will not often be appointed, in particular because the appointment should not be seen, in and of itself, as less restrictive of P's rights and freedoms.

58 [2010] EWHC 1592 (Fam), [2010] 2 FLR 1712.
59 [2010] EWHC 2512 (COP), (2010) 13 CCLR 610.
60 [2011] EWHC 2580 (Fam), [2011] COPLR Con Vol 1095.
61 [2014] EWHC 973 (COP), [2014] COPLR 159.
62 [2019] EWCOP 22, [2019] 1 WLR 5164.
63 [2010] EWHC 1592 (Fam), (2010) 13 CCLR 610.
64 [2010] EWHC 2512 (COP), [2010] 2 FLR 1712.
65 [2019] EWCOP 22, [2019] 1 WLR 5164.
66 At para 8.38. The draft MCA Code of Practice published for consultation in March 2022 reflects the position as set down in this case.

3.132 One advantage of an approach that takes each case on its merits is that a symmetry emerges from the shadows which is consistent with the ethos of the legislation in enabling a judge to advance the best interests of people who have lost capacity. An individual who still had capacity when the Act came into force was or is able to appoint a trusted person such as a spouse or partner to make future decisions for them which they cannot make. What, though, of the person who lost capacity to appoint their spouse or partner before the Act was in force? As in the case of their property, surely the court has the option of appointing as their deputy the person they would have appointed as their attorney. That is, of course, provided on the evidence that the advantages are real and it is in their best interests.

3.133 On this construction, the argument that property and financial affairs deputyship is somehow always different in kind to personal welfare deputyship is artificial. For many incapacitated people, just as many personal welfare decisions as financial decisions are made for them each day or week.

3.134 Ultimately, the decision in each case ought to turn on what is in that person's best interests. It would be strange if the statutory framework is that a judge ought not to appoint a personal welfare deputy even if they are satisfied that it is in the person's best interests. Where does this leave their wishes and feelings? What of their beliefs and values, and the views expressed by the persons consulted? MCA 2005 s4 says that the judge must have regard to these considerations. The position of a spouse or partner of 50 years' duration or the parent of a brain-damaged child who is having their 18th birthday is not the same as that of a paid carer.

3.135 A judge, though, should not appoint someone to be a deputy where the person wants to be appointed not to make decisions, but so that they are listened to by the relevant health and social care professionals – no matter how understandable that desire might be.[67]

Who may be a deputy

3.136 A deputy must be an adult (aged 18 or over) or, in the case of property and affairs deputyships, a trust corporation.[68]

3.137 A person may not be appointed as a deputy without their consent.[69]

67 See *Re CB* [2021] EWCOP 43, [2021] COPLR 549.

68 MCA 2005 s19(1).

69 MCA 2005 s19(3).

3.138 The court may appoint the holder of a specified office or position as the person's deputy,[70] for example the holder of a particular local authority finance office. This avoids the need for a new order when the current holder of the post moves on and is replaced.

Two or more deputies

3.139 The court may appoint two or more deputies to act jointly, jointly or alone ('severally'), or jointly in respect of some matters and jointly or alone in respect of others.[71]

A deputy's powers and duties

3.140 Subject to certain restrictions dealt with below, the court may confer on a deputy such powers and/or impose on them such duties as it thinks necessary or expedient for giving effect to, or otherwise in connection with, their appointment.[72]

3.141 A deputy:

- is appointed to make decisions on the incapacitated person's behalf, not on the court or judge's behalf (in other words, the deputy is deputising for the person concerned, not for the judge or court);
- is to be treated as that person's agent in relation to anything done or decided within the scope of their appointment and in accordance with the Act;[73]
- must act in accordance with the authority conferred by the court.

3.142 With regard to property and affairs deputyships, the court may confer on a deputy powers to:

- take possession or control of all or any specified part of the person's property;
- exercise all or any specified powers in respect of it, including such powers of investment as the court may determine.[74]

70 MCA 2005 s19(2).

71 MCA 2005 s19(4).

72 MCA 2005 s16(5).

73 As a general proposition, whatever P has power to do for themselves (eg request a community care assessment) may be done by their agent and, conversely, what a person cannot do for themselves (eg force a doctor to give a particular drug) cannot be done by their agent.

74 MCA 2005 s19(8).

Interplay between advance decisions and deputyship

3.143 A personal welfare deputy may not consent to treatment which is prohibited by an advance decision because the authority conferred on a deputy is subject to the provisions of the Act.[75] Furthermore, MCA 2005 s20(1) provides that a deputy does not have power to make a decision for the person if they know or have reasonable grounds for believing that the person has capacity to decide the matter, and the advance decision has effect as if the refusal was made with capacity at the time the treatment is proposed.[76]

Restrictions on deputies

3.144 The Act provides that certain powers may not be conferred on or exercised by a deputy:

Powers which a deputy does not have	Powers which the court may not give a deputy
With regard to the person's personal welfare	
A deputy does not have power to make a decision in relation to a matter if they know or have reasonable grounds for believing that the person concerned has capacity in relation to that matter (MCA 2005 s20(1)).	The court may not give a deputy power to prohibit a named person from having contact with the incapacitated person (MCA 2005 s20(2)(a)). Power to prohibit such contact is reserved to judges (and personal welfare attorneys).
A deputy may not refuse consent to the carrying out or continuation of life-sustaining treatment in relation to the relevant person (MCA 2005 s20(5)).	The court may not give a deputy power to direct a professional responsible for the relevant person's health care to allow a different professional to take over that responsibility (MCA 2005 s20(2)(b)).
A deputy may not do an act that is intended to restrain the person unless the four conditions set out in MCA 2005 s20(7) are satisfied.	The court may not give a deputy power to make a decision on the relevant person's behalf which is inconsistent with a decision made, within the scope of their authority and in accordance with the Act, by a donee of a lasting power of attorney (MCA 2005 s20(4)).

75 MCA 2005 s20(6).
76 MCA 2005 s26(1).

A deputy is not authorised to deprive the person of their liberty.	
With regard to the person's property and affairs	
A deputy does not have power to make a decision in relation to a matter if they know or have reasonable grounds for believing that the person concerned has capacity in relation to that matter (MCA 2005 s20(1)).	The court may not give a deputy power to make a decision on the relevant person's behalf which is inconsistent with a decision made, within the scope of their authority and in accordance with the Act, by a donee of an LPA (MCA 2005 s20(4)).
	A deputy may not be given powers with respect to the execution of a will for the person concerned (MCA 2005 s20(3)(b)).
	A deputy may not be given powers with respect to the settlement of any of the person's property, whether for P's benefit or for the benefit of others (MCA 2005 s20(3)(a)).
	A deputy may not be given powers with respect to the exercise of any power (including a power to consent) vested in the person whether beneficially or as trustee or otherwise (MCA 2005 s20(3)(c)).
General limitations imposed by the Act	
The authority conferred on a deputy is subject to the provisions of the Act and, in particular, to MCA 2005 s1 (the principles) and s4 (best interests): MCA 2005 s20(6).	

Powers of deputies compared with donees and the court

3.145 It can be seen that deputies have fewer powers than donees and judges:

	Court	LPA donee	Deputy
Power to refuse life-sustaining treatment	✓	✓	✗
Power to give or refuse consent to other forms of treatment and care	✓	✓	✓

Power to restrain P to give care or treatment	✓	✓	✓
Power to prohibit contact with a named person	✓	✓	✗
Power to allow another person to take charge of P's treatment	✓	✓(?)	✗
Power to deprive P of their liberty	✓	✗	✗

3.146 A donee's powers are subject to any conditions and restrictions in the LPA and any authority to give or refuse life-sustaining treatment is conditional on it being expressly provided for in the LPA. Similarly, a deputy's authority is subject to any duties and conditions specified in the order appointing them. A judge, deputy or personal welfare donee may not make a decision for a person if they know or reasonably believe that the person has capacity to make their own decision. There may be other qualifications in a particular case such as the existence of an advance decision and the table compares the maximum powers which each decision-maker may possess.

More about section 5 ('acts in connection with a person's care or treatment')

3.147 Everyone is liable to an incapacitated person for criminal acts such as ill-treatment or neglect and for negligent treatment or care. MCA 2005 s5 does not affect these liabilities.[77]

3.148 Instead, it provides that a professional or non-professional carer is regarded as having the person's consent for any treatment or care given to them if five conditions are satisfied.

3.149 Because of this presumed consent, the legal effect is that the carer need not worry that technically they may be committing an assault because the person concerned lacks capacity to consent to the operation, treatment or piece of care being provided.[78] Likewise, provided that the conditions are satisfied, the carer is protected even if later it is held that a person who objected to care or treatment did in fact have capacity at the time and a right to refuse it.

77 MCA 2005 s5(3).

78 MCA 2005 s5(2). The person who does the act (D) does not incur any liability in relation to the act that he would not have incurred if P had had capacity to consent in relation to the matter, and had consented to D's doing the act.

3.150 The essential thrust of the provision is that those who care for people without capacity should be protected from legal liability provided that the care is reasonably believed to be in the person's best interests and is performed without negligence.

3.151 Because MCA 2005 s5 is a 'freedom from legal liability' provision, it is of a different kind to those sections of the MHA 1983 which authorise treatment or care without consent but which require applications and medical recommendations to be completed before the power arises.

3.152 There are no statutory forms to complete under section 5, although in non-routine situations it is sensible to keep some kind of written record of the decision. Rather, the section is there to be invoked and relied on as a defence if the carer is later challenged and it is suggested that they are legally liable to the incapacitated person for their act.

<table>
<tr><th colspan="3">THE FIVE SECTION 5 CONDITIONS</th></tr>
<tr><td>1</td><td>The act is one undertaken 'in connection with' another person's care or treatment.</td><td>• This embraces nursing, medical and dental treatment, speech and language therapy, psychological interventions, social work, community care and also personal care such as assistance with washing, dressing, personal hygiene and feeding.
• The phrase 'in connection with' indicates that section 5 also covers diagnostic examinations and tests, assessment procedures, taking a person to see their doctor, arranging the provision of a care service, etc.</td></tr>
<tr><td>2</td><td>The person doing it takes reasonable steps to establish whether the recipient has capacity.</td><td rowspan="2">Unless the carer has given it to the lawyers 'on a plate', they will have taken reasonable steps to establish lack of capacity – which does not necessarily require a formal capacity assessment – and reasonably believe that the person lacks capacity to make this particular treatment or care decision for themselves.</td></tr>
<tr><td>3</td><td>The person reasonably believes that the recipient lacks capacity.</td></tr>
<tr><td>4</td><td>The person reasonably believes that it will be in their best interests for the act to be done.</td><td>• This involves applying the best interests considerations in section 4.
• More than one thing can reasonably be believed and the level of protection to a carer is generous to that extent.</td></tr>
</table>

5	If the person uses restraint, they reasonably believe *both* that it is necessary to do the act in order to prevent harm to the person and that the act is a proportionate response to the likelihood of their suffering harm and the seriousness of that harm.	• The Act states that for these purposes one person restrains another if they a) use, or threaten to use, force to secure the doing of an act which they resist, or b) restrict their liberty of movement, whether or not they resist. • Restricting someone's liberty or using force is always undesirable. If used to give care or treatment, the requirement here is essentially that the care or treatment is necessary and does more good than the restraint does harm; it is the lesser of two evils.

3.153 When providing care or treatment, it may seem tempting to seek to rely on section 5 in all situations, and thereby to avoid the complexities of advance decisions, LPAs and court orders.

3.154 This would be a mistake. For example, the MCA 2005 provides that:

- nothing in section 5 affects the operation of sections 24–26 (advance decisions to refuse treatment);[79] and that
- section 5 does not authorise a person to do an act which conflicts with a decision properly made within the scope of his authority by a donee of a lasting power of attorney or a deputy appointed by the court.[80]

3.155 It is not possible, therefore, simply to leap to section 5 as a way around having to learn the framework. The first step is to consider whether the person made an applicable advance decision or LPA. Only if they did not provide for this situation, or their advance decision or LPA is irrelevant or invalid, does one move on to considering the need for a court application or relying on section 5.

3.156 Furthermore, one cannot reasonably believe that it is in the person's best interests to delay going to court and to continue to provide the care or treatment under section 5 if there is a significant

79 MCA 2005 s5(4).

80 MCA 2005 s6(6). This prohibition does not prevent a person providing life-sustaining treatment, or doing any act which they reasonably believe to be necessary to prevent a serious deterioration in P's condition, while a decision as respects any relevant issue is sought from the court: see MCA 2005 s6(7).

disagreement about whether it is in the person's best interests which cannot be resolved.[81]

A general framework

3.157 It is now possible to set out a framework that is generally applicable to all personal welfare decisions made under the MCA 2005:

	Step	**Example**
1	**The circumstances require a person to make a decision in connection with their own care or treatment**	Mr Smith is being examined at hospital and it is apparent that he has a significant heart condition. Treatment is recommended.
2	**Someone is concerned about whether this person has capacity to make the decision for themselves**	Mr Smith also suffers from quite severe dementia. The doctor is concerned that he appears not to understand the relevant information being conveyed concerning the diagnosis, the treatment which is necessary medically and the prognosis with and without treatment.
3	**The person's capacity to make the particular decision is assessed: is it the case that the person is unable to understand, retain, use or weigh the information relevant to this decision, or to communicate their decision, and is their inability because of an impairment or disturbance of their mind or brain?**	Mr Smith's capacity to make his own decision about whether or not to have the proposed assessment procedures and treatment is assessed.

81 See *An NHS Trust v Y* [2018] UKSC 46, [2018] 3 WLR 751, (2018) 21 CCLR 410, concerning the scope of MCA 2005 s5 in the context of life-sustaining treatment, and also chapter 23.

	Step	Example
4	**If the doctor cannot show reasonable grounds for considering the person to be unable to make the decision, the law regards them as having capacity to make the decision. Who decides? They decide**	On the evidence, the doctor has a reasonable belief Mr Smith lacks capacity to make the treatment decision. He cannot understand, retain and weigh the relevant information because of an impairment of the brain (dementia).
	If the person cannot make the decision themselves, and the decision cannot be postponed, someone will have to decide how to proceed.	
5	**The way the person does this is by applying the MCA 2005. It is an Act which sets out a framework to be used when making a decision for someone who lacks the capacity to make their own decision.**	The doctor applies the treatment and care framework set out in the MCA 2005. The Act contains four mechanisms in relation to providing a person with care and/or treatment. The person must take each in turn and work out which is applicable.
6	**When the relevant person still had capacity to do so, did they make a valid advance decision to refuse this particular treatment?**	There are caveats, but in general terms if Mr Smith did then this is the relevant mechanism to apply.
7	**When the relevant person still had capacity to do so, did they make a (registered) LPA which covers care or treatment decisions of this kind?**	There are caveats, but in general terms if Mr Smith did then this will be the relevant mechanism to apply. Ask the attorney (donee) whether or not they consent to this treatment on Mr Smith's behalf.
8	**If there does not appear to be a relevant advance decision or LPA, is this a situation where it is necessary or appropriate as being in the person's best interests to apply for a court order as to whether the care or treatment should be given?**	If it is such a situation, apply to the court. If not, then there are only four mechanisms and, since three of them are properly 'not in play', there is only one left. Therefore, the care or treatment can be given under the MCA 2005 if the section 5 conditions are satisfied but not otherwise.

	Step	Example
9	**Apply MCA 2005 s5 – are the five section 5 conditions satisfied?**	(a) Is this something connected with the person's care or treatment? (b) Have reasonable steps been taken to establish whether the person has capacity to make their own decision about whether or not to receive this particular piece of care or treatment? (c) Does the person providing the care or treatment reasonably believe that the other person lacks capacity to decide this? (d) Does the person reasonably believe that it will be in their best interests to receive this piece of care or treatment (or for an act connected with it to be done)? (e) If restraint is used to provide the care or treatment, does the person reasonably believe that the care or treatment is necessary and does more good than the restraint does harm (see above for the precise criteria)?

3.158 This gives us a fairly clear framework for providing care and/or treatment to an incapacitated person who has a physical health problem such as a heart or liver disorder. Indeed, once one has learned this basic framework, it can be used in relation to all treatment and care decisions, from helping an incapacitated person to dress to a decision to switch off life-support:

Example 1

3.159 P was recently involved in a car accident and has sustained severe brain injury. P's life is being sustained artificially. There is no prospect of recovery. Medical professionals and family members agree that the situation is hopeless and must now consider whether to stop treatment.

3.160 Taking each of the listed steps in turn:

a) The circumstances require P to make a decision about his care or treatment, ie to consent or refuse consent to what is proposed.
b) Someone is concerned that P lacks capacity to make this decision for himself.

c) P's capacity to make this particular decision is assessed.
d) Because of an impairment or disturbance of P's mind or brain, P is unable to understand, retain or weigh the information relevant to the treatment decision or is unable to communicate his decision.
e) Because P cannot make the decision for himself, someone must decide for P. The way this is done is by applying the MCA 2005 which sets out the framework to be used when making a decision for someone who lacks the capacity to make their own decision.
f) The MCA 2005 contains four mechanisms to consider in turn.
g) If P made a valid advance decision refusing life-sustaining treatment in such circumstances when he had capacity, the general rule is that it must be respected.
h) If P has a registered LPA appointing a trusted person to make decisions for P about life-sustaining treatment in such circumstances, generally that person has the right to decide.
i) If there is no advance decision or LPA which resolves the matter, is this a case where an application to the Court of Protection is necessary or in P's best interests, for a judge to decide whether or not further treatment is hopeless? That would be unusual. Sadly, following serious road traffic accidents, it is not uncommon in intensive care settings for professionals and family members to agree that the situation is now hopeless. A judge would have to decide any application on the evidence and here all of the evidence is consistent and to the same effect. In reality, a court application would simply cause delay and avoidable distress to no benefit.
j) If the first three mechanisms are not applicable, the only one left is MCA 2005 s5.[82]
k) Is this decision something connected with P's care and treatment? Yes.
l) Have reasonable steps been taken to assess P's capacity? Yes.
m) Is it reasonably believed that P lacks capacity to make this decision for himself? Yes.

82 This could apply also if a family member was an attorney, and knew that further treatment was not what P would have wished, but cannot – when it comes to it – face being responsible for refusing further treatment on their behalf. If they made clear that they were simply 'frozen' and could not make any decision, MCA 2005 s5 would provide the route by which the doctors could proceed. It would be wrong to rely upon this route if the family member was, in fact, saying that they thought that P would want treatment to continue: at that point there would be a disagreement which would have to be resolved.

n) Is it in P's best interests to stop treatment? This is the issue. Address it by considering the best interests requirements and considerations in MCA 2005 s4 ('The person making the determination must consider all the relevant circumstances and, in particular, must . . .').

o) The restraint condition adds little here if stopping treatment is in P's best interests. Insofar as this technically involves the use of a degree of restraint, it is reasonable to believe that this is a necessary and proportionate response.

Example 2

3.161 P has developed very advanced dementia and now lives in a care home. Sadly, he seems to have lost the ability to respond to his environment, to speak and to control movement. He cannot sit without support. He requires a wheelchair, is doubly incontinent and needs help with all personal care. He is being taken to a local park and, because it is raining, needs his footwear changing. A care assistant, Ms Q, puts some boots on before taking him out.

3.162 If this was ever challenged then, taking each of the listed steps in turn:

a) The circumstances require P to make a decision about his care or treatment, ie to consent or refuse consent to what is proposed.

b) Based on their long acquaintance, his care assistant's concern is that he no longer has capacity to make this decision for himself, or indeed even to understand that a change of footwear needs to be considered.

c) P's capacity to make this particular decision is assessed. In reality, the care assistant is not aware that she is assessing P's capacity but, if she was ever asked why she acted as she did, she might say that:
   - she knows P and his needs very well;
   - for some time P has been unable to make his own decisions about what to wear because his cognitive decline is now such that he cannot understand or use relevant verbal or visual information;
   - medical and nursing assessments have confirmed this; and
   - P did not demonstrate any awareness of or response to the suggestion or prompt that his footwear was changed.

   In other words, because of an impairment or disturbance of P's mind or brain he is unable to understand, retain or weigh the information relevant to the care decision or is unable to communicate his decision.

d) Because P cannot make this care decision for himself, someone must decide for him. The way this is done is by applying the MCA 2005 which sets out the framework to be used when making a decision for someone who lacks the capacity to make their own decision.
e) The Act contains four mechanisms to consider in turn.
f) Any advance decision which P has made will relate only to treatment, not care, and will not be relevant.
g) If there is a registered LPA appointing a trusted person to make care decisions, then P's care must be consistent with any consents and refusals of consent made by his attorney on his behalf in relation to his care plan.
h) This is not a case where an application is going to be made to the Court of Protection for an order permitting the care assistant to change his footwear. If P already has a personal welfare deputy appointed for him by the court then, as with an LPA, his care must be consistent with any consents and refusals of consent made by his deputy in relation to his care plan.
i) If none of the first three mechanisms are applicable, apply MCA 2005 s5.
j) Is this decision something connected with P's care and treatment? Yes.
k) Have reasonable steps been taken to assess P's capacity? Yes. It is not necessary in the circumstances to do a fresh formal capacity assessment.
l) Is it reasonably believed that P lacks capacity to make this decision for himself? Yes.
m) Is it in P's best interests to have this piece of care? Yes. If the care assistant was ever asked to justify the decision, she might say:
   - that P's care plan is devised to promote his best interests;
   - that it includes visits to local places;
   - that P seems to enjoy the outings and there is a health benefit.

   In section 4 terms, it is in P's best interests to give him this piece of care having regard to his known wishes and feelings, the views concerning his best interests of family members and professional carers and other relevant considerations, such as the care plan which addresses his health and welfare needs.
n) The restraint condition adds little here. If changing P's footwear before going out is in his best interests then, insofar as this tech-

nically involves a degree of force, it is reasonable to believe that it is a necessary and proportionate response.

3.163 The second example may seem rather artificial, although relatives and care home staff are sometimes involved in disagreements about clothing and dressing. Its main function here is to emphasise that once one has learned the above model it can be used as a framework for any situation, from routine care to intensive care. It is therefore worth considering.

Deprivation of liberty

3.164 To recap, the MCA 2005 in its original form included a fairly clear framework in relation to providing care or treatment to an incapacitated person.

3.165 It did not adequately address the problem that an incapacitated person who did not wish to receive this care or treatment was often not permitted to leave the hospital, care home or other place where it was being given.

3.166 In certain circumstances, MCA 2005 s5 permitted a carer to restrict the person's liberty of movement and to use reasonable and proportionate force in order to give the care or treatment. Likewise, if the individual had a personal welfare donee or deputy appointed for them, that person could authorise such restraints in identical circumstances.[83]

3.167 What no one other than a judge of the Court of Protection could do was to authorise depriving the person of their liberty in order to give them the care or treatment. The authority conferred by section 5, deputyship and an LPA was limited to restrictions of liberty which did not amount to deprivation of liberty:

83 MCA 2005 ss11 and 20.

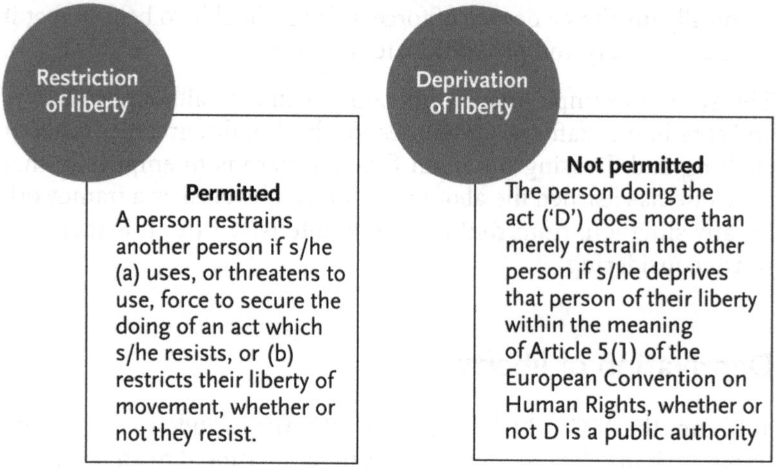
Restriction of liberty
Permitted
A person restrains another person if s/he (a) uses, or threatens to use, force to secure the doing of an act which s/he resists, or (b) restricts their liberty of movement, whether or not they resist.
Deprivation of liberty
Not permitted
The person doing the act ('D') does more than merely restrain the other person if s/he deprives that person of their liberty within the meaning of Article 5(1) of the European Convention on Human Rights, whether or not D is a public authority

3.168 This was a problem for three reasons:

a) First, if the reality was that many care homes were depriving residents of their liberty, it was not practical for them to obtain a court order authorising this for every such resident. They would soon be bankrupt given the relatively modest fees paid by local authorities and the costs involved in applying for court orders.
b) Second, if the reality was that many incapacitated people were being deprived of their liberty in relatives' homes or in supported living accommodation, it was similarly unrealistic to expect families and housing providers to obtain court orders for each person affected.
c) Third, there was uncertainty as to the dividing-line between restricting someone's liberty of movement (permitted without a court order) and depriving them of their liberty (not permitted without a court order). It was not always clear to care providers where the line was, nor therefore whether it had been crossed and a court order was required.

3.169 Even allowing for some uncertainty, it was obvious that a considerable number of incapacitated hospital patients and care home residents were being deprived of their liberty without any proper legal order or authority permitting it, without the use of clear and explicit criteria, with no proper application process and no adequate form of judicial review.

3.170 In essence, this was what was commonly referred to as the 'Bournewood gap' as a result of a famous case in which the European

Court of Human Rights found that this lacuna in English and Welsh law breached the European Convention on Human Rights (ECHR).[84]

3.171 The eventual consequence was that a new scheme was inserted in the MCA 2005 (by the MHA 2007) which enables hospitals and care homes to obtain a legal authority to deprive people of their liberty under the MCA 2005 without having to obtain an order from a court.

3.172 This authority – called a standard authorisation – can be obtained from the relevant local authority (or in Wales, in some cases, the National Assembly), with the incapacitated person having a right to apply to court for a review of the authorisation.[85]

3.173 This 'deprivation of liberty safeguards' scheme – known colloquially as the 'DOLS scheme' – commenced operation on 1 April 2009. The scheme applies only to hospitals and care homes. It seeks to ensure that the relevant person is assessed at least annually by two suitably qualified and independent professionals. They must certify that the care and treatment arrangements made for the incapacitated person are in their best interests, necessary to protect them from harm, proportionate and so forth.

The six requirements

3.174 MCA 2005 Sch A1 provides that deprivation of liberty under the scheme requires that six requirements are satisfied: the age; mental health; mental capacity; best interests; no refusals; and eligibility requirements.

3.175 The purpose of the requirements is the same as in the case of the 'sectioning criteria' in the MHA 1983, ie to prevent people who do not meet the statutory requirements from being deprived of their liberty.

The age requirement

3.176 The age requirement is simply that the person must be an adult. A child may not be deprived of their liberty under a standard authorisation.

84 *HL v UK* (App No 45508/99) [2004] ECHR 471, (2004) 7 CCLR 498, ECtHR ('the Bournewood case').

85 The authorisations are commonly referred to as 'DOLS orders'. Most of the relevant provisions are set out in two schedules at the end of the MCA 2005: Schs A1 and 1A. Even now it is not known publicly who devised the scheme and drafted the schedules, which were not put out to prior consultation.

The mental health requirement

3.177 The second requirement is simply that the person suffers from a mental disorder within the meaning of the MHA 1983 (but disregarding the requirement in the 1983 Act sometimes to demonstrate that a learning disability is associated with abnormally aggressive or seriously irresponsible conduct).

The mental capacity requirement

3.178 The requirement here is that the person lacks capacity to make their own decision about whether or not to be accommodated in the particular hospital or care home in order to receive the care or treatment in question.

The best interests requirement

3.179 This is really four requirements masquerading as one. It is satisfied only if all of the following conditions are satisfied:

1) the person is being detained in the hospital or care home for the purpose of being given care or treatment in circumstances which amount to a deprivation of their liberty;[86]
2) this is in their best interests;
3) this is necessary in order to prevent harm to them; and
4) their detention in the care home or hospital for the purpose of being given care or treatment in circumstances which amount to a deprivation of their liberty is a proportionate response to the likelihood of them suffering harm, and the seriousness of that harm (if they were not so detained).

3.180 If one or more of the four conditions is not satisfied, the person does not meet the best interests requirement; and, because a standard authorisation may only be given if all six requirements are satisfied in their totality, that person may not be deprived of their liberty under the scheme.

86 More precisely, they are a 'detained resident'. By MCA 2005 Sch A1 para 6, a 'detained resident' is 'a person detained in a hospital or care home – for the purpose of being given care or treatment – in circumstances which amount to deprivation of the person's liberty'. If this is not the case, then no authorisation is required, because there is no deprivation that requires authorisation.

The no refusals requirement

3.181 The essence of this oddly phrased requirement is to ensure that the relevant person does not have in place a valid LPA or advance decision which a standard authorisation would breach.

3.182 Specifically, a person may not be deprived of their liberty in a care home or hospital in order to give them treatment or care which by virtue of their advance decision may not be given to them under the MCA 2005.

3.183 Nor may they be deprived of their liberty in order to give them treatment or care which their personal welfare donee under an LPA has refused consent to on their behalf.

3.184 The underlying premise is that one cannot use the MCA 2005 to break the MCA 2005.

The eligibility requirement

3.185 This requirement is concerned with the inter-relationship between the MHA 1983 and the MCA 2005.

3.186 In certain situations where the MHA 1983 is 'in play', detention or compulsory treatment or care takes place under that Act, not the MCA 2005. This requirement is dealt with below, after some relevant provisions of the MHA 1983 have first been considered.

The DOLS scheme and the four mechanisms

3.187 The four care and treatment mechanisms set out in the original MCA 2005, which were explained above, are unaffected by this 'standard authorisation 'DOLS scheme' and are still good law.

3.188 Where a person lacks capacity to consent to treatment or care, their treatment or care is subject to any relevant advance decision, LPA or court order, or is given under the protection of MCA 2005 s5. All that has changed is that if it is necessary and in their best interests to deprive them of their liberty so that this care or treatment can be given, then a standard authorisation is required alongside (or a court order).

3.189 So, for example, a person may be deprived of their liberty at a care home under a standard authorisation in order to give them the care determined to be in their best interests, which in practice most often is provided under the protection of section 5.

The *Cheshire West* and *Re X* cases

3.190 Because the DOLS scheme just described only applies to care homes and hospitals, the absence of a simple equivalent procedure for people deprived of their liberty in other settings such as supported living accommodation or their own homes remained a problem. This gap was considered in the *Cheshire West* case[87] where the Supreme Court found that three incapacitated people were deprived of their liberty in non-care home settings and that they were equally entitled to a proper legal process under ECHR Article 5 (right to liberty and security).

3.191 Following the judgment in *Cheshire West*, a non-statutory 'streamlined procedure' designed to comply with Article 5 was formulated by the then President of the Court of Protection, Sir James Munby, in *Re X and others (deprivation of liberty)*[88] and *Re X (deprivation of liberty) (No 2)*[89] and brought into law as Part 2 of Court of Protection Rules (COPR) Practice Direction (PD) 10AA, now PD 11A.

3.192 Although the President's approach was criticised in some respects by the Court of Appeal in *Re X (Court of Protection practice)*,[90] the '*Re X* Procedure' remains that to follow where authorisation is required under the MCA 2005 for a deprivation of liberty outside hospital or a care home. It involves filing an application form (form COPDOL11) together with certain required information such as a copy of the person's care plan, and paying a fee. If the person affected has not expressed any objection to the care arrangements and application is uncontroversial the judge may authorise the deprivation of liberty 'on the papers', and further identical reviews then take place at least annually.

Three murky streams forming one river

3.193 It can be seen that there are now three different procedures in existence in relation to a deprivation of liberty under the MCA 2005:

- As originally enacted, the MCA 2005 required an application to a judge under MCA 2005 s16 in all cases where authorisation for a deprivation of liberty was sought. This approach is still used for complicated cases where a deprivation of liberty is but one of a

87 *Cheshire West and Chester Council v P* [2014] UKSC 19, (2014) 17 CCLR 5.

88 [2014] EWCOP 25, [2014] COPLR 674, (2014) 17 CCLR 297.

89 [2014] EWCOP 37, (2014) 17 CCLR 464.

90 [2015] EWCA Civ 599, [2015] COPLR 582.

range of issues requiring the court's determination. For example, an application may require the court to determine the relevant person's best interests in relation to deprivation of liberty, residence, family contact, treatment and care.

- There is then the 'DOLS scheme' inserted in the MCA 2005 (by the MHA 2007), which commenced operation on 1 April 2009. This is an administrative procedure which enables a deprivation of liberty in a care home or hospital to be authorised by a local authority, with a right of appeal to a judge of the Court of Protection.
- There is also now a '*Re X* procedure' designed to enable a deprivation of liberty in a setting other than a care home or hospital to be authorised by a judge on the papers in appropriate cases. This is discussed further in chapter 22.

3.194 The reason for this unsatisfactory piecemeal approach is not hard to discern. Twenty years ago, the Department of Health strongly opposed the original 'Bournewood' application and, having eventually lost that case, over many years it has fought hard to minimise the impact.

3.195 As discussed at para 3.236, following a review by the Law Commission, the Mental Capacity (Amendment) Act (MC(A)A) 2019 has now been passed to replace the 'DOLS scheme.'

Ten commandments

3.196 Deprivation of liberty schemes are intended to be protective schemes. Anyone who is deprived of their liberty – that is, who is under another person's complete and effective control and is not free to leave – is vulnerable to abuse.

3.197 The subject is dealt with in detail in chapter 22. However, at this preliminary stage, the relevant domestic and convention law can be understood as imposing ten commandments:

1) Deprivation of liberty requires that the person has been confined in a particular restricted space 'for a not negligible length of time'. This is the 'objective condition'.
2) In addition, a 'subjective condition' must be met before a person is deprived of their liberty. This is that they have not validly consented to their confinement.
3) However, a person cannot consent to being confined if they lack capacity to consent to it.

4) The distinction between deprivation of liberty and restriction of liberty is one of degree or intensity, not one of nature or substance.
5) The starting-point is the specific situation of the individual concerned. Account must be taken of a whole range of factors arising in the particular case, such as the type, duration, effects and manner of implementation of the measure in question.
6) The critical issue is whether the professionals exercise 'complete and effective control' over the person's care and movements, so that the individual is 'under continuous supervision and control and is not free to leave'.
7) The state's obligations under the convention are engaged if a public authority is directly involved in the detention (it is 'imputable to the state'), but also where the state has breached its positive obligation to protect the person against interferences by private persons.
8) This is because ECHR Article 5(1) imposes a positive obligation on the state to protect the liberty of its citizens. The state is obliged to take measures providing effective protection of vulnerable persons, including reasonable steps to prevent a deprivation of liberty of which the authorities have or ought to have knowledge.
9) It is also essential that the person concerned should have access to a court and the opportunity to be heard in person or, where necessary, through some form of representation. Fundamental procedural safeguards are called for in order to protect the interests of detained persons who, on account of their mental disabilities, are not fully capable of acting for themselves.
10) With regard to persons in need of psychiatric treatment in particular, the state is also under an obligation to secure to its citizens 'their right to physical integrity' under ECHR Article 8. Private psychiatric institutions, in particular those where persons are held without a court order, need not only a licence, but also competent supervision by the state on a regular basis of whether confinement and medical treatment is justified.

Detention and deprivation of liberty

3.198 A critical thing to understand is that in law there is a distinction between 'detention' and 'deprivation of liberty'. This is counter-intuitive because most people use these words interchangeably in everyday conversation.

3.199 At first blush, the first commandment appears to be one of those vague legal statements which are of no use to anyone. However, that is not so.

3.200 In our field of interest, the particular restricted space in which the relevant person is confined will often be a hospital, a part of a hospital such as a ward or A&E department, a police station or a care home. A person who is prevented from leaving hospital for a brief period, say for one hour, until he can be assessed by a doctor is being 'detained' there but usually is not in fact being 'deprived of his liberty'. This is because his confinement is, in this sense, for a 'negligible length for time'.

3.201 Compare that with the case of an older person in a care home. Their situation for the next hour may be exactly the same: they are not allowed to leave. However, it may be the case that nor will they be allowed to leave tomorrow or next week or next month. Their confinement in a particular restricted space is 'for a not negligible length of time', in which case the objective condition for a deprivation of liberty is met.

3.202 The doctor's action is an emergency measure which does not carry with it any general claim to a right to control the person's liberty of movement; to prevent that person from being 'at liberty'. It is only in the second case that the 'confiner' claims a general power or right to control the person's liberty of movement to the extent that a right to confine is claimed. Unlike me or you, the concrete reality is that their liberty is no longer theirs and is in the hands of another: they do not decide whether and when to leave, where to go, when if at all to return, what they do when they leave, and so on.

Interplay of the MCA 2005 with the MHA 1983

3.203 The final matter to deal with in any overview of the personal welfare provisions is the interplay between the MCA 2005 and the MHA 1983.

Treating physical disorders

3.204 We have seen that it is relatively easy to understand when the MCA 2005 mechanisms apply in the case of care or treatment for a physical disorder such as a heart or liver disorder:

Physical disorders

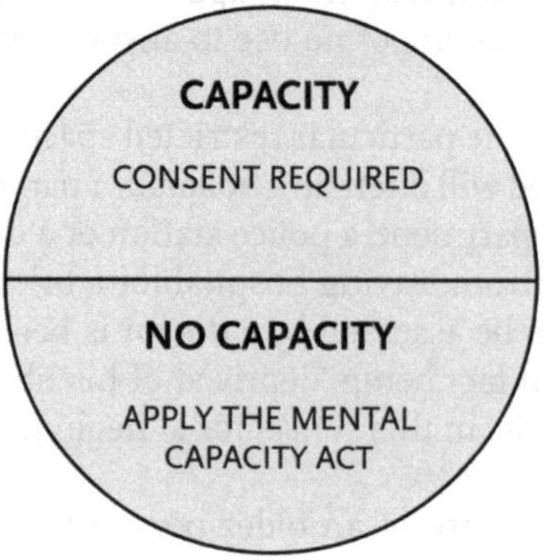

3.205 Because the MHA 1983 is only concerned with the treatment of mental disorders, (subject to one small caveat) the legal position of 'sectioned' patients with regard to treating their physical health problems is exactly the same as for everyone else, and is that set out in the diagram above.

Treating mental disorders

3.206 What then is the legal position where the proposed treatment is treatment for a mental disorder? Does the MHA 1983 or the MCA 2005 apply?

3.207 It is easier to understand the position if one considers first the simpler scheme set out in the MCA 2005 as originally enacted, before considering the modifications introduced by subsequent amendments and recent case-law.

The scheme set out in the original MCA 2005

3.208 The simpler scheme set out in the MCA 2005 as originally enacted was as follows:

- The general rule is (and remains) that the MCA 2005 applies whenever you wish to give care or treatment to an incapacitated person outside the terms of the MHA 1983.
- In other words, if the patient's treatment is covered by the terms of the MHA 1983 then that Act applies.
- If their treatment falls outside the MHA 1983, then the MCA 2005 will apply.

- Treatment may fall outside the MHA 1983 because it is treatment for a physical health problem (see above); or it may fall outside because it is treatment for a mental health problem but the MHA 1983 does not authorise giving it without the person's consent.
- In the second case, one then has to establish whether there is legal authority outside the MHA 1983 to give the treatment without the person's consent, which takes us to the MCA 2005.
- When, then, is treatment for mental disorder without consent not authorised under the MHA 1983? The simple answer is: when the individual is not subject to a section of that Act which authorises psychiatric treatment without consent.
- As is well-known, if a person has been 'sectioned' under the MHA 1983 the fact that the person is 'under a section' may permit professionals to give them psychiatric treatment without consent. If this is the case then the treatment is authorised under the MHA 1983 and it is not necessary to establish whether it is authorised under the MCA 2005.
- However, relatively few sections of the MHA 1983 in fact authorise treating an individual without their consent:

TREATING MENTAL DISORDER WITHOUT CONSENT	
Authorised by the MHA 1983 (or MHA 1983 rules apply)	**Not authorised – apply the MCA 2005**
Section 2 patients (those liable to be detained in hospital for assessment and any necessary treatment for up to 28 days)	Informal patients (those in hospital and in the community who are not presently subject to a section of the MHA 1983)
Section 3 patients (those liable to be detained in hospital for treatment for up to six or 12 months at a time)	Patients detained under the short-term sections of the MHA 1983 that have a maximum duration of 72 hours or less (ss4, 5(2), 5(4), 135, 136)
Patients subject to a Community Treatment Order (in certain circumstances)	Patients subject to guardianship under the MHA 1983 Conditionally discharged restricted patients Persons remanded to hospital by a criminal court for a report on their mental condition under MHA 1983 s35 Persons in prison, eg prison medical units

3.209 Naturally, many people find this confusing. When studying the right-hand column, it seems odd to them that a person may be detained or subject to a MHA 1983 'order' – such as short-term detention or guardianship – but their treatment or care be governed by a different Act, the MCA 2005.

3.210 The reason for this relates to the framework of the MHA 1983 and its interplay with the old common law rules which the MCA 2005 replaced. As enacted, the framework constructed by the MHA 1983 was more liberal than much of today's legislation.

3.211 Subject to complying with various procedural safeguards set out in MHA 1983 Part IV, such as obtaining a second-opinion, persons who were liable to be detained in hospital for up to 28 days (section 2) or for up to six months or more (section 3 and its criminal law equivalents) could be treated without their consent. In their case, their compulsory admission was founded on an application made, in most cases, by an independent approved social worker supported by two medical recommendations, one provided by a specialist.

3.212 People who were not considered to be so unwell as to require detention in hospital for those sorts of period were not liable to treatment without their consent under the Act, and therefore could only be so treated in the limited circumstances then permitted by the common law. These are all the people in the right-hand column now covered by the MCA 2005.

3.213 As can be seen from the right-hand column, the vast majority of people with mental health problems fell within this category, because on any given day relatively few people are subject to one of the more Draconian sections in the left-hand column.

3.214 Looking at who is in the right-hand column, the purpose of the holding sections with a maximum duration of 72 hours or less is to enable a person to be assessed, most often with a view to making an application under section 2 or 3. Because they have not yet been detained on the basis of an application supported by two medical recommendations, the MHA 1983 does not authorise their treatment without consent. Any treatment during this period had to be justifiable under common law.

3.215 The MCA 2005 replaced and replicated the common law in this area; hence the person is detained under one Act but potentially treatable under another.

3.216 Similarly, the MHA 1983 did not authorise giving treatment without consent to persons on community orders such as guardianship and those who had been conditionally discharged. Only patients who were liable to detention were liable to treatment without consent under the Act; and only then if the person was subject to the longer sections and certain legal formalities were observed. Similarly, therefore, any treatment without consent was given under the common law, which now has been replaced by the MCA 2005.

3.217 In diagrammatic form, therefore, the relationship with the MHA 1983 set out in the MCA 2005 in its original form was as follows:

Mental disorders

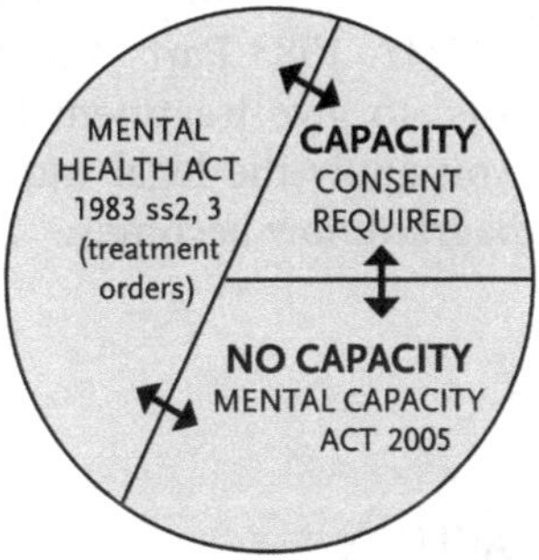

3.218 Looking at the diagram, where it was proposed to give a person treatment for mental disorder – antipsychotics, antidepressants, other medication, ECT (electroconvulsive therapy), etc – that person's situation would come within one of three legal categories, each of which is represented by a segment of the circle:

- If the person was subject to section 2 or one of the treatment orders in the MHA 1983, such as section 3, the rules in (Part IV of) the MHA 1983 applied and, subject to complying with the procedural safeguards set out there, the patient was liable to treatment without their consent.
- If the citizen was not subject to one of those MHA 1983 sections, they retained a citizen's usual rights and were in the same legal position as everyone else. If they had capacity (or, strictly speaking, it could not be established that they lacked it) then treatment required their consent; in short, they could refuse it. If they lacked capacity to make a decision about the treatment then the MCA 2005 applied – unless the patient was 'sectioned' at that point and taken into section 2 of the Act or one of its treatment sections, such as section 3.

3.219 And that is the purpose of the connectors in the diagram. The individual's situation is fluid, not static – the membranes (lines) separating the three segments are permeable and the individual will move across the lines from one segment to another as their mental health and capacity fluctuates, they are sectioned under section 2 or 3 or released from liability to detention under section 2 or 3.

3.220 That was the situation when the MCA 2005 first came into force – but it was then complicated by the MHA 2007.

3.221 There were two main changes to the simpler structure just described.

3.222 *First,* the MHA 2007 inserted a new 'community treatment order' (CTO) in the MHA 1983. The legal rules governing the treatment of patients on a CTO are set out in MHA 1983 Parts 4 and 4A. The general rule is that if it is proposed to give treatment for mental disorder to a person on a CTO you apply the legal framework in MHA 1983 Parts 4 and 4A. Our diagram now becomes:

Mental disorders

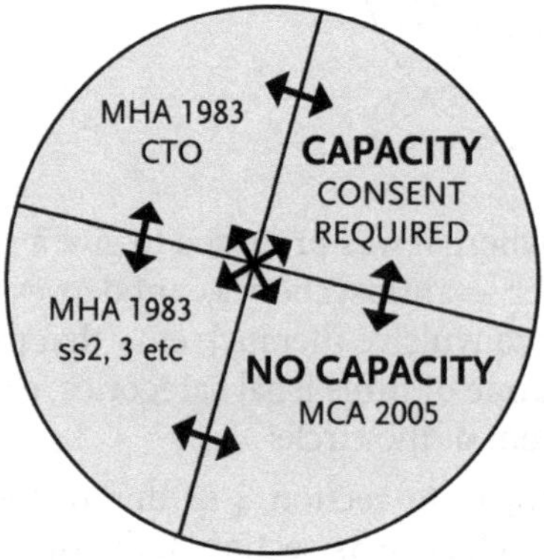

3.223 As can be seen, the individual may now be in one of four groups, and be moving between four groups.

3.224 As with most post-1983 mental health legislation, it is questionable whether the practical benefits justify the extra complexity and the legislation is poorly constructed.

3.225 *The second significant change* related to ECT. As far as antipsychotic and other medication for mental disorder is concerned, sectioning a person under section 2 or 3 still has the same effect as before: the MHA rules apply, not the MCA 2005. Because, as we have seen, the former permit treatment without consent, from a psychiatrist's point of view this may be a 'trump card' in terms of overcoming a patient's refusal to take prescribed medication. (Once the section comes to an end and the patient reverts to informal status, the same problem may of course represent itself.)

3.226 When it comes to ECT, however, taking a person into one of the treatment sections of the MHA 1983 (ss2, 3, etc) no longer necessarily has the effect of 'trumping' or circumventing the protections of the MCA 2005.

3.227 The new ECT rules inserted into the MHA 1983 by the MHA 2007 provide that a section 2 or treatment order patient with capacity cannot be given ECT to which they do not consent unless it can be justified as urgent treatment which is necessary to save their life or immediately necessary to prevent a serious deterioration of their condition.[91]

3.228 Likewise, unless it can be justified as urgent treatment on these terms, an incapacitated section 2 or treatment order patient cannot be given ECT if it would conflict with a relevant advance decision or with a decision made by the Court of Protection, a Court of Protection appointed deputy or a donee appointed under a personal welfare LPA.

3.229 What we see here for the first time is the autonomy provisions in the MCA 2005 starting to infiltrate and cut down the compulsory treatment provisions in the MHA 1983, at least as far as ECT is concerned, and the position is very similar with regard to CTOs.[92]

Deprivation of liberty and the MHA 1983

3.230 Turning to the interplay between the detention provisions in the MHA 1983 and the deprivation of liberty provisions in the MCA 2005, the MHA 1983 only permits detention in a hospital. However, when it comes to deprivation of liberty under the MCA 2005, the local authority standard authorisation scheme applies to hospitals *and* care homes; and under section 16 and the *Re X* procedures the Court of Protection can also authorise deprivation of liberty in any location. However, there are strict rules as to when the MCA 2005 can be used to deprive a person of their liberty in preference to the MHA 1983.

3.231 Where a person requires detention in a hospital for psychiatric treatment, the MCA 2005 is not to be used (in preference to the MHA 1983) if the individual falls within any of the following groups:

- People who are currently detained in a hospital under one of the following sections of the MHA 1983: ss2, 3, 4, 35–38, 44, 45A, 47, 48, 51.

91 For the precise criteria, see MHA 1983 s62.

92 See eg MHA 1983 s64D.

- People who, though not currently detained, are subject to one of these sections or to a CTO, if the care or treatment in question consists wholly or partly of medical treatment for mental disorder in a hospital.
- People who, though not currently detained, are subject to one of these sections, or to a CTO or guardianship, if accommodating them in the hospital or care home under the MCA 2005 would conflict with a requirement imposed on them under their MHA 1983 section.
- People who are subject to guardianship under the MHA 1983, if they object to being accommodated in the particular hospital for the purpose of being given some or all of the proposed medical treatment for their mental disorder (unless they have a donee or deputy who consents to each matter to which they objects).
- People who meet the criteria for being sectioned under MHA 1983 s2 or s3, if they object to being accommodated in the particular hospital for the purpose of being given some or all of the proposed medical treatment for their mental disorder (unless they have a donee or deputy who consents to each matter to which they object).
- Conversely, case-law has conclusively established that detention under the MHA 1983 is limited to detention in hospital. Conditions may not be attached by a tribunal, responsible clinician or the secretary of state under the MHA 1983 to a patient's discharge from hospital that have the effect of depriving the patient of their liberty in the community.
- In the case of CTOs:

  > 29. . . . the MHA does not give the RC power to impose conditions which have the concrete effect of depriving a community patient of his liberty within the meaning of article 5 of the European Convention. I reach that conclusion without hesitation and in the light of the general common law principles of statutory construction, without the need to turn further to the jurisprudence of the European Court of Human Rights . . .[93]

  However, if the patient lacks capacity to make the relevant decisions, it is possible for authority to be given under the MCA 2005 to authorise the deprivation of their liberty.
- In the cases involving the conditional discharge of restricted patients:

  > 38. . . . I conclude that the MHA does not permit either the FtT [Mental Health Tribunal] or the Secretary of State to impose condi-

93 *Welsh Ministers v PJ* [2018] UKSC 66, [2019] 2 WLR 82 per Lady Hale at para 29.

tions amounting to detention or a deprivation of liberty upon a conditionally discharged restricted patient.

33. . . . such a power . . . would be contrary to the whole scheme of the MHA.[94]

- However, if the patient lacks capacity to make the relevant decisions, there is nothing to stop the Mental Health Tribunal (or Mental Health Tribunal for Wales) co-ordinating the discharge of a patient on conditional discharge with the provision of authority under the MCA 2005 to deprive them of their liberty.[95]

Principles of mental health law

3.232 That, then, is the basic relationship between the MCA 2005 and the MHA 1983.

3.233 As a final point, when legislating in this area it is useful to bear the following principles in mind:[96]

1) It is unsatisfactory to seek to determine principles by reason only, without regard for human experience of the world within which principles are formulated and applied. Our value judgments are judgments about experienced objects.[97]
2) There are many reasons to limit state intervention in people's lives: errors in law spread their negative effects throughout the nation as opposed to individual errors that are limited in scope; the damage of erroneous laws affect citizens more than legislators, who are thus less inclined to repeal them; it takes longer to repair the damage done by legislation than the damage done by individuals by their own private choices; because of the constant watch of critics, politicians are less inclined to publicly admit error and undo the damage done; politicians are more inclined than citizens to make decisions based on political gain and prejudice, rather than principle.[98]
3) An effective democratic Constitution separates powers, the aim being to keep executive powers in check and under proper scru-

94 *Secretary of State for Justice v MM* [2018] UKSC 60, [2018] 3 WLR 1784 per Lady Hale at paras 33 and 38.

95 *MC v Cygnet Behavioural Health Ltd and Secretary of State for Justice* [2020] UKUT 230 (AAC), (2020) 23 CCLR 699.

96 A Eldergill, 'Is anyone safe? Civil compulsion under the draft Mental Health Bill', *Journal of Mental Health Law*, January 2003.

97 J Dewey, *The Quest for Certainty*, Milton, Balch & Co, 1929, at p265.

98 Benjamin Constant: *Political Writings*, trans and ed B Fontana, Cambridge University Press, 1988.

tiny, and so to secure good government. This is necessary because the 'whole art of government consists in the art of being honest',[99] and 'it is not by the consolidation, or concentration of powers, but by their distribution, that good government is effected'.[100]

4) Promoting liberty, protecting individuals from harm caused by those at liberty, and those not at liberty from abuse by those who are, alleviating suffering, and restoring to health those whose health has declined, are all legitimate objectives, in that they reflect values embraced by virtually all members of our society.[101]
5) We are, however, 'faced with choices between ends equally ultimate, and claims equally absolute, the realisation of some of which must inevitably involve the sacrifice of others'.[102] Whether individuals 'should be allowed certain liberties at all depends on the priority given by society to different values, and the crucial point is the criterion by which it is decided that a particular liberty should or should not be allowed, or that its exercise is in need of restraint'.[103]
6) When enacting mental health legislation, the legislature has generally sought to erect a balanced legal structure that harmonises three things: individual liberty; bringing treatment to bear where treatment is necessary and can be beneficial; the protection of the public.[104] Those we describe as 'patients' are themselves members of the public, so that the law must seek to ensure that members of the public are not unnecessarily detained, and also that they are protected from those who must necessarily be detained.
7) The purpose of compulsory powers, including 'best interests' interventions, is not to eliminate that element of risk in human life which is a consequence of being free to act and to make choices and decisions. Nor, strange though it may sound, is their purpose to protect an individual from risks which arise when their understanding of substantial risks, or their capacity to control behaviour associated with such risks, is significantly impaired by mental disorder. That is its function but not its

99 Thomas Jefferson: *Rights of British America, 1774. The Writings of Thomas Jefferson*, Memorial Edition, ed, Lipscomb & Bergh, Washington, DC, 1903–04.

100 Thomas Jefferson: *Autobiography, 1821. The Writings of Thomas Jefferson*, Memorial Edition (ed, Lipscomb & Bergh), Washington, DC, 1903–04, 1:122.

101 AC Eldergill, *Mental Health Review Tribunals — Law and Practice*, Sweet & Maxwell, 1997, p45.

102 Berlin, Sir I, *Four Essays on Liberty*, Oxford University Press, 1969, p168.

103 RWM Dias, *Jurisprudence*, Butterworths, 5th edn, 1985, p109.

104 Hansard, H C Vol. 605, col 276.

purpose: compulsory powers are means not ends. The purpose of compulsory powers is to increase human happiness or to reduce human suffering.

8) Consequently, when decision-making for incapacitated people we are seeking the outcome which maximises the individual's happiness not, if different, the one which is safest. All personal welfare decisions involve balancing competing risks of unhappiness of which the risk of physical harm is but one. Deprivation of liberty and compulsory treatment risk the loss of employment, family contact, self-esteem and dignity; unnecessary loss of liberty; institutionalisation; social isolation; and disabling adverse effects.
9) The use of compulsion has been permitted when significant harm is foreseeable if an individual remains at liberty. While we must do our best to assess the risks to a person's physical safety in any decisions we make for them in truth it is difficult to impossible to predict outcomes.
10) Other risks are, constitutionally, matters for citizens to weigh in their own minds. The purpose of compulsion is not to eliminate that element of risk in human life that is simply part of being free to act and to make choices and decisions. A person who obeys our laws is entitled to place a high premium on their liberty, even to value it more highly than their health. Subject to the stated limits, people are entitled to make what others regard as errors of judgement, and to behave in a manner which a doctor regards as not in their best interests, in the sense that it does not best promote health.
11) This desire to determine one's own interests is common to human beings, and so not to be portrayed as an abuse of liberty. On the one hand stands liberty, a right which the legislature and the law should always favour and guard, on the other licence, a wilful use of liberty to contravene the law, which the law must of necessity always punish.
12) Any power given to one person over another is capable of being abused. No legislative body should be deluded by the integrity of their own purposes, and conclude that unlimited powers will never be abused because they themselves are not disposed to abuse them.[105] Mankind soon learns to make interested uses of every right and power which they possess or may assume.[106]

105 Thomas Jefferson: *Notes on Virginia Q.XIII*, 1782, Memorial Edition (supra), 2:164.

106 Thomas Jefferson: *Notes on Virginia Q.XIII*, 1782, Memorial Edition (supra), 2:164.

13) This risk of abuse is multiplied if the individual is not free to escape abuse, is incapacitated or otherwise vulnerable, or their word is not given the same weight as that of others. Children and adults with mental health problems are particularly at risk and the law has usually afforded them special protection.

14) This protection involves imposing legal duties on those with power, conferring legal rights on those in their power, and independent scrutiny of how these powers and duties are exercised. The effectiveness of such schemes depends on whether, and to what extent, they are observed.

15) This is a matter of constitutional importance, for the observance of legal rights and the rule of law are the cornerstones of all liberal democracies. The rule of law 'implies the subordination of all authorities, legislative, executive [and] judicial . . . to certain principles which would generally be accepted as characteristic of law, such as the ideas of the fundamental principles of justice, moral principles, fairness and due process. It implies respect for the supreme value and dignity of the individual.'[107]

16) In any legal system, 'it implies limitations on legislative power, safeguards against abuse of executive power, adequate and equal opportunities of access to legal advice and assistance, . . . proper protection of the individual and group rights and liberties, and equality before the law . . . It means more than that the government maintains and enforces law and order, but that the government is, itself, subject to rules of law and cannot itself disregard the law or remake it to suit itself.'[108]

17) In framing these principles and laws, the legislature has sought to be just, justice being 'a firm and continuous desire to render to everyone that which is his due.'[109]

18) When new laws are necessary, they should impose minimum powers, duties and rights; provide mechanisms for enforcing duties and remedies for abuse of powers; be unambiguous, just, in plain language, and as short as possible.

19) Because there is a long record of experimentation in human conduct, cumulative verifications give these principles a well-

107 David M Walker, *The Oxford Companion to Law*, Clarendon Press, Oxford, 1980, p1093.

108 David M Walker, *The Oxford Companion to Law*, Clarendon Press, Oxford, 1980, p1093

109 Justinian, Inst, 1, 1.

earned prestige. Lightly to disregard them is the height of foolishness.[110]

The future

Liberty Protection Safeguards

3.234 The Law Commission's review of deprivation of liberty (noted at para 3.197 above) included proposals and a draft bill not just to replace the 'DOLS scheme' but also to introduce amendments to the body of the MCA 2005 in part to bring the Act into greater compliance with the UN Convention on the Rights of Persons with Disabilities (discussed further in chapter 25).[111] The government introduced the Mental Capacity (Amendment) Bill in July 2018, including a version of the 'Liberty Protection Safeguards' (LPS) scheme proposed by the Law Commission,[112] but without the proposed amendments to the body of the MCA 2005. The bill had a rocky journey through parliament, in particular because of the substantial role that the government sought to give to care home managers in the assessment process. Their role was significantly watered down during the course of the bill's passage through parliament, which was completed in May 2019. Subsequently, the government has announced that they do not intend to commence the care home manager provisions at all (although were consulting upon this in the context of the wider consultation noted below). At the time of writing, there is no implementation date for the scheme, proposed dates of October 2020 and April 2022 having been postponed. The timeline given by the government in March 2022 as part of its consultation on the draft MCA Code of Practice (see below), did not include a specific date for implementation, but is suggestive of implementation of LPS during the course of 2023, our view being that it is most likely to be October 2023. Updates to the position will be given on the Court of Protection Handbook website.[113]

3.235 In some ways, the new LPS scheme can be seen as a reaction to the fact that the DOLS scheme simply does not cover the gamut of

110 J Dewey, *Human Nature and Conduct*, Allen & Unwin, 1922.

111 Law Commission, *Mental Capacity and Deprivation of Liberty: Report* (March 2017), available at: www.lawcom.gov.uk/project/mental-capacity-and-deprivation-of-liberty/.

112 In a new Sch AA1 to the MCA 2005.

113 A useful source of LPS resources is: www.mentalcapacitylawandpolicy.org.uk/resources-2/liberty-protection-safeguards-resources/.

situations in which a person should be seen to be deprived of their liberty. Most obviously, it applies much more broadly, including to those aged 16 and above,[114] and in any setting (including a person's own home), as opposed to being limited to care homes and hospitals. Other key differences to the DOLS regime are that:

- Responsibility for authorising arrangements will depend (in broad terms) who is responsible for the person's care and treatment. Responsibility will lie with the 'hospital manager' where the arrangements are carried out mainly in an NHS hospital; a CCG or Local Health Board in the case of arrangements carried out through NHS continuing health care (but not mainly in a hospital); and the local authority in all other cases, including in the case of independent hospitals and where care is arranged by the local authority, and where care is provided to people paying for their own care (self-funders).
- The current scheme of 'urgent' authorisations is replaced with a broader approach contained in an amended MCA 2005 s4B, which has no express limit of time.
- The new scheme is intended to be more streamlined, making greater use of already existing assessments and allowing for renewals.[115]
- The scheme crystallises a distinction between those considered to be deprived of their liberty because they cannot consent to arrangements (but who appear to be content), and those who are both deprived of their liberty and are objecting to being required either to live or receive care and treatment at a particular place. The latter cohort will receive additional scrutiny through the mandatory involvement of a so-called 'approved mental capacity professional' (AMCP) before any authorisation can be granted. The former, in general, will not.[116]

114 The Supreme Court in *Re D (A Child)* [2019] UKSC 42, [2019] PTSR 1816 made clear that a parent cannot authorise the confinement of their 16/17-year-old child. If the child lacks capacity to consent to confinement, applying the 'acid test' set down by the Supreme Court in *Cheshire West*, then, until the LPS come into force, an application will be required to court to authorise the deprivation of liberty to which they are subject (unless it is appropriate for an application to made to admit them to hospital under the MHA 1983). See further chapter 22.

115 Initially for a year, then for up to three years at a time.

116 An exception being in the case of independent hospitals where concerns about the treatment of individuals with learning disabilities in private hospitals were repeatedly raised during the passage of the bill through parliament and a government amendment will make AMCP scrutiny mandatory in all such cases.

3.236 At root, however, the LPS scheme, as with DOLS, is based upon the completion of a set of assessments by suitably qualified individuals and their scrutiny by a suitably independent person. The conditions for an LPS authorisation to be granted are that:

- the person who is the subject of the arrangements lacks the capacity to consent to the arrangements;
- the person has a mental disorder; and
- the arrangements are necessary and proportionate to the likelihood and seriousness of harm to the cared-for person.

3.237 The interface between the MCA 2005 and the MHA 1983 in DOLS remains broadly unchanged in principle (although – if possible – more complicated in drafting terms) under the new regime. The LPS cannot therefore be used to authorise admission for treatment for mental disorder where a person objects either to the admission or to all or part of the treatment.

3.238 Much of the detail of how the LPS scheme will work in practice is contained in secondary legislation and a new MCA Code of Practice. In March 2022, the government began a consultation on a new unified MCA Code of Practice, incorporating updated provisions relating to the main sections of the MCA 2005, and new sections relating to the Code. The government also – unusually[117] – consulted upon draft regulations amplifying the provisions of the LPS scheme. The MCA Code of Practice will include guidance as to what arrangements constitute deprivation of liberty and will be reviewed within three years and at five yearly intervals thereafter.[118] This approach represents a compromise proposed by the government after agreement could not be reached on a statutory definition.

Mental Health Act Review

3.239 While the MC(A)A 2019 was going through parliament, the independent Review of the Mental Health Act, commissioned by the Prime Minister, and headed by Sir Simon Wessely, reported in December 2018.[119] For present purposes most relevantly, the Review made recommendations about where the interface should lie

117 Secondary legislation is not usually the subject of consultation.

118 MCA 2005, new s42(2A)–(2B).

119 *Modernising the Mental Health Act Increasing choice, reducing compulsion: Final report of the Independent Review of the Mental Health Act 1983*, December 2018, available at: www.gov.uk/government/publications/modernising-the-mental-health-act-final-report-from-the-independent-review.

between the MHA 1983 and the MCA 2005 and a set of 'confidence tests' to be applied to determine whether the future direction of travel lies in the fusion of mental health and mental capacity legislation.[120] The government published a white paper[121] in response to the MHA Review, together with a consultation which ran from 13 January 2021 to 21 April 2021. On 15 July 2021, in a document[122] summarising its response to the consultation exercise, it made clear that legislation would be brought forward 'when Parliamentary time allows'. On 28 June 2022, a draft Mental Health Bill was introduced, continuing the direction of travel set down in the white paper. As the government had explained would be the case in its consultation response, the draft Bill does not include any changes to the interface between the two regimes. In its July 2021 consultation responses, the government identified that the exercise had:

> . . . made clear there is very limited support for the proposal to change the interface between the Mental Health Act and the Mental Capacity Act in the context of detention. In light of the feedback received, we do not intend to take forward the reform for the interface, as set out in the White Paper, as this time. We will seek to build the evidence base on this issue through robust data collection, to better understand the application of the interface. In addition, we will continue to engage with stakeholders to understand what support and guidance could help improve application of the current interface.[123]

Small payments

3.240 At the time of writing, the Ministry of Justice is considering a 'Small Payments Scheme',[124] which would provide a statutory route (in effect) to enable financial institutions holding the money of a person lacking capacity to manage their affairs to provide that money up to a certain threshold without the need for formal authority from the Court of Protection. The consultation closed in January 2022, and at the time

120 As has happened in Northern Ireland in the Mental Capacity Act (Northern Ireland) 2016, which has yet fully to be implemented.

121 *Reforming the Mental Health Act,* Department of Health and Social Care, published 13 January 2021, last updated 24 August 2021, www.gov.uk/government/consultations/reforming-the-mental-health-act.

122 *Reforming the Mental Health Act: Government response to consultation,* July 2021.

123 *Reforming the Mental Health Act: Government response to consultation,* July 2021, p7.

124 Mental Capacity Act: Small Payments Scheme, Ministry of Justice, 16 November 2021, www.gov.uk/government/consultations/mental-capacity-act-small-payments-scheme.

of writing it is unclear what (if any) steps the Ministry of Justice will take next.[125]

Powers of attorney

3.241 In 2021, the Ministry of Justice launched a consultation on modernising LPAs.[126] The consultation proposals included amendments both to the MCA 2005 and secondary legislation. The consultation closed in October 2021; the government published its response in May 2022. At the time of writing, it is unclear when legislation will be brought forward to amend the provisions of the MCA 2005 to implement the proposals set down in that response.

125 This was development was prompted in significant part by issues relating to now-matured Child Trust Funds where the beneficiary of those funds lacks capacity to manage their property and affairs: see further, Alex Ruck Keene, 'Child Trust Funds – defusing a capacity time bomb', April 20, 2021, www.mentalcapacitylawandpolicy.org.uk/child-trust-funds-defusing-a-capacity-time-bomb/.

126 See: www.gov.uk/government/consultations/modernising-lasting-powers-of-attorney.

CHAPTER 4

The Court of Protection

continued

Introduction and background

4.1 Prior to the Mental Capacity Act (MCA) 2005 coming into force, the Court of Protection's jurisdiction was limited to dealing with an incapacitated person's property and financial affairs.

4.2 The court was an office of the Supreme Court with a full-time Master and nominated officers. The relevant legal provisions were set out in Mental Health Act (MHA) 1983 Part VII, supplemented by Court of Protection Rules[1] (COPR) which regulated its procedures. Appeals from the Master were to the Chancery Division of the High Court.

4.3 Hearings were in London and usually took the form of an inquiry around a conference table rather than a trial. The great advantages were sometimes said to be informality and flexibility, and the perceived disadvantages too much informality and flexibility, in terms of case management, pleadings, advance disclosure and witness statements.

4.4 The Public Guardianship Office (PGO) was responsible for administering the court and it also supervised the affairs of those under the court's jurisdiction.

Establishment and constitution

4.5 The new Court of Protection[2] established by the MCA 2005 is a Superior Court of Record.[3]

4.6 It has 'in connection with its jurisdiction the same powers, rights, privileges and authority as the High Court',[4] for example in relation to witnesses, contempt of court and enforcement.

1 Court of Protection Rules 2001 SI No 824.

2 See: www.gov.uk/courts-tribunals/court-of-protection.

3 According to *Halsbury's Laws of England*, prima facie no matter is deemed to be beyond the jurisdiction of a superior court unless it is expressly shown to be so, while nothing is within the jurisdiction of an inferior court (such as a magistrates' court) unless it is expressly shown on the face of the proceedings that the particular matter is within the cognisance of the particular court: *R v Chancellor of St Edmundsbury and Ipswich Diocese ex p White* [1948] 1 KB 195 at 205–206, [1947] 2 All ER 170 at 172, CA, per Wrottesley LJ.

4 MCA 2005 s47(1).

4.7 Its jurisdiction includes much of the personal welfare and healthcare jurisdiction previously exercised by judges of the Family Division of the High Court, in addition to the property and financial decision-making jurisdiction which it already had under the Mental Health Acts.

4.8 The court is based at First Avenue House, 42–49 High Holborn, London WC1V 6NP. All applications are filed in London. However, where appropriate and convenient, the case can then be transferred to a 'regional hub' to be dealt with by a nominated Court of Protection judge sitting outside London.

4.9 The court has a President and Vice-President and a resident Senior Judge – at the time of writing:

President	Rt Hon Sir Andrew McFarlane, President of the Family Division of the High Court and Court of Protection
Vice-President	The Hon Mr Justice Hayden, Vice-President of the Court of Protection
Senior Judge	HHJ Carolyn Hilder[5]

4.10 Primarily for purposes of identifying appeal routes, judges are now identified as belonging to one of three tiers, with district judges (and equivalent) being Tier 1, circuit judges (and equivalents) being Tier 2, and High Court judges (and equivalent) being Tier 3. This is discussed further in chapter 19, but in practice this terminology is rarely used to describe the level of judge who will hear a particular case.

4.11 All High Court judges are nominated to sit as Court of Protection judges and some applications must be heard by a judge of at least that seniority.

5 Senior Judge Hilder is also, in her own right, entitled to sit as a Deputy High Court judge.

CASES WHICH MUST BE HEARD BY A HIGH COURT JUDGE, etc	
Type of application	**Must be heard by:**
• Cases where a declaration of incompatibility is sought pursuant to Human Rights Act (HRA) 1998 s4; • applications in relation to a case involving an ethical dilemma in an untested area.	The President of the Family Division, the Chancellor or a puisne judge of the High Court (including permission, the giving of any directions, and any hearing): COPR rr12.1, 3.8 and Practice Direction (PD) 3A, PD 12A
• Serious medical treatment cases (terminations, sterilisations, etc) and applications in relation to the lawfulness of withholding or withdrawing artificial nutrition and hydration from a person in a permanent vegetative state, or a minimally conscious state (as to when such applications are required, see *An NHS Trust v Y* [2018] UKSC 46, [2018] 3 WLR 751 and chapter 23)	No PD now but in practice such cases are normally heard by the President of the Family Division, the Chancellor or a puisne judge of the High Court (including permission, the giving of any directions, and any hearing) . See further chapter 23.

Circuit judges and district judges

4.12 The Senior Judge, who has circuit judge rank and is a Tier 2 judge, is supported by resident district judges at First Avenue House in London and by circuit judges and district judges across England and Wales who are nominated ('ticketed') to undertake Court of Protection work as required. In a relatively recent development, it is now possible for deputy district judges to be nominated to undertake Court of Protection work on a part-time basis.

Independence of the judiciary

4.13 Because the office of Lord Chancellor is a political appointment and the holder need not have any legal or judicial qualification or experience, it is the Lord Chief Justice who is responsible for judges and their management, performance and discipline. In terms of their Court of Protection work, the judges are led by, and responsible to, the President.

4.14 In order to further ensure judicial independence and the rule of law, Courts Act 2003 s2(5) provides that: 'The Lord Chancellor may not enter into contracts for the provision of officers and staff to discharge functions which involve making judicial decisions or exercising any judicial discretion'.

HMCTS and court administration

4.15 The Lord Chancellor is under a duty to ensure that there is an efficient and effective system to support the carrying on of the business of the Court of Protection and that appropriate services are provided for it.[6]

4.16 In practice, this duty is discharged day-to-day on the Lord Chancellor's behalf by an agency called Her Majesty's Courts and Tribunals Service (HMCTS).

COURT OF PROTECTION JUDGES	HMCTS
Managed and led by the Lord Chief Justice and the President	A responsibility of the Lord Chancellor
Support system provided by HMCTS	Responsible for ensuring that the judges have the system and support which they require

4.17 The Lord Chancellor may appoint such officers and other staff as appear to them appropriate for the purpose of discharging this general duty.[7]

4.18 HMCTS court staff ('officers') are organised into a number of branches or sections, as described in the table below:

COURT OF PROTECTION – ADMINISTRATION AND CASE WORK	
Branch/Section	**Responsibilities**
• G1 Branch (Receiving and Issuing Applications)	• Making up case files • Issuing applications • Interim directions • Fast-tracking cases • Applications for permission • Issuing applications

continued

6 Courts Act 2003 s1(1)(aa).
7 Courts Act 2003 s2(1).

Branch/Section	Responsibilities
	• Processing fee remissions refunds and payments made using the fee account system • Preparing standard drafts of court orders
• G2 Branch (Processing deputy applications)	• Processing applications to appoint a deputy • Processing routine personal welfare applications • Processing applications from existing deputies • Receiving and processing certificates of service and acknowledgments of service (including objections to applications) • Applications within proceedings • Preparing standard drafts of court orders
• G3 Branch (Issuing Orders team)	• Issuing and dispatching final orders • Dispatching security bond forms • Dealing with bond defaulters • Scanning orders to the Public Guardian
• Judicial Support Team (including the regional and appeals team)	• Ushering hearings • Dealing with cases that require listing for an attended or telephone hearing • Case transfers to and from a regional court • Statutory Will, gift and settlement applications • Issuing most orders and directions made by a judge at a hearing • Dealing with applications to vacate or re-list a hearing • Appeals
• Authorised court officers (ACOs)	• ACOs are civil servants who have been authorised to exercise designated court functions of a purely formal or administrative character which previously were exercised by the judges
• Technical Specialists	• Deprivation of liberty applications • Applications for personal welfare orders • Transfer of welfare cases to regional courts • New trustee applications • Enduring powers of attorney (EPA) and lasting powers of attorney (LPA) objections and directions • Public Guardian applications (now shared with G1 and G2) • Requests for visitor reports under MCA 2005 s49

	• Appointing panel deputies • Orders discharging deputies (recovery/ retirement) • Streamline applications from already appointed court deputies under PD 9D and interim applications in accordance with COPR Part 10 (Band D Technical Specialists)
• Customer Enquiry Service (CES)	• Court's telephone service • General email inquiries • Dispatching court forms to users

Authorised court officers

4.19 A number of civil servants known as ACOs are authorised by the Senior Judge or the President to exercise the jurisdiction of the court in the circumstances set out in PD 2B.[8]

4.20 An authorised officer may not conduct a hearing and must refer to a judge any application or question arising in an application which is contentious or which, in the opinion of the officer, is complex, requires a hearing or for any other reason ought to be considered by a judge. The relevant person concerned ('P'), a party and any other person affected by an order can apply to have an authorised officer's order reconsidered by a judge.

APPLICATIONS THAT MAY BE DEALT WITH BY AUTHORISED COURT OFFICERS (COPR r2.3; PD 2B para 2.1)

2.1 Subject to paragraphs 2.2, 3 and 4.2 an authorised court officer may deal with any of the following applications:

(a) applications to appoint a deputy for property and affairs;

(b) applications to vary the powers of a deputy appointed for property and affairs under an existing order;

(c) applications to discharge a deputy for property and affairs and appoint a replacement deputy;

(d) applications to appoint and discharge a trustee;

(e) applications to sell or purchase real property on behalf of P;

8 COPR r2.3. The power in the rules to authorise court officers to exercise the jurisdiction of the court sits uncomfortably with Courts Act 2003 s2(5), which provides that: 'The Lord Chancellor may not enter into contracts for the provision of officers and staff to discharge functions which involve making judicial decisions or exercising any judicial discretion'.

(f) applications to vary the security in relation to a deputy for property and affairs;

(g) applications to discharge the security when the appointment of a deputy for property and affairs comes to an end;

(h) applications for the release of funds for the maintenance of P, or P's property, or to discharge any debts incurred by P;

(i) applications to sell or otherwise deal with P's investments;

(j) applications for authority to apply for a grant of probate or representation for the use and benefit of P;

(k) applications to let and manage property belonging to P;

(l) applications for a detailed assessment of costs;

(m) applications to obtain a copy of P's will;

(n) applications to inspect or obtain copy documents from the records of the court; and

(o) applications which relate to one or more of the preceding paragraphs and which a judge has directed should be dealt with by an authorised court officer.

4.21 The case management powers of authorised officers are limited to those matters referred to in COPR PD 2B para 3.

Workload and number of applications

4.22 The number of applications to the court increased from 22,583 in 2008 to 35,379 in 2021.[9]

Year	No of applications
2008	22,583
2009	19,093
2010	20,459
2011	23,538
2012	24,877
2013	24,923
2014	26,272
2015	26,722

9 Source: Ministry of Justice, Family Court Statistics Quarterly, www.gov.uk/government/collections/family-court-statistics-quarterly.

2016	29,711
2017	31,332
2018	32,029
2019	34,445
2020	30,635
2021	35,379

4.23 The greatest number of applications has consistently been for appointment of a property and affairs deputy, followed by applications for one-off property and affairs orders. An increasing part of the court's work, especially since 2014, has related to deprivation of liberty matters, whether challenges to authorisations granted under MCA 2005 Sch A1 or applications for judicial authorisation (see further chapter 22). Applications relating to deprivation of liberty, as well as to welfare matters more broadly, occupy a disproportionate amount of court time when it comes to hearings when compared to property and affairs matters.

The court's budget

4.24 Published Ministry of Justice (MoJ) data is quite old, and one can only speculate as to the reasons why. Consequently, it is difficult to establish the court's current budget.[10] What does seem clear is that the MoJ has consistently suffered cuts in funding since 2010, and the effects are felt throughout the court system.

Where to find the law and guidance

Overview

4.25 The relevant law and guidance is found in several places:

- primary legislation: the MCA 2005;
- secondary legislation: orders, rules and regulations made under the authority of the Act;
- practice directions, practice guidance and codes of practice;
- case-law decisions of judges;

10 In line with civil courts generally, the Court of Protection fees are expected to fully cover the cost of administering the court although some funding from central government is inevitable because provision is made for fee exemptions, remission and postponement.

- European Convention on Human Rights (ECHR); and
- textbooks and textbook opinion.

4.26 The precise legal status of these different documents is not always easy to discern. However, the following brief points may help non-lawyers unfamiliar with the various documents and how to refer to them.

Primary legislation

4.27 Acts of Parliament – '*primary legislation*' are divided into sections (s), subsections (subs), paragraphs (para) and subparagraphs (subpara). If a document refers to MCA 2005 s22(3)(a)(i), this is a reference to subparagraph (i) of paragraph (a) of subsection (3) of section 22 of the Act.

Secondary legislation

4.28 Primary legislation takes precedence over '*secondary legislation*', that is over orders, rules and regulations made by the Lord Chancellor or by some other minister with Parliament's permission, ie under the authority of an Act of Parliament.

- The term 'rules' is used for secondary legislation which is concerned with court procedures, eg the COPR. A set of rules is divided into rules (r), paragraphs (paras) and sub-paragraphs (sub-para). Thus, COPR r1.3(2)(b) refers to sub-paragraph (b) of paragraph (2) of rule 1.3 of those rules.
- The term 'regulations' is used for secondary legislation that relates to non-court executive procedures, eg the procedures of the Public Guardian. A set of regulations is divided into regulations (reg), paragraphs (para) and sub-paragraphs (sub-para).
- The term 'order' has no single meaning. In relation to the MCA 2005, it is used for secondary legislation that deals with matters directly relating to the Act's implementation, such as transitional arrangements, consequential provisions and prescribed fees. An order is divided into articles (art), paragraphs (para) and sub-paragraphs (sub-para).

Practice directions, practice guidance and codes of practice

4.29 In recent times, primary and secondary legislation has been augmented by a proliferation of *practice directions, practice guidance and codes of practice*:

- *Practice directions*: MCA 2005 s52 provides that the President of the Court of Protection may, with the concurrence of the Lord Chancellor, give directions 'as to the practice and procedure of the court'. Such directions may not be given by anyone else (for example, by the Vice-President or Senior Judge) without the approval of the President of the Court of Protection and the Lord Chancellor.
- A practice direction cannot establish a legal obligation when none exists already, see *U v Liverpool City Council (Practice Note)*.[11]
- The court in *Bovale Ltd v Secretary of State for Communities and Local Government*[12] considered the status of practice directions and the circumstances in which a judge may depart from them. The issue of a practice direction is the exercise of an inherent power of the court even when made under statutory authority. However, this does not mean that a judge dealing with an application can simply vary practice directions or alter rules with general effect; they are binding on the judge. In particular, a judge's wide case-management powers in individual cases cannot be construed 'as giving the power to individual judges or any court simply to vary the rules or practice directions generally' (*Bovale*, para 26). If there is a gap in the rules and practice directions, there is no impediment to a court making the order that is most appropriate to the case before it under its case management powers, or prescribing or suggesting a procedure which should be followed.
- *Practice guidance*: MCA 2005 s52, cross-referred to Part 1 of Schedule 2 to the Constitutional Reform Act 2005, has the effect that providing providing for practice directions in this way does not prevent the President of the Court of Protection without the concurrence of the Lord Chancellor giving directions which 'contain guidance as to law or making judicial decisions'.
- *Codes of practice*: the two codes (which will in due course become one[13]) do not have statutory force, but professionals and some carers must have regard to their provisions, and the courts must take them into account where relevant. A code of practice cannot create an obligation that does not exist either by virtue of a statute,

11 [2005] EWCA Civ 475, [2005] 1 WLR 2657 at para 48.

12 [2009] EWCA Civ 171, [2009] 1 WLR 2274.

13 See para 3.240.

the common law or the operation of a directly enforceable international treaty (such as the ECHR): see *An NHS Trust v Y*.[14]

Case-law

4.30 *Case-law* – ie judges' decisions that settle or interpret significant points of law – for example, the precise meaning of a section of the Act – may be 'reported', that is published, in one of three historic series of law reports. These are the Official Law Reports; the Weekly Law Reports (WLR); and the All England Reports (All ER). The former should be referred to ('cited') in court if the case is reported in it.

4.31 Transcripts of 'unreported' judgments often appear on the website of the British and Irish Legal Information Institute (Bailii).[15] These transcripts have an uncertain status. They should not usually be cited unless they contain a relevant statement of legal principle not found in reported authority.[16] Many such decisions are simply illustrative of how the law was applied in a novel legal situation or one of obvious public interest. Most often, they are aids to understanding the law and its application rather than legal precedents.

4.32 Many new series of law reports have been established in recent years, the most important of which in this context are the Court of Protection Law Reports.[17] In practice, they are considered to be wholly reliable, and so are relied upon by the court.

European Convention on Human Rights

4.33 The ECHR is essentially a modern-day Magna Carta. So far as is possible, all primary and secondary legislation must be interpreted so as to be compatible with it.

Legal textbooks

4.34 *Legal textbook opinion* may be quoted if it is likely to assist the court as to the meaning of a disputed or difficult legal provision.

14 [2018] UKSC 46, [2018] 3 WLR 751, (2018) 21 CCLR 410, where the Supreme Court analysed the apparent obligation asserted in the then-main Code of Practice to the MCA 2005 to take certain medical treatment cases to court, and found that there was, in fact, no such obligation. See further chapter 23.

15 See: www.bailii.org.

16 PD of 24 March 2012: *Citation of authorities* [2012] 1 WLR 780 at para 10.

17 LexisNexis. See also *Community Care Law Reports* published by LAG covering a significant number of Court of Protection cases.

Mental Capacity Act 2005

4.35 The MCA 2005 consists of 69 sections in three parts. These sections are followed by ten schedules which deal with legal technicalities and formalities that would clog up and make unreadable the main body of the Act if placed there.

Mental Capacity Act 2005		
Part of Act	**Title**	**What it includes**
Part 1	Persons who lack capacity	• Statutory principles • Definitions of incapacity and best interests • Legal protection for professionals and other carers in respect of care and treatment given informally • Payment for necessary goods and services; LPAs • Court declarations and orders • Appointment of deputies by the court • Court's powers in relation to personal welfare matters, property and financial matters, deprivation of liberty, LPAs and advance decisions to refuse treatment (ADRTs) • Research • IMCAS (independent mental capacity advocacy service)
Part 2	The Court of Protection and the Public Guardian	• Establishment, jurisdiction and powers of the Court of Protection and the Public Guardian • Court of Protection visitors
Part 3	Miscellaneous and general	• Scope of the Act • International protection of adults • Interpretation • Making of rules, regulations and orders
Schedule A1	Hospital and care home residents: deprivation of liberty	These schedules set out the 'deprivation of liberty' scheme inserted into the MCA 2005 by the MHA 2007. This schedule will in due course be repealed when the Liberty Protection Safeguards scheme contained in Schedule AA1 comes fully into force.

Schedule AA1	Deprivation of liberty: authorisation of arrangements enabling care and treatment	This schedule sets out the Liberty Protection Safeguards scheme, which will replace the Deprivation of Liberty Safeguards scheme in due course.
Schedule 1	Lasting powers of attorney: formalities	Technicalities and formalities relating to LPAs
Schedule 1A	Persons ineligible to be deprived of liberty by this Act	
Schedule 2	Property and affairs: supplementary provisions	Additional provisions relating to matters such as wills and the effect of the court disposing of part of an incapacitated person's property on the distribution of their estate on their death (either by will or under the intestacy rules)
Schedule 3	International protection of adults	The schedule gives effect in England and Wales to the Hague Convention (the Convention on the International Protection of Adults, 2000). See also MCA 2005 s63
Schedule 4	Provisions applying to existing enduring powers of attorney	The MCA 2005 repealed the Enduring Powers of Attorney Act 1985. Its provisions are, however, repeated here because, although no new EPAs may be made, EPAs made before the new Act continue to have effect, may be challenged in court on the old terms, etc. See also MCA 2005 s66
Schedule 5	Transitional provisions and savings	
Schedule 6	Minor and consequential amendments	
Schedule 7	Repeals	

Note: Schedules A1 and 1A will be repealed when the Mental Capacity (Amendment) Act 2019 comes into force, to be replaced by a new Schedule AA1, subject to transition provisions for the first year of the new regime.

Rules, regulations and orders; practice directions, practice guidance and codes

4.36 The MCA 2005 provides for issuing rules, regulations and orders, and the publication of codes of practice. The following are some of the most important for court users.

Rules	
COPR 2017 SI No 1035	These rules govern the procedures of the court. They are somewhat cumbersome. The rules are in 24 parts and are supplemented by 46 practice directions, numerous prescribed forms and where necessary the Civil Procedure Rules 1998 and Family Procedure Rules 2010.
Practice directions[a]	
The practice directions are essentially of two kinds. Some do no more than repeat in plainer English what is said in a part of the rules; others, such as those on the right, are substantive.	PD 9D – Applications by currently appointed deputies, attorneys and donees in relation to [the person's] property and affairs
	PD 9E: Applications relating to statutory wills, codicils, settlements and other dealings with P's property
	PD 23A: International protection of adults
Regulations and orders	
Lasting Powers of Attorney, Enduring Powers of Attorney and Public Guardian Regulations 2007 SI No 1253	These regulations deal with matters such as the completion and registration of LPAs, the registration of EPAs, the reports required of deputies and the registers maintained by the Public Guardian.
Codes of practice	
There are separate codes on the MCA 2005 as originally passed and the deprivation of liberty provisions added in 2007.	• *Mental Capacity Act Code of Practice* (Department for Constitutional Affairs, 2007)[b]

a See: www.judiciary.uk/publications/court-of-protection-practice-directions/.
b See: www.gov.uk/government/publications/mental-capacity-act-code-of-practice.

	Under review at the time of writing, and to be consolidated into one code with provisions relating to the liberty protection safeguards (LPS).
	Deprivation of liberty safeguards: Code of Practice to supplement the main Mental Capacity Act 2005 Code of Practice (Ministry of Justice, 2008)[c]
	This will cease to be relevant when the deprivation of liberty safeguards (DOLS) provisions are repealed in due course.

Textbooks

4.37 The main textbook on court practice and procedure is LexisNexis' *Court of Protection Practice*, a new edition of which appears annually in the spring. The other four standard publications used by practitioners are:

- *Court of Protection Law Reports* (LexisNexis), which contain decisions made by senior judges on important legal issues;
- *Heywood & Massey: Court of Protection Practice* (looseleaf) (Sweet & Maxwell);
- *Cretney & Lush on Lasting and Enduring Powers of Attorney* (9th edn, LexisNexis, 2022);
- the monthly *Mental Capacity Law Reports* report produced by 39 Essex Chambers, published at www.39essex.com, and by (free) subscription by contacting marketing@39essex.com.

European Convention on Human Rights

4.38 The HRA 1998 makes it unlawful for a public authority, such as the NHS or a local authority, to act in a way which is incompatible with a convention right unless legislation requires it to act in that way. So far as is possible, all primary and secondary legislation must be interpreted so as to be compatible with the ECHR. If this is impossible, one of the higher courts will make a declaration of incompatibility.

4.39 The Articles of the ECHR which are most often 'in play' in Court of Protection proceedings are Articles 5 (right to liberty and security) and 8 (right to respect for private and family life).

c See: http://webarchive.nationalarchives.gov.uk/20130107105354/http://www.dh.gov.uk/prod_consum_dh/groups/dh_digitalassets/@dh/@en/documents/digitalasset/dh_087309.pdf.

4.40 Article 5 is engaged when an incapacitated person is deprived of their liberty. The state is obliged to take effective measures to protect vulnerable persons, including reasonable steps to prevent a deprivation of liberty of which the authorities have or ought to have knowledge. A proper authorisation or court order is required. The person concerned should have access to a court and the opportunity to be heard in person or, where necessary, through some form of representation.

4.41 Article 8 provides a qualified right to respect for one's private and family life, home and correspondence. Any interference with an incapacitated person's family or private life must be authorised by law, proportionate ('necessary in a democratic society') and for a permitted purpose, eg for the protection of their health. The court should consider the nature and strength of the evidence of any alleged risk of harm and there must be a proper, factual basis for such concerns.

Jurisdiction of the Court of Protection

4.42 The court's jurisdiction derives from the MCA 2005 which sets out a number of different types of applications and orders that can be made.

Exempt matters to which the MCA 2005 does not apply

4.43 The MCA 2005 does not apply to some legal situations and cannot be used to authorise certain kinds of interference with a person's life. These exclusions are set out in sections 27–29.

People falling outside the Act

4.44 Depending on the type of decision to be made, the court's jurisdiction may be restricted to adults (eg statutory wills, lasting powers of attorney) or to persons aged 16 or over (eg personal welfare issues).[18]

Family matters falling outside the MCA 2005 (s27)

4.45 Nothing in the MCA 2005 permits a decision on any of the following matters to be made on behalf of a person:

- consenting to marriage or a civil partnership;

18 MCA 2005 s2(5) and (6).

- consenting to have sexual relations;
- consenting to a decree of divorce being granted on the basis of two years' separation;
- consenting to a dissolution order being made in relation to a civil partnership on the basis of two years' separation;
- consenting to a child's being placed for adoption by an adoption agency;
- consenting to the making of an adoption order;
- discharging parental responsibilities in matters not relating to a child's property;
- giving a consent under the Human Fertilisation and Embryology Act 1990.[19]

Mental Health Act matters (MCA 2005 s28)

4.46 MCA 2005 s28 excludes certain MHA matters from being dealt with under the MCA 2005. The precise inter-relationship between the two statutes was considered in chapter 3 above.

Voting rights (MCA 2005 s29)

4.47 Nothing in the MCA 2005 permits a decision on voting at an election for any public office, or at a referendum, to be made on behalf of an incapacitated person.[20]

The range of applications and orders that may be made

4.48 The different types of application and orders that may be made are dealt with in greater detail in the appropriate chapters. However, it is useful at the outset to have an understanding of the range of orders that can be made:

- declarations;
- court orders and decisions under MCA 2005 s16;
- appointing deputies under MCA 2005 s16;
- powers in relation to LPAs;
- powers in relation to advance decisions to refuse treatment (ADRTs);
- powers in relation to EPAs;

19 MCA 2005 s27(1).
20 MCA 2005 s29(1).

- other powers; and
- interim orders.

Declarations

4.49 MCA 2005 s15 provides that the Court of Protection may make declarations as to:

- whether a person has or lacks capacity to make a decision specified in the declaration;
- whether a person has or lacks capacity to make decisions on such matters as are described in the declaration;
- the lawfulness or otherwise of any act done, or yet to be done, in relation to that person.

Section 15(2) provides that the term 'act' includes an omission and a course of conduct.

4.50 As its name suggests, a declaration involves the court declaring the law or a person's rights or interests in relation to a particular matter, historically without any reference to enforcement (see further in this regard para 18.1). It registers what exists and declares what it finds. However, it is not an academic process. There has to be a real issue to resolve between the parties so that declaring something to be lawful or otherwise clarifies for the parties what may and may not be done under the Act. In *Secretary of State for Justice v A Local Authority and others,*[21] Lord Burnett of Maldon noted that, whilst MCA 2005 s15 appeared to give the Court of Protection the power to make declarations about the lawfulness of specific provisions in a care plan, the use of that power to declare lawful conduct which has the potential to be criminal should be confined to cases where the circumstances are exceptional and the reasons cogent. Lord Burnett considered that such an approach applied with equal force in circumstances where the court made a decision reflected in its judgment that certain hypothetical conduct would not amount to a criminal offence.

4.51 Declarations of unlawfulness are rare, but in *Re ND (Court of Protection: Costs and Declarations),*[22] the Court of Protection alighted upon procedural failings by a local authority to comply with directions made to provide care plans to it during the proceedings to ground the making of declarations of unlawfulness under MCA 2005

21 [2021] EWCA Civ 1527, [2021] 3 WLR 1425.

22 [2020] EWCOP 42, [2020] COPLR 808.

s15(1)(c) as to the failures of that authority to discharge its statutory obligations to the subject of proceedings.

4.52 Perhaps slightly surprisingly, it is possible for the Court of Protection to make declarations in relation to someone who currently *has* capacity to make a decision, but only where f is a real risk that they will lose it.[23] This allows the court to make contingency plans for a person. This is most often done in relation to a person who may lose capacity to make decisions about their birth arrangements. See also chapter 23.

Court orders and decisions under MCA 2005 s16

4.53 MCA 2005 s16 applies if a person lacks capacity in relation to a matter or matters concerning their personal welfare or property and affairs.[24] It enables the court by order to make the necessary decisions on their behalf or to appoint a deputy to make those decisions for the person. The powers of the court are subject to the provisions of the Act and, in particular, to sections 1 (the principles) and 4 (best interests).[25] Any order of the court may be varied or discharged by a subsequent order.[26] In *Re MN*,[27] Sir James Munby P suggested the court should usually reflect its determination as to an incapacitated person's best interests not by way of making a declaration, but by making an order under MCA 2005 s16: ie by making a decision on their behalf. Where necessary, such an order can be coupled with a declaration under MCA 2005 s15(1)(c) as to the lawfulness of actions to be taken by others (for instance by medical professionals providing treatment to the individual).

MCA 2005 s16 and personal welfare matters

4.54 The court's section 16 powers as respects an incapacitated person's personal welfare extend in particular to:[28]

- deciding where the person is to live;

23 See *Re R* [2020] EWCOP 4, [2020] 4 WLR 96 and *North Middlesex University Hospital NHS Trust v SR* [2021] EWCOP 58, [2022] COPLR 125.

24 MCA 2005 s16(1).

25 MCA 2005 s16(3).

26 MCA 2005 s16(7).

27 [2015] EWCA Civ 411, [2016] Fam 87, (2015) 18 CCLR 521, endorsed by the Supreme Court [2017] UKSC 22, [2017] AC 549, [2017] COPLR 200 at para 26 per Lady Hale.

28 MCA 2005 s17(1), (2).

- deciding what contact, if any, the person is to have with any specified persons;
- making an order prohibiting a named person from having contact with the person;
- giving or refusing consent to the carrying out or continuation of a treatment by a person providing health care for the person;
- giving a direction that a person responsible for the person's health care allow a different person to take over that responsibility.

4.55 Absent a material change of circumstances, a decision by the Court of Protection as to what is in the person's best interests should be considered as continuing to govern the position thereafter by those working with them.[29]

MCA 2005 s16 and property and financial matters

4.56 The court's section 16 powers as respects an incapacitated person's property and affairs extend in particular to:[30]

- the control and management of their property;
- the sale, exchange, charging, gift or other disposition of their property;
- the acquisition of property in their name or on their behalf;
- the carrying on, on their behalf, of any profession, trade or business;
- the taking of a decision which will have the effect of dissolving a partnership of which the person is a member;
- the carrying out of any contract entered into by the person;
- the discharge of the person's debts and any of their obligations, whether legally enforceable or not;
- the settlement of any of their property, whether for their benefit or for the benefit of others;
- the execution for them of a will (although no will may be made under this power at a time when the person has not reached 18 years of age[31]);
- the exercise of any power (including a power to consent) vested in the person whether beneficially or as trustee or otherwise;
- the conduct of legal proceedings in the person's name or on their behalf.

29 See *An NHS Trust v AF and another* [2020] EWCOP 55, [2021] COPLR 63.

30 MCA 2005 s18(1).

31 MCA 2005 s18(2).

Appointing deputies under section 16[32]

4.57 MCA 2005 s16 provides that the court may:

- by making an order, make the decision or decisions on the person's behalf in relation to the matter or matters, or
- appoint a person (a 'deputy') to make decisions on the person's behalf in relation to the matter or matters.[33]

4.58 Naturally, if the judge can make the decision, it will generally be inappropriate for them to authorise someone else to make it.

4.59 Consequently, the Act provides that a decision by the court is to be preferred to the appointment of a deputy to make a decision; and that the powers conferred on the deputy should be as limited in scope and duration 'as is reasonably practicable in the circumstances': see section 16(4).

4.60 Without prejudice to section 4, the court may make an order or appoint a deputy on such terms as it considers are in the incapacitated person's best interests, and may do so even though no application is before it 'on those terms'.[34]

Who may be a deputy

4.61 A deputy must be an adult (aged 18 or over) or, in the case of property and affairs deputyships, a trust corporation.[35]

4.62 A person may not be appointed as a deputy without their consent.[36]

4.63 The court may appoint the holder of a specified office or position as the person's deputy,[37] for example the holder of a particular local authority finance office. This avoids the need for a new order when the current holder of the post moves on and is replaced.

Two or more deputies

4.64 The court may appoint two or more deputies to act jointly, jointly and separately ('severally'), or jointly in respect of some matters and jointly and separately in respect of others.[38]

32 See further chapter 7.
33 MCA 2005 s16(2).
34 MCA 2005 s16(6).
35 MCA 2005 s19(1).
36 MCA 2005 s19(3).
37 MCA 2005 s19(2).
38 MCA 2005 s19(4).

Appointment of successors

4.65 When appointing a deputy or deputies, the court may at the same time appoint one or more other persons to succeed the deputy or deputies in such circumstances, or on the happening of such events, as may be specified, and for such period as may be so specified.[39]

Property and affairs deputyships

4.66 With regard to property and affairs deputyships, the court may confer on a deputy powers to:

- take possession or control of all or any specified part of the person's property;
- exercise all or any specified powers in respect of it, including such powers of investment as the court may determine.[40]

Restrictions on deputies

4.67 The MCA 2005 provides that certain powers may not be conferred on or exercised by a deputy. These restrictions are described in chapter 3 above.

Security, reports and the Public Guardian

4.68 The court may require a deputy:

- to give to the Public Guardian such security as the court thinks fit for the due discharge of their functions; and
- to submit to the Public Guardian such reports at such times or at such intervals as the court may direct.[41]

Reimbursement and remuneration

4.69 The deputy is entitled:

- to be reimbursed out of the incapacitated person's property for their reasonable expenses in discharging their functions; and
- if the court so directs when appointing them, to remuneration out of the incapacitated person's property for discharging them.[42]

39 MCA 2005 s19(5).
40 MCA 2005 s19(8).
41 MCA 2005 s19(9).
42 MCA 2005 s19(7).

Revoking a deputy's appointment

4.70 The court may revoke the appointment of a deputy or vary the powers conferred on them if it is satisfied that the deputy:

- has behaved, or is behaving, in a way that contravenes the authority conferred on them by the court or is not in P's best interests; or
- proposes to behave in a way that would contravene that authority or would not be in P's best interests.[43]

Ending a deputy's appointment at the request of the deputy

4.71 Once a deputy has been appointed, they can only rescind their appointment by making an application to court.[44] A change of deputy should not be a 'default response' to difficulties in managing a deputyship, as it incurs costs for P 'and risks being perceived as "rewarding" negative behaviour, which in turn undermines the prospects of future stability. Rather the court should probe the actual circumstances, with a view to salvaging working relationships if possible'.[45]

Powers in relation to LPAs[46]

4.72 MCA 2005 ss22 and 23 set out the court's powers where a person has:

- executed[47] or purported to execute a document ('an instrument') with a view to creating an LPA; or
- such a document has been registered as an LPA by the Public Guardian.[48]

Determining whether an LPA exists or still exists

4.73 The court may determine any question relating to:

43 MCA 2005 s16(8).

44 *Cumbria County Council v A* [2020] EWCOP 38, [2020] 1 WLR 4008.

45 *Kambli v The Public Guardian* [2021] EWCOP 53 at para 39.

46 See further chapter 7.

47 'Executed' simply means to sign a document and to complete any other necessary formalities to give it legal effect, such as having it sealed (which does not apply here). The document or 'instrument' is simply the standard LPA form prescribed under the MCA 2005.

48 MCA 2005 s22(1).

- whether one or more of the requirements for the creation of an LPA have been met;[49]
- whether the power has been revoked or has otherwise come to an end.[50]

Impropriety or failure to act in P's best interests

4.74 MCA 2005 s20(4) applies if the court is satisfied:

- that fraud or undue pressure was used to induce the relevant person to execute an instrument for the purpose of creating a lasting power of attorney, or to create a lasting power of attorney; or
- that the donee (or, if more than one, any of them) of an LPA (i) has behaved, or is behaving, in a way that contravenes their authority or is not in the person's best interests, or (ii) proposes to behave in a way that would contravene their authority or would not be in the person's best interests.[51]

4.75 In such a case, the court may:

- direct that an instrument purporting to create the lasting power of attorney is not to be registered; or
- if the person lacks capacity to do so, revoke the instrument or the LPA.[52]

4.76 If there is more than one donee, the court may revoke the instrument or the LPA so far as it relates to any of them.[53]

Powers of court in relation to the operation of lasting powers of attorney

4.77 MCA 2005 s23(1) provides that the court may determine any question as to the meaning or effect of an LPA or an instrument purporting to create one. The court may also:

49 An LPA is not created unless section 10 is complied with, the prescribed document is registered, and the person creating it is an adult who had capacity to execute it: MCA 2005 s9(2). See *The Public Guardian v RI and others* [2022] EWCOP 22 (capacity to execute).

50 MCA 2005 s22(2).

51 MCA 2005 s22(3).

52 MCA 2005 s22(4).

53 MCA 2005 s22(5).

- give directions with respect to decisions which the donee of an LPA has authority to make, and which the person lacks capacity to make;[54]
- give any consent or authorisation to act which the donee would have to obtain from the person if the person had capacity to give it.[55]

4.78 Where the relevant person lacks capacity to do so, the court may:

- give directions to the donee with respect to the rendering by them of reports or accounts and the production of records kept by them for that purpose;[56]
- require the donee to supply information or to produce documents or things in their possession as donee;[57]
- give directions with respect to the remuneration or expenses of the donee;[58]
- relieve the donee wholly or partly from any liability which they have or may have incurred on account of a breach of their duties as donee.[59]

Gifts

4.79 The court may authorise the making of gifts which are not permitted gifts (such as customary birthday presents and charitable donations) within the meaning of MCA 2005 s12(2).[60]

Powers in relation to advance decisions to refuse treatment

4.80 The court may make a declaration as to whether an advance decision exists; is valid; or is applicable to a treatment.[61]

4.81 Nothing in an apparent advance decision stops a person from providing life-sustaining treatment, or from doing any act they reasonably believe to be necessary to prevent a serious deterioration in

54 MCA 2005 s23(2)(a).
55 MCA 2005 s23(2)(b).
56 MCA 2005 s23(3)(a).
57 MCA 2005 s23(3)(b).
58 MCA 2005 s23(3)(c).
59 MCA 2005 s23(3)(d).
60 MCA 2005 s23(4).
61 MCA 2005 s26(4).

the relevant person's condition, while a decision in respect of any relevant issue is sought from the court.[62]

Powers in relation to EPAs

4.82 The court's powers in relation to EPAs are set out in MCA 2005 Sch 4 and derive from the Enduring Powers of Attorney Act 1985. The case-law on that Act therefore continues to be relevant. It is undecided whether and to what extent the main body of the MCA 2005 applies to EPAs.

Objections to the registration of an EPA

4.83 If the Public Guardian receives a valid notice of objection to the registration of an EPA from a person entitled to notice, then they must not register it unless the court directs that it is registered.

4.84 A notice of objection to registration is valid if made on one or more of the following grounds:

1) that the power purported to have been created by the instrument (ie EPA form) was not valid as an EPA;
2) that the power created by the instrument no longer subsists;
3) that the application is premature because the donor is not yet becoming mentally incapable;
4) that fraud or undue pressure was used to induce the donor to create the power;
5) that, having regard to all the circumstances and in particular the attorney's relationship to or connection with the donor, the attorney is unsuitable to be the donor's attorney.

4.85 If any of these grounds is established to the satisfaction of the court, it must direct the Public Guardian not to register the instrument. If the court is not satisfied that any of the grounds are established then it must direct registration.

4.86 If the court directs the Public Guardian not to register an instrument on the fraud, undue pressure or unsuitability ground then it must by order revoke the EPA. This is not necessary under the first two grounds because no EPA exists, and it would be premature under the third ground because it does not rest on a finding of fault and the EPA may require registration in the future.

4.87 In all cases other than the no-fault prematurity ground, the EPA document must be delivered up to the Public Guardian to be

62 MCA 2005 s26(5).

cancelled, unless the court otherwise directs. Again, this is logical. In all of the other cases, the EPA document either has no legal effect (in which case one usually one does not want it circulating in someone's possession) or at best the attorney has been found to be unsuitable (in which case one usually does not want them retaining possession of it).

Powers in connection with a registered EPA

4.88 Once an EPA has been registered, the court may be asked to revoke it or to give directions to the attorney as to the management of the donor's property.

Giving directions concerning the operation of the EPA

4.89 Where an instrument has been registered the court may:

a) determine any question as to the meaning or effect of the instrument;
b) give directions with respect to:
   i) the management or disposal by the attorney of the property and affairs of the donor;
   ii) the rendering of accounts by the attorney and the production of the records kept by them for the purpose;
   iii) the remuneration or expenses of the attorney whether or not in default of or in accordance with any provision made by the instrument, including directions for the repayment of excessive or the payment of additional remuneration;
c) require the attorney to supply information or produce documents or things in their possession as attorney;
d) give any consent or authorisation to act which the attorney would have to obtain from a mentally capable donor;
e) authorise the attorney to act so as to benefit themselves or others otherwise than in accordance with Schedule 4 para 3(2).

Revocation of a registered EPA

4.90 Once an EPA has been registered, because the donor is becoming mentally incapable, it can only be revoked by the donor if the court confirms the revocation. On such an application, the court must confirm the revocation of the power if it satisfied that the donor:

a) has done whatever is necessary in law to effect an express revocation of the power; and

b) was mentally capable of revoking a power of attorney when they did so (whether or not they are still capable of doing so by the time the court considers the application).

Objections to a registered EPA

4.91 The court must direct the Public Guardian to cancel the registration of a registered EPA in any of the following circumstances:

a) on confirming the revocation of the power by the donor (see immediately above);
b) on directing under MCA 2005 Sch 4 para 2(9)(b) that the power is to be revoked (this is where the court makes a deputy order and when doing so directs that a pre-existing EPA shall be revoked);
c) on being satisfied that the donor is and is likely to remain mentally capable;
d) on being satisfied that the power has expired or has been revoked by the mental incapacity of the attorney;
e) on being satisfied that the power was not a valid and subsisting enduring power when registration was effected;
f) on being satisfied that fraud or undue pressure was used to induce the donor to create the power;
g) on being satisfied that, having regard to all the circumstances and in particular the attorney's relationship to or connection with the donor, the attorney is unsuitable to be the donor's attorney.

4.92 If the court directs the Public Guardian to cancel the EPA's registration on one of the fault grounds (fraud, undue pressure or unsuitability) then it must also revoke the EPA itself, ie the EPA document is no longer valid and therefore there can be no future attempts to re-register it.

4.93 In all cases other than the no-fault 'donor is and is likely to remain mentally capable' ground, the EPA document must be delivered up to the Public Guardian to be cancelled, unless the court otherwise directs. Again, this is logical. In all of the other cases, the EPA document either has no legal effect or at best the attorney has been found to be unsuitable.

Other powers

4.94 The court's other main powers relate to COPR r24.5 and MCA 2005 Sch 3.

Applications under COPR r24.5

4.95 The court receives applications from persons subject to a deputyship order for the deputy order to be revoked on the ground that the person concerned no longer lacks capacity in relation to the matter or matters in question and therefore no longer falls within the court's jurisdiction.

Applications under MCA 2005 Sch 3

4.96 The court sometimes receives applications in relation to MCA 2005 Sch 3 which is concerned with the Hague Convention and the international protection of adults with incapacity. For example, a person may apply to the court for a declaration that a protective measure taken in a country other than England and Wales is enforceable in England and Wales. The Convention and Schedule 3 are dealt with in chapter 27.

Interim orders where there is reason to believe person lacks capacity

4.97 The Court of Protection's jurisdiction is directed towards making decisions on behalf of people who lack capacity to make their own decision. By the end of the case there is usually ample evidence on which the judge can determine whether or not the person concerned has that capacity.

4.98 What, though, is the position where it appears that a person lacks capacity to make a decision for themselves, and in consequence is at risk, but that person will not agree to a capacity assessment and the evidence which can be put before the court is incomplete?

4.99 The answer is that the court has power to make interim orders and directions under MCA 2005 s48 if there is reason to believe that the relevant person lacks capacity in relation to the matter and it is in their best interests for the court to do so. This is considered further at para 11.4 onwards below.

Court of Protection procedures

4.100 The court's procedures are dealt with in the relevant chapters. However, it is helpful to emphasise the following points by way of general introduction.

Case Pathways PD 3B

4.101 COPR r3.9 and PD 3B set pathways for health and welfare cases, property and affairs cases, and mixed cases. Not all types of cases are on pathways,[63] but for cases which are, the Case Pathways practice direction places an obligation on applicants to provide improved analysis of the issues at the start of a case, allowing for more robust case management decisions to be taken at the outset and all issues to be identified at the earliest opportunity in proceedings. It also seeks to encourage early resolution of cases, to reduce the number and length of hearings required in contested cases and to promote judicial continuity.

The overriding objective

4.102 COPR r1.1 sets out the overriding objective of the rules which is to enable the court to deal with a case justly 'having regard to the principles contained in the Act'.

4.103 The principles contained in the MCA 2005 are those set out in section 1. So, for example, a person should not be held to lack capacity to make litigation decisions merely because they make what others regard as an unwise decision or until all practicable steps to help them litigate their own case have been taken without success.

Duty of the parties

4.104 COPR r1.4 then provides that 'the parties are required to help the court to further the overriding objective'. Thus, for example, so far as practicable they must help to save litigation expense and deal with the case in ways which are proportionate to the nature, importance and complexity of the issues. In an appropriate case, the penalty for not doing so would be not to allow the party all of their costs in a property and financial affairs case or to require them to contribute to another party's costs in a case involving, eg health and welfare. This is discussed further in chapters 8 and 10.

63 Cases which are not on pathways are: (a) uncontested applications; (b) applications for statutory wills and gifts; (c) applications made by the Public Guardian; (d) applications relating to serious medical treatment; (e) applications in Form COPDOL11 (ie so called '*Re X*' applications for judicial applications of deprivation of liberty) and (f) applications in Form DLA (ie applications challenging deprivation of liberty authorisations under Schedule A1);

Who are the parties to the proceedings?

4.105 Unlike proceedings in other courts, the parties do not define themselves – although they will generally be the applicant(s), any objectors and, in significant personal welfare cases, the person said to be incapacitated. The district judge dealing with a case initially must identify the persons who should be parties and ensure that notice is given to other relevant people to enable them to be joined if they wish.

Involvement of the person concerned

4.106 The reasons why it is important to involve the relevant person in proceedings that involve making decisions about their life and future well-being include the following:

- It is their life and the proceedings are for their benefit.
- Dignity – not allowing or facilitating participation degrades the individual and strips them of their rights as a citizen.
- One of the two basic principles of natural justice is *audi alteram partem*: 'no man is to be condemned unheard'. A legal right of access to courts for citizens whose rights are affected by the litigation is a basic constitutional right.
- Participation provides a procedural safeguard against arbitrariness. The person can ensure that questions are asked of witnesses and that they are challenged on key points.
- The judge understands the emotional context and the importance of the decision to the person.
- It therefore improves the quality of the decision-making.
- It often changes the outcome.

4.107 COPR r1.2 is concerned with the participation of the relevant person. Having considered the issues raised in the case, whether it is contentious and any response of the person on being notified of the application, the court must always consider making one of a number of directions. These directions are joining the person as a party to the proceedings, appointing an accredited legal representative or non-legal representative for them, arranging for them to have an opportunity to address the judge, giving some other appropriate direction, or (having considered the matter) making no direction at all. In practice, the options available to the judge are often severely limited by the unavailability of legal aid and the financial circumstances of the public authorities and family members involved. A flexible approach is necessary which has regard to the person's wishes and feelings and seeks to facilitate their attendance and participation in decisions affecting them. Depending on the particular circumstances, this may be achieved by, for example, their attendance at hearings; telephone hearings; inviting and considering their letters and written representations; the use of advocates; a visit to the person at their home, hospital or place where they are detained; or by a combination of all of these approaches. See further, in this regard, chapters 11 and 16.

WAYS OF INVOLVING A PERSON IN THEIR CASE
By attendance at the hearing
By meeting the judge in their chambers (private room)
By the judge travelling to meet the person
By telephone
By Skype/video
By letter, email exchange or witness statement
Through the Official Solicitor
Through their own solicitor
Through a litigation friend
Through an attorney or deputy
Through their RPR (relevant person's representative) or r1.2 representative
By allowing a McKenzie friend
By commissioning a s49 or independent expert report
By utilising a trusted professional, such as a social worker
Through the evidence of family and friends
By historic documentary evidence of wishes and feelings
By the appointment of an examiner under the rules
By using specialist interpreters
Inferences from behaviour (what makes them happy, etc)

Litigation friends

4.108 Because the COPR are based on the Rules of the Supreme Court, rather than the Mental Health Tribunal Rules, they require the relevant person to have a litigation friend or to be represented by an Accredited Legal Representative if they are made a party to the proceedings (or intend to be a party) and lack capacity to conduct the proceedings.[64] This issue is dealt with in chapter 12.

Case management

4.109 By COPR r1.3, the court is required to further the overriding objective by actively managing cases.

Hearings

4.110 Most hearings take place in court, but they can take place in a hospital, nursing home or other agreed venue where this is necessary in order to enable the relevant person to participate. As now retired District Judge Gordon Ashton OBE has observed on many occasions, the approach may be adversarial, inquisitorial or conciliatory according to the needs of the case.

4.111 Historically, the general rule in the Court of Protection has always been that hearings are held in private. This was considered to reflect the personal, private, nature of the information which the court is usually considering. However, a transparency pilot scheme was introduced on 29 January 2016 (see Court of Protection Practice Direction – Transparency Pilot), which has now become PD 4C.

4.112 COPR Part 4 is concerned with public and private hearings, and PD 4C deals with transparency. The court will ordinarily (and so without any application being made) make an order that any attended hearing shall be in public; and in the same order, impose restrictions in relation to the publication of information about the proceedings, in particular the identity of the person concerned and family members. See further chapter 14.

Legal aid

4.113 For property and affairs cases, public funding is not available. In most kinds of personal welfare cases it is severely restricted, and where available generally means-assessed. This issue is dealt with in chapter 6.

64 COPR r17.2(1).

Personal Support Unit

4.114 The Personal Support Unit (PSU) volunteers at First Avenue House do not give legal advice. However, subject to resources, they may be able to support litigants in person by:

- prompting them to order their thoughts;
- tidying paperwork into a rational order, and indexing it;
- helping them to find out which forms they need to fill in, to complete them if they know what they want to say, and to take the paperwork to the appropriate customer service desk or court office;
- helping people find their way around the court building;
- assisting in discussions with court staff;
- going into court with the person to offer support;
- signposting clients to free legal advice or representation, or to access relevant advice online.

McKenzie friends and lay representation

McKenzie friends

4.115 Litigants who cannot arrange legal representation have the right to have reasonable assistance from a suitable layperson, sometimes called a 'McKenzie friend'.

4.116 A McKenzie friend may:

- provide moral support;
- take notes;
- help with case papers;
- quietly give advice on any aspect of the conduct of the case.

4.117 A McKenzie friend may not act as advocate or to carry out the conduct of litigation. Specifically, they may not:

- act as the litigant's agent in relation to the proceedings;
- manage the litigant's case outside court, for example by signing court documents;
- address the court, make oral submissions or examine witnesses.

See further chapter 6.

Lay representation

4.118 COPR r1.2 provides that the court may appoint a non-legal representative for the relevant person. Their function is to provide the court with information about the person's wishes, feelings, beliefs and values, and to discharge any other functions directed by the court.

4.119 That rule aside, lay representation is not generally allowed. The court should only be prepared to grant a right of audience or a right to conduct litigation to a layperson where there is good reason to do so, taking into account all the circumstances of the case, which are likely to vary greatly. Such grants should not be extended to laypersons automatically or without due consideration, and should not be granted for mere convenience.

4.120 Examples of the type of special circumstances which have been held to justify the grant of a right of audience to a layperson, including a McKenzie friend, are that:

- the person is a close relative of the litigant;
- health problems preclude the litigant from addressing the court, or conducting litigation, and the litigant cannot afford to pay for a qualified legal representative;
- the litigant is relatively inarticulate and prompting by that person may unnecessarily prolong the proceedings.[65]

Appeals

4.121 The appellate court will not interfere with the original decision unless the judge erred in principle or reached a conclusion that was wrong. See further chapter 19.

Enforcement of orders and declarations

4.122 The court has all the powers of the High Court within the scope of its jurisdiction, and the COPR incorporate many of the enforcement provisions contained in the Civil Procedure Rules 1998. See further chapter 18.

65 In this respect, see the practice guidance: *McKenzie friends (Civil and Family Courts)* issued on 12 July 2010 by Lord Neuberger of Abbotsbury (the then Master of the Rolls) and Sir Nicholas Wall (the then President of the Family Division).

CHAPTER 5

Is an application appropriate?

Introduction

5.1 There are many reasons why people 'go to law'. Not all of them are well thought out, and many people have later regretted doing so in haste. It is sensible, therefore, to consider carefully whether an application to the Court of Protection is necessary as a matter of law, or appropriate as being in the person's best interests.

5.2 The matters to think through before applying include the following:

JURISDICTION	
Does the Court of Protection have jurisdiction to consider the proposed application?	• There is little point applying to the court unless it has power to grant the remedy sought. • The court's jurisdiction is defined by the Mental Capacity Act (MCA) 2005. Most obviously, it is a jurisdiction exercisable only over people who lack (or, on an interim basis, appear to lack) capacity as defined by the Act. • Remember that a person must be assumed to have capacity unless it is established that they lack capacity. Furthermore, a person is not to be treated as being unable to make their own decision unless all practicable steps to help them to do so have been taken without success, or merely because they make or propose making an unwise decision. • Even if the person is incapacitated, certain family law matters (such as consenting to the making of an adoption order) and Mental Health Act (MHA) 1983 matters (treatment without consent under that Act) are excluded from its jurisdiction: see sections 27 and 28. • Depending on the type of decision to be made, the court's jurisdiction may be restricted to incapacitated adults (eg statutory wills, lasting powers of attorney (LPAs)), to persons aged 16 or over (eg treatment or care issues) or available to people of all ages (property and financial affairs matters where the child's incapacity is likely to last into adulthood). • Court of Protection Rules 2017[1] (COPR) r13.1 and Practice Direction (PD) 3A contain provisions for disputing the court's jurisdiction.

1 SI 2017 No 1035.

LEGAL NECESSITY	
Is an application necessary?	In various situations, an application is a legal necessity. For example, in the personal welfare sphere, certain cases involving medical treatment (see chapter 23); in the financial sphere, situations where there is a need for someone with capacity to manage an incapacitated person's property.
APPROPRIATENESS	
Is an application appropriate? This is case-specific and depends on many things. For example:	Even if an application is not necessary, it may still be appropriate to apply because an application is reasonably believed to be in the relevant person's best interests. • Whether what is required can be done lawfully and in the person's best interests without the court's involvement (ask what is in their best interests having regard to their legal rights and circumstances). • The person's wishes, feelings, beliefs and values and all of the other relevant circumstances. • The likely benefits for the person concerned (ask in what ways the application will benefit them). • The likely cost for the person concerned, not just financially but emotionally if personal or family discord is likely to result (ask in what ways the application may cause them harm). • The affordability of proceedings for the relevant person. Even relatively modest costs may be unaffordable. The Court of Protection has the same status as the High Court and the fees charged for applications, legal assistance and reports tend to reflect this. It is essential to avoid *Jarndyce v Jarndyce* situations where the costs of litigation approach or exceed the value of the estate. Everyone involved is under a duty to deal with the underlying issues in a proportionate and cost-effective manner. • Who is at risk of bearing the litigation costs. It should not be assumed that whatever the merits of the application each party will pay their own litigation costs or that the costs will be recoverable from the incapacitated person's estate. The rules enable the court to have regard to the conduct of the parties, which includes their conduct before as well as during the proceedings, whether it was reasonable for them to raise, pursue or contest a particular issue, etc.

continued

	• The strength of the evidence and the chances of the application succeeding (is there sufficient evidence in support of it and is the court likely to be persuaded to exercise its powers?). • The suitability and appropriateness of the applicant (ought it to be obvious that another person such as a spouse or partner is better placed to apply and will reasonably object?). • Relevant guidance in the Codes of Practice. • The availability of more appropriate alternative procedures or remedies: – Can the matter wait until the person recovers capacity and is able to take the decision for themselves? – Is this the simplest and most appropriate legal way to address this person's needs? – Can the purpose which the applicant has in mind be as effectively achieved in another way which is less restrictive of the person's rights and freedom of action? – Where relevant, does the person still have capacity to complete an LPA or advance decision? – Can what is proposed lawfully and appropriately be done in the person's best interests under MCA 2005 s5? – Does anyone such as an attorney or deputy already have authority to make this decision for the person? – Is it more appropriate to proceed under a different statute, eg guardianship under the MHA 1983, the Children Act 1989 or public health legislation? – If the matter is contentious, are discussions and negotiations really at an end? Is there a possibility of mediation? Would the appointment of an independent mental capacity advocate (IMCA) or a person with a similar independent role help?
PERMISSION	
If permission to make the application is required, is it likely to be granted?	• In order to prevent applications which are frivolous, vexatious, an abuse of process or otherwise an illegitimate interference with the interests and rights of the relevant person, the court's permission is required to make some applications: see MCA 2005 s50 and COPR rr8.1–8.3. • When deciding whether to grant permission, MCA 2005 s50(3) requires the court to consider:

	(a) the applicant's connection with the person concerned; (b) the reasons for the asking the court to appoint a deputy to make personal welfare decisions for the person concerned; (c) in what ways the person concerned will benefit from having a deputy appointed to make personal welfare decisions for them; (d) whether those benefits can be achieved in any other way. • Even when permission is required, it is simply a filtering stage. Permission ought to be granted where, having regard to these and any other relevant considerations, on the material available to the court the application deserves fuller investigation by it and, realistically, the order sought may be in the best interests of the relevant person.

Maxims and principles

5.3 Opinion varies – otherwise it would not be an opinion. Having acknowledged that, there is a good case for saying that the following common-sense maxims and principles have proved their utility when it comes to reflecting on whether to intervene in someone else's life:

1) First, do no harm – there are many we cannot help, but none we cannot avoid harming. This principle is as important to the practice of law as it is to the practice of medicine.[2]
2) Give due weight to the importance for the person concerned of their liberty and wish to determine their own course in life.
3) In order to avoid disappointment later, be realistic about the proper function of the law and its limits. One can legislate for marriage but not for a happy marriage. The law provides a useful framework for managing conflict, conferring authority, enforcing legal duties and restraining the unlawful exercise of power. It cannot solve family conflict and underlying resentment, that feeling of not being a loved or favoured child, a

2 'The wicked are wicked, no doubt, and they go astray and they fall, and they come by their deserts; but who can tell the mischief which the very virtuous do?,' Thackeray, *The Newcomes*, Book 1 chapter 20. There is a great deal to be said for 'legal homeopathy': the application of minute, sub-clinical, doses of law. That is tongue-in-cheek, but the lightest touch is often the best.

scarcity of resources, the disease process itself or the fact that the person concerned must soon die.

4) Accept that risk cannot be avoided. All personal welfare decisions involve balancing competing risks of which the risk to the person's physical safety is but one. Where appropriate, in order to avoid practising too defensively consider applying (or applying in the alternative) for a declaration that it *is* lawful and in the person's best interests to take the conventional safeguarding risk rather than to avoid it (by, for example, separating them from their life-partner and removing them to a care home). Let the judge take the strain; that is why they are there.
5) Consider the adequacy of your evidence.

Considering the evidence

5.4 Lawyers spend much time discussing new case-law and the nuances of particular sections. However, for every case lost on a point of law, a thousand are lost for want of evidence; and a few more for procedural reasons such as missing time-limits and non-compliance with directions.

5.5 The lawyers' old maxim 'only a fool bags himself as a brief' acknowledges that everyone finds it difficult to be objective about a case in which they have a strong personal interest.

5.6 Much litigation in the Court of Protection is the result of historic family tensions, in particular disagreements between siblings and step-relations. Strained relationships over many years now colour each child's personal assessment of the evidence as to which of them is best placed to take on day-to-day decision-making for an incapacitated parent.

5.7 Where there are longstanding family issues and an application is likely to be opposed, it is sensible to take legal advice on the evidence and merits of a possible application. Litigation is easy to start, often demanding to pursue and sometimes costly to withdraw or settle.

5.8 Given human nature, it is also often quite easy for a person to satisfy themselves that an application for a proposed gift or will in their favour is one in the incapacitated person's best interests. Again, it is prudent to take neutral advice on the weight of the evidence and what to expect before setting out. At this point the question to ask is not 'What do I make of it?' but 'What is a judge likely to make of it?'

5.9 In the case of local authority safeguarding applications, evidential problems often have a different cause. Local safeguarding investigations rarely involve full disclosure, forensic questioning or independent scrutiny. Consequently, in court the findings reached may not withstand that level of scrutiny. See further chapter 24 in relation to the interaction between safeguarding obligations and going to the Court of Protection.

5.10 To summarise, before embarking on litigation that is likely to be contested it is particularly important to assess objectively the strength of one's case and the adequacy of one's evidence.

Example

5.11 Mrs Smith is a 95-year-old widow who suffers from moderate to severe dementia. She lives with her son and daughter-in-law, Ms Jones. She is taken to a day centre three times a week by a paid carer. Staff at the day centre notice that she has a bruise and Mrs Smith says that her daughter-in-law caused it and that she is frightened of her. Wessex County Council are contacted and place Mrs Smith in a care home under a 'DOLS (deprivation of liberty safeguards) order', ie a standard authorisation. Several months later, an adult safeguarding investigation concludes on the balance of probabilities that the bruising was non-accidental. The family start Court of Protection proceedings seeking a declaration that it is in Mrs Smith's best interests to return home.

What is the local authority's submission?	That it is in Mrs Smith's best interests not to return to the family home and that she should remain in the care home.
What is the local authority trying to prove?	Ill-treatment by her family.
How does it prove this?	By evidence.
What is the evidence?	The evidence consists of: i) the fact that bruising was observed by care home staff; and ii) Mrs Smith's statement as to its cause.
How reliable is the evidence?	Given that the family deny ill-treatment, the key evidential questions are: a) What is the evidence that the bruising is of a kind consistent with non-accidental injury?

continued

b) What is the evidence that Mrs Smith is or is not a reliable witness of events, eg that her dementia has not affected her reliability, that she was not led in her account and that she is not motivated by malice?

5.12 As to a), bruising may be related to factors such as age, gender, health status and medication. It is necessary to consider the location, age and pattern of the bruising and any other injuries, the physical indicators of abuse, the behavioural indicators of abuse and the pool of possible perpetrators. Ideally, an applicant requires expert contemporaneous mapping and recording of the injuries by a forensic medical examiner and expert interpretation of the evidence recorded by this examination.

5.13 Although one would never take a child care order application to court without obtaining this evidence, in the case of alleged elder abuse this evidence is very rarely obtained; and by the time the case comes to court, it is too late to obtain it.

5.14 As to b), there are clear evidential problems given the severity of Mrs Smith's dementia, the passage of time, the fact that the allegations are strongly denied and the number of demonstrably inaccurate allegations made by her in respect of other people.

5.15 By the time of the trial, the situation facing the local authority is that there are a number of possible explanations and a pool of possible perpetrators of any non-accidental injury. The alleged perpetrator has no relevant history and Mrs Smith has been living with her family for some years with no previous concerns of this kind being raised. On the evidence, it is accepted that Mrs Smith has made other allegations which must be the result of confusion. The key evidential omission was not obtaining contemporaneous medical evidence and a forensic opinion on the significance (if any) of the bruising.

Analysing one's own case and evidence

5.16 The approach adopted in the following table is not a substitute for analysing the evidence and taking appropriate advice in each particular case. It is merely an example of how one can devise a simple structure to test the quality and internal consistency of one's own case.

	Example 1	Example 2	Example 3	
Type of case	**Place of residence dispute**	**Suitability of a deputy**	**Contact dispute**	
Jurisdiction: can the court do what you want? (the application)	The court may determine P's place of residence (MCA 2005 s17)	The court may revoke a deputy's appointment (MCA 2005 s16)	The court may decide contact issues (MCA 2005 s17)	
The local authority's best interests submission (the submission)	It is in P's best interests to reside at care home X, not at her own home	It is in P's best interests to remove his current deputy	It is in P's best interests not to have unsupervised contact with Y	
What the local authority is alleging/ seeking to prove (the findings sought)	Ill-treatment at home by relatives	The existing deputy has stolen money from P	Sexually inappropriate behaviour by Y	
The evidence for the allegation (the facts which prove the allegation)	Bruising P's oral account	Bank statements Failure to account Failure to explain	Staff observations P's oral account	
Possible alternative explanations which will need to be ruled out on the balance of probabilities (likely defences)	Innocent alternative cause of the bruising P is an unreliable witness	P gifted the money P has capacity P owed the money Money spent on P	P has capacity/consents P enjoys sexual contact Faulty observation	P is an unreliable witness
Evidence re any less restrictive options	Exclude a particular relative or restrict contact with them? Arrange alternative carers or offer additional support?	Retrospective validation of the transaction if no dishonesty, etc	The friendship is in P's best interests	
P = the incapacitated person				

Admissibility and weight of the evidence

5.17 Evidence is discussed in detail in chapter 13, but nowadays there are few strict rules concerning the admissibility of evidence, particularly in the Court of Protection.

5.18 COPR Part 14 deals with evidence and the court's power to control it. Subject to complying with the rules, the court's discretion and the odd caveat, the general position is simply that to be admissible evidence must be relevant. 'Relevance' means relevant to the issues which the court must decide and evidence is relevant if it makes a matter which requires proof more or less probable.[3]

5.19 If evidence is relevant, one must next consider the weight which a court is likely to give it, that is how credible and persuasive it is. The case may consist of a mixture of agreed first-hand evidence (things actually said to or observed by a witness), disputed first-hand evidence, valid and invalid inferences from agreed or disputed first-hand evidence, hearsay (agreed or disputed 'facts' communicated to a witness), inferences from hearsay, assumptions and suspicions ('It must be, or is likely to be, the case that . . .'), professional presumptions, professional opinions, 'independent expert opinions'.

5.20 If a matter is likely to be contested, some of the questions to consider at this stage are:

- Can all of our 'evidence' be used in court? (This often raises issues of confidentiality; the availability, willingness and compellability of witnesses; and the unrepeatability of some suspicions and corridor conversations.)
- What are the gaps in our evidence?
- Assuming the facts are as stated, are the inferences that have been drawn valid?
- What are the weaknesses in our case?
- How impressive are our witnesses and how expert is our expert evidence?
- What will the other side be saying or putting to our witnesses?
- Does the other side have any good points and is their evidence accurate and reliable?
- Even if our witnesses are right, do we have sufficient evidence that we can provide a better alternative for the incapacitated person to the situation which we are trying to remedy?

3 See *Director of Public Prosecutions v Kilbourne* [1973] AC 729 at 756, HL. As Lord Bingham once noted, contested trials last long enough as it is without spending time on evidence which is irrelevant and cannot affect the outcome.

The standard of proof

5.21 The standard of proof in Court of Protection proceedings is always 'the balance of probabilities'. Precisely how this works in the context of the Court of Protection and, in particular, where allegations of abuse or neglect have been made, is examined in chapter 15.

5.22 The balance of probability standard means that a court is satisfied an event occurred if the court considers that, on the evidence, the occurrence of the event was more likely than not. When assessing the probabilities the court will have in mind as a factor, to whatever extent is appropriate in the particular case, that the more serious the allegation the less likely it is that the event occurred and, hence, the stronger should be the evidence before the court concludes that the allegation is established on the balance of probability. Fraud is usually less likely than negligence. Deliberate physical injury is usually less likely than accidental physical injury. A step-father is usually less likely to have repeatedly raped and had non-consensual oral sex with his under-age stepdaughter than on some occasion to have lost his temper and slapped her. Built into the preponderance of probability standard is a generous degree of flexibility in respect of the seriousness of the allegation.

5.23 Although the result is much the same, this does not mean that where a serious allegation is in issue the standard of proof required is higher. It means only that the inherent probability or improbability of an event is itself a matter to be taken into account when weighing the probabilities and deciding whether, on balance, the event occurred. The more improbable the event, the stronger must be the evidence that it did occur before, on the balance of probability, its occurrence will be established. Ungoed-Thomas J expressed this neatly in *In re Dellow's Will Trusts*:[4]

> The more serious the allegation the more cogent is the evidence required to overcome the unlikelihood of what is alleged and thus to prove it.

5.24 This substantially accords with the approach adopted in authorities such as the well-known judgment of Morris LJ in *Hornal v Neuberger Products Ltd*.[5] This approach also provides a means by which the balance of probability standard can accommodate one's instinctive feeling that even in civil proceedings a court should be more sure

4 [1964] 1 WLR 451 at 455, ChD.
5 [1957] 1 QB 247 at 266, CA.

before finding serious allegations proved than when deciding less serious or trivial matters.

5.25 It is also necessary to consider the setting within which the 'evidence' was given; as to this, see the observations of McFarlane J (as he then was) in *Re SA*:[6]

> 68. When looking at evidence from a witness who is engaged in providing therapy to an individual who then, during the course of the therapeutic relationship, makes statements which are then produced as evidence of the truth, the words of Butler-Sloss LJ in *Re D (Child Abuse: Interviews)* [1998] 2 FLR 10 must be borne in mind:
>
> > 'It is essential to distinguish between interviewing the child to ascertain the facts and interviewing to provide the child with help to unburden her worries. The therapeutic interview would seem to me to be generally unsuited to use as part of the court evidence, although there may be rare cases in which it is necessary to use it.'
>
> 69. Often the therapist will alert others to matters of concern arising from the therapeutic interview and the child or vulnerable person may then be subject to an interview aimed at the forensic process – as indeed happened here with the ABE interview. In the event the ABE interview did not provide any evidence to support the local authority case and thus reliance is made on the original statements made to AL. I do not regard AJ's reports as being inadmissible or to be automatically of no weight, but I do have regard to the observations of Butler-Sloss LJ and, the reasons behind them, in being cautious as to the amount of weight that can be attached to the material that originates from the drama therapy sessions.

Evidence meeting

5.26 Time and resources permitting, there is a lot to be said for having an evidence meeting before issuing what is likely to be a contested application.

Possible alternative remedies

5.27 The practice of law is concerned with remedies – people go to a lawyer or a court for the same reason they see a doctor, in order to obtain a remedy.

5.28 Sometimes there will be a more appropriate alternative to making an application to the Court of Protection.

6 [2010] EWHC 196 (Admin), [2010] 1 FLR 1836.

5.29 Most courts deal only with litigious matters. The Court of Protection is unusual in that much of its work, particularly on the property and financial side, is non-litigious. Here there is often a common goal, which is to put in place a protective legal framework for a person who is unable to protect and promote their own personal interests.

5.30 The remainder of this chapter considers or lists possible alternative remedies under the following headings:

- non-contentious property and financial matters;
- contentious property and financial matters;
- non-contentious personal welfare matters; and
- contentious personal welfare matters.

Non-contentious property and financial matters

Steps to take

5.31 Where a person appears to be incapable of managing their property and affairs or a particular transaction, the *first step* is to verify this. Capacity often fluctuates, no one is to be found incapable unless all practicable steps to help them make their own decision have been taken unsuccessfully, the correct legal test must be applied and the answer may depend on the significance and complexity of the matter in hand.

5.32 If the person does lack capacity, the *second step* is to establish if and when they may recover capacity, and whether the decision(s) can be postponed until they are able to act for themselves.

5.33 If a decision is required now, the *third step* is to check whether arrangements are already in place for managing the situation. For example, did the person execute an enduring power of attorney (EPA) or LPA when they had capacity, or has a deputy already been authorised to make decisions of this kind?

5.34 If not, the *fourth step* is the check whether the person's affairs are sufficiently complicated to require the appointment of a deputy or whether an alternative procedure will or may suffice.

5.35 The court process for appointing a deputy is not onerous in most cases. It consists of ensuring that there is adequate evidence of incapacity, information about the person's finances, identifying possible conflicts of interest and ensuring that close family members are notified and have an opportunity to object to the proposed arrangement.

5.36 However, the appointed deputy must then usually take out security, file annual reports with the Public Guardian, pay an annual supervision fee and so forth. It is therefore worth considering whether there are any other suitable ways of managing the person's finances in their best interests which avoid supervision of what hitherto has been the individual's private life and all the expense that goes with that.

5.37 Some of the main options are those given in the following table, which is based on one in Ashton's *Elderly People and the Law*:[7]

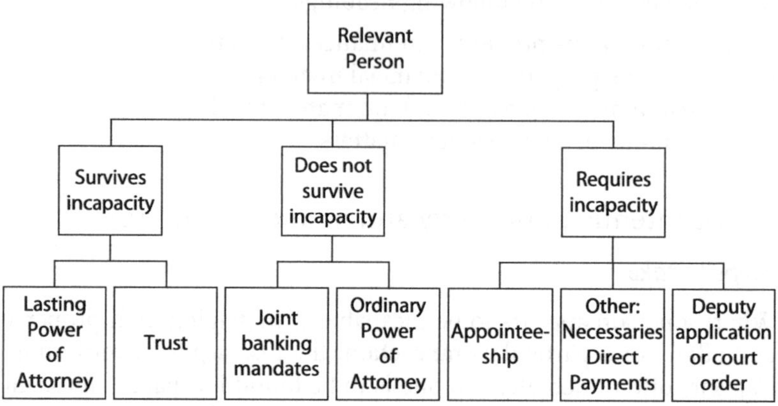

Lasting power of attorney

5.38 The best way of avoiding the need for a court-appointed deputy is for the relevant person to execute an LPA, provided of course that they still have capacity to do so.

5.39 The important point to bear in mind is that a person may lack capacity to manage their property and affairs in a general sense, so that the court could lawfully appoint a deputy to manage their estate, but still have sufficient capacity to execute an LPA.

5.40 In other words, the person concerned may retain sufficient capacity to be able to make their own arrangements for the future management of their estate. If so, they can appoint (say) their spouse or partner as their attorney, which avoids the need for the latter to apply to be appointed as their deputy.

5.41 The possibility arises because capacity is 'issue-specific' and depends on the transaction or decision in hand.

5.42 Because the relevant individual's capacity is borderline in such cases, it is imperative to ensure that the certificate of capacity is completed by an independent professional such as a general

7 G Ashton, *Elderly People and the Law*, Butterworths, London, 1995, p299.

practitioner or solicitor and to establish that close family members and any other key individuals accept the capacity finding.

5.43 Provided there is nothing untoward, the arrangement has clear advantages in terms of maintaining the historic privacy, simplicity and trust of a long-standing relationship. Although there is a fee to be paid for registering an LPA, this is less than the standard court fee payable when filing a deputy application.

Enduring power of attorney

5.44 Once the MCA 2005 came into force on 1 October 2007, it was no longer possible to execute an EPA. However, EPAs made before then were not revoked by the Act and continue to have legal effect, subject to the need for registration if the attorney has reason to believe that the donor is becoming mentally incapable of managing and administering their property and affairs.

Trusts

5.45 It is possible for a person who is concerned that they may be becoming mentally incapacitated to create a trust. This involves transferring money and assets to trustees on terms that require the trustees to manage the trust fund for the benefit of the individual who has created it (and perhaps for the benefit of others also). The relevant test is whether the person has capacity to make the trust at the same time and *Re Beaney*[8] provides some guidance as to this.

5.46 As Ashton noted in 1995, this approach lost some popularity once it became possible for an individual who was beginning to lose capacity to create an EPA. It was then easy for them to enter into a lasting arrangement with a trusted person for the latter to manage the former's property as their agent without the need to create a trust and give up legal ownership of the property to trustees.

5.47 There is usually a tension between the settlor's various objectives. They will often wish to retain ultimate control over the money and to be able to call for it to be spent on them. However, to obtain tax advantages or to avoid it being taken into account in the assessment of means-tested benefits, it is usually necessary to give up any form of control.

5.48 The tax consequences of placing money in trust need to be carefully considered, as do the extent to which the trustees will be legally obliged to maintain the person who created it. In addition, unless the

8 [1978] 1 WLR 770, [1978] 2 All ER 595, ChD.

trust was of a very specific nature, and entered into before there was any reason to believe that the settlor may need residential or nursing care it is extremely unlikely that the trust would be effective at sheltering assets from local authority assessment. Professional advice is essential if a trust is being contemplated. For these reasons the trust is no longer popular as a vehicle for planning for future incapacity.

Banking arrangements

5.49 An account-holder who has mental capacity can authorise someone to access their account, for example because they have physical disabilities. This is called a 'third-party mandate'.[9] A common alternative is for an individual to appoint someone to act as their agent under an ordinary power of attorney. However, neither arrangement survives mental incapacity.

5.50 Joint accounts and other banking arrangements often seem an attractive proposition from a planning point of view compared with other more formal mechanisms. However, as with all mechanisms, they also have limitations and drawbacks. In particular, they can run into the practical difficulty that not all banks and building societies adopt the same procedures when a joint account-holder loses capacity. The degree of flexibility may sometimes depend on their knowledge of the account and their relationship with the account-holders. In some cases, the bank may continue to pay pre-existing direct debits and standing orders for utilities, household bills, residential care fees and living expenses until a deputy has been appointed or a power of attorney has been registered.

Ordinary power of attorney

5.51 An ordinary or general power of attorney can be effective for a specified period of time (for example, to cover a trip abroad) or run indefinitely until the donor brings it to an end by revoking it. The authority granted by the document is automatically revoked if the donor becomes mentally incapacitated.

5.52 Because the donor must be legally competent, an ordinary or general power of attorney does not need to be registered by the Public Guardian.

9 *Guidance for people wanting to manage a bank account for someone else*, AE254, British Bankers' Association (BBA), November 2015, available at: www.gov.uk/government/publications/deputy-and-attorney-guidance-dealing-with-banks.

Appointeeships

5.53 A deputyship may be unnecessary where the person's income consists solely of a state pension or benefits and they have no savings or equity in a house that needs to be sold.

5.54 In such cases, a spouse, partner or other suitable person can apply to the Department for Work and Pensions (DWP) for the pension or benefits to be paid to them as the person's 'appointee'. The appointee is authorised to receive the benefits and manage the benefit income. The appointee has various responsibilities and functions. The appointee:

- must report any change in the person's circumstances that may affect benefit entitlement;
- may sign on behalf of the person if they are a non-taxpayer to enable bank and building society interest to be paid without deducting income tax;
- can only deal with the person's income from benefits, except for small amounts of savings which can be used to meet unforeseen emergencies.

5.55 Once the proposed appointee has completed the usual form, a representative from the DWP may visit the relevant person or ask for evidence confirming that they are no longer able to act on their own behalf.

5.56 Current departmental guidance is that the appointee should, wherever possible, be a close relative who lives with the person or visits them frequently. In certain circumstances, the appointee may be a friend, neighbour or professional carer.

5.57 An appointee who does not wish to continue in the role can resign and the DWP can revoke an appointeeship if it has evidence that the appointee is not acting in the person's best interests.

5.58 The regulations provide that a court-appointed deputy automatically becomes the relevant person's appointee in place of any existing appointee, but are silent as to the effect of registering an EPA or LPA.

Limitations and disadvantages

5.59 The limitations of an appointeeship arrangement are fairly obvious: an appointee does not have authority to deal with capital or with other income belonging to the incapacitated person. A court order and/or the appointment of a deputy will be necessary if authority is required to manage other assets which the relevant person lacks capacity to manage, such as real property, personal possessions, cars, shares and so on.

5.60 Unspent pension and benefits may constitute capital. The general view for some time now has been that a deputy application is unnecessary provided that the appointee only holds a 'reasonable sum' of accrued savings. However, some banks set limits on the amount of money that a person can have in an appointeeship account.

Other options

5.61 A number of other provisions are helpful on occasion.

Payment for necessary goods and services

5.62 MCA 2005 s7(1) provides that: 'If necessary goods or services are supplied to a person who lacks capacity to contract for the supply, he must pay a reasonable price for them.' By subsection (2), 'necessary' means suitable to a person's condition in life and to their actual requirements at the time when the goods or services are supplied.

5.63 This provision combined the old common law rule relating to services with the statutory rule in the Sale of Goods Act 1979 relating to goods. Thus, if the milkman carries on delivering milk to the house of someone who has a progressive dementia, they can expect to be paid. If, however, a roofer puts a completely unnecessary new roof on to that person's house, when all that was required was a minor repair, then the rule will not apply.

Expenditure on the person's behalf

5.64 MCA 2005 s8(1) provides that where someone does an act to which section 5 applies which involves expenditure in connection with another person's care or treatment then it is lawful for them to pledge payment from the person's estate and also to apply money in the person's possession to meet the expenditure.

5.65 Furthermore, if expenditure is borne on the person's behalf by the individual acting under section 5, it is lawful for the latter to reimburse themselves from any money in the person's possession or to be otherwise indemnified by them.

5.66 This restates the common law rules which provided that a person acting as an 'agent of necessity' for another person should not be out of pocket as a result. However, nothing in the clause allows a carer to gain access to the relevant person's funds where they are held by a third party such as a bank or building society.

Direct payments

5.67 Direct payments are local authority cash payments for people who have been assessed as being entitled to help from social services and who would like to arrange and pay for their own, independently contracted, care and support services.

5.68 Where a person with eligible needs lacks capacity to consent to the making of direct payments, a suitable person can be appointed to manage the payments on their behalf.[10] This could be an attorney, deputy, DWP appointee or other person such as a carer.

5.69 The suitable person is the only person who can access and manage the direct payment. The account should be in their name but identified as being held on behalf of the person the payments are for (for example, 'Joan Smith on behalf of Edward Smith').[11]

Personal health budgets

5.70 Since October 2014, people receiving NHS Continuing Healthcare at home have had the right to receive a personal health budget. This can be paid to someone suitable on behalf of an incapacitated person: see regulations 5 and 6 of the National Health Service (Direct Payments) Regulations 2013[12] which are concerned with the appointment of representatives and nominees for incapacitated persons.

Court orders other than deputyship

5.71 Where the authority of the Court of Protection is required, it is not always necessary to appoint a deputy.

5.72 The court is frequently asked to make single orders dealing with matters such as authorising an individual to sign or surrender a tenancy agreement, to litigate on an incapacitated person's behalf, to access their health or social care records, to challenge NHS funding decisions, to ratify a gift and so on. In some cases it ought not to be necessary to obtain a court order, for example in relation to access to records, but the applicant has been frustrated in their attempts to

10 See (in England) Care Act 2014 s32, and the Care and Support (Direct Payments) Regulations 2014 SI No 2871. In Wales, the relevant provisions are contained in the Social Services and Well-being (Wales) Act 2014 s50 and the Care and Support (Direct Payments) (Wales) Regulations 2015 SI No 1815 (W260).

11 *Guidance for people wanting to manage a bank account for someone else*, AE254, British Bankers' Association (BBA), November 2015, available at: www.gov.uk/government/publications/deputy-and-attorney-guidance-dealing-with-banks.

12 SI No 1617, as amended by the National Health Service (Direct Payments) (Amendment) Regulations 2013 SI No 2354 and the National Health Service (Direct Payments) (Amendment) Regulations 2017 SI No 219.

persuade the relevant authority that they are suitable or that the step is in the incapacitated individual's best interests.

Contentious property and financial matters

5.73 Litigation or some formal action may be inevitable if a matter is contentious. The alternative ways forward then need to be explored. Consider the time limits for each possible court action[13] or complaint, the funding options for each and the remedies afforded by each. The aggrieved person needs to be clear about the outcome they wish to achieve – damages, the reversal of a funding decision, better services, disciplinary proceedings, the investigation and deregistration of a care home or service provider, an injunction, a prosecution, an apology, publicity – and who has power to provide that kind of remedy. Remember that the Court of Protection is not a regulatory, investigatory or complaints body, nor is it an inspectorate. Ombudsmen and regulators usually require that a complaint has been investigated locally and the service provider been given a fair opportunity to deal with the situation before considering a complaint.

5.74 Where possible, take professional legal advice or advice from Citizens Advice or a similar organisation. Be fair. Avoid multiple complaints to multiple bodies. This demoralises professionals, creates chaos and delay and damages the complainant's case. Be polite – apart from the fact that unpleasant emails and tweets are upsetting for those concerned, and may constitute a criminal offence, they are damaging when later produced in court and may have a bearing on who pays the litigation costs. Most important of all, if any step is being taken on behalf of an incapacitated person, remember that you must act in their best interests. Therefore apply the MCA 2005 s4 considerations and try to maintain a good relationship, or at least a working relationship, with their professional carers, family members, representatives and friends.

13 Where the claim is not for damages but what is known as equitable relief, for example an injunction, the equitable defence of laches (unreasonable delay in bringing the claim) may be raised.

PROPERTY AND FINANCIAL AFFAIRS – POSSIBLE ALTERNATIVE REMEDIES	
Remedy	**Possible relevance**
	MCA 2005 matters
Best interests meetings	• If the contentious matter is connected with different opinions as to what is in an incapacitated person's best interests with regard to their property and finances, consider whether there is a professional such as a solicitor or a neutral family member who could convene a best interests meeting. Explore what kinds of formal mediation and alternative dispute resolution (ADR) processes are available locally.
Complaints about a deputy or donee	• The Public Guardian supervises court-appointed deputies and deals with representations (including complaints) about the way in which a deputy or donee of an LPA is exercising their powers. These functions may be discharged in co-operation with any other person who has relevant safeguarding functions such as a local authority or the police. • On application by the Public Guardian, the Court of Protection can order that any security bond in place is 'called in' to make good any loss suffered by an incapacitated person as a result of mismanagement by their deputy.
Complaints about court funds	• Contrary to inaccurate press reports, the Court of Protection does not hold or administer funds on behalf of incapacitated people. It is the Court Funds Office (CFO) which provides a banking and administration service for the civil courts throughout England and Wales. See the Court Funds Rules 2011[b] or contact the Court Funds Office, Sunderland SR43 3AB.
	Complaints about an NHS or social services funding decision
NHS	• As to appeals against NHS decisions that a person does not qualify for NHS continuing healthcare, see the section below dealing with personal welfare matters.
Local authority	• As to local authority community care means assessments and charges, see the section below dealing with personal welfare matters.
	Ombudsmen and regulatory bodies
Ombudsmen	• Depending on the nature of the grievance, a number of ombudsmen and regulatory bodies may exercise a relevant function:

continued

b SI No 1734.

Remedy	Possible relevance
	• The Financial Ombudsman Service deals with complaints about banking, insurance, loans, credit and other financial services.
	• The Pensions Ombudsman deals with complaints and disputes about the way that occupational pension schemes and personal pensions are run.
	• The Solicitors Regulation Authority (SRA) is a regulatory body which deals with failures to comply with professional obligations such as the duty to keep the person's affairs confidential or the duty to act honestly and with integrity.
	• The Bar Standards Board (BSB) is the equivalent regulatory body for barristers.
	• The Legal Ombudsman deals with complaints that a poor service has been provided by a barrister, solicitor or legal executive, eg a failure to keep the client properly informed.
	• The Housing Ombudsman Service deals with complaints from people who receive a direct service from registered social landlords in England and certain other landlords who are members of the scheme, including bodies which take over homes transferred from local authorities.
Raising the matter with an elected representative or publicising it	
Member of Parliament (MP)	• A request to the relevant person's MP concerning the provision of a public service often produces positive action. However, MPs cannot properly become involved in litigation issues being dealt with by a court.
Councillor	• Similarly, a request to the person's local councillor about the provision of social services by (or through) the local authority can be effective.
Media/press	• This may be an option but it is a legal minefield and one to be exercised with tremendous caution in relation to someone who lacks capacity to decide for themselves whether to waive their usual right to privacy and confidentiality. Consider their capacity to make the decision for themselves, whether *you* have any legal decision for themselves, whether *you* have any legal right to waive their right to privacy or confidentiality, whether therefore you may be liable to the incapacitated person, the best interests considerations in MCA 2005 s4, the law relating to defamation (libel, slander) and the legal rights and remedies of the other people involved.

Remedy	Possible relevance
Other kinds of legal proceedings (civil)	
Actions relating to vulnerable or incapacitated persons	• As to the enforceability of contracts entered into by an incapacitated person, a contract is not enforceable against them if a) the relevant person was incapable of understanding the nature of the contract they were entering into and b) the other contracting party knew of their incapacity at the time, or knew of such facts and circumstances that they must be taken to have known of the incapacity. A separate rule applies to the supply of necessary goods and services, which is now set out in MCA 2005 s7.
	• A gift made by an incapacitated person may be avoided in the circumstances set out in[c] *Re Beaney*. In the case of a simple and trivial gift, such as giving a small present to a friend, there is not much to it and very little to grasp in order to make a valid gift. More significant transactions – those where the reasonably foreseeable consequences are more significant for the person concerned – by definition require the capacity to understand and weigh the more significant consequences.
	• Unless the commission of a tort (civil wrong) requires specific intention, such as malice, avoiding legal liability may be limited to acts done while in a state of automatism, Although there is a lack of recent authority, in *Mansfield v Weetabix Ltd*,[d] the Court of Appeal said that the question in a road traffic negligence case was whether the defendant did not know and could not reasonably have known of the infirmity which caused the road accident.
	• The common law duties of an attorney include duties a) of utmost good faith, b) to keep accounts, c) to disclose all relevant facts in certain transactions, d) not to make secret profits, e) to discharge duties with reasonable care.
Standard actions	• The relevant person has the usual range of available remedies in relation to breach of trust, breach of contract and torts (other civil wrongs which give rise to a right to a remedy, eg conversion, deceit, trespass to land, trespass to goods, nuisance, negligence).

continued

c [1978] 1 WLR 770, [1978] 2 All ER 595 at 600, ChD.

d [1998] 1 WLR 1263, CA.

Remedy	Possible relevance
	Other kinds of legal proceedings (criminal)
Offences relating to vulnerable or incapacitated persons	• Fraud Act 2006 s4 (abuse of position) makes it a criminal offence where a person intentionally and dishonestly takes advantage of their position.
Standard offences	• Incapacitated persons have the protection of the usual criminal laws relating to property, theft, fraud, false accounting, etc. Where justified, a concerned person may ask for an investigation to be undertaken by the police, the Public Guardian, the local authority adult safeguarding team, the DWP Fraud Investigation Unit or the fraud unit of a bank or other financial institution.

Non-contentious personal welfare matters

5.75 Non-contentious routine care and treatment is usually provided under the protection of MCA 2005 s5 without any application to a court.

5.76 If the relevant person still has capacity to appoint an attorney in relation to their future care and treatment, or some aspect of it, then this mechanism ensures that decisions are always made either with their own consent or that of a trusted person. They may also wish to consider making an advance decision to refuse treatment.

5.77 Direct payments and personal health budgets paid to a suitable person acting for, and hopefully with, the individual also enable care and treatment to be provided in a way which is consistent with the principles of the MCA 2005.

5.78 Guardianship under the MHA 1983 can provide a useful light-touch safety-net for citizens who are vulnerable to self-neglect or abuse.

5.79 The Children Act 1989 provides an alternative age-dependant framework in some cases.

Contentious personal welfare matters

5.80 Most personal welfare litigation in the Court of Protection involves either:

- a public authority (such as a local authority or NHS trust) in dispute with a person alleged to lack capacity and/or one or more family members; or
- a dispute between family members, in particular siblings, as to what personal welfare arrangements are in an incapacitated person's best interests.

5.81 Before commencing court proceedings, it is important to:

- Remember the duty to act in the relevant person's best interests, not one's own.
- Remember that the normal rule in personal welfare proceedings is that each party bears their own legal costs and that the cost of independent expert reports is usually apportioned between the parties. Unless legally aided, the expense can be significant.
- Remember that the Court of Protection cannot review NHS and local authority funding decisions. Provided they do not act so irrationally that it constitutes acting unlawfully, etc, it is for local and other public authorities, not judges, to decide how to allocate their limited resources. Furthermore, the funds available to public authorities, and levels of taxation and public expenditure, are political decisions, that is matters for all of us, ie for voters not judges.
- Consider the likely emotional cost of being involved in prolonged litigation.

PERSONAL WELFARE MATTERS – POSSIBLE ALTERNATIVE REMEDIES[e]	
Remedy	**Possible relevance**
	MCA 2005 matters
Best interests meetings, ADR	• Consider, and where practicable explore, non-litigious ways of resolving the outstanding issues. The court expects those involved in an incapacitated person's care to co-operate wherever possible in seeking to ascertain and promote that person's best interests before asking a court to intervene and rule on the matter. • Where relevant, ask the local authority or NHS body to convene a 'best interests meeting' at which the outstanding issues can be discussed and hopefully a way forward agreed. • Alternatively, or in addition, ask the local authority or NHS body for a professional second opinion as to the matter in dispute and the person's best interests. • Explore what kinds of formal mediation and ADR are available locally.
Remedy	**Possible relevance**
	• Consider whether a neutral family member or professional such as a solicitor not involved in the dispute may be willing and able to mediate.
Alleged unlawful deprivation of liberty	• If an incapacitated person is being deprived of their liberty in a care home or hospital without there existing any legal order or authority which authorises this, consider requesting the relevant local authority to review whether there is an unauthorised deprivation of liberty before applying to the Court of Protection. The non-court procedures relating to unauthorised deprivation of liberty are set out in MCA 2005 Sch A1 paras 67–73.

e Note: for space reasons, this focuses for the most part on the position in England. Many of the alternative remedies relating to such matters as complaints are available, through different channels, in Wales. A very helpful resource in this regard is the website 'Rhydian: Social Welfare Law in Wales', maintained by Ann James and Luke Clements: www.lukeclements.co.uk/rhydian-social-welfare-law-in-wales/.

Remedy	Possible relevance
Deprivation of liberty: requesting a Part 8 review	• An application may be made to the Court of Protection challenging a standard authorisation authorising a deprivation of liberty. An alternative procedure in appropriate cases which does not rule out applying to the court if the outcome is adverse is to ask the local authority to undertake a 'Part 8 review'. In general, it must do so if it receives a request from the person concerned or their representative. The procedure is set out in MCA 2005 Sch A1 Part 8.
Complaints about a deputy or donee	• The Public Guardian supervises court-appointed deputies and deals with representations (including complaints) about the way in which a donee of an LPA or a court-appointed deputy is exercising their powers. These functions may be discharged in cooperation with any other body with relevant statutory functions such as a local authority or police.
Complaints about an NHS or social services decisions in relation to funding and services	
NHS	• 'NHS continuing healthcare' (CHC) refers to a package of ongoing care arranged and funded solely by the NHS where it has been assessed that the individual's primary need is a health need. It can be provided in any setting. In a person's own home, it means that the NHS funds all of the care required to meet the person's assessed health needs. In care homes, it means that the NHS enters into a contract with the care home and pays the fees for the person's accommodation as well as all their care.
Remedy	**Possible relevance**
	• The *National framework for NHS continuing healthcare and NHS funded nursing care*, sets out the principles and processes for determining eligibility.[f] • The initial assessment consists of a screening checklist completed by a healthcare professional or social worker. Depending on the outcome, the relevant person will either be found to be ineligible for NHS continuing healthcare or be referred for a full multi-disciplinary assessment. A 'decision support tool' (ie detailed form) must then be completed which records the person's assessed needs – no needs, low,

continued

f Available at: www.gov.uk/government/publications/national-framework-for-nhs-continuing-healthcare-and-nhs-funded-nursing-care.

Remedy	Possible relevance
	moderate, high, severe, priority – across a number of 'domains' (behaviour, cognition, psychological needs, communication and mobility, etc) in order 'to inform' the final decision as to whether the person does have a primary health need. • There is a three-stage appeals process: *Stage one* involves an appeal to the relevant clinical commissioning group (CCG). *Stage two* involves a request to NHS England for an independent review panel. *Stage three* involves requesting a review by the Parliamentary and Health Service Ombudsman (see below). • NHS continuing healthcare should not be confused with NHS-funded nursing care. A person who lives in a care home who requires care from a registered nurse may be entitled to NHS-funded nursing care (FNC). The standard rate is £187.60 per week.
Local authority	• If the relevant person does not qualify for NHS continuing healthcare, their local authority will be responsible for their care needs and for providing services for which they are eligible. Care services from the local authority are usually means-tested. In other words, if the person is eligible for local authority community care services, their finances are assessed and they may be required to pay some or all of the cost of the services.
Remedy	**Possible relevance**
	• Complaints about community care assessments and services are subject to the Local Authority Social Services and National Health Service Complaints (England) Regulations 2009.[g] • The complaint is made initially to the local authority. A further complaint to the Local Government and Social Care Ombudsman may then be possible if the complainant remains dissatisfied. • The Local Government and Social Care Ombudsman cannot question the merits of community care funding decisions or professional judgements which have been reached properly. However, the Ombudsman can consider how those decisions were reached and whether they have been implemented properly (maladministration and service failure issues).

g SI No 309.

Remedy	Possible relevance
Judicial review	• In some cases, it may be possible to apply to the Administrative Court (a specialist court within the Queen's Bench Division of the High Court) for judicial review of a funding decision on the basis that the decision was unlawful. This might be because the decision of the NHS body or local authority was irrational, procedurally unfair, outside its legal powers, in breach of the Human Rights Act (HRA) 1998 or (albeit less likely now given the UK's departure from the European Union (EU)) in breach of EU law.
Other complaints about the person's treatment or care	
NHS complaints	• The NHS Constitution explains people's rights when it comes to making a complaint. • In England, every NHS organisation must make arrangements for dealing with complaints in accordance with the Local Authority Social Services and National Health Services Complaints (England) Regulations 2009. Regulation 14 imposes a duty on NHS bodies to provide a written response to complaints. • The standard complaints procedure is a two-tier procedure. The complaint must initially be made to the service provider (eg the GP or hospital) or to the commissioner of the service. Since the abolition of primary care trusts (PCTs) in 2013, NHS England commissions most primary care services, such as GP and dental services, while ICBs oversee the commissioning of secondary care such as hospital care and some community services.
Remedy	**Possible relevance**
	• A patient advice and liaison service (PALS) is available in all hospitals. It offers confidential advice, support and information to patients, families and carers. • In addition, an NHS Complaints Advocacy Service was established on 1 April 2013. Local authorities now have a statutory duty to commission independent advocacy services to provide support for people making, or thinking of making, a complaint about their NHS care or treatment. • Where a complaint is not resolved at the first-tier, the complainant may take it to the second stage, which is to refer the matter to the Ombudsman.

continued

Remedy	Possible relevance
	• In England, the Parliamentary and Health Service Ombudsman is the final step for people who want to complain about being treated unfairly or receiving a poor service from the NHS, government departments (including the Ministry of Justice, the Department of Health and Social Care and the DWP) and other public organisations (such as the Care Quality Commission (CQC)). • Much of the primary legislation governing the Ombudsman's remit is set out in the Parliamentary Commissioners Act 1967; Health Service Commissioners Act 1993; Parliamentary and Health Service Commissioners Act 1987; Health Service Commissioners Act 1993; Health Service Commissioner (Amendment) Act 1996.• In Wales, the bodies which the Public Services Ombudsman for Wales may investigate include the Welsh Assembly Government; a local health board; an NHS trust managing a hospital or other establishment or facility in Wales; an independent health provider; and a family health service provider. • See the Public Services Ombudsman (Wales) Act 2005.
Local authority and other care services	• The Local Authority Social Services and National Health Service Complaints (England) Regulations 2009 apply if a local authority provided or commissioned the care service.
Remedy	**Possible relevance**
	• The complainant must normally make the complaint initially to the local authority or to the person or body which provides the commissioned service. If the complaint cannot be resolved at this level, the second stage is to refer it to the Local Government and Social Care Ombudsman. • Where the care is provided under a private contract with the provider, rather than commissioned by a local authority, the CQC requires all registered care providers to have an effective complaints process. The Local Government and Social Care Ombudsman may now also investigate the complaint but expects the complaint to be made to the service provider in the first instance.

Remedy	Possible relevance
	• Provided that (in most cases) the local authority or care provider has had a reasonable opportunity to deal with the matter, the Ombudsman can investigate complaints about issues such as alleged poor-quality care, fees and charges, poor complaint handling, delay, assessments of need, safety and safeguarding. The Ombudsman's remit in some matters extends to personal care at home and supported living services for someone with learning disabilities. • A complaint may be made by a suitable representative if the person is incapable of nominating someone to make it for them. • Much of the relevant primary legislation is set out in the Local Government Act 1974 Parts III and IIIA; Health Act 2009; Regulatory Reform (Collaboration etc between Ombudsmen) Order 2007.[h]
Access to health and social care records	
NHS and social services records	• The Data Protection Act (DPA) 2018 and the UK General Data Protection Regulation (GDPR) now govern these matters following the exit of the UK from the EU.
Remedy	**Possible relevance**
	All organisations that hold information about an individual must follow the seven principles set out in the UK GDPR. These principles are: • lawfulness, fairness and transparency • purpose limitation; • data minimisation; • accuracy; • storage limitation; • integrity and confidentiality (security); accountability • The 'right of access' to data, commonly referred to as subject access, gives individuals the right to obtain a copy of their personal data. Record holders cannot charge for accessing records. The only exception is where requests are 'manifestly unfounded or excessive'. In these cases, the data controller can charge a reasonable fee to cover the administrative costs or refuse to act on the request.

continued

h SI No 1889.

Remedy	Possible relevance
	• There are certain circumstances in which full access to a patient's health records may be denied. These include cases where the release of health records is likely to cause serious harm to the physical or mental health of the subject or another individual. • Where records do disclose information related to another individual, the data controller is not obliged to release the information, except in the following circumstances: – The third party is a health professional who has compiled or contributed to the health records or who has been involved in the care of the patient; – The third party, who is not a health professional, gives their consent to the disclosure of that information; – It is reasonable to disclose without that third party's consent. • The Access to Health Records Act 1990 applies to records of deceased persons created since 1 November 1991.
Remedy	**Possible relevance**
	• The Access to Medical Reports Act 1988 concerns medical reports prepared for employers and insurance companies. • Complaints that information has been disclosed to a third-party without a court order requiring or authorising this usually turn on whether there has been an unlawful breach of confidentiality or privacy or a breach of the DPA 2018 principles in relation to processing personal data fairly and lawfully.
The Information Commissioner	• The Information Commissioner enforces and oversees the DPA 2018, the UK GDPR and the Freedom of Information Act 2000, for both England and Wales. A person denied access to records may complain using the NHS and local authority complaints procedures and then, if a local resolution is not achieved, to the Information Commissioner's Office.
	Regulatory bodies
NHS hospitals, local authority care services, private and voluntary sector	• The CQC is the regulator of health and social care in England. In general terms, it registers and inspects all health and social care provision and seeks to ensure that they meet essential standards of quality and safety.

Remedy	Possible relevance
	• The Health and Social Care Act 2008 (Regulated Activities) Regulations 2014[i] set out the essential standards of quality and safety expected from service providers of regulated activities, such as care homes. These are set out in regs 8–24 and are supported by compliance guidance.
Remedy	**Possible relevance**
	• The CQC deals with complaints about the standards of care homes, hospitals and other registered services as a whole rather than with the kind of individual complaint of poor service dealt with by ombudsmen. • NHS England and NHS Improvement oversees, amongst other things, foundation Trusts and NHS trusts, as well as independent providers that provide NHS funded care. • The Care Inspectorate Wales (CIW) is the body equivalent to the English CQC. It regulates and inspects domiciliary services and care homes for adults including those providing nursing care in order to ensure that they meet national minimum standards. The Regulated Services (Service Providers and Responsible Individuals) (Wales) Regulations 2017[j] set out the requirements for providers and responsible individuals in relation to regulated services.
Individual practitioners	• The General Medical Council (GMC) regulates doctors.
	• The Nursing and Midwifery Council (NMC) regulates nurses and midwives.
	• The Health and Care Professions Council (HCPC) regulates psychologists, social workers in England (in Wales, this is done by Social Care Wales) and speech and language therapists.

continued

i SI 2017 No 2936.
j SI 2017 No 1264 (W295).

Remedy	Possible relevance
Other 'avenues' for complaints and grievances	
MPs, local authority councillors, media/ press	• As to these options, see the section above dealing with property and financial affairs.
Remedy	**Possible relevance**
Other kinds of legal applications and proceedings (civil)	
The relevance of these options depends on whether a public authority or family member is seeking a safeguarding-type remedy or an incapacitated person (or someone on their behalf) is seeking to enforce their legal rights.	
Possible remedies for public authorities[k]	
Application under the High Court's inherent jurisdiction	• The exercise of the High Court's inherent jurisdiction may be used to obtain appropriate orders where a person not incapacitated by mental disorder or mental illness is vulnerable and is reasonably believed to be (i) under constraint; or (ii) subject to coercion or undue influence; or (iii) for some other reason deprived of the capacity to make the relevant decision, or disabled from making a free choice, or incapacitated or disabled from giving or expressing a real and genuine consent. See *DL v A Local Authority*[l] and chapter 28.
MHA 1983 powers	The MHA 1983 includes various provisions relating to compulsory admission to hospital, in particular sections 2, 3 and 4. The community provisions include reception into guardianship and sections 115 (entry to and inspection of private premises); 135 (warrants to search private premises and to remove to a place of safety persons suspected to suffer from mental disorder); and 136 (removal by police to a place of safety of persons in public places who appear to be suffering from mental disorder and to be in immediate need of care or control).

k See also the guide published by the Social Care Institute for Excellence: *Gaining access to an adult suspected to be at risk of neglect or abuse* (www.scie.org.uk/safeguarding/adults/practice/gaining-access) addressing an issue which often arises in the context of the discharge of safeguarding obligations under the Care Act 2014 (in England) or the Social Services and Well-being (Wales) Act 2014 (in Wales).

l [2012] EWCA Civ 253, (2012) 15 CCLR 267.

Remedy	Possible relevance
Protecting the person's moveable property under the Care Act 2014 (England)	• The Care Act 2014 applies when a person is provided with accommodation under the Care Act 2014 or admitted to hospital. • It imposes a statutory duty on the relevant local authority to take reasonable steps to prevent or mitigate loss or damage to the person's movable property if the person is unable to protect or deal with it and no other suitable arrangements are in place. • A power is given to the local authority to enter the person's premises in order to take the steps necessary to protect their moveable property. Any reasonable expenses incurred in protecting the property are recoverable from the person concerned.
Emergency police powers to save life, limb, etc	Police and Criminal Evidence Act (PACE) 1984 s17(1)(e) authorises a police constable to enter and search any premises for the purpose of saving life or limb or preventing serious damage to property.
Public health remedies	• Public Health Act 1936 s83 allows the local authority to require the cleansing (by disinfecting and decorating) of any premises which are in such a filthy or unwholesome condition as to be prejudicial to health or are verminous. • Sections 84 and 85 contain supplementary provisions concerning the 'cleansing or destruction of filthy or verminous articles' and the 'cleansing of verminous persons and their clothing'. • Environmental Protection Act 1990 Part 3 provides local authorities with abatement powers in relation to 'premises in such a state as to be prejudicial to health or a nuisance'. • Powers of entry, if need be under warrant, are contained in Public Health Act 1936 s287 and Environmental Protection Act 1990 Sch 3. • Local authorities and social landlords may take action under the no-nuisance terms in tenancy agreements. • See *Professional Practice Note: Hoarding and how to approach it – Guidance for Environmental Health Officers and others*, Chartered Institute of Environmental Health, 3rd Revision, June 2015 (available at the institute's website).

Possible remedies for the incapacitated person

continued

Remedy	Possible relevance
Damages claim in the civil courts	Under English law, an individual may be entitled to compensation if they have been injured as a result of the negligence of another person. Other actionable civil wrongs include trespass to the person (assault, battery), nuisance, breach of privacy and breach of confidentiality.
HRA 1998 claim	The HRA 1998 makes it unlawful for a public authority to act incompatibly with the rights conferred by the European Convention on Human Rights. It allows a case to be brought in a UK court or tribunal against the authority if it does so. However, a public authority will not have acted unlawfully under the Act if as the result of another Act of Parliament it could not have acted differently. The Act extended the power to award damages for the breach of a convention right to any court that has the power to order payment of damages or compensation in a civil case.
Equality Act (EqA) 2010	• The EqA 2010 provides that a person is disabled if they have a physical or mental impairment which has a substantial and long-term adverse effect on their ability to carry out normal day-to-day activities. All employers and service providers in England, Wales and Scotland must follow the EqA 2010. • A person (A) discriminates against a disabled person (B) if: (a) A treats B unfavourably because of something arising in consequence of B's disability, and (b) A cannot show that the treatment is a proportionate means of achieving a legitimate aim. • This prohibition does not apply if A shows that A did not know, and could not reasonably have been expected to know, that B had the disability. • EqA 2010 s19 deals with indirect discrimination, section 26 with the harassment of disabled people, section 27 with victimisation and Part 3 of the Act with the provision of services.

Remedy	Possible relevance
Family law remedies	• The Family Law Act 1996 allows non-molestation orders and occupation orders to be made in respect of 'associated persons' such as married persons, civil partners, cohabitants, relatives, parties to family proceedings and persons who have or have had an intimate personal relationship. • A power of arrest may not be attached to a non-molestation order. However, breach of such an order without reasonable excuse is a criminal offence and also a contempt of court. • An occupation order is an order by which the court regulates occupation of the home by declaring a person's entitlement to occupy it, prohibiting someone's right to occupy it and so on. Such orders may be made in respect of associated persons who share, have shared or intend to share a dwelling house as their home. • It is sometimes said that the Court of Protection cannot prohibit the rights of occupation of capacitated people and cannot therefore exclude a joint owner or spouse from a dwelling-house. However, there is no case in point. • A power of arrest may be attached to an occupation order and breach of such an order is also a contempt of court.
Anti-harassment injunction	• The High Court and the county court have jurisdiction to grant an injunction under the Protection from Harassment Act (PHA) 1997. • Section 1 provides that a person must not pursue a course of conduct: (a) which amounts to harassment of another, and (b) which the person knows or ought to know amounts to harassment of the other. • An actual or apprehended breach may be the subject of a claim in civil proceedings. An injunction may be made and the court may also award damages for (among other things) any anxiety caused by the harassment and any financial loss resulting from it. (A person who pursues a course of conduct in breach of section 1 also commits a criminal offence.)

continued

Remedy	Possible relevance
Common law injunctions	It is still possible to obtain a common law injunction in the context of common law proceedings for torts such as assault, battery, trespass to the person and nuisance. However, it is relatively unusual for a situation not to be covered either by the Family Law Act 1996 or by the PHA 1997, eg where the behaviour complained of does not amount to a course of conduct involving associated persons.
Compensation for criminal injuries	Victims of violent crimes can apply to the Criminal Injuries Compensation Authority (CICA) for compensation. It does not matter that a prosecution was not brought or that the perpetrator could not be held responsible because they were suffering from a mental disorder. The claim must be brought within two years from the date of the incident. A responsible person can make a claim on behalf of an incapacitated victim.
Other kinds of legal proceedings (criminal)	
A remand in custody, bail conditions and/or term of imprisonment may serve to protect an incapacitated person.	
Offences relating to vulnerable or incapacitated persons	• MCA 2005 s44 created an (ambiguous) offence of ill-treatment or wilful neglect. It applies to deputies, donees (LPA or EPA) and anyone who has the care of a person who lacks capacity or whom the carer reasonably believes lacks capacity. • Criminal Justice and Courts Act 2015 s20 created an offence for a paid care worker to ill-treat or wilfully to neglect an individual for whom they are caring. A care worker also includes those with managerial responsibility and directors (of equivalents) of organisations providing such care. A separate offence under section 21 exists in relation to care providers in respect of serious management failures giving rise to offences committed by care providers within their employ. • Domestic Violence, Crime and Victims Act 2004 s5 makes it an offence where a vulnerable adult dies or suffers serious physical harm as a result of the unlawful act of a person who was a member of the same household as the victim and had frequent contact with them.

Remedy	Possible relevance
	• MHA 1983 s127 makes it an offence for an officer or employee of an NHS hospital, independent hospital or care home to wilfully neglect or ill-treat a person who suffers from or appears to be suffering from a mental disorder. A like offence is committed if someone who has such a person in their custody or care ill-treats or wilfully neglects them. • The Sexual Offences Act 2003 includes various relevant offences such as sexual activity with a person with a mental disorder impeding choice and sexual activity by a care worker with a person with a mental disorder.
Standard offences	Incapacitated persons are also protected by the general criminal law (eg the Offences Against the Person Act 1861 and public order offences) but the likelihood of a successful prosecution may be affected by their inability to give evidence at trial.
Harassment and malicious communications, etc	• PHA 1997 s1 is dealt with above. • Criminal Justice and Police Act 2001 s42A makes it an offence to harass a person in their home. • The Malicious Communications Act 1988 provides that persons who send letters, electronic communications or make telephone calls with intent to cause distress or anxiety are guilty of a criminal offence. • Communications Act 2003 s127 makes it an offence to send a message which the perpetrator knows to be indecent, obscene, of a menacing character or grossly offensive for the purpose of causing annoyance, inconvenience or needless anxiety.

CHAPTER 6

Funding and representation

Introduction

6.1 This chapter looks at sources of advice, funding and legal representation to parties in the Court of Protection.

6.2 It will provide an overview of the sources of support available in the absence of formal legal representation. It then considers the sources of legal advice and how these can be funded.

6.3 It will then provide an explanation of the legal aid scheme as it applies in the Court of Protection. The aim of this section is to assist both practitioners and their clients in navigating the scheme and in understanding the impact of the relevant legislation and guidance.

6.4 Issues concerning the representation of P and other protected parties are considered in detail in chapter 12.

General

6.5 The importance of accessing legal advice and representation in the Court of Protection cannot be underestimated. This is particularly so given the complexity of some of the issues and the impact on people's lives. Many cases may be resolved without full legal representation but access to advice at the right time at the right level is crucial.

6.6 The Mental Capacity Act (MCA) 2005 is a relatively new jurisdiction as far as health and welfare matters are concerned. Prior to the MCA 2005, the cases before the court concerned financial disputes which were in the main outside the scope of legal aid. However this changed radically with the implementation of the new statutory scheme.

6.7 It is vital that all legal practitioners, and those working in the health and social care spheres are aware of the availability of legal aid where appropriate. In particular practitioners whose expertise lies in litigating financial disputes need to apprise themselves of the availability of legal aid for health and welfare issues, and also other issues such as the validity of lasting powers of attorney (LPAs). Failure to advise a client about the possible availability of legal aid may give rise to regulatory concerns, a complaint or a claim for negligence. It is incumbent on all parties working in this jurisdiction to be aware – and if unable to assess the client's eligibility themselves,[1] to make the

1 Note, for those who do not regularly encounter legal aid, an important tool is the Legal Aid Checker (replacing the previous legal aid eligibility calculator), available at: www.gov.uk/check-legal-aid.

necessary referral or to signpost the client to a practitioner with a legal aid contract to assess their eligibility.

Being a litigant in person

6.8 There is no obligation to instruct a lawyer in court proceedings in England and Wales. A person who is a party to proceedings without a legal representative is known as a 'litigant in person', sometimes referred to as 'LiP' or an 'unrepresented party'. They can conduct the preparation of the case without a legal representative and also have the right to address the court directly. The Court of Protection Rules 2017[2] (COPR) require the court to 'have regard' to the fact that at least one party is unrepresented in exercising its case management powers.[3] This may include, for example, the judge finding out what questions a litigant in person may wish to put to a witness, and either putting them to the witness directly or causing the questions to be put.[4]

6.9 Litigants in person have the same responsibilities to the court as represented parties to help the court further what is described as 'the overriding objective' (see further paras 11.8–11.12). This means dealing with the case justly, and at proportionate cost, having regard to the principles contained in the MCA 2005.[5] This includes complying with orders, keeping to timetables, and being full and frank in their disclosure to the court and the parties of information and documents. The COPR imposes a specific duty on litigants in person to engage with the court process, to co-operate with the court and the parties, to present their case fairly and to seek early resolution of disputes where practicable.[6] Parties who fail to comply with their duties risk being ordered to pay costs.[7]

6.10 We suggest that it is wise for anyone involved in Court of Protection proceedings at least to consider the possibility of obtaining legal advice. Court of Protection judges will sometimes make a specific recommendation to a litigant in person that they should seek legal advice. This should be followed up where possible. Furthermore,

2 SI 2017 No 1035.
3 COPR r3.2(2).
4 COPR r3.2(4).
5 COPR r1.1(1).
6 COPR r1.6.
7 COPR r4.3.

legal advice is likely to be more effective if it is provided early on in the case, and obtaining legal advice at the outset may mean that it is possible to narrow the issues in the case or focus them so that either the case can be brought to a close more quickly, or a litigant in person may then be in a better position to deal with those remaining issues themselves.

6.11 Sources of support available to litigants in person[8] are limited as welfare cases in the Court of Protection are a relatively recent addition and the expansion of the scope of the Court coincided with the legal aid cuts which removed many practitioners and advice centres. The services which are available include the Support Through Court (formally the Personal Support Unit (PSU))[9] which is an independent charity, staffed by volunteers. It operates in 20 courts around England and Wales. Its aim is to help those facing civil proceedings unrepresented manage their cases better. Support Through Court volunteers will not offer legal advice and cannot provide representation but can sometimes put litigants in touch with relevant agencies. Support Through Court volunteers are able to offer practical support including guidance round the court building, help with organising documentation and can offer emotional support. Information about the PSU is prominently displayed in the courts where it operates.

6.12 A 'McKenzie friend' is someone who is not a qualified lawyer and who provides reasonable assistance to a litigant in person. A McKenzie friend does not represent the litigant, but can sit beside them in court hearings and 'quietly assist'.

6.13 In the light of an increase in the number of litigants in person, the Master of the Rolls and the President of the Family Division issued *Practice Guidance on McKenzie friends* on 12 July 2010.[10] This has been held to apply in the Court of Protection (*LBX v TT*[11]). The following points should be noted:

8 A guide for litigants in person in the courts system more generally was prepared by the judiciary in 2013, and is available at: www.judiciary.uk/publications/handbook-litigants-person-civil-221013/.

9 See: www.supportthroughcourt.org/.

10 *Practice Guidance: McKenzie friends (Civil and Family Courts)* ('Practice Guidance'), 12 July 2010; available at: www.judiciary.gov.uk/wp-content/uploads/JCO/Documents/Guidance/mckenzie-friends-practice-guidance-july-2010.pdf.

11 [2014] EWCOP 24, [2014] COPLR 561.

- A McKenzie friend can only act on behalf of a person with litigation capacity.[12]
- Litigants in person can receive reasonable assistance from a McKenzie friend, subject to the discretion of the court. The court may refuse to permit assistance by a McKenzie friend if satisfied that the interests of justice and fairness do not require it.[13]
- A litigant seeking assistance from a McKenzie friend should seek the court's permission as soon as possible and the McKenzie friend should submit a short CV and confirm their independence of the case and their understanding of their duty of confidentiality.[14]
- A McKenzie friend *may*: provide moral support; take notes; help with case papers; quietly give advice on any aspect of the conduct of the case.[15]
- A McKenzie friend may *not*: act as the party's agent; manage the case outside court for example by signing documents; address the court; make submissions or examine witnesses.[16]
- The right to a fair trial is engaged by the decision whether to permit a McKenzie friend, and the litigant should be given the chance to argue the point. Unless the proceedings are in private, the proposed McKenzie friend should be allowed in court to help the litigant. If the case is being heard in private, then it is for the litigant to justify the proposed McKenzie friend's presence in court.[17]
- Refusal to allow a McKenzie friend would not be justified simply because the case is straightforward, or because the proposed McKenzie friend belongs to an organisation that promotes a particular cause, or that the proceedings are confidential. Refusal could be justified if the assistance might undermine or has undermined the efficient administration of justice. Examples might include that the assistance was being used for an improper purpose; or the assistance is unreasonable in nature or degree; or the McKenzie friend was using the litigant as a 'puppet'; was

12 This is not stated in the Practice Guidance, but it is suggested from the scope of the role of such a friend as an assistant to the litigant.

13 Practice Guidance paras 2 and 5.

14 Practice Guidance para 6.

15 Practice Guidance para 3.

16 Practice Guidance para 4.

17 Practice Guidance paras 8 and 9.

directly or indirectly conducting the proceedings or does not appear to understand the duty of confidentiality.[18]

- Rarely, courts may grant rights of audience, or the right to conduct litigation, to McKenzie friends.[19]
- Litigants may agree to pay fees to McKenzie friends for the provision of reasonable assistance, and these costs cannot be recovered from the opponent. If the court has granted the McKenzie friend the right to conduct litigation or a right of audience, then costs incurred in these activities are in principle recoverable from the litigant, and may be recoverable from the opponent as a disbursement.[20]

6.14 The role of the McKenzie friend in Court of Protection proceedings, and the risk of conflicts of interest, was considered in *HBCC v LG*.[21] Eleanor King J had permitted P's daughter to receive assistance from CP, a McKenzie friend who was also a local councillor. The judge described the positive contribution that McKenzie friends can make:

> 141. This court is always keen to welcome McKenzie friends; they give time and support of inestimable value to the litigant they have agreed to assist. McKenzie friend[s] come from all walks of life: often they are personal friends or connections of the litigant; sometimes they are 'professional' McKenzie friends. Sometimes, as here, they are respected members of the community who have been approached by a litigant for support and advice. Each has their place.

6.15 The judge considered that C had exceeded his role as McKenzie friend, not in his conduct during the trial itself, but in his behaviour outside court which she described as inflammatory, including his 'dogged maintenance of his stated position' in correspondence which had gone beyond what was proper. She commented that:

> 147. . . . I understand that democratically elected representatives be they Members of Parliament or local Councillors will often, appropriately, take up issues on behalf of their constituents. It follows that any elected representative must be cautious that in doing so they do not find themselves in conflict with their role as a McKenzie friend.

6.16 Following the rise in numbers of unrepresented parties in court proceedings, there has been a corresponding increase in organisations and individuals offering a McKenzie friend service. While there are many excellent McKenzie friends, there are stark examples of

18 Practice Guidance paras 12 and 13.

19 Practice Guidance paras 18–26.

20 Practice Guidance paras 27–30.

21 [2010] EWHC 1527 (Fam), [2011] 1 FLR 463.

poor practice. In a judgment in a children's case from 2017, Her Honour Judge Atkinson stated:[22]

> Nothing in this Judgment is to be taken as intended to undermine the value to the courts of third parties who offer support and assistance to litigants in family proceedings. There are many occasions where the help and support of a McKenzie Friend can greatly assist. That is why the family courts in particular have generally welcomed McKenzie Friends. However, with the withdrawal of public funding there has been a marked increase in the use of 'professional' McKenzie Friends, as here, and there is a danger that the boundaries between the regulated and non-regulated representative is becoming blurred. The facts of this case illustrate how significant the impact can be where there is no clear understanding of, or respect for, the limitations on their role by the third party offering non-regulated legal assistance. Meanwhile, the person left to police the non-regulated representative is the Judge with the result that precious and hard pressed judicial time is diverted to matters of third party involvement when the focus should be the children.
>
> . . .
>
> . . . [D]uring this case the McKenzie Friend in question has on occasions described his role as 'quasi-solicitorial'. There is no such thing as 'almost' a solicitor. You are either a solicitor or you are not. Significantly, if you are, you are bound by your professional duties and you are externally regulated. Whilst a 'professional McKenzie Friend' is not subject to regulation in the way that barristers and solicitors are, the powers utilised by DJ Major in this case are available to ensure that the limits within which non-regulated third parties are permitted to operate are respected and the absence of professional rules does not permit the interference with justice . . . Nevertheless this has taken up hours of court time when the focus of the litigation should have been the two children subject to the applications. If 'professional' McKenzie Friends are to assist parents in such emotionally fraught cases they must be sensitive to these issues and mindful of the dangers of becoming an irritant hindering the process rather than giving the assistance that the courts have been used to in the past.

6.17 The long-awaited response from the office of the Lord Chief Justice to the consultation into the role of McKenzie friends was published in February 2019.[23]

22 *Re H (Children: exclusion of McKenzie friend)* [2017] EWFC B31 at paras 3 and 70.

23 *Reforming the courts' approach to McKenzie Friends: Consultation response*, February 2019, available at: www.judiciary.uk/publications/consultation-reforming-the-courts-approach-to-mckenzie-friends/ .

6.18 The Judicial Executive Board (JEB) considered that the expansion of McKenzie friends had to be seen in the context of the government's policy regarding reduction to legal aid, and that the responsibility for ensuring that litigants in person had sufficient support lay with the Lord Chancellor and not the judiciary.

6.19 The JEB recommended the updating of the 2010 Practice Guidance for McKenzie Friends and the publication of a plain English guide for litigants in person. Importantly, the consultation response highlighted serious concerns:

> The JEB remain deeply concerned about the proliferation of McKenzie Friends who in effect provide professional services for reward when they are unqualified, unregulated, uninsured and not subject to the same professional obligations and duties, both to their clients and the courts, as are professional lawyers. The statutory scheme was fashioned to protect the consumers of legal services and the integrity of the legal system. JEB's view is that all courts should apply the current law applicable to McKenzie Friends as established by Court of Appeal authority.[24]

6.20 At the time of writing, it is unclear whether there will be any response to this report. It may, however, be useful to ask the following questions to anyone offering services as a McKenzie friend:

- How are charges worked out, and what is the likely cost of support for the case in question? It may be that the charges are more than those of a legal professional.
- What is the professional background of the proposed McKenzie friend? A CV should be requested.
- What experience does the McKenzie friend have? Are they able to supply references?
- Have they been involved in cases previously and has there been any praise or criticism of their services?
- Does the McKenzie friend hold a particular view about the issues involved in the case – for example, are they involved in relevant campaigns? This does not mean that they cannot act as McKenzie friend; but it may have a bearing on the advice they provide.

24 *Reforming the courts' approach to McKenzie Friends: Consultation response*, p3.

Legal representation

6.21 Unless the court (unusually) gives permission for a McKenzie friend to conduct the litigation,[25] legal representation in the Court of Protection will be by a qualified lawyer, who will be a solicitor, a barrister, or in some cases a Fellow of the Institute of Legal Executives. These lawyers are all regulated by professional bodies. They have to meet quality standards as well as being properly insured to protect the interests of the public.

6.22 As we have seen, cases in the Court of Protection may be heard by district judges, circuit judges or judges of the High Court. Until 29 January 2016, most Court of Protection hearings took place in private, sometimes referred to as 'in chambers'. The exception to this rule were serious medical treatment cases, which have usually been heard in public.

6.23 The Transparency Pilot, now cemented into the practice of the court, reversed the default position so that cases are now normally heard in public, with reporting restrictions to protect the identity of P and members of P's family.[26] The Transparency Practice Direction, COPR PD 4C[27] provides that legal representatives with rights of audience in private proceedings in the Court of Protection can continue to appear in Court of Protection cases when they were heard in public, unless there is 'good reason' not to allow them to do so.[28]

6.24 Solicitors' firms are regulated by the Solicitors Regulation Authority (SRA) and barristers are regulated by the Bar Standards Board (BSB). Traditionally barristers are instructed by solicitors, but those who have been through suitable training can now receive instructions directly from members of the public (referred to as 'public access' or 'direct access').[29]

6.25 Fellows of the Chartered Institute of Legal Executives (CILEx) are regulated by Cilex Regulation and may appear at hearings in chambers before the district court, circuit court and High Court. They may address the court on unopposed applications for adjournment or to enter judgment by consent.

25 As it could do – see para 19 of the Practice Guidance referred to above.

26 See further chapter 14.

27 COPR PD 4C para 2.6.

28 See the model order on the Court of Protection Handbook website at para 11.

29 The Bar Council operates a website to assist in finding a direct or public access barrister, available at: www.directaccessportal.co.uk.

Finding a lawyer

6.26 For members of the public seeking legal advice about Court of Protection cases, the following may be useful sources of information:

- The Law Society maintains a register of qualified solicitors and firms. This can be accessed through the 'Find a Solicitor' page in the Law Society's website.[30]
- In response to demand, the Law Society has created a Mental Capacity Health and Welfare accreditation scheme for solicitors undertaking welfare cases in the Court of Protection. Members of the scheme are required to show, through a training and examination/interview process, as well as having had experience of a wide variety of Court of Protection cases that they meet the high standards required. Members who qualify can act as 'accredited legal representatives' or ALRs, and be directly appointed by the court as representing P.[31] Members of the scheme have a 'Kitemark' showing that they have demonstrated experience in this area of law. This is an important development given the complexity of this area of law and the vulnerability of many of the parties involved in litigation.
- The Law Society's Lexcel accreditation scheme is a practice management standard.[32] Firms with Lexcel accreditation have to show that they have met certain standards in client care, risk management and case management.
- The Bar Council maintains a list of all barristers, and a further list of those offering public access, on its website.[33] There is a dedicated telephone number for questions about public access: 020 7611 1472.
- Some publications provide information about solicitors and barristers practising in the Court of Protection, for example *Chambers and Partners* and the *Legal 500*.

6.27 Solicitors and barristers acting on a direct public access basis are also obliged to provide information about their charges and the likely costs of the case at the outset of a case.

30 See: www.lawsociety.org.uk.

31 See: www.lawsociety.org.uk/support-services/accreditation/mental-capacity/ and also paras 12.84–12.100 below.

32 See: www.law.society.org.uk/accreditation/lexcel.

33 See: www.barcouncil.org.

6.28 Legal aid is available for certain cases in the Court of Protection subject to merits and financial limits, as is discussed further in the next section.

6.29 Where legal aid cannot be secured, clients will have to pay privately for legal representation. Providing privately funded representation in contested welfare cases can bring challenges, because of the difficulties in predicting the costs that will be incurred and because many cases are so complex that high costs can be involved.

6.30 In some cases, legal practitioners may be able to take on cases under a partial retainer – sometimes referred to as 'unbundling'. The Law Society has issued a practice note about partial retainer cases.[34] Practitioners considering this option should consider the advice given in the practice note. The professional obligations of the solicitor on a partial retainer are significant and include a greater responsibility to clients of unbundled services to clearly set out the responsibilities of both solicitor and client. The practice note does not recommend a partial retainer in cases of 'great complexity or where you have concerns that the client does not have the intellectual or emotional capacity to carry out tasks that fall within their responsibility. In such cases you should carefully consider whether and to what extent it is in your client's interests to provide an unbundled service'.[35]

Legal aid in the Court of Protection

6.31 This section focuses on legal aid for Court of Protection cases. It is not an exhaustive description of the legal aid scheme generally, and readers are referred to the *LAG Legal aid handbook* for a comprehensive guide and overview and to the Legal Aid Agency website itself.[36]

34 See: www.lawsociety.org.uk/support-services/advice/practice-notes/unbundling-civil-legal-services (the most recent version dating from April 2022).

35 Para 3.2.

36 V Ling and S James (eds), *Legal aid handbook 2022/2023* (LAG) available at www.lag.org.uk; https://www.gov.uk/government/organisations/legal-aid-agency/.

Resources

6.32 There is no single document which describes the legal aid scheme. Below is a list of the materials referred to, to which practitioners will need to access from time to time.

Primary legislation

- Legal Aid, Sentencing and Punishment of Offenders Act 2012 (LASPO) Sch 1.

Secondary legislation

- Civil Legal Aid (Merits Criteria) Regulations ('Merits Regs') 2013[37] (as amended);
- Civil Legal Aid (Financial Resources and Payment for Services) Regulations 2013[38] (as amended);
- Civil Legal Aid (Statutory Charge) Regulations 2013;[39]
- Civil Legal Aid (Procedure) Regulations 2012.[40]

Guidance

- *Lord Chancellor's Guidance under section 4 of the Legal Aid, Sentencing and Punishment of Offenders Act 2012;*[41]
- HCC (High Cost Cases): a solicitor's information pack (non-family) (2017) and a barrister's information pack.[42]

Legal Aid Agency contracts

- Standard Civil Contract 2018;
- 2013 Individual Case Contract (High Cost Cases) Specification.

37 SI 2013 No 104.
38 SI 2013 No 480.
39 SI 2013 No 503.
40 SI 2012 No 3098.
41 August 2021, https://assets.publishing.service.gov.uk/government/uploads/system/uploads/attachment_data/file/1008832/210804_Lord_Chancellor_s_s4_Guidance_-_FINAL.pdf.
42 See: https://assets.publishing.service.gov.uk/government/uploads/system/uploads/attachment_data/file/651806/vhcc-solicitors-information-pack-non-family.pdf.

Legal Aid, Sentencing and Punishment of Offenders Act 2012

6.33 Publicly funded advice and representation ('legal aid') is governed by LASPO, which came into force on 1 April 2013 and removed a number of areas of law from the scope of legal aid. The Legal Services Commission (LSC), which had previously administered legal aid in England and Wales, was replaced by the Legal Aid Agency (LAA) by the Act. The LAA is headed by the Director of Legal Aid Casework.

6.34 LASPO Sch 1 lists those areas of law where advice and/or representation can be provided under legal aid. If an area of law is not in Schedule 1, then no legal aid in any form may be provided to a client seeking help in this area of law unless it is necessary because to deny legal aid would be a breach of the European Convention on Human Rights (ECHR).[43]

6.35 Those areas of law listed in Schedule 1 are then subject to further exclusions and criteria which appear in the regulations. These should be considered in order to ascertain whether a client presenting with a particular case is eligible to receive legal aid for their problem, and what form of legal aid should be provided.

6.36 The purpose of LASPO has been described by the Supreme Court as:

> . . . in very summary terms, to channel civil legal aid on the basis of the nature and importance of the issue, an individual's need for financial support, the availability of other funding, and the availability of other forms of dispute resolution.[44]

6.37 Since LASPO was implemented, report after report has criticised its effect and questioned whether its aims, other than simply reducing the budget overall, have been met. Many reviews – including the government in its now-published Post Implementation Review of LASPO[45] – now recognise that the legal aid reforms have not achieved

43 Under LASPO s10, legal aid (Legal Help and certificates) may be made available notwithstanding that it does not appear in the list in LASPO Sch 1 on an 'exceptional' basis if it is necessary under the ECHR. The threshold for such exceptional case funding (ECF) is extremely high, requiring the applicant to show that to deny them legal aid would be a breach of the ECHR. While the number of applications which have been granted have increased following a challenge to the way that the ECF operates, it remains a fraction of those which was anticipated. There is no legal aid funding to cover the work for making the application for exceptional funding unless and until it is actually granted.

44 *R (Public Law Project) v Lord Chancellor* [2016] UKSC 39, [2016] 3 WLR 387 at para 37.

45 See: www.gov.uk/government/publications/post-implementation-review-of-part-1-of-laspo.

many of the other goals, and that the cuts to legal aid have also resulted in consequential expenditure elsewhere in statutory services such as the NHS, social services, etc.

Legal aid contracts

6.38 All providers of legal aid must hold a contract with the LAA which covers the areas of law which they offer. The provider must at all times comply with the terms of the contract. These include the duty on both the provider and the LAA to act in good faith in relation to the contract.[46] Providers of legal aid who hold contracts in the areas of either mental health or community care may offer a legal aid service in cases arising under the MCA 2005. Currently the position is governed by the 2018 Standard Civil Contract and the associated category specifications.[47]

6.39 As from April 2016, practitioners have been required to make use of the digital online Client and Cost Management System (CCMS) when submitting applications to the LAA, with a new digital system ('Apply') under test at the time of writing.

The different levels of legal aid

6.40 Legal aid is provided at different levels. Unless legal proceedings are already underway requiring an immediate legal aid certificate the usual first level of legal aid funding is Legal Help. This kind of legal aid will cover an adviser taking instructions at the start of a case, writing letters and advising whether further action is required. Legal Help does not cover representation of a client in court proceedings or taking any steps to conduct proceedings on a client's behalf. If the practitioner wishes to represent the client in the Court of Protection, a legal aid certificate must be obtained, which is linked to the specific proceedings.

Obtaining legal aid

6.41 In order to qualify for any form of legal aid, including Legal Help, the following criteria have to be met. Each of these is addressed in more detail below:

- The client's case must be within 'scope' of legal aid.

46 General Terms, 2014 Standard Contract, 2.1.

47 A new contract is expected (at the time of writing) from August 2023.

- The client's case must meet the 'merits test' as to whether legal aid is justified.
- The client must meet the 'means test' and be financially eligible for legal aid (unless the case is a MCA 2005 s21A challenge, and the client is either P or the relevant person's representative (RPR)).
- The client must produce the relevant evidence of their means (benefits, bank statements etc) to satisfy the requirements of the LAA.

Scope of legal aid

6.42 The relevant paragraph of LASPO Sch 1 Part 1 for cases where the Court of Protection has jurisdiction is para 5, which provides that civil legal services can be provided 'in relation to matters arising under the Mental Capacity Act 2005'.[48]

6.43 This means that legal aid can – provided all the other criteria are met – be provided in respect of legal issues arising under the MCA 2005.

6.44 This is subject to certain exclusions. No legal advice at all can be provided about:

- creating LPAs under the MCA 2005; or
- the making of advance decisions under that Act.[49]

6.45 Therefore, practitioners may not provide any advice at all under legal aid to a client who wishes to prepare an LPA (whether financial or welfare) or an advance decision. Such clients will have to pay privately for advice. However, if a client requires advice or representation about a case before the Court of Protection which concerns determinations and declarations about the effect, meaning, validity or applicability of a LPA or advance decision, then it may be possible to provide legal aid, in some form, assuming that all other criteria are satisfied.[50] Cases where the validity of a LPA, most commonly where capacity to make the LPA is disputed, can therefore be within scope of the legal aid system.

6.46 Advocacy services can be provided in the Court of Protection[51] if the case concerns at least one of the following issues:

48 LASPO Sch 1 Part 1 para 5(1).
49 LASPO Sch 1 Part 1 para 5(3).
50 LASPO Sch 1 Part 1 para 5(4).
51 LASPO Sch 1 Part 3.

- a person's right to life;
- a person's liberty or physical safety;
- a person's medical treatment (within the meaning of the Mental Health Act (MHA) 1983),
- a person's capacity to marry, to enter into a civil partnership or to enter into sexual relations; or
- a person's right to family life.[52]

The inherent jurisdiction

6.47 Civil legal services can be provided in relation to the 'inherent jurisdiction' of the High Court in relation to children (persons under the age of 18) and vulnerable adults (persons aged 18 and over), subject to the merits and means test.[53]

Breaches of ECHR rights by a public authority

6.48 Claims for damages in respect of acts and omissions by public authority remain in scope of legal aid, if these involve a 'significant breach' of ECHR rights. As explained in para 6.67 below, the LAA has accepted that such claims can be litigated in the Court of Protection. The LAA position statement referred to at para 6.90 below, while applicable to care proceedings is of direct relevance to Court of Protection proceedings. The logical conclusion is that if there is a separate damages claim to the welfare proceedings the statutory charge will not apply to the damages award or settlement. See also para 26.7 below.

The merits test

6.49 Once it has been established that the case is within the scope of legal aid, the next matter to be considered is whether the case meets the merits criteria. If it does not, legal aid will not be available for advice, or in the case of representation in court proceedings, granted.

6.50 The relevant merits tests are set out in the Merits Regs 2013.[54] These include definitions of the tests of prospects of success (regs 4–5); public interest (reg 6); reasonable private paying individual (reg 7); and proportionality (reg 8).

52 LASPO Sch 1 Part 3.

53 LASPO Sch 1 Part 1 para 9.

54 SI 2013 No 104.

6.51 The criteria for the grant of Legal Help are not the same as the criteria for the grant of full representation, so these are considered separately.

The merits test for Legal Help

6.52 The criteria for qualification for Legal Help are set out at Merits Regs 2013 reg 32 (as amended). They are that it must be reasonable to provide Legal Help having regard to other potential sources of funding and that there will be sufficient benefit to justify the cost of Legal Help. A person's conduct is relevant to whether it is reasonable to provide legal services (including Legal Help).[55]

6.53 It will be seen from para 6.33 above that advice about any matter arising under the MCA 2005 could be provided under Legal Help, apart from those areas excluded by LASPO Sch 3 para 5(1), (3). This could include advice to a representative under COPR r1.2(2)(c) about how to discharge their role.

The merits test for Legal Representation (a legal aid certificate)

6.54 Legal representation may only be provided if the relevant merits tests are met and it is reasonable in the light of the person's conduct (Merits Regs 2013 reg 11(7)).

6.55 There are standard criteria which apply in a number of categories of civil proceedings, and then specific criteria which are relevant in the Court of Protection. The standard criteria are set out in reg 39 below. If they are not all satisfied, the individual will not obtain legal aid:

> 39. An individual may qualify for legal representation only if the Director is satisfied that the following criteria are met–
> (a) the individual does not have access to other potential sources of funding (other than a conditional fee agreement) from which it would be reasonable to fund the case;
> (b) the case is unsuitable for a conditional fee agreement;
> (c) there is no person other than the individual, including a person who might benefit from the proceedings, who can reasonably be expected to bring the proceedings;
> (d) the individual has exhausted all reasonable alternatives to bringing proceedings including any complaints system, ombudsman scheme or other form of alternative dispute resolution;
> (e) there is a need for representation in all the circumstances of the case including–

55 Merits Regs 2013 reg 11(7).

(i) the nature and complexity of the issues;
(ii) the existence of other proceedings; and
(iii) the interests of other parties to the proceedings; and

(f) the proceedings are not likely to be allocated to the small claims track.

6.56 The impact of the test in reg 39(c) was considered in *R (Moosa) v Legal Services Commission*.[56] This case was brought prior to LASPO, but the same test had formed part of the previous merits criteria. The case concerned a dispute between a family and local authority as to where their son who had significant difficulties would live. The son was being cared for in residential care. The family wanted him to return home. The local authority commenced proceedings in the Court of Protection to determine P's best interests in terms of his residence. His mother was a respondent on the Form COP1 and pursuant to COPR r73 she automatically became a party. She was financially ineligible for legal aid as she had an amount of equity in her home (where she hoped to accommodate P) that took her over the capital limits. Charles J agreed to join P's brother as a party. P's brother was a student and was financially eligible for legal aid. It was made clear to the Court of Protection that the reason for joining the brother was to ensure that there was one family member who was eligible for public funding. That member would then become the voice of the family.

6.57 The LSC (the predecessor to the current LAA) refused the brother funding on the basis that the mother could reasonably bring the case. The refusal was challenged. It was argued that a refusal to fund the brother simply made it impossible for anyone to argue the family's position with the benefit of legal aid, because the mother could not access the equity in her home, and the home was the place where the family wished to accommodate their son. It was unrealistic to consider for example the sale of that property to allow the mother to realise some of her capital. While the judge expressed some sympathy to the family the application for judicial review was refused.

6.58 The *cost-benefit* criteria and the *prospects of success* test must also be met.[57]

6.59 The cost-benefit criteria require the Director to be satisfied that (assuming the case is not for damages, or of significant wider public interest) the reasonable private paying individual test is met. If the

56 [2013] EWHC 2804 (Admin).

57 Merits Regs 2013 reg 41.

case is of significant wider public interest then the proportionality test must be met (reg 42).

6.60 The prospects of success test is as follows.[58] The test will be met where the Director is satisfied that the prospects of success are very good, good or moderate. All other cases must be classified as one of the following:

- 'marginal' – where there is between 45 and 50 per cent chance of a successful outcome;
- 'borderline' – where it is not possible to say whether there is a greater than 50 per cent chance of success or whether the prospects of success should be classified as poor or marginal, because of disputed law, fact or expert evidence;
- 'poor' – where there is less than 50 per cent chance of obtaining a successful outcome.

6.61 The test will not be met where the prospects of success are poor but may in some cases be met where the prospects are marginal or borderline, for example because the case is of overwhelming importance to the individual or of significant wider public interest.

6.62 If all the criteria above are met, a further test still needs to be carried out if the case is being heard in the Court of Protection. This is set out in reg 52 and provides that full representation will only be granted if *two further tests* are met.[59] The *first test* is that the Court of Protection has ordered or is likely to order an oral hearing, *and* that it is necessary for the individual to be provided with full representation in the proceedings.[60] This therefore excludes uncontentious 'streamlined' applications for authority to deprive P of their liberty which are usually dealt with on the papers without a hearing – the so-called '*Re X*' applications.[61] Legal Help however may be available to parties to such cases, or to a person who has been appointed to represent P under COPR r3A(2)(c) but it is important to recognise that Legal Help cannot extend to steps which amount to conducting proceedings.

6.63 The Lord Chancellor's guidance as to when it is 'necessary' to provide representation is considered below at para 6.64.

58 See: www.gov.uk/government/news/civil-news-merits-criteria-regulations-amended-from-22-july/.

59 Note that reg 52 does not apply to cases heard under the 'inherent jurisdiction' – see chapter 28.

60 Merits Regs 2013 reg 52(2).

61 Discussed in more detail in chapter 21.

6.64 The inclusion of a requirement for an oral hearing (or the likelihood of an oral hearing being listed) has resulted in reports of additional hearings having to be listed at a time when resources are already stretched. There are ongoing discussions about the logic of equating the need for an oral hearing with the need for P to be represented. Many cases are complex and P requires to be a party and represented, but directions can be agreed between the parties without the need for an oral hearing to be listed, particularly at the earlier stages of a case. The linking of the requirement for an oral hearing to availability of legal aid for representation is considered by the authors to need urgent review.

6.65 The *second test* is that the case relates to:

a) a person's right to life;
b) a person's liberty or physical safety;
c) a person's medical treatment (within the meaning of the MHA 1983);
d) a person's capacity to marry, to enter into a civil partnership or to enter into sexual relations; or
e) a person's right to family life.

6.66 From the list above it can be seen that cases which concern a person's psychological safety alone, or right to respect for their home or for their private life and which may also engage rights under ECHR Article 8 could, if there are no other factors involved fall outside the merits criteria.

6.67 In *R (SL) v Director of Legal Aid Casework and Cambridgeshire County Council*[62] the LAA conceded that legal aid funding is available to P to bring a claim for damages under the Human Rights Act (HRA) 1998 in the Court of Protection. Such claims can be brought in relation both to ongoing and historic violations of P's rights under the ECHR.

The Lord Chancellor's Guidance

6.68 It is important to be aware of the Lord Chancellor's Guidance,[63] which sets out the approach that will be taken to questions such as

62 Unreported, CO/5916/2015.The sealed order can be viewed at https://courtofprotectionhandbook.com/sealed-final-order-04-04-16/.

63 *Lord Chancellor's Guidance under section 4 of the Legal Aid, Sentencing and Punishment of Offenders Act 2012*, August 2021, https://assets.publishing.service.gov.uk/government/uploads/system/uploads/attachment_data/file/1008832/210804_Lord_Chancellor_s_s4_Guidance_-_FINAL.pdf.

what 'other sources of funding' might be (para 7.14); and when a case is unsuitable for a conditional fee agreement (CFA) (para 7.16). Paragraph 7.24 of the guidance deals with when it will be 'necessary' to represent an applicant for legal aid, and comments:

> It should not be necessary for there to be more parties legally represented than there are positions to be argued. This may be particularly relevant in a welfare case in the Court of Protection where an additional member of the family of the subject of the proceedings seeks representation.

6.69 Section 9 of the Lord Chancellor's Guidance deals with mental health cases, and includes the following relevant provisions:

- Legal representation (ie a legal aid certificate) may be refused if it is premature or if legal help is more appropriate (para 9.5).
- For Court of Protection work, the expectation will be that 'support will be available through legal help' (para 9.8).[64]
- Accommodation cases will only be in scope if they affect P's family life.
- Although legal help is not available to create an advance decision or LPA, it is available to advise on potential or actual proceedings about the validity or applicability of an LPA.

Financial eligibility (means test)

6.70 The means test is governed by the Civil Legal Aid (Financial Resources and Payment for Services) Regulations 2013.[65]

6.71 There is only one exception to the rule that the client must satisfy the means test before getting legal aid in the Court of Protection. This is where a person is deprived of their liberty under an urgent or standard authorisation under MCA 2005 Sch A1 and there is an appeal against the authorisation under MCA 2005 s21A. In this case, the person detained under the authorisation can obtain legal aid without their means being assessed, and so can their 'relevant person's representative' (RPR) ie 'non- means-tested legal aid'.

6.72 The relevant regulation (reg 5(1)(g)) is below and shows when legal aid can be provided without the applicant satisfying the means test:

64 This appears to ignore that proceedings cannot be conducted under Legal Help.

65 SI 2013 No 480.

(g) legal representation in relation to a matter described in paragraph 5(1)(c) (mental capacity) of Part 1 of Schedule 1 to the Act to the extent that–
  (i) the legal representation is in proceedings in the Court of Protection under section 21A of the Mental Capacity Act 2005; and
  (ii) the individual to whom legal representation may be provided is–
    (aa) the individual in respect of whom an authorisation is in force under paragraph 2 of Schedule A1 to the Mental Capacity Act 2005; or
    (bb) a representative of that individual appointed as such in accordance with Part 10 of that Schedule;

6.73 From this it will be seen that the exemption from the means test relates to legal representation only. Legal Help could only be provided in relation to an MCA 2005 s21A case if the client satisfied the means test. There is therefore an inconsistency in approach which is unlikely to be justified if challenged.

6.74 Guidance from Charles J in *Re HA*[66] (determined before the regulations came into effect) encouraged judges in section 21A cases to make interim orders depriving P of their liberty under MCA 2005 s16. The authorisation would then fall away and P's entitlement to non-means tested legal aid would be lost. In *UF v (1) A Local Authority (2) AS (3) Director of Legal Aid Casework (4) Ministry of Justice.*[67] UF appealed against a standard authorisation. The district judge made orders depriving UF of her liberty under MCA 2005 s16. On the expiry of the standard authorisation, UF was advised by the LAA that her means would now be assessed because she no longer came within reg 5(1)(g)(ii)(aa) above. UF's means would have made her ineligible for legal aid. She applied to the court to vary the court's order so that the court's authorisation of her deprivation of liberty would be set aside. Charles J held that in the vast majority of cases the court could exercise its powers under MCA 2005 s21A(3)(a) to vary the standard authorisation; and could extend an extant authorisation pursuant to MCA 2005 s21A(2)(b).

6.75 The Director of Legal Aid Casework and Ministry of Justice assured Charles J that if a court adopted either of the courses in a) or b) or the course adopted in that of *UF*, it would not treat the orders as contrivances and refuse public funding for that reason when applying the merits test for public funding. The effect of these concessions is that it is clear that non-means tested legal aid should

66 [2012] EWHC 1068 (COP), [2012] COPLR 534.

67 [2013] EWHC 4289 (COP), [2014] COPLR 93.

remain available on any application under MCA 2005 s21A for so long as P is deprived of their liberty under an authorisation, including under orders of the court which are framed as set out in *UF*. An example is set out below:

Example

P brings proceedings a) challenging a standard authorisation and b) seeking declarations that his Article 5 rights have been breached by an act done in relation to the standard authorisation. At the first hearing the authorisation is about to expire but the judge varies the standard authorisation by extending it to the next hearing. P will continue to be eligible for non-means tested legal aid. At the second hearing the judge terminates the standard authorisation and P returns home. The proceedings continue while P seeks declarations about the lawfulness of the authorisation. P will no longer be eligible for non-means tested legal aid.

6.76 In *UF*, Charles J also indicated that, where the court varied the standard authorisation by extending it, the court may need to consider making an order under MCA 2005 s21A(6) exonerating the supervisory body from liability for the extended period as the court would have assumed the responsibility for the deprivation of liberty. Importantly, the court may only extend a standard authorisation before its expiry and close attention should be paid to renewal dates otherwise a new standard or urgent authorisation may be required to avoid a gap in legal aid cover. If P's legal aid is jeopardised because of a delay in putting a valid authorisation in place then there is a risk that costs may be sought against the supervisory body for the legal costs of any period which is not covered by legal aid. Care should therefore be taken that any standard authorisation of a deprivation of liberty is extended by the court before its expiry or alternatively properly renewed on time. It is also important to note that it is extremely unlikely that the Court of Protection has the power to extend an authorisation for longer than a year (as the maximum period allowed for by statute).[68] If proceedings are protracted, practitioners will need to make sure that the relevant supervisory body has taken steps to get a new authorisation in place before the end of the year period. If not, many Ps will be left without legal representation at all (as they will be

68 See *UF* at paras 35 and 36 and *N v A Local Authority* [2016] EWCOP 47.

ineligible for means tested legal aid) or if they are eligible for means tested legal aid, they will be liable to pay a large contribution towards their legal aid. It can also give rise to serious practical problems where an expert has been instructed prior to the expiry of the authorisation, but has yet to report. Disputes about costs of P's representation arising from lapsed standard authorisations are increasingly common, and these could be avoided by prompt action on the part of supervisory bodies.

6.77 The question of the availability of legal aid in serious medical treatment cases where the dispute between the parties was not solely concerned with deprivation of liberty but whether the treatment was in P's best interests was considered in *Director of Legal Aid Casework v Briggs*.[69] The LAA sought to narrow the scope of non-means tested legal aid and argued that as long as there was a proper assessment and care plan the scope of the section 21A enquiry was not to its content:

> . . . under Schedule A1, all that is required within the best interests assessment is for the assessors to satisfy themselves that there is in fact a care plan and a needs assessment in place. No further detailed examination or consideration of the contents is . . . either required or appropriate.[70]

6.78 The Court of Appeal rejected this argument and confirmed that:

> 93. . . . There are many issues which relate to a deprivation of liberty which need appropriately to be considered by the assessor and which may be reflected in recommendations for conditions in the assessor's report and which may even be determinative of whether a standard authorisation is made.
>
> 94 Where a dispute is referred to the court under s21A, the issue is often in relation to P and the family's wish for P to go home, set against the assessor's view that it is in P's best interests to be placed in a care home and consequently deprived of his or her liberty. [The Official Solicitor] has helpfully provided the court with a table of cases where applications have appropriately been made under s21A; on closer examination, each of them has involved a dispute as to whether P should reside in some form of care home or return to either his home or to live with a family member in the community. Such cases are focused specifically on the issue as to whether P should be detained and are properly brought under s21A. Proper consideration of those cases by the assessor in compliance with the guidance in the DOLS Code, requires far more of an extensive consideration of the relevant circumstances than that which is suggested by [the LAA],

69 [2017] EWCA Civ 1169, [2018] Fam 63, [2017] COPLR 370.

70 *Briggs* at para 73.

> namely simply ensuring a care plan and needs assessment is in place without further consideration as to the content.
> 95 Contact, for example, is an issue capable of going to the heart of whether being detained is in a person's best interests; it may be that in an ideal world P's best interests would be served by a deprivation of liberty in the form of her living in a care home properly looked after, where the appropriate medication regime will be adhered to and P will have a proper balanced diet. Desirable as that may be, and such a regime may well provide the optimum care outcome for P, but it may also be the case that unless, regular contact can be facilitated to a particular family member, the distress and confusion caused to P would be such that it would be no longer in her best interests to be detained, and that what might amount to sub optimum physical care would ultimately be preferable to no, or insufficient contact. The weighing up of such options are part of the best interests assessment process in relation to which the professionals who are eligible to be assessors are peculiarly qualified to conduct.

6.79 Non-means tested legal aid is not available if P is only deprived of their liberty through an order of the court without an urgent or standard authorisation being in place, or because P lives in a setting where MCA 2005 Sch A1 (DOLS) cannot be used eg a supported living setting which is not a care home or hospital.

6.80 In both *Re NRA*[71] and *Re JM*,[72] Charles J considered the position of an uncontentious application is made for orders depriving P of their liberty (so-called '*Re X*' cases)[73] under MCA 2005 s16. Such cases rarely involve an oral hearing and therefore do not satisfy the merits test (see para 6.46 above); Legal Help would also only be available if P were financially eligible and would not cover the conduct of proceedings. He encouraged the secretary of state to consider whether to amend the legal aid scheme for such cases. Charles J found in *Re JM* that the 'minimum procedural requirements' to satisfy Article 5 necessitated 'some assistance from someone on the ground who considers the care package through P's eyes'.[74] A litigation friend (or an accredited legal representative (ALR): see para 12.7) could fulfil that role, and non-means tested legal aid in such cases would make this a potential solution to the dearth of representatives for P in '*Re X*' cases. However as at the time of writing, there has been no change in policy to reflect these observations. This

71 [2015] EWCOP 59, [2015] COPLR 690.

72 [2016] EWCOP 15, [2016] COPLR 302.

73 See further para 22.61 onwards.

74 *Re JM* at para 140.

position is deeply problematic; even more problematic is the situation where the application for authorisation **is** contentious. On one view, it might be said that the person does not need to exercise their ECHR Article 5(4) rights because the deprivation of their liberty is being authorised from the outset by a court, as opposed to being authorised by an administrative mechanism against which there should lie a right of challenge. However, we suggest that this is unduly narrow, because it means, unless the individual satisfies the means test, they have no ability to instruct lawyers to review or challenge the making of the order in the first place by the court. It would be a perverse position, we suggest, were the person to be a worse position as regards their ability to make representations (via a lawyer) as to whether Article 5 is satisfied (the burden always lying upon the state) because a court is involved at the outset than they would be if the court were involved at a later date.

6.81 There are therefore still two groups of mentally incapacitated persons deprived of their liberty who are arbitrarily treated completely differently as far as access to legal representation is concerned. This creates huge inequality and is unacceptable. Given the delay to the implementation of the liberty protection safeguards (LPS), which would cover many of those in this situation,[75] we suggest that the differential, discriminatory, position is one that is ripe for challenge by way of judicial review.

Evidence of financial eligibility

6.82 In some cases, if the applicant for legal aid is in receipt of certain means tested benefits, then they will be 'passported' for income and their income will not need to be further assessed.[76] However, in all cases at all levels of legal aid, an applicant for legal aid must always also have their capital assessed.

6.83 Since 2013, all applicants for legal aid are also subject to a capital test, even if they are in receipt of 'passporting benefits' where the Department for Work and Pensions (DWP) has already undertaken an assessment of their capital in order to decide that they qualify for income related state benefits.

75 See chapter 22. It is important to note, however, that the same disparity will exist even after the introduction of the LPS in any case where the relevant public body seeks authorisation from the court, rather than via the mechanism of the LPS.

76 Civil Legal Aid (Financial Resources and Payment for Services) Regulations 2013 SI No 480 reg 6.

6.84 The threshold for eligibility for legal aid is different to that for welfare benefits, with the capital limit for legal aid being much lower than for benefits. Therefore a person can be assessed by one department of the state as being so impecunious as to be eligible for benefits, while at the same time not being entitled to legal aid.

6.85 In addition, the capital assessment for legal aid does not (unlike other means tested benefits) disregard the value of the client's main dwelling house. Whilst the legal aid assessment does allow for some equity in any property to be disregarded, this is often exceeded in practice, particularly in the case of older persons. The person is treated as having capital sums to pay for legal representation which is simply not there in practice and where the person has no real prospect of being able to raise any funds from a bank in respect of the equity. The result is that the person is not eligible for legal aid at any level. This is particularly concerning in cases of deprivation of liberty under MCA 2005 s16 which are means tested, as against deprivation of liberty cases under MCA 2005 s21A which are non-means-tested.

6.86 The difficulty of inaccessible capital, sometimes described as 'trapped capital', was raised in *R (GR) v Director of Legal Aid Casework*,[77] a judicial review of the decision of the LAA to treat a victim of domestic abuse as having capital in her former home in assessing her eligibility for legal aid. Pepperall J commented that if there was no discretion to reduce the value or ascribe no value to capital assets that applicant cannot access to fund representation 'then I am satisfied . . . would prevent some people on low incomes who cannot access the equity in their homes from having fair and effective access to justice'.[78] The case was remitted to the Director of Legal Aid Casework for a new decision.

6.87 It is not difficult to see how the treatment of capital in the legal aid system means that assessment can exclude a person from legal aid, particularly where they have property in later life – yet such capital is clearly often inaccessible to the person, not least because of their mental incapacity. Despite the judgment in *GR*, there continue to be issues in accessing legal aid because of the way that capital is treated.[79]

6.88 When acting for P, or a protected party, it is P's means which must be assessed, and not those of any litigation friend. The LAA

77 [2020] EWHC 3140 (Admin), [2021] 1 WLR 1483.

78 *GR* at paras 73 and 75.

79 See, for instance, the Public Law Project's 2022 report on trapped capital available at: https://publiclawproject.org.uk/resources/trapped-capital-still-barrier-to-legal-aid-research-shows/.

encourages practitioners having difficulty obtaining evidence of means in these cases to email: contactcivil@legalaid.gsi.gov.uk with the heading 'Vulnerable Client Means Assessment'.

Legal Aid Means Test Review

6.89 At the time of writing, the Ministry of Justice had published for consultation its long-awaited review of the means test.[80] Many of the proposed changes are long overdue, such as removing the housing costs cap, increasing disposable capital and income levels, and allowances for dependents.

6.90 However, there are some notable omissions. Legal Help for mental capacity issues should be non-means-tested, if not for all cases, then for all deprivation of liberty cases. Early legal advice can help to resolve disputes before more expensive and polarising court proceedings are even started. Additionally, non-means-tested legal aid certificates should be available to challenge not only an existing deprivation of liberty, but also any proposal to deprive a person of their liberty. It seems illogical, let alone unjust, for a person to be eligible for non means tested legal aid only at the stage when they have already been removed from their home into a care placement, but not at the stage where they are facing removal.

Practical issues

6.91 Although it will be P's means which are assessed for the purpose of an application for legal aid, legal aid forms should be signed by the litigation friend (if appointed) or, if there are no proceedings on foot, by the person who intends to act as litigation friend. The Civil Legal Aid (Procedure) Regulations 2012 permit the signature of applications for legal services on behalf of a protected party by a person acting or proposing to act as litigation friend; or by any other person where there is good reason why the litigation friend or proposed litigation friend cannot make the application. This does not include the provider of legal services.[81] The Standard Civil Contract authorises a third party to sign forms on behalf of a protected party where there is sufficient connection between the protected party and the third party to ensure that the third party is likely to act reasonably; and when the

80 See: www.gov.uk/government/consultations/legal-aid-means-test-review/legal-aid-means-test-review, the consultation closing on 7 June 2022.

81 Civil Legal Aid (Procedure) Regulations 2012 SI No 3098 reg 22.

third party has sufficient knowledge of the protected party's means to provide instructions.[82] Temporary contingency arrangements were made during the pandemic to ease the requirements, but these were removed with effect from May 2022.

6.92 The appointment of an ALR does not bring funding with it. ALRs will need to be authorised by the court to investigate P's means to assess their eligibility for legal aid.

6.93 The regulations do not on their face currently cater for ALRs to sign legal aid forms on behalf of P. The LAA has, however, indicated that it will exercise its discretion to allow ALRs to sign a legal aid application form, which will need to be requested individually in each case. It is suggested that until such time as the regulations are amended, courts appointing ALRs should also specifically authorise the ALR to sign the application form on behalf of P. There is currently no power for an ALR to sign a Legal Help form for P to obtain initial advice, which is another anomaly which needs attention.

The statutory charge

6.94 The statutory charge applies to property which is recovered or preserved as a result of a person being in receipt of legal aid for the proceedings. This effectively converts the legal aid funding for the case into a loan for the person, which has to be repaid as a first charge on any property/compensation which is awarded or preserved.

6.95 LASPO s25(1) provides that the LAA's charge attaches to:

(a) any property recovered or preserved by the individual in proceedings, or in any compromise or settlement of a dispute, in connection with which the services were provided (whether the property is recovered or preserved for the individual or another person), and
(b) any costs payable to the individual by another person in connection with such proceedings or such a dispute.

6.96 The definition above is wide and is not limited to property recovered or preserved in the same set of proceedings in which legal aid was made available.

6.97 The Civil Legal Aid (Statutory Charge) Regulations 2013[83] give the Lord Chancellor discretion to waive all or part of the statutory charge in limited circumstances.[84] Regulation 8 applies when the statutory

82 Standard Civil Contract 2014, General Specification, para 3.12.
83 SI 2013 No 503.
84 Civil Legal Aid (Statutory Charge) Regulations 2013 regs 8 and 9.

charge is in favour of a provider of legal aid services. The Lord Chancellor can permit the provider, whether in individual cases or generally, to waive all or part of the charge when it would cause grave hardship or distress to a legally aided party to enforce the charge; and when enforcing the charge would be unreasonably difficult because of the nature of the property. Regulation 9 allows the Lord Chancellor to waive all or part of the charge when it is equitable to do so and where at the time of granting legal aid, the Director of Legal Aid Casework had been satisfied that the proceedings has a significant wider public interest and that there were other claimants or potential claimants who might benefit from the proceedings.

6.98 In *R (Faulkner) v Director of Legal Aid Casework*[85] Mostyn J rejected a challenge to the (then) Legal Services Commission not to waive the statutory charge which would have the effect of eliminating the damages awarded to Mr Faulkner for breach of ECHR Article 5. He held that damages for Convention breaches do not bring immunity with them and are subject to the same costs regime as any other damages.

6.99 There has been considerable debate around the approach by the LAA to damages claims under the HRA 1998 and whether damages awarded in care proceedings and in Court of Protection proceedings attract the charge. In February 2018 the LAA published its policy position in the form of a position statement.[86] In July 2018, the LAA also confirmed that the application of the statutory charge in respect of the costs incurred in welfare proceedings can be avoided by ensuring that damages are not pursued or awarded within the welfare proceedings and by keeping the costs of pursuing the damages claim separate.[87] This is a welcome clarification for practitioners and clients alike in that any damages in Court of Protection proceedings will not be payable to the LAA via the charge but can be retained by the person subject to the damages claim being dealt with separately from the general welfare proceedings.

85 [2016] EWHC 717 (Admin), [2016] 2 Costs LR 237. Available at: https://assets.publishing.service.gov.uk/government/uploads/system/uploads/attachment_data/file/724127/LAA_statutory_charge_position_statement.pdf.

86 Available at: https://assets.publishing.service.gov.uk/government/uploads/system/uploads/attachment_data/file/724127/LAA_statutory_charge_position_statement.pdf.

87 See the letter from the LAA to Miles and Partners dated 20 July 2018, available at: https://courtofprotectionhandbook.com/2018/07/28/hra-claims-the-court-of-protection-and-the-statutory-charge-certainty-at-last/.

Experts' fees

6.100 This section should be read in conjunction with paras 13.66–13.80, which discuss the tests that the court will apply in deciding whether to allow the instruction of an expert and on what terms.

6.101 Experts' fees can be claimed as a disbursement on a party's legal aid certificate. The LAA sets standard rates which it will agree to pay experts. The current rates were set on 2 December 2013 and have not increased in line with inflation.[88] If a certain type of expert is not listed in the remuneration regulations, they will be remunerated at a rate determined by the LAA, which will have regard to the codified rates in setting such a rate. The LAA published guidance on the remuneration of experts in September 2014.[89] Practitioners will need to be aware of this guidance, which includes indications of typical hours spent in various types of work.

6.102 If an expert charges a rate in excess of the current codified rate, the LAA will only pay this if it considers it is reasonable to do so in exceptional circumstances *and* it has granted prior authority in response to an application. The LAA considers the following to be exceptional circumstances:

- the expert's evidence is key to the client's case, and either
- the complexity of the material is such that a high level of seniority is required, or
- the material is of such a specialised nature that only very few experts are available to provide the necessary evidence.[90]

6.103 Practitioners considering instructing an expert who charges above the codified rates must therefore obtain prior authority before instructing the expert, which has the effect of guaranteeing that the cost of the expert will be covered.[91] Practitioners will be expected strictly to demonstrate that the request for prior authority comes within the conditions set out above.

88 Civil Legal Aid (Remuneration) (Amendment) Regulations 2013 SI No 2877 Sch 2.

89 Available at: www.gov.uk/government/uploads/system/uploads/attachment_data/file/420106/expert-witnesses-fees-guidance.pdf.

90 Standard Civil Contract 2018 para 6.60.

91 Assuming that incorrect information has not been provided in the application and /or there has been a material change between the grant of authority and the costs being incurred: Standard Civil Contract 2018 para 5.11.

6.104 Where the expert charges the rate set by the LAA prior authority may be sought if the item of costs is unusual in size or nature; or if there are no codified rates set for a particular expert.[92]

6.105 In all cases where an expert is instructed it is helpful to invite the court to approve the instructions of the particular expert when the court gives permission for the expert to be instructed. Precedents can be found on the Court of Protection Handbook website: www.courtofprotectionhandbook.com. The order should make clear that evidence is *necessary* to assist the court to resolve the issues in the proceedings and cannot otherwise be provided[93] (see further in this regard para 13.72).

6.106 While the LAA's starting point will frequently be to expect costs of experts to be apportioned equally and therefore not to allow a legally aided party's share to exceed that of the other parties, the case of *JG v Lord Chancellor and others*[94] is a useful reminder that equal apportionment of experts' fees is not inevitable and will depend on the facts of the case including for whose benefit the report is sought. Black LJ's judgment contains a review of Strasbourg cases where the securing of expert evidence engaged rights under ECHR Articles 6 and 8. The guidance on remuneration recognises that equal apportionment will not always be the norm in public law children cases, because some parties may have limited involvement in the case (such as an intervenor),[95] or because the case concerns children with different fathers and the issue relates to one child only. There are potential analogies in Court of Protection cases. A Trust may be providing inpatient care for P and may thus be a party to an application; but may not have an interest in P's care arrangements after discharge.

6.107 In *Re AB (a child) (temporary leave to remove from jurisdiction: expert evidence)*,[96] a family case involving the instruction of an expert in Indian law, HHJ Bellamy noted that neither the Civil Legal Aid (Remuneration) Regulations 2013 nor the LAA's contract defined the term 'expert'. He commented:

92 Guidance on the Remuneration of Expert Witnesses 4.2, 4.14, 4.15. The LAA's Central Legal Team also published guidance on prior authority in January 2021: https://assets.publishing.service.gov.uk/government/uploads/system/uploads/attachment_data/file/953010/Guidance_on_authorities_and_legal_aid_for_cases_in_courts_outside_England_and_Wales_Jan2021.pdf.

93 Ie the test in COPR r15.3(1) is met.

94 [2014] EWCA Civ 656, [2014] 2 FLR 1218.

95 Guidance on the Remuneration of Expert Witnesses, 4.5.

96 [2014] EWHC 2758 (Fam), [2015] 1 FCR 164.

> That is unsurprising. The determination of whether expert evidence is necessary in order to resolve a case justly and whether a particular witness 'is qualified to give expert evidence' (s3(1) of the Civil Evidence Act 1972) are issues for determination by the court not by the LAA. I am concerned that in this case the LAA should have disregarded a decision by the court that Mr Kumar is an expert. In my judgment it was not open to the LAA to disregard a judicial decision on this issue.[97]

High cost cases

6.108 High cost cases (HCCs) are defined in Civil Legal Aid (Procedure) Regulations 2012[98] reg 54(3). These cases are managed under an individual contract which is agreed between the practitioners (solicitor and barrister) and the LAA. For the purpose of Court of Protection cases, the HCC provisions will apply when the Director of Legal Aid Casework has reason to believe that the actual or likely costs of the case are likely to exceed £25,000 (ie the fees of the solicitor(s) and barrister(s) and disbursements, excluding VAT).

6.109 Practitioners will keep the overall costs of any certificated case under careful review. If it appears that the likely costs of the case – taking into account counsel's fees and disbursements – are likely to exceed £25,000, then the practitioner must follow the steps set out in the LAA's information pack, *HCC – A solicitor's information pack (non-family)* ('Solicitors Information Pack').[99] There is an equivalent pack for barristers.

6.110 Once the threshold for a High Cost Case contract is reached (ie where the costs are likely to exceed £25,000), the legal team must complete a pro forma case plan which predicts all the work which is likely to be required in the case, up to the next stage (usually work in preparing for and attending a hearing). The stage must be agreed between the legal team and the LAA and further stages are then submitted for prior agreement. Where the criteria are met (unusual rates or amounts of work) prior authority applications should still be made for the cost of experts, in addition to the work being included in the case plan. Critics report that the approach to high cost case contracts is very time consuming and delays in finalising the

97 *AB* at para 64.

98 SI 2012 No 3098.

99 See: www.gov.uk/government/publications/high-cost-cases-non-family-civil.

contracts are common. This results in practitioners working at risk, which is not the way that the system is intended to operate.

6.111 It is not difficult for a contested Court of Protection case to become a HCC, particularly if the case is complex, there are substantial interim hearings and/or experts are used.

CHAPTER 7

Making an application: property and affairs cases

Introduction

7.1 The majority of the applications dealt with by the Court of Protection concern property and affairs.

7.2 This chapter looks first at the application process for property and affairs applications, focussing on a deputyship application. It then goes on to look at issues relating to deputyship and other types of applications to the court as well as the court's powers in relation to lasting and enduring powers of attorney (LPA/EPA). Chapter 8 then looks at responding to an application and the procedure when an application is contested.

7.3 A flowchart summarising the procedure is set out at the end of this chapter. The very significant majority of applications concerning P's property and affairs are not contested, and are necessary simply because court authority is needed lawfully to make the necessary decisions.

Preliminary matters

Initial considerations

7.4 Before making an application to the court it is worth considering if other less costly and cumbersome options could offer a solution (see also in this regard, chapter 5). Where P's life expectancy is short or funds are very limited then an application may not be appropriate. If the prospective applicant is aware that there is any possibility that the application could be contentious it is wise to try to consult with P's family and wider support network to establish if a consensus can be achieved before taking matters before the court.

7.5 If the appointment of a deputy is necessary there are particular considerations as to the choice of deputy, these can be found below at para 7.40.

Application procedure

7.6 All property and affairs applications begin following the same procedure. Permission is not required to make any application concerning P's property and affairs, whether for the appointment of deputy or any other issue.[1]

1 Court of Protection Rules (COPR) r8.2(2)(a).

7.7 The core application documents for property and affairs applications are:[2]

- COP1 Application form;
- COP1A Supporting evidence for property and affairs; and
- COP3 Assessment of capacity.

Sample COP1 and COP1A forms have been published on the gov.uk website for applications relating to a matured Child Trust Fund held on behalf of a person lacking capacity to manage property and affairs.[3] They are equally applicable to other situations where a relatively small sum of money is in play.

7.8 Court of Protection Rules 2017[4] (COPR) Part 9 deals with beginning proceedings. Practice Direction (PD) 9A provides guidance on completing the COP1, which is the main application form for starting proceedings. The COP1 form sets out the order or decision that the court is being asked to make, why the decision needs to be made and how it is in P's best interests to make the decision.

7.9 All applications relating to property and affairs (unless made by an existing deputy or attorney under the procedure set out in PD 9D) require a COP1A form to provide the court with P's financial context. It is important to give as much information as possible to ensure that the order ultimately made by the court suits P's circumstances. Where the application is for the appointment of a deputy this information will be used by the court to set the appropriate guarantee bond and set such restrictions as it deems appropriate. Typical restrictions might include a limit on how much the deputy may access of P's funds in any given year without further authority, or limiting the deputy's ability to sell P's property without a further order. This ensures that the court does not unnecessarily curtail the deputy's authority or leave P exposed by the deputy being under-bonded. In other applications relating to P's property and affairs the question of affordability is often key to any decision to be made so it is essential to robust decision making that all parties have detailed financial information.

7.10 The COP1A form also identifies who is a respondent to the application and who is to be notified. A respondent is 'any person

2 Court of Protection forms and guidance are available at: www.gov.uk/government/collections/court-of-protection-forms.

3 See:www.gov.uk/government/publications/apply-to-make-decisions-on-someones-behalf-form-cop1 and www.gov.uk/government/publications/apply-to-make-decisions-on-someones-behalf-property-and-finance-form-cop1a.

4 SI 2017 No 1035.

(other than P) whom the applicant reasonably believes to have an interest which means he ought to be heard in relation to the application (as opposed to being notified of it)'.[5] The applicant should attempt to identify at least three people to notify of the application.[6] People to be notified are people who have a reasonable interest in being notified of the application. Those who are notified of an application may apply to be joined as parties.[7] There is a presumption (which can be displaced) that close members of P's family will have such an interest and PD 9B para 7 lists those who should ordinarily be notified, in descending order of closeness to P.[8] If someone in that list is not notified, then the application form should explain the reasons for their omission.

7.11 Form COP3, under review at the time of writing, provides the court with an assessment of P's mental capacity in relation to the specific decision to be made by the court. It is usually completed by a medical practitioner, social worker or other suitably qualified professional. The Court of Protection's jurisdiction is only engaged where there is evidence that on the balance of probabilities it is more likely than not that a person is not capable of making certain decisions for themselves because of a lack of capacity (see further paras 3.33–3.39). When completing Part A of the form, advisers should ensure that they have correctly identified the issue or issues in respect of which P's decision-making capabilities need to be assessed. The tests in relation to statutory wills and gifts are touched on below at para 7.91 onwards and are addressed in detail in the British Medical Association (BMA)/Law Society's *Assessment of Mental Capacity*.[9] At this stage the applicant may wish to ask the professional assessing capacity to provide guidance as to the decisions that P *can* make or could make with appropriate support. The present COP3 focuses on where P lacks capacity but the Mental Capacity Act (MCA) 2005 requires that deputies take steps to support P's decision making and in our experience, it can be invaluable to have advice as to how this can be achieved in the case of the actual P the subject of the application.

7.12 Occasionally there will be uncertainty as to a person's capacity or lack of capacity. If there is conflicting evidence all relevant evidence

5 COPR r9.3(c)(iii).
6 COPR r9.10 and PD 9B para 4.
7 COPR r9.12(6) and (8); PD 9C para 4.
8 COPR PD 9B para 7.
9 5th edn, 2022.

as to capacity should be put before the court for consideration.[10] The court's jurisdiction to make interim decisions is engaged at a lower threshold – namely that there reason to believe that the person lacks capacity.[11] The judge can then consider the evidence available and make a decision or give directions to resolve the issue of P's mental capacity. This may be by way of an oral hearing.

7.13 If the court is not satisfied with the medical evidence available, or if there has been some difficulty in having P's capacity assessed, the court is able to order under MCA 2005 s49 that a Special Visitor meets P to assess their capacity (see further in respect of section 49 reports, paras 13.47–13.55). A Special Visitor is a member of a panel appointed by the Lord Chancellor, with a medical qualification and special knowledge of and experience in cases of impairment of or disturbance in the functioning of the mind or brain;[12] one of their roles is to carry out assessments of capacity in these more difficult or unusual cases.

7.14 Medical evidence must be recent. If the court deems that the evidence is too old it may order that an updated assessment of capacity needs to be carried out which will delay the application. There is no specific guidance on when the court will consider that a COP3 need to be updated before a decision can be made but our experience is that, if the COP3 form is dated more than six months before the application, then the court is likely to ask for an updated assessment.

7.15 Additional forms are required depending upon the particular application to be made:

- deputy application – COP4 deputy's declaration;
- authorisation of a statutory will, codicil, gift or other disposition of P's property – COP1C;
- applications to appoint or discharge a trustee – COP1D;
- applications by an existing deputy or attorney – COP1E;
- applications relating to the validity or operation of an EPA/LPA – COP1F.

Applicants are directed to these additional forms when completing the COP1.

7.16 Form COP4 is the prospective deputy's declaration that they are a fit and suitable person to act, and their acknowledgement that they

10 See, by analogy, *Loughlin v Singh and others* [2013] EWHC 1641 (QB), [2013] COPLR 371.

11 MCA 2005 s48. See also paras 4.94–4.100.

12 MCA 2005 s61(2).

recognise the main duties and responsibilities of a deputy. Each person who wishes to be appointed as deputy must compete a copy of this form.

7.17 Forms COP1C, COP1D, COP1E and COP1F each use a check-list approach to ensure that the applicant has provided all the information that the court will need to reach a decision for the specified matter.

7.18 In most applications other than a straightforward deputy application a COP24 witness statement will also be required. This allows applicants to explain more fully the matter they wish the court to decide and to set out the evidence available and the reasons for the decision proposed being in P's best interests. The rules relating to evidence are explored in more detail in chapter 13.

Process

7.19 The completed documents must be submitted (the address is in appendix G below) along with the appropriate application fee. In some circumstances a fee remission may be available. Details of fees and remissions are to be found in appendix F below.

7.20 For a straightforward application, such as that for the appointment of a deputy, the application form will usually be sealed and issued without the need for it to be referred for judicial scrutiny. To issue an application the court logs the details of the applicant and P on their system, allocates a case reference and makes up the court's paper file. A copy of the COP1 form, stamped with the date of issue and with the court reference number completed, will be returned to the applicant to carry out service.

7.21 In some cases the application will need to be referred to a judge before it is issued. This may be where there is conflicting evidence as to P's capacity, if some information is incomplete, interim directions have been requested or the application is for a statutory will or gift for example. Depending upon the circumstances or the nature of the application the court may make enquiries or issue initial directions to obtain further information before issuing the requested application. Where the application is for a statutory will or gift the court will make an order at this stage joining the Official Solicitor to represent P. If the applicant is aware that there is a potential for a hearing at any stage in the proceedings, it is important to identify (most obviously in the COP24) whether there are any specific factors the court need to consider in deciding whether to hold such hearings in-person or remotely (or on a hybrid basis).

7.22 Once the applicant receives back the issued COP1 form and any initial directions, the next step is to deal with service and notification.

Service and notification

7.23 The applicant is responsible for serving anyone named as a respondent[13] or anyone who is to be notified of the proceedings.[14] The applicant must serve the respondents, and those to be notified of the issue of proceedings, within 14 days of the date of the issue of the application.[15] The provisions as to service appear in COPR Part 6, supported by PD 6A, which sets out how service should be effected (for example, by document exchange or electronically). Rule 6.4 explains the provisions for service on children or protected parties.

7.24 When serving respondents[16] the applicant must send each of them a copy of the following documents:

- a copy of the issued application form;
- a copy of any documents filed with the application form (for example, the COP1A, COP3, COP4 if the application relates to a deputyship, any witness statements);
- a copy of any orders made by the court;
- notice of acting (if this has not been served) – COP30;
- COP5 acknowledgment of service for the individual to complete.

7.25 Those who are notified of an application do not need to be served with a full copy of the application papers. When serving those notified the applicant must send them:

- COP15 notice that an application has been issued, this provides details of the applicant and the order sought;
- COP5 acknowledgement of service for the individual to complete.

7.26 When carrying out service, the applicant or their legal adviser should consider whether to include documents or information other than those required by the procedure. For instance, it is good practice to include information about the general rule as to costs should the party notified wish to take independent legal advice.

13 COPR r9.6.
14 COPR r9.10.
15 COPR r9.6(1).
16 See para 8.5.

7.27 Once the applicant has served all those who are to be served or notified she must complete form COP20B confirming that dates or service and notification and return this to the court.

Dispensing with service

7.28 There are certain circumstances under which service can be dispensed with, either upon application to the court or of the court's own motion.[17] It has been held that a decision to dispense with service is not an act done or decision made on behalf of P, such that the principles of the MCA 2005 do not strictly apply to the decision: *I v D*.[18] The (limited) case-law on dispensing with service has mostly focused on the position in statutory will cases discussed at para 7.91 and following below.[19]

Service abroad

7.29 Service outside the jurisdiction is dealt with at COPR rr6.11–6.19. These rules supported by PD 6B. We do not address the issue of such service further here because it is an issue which only arises infrequently, and because PD 6B is comprehensive in its guidance.

Notifying P

7.30 The applicant is responsible for notifying P of the issue of an application, within 14 days of the issue of the application, unless P has already been made a party.[20] Decisions about whether to join P and, if P is joined, how P will be represented are governed by COPR r1.2, which is discussed in detail in chapter 12. If P has been made a party, then the court will decide how service should take place.[21] If P has not been made a party, then P must be provided with the information personally, in a manner that is appropriate to P's circumstances, for

17 COPR r6.10.

18 [2016] EWCOP 35, [2016] COPLR 432, endorsing an earlier decision of District Judge Batten in *A v B* [2013] EWHC B39 (COP).

19 An exception is the decision of District Judge Beckley in *LCN v CJF* [2019] EWCOP 1, concerning an urgent application for settlement of property on trust in respect of a 13-year-old who had a life expectancy of only a matter of weeks. District Judge Beckley applied the approach adopted in statutory will cases to determine whether to dispense with service on P's biological father who had denied paternity and played no part in P's life: see paras 36–40.

20 COPR r7.8.

21 COPR r6.5(1).

example using simple language or visual aids.[22] P must be given a form COP14, which should explain clearly the matter which the court has been asked to decide, and a COP5 (acknowledgement of service).[23] Once this has been done, form COP20A must be completed by the person who carried out the notification and filed with the court by the applicant.

7.31 If at all possible, it is good practice for a prospective deputy – especially one acting in a professional capacity without personal knowledge of P – to meet P and take steps to discuss the proposed application *prior* to making any application.

7.32 COPR r7.11 allows an applicant or appellant or anyone directed to effect notification on P to apply to the court for an order dispensing with the requirement to comply with the provisions relating to the notification of P or requiring some other person to comply with those provisions. Moreover, the court can in any case, either on its own initiative or on application, direct that he must not be notified of any matter or document, or provided with any document.[24] The court might dispense with the requirement to notify P if P were in a permanent vegetative or minimally conscious state, or if notification by the applicant is likely to cause significant and disproportionate distress to P.[25]

Next steps

7.33 Unless a specific application has been made on the basis of particular urgency, the court will take no steps during the 14-day period during which those who have been notified must make their response.[26]

7.34 If no objections are received by the court during this period, the file will be referred back to the court for consideration, either by a judge or authorised court officer (depending on the nature of the application). If everything is in order at this stage, then the order will usually be made. If the application concerned the appointment of a deputy the applicant, or their legal adviser, will receive a letter notifying them that the court has made an order appointing them as

22 COPR r7.8.
23 PD 7A para 6.
24 COPR r7.1(3).
25 PD 7A para 9.
26 COPR r9.12 allows 14 days after service for acknowledgment of the application by the person upon whom the application is served.

deputy and advising them that the order will be released to them on the security bond has been put in place.

7.35 If the application is urgent or contested further guidance as to the procedure is provided below in chapter 8.

Deputyship applications

When is a deputy needed?

7.36 If a person loses their capacity to make some decisions about their finances and they have not planned for this eventuality by making an EPA (before 1 October 2007) or an LPA for property and affairs (from 1 October 2007 onwards) then it may be necessary for an application to be made to the court for the appointment of a property and affairs deputy. Without an attorney or deputy, the general rule is that no transactions concerning P's property or finances can be validly undertaken.

7.37 When deciding if an application for the appointment of a deputy is necessary, the nature of P's assets and income should be considered. If the only income of the person concerned is state benefits then the appointment of a deputy may be disproportionate and costly, an application can be made by an individual (such as a family member) or an organisation (eg a council) to the Department for Work and Pensions (DWP) to be made their appointee to manage those benefits. This does not require an application to the court.[27]

7.38 If, however, there are other assets or income that need to be managed, then it is likely that a deputy will need to be appointed. This would include situations such as P owning a property or savings and investments that needed to be sold or accessed, for example to pay for the costs of a care home or to meet P's day-to-day expenses or regular payments.

7.39 It is important to keep in mind that under the MCA 2005 capacity is 'decision-specific', there are no absolutes in terms of a person's decision-making capabilities (see paras 3.33–3.64). There is no contradiction between having a deputy and retaining the ability to make some decisions. For example, a deputy may need to make decisions about investing a large sum of money while P retains the capacity to manage their weekly income to buy groceries and personal items. As mentioned above it may be prudent to obtain specific

27 See: www.gov.uk/become-appointee-for-someone-claiming-benefits.

guidance about P's capabilities and how to support their decision-making abilities.

Choice of deputy

7.40 The MCA 2005 does not set out any order for individuals to be considered for the role of deputy. The choice of who would be a suitable deputy will depend largely upon P's family and circumstances.

7.41 In *Re M; N v O and P*[28] former Senior Judge Lush noted that pre-MCA 2005 authorities were still pertinent to the question of who to appoint as a deputy, and set out an 'order of preference' in which P's family was to be preferred by the court over strangers such as professional advisers or statutory bodies. Senior Judge Lush observed that:

> The court prefers to appoint a family member or close friend, if possible, as long as it is in P's best interests to do so. This is because a relative or friend will already be familiar with P's affairs, and wishes and methods of communication. Someone who already has a close personal knowledge of P is also likely to be better able to meet the obligation of a deputy to consult with P, and to permit and encourage him to participate, or to improve his ability to participate, as fully as possible in any act done for him and any decision affecting him. And, because professionals charge for their services, the appointment of a relative or friend is generally preferred for reasons of economy. There are, of course, cases in which the court would not countenance appointing a particular family member as deputy. For example, if there had been physical or financial abuse; if there is a conflict of interests; if the proposed deputy has an unsatisfactory track record in managing his own financial affairs; and if there is ongoing friction between various family members that is likely to interfere with the administration of P's affairs. This list is not exhaustive.[29]

7.42 In this case, in applying the balance-sheet approach, the various factors the court considered in assessing the merits of the two proposed deputies were:

- ability to act;
- willingness to act;
- qualifications;
- place of residence;
- security;
- conduct before and during the proceedings;
- nature of relationship with M;

28 [2013] COPLR 91.
29 Para 39.

- M's wishes and feelings;
- views of others;
- effect of hostility;
- conflicts of interest;
- remuneration; and
- the terms of M's will.

7.43 Senior Judge Lush found that the two factors of 'magnetic importance' in deciding who the court should appoint as deputy for P, where there were competing candidates for the role were 'M's past and present wishes and feelings and the unanimous views of others, who are particularly close to him, as to what would be in his best interests'.[30] He went on to comment that there were also cases in which the court would not appoint a family member, such as where P has recovered damages in personal injury litigation specifically to fund a professional deputy appointment.

7.44 Some individuals will be considered as unsuitable to act as deputy. In *Re BM; JB v AG*[31] and again in *Re PAW*[32] former Senior Judge Lush set out a list of those the court would not consider appointing, this list includes:

a) a proposed deputy who has physically, emotionally or financially abused P;
b) where there is a need to investigate dealings with P's assets prior to the matter being brought to the court's attention, and the proposed deputy's conduct is the subject of that investigation;
c) where there is an actual conflict of interests, rather than simply a potential conflict;[33]
d) the proposed deputy has an unsatisfactory track record in managing their own financial affairs;
e) when there is ongoing friction between various family members, which is likely to interfere with the proper administration of P's affairs; and
f) if there is a need to ensure that P is free from undue influence, particularly the influence exerted by the person who is seeking to be appointed as deputy.[34]

30 Para 78.
31 [2014] EWCOP B20.
32 [2015] EWCOP 57, [2015] WTLR 1785.
33 For comments on the court's approach to managing conflict see *Re JW* [2015] EWCOP 82, [2016] COPLR 36.
34 *Re PAW* [2015] EWCOP 57, [2015] WLTR 1785 at para 26.

Other factors that may influence the decision about who should be appointed as deputy include locality, health, family and work commitments.

7.45 In *DGP Law v DGHP and others*,[35] the previous position was reversed with regard to appointing a deputy who lives outside the jurisdiction. In this case former Senior Judge Lush appointed a deputy who lived in the USA. In his judgment, Senior Judge Lush observed that 'in the two decades since Justice Cunningham delivered his judgment there have been further technological advances in communications, such as online banking, digital reporting, mobile phone, email and Skype, and cheaper air travel as a result of a proliferation of budget airlines'.[36]

7.46 The court has also considered the situation where a deputy has limited command of English in the case of *Re FH*[37] and concluded that this is not an absolute bar to being appointed deputy.

7.47 These may be cases that need to be looked at on their facts as in each case features existed that mitigated the disadvantage suffered by the proposed deputy. In the first case the proposed deputy had access to up to date technology which facilitated administration of P's affairs and in the second a close family member was available to translate for the proposed deputy. Once again, we suggest that the court will look at all the circumstances of P and the proposed deputy when coming to a decision.

7.48 It is possible for an application to be made for joint deputies to be appointed. This can help to share the burden but does require good communication to work efficiently. The current application forms make it simple to make a joint application, providing spaces to specify up to four prospective deputies.

7.49 Most deputies appointed are lay deputies, ie private individuals acting as deputy, usually for a family member. There are, however, professionals who specialise in this area of work and whose appointment is appropriate in some circumstances. Many local authorities continue to have a deputyship department but they will often only act as deputies of last resort where a suitable relative cannot be traced to undertake the role. A professional deputy is usually appointed where P has received substantial funds in compensation for a personal injury, or where P has complex or very high value personal finances or if the court concludes that is in P's best interests for a neutral

35 [2015] EWCOP 58.

36 *DGP Law* at para 47.

37 [2016] EWCOP 14, [2016] COPLR 287.

professional to undertake the role, usually where there is discord within a family. The Public Guardian maintains a panel of deputies to whom cases can be referred to as a deputy of last resort (see also paras 21.43–21.44). Panel deputies are often appointed to act where there has been significant friction within the family about who should act as deputy for P. If the court believes that ongoing family friction would impact upon the proper management of P's finances a panel deputy will be invited to take on the role.

7.50 The court's approach to deciding among competing professionals has developed since *Re RP; Z v SP*[38] when the court first looked at the appointment of competing professionals. The choice of a suitable professional deputy was at issue in *NKR and another v The Thomson Snell and Passmore Trust Corporation Ltd.*[39] In this case, the family of NKR proposed that a direct access barrister be appointed as deputy, while the deputy wishing to be discharged favoured the appointment of a new panel deputy. The court confirmed that in principle a barrister could be a deputy (subject to suitable insurance being in place and treated as a business overhead not charged to P) but on the facts in the case the decision was made to appoint a new panel deputy due to their greater experience of acting as a deputy. In *KKL Executor & Trustee Company Ltd v Harrison,*[40] two professional deputies had applied to be appointed to act for OT. One applicant was an experienced solicitor deputy to whom the local authority referred work, and the other a charity which had a long-standing relationship with OT. Accusations were made on both sides of a conflict of interest. The court considered the factors in the case and concluded that the existing relationship with the charity was outweighed by the need for the deputy to be able to investigate whether the charity's previous behaviour amounted to a breach of the Fundraiser's Code. It is worth noting that these cases show a leaning in favour of experience as an important factor when deciding who to appoint where there is a disagreement.

7.51 The appointment of a panel deputy may not always solve the problem of friction between the deputy and P's family, a situation

38 [2016] EWCOP 1.
39 [2019] EWCOP 15, [2019] COPLR 420.
40 [2020] EWCOP 25, [2020] COPLR 597.

considered by Senior Judge Hilder in in *Kambli v The Public Guardian*.[41]

7.52 In appropriate cases, an office holder can be appointed rather than a named individual as a deputy to manage property and affairs.[42] An order appointing an office holder should include a requirement that the holder at the date of appointment notifies the Public Guardian if they cease to hold that office. The Public Guardian will then be in a position to refer the matter to the court if he considers that appropriate. A single application could be made in respect of one P, and in the light of the conclusion in that application, the court may be invited 'of its own motion' to review all other deputyships held by the office in question.[43]

7.53 In recent years it has become increasingly common for a trust corporation can be appointed to be a property and affairs deputy (but not a health and welfare deputy). The reasons for the use of trust corporations, instead of personal appointments, are essentially flexibility and convenience. A trust corporation may be established with a number of Directors who are able to exercise the duties of a deputy. If an individual is appointed as deputy, there may be difficulty if they are absent for any reason. Using a trust corporation avoids these issues, and also provides greater stability and continuity in succession for example when a professional wishes to retire.[44] The issue of the appointment of trust corporations was first examined by Senior Judge Hilder in *Various Incapacitated Persons and the Appointment of Trust Corporations as Deputies*.[45] In this judgment, Senior Judge Hilder detailed the information required by the court for it to be satisfied that a trust corporation is a proper legal person to hold the appointment of deputy. The judgment also refers to how the level of security bond should be set. The relevant considerations are:

41 [2021] EWCOP 53, [2022] COPLR 113 where the panel deputy sought to be discharged given the frictions involved. She emphasised at para 39 that a change of deputy should not be a 'default response' to difficulties in managing a deputyship, as it incurs costs for P and risks being perceived as 'rewarding' negative behaviour, which in turn undermines the prospects of future stability. Rather, the court should probe the actual circumstances, with a view to salvaging working relationships if possible.

42 *Re SH* [2018] EWCOP 21, [2018] COPLR 522.

43 *Re SH* at para 27.

44 MCA 2005 s19(1)(b).

45 [2018] EWCOP 3, [2018] COPLR 239.

1) whether the trust corporation can lawfully act as a deputy;
2) whether its internal management, supervision and controls are appropriate;
3) the applicable external regulation (apart from the supervision of the Office of the Public Guardian (OPG));
4) the amount of protected persons' assets and funds held; and
5) the level of insurance cover which the trust corporation has

7.54 In *Re TWAH*,[46] the court has also considered the approach to be taken where a trust corporation that is also a registered charity wishes to be appointed as property and affairs deputy. Having considered and been satisfied with the insurance arrangements, and that registration with the Charity Commission was a sufficient safeguard the court set out a process for these cases, similar to that set out above for other trust corporations.

7.55 The procedure in these cases is for the additional information to be provided as a page supplementing the COP4.

Security bond

7.56 The court has discretion to require a deputy to provide security for the discharge of the functions conferred upon them.[47] Generally, all deputies, whether lay or professional, are required to provide security by way of a bond, with the exception of local authority deputies. The level of the bond and the premium charged for it is determined by the court in reference to P's assets and the amount of money to which the deputy has access.[48] The security bond is to protect P from financial loss caused by the deputy, whether deliberately or by negligence. There is a bond arrangement in place which deputies can use or they may wish to try to obtain their own cover. Once the bond is in place, the court will be notified and sealed copies of the order will be sent out to the deputy.

7.57 Deputies and their legal advisers should note that they must apply to the court as circumstances change for the level of the security bond to be reviewed. During P's lifetime the nature and extent of their assets will alter and therefore the appropriate level of bond should be reviewed at regular intervals.

46 [2019] EWCOP 36, [2019] COPLR 488.

47 MCA 2005 s19(9); see also COPR r24.3.

48 *Re H (a minor and incapacitated person); Baker v H and the Official Solicitor* [2009] COPLR Con Vol 606, (2009) 12 CCLR 695.

Supervision

7.58 When a new deputy is appointed, the OPG will be notified by the court. The OPG will then provide a suitable programme of supervision to the deputy depending upon P's circumstances. The OPG requires that every deputy submit an annual report detailing how P's funds have been spent in the previous year and how any capital is invested. They check that the deputy obtains appropriate financial advice and acts upon it and they will schedule a visit by a court visitor to check that the deputy is coping with the new role. Professional deputies can expect a period assurance visit to review internal procedures. For more information on the role of the OPG, see chapter 21.

Restrictions

7.59 It is not uncommon for a deputy order to contain restrictions to the deputy's authority. When a new order is received, the deputy or their legal adviser should read it carefully and note any limits to their authority. Common restrictions include preventing the sale of a property without a further application to the court, or a limit to the amount of money that a deputy can spend in a year. If any of the restrictions are going to prove problematic, then so long as the application is made within 21 days of the order being served, a request can be made for a reconsideration under the provisions of COPR r13.4 (see further paras 19.3–19.6). Such a request can be made without incurring a further application fee.

7.60 A deputy order cannot be exhaustive in setting out what a deputy is and is not authorised to do; the new deputy, or their legal adviser, should ensure that they are aware of the limits to the scope of the powers that they may exercise without further authorisation of the court.

Powers and duties of a deputy

7.61 The order made by the court will set out the deputy's powers and their limits; typical orders are to be found on the Court of Protection Handbook website.[49]

7.62 A deputy has what is known as a fiduciary duty towards P. This means that there is a relationship of utmost trust and confidence between the deputy and P. Where a fiduciary relationship exists,

49 See: https://courtofprotectionhandbook.com/precedents/.

money and property must be managed in P's best interests, without regard to any interest of the deputy. This means (among other things) that the deputy cannot profit personally by acting as P's deputy and the funds and assets of P must be kept entirely separate from those of the deputy. In relation to property, the deputy cannot sanction a sale to themselves, or a family member, particularly for less than full market value, without the additional approval of the court. It is also not appropriate for the deputy to receive any of P's funds into an account in their own name. All of P's assets and funds must be clearly in P's name at all times. Most bank accounts and other assets should be named 'A as deputy for Y' so that it is immediately clear who the asset belongs to.

7.63 A discussion of the full range of a deputy's powers and duties falls outside the scope of this chapter, and indeed of this book. However, any person considering putting themselves forward as a deputy would be well advised to familiarise themselves with the Code of Practice to the Mental Capacity Act 2005,[50] the principles of the MCA 2005 and the COPR. There has been a range of cases[51] which demonstrate that the court will not be lenient on deputies, or attorneys, who simply do not understand the true nature and scope of the role. They should also familiarise themselves with the likely remuneration that they can expect: see further para 17.11.

7.64 We suggest the following by way of good practice upon the initial appointment of a deputy:

- The deputy should begin their task by circulating the deputy order to all the financial institutions with whom P has a relationship. It is good practice to ask for an up-to-date statement or valuation and consider updating the court if it becomes clear once appointed that P had considerably more or fewer assets than were detailed in the COP1A. If P is living independently, the deputy should ensure as far as possible that their actions do not jeopardise P's day-to-day activities. If P relies upon a particular current account to access a pension to buy groceries, the deputy should make it clear to the bank and the DWP at the time of notifying

50 Available at: www.gov.uk/government/publications/mental-capacity-act-code-of-practice.

51 See *Re GM* [2019] EWHC 2966 (COP), [2013] COPLR 290; *Re Buckley* [2013] EWHC 2965 (COP), [2013] COPLR 39; *Re AB* [2014] EWCOP 12, [2014] WTLR 1303, [2014] EWCOP 12; *The Public Guardian v AW and DH* [2014] EWCOP 28, [2014] WTLR 1705 and *The Public Guardian v DA, YS and ES* [2015] EWCOP 41, [2015] WTLR 1647.

them of the deputy order that they do not want any changes to the present arrangement.

- Ensure that P is receiving all the income to which they are entitled (and none that they are not). This means that an early task for any new deputy is to review P's benefits and make sure that claims are up-to-date. Benefits will need to remain under review by the deputy in the event of P's circumstances changing.
- Check that insurance policies are updated and relevant to P's circumstances. If the deputy has been appointed because of an accident sustained by P, it may be, for instance, that P has a critical illness policy which would pay out a sum to P.
- If P lives in their own home, the deputy should visit and check how well-maintained it is. If repairs or adaptations are needed, the deputy should seek quotes and take professional advice about the suitability of any changes. If there is a property that needs to be sold, the deputy should check that the deputy order allows sale without further court approval, and if so, then approach estate agents to get a range of valuations before choosing whom to market a property with. If not, the deputy should seek specific approval from the court.
- Consider P's care arrangements and how they are funded. Explore options to maximise funding for example having an assessment for NHS Continuing Care or applying to the local authority for an assessment of P's needs. If family members are being paid for caring for P from P's funds the new deputy should follow the court's guidance in *Re HC* which is discussed below at para 7.64.
- Consider requesting disclosure of P's will to ensure that the deputy's actions do not interfere with P's successions plans.[52] The deputy should have regard to the guidance issued by the Law Society on the release of a will to attorneys of deputies where P has lost capacity.[53]

Investment

7.65 A deputy should take care to review P's finances and investments, preferably with the assistance of a suitably qualified independent financial adviser (IFA). This is true not simply of new deputies but equally applies to long-standing appointments. P's needs and circum-

52 See *Re Treadwell* [2013] EWHC 2409 (COP), [2013] COPLR 587 at paras 81–88.

53 Available at: www.lawsociety.org.uk/support-services/advice/practice-notes/access-and-disclosure-of-an-incapacitated-persons-will/.

stances will alter over time and the deputy should be alive to these changes.

7.66 In *Re Buckley*[54] former Senior Judge Lush took the opportunity to look at the investment responsibilities of an attorney, noting that:

> 20. There are two common misconceptions when it comes to investments. The first is that attorneys acting under an LPA can do whatever they like with the donors' funds. And the second is that attorneys can do whatever the donors could – or would – have done personally, if they had the capacity to manage their property and financial affairs.
>
> 21. Managing your own money is one thing. Managing someone else's money is an entirely different matter.
>
> 22. People who have the capacity to manage their own financial affairs are generally not accountable to anyone and don't need to keep accounts or records of their income and expenditure. They can do whatever they like with their money, and this includes doing nothing at all. They can stash their cash under the mattress, if they wish and, of course, they are entitled to make unwise decisions.
>
> 23. None of these options are open to an attorney acting for an incapacitated donor, partly because of their fiduciary obligations and partly because an attorney is required to act in the donor's best interests. The Mental Capacity Act 2005, section 1(5), states that, 'an act done, or decision made, under this Act for or on behalf of a person who lacks capacity must be done, or made, in his best interests.'
>
> . . .
>
> 25. Attorneys hold a fiduciary position, which imposes a number of duties on them. Like trustees and other fiduciaries, they must exercise such care and skill as is reasonable in the circumstances when investing the donor's assets and this duty of care is even greater where attorneys hold themselves out as having specialist knowledge or experience.
>
> 26. Although it does not expressly apply to attorneys, the Trustee Act 2000, section 4, requires trustees to have regard to what are known as the 'standard investment criteria' when exercising any power of investment. [Senior Judge Lush then set out how these investment criteria apply]

7.67 This guidance was given in the context of a case concerning an LPA, but both the comments should be read as being equally applicable to a property and affairs deputy.

7.68 The investments made by the deputy (or attorney) on behalf of P must be in P's best interests, and in line with any other restrictions set out in the deputy order.

54 [2013] EWHC 2965 (COP), [2013] COPLR 39.

Family care payments: 'gratuitous care'

7.69 In the case of *Re HC*[55] the court considered the issue of family members being paid for care from P's funds. This is usually known as 'gratuitous care', as it refers to a situation where the person being paid (often one of P's parents) provides care out of love and affection for P but in doing so they save P considerable money on the provision of commercial care arrangements and also make a sacrifice of their own career and earning potential. In these circumstances gratuitous care payments can be made to the carer to recognise their contribution, so long as court authority is obtained.

7.70 A deputy order does not automatically allow a lay deputy to make payments to themselves or a close relative for providing care to P. A lay deputy wishing to make gratuitous care payments should follow the steps set out in *Re HC* for ascertaining the appropriate level of payment:

1) establish the commercial value of the care that the family member provides;
2) the ceiling for a gratuitous care payment is the value of commercial care reduced by 20 per cent to reflect the savings of tax and National Insurance;
3) consider if the proposed payment affordable for P?

The case also sets out a mechanism for increasing the payment each year on the anniversary of the order.

7.71 The method for deciding the commercial value of the care provided will differ depending upon the circumstances of each particular case. Some applicants may need to commission a report from a care expert to assist with this point. The issue of affordability will also be highly variable from case to case and to be able to make decision about what is in P's best interests the court will require up to date information about all P's capital, income and expenditure as well as the proposed gratuitous care payment and the impact this will have as well as medical information about P's life expectancy.

7.72 The case of *Re HNL*[56] saw the court examine the situation of families where care payments commenced under pre-MCA 2005 arrangements and were continued by the lay deputy. In this case the court had sufficient information to give retrospective approval to payments that had been made and to authorise the continuation of

55 [2015] EWCOP 29.
56 [2015] EWCOP 77.

payments in future. It is not uncommon for lay deputies to have begun making gratuitous care payments without being aware that court authorisation was required. It is clear now that the court will look to regularise these situations when they come before it.

7.73 A deputy making gratuitous care payments would also be wise to notify HM Revenue and Customs (HMRC) of the arrangement to ensure that the payments will not be subject to income tax. The recipient of the payments should be made aware that unlike paid employment they will be responsible for their own National Insurance payments and they may wish to take independent financial advice about the likely impact on their state pension entitlement.

7.74 The OPG has produced a Practice Note on gratuitous care, taking into account decisions such as those set out above.[57]

Deputyship in personal injury award cases

7.75 Many of the highest value deputyships arise from claims for personal injury where P has sustained a brain injury. As mentioned above, in these cases the court will usually prefer a professional deputy. They raise specific considerations which merit brief highlighting here.

7.76 An applicant in this type of case should also be aware of the decision in *Watt v ABC*[58] which considered the question of when damages should be managed by a deputy and when the creation of a personal injury trust would be appropriate. Charles J commented that when a decision is made as to the best vehicle for future management of P's funds, those making this decision should not proceed on the basis that there is a strong presumption that the Court of Protection would appoint a deputy and would not make an order that a trust be created of the award.

7.77 The deputy will usually become involved at a stage of the litigation where there has been an interim payment, or liability has been settled and an interim payment is anticipated. More rarely, a deputy is needed well before liability is established – for example, where P had an insurance policy that has paid out to a sole name account and their family need to access it to meet day-to-day bills.

7.78 If a referral is made before liability is established or any funds are available, the deputy must act cautiously; there is the possibility that

57 See: www.gov.uk/government/uploads/system/uploads/attachment_data/file/524111/PGnote_2016_05_family_care_payments.pdf.

58 [2016] EWCOP 2532, [2017] 4 WLR 24, [2016] COPLR 605.

the claim will fail and they should bear in mind how the court and other fees are to be funded. It may be necessary to advise the family of P on other options, eg appointeeship to claim benefits, local authority funding etc.

7.79 Once liability has been settled and an interim payment is made, the deputy should take steps to ensure that they know the terms of the payments made and the professional recommendations for P's care and case management. In cases of this sort, interim payments will be made for a particular purpose and a failure to manage funds in line with these purposes can have an adverse impact on the overall value of P's claim. The deputy needs to ensure that they have regular communication with the litigation team. The deputy should consider asking for certain litigation documents such as a copy of any order relating to interim payments as these are useful to have on the file to refer back to in the future.

7.80 Reports obtained in the course of litigation can also include valuable guidance as to how it is recommended that P's funds be applied, as well as how best to communicate with P to maximise their understanding and participate in decision-making. Professionals engaged to provide services to P such as case managers, physiotherapists, occupational therapists and neuropsychologists will all provide costs estimates for their intervention. All this information can then be used by the deputy to formulate a proposed budget for the management of P's funds. It has generally been understood that compliance with the MCA 2005 and involving P in decision making around his finances would necessarily include advising them about the full extent of his wealth. However, the question of when it might be in P's best interests to withhold this information in the context of a significant compensation settlement was considered in *EXB v FDZ*.[59] In this case, there was evidence that this approach would not be in P's best interests due to pressures on P and his own vulnerabilities. Although he lacked capacity to manage his property and affairs, P was aware of his deficits, and agreed with the approach that he should not be told the exact value of his settlement. It remains to be seen how the court would approach this question in the case of a person who wished to know the full value of his settlement but who would be made more vulnerable to financial exploitation if he were to know.

7.81 When establishing a budget, the deputy will typically communicate with family members or care-providers depending upon P's

59 [2018] EWHC 3456 (QB). See also *PBM v TGT* [2019] EWCOP 6, [2019] COPLR 427, for a slightly different approach.

circumstances. Sadly it is often the case that a family will be under a huge amount of financial pressure if they have managed for some years without P's financial contribution or they have been frequently travelling to a distant hospital to visit P. The deputy may be able to consider alleviating some of this pressure by reimbursing some of these past losses. The legal team involved in running the personal injury claim will be able to guide on this point, and in some cases the order obtained in the personal injury claim approving the interim payment will make specific allowance for a sum to be paid to the family for these costs.

7.82 Clarity is important at this stage, first because whoever is paying sums out needs to be clear about the authority to make those payments; and second, because litigation can take many years to settle, it is important to make sure that everyone understands and records accurately what each payment is for.

7.83 In many personal injury cases insufficient funds are made available at the interim payment stage to implement all of the recommendations made to the claimant's litigation team. In an appropriate case, the deputy should consider exploring other funding avenues such as local authority funding in the form of direct payments.

7.84 The deputy is responsible for scrutinising the quality of the services they pay for on behalf of P. If a service or treatment provider is falling below an acceptable standard, or not providing what has been recommended for P, then there may be the risk that the cost of the service or treatment is disallowed when the damages are assessed.[60]

7.85 Occasionally the deputy may feel that they are being asked to perform a role outside that of simply managing P's property and affairs. If the deputy is being asked to make a decision that goes beyond the financial and budgetary, this is beyond the scope of the deputy's authority. For example, if P wants to go on holiday, the deputy would be expected to set a suitable budget with reference to affordability and make sure that the costings include all the expected items. It is best practice for the deputy to work closely with other professionals involved with P to establish what is in their best interests overall. However, the property and affairs deputy should be mindful that they not use their role to effectively take welfare decisions by their funding decisions.

7.86 The case of *Re SRK* placed the additional responsibility on a professional deputy, in cases where P benefits from a private care

60 *Loughlin v Singh and others* [2013] EWHC 1641 (QB), [2013] COPLR 371.

regime at home, to make contact with the local authority if they are of the view that P's care regime could amount to an objective deprivation of liberty to which P cannot consent.[61] This case concluded that where there is a court appointed deputy this is sufficient state involvement to engage the state's obligations to secure the person against arbitrary deprivation of their liberty. A professional deputy in this position would be well advised to familiarise herself with the case.

7.87 Depending upon the level of funds available and the expected expenditure where there is ongoing litigation, the deputy will usually want to consider putting in place regular budget updates. This allows the deputy to see if funds are being spent in accordance with recommendations and if budgets are being kept to. If P's funds are going to be exhausted it is important to notify the litigation team in good time that a further interim payment will be needed. P's circumstances, and the recommendations for their care, can change rapidly; the deputy should keep pace with these changes.

7.88 Once a claim for compensation is settled the deputy will need to review the financial position P has been left in and begin to make plans for the longer term. Many cases settle for a lump sum plus periodical payments to meet P's care needs. The deputy will typically want to focus on investing the lump sum in such a way that P's needs are met now and in the future. A deputy should work with a suitably qualified and experienced financial advisor on establishing appropriate investments for P.

7.89 It is worth mentioning here the decision of *Re ACC, JDJ and HPP*.[62] In this case, three professional deputies brought applications concerning the extent to which the orders appointing them authorised expenditure from P's estate in respect of obtaining legal advice and conducting proceedings on P's behalf. Senior Judge Hilder set out detailed guidance as to the authority of deputies in this regard. The OPG then issued (on 22 January 2021) guidance for court-appointed deputies to comply with the judgment. For any property and affairs deputy considering taking legal advice on behalf of P it is essential to carefully consider this case, and the guidance and to proceed cautiously to comply with it.

7.90 Other matters that the deputy should consider once any personal injury litigation has been finalised will include reviewing P's testamentary provision.

61 [2016] EWCA Civ 1317, [2017] Fam 278, [2017] COPLR 120. See further in this regard chapter 22.

62 [2020] EWCOP 9, [2020] COPLR 406.

Statutory wills and gifting

7.91 The Court of Protection has the power under MCA 2005 s18 to authorise the execution of a will (or a codicil) on behalf of a person who lacks the relevant capacity, and also to authorise gifts on behalf of P that fall outside the very limited scope to gift that is enjoyed by deputies and attorneys alike. These applications raise particular issues which fall outside the scope of this book to discuss fully.[63] What follows is a summary of the key points that arise.

7.92 In each case the applicant should obtain specific medical evidence as to P's capacity in relation to the decision that the court will be invited to make. There are different tests for each decision.

1) In *A, B and C v X and Z*,[64] Hedley J held that the test of testamentary capacity before the Court of Protection is the common law test formulated in *Banks v Goodfellow*,[65] ie that:

   > It is essential . . . that a testator shall understand the nature of the act [of making a will] and its effects; shall understand the extent of the property of which he is disposing; shall be able to comprehend and appreciate the claims to which he ought to give effect, and . . . that no disorder of mind shall poison their affections, pervert his sense of right, or prevent the exercise of his natural faculties – that no insane delusion shall influence his will in disposing of his property and bring about a disposal of it which, if his mind had been sound, would not have been made.

   However, the test in *Banks v Goodfellow* in fact differs from the approach adopted under MCA 2005 ss2–3 (see further paras 3.33–3.64), in particular because it does not allow the reliance on supported decision making that applies to all other decisions under the MCA 2005.[66] The civil courts may well continue to apply the 'pure' common law test,[67] but the Court of Protection is required by statute to apply the test in MCA 2005, so the evidence put before it must meet the criteria in sections 2–3.

63 For more detail, readers are referred to Baker LJ et al, *Court of Protection Practice* (annual) LexisNexis s, chapter 5, and D Rees QC, general editor, *Heywood & Massey: Court of Protection Practice* (looseleaf), Sweet & Maxwell, chapters A20 (wills) and A21 (settlements and gifts).

64 [2012] EWHC 2400 (COP), [2013] COPLR 1.

65 (1870) LR 5 QB 549, [1861–1873] All ER 47.

66 See for further discussion, Alex Ruck Keene and Annabel Lee, 'Testamentary capacity' [2013] Eld LJ 272.

67 See, for instance, *Clitheroe v Bond* [2021] EWHC 1102 (Ch), [2021] COPLR 380.

2) The test for the capacity to make a gift is – again – derived from the common law, this time from the test in *Re Beaney*.[68] The essence of this test is that it is calibrated to the circumstances of the gift, in particular the size of the gift in question in relation to the donor's assets.

7.93 The application for the court to approve a statutory will or gift is subject to the procedures outlined in COPR PD 9E. In essence, it proceeds in the same fashion as outlined above for the basic application, with the addition of a detailed witness statement on the part of the applicant setting out:

- proposed draft will (for an application to approve a will) or details of the gift(s) proposed;
- details of previous wills (if applicable);
- schedule of capital;
- schedule of income;
- schedule of expenditure;
- family tree;
- schedule showing impact of inheritance tax and distribution of estate with and without proposed will or gift;
- the reasoning behind the proposals and why it is in the best interests of P.

7.94 The case of *Re P*[69] sets out in some detail the relevant jurisprudence and the tests that will be applied by the court in deciding if a statutory will should be approved. Further helpful comments can also be found in *Re Peter Jones*.[70]

7.95 Careful consideration needs to be given to ensuring that the correct parties are identified and served as respondents in this type of application. If a person is named as a residuary beneficiary in an existing will of P they will need to be named as a respondent in any application to approve a statutory will. A pecuniary or specific legatee under P's will, whose entitlement would be unchanged by the proposed will, can be named as a person to be notified. If P is intestate (ie they have never made any testamentary provision) then the deputy will need to ascertain their family tree to establish who would inherit from P under the Intestacy Rules set out in Administration of Estates Act 1925 ss46–47. Anyone who would inherit under P's intest-

68 [1978] 1 WLR 770, [1978] 2 All ER 595, Ch D; see also *Re P (capacity to tithe inheritance)* [2014] EWHC B14 (COP).

69 [2009] EWHC 163 (Ch), [2010] Ch 33.

70 [2014] EWCOP 59, [2016] WTLR 661.

acy must be notified as a respondent in any application to approve a statutory will.[71]

7.96 The courts have drawn a distinction between actual beneficiaries who are likely to be materially or adversely affected by the application, and potential beneficiaries who have a less certain prospect of inheriting under an intestacy and therefore being affected by the proposed will

- In the former category, it will only be in exceptional cases that it would be appropriate to dispense with service on an individual (or individuals) who is directly and adversely affected by an application. An applicant who is considering making an application to dispense with service is advised to familiarise themselves with the decision in *I v D* and to note the warning set out in the final paragraph that the Official Solicitor may well, on behalf of P, seek a costs order against an applicant who, in unexceptional circumstances and for no compelling reason, apply to dispense with service on someone who is materially and adversely affected by an application for the execution of a statutory will.
- The latter category was considered by Senior Judge Hilder in *M and H v P*.[72] In that case, P's son was not likely to be materially or adversely affected by the proposed statutory will. Distinguishing *I v D*, Senior Judge Hilder observed that the balancing exercise of procedural fairness was differently weighted where the person was not likely to be materially or adversely affected. However, she noted that there was still the disadvantage that the court may have to determine the substantive application without all relevant material.[73]

7.97 Deputies and attorneys who are considering making a gift from the estate of the person they act for are wise to check and understand their powers in this area. In general deputies and attorneys have limited power to make gifts on behalf of P. The standard wording of a deputy order gives the power to make gifts of 'a seasonal and customary nature' (see appendix D below). The case of *Re GM*[74] addressed the scope of a deputy's powers to make gifts from P's assets and former Senior Judge Lush took the opportunity to provide some guidance on this topic. Having noted that the deputyship order permitted the

71 *Re D* [2016] EWCOP 35, [2016] COPLR 432.

72 [2019] EWCOP 42, [2020] COPLR 305.

73 On the particular facts of the case, including the risks posed by the son to P, Senior Judge Hilder dispensed with service.

74 [2013] EWHC 2966 (COP), [2013] COPLR 290.

deputies to make gifts 'on customary occasions to persons who are related to or connected with them, provided that the value of each such gift is not unreasonable having regard to all the circumstances and, in particular, the size of their estate' and that 'a customary occasion' is defined in MCA 2005 s12(3) as 'an anniversary of a birth, a marriage or a civil partnership, or any other occasion on which presents are customarily given within families or among friends or associates' and also that 'the value of the gift must be 'not unreasonable' (s12(2)). Senior Judge Lush set out very clearly the approach to be followed in determining what is reasonable in a given case:

> First, regard must be had to the totality of P's current and anticipated income and capital, expenditure and debts.
>
> Second, consideration must be given to P's best interests, including the following factors:
>
> - the extent to which P was in the habit of making gifts or loans of a particular size or nature before the onset of incapacity;
> - P's anticipated life expectancy;
> - the possibility that P may require residential or nursing care and the projected cost of such care;
> - whether P is in receipt of aftercare pursuant to section 117 of the Mental Health Act 1983 or NHS Continuing Healthcare;
> - the extent to which any gifts may interfere with the devolution of P's estate under their or their will or intestacy; and
> - the impact of Inheritance Tax on P's death.
>
> Third, any gift that is not de minimis, must be approved in advance by the Court of Protection. A de minimis gift is to be construed as follows:
>
> 'covering the annual IHT exemption of £3,000 and the annual small gifts exemption of £250 per person, up to a maximum of, say, ten people in the following circumstances:
> (a) where P has a life expectancy of less than five years;
> (b) their estate exceeds the nil rate band for Inheritance Tax ('IHT') purposes, currently £325,000;
> (c) the gifts are affordable having regard to P's care costs and will not adversely affect P's standard of care and quality of life, and
> (d) there is no evidence that P would be opposed to gifts of this magnitude being made on their behalf.'

7.98 Bearing this very clear guidance in mind, if a deputy thinks that:

a) a more significant gift should be made on behalf of P;
b) that to do so would be in P's best interests; and
c) the gift is affordable in P's circumstances;

the deputy must apply to the court for approval *before* the gift is made.

7.99 The question of the extent to which a donor could include within their LPA valid instructions to the attorney to benefits someone other than the donor was considered in *Re Various Lasting Powers of Attorney*.[75] Senior Judge Hilder departed from the approach taken previously by former Senior Judge Lush and held that:

1) a donor cannot authorise a gift within the meaning of MCA 2005 s12 so as to extend the attorney's powers to make gifts in circumstances covered by that section;
2) provisions that authorise the benefitting of another are not rendered valid simply by reason of the fact that the donor owes a legal obligation towards that other for that other's maintenance;
3) a provision that provides for the donee to use the donor's funds to benefit another person may be valid so long as it is a precatory provision. If it is mandatory, it is ineffective;
4) a provision that authorises the benefitting of the donee is not invalid simply because the donee is in a fiduciary position vis-a-vis the donor;
5) such a provision is also not invalid simply because of a conflict of interests as such has been authorised by the donor and in any event the donee is obliged to act in the donor's best interests.

7.100 In an unusual step, recognising that most attorneys are laypeople managing finances on behalf of a relative, Senior Judge Hilder included a very helpful decision-tree with her judgment in this case.

7.101 In cases concerning the approval of a will or substantial gifting, P will usually be joined to proceedings as a party, and be represented by the Official Solicitor.

Powers of attorney

7.102 Prior to the implementation of the MCA 2005 on 1 October 2007, an EPA allowed a donor (the person who wishes to make arrangements for someone else to look after their finances if they are unable to do so in future) to appoint an attorney (or attorneys) to deal with their finances both immediately after the signing of the document and in the future, should the donor lose their capacity. An EPA could only be made to cover the donor's financial affairs; no power was conferred

75 [2019] EWCOP 40, [2020] COPLR 171.

by it to allow decision-making with regard to health or welfare matters.[76]

7.103 To be valid, an EPA must be in the prescribed format and have been signed by all parties on or before 30 September 2007.[77] The attorneys named in an EPA are under a duty to register the document with the OPG when the donor has lost, or is losing their capacity. It is now extremely rare to see an EPA in practice. The authors are aware of anecdotal evidence that banks and other financial institutions are unwilling to accept an unregistered EPA.

7.104 LPAs were introduced by the MCA 2005 and come in two varieties:

1) health and welfare; and
2) property and affairs.

The property and affairs LPA is similar in function to the old EPA, but crucially it cannot be used until it has been registered with the OPG.

7.105 The special feature enjoyed by both the EPA and LPA is that the authority conferred by them continues even after the donor has lost their capacity. All other types of power of attorney (usually referred to as a 'general power of attorney') are automatically revoked by the donor's incapacity.

7.106 The OPG has a range of documents available to download[78] that can take the prospective donor through the process of making an LPA, and registering it. Mencap has also published a suite of 'easy read' guides to the making and use of health and welfare LPAs.[79] The process of making and registering an LPA is an administrative process, falling outside the scope of this book, with one important exception detailed in the bullet points below:

- The process of registration requires notification to any person named in the LPA for that purpose on a form LPA001.[80] If a person notified wishes to object to the registration of an LPA on a prescribed ground,[81] ie most obviously, that either fraud or undue pressure was used to execute an instrument for the

76 For more detail on EPAs and LPAs, see chapter 3; and C Bielanska and D Lush, *Cretney & Lush on Lasting and Enduring Powers of Attorney*, 9th edn, LexisNexis, 2022.

77 Provisions relating to EPAs can now be found in MCA 2005 Sch 4.

78 See: www.justice.gov.uk/forms/opg.

79 Available at: www.mencaptrust.org.uk/guides-lasting-power-attorney.

80 MCA 2005 Sch 1 para 6.

81 MCA 2005 Sch 1 para 13(3), referring to MCA 2005 s22(3).

purpose of creating an LPA or to create a LPA,[82] then they must within three weeks from the date on which notice is given make an application to the Court of Protection in a form COP7 (not a COP1), and notify the OPG of their application in a form LPA008. There is no fee payable. The COP7 form will then be issued by the court; it must then be served as soon as practicable and in any event within 14 days; the COP7 form must be accompanied with a COP5 form for the person upon whom it is served to respond, and a certificate of service will be required under COP20. Taking these steps will have the effect of preventing the OPG from registering the LPA until the court has determined the application and directed the OPG to do so.[83]

- If the person who wishes to object to the registration was not a person notified on a LPA001 form, the application is made not on an COP7 form, but on a COP1 form; the OPG must also be notified. There is a fee payable in such case (see appendix F below). This will also apply if the LPA has already been registered, but the person wishes the power to be cancelled.

7.107 The Court of Protection has a range of powers in relation to determining both the validity of LPAs[84] and their operation.[85] The most relevant for present purposes are those related to the jurisdiction that the court exercises over the conduct of attorneys (which also extends to the conduct of attorneys under EPAs[86]); see further paras 7.117–7.119 below.

7.108 The court may determine the validity of an LPA[87] and if it finds that it was not properly created may order that the instrument is not registered. Other powers of the court include severing the appointment of an attorney under an LPA if there is more than one appointed. For example, if only one attorney were found to be in breach of their duties this would in itself not invalidate the appointment of any other attorney validly appointed in the same instrument. The court

82 MCA 2005 s22(3)(a). It is also possible to object on the basis that the proposed attorney proposes to behave in a way that would contravene there authority or would not be in P's best interests (MCA 2005 s22(3)(b)): see *Re KC* [2020] EWCOP 62, [2021] COPLR 195 (pre-emptive refusal to register on the basis that the proposed attorneys were at loggerheads and would not be able to work together in the best interests of the donor).

83 MCA 2005 Sch 1 para 13(4).

84 MCA 2005 s22.

85 MCA 2005 s23.

86 Under the – slightly different – provisions in MCA 2005 Sch 3 para 16.

87 MCA 2005 s22(2)(a).

considered the issue of severance in a range of circumstances in *Re Public Guardian's Severance Application*.[88]

7.109 The court also has powers to require attorneys to provide accounts or other information if the donor lacks the capacity to call for these themselves,[89] as well as giving directions about the remuneration of a donee[90] or alleviating them from liability for any breach of their duty as attorney.[91]

7.110 The court also has jurisdiction to authorise gifts that fall outside of the attorney's existing powers under the LPA, see para 7.91 above. The court's power to revoke an LPA is discussed below at para 7.114.

Jointly owned property and other trustee matters

7.111 In cases where P is a trustee, a deputy may not be given power to exercise P's functions as a trustee.[92] An application will need to be made to the court for the appointment of a new trustee to act in P's place.

7.112 This is most commonly found where P is the co-owner of real property as this is a form of trusteeship. P will usually need to be removed from the title to the land and a new trustee appointed in order for a sale of the land to take place.

7.113 An application to the court to appoint a trustee can be made by reference to COPR PD 9F. This sets out the information that the court will require in order to consider the application.

Removal of attorney or deputy

7.114 A deputy or attorney may retire from their role and cease to act if circumstances change. An attorney may do this by disclaiming the role, a deputy will need to apply to the court for an order to appoint an alternative. There are, however, occasions when another will apply to the court for the removal of a deputy or attorney. The MCA 2005 gives the court the power to revoke an LPA if P is unable to do so and the attorney:

88 [2017] EWCOP 10, [2017] WTLR 1145.
89 MCA 2005 s23(3)(a).
90 MCA 2005 s23(3)(c).
91 MCA 2005 s23(3)(d).
92 MCA 2005 s20(3).

a) has behaved, or is behaving, in a way that contravenes their authority or is not in P's best interests; or
b) proposes to behave in a way that would contravene their authority or would not be in P's best interests.'[93]

7.115 The Court of Protection can also revoke the appointment of a deputy if it is satisfied that the deputy:

a) has behaved, or is behaving, in a way that contravenes the authority conferred on them by the court or is not in P's best interests; or
b) proposes to behave in a way that would contravene that authority or would not be in P's best interests.[94]

7.116 An application may be made by the OPG (following an investigation – see chapter 20),[95] local authority safeguarding team if there are fears about financial abuse or by someone interested in P's welfare that has well-founded fears about the management of P's finances.

7.117 As more cases continue to be reported, there is more guidance emerging about what the court considers to be behaviour that justifies the removal of either an attorney or a deputy.

7.118 The cases of *Re J*[96] and *Re Harcourt*[97] both comment upon the relevant behaviour to be taken into account when considering applications of this type. In *Re J* HHJ Marshall QC considered the question of what conduct of the attorney would be of relevance to the question of revocation, holding that:

> . . . on a proper construction of s22(3), the court can consider any past behaviour or apparent prospective behaviour by the attorney, [and], depending on the circumstances and apparent gravity of any offending behaviour found, it can then take whatever steps it regards as appropriate in P's best interests (this only arises if P lacks capacity), to deal with the situation, whether by revoking the power or by taking some other course.[98]

7.119 Former Senior Judge Lush commented in *Re Harcourt* that: 'Essentially, the Lasting Powers of Attorney scheme is based on trust and envisages minimal intervention by public authorities.'[99] He went

93 MCA 2005 s22(3)(b).
94 MCA 2005 s16(8).
95 See, for instance, *Public Guardian v JM* [2014] EWHC B4 (COP).
96 [2011] COPLR Con Vol 716.
97 [2013] COPLR 69, [2012] WTLR 1799.
98 Para 13.
99 Para 39.

on to note that: 'The factor of magnetic importance in determining what is in Mrs Harcourt's best interests is that her property and financial affairs should be managed competently, honestly and for her benefit.'[100]

7.120 In *Re AB*[101] the court sets out the different test that applies in the revocation of an EPA as opposed to that of an LPA. In *The Public Guardian v PM and SH*[102] the court commented upon the different approach that would be taken when asked to revoke an LPA for property and affairs and an LPA for health and welfare.

7.121 The cases of *Re Buckley* and *Re GM* discussed above also resulted in the removal of the deputies involved. Other examples of the type of behaviour that will result in the removal of the attorney or deputy can be found in *Re AB*;[103] *The Public Guardian v AW and DH*[104] and *The Public Guardian v DA, YS and ES*.[105] Finally, while *Re DB*[106] is a decision relating to costs, the case is also of note for the approach taken by the court to the suitability of a proposed deputy. Professional deputies should be aware of the issues raised in *Public Guardian v Matrix Deputies Ltd and Enfield LBC*.[107] In this case, a firm of professional deputies were removed from all their deputyships because of a range of issues including incorrect billing and conflicts of interest.

7.122 The process for making an application for the removal of an attorney or deputy follows that of all other applications relating to P's property and affairs. Firstly, the applicant should obtain an assessment of capacity addressing the questions to be put before the court. Depending upon the situation the questions to be considered may include:

- whether P lacks the capacity to revoke their LPA;
- whether P can validly enter into a new LPA;
- whether P lacks capacity to request accounts from their attorney;
- whether P lacked the capacity to make a gift (or other relevant detrimental financial decision) at the relevant time.

100 Para 60.
101 [2014] EWCOP 12, [2014] WTLR 1303.
102 [2016] EWCOP 25, [2016] COPLR 488.
103 [2014] EWCOP 12, [2014] WTLR 1303.
104 [2014] EWCOP 28, [2014] WTLR 1705.
105 [2015] EWCOP 41, [2015] WTLR 1647.
106 [2014] EWHC 483 (COP), [2014] COPLR 275.
107 [2017] EWCOP 14, [2017] COPLR 415.

7.123 The applicant would be wise to consider the outcome for P that would be achieved through making the application, if an LPA is to be revoked and P lacks capacity to enter into a new LPA, who will manage P's finances? It may be appropriate to ask the court, for example, not only to revoke the appointment of an attorney but to order the appointment of a neutral panel deputy.

7.124 The applicant may find that they do not have access to all the information that they need to support their application. P's financial documents are likely to be kept by the attorney or deputy. In these cases it may be preferable to approach the OPG to investigate and use its powers to obtain documents and to make any necessary application. If the applicant has access to sufficient evidence that the deputy or attorney may be acting in such a way that the court should consider their removal, then proceeding straight to apply to the court will be the quickest route to take.

7.125 The applicant may consider asking for immediate directions to protect P's position, but these are rarely granted in cases that solely concern P's property and affairs.

Redress

7.126 As mentioned earlier in this chapter, every deputy (with the exception of a local authority deputy) must purchase a security bond, which is in effect an insurance against them causing financial loss to P. If the court removes a deputy in circumstances in which their actions have caused loss to P, then it is possible to recover those funds for P, up to the value of the relevant security bond if the court orders it. In *Re Meek*[108] HHJ Hodge QC considered when to call in a bond. The issue was re-visited in *Re M*[109] and *Enfield LBC v Matrix Deputies Ltd, DW, OM and the Public Guardian.*[110] In the latter case Senior Judge Hilder clarified the information that the court needs in order to call in a guarantee bond. It should be noted that the latter decision does not address what might happen in later proceedings against the former deputy by the bond-holder if it was established that P had suffered no loss. The agreement between the bond provider and the deputy is that the bond provider guarantees to pay the amount of any loss by the deputy as determined by the Court of Protection. In any

108 [2014] EWCOP 1, [2014] COPLR 535.
109 [2017] EWCOP 24.
110 [2018] EWCOP 22, [2018] COPLR 451.

subsequent proceedings to enforce recovery in the civil courts it may be the case that the bond provider can proceed on the basis that the Court of Protection decision is equivalent to a judgment debt which the cannot be challenged.

7.127 It may be possible to make an application for a security bond to be called in within the course of the proceedings to remove the deputy. If there is insufficient information at the time of the removal proceedings about the full scale of P's financial loss, a later application can be brought by the new deputy on behalf of P.

7.128 If P has suffered financial loss through the actions of their attorney, or if this loss caused by their deputy exceeds the value of the security bond, the only remedy open is for the new deputy acting on behalf of P is to take civil action against the former attorney or deputy personally. Before considering this step (which would require the endorsement of the Court of Protection), the deputy would need to be sure that the removed attorney or deputy had sufficient resources to meet any liability. Where the defaulting deputy is a professional, there will usually be recourse to their indemnity insurance.

7.129 There is increasing awareness of financial abuse as a crime. Financial abuse covers a range of actions aimed at obtaining money or property from vulnerable individuals. A deputy appointed in the wake of known or suspected financial abuse will want to consider reporting their findings to the police, with a view to supporting a prosecution.

Recovery of capacity

7.130 The Court of Protection's jurisdiction only extends to those who lack capacity to make certain decisions. It follows, therefore, that if P ceases to lack capacity in relation to their property and affairs, an application should be made for the discharge of the deputy.[111]

7.131 If a deputy believes that P has regained their capacity to manage their property and affairs, they should obtain updated medical evidence to this effect and then apply to the court, following the procedure described above, to approve the discharge of the deputyship.

7.132 The court will consider the evidence and if the application is approved will make an order for final accounts to be submitted, the

111 See COPR PD 24B para 5.

ending of the security bond, the transfer of all assets to P's name and for final costs to be dealt with.[112]

Death of P

7.133 The death of P automatically ends both the valid appointment of a deputy and also that of an attorney. The deputy should liaise with the personal representatives of P's estate to make information available to allow them to administer P's estate. A professional deputy will be entitled to final costs for winding up the deputyship. The deputy should notify the OPG of the death of P, by submitting a copy of the death certificate. Other matters for a deputy to deal with will include submitting a final report to the OPG and discharging the security.

Mixed applications

7.134 During the course of proceedings, issues may arise that go beyond those concerning P's property and affairs, to touch on health and welfare issues as well. A common scenario is a dispute arising within a family about who should act as attorney or deputy for an incapacitated relative that also includes an aspect about where the individual should reside or the care they should receive.

7.135 Parties and their advisers need to be clear as to the differences between the two sets of issues. For welfare matters, permission will only need to be sought for the part of the application where permission is required.[113] For the procedure for obtaining permission in relation to health and welfare decisions, see chapter 9.

7.136 Advisers should also be aware of the differing costs regimes in property and affairs matters and health and welfare matters. Details on the appropriate treatment of costs in mixed applications can be found in chapter 17.

7.137 Mixed applications will also be subject to case management on the relevant pathways as described in chapters 8 and 10. There are two stages before the court decides which pathway, or mixture of the two, is most appropriate:

112 See COPR PD 24B, COPR r19.3, and the Lasting Powers of Attorney, Enduring Powers of Attorney and Public Guardian Regulations 2007 SI No 1253 regs 37 and 40. See also chapter 17.

113 COPR r8.3.

1) Pre-issue stage – where potential parties are to identify most appropriate pathway and comply with the requirements and seek to resolve issues.
2) Point of issue of application – where the parties must file a list of issues to allow the court to identify the appropriate pathway or mixture of the two.[114]

7.138 Where an application contains both welfare and property and affairs issues, the papers will be placed before a judge for initial case management who will either:

1) order allocation to a pathway and give directions accordingly; or
2) give directions as to which elements of each pathway are to apply and procedure to follow.[115]

Bulk applications

7.139 Following comments made in the *The Friendly Trust's Bulk Application*,[116] previous guidance about bulk applications was withdrawn. It had been thought possible to make a bulk application where the same issue affected all or many of the deputyships held by one deputy. Attention is now drawn to the fact that the COPR make no provision for bulk applications. Charles J confirmed this approach in *Re AR*,[117] commenting that in the past the court had erred too far in favour of administrative convenience.

114 COPR Case Pathways PD 3B para 4.1(2).
115 COPR Case Pathways PD 3B para 4.1(3).
116 [2016] EWCOP 40.
117 [2018] EWCOP 8, [2018] COPLR 274.

CHAPTER 8

Responding to an application and contested applications: property and affairs

Introduction

8.1 Most applications concerning P's property and affairs are not contested and are dealt with 'on the papers', ie without a hearing. However, some will meet with disagreement. This chapter looks at the steps that are necessary when responding to an application, whether the decision is to consent to it or the party served or notified wishes to oppose it or suggest an alternative order.

8.2 Those who are served with application papers, or notified of an application, should consider (where necessary with the benefit of legal advice) as soon as possible how they wish to respond and what part they wish to play in the proceedings. The Court of Protection Rules 2017[1] (COPR) provide for a number of variations, which will have different consequences for the shape of any proceedings.

8.3 All parties should bear in mind the impact of their behaviour on the costs of the matter, as a timely response will be most effective at curbing costs.

Initial steps

8.4 Permission is not required prior to making an application to the court about a matter concerning P's property and affairs.[2] Service or notification that an application form has been issued will therefore usually be the first information that a respondent or a person notified will have of proceedings.

8.5 A respondent will be served (by the applicant) with a copy of the COP1 form[3] (application to make decisions on someone's behalf as a deputy) as issued by the court, as well as a copy of the complete application papers and any orders made by the court, a COP5 acknowledgement of service or notification will also be provided. A person notified will be served (by the applicant) with a COP15 notice of proceedings and a COP5.

8.6 Those who are served or notified of proceedings should consider taking appropriate legal advice about their response to the application as soon as possible. The general rule about funding in property and affairs cases[4] is that P's estate pays the costs of all parties. There

1 SI 2017 No 1035.

2 COPR r8.2(a).

3 Available at: www.gov.uk/government/collections/court-of-protection-forms.

4 COPR r19.2.

is no public funding available for property and affairs cases. For more information on the treatment of costs see chapter 17.

8.7 There can be significant variations in the amount of detail provided within an application. The receipt of the application will, however, offer the respondent an opportunity to consider the issues raised by the application and how they may be able to counter them. This is all part of the vital exercise of ensuring the actual issues in the case are identified as quickly and precisely as possible. The receipt of the application may be a useful time to consider not only the evidence that the respondent may be able to provide, but whether there are others in P's life who will be able to provide a helpful perspective as well. See further in this regard para 8.19 onwards below.

8.8 It is vital that the matters are not set in stone at the outset. In other words, those served with the application as much as the person or body bringing the application should remain flexible as to the possible outcome of the application. Parties' views will alter as evidence is gathered and others may have a very markedly different opinion as to P's best interests.

Consenting to an application

8.9 If a person notified, or a respondent, considers that the application is one which is reasonable and which they support, then they can indicate this simply by completing and filing the COP5 form to the effect that they agree with the application proposed. This response should be filed the court within 14 days of service.[5]

8.10 There is no obligation on the part of a person notified or a respondent to make any response to the application, but a failure to do so will not prevent the making of the order that is sought. Respondents or those notified who do not respond will still be bound by the decision of the court as if they had been a party.[6]

8.11 A person who has been notified will not become a party to the proceedings simply by filing a COP5 form consenting to the application. However, if a person notified has taken legal advice before reaching the conclusion that they wish to consent to the application as proposed, it would be appropriate to seek a direction that they be joined as a party to the proceedings only for purposes of seeking to

5 COPR r9.12.

6 COPR r9.14(2), emphasised in *Mrs P v Rochdale BC* [2016] EWCOP B1 at para 26.

recover their costs.[7] This is likely only to be of relevance in property and affairs case where the costs are in principle recoverable from the estate of P.[8]

8.12 By contrast with proceedings in some other courts, there is no such category as 'interested party' in proceedings before the Court of Protection. A person (or body) is either a party or they are not.[9]

Becoming a party

8.13 A person who has been served as a respondent will automatically become a party to proceedings by filing a COP5 form.[10]

8.14 If a respondent wishes to oppose the application or to propose an alternative order, then the acknowledgement of service should be accompanied by a witness statement which contains any evidence upon which the respondent intends to rely.[11] In practice, however, it is not always appropriate or indeed possible to serve a witness statement along with the COP5 form. The respondent may not have access to documents that would support their position. In these circumstances, directions should be sought for the provision of any information that the respondent requires, for example (for instance, in a financial case) bank statements or other financial information.

8.15 If a person who is notified wishes to oppose the application, or to propose an alternative order, they must apply to be joined as a party to proceedings. The person does this by indicating their wish to be joined as a party on the COP5 and filing this response with the court within the appropriate timescale. The COP5 must set out the person's reasons for wishing to be a party, and should be accompanied by a witness statement setting out their interest in the proceedings. The court will decide whether or not to join that person as a party.[12] The relevant test for whether a person should be joined as a party is whether the court considers it desirable for the purpose of deciding the application.[13] If the court approves the application, then the person notified will be made a party to proceedings and the applicant

7 COPR r19.12.
8 COPR r19.2; see further chapter 17.
9 See *Re SK* [2012] EWHC 1990 (COP), [2012] COPLR 712 at para 21.
10 COPR r9.13(1)(b).
11 COPR r9.12(5).
12 COPR r9.12(8).
13 COPR r9.13(2).

will be required to serve them with a copy of the full application papers.

8.16 A person who subsequently becomes aware of an application may apply to become a party. To do so, they must demonstrate 'sufficient interest' in the proceedings.[14] That interest must be a sufficient interest in the proceedings themselves – ie 'the ascertainment of the incapacitated person's best interests' – as opposed to any commercial (or other interest) of the applicant's own.[15] This approach was approved by the former President in *Re G*.[16]

8.17 A person who wishes to be joined as a party must file an application notice (COP9) and a statement explaining their interest in the proceedings and – if they intend to ask the court to make an order that is different to the order sought by the applicant – the evidence on which they rely.[17] The person seeking to join should send enough copies of the application for all the parties and the court will serve it.[18] Again, the test will be whether it is desirable to join the person to the proceedings for the purpose of dealing with the application.[19]

Being removed as a party

8.18 It is convenient here to deal with when a party might be removed. There are two circumstances under which a party could be removed:

1) The party themselves might want to be. In such case, they should apply using form COP9.[20] There is no guidance in either the COPR or the accompanying Practice Directions (PDs) as to the test that the court will apply (nor are there any reported decisions on the point), but logic suggests that the application will be granted only if the court considers that the continued participation of the person as a party is no longer desirable for the purpose of dealing with the application. As a half-way house, and in line with the overriding objective in COPR r1.1, courts will

14 COPR r9.15(1).

15 *Re SK* [2012] EWHC 1990 (COP), [2012] COPLR 712 at paras 41–43 per Bodey J (refusing application by defendant to personal injury proceedings brought by P to be joined to Court of Protection proceedings concerning P).

16 *Re G, London Borough of Redbridge v G (by her litigation friend the Official Solicitor), C and F* [2014] EWCOP 1361, [2014] COPLR 416.

17 COPR r9.15(3).

18 COPR r9.15(4).

19 COPR r9.13(2).

20 COPR r9.16.

sometimes allow parties to cease to play any active steps for certain stages in the proceedings where their contribution will not be required at all points (or will provide that the party in question only need file documentation or attend directions hearings 'if so advised').

2) Separately, the court has the power to discharge a party on application from *another* party, or if its own motion. However, this power should be exercised with care, especially if the power is to be exercise without notice to the party whose discharge is being completed.[21] Although not, strictly, a decision governed by Mental Capacity Act (MCA) 2005 s1(5), whether P's interests will be served or harmed by the person remaining a party will be major factor in the court's consideration.[22]

Contesting an application

8.19 Careful consideration should be given to the available evidence when considering whether to contest an application, or to suggest an alternative order. In property and affairs cases, which commonly concern the management or movement of money or property within families it is important for each party to remain focused on what is in P's best interests and what is realistically achievable. Any party considering contesting an application should ensure that they are familiar with and adhere to the overriding objective[23] which places emphasis on controlling costs through compliance with procedure in order to resolve issues quickly and fairly. Parties have explicit duties[24] designed to further the overriding objective. There are additional duties imposed upon legal representatives and unrepresented litigants.[25]

8.20 The grounds on which an application may be contested will depend upon the facts of the case and the evidence available. For

21 See *Re P (Discharge of Party)* [2021] EWCA Civ 512, [2021] 1 WLR 3098 at para 65, per Baker LJ.

22 *Re P (Discharge of Party)* [2021] EWCA Civ 512, [2021] 1 WLR 3098 at para 53 per Baker LJ. The subsequent decision in this case, reconsidering the question of the discharge of the party in question (*London Borough of Southwark v P and others* [2021] EWCOP 46) shows the working out of this approach.

23 COPR r1.1.

24 COPR r1.4.

25 COPR rr1.5 and 1.6; see further chapter 12.

details about a range of specific applications and situations see chapter 7.

8.21 In property and affairs cases, if there is a dispute, it is often likely to be between family members, rather than family members and a statutory body. In such cases – and especially given that the general rule as to costs is that the costs (of all parties) will be payable out of P's estate[26] – the temptation must be resisted for respondents to oppose applications on the basis of a point or points that do not relate to the issues in the case and which will serve no purpose but to increase the cost to P. The court will primarily be concerned with P's present circumstances, and the resources of the court do not exist to allow the ventilation of unrelated allegations of the nature that can, sadly, often arise in the case of family disputes. Parties must remain focussed on the issues that are before the court and the relevance of the information they wish to put before the court both in the application and in any potential response.

8.22 Parties should maintain a flexible approach, focused on P's best interests and avoid entrenched positions as far as possible. This allows alternative options to be explored by way of mediation and other forms of alternative dispute resolution (ADR) (see chapter 20), and may help to avoid incurring the expense of attended court hearing(s).

8.23 Advisers should, however, be alert to the danger of attempting to persuade parties to take an approach that fundamentally they do not agree with.

8.24 If the parties are able to reach a negotiated way forward that represents a compromise between the position advocated by the applicant and that desired by the respondent(s), the court should be notified and a consent order submitted, with each party or their legal representative confirming their consent to the order as agreed: see further para 11.56.

8.25 If the parties cannot agree a negotiated way forward within a reasonable timescale, the court will proceed to determine how best to put itself in a position to reach a conclusion. This means that the case will usually proceed on the basis of directions given when the case becomes contested, allowing the parties time to attempt to reach a negotiated agreement before a final hearing is listed.

26 COPR r19.2; see also chapter 17.

Contested applications – the Case Pathways Practice Direction

8.26 The COPR Case Pathways PD 3B sets out the pathways which the court will use to manage applications which are contested. All property and affairs applications will be subject to the property and affairs procedure set out in the Case Pathways PD 3B except for:

- uncontested applications;
- applications by the Public Guardian; and
- applications for the approval of statutory wills and gifts.

8.27 It may appear from these exclusions that requirements set down in the relevant parts of the property and affairs pathway will affect only the minority of applications. However, in practice the courts are likely to use the property and affairs pathway to case manage *all* cases which are contested and where it appears that the parties are not able to refine the issues and work towards a negotiated agreement in a reasonable timescale.

8.28 It is important that all applicants and respondents are aware of the procedure as property and affairs applications tend not arise out of an existing disagreement and the applicant will only become aware at a later stage that that the application is opposed, or a different order sought.

The stages of the property and affairs pathway

8.29 The property and affairs pathway[27] set out in PD 3B comprises four stages:

1) when the application becomes contested;
2) case management on allocation to the pathway;
3) the dispute resolution hearing; and
4) the final hearing.

When the application becomes contested

8.30 The property and affairs pathway begins at a later stage than the personal welfare pathway, and has no pre-issue stage. Until it is contested, all property and affairs applications will follow the procedure in chapter 7 at para 7.6 onwards. The *first stage* therefore

27 COPR r3.9.

commences when court is notified by one of the respondents or those notified returning a completed COP5 form indicating that the application is opposed or a different order sought. When this happens, the case will be allocated to the pathway. The court will then serve on the applicant a copy of the COP5 form and an order allocating the case to the pathway.

Case management on allocation to the pathway

8.31 At the *second stage*, the papers are placed before a judge, who will either:

a) list for a dispute resolution hearing; or
b) transfer case to the most appropriate regional court for listing of the dispute resolution hearing.

At this stage the respondent may also be ordered to file a summary of reasons for opposing the application or seeking different order, if this is not clear from their COP5.

Dispute resolution hearing

8.32 The *third stage*, the dispute resolution hearing (DRH),[28] is modelled upon the financial dispute resolution (FDR) hearing found in the family courts. The purpose of the hearing is to enable the court to determine if the case can be resolved and avoid unnecessary litigation, and by extension costs.

8.33 The DRH will usually take place before a district judge. All parties must attend unless the court directs otherwise, and are to approach the hearing 'openly and without reserve'.[29] The content of the hearing is not to be disclosed and evidence of anything said or admission made at the hearing will not be admissible in evidence at a final hearing. The exception to this being at a trial for an offence committed at the hearing.

8.34 Parties attending a DRH are likely to find that the process will involve negotiations between the representatives of the various parties, and unrepresented parties if there are any, coupled with the making of offers and counter-offers. Positions adopted and concessions made will be treated as being made 'without prejudice' to allow parties to make genuine attempts to reach an agreement.

28 COPR Case Pathways PD 3B para 3.4.
29 COPR Case Pathways PD 3B para 3.4(3)(a).

8.35 The parties will be expected to appear before the court when the judge will wish to be advised on the progress towards refining the issues and reaching agreement, and also the areas where this has not been possible. At the hearing the court will give a view on the likely outcome of the matter if it were to proceed to a final hearing. This allows the parties to consider the strengths and weaknesses of their respective positions and to make further offers in the light of this.

8.36 If the parties are able to reach an agreement at this stage, the court will make a final order if it is in P's best interests to do so. If the parties are unable to reach an agreement at the DRH, the court will make directions for further case management up to the final hearing.

8.37 It should be noted that DRHs are not an attended hearing for purposes of the Transparency Practice Direction.[30]

8.38 The court may turn to either the Civil Procedure Rules (CPR) or Family Procedure Rules (FPR) in cases where the COPR do not provide express guidance,[31] and given that DRHs are modelled upon FDRs, we consider that it is likely that the courts will draw upon those parts of the FPR which apply to FDRs. Until and unless specific guidance is given, we suggest that parties preparing for a DRH should therefore turn to FPR rr9.14 and 9.17 as a guides. These set out the requirements on parties preparing for the first appointment and FDR appointment in family proceedings. The COPR do not provide for the equivalent of a first appointment, but the court would be greatly assisted by the provision of the documents required by those rules, including:

- a chronology;
- a list of the issues between the parties; and
- details of all offers and proposals, and responses to them.

These must be filed at court at least seven days before the hearing. The court would welcome the provision of these documents as part of a bundle which also includes copies of all the application papers and any orders.

8.39 At the conclusion of the DRH, any documents containing details of the offers and proposals, and any filed documents referring to them, must, at the request of the party who filed them, be returned to that party and not retained on the court file. This is not express from

30 COPR Transparency PD 4C para 2.2.

31 COPR r2.5.

the provisions of the Case Pathways PD, but we suggest must flow from the analogous position prevailing in relation to FDRs.[32]

8.40 If an agreement is not reached at a DRH, a final hearing is not inevitable. It is possible for the parties to go away and reflect upon the indication given by the court and to make other offers before reaching a final hearing. Sometimes parties need more time than is available in the day to reflect upon the developments at the DRH.

8.41 In a case where one party considers that an offer made at the DRH was unreasonably refused, there is considerable merit in that offer being repeated following the DRH in correspondence reflecting the terms of the offer made at the DRH. That offer[33] cannot refer to the contents of the negotiations at the DRH. However, if, at the conclusion of the proceedings, the court reaches a conclusion that is broadly in line with (or, where relevant) more favourable (in whatever way) than the offer, it would then be entirely proper to refer to the offer when submissions are made as to costs (see further chapter 17).

Final hearing

8.42 The final hearing will be listed before a different judge to that who heard the DRH. This is a necessary consequence of the nature of a DRH, but this may cause practical difficulties in some areas where there are only very few 'ticketed' Court of Protection judges.

8.43 The final hearing will proceed in accordance with the directions given at or following the DRH. The applicant will usually be required to prepare the bundle for the hearing, although the court may make a different order to vary this if the applicant is unrepresented. For more detail on preparing for and conducting the final hearing please see chapter 16 below.

Costs

8.44 At the conclusion of the case, whether by consent or by judicial decision, the court will deal with costs. For a full discussion of costs, see chapter 17.

8.45 Parties who proceed to a final hearing should be clear as to the potential costs implications and prepare accordingly. Parties who

32 See FPR r9.17(5).

33 Which could be made on a without prejudice or an open basis depending on the circumstances (the former meaning, in essence, that it could not be put before the court until the conclusion of the substantive proceedings).

proceed to a final hearing must be sure that their opposition is objectively in P's best interests.

Urgent applications

8.46 Urgent applications in property and affairs matters are rare, and the court will only treat a matter as urgent if P's life expectancy is very short and the matter must be resolved before their death, for example to make a statutory will, or a settlement (a rare example of which can be seen in the case of *LCN v CJF*).[34]

8.47 The Case Pathways PD sets out[35] how the court will approach a property and affairs application which is urgent from the outset. Parties are reminded of the requirement in the COPR to co-operate.[36] The applicant must include the following with the application papers:

- an explanation of why the case is urgent and what the consequences will be if the case is not treated as urgent;
- if the application is made without notice, an explanation why it was not possible to make the application on notice, and what the consequences would be if the application were to proceed on notice and the order or an interim order were not made immediately;
- confirmation of any specific deadline;
- information identifying and separating the issues which are urgent from those which are not urgent.

8.48 The court will consider the papers and on issue will, if the matter appears or is confirmed to be contentious, either order:

a) the case will proceed to a DRH but listed urgently; or
b) the case may be listed for an interim hearing to decide the urgent matter or matters in the case, and the court can decide at that hearing whether any further hearing is necessary and if so, whether that further hearing should include a DRH or not.

8.49 Applications which are not contentious but are urgent can be dealt with on the papers if all the relevant consents have been received by the court.

8.50 Sometimes applications are not urgent at the time they are commenced but become so as matters proceed. This is especially likely to be the case in statutory will applications where P's health

34 [2019] EWCOP 1, [2019] COPLR 262.
35 COPR Case Pathways PD 3B para 3.6.
36 COPR r1.4(2)(c).

may decline suddenly making the issue of their will more urgent. Where this occurs it is important to advise the court and other parties of the change in circumstances as soon as possible and to share any available medical evidence. The court will then be able to take steps to consider the matter urgently and decide if a final order can be made or if a hearing should be listed urgently.

CHAPTER 9

Making an application: health and welfare cases

Introduction

9.1 This chapter considers the process of initiating a case in the Court of Protection which concerns P's health or personal welfare. It examines the 'personal welfare pathway,' and goes on to provide guidance on completing the relevant COP forms, obtaining permission and dealing with service. It then discusses how to respond to an application. A flowchart summarising the procedure is set out at the end of this chapter. It should be read with chapter 11 on interim hearings and interim applications, because that chapter takes the life of the application forward.

Before making an application

9.2 In chapter 5 we consider how to decide when an application is appropriate in the context of P's health or personal welfare. In chapter 20 we consider mediation and other forms of alternative dispute resolution (ADR). Readers are advised to refer to those chapters before commencing litigation, and should also bear in mind that the Mental Capacity Act (MCA) 2005 Code of Practice anticipates that attempts will be made to resolve disputes outside the court arena in the first instance.[1]

9.3 There are broadly three types of case where a health or welfare application to court will need to be made:

1) First, certain types of medical treatment cases, considered in chapter 23.
2) Second, (at least until the liberty protection safeguards (LPS) come into effect) where the court's authority is needed because P's care plan deprives them of their liberty, in a placement which is not a hospital or care home. These cases are considered in chapter 22.
3) The third is where there is a genuine dispute as to either P's capacity or best interests.

1 Mental Capacity Act 2005 Code of Practice chapter 15 (the code is under revision at the time of writing), available at: www.gov.uk/government/publications/mental-capacity-act-code-of-practice; and *G v E (Deputyship and Litigation Friend)* [2010] EWHC 2512 (Fam), (2010) 13 CCLR 610.

9.4 If one of the parties is a public body, then that body will be expected to take the initiative in bringing the matter before the court.[2] Parties should be aware that their conduct before proceedings start can be taken into account if the court is considering departing from the general rule in health and welfare cases that the parties should bear their own costs.[3]

Types of application

9.5 It is important to decide before making an application both whether an application should be made at all, and precisely what declarations and/or orders should be sought: see further chapter 5.

9.6 In general, applications in relation to P's welfare will be for specific declarations and/or decisions, rather than for the appointment of a deputy. As set out in chapter 3, the court has the power to make decisions on P's behalf[4] or appoint a deputy to make them for P.[5] However, it is clear that a decision of the court is preferred to the appointment of a deputy[6] and the powers conveyed upon a deputy should be as limited as possible.[7] These powers are limited by MCA 2005 s20. For example, a deputy cannot prohibit contact between P and a named person,[8] or refuse consent to life-sustaining treatment.[9] In *Re Lawson, Mottram and Hopton (appointment of personal welfare deputies)*,[10] Hayden J held that:

- The MCA Code of Practice was wrong insofar as it suggested[11] that the starting-point is that personal welfare deputies should only be appointed in the most difficult cases.

2 *Hillingdon LBC v Neary* [2011] EWHC 1377 (COP), [2011] COPLR Con Vol 632; also (by way of example of the approach adopted by district judges): *A Local Authority v Mrs D and another* [2013] EWHC B34 (COP) and *Re RR (Costs)* [2014] EWCOP 34. See also chapter 5.

3 Court of Protection Rules 2017 (COPR) SI No 1035 r19.5.

4 MCA 2005 s16(1).

5 MCA 2005 s16(2).

6 MCA 2005 s16(4)(a).

7 MCA 2005 s16(4)(b).

8 MCA 2005 s20(2) and *Re TZ (No 2)* [2014] EWHC 973 (COP), [2014] COPLR 159 at para 83.

9 MCA 2005 s20(5).

10 [2019] EWCOP 22, [2019] 1 WLR 5164.

11 At para 8.38. The Code of Practice is under revision at the time of writing.

- Each case fell to be decided on its merits, and by reference to whether an appointment is in the best interests of the person.
- The person's wishes and feelings will form an aspect of that decision (for instance, if it is clear that P would wish a family member to be appointed to be their personal welfare deputy).
- The proper operation of MCA 2005 ss4 and 5 means that, in practice, personal welfare deputies will not often be appointed, in particular because the appointment should not be seen, in and of itself, as less restrictive of P's rights and freedoms.[12]

9.7 A welfare deputyship should not be sought if the underlying decision that the deputy wishes to make is a 'one off' decision, such as a change of residence. In many cases, the reason deputyship might be sought is because of a history of a failure by statutory services to take due account of the views of (say) P's parent in decision-making under MCA 2005 s5. In any such application, it will be important to identify why such a failure impacts upon P's best interests. It will also be important to identify why and how the proposed deputy will make decisions on P's behalf – the courts have made clear that simply (if understandably) wanting to be a deputy so that health and social care professionals will listen is not an appropriate basis for appointment.[13]

9.8 In many cases, the issues that the court needs to address will relate both to P's health and welfare and to P's property and affairs. These 'mixed' applications are addressed in paras 7.134–7.138.

The Case Management Pathways

9.9 The COPR Case Pathways Practice Direction (PD) 3B provides that health and welfare applications are allocated to a dedicated personal welfare pathway with limited exceptions, namely (for these purposes): uncontested applications; applications using form COPDOL11 (so-called *Re X* applications);[14] and applications using form DLA (applications under MCA 2005 s21A).[15] It should be noted that all

12 This is borne out in practice. In 2021 (the last full year for which statistics are available), for instance, 382 health and welfare deputies were appointed. By contrast, 12,846 property and affairs deputies were appointed. See: www.gov.uk/government/collections/family-court-statistics-quarterly.

13 See *Re CB* [2021] EWCOP 43, [2021] COPLR 549.

14 See chapter 22.

15 See chapter 22.

medical treatment cases are now treated as personal welfare cases, although, as discussed in chapter 23, the procedure adopted in practice will usually differ from other cases on the welfare pathway.

9.10 The personal welfare pathway has four stages: pre-issue, the point of issue; case management on issue; the case management conference; the final management hearing and the final hearing. There are requirements at each stage: this chapter concerns the pre-issue and issue stages; case management thereafter is dealt with in chapter 11 and the final hearing in chapter 16.

9.11 The pre-issue stage puts an explicit obligation on the applicant in non-urgent cases to identify and engage with potential respondents and set out proposals for resolving the issue outside the court arena. We will consider the requirements in more detail as we discuss the process of making and (in chapter 10) responding to an application.

9.12 It is important for both potential applicants and potential respondents to be aware that the court will take into account in deciding whether or not to depart from the general rule as to costs (ie in welfare proceedings, that each party bears their own) the conduct of the parties *before* as well as during the proceedings.[16] This rule has been on the statute books for some time, but it is likely that greater attention will be paid to it given the express introduction of a pre-issue stage in welfare applications, to which we now turn.

The personal welfare pathway: the pre-issue stage

9.13 The COPR Case Pathways PD 3B requires the applicant to 'take all necessary steps'[17] to identify all potential respondents and interested parties[18] and inform them and (if possible) P of the applicant's intention to start proceedings unless the matters which the court may be asked to determine can be resolved. The applicant must set out the nature of the proceedings that the applicant intends to commence and the issues concerned. Importantly the applicant must set out proposals for resolving the issues and engage with the potential respondents in order to do so. Thus the focus is on narrowing the issues from an early stage and aiming to resolve as much as possible without litigation.

16 COPR r19.5(2)(a).

17 COPR Case Pathways PD 3B para 2.2(1).

18 This not a category of person defined in the COPR, so it must be given a common sense interpretation.

9.14 Applicants may find it useful to send a pre-issue letter, and a suggested example appears at appendix D. The tone of any such letter should reflect the priority attached to the resolution of issues without litigation. Equally, potential respondents receiving such communication from applicants should ensure that they engage with the pre-issue stage, in keeping with their own duties.

9.15 An urgent application should only be made once the applicant has given thought to the consequences if the case is not treated as urgent; the consequences of not carrying out pre-issue steps; whether there is a specific deadline and if so what that deadline is.[19] An applicant who then goes ahead without complying with the pre-issue requirements will have to explain any omissions on issue.[20]

How to make an application

9.16 The majority of applications in health and welfare cases (including for the appointment of a deputy) will require permission from the court.[21] Permission for such cases is not required where an application is made by:

- a person who lacks, or is alleged to lack, capacity;[22]
- a person with parental responsibility for someone under 18 who lacks or is alleged to lack capacity;[23]
- the donor or donee of a lasting power of attorney (LPA) to which the application relates;[24]
- a deputy appointed for P;[25]
- a person named in an existing order, where the application relates to that order;
- an application under MCA 2005 s21A by the relevant person's representative (RPR);[26]
- the Official Solicitor or Public Guardian.[27]

19 COPR Case Pathways PD 3B para 2.2(2).
20 COPR Case Pathways PD 3B para 2.3(2); also para 9.22 onwards.
21 MCA 2005 s50.
22 MCA 2005 s50(1)(a).
23 MCA 2005 s50(1)(b).
24 MCA 2005 s50(1)(c).
25 MCA 2005 s50(1)(a).
26 MCA 2005 s50(1)(c).
27 COPR r8.2(a).

9.17 Nor is the court's permission required to apply for an order under MCA 2005 s16(2)(a) the purpose of which is to authorise the deprivation of P's liberty,[28] as to which see further chapter 22.

9.18 The following forms will be needed to commence an application for health and welfare declarations and decisions:[29]

- COP1 – the application form;
- COP1B – supporting information for health and welfare applications;
- COP3 – capacity assessment.

9.19 The following forms will be needed to commence an application for a health and welfare deputyship:

- COP1 – the application form;
- COP1B – supporting information for health and welfare applications;
- COP3 – capacity assessment;
- COP4 – deputy's declaration.

9.20 All the relevant forms can be found via the Court of Protection Handbook website.[30] In both cases, supporting evidence should be provided either in the body of the COP1 or, more usually, by way of a witness statement in form COP24 (witness statements are addressed in para 13.14 onwards).

9.21 Following the 2015 rule changes, there is now no separate permission form. Where permission is required, it should be addressed in the relevant part of the COP1 form (section 6).

9.22 Once these forms have been completed, they must be sent either to the Court of Protection at First Avenue House in London, or to the relevant 'hub' for the region where P resides together with the appropriate fee.[31] For applications made to regional hubs, the applications to be made electronically, unless the applicant is unable to submit electronic applications. The full address of the court and the contact

28 COPR r8.2(d).

29 Court of Protection forms are available at the Court of Protection Handbook website: https://courtofprotectionhandbook.com/legislation-codes-of-practice-forms-and-guidance/; and the gov.uk website: www.gov.uk/government/collections/court-of-protection-forms.

30 See: https://courtofprotectionhandbook.com/legislation-codes-of-practice-forms-and-guidance/.

31 Regional hubs can only issue applications relating to health and welfare (or MCA 2005 s21A challenges: see chapter 22). Applications relating to property and affairs have to be issued by the Court of Protection in London.

details of the regional hubs appear at appendix G below, together with the telephone contact details.

Completing the forms and supporting information

9.23 COPR Part 9 deals with starting proceedings. COPR PD 9A provides guidance as to how to complete the application form (COP1). In addition, the Case Pathways PD 3B sets out in para 2.3 a broadly comprehensive list of the information that the applicant must include either within the application itself, or must refer to in the application and which must be filed alongside it. The checklist is designed, in particular, to ensure that such matters as the available options for P are identified as soon as possible. It is therefore advisable to use Case Pathways PD 3B para 2.3 as a checklist to ensure that everything the court is likely to need has been included.

9.24 One matter that is not covered in PD 3B para 2.3, drafted as it was before the COVID-19 pandemic, is the question of whether any hearings in the case should be held in-person or remotely (or on a hybrid basis). If there are specific factors the court will need to consider when listing the first case management hearing, it is important to include these in the materials provided at the outset.

Form COP1

9.25 This form is not complex. However, the following issues need to be considered with particular care.

9.26 Section 4 of the form requires the applicant to set out the order that they are asking the court to make. Ideally, pre-issue correspondence and engagement will have helped to narrow the issues. In any event it is helpful to focus here on precisely what the court will need to determine. The more precision that can be brought to bear the better. For cases on the personal welfare pathway, COPR Case Pathways PD 3B para 2.3(1)(a) requires a draft order or an explanation of the order that is sought.

9.27 It is of course essential to draft the form in a balanced manner and not to ask for inappropriately broad orders or powers.[32] The application form and the permission form contain a statement of truth, and proceedings for contempt of court may be brought if a

32 *Hillingdon LBC v Neary* [2011] EWHC 1377 (COP), [2011] COPLR Con Vol 632.

person makes a false statement in a document verified by a statement of truth.[33] All litigants are 'required to help the court to further the overriding objective',[34] as are their lawyers.[35] Solicitors are further subject to the mandatory principles of the Solicitors Regulation Authority (SRA) Standards and Regulations[36] in a way that upholds public trust and confidence in the solicitors' profession and in legal services provided by authorised persons, as well as to act with integrity.

9.28 In a complex case, there is no reason why this section cannot be drafted in a separate document to which the COP1 can refer. A useful rule of thumb is to ask whether it will be easier for the judge reading the 'package' of materials in the application to understand what is being asked for, and why, by reference to one standalone document, rather than having to navigate between different forms.

9.29 COP1 section 5.1 provides that respondents to the application should be listed, together with their relationship to P and full postal address. Individuals listed here will automatically become parties[37] unless the court orders otherwise. PD 9A requires that the applicant must list as a respondent 'any person (other than P) whom the applicant reasonably believes to have an interest which means he ought to be heard in relation to the application (as opposed to being notified of it)'.

9.30 It may seem anomalous that P does not become a party automatically given that P's future is at stake in the application. COPR r9.13(4) provides that P should not be named as a respondent to any proceedings without the leave of the court. COPR r1.2 attempts to offer the court a range of options in ensuring the participation of P and the implications are considered at para 12.6 onwards. To this end, for cases on the personal welfare pathway, COPR Case Pathways PD 3B para 2.3(1)(o) requires the applicant to address how it is proposed that P will be involved in every case. It should be noted that P is bound as if P were a party by orders of the court in any event.[38]

9.31 Specific issues arise in relation to the ability of P themselves to bring proceedings. The MCA 2005 provides that P can make an

33 COPR r5.6.

34 COPR r1.4.

35 COPR r1.5.

36 Available at: www.sra.org.uk/solicitors/standards-regulations/.

37 COPR r9.13(1)(b).

38 COPR r9.14(2)(a).

application without permission.[39] However, if P lacks capacity to conduct the proceedings, they must have a litigation friend.[40] See chapter 12 for a full discussion of the role of litigation friend; this is also considered in the context of applications under MCA 2005 s21A in chapter 22.

9.32 Practical difficulties can arise if the adviser has represented P directly – perhaps in a forum such as a mental health tribunal where patients are represented without an intermediary – and an issue has arisen which the adviser reasonably believes requires resolution by the Court of Protection. The Official Solicitor will not normally accept an invitation to act unless proceedings have already started. If P has a family member or friend who might be willing to act as litigation friend, or an advocate who is willing to support P, that individual should be approached. In *Re UF*,[41] Charles J recognised that it may be necessary for pragmatic reasons for an interim litigation friend to be named in order to commence proceedings, but for the court at a later stage to invite the Official Solicitor to act.

9.33 In some cases P may lack capacity to conduct the proceedings, but may have capacity to decide to make the application in the first place. This may allow P to make the application in their own right. See para 12.12 for further discussion.

9.34 There will be some cases where there really is no individual who is willing to act as litigation friend, even for a limited period. In some cases this may mean that it is not possible to take the matter forward to the court, unless another party – for example, the relevant local authority – can be persuaded to issue proceedings. There may be some cases where the adviser reasonably considers that P's best interests will be seriously compromised if proceedings cannot be brought. In such cases, which will be rare, we consider the adviser could act as litigation friend, solely in order to bring the case to court. The adviser should prepare a detailed witness statement in which the attempts to locate a suitable litigation friend are described. This is not entirely without precedent, as a solicitor was appointed litigation friend to a protected party whom he knew well.[42] Advisers may find it

39 MCA 2005 s50(1)(a).

40 COPR r1.2(4). It would not be possible, we suggest, for P to bring proceedings by an Accredited Legal Representative because such will only ever be appointed 'reactively' by the court.

41 [2013] EWHC 4289 (COP), [2014] COPLR 93.

42 *Re RGS* [2012] EWHC 4162 (COP).

useful to refer to the Law Society's guidance notes: *Meeting the needs of vulnerable clients*[43] and *Working with clients who may lack capacity*.[44]

9.35 In addition to listing respondents, section 5.1 of form COP1 requires the applicant to list the people who will be notified of the application, once it has been issued by the court. PD 9B requires the applicant to try to identify at least three people who have an interest in being notified that the application has been issued.[45] Such individuals will have the opportunity of asking to be joined as parties.[46] They will be bound by the court's orders as if they were parties.[47] There is a presumption (which can be displaced) that close members of P's family will have such an interest and the Practice Direction lists those who should ordinarily be notified, in descending order of closeness to P.[48] If someone in that list is not notified, then the reasons must be explained. (For example, P may have several siblings, only one of whom has any contact or involvement with P. There might in that case be good reason not to notify the remaining three.)

9.36 In addition to P's family, the following persons should generally be notified:[49]

- if P is under 18, anyone with parental responsibility for P;
- any person – including a legal entity such as a trust or local authority – likely to be affected by the outcome of the application;
- a deputy or attorney whose powers relate to the issue involved in the application.

9.37 Form COP1 section 6 deals with the question of permission. This section asks three questions:

1) What is the matter you want the court to decide?
2) Please state the order you are asking the court to make?
3) How would the order benefit the person to whom the application relates?

43 Available at: www.lawsociety.org.uk/en/topics/client-care/meeting-the-needs-of-vulnerable-clients.

44 Available at: www.lawsociety.org.uk/topics/client-care/working-with-clients-who-may-lack-mental-capacity.

45 COPR PD 9B para 4.

46 COPR r9.12(6), (8); PD 9C para 4.

47 COPR r9.14(2)(b).

48 COPR PD 9B para 7.

49 COPR PD 9B para 10.

9.38 The test for the grant of permission is not set down either in the MCA 2005 or in the COPR. The questions at section 6 reflect the guidance in *NK v VW and others*.[50]

9.39 There is no requirement to send proposed respondents copies of the application before it is issued, but it is good practice to do so, especially as the proposed parties should have been in correspondence in any event during the pre-issue stage.

9.40 Form COP1B requires some additional supporting information. This form is largely self-explanatory.

Evidence of capacity

9.41 Form COP3 is the assessment of capacity. It is important to note that this does not need to be completed by a medical practitioner – it can be completed by a:

- medical practitioner, for example the GP of the person to whom the application relates;
- psychiatrist;
- approved mental health professional (AMHP);
- social worker;[51]
- psychologist;
- nurse; or
- occupational therapist.

9.42 The form also makes clear that in some circumstances it might also be appropriate for a registered therapist, such as a speech therapist or occupational therapist, to complete the form.

9.43 Some medical practitioners, in particular GPs, will charge to complete a COP3. There is a good argument that it should fall within the scope of the medical services that they provide to P, and advisers should always seek to query the basis upon which any charge is made before simply agreeing to pay.

50 [2012] COPLR 105. The permission threshold was analysed in *Re D (a young man)* [2020] EWCOP 1, [2020] 1 WLR 2765. In it, Mostyn J considered that the threshold was the same as that applicable in the field of judicial review: i.e. that the applicant must demonstrate that there is a good arguable case.

51 In *A local authority v SY* [2013] EWHC 3485 (COP), [2014] COPLR 1, decided before the change in the COP3, the COP3 had been completed by a social worker; Keehan J noted that: 'The assessment in this case demonstrates that an appropriately qualified social worker is eminently suited to undertake such capacity assessments. I commend the practice which I hope will be followed in appropriate future cases' (para 22).

9.44 Whoever completes the COP3 form, it is important that the practitioner completes the COP3 correctly and provides an appropriate level of detail. In particular, section 7.1 requires the practitioner to set out the areas of decision-making where P lacks capacity. These might, for example, be P's place of residence, P's care arrangements and contact with others. When the practitioner completes the rest of the form, they must ensure that evidence of lack of capacity is set out in respect of all those three areas of decision-making. The COP3, under review at the time of writing, does not ask about capacity to conduct the proceedings but if the assessor can also provide a view on this question, this will assist when the court considers P's participation in the proceedings at a later stage (see below, para 12.6).

9.45 COPR PD 9A, para 14 explains that if the applicant cannot complete a COP3 ('for example, where P does not reside with the applicant and the applicant is unable to take P to a doctor, or where P refuses to undergo the assessment'), then the applicant should file a witness statement explaining why they cannot obtain an assessment of capacity, what attempts have been made to do so and why they believe that P lacks capacity to make a decision that is relevant to the application. It is worth bearing in mind that the test for the engagement of the MCA 2005 is lower than that for the making of final determinations by the court: see para 11.5.

Supporting evidence

9.46 COPR r9.4 provides that the evidence which supports the application should be filed at court with the application. PD 9A states that this can be provided in the form COP1, provided it is verified by a statement of truth, or by way of a witness statement in form COP24. It is suggested that in most cases it will be desirable for the applicant to provide a witness statement explaining the background to the case in appropriate detail. Questions of evidence are addressed in greater detail in chapter 13.

Human rights issues

9.47 Any claim for remedies under the Human Rights Act 1998 must be clearly pleaded and particularised. This issue is considered in chapter 26.

Fees

9.48 There is a fee for making an application. The current fees at the time of writing are set out in appendix F below.

Confidential matters

9.49 There may be cases where a party does not wish to reveal certain personal details to some or all of the other parties. The position is governed by COPR r5.7. This provides that if a party does not wish to reveal their home or business address or telephone number, or P's address or telephone number, or details of a person with whom P is living, then those details must be provided to the court in any event. These details will, however, not be provided to any other party unless the court directs this. The party must provide an address for service that it within the jurisdiction of the court.

9.50 Anyone who does not wish to reveal the details set out above should explain their reasons in a witness statement. If the party wishes to withhold more details than this, then it will be necessary to follow the procedure discussed at paras 13.106–13.115 (withholding of disclosure).

Urgent applications

9.51 There will be some cases which are so urgent that it is not possible to carry out all the steps set out above or to wait for the court to grant permission. The majority, though not all, will be cases involving serious medical treatment, and are considered in chapter 23. There is provision for urgent cases to be heard without notice, sometimes out of hours, where this is strictly necessary. COPR PD 10B provides guidance as to how to contact the court to set up an urgent hearing. Further discussion of urgent hearings can be found at para 11.66 below. For cases falling within the personal welfare pathway, COPR Case Pathways PD 3B para 2.3(2) requires the applicant to:

- explain why the case is urgent;
- explain why any of the steps in the 'checklist' at COPR Case Pathways PD 3B para 2.3(1) have not been taken, and the consequences (presumably in terms of delay) if they had been taken;

- confirm any specific deadline; and, importantly,
- separate the issues that are urgent from those which are not.

Issue of the proceedings

9.52 There is no longer a separate permission stage, and the court will issue the application form as soon as practicable after the application form is filed.[52] The court will seal the application form and stamp it with the date of issue. This is the date on which the proceedings formally commence.[53] The application form will be returned to the applicant for the applicant then to serve the proceedings in accordance with the procedure set out below. Issue is the trigger for the start of the 28-day period within which a case management conference must be held for cases on the personal welfare pathway within the COPR Case Pathways PD 3B (unless one is required within a shorter period in cases of urgency).[54]

Service and notification

9.53 The applicant is responsible for serving anyone named as a respondent or anyone who is to be notified of the proceedings,[55] as well as notifying P. This is dealt with in paras 7.23–7.32, the procedure being the same, in principle, for all applications.

52 COPR r9.5.
53 COPR r9.2.
54 COPR Case Pathways PD 3B para 2.4(1)(b).
55 COPR r9.6.

Health and welfare applications

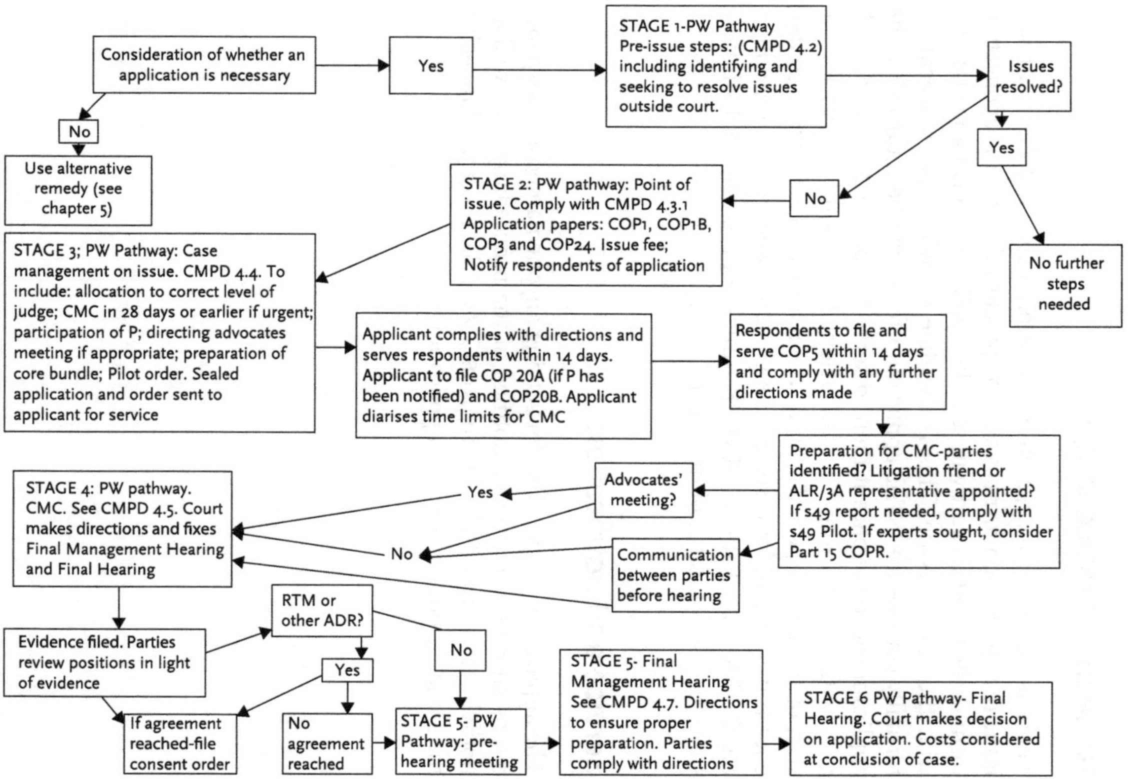

Consideration of whether an application is necessary
Yes
No
Use alternative remedy (see chapter 5)
STAGE 1-PW Pathway Pre-issue steps: (CMPD 4.2) including identifying and seeking to resolve issues outside court.
Issues resolved?
Yes
No further steps needed
No
STAGE 2: PW pathway: Point of issue. Comply with CMPD 4.3.1 Application papers: COP1, COP1B, COP3 and COP24. Issue fee; Notify respondents of application
STAGE 3; PW Pathway: Case management on issue. CMPD 4.4. To include: allocation to correct level of judge; CMC in 28 days or earlier if urgent; participation of P; directing advocates meeting if appropriate; preparation of core bundle; Pilot order. Sealed application and order sent to applicant for service
Applicant complies with directions and serves respondents within 14 days. Applicant to file COP 20A (if P has been notified) and COP20B. Applicant diarises time limits for CMC
Respondents to file and serve COP5 within 14 days and comply with any further directions made
Preparation for CMC-parties identified? Litigation friend or ALR/3A representative appointed? If s49 report needed, comply with s49 Pilot. If experts sought, consider Part 15 COPR.
Advocates' meeting?
Yes
No
Communication between parties before hearing
STAGE 4: PW pathway. CMC. See CMPD 4.5. Court makes directions and fixes Final Management Hearing and Final Hearing
Evidence filed. Parties review positions in light of evidence
RTM or other ADR?
Yes
No
If agreement reached-file consent order
No agreement reached
STAGE 5- PW Pathway: pre-hearing meeting
STAGE 5- Final Management Hearing See CMPD 4.7. Directions to ensure proper preparation. Parties comply with directions
STAGE 6 PW Pathway- Final Hearing. Court makes decision on application. Costs considered at conclusion of case.

CHAPTER 10

Responding to an application: health and welfare cases

Introduction

10.1 This chapter looks at the steps that are necessary when responding to an application, whether the decision is to consent to it or the party served or notified wishes to oppose it or suggest an alternative order.

10.2 Those who are served with application papers, or notified of an application, should consider (where necessary with the benefit of legal advice) as soon as possible how they wish to respond and what part they wish to play in the proceedings. The Court of Protection Rules 2017[1] (COPR) provide for a number of variations, which will have different consequences for the shape of any proceedings.

10.3 All parties should bear in mind the impact of their behaviour on the costs of the matter – a timely response will be most effective at curbing costs.

Responding to an application

10.4 In proceedings relating to health and welfare, a respondent, or person notified of proceedings, should already be aware of the possibility of proceedings, given the pre-issue obligations imposed upon potential applicants by the COPR Case Pathways Practice Direction (PD) 3B.[2]

10.5 There can, however, be significant variations in the amount of detail provided within an application. The receipt of the application will offer the respondent an opportunity to consider the issues raised by the application and how they may be able to counter them. This is all part of the vital exercise of ensuring the actual issues in the case are identified as quickly and precisely as possible. The receipt of the application may be a useful time to consider not only the evidence that the respondent may be able to provide, but whether there are others in P's life who will be able to provide a helpful perspective as well.

Consenting to an application

10.6 If a person notified, or a respondent, considers that the application is one which is reasonable and that they support, then they can indicate this simply by completing and filing the COP5 form to the effect that

1 SI 2017 No 1035.

2 See: www.judiciary.uk/publications/court-of-protection-practice-directions/.

they agree with the application proposed. This response must be filed with the court within 14 days of service.[3]

10.7 There is no obligation on the part of a person notified or a respondent to make any response to the application, but a failure to do so will not prevent the making of the order that is sought. Respondents or those notified who do not respond will still be bound be the decision of the court as if they had been a party.[4]

10.8 A person who has been notified will not become a party to the proceedings simply by filing a COP5 form consenting to the application. However, if a person notified has taken legal advice before reaching the conclusion that they wish to consent to the application as proposed, it may be appropriate to seek a direction that they be joined as a party to the proceedings only for purposes of seeking to recover their costs,[5] although given that costs are generally not recoverable in welfare proceedings, the circumstances under which it would be sensible to seek such a direction are limited.

10.9 By contrast with proceedings in some other courts, there is no such category as 'interested party' in proceedings before the Court of Protection. A person (or body) is either a party or they are not.[6]

Disputing the court's jurisdiction

10.10 Disputes as to whether permission should be granted are rare, and given that there is now no separate permission stage, it would be an unusual case where it was possible to raise an argument as to permission prior to the court's consideration of the issue. An – unusual, but important – example of where it is appropriate to contest permission is where a proposed party wishes to apply under COPR r13.1 for an order that either (a) the Court of Protection has no jurisdiction to hear an application; or (b) the Court of Protection will not exercise its jurisdiction. Such an application is governed by COPR PD 13A: it should be made on a COP5 form and be accompanied by witness

3 COPR r9.12. Court of Protection forms are available at the Court of Protection Handbook website: https://courtofprotectionhandbook.com/legislation-codes-of-practice-forms-and-guidance/; and the gov.uk website: www.gov.uk/government/collections/court-of-protection-forms

4 COPR r9.14(2), emphasised in *Mrs P v Rochdale BC* [2016] EWCOP B1 at para 26.

5 COPR r19.12.

6 See *Re SK* [2012] EWHC 1990 (COP), [2012] COPLR 712 at para 21.

evidence.[7] One reported example of an application under both of these grounds being made (and succeeding, in fact, on both of these grounds in relation to different aspects of the proceedings that the applicant wished to bring) is that of *Re PO*,[8] a cross-border case (discussed further in chapter 26) in which the local authority in the 'foreign' (Scottish) jurisdiction to which the person in question had been moved wished to dispute the jurisdiction of the Court of Protection on the basis that the person was no longer habitually resident in England and Wales.

10.11 It is possible to make an application under rule 13.1 even after the grant of permission if this was done without a hearing; in this case, the party wishing to make the application would need also to seek a reconsideration of the order under rule 13.4 (see chapter 19). Most applications under rule 13.1 are likely to take such a form; the court would then consider how and when such application should be determined at the case management hearing. It would be open to a party to seek to make an application under rule 13.1 later during the course of proceedings, but the court would wish to see clear evidence as to why the issue was not taken at the outset. An example when this might be appropriate is where it is said that P has either gained or regained the capacity to make the decisions in question: see further paras 12.53–12.56.

Becoming a party

10.12 A person who has been served as a respondent will automatically become a party to proceedings by filing a COP5 form.[9]

10.13 If a respondent wishes to oppose the application or to propose an alternative order, then the acknowledgement of service should be accompanied by a witness statement which contains any evidence upon which the respondent intends to rely.[10] In practice, however, it is not always appropriate or indeed possible to serve a witness statement along with the COP5 form. The respondent may not have access to documents that would support their position. In these circumstances, directions should be sought for the provision of any information that the respondent requires.

7 COPR PD 13A paras 2 and 8.
8 [2013] EWHC 3932 (COP), [2014] COPLR 62.
9 COPR r9.13(1)(b).
10 COPR r9.12(5).

10.14 If a person who is notified wishes to oppose the application, or to propose an alternative order, they must apply to be joined as a party to proceedings. The person does this by indicating their wish to be joined as a party on the COP5 and filing this response with the court within the appropriate timescale. The COP5 must set out the person's reasons for wishing to be a party and should be accompanied by a witness statement setting out his or her interest in the proceedings. The court will decide whether or not to join that person as a party.[11] The relevant test for whether a person should be joined as a party is whether the court considers it desirable for the purpose of deciding the application.[12] If the court approves the application then the person notified will be made a party to proceedings and the applicant will be required to serve them with a copy of the full application papers.

10.15 A person who subsequently becomes aware of an application may apply to become a party. To do so, they must demonstrate 'sufficient interest' in the proceedings.[13] That interest must be a sufficient interest in the proceedings themselves – ie 'the ascertainment of the incapacitated person's best interests' – as opposed to any commercial (or other interest) of the applicant's own.[14] This approach was approved by the former President in *Re G*.[15]

10.16 A person who wishes to be joined as a party must file an application notice (COP9) and a statement explaining his or her interest in the proceedings and – if he intends to ask the court to make an order that is different to the order sought by the applicant – the evidence on which he relies.[16] The person seeking to join should send enough copies of the application for all the parties and the court will serve it.[17] Again, the test will be whether it is desirable to join the person to the proceedings for the purpose of dealing with the application.[18]

11 COPR r9.12(8).
12 COPR r9.13(2).
13 COPR r9.15(1).
14 *Re SK* [2012] EWHC 1990 (COP), [2012] COPLR 712 at paras 41–43 per Bodey J (refusing application by defendant to personal injury proceedings brought by P to be joined to Court of Protection proceedings concerning P).
15 *Re G, London Borough of Redbridge v G (by her litigation friend the Official Solicitor), C and F* [2014] EWCOP 1361, [2014] COPLR 416.
16 COPR r9.15(3).
17 COPR r9.15(4).
18 COPR r9.13(2). For an example of an application being refused in the context of a welfare case, see *KK v Leeds City Council* [2020] EWCOP 64, [2021] COPLR 96, in which Cobb J noted that it would be 'relatively uncommon' for such an application to be refused (see para 48(i)).

Being removed as a party

10.17 It is convenient here to deal with when a party might be removed. There are two circumstances under which a party could be removed:

- The person themselves might want to be. In such a case, they should apply using form COP9.[19] There is no guidance in either the COPR or the accompanying practice directions as to the test that the court will apply (nor are there any reported decisions on the point), but logic suggests that the application will be granted only if the court considers that the continued participation of the person as a party is no longer desirable for the purpose of dealing with the application. As a half-way house, and in line with the overriding objective in COPR r1.1, courts will sometimes allow parties to cease to play any active steps for certain stages in the proceedings where their contribution will not be required at all points (or will provide that the party in question only need file documentation or attend directions hearings 'if so advised').
- Separately, the court has the power to discharge a party on application from *another* party, or if its own motion.[20] However, this power should be exercised with care, especially if the power is to be exercise without notice to the party whose discharge is being completed.[21] Although not, strictly, a decision governed by Mental Capacity Act (MCA) 2005 s1(5), whether P's interests will be served or harmed by the person remaining a party will be major factor in the court's consideration.[22]

Contesting an application

10.18 Careful consideration should be given to the available evidence when considering whether to contest an application, or to suggest an alternative order. Given that the initial case management conference will take place within 28 days of the issue of the proceedings, speed is of the essence here.

19 COPR r9.16.

20 COPR r9.13(2).

21 See *Re P (Discharge of Party)* [2021] EWCA Civ 512, [2021] 1 WLR 3098 at para 65, per Baker LJ.

22 *Re P (Discharge of Party)* [2021] EWCA Civ 512, [2021] 1 WLR 3098 at para 53 per Baker LJ. The subsequent decision in this case, reconsidering the question of the discharge of the party in question (*London Borough of Southwark v P and others* [2021] EWCOP 46) shows the working out of this approach.

10.19 The grounds on which an application may be contested will depend upon the facts of the case and the evidence available. In welfare cases, costs will always be a consideration, as the costs of any contested hearings will (most likely) be met out of the resources of the parties themselves.[23] This does not mean that genuinely contested applications should not be fully explored and prepared. Clearly, if after careful investigations and taking material from potential witnesses the adviser reaches the view that contesting an application will not succeed, then the adviser must give their client the appropriate advice. However, in welfare cases, families seeking to oppose the removal of P – or to seek P's return – must be given the opportunity fully to put their case to the court or their own rights under the European Convention on Human Rights (ECHR) Articles 8 (right to respect for private and family life) and indeed 6 (right to a fair trial) may be compromised. In deciding whether the case is one that should be contested, it is in the authors' experience often useful to look outside the areas of dispute between the applicant, often a statutory body, and the respondent(s), often family member(s) caring for P. In such a case, the following questions can usefully be considered at this very early stage:

- What does the party think that P would want to happen?
- What were the care arrangements for P before the dispute arose? Has anything changed (for example, was additional support given by another carer who has died or moved away)?
- Has there been any change in the amount of support provided to P by the relevant statutory bodies?
- Who are the other important individuals in P's life apart from the respondent and members of the relevant statutory body? Can any of them provide evidence about positive aspects of P's care (past or current)? What, if anything, can they say about P's likes and dislikes and what is important to P?
- If the relationship between the respondent and the statutory body is currently poor, has this always been the case? Is the respondent in contact with any professionals with whom they have worked well in the past?
- Is evidence needed about any cultural issues or expectations? Who might be able to provide such evidence?
- Are there likely to be significant disputes of fact? If so, what evidence needs to be gathered to corroborate the respondent's case?

23 COPR r19.3; see also chapter 16.

- Is it likely that expert evidence may be needed? It may not be possible on receipt of an application to make this judgment. However, once the need for an expert is identified by any party, they would be well advised to make enquiries as soon as possible about the costs and availability of suitable experts. This subject is discussed in detail in chapter 13.

10.20 In all cases, the relevance of the information put before the court both in the application and in any potential response should always be considered.

10.21 The authors further suggest that parties should seek to maintain a flexible approach, focused on P's best interests and avoid entrenched positions as far as possible. This allows alternative options to be explored by way of mediation (see chapter 20), and may help to avoid incurring the expense of attended court hearing(s).

10.22 Advisers should, however, be alert to the danger of attempting to persuade parties to take an approach that fundamentally they do not agree with. In a welfare case, for instance, a family carer recently served with an application seeking a draconian step in relation to P should of course be given the opportunity to consider the benefits of consenting at an early stage. However, advisers will not at that stage have gathered all the available evidence that might point away from the application. It is important that advisers are scrupulous in following their client's instructions and gathering evidence that may support their position. Advisers will need to be astute to making clear to the court at the case management conference why more time may be required, and to giving a clear time-frame within the task is to be carried out.

10.23 If the parties are able to reach a negotiated way forward that represents a compromise between the position advocated by the applicant and that desired by the respondent(s), the court should be notified and a consent order submitted, with each party or their legal representative confirming their consent to the order as agreed: see further in this regard para 11.56.

10.24 If the parties cannot agree a negotiated way forward, the court will proceed to determine how best to put itself in a position to reach a conclusion. This is discussed in chapter 11.

CHAPTER 11

Interim hearings and interim applications

continued

Introduction

11.1 In all applications which require consideration by a judge at a hearing (as opposed to a decision made on the papers), there will be at least one and often several, hearings before a final decision is made. At these hearings, the court will both be:

- setting down the steps necessary for the determination of the central issues in the case; and
- making such interim declarations and decisions under the provisions of Mental Capacity Act (MCA) 2005 s48[1] as are necessary to secure P's interests pending the final determination of those central issues.

11.2 This chapter addresses both aspects of such hearings, as well as addressing the (related) issue of making applications during the course of proceedings. It focuses on the procedures applicable to interim hearings in cases allocated to a pathway under the Court of Protection Rules 2017[2] (COPR) and Case Pathways Practice Direction (PD) 3B.[3] The main categories of case in which interim hearings are likely and which are not on a pathway are deprivation of liberty (covered in chapter 22). Cases relating to serious medical treatment are also approached differently even if they are, strictly, on the welfare pathway. The specific issues that arise in relation to such cases are addressed in the relevant chapter. The nature of both types of case is that the urgency of the circumstances giving rise to the application may make compliance with the pre-issue stage in COPR PD 3B impossible. However, in all cases the pre-issue requirements represent good practice and should be adhered to where possible.

11.3 The chapter does not address dispute resolution hearings (DRHs), which are an important feature of the property and affairs pathway.[4] These are covered at para 8.32 onwards.

1 See para 11.6 below.

2 SI 2017 No 1035.

3 See: www.judiciary.uk/publications/court-of-protection-practice-directions/.

4 COPR Case Pathways PD 3B para 3.4.

The jurisdiction of the court to make interim orders and give directions

11.4 Where an application has been made, the court has jurisdiction to exercise its powers on an interim basis to make orders and give directions where:

- there is reason to believe that P lacks capacity in relation to the matter;
- the matter is one to which its powers under the MCA 2005 extend; and
- it is in P's best interests to make the order, or give the directions, without delay.[5]

11.5 There has been conflicting case-law in relation to the first of these requirements.[6] The case-law was reviewed by Hayden J in *DP v Hillingdon LBC*.[7] He made clear that the words in MCA 2005 s48 require no gloss, such that the question remains throughout: is there reason to believe that the person lacks capacity? That question, he observed at para 62, stimulates 'an evidential enquiry in which the entire canvas of the available evidence requires to be scrutinised', and in which the presumption of capacity applies with equal force. He further distinguished between the test in MCA 2005 s48 and the test in section 15. The former, he considered, requires a focus on whether the evidence establishes reasonable grounds to believe that the person lacks capacity. The latter requires an evaluation as to whether the person, in fact, lacks capacity.

11.6 If the court makes an order under MCA 2005 s48, it should use the following recital:[8]

> The Court is satisfied that there is reason to believe, for the purposes of section 48 of the Mental Capacity Act 2005, that [P] lacks capacity to:
> (1) conduct these proceedings;
> (2) make decisions about . . .
> and that it is in [P]'s best interests to make this order without delay.

5 MCA 2005 s48(a)–(c).

6 A particular tension being between *Re F* [2009] EWHC B30 (COP), [2009] COPLR Con Vol 390; and *London Borough of Wandsworth v M and others* [2017] EWHC 2435 (Fam), [2017] 4 WLR 180, [2018] COPLR 71.

7 [2020] EWCOP 45, [2020] COPLR 769.

8 See also the precedent orders on the Court of Protection Handbook website: https://courtofprotectionhandbook.com/precedents/.

11.7 While MCA 2005 s48 only talks of 'orders' and 'directions', this includes decisions as to such matters as to where P should live or who P should have contact with. In that the threshold is crossed, the court can – and will very often – make interim decisions to 'hold the ring' pending the final determination of the application before it. To emphasise the limited basis upon which they are made, orders made under section 48 should be phrased on the following basis:

> The Court is satisfied that there is reason to believe, for the purposes of section 48 of the Mental Capacity Act 2005, that [P] lacks capacity to:
> (1) conduct these proceedings;
> (2) make decisions about . . .
> and that it is in [P]'s best interests to make this order without delay.

11.8 There have sometimes been questions about whether it is possible to appeal against the court's interim inclusion as to the person's decision-making capacity. However, the recording of the section 48 'precondition' in the order should suffice to enable any appeal to be brought against the court's conclusion in this regard. In any event, in most cases, any appeal would be unlikely to be against the interim conclusions as to capacity, but any substantive orders made on the basis of that conclusion.

11.9 While, in practice, it is often the case that orders made under section 48 will be in place for a sustained period of time, the fact remains that they are made without a final determination of whether or not P lacks capacity to make the decisions in question. Care should always be taken to ensure that they give rise to the most minimal intrusion possible into P's life consistent with securing their interests.[9]

Case management

The overriding objective

11.10 COPR Part 1 has significantly strengthened the duties upon the court and the parties (and their legal representatives) to secure the overriding objective of enabling the court to deal with a case justly. It has also introduced a new element to the overriding objective of enabling the court to deal with cases at proportionate cost.

9 See, in the medical treatment context; *University Hospitals of Derby and Burton NHS Foundation Trust and Derbyshire Healthcare NHS Foundation Trust v MN* [2021] EWCOP 4.

11.11 There are now specific duties to further the overriding objective upon the court, the parties, legal representatives and unrepresented litigants, each of which we examine briefly in turn.

11.12 The **court** has a duty under COPR r1.3 actively to manage cases at all times, and in particular at certain key points such as the referral of the case file to a judge, at every hearing, and at all stages of a final hearing.[10] Key aspects of the duty include:

- ensuring that the appropriate judge is allocated to the case and judicial continuity so far as practicable;
- avoiding delay and keeping costs down;
- encouraging the parties to co-operate with each other in the conduct of the proceedings;
- identifying at an early stage the issues and who should be a party to the proceedings;
- deciding promptly which issues need a full investigation and hearing and which do not, and the procedure to be followed in the case;
- deciding the order in which issues are to be resolved;
- encouraging the parties to use an alternative dispute resolution procedure if the court considers that appropriate;
- fixing timetables or otherwise controlling the progress of the case;
- considering whether the likely benefits of taking a particular step justify the cost of taking it;
- dealing with as many aspects of the case as the court can on the same occasion;
- dealing with the case without the parties needing to attend at court;
- making use of technology; and
- giving directions to ensure that the case proceeds quickly and efficiently.

11.13 The avoidance of delay has been identified as being of particular importance. As Hayden J identified in *London Borough of Southwark v NP and others*:[11]

> Though the avoidance of delay is not prescribed by the Mental Capacity Act 2005, the precept should be read in to the proceedings as a facet of Article 6 ECHR [European Convention on Human Rights . . . Any avoidable delay is likely to be inimical to P's best interests.

10 COPR r1.3(2).

11 [2019] EWCOP 48, [2019] 4 WLR 141 at para 31.

11.14 The **parties** have a duty to help the court further the overriding objective,[12] a particularly important aspect of which is the requirement actively to ask the court to take steps to manage a case if it appears that an order or direction of the court appears not to deal with an issue, or a new circumstance, issue or dispute arises of which the court is unaware.[13] It is important to note that the court can take into account a failure without reasonable excuse to comply with the duty imposed by COPR r1.4 when deciding whether or not to depart from the general rules as to costs (see further chapter 17).

11.15 **Legal representatives** have their own specific duty to help the court further the overriding objective.[14] This does not override their duty to their clients, but does emphasise the extent to which they have obligations to the court as to how they conduct the proceedings.[15]

11.16 **Unrepresented litigants** are under a duty to help the court further the over-riding objective. This includes engaging with the process which is applicable to the case; co-operating with the court and other parties; seeking the court's direction if an issue or dispute arises and presenting their case fairly.[16]

The powers of the court

11.17 To enable it to further the overriding objective, the court is given general powers of case management by COPR r3.1 which details a wide-ranging suite of tools that judges can deploy, tools which (unsurprisingly) match closely the obligations imposed by COPR r1.3. COPR r3.2 addresses how the fact that one or more party may be unrepresented may affect the steps the court takes to further the over-riding objective. Judges are given added flexibility by COPR r3.6, which provides that, in addition to its general powers and those listed in COPR r3.1, the court may dispense with the requirement of any rule. COPR r3.7 then provides the court with specific powers to make directions.

11.18 The powers of a court at a directions hearing are therefore very wide. They extend as far as determining a case summarily upon its

12 COPR r1.4.

13 COPR r1.4(2)(a).

14 COPR r1.5.

15 See also in this regard *R v Farooqi and others* [2013] EWCA Crim 1649, [2014] 1 Cr App R 69 at para 108 and also para 15.32.

16 COPR r1.6.

own motion, but that jurisdiction 'must be exercised appropriately and with a modicum of restraint': *KD and LD v Havering LBC*,[17] in which an appeal was allowed where the district judge brought proceedings to an end summarily before a best interests report (which the judge had previously directed be prepared) was filed.

11.19 Authorised officers of the court may exercise certain case management powers in (broadly) non-contentious applications relating to property and affairs.[18] Authorised court officers may not conduct a hearing, and must refer to a judge any application or any question arising in any application which is contentious or which, in the opinion of the officer:

- is complex;
- requires a hearing; or
- for any other reason ought to be considered by a judge.

As this chapter is for the most part concerned with case management hearings, the powers of authorised officers are not addressed further here.

Initial case management

11.20 Judges will make a significant number of initial directions upon consideration of the papers (and, where the grant of permission is required, at the same time as granting permission).[19] For cases on the personal welfare pathway, the COPR Case Pathways PD 3B specifically provides for judges to make a number of important decisions on the papers at the point of issues, including:

- gatekeeping (ie allocating the case to the right level of judge);[20]
- listing for a case management conference within 28 days, unless the matter is urgent, in which case consideration must be given as to whether it is a case which should be allocated to a Tier 3[21] (ie a High Court or equivalent) judge;

17 [2009] COPLR Con Vol 770, (2009) 12 CCLR 671 at para 28 per HHJ Horowitz QC.

18 COPR r2.3.

19 The express power to do so is contained in COPR r3.7(1)(a).

20 For example, in *Manchester City Council Legal Services v LC and KR* [2018] EWHC 2849 (Fam), [2019] COPLR 38 at para 24, Hayden J said that cases concerning measures in areas where P lacks capacity which impinge on P's autonomy in areas where P *has* capacity should be heard in the High Court.

21 See para 19.11 in relation to the tiering of judges in the Court of Protection.

- considering whether it is necessary that P be joined as a party (as to which see further chapter 12 below) and if so make decisions about what details of P's estate should be disclosed for funding purposes;
- considering whether an advocates meeting is required before the case management hearing and ordering such a meeting if appropriate; and
- ordering the preparation of a core bundle (not usually to exceed 150 pages) for the case management conference.[22]

11.21 For cases on the property and affairs pathway, the judge will list the case for a Dispute Resolution Hearing (see further chapter 8 above), or transfer the case to the most appropriate regional court outside the Central Office and Registry for listing of the Dispute Resolution Hearing and future case management.[23] The judge will also order the respondent(s) to file a summary of the reasons for opposing the application or for seeking a different order if the reasons are not clear from the COP5 form submitted.[24] Where the matter is urgent, the judge may either list for an urgent DRH, or list an interim hearing to decide the urgent matter(s) in the case.[25]

11.22 In mixed cases, the judge will on the papers either allocate it to a specific pathway, and give directions accordingly, or give directions as to which elements of each pathway are to apply and the procedure that the case will follow.[26]

11.23 Anyone affected by an order made without a hearing has an automatic right to seek review of such orders by virtue of COPR r13.4 (see paras 19.3–19.8), but such review will inevitably add delay and expense. So as to avoid unnecessary delay, it is therefore important when making an application to ensure that it is clear on the face either:

- any of the 'standard' directions are inapplicable; or
- any unusual directions are required at the outset.

Case management on the personal welfare pathway

11.24 The court must list a case management hearing within 28 days (unless the matter is urgent, as to which see further paras 11.74–11.81

22 COPR Case Pathways PD 3B para 2.4(1).
23 COPR Case Pathways PD 3B para 3.3(1).
24 COPR Case Pathways PD 3B para 3.3(2).
25 COPR Case Pathways PD 3B para 3.6(3).
26 COPR Case Pathways PD 3B para 4.1(3).

below).[27] The COPR Case Pathways PD 3B then specifies in some detail what the court is expected to do at that Case Management Conference.[28] The most important tasks for the judge include:

- Decide – and record – which issues are in dispute, what has been agreed between the parties, and what issues are not to be the subject of adjudication.[29] The then-President of the Court of Protection, Sir James Munby, called for a 'culture change' in the Court of Protection[30] and judges have been under significant pressure to be much more robust about only allowing the key issues in any case to go forward for determination. The importance of avoiding delay was noted at para 11.11 above. Judges are astute to the fact that a:

  > . . . common driver of delay and expense is the search for the ideal solution, leading to decent but imperfect outcomes being rejected . . . the requirement in Section 1(5) of the Mental Capacity Act 2005 that 'An act done, or decision made, under this Act for or on behalf of a person who lacks capacity must be done, or made, in his best interests' calls for a sensible decision, not the pursuit of perfection.[31]

  - To take a practical example: if the application is for a decision that an adult with learning disabilities should no longer live at the family home but in a residential placement, the key issues for the court will be the 'macro' issues of 1) the adult's future residence; and 2) (likely) whether they should have contact with their family. The judge will not be expected to wish to list for determination the 'micro' elements of the day-to-day care arrangements for the adult at the placement.
- Allocate a judge to the case, judicial continuity being recognised as one of the key drivers to ensuring that cases are resolved proportionately.
- Decide how P is to participate in the proceedings (see further chapter 12). If that participation is to include a visit by the judge to P, specific considerations will arise, addressed in chapter 16.[32]

27 COPR Case Pathways PD 3B para 2.4(1)(b).

28 COPR Case Pathways PD 3B para 2.5.

29 COPR Case Pathways PD 3B para 2.5(a)–(e).

30 *Re MN* [2015] EWCA Civ 411, [2016] Fam 87, (2015) 18 CCLR 521.

31 *Re A and B (Court of Protection: Delay and Costs)* [2014] EWCOP 48, [2015] COPLR 1 at para 14. See also *Hounslow LBC v A Mother and A Father* [2018] EWCOP 23.

32 See also *Practice Guidance (Court of Protection: Judicial visits)* [2022] EWCOP 5, [2022] 1 WLR 1445 and *Re AH (Serious Medical Treatment)* [2021] EWCA Civ 1768, [2022] COPLR 253.

- Consider the evidence required, and in particular, whether an MCA 2005 s49 report or a COPR r1.2 representative (see para 12.6) could achieve a better result than an expert. (As to evidence see chapter 13).
- Fix a date for the final management hearing and set a target date for the final hearing (or a trial window).

11.25 The personal welfare pathway also provides that there should be a final management hearing at which the court can decide whether the case can be resolved, and, if not, to give directions for the proper preparation of the final hearing.[33] Importantly, at least five days before the final management hearing, COPR Case Pathways PD 3B expects that a meeting will take place between the advocates and (so far as practicable) any unrepresented parties with the purpose of resolving or narrowing the issues to be decided at the final management hearing.[34] Unless otherwise directed, a further advocates' meeting is then to be held no less than five days before the final hearing.[35] Advocates' meetings are discussed in more detail at paras 11.52–11.56.

Applications during proceedings

11.26 Even within the much tighter structure envisaged by the COPR Case Pathways PD 3B, a party may well need to make an application during the proceedings either for additional directions, or for interim relief, most usually by way of declarations or decisions relating to P (interim relief is considered further at para 11.67 onwards below). Not all applications will need to be determined at a hearing, many can be made on the papers (often by consent).

11.27 The procedure for making an application within proceedings is set out in COPR Part 10, as well as in PD 10A. Note that an application under Part 10 may be made by a person who is not yet a party (but who, for example, wishes to be joined as one).[36] Part 10 of the Rules also covers the position in respect of urgent applications (as to which, see further para 11.74 onwards below). In short, when making an application, it is necessary to file an application notice (on a form COP9)[37] setting out the order or direction the applicant seeks and the

33 COPR Case Pathways PD 3B para 2.6(1).
34 COPR Case Pathways PD 3B para 2.6(2).
35 COPR Case Pathways PD 3B para 2.7(1).
36 COPR r10.1(2), PD 10A.
37 COPR r10.2(1).

grounds on which it is sought.[38] Where an unusually long or complex order is sought, an electronic copy should be provided; COPR PD 10A provides that this should be done on a disk:[39] almost invariably, however, email is now used. The applicant should also file the evidence upon which they rely unless it is already before the court.[40] The court has the power to dispense with the need to file an application notice (for instance, by treating a letter sent during the currency of proceedings as if it were an application).[41]

11.28 As a general rule, it is necessary for the applicant to serve a copy of the application notice on anyone named as a respondent in the application notice, every party to the proceedings and on any other person directed by the court, as soon as practicable and in any event within 14 days of service.[42] The application notice must be accompanied by a copy of the evidence filed in support,[43] and the applicant must file a COP20 certificate of service within seven days of the date on which documents were served;[44] where a person has already been served with evidence, the applicant does not need to file a further copy of such evidence but should instead give notice of the evidence upon which they intend to rely.[45] The applicant can dispense with service only where there is exceptional urgency, where the overriding objective is best served by so doing, by consent of all the parties, with the permission of the court, or where a rule or other practice direction permits (the material practice direction here being COPR PD 10B).[46] Where the applicant has dispensed with service, the court can nonetheless still direct that service should be effected and specify who should be served with or notified of the application.[47]

11.29 Wherever possible, an application should be made so as that it can be considered at a hearing which is already listed.[48] If a hearing

38 COPR r10.3. COPR r10.3(c) refers to information being required by a practice direction; PD 10A provides that certain basic information (for instance, the case number) is required, but does not materially add to the requirements.

39 COPR PD 10A para 4.

40 COPR r10.2(2).

41 COPR r10.2(5).

42 COPR r10.4(1).

43 COPR r10.4(2).

44 COPR r10.4(3).

45 COPR r10.4(4).

46 COPR PD 10A para 9.

47 COPR PD 10A para 11.

48 COPR PD 10A para 15.

date has already been fixed and a party wishes to make an application at that hearing but does not have sufficient time in which to file an application notice, COPR PD 10A provides that the applicant should inform the court (in writing if possible) and, if possible, the other parties as soon as they can of the nature of the application and the reason for it, and should then make the application orally at the hearing.[49]

11.30 Parties should also be aware of the power under COPR r3.7(4)[50] to vary the time specified for a person to 'do any act' either by the rules or the practice directions or the court, by the written agreement of the parties. This cannot be used to vary the date of a final hearing or to vary the period within which a final hearing can take place. This will always require an application to the court.[51] Nor can it be used if the outcome of the variation would require variation of the date of the final hearing or the period in which the final hearing takes place.[52] However if – for example – it becomes clear that the timetable set by the court for the filing of evidence is unlikely to be met, and the parties agreed to vary it, a consent order recording that agreement pursuant to COPR r3.7(4)[53] could be filed at court, thus avoiding the need for an application.

Interim hearings: general provisions

11.31 However they have been listed, interim hearings will usually be listed for between 30 minutes and one hour, and it is very common for a direction to be made that parties are to attend one hour before for purposes of discussions. As set out further below, such discussions can be immensely productive, and every effort should be made to attend in good time for such discussions. In the case of final management hearings on the personal welfare pathway, this requirement has been strengthened by the introduction of mandatory meetings between advocates (and, so far as practicable, any unrepresented parties) in advance of the hearing.[54]

49 COPR PD 10A para 16.
50 COPR r3.7(4).
51 COPR r3.7(5).
52 COPR r3.7(6).
53 COPR r3.7(6)
54 COPR Case Pathways PD 3B para 2.6(2).

11.32 Interim hearings can also take place by telephone or video-link.[55] The vast majority took place remotely during the COVID-19 pandemic; at the time of writing, and as the public health factors pointing towards remote hearings have changed, the court is still calibrating its position. It is likely, however, that interim hearings will be remote in many cases. We deal separately with the considerations that arise in relation to both in-person and remote hearings below (at paras 11.58–11.60 and 11.61 respectively). It is particularly important to draw to the court's attention any specific matters that may militate towards either a remote or an-person hearing being limited.

11.33 Any interim hearing on a case falling within the COPR Transparency PD 4C (as to which, see further chapter 14) will be held in public.

Practice Direction 4B

11.34 COPR Court Bundles PD 4B deals with court bundles and applies expressly to final management hearings.[56] It will also apply whenever a hearing is listed for more than an hour before a district or circuit judge, and whenever it is listed before the President of the Family Division, the Chancellor or a High Court Judge sitting as a judge of the Court of Protection. The practice direction applies to directions hearings, interim hearings and also final hearings, with the exception of any urgent application if and to the extent that it is impractical to comply with it. Even where the practice direction does not strictly apply (for instance, in relation to a 30-minute directions hearing before a district judge), the principles that it sets down should still be adhered to where possible so as to maximise the effectiveness of the hearing.

11.35 Where PD 4B does apply, para 12 of the practice direction makes clear the penalty for failure to comply with any part of it may result in the judge removing the case from the list or moving it further back in the list, as well as adverse costs orders.

11.36 For present purposes, the two most important aspects of PD 4B are those relating to the preparation of the bundle, and the preparation of the so-called preliminary documents to accompany the bundle. Each of these is discussed in turn below.

55 COPR r3.1(2)(d). See also PD 10A paras 18–21 in respect of applications made within proceedings.

56 COPR Case Pathways PD 3B para 2.6(3).

Bundles

11.37 The general rule is that the party which is the applicant at the hearing (or the first applicant if there is more than one application) has the responsibility for producing the bundle for the use of the court at that hearing.[57] However, if that person is a litigant in person, then subject to any direction by the court, the responsibility falls upon the first listed respondent who is not a litigant in person or P.[58] If the first named respondent is P and they are represented by the Official Solicitor, the responsibility for preparing the bundle will fall to the next named respondent who is represented.[59] It is suggested that the same should apply if a litigation friend other than the Official Solicitor has been appointed to act on P's behalf.

11.38 If possible, the contents of the bundle must be agreed by all parties.[60] This can cause difficulties where one or more of the parties is a litigant in person (especially if they do not have access to a computer for purposes of reviewing and commenting upon a draft index). In such cases, while reasonable steps should be taken to try to agree the index with the litigant in person, a decision will need to be taken as to a cut-off point after which the process of agreement should be completed by the represented parties. PD 4B provides a timetable for the process of preparing and lodging the bundle, thus:

- The party preparing the bundle must (whether or not it has been agreed) provide a paginated index and, where practicable, paginated copies of material additional to that provided with the original application, to all other parties not less than five working days before the hearing.[61] It should be noted that this does not mean that a new, complete, bundle be supplied to each party in advance of a hearing, but experience has taught that it is much better for paginated copies of additional material to be supplied rather than relying upon parties to paginate their additional documents themselves. In such cases, it is almost invariably the case that at least one of the parties will end up operating from a differently paginated bundle at the hearing, with consequential delays and judicial frustration.

57 COPR PD 4B para 3.1.
58 COPR PD 4B para 3.1.
59 COPR PD 4B para 3.1.
60 COPR PD 4B para 3.3.
61 COPR PD 4B para 6.1.

- Where counsel is to be instructed at any hearing, then if the bundle is not already in counsel's possession, the bundle must be provided to counsel by the person instructing that counsel not less than four working days before the hearing.[62]
- The bundle (with the exception of the preliminary documents if they are not then available) must be lodged with the court not less than three working days prior to the hearing, unless some other time has been specified by the judge.[63] Specific provisions are set out as to the appropriate office for lodging the bundle dependent on where the case is to be heard. It is always strongly advisable to confirm by telephone the day before the hearing with the relevant office whether the bundle has been received,[64] as it is sadly very common for bundles to go astray in the system.

11.39 Bundles should contain copies of all documents relevant to the hearing in chronological order, indexed and divided into separate sections.[65] They should also be paginated, either within the sections or separately – it is much better to paginate within sections because this allows for easier updating of the bundle. The sections required are as follows:

- preliminary documents (discussed at para 11.33 below);
- case management documents required by any other practice direction (in practice, at present, there are no such documents);
- applications and orders including all Court of Protection forms filed with the application;
- any registered, enduring or lasting power of attorney;
- any urgent or standard authorisation given under MCA 2005 Sch A1 (ie authorising a deprivation of P's liberty in a hospital or care home);
- statements and affidavits (which must state on the top right-hand corner of the front page the date when it was signed or sworn[66]);
- care plans (where appropriate[67]);
- experts' reports and other reports;[68]
- other documents, divided into further sections as may be appropriate.

62 COPR PD 4B para 6.2.
63 COPR PD 4B para 6.3.
64 Useful telephone numbers are given in appendix G below.
65 COPR PD 4B para 4.1.
66 See further para 13.14.
67 See further para 13.14 and appendix E.
68 See further para 13.56.

11.40 Physical bundles should be contained in one or more A4-size ring-binders or lever-arch files (each lever-arch file being limited to 350 pages), clearly marked on the front and the spine with the title and the number of the case, the court where the case has been listed, the hearing date and time, (if known) the name of the judge hearing the case, and where there is more than one ring-binder or lever-arch file, a distinguishing letter or number and confirmation of the total number of binders or files (eg '1 of 3' etc).[69] It is *not* advisable to prepare even short bundles using treasury tags, because it makes it very difficult for the parties and the judge to take out or insert documents.

Electronic bundles

11.41 The COVID-19 pandemic has accelerated the move towards electronic bundles. Used properly, they can be extremely helpful, but they bring with them their own problems. The Vice-President issued guidance in March 2020 which continues to govern the position in default of an updated practice direction.[70] Its key provisions are as follows:

- Electronic bundles are the default for remote hearings, with no requirement for a physical bundle to be lodged.[71]
- The parties must agree, and the lead party must prepare and send to the court, an electronic bundle of documents for each remote hearing. The electronic bundle must be prepared by somebody with adequate knowledge of the case.
- The following requirements must be followed:[72]
  - PDF format is to be used;
  - all documents are to be contained, if possible, within one single PDF file and with pagination;
  - electronic bundles should contain only documents and authorities that are essential to the issues required to be decided at the remote hearing;
  - the electronic bundle must be filed with the court by email;

69 COPR PD 4B paras 5.1–5.2.

70 Available at: www.judiciary.uk/coronavirus-covid-19-advice-and-guidance/20200331-court-of-protection-remote-hearings-2/.

71 Paras 90–91, the template orders being made by the Court of Protection at the outset of proceedings disapplying COPR PD 4B paras 5, 7 and 8.

72 Para 93.

  - o all position statements/skeleton arguments should also be separately filed by email in a Microsoft Word format (see para 11.44 below for position statements).
- Where it is practical, the court's preference is that:[73]
  - o pagination be computer generated within the PDF, not hand-written;
  - o each section of the bundle, and each individual document referenced in the index, should be separately bookmarked;
  - o the PDF file be searchable;
  - o the index should be hyperlinked to the documents.

11.42 While an electronic bundle is almost invariably used, consideration should always be given to whether this will have the effect of excluding any of the parties, especially those in person. In practice, either the relevant statutory body or P's Accredited Legal Representative or litigation friend will usually arrange provision of a paper bundle if this is the only way an unrepresented party will be able to have meaningful access to it.

11.43 Whether physical or electronic, the key principle is that the bundle should contain those documents relevant to the specific hearing in question, but should not contain *more* than those documents. Especially where a matter has been ongoing for a considerable period of time, the documents generated in the proceedings can start to run to a (significant) number of lever-arch files: it may very well not be necessary for all of the documents in all of the files to be before the court on each occasion, and having too many before the court will slow the process down. In this regard, it is useful to have in mind that for cases on the welfare pathway under the Case Pathways PD 3B, the bundle prepared for the final hearing in the case must ultimately not only comply with these provisions, but also must: (1) not generally exceed 350 pages; and (2) in any event must not contain more than one copy of the same document.[74]

Preliminary documents and position statements

11.44 For directions and interim hearings to which COPR PD 4B applies, each party (ie not just the applicant) *must* prepare a document (or documents) which sets out – either within the document(s) or by

73 Para 93.

74 COPR Case Pathways PD 3B para 2.7(2).

cross-reference to another document that will be in the bundle before the court:

- a case summary;
- a chronology of relevant events;
- the issues for determination at the hearing;
- an outline of the likely factual and legal issues at the trial of the case;
- the relief sought at the hearing; and
- a list of essential reading.[75]

11.45 In practice, this information is most usually set out in a 'position statement' (a term which does not appear in PD 4B, but which is common currency before the court and will be used here). Position statements are vital documents, and should be prepared even if PD 4B does not strictly apply.

11.46 Directions regularly provide that position statements should be limited, often to no more than a page. Especially in the case of a position statement prepared on behalf of the applicant at a hearing, it can, though, frequently be difficult properly to encapsulate the necessary information in so short a space. If the position statement runs to more than two or three pages, a clear introduction should be given which sets out a route map so that the judge can identify clearly where the necessary information will be found in the statement. A sample position statement is to be found at appendix D below.

11.47 COPR PD 4B goes on to provide that 'where appropriate', the preliminary documents for a directions or interim hearing should include:

- a description of relevant family members and other persons who may be affected by or interested in the relief sought;
- a particularised account of the issues in the case;
- the legal propositions relied on, and in particular whether it is asserted that any issue is not governed by the MCA 2005;
- any directions sought concerning the identification and determination of the facts that are agreed, the facts the court will be invited to find and the factors it will be invited to take into account based on such agreed facts or findings of facts;
- any directions sought concerning the alternatives the court will be invited to consider in determining what is in P's best interests;

75 COPR PD 4B para 4.2. Case Pathways PD 3B para 2.6(3) draws the particular attention of those preparing for final management hearings to these provisions.

- any directions sought relating to expert evidence;
- any other directions sought; and
- a skeleton argument.[76]

11.48 These requirements stem from the judgment of Charles J in *A Local Authority v PB and P*,[77] in which the judge made clear that the direction of preparation of position statements and skeleton arguments 'at an appropriate stage' containing this information will be necessary in most welfare cases.[78] The *PB and P* case raised complex questions as to the scope of the jurisdiction of the Court of Protection, and the directions that were made in it therefore were arguably more extensive than will be required in many cases. Nonetheless, where PD 4B applies, it is incumbent upon the person preparing the preliminary document to consider whether it is appropriate to include each of the types of information set out above.

11.49 In almost all cases, and whether or not PD 4B strictly applies, it is advisable for the position statement to be accompanied by a draft of the directions that the court will be asked to make. This will be important not just so that the court can see precisely what is being asked of it, but also so that the other parties can have sight in advance of the draft of the directions and – potentially – so that agreement can be reached upon the basis of one of the drafts.

11.50 Whenever a directions hearing has been listed, the directions will usually provide a specific point by which the preliminary documents should be filed (whether by reference to a specific date or the period before the hearing). It is always advisable, wherever possible, for the preliminary documents to be served upon the other parties in advance of this deadline so that the process of negotiation can begin quickly.

11.51 For final management hearings, the core bundle complying with the requirements of PD 4B must be filed no later than three days before the hearing.[79] Otherwise, where PD 4B applies, the preliminary documents (and any documents referred to in them which are not already in the bundle) must be lodged with the court no later than 11am on the day before the hearing.[80] PD 4B provides that they should also be sent by email to the judge's clerk where the hearing is before a High Court judge and the judge's name is known;[81] most of

76 COPR PD 4B para 4.3.
77 [2011] EWHC 502 (Fam), [2011] COPLR Con Vol 166.
78 Para 46.
79 COPR Case Pathways PD 3B para 2.6(3).
80 COPR PD 4B para 6.4.
81 COPR PD 4B para 6.4.

the courts in which directions hearings are heard now also have dedicated email addresses for this purpose.[82] It is always better to err on the side of caution as regards lodging preliminary documents and to seek to ensure (for instance) that they have been sent both by fax and by email. Even where PD 4B does not apply, it is in any event *strongly* advisable that care is taken to make sure that the documents are with the court by 11am the day before.

Making effective use of court time

The advocates' meeting

11.52 The COPR Case Pathways PD 3B has introduced a specific requirement for advocates' meetings for cases on the personal welfare pathway.[83] Such meetings are to be held both with the legal representatives for the parties and, wherever practicable, any unrepresented parties. Their specific purpose is:

- to resolve or narrow the issues to be determined at the final management hearing, to address the case and bundle preparation matters set down in PD 4B (see above) and to produce a draft order;[84]
- to resolve or narrow the issues to be determined at the final hearing.[85]

11.53 Experience suggests that advocates' meetings are likely to be most effective where:

- the advocates instructed are those with conduct of the case;
- one party's representative (often that instructed by the Official Solicitor if the Official Solicitor is acting on behalf of P) takes the lead in setting the agenda by identifying areas of agreement and disagreement;
- one party's representative takes the lead in taking a note of the order as it evolves;
- areas where agreement will not be reached are parked quickly, with an agreement to raise them before the judge;

82 Useful addresses are given in appendix G below.
83 COPR Case Pathways PD 3B para 2.6(2).
84 COPR Case Pathways PD 3B para 2.6(2).
85 COPR Case Pathways PD 3B para 2.7(1). Note that an advocates' meeting must be held at least five days prior to the final hearing unless the court orders to the contrary.

- arrangements have been made in advance to make sure that, where information may be needed from (for instance) a social worker that social worker will be easily contactable so that information can be provided quickly;
- where interim relief is being negotiated (for instance, as to contact restrictions or the interim management of P's property and affairs), a clear distinction is drawn between discussions as to the progression of the case and negotiations as to such relief and sufficient time is allocated to both. In many cases, what (say) the family members will be most concerned about will be about the interim relief, whereas what will actually be most important for the speedy resolution of the application as a whole will be negotiations as to case management orders. If all parties are represented by solicitors and counsel, it can sometimes be possible for both sets of negotiations to be taking place simultaneously, but in such circumstances it is important that all those involved in one set of negotiations are clear as to what the other part of the legal team will be doing.

11.54 Careful thought and preparation – and chairing – will be required wherever one or more of the parties attending is unrepresented. It may in such cases be sensible to have a 'pre-meeting' beforehand between the legal representatives.

11.55 Advocates' meetings can take place remotely but the following additional points need to be considered:

- ensuring that any unrepresented party is able meaningfully to take part; and
- ensuring that sufficient time is allowed.

11.56 If complete agreement is reached, then a consent order should be submitted for endorsement. Such a consent order should be submitted with an application on COP9 outlining a short background summary of the case, the written details of each party who consents, and enough information to allow the court to decide whether to take the case out of the list and whether to make the proposed order.[86] Where not all parties consent, an order can still be submitted together with details of the steps taken to obtain that party's consent and, where known, an explanation of why that consent has not been given.[87] The likelihood of the court endorsing an order in such

86 COPR PD 4B para 11. This will apply by analogy given the wording of Case Pathways PD 3B para 2.6(2).

87 COPR PD 4B para 11.

circumstances will depend greatly on whether: a) it has not been possible to contact the person to obtain their consent (for instance, because they are a litigant in person who has not given the proper contact details); or b) the person is actively objecting to all or part of the order. It is good practice to ensure that, in a case where agreement is likely, the consent order is lodged in good time before the hearing. Otherwise, if the court is not able to consider it immediately costs will be incurred unnecessarily preparing for a hearing which will never take place.

Before the directions hearing

11.57 Even where an advocates' meeting is not strictly required, it nonetheless remains the case that it is sensible to seek to agree as many of the directions as possible or, at a minimum, to outline the key areas of agreement and disagreement. The process at para 11.56 above should be followed as regards providing a consent order to the court recording either partial or complete agreement as to the directions that are to be required, and the court should also be notified by telephone.[88] If the directions hearing is not going to be effective for any other reason PD 4B (where it applies) mandates the same notification procedure, by telephone and letter. It is suggested that it is sensible to follow as much of PD 4B as is possible whether or not it strictly applies.

The day of the hearing: in person hearings

11.58 If the hearing is to take place in person, then (as noted above at para 11.31), it will often be the case that the parties are directed to attend one hour beforehand for discussions. It is in any event very sensible to try to agree with the other parties to attend (at least) one hour before. Depending on how busy their list is, judges are usually happy to give parties additional time to discuss matters, especially if this means that it is more likely that a consent order can be submitted for endorsement, but it is much better to start the discussion process sooner rather than later.

11.59 Finding suitable rooms for discussions at court can often be difficult, especially as it will usually be the case that more than one will be needed so that instructions can be taken in private away from the negotiations. This is another good reason to be at court earlier rather

88 COPR PD 4B para 11.

than later, as this will maximise the chances of obtaining suitable numbers of conference rooms.

11.60 Much the same approach as that set out above in relation to advocates' meetings also applies in relation to productive discussions outside court. Two further points apply:

- More and more judges are in a position (and happy) to receive drafts of orders by email directly and/or it may be possible to persuade the court office to print off copies of the draft orders generated as a result of discussions. If it is possible for one of the parties' representatives to bring a laptop with internet access, therefore, it may well be possible for a draft order to be produced during the course of discussions and for it then either to be emailed to the judge or provided in printed form. If this is not possible, then the choice of representative to chair the discussions is likely to be dictated by the individual with the best handwriting;
- In many cases, especially those brought by public bodies concerning P's health and welfare, it is a productive use of staff resources for the relevant professionals to attend (at least the first) directions hearing, ie the case management hearing for cases on the welfare pathway. This is for two reasons: 1) because it will allow instructions to be received rapidly from the professionals involved; and 2) because of the importance of the interim declarations and decisions that are likely to be made at that hearing 'holding the ring' pending the final determination by the court of the application. Further, where (as is often the case) the underlying issues involve those of trust as between family members and the relevant public authorities, having the opportunity for the professionals to meet with the family members outside court can provide a surprisingly productive forum for discussions: if nothing else, knowing that a judge will be scrutinising whatever agreements are reached or reaching (interim) decisions upon any areas of disagreement serves very usefully to focus the minds of those attending.

The day of the hearing: remote hearings

11.61 If the hearing is to take place remotely, then the following considerations need to be taken into account:

- practical arrangements – e.g. allowing time for logging in, setting up a means of communication during the hearing such as a WhatsApp group;
- ensuring the ability of litigants in person to attend and take part;

- participation of P

Practitioners may be assisted by guidance on the effective conduct of remote hearings produced by the Court of Protection Bar Association.[89]

The hearing

11.62 Whilst the hearing is likely to be relatively informal, especially before a district judge, the Case Pathways PD 3B is prescriptive as regards the matters that will require consideration and resolution at both case management and final management hearings on the personal welfare pathway (see further paras 11.20–11.21) above, and parties should therefore be prepared to address the relevant matters set down in the practice direction for the particular hearing in question.

11.63 In any hearing with members of the press or public present, judges will often invite the applicant's representative to give an outline of the case. This need not be lengthy; being able to sketch the key issues in the case is also a good discipline to ensure that the representative themselves understands them. It is unusual for evidence formally to be given in a directions hearing (as to the requirements in this regard, see para 13.14), but it is not uncommon for a judge to want to hear information directly from those with possession of it rather than through a legal representative. This is another reason why it makes sense in cases involving social services that the relevant social worker for the individual in question attends court (or is in a position to attend remotely).

After the hearing: the order

11.64 It is now very common for the judge to ask the representative for one of the parties (usually either the applicant, if legally represented, or the party represented by the Official Solicitor if the Official Solicitor is acting as litigation friend) to submit an order to the court reflecting the directions made during the hearing. Some judges will in essence dictate the order down to the last detail, such that the task of drawing together the order for submission is relatively straightforward. Some judges will identify the broad thrust of their directions and leave it to the parties to agree the details to be put into an order for endorsement.

89 Available at: www.cpba.org.uk/wp-content/uploads/2020/07/CPBA-Effective-Remote-hearings-7.7.2020.docx.

11.65 It is clear that, if a party is charged with drawing up an order it is the duty of its solicitors and counsel to produce a draft that fairly reflects what they think the judge decided or directed.[90] Experience has shown that the more that details are left to be discussed by the parties after the hearing, the more room there can be for difficulties, in particular if one or more of the parties starts (in essence) re-running matters discussed during the hearing or (even worse) raising entirely new matters. While it is not always practical to do so, especially if the hearing has run late in the day, it is always a good idea to try to agree as many of the points in the order as possible before parties leave the court building (or log off from the hearing) because face-to-face discussion is almost invariably more effective in resolving debates than emails sent on the next or subsequent days. It is also likely to be more efficient in the majority of cases where disputes arise *not* to spend the subsequent days/weeks re-arguing the points between the parties, but rather to put two (or if necessary) more versions of the order to the judge by email so that the judge can decide. It is also suggested that unreasonable conduct in the post-hearing period is capable of attracting a costs sanction (ie it represents a basis under COPR r19.5 for departing from the normal costs rules set out in rr19.3–19.4: see further, chapter 17 below).[91]

11.66 One specific wrinkle arises in respect of cases in which the Official Solicitor is instructed to act as litigation friend for P. The Official Solicitor's caseworker – ie the member of the Official Solicitor's office with delegated responsibility for giving instructions on behalf of the Official Solicitor – often requires sight of an order for purposes of giving approval. This can sometimes give rise to difficulties where matters have taken an unanticipated turn at the hearing and the Official Solicitor's caseworker (not having been present) takes the view that a different order to that set down by the judge should have been made. In such circumstances, and assuming that the provision in question reflects a direction made by the judge, the proper course of action is for the Official Solicitor to seek leave to appeal the direction, rather than re-open matters in post-hearing correspondence.

90 See, by analogy, *Webb Resolutions Ltd v JT Ltd* [2013] EWHC 509 (TCC), [2013] TCLR 6 at para 19 per Edwards-Stuart J.

91 See, by analogy, *Webb Resolutions* at para 23.

Interim relief and interim hearings

11.67 On very many occasions that the court is considering making directions, it will also be considering what interim declarations or decisions are required to 'hold the ring' prior to the determination of the underlying application before it. For instance, in welfare cases, it will usually be necessary for the court to make interim declarations and decisions as to where P should live and with whom they should have contact prior to the final hearing. In property and affairs cases, it will very often be necessary to identify on an interim basis who should administer P's assets so as to secure them prior to a final determination of the application.

11.68 In some situations, especially those urgent ones discussed further at para 11.74 below, the primary focus of the hearing will be to consider the question of interim relief. As discussed at the outset, such hearings should technically be called interim hearings. Even in such hearings, though, the court is very likely to make directions as to the further consideration of the issues that have arisen or matters that flow in consequence of the decisions made.

11.69 Whenever interim relief is sought during the course of proceedings, the process for doing so is the same as set out above at paras 11.26–11.30 in relation to seeking directions.

11.70 The court has the power to enforce its interim decisions. Enforcement is dealt with at chapter 18 below, but in addition to the general powers granted the court under MCA 2005 s48, COPR r11.10 confirms that the court has the power to grant an interim injunction, an interim declaration or any other interim order it considers appropriate.

11.71 Any order for an interim injunction must set out clearly what the person to be subject to the injunction must or must not do. The courts have repeatedly emphasised the importance of clarity in this regard, together with the importance of ensuring that any injunction must not require the person subject to it to cross-refer to other material so as to understand their obligations: see, in particular, the comments of Munby LJ in *Re X and Y (children)*.[92]

11.72 Judges will usually seek, at least at the outset of proceedings, not to make injunctions (for instance) restricting contact between P and family members, but rather to seek undertakings from the family members in question to abide by contact restrictions. Negotiating the

92 [2012] EWCA Civ 1500, [2013] Fam Law 148 at paras 61–63. See also *Re Whiting* [2013] EWHC B27 (Fam), [2014] COPLR 107 at para 12(7),

terms of such undertakings will often represent some of the most important, if difficult, work done outside court at the hearing. It may not always be appropriate to proceed in such a way, most obviously if the proposed subject of the restriction is not present at the hearing; indeed, if they are represented but not actually present, some judges will not accept an undertaking because they consider it necessary to accept the undertaking personally from the individual and to explain its significance.

11.73 COPR PD 10B provides that an interim injunction can be varied or discharged by any judge of the Court of Protection.[93] In other words, it is not necessary that the matter be brought back before the same judge, or even the same level of judge. It is important to note, however, that an appeal against a decision to grant an injunction must follow the usual appeal routes[94] – in other words, a district judge could consider an application to vary an injunction granted by a High Court judge, but could not consider the basis upon which it was granted in the first instance.

Urgent applications

11.74 COPR PD 10B emphasises[95] that applications that become urgent merely because steps were not taken sufficiently promptly at an earlier stage should be avoided. Further, an application which becomes urgent as a result of professional delay in decision-making is a 'professional failure which always militates against the interests of P'.[96] However, the court has the ability to deal with truly urgent applications 24 hours a day throughout the year. During court hours (ie weekdays between 10.30 and 16.30), it will usually be necessary for the application to be made before the judge at court, most frequently before the Urgent Applications judge in the Family Division.[97] Out of hours, or in the case of extreme urgency, applications can be made by telephone. Not all urgent applications will require a hearing, but in the majority of cases applications which are

93 COPR PD 10B para 15.

94 See chapter 19.

95 COPR PD 10B para 4. See also *Sandwell and West Birmingham Hospitals NHS Trust v CD and others* [2014] EWCOP 23, [2014] COPLR 650, (2014) 17 CCLR 395, (medical treatment case not brought to court in sufficiently good time to enable proper participation by family members).

96 *Bagguley v E* [2019] EWCOP 49, [2020] Fam 267 at para 44.

97 Contact details are contained at appendix G below.

properly characterised as urgent will carry with an element of complexity which will necessitate one being arranged in short order.

11.75 If sufficiently urgent, an application can be determined even though an application form has not been issued, or even filed;[98] in all circumstances, the defining characteristic of an urgent application will be that the respondent will not have been formally notified of it. It is always necessary to explain in the application form (or, if none is being filed, in clear terms to the court office or – if out of hours – the security office at the Royal Courts of Justice) precisely how urgent the application is, what level of judge is required to determine it and whether it requires a hearing.[99] It is necessary to provide 'clear and cogent' evidence of the urgency, as a professional obligation on all professionals concerned, but in particular the lawyers involved in bringing the application.[100]

11.76 The guiding principle as regards urgent applications is that, as far as possible, the provisions relating to applications made on notice set out at paras 11.26–11.30 above should be complied with.[101] In other words, the court and the respondent(s) should be provided with as much information as soon as possible (unless, in the respondent's case, to do so would be to defeat the purpose of the application), and that, as a minimum, steps should be taken to inform the respondent of the application by telephone or in writing.[102] The rationale for this is obvious. It means that, even if the respondent cannot properly be said to have been notified of the application, the respondent may still be able to advance their views to the court at the hearing of the application, even only in writing.

11.77 The courts have repeatedly emphasised the stringency of the requirements upon those appearing before them on without notice applications and the care that must be exercised by judges in scrutinising them. These can be summarised thus:

- The grant of an order without notice is an exceptional remedy, and will normally be appropriate only if the case is genuinely

98 COPR PD 10B paras 1 and 6–7.

99 COPR PD 10B para 13; although this is in discretionary terms, the reality is that these obligations are mandatory.

100 *Bagguley v E* [2019] EWCOP 49, [2020] Fam 267 at para 44.

101 COPR PD 10B para 7.

102 COPR PD 10B para 5.

urgent (and even then some kind of informal notice should be given).[103]

- A party who applies for an order without notice to another party must provide the court with their reasons for taking that course.[104]
- Applicants and the court should ensure that sufficient appreciation is shown for the exceptional nature of relief granted without notice and the impact it has on the 'rights, life and emotions of the persons against whom [and in respect of whom] it is granted'.[105]
- Those who seek relief without notice are under a duty to make full and frank disclosure. This extends to all relevant matters, and the duty includes a duty to make proper inquiries before making the application.[106] In other words, full and frank disclosure must be of what is known and what should be known or would be known if proper inquiries had been made.[107] The duty involves more than including relevant documents in the court bundle: it involves specifically identifying all relevant documents and taking the judge to the particular passages in the documents which are material and taking appropriate steps to ensure that the judge correctly appreciates the significance of what he is being asked to read.[108] In a paper application the judge must not be left to consider on their own a pile of undigested exhibits; the representative must draw the significance of a particular document to the attention of the court, particularly where they have knowledge that enables them to do so.[109] A failure to comply with the duty of full and frank disclosure can give rise to a liability in costs, including on an indemnity basis (see chapter 17).
- Representatives must identify the crucial points for and against the application and not rely on general statements or the exhibiting of numerous documents. They must identify any likely defences. Fairness demands that the applicant provide the court

103 *R (Lawer) v Restormel BC* [2007] EWHC 2299 (Admin). See also *Mazhar v Birmingham Community Healthcare Foundation NHS Trust and others* [2020] EWCA Civ 1377, [2021] 1 WLR 1207 at para 74.

104 *Mazhar v Birmingham Community Healthcare Foundation NHS Trust and others* [2020] EWCA Civ 1377, [2021] 1 WLR 1207 at para 74.

105 *B BC v S (by the Official Solicitor)* [2006] EWHC 2584 (Fam), [2007] 1 FLR 1600 at paras 37 and 41.

106 See In *re S (a child) (Family Division: without notice orders)* [2001] 1 WLR 211 at paras 219–221.

107 *Brink's Mat Ltd v Elcombe* [1988] 1 WLR 1350 at 1356 and 1358.

108 *R (Lawer) v Restormel BC* [2007] EWHC 2299 (Admin) at para 69.

109 *R (Khan) v Secretary of State for the Home Department* [2016] EWCA Civ 416 at paras 32 and 40.

with a balanced, fair and particularised account of the events leading up to the application, which in many cases should include a brief account of what the applicant thinks the respondent's case is, or is likely to be. It should not be based on largely unparticularised assertions by one side of serious allegations without any third-party material to support them.[110]

11.78 COPR PD 10B provides that, where an order is made without notice to any party, the order should ordinarily contain:

- an undertaking by the applicant to serve the application notice, evidence in support and any order made upon the affected parties as soon as possible or as ordered by the court; and
- a return date for a further hearing at which the other parties can be present.[111]

11.79 COPR r11.5 further provides that a copy of the application notice, the order and the evidence in support is to be served by the applicant on anyone named as a respondent in the application notice (if not otherwise a party to the proceedings), every party to the proceedings and any other person directed by the court, such service to take place as soon as practicable or within such date as the court may direct. Where the application has been made in a situation of exceptional urgency and no application form has been issued, an undertaking will be required that the application form in the terms of the oral application be filed on the next working day, or as required by the court.[112]

11.80 While PD 10B is silent on the subject, it is necessary for a detailed note to be made of submissions made to the judge when the respondent is not present or represented, and of the reasons given by the judge for making (or not making) the order sought.[113] The court will often order that such a note be filed in advance of the return date; in any event, without such a contemporaneous note it can be very difficult at any later date to identify with clarity precisely how any without notice order came to be made.

11.81 Where a hearing of an urgent application takes place by telephone, PD 10B envisages that, where practicable, that hearing will

110 *A Local Authority v B (Emergency Protection Orders)* [2004] EWHC 2015 (Fam), [2005] 1 FLR 341 at para 53.

111 COPR PD 10B para 6.

112 COPR PD 10B para 9.

113 See *In re S (a child) (Family Division: without notice orders)* [2001] 1 WLR 211 at paras 219–221.

take place by way of a conference call arranged (and in the first instance, paid for) by the applicant through a service provider (such as BT Connect or Multivoice), and that the service provider will record the call. In such situations, the applicant should order a transcript of the hearing from the service provider.[114] If it is genuinely not possible to arrange for the call to be recorded, the obligation on the applicant's representative to take a proper note of relevant matters is particularly onerous.

114 COPR PD 10B para 12.

CHAPTER 12

P, protected parties and children

continued

Introduction

12.1 This chapter addresses the participation and representation of P before the Court of Protection, which has been the subject of some of the most significant developments (in both legislative and case-law terms) since the first edition of this book was published in 2014. While it will remain the case that P will not be joined as a party to the majority of applications, P is now able to participate through a wider range of options than was the case when the first edition of this book was written.

12.2 The chapter will also address the position where a party to the proceedings is a protected party (ie they are an adult who lacks litigation capacity) or they are a child, as in both cases they will require a litigation friend (in the case of a child, unless the court orders otherwise).

Participation of P

Background

12.3 By 2014, the participation of P had become a particular issue for two main reasons:

- A line of cases decided in the European Court of Human Rights[1] (ECtHR) had made it increasingly clear that the proper participation of the subject of proceedings for declarations as to their capacity was necessary so as to secure their rights under both Articles 6 and 8 of the European Convention on Human Rights (ECHR).
- More pressingly, the decision of the Supreme Court in *Cheshire West*[2] (see further para 22.6) led to a perception that there would be an enormous increase in the number of applications to the Court of Protection for judicial authorisation of deprivations of liberty outside care homes and hospitals. The question then arose as to whether the person concerned had to be a party to such

1 *X and Y v Croatia* (App No 5193/44009, decision of 3 November 2011), *Shtukaturov v Russia* (App No 44009/05), [2008] ECHR 223, (2008) 11 CCLR 44009 and *Lashin v Russia* (App No 33117/02, decision of 22 January 2013). See also, subsequently *Ivinovic v Croatia* (App No 13006/13, (2017) 65 EHRR 23 and *AN v Lithuania* (App No 17280/08, decision of 31 May 2016). See also the paper by Lucy Series entitled 'The participation of the relevant person in proceedings before the Court of Protection' available at http://sites.cardiff.ac.uk/wccop/files/2014/09/ Briefing-on-Personal-Participation-in-the-CoP-v1-2.pdf.

2 *Cheshire West and Chester Council v P* [2014] UKSC 19, [2014] COPLR 313, (2014) 17 CCLR 5.

proceedings in all cases and, if they were not to be a party, how their participation could be sufficiently ensured so as to secure their rights under ECHR Article 5. How the courts then grappled with that issue is addressed further in chapter 22.

12.4 The ad hoc Rules Committee which met in late 2014/early 2015 with a remit to focus upon the most pressing issues that had been identified as requiring changes in the practice and procedures of the Court of Protection therefore devoted the majority of its energies to addressing the participation of P. The result of their work was a significant recasting of the previous approach, and is now to be found in Court of Protection Rules 2017[3] (COPR) r1.2 (referred to as rule 3A in the 2015 numbering).[4]

The menu of options

12.5 The participation of P is provided for in COPR r1.2.[5] This rule requires in each case the court to consider, either on its own initiative or on the application of any person, whether it should make one or more directions relating to P's participation set down in a 'menu' provided by the rule. Consideration of P's participation is expressly required at the first case management hearing for cases falling under the personal welfare pathway under the COPR and Case Pathways Practice Direction (PD) 3B (see para 11.20).

12.6 The menu of options for P's participation includes:

- P being a party;[6]
- P's participation being secured by the appointment of an accredited legal representative (ALR) to represent P in the proceedings and to discharge such other functions as the court may direct. The position of such ALRs is considered at paras 12.84–12.99 below;[7]
- P's participation being secured by the appointment of a representative whose primary function is to give P a 'voice' by relaying information as to P's wishes and feelings. The position of such representatives is considered at para 12.75 below;[8]

3 SI 2017 No 1035.
4 For more detail of the background to the amendments, see Alex Ruck Keene, *The next stage of the journey – the Court of Protection (Amendment) Rules 2015* [2015] 2 Eld LJ 150.
5 The accompanying Practice Direction is PD 1A.
6 COPR r1.2(2)(a).
7 COPR r1.2(2)(b).
8 COPR r1.2(2)(c).

- specific provision for P to address (directly or indirectly) the judge determining the application;[9] or
- no direction or an alternative direction (meeting the overriding objective) if P's interests and position can properly be secured.[10]

12.7 Which of the directions set out above is made is a decision for the court having regard to a) the nature and extent of the information before the court; b) the issues raised in the case; c) whether a matter is contentious; and d) whether P has been notified in accordance with the provisions of Part 7 of the COPR (see further chapters 7 and 9) and what, if anything, P has said or done in response to such notification. In practice, a further important consideration is the limited availability of funding for representatives (of whatever kind). This is a particular issue in relation to applications for authorisation of deprivation of liberty, and is addressed further in chapter 22.

12.8 COPR PD 1A, which accompanies these provisions, envisages that in many cases no sort of representative will be needed because these are non-contentious property and affairs cases and 'experience has shown that they can be dealt with on paper and without joining P as a party or appointing anyone to represent P'.[11] The practice direction comments that as a result of COPR r1.2 the court 'is both enabled and required to tailor the provision it directs for P's participation and representation to the circumstances of the individual case'.[12]

12.9 Practical guidance to enhance the participation of P was issued by the former Vice-President of the Court of Protection, Charles J in 2016, and reissued by the current Vice-President in 2022.[13] Researchers on the Arts and Humanities Research Council (AHRC) funded project, *Judging values and participation in mental capacity law*,[14] based at the Institute for Crime and Justice Policy Research (ICPR), Birkbeck School of Law, have produced two training films for specialist lawyers who work in the Court of Protection, 'Communication and participation in the Court of Protection', available on YouTube.[15] The first video, developed in association with VoiceAbility, utilises role-plays and

9 COPR r1.2(2)(d). See further para 16.34 and onwards below.

10 COPR r1.2(2)(e).

11 COPR PD 1A para 3.

12 COPR PD 1A para 6.

13 As an annex to *Practice Guidance (Court of Protection: Judicial visits)* [2022] EWCOP 5, [2022] 1 WLR 1445.

14 See: www.icpr.org.uk/theme/courts-court-users-and-judicial-process/judging-values-and-participation-mental-capacity-law.

15 See: www.youtube.com/watch?v=WuEtw2rnqBw.

roundtables with lawyers and people with learning disability and autism to demonstrate how to enhance communication and achieve better quality evidence for the court.[16] The second video, also produced in association with Voiceability, uses similar techniques to demonstrate how to make P's values matter before the Court of Protection.[17] These issues are also considered further in chapter 16.

12.10 Where P is to be a party and does not have capacity to conduct the proceedings, the court must either appoint a litigation friend to act on their behalf,[18] or appoint an ALR to act without a litigation friend being appointed to act for P.[19] The appointment and duties of litigation friends are considered at paras 12.26–12.52 below; the appointment and duties of ALRs are set out at paras 12.87–12.102 below. An order joining P as a party will only take effect where either a litigation friend or an ALR has been appointed.[20] If the court has directed that P should be joined as a party but it has not taken place because no litigation friend or ALR has been appointed, the court must record in a judgment or order the fact that one has not been appointed, and the reasons given as to why not.[21] This is designed to 'flush out' situations in which funding has not been forthcoming to enable such appointments to take place.

12.11 In deciding whether P has capacity to conduct the proceedings (often called 'litigation capacity'), the court will apply Mental Capacity Act (MCA) 2005 ss2–3. A detailed examination of the issue of litigation capacity lies outside the scope of this work.[22] In summary, however:

1) the *test* that the court will apply is that under MCA 2005 ss2–3 (see further para 3.33 onwards), which means – importantly – that it must have regard to the principles of the presumption of capacity and that all practicable support must have been given to the person without success before they can be found to lack capacity. What this means in practical terms for those representing P is set out in the guide at the end of this chapter.

16 See: www.youtube.com/watch?v=WuEtw2rnqBw.
17 See: www.youtube.com/watch?v=IfSmzITspzs.
18 COPR r1.2(4)(a).
19 COPR r1.2(2)(4)(b).
20 COPR r1.2(4).
21 COPR r1.2(5).
22 For a more detailed discussion, see chapter 9 of the Law Society/British Medical Association's *Assessment of mental capacity: a practical guide for doctors and lawyers*, 5th edn, 2022.

2) In applying that test, the court will have regard to cases decided under the common law as to the key *information* that the person must be able to retain, understand, use and weigh. In particular, in *A, B and C v X and Z*,[23] Hedley J considered that the 'heart of the test' were the observations of Chadwick LJ at para 75 of *Masterman-Lister*[24] that:

   [T]he test to be applied, as it seems to me, is whether the party to the legal proceedings is capable of understanding, with the assistance of proper explanation from legal advisers and experts in other disciplines as the case may require, the issues on which his consent or decision is likely to be necessary in the course of those proceedings. If he has capacity to understand that which he needs to understand in order to pursue or defend a claim, I can see no reason why the law – whether substantive or procedural – should require the interposition of a next friend.[25]

12.12 Three points are particularly important when it comes to considering litigation capacity:

1) The question of capacity to litigate is not something to be determined in the abstract: it is always necessary to ask whether P has the capacity to litigate in relation to the particular application before the court.[26]
2) P may have capacity to conduct the proceedings even though it is asserted that they do not have capacity to make the decisions in question.[27] There is something of a division between the judges as

23 [2012] EWHC 2400 (COP), [2013] COPLR 1.

24 *Masterman-Lister v Brutton & Co, Masterman-Lister v Jewell and another* [2002] EWCA Civ 1889, [2003] 1 WLR 1511, (2004) 7 CCLR 5. The approach adopted in *Masterman-Lister* was endorsed by the Supreme Court in *Dunhill v Burgin (Nos 1 and 2)* [2014] UKSC 18, [2014] WLR 933, (2014) 17 CCLR 203.

25 *A, B and C v X and Z* [2012] EWHC 2400 (COP), [2013] COPLR 1 at para 42. See also *Brent LBC v SL* [2017] EWCOP 5 where District Judge Glentworth (at para 35) identified the need for P to be able to 'make decisions and give instructions in relation to matters which are integral to the process of this litigation.'

26 *Sheffield City Council v E and another* [2004] EWHC 2808 (Fam), [2005] Fam 326, at para 38. In the context of Court of Protection proceedings see *Brent LBC v SL* [2017] EWCOP 5.

27 See, for instance *Re SB* [2013] EWHC 1417 (COP), [2013] COPLR 445 and *CC v KK, STCC* [2012] EWHC 2136 (COP), 2808 (Fam), [2005] Fam 326 [2012] COPLR 627, both cases in which the court ultimately held that the person did have the capacity to make their own decisions.

to whether a person who lacks "subject matter capacity" can ever truly have capacity to conduct proceedings.[28]

3) P may well have capacity to wish to challenge a decision but lack the capacity to conduct the entirety of the consequent proceedings. This is particularly relevant in the context of applications under MCA 2005 s21A,[29] discussed further in chapter 22.

12.13 Where P is aged 16 or 17,[30] it is suggested that the court should approach them *as if* they were an adult P for the purposes of deciding their capacity to conduct the proceedings and therefore apply the capacity test set down in MCA 2005 ss2–3. This would be in line with the approach taken to other decisions made by 16/17-year-olds.[31] Further, if the situation is one where the concern is solely about the young person's age, rather than any cognitive impairment, the Court of Protection could not make any substantive decisions on behalf of the young person.[32] It

28 Mostyn J has expressed the view that such situations should be as 'rare as a white leopard': *An NHS Trust v P* [2021] EWCOP 27, [2021] COPLR 450, although Hayden J robustly defended the potential for such a situation to exist in *Lancashire and South Cumbria NHS Foundation Trust v Q* [2022] EWCOP 6, [2022] COPLR 315; an example of one is *Islington LBC v QR* [2014] EWCOP 26, (2014) 17 CCLR 344.

29 *RD v Herefordshire Council* [2016] EWCOP 49; [2017] 1 WLR 1723, [2017] COPLR 87 at para 86(1), in the context of a MCA 2005 21A challenge, where Baker J held that the question was whether P had capacity to issue proceedings: '[t]his simply requires P to understand that the court has the power to decide that he/she should not be subject to his/her current care arrangements. It is a lower threshold than the capacity to conduct proceedings'. See also (by analogy) *SM v Livewell Southwest Community Interest Co* [2020] UKUT 191 (AAC), [2020] 1 WLR 5171, concerning applications to the Mental Health Tribunal.

30 MCA 2005 provides for the Court of Protection to make certain types of decision in respect of those between the age of 16 and 18, and indeed, in respect of those below 18, to make any decision relating to P's property and affairs save for the making of a will, if the court considers it likely that P will still lack capacity to make decisions in respect of that matter when he reaches 18: MCA 2005 ss2(5) and 18(3).

31 See *Re D (a child) (residence order: deprivation of liberty)* [2019] UKSC 42, [2020] COPLR 73 (consent to confinement) and *Re X (a child) (No 2)* [2021] EWHC 65 (Fam), [2021] COPLR 626 (medical treatment).

32 Theoretically, it might be possible for the concern in relation to the ability to make the underlying decisions to be impairment related, and the concern in relation to the ability to conduct the proceedings about those decisions to be purely age-related. In such a case, the young person could possibly be MCA 2005 capacitous to conduct the proceedings, but might lack so-called *Gillick* competence to do so (after *Gillick v West Norfolk and Wisbech Area Health Authority* [1985] UKHL 7, [1986] 1 AC 112). It is almost impossible to imagine such a situation arising in practice, because a young person given appropriate time and support who is still unable to make the decisions necessary to conduct the proceedings would all be inevitably be identified as having an impairment or disturbance in the functioning in their mind or brain, bringing the MCA 2005 into play.

would be necessary to go either to the Family Court or the Family Division of the High Court. This is not addressed further here.[33]

Protected parties

12.14 An adult other than P who lacks capacity to conduct the proceedings is called a 'protected party'.[34] A protected party requires a litigation friend.[35]

12.15 The same principles as set out in relation to P above apply to the determination of the litigation capacity of an adult party. However, because the focus of the proceedings will not initially be upon the litigation capacity of the adult party, it is often the case that it will only become apparent after proceedings have started that they lack litigation capacity. This gives rise to practical issues as to what should happen in such a case.

12.16 In some ways the situation is relatively straightforward if the person has legal representation – it is clear that a responsible solicitor who has concerns as to the capacity of their client should take steps to address that concern. In most cases, that is likely to require seeking clinical input.[36] If the solicitor's concerns are not allayed, they should take steps to ensure that a litigation friend is appointed before proceeding further.[37]

33 For more on decision-making and remedies in relation to children, see chapters 7 and 11 respectively Broach et al, *Disabled Children: a legal handbook*, Legal Action Group, 3rd edn, 2021, also available (free) at https://councilfordisabledchildren.org.uk/. See also Camilla Parker, *Adolescent Mental Health Care and the* Law, Legal Action Group, 2020.

34 COPR r2.1.

35 COPR rr17.2(2) and 2.1.

36 Whether that is from a GP, a psychiatrist or a psychologist will depend upon the circumstances of the case. Note, however, that there is no absolute requirement that medical evidence is obtained before steps are taken to apply for the appointment of a litigation friend: see, by analogy *Hinduja v Hinduja and others* [2020] EWHC 1533 (Ch), [2020] 4 WLR 93. Logically, therefore, it may possible for a solicitors' concerns as to litigation capacity to be allayed without the need for medical input.

37 See *Masterman-Lister v Brutton & Co Masterman-Lister v Jewell and another* [2002] EWCA Civ 1889, [2003] 1 WLR 1511, (2004) 7 CCLR 5 at para 30. For more on the duties of solicitors here, see the Law Society's Guidance Note: *Meeting the needs of vulnerable clients* (www.lawsociety.org.uk/en/topics/client-care/meeting-the-needs-of-vulnerable-clients); and Practice Note: *Working with clients who may lack capacity* (www.lawsociety.org.uk/topics/client-care/working-with-clients-who-may-lack-mental-capacity).

12.17 If the person is acting for themselves, however, then a difficult question can arise. It is ultimately a judicial question whether an individual is or is not a protected party.[38] If the court is in possession of information raising a question as to the capacity of a litigant in person to conduct the litigation, how is it to satisfy itself as to whether the person has the requisite capacity? At that stage, it is clear that there are a series of elephant traps,[39] that the court should avoid, including:

- failing to grasp the nettle fully and early;
- ignoring information or evidence that a party may lack capacity;
- relying upon the presumption of capacity in circumstances where capacity has been questioned;
- making directions addressing the capacity issue, but discharging them or failing to comply with them and thereby leaving the issue inadequately addressed;
- failing to obtain evidence (expert or otherwise) relevant to capacity;
- use of 'unless' orders against the party;
- similarly, using personal service or 'warning notices' on that party;
- relying on non-engagement by that party either with assessments or the proceedings;
- proceeding with any substantive directions, let alone making final orders, in the absence of adequate enquiry and proper determination of the capacity issue;
- treating a party as having provided consent to any step, let alone a grave and possibly irrevocable final step, where capacity has been questioned but the issue not determined.

12.18 It may be that the litigant in person is prepared to agree to undergo a medical examination, but what if they refuse? A party to proceedings cannot be ordered to undergo a medical examination[40] and the

38 See *Carmarthenshire CC v Lewis* [2010] EWCA Civ 1567 at para 8 per Rimer LJ.

39 These are taken from *Mr and Mrs Z v Kent CC* [2018] EWFC B65, [2019] COPLR 79 at para 40.

40 See also para 4.59 of the Code of Practice accompanying the MCA 2005: 'Nobody can be forced to undergo an assessment of capacity' (www.gov.uk/government/publications/mental-capacity-act-code-of-practice). Although see *Re SA* [2010] EWCA Civ 1128 where the court sought to require both P and her mother to cooperate in the carrying out of a capacity assessment upon P (for purposes of determining her capacity to make the underlying decisions in the case). On a proper analysis, there was an element of bluff deployed here because there was a strong suggestion that P was being influenced in her refusal by her mother.

court is therefore faced with a difficult dilemma. In *Baker Tilly (a firm) v Makar*,[41] Sir Raymond Jack made clear that:

> The absence of medical evidence cannot be a bar to a finding of lack of capacity but where most unusually circumstances arise in which medical evidence cannot be obtained, the court should be most cautious before concluding that the probability is that there is a disturbance of the mind. Section 2(3)(b) of the [Mental Capacity] Act must be kept in mind. A finding of lack of capacity is a serious matter for both parties. It takes away the protected party's right to conduct their litigation. It may constitute, and here would constitute, a serious disadvantage to the other party.

12.19 It is possible for the court to make an interim declaration of lack of litigation capacity, especially if that would enable proper investigation of the matter.[42] In an appropriate case, further, the court can – and should – make findings as to litigation capacity even where a party refuses to attend a medical examination where there is sufficient evidence. Such evidence may emerge from a variety of sources. In *Re RGS*,[43] for instance, the court had limited medical information about RBS, P's son, who was known to have a history of contact with psychiatric services but who refused to attend a medical examination. The court found RBS to lack litigation capacity. The court found that such information as there was from the professional witnesses and RBS' own account founded the conclusion that RBS had an impairment or disturbance of the mind or brain. RBS' own conduct during the proceedings gave rise to the finding that the impairment/disturbance had compromised his ability to understand, retain and weigh the information relevant to the litigation.

12.20 In extreme cases, where a litigant in person refuses to take part in a medical examination, the court may be able to direct disclosure of the litigant's medical records to an independent medical examiner who could then prepare a report based on the clinical record. A party's medical records are confidential, but in *Bennett v Compass Group*[44] (a

41 [2013] EWHC 759 (QB), [2013] COPLR 245. These comments were made in the context of adversarial civil proceedings, but it is suggested that they are equally applicable before the Court of Protection.

42 See by analogy *CS v FB* [2020] EWHC 1474 (Fam), [2020] COPLR 762, proceedings concerning a child, in which an interim declaration of lack of litigation capacity was made to enable the Official Solicitor to be appointed as the mother's litigation friend, legal aid to be secured, and for the Official Solicitor to investigate for final determination the mother's capacity to conduct these proceedings.

43 [2012] EWHC 4162 (COP), [2012] EWCOP 4162.

44 [2002] EWCA Civ 642, [2002] CP Rep 58.

case relating to the disclosure of medical records in a personal injury case where the claimant's capacity was not in issue), comments made by both Chadwick LJ[45] and Pill LJ[46] would suggest that a (civil) court could make an order requiring a GP or hospital to disclose records directly to a party to the litigation without the consent of the person in question, although it is clear from the comments made in that case that such an order would be wholly exceptional. There is no reason in principle why such an approach could not be adopted by the Court of Protection, albeit after a very careful balancing exercise between the litigant's rights to maintaining the confidentiality of their medical records under ECHR Article 8 (right to respect for private and family life)[47] and the potential benefits to them of being represented by a litigation friend.

Children

12.21 A child – ie someone under 18[48] – who is a party to proceedings but is not P, will require a litigation friend unless the court orders otherwise.[49] An application must be made for the court to make such an order; if the application is made by the child, then if a litigation friend has already been appointed to act on their behalf, it must be made on notice to that litigation friend.[50] It may otherwise be made without notice.[51] There is no guidance in the MCA 2005, the COPR or PD 17A as to the circumstances under which a court will permit a child to conduct proceedings without a litigation friend.

12.22 There are two bases upon which a child may lack the legal capacity to conduct proceedings. The first is on the basis that they are not '*Gillick* competent,'[52] which is essentially simply a function of the child's age. This approach undoubtedly holds good in relation to those under 16. However, in respect of a child aged 16 or 17, and by parity of reasoning with the approach relating to 16/17 year olds

45 At paras 67–68.
46 Para 88.
47 See in this regard *Z v Finland* (1998) 25 EHRR 371 at para 95.
48 COPR r2.1.
49 COPR r17.2(3)–(4).
50 COPR r17.2(5)(b).
51 COPR r17.2(5)(c).
52 Ie they do not have sufficient maturity and intelligence to understand the nature and implications of the proposed decision: *Gillick v West Norfolk and Wisbech Area Health Authority* [1985] UKHL 7, [1986] AC 112. See also para 12.13 above.

more broadly (see para 12.13 above) it is suggested that the starting point would not be the test of *Gillick* competence, but rather that of mental capacity under the MCA 2005.

12.23 If the concern in respect of the child arises not because of a suggestion that they are in some way suffering from a disability, but rather simply because of their age, then it is suggested that useful guidance can be found in the approach adopted in the Family Procedure Rules (FPR) 2010,[53] which also contain a provision for the court to dispense with the requirement that a child be represented by a litigation friend (or a children's guardian) in certain circumstances. The FPR provide that an application by the child will be granted 'if [the court] considers that the child has sufficient understanding to conduct the proceedings concerned or proposed without a litigation friend or children's guardian'.[54] The FPR contain differences to the COPR, not least as they provide that the court can nonetheless require the litigation friend or guardian to continue to play a part in the proceedings, but it is suggested that the approach set down in the FPR is likely to be adopted before the Court of Protection. Purely age-related concerns are likely to be of less relevance as the child gets older, and it is suggested that it would be a relatively unusual situation in which a 16- or 17-year-old could be said to lack capacity to conduct litigation purely on age-related grounds. In such a situation, it is more likely that the concern would be one related to disability.

12.24 If the concern in respect of the child's ability to participate in the proceedings arises out of a concern that they are suffering from a disability affecting their ability to conduct litigation, it is suggested that:

- for a child below the age of 16, the approach is likely to be very similar to that under the FPR;
- for a child aged 16 or 17, the primary considerations should be those set out at paras 12.11–12.12 above in relation to adults.

12.25 Even where an order has been made permitting a child to act without a litigation friend, the court retains the power to appoint a litigation friend if it subsequently appears to the court that it would be desirable for such a litigation friend to conduct proceedings on the child's behalf. There is no guidance in the MCA 2005, the COPR or PD 17A as to when such a step would be desirable. At least where the appointment of a litigation friend for a child has taken place on the basis out

53 SI 2010 No 2955, as amended.

54 FPR r16.6(6).

of a concern that they are not sufficiently mature, then by analogy with the FPR[55] it is suggested that a court should be slow to re-appoint a litigation friend save where it has become clear that the child, in fact, lacks the understanding to conduct the proceedings. To do otherwise – for instance, on the basis that the child's conduct is disruptive – would be to risk depriving the child of a voice in the proceedings; the court has other mechanisms to control such disruptive conduct by way of its case management powers granted it under COPR rr3.1 and 3.7 (or COPR Part 3 where this applies).

Litigation friends

Pre-appointment

12.26 The COPR are silent as to what the court may or may not do as regards the proceedings generally where a party who requires a litigation friend (including P) has not yet had one appointed. It is suggested that the court does have the power to proceed, either under its general case management powers in COPR r3.1 and/or, if required, by importing the provisions of the Civil Procedure Rules 1998 (CPR) r21.3(3) through the provisions of COPR r2.5(1),[56] enabling it to give permission to the other parties to proceed to take steps in the proceedings absent the relevant appointment. The court will seek to do the minimum possible to 'hold the ring', pending such an appointment, especially in relation to P, although if needs be the court can proceed simply to make decisions in a suitably urgent case.[57]

Appointment

12.27 There are two ways in which a litigation friend can be appointed: without a court order and with one. A litigation friend can never be appointed for P without a court order.

55 FPR r16.6(8).

56 Which provide that: 'In any case not expressly provided for by these Rules or the practice directions made under them, the Civil Procedure Rules 1998 (including any practice directions made under them) may be applied with any necessary modifications, insofar as is necessary to further the overriding objective'.

57 See, for instance, *Newcastle-upon-Tyne Hospitals, Foundation Trust v LM* [2014] EWHC 454 (COP), [2015] 1 FCR 373, where the medical treatment decision had to be taken in circumstances where it was not possible (in the time available) to appoint the Official Solicitor to act as P's litigation friend.

Appointment without a court order

12.28 A deputy appointed with the specific power to conduct legal proceedings in the name of the protected party is entitled to act as litigation friend without a further order if their power extends to the proceedings in question.[58] In this regard, it is important to understand that:

> Specific authority is required to conduct litigation on behalf of P ... *except* where the contemplated litigation is in the Court of Protection in respect of a property and affairs issues ... or to seek directions in respect of a welfare issue ...[59]

If a deputy is to act as litigation friend, the deputy must file and serve an official copy of the order on the other parties (or, if a party is represented by a litigation friend, upon that party's litigation friend).[60]

12.29 If there is no deputy, a person can become a litigation friend for a protected party or for a child (but not for P[61]) without a court order if they file a certificate of suitability (with a statement of truth[62]) on a form COP22[63] stating (among other things) that:

- they can fairly and competently conduct proceedings on behalf of the individual in question;[64]
- they have no interests adverse to the individual in question;[65]
- that the litigation friend knows or believes that the child or protected party lacks capacity to conduct the proceedings themselves;[66]
- the grounds of the belief set out above (and, if the belief is based upon medical opinion, or the opinion of another suitably qualified expert, attach any relevant document to the certificate).[67] There is no absolute requirement that an application to be made a litigation friend is supported by medical evidence,[68] but it is likely that a court would wish to consider carefully any situation

58 COPR r17.3(2).
59 *Re ACC and others* [2020] EWCOP 9, [2020] COPLR 406, Appendix, para 4.
60 COPR r17.3(4) and PD 17A para 5.
61 COPR r17.3(1)(a).
62 COPR PD 17A para 8.
63 Which will serve as the requisite consent for purposes of COPR PD 17A para 7(a).
64 COPR r17.3(3)(a) read together with COPR r17.1(1)(a).
65 COPR r17.3(3)(a) read together with COPR r17.1(1)(b).
66 COPR PD 17A para 7(b).
67 COPR PD 17A para 7(c).
68 See, by analogy *Hinduja v Hinduja and others* [2020] EWHC 1533 (Ch), [2020] 4 WLR 93.

in which a litigation friend had been appointed pursuant to this process absent medical evidence.[69]

12.30 The first two bullet points are discussed further at para 12.46 onwards below.

12.31 The proposed litigation friend must serve the certificate of suitability on the other parties (or, if a party is represented by a litigation friend, upon that party's litigation friend).[70] Unless the court directs otherwise, the proposed litigation friend does not need to serve any document relating to the medical or other opinion noted at the last bullet point above.

12.32 The proposed litigation friend must then file the certificate of suitability together with a certificate of service on a COP20 form when they first take a step in the proceedings.[71]

12.33 The procedure set out above cannot be used if the court has previously appointed a litigation friend,[72] because in such situations an order will be required to terminate the appointment of the existing litigation friend (see further para 12.53 onwards below). It also cannot be used by the Official Solicitor[73] (perhaps because the Official Solicitor is to be taken automatically to satisfy the suitability requirement and hence should not be required to file such a certificate).

Appointment with a court order

12.34 An order appointing a person as a litigation friend for a protected party, a child or – importantly – P (if P is joined to the proceedings) can be made either at the court's own initiative or upon application by any person (ie not just by the proposed litigation friend).[74] Any application must be made by filing a COP9[75] and be supported by evidence[76] that will allow the court to be satisfied (as it must also be satisfied if it is contemplating making the order of its own initiative) that:

69 Whether that is from a GP, a psychiatrist or a psychologist will depend upon the circumstances of the case. See *Masterman-Lister v Brutton & Co, Masterman-Lister v Jewell and another* [2002] EWCA Civ 1889, [2003] 1 WLR 1511, (2004) 7 CCLR 5 at para 17.

70 COPR r17.3(3)(b) and PD 17A para 9.

71 COPR PD 17A para 12.

72 COPR r17.3(1)(b).

73 COPR r17.3(1)(c).

74 COPR r17.4(2).

75 COPR PD 17A para 13. See further para 11.26 for applications within proceedings.

76 COPR r17.4(1).

- the proposed litigation friend can fairly and competently conduct proceedings on behalf of the individual in question;[77]
- the proposed litigation friend has no interests adverse to the individual in question;[78]
- the proposed litigation friend consents to the appointment.[79]

12.35 The last of these criteria is self-evident, although note that a litigation friend can make their consent (and continuing consent) contingent on receiving appropriate funding (see para 12.40 below); the first two are discussed at para 12.46 onwards below. Because the evidence matches that set out in a COP22 certificate of suitability, there is no requirement to file such a certificate where an application is being made.

12.36 As noted above, a court order is required in order to appoint the Official Solicitor as litigation friend for a protected party, a child or P.[80] Although the COPR are silent on this, it would seem that the Official Solicitor is automatically taken to meet the suitability criteria and the Official Solicitor would never be required to file evidence to address these criteria.

12.37 If the court considers that it requires further evidence before it can grant an application to be appointed as litigation friend, or if it appears to the judge during the course of proceedings that a party (other than P) may require a litigation friend, but that further evidence is required, directions can be made.[81] If P has previously made a successful application to be allowed to instruct representatives directly (see further paras 12.53–12.55 below) but it then appears that the position has changed subsequently, then the same provisions will apply.

12.38 The court has the power, exercisable on its own initiative or at the application of any person (whether or not that person is a party) to prevent someone acting as a litigation friend (for any party).[82]

12.39 Where the application is made on the basis of the proposed litigation friend's conduct, it must be supported by evidence.[83] Where the application is made on the basis that the person (whether that is P, a

77 COPR r17.1(1)(a).
78 COPR r17.1(1)(b).
79 COPR r17.3(2).
80 COPR r17.3(1)(c).
81 COPR r17.4(5). The position where it appears that an adult party other than P may require a litigation friend is addressed at paras 12.14–12.20 above.
82 COPR r17.5(1).
83 COPR r17.5(2).

protected party, or a child) does not require a litigation friend because they, in fact, have the capacity to litigate (or in the case of a child, that one is unnecessary having regard to the factors set out at para 12.21 above), no evidence is required. This is addressed further below at para 12.53 onwards.

Who may be appointed as a litigation friend?

For P

12.40 Many default immediately to thinking of the Official Solicitor as the litigation friend for P. However, the Official Solicitor describes herself[84] and because of resource constraints takes very seriously her position as, litigation friend of last resort. This means that she will only consider acting where no suitable and willing person can be identified to act. Further, and save in the case of serious medical treatment cases (as to which, see chapter 22), even assuming that there is no other suitable and willing person, the Official Solicitor will only accept an appointment to act subject to being given suitable security for a) the costs of any external solicitors she retains to act for P; or b) where she acts as solicitor and conducts the litigation, those costs of so acting. In other words, and while the Official Solicitor does not seek to recover her costs of acting as litigation friend, she must be satisfied that the costs incurred either by external solicitors or by her staff in acting as solicitors will be met, whether that be from P's own assets or by way of legal aid. If the Official Solicitor is not given this security, she will not act, and if it emerges during the course of proceedings that her legal costs can no longer be met, she will stop acting – and cannot be compelled to continue to act.[85]

12.41 It is therefore extremely important in any case both to identify whether another person may be suitable to act as a litigation friend and, if it would appear that the Official Solicitor may be the only candidate, to identify the basis upon which the Official Solicitor can be satisfied that her legal costs will be met. There is a standard order permitting the Official Solicitor to investigate P's financial position for costs purposes,[86] and if ineligible for legal aid for her costs of

84 Sarah Castle, appointed in 2019, is the first female holder of the post. Her approach her mirrors that of her male predecessors.

85 See *Bradbury and others v Paterson and others* [2014] EWHC 3992 (QB), [2015] COPLR 425. This was a decision in civil proceedings, but the same approach would be applied before the Court of Protection.

86 Available at: https://courtofprotectionhandbook.com/precedents/.

representation of P to be paid from P's estate at the conclusion of the proceedings, to be subject to detailed assessment if not agreed. Where P is not eligible for legal aid then an assessment will need to be carried out as to whether P's funds are sufficient to cover the costs of representation. This may depend on how P's assets are held, and difficulties can arise where P's only asset is a property whose value exceeds the threshold for eligibility for legal aid but where otherwise there is no available capital. In some cases statutory bodies who are parties have taken the view that it is sensible and cost effective for them to fund part or all of P's representation by way of undertakings, to allow the proceedings to progress, particularly where there is a risk that the proceedings may stall because there is no independent representation for P.

12.42 The Official Solicitor has also published two Practice Notes setting out important practicalities relating to her appointment as litigation friend of P in the Court of Protection and requests by the court to the Official Solicitor to act as, or appoint counsel to act as an advocate to the court.[87]

12.43 The appointment of family members, friends and advocates (such as independent mental capacity advocates (IMCAs)[88]) as P's litigation friend has become increasingly common over the past few years, especially in the context of applications in relation to deprivation of liberty (discussed further in chapter 22). Detailed guidance for such individuals considering acting as a litigation friend was commissioned in 2014 by the Department of Health,[89] but the following points are of particular importance in relation to such appointments:[90]

87 One deals with health and welfare proceedings (www.gov.uk/government/publications/appointment-of-the-official-solicitor-in-welfare-proceedings-practice-note); the other with property and affairs proceedings (www.gov.uk/government/publications/appointment-of-the-official-solicitor-in-property-and-affairs-proceedings-practice-note).

88 See, for instance, *Re M* [2013] EHWC 3456 (COP), [2014] COPLR 35.

89 See: www.39essex.com/wp-content/uploads/2015/01/Acting-as-a-Litigation-Friend-in-the-Court-of-Protection-October-2014.pdf. This guidance has been superseded to some extent by events, and should be read subject to the discussion below as to the duties of litigation friends, and also the ability of a litigation friend to act without instructing lawyers.

90 The case of *Hinduja v Hinduja and others* [2020] EWHC 1533 (Ch), [2020] 4 WLR 93 suggests that there may be a difference in approach between the criteria for appointment of a litigation friend in adversarial civil proceedings and inquisitorial Court of Protection Proceedings (see, in particular, paras 56–60). Caution should therefore be placed upon reliance upon authorities on this issue determined in the civil context.

- The mere fact that a person (for instance, a family member) has strong views as to where P's best interests lie does not automatically disqualify them from acting as P's litigation friend. Indeed, a person with strong and vocal views may very well be the best 'champion' for P.[91]
- However, where there is a family dispute concerning P's best interests, it would be rare for it to be appropriate for a family member to be appointed as P's litigation friend in proceedings relating to that dispute. If they were to be so appointed, they would have 'to demonstrate that he or she can, as P's litigation friend, take a balanced and even-handed approach to the relevant issues'.[92]
- Having religious beliefs which may colour the view of the litigation friend as to the right outcome will not automatically disqualify them from acting if they are capable of taking an objective view of the proceedings.[93]
- In the case of those subject to the deprivation of liberty safeguards (DOLS) regime (see further chapter 22 below), the courts have specifically endorsed the appointment of P's relevant person's representative (RPR) as their litigation friend: see *AB v LCC (a local authority) and the Care Manager of BCH*.[94] In *Re UF*, Charles J, endorsing *AB*, suggested that the possibility of whether the RPR could act as a litigation friend should 'often' be investigated.[95]
- Although it would be unusual for a solicitor to be appointed as litigation friend, this has happened in one publicly available case.[96]
- A litigation friend can act in person (ie without instructing legal representatives).[97] However, in all cases, a litigation friend should consider very carefully whether they can properly discharge their

91 See *Re NRA and others* [2015] EWCOP 59, [2015] COPLR 690, (2015) 18 CCLR 392 at paras 163–164.

92 *Re UF* [2013] EWHC 4289 (COP), [2014] COPLR 93, (2014) 17 CCLR 445 at para 23 per Charles J. See also *Re NRA and others* at para 169. In *Re D (appointment of litigation friend)* [2016] EWCOP 67, Baker J held that the principles identified by Charles J in *Re UF* applied in all cases where the court is considering whether a family member can act as a litigation friend.

93 *R (Raqeeb) v Barts NHS Trust* [2019] EWHC 2976 (Admin) at para 30 (by analogy, the case concerning a child).

94 [2011] EWHC 3151 (COP), [2012] COPLR 314.

95 *Re UF* at para 19.

96 *Re RGS* [2012] EWHC 4162 (COP).

97 *Re NRA and others* [2015] EWCOP 59, [2015] COPLR 690, (2015) 18 CCLR 392 at para 135.

obligation to conduct the proceedings competently without the assistance of legal representatives. If they consider that they cannot, then there would be nothing improper for the person to decline to act absent receiving appropriate security for cost of instructing legal representatives. The terms of the orders that would then be made would be very similar to those made in cases where the Official Solicitor consents to act.

- To act properly as a litigation friend can be an onerous undertaking. Where a paid RPR or an IMCA employed by an advocacy provider acts, it is important therefore that both they and – more importantly – their organisation are aware of the potentially significant amounts of time that may be required on their part properly to conduct litigation on P's behalf. Specific arrangements will also need to be made to ensure that their costs of acting as P's litigation friend (and, where appropriate, of instructing legal representatives) are met. The question of the basis upon which RPRs and IMCAs are entitled to reimbursement of their costs is addressed below at paras 12.70–12.71, but for present purposes it is important to note that there is a difference between an entitlement to reimbursement and a guarantee that they will not be left out of pocket – ie security for their costs. It should also be remembered that when considering an application for legal aid it is P's means, and not those of the litigation friend, which will be assessed (see further, chapter 6).

12.44 The MCA 2005, the COPR and the practice directions are silent as to whether it must be an individual who acts as litigation friend, or whether the responsibility can be taken on by a body. This is of particular relevance in the context of the involvement of RPRs and statutory advocates who may well – understandably – feel more comfortable (and more sure of themselves in demanding proper time to discharge their roles) if the formal responsibility for acting as litigation friend lies with their organisation, rather than resting solely upon their shoulders. The natural reading of the relevant provisions of the COPR would suggest that the draftsman had in mind the appointment of individuals, rather than organisations, but the position is not entirely clear.[98] We would strongly suggest that if any application to be appointed as a 'corporate' litigation friend is advanced, then it is made very clear in that application precisely who will have day-to-day responsibility for the conduct of the case on P's behalf[99] and what arrangements are in place to ensure continuity of consideration in the event that that individual is unavailable.

Acting for a child or a protected party other than P

12.45 Essentially the same considerations as set out above in relation to P also apply in terms of the appointment of a suitable litigation friend to represent children or adult protected parties other than P. In particular, it should be noted that it is not unheard of for the Official Solicitor to act for other parties in addition to P: the authors have experience of at least one case in which the Official Solicitor was acting for two other family members as well as P. In such cases, where it is quite possible that it is necessary that different individuals have different cases advanced on their behalf, the Official Solicitor will put in place 'Chinese walls' to ensure that such can be carried out ie, strict rules to ensure that each caseworker only sees the information relevant to their case.

Duties of the litigation friend

General

12.46 The COPR draws no distinction between the roles of a litigation friend depending upon whether they are acting on behalf of P or on behalf of a protected party (or, indeed, a child, a position addressed further at paras 12.50–12.52 below). In all cases, a litigation friend must (in order to be appointed) be able fairly and competently to conduct the proceedings.[100] The role of the litigation friend for P has

98 A trust corporation can be appointed as a deputy to manage P's property and affairs: MCA 2005 s19(1)(b). It is also possible for an office holder rather than a named individual to be appointed as a deputy to manage property and affairs (*Re SH* [2018] EWCOP 21, [2018] COPLR 522). Management of property and affairs is specifically said to extend to the conduct of legal proceedings on P's behalf (MCA 2005 s18(1)(k)). If appointed as deputy, therefore, and if the relevant order included specific provision relating to legal proceedings, a trust corporation or an office holder could therefore properly bring proceedings on P's behalf as P's litigation friend.

99 See, by analogy, *Re SH* at para 26 (in the context of office-holders discharging the functions of deputy).

100 COPR r17.1(1).

been held to be to form a view as to what is in the person's best interests and then advance that view to the court, although it may not accord with what the person is asserting.[101] The 'solution' that they must advance on P's behalf is the substantive outcome that they consider would best meet P's interests. Moreover, whether acting for P or for another party (or child) the litigation friend is not required to advance a case that would accord with the person's wishes if they consider that to do so would be unarguable, on the (to us the questionable) basis that such would not be in their best interests.[102] However, in all cases, the litigation friend must take all necessary steps to relay the individual's wishes and feelings to the court upon the relevant issues in the case.[103]

12.47 Where a professional has been appointed to act as litigation friend, the professional (and any representatives they appoint) should be sensitive to the concerns of parties such as P's family or others close to P that a stranger has been appointed to act for P. This is understandable, especially for parents of young adults who are used to being asked to speak on behalf of their son or daughter. A transparent approach will assist. If family members are unrepresented, we recommend a letter at the time of appointment in clear, non-technical language explaining the role of the litigation friend. It may be useful to include an explanation of other features of the Court of Protection which are likely to be unfamiliar, for example the role of the Transparency order (see further, chapter 14).

12.48 It is also very important for those acting for P to keep the other parties (whoever they are) up-to-date as to P's expressed wishes and feelings. Practitioners should prepare a full attendance note after all meetings with P. Such attendance notes should, if at all possible, contain a verbatim account of what P has actually said, so that the court and the parties hear P's voice directly rather than mediated

101 *Re NRA and others* [2015] EWCOP 59, [2015] COPLR 690, (2015) 18 CCLR 392 at para 170. This is also the approach adopted by the Official Solicitor: see fn 3 of her Practice Note: Appointment as Litigation Friend in Personal Welfare Proceedings in the Court of Protection (www.gov.uk/government/publications/appointment-of-the-official-solicitor-in-welfare-proceedings-practice-note).

102 *Re NRA and others* [2015] EWCOP 59, [2015] COPLR 690, (2015) 18 CCLR 392 at para 144, citing *RP v UK* (App No 38245/08, decision of 9 October 2012), [2013] 1 FLR 744, (2013) 16 CCLR 135. As to why we say 'questionable,' see Alex Ruck Keene, Peter Bartlett and Neil Allen, *Litigation friend or foe? Representation of P before the Court of Protection* (2016) Medical Law Review, Volume 24, Issue 3, 1 pages 333–359.

103 See, by analogy, *RP v UK* (App No 38245/08, decision of 9 October 2012), [2013] 1 FLR 744, (2013) 16 CCLR 135.

through the practitioner. Unnecessary anxiety or even suspicion can arise if parties are aware that a meeting with P has taken place without disclosure of the contents. For this reason we recommend that the court's permission is sought for the litigation friend to file and serve COP24 witness statements with attendance notes following meetings with P. If this approach is not appropriate in the case in question, alternative directions should be sought.

Deprivation of liberty cases

12.49 It is suggested that litigation friends should proceed with particular caution where P's right to liberty under ECHR Article 5 is engaged, and in particular in cases brought under MCA 2005 s21A in relation to authorisations granted under the DOLS regime (see further chapter 22). There is a considerable body of case-law from the ECtHR emphasising the importance of ensuring that the right to challenge a deprivation of liberty under Article 5(4) is effective.[104] In the light of that case-law, it is suggested that in a case involving a deprivation of liberty:

- A litigation friend for P must *always* consider testing whether it is correct that the assertion implicit in a request that the court uphold an authorisation or otherwise approve a deprivation of liberty that the regime in question is the least restrictive option. In other words, and to use the language of the ECtHR, the litigation friend must consider testing whether other, less severe measures have been considered and found to be insufficient to safeguard the individual or public interest which might require that the person concerned be detained.[105]
- Where P wishes to challenge that deprivation, then we would suggest that the litigation friend is, in fact, *obliged* to do so unless satisfied, after the most careful deliberation, that there truly is no properly arguable case that the deprivation of liberty does not

104 Summarised in *AJ (Deprivation of Liberty Safeguards)* [2015] EWCOP 5, [2015] Fam 291, (2015) 18 CCLR 158 at para 35. See also, subsequently, the decision of the ECtHR in *AN v Lithuania* (App No 17280/08, decision of 31 May 2016). See also *N v Romania* (App No 59152/08), (2017) 65 EHRR 23, where the ECtHR criticised the fact that N was represented by different lawyers at each procedure, and that there was a 'complete absence of consultation' with N at and between hearings.

105 As, for instance, did the Official Solicitor in *Y County Council v ZZ* [2012] EWHC B34 (COP), [2013] COPLR 463, in which ZZ vigorously disputed the necessity for the restrictions imposed upon him – primarily so as to secure against the risk that he would commit sexual offences against children.

represent the least restrictive requirement. If this is the case, then we would further suggest that it would never be appropriate for the litigation friend actively to concede that the deprivation of liberty was in P's best interests. At most, we would suggest, the litigation friend could leave it to the judge to decide (having ensured that P's views were relayed to the court). We suggest this is likely in most cases also to require an oral hearing.

Litigation friends acting for a child

12.50 A litigation friend acting on behalf of a child over the age of 16 who suffers from a material disturbance of the mind or brain giving rise to a lack of litigation capacity is, we suggest, in the same position as a litigation friend acting on behalf of an adult protected party.

12.51 The same does not necessarily go for:

- a litigation friend acting on behalf of a child under the age of 16 who suffers from a material disturbance or impairment of the mind or brain, as the MCA 2005 could never apply to the litigation friend's actions;[106]
- (assuming that such a category still exists) a litigation friend acting on behalf of a 16- or 17-year-old who requires a litigation friend because of their age and lack of maturity.

12.52 In either of these circumstances, it is suggested that a litigation friend acting for a child takes their duties from COPR r17.1. However, (by analogy with the situation where a litigation friend is appointed for a child in family proceedings), all steps and decisions the litigation friend takes in the proceedings must be taken for the benefit of the child.[107]

Terminating the appointment of a litigation friend

Litigation friend acting on behalf of P: capacity gained or regained

12.53 Any person – including P themselves – can apply to discharge the appointment of P's litigation friend if P has 1) gained, 2) regained or 3) asserts that they have always had capacity to conduct the proceedings.[108] By contrast to the position where an application is brought to

106 See MCA 2005, s2(5), which provides that no power may be exercised by a person under the MCA 2005 in relation to a person who lacks capacity under the age of 16; the exception in section 18(3) would not apply.

107 FPR PD 16A para 2.1.

108 COPR r17.5(1).

terminate the appointment of the litigation friend on the basis of their conduct, there is no need to file evidence with the application.[109] The court will no doubt decide what evidence is required in any given case, bearing in mind the presumption of capacity contained in MCA 2005 s1(1). The appointment of the litigation friend will continue in force until the court brings it to an end by an order,[110] in which it will no doubt make appropriate directions consequential upon the termination of the appointment (for instance as to where documents are to be sent to P in circumstances where they are no longer to be sent to the litigation friend).

12.54 Reported examples of applications made by or on behalf of P to discharge a litigation friend appointed to act on their behalf are (perhaps disappointingly) rare. An example is the medical treatment case of *Re SB*,[111] where the Official Solicitor applied successfully to be discharged on the basis of expert evidence that P had litigation capacity.[112]

12.55 However, save in a case where it is entirely clear that P can never have litigation capacity because of the severity of their underlying disability, the litigation friend acting on P's behalf should be very astute to keep P's capacity to conduct the litigation under review and, if it appears that they may have regained it, take immediate steps to bring matters before the court in short order.

12.56 If P has either gained or regained capacity in relation to the matter or matters to which the application relates, then the court will have no jurisdiction under the MCA 2005 and an application should be made to bring the proceedings to an end[113] (see further chapter 16). Such an application must be supported by evidence.[114]

Litigation friend acting on behalf of an adult protected party: capacity gained or regained

12.57 Where an adult protected party ceases to lack capacity to conduct the litigation, an application can be made for the litigation friend's appointment to be discharged, in the same way as discussed above in

109 The silence in COPR r17.5(2) in this regard is deliberate.

110 COPR r17.5(4).

111 [2013] EWHC 1417 (COP), [2013] COPLR 445.

112 See paras 27–30.

113 Under COPR r13.1, the application being made on a COP9 form (see further para 10.21 for applications within proceedings).

114 COPR r13.1(2)(b).

respect of P themselves[115] (para 12.53 above). Any person may make such an application, including the protected party themselves.[116] There is no need for evidence to be filed to support such an application.

Litigation friend acting on behalf of a child: capacity gained or regained

12.58 An application can be made during the currency of proceedings that a child no longer requires a litigation friend to conduct the proceedings on their behalf.[117] This would be appropriate if, for instance, the litigation friend considers that a child not suffering from any disability but previously requiring a litigation friend because they were not *Gillick*-competent[118] has now matured sufficiently to understand and conduct their own litigation. Formally, there is no requirement for evidence to support such an application, but it is suggested that the court would be likely to wish (at a minimum) a statement from the litigation friend explaining the basis upon which they consider that the child is now *Gillick*-competent.

Litigation friend acting on behalf of a child: child reaching majority

12.59 When a child party to proceedings turns 18, then, if they are not a protected party (ie an adult without litigation capacity), the appointment of the litigation friend will come to an end automatically.[119] The child must, though, serve notice on every other party stating that they have reached full age, that the appointment of the litigation friend has ended, and providing their address for service.[120]

Any litigation friend: other situations

12.60 Any litigation friend can also be removed by the court:

- on their own application (if, for instance, P is no longer eligible for public funding and the litigation friend cannot continue to

115 COPR r17.5(1).

116 COPR r17.5(1).

117 Ie for an order under COPR r17.5(1).

118 *Gillick v West Norfolk and Wisbech Area Health Authority* [1985] UKHL 7, [1986] 1 AC 112. This is subject to the discussion at para 12.13 above.

119 COPR r17.7.

120 COPR r17.7.

discharge their functions without such funding to pay for legal advice and representation);[121]

- on the application of any person (including, logically, both any party or indeed P); or
- of the court's own motion.[122]

12.61 Where the application is brought on the basis of the litigation friend's conduct, the application must be supported by evidence.[123]

12.62 COPR r17.5 does not place any limit on the power of the court to terminate the appointment of a litigation friend. In *Re A (conjoined twins: medical treatment) (No 2)*,[124] Ward LJ commented on the:

> . . . particular situation in which the court is asked to replace a guardian ad litem because the guardian has in the conduct of litigation taken a course of action (in which we include an omission), or is about to take a course of action, which is manifestly contrary to the best interests of the child whose interests it is the guardian's duty to safeguard. If the guardian (or litigation friend) does act manifestly contrary to the child's best interests, the court will remove him even though neither his good faith nor his diligence is in issue.

12.63 It is suggested that a similar approach would be adopted in the Court of Protection (subject to the discussion at paras 12.45–12.48 above as to the precise scope of the litigation friend's duties).

12.64 A solicitor who is acting for a protected party is likely under an obligation to inform the court of any concern that the litigation friend is not acting properly. In such circumstances, the court must be entitled to rely on the assessment of the legal team when considering the extent to which it can be established that the litigation friend has or is pursuing an interest adverse to that of the child.[125]

12.65 In any case where a litigation friend's appointment is terminated, the court will strive, if at all possible, to appoint a suitable person to act as replacement litigation friend[126] so that the proceedings can continue in an uninterrupted fashion.

121 See by analogy *Bradbury and others v Paterson and Others* [2014] EWHC 3992 (QB), [2015] COPLR 425.

122 COPR r17.5(1).

123 COPR r17.5(2).

124 [2000] EWCA Civ 254, [2001] 1 FLR 267.

125 *R (Raqeeb) v Barts NHS Trust* [2019] EWHC 2976 (Admin) at para 37 (by analogy, the case concerning a child).

126 COPR r17.5(1)(c), the substitute litigation friend being required to fulfil the conditions set by COPR r17.1(1): COPR r17.5(3).

After the hearing

12.66 In all cases, those who represent P should give careful thought to the likely impact of the conclusion of the proceedings on P. Once the case has ended, P's legal team's involvement will almost certainly end too, and in some cases this may remove a source of support for P. If P has an RPR or advocate, it may be helpful to speak to them before ending the legal team's involvement.

12.67 In a case where it is known that P is going to be very distressed by the outcome (for example an unsuccessful section 21A application) and where there is a real risk that this may lead to a deterioration in P's mental health, judges have been willing to approve orders directing a care plan addressing how this can be mitigated in the aftermath of the hearing.

Costs and the litigation friend

Costs incurred by the litigation friend

The Official Solicitor

12.68 The Official Solicitor is placed in a special position by virtue of COPR r19.9, which provides that her costs (if they are not met by payments made out of P's estate, by P's deputy, donee or attorney) shall be paid by such person or out of such funds as the court may direct. As noted above (see para 12.40), the Official Solicitor will not accept an invitation to act as litigation friend if she is not satisfied that there is provision for the (in-house or external) litigation costs to be met.

12.69 Largely for historical reasons, the Official Solicitor receives sufficient central government funding to conduct (in-house) proceedings relating to serious medical treatment cases (as to which, see further chapter 22), and conventionally seeks and is awarded half the costs of so doing against the relevant NHS body: see *An NHS Trust v D*.[127] The Official Solicitor will in general decline to act in such cases until an undertaking to meet half of her costs has been received from the NHS body in question. For these purposes, 'costs' include any of her costs incurred before the application is formally issued and also

127 [2012] EWHC 886 (COP), [2012] COPLR 499. This position is recorded also in the court's Serious Medical Treatment Guidance [2020] EWCOP 2, [2020] WLR 641 at para 21(b) and the Official Solicitor's Practice Note: *Appointment as litigation friend in personal welfare proceedings in the Court of Protection* (www.gov.uk/government/publications/appointment-of-the-official-solicitor-in-welfare-proceedings-practice-note) at para 15.

those which may arise from any subsequent appeal or applications to review orders which may be brought by any of the other parties.[128] Note that the relevant NHS body will usually be the body which has brought the proceedings as the applicant but in cases where the applicant is a private individual(s) this may be one or more of the public bodies acting as respondent.[129] The Official Solicitor does not seek to recover costs from P's own funds for acting in cases concerning serious medical treatment.

Other litigation friends

12.70 There are no equivalent statutory provisions to those relating to the Official Solicitor to guarantee reimbursement for others who act as litigation friend (whether for P or another individual requiring such representation). In *B v B*,[130] a case concerned with the ability of the Official Solicitor to recover her costs of acting as the litigation friend of an adult in matrimonial proceedings, Bennett J held that a litigation friend acts as the agent of the protected party and is entitled to be reimbursed by the protected party for the properly incurred costs of so acting.[131]

12.71 It is suggested that this principle holds true in Court of Protection proceedings for all litigation friends. There is, though, a difference between an entitlement to reimbursement and security for costs – ie a guarantee that the costs incurred (if properly incurred) will be repaid. As set out at para 12.43 above, it is suggested that – as with the Official Solicitor – it is entirely proper for a litigation friend such as an IMCA or family member to decline an invitation to act without sufficient security for their costs of so doing.

Costs payable to other parties

12.72 A curious feature of the COPR is that (unlike the CPR[132]) they do not provide any circumstance under which the litigation friend is

128 Official Solicitor's Practice Note: Appointment as Litigation Friend in Personal Welfare Proceedings in the Court of Protection (www.gov.uk/government/publications/appointment-of-the-official-solicitor-in-welfare-proceedings-practice-note) at para 15.

129 Official Solicitor's Practice Note: Appointment as Litigation Friend in Personal Welfare Proceedings in the Court of Protection (www.gov.uk/government/publications/appointment-of-the-official-solicitor-in-welfare-proceedings-practice-note) at para 15.

130 [2010] EWHC 543 (Fam), [2012] COPLR 480.

131 Paras 15, 30 and 41.

132 CPR 21.4(3)(c).

required personally, as a condition of acting, to undertake to pay the costs incurred by other parties in proceedings before the Court of Protection. That most likely reflects the general rules on costs in such proceedings which are to the effect that either a) P is to pay the costs of proceedings relating to their property and affairs;[133] or b) there should be no order as to costs in proceedings relating to P's health and welfare[134] (see further chapter 17 below).

12.73 It is clear, however, that the party on whose behalf the litigation friend acts can be made the subject of a costs order – and, indeed, at present, the general rule in property and affairs proceedings is that P will be required to pay the costs of those proceedings (including those costs incurred by others).[135] There is no reason in principle why a child or an adult protected party could not also be made the subject of a costs order. It would be the responsibility of the litigation friend to take appropriate steps to ensure that these costs are met (it is suggested as part of their duties to the court in the conduct of the litigation). It is not clear, however, that this would, formally give rise to a personal liability on the part of the litigation friend to meet the costs.[136] Even if it did, however, it is suggested that the litigation friend can look to the individual to reimburse them, at least if the proceedings have been properly conducted on the part of the litigation friend.[137]

12.74 Any litigation friend (theoretically including the Official Solicitor) is, however, potentially at risk of being ordered to pay costs *themselves*. Even though they are not, themselves, a party to proceedings, the COPR has provision for costs orders to be made against non-parties.[138]

12.75 In the absence of further guidance to clarify the scant provisions of the COPR as they relate to litigation friends other than the Official Solicitor, it has become an increasing practice for RPRs and IMCAs in welfare proceedings to make their agreement to act as litigation friend conditional on the giving of an undertaking on the part of the relevant public authority that they will not seek their costs against the

133 COPR r19.2.

134 COPR r19.3.

135 COPR r19.2.

136 It may be that the obligation arises at common law, see *Re Brocklebank* (1877) 6 Ch D 358 at 360, CA.

137 See, by analogy, *Re E (mental health patient)* [1984] 1 WLR 320 at 324H per Sir Robert Megarry V-C, COP, and also *B v B* [2010] EWHC 453 (Fam), [2012] COPLR 450.

138 COPR r19.12.

RPR/IMCA. It is suggested that this is a useful mechanism by which RPRs/IMCAs can be given reassurance in the discharge of what is an important public function, although it cannot (and would not be seen by the court as) acting as a carte blanche to the RPR/IMCA acting as litigation friend to depart from the proper and proportionate conduct of litigation.

12.76 There are no reported cases in which a litigation friend has themselves been made the subject of a costs order in the Court of Protection, and it is suggested that such an order would only be made in the event of serious misconduct on the part of the litigation friend, especially if such misconduct had the consequence of increasing the costs of the proceedings. In the event of such misconduct, it is further suggested that a local authority that had given an undertaking of the nature described in the paragraph immediately above would readily be relieved of its obligation by a judge and given permission to seek their costs as against the litigation friend personally.

COPR r1.2 representatives

Appointment

12.77 As set out at para 12.6 above, one of the options that the court can adopt to ensure the participation of P is to appoint a representative for them 'to provide the court with information as to the matters set out in section 4(6) of the Act [ie P's wishes, feelings, beliefs and values] and to discharge such other functions as the court may direct'.[139] It would, in principle, be possible to appoint such a representative even where P is joined as a party to proceedings, but in practice it is likely that a representative will only be appointed where the court has decided that P's participation can be secured other than by joining them. These representatives are known as 'rule 1.2 representatives' for purposes of the COPR. They are sometimes referred to as 'rule 3A representatives', after the original 2015 rule which created them. This term can give rise to some confusion, because rule 1.2 is the over-arching enabling power under which the court also appoints litigation friends and ALRs.[140] For the avoidance of doubt, this section of the chapter refers to representatives appointed under COPR r1.2(2)(c).

139 COPR r1.2(2)(c).
140 As is made clear by COPR r17.9.

12.78 The court may appoint a COPR r1.2 representative of its own motion or on the application of any person, but only with the consent of the representative.[141] Such an application must be made using form COP9[142] and must be served on all parties, as well as on any current representative or ALR and the proposed representative.[143] The representative must be able to discharge their functions[144] 'fairly and competently'.[145]

Duties

12.79 COPR PD 1A envisages a COPR r1.2 representative as being someone with knowledge of P, such as a family member or friend, or an IMCA or Care Act 2014 advocate.[146] Whilst, in theory, a legally qualified person could be appointed, it is suggested that they would not – if appointed as such a representative – be discharging any functions as a lawyer. If the court wished to appoint the person to act as a lawyer, then it would be required to do so under the provisions relating to ALRs, addressed further below.

12.80 In *Re NRA and others*,[147] Charles J approved the appointment of family members or friends of P, who have 'fought P's corner' over the years, in uncontentious cases where a statutory body applies to the court under MCA 2005 ss15 and 16 for authority to deprive P of their liberty (known as '*Re X* cases') (see further chapter 22). As he indicated, such appointments provide a means of:

(i) eliciting P's wishes and feelings and making them and the matters mentioned in s 4(6) of the MCA known to the court, without causing P any or any unnecessary distress, and
(ii) critically examining from the perspective of P's best interests, and with a detailed knowledge of P, the pros and cons of a care package, and whether it is the least restrictive available option.[148]

12.81 In the context of *Re X* cases, Charles J drew an express analogy between the role of a COPR r1.2 representative and the role of the Relevant Person's Representative under Schedule A1.[149] In other

141 COPR r17.10(2); PD 1A para 8.
142 COPR PD 17B (3).
143 COPR r17.13.
144 See COPR r1.2(2)(c) and the paragraph above.
145 COPR r17.9.
146 COPR PD 1A para 12.
147 [2015] EWCOP 59, [2015] COPLR 690 at para 234.
148 *Re NRA* at para 164.
149 *Re NRA* at para 112.

words the role requires a continuing commitment to the representation of P's wishes and feelings and the scrutiny of P's circumstances. In *Re VE*,[150] Charles J set out an extensive list of functions that would be expected of the representative including:

- checking the court documentation for accuracy;
- discussing points of difference with the statutory body making the application;
- discussing the package of care and support and the application to the Court with P in so far as P is able to understand them; and ascertaining P's views if this can be done without unnecessary distress including asking P what he thinks about the package of care and support
- deciding whether to support the application;
- considering how P should participate in the application; and
- preparing a statement to set out all of the above matters.

12.82 However, and especially outside the context of cases involving the authorisation of deprivation of liberty, the appointment of a representative will not always require the long-term involvement envisaged in *Re NRA* and *Re JM*.[151] Such an appointment could be limited to a single report to the judge in, for example, a property and affairs case where the judge does not wish to join P to save P the legal costs but wants to ensure that they have heard a neutral voice relaying P's views to the court.

12.83 The COPR do not prohibit a COPR r1.2 representative seeking to instruct a lawyer to assist them in the discharge of their duties. As discussed in chapter 6, public funding in the form of Legal Help is in principle available to assist a COPR r1.2 representative who is, themselves, financially eligible for such assistance, and a family member wishing to understand their duties may well wish to enlist legal advice by way of Legal Help. It would also be possible – by analogy with the position in relation to litigation friends (see para 12.71) for a person to decline to consent to be a COPR r1.2 representative without being given the necessary funds to instruct a lawyer. However, we suggest that a COPR r1.2 representative who finds that they are needing recourse to more than outline advice as to the nature of the duties (and, for instance, how to draft a witness statement) should consider very carefully whether it is in fact appropriate for them to continue in their role, or whether they should not take the matter

150 [2016] EWCOP 16, [2016] COPLR 406.
151 [2016] EWCOP 15, [2016] 4 WLR 64.

back to court for further directions under the provisions discussed in the following paragraph.

Directions and variation or termination of appointment

12.84 COPR r17.11 allows any representative appointed under COPR r1.2 to apply to the court for directions at any time, and does not require notice to be given to the parties (this of course includes ALRs). The directions sought may concern the 'performance, terms of appointment, or continuation of the appointment.' An application by the representative must be made on form COP9.[152] PD 1A recognises the possibility that representatives may find themselves in either a personal or professional position where they cannot properly represent P, or provide the court with information about P or carry out functions directed by the court.[153]

12.85 Other persons may also apply for the appointment of a representative to be brought to an end or varied; and may also apply for orders that a person does not act as a COPR r1.2 representative, or for an order that the representative is replaced.[154] If any such application is based on the conduct of the representative then this must be supported by evidence.[155] The court can also make any such order on its own initiative.[156] The court must bring the appointment of a representative to an end if P has capacity to appoint a representative and does not wish the appointment to continue.[157]

Funding

12.86 Many COPR r1.2 representatives will be family members who would be expected to act as a representative without recompense. However, as noted above, it is also entirely possible for an IMCA or another statutory advocate to act as such a representative. Charles J confirmed

152 COPR PD 17B para 2.
153 COPR PD 1A para 13.
154 COPR r17.12(1).
155 COPR r17.12(2).
156 COPR r17.12(2).
157 COPR r17.12(5). In *Central and North West London NHS Trust* [2015] UKUT 37 (AAC), Charles J held (at para 8) that to have capacity to appoint a representative for the purpose of an application to the Mental Health Tribunal required an appreciation of the patient's inability to conduct the proceedings unaided. It is suggested that this test should be applied for the purpose of COPR r17.12(5).

in *Re JM and others*[158] that local authorities are under no statutory duty, and cannot be compelled, to fund advocates to act as COPR r1.2 (formerly 'rule 3A') representatives. By analogy with a litigation friend (see paras 12.40–12.43 above), we suggest that a statutory advocate can decline to consent to act as a COPR r1.2 representative absent confirmation that they will be recompensed for their time, or withdraw their consent if it suitable funding is no longer available.

Accredited Legal Representatives

Definition

12.87 An ALR is defined in COPR r2.1 as 'a legal representative authorised pursuant to a scheme approved by the President to represent persons meeting the definition of P in this rule in proceedings before the Court'. A legal representative is also defined in COPR r2.1 as one of a number of categories of legally qualified individuals who has been instructed to act for a party in relation to any application.[159]

12.88 The Law Society maintains an accreditation scheme for ALRs, membership of which qualifies the practitioner to be appointed by the Court of Protection under COPR r1.2(1)(b).[160] The scheme is open to solicitors, barristers and Fellows of the Chartered Institute of Legal Executives (CILEx). The list of members is provided to the Court of Protection and is updated monthly.

12.89 It is important to note that, at present, the scheme only provides accreditation in relation to cases concerning P's welfare. As there is no scheme approved by the President in relation to cases concerning P's property and affairs, there is no power to appoint an ALR in a case concerning P's property and affairs.

158 [2016] EWCOP 15, [2016] 4 WLR 64, [2016] COPLR 302. See also *Re KT (incapacitated persons) (deprivation of liberty: general visitor)* [2018] EWCOP 1, [2018] 4 WLR 21, [2018] COPLR 185.

159 The reference to 'being instructed to act' is not strictly accurate in the context of ALRs, and it is likely that this will be amended in due course to 'being appointed for' or 'being appointed on behalf of.'

160 Details available at: www.lawsociety.org.uk/support-services/ accreditation/ mental-capacity/.

When will an ALR be appointed?

12.90 COPR PD 1A gives the judge 'pointers' when considering which of the options in COPR r1.2 to select. In light of the relative novelty of the role, paras 9–12 are set out below.

> 9. An accredited legal representative is defined in rule 2.1. When such representatives exist one can be appointed whether or not P is joined as a party and this may be of assistance if urgent orders are needed, particularly if they are likely to have an impact on the final orders (eg an urgent order relating to residence).
>
> 10. When P lacks capacity to conduct the proceedings and is made a party an accredited legal representative is not intended as a substitute for a litigation friend, but as an alternative in a suitable case (or in the early stages of the case).
>
> 11. When P lacks capacity to conduct the proceedings and an order that he is to be a party is made factors relevant to the choice between appointing a litigation friend and an accredited legal representative to represent him as a party will include –
>
> - Whether there will be a need for expert or other evidence to be obtained and filed, or other material gathered, on P's behalf;
> - The nature and complexity of the case;
> - The likely range of issues.
>
> 12. In other cases their nature and complexity, the issues raised or likely to be raised in them and the stage they have reached could mean that the assistance of an accredited legal representative is not required or is inappropriate and that P's participation is best secured and the court will be properly informed by the appointment of a representative under rule 1.2(2)(c) (who could be a friend, an IMCA, an advocate appointed under the Care Act 2014, a family member or anyone with relevant knowledge) or by directions being made under rule1.2(2)(d) or (e).

12.91 While COPR r1.2(2)(b) envisages that an ALR can be appointed to represent P in the proceedings without P being joined as a party, we anticipate that this form of appointment will be relatively rare; rather, we anticipate that ALRs will be more usually appointed where the court considers that P's participation requires them to have party status but P does not have the capacity to conduct the proceedings. At that point, and as set out at para 12.10 above, the court must either appoint an ALR or a litigation friend.[161]

12.92 It is also clear that the court does not envisage that ALRs will lead to litigation friends becoming redundant. Paragraph 11 explains the

161 COPR r1.2(4).

factors which the court would consider when deciding between an ALR and a litigation friend:

- whether there will be a need for expert evidence or other evidence to be obtained or filed, or other material gathered, on behalf;
- the nature and complexity of the case; and
- the likely range of issues.

12.93 This suggests that the court is more likely to appoint an ALR in a case where the issues are relatively defined. Paragraph 10 suggests that there may be cases where an ALR is appointed in the early stages of the case but that subsequently a litigation friend is needed because – for example – the case is more complex than first appeared. See further paras 12.97–12.99 below.

12.94 Although ALRs have now existed for a number of years, there remains limited case-law to assist in terms of their potential duties and role. By way of somewhat niche exception, in *Re PD* Baker J held that in an application for recognition and enforcement of a foreign order (see further chapter 27), P does not always need to be a party but could participate through an ALR who could 'facilitate a quick but focussed analysis of the particular requirements of Schedule 3'.[162] In *Re KL*,[163] Senior Judge Hilder considered the – limited – role for ALRs in proceedings to authorise the deprivation of liberty of a 16–17 year old (see also chapter 22).

12.95 It had been hoped that the availability of ALRs might reduce the pressure on the Official Solicitor's office, especially in urgent cases. It is not always possible to identify other paid litigation friends (eg IMCAs, RPRs) because of capacity and funding issues. There was vivid evidence of the pressure on advocacy services from some of the statutory bodies in *Re JM*.[164] It is the authors' experience that ALRs are increasingly acting in section 21A appeals, where P is entitled to non-means-tested legal aid (see chapters 6 and 22), even those raising complex issues.[165]

Requirements for appointment as an ALR

12.96 COPR r17.9 provides that a COPR r1.2 representative (including an ALR) must be able to discharge their functions in relation to P 'fairly

162 [2015] EWCOP 48, [2015] COPLR 544.
163 [2022] EWCOP 24.
164 [2016] EWCOP 15, [2016] 4 WLR 64 at para 96.
165 See, for example, *DP v Hillingdon LBC* [2020] EWCOP 45, [2020] COPLR 769.

and competently'. COPR r17.10 requires the consent of the COPR r1.2 representative before they are appointed.

Appointment

12.97 COPR r17.10 provides that the court may appoint an ALR at any time, either on its own initiative or on the application of any person,[166] provided it is satisfied that the person to be appointed satisfies the requirements of COPR r17.9 (see para 12.34 above). The same requirements apply as regards the appointment of ALRs as they do COPR r1.2 representatives (see para 12.77 above).

Duties

12.98 An ALR has the following responsibilities:

- a duty to the court to comply with COPR r1.2/COPR r3A and to help the court to further the overriding objective;[167]
- Professional responsibilities to the client and others in line with the relevant regulatory framework applicable to the relevant category of legal representative;[168] and
- (In legal aid cases) a duty to the Legal Aid Agency (LAA) to comply with the contracting arrangements (see further chapter 6).

12.99 The Law Society has produced a Practice Note for ALRs. It can be found on the Law Society's website.[169] ALRs should adhere to the guidance in the Practice Note. It may also be useful for practitioners:

- when instructed by the Official Solicitor;
- when instructed by another litigation friend;
- (In rare cases) instructed by P directly where P has litigation capacity.

12.100 In the absence of guidance from the courts on the use of ALRs, we note that COPR PD 1A recommends a cautious approach to the use of ALRs and concludes with the following paragraph (para 13):

> A rule 1.2 representative must be able to discharge his or her functions fairly and competently It is possible that a rule 1.2 representative

166 COPR r17.10(2).

167 COPR Part 4/COPR r1.4.

168 For instance the SRA Code of Conduct for solicitors or the BSB Code of Conduct for barristers.

169 See: www.lawsociety.org.uk/en/topics/advocacy/accredited-legal-representatives-in-the-court-of-protection.

may be in, or find himself or herself in, a personal or professional position in which he or she cannot properly represent P, provide the court with information about P or carry out other functions directed by the court. In such a case, Section 2 of Part 17 allows for the court to vary the terms of the appointment with a view to resolving the difficulty, or to discharge the appointment altogether (in which case the court will consider afresh whether it should make one or more of the directions in paragraph (2) of rule 1.2.

12.101 This suggests in turn that ALRs (or COPR r1.2 representatives) should not attempt to 'soldier on' if they find themselves in difficulty discharging the various duties they owe. We suggest that the circumstances in which the ALR should consider approaching the court will include cases where there is a divergence between the ALR's view of P's best interests and P's wishes, and where the ALR is satisfied that P lacks capacity to make the decision.

12.102 ALRs may therefore wish to apply a relatively low threshold for approaching the court under Part 17. The court will then have a range of rule 1.2 options open to it, including the appointment of a litigation friend who could then instruct the former ALR in the usual way. In their article referred to at footnote 102 above, Alex Ruck Keene and others suggest the appointment of an advocate to the court in such cases, allowing the ALR to argue P's wishes without reservation.

Directions and variation or termination of appointment

12.103 The relevant provisions apply in relation to ALRs in this regard as they do in relation to COPR r1.2 representatives: see para 12.84 above.

CHAPTER 13

Evidence and disclosure

Introduction

13.1 This chapter deals with the process by which sufficient evidence is obtained and put before a judge to enable them to decide upon the application before them. It deals, in particular, with the different categories of evidence that may be necessary, whether that be factual evidence or expert evidence. It addresses questions relating to hearsay evidence. It then turns, finally, to disclosure, in particular the questions of when and how disclosure is or should be withheld.

13.2 The matters covered in this chapter are very wide-ranging, and space precludes detailed discussion of the intricacies of such matters as the law relating to hearsay evidence. The reader is directed to such works as *Phipson on Evidence*;[1] there is also valuable commentary to be found about the application of the principles to public law proceedings relating to children (which bear certain analogies to proceedings relating to incapacitated adults) in works such as *Hershman and McFarlane: Children Law and Practice*.[2]

Evidence

The powers of the court

13.3 The provisions of Court of Protection Rules 2017[3] (COPR) Part 14 amplified by Practice Direction (PD) 14, set out a detailed framework by which the court can ensure that (ideally) it has before it that evidence, but only that evidence, which it needs to make the decision(s) it is asked to make.

13.4 The heart of COPR Part 14 is rule 14.2 'Power of court to control evidence', which provides that:

> (1) The court may–
> (a) control the evidence by giving directions as to:
> (i) the issues on which it requires evidence;
> (ii) the nature of the evidence which it requires to give those issues; and
> (iii) the way in which the evidence is to be placed before the court;
> (b) use its power under this rule to exclude evidence that would otherwise be admissible;

1 Sweet & Maxwell, 20th edn, 2021.
2 Bloomsbury, looseleaf, Section 7.
3 SI 2017 No 1035.

(c) allow or limit cross-examination;
(d) admit such evidence, whether written or oral, as it thinks fit; and
(e) admit, accept and act upon such information, whether oral or written, from P, any protected party or any person who lacks competence to give evidence, as the court considers sufficient, although not given on oath and whether or not it would be admissible in a court of law apart from this rule.

13.5 The powers granted to judges under this rule are in addition to the general case management powers granted them by COPR rr3.1 and 3.7. They are very broad, and reflect the fact that a very wide range of cases come before the Court of Protection, requiring a carefully calibrated approach so as to ensure that (in line with the overriding objective set down in rule 1.4) evidence is obtained – and limited – in a proportional fashion.

What evidence is required?

13.6 The Mental Capacity Act (MCA) 2005 and COPR are silent as to the evidential requirements that must be satisfied before the court can decide the application(s) before it. There are, though, two obligations of particular importance that are imposed upon the court:

- to act in the best interests of the adult without capacity if the decision it is being asked to make is one falling within the scope of MCA 2005 s1(5), which requires that an act done or decision made under the MCA 2005 for or on behalf of a person who lacks capacity 'must be done, or made, in his best interests';
- to act compatibly with the rights under the European Convention on Human Rights (ECHR) of the adult without capacity (and, to the extent relevant, the rights of the other parties to the application or potentially affected by its decision) (see further chapter 26).[4]

13.7 Determining the nature and scope of the evidence required by the court is a matter that is complicated by the fact that:

> The processes of the Court of Protection are essentially inquisitorial rather than adversarial. In other words, the ambit of the litigation is determined, not by the parties, but by the court, because the function of the court is not to determine in a disinterested way a dispute brought to it by the parties, but rather, to engage in a process of

4 Human Rights Act (HRA) 1998 s6(1), read together with s6(3).

assessing whether an adult is lacking in capacity, and if so, making decisions about his welfare that are in his best interests.[5]

13.8 That having been said:

- In all cases, the burden lies upon the party asserting that P lacks capacity to take the material decisions in question to establish that they lack such capacity, on the balance of probabilities.[6]
- Further, it may be necessary that a party prove a particular fact or facts in a way akin to conventional civil litigation:
  - In *LBB v JM, BK and CM*[7] Hedley J held that, where the intervention of the court would engage a potential breach of rights under the ECHR, as is particularly likely in welfare cases, it is incumbent upon the applicant to establish a factual basis upon which the court can be satisfied both that the jurisdiction should be exercised and that any interference is lawful.
  - Another (not uncommon) scenario is where it is said that a deputy or attorney has behaved in a way which justifies the intervention of the court; in such instance, it will fall to the party asserting such misconduct to establish it upon the basis of appropriate evidence.

13.9 Questions of the resolution of disputed facts are addressed further in chapter 15 below. The resolution of disputes as to capacity is addressed further in the context of the final determination of proceedings at chapter 16 below.

13.10 Further, even if a judge is presented with a consent order for approval by parties to an application, the judge is required to consider for themselves as an independent matter whether they can properly endorse that order, and must do so by reference to the evidence before them. In a contested application, one of the first questions for the court will be to determine as precisely as possible what evidence it will require before it can make any final decision(s) (in this regard see also chapter 11, on interim hearings).

13.11 A failure to bring proceedings upon the basis of proper evidence can lead to substantial costs consequences. A good example of this is

5 *Cheshire West and Cheshire Council v P and M* [2011] EWHC 1330 (Fam), [2011] COPLR Con Vol 273 at para 52 per Baker J, endorsed by Sir James Munby P in *Re G (An Adult)* [2014] EWCOP 1361, [2014] COPLR 416 at para 26, see also *N v ACCG* [2017] UKSC 22, (2017) 20 CCLR 133 at para 43.

6 MCA 2005 ss1(2) and 2(4). See also *PH v A Local Authority and others* [2011] EWHC 1704 (Fam), [2012] COPLR 128 at para 16, per Baker J.

7 [2010] COPLR Con Vol 779.

A Local Authority v HS and others,[8] in which the local authority maintained allegations that P's brother had sexually abused her but then withdrew them shortly before a hearing was to take place to determine them, on the basis that it accepted that it would not be able to establish them. The local authority applicant was ordered to pay all of the costs claimed by the Official Solicitor on behalf of P and of P's brother in respect of the steps taken towards the determination of the allegation up to and including the point that the local authority withdrew the allegation. As the court noted: 'Cogent evidence never existed. It should have been obvious long before these proceedings were commenced . . . that there was never any cogent evidence'.[9] Those costs amounted (together) to some £88,000. See also in this regard chapter 24 on safeguarding and the Court of Protection.

Admissions

13.12 The COPR provide for the making of admissions by a party of the truth of the whole or another part of another party's case by giving notice in writing.[10] This provision is, in the authors' experience, rarely invoked, but it serves as a formal mechanism by which factual matters can be agreed between the parties and advanced to the court as an agreed basis upon which it can then be invited to take a decision. There is no necessary formality to the notice that is required (nor is it necessary that the notice be filed at court), but it is prudent to ensure that, where an admission is being made, express reference is made to the provisions of COPR r14.1(1) and care is taken to ensure that the precise scope of what is being admitted is defined.

Factual evidence

Overview

13.13 Very broadly, most evidence before the court will fall into one of two categories: factual evidence and expert evidence. The latter is discussed at para 13.56 onwards below. The former constitutes a range of different types of material, the most obvious being evidence from witnesses as to facts relevant to the decision(s) that the court is

8 [2013] EWHC 2410 (COP).

9 Para 185, per District Judge Eldergill.

10 COPR r14.1(1). The court may allow a party to amend or withdraw an admission: COPR r14.1(2).

being asked to take. The different categories of such evidence are discussed below.

Witness statements: formalities and contents

13.14 The general rule is that any fact that needs to be proved by the evidence of a witness must be proved by the oral evidence of that witness if there is a final hearing, and by their evidence in writing at any other hearing (or if there is no hearing).[11] It would appear that a permission form, an application form or an application notice can stand as evidence at a hearing other than a final hearing if verified by a statement of truth.[12]

13.15 Almost without exception, and in line with the position that prevails in civil litigation and proceedings involving children, a witness will be required to provide a witness statement in advance of the final hearing, which will stand (if they are to give oral evidence) as their evidence in chief.[13] In other words, the court will accept their statement (if it complies with the formal requirements discussed below) at a final hearing *as if* they had given its contents orally in response to questions from the representative of the party on whose behalf the witness has been called. The corollary of this is that a witness will only be allowed to amplify their statement and/or to give evidence relating to new matters if there is good reason to do so.[14] The latitude granted by judges to witnesses to go beyond the contents of their witness statement in oral evidence will depend greatly upon the circumstances of the case, but as a general rule it is prudent to proceed on the cautious basis that the main opportunity that the witness will get to give oral evidence will be in response to questions asked in cross-examination by other parties or to questions asked by the judge.

13.16 While permission is not required to serve written evidence with an application (including an interim application) or in response to an application (and indeed, it is in some circumstances mandatory to file such evidence[15]), as a general rule it is only possible to rely upon

11 COPR r14.3(1).
12 COPR r5.2(3)(a).
13 COPR r14.3(2).
14 COPR r14.3(3)–(4).
15 For instance, a party served with an application who opposes it or seeks a different order must file a witness statement with their acknowledgment of service containing any evidence upon which they intend to rely: COPR r9.12(5); an interim application must also be accompanied by evidence if it the evidence not already before the court: COPR r10.2(2).

written evidence filed subsequently if permission has been given by the court.[16] As noted above (and discussed further in chapter 10), one of the primary questions for the court as part of its case management functions will be to decide whether to grant such permission; indeed, it is required by the COPR to give directions as to the service of witness statements in advance of the final hearing.[17] Judges will be astute in deciding whether to grant permission to ensure – insofar as possible – that the written evidence filed only goes to the issues in question.

13.17 Witness statements to be used at a final hearing are the subject of particular requirements. They must contain a statement of truth and comply with the requirements of COPR PD 14A paras 33–50.[18] While, strictly, witness evidence prepared for other purposes (for instance, at an interim hearing), does not need to comply with these requirements, it is advisable that, wherever practicable, witness evidence is put before the court in a form that can stand, if necessary, at the final hearing.

13.18 A sample witness statement is to be found in appendix D below. The most important points to emphasise in relation to the preparation of witness statements are as follows:

- Witness statements should be clearly headed so that it is immediately obvious who is giving the statement, on whose behalf they are giving it, whether it is the first statement that they are making (and, if not, which number it is), and the date upon which it was made.
- While witness statements must be attached to a COP24 form, it is not necessary that they are included in the form itself. The form is unwieldy; unless the statement is very short, it is often much better to prepare the statement as a stand-alone document and attach it to a COP24. If this is done, then it is advisable to include a statement of truth at the end of the stand-alone document as well as in the box contained in the COP24.
- Only evidence that is relevant to the issue(s) before the court should be included. Indeed evidence that is not relevant is strictly not admissible.[19] For cases on the welfare pathway under the Case

16 COPR r14.4(c).

17 COPR r14.6(2).

18 COPR r14.7 read together with PD 14A. PD 5B makes detailed provisions relating to statements of truth.

19 *Hollington v Hewthorn and Co Ltd* [1943] KB 587 at 594. For a detailed discussion of questions of relevance and admissibility, see *Phipson on Evidence*, chapter 7.

Pathways PD 3B (see further para 4.101), specific tasks for the judge at the case management conference include recording the issues in dispute, what has been agreed between the parties, and which issues are not to be the subject of adjudication in the case.[20] Care should be exercised not to include in the witness statement evidence that goes to issues that have been specifically recorded as not being the subject of adjudication, otherwise (at a minimum) judicial criticism will be likely.

- It is important clearly to distinguish in the statement between facts that are directly within the knowledge of the person making the statement and those which are matters of information or belief (and, where the latter, the source for those matters). While it may be quite proper for a witness statement to contain hearsay evidence (ie evidence relating to matters that they have not witnessed directly, discussed further below at para 13.23 below), it is necessary that this is clearly identified.
- Any exhibits should be clearly referenced in the statement by the witness; where the witness gives more than one statement, the numbering of the exhibits should run consecutively throughout, rather than starting again with each statement. The mechanics of exhibiting documents (and other items) to a witness statement are set out at PD 14A paras 20–31.[21]

13.19 A common error in statements prepared by public bodies in welfare proceedings is that they do not set out in sufficient detail what is proposed for P, why the proposed option is considered to be in P's best interests and how, if there is to be a change in the arrangements for P (for instance a move) how any transition is to be managed. It is (often) the case that further investigation in fact reveals that the necessary issues have been considered, but that the analysis underpinning the conclusions set out in the statement is not set out in sufficient detail. A checklist for the preparation of such statements is to be found at appendix E.

13.20 By the same token, if any other party wishes to advance an alternative suggestion as to what is in P's best interests in welfare proceedings (or, indeed, suggestions are being advanced as to P's best interests in proceedings relating to property and affairs), it is suggested that the maxim of 'show your workings' in terms of outlining the

20 COPR Case Pathways PD 3B para 2.5(a)–(c).

21 Which apply not to just to affidavits, as suggested by their placement in the practice direction, but also to witness statements: see COPR PD 14A para 39.

reasons why the course of action advanced is in P's best interests will always serve well.

Witness statements – timing

13.21 The court will usually consider, when giving directions as to service of witness statements, the order in which they are to be served.[22] Where P is a party to the proceedings, and the Official Solicitor acts as their litigation friend, it is usual for the Official Solicitor to serve his evidence last. That evidence (save in the most straightforward of cases) takes a standard form and is not, formally, a witness statement, but simply a statement, as the Official Solicitor does not have direct knowledge of the facts and matters in question. It is prepared by the solicitors instructed on the Official Solicitor's behalf (or by a lawyer or case-worker in the Official Solicitor's office if the matter is being handled in-house), but will be signed by the Official Solicitor or one of their deputies. It will set out the Official Solicitor's summary of the relevant background to and the procedural developments in the proceedings, and setting out the Official Solicitor's views as to P's best interests in the light of the evidence as it stands as at the time of the statement. Such views are almost invariably expressed as being subject to the caveat that they will be the subject of further consideration at the conclusion of the hearing, to cater for unanticipated developments at the hearing. It is suggested that a broadly similar approach should also be followed where another litigation friend or ALR is appointed to act on P's behalf. In addition to filing such a statement before the final hearing, we recommend that those acting for P should keep the court and parties up-to-date following attendances with P. See discussion at para 12.47.

13.22 In some circumstances, it is not possible for witness statements to be prepared and served in the way outlined above. There are two potential scenarios:

- The party wishing to rely upon the evidence of the witness may not be able to take the formal steps required to enable the witness to give their statement (for instance, because the witness is unwell at the time). In such circumstances, the party can apply without notice to be permitted to file a witness summary, which is a summary of a) the evidence, if known, which would otherwise be included in a witness statement; or b) if the evidence is not known, the matters about which the party proposes to question the

22 COPR r14.6(3).

witness.[23] Unless the court directs otherwise, the summary must include the name and address of the intended witness, and the summary must be filed within the period in which the statement would have had to be filed.[24] The court will then apply, as far as practicable, the provisions relating to the amplification of witness statements discussed at para 13.15 above and also the provisions relating to the service of witness statements (for instance, as to the order in which the summary is to be served).[25]

- It may become clear shortly before a hearing that a witness is able to give evidence necessary to the resolution of the matters before the court, but permission has not previously been granted to the relevant party to rely upon the evidence of the witness. In such circumstances, it is strongly advisable to notify the other parties and the court as soon as possible of the existence of the witness and the nature of the evidence that they will be able to give if permission is granted to rely upon their evidence at the hearing. Depending upon the timing, it may be possible for the question of permission to be determined in advance of the hearing; it may well, however, be necessary for the question to be decided at the outset of the hearing. If it will not be possible for the question of permission to be decided before the hearing, it is advisable that as full a statement as possible is obtained from the witness and served upon the other parties so as to reduce any element of surprise. The statement should also be filed with the court, but it is particularly important to flag up in any list of pre-reading prepared for the judge that permission has not been granted to rely upon the statement; if any party has indicated that they will object to the late service of the statement and/or the giving of evidence by the witness, the judge should not be invited to read the statement prior to the hearing.

Hearsay evidence

13.23 Space precludes a detailed discussion of the law relating to hearsay evidence, ie statements made otherwise than by a person while giving oral evidence in the proceedings which are tendered as evidence of the matters stated.[26] In contrast to the statutory schemes for

23 COPR r14.8(1)–(2).
24 COPR r14.8(3)–(4).
25 COPR r14.8(5).
26 The statutory definition contained in Civil Evidence Act (CEA) 1995 s1(2)(a). A detailed discussion can be found in chapter 29 of *Phipson on Evidence*.

both civil and family proceedings, the MCA 2005 and COPR make no express reference to hearsay. However, in *Enfield LBC v SA and others*,[27] McFarlane J held that Court of Protection proceedings under the MCA 2005 fall within the very wide definition of 'civil proceedings' under the CEA 1995. The CEA 1995 therefore applies to such proceedings, and hearsay evidence is admissible in accordance with the provisions of the CEA 1995.[28]

13.24 In the light of the decision in *SA*, the formal position is that:

- If a party wishes to rely upon hearsay evidence, they must give to the other party or parties such formal notice of and (on request) such particulars of or relating to the evidence, as is required to enable them to deal with any matters arising from its being hearsay.[29] It would appear that there is no requirement to give notice to rely upon a hearsay statement contained in a document within the agreed bundle (see paras 13.30–13.33 below).[30] In any event, in light of the flexibility granted by COPR r14.2(d), it is unlikely that a judge would decline to consider hearsay evidence in respect of which formal advance notice had not been given. The judge would, however, no doubt consider the extent to which the other party or parties had been disadvantaged by the fact that the maker of the original statement had not been produced for cross-examination.
- In estimating the weight (if any) to be given to the hearsay evidence the court shall have regard to any circumstances from which any inference can reasonably be drawn as to the reliability or otherwise of the evidence, and, in particular, may have regard to:
  - whether it would have been reasonable and practicable for the party by whom the evidence was adduced to have produced the maker of the original statement as a witness;
  - whether the original statement was made contemporaneously with the occurrence or existence of the matters stated;
  - whether the evidence involves multiple hearsay;
  - whether any person involved had any motive to conceal or misrepresent matters;
  - whether the original statement was an edited account, or was made in collaboration with another or for a particular purpose;

27 [2010] EWHC 196 (Admin), [2010] COPLR Con Vol 362.

28 *SA* at paras 29–30.

29 CEA 1995 s2(1).

30 By analogy with *Charnock v Rowan* [2012] EWCA Civ 2, [2012] CP Rep 18.

- whether the circumstances in which the evidence is adduced as hearsay are such as to suggest an attempt to prevent proper evaluation of its weight.[31]

13.25 One type of hearsay evidence that has assumed increasing prominence, often (but not exclusively) in medical treatment cases, are recordings. These have caused considerable concern to the judiciary:

- The Vice-President, Hayden J, has expressed unease with the use of video recording by family members of P for purposes of investigating or assessing capacity or best interests, observing in *Abertawe Bro Morgannwg University Local Health Board v RY and another*[32] that:

  > It is axiomatic that they are highly invasive of [P's] privacy and that he has no capacity to consent to them. They have been viewed by a variety of professionals. . . ., I do not consider that video recordings should ever be regarded as a routine investigative tool. Both the videoing and their distribution will require strong and well-reasoned justification.

- In *Z v University Hospitals Plymouth NHS Trust and others*[33] Cohen J observed that:

  > Although I have not heard any detailed argument, it seems to me arguably unlawful and in breach of the rights of both [P] and the Trust for the niece to film a visit made to [P] without the consent of [P], his next of kin or the hospital authorities.

If video evidence is to be relied upon, then it is important that matters are raised with the court as early as possible so that appropriate consideration can be given as to 1) why it is required; 2) how it is to be obtained; 3) how its circulation is to be appropriately limited; and 4) what information the court may require in order to be able to place any such evidence in its appropriate context.

13.26 If a witness is not competent to give evidence, information can be received as hearsay. COPR r14.2(e) makes clear that the court can accept hearsay evidence (in the form of 'information') from P, any protected party or any person who lacks competence to give evidence.[34] Competence to give evidence should not be confused with capacity to conduct proceedings: the test for competence is whether the witness is capable of understanding the nature of an oath and of

31 CEA 1995 s4.

32 [2017] EWCOP 2, [2017] COPLR 143 at para 52.

33 [2020] EWCOP 69 at para 23.

34 See also *A County Council v AB and others (Participation of P in Proceedings)* [2016] EWCOP 41.

giving rational testimony.[35] A person may not be able to conduct proceedings and require a litigation friend, but be entirely competent to give evidence.[36]

13.27 However, even if the evidence from a witness who is not competent to give evidence is admissible, as McFarlane J noted in *SA*:

> Admissibility is one thing, and the weight to be attached to any particular piece of hearsay evidence will be a matter for specific evaluation in each individual case. Within that evaluation, the fact that the individual from whom the evidence originates is not a competent witness will no doubt be an important factor, just as it is, in a different context, when the family court has to evaluate what has been said by a very young child.[37]

13.28 The position in respect of hearing from P is addressed at paras 16.38–16.49.

Affidavits

13.29 The COPR and PD 14A both make reference to the giving of evidence by witnesses within the jurisdiction by way of affidavit instead of or in addition to a witness statement.[38] Save for the making of an application for an order for committal to prison for contempt of court,[39] there are no rules or practice directions (or other enactments) which require that evidence be given in such a form. A judge may require such to be given, but such is in practice unusual, especially given that proceedings for contempt of court can be brought against a person who makes or causes to be made a false statement in a witness statement verified by a statement of truth without an honest belief in its truth.[40]

Documentary evidence

13.30 COPR PD 14 provides both that a court may give directions requiring the parties to use their best endeavours to agree a bundle or

35 *Phipson on Evidence*, Sweet & Maxwell, 20th edn, 2021, para 9–08.

36 See by analogy *Milroy v British Telecommunications plc* [2015] EWHC 532 (QB), in which the claimant in personal injury proceedings did not have capacity to litigate those proceedings, but was competent to give evidence as the training he had received and the circumstances under which he had suffered the material injury.

37 *Enfield LBC v SA and others* [2010] EWHC 196 (Admin) at para 36.

38 COPR rr14.9–14.10; PD 14A paras 1–19. The position of witnesses outside England and Wales is considered separately at para 13.43 below.

39 COPR r21.15(1) and PD 21A.

40 COPR r5.6.

bundles of documents for use at any hearing,[41] and that all documents contained in such bundle(s) shall be admissible at that hearing as evidence of their contents unless a) the court orders otherwise; or b) a party gives written notice of objection to the admissibility of particular documents.

13.31 In practice, it is routine in welfare cases for a direction to be made at an early stage in the proceedings that social services and/or medical records relating to P be provided by the relevant public authorities to the litigation friend appointed to act on behalf of P, most usually the Official Solicitor. It is then not uncommon for parts of those records to be included (whether by the public authority or those acting on behalf of P) in the bundles before the court, and then to form a significant part of the evidence upon which the court will make its decision. It is therefore important that if a family member (say) wishes to object to the admissibility of any or all or those documents that this is made very clear in the preparation of the agreed bundles before the final hearing. Questions of the wider disclosure of such records during the currency of proceedings and (in particular) the circumstances under which such disclosure can be withheld raise difficult issues that are discussed further below at para 13.103.

13.32 Another mechanism by which factual information can be put before the court is by the power granted under COPR r14.14 to the court to direct that a party with access to information which is not reasonably available to another party to direct the former to prepare and file a document recording the information and to serve it on the other party (or parties). Any document prepared pursuant to this rule must include sufficient details of all the facts, tests, experiments and assumptions which underlie any part of the information to enable the party on whom it is served to make, or to obtain, a proper interpretation of the information and an assessment of its significance.[42] This provision is rarely, if ever, invoked, but can serve a purpose if one party has information which is not reduced to documentary form which can and should properly be provided to the other parties to the court in a document which can be the subject of proper scrutiny. Rule 107 does not, itself, provide that a document produced under the provision is evidence of its contents, but if it is included within

41 For welfare cases on the personal welfare pathway under the Case Management Pilot, specific provision is made in relation to the preparation of bundles for the case management hearing, final management hearing and the final hearing (see COPR Case Pathways PD 3B paras 2.4(1)(h), 2.6(3) and 2.7(2) respectively and chapter 10).

42 COPR PD 14A para 54.

the agreed bundle for a hearing, the rule discussed at para 13.30 above will apply.

Notarial acts and instruments

13.33 A notarial act or instrument may, without further proof, be received in evidence as duly authenticated in accordance with the requirements of law unless the contrary is proved.[43] Such acts or instruments will, in most cases, originate from a foreign country in which notaries play an important role in authenticating documents.

Witness summons

13.34 A party can apply for the issue of a witness summons requiring a named individual to attend court and give oral evidence or to produce a document.[44] Permission to issue such a summons must be sought upon application using a COP9 form (see further para 11.26 onwards), and the application notice must include particulars of the applicant, the proposed witness, any document which the proposed witness is required to produce, and the grounds upon which the application is made.[45] A witness summons can also be issued by the court of its own motion, and in *Re NRA*, Charles J noted the use of such summons as one of the tools that the court should consider using as part of its 'investigatory jurisdiction'.[46]

13.35 A summons to produce documents to the court must either identify the individual document(s) or by reference to a specific category or event, but 'with sufficient certainty to leave no real doubt in the mind of the person to whom the summons is addressed about what they are required to do'.[47]

13.36 If the application is granted, the witness summons will then be prepared by the court[48] (PD 14D provides for the correction of errors in the name or address of the person to be summoned prior to service). The usual rule is that the party that made it must serve the

43 COPR r14.12.

44 COPR r14.13.

45 COPR r14.13(2); PD 14D para 3.

46 *Re NRA and others* [2015] EWCOP 59, [2015] COPLR 690, (2015) 18 CCLR 392 at para 261.

47 *Tajik Aluminium Plant v Hydo Aluminium AS* [2005] EWCA Civ 1218, [2006] 1 WLR 767 at para 28 per Moore-Bick LJ. The court added that doubts about the adequacy of the description should generally be resolved in favour of the witness.

48 COPR PD 14D para 4.

summons; at the time of service, the party must be offered or paid a) a sum reasonably sufficient to cover his travelling expenses to and from court; and b) compensation for his loss of time.[49] Both of these sums are fixed by reference to those payable in criminal cases;[50] compensation for ordinary witnesses (ie those who are neither experts nor professionals) is capped at £33.50 for a period of absence not exceeding four hours and £67.00 for a longer period.[51] The court can also order that a witness be paid such general costs as it considers appropriate.[52] Although the COPR and the accompanying practice direction (PD 14D) are silent as to who should pay, the silence suggests that payment should be made by the party who sought the application.

13.37 In general, a witness summons is only binding if a) it is served more than seven days prior to the date on which the witness is required to attend court; and b) the requirements as to offering or paying compensation have been met.[53] It is possible, though, for the court to shorten the time period in an appropriate case (although not to dispense with the compensation requirements).[54]

13.38 Where the summons is issued solely so as to obtain documents and prove their authenticity, it is suggested that the same practice as is used in civil proceedings would be followed, ie that the summons specify a date for the production of the documents that is in advance of the substantive hearing.[55] This power is of little application in terms of documents held by the parties, because of the operation of COPR r14.14 (see above, para 13.32).

13.39 It should be noted, finally, that witness summons are not issued solely to comply reluctant witnesses to attend court, but also as a

49 COPR r14.13(6)(a) and (b).

50 COPR PD 14D para 10 and the Costs in Criminal Cases (General) Regulations 1986 SI No 1335 (made under the Prosecution of Offenders Act 1985 (as amended)).

51 Annex A to the *Guide to Allowances under Part V of the Costs in Criminal Cases (General) Regulations 1986*, 2016; available at: https://assets.publishing.service.gov.uk/government/uploads/system/uploads/attachment_data/file/592291/guide-allowances-under-part-v-costs-criminal-cases-general-september- 2016.doc.

52 COPR r14.13(7).

53 COPR r14.13(3).

54 COPR r14.13(4).

55 See *Khanna v Lovell White Durrant* [1995] 1 WLR 121 and the *White Book 2022*, at para 34.0.3.

mechanism by which (for instance) an employer can be forced to allow an employee to attend to give evidence.[56]

13.40 The COPR are silent as to the sanctions that follow a failure to comply with a witness summons. It is suggested, however, that, by analogy with the position that prevails in the High Court, such a failure can be punished as a contempt of court: see further chapter 18 below.

Depositions

13.41 It is possible for an order to be obtained for a person to be examined on oath before the relevant hearing takes place. Such an order must be sought upon application using a COP9 form (see further para 11.26 onwards), although it is not necessary that it be made on notice to the other parties.[57] The deponent can be examined before a circuit judge or a district judge (whether or not nominated as a judge of the Court of Protection), an examiner of the court or such other person as the court appoints,[58] and the order can require the production of any document which the court considers is necessary for the purposes of the examination.[59] The court can also order that the party who obtained the order to file a witness statement or witness summary in relation to the evidence to be given by the person be examined.[60]

13.42 A deposition that has been ordered under COPR r14.15 may be put in evidence at a hearing unless the court orders otherwise.[61] If a party intends to put such a deposition in evidence, they must file notice of their intention to do so with the court and serve it on every other party; absent order to the contrary, they must file such notice at least 14 days before the hearing date.[62] The court can require the deponent to attend the hearing and give evidence orally.[63]

13.43 Detailed provisions relating to the conduct of depositions to be taken in England and Wales are set out in PD 14B,[64] aimed primarily

56 In *Re CD* [2021] EWFC 112, a family case, the judge even resorted to issuing (of her own motion) a witness summons to seek to compel the attendance of an expert who had, in effect, disappeared.

57 COPR r14.15(1); PD 14B para 9.

58 COPR r14.15(3); 'examiners of the court' are appointed by the Lord Chancellor: see COPR r14.18.

59 COPR r14.15(4).

60 COPR r14.15(7).

61 COPR r14.15(1).

62 COPR r14.20(2)–(3).

63 COPR r14.20(4).

64 COPR PD 14B paras 1–15.

at ensuring the creation of an accurate record of the questions put and the answers given, and also at setting out the consequences of a failure of a deponent to attend the examination or a refusal to be sworn, answer any lawful question or produce any document. They are not addressed further here because the process is so rarely invoked before the Court of Protection.

Witnesses outside the jurisdiction

13.44 The COPR and PD 14A contain detailed provisions relating to the obtaining of evidence from witnesses outside England and Wales; they also (along with PD 14B) contain provisions relating to the taking of depositions outside England and Wales. In summary:

- a person may make an affidavit outside England and Wales in the same (limited) circumstances as provided for within England and Wales, or as in accordance with the law in the place where they make the affidavit;[65]
- the procedure for taking evidence outside the jurisdiction is set out in the COPR and PD 14B.[66] As a result of the UK's departure from the European Union (EU), there is no longer any difference if the person in question is or is not in an EU member state;[67]
- the same procedural requirements apply in relation to the putting before the court of evidence obtained outside the jurisdiction as do in relation to depositions taken from witnesses in England and Wales.[68]

13.45 Where a witness is outside the jurisdiction, it is more likely that steps will be taken to enable them to give any oral evidence required by way of video link, as provided for at COPR r14.5, and discussed further at paras 16.59–16.60.

Documents held by the police

13.46 Where the police force of a particular area is not a party to the proceedings, but where the court agrees that documents are required from the police, the police normally require that any order be made

65 COPR r14.11.

66 COPR r14.23; PD 14B paras 16–22. Paras 23-32 of PD 4B are no longer relevant.

67 The relevant provisions of the COPR having been removed by the Family Procedure Rules 2010 and Court of Protection Rules 2017 (Amendment) (EU Exit) Regulations 2019 SI No 517 reg 32.

68 COPR r14.20.

in terms that a) are directed to the chief constable of the force in question; b) invite, rather than require, the production of documents; and c) include the full name and date of birth of the person to whom they relate. Many police forces have in place local protocols with local authorities for the disclosure of documents in proceedings relating to children; it is usually easiest if such protocols (modified as necessary) are adopted in proceedings relating to incapacitated adults. A model order can be found at www.courtofprotectionhandbook.com precedents.

Section 49 reports

13.47 The court has the power under MCA 2005 s49 to call for a report in respect of such matters relating to P as it may direct from:

- the Public Guardian;
- a Court of Protection Visitor, appointed by the Lord Chancellor to one of two panels, Special Visitors and General Visitors, the former requiring a medical qualification and special knowledge of and experience in cases of impairment of or disturbance in the functioning of the mind or brain;[69]
- a local authority or NHS body (such report to be produced by one of its officers or employees or such other person other than that the Public Guardian or a Court of Protection Visitor as the authority/NHS body considers appropriate).

13.48 There are specific provisions in MCA 2005 s49 and COPR r14.24 relating to the powers of those charged with producing such reports (which are normally, but not necessarily, provided in writing[70]). In summary:

- The Public Guardian or a Court of Protection Visitor is entitled, at all reasonable times, to examine and take copies of any health record, any record of or held by a local authority and compiled in connection with a social services function, and any record held by a person registered under Care Standards Act 2000 Part 2 or Health and Social Care Act 2008 Part 1 Chapter 2 (broadly, records held by those managing private residential and nursing homes) relating to P.[71]

69 MCA 2005 s61(2).

70 MCA 2005 s49(6). The model order attached to PD 14E (see further below) provides alternative wording for oral and written reports: see para 4.

71 MCA 2005 s49(7).

- Any person compiling a report can inspect and take copies of any document in the court records, unless the court orders to the contrary (or orders that they may only have access to the information on an edited basis).[72]
- A Public Guardian or Court of Protection Visitor can interview P in private for purposes of producing a report.[73]
- A Special Visitor can, if the court directs, carry out a private medical, psychiatric or psychological examination of P's capacity and condition.[74]
- An officer or an employee of a local authority or NHS body (or person reporting on their behalf) is expected to contact or seek to interview such persons as he thinks appropriate or the court directs, but is not granted any specific power to interview or examine P for purposes of producing a report.[75]

13.49 Section 49 reports, especially those produced by Court of Protection Visitors, bear a strong resemblance to expert reports, in that they will include both discussion of factual matters and also opinions reflecting the expertise of the maker of the reports. Both those providing reports under MCA 2005 s49 and experts reporting to the court owe a duty to the court (rather than to the parties) to assist on the matters within their expertise.[76] However, even though many section 49 reports are in substance identical to expert reports, they are treated distinctly to such reports for purposes of the COPR,[77] and therefore conceptually occupy a somewhat curious position in the conventional categorisation of evidence. In an extension of the use of section 49 reports to meet the shortage of COPR r1.2 representatives, Charles J concluded in *Re KT (incapacitated persons) (deprivation of liberty: general visitor)*[78] that a report by a special visitor could provide a 'voice' for P in cases where a welfare order authorising the deprivation of P's liberty is sought.

72 COPR r14.24(5) and (7).
73 MCA 2005 s49(8).
74 MCA 2005 s49(9).
75 COPR r14.24(3)(a).
76 COPR r14.24(2) (reports under MCA 2005 s49); COPR r15.4 (experts). The maker of a section 49 report must also give a statement of truth that relates both to the facts contained within their report and the expression of their professional opinions: PD 14E para 23(e).
77 By COPR r15.1(b), an expert does not include any person instructed to make a report under MCA 2005 s49.
78 [2018] EWCOP 1, [2018] 4 WLR 21, [2018] COPLR 185.

13.50 The power exercisable under MCA 2005 s49 can provide a proportionate mechanism for obtaining information about P from a statutory body which has knowledge of P and need not be joined as a party. In many circumstances, however, the power serves as an effective route by which the court can obtain independent evidence as to matters relevant to the application, and thus as an alternative to the grant of permission to the parties to instruct (jointly or separately) an expert to give evidence. For welfare cases falling within the Welfare Pathway the court must actively consider whether such a report[79] could achieve a better result than an expert.[80]

13.51 There is one substantial advantage to the parties in the obtaining of such a report, namely that the MCA 2005 and the COPR make no express provision for the payment of any fees. This is in contrast to the position in relation to experts where the default position is that the instructing parties are jointly and severally liable for the payment of the expert's fees and expenses[81] (see further para 13.76 below). In practice, this means that the costs fall upon the body required to produce the report (in the case of Special and General Visitors, they are remunerated for their work by Lord Chancellor, including for the provision of section 49 reports[82]).

13.52 In part because of concerns expressed by NHS bodies at the burdens being placed upon them by orders to provide section 49 reports (especially in relation to individuals with whom they had had no previous contact),[83] and in part also because of practical difficulties that were being encountered on a regular basis in obtaining timely and appropriately detailed section 49 reports from public bodies, PD 14E was introduced and applies to all cases where a section 49 report is ordered. In *DL v Enfield LBC*[84] Senior Judge Hilder emphasised that the powers under section 49 are a 'vital tool' in the armoury of the Court of Protection, but that compliance by both the court and the parties with the requirements of the practice

79 Or from a COPR r1.2 representative (see further chapter 11).

80 COPR Case Pathways PD 3B para 2.5(m).

81 COPR r15.13(6).

82 MCA 2005 s61(4).

83 See *RS v LCC and others* [2015] EWCOP 56, in which District Judge Bellamy emphasised that there is no provision is made within MCA 2005 s49 for fees or expenses incurred by the relevant public bodies, but that '[w]hat the court will do is to carefully consider resources and listen to any argument from the [public body] particularly in relation to the time for compliance and the scope of the work to be undertaken. That would appear to be both a reasonable and proportionate approach'.

84 [2019] EWCOP B1, [2020] COPLR 128.

direction is important given the burden that such reports impose upon other parties.

13.53 The section 49 PD 14E contains detailed guidance both as to when a section 49 report is likely to be ordered, and also as to the contents of the report. It also contains details as to the steps that should be taken by a party before applying for an order for a section 49 report directed against a public body, in particular as to the identification of a suitable person ('the senior officer') at the local authority or NHS body in question who will be in a position to receive the order and take action upon it. There is also a detailed model order attached to COPR PD 14E, which includes specific provisions for such matters as the contents of the report, persons to whom it is likely to be disclosed and access to records.

13.54 For purposes of PD 14E the rule of thumb will therefore be to prepare *as if* an expert is being instructed (see further below para 13.81 onwards). In other words:

- If the report is to be provided by a public body and requires any specific expertise (for instance the preparation of a report addressing P's capacity), an individual should, if possible, be identified at the relevant body with that expertise; alternatively, a particular category of individual (for instance a psychologist, or psychiatrist). Whilst MCA 2005 s49 provides for a report to be provided by the public body, rather than by a specific person within the public body,[85] if an appropriate person can be identified and agreed with the 'senior officer' then this will speed matters up considerably as regards the preparation of the report.
- A realistic time-frame should be identified within which the report can be prepared.
- A draft letter of guidance should be prepared for consideration by the court,[86] which contains a summary of the relevant background matters (including, in many cases, relevant documentation); and a summary of the relevant legal tests to apply (including not just the provisions of the MCA 2005 but any relevant cases). It should also ask detailed and specific questions. This does not apply just to situations where the report is being sought of a public body, but also of a Court of Protection Visitor: experience has taught that both General and Special Visitors can on occasion be asked to

85 And COPR PD14E provides for how the public body is to nominate the person to prepare the report: paras 11–12.

86 This is a specific requirement: COPR PD14E para 8.

report in extremely vague terms, producing in consequence extremely vague – and unhelpful – reports.

13.55 A report made in response to an order under MCA 2005 s49 is made to the court, rather than to the parties. It will then be sent by the court to the parties; it can also be sent to such other persons as the court may direct.[87] A party (but not another person to whom the report has been sent) can apply for permission to put written questions to the maker of the report.[88] Such questions must be directed via the court, which will make such amendments as it sees fit; the court will then send the replies received to the parties and such other person as it may direct.[89]

Expert evidence

Overview

13.56 More than in many other types of proceedings, judges sitting in the Court of Protection will often require assistance from suitably qualified individuals as to such matters as:

- whether P has or lacks capacity to take the decision(s) in question; and
- what course of action is in P's physical and/or psychological best interests, especially if there are specific clinical or social work concerns. The breadth of the areas on which expertise might be required is wide: see, for instance, *Re IH (Observance of Muslim Practice)*,[90] in which an expert was instructed to assist the court on Islamic religious observance for those without capacity.

13.57 That evidence will go beyond evidence of fact and, indeed, it will be of value to the court predominantly insofar as it constitutes evidence of opinion based upon the expertise of the individual in question. As such evidence would not otherwise be admissible, the MCA 2005 and COPR Part 15 contain provisions enabling such evidence can be put before the court in a proportionate fashion.[91] COPR Part 15 is

87 COPR r14.24(4). Paragraph 12 of the model order attached to PD 14E directs the minds both of the parties and the court to identifying whom the report is to be disclosed to other than the parties.

88 COPR r14.25(1).

89 COPR r14.25(2)–(3).

90 [2017] EWCOP 9, [2017] COPLR 281.

91 Space precludes a detailed discussion of the law relating to expert evidence; the reader is referred to *Phipson on Evidence* at para 33-09 onwards.

accompanied by a practice direction (PD 15A); this is very much less detailed than the suite of practice directions that are now in force accompanying the Family Procedure Rules (FPR) 2010[92] Part 25, the equivalent provisions in proceedings relating to children. At present, there is no immediate prospect of PD15A being amended to introduce a similar degree of detail.

13.58 Slightly oddly, neither the MCA 2005 nor the COPR provide any definition of an 'expert',[93] but it is suggested that for these purposes an 'expert' is a person qualified to express an expert opinion upon a relevant matter by virtue of their qualifications or experience upon such matters. By analogy, Civil Evidence Act (CEA) 1972 s3 provides that where a person is called as a witness in any civil proceedings, the person's opinion on any relevant matter on which they are qualified to give expert evidence shall be admissible in evidence, and that 'a relevant matter' includes an issue in the proceedings in question. It is suggested that proceedings before the Court of Protection are 'civil proceedings' for these purposes (by analogy with *Enfield LBC v SA and others*[94]).

13.59 It is further suggested that an expert is a person who must have a degree of independence from P,[95] such that a family member could not properly qualify as an expert for these purposes. In the ordinary run of events, it would be unusual for a treating clinician (or a social worker involved with P's case) to be asked to provide expert evidence falling within the scope of COPR Part 15. However, in *O-M and others v The Local Authority and others*,[96] the Court of Appeal held that there is no blanket rule which prevents, in an appropriate case, a treating doctor becoming a jointly instructed expert in public law proceedings relating to children. It is suggested that there is no reason in principle why the same approach could not apply in proceedings in relation to adults.

13.60 In any event, 'specialist' professional witnesses employed or acting on behalf of a public body party to proceedings often give evidence that contains both evidence of fact and what would in layper-

92 SI 2010 No 2955.

93 Although, as noted above, it cannot be a person who gives a report under the provisions of MCA 2005 s49.

94 [2010] EWHC 196 (Admin), [2010] COPLR Con Vol 362, discussing the CEA 1995, which contains the same definition of 'civil proceedings'. See CEA 1972 s3; compare CEA 1995 s11.

95 See COPR PD 15A paras 3–4, discussed further below.

96 [2009] EWCA Civ 1405, [2010] 2 FLR 58. See also *Hershman and McFarlane: Children Law and Practice*, at para 3060-1.

son's terms be considered to be expert opinion evidence. For instance, a social worker will very often both relate events that they have witnessed directly (or have knowledge of from their reading of social services records) and then also express their professional opinion as to where P's best interests may lie on the basis of their perception of those events. That opinion may well be due (and be given) significant weight by the court. As noted extra-judicially by the former President of the Family Division and Court of Protection, Sir James Munby P (in comments relating to care proceedings but of equal relevance to proceedings under the MCA 2005):

> Social workers may not be experts for the purposes of FPR Part 25 [the equivalent of COPR Part 15], but that does not mean that they are not experts in every other sense of the word. They are, and we must recognise them and treat them as such.[97]

13.61 There are two important consequences to this:

1) As discussed below, where there is evidence before the court from a witness such as a social worker on behalf of a public authority, this will factor into the question of whether expert evidence falling within the scope of COPR Part 15 is in fact required.
2) An important further corollary of this is as regards the duties upon those giving evidence in this quasi-expert guise. In *London Borough of Southwark v NP and others*[98] the Vice-President, Hayden J, observed that:

   > . . . the court will frequently be asked to take evidence from treating clinicians. Invariably, (again especially at Tier 3), these will be individuals of experience and expertise who in other cases might easily find themselves instructed independently as experts. Treating clinicians have precisely the same obligations and duties upon them, when preparing reports and giving evidence as those independently instructed.

13.62 It is also vital as a preliminary point to remember in respect of all expert evidence (both that falling within the scope of Part 15 and that of the quasi-expert nature discussed immediately above) that:

- where the opinion of an expert is based upon the report of facts, those facts, unless within the expert's own knowledge, must be proved independently;

97 Sir James Munby P, 'View from the President's Chambers (3) The process of reform: expert evidence' [2013] Fam Law 816.

98 [2019] EWCOP 48, [2019] 4 WLR 141, at para 31(vi).

- an expert may (in an appropriate case) give evidence upon 'ultimate questions' going to factual matters, for instance as to the accuracy or truthfulness of a witness, but the final decision remains that for the judge;[99]
- likewise, the 'ultimate' questions of whether P has capacity and as to what is in their best interests are matters for the court.[100]

13.63 In other words, and as Charles J observed in *A County Council v K, D and L*,[101] after a detailed review of the authorities:

> . . . it is important to remember (i) that the roles of the court and the expert are distinct; and (ii) it is the court that is in the position to weigh the expert evidence against its findings on the other evidence . . . the judge must always remember that he or she is the person who makes the final decision.

13.64 Allied to this is the fact that the judge is not limited in their determination even of questions upon which expert evidence might be thought to be of particular weight solely to consideration of that evidence. In particular, it is clear that capacity is a question ultimately to be determined by the court, and it must do so on the basis of:

> . . . all the relevant evidence. Clearly, the opinion of an independently-instructed expert will be likely to be of very considerable importance, but in many cases the evidence of other clinicians and professionals who have experience of treating and working with P will be just as important and in some cases more important.[102]

13.65 A corollary of the matters set out above is that the judge is entitled to depart from the expert evidence put before them, as happened in the *CC* case referred to above, where Baker J held in the face of all the professional and expert evidence before him that P had the capacity to decide where she wished to reside, largely (it appears) on the basis

99 See, by analogy, *Re M and R* [1996] 2 FLR 195, CA at 205–213 per Butler-Sloss LJ and *Re M (sexual abuse allegations: interviewing techniques)* [1999] 2 FLR 92 per Sir Stephen Brown P. See also the discussion in *Hershman and McFarlane: children law and practice*, at para 3056.

100 *CC v KK and STCC* [2012] EWHC 2136 (COP), [2012] COPLR 627 at para 24 per Baker J.

101 [2005] EWHC 144 (Fam), [2005] 1 FLR 851 at paras 39 and 44. This case related to an application for a care order under the Children Act 1989, but its principles were held to be equally applicable to proceedings under the MCA 2005 by Baker J in *CC v KK and STCC* [2012] EWHC 2136 (COP), [2012] COPLR 627 at para 24.

102 *PH v A Local Authority and others* [2011] EWHC 1704 (Fam), [2012] COPLR 128 at para 16(xiii) per Baker J. See also, in a 'delicately balanced' case involving bulimia, *Re Q* [2022] EWCOP 6.

of his own assessment of P when she appeared before him. See further in this regard para 16.38. By analogy with the position that prevails in relation to children, it is suggested that a departure where it concerns the potential level of risk to the welfare of P must be accompanied by appropriately detailed reasons.[103]

Permission

13.66 Although it is not necessary to obtain permission to file expert evidence as to capacity and/or best interests with the initial application to the court,[104] the court's permission must be obtained before filing any subsequent expert evidence[105] (and evidence filed with the application can only be relied upon to the extent and for the purposes that the court allows).[106] The important of compliance with these provisions was emphasised by the Court of Appeal in *Z v University Hospitals Plymouth NHS Trust.*[107]

13.67 COPR rr15.5(2)(a)–(f) sets out the requirements for an application for permission to instruct an expert, requiring the party applying for permission to:

- identify the field in respect of which that party wishes to rely upon expert evidence, and the issues to which the expert evidence is to relate;
- where practicable, identify the expert in that field upon whose evidence the party wishes to rely;
- provide any other material information about the expert;
- state whether the expert evidence could be obtained from a single joint expert;
- provide any other information or documents required by a practice direction; and
- provide a draft letter of instruction to the expert. In our experience, judges may be sympathetic if it has not been possible to comply this requirement if it can properly be said to do so would be disproportionate in the circumstances.

13.68 The court will require considerable persuasion to allow the appointment of more than one expert to report upon a single issue. It is

103 See *Re B (care: expert witnesses)* [1996] 1 FLR 667, CA and *Hershman and McFarlane: children law and practice* at para 3056.

104 COPR r15.2(1)(a)–(b).

105 COPR r15.2(1).

106 COPR r15.2(2).

107 [2021] EWCA Civ 22, [2021] COPLR 342.

worth noting that there are advantages to the instruction of single joint experts other than those of proportionality and cost-saving. As Ryder J (as he then was) noted after a review of the authorities in *JG (a child) v Legal Services Commission and others*[108] (in the context of a discussion of the principle of the equal apportionment of the costs of joint expert evidence (see further para 13.76 below)):

> 47. There are sound reasons, recognised in the decided cases, why there should be apportionment of costs in cases where there is joint expert evidence. Such evidence will:
>
> (a) be something which each party has an interest in making available to the court . . .;
>
> (b) be something from which each party has the potential to benefit (whether or not they ultimately do so) . . .; and
>
> (c) inform the positions of the parties . . .
>
> 48. These points do not apply to evidence obtained, and paid for, on a single party's behalf. In *Lambeth*,[109] the court approved (at para [59](viii)) the comment of Bodey J in *Calderdale*[110] (at para [37](e)) in relation to the cost of a joint report prepared for care proceedings brought by a local authority that:
>
> '. . . there is much force in the Local Authority's point that parents need to know that reports which may prove to have a "preponderant influence" (per Munby J at paragraph 113(ii) of *Re L*) are not being prepared at the sole expense of the Local Authority – in which event they may feel that the Local Authority calls the tune.'

13.69 These comments were made in the context of a discussion of expert evidence in private law proceedings concerning a child, but it is suggested that they are equally applicable in proceedings under the MCA 2005.

13.70 The requirement to obtain permission is an important tool in the court's case management armoury. The court's duty is to restrict expert evidence to that which is necessary to assist the court to resolve the issues in the proceedings, and the court may only give permission to file or adduce expert evidence if it is satisfied that it is both necessary and cannot otherwise be provided.[111]

108 [2013] EWHC 804 (Admin), [2013] 2 FLR 1174. This decision was reversed on appeal: [2014] EWCA Civ 656 but these dicta remain valid.

109 *Lambeth LBC v S, C, V and J (by his guardian); Legal Services Commission (intervening)* [2005] EWHC 776 (Fam), [2005] 2 FLR 1171.

110 *Calderdale MBC v S and the Legal Services Commission* [2004] EWHC 2529 (Fam), [2005] 1 FLR 751.

111 COPR r15.3.

13.71 In deciding whether to give permission to file or adduce expert evidence, the court must have specific regard to (a) the issues to which the expert evidence would relate; (b) the questions which the expert would answer; (c) the impact which giving permission would be likely to have on the timetable, duration and conduct of the proceedings; (d) any failure to comply with any direction of the court about expert evidence; and (e) the cost of the expert evidence.[112] Additionally, the Case Pathways PD 3B provides that for cases on the welfare pathway, the court must at the case management hearing (see further para 11.24) actively consider whether a section 49 report[113] could achieve a better result than the use of an expert.[114]

13.72 The test introduced into the COPR 2017 echoes that to be found in the Family Procedure Rules.[115] 'Necessity' was interpreted in the context of those rules in *Re H-L (A Child) (Expert Evidence: Test for Permission)*[116] as having 'the connotation of the imperative, what is demanded rather than what is merely optional or reasonable or desirable'.[117] It may also be that the bar is even higher in challenges to deprivation of liberty authorisations brought under section 21. In *DP v Hillingdon LBC*,[118] Hayden J noted (at para 41) his 'doubt' that it was necessary to instruct an expert to report upon capacity when a report had already been prepared for authorisation purposes.

13.73 A further hurdle to the obtaining of expert evidence in cases in which one or more parties are in receipt of public funding is the increasing reluctance of the Legal Aid Agency (LAA) to fund expert evidence (whether at the particular rate sought by the expert, or indeed at all). That the LAA has the power to refuse all or part of the instruction, even if permission has been granted by the court was confirmed by Collins J in *R (T) v Legal Aid Agency*.[119]

112 COPR r15.5(3).

113 Or from a COPR r1.2 representative (see further chapter 11).

114 COPR Case Pathways PD 3B para 2.5(m).

115 FPR r25.1 as amended by the Family Procedure (Amendment) (No 5) Rules 2012 SI No 3061.

116 [2013] EWCA Civ 655, [2014] 1 WLR 1160 at para 3 per Sir James Munby P; see also Sir James Munby P, 'View from the President's Chambers (3) The process of reform: expert evidence' [2013] Fam Law 816.

117 [2013] EWCA Civ 5, [2013] 1 FLR 1250, at para 30 per Sir James Munby P. the approach taken in the family courts is now summarised pithily in the President of the Family Division's 2021 Memorandum: Experts in the Family Court.

118 [2020] EWCOP 45, [2020] COPLR 769.

119 [2013] EWHC 960 (Admin), [2013] Fam Law 805.

13.74 It is strongly advisable that (in line with the approach that applies in family proceedings[120]):

- Where the court takes the view that the expert's report is necessary for the resolution of the case, it should say so and should give reasons (and should do so even if the order is a consent order being endorsed by the court, as it is still a judicial decision).
- While the reasons need not be lengthy or elaborate, they must, however, explain to anyone reading them why the decision-maker has reached the conclusion they have, particularly if the expert's rates exceed the maximum rates ordinarily allowable. This can be done by way of preamble to the order, or in an appropriate case by a short judgment, delivered at dictation speed or inserted by the parties with the judge's approval. It is suggested that the preamble or judgment should include (and hence the material put to the court must indicate clearly):
  - what relevant papers it has read;
  - the reasons why it considers that the expert evidence is necessary to resolve proceedings, which should include the reasons why the evidence would not otherwise be available to it as part of the proceedings (for instance, from a social worker or a treating clinician who has given evidence on behalf of a public body);
  - the reasons why the volume of work is required, if it is a particularly complex report;
  - (if one or more parties is publicly funded) the reasons for why there is any need to exceed the maximum rates usually allowable by the LAA; and
  - the reasons why there is any departure from: i) the principle that the costs of a single joint expert will be shared equally between the instructing parties, particularly if this has the effect of placing a disproportionately high cost burden on a party or parties in receipt of public funding (this should include a robust scrutiny of the means of any party claiming to be unable to afford the cost of the instruction); or ii) the principle that the instructing parties are to be jointly and severally liable for the costs of single joint expert.

13.75 The last point above requires some amplification because a question that arises relatively often is whether all the parties to proceedings

120 *A Local Authority v S and others* [2012] EWHC 1442 (Fam), [2012] 1 WLR 3098 at para 45 per Sir Nicholas Wall P.

need to join in the instruction of an expert and, if they do not, what, if any a) right do they have to have input into the instruction; and b) obligation do they have to pay the costs of the expert report?

13.76 The starting point in respect of both is simple: only a party who wishes to submit expert evidence is an 'instructing party';[121] only such a party has the right (but not the duty) to give instructions to the expert;[122] and the status of instructing party carries with it the obligation to meet jointly and severally the expert's fees and expenses.[123] The Court of Protection cannot force a party to join in the instructions; if a party refuses to do so, it is suggested that this should be recorded on the face of the directions giving permission to other party or parties to instruct the expert in question.

13.77 Conversely, especially where one party is a litigant in person and/or is of limited means, the argument is often run that the letter of instruction should be circulated to the relevant party for their input and comment, but that they should not then be required to meet any part of the costs of the report. There is undoubtedly a pragmatic attraction to this, not least as written questions can be put to an expert by any party, not just an instructing party, and the presumption is that the costs of producing the replies will in the first instance be met by the instructing party or parties.[124] It may therefore be thought easier to ensure that the expert is asked to consider all matters compendiously, rather than having to respond to subsequent questions by a party who has not taken part in the instruction. Care needs to be exercised, however, both by the parties and the court, if this course is adopted. This is in part because it offends against the principle of the joint apportionment of costs which is enshrined in COPR r15.7(7). It is also, pragmatically, a course which is likely to lead to substantial problems if the LAA consider that there has been any degree of 'loading' of the costs of an expert report upon a public funding certificate for any party.

13.78 However, the position may be somewhat more flexible at least where one (or more) parties is of limited means and one party is publicly funded following the decision in *JG v Lord Chancellor and others*.[125] This case was decided in the context of a private law dispute involving a child, but the central principles are equally applicable

121 COPR r15.2(2).

122 COPR r15.3(1).

123 COPR r15.3(5).

124 COPR r15.7(1) and (7). See further para 13.91 below.

125 [2014] EWCA Civ 656, [2014] 2 FLR 1218.

before the Court of Protection (see also the discussion of this case at para 13.68 onwards). In this case, the Court of Appeal made a number of general observations, including that:

- no party could be compelled to join in instructing an expert (under the FPR – this also applies to the COPR);
- the involvement of other parties will not necessarily convert an expert instructed on behalf of one party into a single joint expert;
- there are good practical reasons to be cautious about treating an expert as a joint expert, as it would be undesirable for non-instructing parties to be deterred from contributing to an expert's instruction, and thus from providing useful information to an expert, for fear they will be treated as a joint expert;
- if, on proper analysis, the expert is a joint expert, the possible grounds for departing from the principle of equal apportionment could be a) impecuniosity, b) the need to avoid a breach of the ECHR[126] and c) a 'very exceptional case'. If it is established that a lack of an expert report would breach an individual's rights under the ECHR, there was no need to consider exceptionality as an additional requirement.

13.79 It is important to remember that the pressure of work means that a judge at a case management hearing may not have time to master the details of the documents in the case. This means that it is particularly important to flag up all relevant matters clearly (and succinctly) for the judge, ideally in the position statement filed in advance of the hearing (discussed further at para 11.44 onwards).

13.80 Wherever practicable, the court being invited to grant permission to instruct an expert should be asked to give permission to instruct a specific expert, rather than a category of expert. In other words, and as the COPR provide,[127] the identity of the expert together with the professional qualifications should be made clear to the judge at the time that permission is sought, rather than permission being sought to rely upon (say) a consultant psychiatrist to report upon P's capacity in one or more domains. This has two advantages:

- The court can make clear in its reasons for the grant of permission that it has considered the value that the specific expert proposed can add (assuming that such expert is endorsed by the court; if the expert is not, then appropriate steps can then be direc-

126 A failure by the court to allow expert evidence can be a violation of ECHR Article 8 (see *Elsholz v Germany* (2002) 34 EHRR 58).

127 COPR r15.5(2)(b).

ted to put forward a suitable alternative for judicial endorsement).

- Where more than one party is to be involved in the instruction of the expert, the order appointing that expert will name them. In the authors' experience, while there is a mechanism in the COPR for the resolution by the court of disputes as to the identity of the expert between joint instructing parties,[128] leaving matters open in the order can give rise to unhelpful and time-consuming debates subsequently that can be avoided by ensuring that any such discussions take place prior to the making of the order.

Instructing the expert

13.81 An expert must be instructed before they can report. In other words, they must be provided with:

- a summary of the background to the case;
- a summary of the relevant legal provisions (and of any relevant case-law); and
- relevant documentation.

13.82 The questions upon which their opinion is sought must also be set out with clarity. A sample letter of instruction is included at appendix D below, but particular points to emphasise are that:

- As noted above, the presumption is that expert evidence will be provided by way of an expert jointly instructed by all those parties who wish to submit expert evidence upon a particular issue or issues. In such circumstances, and while the COPR provide for separate instructions to be given by the instructing parties to the expert,[129] courts are in practice astute to seek to ensure that only one letter of instruction is sent, and will use their general case management powers to bring about (if all possible) one letter, agreed, if possible between the instructing parties. This means, in practice, that the solicitors for one of the parties should take the lead in drafting the letter and then circulate it to the other instructing parties for comment. Wherever the Official Solicitor is instructed as P's litigation friend and is participating in the instruction, it is conventional that the solicitors instructed by the Official Solicitor take on the task of producing the first draft. This is

128 COPR r15.12(3) providing that the court can either select the expert from a list prepared or identified by the instructing parties or direct the manner by which the expert is to be selected.

129 COPR r15.2(2).

usually the arrangement in cases where an alternative litigation friend such as an RPR acts. If agreement cannot be reached as to the terms of the letter, it is almost invariably quicker if rival drafts (with the differences clearly marked) are provided in writing along with submissions to the merits of the different drafts to the judge who made the original order granting permission for the judge to make the final decision as to the terms of the letter, rather that engaging in protracted rounds of correspondence. COPR r15.13(2) provides, expressly, that, where instructions are to be contained in a jointly agreed letter, in default of agreement the instructions may be determined by the court on the written request of any instructing party copied to the other instructing parties.

- Where an expert is jointly instructed, the expert must be reminded that any communications that they have with one instructing party should be copied to the others; there is a real risk, otherwise, that the independence of the expert will (even if only apparently) be compromised.[130]
- Thought must be given as to the documentation that it is necessary that the expert reviews in order to give their report, and the mechanics by which the expert can review that documentation. In this regard two considerations arise, in particular:
  - The expert may well not need to see the entirety of files held upon P by relevant public bodies, but must be entitled to inspect and/or be provided with copies of sufficient documents in order to be able to reach their conclusions.[131]
  - It is quite possible that the expert will need to see documents relating to P (for instance, their social services files) to which the other parties in the proceedings (most obviously family members) may well not have had sight of and which there are legitimate reasons to suggest the other parties should not see. In *Re L (care assessment: fair trial)*, Munby J (as he then was) held in relation to care proceedings that there might be a

130 See in this regard *SMBC v WMP* [2011] EWHC B13 (COP), (2011) 14 CCLR 413, [2011] COPLR Con Vol 1177 at para 57(vii) per HHJ Cardinal (discussions between the Official Solicitor's solicitor and the expert).

131 See *London Borough of Southwark v NP and others* [2019] EWCOP 48, [2019] 4 WLR 141 at para 31(vi): 'it is the obligation of the lawyers to ensure that [expert] witnesses are furnished with all relevant material which is likely to have an impact on their views, conclusions and recommendations . . . This should not merely be regarded as good litigation practice but as indivisible from the effective protection of P's welfare and autonomy'.

breach of ECHR Article 6 (right to a fair trial) where a jointly instructed or other sole expert's report was 'likely to have a preponderant influence on the assessment of the facts' by the court, if a litigant were denied the opportunity, before the expert produced his report, a) to examine and comment on the documents being considered by the expert and b) to cross-examine witnesses interviewed by the expert and on whose evidence the report was based, and hence to participate effectively in the process by which the report was produced.[132] It is suggested that the same principle applies in relation to proceedings under the MCA 2005; this does not necessarily mean that an expert cannot have sight of documents withheld from other parties – rather, it means that consideration must be given to the basis upon which those documents are withheld both by the party wishing to withhold those documents and the court. These difficult issues are examined further at para 13.106 onwards below.

- Arrangements must be made for the expert to be able to visit P (which will, in the majority of cases, be necessary for them to be able to form any proper conclusion as to their capacity and/or best interests[133]), and interview any individuals such as carers or family members whom the expert considers necessary in order to be able to produce a sufficiently rounded picture. If an expert is unable to obtain access to see P because of the actions of a family member, this is something that should be raised with the court at the earliest possible opportunity so that – if appropriate – steps can be taken to consider the making of injunctions (and, ultimately, initiating proceedings for contempt of court).
- While the court is likely to have indicated in the order granting permission the matters to be covered in the report,[134] it is unlikely that the order will set down the questions in detail (nor, in the ordinary run of events, is it likely that the judge making the order will have had sight of the letter of instruction before it is sent out). It is therefore important that care is taken to formulate the

132 [2002] EWHC 1379 (Fam), at paras 113–118, applying *Mantovanelli v France* (App No 21497/93) (1997) 24 EHRR 370.

133 As an independent consultant neuro-psychiatric expert noted in *Wandsworth CCG v IA and TA* [2014] EWHC 990 (COP): 'assessment of capacity based on case notes is of necessity a relatively inadequate substitution for the complex assessments that occurs in a clinical interview' (*IA* at para 43).

134 COPR r15.8(1) provides that the court may give directions as to the matters to be covered in such a report.

questions so as to direct the expert's attention to answering the issues that actually fall for consideration in the case. In the authors' experience, unclear reports are very frequently the result of unclear questions having been asked in the first place (and it is also difficult to 'salvage' such an unclear report by way of questions asked upon receipt of the report, discussed further at para 13.88 below).

- The expert should be reminded that they should exercise extreme care before expressing any provisional views to P: in *SC v BS and A Local Authority*,[135] the expert was criticised for having given an indication to P that he thought she had capacity in the material domains without having read the very extensive records. As Baker J noted: 'Although his comments to her were hedged with qualifications, it was highly probable that [P]'s hopes were raised that she would shortly be allowed to leave her current accommodation.'[136] No expert should give a patient a 'provisional' view of the patient's capacity without reading the patient's history.
- The expert should be reminded that they have the right to ask the court for directions to assist them in carrying out their functions as an expert.[137] While in the first instance, an expert would usually be expected to look to the representatives of the instructing parties to assist them to overcome any logistical difficulties, experts must, themselves, take responsibility for ensuring that they are satisfied that they have obtained the information necessary to report to the court. In *SMBC v WMP*, HHJ Cardinal indicated that, as a matter of good practice: 'An expert . . . ought . . . to seek clarifications and raise questions under [COPR r15.11] before completing a report referring to lacunae in the information before him.'[138]
- Instructions to an expert are not privileged against disclosure:[139] in other words, nothing should be put to an expert in a letter of instruction which cannot properly be seen by all the other parties to the proceedings.

135 [2012] COPLR 567.

136 Para 39.

137 COPR r15.11(1). Any such application must (in the absence of direction to the contrary) be provided in advance to the instructing party and to the other parties to the proceedings.

138 *SMBC v WMP* [2011] EWHC B13 (COP), [2011] COPLR Con Vol 1177, (2011) 14 CCLR 413, at para 57(i). See also *London Borough of Southwark v NP and others* [2019] EWCOP 48, [2019] 4 WLR 141 at para 31(v).

139 COPR r15.8(5).

The duties upon an expert

13.83 The expert must assist the court on the matters within his or her expertise.[140] This encompasses two equally important aspects:

- No matter who the expert is instructed by or who pays them, the expert does not owe their duty to any party or parties, but to the court (and, to that end, their report is to be addressed to the court, rather than to any party from whom they have received their instructions[141]). An expert whose report lacks objectivity may themselves be at risk not just of having all or part of their fees disallowed, but may, themselves, be at risk of having to pay costs incurred by other parties in consequence of their report.[142]
- The expert must only advise upon the matters within their expertise, and make clear if a matter upon which their opinion is sought lies outside their expertise.[143] While this is in large part, a matter for the expert, it also reflects the need to ensure that the right person is chosen by the instructing parties. In *SC v BS and A Local Authority*,[144] the court (in granting permission for another expert to be instructed to report upon capacity, where the first expert, although a nationally recognised expert on autism, had not demonstrated the requisite degree of knowledge of the MCA 2005 but offered to undergo training) noted that: 'It cannot be satisfactory to seek the expert opinion from someone who perceives the need to undergo training before he can give that opinion.'[145] If a conclusion cannot be reached without carrying out appropriately structured investigations, the expert must not purport to reach a conclusion without having carried out those investigations.[146]

140 COPR r15.4.

141 COPR PD 15A para 8.

142 See, by analogy, *Phillips v Symes* [2004] EWHC 2330 (Ch), [2005] 1 WLR 2043. COPR r19.12 provides for costs orders to be made against non-parties.

143 COPR PD 15A para 6(a). See also in this regard *A Local Authority v M and others* [2014] EWCOP 33, [2015] COPLR 6 at 88 per Baker J: 'in assessing the expert evidence . . . the court must be careful to ensure that each expert keeps within the bounds of their own expertise and defers where appropriate to the expertise of others – see the observations of Eleanor King J in *A Local Authority v S* [2009] EWHC 2115 Fam.' See also *London Borough of Southwark v NP and others* [2019] EWCOP 48, [2019] 4 WLR 141 at para 31(v).

144 [2012] COPLR 567.

145 *SC* at para 37 per Baker J.

146 *Z v University Hospitals Plymouth NHS Trust and others* [2020] EWCOP 69 (diagnosis of Minimally Conscious State absent appropriate testing). The conduct of the expert, and of the family members instructing him, were the subject of serious criticism by both Cohen J and the Court of Appeal (*Z and others v RS* [2021] EWCA Civ 22, [2021] COPLR 342).

The expert's report – content

13.84 COPR PD 15A, amplifying COPR r15.8(2)–(4), sets out in some detail the requirements that apply both as to the form and the content of an expert's report, and they are not rehearsed here, save to emphasise that an expert report which does not comply with the requirements of para 9 is unlikely to be accepted by the court, not just because of the formal defects, but more importantly because para 9 sets out the 'route map' by which an expert can produce a report that establishes the proper building blocks by which reliable conclusions can be reached. As Henderson J put it in *Re S*: 'The rules are there for a good reason, and if they are not complied with a report, even from the most eminent of experts, is likely to lack the transparency and objectivity which the court rightly insists upon in expert evidence.'[147]

13.85 Further, and as set out above (para 13.62), an expert must be very careful in their report not to seek to determine factual issues that are outside their direct experience. If – as is regularly the case in reports relating to best interests – the view of the expert as to where P's best interests will lie will vary depending upon which interpretation of the facts is preferred, the proper course of action is for the expert to set out both alternative chains of reasoning from factual scenario to opinion as to best interests. In other words, the expert should give their opinion as to where P's best interests will lie depending on whether the court accepts that the particular factual issue(s) is/are made out. The most obvious example is where the allegation is made that a named individual has abused or otherwise caused harm to come to P; in such a case, the expert should give their view as to (say) contact between P and that individual based upon either a) the allegation being established; or b) the allegation not being established (see chapter 15 below for further discussion of the resolution of factual disputes).

13.86 One of the contexts in which expert evidence is most often called upon is in relation to capacity. In *AMDC v AG and another*[148] Poole J provided a useful summary of the core requirements for an expert reporting upon capacity, emphasising that '[a]n expert report on capacity is not a clinical assessment but should seek to assist the court to determine certain identified issues. The expert should therefore pay close regard to (i) the terms of the Mental Capacity Act and

147 [2010] EWHC 2405 (COP), [2010] COPLR Con Vol 1112 at para 146.

148 [2020] EWCOP 58, [2020] 4 WLR 166. The case also provides helpful guidance as to what to do where the expert finds it difficult to engage with P.

Code of Practice, and (ii) the letter of instruction'.[149] There are two particular risks that the courts have identified that experts must guard against in the assessment of capacity:

- The first, which applies equally (if not with greater force) to those involved in the ongoing care and treatment of P, is succumbing to the 'protection imperative', namely feeling 'drawn towards an outcome that is more protective of the adult and thus . . . fail[ing] to carry out an assessment of capacity that is detached and objective'.[150]
- The second is not paying sufficient weight to the fact that (as necessarily occurs in most cases) the expert only has the benefit of a limited exposure to P by comparison with the more 'longitudinal' picture enjoyed by other professionals with longer-term contact with P. While on the one hand, this may make it easier to produce a detached report, the risk is that the resulting report will represent a snapshot alone.[151] There is, in reality, unlikely to be any way in which this risk can be entirely avoided; the best that can be done is to ensure that the expert is alive to its existence.

Once the report has been provided

13.87 An expert report disclosed by a party can be used by any party as evidence at any hearing in the proceedings. The report cannot be used by a party to whom it has been disclosed for any other purpose, unless:

- the document has been read to or by the court or referred to at a public hearing; or
- the court otherwise permits.[152]

13.88 As noted above, any party (not just an instructing party) can put written questions to an expert.[153] That entitlement is limited in that

149 *AMDC* at para 28(a).

150 *PH v A Local Authority and others* [2011] EWHC 1704 (Fam), [2012] COPLR 128 at para 16(xiii) per Baker J. See also *CC v KK and STCC* [2012] EWHC 2136 (COP), [2012] COPLR 627 and also *X and Y v Croatia* (App No 5193/09, decision of 3 January 2011) (criticism by the ECtHR of the fact that the psychiatrist charged with determining X's capacity saw her for only 20 minutes, at a time when she was 'tired and under the influence of medication' (para 87)).

151 *PH* at para 56.

152 COPR r5.10.

153 COPR 15.7(1).

(subject to a different order of the court or the agreement of all the relevant parties[154]):

- the questions can only be put once;
- must be put within 28 days beginning with the date upon which the report was served; and
- can only be for purpose of clarification of the report.[155]

This last restriction is particularly important – courts take a very dim view of attempts to cross-examine experts in writing. Both to try to stop such questions being put and also so as to ensure that the expert is not bombarded with a sequence of questions from different parties, judges sometimes direct that any questions are to be put via the solicitors for one of the parties, most obviously those instructed on behalf of the Official Solicitor where P is a party and represented by the Official Solicitor.

13.89 The COPR imposes a further obligation in relation to putting written questions to an expert, namely that the question must be copied and sent to the other parties at the same time as they are sent to the expert.[156]

13.90 If an expert fails to respond to a question put to them under the procedure put to them, then the court may order:

- that the instructing party or parties may not rely on the evidence of the expert; and/or
- that the party may not recover all or part of the fees and expenses of the expert or part from any other party.[157]

13.91 Any answers given by the expert to questions put under the procedure set out above are treated as part of their report,[158] and subject to any different order of the court or final costs order, the instructing party or parties are responsible for meeting the costs both of the original report and of the answers.[159]

13.92 If permission has been granted to two (or more) experts to report upon an issue, then specific powers are granted to the court in addition to its general case management powers contained in COPR r3.1 and r3.7. The court may at any stage direct that the experts meet for

154 COPR r15.7(3) also provides for a practice direction to make alternative provision; none at present does so.

155 COPR r15.7(2)–(3).

156 COPR r15.7(2)(d).

157 COPR r15.7(5)–(6).

158 COPR r15.7(4).

159 COPR r15.7.

purposes of identifying and discussing the expert issues in the proceedings and, where possible, reaching an agreed opinion on those issues.[160] The court can specify the issues the experts must discuss, and can direct that the experts prepare a joint statement for the court setting out issues upon which they agree and issues upon which they disagree (together with a summary of their reasons for disagreeing).[161] Whether contained in a statement or otherwise, the contents of the discussions may, absent order to the contrary, be referred to at any hearing or at any stage in the proceedings (including, although the COPR do not say so expressly, for purposes of considering the conduct of any party for purposes of determining the final allocation of costs).[162] Permission to appoint two experts is unusual. Much more usual is the situation would be the situation where one of the parties before the court relies upon the quasi-expert evidence of (for instance) a treating clinician: see further para 13.58. In such a situation, consideration should also be given to holding a meeting as to share information and to identify areas of agreement and/or disagreement.[163]

13.93 If more than one expert or quasi-expert witness is involved,[164] then consideration should be given to holding an experts' meeting as to share information and to identify areas of agreement and/or disagreement.[165]

13.94 The MCA 2005 and COPR are silent as to what should happen in the event that a party who has taken part in a joint instruction is dissatisfied with the expert report. By analogy with the position that prevails under the Civil Procedure Rules (CPR), it is suggested that:

> If having obtained a joint expert's report, a party, for reasons which are not fanciful, wishes to obtain further information before making a decision as to whether or not there is a particular part (or indeed the whole) of the expert's report which he or she may wish to challenge,

160 COPR r15.10(1).

161 COPR r15.10(2)–(3).

162 COPR r15.10.

163 *London Borough of Southwark v NP and others* [2019] EWCOP 48, [2019] 4 WLR 141 at para 31(vii).

164 This could be because, unusually, two independent experts have been instructed. Much more common would be the situation where one of the parties before the court relies upon the quasi-expert evidence of (for instance) a treating clinician.

165 *London Borough of Southwark v NP and others* [2019] EWCOP 48, [2019] 4 WLR 141 at para 31(vii).

> then they should, subject to the discretion of the court, be permitted to obtain that evidence.[166]

In the light of the statutory provisions and authorities discussed above, it is clear that the court will be astute to ensure that every other avenue is explored first before such permission is granted.

Disclosure

Overview

13.95 COPR Part 16 contains provisions relating to disclosure which are based upon those in CPR Part 31. In both, a party discloses a document by stating that it exists or has existed;[167] the CPR defines a 'document' broadly as 'anything in which information of any description is recorded.'[168] While no equivalent description is given in the COPR, it is suggested that the same definition should apply.

13.96 Because proceedings before the Court of Protection are, at heart, inquisitorial rather than adversarial,[169] it has become increasingly apparent that the provisions of COPR Part 16 are not altogether well-suited to the requirements of applications under the MCA 2005. In *Enfield LBC v SA and others*,[170] McFarlane J (as he then was) commented adversely on the fact that the rules contained in COPR Part 16 were based upon:

> . . . ordinary civil litigation with the expectation that disclosure will be based on whether documents 'adversely affect [a party's] own case' or 'support another party's case' (COPR r133(2)(b))[171] whereas the approach of the family court is that there is a duty to give *the court* all relevant material.[172]

He continued that there could be:

> . . . no justification for there being a difference of this degree on the issue of disclosure between the family court and the Court of

166 *Daniels v Walker (practice note)* [2000] 1 WLR 1382 at 1387 per Lord Woolf MR.

167 CPR 31.1; COPR r16.1.

168 CPR 31.4.

169 *Re G* [2014] EWCOP 1361, [2014] COPLR 416 at para 26 per Sir James Munby P, endorsing *Cheshire West and Cheshire Council v P and M* [2011] EWHC 1330 (Fam), (2012) 15 CCLR 48, [2011] COPLR Con Vol 273 at para 52 per Baker J.

170 [2010] EWHC 196 (Admin), [2010] COPLR Con Vol 362.

171 Now COPR r16.2 92)(b), but the wording is unchanged.

172 *SA* [2010] EWHC 196 (Admin) at para 57 (emphasis in original).

> Protection in fact finding cases of this type where really the process and the issues are essentially identical whether the vulnerable complainant is a young child or an incapacitated adult. For the future in such cases in the Court of Protection it would seem to be justified for the court to make an order for 'specific disclosure' under COPR 2007 r133(3)[173] 16.2(3)] requiring all parties to give 'full and frank disclosure' of all relevant material.[174]

See further in this regard para 13.103 below.

13.97 Because they essentially do not 'fit' the approach of the Court of Protection, the majority of the provisions relating to disclosure in COPR Part 16 will not be invoked in most applications. The Case Pathways PD 3B directs that the court must in relation to cases on the welfare pathway give specific consideration to disclosure at the case management hearing (see further para 11.24), but in the authors' experience this has not led to an increase in the use of COPR Part 16.[175] Therefore these provisions are not discussed in detail in this chapter, the focus rather being upon the disclosure issues that arise most commonly in practice.

Disclosure issues in practice

13.98 It is important to note that disclosure issues can arise at the very outset of proceedings in (at least) two ways.

13.99 First, if an application is brought on an ex parte basis (ie in the absence of the respondent) then, as discussed at para 11.77 above, there is a duty upon the advocate making that application to give full and frank disclosure of all relevant matters, including those tending to suggest that the application should not be brought.

13.100 Second, the decision in *Loughlin v Singh and others*[176] stands as a clear endorsement of the propositions:

- that the rules that apply in civil proceedings as regards the privileged status of expert reports do not apply before the Court of Protection (see further para 13.116 below); and
- (in consequence) that there is a duty to bring relevant material contained in expert evidence within the possession of the applicant to the attention of the court at the outset of proceedings.

173 Now COPR r16.2(3).

174 *SA* at para 58.

175 Case Pathways PD 3B para 2.5(l).

176 [2013] EWHC 1641 (QB), [2013] COPLR 371.

13.101 In that case, an application had been made to the Court of Protection for a professional deputy to be appointed to manage the property and affairs of an adult who had suffered a number of serious injuries in a road traffic accident. The solicitors making the application were in possession of expert evidence which suggested that he *had* the requisite capacity, but did not bring this to the attention of the court. A district judge appointed the deputy without a hearing. In subsequent personal injury proceedings, the issue of the man's capacity to manage his property and affairs was hotly contested by the defendant. Kenneth Parker J found – on a fine balance[177] – that the claimant lacked capacity, such that there was ultimately no inconsistency between his decision and that which underpinned the appointment of the deputy. The judge was, however, highly critical of the actions of the solicitors, noting in an appendix to his judgment that:

> 14. In my view, this was a case where *all* available medical evidence relevant to the issue of capacity should have been disclosed to the court [of Protection] . . . It is then almost certain that the court, faced with this welter of conflicting medical opinion and aware [of other unsatisfactory aspects of an expert's report] would have refused to determine the application on paper, but would have insisted on an oral hearing at which the issue could have been fully and properly considered. I am unwilling to speculate as to what the outcome might have been if a proper procedure had been followed at that time, but the possibility cannot be ruled out that the court might at that time have found that the claimant had capacity. In the light of my own conclusion such a finding, although not unreasonable, would have been incorrect.
>
> 15. All I need add is that the lamentable failures that occurred here, and the invidious position in which the judge in the Court of Protection was unwittingly placed, must never be repeated. The issue of capacity is of very great importance, and all involved must ensure that the Court of Protection has all the material which, on proper reflection, is necessary for a just and accurate decision.

13.102 While the decision in *Loughlin v Singh* is not, strictly, binding on practitioners appearing before the Court of Protection, as it was a decision taken in the Queen's Bench Division, nor do these passages appear to reflect argument advanced to the court based upon analysis either of the MCA 2005 or of the COPR, it is suggested that the passages set out above are entirely correct in their approach and should be followed.

177 Para 45.

13.103 Once proceedings are under way, it would appear that the injunction given by McFarlane J in *SA* discussed at para 13.96 above is routinely ignored, orders for full and frank disclosure in welfare proceedings being made very rarely (if at all). In any situation in which it appears that one (or more) parties may need reminding of their ongoing duties to bring material information to the court, it is suggested that an order can and should be made, and compliance with it revisited at each case management hearing.

13.104 It is also unusual for the Court of Protection routinely to make an order for general disclosure, ie for each party to disclose those documents on which they rely, and documents which adversely affect their own case; adversely affect another party's case; or support another party's case. Indeed, in some cases, no disclosure orders will be made at all.

13.105 In welfare cases, however, orders are commonly made for the provision of specific categories of documents (for instance of medical or social services records), not to all the parties to the proceedings, but rather only to those with a specific need to have sight of them. This happens most obviously where P is a party to the proceedings and orders are made requiring (for instance) either all or part of the records held by the local authority's social services department relating to P to be provided to their litigation friend (and frequently on the basis that subsequent onward disclosure is made by the litigation friend). The authors' experience is that these orders are made without judicial examination of the basis of the power under which they are made.

Withholding disclosure on confidentiality/welfare grounds

13.106 No matter the power under which such orders are made, one question arises with some regularity, namely the extent to which it is permissible for orders to be made allowing for documents to be seen by one party but not by others. Orders are regularly made providing (for instance) that social services records relating to P are to be provided to P's litigation friend (and can, in turn, be provided to any independent expert instructed to report to the court), but either making no provision for those records to be provided to other parties to the proceedings, or giving P's litigation friend a 'vetting' role so as to allow their litigation friend to determine which documents should be provided to other parties. The COPR do not contain any test or threshold for denying disclosure (whether to one or to more than one party), rule 16.7 merely providing in material part that:

(1) A party who wishes to claim that he has a right or duty to withhold inspection of a document, or part of a document, must state in writing –
(a) that he has such a right or duty; and
(b) the grounds on which he claims that right of duty.

13.107 Moreover, as COPR r16.7 can only be invoked at the time that a disclosure list is provided,[178] and as such disclosure lists are rarely, if ever, in fact used in the Court of Protection, it would appear that rule 16.7 does not, in fact, serve as the basis upon which disclosure of such materials as social work records is limited. The precise basis upon which such orders are made is therefore not entirely clear.

13.108 Following the decision of Sir James Munby P in *RC v CC and X Local Authority*,[179] it is, however, clear that the court does have the power to withhold disclosure of reports or records. *RC* did not spell out the basis upon which the power arose,[180] but it is suggested that it is perhaps most obviously under the court's general powers under COPR r3.1.

13.109 The decision in *RC* also set out the test for the circumstances under which such orders can be made where a party wishes to withhold documents on the basis of their confidentiality and/or their adverse impact upon P (the position where disclosure is withheld on the basis of privilege is discussed at para 13.116 onwards below).

13.110 Before addressing the decision in *RC*, it is worth noting the competing principles in play, in particular:

- P's right to the maintenance of confidentiality in relation to what will often be highly sensitive personal data (a right which is recognised at common law and by ECHR Article 8 right to respect for private and family life), and is enshrined in statutory provisions such as the Data Protection Act 1998). In the case of children, there has also been a historical acceptance that the particular circumstances in which social services records are created give rise to a presumption that they should be immune from disclosure on a public interest basis.[181]
- The rights of other parties to have sight of, and the ability to respond to, information contained in those documents if any reliance is to be placed by the court upon that information, whether

178 COPR r16.7(2).
179 [2014] EWHC 131 (COP), (2014) 17 CCLR 127.
180 See para 20.
181 *Re M (a minor) (disclosure of material)* [1990] 2 FLR 36. This case must now be treated with caution: *Dunn v Durham CC* [2012] EWCA Civ 1654, [2013] 1 WLR 2305 at para 45 per Munby LJ.

that reliance is to be direct – ie the judge himself reading the documents – or indirect – ie an expert reporting to the court based upon the documents. The proper exercise of those rights is integral to enabling the fairness of the proceedings, a principle enshrined both at common law and in ECHR Article 6.[182]

13.111 In *RC*, Sir James Munby P drew direct analogies between the position that prevailed in proceedings in relation to children and those that should apply in the Court of Protection. He placed particular reliance upon three decisions,[183] and his conclusions can be summarised thus:

- It is a fundamental principle of fairness that a party is entitled to the disclosure of all materials which may be taken into account by the court when reaching a decision adverse to that party.
- When deciding whether to direct that a party referred to documentation should not be able to inspect the part which refers to them, the court should first consider whether disclosure of the material would involve a real possibility of significant harm to P.
- If it would, the court should next consider whether the overall interests of P would benefit from non-disclosure, weighing on the one hand the interest of P in having the material properly tested, and on the other both the magnitude of the risk that harm will occur and the gravity of the harm if it does occur.
- If the court is satisfied that the interests of P point towards non-disclosure, the next and final step is for the court to weigh that consideration, and its strength in the circumstances of the case, against the interest of the parent or other party in having an opportunity to see and respond to the material. In the latter regard the court should take into account the importance of the material to the issues in the case.
- In all cases, the test for non-disclosure is whether it is strictly necessary to meet the risk identified by the court.[184]

182 In *KK v Leeds City Council* [2020] EWCOP 64, [2021] COPLR 96, Cobb J considered the position of a potential party, and noted (at para 41(v)) that: 'While the principles of natural justice are always engaged, the obligation to give full disclosure of all information (including sensitive information) to someone who is not a party is unlikely to be as great as it would be to an existing party'.

183 *In re D (minors) (adoption reports: confidentiality)* [1996] AC 593, [1995] 3 WLR 483, HL; *Re B (disclosure to other parties)* [2001] 2 FLR 1017, [2002] 2 FCR 32, Fam; and *Dunn v Durham CC* [2012] EWCA Civ 1654, [2013] 1 WLR 2305.

184 See paras 15–17.

13.112 Sir James Munby P also noted in *RC* that consideration should always be given to the fact that disclosure is never a binary exercise, and a proper evaluation and weighing of the various interests may lead to the conclusion that i) there should be disclosure but ii) the disclosure needs to be subject to safeguards such as limits to the use that may be made of the documents, in particular so as to limit the release into the public domain of intensely personal information about third parties. Further, he emphasised, the position initially arrived at is never set in stone; it may be appropriate to proceed one step at a time.[185]

13.113 A further factor that did not arise in *RC* but may well do in a future case is where P themselves has views as to whether or not information should be disclosed to a particular party or parties. Whilst those views will not be determinative, it is likely that considerable weight will be placed upon them by analogy with the position adopted in *Local Authority X v HI*,[186] concerning whether sensitive information revealed by a boy subject to care proceedings which he did not wish disclosed to his parents or stepmother.

13.114 *RC* is also of significance because Sir James Munby P confirmed that the first instance judge had had the power to direct that some documents could be disclosed solely to the advocate for a party, with a direction that the representative could not disclose or discuss it with the client.[187] However, Sir James made it clear that such limited disclosure can only be ordered if there is clear and express consent on the party of the affected party's legal representative, who should only give such consent if they are satisfied that they can do so without harming their client's case.[188]

13.115 Notwithstanding the endorsement by Sir James Munby P of 'confidentiality rings', it is suggested that any legal adviser should be very cautious before advancing or agreeing to one. The 'very serious problems' it creates between lawyer and client have led to doubts being placed upon the decision in *Mohammed* upon which Sir James Munby P relied.[189] The decision in *RC* may therefore not necessarily be the end of the story in this regard. Another possible alternative,

185 See paras 18–19.

186 [2016] EWHC 1123 (Fam).

187 See paras 21–23. The appeal was allowed in this regard because of a doubt as to the basis upon which the power had been exercised.

188 *RC* at para 38, endorsing dicta of Moses LJ in *R (Mohammed) v Secretary of State for Defence* [2012] EWHC 3454 (Admin), [2014] 1 WLR 1071.

189 *AHK, AM, AS, FM v Secretary of State for the Home Department* [2013] EWHC 1426 (Admin) at paras 20–28 per Ouseley J.

that of appointing a special advocate (ie an advocate who can see all of the material, but on the basis that they do not communicate any of it, or its gist, to the client's representatives, might be appropriate, but only in sufficiently unusual circumstances.[190]

Privilege

13.116 Disclosure of documents can also be resisted on the basis that they are subject to legal professional privilege: ie that they represent 'protected' communications between lawyer and client (and, in certain circumstances, with third parties).

13.117 This is a very large topic. Space precludes a detailed discussion of it here,[191] but the position is set out in summary form in the paragraphs that follow. These paragraphs must be read subject to the caveat that, with the limited exception of the case of *Loughlin v Singh* discussed above (para 13.101), there has been no reported judicial consideration of the application of the law of privilege to proceedings before the Court of Protection. The paragraphs below therefore represent the authors' view that the closest analogy to such proceedings are those involving children, and that the principles derived in those proceedings can and should be applied before the Court of Protection.

13.118 There are two forms of legal professional privilege: legal advice privilege and litigation privilege.

- **Legal advice privilege** protects confidential communications between a client and their professional legal adviser that is made for the purpose of seeking or giving any legal advice or related legal assistance. It is not necessary for it to apply that there is litigation in prospect.[192]
- **Litigation privilege** protects confidential communications between either the client or their legal adviser or their legal adviser and a third party (such as a factual or an expert witness), where such communications come into existence for the dominant purpose of being used in connection with actual, pending or contemplated litigation.[193]

190 See *Re P (discharge of party)* [2021] EWCA Civ 512, [2021] 1 WLR 3098.

191 The reader is directed, in particular, to C Passmore *Privilege*, Sweet & Maxwell, 4th edn, 2019; also see *Phipson on Evidence*, Sweet & Maxwell, 20th edn, 2021, chapter 23.

192 Passmore, *Privilege*, para 1-002.

193 Passmore, *Privilege*, para 1-002.

13.119 Where a litigation friend has been appointed to act on behalf of a party (whether that be P or a protected party: see chapter 12), and whilst there is no reported case from the Court of Protection on the point, it is suggested that for these purposes the litigation friend stands in the shoes of the client. By analogy, we note that the Court of Appeal accepted in *RP v Nottingham City Council* (it appears without argument) that the file maintained by a solicitor retained by the Official Solicitor where he was acting as litigation friend for a protected party in care proceedings contained privileged material.[194]

13.120 Litigation privilege is 'essentially a creature of adversarial proceedings'; it does not therefore extend to protect expert reports obtained in the context of care proceedings involving children.[195] It is suggested that this applies equally in the context of proceedings under the MCA 2005. Indeed, this would appear to be (albeit implicitly rather than expressly) the basis upon which Kenneth Parker J held in *Loughlin v Singh* (para 13.101 above) that all relevant expert reports in the possession of the claimant's solicitors should have been disclosed to the Court of Protection when making an application for the appointment of a deputy to manage his property and affairs. It should also be noted that it is clear from the COPR that *instructions* to an expert are not privileged against disclosure.[196]

13.121 It would, further, appear that it may well be the case that litigation privilege cannot be claimed in the context of other classes of documents or correspondence created in the context of proceedings before the Court of Protection.[197] Moreover, even if litigation privilege can be claimed, a number of family law cases have suggested this may be overridden by a duty to disclose documents where the court must determine what is in the best interests of the child.[198] It is suggested that such an approach would be likely also to be taken by the Court of Protection.

13.122 The position as regards legal advice privilege, however, is very different. Save for rare exceptions involving fraud or misconduct, the privilege has been held to be an absolute one even in respect of proceedings involving the determination of the best interests of chil-

194 [2008] EWCA Civ 462, (2008) 11 CCLR 316 at paras 34–35, per Wall LJ.

195 *Re L (a minor) (police investigation: privilege)* [1997] AC 16 at 27 per Lord Jauncey.

196 COPR r15.8(5).

197 Following the approach adopted by the House of Lords in *Three Rivers (No 6)* [2004] UKHL 48, [2005] 1 AC 610.

198 See, in particular, *Oxfordshire CC v M* [1994] Fam 151, [1994] 2 WLR 393, CA.

dren.[199] It is suggested that the same applies in proceedings under the MCA 2005 so as to protect lawyer-client communications, communications between a litigation friend appointed to act on behalf of P (or a protected party other than P, or a child) and the lawyers that that litigation friend has retained.

13.123 It should be emphasised that the mere fact that a person lacks capacity to conduct the proceedings does not mean that they should not be afforded the same protections as would be afforded to others. This means that, for instance, a litigation friend and lawyers instructed on behalf of P (or a protected party other than P or a child) must be very careful before putting before the court, whether by way of attendance notes of visits or otherwise, material that might incriminate their client if factual allegations are made against the individual in question.[200]

199 *AB (care proceedings: disclosure of medical evidence to police)* [2002] EWHC 2198 (Fam), [2003] 1 FLR 579.

200 See, by analogy, *Re E (a child)* [2016] EWCA Civ 473, [2016] WLR 105.

CHAPTER 14

Publicity, privacy and confidentiality

Introduction

14.1 The Court of Protection's approach to public and media access has undergone dramatic changes since the first edition of this book in 2014. In 2014, most hearings were held in private, the sole exception being serious medical treatment cases, and stories were repeatedly run in the press about the so-called 'secret court'. The then-President, Sir James Munby, had made clear that he wanted the position to change, firstly by securing greater publication of judgments.[1]

14.2 Limited changes were made in July 2015 through amendments to Court of Protection Rules 2007 r91, and to then Practice Direction (PD) 13A. More fundamental change was implemented with the (initially) six-month Transparency Pilot in January 2016, establishing a presumption that hearings will take place in public, with reporting restrictions to protect the identity of P and P's family, unless there is 'good reason' to order otherwise. The Transparency Pilot was extended in July 2016 to last until 31 August 2017. On 1 December 2017, the Court of Protection Rules 2017[2] (COPR) and accompanying practice directions cemented the Transparency Pilot into the practice and procedure of the court.

14.3 After a little over two years of (crudely) a court sitting in public but very few members of the public attending, the COVID-19 pandemic led to yet further changes in 2020 as a result of the court having to transition rapidly to sitting remotely. The Vice-President of the Court of Protection made clear, early on, his commitment to seeking to maintain the 'culture' of transparency.[3] As Lieven J observed almost two years later:

> The volume and necessity of remote hearings brought about by the COVID-19 pandemic has presented a challenge to the extent to which this 'ordinary' course can be followed but the need for transparency has not abated.[4]

14.4 One unanticipated consequence of the move to remote hearings was that at a stroke, it became – oddly – significantly easier, at least in

1 See the guidance published in January 2014 entitled *Transparency in the Court of Protection: publication of judgments*, available at: www.judiciary.gov.uk/Resources/JCO/Documents/Guidance/transparency-in-the-cop.pdf.

2 SI 2017 No 1035.

3 *Remote access to the Court of Protection guidance*, 31 March 2020, para 54, available at www.judiciary.uk/wp-content/uploads/2020/04/20200331-Court-of-Protection-Remote-Hearings.pdf.

4 *Kent County Council v P* [2022] EWCOP 3 at para 11.

principle, for members of the public to attend, by simple virtue of being sent the relevant link to the hearing or the telephone number. Capitalising on this, Professor Celia Kitzinger and Gill Loomes-Quinn founded the Open Justice Court of Protection Project,[5] which both facilitates access by non-parties to hearings being held remotely and hosts on its website numerous blogs by observers reporting upon hearings. The Project team and the observers who have sat in on hearings have asked searching and important questions about the practices and processes of the court. However, it is also legitimate to identify that facilitating that access has come at some cost in terms of the (scarce) resources of the court.[6] It is also legitimate to identify that there are some situations in which insufficient focus has been paid to the impact upon P of (in effect) broadcasting – or at least, narrowcasting – a hearing. Calibrating these matters will be an important task for the court as it moves back to a position where more hearings are held either in person or in a hybrid fashion.

14.5 In this chapter, we:

- set out the relevant provisions of the Administration of Justice Act (AJA) 1960;
- set out the rules and explain the modifications as a result of the rule changes in 2015;
- explain the implications of the COPR PD 4C ('the Transparency PD');
- consider the position in cases which fall outside the Transparency PD (ie committal proceedings);
- consider the effect of the Courts Act 2003 s85A;
- consider specific issues arising in relation to remote hearings; and
- consider the issues that may arise in relation to anonymisation.

The Administration of Justice Act 1960

14.6 It is important to be aware of AJA 1960 s12, as amended by Mental Capacity Act (MCA) 2005 Sch 6 para 10. The relevant part of section 12 reads:

5 See: https://openjusticecourtofprotection.org/.

6 In particular in the case of Tier 1 (district judges) who do not as a general rule have clerks, and are therefore themselves regularly having to deal with the emails requesting access whilst preparing for hearings.

12 Publication of information relating to proceedings in private

(1) The publication of information relating to proceedings before any court sitting in private shall not of itself be contempt of court except in the following cases, that is to say–

(a) where the proceedings–
  (i) relate to the exercise of the inherent jurisdiction of the High Court with respect to minors;
  (ii) are brought under the Children Act 1989 or the Adoption and Children Act 2002; or
  (iii) otherwise relate wholly or mainly to the maintenance or upbringing of a minor;

(b) where the proceedings are brought under the Mental Capacity Act 2005 or under any provision of the Mental Health Act 1983 authorising an application or reference to be made to the First-tier Tribunal, the Mental Health Review Tribunal for Wales or the county court . . .

14.7 Therefore it is a contempt of court to publish information relating to Court of Protection proceedings when the court is sitting in private. This applies whether or not the court has made any order restricting publication of information about a specific case.

The Court of Protection Rules

14.8 COPR Part 4 deals with hearings. It is supported by two Practice Directions: PD 4A 'Hearings' and PD 4C 'Transparency'.

14.9 As it will be seen, the rules provide the 'general rule' that hearings are heard in private. The rules contain a degree of flexibility with judges having discretion to allow the publication of information or the attendance of members of the public or the media. Departure from the general rule requires 'good reason'.[7] These rules are still in technically in force, but in practice have been fundamentally altered by the Transparency PD, and also by the routine making of orders providing for remote hearings (as to which see para 14.47 below).

COPR PD 4A

14.10 Before we address the COPR Transparency PD, it is important to note that PD 4A allows – in all cases – for the communication of information without the need for formal authorisation by the court, for example by a party to their GP, to enable them to receive confid-

7 COPR r4.4(1).

ential support, or their MP to pursue a complaint. PD 4A para 31 makes clear that communication for these purposes will not constitute contempt of court. The court can make a specific direction limiting communication of information if it considers that such is required in a particular case.[8] Conversely, the court can also make a direction expanding the scope of such disclosure: one area that it is important for practitioners to be aware of is that the provisions relating to healthcare professionals in PD 4A only relate to disclosure for purposes of obtaining healthcare or counselling. If it is likely that those professionals will need to have sight of information within the proceedings for other purposes, a specific direction is required.

14.11 COPR PD 4A para 33 sets out the circumstances in which information about proceedings can be released, for example to a party, a party's legal representative or accredited legal representative (or ALR, see chapter 10), an expert or author of a report directed under MCA 2005 s49 (see para 13.47) as well as the Director of Legal Aid casework.

14.12 COPR PD 4A para 34 reads:

> **Communication of information for purposes connected with the proceedings**
>
> 34(1) A party or the legal representative of a party, on behalf of and upon the instructions of that party, may communicate information relating to the proceedings to any person where necessary to enable that party–
>
> (a) by confidential discussion, to obtain support, advice or assistance in the conduct of the proceedings;
>
> (b) to engage in mediation or other forms of non-court dispute resolution;
>
> (c) to make and pursue a complaint against a person or body concerned in the proceedings; or
>
> (d) to make and pursue a complaint regarding the law, policy or procedure relating to proceedings in the Court of Protection.

14.13 There are restrictions on onward disclosure. It should be noted that if information is communicated under PD 4A para 34(1)(a) – perhaps to a party's GP or counsellor – the person who receives the information must not pass it on to anyone else. Further communication is permitted where the initial disclosure is made under para 34(1) (b), (c) or (d), either to take part in some form of alternative dispute resolution (ADR) or to make a relevant complaint. In these cases successive communication is permitted but only with the agreement of the party who communicated the information in the first place and for the original purpose. The provisions for onward disclosure appear at PD 4A para 35.

8 COPR PD 4A para 31.

The Transparency PD

14.14 The Transparency PD provides that the court will ordinarily make an order that the hearing shall be in public and at the same time impose reporting restrictions.[9] Thus, it reverses the presumption that hearings will be in private. Now the default position is that they will be in public with standard orders.[10]

14.15 The practice direction applies to hearings in all proceedings except applications for a committal order (addressed at paras 14.51–14.55 below). Transparency PD para 2.1 explains that the court will ordinarily direct that any attended hearing shall be in public and will make a standard order in relation to the publication of proceedings. So, once the transparency order has been made it is in place for the remainder of the case and all attended hearings will be in public. There is therefore no need for the court to make more than one Pilot order. A 'dispute resolution hearing' for a case on the property and affairs pathway is not considered to be an attended hearing for the purpose of the Transparency PD.[11]

14.16 Transparency PD para 2.4 allows the court not to make an order under para 2.1, but only if it considers there is 'good reason' for not making the order.

14.17 Transparency PD para 2.5 sets out some of the factors that the court will consider when deciding if there is 'good reason' not to make an order that the hearing should be in public. These are:

(1)(a) the need to protect P or another person involved in the proceedings;
(b) the nature of the evidence in the proceedings;
(c) whether earlier hearings in the proceedings have taken place in private;
(d) whether the court location where the hearing will be held has facilities appropriate to allowing general public access to the hearing, and whether it would be practicable or proportionate to move to another location or hearing room;
(e) whether there is any risk of disruption to the hearing if there is general public access to it;
(f) whether, if there is good reason for not allowing general public access, there also exists good reason to deny access to duly accredited representatives of news gathering and reporting organisations.

9 Transparency PD para 2.1.
10 Transparency PD para 1.1.
11 Transparency PD para 2.2, see further para 8.36.

> (2) In sub-paragraph (1)(f), 'duly accredited' refers to accreditation in accordance with any administrative scheme for the time being approved for the purposes of this practice direction by the Lord Chancellor.

14.18 It should be noted, however, that the court is not expected to take a binary approach and either make a standard order or no such order at all. Instead, para 2.4 provides that the court should always consider as an alternative making an order under that only part of the hearing will be in public or that some persons or classes of persons should be excluded.

14.19 Transparency PD para 2.6 provides that:

> Where the court makes an order pursuant to paragraph 2.1 or 2.4 that an attended hearing or part of it is to be in public, the court will grant, to any person who would have been entitled under the Legal Services Act 2007 to exercise rights of audience at that hearing if such an order had not been made and the hearing was held in private (and who is not otherwise entitled to exercise such rights), the equivalent rights of audience at that attended hearing and any further attended hearing, unless the court is satisfied that there is good reason not to do so.

14.20 This was a late addition to the scheme, after it was pointed out by several solicitors who had seen the documentation in its draft form that the effect of holding public hearings would be to deprive them of their rights of audience in the Court of Protection. The new provision does, however, give rise to the question of when there might be good reason not to allow a solicitor to appear in a public hearing in the Court of Protection. We are not aware of any reported cases in which this has been considered.

14.21 The approach of the court to the (linked) question of the importance of enabling the press to report upon the work of the court is considered at para 14.57 below. It is important, however, to recognise that the provisions of the Transparency PD apply even where there is no suggestion that the press might report upon the case. In *Re P (Court of Protection: Transparency)*[12] Keehan J emphasised that:

> The importance of public justice, . . . is a central tenet of the Court of Protection. It should only be overridden when the circumstances of the case compellingly, and on the basis of cogent evidence, require the proceedings to be heard in private[13]

14.22 It should be noted that the views of P themselves, when they can be elicited, are an important factor. By way of example, in a case concerning anorexia, Moor J in directing the hearing to take place in private 'in particular, because of the express wishes of RD that the intensely

12 [2019] EWCOP 67.

13 Para 16.

personal matters that are being discussed in relation to her health should not take place in public'.[14]

14.23 It is important to identify that the balance may shift over time. In *Kent County Council v P and another*,[15] it became clear that there would in the particular circumstances of P's case be little risk of any distress being caused to her by her case being heard in public, and potentially reported upon. In that case, the police also argued that allowing the press to attend and report on the Court of Protection proceedings might undermine the integrity of the criminal trial. However, Lieven J considered such a risk to be merely notional, rather than real.[16]

The Transparency Order

14.24 Transparency PD para 2.2 contemplates that Transparency Orders will be made in standard form, approved by the President of the Court of Protection and published on the judicial website at: www.judiciary.gov.uk/publication-court/court-of-protection. At the time of writing, the model order is out of date, referring to the Transparency Pilot and the previous Rules; an updated version is on the Court of Protection Handbook website.[17]

14.25 The wording of the Order is complex, reflecting primarily the fact that, absent amendments to the COPR (and potentially primary legislation) careful navigation is required by the court to ensure that it does not, by listing a hearing as a public hearing, thereby lose the ability to ensure that private information relating to P is kept private. Repeated proposals have been advanced for the simplification of the order, a need made more pressing by the complexities of operating with them in the context of remote hearings, but as yet they have not borne fruit.[18]

14.26 The Transparency Order is a public document and therefore P's full name should no longer appear in full in it. Likewise the names of the parties should be 'appropriately anonymised'; although as with judgments[19] public bodies should be named in full. However, this

14 *RD (anorexia: compulsory treatment)* [2021] EWCOP 36 at para 1.

15 [2022] EWCOP 3.

16 Applying *Jefferson v Bhetcha* [1979] 1 WLR 898.

17 See: https://courtofprotectionhandbook.com/.

18 The Vice-President, Charles J, explained the basis for the order – and then its differences to those made in serious medical treatment cases in a schedule to the judgment he gave in *V v Associated Newspapers Ltd and others* [2016] EWCOP 21, [2016] COPLR 236. As discussed in chapter 23, there is now no specific category of serious medical treatment cases.

19 See *Transparency and the Court of Protection: publication of judgments*, para 20.

should not take place if the naming of the public body could give rise to 'jigsaw identification' of P.[20] By way of pre-Transparency PD example, in *NHS Trust and others v FG*,[21] Keehan J held that it was not in P's interests for the hospital, the responsible trust or the county in which she resided to be identified. This was because he accepted there was 'a real risk that if the latter were made public it is highly likely [P] and /or her baby would be identifiable given the most unusual circumstances of this case'.[22]

14.27 The standard order will provide for the next hearing and any further hearing to be in public. Paragraph 2 makes it clear however that admission to hearings will be dependent on the attendees signing a document before they go into court which will give their details and will confirm that they have been given a copy of the order and are aware of its terms. In the context of remote hearings, this provision is inoperative.

14.28 The standard order contains some basic details of the issues that the case concerns, from a list of standard descriptions. These are also included in a daily cause list. These are:

a) where P should live;
b) contact with specified persons;
c) prohibiting contact with P;
d) healthcare;
e) capacity to marry or to consent to sexual relations;
f) appointment of deputy for personal welfare;
g) varying or terminating an urgent or standard authorisation under the Deprivation of Liberty Safeguards;
h) authorising a deprivation of liberty (in relation to . . . eg care and residence arrangements);
i) appointment of deputy for property and affairs;
j) discharge or conduct of deputy;
k) will, codicil, gift or settlement of property;
l) registration of enduring or lasting power of attorney;
m) discharge or conduct of deputy or attorney (application by Public Guardian/delete as necessary);
n) recognition and enforcement of a protective measure under the law of [name country]; and
o) publication of information about proceedings.

20 The President of the Family Division, Sir Andrew McFarlane has issued practice guidance on anonymisation for use in cases involving children, but applicable in principle to the Court of Protection, available at: www.judiciary.uk/wp-content/uploads/2018/12/anonymisation-guidance-1.pdf.

21 [2014] EWCOP 30, [2015] 1 WLR 1984.

22 Para 67.

14.29 This should have the effect of making research into the types of cases which come before the courts much easier.

14.30 Paragraph 5 is the injunctive provision and reads as follows:

The following persons (the Persons Bound by this Injunctive Order) are bound by this injunctive order:

i) the parties and their representatives,
ii) the witnesses,
iii) all persons who attend all or any part of an attended hearing,
iv) all persons who by any means obtain or are given an account or record of all or any part of an attended hearing or of any order or judgment made or given as a result of an attended hearing,
v) all persons who are provided with or by any means obtain documents and information arising from this application, and
vi) any body, authority or organisation (and their officers, employees, servants and agents) for whom any such person works or is giving evidence.

14.31 Paragraph 6 sets out the material and information (the Information) covered by this injunctive order:

i) any material or information that identifies or is likely to identify that
   (a) [*INITIALS TO IDENTIFY P NOT NAME*] and members of [*SAME INITIALS TO IDENTIFY P*]'s family are respectively the subject (and so a P as defined in the Court of Protection Rules 2007) or members of the family of a subject of these proceedings, or that
   (b) [*ANONYMISED PERSON*] [. . . *ANONYMISED REFERENCE TO ANY OTHER PARTY* . . .] is a party to these proceedings, or that
   (c) [*ANONYMISED PERSON*] [. . . *ANONYMISED PERSON WHOSE IDENTITY SHOULD NOT BE PUBLISHED* . . .] (who the Court has so identified to the parties in private) [. . . has taken a part in/or been referred to in . . .] these proceedings; and
ii) any material or information that identifies or is likely to identify where any person listed above lives, or is being cared for, or their contact details.[23]

14.32 Paragraph 7 explains what the order prevents:

23 It is particularly important that the court is made aware of any information about P which is already in the public domain: see *Manchester University NHS Foundation Trust v Verden and others* [2022] EWCOP 4.

> Subject to further order of the Court and save as provided by sub-paragraph (D) the Persons Bound by this Injunctive Order shall not by any means directly or indirectly:
> i) publish the Information or any part or parts of it, or
> ii) cause, enable, assist in or encourage the publication of the Information or any part or parts of it.

14.33 Paragraph 8 deals with the duration of the injunction. The options are either until further order, or until a specified period after the death of P (reflecting the use of the order in medical treatment cases).

14.34 Paragraph 9 sets out the limitations of the order:

> Subject to further order of the Court this injunctive order does not prevent the Persons Bound by this Injunctive Order from communicating information relating to these proceedings on the basis that Part 3 of Practice Direction 13A to the Court of Protection Rules 2007 (which relates to proceedings held in private) applies to these proceedings.

14.35 It will be noted that members of the media are not specifically listed. The media must be given notice of an order restricting the media from reporting what happens in a given case.[24] Charles J explained in the note accompanying the launch of the Pilot that to give the media formal notice on each occasion that an Order was made would be impracticable and would cause delays. His view was that this was not necessary anyway as if a member of the media attends a hearing they will be bound by the terms of the order. The possibility that someone who attends the hearing subsequently breaches the Transparency Order and provides information to a third party is catered for by sub-para 5(iv) which binds the third party.

14.36 Paragraph 6 sets out the information which is covered by the injunction. This broadly protects the identity of:

- P and members of P's family;
- other parties;
- other persons involved or referred to.

14.37 The injunction does not prevent disclosure of information under PD 4A Part 3 (see para 14.10 above) (see para 5D).

14.38 Paragraph 11 requires any transcripts of judgments as well as orders to be anonymised, but is subject to the position in relation to third party orders addressed below.

14.39 Paragraph 12 provides that the court may at any time give such directions as it thinks fit (including directions relating to anonymisation, payment, use, copying, return and the means by which a copy of

24 COPR PD 4A para 10.

a document or information may be provided) concerning the provision of information or copies of documents put before the court and the terms on which they are to be provided to any person who attends an attended hearing (and is not a person to whom the document can be provided under Part 3 of PD4A).

14.40 Paragraph 13 provides for a record of that information which the court has determined should not be released to be kept and referred to as 'the Record'. This information may be made available 'on such terms as the court thinks fit' to anyone who attends the hearing (para 13) or makes an application supported by evidence (para 14). It is the Record which will contain the full names of the parties.

14.41 Paragraph 10 gives the parties and anyone affected by the order liberty to apply to vary or discharge it. The Vice-President's Note[25] makes it clear that such applications must be supported by evidence, although this is not in the practice direction or the draft order.

14.42 Paragraph 15 deals with the question of rights of audience, discussed at paras 6.23–6.25.

14.43 Care should be taken in preparing third party orders (ie orders directed to a person or body who is not a party to proceedings and was not present at the hearing at which they were made – an example being an order for disclosure of records held by a public body). Orders are public and should be endorsed with the following notice:

> This order is covered by the terms of the transparency order served herewith which imposes restrictions upon the identification of the parties. If any person disobeys that order in paragraph (5) they may be found guilty of contempt of court and may be sent to prison, fined or have their assets seized. They have the right to ask the court to vary or discharge the order.

14.44 Because the third party order will be anonymised, para 6 makes clear that a confidential schedule will also need to be prepared, providing the necessary identification. The schedule should also contain the notice in the paragraph above.[26]

Assessment

14.45 No formal report was ever published as to the success (or otherwise) of the Transparency Pilot, but readers may find the comments of the Transparency Project, whose authors were following the Pilot, to be

25 See: www.judiciary.gov.uk/wp-content/uploads/2016/01/CoP-Transparency-Pilot-Note-from-the-VP–11Dec15final.pdf.

26 Model Order.

of interest.[27] Anecdotal evidence suggests that, prior to the COVID-19 pandemic, there were very limited take-up of the opportunity to attend hearings both by members of the public and by media representatives. In part, this was because of considerable inconsistency as to the information provided in and the timing of the listing of cases. As noted above, the fact that many hearings are now held remotely means that access is, curiously, easier. The Open Justice Court of Protection Project has also provided, in effect, an (informal) listing service which, again, makes public access easier. As valuable as this service is, the members of the Project are entirely within their rights to observe (as they do, repeatedly) that this is something that should be done by HM Courts and Tribunals Service.

14.46 A particular problem identified both before and during the COVID-19 pandemic is the fact that there is inconsistency in practice as regards explanation of PD 4A to those who do attend the hearing, as well as inconsistency in identifying whose task it is to explain the practice direction and its effects. Most judges will provide an explanation of the order at the start of a hearing, but given its complexity and the fact that it is cast in injunctive terms, it is unsurprising that the use of the orders has been the subject of considerable criticism by those attending remote hearings. These criticisms can be found from any perusal of the Open Justice Court of Protection Project website. In consequence of one incident involving the Project, Roberts J reiterated that any order should not be drafted as to include any reporting restriction order should not be drafted to include any prohibition of information which is already properly and lawfully in the public domain.[28]

Remote hearings and remote access

14.47 One of the difficulties in remote hearings is that there is some inconsistency in the approach of the courts in remote hearings as to whether the court is sitting in private, with permission being given to commentators, legal bloggers or members of the public to attend (as anticipated by the model Remote Hearing Order);[29] or whether the court is sitting in public. Does the fact that a member of the public can request a link to attend a hearing equate to the ability to enter the court as of right, or is the reality that the hearing is in private but that access is routinely being granted?

27 See: www.transparencyproject.org.uk/category/cop/.

28 *Re BU* [2021] EWCOP 54, [2022] COPLR 46.

29Featured in the Remote Hearing guidance promulgated by Hayden J in March 2020.

14.48 A further difficulty is that the model Remote Hearing Order does not include the usual injunctive provisions in para 6 (see para 5.34 above). These are sometimes imported into the Remote Hearing Order, but not invariably.

14.49 It is to be hoped both of these issues can be addressed as part of the consideration of the post-pandemic Working Group's report discussed in chapter 1.

14.50 With effect from 28 June 2022, a new framework governing remote access by non-participants to proceedings was introduced by the Police, Crime, Sentencing and Courts Act 2022 – introducing a new sections 85A and 85B into the Courts Act 2003 – and the Remote Observation and Recording (Courts and Tribunals) Regulations 2022.[30] This framework is explained in the Practice Guidance issued by the Lord Chief Justice and the Senior President of Tribunals on 28 June 2022.[31] It applies whether the court is sitting in person, but enabling remote observation, or if the court is, itself, sitting remotely. In broad terms, its effect is to:

- provide judges with the power to make directions to enable members of the public to observe proceedings remotely (by video or audio);
- set down a series of considerations for judges to apply when deciding whether to make such a direction;
- make it (by the Courts Act 2003 s85B) a criminal offence to make an unauthorised recording during any such remote observation.

It is likely that the Remote Hearings Guidance issued by the Vice-President, Hayden J, in March 2020 will be updated in due course to address the provisions of this new framework, not least as the provisions of the template order attached to that guidance now require updating to reflect that there is now no need to injunct observers from making unauthorised recordings, as this is covered by the offence under Courts Act s85B. It should be noted, though, that this new framework stands alongside, rather than replacing, the provisions of the Transparency Practice Direction: the latter provides the mechanism by which the court decides whether the matter should be held in public (and subject to what limitations as to

30 SI 2022 No 705. The introduction of the new framework places matters on a clearer statutory footing than previously; whilst judges had grappled with the problem of recording of remote observations (see *Re TA (recording of hearings; communication with court office)* [2021] EWCOP 3), they had been doing so in circumstances where the powers to prevent recording were perhaps not entirely obvious.

31 Available at https://www.judiciary.uk/wp-content/uploads/2022/06/Practice-Guidance-on-remote-observation-final.pdf/.

identification of P; the former the mechanism by which the public may be given remote access to the hearing(s).

Contempt of court

14.51 Special considerations arise in cases involving contempt of court. A practice direction[32] issued on 26 March 2015 applies in all proceedings. It draws attention to the fundamental principle of the administration of justice in England and Wales that applications for committal for contempt should be heard and decided in public, that is, in open court. Any derogation must be strictly justified.[33] The practice direction specifies how the case should be listed.[34]

14.52 Importantly, the practice direction makes it clear that 'the fact that the hearing may involve disclosure of material which ought not to be published does not of itself justify hearing the application in private if such publication can be restrained by an appropriate order'.[35] Thus, P's details could be anonymised in any order or judgment, and the hearing could proceed in public.

14.53 If the court is considering holding a committal hearing in private the media should be notified.[36] A reasoned public judgment must explain any decision to hear a committal hearing in private.[37] If, in an exceptional case, a committal application is heard in private and the court finds that a person has committed a contempt of court it must state in public:

a) the name of that person;
b) in general terms the nature of the contempt of court in respect of which the committal order [committal order for this purpose includes a suspended committal order] is being made; and
c) the punishment being imposed.

14.54 In addition, it is mandatory for the above information to be notified to the national media. There are no exceptions. The practice direction states that:

> There are never any circumstances in which any one may be committed to custody without these matters being publicly stated.[38]

32 Practice Direction of 26 March 2015 Committal for Contempt of Court – Open Court.

33 Practice Direction para 4.

34 Practice Direction para 5.

35 Practice Direction para 9.

36 Practice Direction para 8, also see Practice Guidance June 2015 para 2.

37 Practice Direction para 10.

38 Practice Direction para 14.

14.55 Applications for committal for contempt are discussed in full at para 18.13 onwards.

The approach of the court to reporting restrictions

14.56 As we have seen, the default position now is that there will be open access to hearings, but with restrictions aimed at protecting the identity of P and of P's family. This is the thrust of the injunctive provisions in the Transparency Order,[39] as well as COPR PD 4A.[40]

14.57 The tension between protecting P's European Convention on Human Rights (ECHR) rights and the freedom of the press has been considered in several judgments since the Court of Protection acquired its welfare jurisdiction. A detailed examination of these judgments is beyond the scope of this book and what follows is only a summary of the key cases. In *Independent News and Media Ltd v A*,[41] the Court of Appeal approved the approach that Hedley J had taken at first instance. He had taken a two-stage approach to the application for an order under COPR r4.2. The first stage was to ascertain whether there was good reason to permit the application. If this is established, the court should proceed to weigh up the competing factors. The Court of Appeal noted the paradox whereby matters in respect of which adults with capacity would take their privacy for granted come before the Court of Protection: the incapacitated adult faces a risk to their privacy (because the relevant decisions are being taken by the court) that an adult with capacity would never face. As the Court of Appeal noted, adults with capacity make decisions about their personal lives all the time, and take their privacy in doing so for granted, but that a person who needs the court to make these decisions, because the person cannot, faces the potential loss of that privacy as a result.

14.58 In *Hillingdon LBC v Neary*,[42] Peter Jackson J again noted the salutary impact that publication of information could have, commenting that:

> There is a genuine public interest in the work of this court being understood. Not only is this healthy in itself – the presence of the media in appropriate cases has a bracing effect on all public servants, whether in the field of social services or the law – but it may also help to dispel misunderstandings. It is not in the interests of individual litigants, or of society at large, for a court that is by definition devoted

39 Considered in para 14.26 above.

40 COPR PD 4A para 27.

41 [2010] EWCA Civ 343, [2010] 1 WLR 2262.

42 [2011] EWHC 413 (COP), [2011] COPLR Con Vol 677.

to the protection of the welfare of disadvantaged people to be characterised (including in a report about this case, published as I write this judgment) as 'secretive'. It is part of our natural curiosity to want to know other people's secrets, and using pejorative descriptions of this kind may stimulate interest. The opportunity, in appropriate cases, to follow a process that has welfare, not secrecy, at its heart can only help the media to produce balanced reporting, and not fall back on clichés.[43]

14.59 Steven Neary's name and circumstances had been in the public eye before proceedings had started but there was no evidence that the publicity had or was likely to harm him. Stories about named individuals may hold more interest than those about unidentified people.[44] Individuals should not be named at the outset of a case if there is a real possibility that at the end of the case the court would not allow publication; but it would be stultifying to withhold information when it was already in the public domain, as in this case.

14.60 This approach is consistent with PD 4A para 28, which, as we have seen, provides that orders will not normally restrict the publication of information that is already in the public domain, apart from in exceptional cases. These could include circumstances where there would be a 'qualitative difference' between the level of intrusion that would result from unrestrained publication and the current level.[45]

14.61 *W v M (reporting restriction order)*[46] concerned the proposed withdrawal of artificial nutrition and hydration from a M, a minimally conscious patient. In accordance with PD 9E (as it then was), Baker J directed that hearings should take place in open court. Orders were granted restricting publication which could identify M, her family and care staff, but also restraining the media –who were not represented – from contacting anyone on a list of 65 persons involved in caring for M. Baker J agreed to reconsider the order on receipt of a letter from Times Newspapers Ltd expressing concern that the media had not been notified of the full nature of the orders to be sought and had therefore been unable to make representations.

14.62 Baker J held that:

- While COPR PD 13A[47] does not require the applicant to serve a draft order, it is essential for the applicant to give an outline of the

43 Para 15.

44 As emphasised in *Re Guardian News and Media Ltd* [2010] UKSC 1, [2010] 2 AC 697.

45 For example as in *PJS v News Group Newspapers Ltd* [2016] UKSC 26, [2016] AC 1081.

46 [2011] EWHC 1197 (COP), [2011] COPLR Con Vol 1205.

47 Now COPR PD 4A.

orders sought and the applicant must indicate the categories of people whose identities it is proposed will be kept confidential.

- If the applicant seeks restrictions on contact by the media with individuals or categories of persons, the application must make this clear.
- There is no automatic precedence between the ECHR Article 8 rights of P or P's family and the Article 10 rights of the media organisations.
- There must be a proper evidential basis for concerns about the risk of harm from an interference with the Article 8 rights of P or P's family.
- The public interest in freedom of expression in medical cases will usually lie in information being available about the general issues rather than the identity of individuals.
- There is a public interest in the practices of the Court of Protection being better understood and the urge to take an over-protective stance should be resisted.
- Celebrity cases and super-injunctions involve balancing the same convention rights, but the circumstances of the individuals concerned are so different that decisions in the two types of cases are unlikely to be relevant to each other.

14.63 Particular issues can arise in respect of anonymisation. The expectation is that statutory bodies will be identified, although not if this can risk 'jigsaw identification' (see para 14.26) above. It will be an unusual case in which P themselves is identified, although an example is *Westminster City Council v Sykes*[48] (which pre-dated the Transparency Pilot) DJ Eldergill decided to allow the publication of the names of Manuela Sykes and the local authority where she had once been a councillor and which was at the time depriving her of her liberty. Ms Sykes had been a political campaigner all her life and had always wanted to be heard. On learning of her diagnosis of dementia she had shared her experiences on the internet, campaigning for the rights of those with the condition. Her personality and wishes were a magnetic factor in the balancing exercise.

14.64 Another example is that of *PH and RH v Brighton and Hove City Council and others*,[49] where very significant amounts of information was already in the public domain, including P's name. Senior Judge Hilder identified that:

> I am concerned that where the facts of this matter are much known about in advance, and are likely to be known about if and when proceedings come to an end, that the maintaining of the Transparency

48 [2014] EWHC B9 (COP), (2014) 17 CCLR 139.

49 [2021] EWCOP 63.

> Order at this point effectively creates a 'black hole' of information which, in some, invites misinterpretation rather than accurate information and debate.[50]

PH is an example of a case where family members wanted P's name to be in the public domain to support a campaign on his behalf. Similarly, publicity – including the reporting of P's name – was sought (and, in effect, endorsed by the court) in *Manchester University NHS Foundation Trust v Verden and others*[51] as part of a campaign to identify a potential kidney donor. However, the court will be very alive to the possibility that publicity is being sought for purposes that may be adverse to P's interests.[52]

14.65 Anonymisation is increasingly an issue in relation to those involved in the care of P. In *PH* (above), Senior Judge Hilder also considered the decision of the Court of Appeal in *Abbasi v Newcastle upon Tyne Hospitals NHS Foundation Trust*,[53] which she summarised pithily as being a decision:

> . . . where the current President of the Family Division roundly says that the decision in *Re Ward (a Child)* [2010] 1 FLR 1497 is wrong, and asks why should the law tolerate and support a situation in which conscientious professionals who are not found in fault in any manner are at risk of harassment and vilification?[54]

The increased risk of such harassment and vilification, especially on social media, is a factor that points strongly towards the anonymisation of individual professionals, but not necessarily towards anonymisation of organisations.

14.66 If an application to extend anonymisation is made in a case where an order has already been made under the Transparency PD, then it will be necessary to notify the media as a result of PD 4A para 10.

Restrictions after P's death

14.67 COPR PD 4A specifies that reporting restriction orders should last only as long as necessary to achieve their purpose.[55] Some orders

50 Para 29(iii).

51 [2022] EWCOP 4.

52 See, for instance *LF v An NHS Trust and others* [2022] EWCOP 8.

53 [2021] EWHC 1699 (Admin), [2022] Fam 180.

54 Para 30.

55 COPR PD 13A para 28. See also *W v M and S (reporting restrictions)* [2011] EWHC 1197 (COP), [2011] COPLR Con Vol 1205 (injunctions were made in support of reporting restrictions that prevented contact being made with the laypeople at the heart of a high-profile medical treatment case were expressed so as to last for the lifetime of P).

may need to last until P's death; and in some cases longer.[56] Three cases have considered the question of anonymity after P's death.

14.68 In *V v Associated Newspapers Ltd*[57] Charles J considered an application following the death of C whose case had come before the Court of Protection for determination as to her capacity to consent to renal dialysis.[58]

14.69 A reporting restrictions order was made at the outset of the proceedings restricting reporting of information leading to the identification of C and her adult daughters. The order was expressed to have effect during C's lifetime. After a hearing at which it was determined that C had the capacity, such that the Court of Protection had no jurisdiction, C died.

14.70 The case was the subject of considerable media interest, and both the tactics adopted by some reporters and the style of some reporting caused distress to C's family. The adult daughters applied for a continuation of the reporting restriction order; by the time that the matter came finally to be determined by Charles J, the relevant media organisations did not contest that the order should be continued to the 18th birthday of C's teenage daughter, although raised an issue as to whether the order could be made by Charles J as a Court of Protection judge (as opposed to a High Court judge). Subsequent to the hearing, a further application was made that the order be extended to cover C's inquest, which the media organisations did not resist, and which Charles J found to be justified on the particular facts of the case, especially given the prurient nature of the reporting that had taken place.

14.71 Much of the judgment, therefore, consisted of determination of general principles for future guidance, rather than the resolution of a contest as to how they should apply upon the facts of the instant case. The following conclusions he reached are key.

14.72 First: the Court of Protection has jurisdiction to make a post-mortem reporting restrictions order (although in the instant case, and on a 'belt and braces approach,' Charles J also made the order as a High Court judge to avoid any future jurisdictional arguments). Further, reporting restrictions orders in serious medical treatment cases can extend beyond the death of the subject of those proceedings and there is no presumption or default position that such orders should end on P's death.

56 COPR PD 4A para 29 where it applies.

57 [2016] EWCOP 21, [2016] COPLR 236.

58 *King's College NHS Foundation Trust v C and V* [2015] EWCOP 80, [2016] COPLR 50.

14.73 Second: the Court of Protection should generally address the following questions:

- Are there good reasons for the hearing to be in public?
- If there are, should that public hearing be ordered with or without reporting restrictions? As part of that determination, how effective are any such reporting restrictions likely to be in protecting and promoting the relevant ECHR Article 8 rights and how restrictive are they likely to be of the relevant Article 10 rights having regard to the factors, propositions and public interests that underlie and promote those competing rights?
- In the light of the conclusions as to these questions, and applying the ultimate balancing test required by *Re S (a child) (identification: restrictions on publication)*,[59] should the hearing be in private or in public? If in private, which documents (with or without redactions and anonymisation) should be made public (and when and how should this be done)? If in public, what reporting restrictions order / anonymity order should be made?

14.74 Third, the answer to the first question is almost always going to be 'yes' because of the benefits of open justice and so almost always the *Re S* exercise will be engaged by addressing the second and third questions.

14.75 Fourth: a distinction can be made between a) cases where pursuant to the default or general position under the relevant rules or practice directions the court is allowing access (or unrestricted access) to the media and the public, and b) cases in which it is imposing restrictions and so where the court is turning the tap on rather than off. However, Charles J emphasised that this distinction only reflects the strength of the reasoning underlying those rules and practice direction that in many, perhaps most, cases the important safeguards secured by a public hearing can be secured without the press publishing or the public knowing the identities of the people involved. The distinction therefore provides weight to the general arguments for anonymity to promote the administration of justice by the court generally and in the given case. The distinction therefore does not undermine the general proposition that naming people has a valuable function of rendering news stories personal and therefore effective as journalism.[60]

14.76 Fifth, the weight to be given to the 'naming proposition' and the conclusion as to what generally best promotes the administration of justice will vary from case to case, and may require specific consider-

59 [2004] UKHL 47, [2005] 1 AC 593.

60 See *Re Guardian News and Media Limited* [2010] UKSC 1, [2010] 2 AC 697.

ation (and reasons) in specific cases. Charles J gave some useful examples of how these considerations might apply in different cases:

- If the case involves a celebrity but otherwise is not out of the ordinary, the court will be exercising a well-known decision making process, and the difficulty or impossibility of providing effective anonymisation may found a decision not to order a public hearing. The question for the trial judge will therefore be what (if any) document or judgment should be made public;
- If the case involves a celebrity but raises new or unusual points and so is out of the ordinary this may found a decision for a public hearing with no (or unusual) reporting restrictions;
- Where findings of serious mistreatment or malpractice are sought or when a member of a family wants (or has initiated) publicity that identifies P and family members issues will arise whether: 1) there should be a public hearing with no reporting restrictions (so the rival arguments and assertions are made public and linked to identified individuals); or 2) whether there should be a private hearing (with disclosure to relevant bodies or persons).

14.77 In *University College London Hospitals NHS Foundation Trust v G*,[61] Peter Jackson J refused an application by the treating Trust and supported by G's family, to extend a reporting restriction order in relation to G, which was to end a month after her death. Noting that the names of those who are born and those die are a matter of public record the judge found that although the circumstances of G's death were understandably distressing, there was no evidence that her identification would harm family members or significantly infringe their privacy. Hayden J reached a similar view in *M v Press Association*,[62] addressing himself to the questions which Charles J had formulated in *V v Associated Newspapers*. He did not consider that M or her family were at risk of intrusive commentary, and noted that intrusion by the media on the family's grief would breach the Independent Press Standards Organisation (IPSO) Code of Conduct. He took the unusual step in his judgment of providing details of IPSO's website.[63]

Restrictions on disclosure of documents

14.78 A final, related, series of points should be noted as regards witness statements and/or other documents filed on behalf of a party. First,

61 [2016] EWCOP 28.

62 [2016] EWCOP 34, [2016] COPLR 592.

63 See: www.ipso.co.uk/IPSO/harassment.html.

where a document has been filed or disclosed, a party to whom it was provided may only use it for the purpose of the proceedings in which it was filed or disclosed, except where:

a) the document has been read to or by the court or referred to at a public hearing (NB, which is now the majority of hearings in proceedings under the MCA 2005); or
b) the court otherwise permits.[64]

14.79 Second, a party to proceedings may (subject to any order to the contrary) inspect or obtain from the records of the court a copy of any document filed by a party to the proceedings.[65]

14.80 Third, where the application has been for the appointment of a deputy or the variation of the order under which the deputy was appointed, the Public Guardian is entitled to be supplied with copies (among other things) of documents filed in the proceedings relevant to the decision to appoint the deputy, any powers conferred upon him, any duties imposed on him if the Public Guardian reasonably considers it necessary for him to have regard to them for purposes of the discharge of his statutory functions in relation to the supervision of deputies. The court can limit disclosure of particular documents or categories of documents or direct that the documents are provided on an edited basis.[66]

14.81 Finally, upon application, the court may authorise a person who is not a party to proceedings to inspect documents in the court records or to obtain a copy of any such documents or extracts from such documents.[67] The court must consider whether to provide any document on an edited basis.[68]

14.82 The provisions of COPR r.5.9 were considered in *Re Z*,[69] in which Morgan J confirmed a decision whether to disclose a document to a non-party is not governed by MCA 2005 s1(5), but that the legitimate interests of P and any need they may have to be have to be protected from any consequences of the order sought are relevant considerations. Morgan J also confirmed that the court was required by COPR r1.1(3)(b), so far as practicable, to ensure that P's interests and position are properly considered.

64 COPR r5.10.
65 COPR r5.8.
66 COPR r5.12(1)–(6).
67 COPR r5.9(2).
68 COPR r5.9(4).
69 [2019] EWCOP 55, [2020] COPLR 367.

14.83 In *AB (Court of Protection: police disclosure)*,[70] Keehan J considered an application by the police for disclosure of psychological reports in relation to the subject of Court of Protection proceedings. He applied the approach set down in children cases set down in *Re C (a minor) (care proceedings: disclosure)*,[71] with appropriate modifications. He observed:

> . . . the singular importance in cases before the Court of Protection of those who are the subject of the proceedings being frank in their discussions and their cooperation with professionals. It is vital that those who are the subject of proceedings in the Court of Protection have confidence in the confidentiality of the proceedings and, in particular, the confidentiality of assessments undertaken of them for the purposes of determining whether or not they have capacity in the various relevant domains.[72]

14.84 Ultimately, the application was refused in large part because the reports were considered to be irrelevant to the purposes for which the police were seeking. It is, though, with respect, not entirely obvious that the importance of frankness upon which such weight was placed by Keehan J quite plays out in the same way in proceedings before the Court of Protection as it does in relation to children. The *C* case was not concerned so much with potential incrimination by the child themselves, as by those who might potentially have committed offences against the child. There may, perhaps, be some more links required in the logical chain before the position in relation to the subject of proceedings before the Court of Protection is reached. Perhaps another, more satisfactory way, of framing this would have been to identify that the Court of Protection would be substantially hindered in its ability to discharge its inquisitorial functions if it were deprived of its ability to obtain the best information in relation to the subject of proceedings.

14.85 The decision does, however, set up an interesting – and unresolved – tension as between the Court of Protection's functions in considering the best interests of the person, and the wider societal interest in determining both whether that person has committed an offence and, if they have, their responsibility. It is not impossible to imagine a case in which this tension cannot be avoided on the basis of the irrelevance of the information being sought by the police.

70 [2019] EWCOP 66, [2021] 4 WLR 34.

71 [1997] Fam 76, [1997] 2 WLR 322, CA.

72 At para 11.

CHAPTER 15

Fact-finding

Introduction

15.1 Proceedings before the Court of Protection are primarily inquisitorial, not adversarial.[1] However, there will be circumstances in which it is necessary for the court to reach determinations upon contested facts before it is possible for it then to go on to consider where P's best interests lie (or to make other decisions/declarations open to it). It is open to a judge, in the exercise of their case management powers under Court of Protection Rules 2017[2] (COPR) Part 3 (see further chapter 4), to decide that it is necessary that such a determination of fact take place.

15.2 This chapter discusses the question of when and how disputes of fact are resolved in the Court of Protection. It addresses, in particular, the circumstances under which a separate fact-finding hearing will be listed (a so-called 'split trial'), and the particular steps required to prepare for such hearings. The issues that it raises are likely to be of most relevance in applications concerning P's welfare, and, in particular, in cases brought by local authorities in the discharge of their safeguarding obligations owed to adults at risk (as to which, see chapter 24 below).When is fact-finding necessary?

15.3 Unlike in applications for care or supervision orders under Children Act (ChA) 1989, the local authority (or other applicant) does not need to establish that the adult in question is suffering or is likely to suffer significant harm[3] before the court can move on to the second stage of considering whether making the order sought will promote the welfare of the adult. 'The Mental Capacity Act does not contain provisions equivalent to the threshold provisions under [ChA] s31(2). Nor should any such provisions be imported in it as clearly Parliament intended that they should not be.'[4]

15.4 However, that does not mean that the court can necessarily gloss over disputes of fact as to the conduct of those suspected of acting in a way adverse to the adult in favour of a broader-brush analysis of where their best interests may lie. This is for several reasons, the most important of which are that:

1 *Re G* [2014] EWCOP 1361, [2014] COPLR 416 at para 52 per Sir James Munby P, endorsing *Cheshire West and Cheshire Council v P and M* [2011] EWHC 1330 (Fam), [2011] COPLR Con Vol 273 at para 52 per Baker J.

2 SI 2017 No 1035.

3 ChA 1989 s31(2). The threshold criteria go further than this, but this requirement is at their core.

4 *LBB v JM, BK and CM* [2010] COPLR Con Vol 779 at para 8 per Hedley J.

- In order for any best interests decision to be made, the court needs to be satisfied as to 'all [of] the relevant circumstances' for purposes of the application of the checklist set down in Mental Capacity Act (MCA) 2005 s4. If those circumstances are disputed, it may well be necessary for the dispute to be resolved as a preliminary step to the determination of where the adult's best interests lie. For instance, if the allegation has been made that a family member has mistreated the adult, it is likely to be necessary for the court to determine whether that allegation is made out in order before it can make any best interests decision about contact with that family member.
- As Hedley J made clear in *LBB v JM, BK and CM*:[5] 'an intervention with parties' rights under [European Convention on Human Rights (ECHR)] Article 8 is a serious intervention by the State which requires to be justified under Article 8(2). If there is a contested factual basis it may often be right . . . that that should be investigated and determined by the court'.[6]

15.5 In *Re AG*,[7] Sir James Munby set down when it is necessary to have fact-finding proceedings in the Court of Protection, expressly endorsing the approach adopted by Wall J (as he then was) in the pre-MCA 2005 case of *Re S (adult's lack of capacity: carer and residence)*.[8] In this case, concerning a 33-year-old woman, S, the relevant local authority sought declarations as to S's capacity and best interests as regards her residence, care arrangements and contact with her father. The catalyst for the local authority's application was an alleged incident of assault by S's father upon her; it was also alleged that her father had on a number of occasions been drinking and had been unfit through drink to care for her. The father strongly denied both allegations. In a detailed discussion of the relevant legal principles, Wall J directed himself that:

5 [2010] COPLR Con Vol 779.

6 It is suggested that this approach holds good notwithstanding the subsequent decision of the Court of Appeal in *K v LBX and others* [2012] EWCA Civ 79, [2012] COPLR 411, (2012) 15 CCLR 112, that the consideration of ECHR Article 8 rights follows on from the application of the MCA 2005 s4 checklist; the Court of Appeal was considering a different question: see para 2 of the judgment.

7 [2015] EWCOP 78, [2016] COPLR 13 at para 30.

8 [2003] EWHC 1909 (Fam), [2003] 2 FLR 1235. That approach was also set down as being the correct test in the first edition of this work (at para 15.7 onwards).

> . . . unlike care proceedings under the Children Act 1989, the exercise of the jurisdiction over mentally incapable adults is not dependent upon any threshold criteria apart from the fact of incapacity and the existence of what Dame Elizabeth Butler-Sloss P described in *Re F (No 2)*[9] . . . [at 47 and 521 respectively] as 'a serious justiciable issue' which requires the court's adjudication.[10]

15.6 Applying *Re A (male sterilisation)*,[11] Wall J further directed himself that the central question for the court was as to what outcome was in the best interests of the adult.[12] He continued that both of the factors outlined immediately above, but in particular the absence of any threshold criteria, raise 'the question as to the extent to which (if at all) it is necessary, for the purposes of exercising the jurisdiction and deciding which course of action is in the best interests of S, to make findings of fact relating in particular to disputed historical issues'.[13]

15.7 Importantly, Wall J rejected the submission made on behalf of the father to the effect that absent findings of fact which warranted her removal from her father's care, the local authority would not have made out a case for such removal, and that she should therefore be returned, stating that:

> I do not accept that argument. I agree that there must be good reason for local authority intervention in a case such as the present. Equally, if there are disputed issues of fact which go to the question of Mr S's capacity and suitability to care for S, the court may need to resolve them, if their resolution is necessary to the decision as to what is in S's best interests. Findings of fact against Mr S on the two issues identified [above] would plainly reflect upon his capacity properly to care for S. But it does not follow, in my judgment, that the proceedings must be dismissed simply because the factual basis upon which the local authority instituted them turns out to be mistaken, or because it cannot be established on the balance of probabilities. What matters (assuming always that mental incapacity is made out) is which outcome will be in S's best interests. There will plainly be cases which are very fact specific. There will be others in which the principal concern is the future, and the relative suitability of the plans which each party can put forward for both the short and long term care of the mentally incapable adult. The instant case, in my judgment, is one of the cases in the latter category.[14]

9 *Re F (Adult: court's jurisdiction)* [2001] Fam 38, (2000) 3 CCLR 210, CA.
10 Para 13.
11 [2000] 1 FLR 549, [2000] 1 FCR 193, CA.
12 Para 15.
13 [2003] EWHC 1909 (Fam), [2001] Fam 38 para 15.
14 Para 18.

15.8 Wall J continued:

> Whilst I acknowledge that in a relatively untried jurisdiction there are dangers in too relaxed an approach to historical issues, I am unable to accept the proposition that the approach to best interests is fettered in any way beyond that which applies to any judicial decision namely that it has to be evidence based; that it excludes irrelevant material; and that it includes a consideration of all relevant material. In a field as complex as care for the mentally disabled, a high degree of pragmatism seems to me inevitable. But in each case it seems to me that the four essential building blocks are the same. First, is mental incapacity established? Secondly, is there a serious, justiciable issue relating to welfare? Thirdly, what is it? Fourthly, with the welfare of the incapable adult as the court's paramount consideration, what are the balance sheet factors which must be drawn up to decide which course of action is in his or her best interests?[15]

15.9 In this regard, it is, further, important to emphasise that proceedings under the MCA 2005 do not exist as a forum to canvass allegations of misconduct save and to the extent it is necessary that such allegations are determined in order to allow the judge properly to determine the application before them. As has been said in the context of private law proceedings under the ChA 1989: 'the finite resources of the court do not exist simply to provide a free-standing medium for one party to obtain, for no reason other than vindication, findings of matrimonial misconduct against the other'.[16] The same holds equally true of allegations of misconduct towards the adult without capacity.

15.10 In order to assist the court to determine whether a fact-finding exercise: a) will be necessary; and b) (if it is) should be listed as the first part of a split trial process, it is incumbent upon the parties to identify at an early stage precisely what the issues are and precisely what factual findings will be required from the court in order to ground the relief that is sought. This point is discussed further in chapter 11 above. With the drive towards speedier determination of welfare cases before the Court of Protection it is likely that courts will now require some persuasion that a split trial is necessary given the inevitable delay that this will build in to the final resolution of the application.

15 Para 21.

16 *AA v NA (appeal: fact-finding)* [2010] EWHC 1282 (Fam), [2010] 2 FLR 1173 at para 18 per Mostyn J.

Preparing for a fact-finding hearing

15.11 Fact-finding hearings are most commonly directed by the court (either separately or as part of the final hearing) in what might be termed safeguarding cases brought by local authorities (see further chapter 24). In such cases, it is usually the case that the local authority will be seeking adverse findings against an individual or individuals to support its contention that (for instance) their contact with P should be limited, or that P should live other than in the family home.

15.12 In such cases, the practice has developed of requiring the local authority applicant to draw up a so-called '*Scott* schedule'[17] of allegations, in other words a table setting out:

- the specific allegation made (for instance that 'X failed to provide adequate care to P');
- the particulars of the allegation (for instance that 'On 9 September 2021 X failed to change P's incontinence pad for a period of 12 hours'); and
- a cross-reference (or cross-references) to the evidence relied upon in support of the particulars of the allegation (for instance 'paragraph 9 of the witness statement of Ms Y, social worker, dated 20 October 2021').

15.13 It is conventional then for the subject of the allegation to be required to set out in the same table their response to the allegation and, if it is denied, cross-references to the evidence upon which they rely in support of their denial. The local authority is then usually permitted to reply to the response, again in the same format. A column can then be provided in which the court can in due course record its finding against each allegation. The end result is a table which (ideally) makes it easier for preparations to be made for the fact-finding hearing by bringing into sharp focus the allegations, whether the allegations are disputed (and, if so, whether in whole or in part) and the scope of the evidence that will be called by the parties.

15.14 Experience shows that the process of preparing and responding to *Scott* schedules serves significantly to focus the minds of both applicants and respondents as to the issues in the case and the strength of the evidence. Conversely:

17 So-called because the original schedule was devised by George Alexander Scott, who held the post of Official Referee (ie judge in what is now the Technology and Construction Court) in the 1920s.

- experience has also shown that it is very common for applicants to produce *Scott* schedules that run to many pages of allegations when, in reality, the court need only determine a limited number in order to be able to have a secure foundation upon which to determine where P's best interests lie;
- The use of *Scott* schedules may not be appropriate in cases where the real concern is about the cumulative effect of individual incidents. This is particularly so in the context of coercion and control.[18]

15.15 An important function of the final case management hearing prior to the fact-finding hearing will therefore be to ensure that 1) it is in fact appropriate to use the *Scott* schedule approach; and 2) if it is, only those allegations that it is truly necessary for the court to determine are set down for resolution at that latter hearing.

15.16 COPR Practice Direction (PD) 4B 'Court Bundles',[19] in turn, makes clear that at the start of any bundle prepared for the fact-finding hearing, there must be inserted a document or documents prepared by each party which should set out (either within the document(s) themselves or by cross-referring to another document that is, or will be, within the bundle):

- the findings or fact that the court is being asked to make; and
- cross-references to the evidence relied upon to found those findings

(in other words, a *Scott* schedule).[20]

15.17 Where appropriate, the preliminary documents for a fact-finding should also include:

- a chronology;
- a skeleton argument; and
- a description of relevant family members and other persons who may be affected by or interested in the relief sought.[21]

15.18 Where (as is often the case) the documents in the case run to several lever-arch files, it is also strongly advisable for the applicant to prepare (on an agreed basis if possible) a core bundle which contains:

18 See, by analogy, *H-N and others (Children) (domestic abuse: finding of fact hearings)* [2021] EWCA Civ 448, [2022] 1 WLR 1681, and *F v M* [2021] EWFC 4. Hayden J addressed the question of coercion and control in the context of adults with impairments in *A County Council v LW and another* [2020] EWCOP 50, [2020] 4 WLR 164. See also *MB v PB and others* [2022] EWCOP 14.

19 Discussed in greater detail at para 11.30 onwards.

20 COPR PD 4B para 4.4.

21 COPR PD 4B para 4.5.

- any relevant directions made by the court;
- the completed *Scott* schedule;
- a chronology of relevant dates;
- the witness statements of the relevant witnesses; and
- any documents to which those witnesses are likely to have to be taken for purposes of giving evidence.

15.19 For welfare cases under the COPR Case Pathways PD 3B, the expectation is that the bundle for the final hearing (and it is suggested, by analogy, for any 'split' fact-finding hearing) should run to no more than 350 pages into total.[22]

15.20 Preparing for a fact-finding hearing involves ensuring that those against whom findings are sought are carefully taken through the evidence by their representatives so that they can properly respond. Where both solicitors and counsel are involved, both need to work together to this end. The consequences of cutting corners in the preparatory stages can be devastating. In *Re K and C (children finding of fact)*[23] (a family case, but wholly applicable to the Court of Protection) HHJ Moradifar said:

> Families are the building blocks of our society and in Public Law Proceedings, the Courts deal with some of the most vulnerable families. Professionals who work in the Family Justice System are highly skilled specialists who often work on complex cases involving serious intricate forensic issues. Their skill set and professional standards are essential for those who represent the parties in Public Law Proceedings. It is incumbent on those representing the parties facing serious allegations to ensure they have seen, read and understood all the evidence in the case and to ensure that the party who they represent has been able to participate meaningfully in the court process.
>
> I note that in this case, neither the parents nor their Counsel were aware that there were coloured photographs of the injuries that were commented upon in detail in the written report of the jointly instructed expert. Until she was partway through giving oral evidence, the Mother had never seen the transcript of her police interview. Despite being in possession of Y's photograph, the mother's solicitors failed to mention this to the local authority or their own private investigator, resulting in much embarrassment when the wrong person was witness summonsed and attended Court. Counsel for the parents have both informed me that they are immigration specialists, consequently the other professionals have had to work very hard to make sure that the hearing could be fair and effective. The mother's evidence has taken

22 COPR Case Pathways PD 3B para 2.7(2)(b).

23 [2018] EWFC B85 at postscript.

much longer than necessary, which can only have made it more stressful than it needed to be. There is no room in the Family Court for such a lack of care and lackadaisical approach to case preparation.

15.21 A further, important, point needs to be made in this regard. As discussed at para 13.98 onwards, the provisions relating to disclosure in the COPR are not regularly applied. However, in *Enfield LBC v SA and others*,[24] McFarlane J (as he then was) considered a situation that had arisen where, during the course of a fact-finding hearing held to determine allegations of abusive parenting against a learning disabled woman, it emerged that the police had already conducted an 'achieving best evidence' (ABE) interview with the woman, in which the woman had denied that she had been abused, and had repeatedly asked to go home or to see her parents, and that the authority had a copy of this interview. The local authority had informed the Official Solicitor afterwards that the interview had taken place, but, having signed a police disclaimer, had not disclosed the interview, on the basis that it decided not to rely upon the content of the interview. McFarlane J was highly critical of the local authority, and his reasoning is sufficiently important to merit reproduction in this chapter almost in full (emphasis in original):

> 55. . . . [I]t would seem that in this case they have provided the disclosure that was required of them [under the directions made], yet the result, from the perspective of a judge who is embedded in the procedure and culture of child protection proceedings under the Children Act 1989, is totally unacceptable. In a fact-finding process, where the case is largely based upon what a vulnerable adult ('P') has said and the aim of the court in due course is to make orders to meet P's best interests, how can it be appropriate, fair to the interests of all parties (but particularly P) or in any way acceptable for the applicant local authority to take part in arranging a formal ABE interview of P and subsequently take possession of a DVD recording of the interview yet be under no duty to inform the other parties or the court that that is the case?
>
> 56. The position in family proceedings is that 'it is a duty owed to the court both by the parties and by their legal representatives to give full and frank disclosure in ancillary relief applications and also in all matters in respect of children' [*Practice Direction (Family Proceedings: Case Management*) [[1995] 1 WLR 332, [1995] 1 All ER 586, sub nom Practice Direction: Case Management (31 January 1995) [1995] 1 FLR 456]]. If these were proceedings relating to children, then there is absolutely no doubt that the local authority, under the duty to give 'full and frank disclosure', would have been required to inform the parties

24 [2010] EWHC 196 (Admin), [2010] COPLR Con Vol 362.

> and the court of the occurrence of the interview and to disclose the DVD record (subject to the court's power to limit or control disclosure on a case specific basis). Given that the aim of protection is common between child protection proceedings under the [ChA] 1989, Part 4 and proceedings such as the present which aim to investigate allegations of harm to P and, if necessary, protect her, how can it be a requirement in one process for the applicant to disclose the existence of an ABE interview, yet not a requirement, absent of an express order from the court [in the other process]?
>
> 57. The apparent difference in the approach to disclosure as between the family courts and the Court of Protection may well arise from the fact that the rules for the latter are based upon ordinary civil litigation with the expectation that disclosure will be based on whether documents 'adversely affect [a party's] own case' or 'support another party's case' [COPR r16.2(2)(b)] whereas the approach of the family court is that there is a duty to give *the court* all relevant material.
>
> 58. There can, in my view, be no justification for there being a difference of this degree on the issue of disclosure between the family court and the Court of Protection in fact-finding cases of this type where really the process and the issues are essentially identical whether the vulnerable complainant is a young child or an incapacitated adult. For the future in such cases in the Court of Protection it would seem to be justified for the court to make an order for 'specific disclosure' under [COPR 2017 r16.2(3)] requiring all parties to give 'full and frank disclosure' of all relevant material. If such a direction had been made in the present case, the local authority would have been under a duty to disclose the DVD of the ABE interview, and any other records relating to it, once they came into their possession.

15.22 An important issue to be addressed at the final case management hearing before the fact-finding hearing, if not before, is whether the fact-finding hearing is to take place in person, remotely or in a hybrid manner. There have been no recorded judgments in which the Court of Protection has addressed this question, but it is one that has troubled the courts considerably in relation to children during the COVID-19 pandemic. The starting-point is the decision of the Court of Appeal in *Re A (children) (remote hearings)*,[25] and a useful summary of the position can be found in *A Local Authority v A Mother*,[26] in which Lieven J identified that an important factor in deciding whether to proceed with a remote hearing in a fact-finding case is whether the judge will be in a less good position to judge whether or not the witnesses are telling the truth if the case is conducted remotely. The

25 [2020] EWCA Civ 583, [2020] 1 WLR 4931.

26 [2020] EWHC 1086 (Fam), [2020] Fam Law 678.

Court of Appeal has also identified that, if a witness has a cognitive impairment, remote examination can, itself, serve to impair the ability of the person to give evidence.[27] As the Court of Appeal identified with some understatement in July 2021, 'experience is increasingly demonstrating that fact-finding hearings of any degree of complexity that are conducted remotely are sub-optimal'.[28]

15.23 A final question which must be asked is whether any of the parties[29] have cognitive or other difficulties which need to be addressed to ensure that they are in a position to give the best quality evidence. The obligation lies upon both legal representatives to identify this as a possibility, and upon the court to be alive to the situation.[30]

The determination of contested facts

15.24 As noted at the outset to this chapter, the processes of the Court of Protection are essentially inquisitorial, which means that questions of the burden of proof are not relevant to some of its tasks. Questions of the burden of proof are, for instance, not relevant to the question of what is in P's best interests, which is 'primarily an inquiry by the courts, weighing into the balance various factors. No party is under a burden of proof; rather the court, after investigating best interests, decides that issue on a balance of probability'.[31]

15.25 However, the court nonetheless proceeds on the basis of conventional civil principles when it comes to the determination of a fact or facts that one party must prove in order to obtain the relief that it

27 See *S (vulnerable parent: intermediary)* [2020] EWCA Civ 763, [2020] 4 WLR 97 at para 28 (the parent in question having a learning disability).

28 *Re YW (a child) (adequacy of reasons)* [2021] EWCA Civ 1174, [2022] 1 FCR 724 at para 53 per Baker LJ.

29 The participation of P themselves is addressed at para 16.38 and following below.

30 See, by analogy, *Re S (vulnerable party: fairness of proceedings)* [2022] EWCA Civ 8, [2022] 1 FCR 626. Although the Court of Appeal here was considering the specific provisions within the Family Procedure Rules (FPR) concerning vulnerable persons, which are not (oddly) directly replicated in the COPR 2017, those provisions make express underlying principles which apply equally in the Court of Protection: see also para 16.50.

31 *A Local Authority v M and another* [2014] EWCOP 33, [2015] COPLR 6 per Baker J.

seeks (properly called 'facts in issue'). These principles have been summarised thus:[32]

> 83. First, the burden of proof lies with the local authority. It is the local authority that brings these proceedings and identifies the findings that they invite the court to make. Therefore, the burden of proving the allegations rests with them.
>
> 84. Secondly, the standard of proof is the balance of probabilities: *Re B (Children)* [2008] UKHR 35. If the local authority proves a fact on the balance of probabilities, this court will treat that fact as established and all future decisions concerning M's future will be based on that finding. Equally, if the local authority fails to prove any allegation, the court will disregard that allegation completely. In her written submissions on behalf of the local authority, Miss Bretherton contended that the court should apply the principle that
>
> > the more serious the allegation the more cogent is the evidence required to overcome the unlikelihood of what is alleged and thus to prove it.'
>
> This principle, originally stated by Ungoed-Thomas J in *Re Dellows Will Trust* [1964] 1 WLR 451, was at one time applied by the courts considering allegations of child abuse in family proceedings under the Children Act 1989. In *Re B*, however, the House of Lords emphatically rejected that approach. Baroness Hale of Richmond, with whose judgment the other four Law Lords agreed, having analysed the case law, stated at paragraphs 70 to 72:
>
> > '70 I would announce loud and clear that the standard of proof in finding the facts necessary to establish the threshold under s31(2) or the welfare considerations of the 1989 Act is the simple balance of probabilities – neither more nor less. Neither the seriousness of the allegation nor the seriousness of the consequences should make any difference to the standard of proof to be applied in determining the facts. The inherent probabilities are simply something to be taken into account, where relevant in deciding where the truth lies.
>
> 71. As to the seriousness of the consequences, they are serious either way. A child may find her relationship with her family seriously disrupted or she may find herself still at risk of suffering serious harm. A parent may find his relationship with his child seriously disrupted or he may find himself still at liberty to maltreat this or other children in the future.
>
> 72. As to the seriousness of the allegation, there is no logical or necessary connection between seriousness and probability.'

32 *A Local Authority v M and another* [2014] EWCOP 33, [2015] COPLR 6 per Baker J.

In my judgment, the same approach must surely apply in the Court of Protection where the court is carrying out a similar exercise in determining the facts upon which to base decisions as to the best interests of an incapacitated adult.

85. Thirdly, findings of fact in these cases must be based on evidence. As Munby J (as he then was) observed in *Re A (A Child: Fact-finding hearing: speculation)* [2011] EWCA Civ 12:

> 'It is an elementary proposition that findings of fact must be based on evidence, including inferences that can properly be drawn from the evidence, and not on suspicion or speculation.'

86. Fourth, the court must take into account all the evidence and, furthermore, consider each piece of evidence in the context of all the other evidence. As Dame Elizabeth Butler-Sloss, President, observed in *Re T* [2004] EWCA Civ 458, [2005] 2 FLR 838, at paragraph 33:

> 'Evidence cannot be evaluated and assessed in separate compartments. A judge in these difficult cases must have regard to the relevance of each piece of evidence to the other evidence and to exercise an overview of the totality of the evidence in order to come to the conclusion whether the case put forward by the local authority has been made out to the appropriate standard of proof.'

87. Fifth, whilst appropriate attention must be paid to the opinion of medical experts, those opinions need to be considered in the context of all the other evidence. The roles of the court and the experts are distinct. It is the court that is in the position to weigh up expert evidence against the other evidence: *A County Council v K, D and L* [2005] EWHC 144 Fam, [2005] 1 FLR 851 per Charles J.

88. Sixth, in assessing the expert evidence, which involves a multidisciplinary analysis of the medical information conducted by a group of specialists, each bringing their own expertise to bear on the problem, one important consideration – and of particular relevance in this case – is that the court must be careful to ensure that each expert keeps within the bounds of their own expertise and defers where appropriate to the expertise of others – see the observations of Eleanor King J in *Re S* [2009] EWHC 2115 Fam.

...

90. Eighth, it is not uncommon for witnesses in these cases to tell lies, both before and during the hearing. The court must be careful to bear in mind that a witness may lie for many reasons – such as shame, misplaced loyalty, panic, fear and distress – and the fact that a witness has lied about some matters does not mean that he or she has lied about everything – see *R v Lucas* [1981] QB 720. The assessment of the truthfulness is an important part of my function in this case.

15.26 In *Re A (children: findings of fact) (No 2)*,[33] concerning children, but applicable by analogy, the Court of Appeal rehearsed similar points to those above, and also emphasised that:

- The court is not bound by the cases put forward by the parties, but may adopt an alternative solution of its own.[34] Judges are entitled, where the evidence justifies it, to make findings of fact that have not been sought by the parties, but they should be cautious when considering doing so.[35]
- It is an elementary feature of a fair hearing that an adverse finding can only be made where the person in question knows of the allegation and the substance of the supporting evidence and has had a reasonable opportunity to respond. With effective case-management, the definition of the issues will make clear what findings are being sought and the opportunity to respond will arise in the course of the evidence, both written and oral;[36]
- Where, during the course of a hearing, it becomes clear to the parties and/or the judge that adverse findings of significance outside the known parameters of the case may be made against a party or a witness consideration should be given to the following:
  - ensuring that the case in support of such adverse findings is adequately 'put' to the relevant witness(es), if necessary by recalling them to give further evidence;
  - prior to the case being put in cross examination, providing disclosure of relevant court documents or other material to the witness and allowing sufficient time for the witness to reflect on the material;
  - investigating the need for, and if there is a need the provision of, adequate legal advice, support in court and/or representation for the witness.[37]

15.27 The following observations of Mostyn J[38] are also important:

> ii) The law operates a binary system in which the only values are 0 and 1. The fact either happened or it did not. If the court is left in doubt, the doubt is resolved by a rule that one party or the other carries the

33 [2019] EWCA Civ 1947, [2020] 1 FLR 755 at paras 93–99.

34 *Re S (a child)* [2015] UKSC 20, [2015] 1 WLR 1631 at para 20.

35 *Re G and B (fact-finding hearing)* [2009] EWCA Civ 10, [2009] 1 FLR 1145.

36 *Re B (a child)* [2018] EWCA Civ 2127, [2019] 1 FCR 120.

37 *Re W (a child)* [2016] EWCA Civ 1140, [2017] 1 WLR 2415.

38 *Re D (a child)* [2014] EWHC 121 (Fam), [2014] Fam Law 421 at para 31 per Mostyn J. This was a care case, but the principles are of general application.

burden of proof. If the party who bears the burden of proof fails to discharge it, a value of 0 is returned and the fact is treated as not having happened. If he does discharge it, a value of 1 is returned and the fact is treated as having happened: *Re B (Care Proceedings: Standard of Proof)*, at para [2] per Lord Hoffmann.

. . .

iv) Sometimes the burden of proof will come to the judge's rescue: the party with the burden of showing that something took place will not have satisfied him that it did. But generally speaking a judge ought to be able to make up his mind where the truth lies without needing to rely upon the burden of proof: *Re B (Care Proceedings: Standard of Proof)* at paras [2] and [32]; *Rhesa Shipping Co SA v Edmond and Another: The Popi M* [1985] 1 WLR 948.

v) It is impermissible for a judge to conclude in the case of a series of improbable causes that the least improbable or least unlikely is nonetheless the cause of the event: *Rhesa Shipping Co SA v Edmond and Another: The Popi M; Ide v ATB Sales Ltd; Lexus Financial Services t/a Toyota Financial Services (UK) plc v Russell* [2008] EWCA Civ 424 at para [4].

vi) There is no pseudo-burden or obligation cast on the respondents to come up with alternative explanations: *Lancashire County Council v D and E* [2010] 2 FLR 196 at paras [36] and [37]; *Re C and D (Photographs of Injuries)* [2011] 1 FLR 990, at para [203].

vii) The assessment of credibility generally involves wider problems than mere 'demeanour' which is mostly concerned with whether the witness appears to be telling the truth as he now believes it to be. With every day that passes the memory becomes fainter and the imagination becomes more active. The human capacity for honestly believing something which bears no relation to what actually happened is unlimited. Therefore, contemporary documents are always of the utmost importance: *Onassis and Calogeropoulos v Vergottis* [1968] 2 Lloyd's Rep 403, per Lord Pearce; *A County Council v M and F* [2011] EWHC 1804 (Fam) [2012] 2 FLR 939 at paras [29] and [30].

15.28 It is worth amplifying point ii): if a party decides not to advance an allegation (or withdraws it) because it does not consider that it can properly make out the relevant facts supporting that allegation, for purposes of the court's determination of the issues to which the allegation goes, it must proceed on the basis that the facts did not happen.

15.29 Further, where the court is asked to determine allegations of harm it is suggested that, by analogy with the position that prevails in care proceedings relating to children, a conclusion that an adult has suffered from harm at the hands of another must be based upon facts, not just suspicion.[39] It is further suggested that a real possibility alone would not be sufficient.[40]

P's participation in fact-finding hearings

15.30 The participation of P generally in final hearings is discussed at paras 16.3–16.49, and the same approach will apply where there is a separate fact-finding hearing: the case study at the end of chapter 16 relates to P's participation in such a hearing.[41] For present purposes, it is important to emphasise the following points:

- If P has a litigation friend, then it is for the litigation friend in the first instance to decide whether P should decide whether P should attend a hearing and participate.[42]
- The fact that P does not have capacity to conduct the proceedings does not mean that P necessarily lacks the competence to give evidence as to factual matters (see further para 13.26).
- The fact that P is not competent to give evidence as to factual matters would not preclude the court from receiving 'information' from P under (now) COPR r14.2(e) (see further para 13.26). A court may well, however, proceed with caution in assessing the weight to be placed upon such information when deciding whether a serious factual allegation against a party is made out.

Fact-finding and future risk

15.31 'Safeguarding' cases are sometimes brought, not on the basis that an adult *has* suffered harm at the hands of another, but rather on the basis that they are *likely* to do so absent preventative action on the part of the court. In care proceedings, the approach that the court must take has been set down by the Supreme Court thus:

> 8. . . . [I]f the case is based on the likelihood of future harm, the court must be satisfied on the balance of probabilities that the facts upon

39 *Re H (minors) (sexual abuse: standard of proof)* [1996] AC 563 at 591E, HL, per Lord Nicholls.

40 *In Re B (children) (sexual abuse: standard of proof)* [2008] UKHL 35, [2009] 1 AC 11 at para 70 per Baroness Hale.

41 Drawing on *A county council v AB and others (participation of P in proceedings)* [2016] EWCOP 41, [2016] COPLR 576.

42 *A County Council v AB and others (participation of P in proceedings)* [2016] EWCOP 41, [2016] COPLR 576.

which that prediction was based did actually happen. It is not enough that they may have done so or that there was a real possibility that they did ... [H]owever, if the case is based on the likelihood of future harm, the court does not have to be satisfied that such harm is more likely than not to happen. It is enough that there is 'a real possibility, a possibility that cannot sensibly be ignored having regard to the nature and gravity of the feared harm in the particular case', [*In re H (Minors) (Sexual Abuse: Standard of Proof)* [1996] AC 563] per Lord Nicholls of Birkenhead, at p 585f.

9. Thus the law has drawn a clear distinction between probability as it applies to past facts and probability as it applies to future predictions. Past facts must be proved to have happened on the balance of probabilities, that is, that it is more likely than not that they did happen. Predictions about future facts need only be based upon a degree of likelihood that they will happen which is sufficient to justify preventive action. This will depend upon the nature and gravity of the harm: a lesser degree of likelihood that the child will be killed will justify immediate preventive action than the degree of likelihood that the child will not be sent to school.[43]

15.32 This approach was also adopted prior to the coming into force of the MCA 2005 in the exercise of the inherent jurisdiction of the High Court to protect vulnerable adults,[44] and has, in turn, been expressly endorsed within the Court of Protection.[45]

Fact-finding: consequences

15.33 Although, as noted above, fact-finding can (and often will) take place at essentially the same time as the determination of the substantive best interests questions relating to P, where the fact-finding takes place separately it would be usual for the court to give a separate judgment in relation to the fact-finding hearing in order for the parties to take stock prior to the second stage. Part of this taking stock might well be to consider – in an appropriate case – the instruction of the relevant expert to report upon P's best interests. Experience

43 *Re S-B (children)* [2009] UKSC 17, [2010] 1 AC 678 at para 8 per Baroness Hale.

44 *Re MM; Local Authority X v MM (by the Official Solicitor) and KM* [2007] EWHC 2003 (Fam), [2009] 1 FLR 443 at para 119 per Munby J (as he then was).

45 *A Local Authority v TZ (by his litigation friend the Official Solicitor) (No 2)* [2014] EWHC 973 (COP), [2014] COPLR 159 per Baker J (as he then was), endorsing the approach in *MM*.

has taught that it is frequently helpful to delay the instruction until this stage so that the expert can proceed upon the basis of clearly established facts, rather than having to give alternative conclusions upon the basis of what may be found in due course to have occurred (it being clear that an expert cannot seek to determine contested facts for themselves: see para 13.62).

15.34 Importantly, as there is no difference in principle between the approach to be adopted to split hearings in the Court of Protection (at least in welfare cases) and public law child protection proceedings, the decision of the House of Lords in *Re B*[46] applies so as to require that once findings of fact have been made the case is part heard and the trial should not resume before a different judge.[47]

15.35 Finally, it should be noted that it is clear that a judge may subsequently revisit the conclusions reached at a fact-finding hearing if subsequent evidence warrants it.[48]

46 *Re B (children) (sexual abuse: standard of proof) (CAFCASS intervening)* [2008] UKHL 35, [2009] 1 AC 11 at para 2 per Lord Hoffmann.

47 *Enfield LBC v SA and others* [2010] EWHC 196 (Admin), [2010] COPLR Con Vol 362 at para 113 per McFarlane J (as he then was).

48 *In re L and another (children) (preliminary finding: power to reverse)* [2013] UKSC 8, [2013] 1 WLR 634 at para 34; see also *In re S-B (children) (care proceedings: standard of proof)* [2009] UKSC 17, [2010] 1 AC 678 at para 46.

CHAPTER 16

The final determination of the application

Introduction

16.1 This chapter deals with how applications are finally disposed of by the court. After touching on the disposal of applications without a final hearing, the focus is on the steps required effectively to prepare and to conduct final hearings, as well as dealing with the subsequent steps of receiving the judgment and drawing up the final order. Because the issues of principle are the same, the chapter covers both proceedings relating to P's property and affairs, and P's health and welfare; many of the examples will, though, be drawn from applications relating to health and welfare because they form the bulk of the reported cases.

16.2 This chapter must be read alongside the preceding chapters, and in particular those relating to directions hearings (chapter 11), evidence and disclosure (chapter 13) and (in an appropriate case) fact-finding (chapter 15). It is clear from the reported cases[1] that matters will very rapidly go awry in a contested case unless a proper focus is maintained by all parties – and the court – upon the final destination of the proceedings and of the steps required along the route.

Determining an application without a final hearing

16.3 The vast majority of applications to the Court of Protection are disposed of without any hearing at all.

16.4 Moreover, many applications which start out hotly contested end up being resolved by consent without the need for a final hearing. This can be, for instance, because an independent expert has provided a report making entirely clear where P's interests lie which is accepted by all parties and encapsulated in a proposal put to the court to be endorsed as a consent order. In other cases, mediation or some other form of alternative dispute resolution (discussed further in chapter 20) can achieve a resolution to the issues dividing the parties that they consider that they can properly put to the court as being in P's best interests.

16.5 As discussed above (para 11.56), where parties have reached agreement, they are required to notify the court as soon as possible. Where a consent order has been submitted for approval which finally disposes of all the issues in the case, the starting position will be that the court will only convene a hearing a) if insufficient notice has been

1 See, for instance, *Re A and B (Court of Protection: delay and costs)* [2014] EWCOP 48, [2015] COPLR 1.

given; or b) there is some specific feature which the court considers it must deal with at an attended hearing. In some cases the information provided with the consent order is not sufficient to satisfy the judge that they can endorse it without further clarification that the decisions/declarations set out are properly in P's best interests. In other cases, P may have such strong views about the final outcome that the parties agree that they should be given the opportunity to speak to the judge, even where there is no disagreement. This is perhaps most likely to occur in section 21A applications (under the Mental Capacity Act (MCA) 2005), discussed in detail in chapter 22).

16.6 It should be remembered that wherever the court makes an order without a hearing, Court of Protection Rules 2017[2] (COPR) r13.4 applies so as to allow P, any party to the proceedings, or any person affected by the order to apply for reconsideration. Reconsideration is addressed further in chapter 19, but is unlikely to be relevant where the court is endorsing a consent order submitted by the parties for approval.

16.7 In some cases, the applicant may decide that they wish to withdraw proceedings. For instance, the safeguarding concern that underpinned a local authority's application to the court for draconian welfare orders (eg removing the person from their own home and restricting contact with a family member) has now been sufficiently alleviated that the relevant local authority no longer considers that they are justified. Or it may become clear that it will not be possible to establish a sufficient factual basis upon which to seek such orders (as to which see further chapter 15). With the introduction of COPR 2007 Part 87A in July 2015 (now COPR 2017 r13.2), permission is now required to withdraw proceedings. An application must be made on a COP9 form,[3] following the normal procedure for applications made within proceedings (see para 11.26). It is suggested that a decision upon an application to withdraw proceedings is not a decision falling within MCA 2005 s1(5): ie it forms part of the court's 'extensive case management powers'[4] rather than a decision taken for or on behalf of P (and therefore not a 'best interests' decision under MCA 2005 s16), albeit that the court will have P's welfare interests squarely in mind.[5]

2 SI 2017 No 1035.

3 COPR r13.2(2).

4 See *N v ACCG* [2017] UKSC 22, [2017] AC 549, [2017] COPLR 200 at para 40 per Lady Hale.

5 See, by analogy, *Re W (Care Proceedings: Functions of Court and Local Authority)* [2013] EWCA Civ 1227, [2014] 2 FLR 431 at para 40.

16.8 As discussed further in para 24.18, while the court is likely to endorse an order to withdraw proceedings where it is clear that the underlying basis for the concern motivating the application is no longer present, it is likely that the court will take a dim view of attempts to withdraw proceedings on the basis that the public authority which has brought proceedings now takes a different view of where the person's interests lie than it is likely that the court will do. Indeed, the public body may well find itself directed to file evidence (including care plans), even though the plan's contents may not or do not reflect its formal position.[6] Where the public body decides, in the discharge of its public law obligations relating to funding of care and treatment, that a particular option is no longer on the table, the position is different, and is discussed in chapter 25.

Finalising the issues and the evidence; timetabling

16.9 As discussed in detail in chapter 11 above, and has been given renewed emphasis by the COPR Case Pathways Practice Direction (PD) 3B, one of the key case management tasks of the court is to ensure that the issues in the case are identified at an early stage, in large part so that directions can be made to ensure that the evidence (but only the evidence) necessary to resolve those issues will be before the court. It is worth emphasising, however, that the issues can – and frequently do – evolve during the currency of proceedings. For instance, if P is an older person, their health may deteriorate and different priorities may assert themselves when it comes to their best interests. A case brought before the court on an urgent basis arising out of a safeguarding concern may evolve dramatically if further investigation reveals that the concern is in part not borne out. If a separate fact-finding hearing has been listed (see chapter 15 above), the court may in giving its judgment upon the matters considered at that hearing make findings which require one or other party to take stock of how it wishes to present its case at the subsequent hearing to determine the substantive best interests questions. Alternatively, expert evidence may be directed following such a fact-finding hearing which puts a different complexion upon the best interests exercise. It can also be the case that trial periods of contact (for instance) directed at an interim hearing have proceeded sufficiently successfully

6 *Re W*, see also *Re MN (Adult)* [2015] EWCA Civ 411, (2015) 18 CCLR 521, [2016] Fam 87 at para 37.

that a local authority applicant decides that it can adopt a more 'relaxed' position at the final hearing. Finally, it may be the case that it has become sufficiently clear that one of the options advanced is simply not realistic that the court is in a position simply to rule it out in advance of a final consideration of what is in P's best interests.[7]

16.10 By the same token, it can also frequently be necessary for provision to be made for the filing of updating evidence relating to P's circumstances: the court will be determining what is in P's best interests *as at* the time of the final hearing, so it is necessary that it is provided with the most up-to-date evidence possible. While witnesses can amplify their written evidence in the witness box (see further, para 16.32 below), it is desirable to ensure that that written evidence is as current as possible.

16.11 So as to ensure that final hearings are successful in terms of leading to a determination of the issues on the basis of the necessary evidence, the Case Pathways PD 3B has introduced a final management hearing for cases on the welfare pathway (see further, para 11.25). Even though there is no formal requirement for a final management hearing for cases on the property and affairs pathway, it is likely that an equivalent hearing would be listed in the event that the case was of any complexity.

16.12 A final management hearing will follow the pattern of directions hearings discussed in chapter 11, but with a particular focus on ensuring that both the issues and the evidence have been finalised insofar as possible in advance of the final hearing. To that end, the Case Pathways PD 3B provides that a meeting should take place five days before the final management hearing between advocates, and, insofar as practicable, any unrepresented parties, with the purpose of resolving and narrowing the issues to be determined at the hearing, addressing each of the matters required by PD 4B 'Court Bundles' (see further, paras 11.34–11.36) and, critically, preparing a draft order.[8] The applicant or (if the applicant is not represented but the respondent is) must also file a core bundle complying with the provisions of PD 4B including, in particular, those provisions set out at para 11.38).[9]

16.13 The judge at the final management hearing will want to see, in particular:

7 See *A North East Local Authority v AC and another* [2019] EWCOP 44. The ruling out in this case took place at the final hearing, but it could in principle have taken place at an earlier stage.

8 COPR Case Pathways PD 3B para 2.6(2).

9 COPR Case Pathways PD 3B para 2.6(2); and PD 4B paras 4.2 and 4.3.

- an agreed time estimate for the final hearing made on the basis of separate provision being made for 1) judicial pre-reading; 2) hearing all the evidence and submissions; and 3) preparation and delivery of judgment.[10] Experience suggests that estimates given by legal representatives often underestimate the time for 2) and almost invariably do not give sufficient time for either 1) or 3);
- a draft witness template identifying precisely who will be giving evidence when and specific arrangements that may be required in relation to any particular witness (see further para 16.45 onwards for particular considerations that may apply in relation to vulnerable witnesses or where a person is giving evidence by video-link). It is important to be realistic as to how quickly it is possible to hear from each witness, and also to schedule witnesses appropriately, especially where (for instance) clinicians will need to re-arrange clinics in order to attend; and
- specific consideration as to any practical issues that may arise in relation to hearing from P. See further below, para 16.34 onwards.

16.14 The preparation of bundles for directions hearings is discussed in detail at para 11.33 onwards above. The same practical requirements set out in PD 4B will apply to almost all final hearings as they do to interim hearings (including as to the timing for lodging them), and they are not repeated here. There are, though, specific requirements that apply to the preliminary documents that must appear in the bundle, addressed in the paragraphs which follow.

16.15 At the start of the bundle there must be inserted a document or documents prepared by each party ('the preliminary documents for a final hearing') which should set out (either within the preliminary documents themselves, or by cross-reference to what is set out in another document that is in, or is to be put in the bundle):

- the relief sought;
- a skeleton argument.[11]

16.16 Where appropriate, the preliminary documents for a final hearing should include:

- a chronology;
- the findings of fact that the court is being invited to make and the factors based on such findings or agreed facts that the court is being invited to take into account;

10 COPR PD 4B para 10.1.
11 COPR PD 4B para 4.6.

- an appropriately particularised description of the alternatives the court is being invited to consider; and
- a description of relevant family members and other persons who may be affected by or interested in the relief sought.[12]

16.17 Each of the preliminary documents must state on the front page immediately below the heading the date when it was prepared and the date of the hearing for which it was prepared.[13] All case summaries, chronologies and skeleton arguments contained in the preliminary documents must be cross-referenced to the relevant pages of the bundle.[14]

16.18 Where the nature of the hearing is such that a complete bundle of all documents is unnecessary – for instance, because the relief now being sought by the applicant has been refined significantly – the bundle (which need not be repaginated) may comprise only those documents necessary for the hearing, but i) the preliminary documents must state that the bundle is limited or incomplete; and ii) the bundle must if reasonably practicable be in a form agreed by all parties.[15]

16.19 One injunction which is regularly honoured more in the breach, but which is actually of some importance, is that, where a bundle has been taken away after a directions hearing and is then re-lodged, the bundle must be updated and superseded documents must be *removed*.[16] Judges – understandably – become very impatient with bundles that contain numerous iterations of documents: it is very rarely necessary for any but (for instance) the most recent version of the care plan for P to be contained in the bundle.

16.20 For the final hearing (as opposed to the final management hearing), a further requirement is imposed in relation to the court bundle for welfare cases falling within the Case Pathways PD 3B: the bundle should not normally be more than 350 pages, and should in any event not contain more than one copy of any document.[17]

16.21 Where witnesses are to give evidence at the final hearing, it is important that a separate copy of the bundle is provided which can be put into the witness box for them to use during the course of the hearing. It is equally important (but sadly not always the case) that this bundle matches the pagination of the bundles being used by the parties and the judge to avoid unnecessary delays during the hearing.

12 COPR PD 4B para 4.7.
13 COPR PD 4B para 4.8.
14 COPR PD 4B para 4.9.
15 COPR PD 4B para 4.10.
16 COPR PD 4B para 4.11.
17 COPR Case Pathways PD 3B para 2.7(2)(b).

Skeleton arguments

16.22 As noted above (para 16.15), COPR PD 4B 'Court Bundles' envisages that the parties will each provide skeleton arguments in advance of the final hearing. The courts have repeatedly emphasised that skeleton arguments should be just that – ie skeletal. In the course of a judgment given in the Court of Appeal, but of equal relevance to proceedings before the Court of Protection, Mummery LJ emphasised that:

> . . . skeleton arguments should not be prepared as verbatim scripts to be read out in public or as footnoted theses to be read in private. Good skeleton arguments are tools with practical uses: an agenda for the hearing, a summary of the main points, propositions and arguments to be developed orally, a useful way of noting citations and references, a convenient place for making cross references, a time-saving means of avoiding unnecessary dictation to the court and laborious and pointless note-taking by the court.[18]

The hearing

The day of the hearing: in-person hearings

16.23 Even more than is the case with directions hearing, it is important to get to court early on the day of the final hearing. This will allow for any last-minute discussions to take place and for steps to be taken in the event of any logistical problems (a common one being that the bundle provided for the witnesses has not found its way into the witness box). If witnesses are to give evidence, it will also allow time to take their details and give them to court staff – who need to know, in particular, whether the witness will swear on the Bible or other Holy Book, or affirm.

16.24 Both in relation to witnesses of fact and expert witnesses, making sure that they are familiar with the layout of the court room is important: wherever possible they should be taken in and shown where they are to sit, where the witness box is and where the judge will sit. It is important to understand that for most witnesses, even social or health care professionals, a court room is an alien and often forbidding environment; much can be done by way of simple familiarisation with that environment. It is also important – and is not

18 See *Raja v Van Hoogstraten (No 9)* [2008] EWCA Civ 1444, [2009] 1 WLR 1143 at para 126 per Mummery LJ.

(impermissible 'coaching') – to explain to a witness the process of being questioned: one particularly useful tip being to address the answers to any question being asked in cross-examination to the judge so as to avoid the natural tendency to feel that cross-examination represents a personal attack upon the witness by the person conducing the questioning.

The day of the hearing: remote hearings

16.25 The same level of preparation will be needed for a remote hearing as for an in person hearing.[19] Given that witnesses may be dialling in from a variety of locations, it is essential to ensure that all witnesses have access to an electronic copy of the up to date bundle and will be able to navigate it without assistance.

16.26 Provision will need to have been made well in advance to enable participants to the hearing to access a platform on which any final discussions can take place. If members of a team are not dialling in from the same location, consider how instructions will be taken during the course of the hearing (for example, via a WhatsApp group).

16.27 Remote hearings can be tiring for parties and witnesses and advocates should not hesitate to request breaks where necessary.

16.28 Careful thought will need to be given to P's attendance. If P is joining remotely, it is essential to ascertain what arrangements are in place in order to provide support to P, not only during but in the immediate aftermath of the hearing.

Public or private?

16.29 As discussed in greater detail in chapter 14, final hearings will take place in the majority of cases in public.

Opening speeches

16.30 In any hearing with members of the press or public present, judges will often invite the applicant's representative to give an outline of the case. However, especially where full skeleton arguments have been provided, it is unlikely that the judge will want to hear lengthy

19 See also the guidance on remote hearings produced by the Court of Protection Bar Association, available at: www.cpba.org.uk/wp-content/uploads/2020/07/CPBA-Effective-Remote-hearings-7.7.2020.docx.

opening speeches from any of the legal representatives. Matters will then proceed very rapidly (often within a matter of minutes) to the calling of the first witness for the applicant.

Witness evidence

16.31 Proceedings before the Court of Protection are formal proceedings, such that witnesses will be required to swear on the Bible or other Holy Book, or affirm as to the truth of their evidence.

16.32 The importance of preparing a thorough witness statement cannot be over-emphasised. As discussed at para 13.15 above, a witness statement will stand as the evidence-in-chief of a witness, such that they will only be permitted to give supplementary evidence in answer to questions from the party on whose behalf they appear with the permission of the court. How readily this will be granted will depend upon the nature of the case; it can, though, be the case that a witness will have done no more than confirm their name and address and that the contents of their statement are true before they are answering questions put by the other parties. This can be disconcerting for the witness, and, where it can properly be done, it is usually advisable for the legal representative for the party calling the witness to ask at least one 'settling in' question. What this question will be will depend upon the context, but most usually it will consist of inviting the witness to update the court as to any developments since the witness statement was prepared.

16.33 A witness called on behalf of a party will then be cross-examined by the other parties, and can then be re-examined by the party on whose behalf they have given evidence. They can also be asked questions by the judge: especially given the inquisitorial nature of the Court of Protection's processes, it is quite frequently the case that many of the questions that are put to the witness in the court are, in fact, asked by the judge. The judge should then give the chance to the parties to ask any further questions of the witness arising out of their questions.

16.34 The usual practice is for all the witnesses of fact to give their evidence, first those called on behalf of the applicant, then those called on behalf of the first respondent, and so forth, before any expert witness gives their evidence. Ideally, an expert witness such as an independent social worker will have had the chance to hear the evidence of the witnesses of fact so that they are able to consider this evidence when giving their opinion to the court; if the hearing is lengthy, however, it may well be too expensive and/or logistically impracticable for the expert to attend all the days of the hearing. In such a case, then the party calling the expert (which will, if the Official Solicitor has been instructed on behalf of P, almost invariably be the Official Solicitor) should make sure that they give a summary to the expert of any relevant evidence given in their absence.

16.35 Space precludes a detailed discussion of the principles of witness handling, the principles of which are the same before the Court of Protection as they are before any other court or tribunal.[20] In very brief summary, *preparation* and *politeness* are the two watchwords that will perhaps most usefully serve. What the judge wants is to have brought out before them the evidence upon which they can:

a) determine any facts in issue; and
b) determine whether
   - P has or lacks the requisite decision-making capacity; and
   - (if P lacks capacity), where P's best interests lie.

It is only by being clear as to what submissions will be made in closing arguments as to the evidence going to a) and b) that proper lines of questioning can be developed. Further, while it can frequently be necessary to be robust in cross-examination, and it is important that particular points of contention are put to the witnesses so that they can properly respond, judges respond very negatively to discourtesy in questioning. This is particularly so when it comes to the cross-examination of independent experts, whose duty it is to assist the court rather than one of the parties (see para 13.81 onwards). Moreover, experience teaches that it is generally extremely unlikely that 'badgering' an expert under cross-examination will lead them to recant their opinions. It is generally far more productive for an advocate to treat the expert as a fellow professional and, in essence, to engage with them upon their own terms so as to tease out the nuances in their views. What is often effective is to examine with the experts the factual premises upon which they have based their opinions, because a good expert will always reassess their opinion if they are given new or different factual information upon which to base that information. As discussed at para 13.62 above, an expert should not be determining the factual matters in issue in the case, so where there are still factual matters that are not determined, it is entirely appropriate to invite an expert to give their opinion on the basis that 'if the court were to find that X took place, how would your opinion differ?'.

20 And are pithily summarised by Parker J in *NCC v PB and TB* [2014] EWCOP 14, [2015] COPLR 118 at paras 140–146.

16.36 One point cannot be emphasised enough. As obvious as it seems, it is vital to recall that the focus of the hearing will be upon P's capacity and best interests, a matter in respect of which there are no winners or losers. The court will therefore be very impatient with questions that are directed to the canvassing of allegations of misconduct or poor practice save and to the extent necessary for the court to be able to determine where the interests of P lie (see also para 15.9). This can place advocates in particular difficulties where they are being pressured by their lay clients to put questions to others because they want grievances aired. Those grievances – for instance, as to how another family member or a local authority social worker has conducted themselves – may well be very deeply felt, but unless they relate to the issues actually before the court they should not be advanced by way of questioning. In this regard, it is useful to recall the strong guidance given by the Court of Appeal that:

> Something of a myth about the meaning of the client's 'instructions' has developed . . . . the client does not conduct the case. The advocate is not the client's mouthpiece, obliged to conduct the case in accordance with whatever the client, or when the advocate is a barrister, the solicitor 'instructs' him. In short, the advocate is bound to advance [his client's] case on the basis that what his client tells him is the truth, but save for well-established principles [relating specifically to criminal cases] the advocate, and the advocate alone remains responsible for the forensic decisions and strategy. That is the foundation for the right to appear as an advocate, with the privileges and responsibilities of advocates and as an advocate, burdened with twin responsibilities, both to the client and to the court.[21]

This guidance was given in the context of criminal proceedings, but it is equally applicable to proceedings before the Court of Protection.[22]

16.37 Finally, it should be noted that it is very important to keep a proper note of the evidence given by witnesses; while proceedings before the Court of Protection are recorded, such recordings a) can sometimes contain gaps at the vital moments; b) can take some time to transcribe; and c) will usually only be transcribed upon payment of a fee by the party requesting the transcription.

21 *R v Farooqi and others* [2013] EWCA Crim 1649, [2014] Cr App R 8 at para 108.
22 *Re PB* [2014] EWCOP 14, [2015] COPLR 118 at paras 140–146.

Witnesses: special cases (1) hearing from P

16.38 As discussed in chapter 4, there is an increasing trend for judges to hear from P, and judges are now required specifically to consider whether they should do so as part of determining how P is to participate in the proceedings (see para 12.5).

16.39 In light of what is now a considerable body of case-law from the European Court of Human Rights (ECtHR) outlining what some have called the 'rule of personal presence',[23] there is in the authors' view, a strong argument that the presumption should be that the judge determining any case in which either P's capacity or best interests is in issue should take steps to ensure that they have had personal contact with P.[24]

16.40 'Personal contact,' however, can take various forms, not all of which will necessarily involve P participating as a witness, ie giving information to the court in a formal fashion in the presence of the parties and being questioned by the parties. The use of the word 'information' here is deliberate: P may well not be competent to give evidence (see further, para 13.26), but following the introduction in July 2015 of COPR 2007 r95(e) (now COPR 2017 r14.2(e)), the court can 'admit, accept and act upon such information, whether oral or written, from P . . . as the court considers sufficient, although not given on oath and whether or not it would be admissible in a court of law apart from this rule'.[25]

16.41 Even if P does give information in open court, it would be an unusual case in which P was cross-examined in a conventional fashion by the representative of a party (and, we suggest, an extremely unusual case in which the court would allow such questioning by an unrepresented party).[26] The main circumstances where we suggest

23 Summarised in *AN v Lithuania* [2016] ECHR 462. See also Lucy Series, 'The participation of the relevant person in proceedings in the Court of Protection: A briefing paper on international human rights requirements,' available at http://sites.cardiff.ac.uk/wccop.

24 This argument is reinforced by considerations arising out of the UN Convention on the Rights of Persons with Disabilities: see chapter 26.

25 See also *A County Council v AB and others (participation of P in proceedings)* [2016] EWCOP 41.

26 In *Lancashire and South Cumbria NHS Foundation Trust v Q* [2022] EWCOP 6, [2022] COPLR 315 for instance, a finely balanced capacity decision relating to bulimia, Hayden J noted (at para 56) that Q gave evidence 'because she wanted to and, by that stage, I had already concluded that she had litigation capacity. Her evidence was not structured in a way as to require her to assert her capacity on the central issue nor was she challenged on this by this experienced team of advocates'.

that such might be permissible – and possibly even in some circumstances required – is where P is giving information as to factual matters which have to be determined before the court can make determinations as to best interests, most obviously where the court has to resolve factual allegations against one or more parties. In some (rare) cases, most obviously where the allegation is one that essentially relates to P's word against that of another, P may well have to be cross-examined. In such a case, however, we suggest that the court will proceed with extreme care and will follow the guidance we discuss in relation to vulnerable witnesses below in controlling the questioning process.

16.42 The courts have not yet authoritatively determined exactly what is happening where P is giving information to a court which is determining their capacity. However, in *CC v KK and STCC*, Baker J proceeded on the basis that KK was able to give evidence as to her own capacity which he both and should weigh up alongside all the other evidence (including that from the experts instructed). This was in some ways an unusual case because KK had been found to have capacity to conduct the proceedings, and it is also clear that KK was cross-examined as to her evidence as to (or possibly, strictly, her assertion of) her own capacity.[27]

16.43 Nor have the courts authoritatively determined whether P can give evidence (or information) going to their best interests. The determination of P's best interests is not the determination of a fact, but an evaluative exercise.[28] As the identification of and giving suitable respect to P's wishes and feelings assumes greater importance in decision-making under the MCA 2005 (see further chapter 3), it is clear that the courts are becoming increasingly alive to the need to hear those wishes and feelings, wherever possible, directly from P. Strictly, the court is in doing so probably not taking information or evidence in any conventional sense, but rather discharging its obligation under MCA 2005 s4(4) to 'permit and encourage [P] to particip-

27 [2012] EWHC 2136 (COP), [2012] COPLR 627. See para 49. In *Q*, Hayden J identified that: 'For good measure, all who heard Q in Court, regarded her as having engaged confidently and articulately with the Court process. The latter is an extraneous lay observation and requires to be identified as such. It is nonetheless part of the broad canvas of the evidence' (para 41).

28 See *Aintree University Hospitals NHS Foundation Trust v James* [2013] UKSC 67, [2013] 1 WLR 1911, (2013) 16 CCLR 554 at para 42.

ate . . . as fully as possible in any act done for him or any decision affecting him'.[29]

16.44 However it is characterised, the judge seeing P will in the right circumstances give a very valuable picture which may be very different to that presented at second hand on the papers by others.[30] It cannot be emphasised enough that this must be in the right circumstances: it may well be entirely inappropriate, if not actively counterproductive and damaging, to bring P from their home or care placement to court.[31] Rather, it may well be necessary for the judge to visit P – including, for instance, at P's bedside – and in the presence of only a limited number of representatives so as to minimise any pressure upon P.

16.45 The importance of identifying 1) the purpose of the visit and 2) the practicalities of the visit was emphasised by the Court of Appeal in *Re AH (serious medical treatment)*.[32] Following that decision, the Vice-President, Hayden J, issued guidance addressing the principles and practicalities to be considered.[33] As regards the principles, the guidance emphasises[34] that:

> I. A judge meeting with P can achieve a number of important objectives, including (where P lacks capacity) their participation in 'best interests' decision-making, as required by s.4(4) Mental Capacity Act 2005. Which provides:
>
> > (4) He *must*, so far as reasonably practicable, permit and encourage the person to participate, or to improve his ability to participate, as fully as possible in any act done for him and any decision affecting him.
>
> It is important to emphasise the mandatory nature of this obligation.
> II. A decision to meet P is one which must be taken by the judge, having listened to any representations made on behalf of the parties. In particular, there should be discussion directed towards identifying a clear understanding, of the scope and ambit of the visit.
> III. However, it is in the nature of such visits that the parameters may become unsettled or expanded by events and exchanges. It is, important to emphasise that:

29 See *Wye Valley NHS Trust v B Court of Protection* [2015] EWCOP 60, [2015] COPLR 843, (2015) 18 CCLR 733 at para 18.

30 See in this regard *A Hospital NHS Trust v CD and another* [2015] EWCOP 74, [2016] COPLR 1 at para 31.

31 See the comments in *Re M* [2013] EWHC 3456 (COP), [2014] COPLR 35 at para 42.

32 [2021] EWCA Civ 1768, [2021] COPLR 253.

33 *Practice Guidance (Court of Protection: Judicial visits)* [2022] EWCOP 5, [2022] 1 WLR 1445 (emphasis in original).

34 At para 6.

i. a judge meeting P will not be conducting a formal evidence-gathering exercise;
ii. a visit may serve further to highlight aspects of the evidence that the Judge has already heard, in a way which reinforces oral evidence given by either the experts or family members;
iii. a visit may sometimes lead the Judge to make further enquiries of the parties, arising from any observations during the visit;
iv. at any visit the Judge *must* be accompanied, usually, by the Official Solicitor or her representative (at Tier 1 and 2 this will usually be the instructed solicitor);
v. it will be rare for a member of P's family to be present at a Judicial visit. In principle, this should usually be avoided;
vi. a note *must* be taken of the visit and quickly made available to the Judge for his or her approval. That note should be circulated to the parties for them to consider and where appropriate to make any representations arising from it;
vii. where the Judge considers that information from, or the experience of, visiting P may have had or might be perceived to have had an influence on the 'best interests' decision, the Judge must communicate that to the parties and, where appropriate, invite further submissions.

16.46 Wherever a judge is seeing P other than in the presence of the parties, a proper record should be kept of any discussion, usually by the representative of the Official Solicitor if instructed on P's behalf. It is also important that P is assisted insofar as possible to understand both nothing that P says to the judge can be kept confidential as between P and the judge, and also that the judge will have to reach their decision on the relevant issues on the basis of everything that they have heard, not just the information that P has given them.

16.47 A further reason for the judge to see P has nothing, strictly, to do with the gathering of evidence, but is simply to allow P to feel 'connected' to the proceedings.[35] There is also a risk that this can come across as both patronising and demeaning, but it can be extremely important to allow P to understand who it is who is taking often very significant decisions in their life. Many, even with relatively severe levels of cognitive impairment, have a concept of a 'judge', and to see the judge who will be deciding the case can be extremely important for them.

16.48 Wherever it is suggested that the judge should see P, consideration will always need to be given to the practicalities, and to plan ahead so that arrangements can be put in the judge's diary well in advance of the hearing. For instance, it may well not be appropriate

35 *Re M* [2013] EWHC 3456 (COP), [2014] COPLR 35 at para 42.

for P to be brought into the well of a large and intimidating court room, but the judge might well be able to see P in a smaller conference room. It may well also be a good idea, if such is practicable, for P to be brought to the court before the day of hearing so that they are familiar with the journey and reassurance can be given as to the practical arrangements: a small but important example being whether tea is available: the calming power of a cup of tea can never be overestimated. If the judge is to visit P in their care home or day centre, then suitable arrangements will need to be made for somewhere private to be made available for the relevant meeting to take place. If the judge is to visit P in their own home, court security staff will need to visit first to carry out a risk assessment.

16.49 See further the end of this chapter for practical examples of steps taken in a case to maximise P's participation in the proceedings.[36]

Witnesses: special cases (2) vulnerable witnesses

16.50 Although it is likely to be rare that the court will need to hear from a witness who themselves is vulnerable (by reason of age, disability or otherwise), the possibility cannot be ruled out. It also important to identify in advance of the hearing whether such a witness requires steps to be taken to put them in a position to give the best quality evidence.[37] The obligation lies upon both legal representatives to identify this as a possibility, and upon the court to be alive to the potential. Perhaps oddly, there are no specific provisions in the COPR to cater for the putting in place of special measures to cater for vulnerable witnesses; however, there are a suite of such measures that are regularly deployed in family proceedings[38] that can be pressed into service by the court.[39] Some of these steps include:[40]

36 See also the guidance issued by Charles J reissued as an annex to Hayden J's *Practice Guidance (Court of Protection: Judicial visits)* [2022] EWCOP 5.

37 See by analogy *Re S (vulnerable party: fairness of proceedings)* [2022] EWCA Civ 8, [2022] 1 FCR 626. Although the Court of Appeal here was considering the specific provisions within the Family Procedure Rules (FPR) concerning vulnerable persons, which are not (oddly) directly replicated in the COPR 2017, those provisions make express underlying principles which apply equally in the Court of Protection.

38 Contained in FPR Part 3A.

39 Using, in particular, COPR rr1.1 and 14.2(a)(iii).

40 For more detail, see Alex Ruck Keene, Penny Cooper and Claire Hogg, 'Special measures in the Court of Protection' [2016] Eld LJ 62.

- Using a live video-link so that the witness can give evidence remotely, most usually so that they can give evidence other than in the presence of a person who may be subjecting them to intimidation. It should be noted, however, that if the difficulties for the person arise in consequence of cognitive impairments, remote examination can, itself, serve to impair the ability of the person to give evidence.[41]
- Pre-recording evidence, whether evidence in chief, or (in special cases) cross-examination.[42]
- Using an intermediary, whose function is to communicate a) to the witness, questions put to the witness, and b) to any person asking such questions, the answers given by the witness in reply to them, and to explain such questions or answers so far as necessary to enable them to be understood by the witness or person in question.[43] Although originally a development in the criminal sphere, intermediaries are seeing increasing use in the family as well as criminal courts, where they have received praise for their effectiveness in facilitating communication. In *Newcastle City Council v WM and others*,[44] Mr Justice Cobb described the two intermediaries as 'excellent', and as having performed their role 'with great skill and discretion'. He found himself to be 'indebted' to the intermediary service for enabling the mother, who suffered from learning disabilities and spoke English as a second language, 'to participate in the process as fully and effectively as could possibly be achieved'.[45]

16.51 Perhaps the most crucial step is recognising that both the court and the advocates must adjust their approach to questioning so as to ensure that the witness is enabled to give their best, most accurate and most coherent account. This can be facilitated by:

- The use of Ground Rules Hearings, which are established practice in the criminal sphere, and at which specific, advance, consideration can be given to the approach to take to questioning so as to ensure both fair treatment and proper participation.[46] In a welfare case falling under the COPR Case Pathways PD 3B (see further chapter 4), we would suggest that the final management

41 See *Re S (vulnerable parent: intermediary)* [2020] EWCA Civ 763, [2020] 4 WLR 97 at para 28.

42 See in the criminal context, Youth Justice and Criminal Evidence Act 1999 s27.

43 Youth Justice and Criminal Evidence Act 1999 s29(2).

44 [2015] EWFC 42, [2016] 2 FLR 184.

45 At paras 5–6.

46 *R v Lubemba (Cokesix)* [2014] EWCA Crim 2064, [2015] 1 WLR 1579.

hearing should also, where appropriate, include the relevant ground rules determination (although we also suggest that adapting to the particular needs of relevant witnesses and – especially – P is something that starts much earlier in the process, from the first case management hearing).

- Prior vetting of the planned examination or cross examination. Where examination is necessary, advocates may submit their proposed questions in advance to an individual (often an intermediary) who is well placed to advise on vocabulary, order of questioning and general approach in light of the needs and limitations of the vulnerable witness.
- A collaborative rather than adversarial approach to questioning.

16.52 A particularly useful recourse in this regard is The Advocate's Gateway, a free resource designed to assist in the questioning of vulnerable witnesses, including specific resources to assist in (for instance) the questioning of those with learning disability.[47]

16.53 It should be noted, finally, that, while appropriate measures must be taken to secure the ability of vulnerable witnesses to take part in the proceedings, taking such measures should not affect the weight to be placed upon their evidence:

> . . . many vulnerable witnesses are just as likely as anyone else either to tell the truth or to lie deliberately or misunderstand events. It would be unfair and discriminatory to discount a witness's evidence because of their inherent vulnerabilities (including mental and cognitive disabilities) and it would be equally wrong in principle not to apply a rigorous analysis to a witness's evidence merely because they suffer from mental, cognitive or emotional difficulties. To do otherwise would, in effect, attenuate the standard of proof when applied to witnesses of fact with such vulnerabilities.[48]

Witnesses: special cases (3) interpreters

16.54 Her Majesty's Courts and Tribunals Service (HMCTS) will meet the reasonable costs of interpreters for deaf and hearing-impaired litigants for hearings in civil proceedings, including those before the Court of Protection.[49] If an interpreter is needed, the court will make arrangements for an interpreter to attend.

47 See: www.theadvocatesgateway.org/.

48 *Re C (female genital mutilation and forced marriage: fact finding)* [2019] EWHC 3449 (Fam).

49 See: www.justice.gov.uk/newsite/courts/interpreter-guidance.

16.55 Although some people will have a friend or relative who is willing to interpret for them, unless the relative or friend has a recognised qualification in relaying information between deaf and hearing people, it may be better to use a qualified interpreter, particularly at a final hearing. The friend or relative may still be able to attend and provide support, but permission should be sought from the judge first.

16.56 Language interpreters will be arranged at public expense in certain limited circumstances:

- proceedings for committal for contempt of court (see further chapter 18), where the subject of the application cannot understand or speak the language used in court;
- where it is the only way in which a litigant can take part in proceedings, ie where the person:
  - cannot speak or understand the language of the court well enough to take part in the hearing;
  - cannot get public funding;
  - cannot afford to fund an interpreter privately; and
  - has no family member, or friend, who can attend to interpret for them and who is acceptable to the court;
- where a party is exercising the right given by the Welsh Language Act 1993 to any party to speak Welsh in legal proceedings in Wales.

16.57 It is vital to give as much notice as possible wherever an interpreter will have to be arranged by the Courts Service, especially where the services are required for interpretation to and from an unusual language. Regrettably, it is not unusual for booking arrangements by HMCTS to break down.

16.58 It will also be necessary to factor in extra time for the giving of evidence whenever the services of an interpreter is required – a rough rule of thumb is that it is sensible to double the time-estimate for any given witness because of the inevitable impact upon the speed at which questions can be put and answered.

Witnesses: special cases (4) 'remote' evidence giving

16.59 COPR r14.5 provides that the court can allow a witness to give evidence through a video-link or other communication technology. In consequence of the COVID-19 pandemic, it is now a routine procedure. In principle, a formal application is required,[50] but in practice this is a matter which would now be considered routinely at a case management hearing in advance of the final hearing. COPR PD 14A gives some detailed guidance – which remains largely relevant – as to the practical considerations that arise when taking evidence by video, in particular given the 'lag' that can arise between receipt of the picture and accompanying sound, and also as to how to ensure that the person giving evidence has access to the same documents as those in the courtroom with the judge.[51]

16.60 In urgent medical treatment cases (see further, chapter 23), it is not uncommon for evidence to be given by the treating clinicians by telephone; the courts discourage the use of telephone evidence in final hearings in other cases, and it would be very unusual indeed for it to be acceptable for a witness giving evidence as to contested facts to give telephone evidence because of the difficulties to which this gives rise in terms of assessing their credibility absent the ability to see their face and body language. If it is proposed that evidence should be taken from a witness by telephone in anything other than the most urgent hearing, a detailed application for permission should be submitted on a COP9 form in good time. Wherever telephone evidence is taken, particular care must be taken to ensure that the loudspeaker on the telephone in the court room is set to a sufficiently loud volume to be able to be picked up by the tape transcription of the proceedings.

Closing arguments

16.61 The normal practice with regard to closing arguments is that the applicant will make their closing submissions first, followed by the respondent(s), and then the applicant will have the last word by way of a reply.

16.62 Where P is a party, the court will usually wish to hear from the litigation friend after all of the other respondents. As noted at para 13.21 above, in many cases the litigation friend will have filed a statement in advance of the final hearing, setting out a summary of the relevant background to and the procedural developments in the proceedings, and setting out the litigation friend's views as to P's best interests in the light of the evidence as it stands as at the time of the

50 See COPR PD 14A Annex 2.

51 See also the guidance on remote hearings produced by the Court of Protection Bar Association, available at: www.cpba.org.uk/wp-content/uploads/2020/07/CPBA-Effective-Remote-hearings-7.7.2020.docx.

statement. Such views are usually expressed as being subject to the caveat that they will be the subject of further consideration at the conclusion of the hearing, to cater for unanticipated developments at the hearing. The court will therefore be particularly keen to understand from the litigation friend what their final position is as to P's best interests in the light of all the evidence heard.

Negotiations during the hearing

16.63 It is very common for the positions of parties to shift during the course of a final hearing, especially if it lasts any length of time. This is particularly so if the evidence given by a witness (or witnesses) is either particularly compelling or is demonstrated to be particularly weak by way of cross-examination. It is important always to keep in mind that there is no reason why agreement in such circumstances cannot be reached upon part (or even the whole) of the application. While judges are reluctant to risk letting a case overrun by granting too many adjournments, it is usually the case that a judge will be happy to retire to allow discussions to take place during the time set aside for the final hearing if they can be satisfied that constructive progress is being made.

Judgment

16.64 In some cases, the judge will be in a position to give an oral judgment immediately following the close of oral arguments or after a short period of reflection. Judgments given orally (known as ex tempore judgments) are recorded; again, though, it is important for as full as possible a note to be taken. If permission to appeal the judgment is to be sought from a higher court (as to which, see chapter 19 below), the time limits are sufficiently short that it can frequently be necessary to seek permission from that higher court before a transcription can be prepared. This makes it particularly important that a proper note be taken of the judgment so that, if necessary, it can be filed with the application for permission to appeal.[52]

16.65 In cases of any complexity, it is likely that the judgment will be 'reserved': in other words, the judge will take a longer period of time

52 Note also that there can be a duty upon an advocate for the respondent to any application to appeal to provide their note promptly and free of charge to an unrepresented appellant: see para 19.29 below.

to deliberate and will then, most often, prepare their judgment in written form. Where judgments are given in writing, the practice increasingly is for a draft to be circulated to the legal representatives in advance. The purpose of so doing 'is to introduce an orderly procedure for the delivery of reserved judgments, whereby the parties' lawyers can have time to consider and agree the terms of any consequential orders they may invite the court to make and the process of delivering judgment can be abbreviated by avoiding the need for the judge to read the judgment orally in court'.[53] Such draft judgments must be kept strictly confidential to the parties' lawyers.[54] While judges will normally invite the submission of corrections of typographical errors, the circulation of a draft judgment is not intended to afford an opportunity to the parties to re-argue their case.[55] Where a party or parties are not legally represented, the practice commonly adopted is not to circulate a draft judgment for correction, but rather to hand down a draft judgment 'subject to editorial corrections', allowing for any revisions to be incorporated before a final approved version is handed down.[56]

16.66 One matter that will usually have to be resolved after judgment has been given is as to costs. This is addressed further at chapter 17 below.

Final orders

16.67 The precise nature of the relief that the court can grant is discussed at para 4.48 onwards. The actual decision of the court, whatever it may be, must be recorded in an order.

16.68 If the judgment has been circulated in draft ahead of it being handed down, the judge will expect that the parties will have tried to agree the terms of that order. If the judgment has been given orally, and if the order records anything more than a simple decision/declar-

53 *Prudential Assurance Company v McBains Cooper and others* [2000] 1 WLR 2000 at 2008E–F, CA, per Brooke LJ. See also Civil Procedure Rules (CPR) PD 40E (Reserved judgments).

54 Reiterated in ringing terms by the Court of Appeal in *R (The Counsel General for Wales) v The Secretary of State for Business, Energy and Industrial Strategy* [2022] EWCA Civ 181, [2022] 1 WLR 1915.

55 See *Egan v Motor Services (Bath) Ltd* [2007] EWCA Civ 1002, [2008] 1 All ER 1156 and *G v A* [2009] EWHC 11 (Fam), [2009] 1 WLR 1621.

56 See, by analogy, *R (S) v General Teaching Council for England* [2013] EWHC 2779 (Admin) at para 5.

ation, then it may well prove difficult for all the details of the order made to be finalised at the end of what is likely to have been a long court day. For similar reasons as discussed at para 10.55 above in relation to directions hearings, however, every effort should be made to ensure that the broad outlines of the order have been agreed and (if possible) endorsed by the judge before the parties leave for the day to avoid lengthy – and expensive – debates in the ensuing days via correspondence as to the terms of the order.

16.69 One oddity of proceedings under the MCA 2005 is that it is far from unusual that an order made at what all parties and the court treat as final hearing will not, in fact, be a final order. A good example of this is where the court has, itself, authorised the deprivation of P's liberty (for instance, because P is deprived of their liberty in supported accommodation, so cannot be made the subject of the deprivation of liberty safeguards (DOLS) regime discussed in chapter 22 below). In such a case, it is necessary in order to secure P's rights under European Convention on Human Rights (ECHR) Article 5 (right to liberty) that the court undertakes regular reviews of that deprivation.[57] In such cases, particular care needs to be paid to the way in which the order made at the hearing provides for the payment of the costs of any publicly funded party so as to ensure that such funding is readily available for purposes of any further review by the court. Such orders are likely to become less frequent following the implementation of MCA 2005 Sch AA1 through the Mental Capacity (Amendment) Act 2019.

16.70 A final point should be made here. In many cases, the court will be asked to take a one-off decision on P's behalf. In other cases, the court will be asked to make a declaration under MCA 2005 s15 as to P's capacity in respect of a particular decision, or to decide on P's behalf (for instance) where to live. It is quite possible that circumstances will change after the hearing, however, such that P's best interests may dictate a different course of action. The question that arises immediately in this regard is whether it is necessary to return the matter to court, or whether the parties to the proceedings are bound by the declaration(s) and decisions contained in the final order.

57 *Cheshire West and Chester Council v P* [2011] EWCA Civ 1257, [2012] COPLR 37, (2012) 15 CCLR 48 at para 4 per Munby LJ. This aspect of the judgment of the Court of Appeal was not contested before the Supreme Court on the Official Solicitor's (successful) appeal against the decision.

16.71 Although the question has not yet come before the courts to be determined (at least in any recorded cases),[58] it is suggested that, by analogy with the position that prevails in respect of decisions taken by mental health tribunals, the parties must consider themselves bound by the decision unless they reasonably and in good faith consider that they have information unknown to the court 'which put a significantly differently complexion on the case as compared with that before the [court]'.[59] If there has not been such a material change of circumstances, but the circumstances are such that they nonetheless require revisiting by the court then, depending upon the length of time since the original proceedings were concluded (and especially if all questions relating to costs have been resolved), it may be necessary for a fresh application to be made. If a fresh application has to be made, then it would be prudent for the applicant to make clear that the proceedings were previously before the court and to seek an order at the first directions hearing that (if the court bundle from the previous proceedings is still in readily accessible form and remains relevant) that the documents contained in the bundle stand as evidence in the new proceedings, so as to ensure that all relevant materials are before the court in the new proceedings.

16.72 The position where P regains capacity after the proceedings have come to an end is covered by COPR PD 24B (primarily concerned with property and affairs). Where P ceases to lack capacity after proceedings have concluded, an application may be made to the court to discharge any orders made (including an order appointing a deputy or an order in relation to a security bond) by filing a COP9 application notice, together with any evidence in support of the application. The application notice should set out details of the order or orders the applicant seeks to have discharged, and should in particular be supported by evidence that P no longer lacks capacity to make

58 Although it was considered indirectly in *An NHS Trust v AF* [2020] EWCOP 55, [2021] COPLR 63, dealing with the question of what the court should if asked to make a best interests decision only a few months after another court has done so. Poole J adopted, in effect, the approach set out in this paragraph. In *Z and others v RS (by his litigation friend, the Official Solicitor) and another* [2021] EWCA Civ 22, [2021] COPLR 342, the Court of Appeal confirmed that the Court of Protection (as with courts hearing cases in relation to children) will review an earlier best interests decision, such a reconsideration being undertaken 'on the grounds of compelling new evidence' but not on 'partially informed or ill-informed opinion'. The decision of the Court of Appeal was a permission decision, so strictly does not have precedent value.

59 *R (von Brandenburg) v East London and City NHS Trust* [2003] UKHL 58, [2004] 2 AC 280, (2004) 7 CCLR 121 at para 10 per Lord Bingham.

decisions in relation to the matter or matters to which the proceedings relate.[60] Note that if the Court Funds Office is holding funds or assets on behalf of P, it will require an order of the court to the effect that P no longer lacks capacity to make decisions with regard to the use and disposition of those funds or assets before any funds or assets can be transferred to him.[61]

P regains capacity or dies

16.73 There are two other events that will bring about a final determination of the proceedings in a way other than provided for in the balance of this chapter, namely P regaining the relevant capacity to take the decision(s) in question during the course of the proceedings, or P dying. What should happen in these circumstances is, in part, set out in COPR PD 24B, and in part in PD 13A.

16.74 If P regains capacity (or, to use the terminology of PD 24B, 'ceases to lack capacity'), then steps should be taken forthwith to end the proceedings and discharge any orders made in respect of P. While PD 24B refers to an order being sought under COPR r24.5 (disposal of property where P ceases to lack capacity), PD 13A makes clear that an order may also be sought under COPR r13.1(1)(b) for the court to declare that it no longer has jurisdiction over P.[62] Such an application can be made by P, their litigation friend or any other person who is party to the proceedings, and should be made on a COP9 form together with, in particular, evidence that P no longer lacks capacity to make decisions in relation to the matter or matters to which the proceedings relate.[63]

16.75 If P dies during the currency of proceedings (which is, sadly, not an altogether unusual experience), then this should be brought to the attention of the court as soon as practicable. At that point, proceedings will come to an effective halt,[64] although the court retains a residual jurisdiction in respect of matters such as:

- costs;[65]
- the remuneration of a deputy, donee or attorney;[66]

60 COPR PD 24B para 5.
61 COPR PD 24B para 6.
62 COPR PD 13A para 5.
63 COPR PD 24B paras 3–4, PD 13A paras 5–7.
64 See *Re RC (deceased)* [2011] 1 FLR 1447, [2010] COPLR Con Vol 1022 at paras 50–54 per Senior Judge Lush.
65 COPR r19.11 and PD 24B para 10.
66 COPR r19.13.

- fees;
- the discharge of security;[67]
- (if a deputy has been appointed), the deputy's final report on the termination of his appointment;[68] and
- the transfer and delivery of funds.[69]

16.76 The court will also have a jurisdiction to take necessary steps as regards the protection of P's identity: see further chapter 14.

Case study: facilitating participation of 'P' in Court of Protection proceedings

16.77 In the body of this chapter, we set out some of the ways in which practice has begun to change within the Court of Protection to ensure that the court and representation process is looked at through P's eyes, rather than just adding P as an afterthought. Practical guidance to enhance the participation of P was issued by the former Vice-President of the Court of Protection, Charles J in 2016, and reissued by the current Vice-President in 2022,[70] and we commend that guidance to readers. We also commend to readers the films produced by researchers on the Arts and Humanities Research Council (AHRC) funded project, *Judging values and participation in mental capacity law*,[71] based at the Institute for Crime and Justice Policy Research (ICPR), Birkbeck School of Law, available on YouTube.[72]

As a case study, we set out here measures which were implemented to facilitate P's participation in a fact-finding hearing listed to determine allegations of abuse at the hands of his parents.[73]

67 Lasting Powers of Attorney, Enduring Powers of Attorney and Public Guardian Regulations 2007 SI No 1253 reg 37.

68 Lasting Powers of Attorney, Enduring Powers of Attorney and Public Guardian Regulations 2007 reg 40.

69 COPR PD 23B para 11.

70 As an annex to *Official Judicial Visits to P (Guidance)* [2022] EWCOP 5.

71 See: www.icpr.org.uk/theme/courts-court-users-and-judicial-process/judging-values-and-participation-mental-capacity-law.

72 See: www.youtube.com/watch?v=WuEtw2rnqBw (on communication) and https://www.youtube.com/watch?v=IfSmzITspzs&feature=youtu.be (on making values matter).

73 *A County Council v AB and others (participation of P in proceedings)* [2016] EWCOP 41, [2016] COPLR 576. This case study is written by Nicola Mackintosh QC (Hon), who acted as P's solicitor, instructed by the Official Solicitor as his litigation friend.

P had expressed a wish to attend Court to come to the fact finding hearing to listen to what his parents and other witnesses were saying, as well as to 'tell his story' to the court. This was opposed by both his parents and the local authority, but the court ruled that he should attend. The court also ruled that, whilst P was:

> . . . almost certainly not competent to give evidence [this is] is no reason not to seek with appropriate help to elicit 'information' from him via a skilled intermediary . . . using Rule 95 (e) [now Rule 14.2(e)] the Court may admit the information but there is no guarantee that it would accept or act upon it . . . . the Court's ability to have information provided by P is wide and flexible . . .[74]

In the light of the judgment, the practical arrangements which had already been made were implemented. These steps show clearly how vital it is when securing and enhancing P's participation that each and every detail of the arrangements is planned from P's perspective and not simply limited to a meeting with the judge (important as that is). This involved the following:

1) P's lawyers meeting with P and securing appropriate speech and language therapy support to prepare for the hearing by exploring concepts such as the following:
   a) 'What is happening in court, what is a case, why is your case in court, what is the case about?'
   b) 'What is a judge, what will the judge be deciding, why is it important to you?'
   c) 'What will happen at the hearing, who will speak when, how long will it take etc?'
   d) 'How can I tell my story?'
2) Considering which court location would best meet the needs of the case, taking into account all physical facilities, travel time for P and others etc.
3) As the court's video facilities did not allow for P to be in an adjacent room viewing the proceedings from a distance so as to minimise distress, an alternative facility was found nearby which could provide a video link to the court. Arrangements were made for this between the IT specialists of the court and the other facility, and for the video link to be tested in advance to ensure it was working. In the event this facility was not used as P remained in court throughout the proceedings.

74 *A County Council v AB and others (participation of P in proceedings)* [2016] EWCOP 41, [2016] COPLR 576 at para 45

4) (With consent) taking photographs of the judge, the courtroom and all the lawyers involved in the proceedings to explain to P the physical location and the identity of all involved in advance of the hearing.
5) Before the hearing, arranging a visit by P to the courtroom when the court was not sitting to see the layout, and also to meet the court clerk who was to be allocated to the hearing days.
6) Deciding where it was best for P to sit in his wheelchair in the courtroom to listen to the proceedings, taking into account the position of other parties and 'lines of sight' with others.
7) Arranging for P to be supported by staff regarding personal care, and ensuring mobile hoists were provided for P in both locations for care.
8) Ensuring that there was enough physical space in the court complex so that P had a separate room just next to the courtroom, with a fan (P being a wheelchair user had reduced temperature control).

The first day of the hearing was listed as a Ground Rules Hearing, as provided for in the Advocates' Gateway (see para 16.51). On the first day, as planned, the judge met with P in a side room next to the courtroom. P's solicitor was present, and P's speech and language therapist (SALT) also assisted by explaining to the judge that P was able to respond 'yes, no, happy and sad' through different Makaton signs. P showed the judge how he communicated each of these expressions, enabling the judge better to understand how to interpret P's wishes and reactions.

Although the fact finding hearing was listed for nine days, after the initial part of the first day of the hearing (P being present in court with his carers and intermediary) the parties set out their updated positions which then resulted in negotiations to see if a settlement could be reached without the need for the fact finding process. This lasted the first day and the terms of an order were agreed on the second day of the hearing. P was present during all discussions between lawyers and the court, and communicated his wish to continue to be involved and to listen to the proceedings. Between updates to the court he was permitted by the judge to remain in the courtroom with his support workers, watching a DVD. This reduced the need for him to be taken in and out of the courtroom, waiting for long periods in a small stuffy side room, and was invaluable. This could not have been arranged without the court's co-operation and flexibility of the court staff.

Once agreement had been reached in principle between the parties as to the core issues in the case, it was considered vital for P's wish to 'tell his story' to be facilitated. A very careful consideration of the issues raised, and the broad themes set out in the fact finding schedule was undertaken. Questions of P were drafted by P's legal representatives with the assistance of P's SALT and intermediary. As P's communication was limited to responses such as 'yes, no' etc, it was necessary for leading questions to be posed however these were broken down into questions so that the leading element was minimised. Examples of questions included 'Do you want to talk about when you were living at home?', 'How did you feel when you were living at home?', When you were living at home did anyone do X to you?', and if the answer was affirmative, 'How did it make you feel?' These questions were devised to ensure that P's broad wishes were communicated to the court notwithstanding the agreement between the parties, so that P felt that he had been listened to by the parties and the judge, but avoiding detailed questioning on the fact finding schedule which eventually proved to be unnecessary.

The question and answer sessions were broken down into more than one session to allow P to rest and refocus. With agreement they were filmed on a mobile phone and then played to the judge in his chambers. They were then also played to the other parties. This flexibility avoided all the delays and organisational problems associated with using the court video facilities.

By the end of the second day, agreement had been reached in the form of a detailed order. The judge held a further short hearing and again explained the outcome to P, coming into the courtroom and sitting by P to confirm what was going to happen. P was repositioned in his wheelchair to be solely in the line of sight of the judge and not the other parties.

In conclusion, P's wishes and story had been communicated to the judge, and P had been present throughout the proceedings in accordance with his wishes. P communicated that he felt he had 'told his story', and he did not need to say anything more. He was clearly excited by the eventual outcome (that he could return to his own home, without his parents, but having regular contact), and felt that he and his wishes had been central to the process.

CHAPTER 17

Costs

Introduction

17.1 This chapter sets out how costs are dealt with in the Court of Protection. The costs rules that apply are unique to the court, balancing as they do a number of interests that are not necessarily in play in other forms of litigation. They also make different provisions for applications involving property and affairs on the one hand, and health and welfare on the other. This chapter addresses both categories of application, together with the (common) scenario where the two are mixed.

17.2 Costs in Court of Protection proceedings, especially in complex cases, can be high. Proceedings may continue for an extended period of time, even many years.

17.3 At all times the parties and their legal advisers must take care to ensure that only those matters which need to be determined by the court are the subject of proceedings. During the course of proceedings, the parties and their legal advisers must pay close attention to the proportionality of the costs and time expended, and importantly the effect on P of how the proceedings are conducted. This may include litigation conduct which has the effect of delaying important decisions which need to be made in P's best interests, and litigating/disputing matters which are of less vital importance to P than to the other parties. The parties and their advisers must co-operate.[1] The court also has an important case management role in ensuring that the overriding objective is achieved.[2]

The statutory provisions

Mental Capacity 2005

17.4 Mental Capacity (MCA) 2005 s55 provides as follows:

55 Costs

(1) Subject to Court of Protection Rules, the costs of and incidental to all proceedings in the court are in its discretion.

(2) The rules may in particular make provision for regulating matters relating to the costs of those proceedings, including prescribing scales of costs to be paid to legal or other representatives.

1 Court of Protection Rules 2017 (COPR) SI No 1035 r1.4(2)(c)–(g).

2 COPR r1.3(3). See *Re A and B (Court of Protection: delay and costs)* [2014] EWCOP 48, [2015] COPLR 1.

(3) The court has full power to determine by whom and to what extent the costs are to be paid.
(4) The court may, in any proceedings–
  (a) disallow, or
  (b) order the legal or other representatives concerned to meet, the whole of any wasted costs or such part of them as may be determined in accordance with the rules.
(5) 'Legal or other representative', in relation to a party to proceedings, means any person exercising a right of audience or right to conduct litigation on his behalf.
(6) 'Wasted costs' means any costs incurred by a party–
  (a) as a result of any improper, unreasonable or negligent act or omission on the part of any legal or other representative or any employee of such a representative, or
  (b) which, in the light of any such act or omission occurring after they were incurred, the court considers it is unreasonable to expect that party to pay.

17.5 Practitioners should be aware of the powers in MCA 2005 s55(3)–(6) to use costs sanctions against legal representatives when the court considers this to be justified. These powers replicate the powers in Senior Courts Act 1981 s51(6), and will be deployed according to the same criteria.[3]

Court of Protection Rules

17.6 COPR Part 19 sets out the general provisions dealing with costs. We set out the key provisions below.

Application of other statutes and the Civil Procedure Rules

17.7 Some of the provisions in the Civil Procedure Rules 1998 (CPR) apply to Court of Protection cases, with modifications.[4]

3 *Sharma and Judkins v Hunters* [2011] EWHC 2546 (COP), [2012] COPLR 166.

4 COPR r19.6, Practice Direction (PD) 19A. Further, by virtue of provisions contained in the Legal Aid, Sentencing and Punishment of Offenders Act 2012 (LASPO), a costs order can be made against a party who holds a legal aid certificate, but these cannot exceed the amount which it is reasonable for that party to pay, having regard to the circumstances including the conduct and financial resources of all the parties. If a legally aided party is ordered to pay an amount of costs which is less than the costs incurred by the receiving party, then the receiving party may apply for an order that the shortfall is met by the Lord Chancellor. There is no reason why, in principle, such an order could not be made in favour of a public body. See LASPO s26 and the detailed guidance notes on the application of s26(1) by the Senior Costs Judge.

The general rule

17.8 The COPR currently sets out two very different general rules depending on whether a case is health/welfare or property and affairs:

- The general rule in cases concerning P's welfare is that there will be no order as to the costs of the proceedings, or of that part of the proceedings that concerns P's welfare.[5] This means that in 'pure' welfare cases, each party should expect to bear their own costs and there will be no costs order as between one party and another. Clients who are not legally aided therefore need to be advised that they cannot, save in circumstances which are highly unlikely to be clear at the start of a case, expect to recover costs they incur in those proceedings.
- In respect of cases concerning P's property and affairs, the general rule is that all the costs of the proceedings will be met from P's estate.[6] At the time of writing (and indeed, for several years now) a consultation is likely as to whether to amend this general rule (see paras 17.40–17.41 below).

17.9 In *Re E*,[7] Senior Judge Lush considered the origin of the 'general rules' in COPR rr19.2–19.3 and commented:

> 34. The origin of the general rule in property and affairs cases goes back to the decision of the Lords Justices in Lunacy in *Re Windham* (1862) 4 De G F & J 53, following which the Lunacy Amendment Act 1862 conferred upon the court a wide discretion as to costs.
>
> 35. As both Mr Holland and Miss Hughes observed, the current rule 156 is largely a replication of the principles laid down by the Court of Appeal in *Re Cathcart* [1892] 1 Ch 549, with a few exceptions, such as a requirement in *Re Cathcart*, which does not appear in the Court of Protection Rules 2007, to have regard to the respective means of the parties.
>
> 36. By contrast, the general rule in personal welfare cases is of recent origin, dating from 1989, and reflects the fact that most personal welfare cases are of a public law nature.

5 COPR r19.3. Note that this is, in effect, the same rule that will apply in relation to cases brought under the inherent jurisdiction in respect of vulnerable adults, to which the Family Procedure Rules 2010 (FPR) will apply: see *Re T and another v L and others (inherent jurisdiction: costs)* [2021] EWHC 2147 (Fam) and chapter 28.

6 COPR r19.2.

7 [2014] EWCOP 27, [2014] Med LR 417.

17.10 Many cases involve a mixture of welfare and property and affairs issues. It is important to differentiate between the different elements of the case to ensure that there is clarity as to who is responsible for which costs. The court will, insofar as possible, apportion the costs between the issues.[8]

Deputies

17.11 Special provisions apply in relation to deputies, starting with appointment:

- An order appointing a property and affairs deputy will deal with both with any legal costs incurred by the deputy in making the application and the expenses incurred by the deputy in the discharge of their functions.
- Where a lay deputy is appointed, the costs will be limited to reasonable out-of-pocket expenses.[9]
- Where a professional is appointed, either as a sole appointment or jointly with a lay deputy, a clause will be included in the appointment order to permit fixed costs to be taken,[10] or for the costs to be assessed by the Senior Court Costs Office (SCCO).
- Health and welfare deputies should be aware that there is no guarantee that they will be able to recover either the legal costs of making the application[11] or of the majority of the expenses incurred in discharging their functions. Professional deputies are – rarely – appointed to act as health and welfare deputies. COPR PD 19B provides that the costs of a professional health and welfare deputy may be paid 2.5 per cent of the net assets of P up to a maximum of £555 per annum,[12] although the proposed consultation on costs in the Court of Protection may revisit this.

8 COPR r19.4.

9 MCA 2005 s19(7).

10 COPR r19.10, PD 19B.

11 See *Re CB* [2021] EWCOP 43, [2021] COPLR 549 (where P's sister was, in fact, not appointed as the deputy).

12 COPR PD1B para 10.

Costs of professional deputies

17.12 The rates that can be charged by a professional deputy are usually subject to the Guideline Hourly Rates.[13] These may be departed from if justified. If P's estate is less than £16,000 the option for detailed assessment by the SCCO will only arise if the court has made a specific order to that effect.[14] Where an hourly rate is authorised, COPR PD 19B 'Fixed costs in the Court of Protection' provides that solicitors will ordinarily be entitled to a higher rate than local authorities. The practice direction explicitly leaves to the court's discretion in each case the issue of whether and how to apply its provisions to a not-for-profit organisation deputy or to a deputy from another discipline, such as an accountant. For a detailed exposition of the law and practice on this point, see *The Friendly Trust's Bulk Application*[15] and also PD 19B. in *Riddle v Public Guardian*,[16] Lieven J refused the deputy permission to appeal from the judgment of Senior Judge Hilder, which considered at (necessary) length the ability of a professional deputy who is not a solicitor to charge fees at the solicitors' rate, concluding, broadly, that the non-solicitor deputy could not.

17.13 The usual practice is that professional deputies obtain limited payments on account of their costs from P's funds during each year of their appointment pending their costs being assessed. They are required by the Office of the Public Guardian (OPG) to provide a

13 These will be subject to revision in light of the report of the Civil Justice Council on the subject in 2021: *Guideline hourly rates: final report* available at: www.judiciary.uk/wp-content/uploads/2021/07/Civil-Justice-Council-final-report-on-guideline-hourly-rates.pdf. Note that that the report makes clear that the rates set out by Costs Judge Whalan in the case of *Re PLK, Thakur, Chapman and Tate* [2020] EWHC B28 (Costs), [2021] COPLR 163 are no longer to be applied. Costs Judge Whalan had, in effect, sought to effect an increase in the (very out of date) guideline rates applicable from 2011 amid concerns about the sustainability of the provider base.

14 *Penn Trust Ltd v A Local Authority and another* [2020] EWCOP 48, [2021] COPLR 142. In that case, the issue was the valuation of P's net estate and whether P's property was to be included. The court concluded that it should be so included and that net assets should have its ordinary meaning of total assets less total liabilities.

15 [2016] EWCOP 40. See also *London Borough of Enfield v Matrix Deputies Ltd and others (No2)* [2018] EWCOP 22, [2018] COPLR 451 confirming that, if a deputy order authorises 'fixed costs' without specifying at what rate, that necessarily implies the lower, public authority rate; and that if an order authorises 'fixed costs' without specifying at what rate but also authorises the deputy to seek assessment from the SCCO, that does not imply the higher, solicitors' rate.

16 [2021] EWCOP 38. See also Mr Riddle's second (unsuccessful) attempt before Hayden J: [2022] EWCOP 18.

breakdown of costs incurred and to estimate their costs for the forthcoming year.[17] An application could also be made for an order for payment of limited costs prior to appointment but subject always to the court being satisfied that P's funds are sufficiently safeguarded (including repaying any sums to P's estate if necessary).

Deputies – practice points

17.14 Good practice guidance on professional costs incurred by deputies in the discharge of their duties was issued by the OPG and the SCCO in July 2016.[18] See further chapter 21.

17.15 Where the court has appointed a deputy to manage P's property and affairs, care should be taken in relation to costs of any step which are beyond the deputy's powers and which may result in P incurring two sets of legal costs unnecessarily. In an unreported case in the authors' experience, the court decided, unusually, that the legal costs incurred by a professional deputy for property and affairs after the issue of welfare proceedings should be disallowed and not paid from P's money. This was because the deputy had not obtained an order for payment of their costs in issuing the welfare proceedings. Moreover, the Official Solicitor had then been appointed to act as P's litigation friend and once the appointment had been made there was no need for the deputy to continue to be an additional party to the proceedings and to incur costs from P's funds which would amount to unnecessary duplication.

17.16 Care should also be taken to avoid any perceived or actual conflict of interests when a solicitor deputy is appointed and separate issues arise which require the legal advice for P (this might be in relation to property transactions, employment advice, for example). In *ACC and others (property and affairs deputy; recovering assets costs for legal proceedings)*,[19] Senior Judge Hilder set out the scope of the 'general authority' of the deputy in relation to both property and affairs and also health and welfare issues, and where specific authority would be required to take certain steps including commencing litigation. The judgment also sets out core principles to ensure that solicitor deputies were not in a position of conflict in instructing their own firm to advise and litigate including seeking of directions or prior authority to take certain steps.

17 See: www.gov.uk/government/publications/professional-deputy-costs.

18 See: www.gov.uk/government/publications/professional-deputy-costs.

19 [2020] EWCOP 9, [2020] COPLR 406.

Serious medical treatment cases

17.17 While the general rule in health and welfare cases is as set out above, it is important to note that the courts had recognised what amounts to a further general rule in cases relating to serious medical treatment (see further in respect of such cases, chapter 23). It had been the standard practice for the NHS Trust that made the application to pay half of the costs of the Official Solicitor (who will, in most cases where P is made a party – ie almost all[20] – act as P's litigation friend).[21] That practice continues even though there is now, strictly, no such category of case as 'serious medical treatment'.[22] For these purposes, 'costs' include any of the Official Solicitor's costs incurred before the application – which may be brought by any of the other parties – is formally issued and also those which may arise from any subsequent appeal or applications to review orders. Note that the relevant NHS body will usually be the body which has brought the proceedings as the applicant but in cases where the applicant is a private individual(s) this may be one or more of the public bodies acting as respondent.[23] The Official Solicitor does not seek to recover costs from P's own funds for acting in cases concerning serious medical treatment. Note that, given that there is no longer strictly any such category of case, there is a lurking issue as to the point at which the Official Solicitor (or an NHS body) might take the view that a particular treatment is medical treatment, but not serious medical treatment, such that this practice should not be followed. To date, the issue has not yet reached the point of determination or recording in a reported case.

17.18 Costs may need to be apportioned in those occasional cases which involve a specific serious medical treatment issue but are otherwise general welfare proceedings, and it is sensible in such cases to keep a separate record of costs for each category of issue.

20 Essentially the only exception being where urgency makes this impossible: for an example, see *Newcastle-upon-Tyne Hospitals Foundation Trust v LM* [2014] EWHC 454 (COP), [2015] 1 FCR 373.

21 *Re D (Costs)* [2012] EWHC 886 (COP), [2012] COPLR 499.

22 This position is recorded in the court's *Serious Medical Treatment Guidance* [2020] EWCOP 2, [2020] WLR 641 at para 21(b) and the Official Solicitor's Practice Note: *Appointment as litigation friend in personal welfare proceedings in the Court of Protection* (www.gov.uk/government/publications/appointment-of-the-official-solicitor-in-welfare-proceedings-practice-note) at para 15.

23 As per the previous footnote.

Departing from the general rule

17.19 As COPR r19.5 makes clear, the court can depart from rules set out above (rr19.2–19.3) if the circumstances so justify. Rule 19.5 provides that:

> **19.5 Departing from the general rule**
> (1) The court may depart from rules 19.2 to 19.4 if the circumstances so justify, and in deciding whether departure is justified the court will have regard to all the circumstances, including–
> (a) the conduct of the parties;
> (b) whether a party has succeeded on part of his case, even if he has not been wholly successful; and
> (c) the role of any public body involved in the proceedings.
> (2) The conduct of the parties includes–
> (a) conduct before, as well as during, the proceedings;
> (b) whether it was reasonable for a party to raise, pursue or contest a particular issue;
> (c) the manner in which a party has made or responded to an application or a particular issue;
> (d) whether a party who has succeeded in his application or response to an application, in whole or in part, exaggerated any matter contained in his application or response; and
> (e) any failure by a party to comply with a rule, practice direction or court order.
> (3) Without prejudice to rules 19.2 to 19.4 and the foregoing provisions of this rule, the court may permit a party to recover their fixed costs in accordance with the relevant practice direction.

17.20 It will be seen that the court retains a broad discretion to award costs and to take into account the parties' behaviour before and during the proceedings. Given the pre-issue obligations imposed upon potential parties to welfare proceedings under the COPR Case Pathways PD 3B Case Management Pilot (see further, chapter 11), it is likely that greater focus is going to be placed in due course upon the conduct of parties before litigation concerning P's welfare is started.

17.21 COPR r1.4 imposes a duty on the parties to help the court to further the overriding objective, and sets out a non-exhaustive list of expectations, considered at para 11.8 onwards. These include, amongst others, full and frank disclosure[24] and co-operation in all aspects of the proceedings, including the preparation of bundles.[25]

24 COPR r1.4(2)(f).
25 COPR r1.4(2)(g).

The COPR also introduce duties upon legal representatives[26] and also upon unrepresented parties,[27] both discussed in chapter 11.

17.22 COPR r1.4(3) provides, in a warning clearly intended to focus the minds of parties and their advisers on the importance of compliance, that:

> If the court determines that any party has failed without reasonable excuse to satisfy the requirements of this rule, it may under rule 19.5 depart from the general rule about costs in so far as they apply to that party.

17.23 In this regard, it is important to emphasise that case management directions are not guidance; they are orders of the court which are expected to be complied with. If a party considers that it cannot comply with a direction in an order by the date specified then an application to vary the order should be submitted for the court's consideration.[28] It is not sufficient simply to notify the parties or to stand by while the court timetable drifts.[29]

17.24 It is also the experience of the authors that with more hearings taking place in the regions local judges are more willing to exercise their powers to undertake a summary assessment of costs. Advisers need to be alert to these issues which should be drawn to clients' attention in the appropriate client care letter and/or terms and conditions.

Conduct issues

17.25 The court can use its powers under the COPR to mark its displeasure not just at the conduct of the proceedings, but also the underlying conduct of the parties. By way of example:

26 COPR r1.5.

27 COPR r1.6.

28 It is always prudent where possible to seek the parties' agreement to an extension of time in a draft consent order which can be submitted to the court for approval, and at the same time to review the remainder of the court timetable to see if any further consequential adjustments need to be made.

29 See *Re ND (Court of Protection: costs and declarations)* [2020] EWCOP 42, [2020] COPLR 808, where Keehan J directed part payment of costs resulting from the local authority's failure to comply with directions; and *A Local Authority v ST (costs application)* [2022] EWCOP 11, [2022] Costs LR 763 where HHJ Burrows ordered the payment by the local authority of 85 per cent of the Official Solicitor's costs on various grounds including that a hearing was ineffective due to the authority's noncompliance with directions.

- In *London Borough of Lambeth v MCS and another*,[30] Newton J was very troubled at the conduct of both the clinical commissioning group and the local authority in allowing P to languish in hospital for an extended period of time and directed that they should pay the entire costs of the proceedings between them. The case concerned P, originally from Colombia, who following a brain injury in 2014 clearly wished to return there. However, she spent three years waiting for the practical arrangements to be made by the statutory agencies[31] before she eventually returned. In reaching his decision as to costs, the judge criticised the 'disorganised, muddled and unfocused decision making' of the statutory authorities which at time verged on an 'arrogance'.[32]
- In *London Borough of Harrow v AT and DT* where a local authority failed to comply with the provision in an order made authorising a deprivation of liberty requiring it to bring the matter back to court, SJ Hilder noted:

  the purpose of the review requirement is to provide procedural safeguards to prevent arbitrary deprivation of liberty and so avoid a violation of the State's positive obligations under the European Convention of Human Rights. If a local authority fails to comply with a requirement (by court order) to apply for review, the effectiveness of any safeguards is seriously undermined. Such conduct on the part of a public body cannot be overlooked.[33]
- In *Re A (fact-finding)*,[34] HHJ Clayton made a costs order against the relevant public bodies for resisting an application made by former professional carer of P to be appointed as P's welfare deputy, which had only been made 'as a result of P's rights being violated and her despair at the failings of the system'.
- In *Re JBN*,[35] HHJ Marin departed from the general rule to require the Public Guardian to pay half of the costs of an attorney after an application to remove him following an investigation had been refused. HHJ Marin was critical of the fact that the proceedings were commenced 'solely on the basis of the desk-top evaluation of the case carried out by an investigator. I am clear that this led to proceedings being issued which went beyond what was necessary

30 [2018] EWCOP 14, [2018] COPLR 484.
31 Incidentally at significant cost to the taxpayer (around £2,000 a week).
32 Para 9.
33 [2017] EWCOP 37, [2018] COPLR 412 at para 24.
34 [2019] EWCOP 58 at para 28.
35 [2019] EWCOP 62, [2020] COPLR 587.

and reasonable'.[36] He was particularly concerned also that the Public Guardian sought without notice orders of a very serious nature, namely the suspension of the lasting power of attorney (LPA) and the appointment of an interim deputy, which completed ignored the fact that the attorney was cooperating. HHJ Marin was also troubled by the fact the Public Guardian had not responded to attempts by the attorney to settle; he observed that: 'the rules of court apply equally to all court users including the Public Guardian. COPR 2017 r1.4 imposes a duty on litigants to help further the overriding objective and this includes co-operating with the other party'.[37] It appeared at the time of the hearing that the OPG might have a policy of not negotiating in cases brought before the court; the OPG confirmed subsequently to the court that this was not the case.

- In *JB (costs)*[38] the local authority's application for an injunction was considered to be totally without merit and it was ordered to pay not only the costs of the residential placement but also P's mother and the Official Solicitor in responding to the application.

17.26 Where the court is looking at the proceedings themselves, a particular concern is proportionality.[39] In some cases, both sides can lose sight of the requirement. A good example is *Hounslow LBC v A Father and a Mother*.[40] Here, the court was concerned with an application by the local authority to be appointed as deputy for property and affairs of P, whose only income was welfare benefits. Allegations of dishonesty were made against the appointee father and the mother which needed to be addressed; however, the allegations were not spelled out clearly as the authority relied (incorrectly) on public interest immunity in providing details. During the proceedings both parties and their legal representatives escalated the dispute and the costs were wholly disproportionate to the matters in issue. On the day of the hearing, the applicant authority withdrew its application. District Judge Eldergill was minded to order that the costs of the proceedings should be paid entirely by the authority but given the conduct of the father's legal advisers (about which he was almost equally critical) he directed

36 Para 49.

37 Para 60.

38 [2020] EWCOP 49, [2021] COPLR 88.

39 See *Re A and B (Court of Protection: Delay and Costs)* [2014] EWCOP 48, [2015] COPLR 1 and *A Local Authority v ED* [2013] EWHC 3069 (COP), (2013) 16 CCLR 597.

40 [2018] EWCOP 23.

that 90 per cent of the costs be paid. In respect of the mother's position as a litigant in person, see paras 17.30–17.31.

17.27 The court can also mark its displeasure at how a party has approached a particular stage of proceedings, either because it has conducted itself in accordance with the COPR or required costs to be incurred unnecessarily. Examples include from unreported cases in the experience of the authors:

- Where a delay in providing information regarding P's eligibility for legal aid has required P to incur additional unnecessary funds in paying privately for legal advice when they could and should have been eligible for legal aid at an earlier stage. This principle would apply equally in MCA 2005 s21A proceedings if a standard authorisation expired without a new one being made promptly by the relevant authority so that there is no gap (which would result in a corresponding gap in non-means-tested legal aid).
- Where directions for disclosure of financial information from banks have not been complied with resulting in delays in obtaining legal aid for P, and costs incurred as a result.
- Where an invitation to vacate a hearing by consent was met with no response from the applicant statutory authority and preparation for and attendance at an unnecessary hearing was the result (the court directed that the costs of and occasioned by the hearing should be paid by the applicant).

Costs of the Official Solicitor

17.28 How the legal costs of the Official Solicitor are provided for is addressed in paras 12.40–12.41. At the conclusion of the proceedings, where P's representation is to be paid privately from P's estate, the SCCO will usually carry out a detailed assessment of the costs. These costs are essentially akin to solicitor and own client costs in that they are the Official Solicitor's costs of P's representation rather than costs being assessed on a party and party basis. In an unreported case Master Whalan has confirmed that whilst not automatically determinative of reasonableness, where the hourly rates for solicitor and barrister are agreed by the Official Solicitor then this creates a factual presumption of reasonableness. This is similar to the usual provision in CPR 46.9 that where a client agrees a rate and items of expenditure with their legal advisers then there will be a presumption of reasonableness in the assessment of those costs, which would in that case be on the indemnity basis and not on the standard basis and only disallowed if shown to be unreasonable.

17.29 The particular role of the Official Solicitor and her representatives was also raised in another unreported judgment of Master Whalan, where it was confirmed that rates to be allowed for work done should not be subject to arbitrary (in that case significantly lower) rates bearing no reference to guideline rates or rates agreed with the Official Solicitor – either the work was reasonably incurred in which case it should be allowed in full or it was not reasonable and should be disallowed. Moreover, the intensive nature of some welfare litigation and the particular role of the Official Solicitor could warrant the attendance of more than one fee earner at a hearing, particularly where there were unrepresented parties who needed to be updated and given explanations during the course of the hearing.

Costs of a litigant in person

17.30 In *Hounslow LBC v A Father and A Mother*[41] (see para 17.26 above), District Judge Eldergill carried out a detailed analysis of the relevant provisions regarding entitlement of litigants in person to costs. The court found that:

> The intention of the [Court of Protection Rules] is that a litigant in person is entitled to be reimbursed for their reasonable expenses but is not entitled to a fee or to remuneration. The intention of the rules seems to be that expenses but not fees, charges and remuneration are permitted and this is consistent with the disapplication of both CPR Rule 46.5 and the Litigants in Person (Costs and Expenses) Act 1975.
>
> Given a general rule in financial proceedings that costs are payable from the incapacitated person's estate, the intention underlying the rules seems to be that litigants in person such as family members who have not incurred any legal costs should not charge a fee for assisting an incapacitated person and the court, for example to cover loss of earnings for attending court, reading documents and preparation. In many cases, such as statutory Will, LPA and disputed deputyship applications, several family members may wish to participate and join the proceedings as parties without being represented. The record I have seen, in a statutory Will case, is nineteen. If all of them were entitled to, for example, loss of earnings for attending and preparing for court, the additional costs would be significant.

17.31 District Judge Eldergill noted, however, that:

41 [2018] EWCOP 23.

> [This is an] unfortunate finding in the mother's case and one which, in my view, leads to an injustice. A serious allegation was made against her which necessarily she was bound to defend. It proved to be an unfounded allegation. Her conduct has been reasonable and I have no reason to doubt that her loss of earnings in defending her reputation is real. Naturally I am tempted to hold that section 55(1) is sufficiently broad that I have a discretion to award her costs but the section is subject to the rules and in my view the intention of Rule 19(1) is that litigants in person, like family member deputies, cannot charge or recover loss of earnings or hourly fees.

17.32 A different – more generous – view was taken by HHJ Evans-Gordon in *JMH v CFH and SAP (costs: the Chorley principle, litigants in person)*,[42] in which he held that a litigant in person is entitled to some costs for their time with COPR r46(5) as a guide without it being of direct application. HHJ Evans-Gordon also clarified that a solicitor party is entitled to charge for their time as a solicitor pursuant to the so-called *Chorley* principle[43] and set out what such a solicitor needs to do to be able to do so.

Alternative dispute resolution / mediation – costs consequences

17.33 There is an increasing emphasis upon forms of alternative dispute resolution (ADR) including mediation as a way both to prevent disputes reaching the Court of Protection and to bring about a speedier resolution to proceedings if they do. This is discussed in more detail in chapter 20. As noted in that chapter, the court has no power to require parties to engage in a form of ADR, and there are of course particular difficulties in ensuring that P's position is properly protected in any mediation process. We suggest, however, that, by analogy with the approach adopted in family proceedings,[44] and in judicial review proceedings an unreasonable failure to engage in ADR in a suitable case might give a basis for departure from the general rule.

17.34 In *Rolf v De Guerin*[45] Lord Justice Rix stated that:

42 [2020] EWCOP 63, [2021] COPLR 428. One unusual aspect of this case was that the solicitor in question was acting in three roles: as a solicitor, as a solicitor retained to represent P, and a litigant in person.

43 After *London Scottish Benefit Society v Chorley* [1884] 13 QBD 872, CA.

44 Eg *Mann v Mann* [2014] EWHC 537 (Fam), [2014] 1 WLR 2807.

45 [2011] EWCA Civ 78.

> Parties should respond reasonably to offers to mediate or settle and ... their conduct in this respect can be taken into account in awarding costs.

17.35 In *PGF*[46] a lack of a response to an invitation to mediate was held to be unreasonable conduct. Lord Justice Briggs stated:

> In my judgment, the time has now come for this court firmly to endorse the advice given in Chapter 11.56 of the ADR Handbook, that silence in the face of an invitation to participate in ADR is, as a general rule, of itself unreasonable, regardless whether an outright refusal, or a refusal to engage in the type of ADR requested, or to do so at the time requested, might have been justified by the identification of reasonable grounds ... this case sends out an important message to civil litigants, requiring them to engage with a serious invitation to participate in ADR, even if they have reasons which might justify a refusal, or the undertaking of some other form of ADR, or ADR at some other time in the litigation.

17.36 For the particular issues which arise in mediating Court of Protection proceedings see chapter 20.

Wasted costs orders

17.37 It is important that legal advisers are clear that case management directions must be complied with- even when it is another party who has been directed to take the steps in question. By way of analogy, in *Re L (case management: wasted costs)*[47] HHJ Bellamy made wasted costs orders against all the legal representatives in a care case, finding that they were all negligent for the purpose of Senior Courts Act 1981 s51, so as to give rise to the power to make a wasted costs order. The local authority had failed to disclose relevant material and bore the brunt of the responsibility: but the other parties should have noticed this and were negligent in 'failing to take pro-active steps in drawing the omission to the attention of the local authority and court'. Given the express duty on all parties to ask the court to make directions if an issue arises 'of which the court is unaware,[48] and the duty on legal representatives to comply with the rules,[49] it is entirely possible to imagine a similar approach being taken in the Court of Protection.

46 *PGF II SA v OMFS* [2013] EWCA (Civ) 1288, [2014] 1 WLR 1386.
47 [2016] EWFC B8.
48 COPR r1.4(2)(a).
49 COPR r1.5(2)(a).

17.38 In *Re M (costs)*[50] applications for costs were made following long-running and complex welfare proceedings. The main welfare issues concerned whether P should return to the care of his parents, where the court had previously found, following an extensive fact finding hearing that P's mother had harmed him. An application for wasted costs was made by the parents against the local authority and also against the legal representatives of P (in that case P was represented by the Official Solicitor). That application was dismissed as being 'hopeless and totally without merit'.[51] Orders were made regarding the contribution by the parents towards the costs of the experts which had led to the court deciding that P's mother had symptoms of factitious disorder imposed on another (FDIA)[52] and aspects of various personality disorders.

Appeals

17.39 Appeals are dealt with in chapter 19. It should be noted, however, that the Court of Appeal has made clear that the bar for appealing a costs order is set high. In *Re G (an adult) (by her litigation friend the Official Solicitor) (costs)*,[53] Lord Justice Ryder noted that 'an appeal against the exercise of by a judge of his discretion [in making a decision as to costs] faces a high hurdle', and that the Court of Appeal will only interfere if the judge exceeds the generous ambit of his discretion. The same approach will also prevail in respect of appeals within the Court of Protection (ie from a lower 'tier' of judges to a higher 'tier': see further para 19.11).

The future of costs in property and affairs cases

17.40 At the time of writing, a consultation is expected (and indeed has been expected for some time) to ascertain views about changing the general rule as to costs in property and affairs cases to encourage settlement and to discourage litigation at P's expense where this may be unjustified. It is easy to see that in many cases where several family members are in dispute about aspects of P's property and

50 [2015] EWCOP 45.

51 Para 16.

52 Previously referred to as 'Munchausen syndrome by proxy'.

53 [2015] EWCA Civ 446, [2015] COPLR 438 at para 22.

affairs, it is unfair that P should bear the entire cost of all parties regardless of the outcome or the merit in the parties' positions. This is particularly so when an application for a gift of money from P's estate may be made by the proposed donee, all at P's expense.

17.41 A consultation on principles which should apply to property and affairs cases is likely to include suggestions that initial legal advice may be payable from P's estate but that when any application becomes contested, parties may be more at risk on costs. The intention behind such a proposal is that this would focus the parties' minds on the issues and make them more aware that they cannot always litigate at P's expense regardless of costs, whilst also ensuring that where disputes do properly arise, the court will be available to determine them in P's best interests. In the authors' view, it is also important that consideration be given to revisiting the provisions of COPR PD 19B relating to costs incurred by health and welfare deputies, so that there is an appropriate pool of people willing to be appointed for those cases where such a deputy is required.

Summary and practice points

17.42 The following practice points should be borne in mind:

- It is essential for anyone embarking on litigation, however it is to be funded, to be properly advised about the likely costs risks at the start of the case and throughout it.
- Any decision to depart from the general rule will turn on the facts of the individual case but is not reserved for 'exceptional' cases.

17.43 Costs can be directed to be paid by another party for the entire case or for a particular period of time or in relation to litigating a particular issue:

- The fact that a party seeking costs is legally aided is not relevant.[54]
- Costs do not necessarily follow the outcome of the case, although they may do.[55]

54 *WBC v CP* [2012] EWHC 1944 (COP).

55 *G v E (by his litigation friend the Official Solicitor) and F* [2010] EWHC 3385 (Fam), (2011) 14 CCLR 140, [2010] COPLR Con Vol 454; *Hillingdon LBC v Neary* [2011] EWHC 3522 (COP), [2011] COPLR Con Vol 632; *AH v (1) Hertfordshire Partnership NHS Trust, (2) Ealing Primary Care Trust* [2011] EWHC 3524 (COP), [2012] COPLR 327.

- Bad faith is not necessary to establish a reason to depart from the general rule.[56]
- Parties should consider whether the issue of proceedings is necessary, whether it is necessary to pursue each and every issue and to avoid duplication of costs at P's expense.
- Refusal to co-operate or a lack of co-operation prior to the issue of proceedings including in relation to pre issue disclosure of relevant documents may be relevant to costs at the conclusion of the case.[57]
- A failure to comply with the provisions of the MCA 2005 or other statutes or guidance may be relevant to the question of costs.[58]
- Failure to comply with the rules or the court's case management directions may justify the court in departing from the general rule.[59] There may be a risk of a costs order in relation to a particular hearing or a particular stage of the proceedings.
- A party that refuses to modify its position in the face of the evidence may be vulnerable to a costs order.[60]
- Public bodies can be expected to know the risks of litigation and warnings are not necessary pre-conditions for costs orders against public bodies, though warnings may be appropriate before costs are awarded against private individuals, especially those acting in person.[61]
- There are particular obligations on public bodies bringing applications in the context of safeguarding concerns, and failure to take appropriate steps to consider the evidential basis for such applications can give rise to an award of costs against them: see further chapter 24.
- The risk of a costs order should not deter applicants from bringing disputes to the court for resolution in appropriate cases.[62]

56 *G v E* [2010] EWHC 3385 (Fam), (2011) 14 CCLR 140, [2010] COPLR Con Vol 454; *AH and others* [2013] EWHC 2410 (COP).

57 *AH and others* [2013] EWHC 2410 (COP).

58 *AH and others* [2013] EWHC 2410 (COP); *WBC v CP* [2012] EWHC 1944 (COP).

59 COPR r1.4(3).

60 *AH and others* [2013] EWHC 2410 (COP); *A Local Authority v HS* [2013] EWHC 2410 (COP).

61 *AH and others* [2013] EWHC 2410 (COP); *SC v LBH* [2010] EWHC B29 (COP), *sub nom Re RC (deceased)* [2011] 1 FLR 1447, [2010] COPLR Con Vol 1022.

62 *G v E* [2010] EWHC 3385 (Fam), (2011) 14 CCLR 140, [2010] COPLR Con Vol 454; *AH and others* [2013] EWHC 2410 (COP); *Re HS* [2013] EWHC 2410 (COP).

- Failure to bring a dispute to court in a timely fashion may be a relevant factor leading to a costs order.[63]
- An unreasonable refusal to engage in ADR may leave a party vulnerable to a costs order.[64]
- Legal representatives should be alert to the need to advise the court and seek directions when another party has failed to take necessary steps which might put a hearing at risk.[65]

63 *Hillingdon LBC v Neary* [2011] EWHC 3522 (Fam), [2011] COPLR Con Vol 632; *AH and others* [2013] EWHC 3524 (Fam).

64 *Mann v Mann* [2014] EWHC 537 (Fam), [2014] 1 WLR 2807; *PGF II SA v OMFS* [2013] EWCA Civ 1288, [2014] 1 WLR 1386.

65 *Re L* [2016] EWFC B8.

CHAPTER 18

Enforcement

Introduction

18.1 Previous chapters in this book have set out the steps by which a judge can be placed in a position to determine applications relating to P (and to grant interim relief pending such final determination). Sometimes, all the court will be required to do is to grant a declaration, either as to P's (lack of) capacity or that a course of action is lawful,[1] and no substantive decisions will be taken by the court that will require enforcement. In such situations, there would be no need for the judgment and the accompanying order of the court to be enforced. Indeed, it would appear that a declaration alone is not capable of being enforced by way (for instance) of committal proceedings.[2]

18.2 However, on occasions, one (or more) of the parties to the proceedings may be required either to take or to refrain from taking specific actions. This requirement can arise in three main ways:

1) by way of case management directions made so as to secure the effective resolution of the application;
2) as a necessary consequence of a decision (for instance, that P is to be moved from their home into a care home), which can only be given effect by one or more of the parties;
3) by the court making an injunction specifically requiring one of the parties to do something or not to do something (for instance, not to have contact with P save under specified circumstances).

18.3 Court of Protection judges are well aware (especially in welfare cases) that:

> ... the mere fact that a litigant, perhaps in the heat of a frenzied battle, may breathe defiance is not to be taken by the court as necessarily an accurate reflection of what will happen in the future. The court assumes, is entitled to assume, has to assume, because otherwise the road leads to anarchy, that its orders will be complied with.[3]

18.4 Absent the ability to enforce decisions falling into the categories set out above, the Court of Protection would be toothless. This chapter discusses the mechanisms by which the court can enforce its judgments and its orders as well as its own processes.[4]

1 Under Mental Capacity Act (MCA) 2005 s15(1)(a) or (c) respectively.

2 See *MASM v MMAM and others* [2015] EWCOP 3, [2015] COPLR 239 and *Re MN (An Adult)* [2015] EWCA Civ 411, [2015] COPLR 505 at paras 87–91.

3 *Re SA* [2010] EWCA Civ 1128 at para 52 per Munby LJ.

4 The limits of those powers, especially in the context of cases where P has been removed from the jurisdiction, are explored in the judgment of Munby LJ in *Kirk v Devon County Council and another* [2017] EWCA Civ 34.

The powers of the Court of Protection

Powers drawn from those of the High Court

18.5 Before turning to the detail of the enforcement mechanisms set out in Court of Procedure Rules 2017[5] (COPR) Part 21, it is necessary first to discuss the more general powers of the Court of Protection. The Court of Protection is a superior court of record,[6] which has 'in connection with its jurisdiction the same powers, rights, privileges and authority as the High Court'.[7] This has the following consequences:

- A judge sitting in the Court of Protection can grant an injunction so as to give effect to their decision and to secure the best interests of the adult.[8] Senior Courts Act 1981 s37 provides that 'the High Court may by order (whether interlocutory or final) grant an injunction . . . in all cases in which it appears to the court to be just and convenient to do so'. The Court of Protection is, by MCA 2005 s47(1), given these same powers.[9] Such an injunction will either require a person to do a specified act or (more usually) not to do a specified act or acts. Its terms must be clear and unambiguous in order for it to be effective,[10] and the person to whom it is addressed must have proper notice of its terms.[11]

5 SI 2017 No 1035.

6 MCA 2005 s45(1).

7 MCA 2005 s47(1). See also *MASM v MMAM and others* [2015] EWCOP 3, [2015] COPLR, (2015) 18 CCLR 80 at para 13. Note that, as this work was going to press, Hayden J delivered judgment in *An NHS Foundation Trust v G and others* [2022] EWCOP 25, in which he proceeded on the basis that the court's powers derived from MCA 2005 s16(5). The correctness of this analysis is likely to be tested in due course, not least as it leads to the somewhat paradoxical outcome that the Court of Protection would appear (by this route) to have considerably wider powers to make injunctive orders than does the High Court, despite the provisions of MCA s47(1) expressly providing that it has the same powers.

8 The authorities relating to the power of the Court of Protection to grant an injunction were reviewed by Keehan J in *Re SF (injunctive relief)* [2020] EWCOP 19, [2020] COPLR 683, who confirmed that it does have such a power, and also touched upon – but did not address in terms – the power of the court to make an injunction against persons unknown. It is suggested that the court does have such a power in an appropriate case: see, by analogy, *Barking and Dagenham LBC v Persons unknown* [2022] EWCA Civ 13, [2022] 2 WLR 946.

9 *W v M and S (reporting restriction order)* [2011] EWHC 1197 (COP), [2011] COPLR Con Vol 1205 at para 21.

10 *Iberian Trust Ltd v Founders Trust and Investment Co Ltd* [1932] 2 KB 87, KBD; *R v City of London Magistrates' Court ex p Green* [1997] 3 All ER 551. See also the commentary in *Halsbury's Laws* Volume 22 (5th edn, 2012), at para 75, and *Re Whiting* [2013] EWHC B27 (Fam), [2014] COPLR 107 at para 12.

11 *R v City of London Magistrates' Court ex p Green* [1997] 3 All ER 551. See also the commentary in *Halsbury's Laws*, Volume 22, 5th edn, LexisNexis, 2012, at para 75.

- That the High Court would use its powers to grant an injunction so as to secure the interests of an adult without capacity (at least pending the final resolution of the application) had been established prior to the coming into force of the MCA 2005.[12] The power to grant an interim injunction has been codified in the Court of Protection Rules 2017,[13] and is regularly exercised so as to 'hold the ring' pending the determination of an application.
- It is also possible to grant an injunction that will continue in force after the end of proceedings. In *W v M*, a high-profile case regarding the withdrawal of treatment from M, a person in a minimally conscious state, injunctions were made in support of reporting restrictions that prevented contact being made with the lay people at the heart of the case; those injunctions were expressed so as to last for M's lifetime.[14] An analogy can also be drawn with the circumstances of *Re SA (vulnerable adult with capacity: marriage)*,[15] a case decided under the inherent jurisdiction of the High Court. In this case,[16] Munby J (as he then was) made final orders prohibiting the family members of a vulnerable adult from either themselves or by others removing her from the jurisdiction and/or arranging for her marriage save in very clearly defined circumstances. A time-limited power of arrest was attached to one provision (relating to the use of violence), but the remainder of the injunctions were expressed to run on an indefinite basis.[17]
- An order made by a Court of Protection judge (of no matter what level) has the same status as that made by a High Court judge.
- A breach of an order made by a Court of Protection judge, whether for purposes of case management or for purposes of giving effect to a judgment, can amount to a contempt of court and the court has the power to punish such contempt.[18] There are detailed

12 See, for example, *Re S (hospital patient: court's jurisdiction)* [1996] Fam 1, [1995] 1 FLR 1075 and the commentary in Ashton et al *Court of Protection Practice 2016*, Jordans, at para 1.40.

13 COPR r10.10(1)(a). See further para 10.58 onwards above.

14 *W v M* at para 70. It may be possible for reporting restrictions to continue after P's death: *Press Association v Newcastle upon Tyne Hospitals Foundation Trust* [2014] EWCOP 6, [2014] COPLR 502 and *V v Associated Newspapers Ltd and others* [2016] EWCOP 21, [2016] COPLR 236.

15 [2005] EWHC 2942 (Fam), [2006] 1 FLR 867.

16 Which pre-dated the MCA 2005 and concerned an adult with capacity, but who was vulnerable to coercion.

17 Paras 136–137.

18 See, for a discussion of the relevant powers of the High Court, *Halsbury's Laws*, Volume 24, at paras 65ff, and the commentary in the *White Book 2022* at section 3C.

provisions in COPR Part 21 relating to the procedural steps for applications for committal to prison for contempt of court, addressed further at para 18.13 onwards below. It is suggested that the underlying power to commit a person to prison (or to fine them) does not derive from the COPR, but rather, from MCA 2005 s47(1) and, in turn, the inherent, common law power of the High Court both to control its own processes[19] and to enforce compliance with its decisions.[20] Note that it would be entirely possible, in principle, for the court to hold a public authority in contempt for failing to comply with an injunction.[21]

18.6 The range of orders that the court can make under its general powers so as to compel compliance with its decisions is extensive. By way of example, in *Re HM*,[22] a case involving the abduction of an adult with impaired capacity, PM, from the jurisdiction to Israel, orders were made including:

- injunctive orders directed to PM, HM's father, including a collection order;
- orders inviting the assistance of both domestic and foreign public (including judicial) authorities;
- orders seeking information from various individuals, friends or associates of HM (including summonses to court to give evidence), from various banks, insurers and travel agents, from an airline, various telephone and email service providers and the DVLA, and from others thought to be holding monies for PM;
- freezing orders, some directed to specific individuals in relation to specific assets held by them, the other a general freezing order in respect of all of HM's assets which had been renewed from time to time;
- orders permitting frozen funds to be used to fund living expenses and to fund not merely PM's legal costs in this country and in

19 See *Days Healthcare UK Ltd (formerly known as Days Medical Aids Ltd) v Pihsiang Machinery Manufacturing Co Ltd* [2006] EWHC 1444 (QB), [2007] CP Rep 1 at paras 20–23 per Langley J.

20 See *Griffin v Griffin* [2000] 2 FLR 44 at para 21, CA per Hale LJ.

21 See, by analogy, *JS v Cardiff City Council* [2022] EWHC 707 (Admin), [2022] ACD 54 in which Cardiff City Council was held in contempt of court for failing to comply with a mandatory injunction to complete care planning for the adult in question.

22 *Re HM (Vulnerable adult: abduction)* [2010] EWHC 870 (Fam), [2010] 2 FLR 1057. Although HM lacked the material decision-making capacity, this case was decided under the inherent jurisdiction of the High Court essentially as an accident of history. It is clear that similar relief can be granted by the Court of Protection, and the authors are aware of unreported cases in which such has been done.

Israel but also the living costs of HM and her mother (KH), costs both in England and Israel and the costs of HM's guardian in Israel, together with directing a third party to transfer monies from an account in his name to an account in the name of the Official Solicitor's solicitors, directing the relevant bank to honour those instructions whatever contrary instructions they might have from PM, and subsequently directing the solicitors as to the utilisation of funds in that account; and

- orders designed to prevent PM knowing what was going on, though at the same time permitting appropriate disclosure to others.

18.7 Other examples of situations in which the court has deployed its powers under MCA 2005 s47 include:

- *The Public Guardian v XR and others*,[23] in which an order was made requiring the removal of 'any video, audio, still photography of [P] or any other person and any other written material of whatever sort, which includes content relating to the [Court of Protection] proceedings posted on social media, YouTube, or any other platform accessible to third parties forthwith'.[24]
- *Re TA (recording of hearings: communication with court office)*,[25] in which Cobb J had recourse to MCA 2005 s47 to injunct a party to proceedings from communicating with the court by email and telephone, stating that although such a course was exceptional it was proportionate to the facts of the case.

Specific powers contained in the COPR

18.8 The COPR[26] contain specific provisions relating to the enforcement powers of the Court of Protection. In particular:

- The court is given a specific power to direct that a penal notice be attached to any order. Such a notice makes clear that any person upon whom a copy of the order is served that disobedience would be a contempt of court punishable by imprisonment or a fine.[27] It should be made in the following terms: 'If you the within-named [. . .] do not comply with this order you may be held to be in

23 [2019] EWCOP 65; the case does not have precedent value, but serves as a useful example.

24 Para 34.

25 [2021] EWCOP 3, [2021] COPLR 459.

26 See also MCA 2005 s51(2)(j), providing specific authority for rules to be made for the enforcement of orders made and directions given in proceedings.

27 COPR r21.9(1).

contempt of court and imprisoned or fined or your assets may be seized.'[28] In practice, such penal notices – which are not infrequently used in welfare cases – usually also specify the precise paragraphs of the order which contain the particular act(s) that the person in question must do or not do.

- If the court does not make a penal notice direction, then a penal notice may not be attached to the order. It should be noted, however, that this does not mean that – in a suitable case – the court cannot consider whether disobedience of the order represents a contempt of court: this flows both from the provisions of the COPR themselves[29] and also from the wide powers granted to the court by MCA 2005 s47.

18.9 Further, COPR r24.2 imports into the COPR the material provisions of the Civil Procedure Rules (CPR). These provide a suite of tools which are, in practice, relatively infrequently used by the Court of Protection. They enable the party entitled to enforce a judgment or order ('the judgment creditor') to enforce such a judgment or order against another party ('the judgment debtor'). As the use of the terms 'creditor' and 'debtor' suggest, these tools are primarily directed to the enforcement of judgments or orders in relation to property and affairs. They are applicable also to enforce undertakings given to the court.

18.10 In summary, these tools (all of which are only applicable at the instigation of the judgment creditor, and in some cases only with the permission of the court) are as follows:

- The Court of Protection can transfer enforcement proceedings to the county court.[30]
- The court may make an order requiring the judgment debtor to provide specific information to court about such matters as their means.[31]
- The court may make an order requiring a third party to pay a judgment creditor a specified sum.[32]
- The court may make a charging order (which is the equivalent of a mortgage) in favour of the judgment creditor over land or other property owned by the judgment debtor.[33]

28 COPR Practice Direction (PD) 21A para 1.
29 In particular COPR r21.2(3).
30 COPR r24.2(a); CPR Part 70; 70.3.
31 COPR r24.2(a); CPR Part 71.
32 COPR r24.2(a); CPR Part 72.
33 COPR r24.2(a); CPR Part 73.

- The court may prevent certain steps being taken (by way of a stop order and stop notice) in relation to securities and funds held by the judgment debtor.[34]
- The court may issue a writ or warrant of control to enable the taking control and sale of the debtor's goods.[35]
- The court may make other provision for enforcement by way of taking control of the debtor's goods.[36]

18.11 It should be noted that CPR Part 89 (attachment of earnings), is not incorporated into the CPR. However, this makes little difference as the county court has sole jurisdiction to make an order under the Attachment of Earnings Act 1971, so a transfer to the county court would have been all but inevitable under CPR 70.3, incorporated by COPR r24.2(a).

18.12 Space precludes a discussion of the procedural steps required to invoke enforcement proceedings, but the central steps are set out clearly in CPR PD 70 (Enforcement of judgments and orders). They are, in the authors' experience, rarely invoked.

Committal proceedings

Bringing proceedings

18.13 The COPR contains detailed provisions[37] (accompanied by a practice direction[38]) relating to the procedure that applies when an application is made to a Court of Protection judge to commit a person for contempt of court. Such an application can be made in a range of circumstances, including where the person has: a) refused or neglected to do an act required by a judgment or an order within the specified time; b) disobeyed a judgment or order requiring them to abstain from doing a specific act; or c) breached the terms of an undertaking given to the court.[39] With one exception, no permission is required to bring such an application. That exception is where the application is brought on the basis that made or caused to be made a false statement in a document verified by a statement of truth (such

34 COPR r24.2(a); CPR Part 73.
35 COPR r24.2(a); CPR Part 83.
36 COPR r124.2(a); CPR Part 84.
37 COPR r21.10.
38 COPR PD 21A.
39 COPR PD 21A para 8.5.

as a witness statement). Such an application can only be brought by the Attorney-General and with the permission of the court.[40]

18.14 The provisions of the COPR do not govern the *power* to commit a person who has committed contempt (referred to as a 'contemnor') to prison. As discussed at para 18.5 above, this power is derived (via MCA 2005 s47(1)) from the High Court's common law powers in this regard. Rather, the provisions of the COPR govern the *procedure* for such applications.

18.15 The provisions of the COPR r21.10 are largely self-explanatory, requiring as they do the filing of an application notice on a COP9, accompanied (unusually) by an affidavit containing specific details set out in COPR PD 21A, most importantly of the alleged act(s) of contempt.[41]

18.16 In *Re Whiting*,[42] an application for committal for alleged breaches of orders made by the Court of Protection, Hayden J emphasised some crucial features of the committal process:

(1) the procedure has an essentially criminal law complexion. That is to say, contempt of court must be proved to the criminal standard, i.e. so that the judge is sure. The burden of proof rests throughout on the applicant (see: *Mubarak v Mubarak* [2001] 1 FLR 698);
(2) contempt of court involves a deliberate contumelious disobedience to the court (see: *Re A (A Child)* [2008] EWCA Civ 1138);
(3) it is not enough to suspect recalcitrance; it must be proved (see: *London Borough of Southwark v B* [1993] 2 FLR 559);
(4) committal is not the automatic consequence of a contempt, though the options before the court are limited – for example: (a) do nothing; (b) adjourn where appropriate; (c) levy a fine; (d) sequester assets; (e) where relevant, make orders under the Mental Health Act (see: *Jamie Malcolm Hale v Rachel Tanner* [2000] 2 FLR 879);
(5) the objectives of the application are usually dual, ie to punish for the breach and to ensure future compliance;
(6) bearing in mind the dual purpose of many committal proceedings, they should be brought expeditiously, whilst primary evidence is available and the incidents are fresh in the mind of the relevant witness. This is particularly important in the Court of Protection where there may be reliance on a vulnerable witness and where capacity might have to be assessed.
(7) It follows, therefore, that where injunctive orders are made, they should be clear, un-ambivalent and drafted with care. In my judg-

40 COPR r5.6(2)(a).

41 COPR r21.15(1).

42 [2013] EWHC B27 (Fam), [2014] COPLR 107.

ment, simplicity should be the guide.[43] Similarly, where breaches are alleged, they should be particularised with care, both so that the alleged contemnor knows exactly what, where, when and how it is contended that he is in breach, so as to be able to marshal his defence, but also to help the applicant focus on what evidence is likely to be required to establish the breach to the requisite standard of proof.[44]

18.17 In the same case, and criticising the vagueness of the evidence advanced by the local authority which brought the application for committal for contempt, Hayden J, further, emphasised that:

> What is required ... is an intellectually rigorous relationship between the lawyers and the social workers in every aspect of the Court of Protection, of course, but particularly on an application of this kind. The lawyers preparing the case must realise that establishing breaches to the criminal standard of proof requires forensic precision and the careful identification of evidence to support each of the particulars of the breach ... The process requires the lawyer and the social worker to work closely together to look at the order, to identify the breach and to marshal the material as if proving the constituent parts on a count on an indictment. Nothing less will do where the liberty of the individual is at stake.[45]

The hearing

18.18 COPR r21.27(2) makes clear that, even if the underlying proceedings are (or were) taking place in private, applications for committal are to be heard in public unless the court directs otherwise. The position is also confirmed by the Lord Chief Justice's Practice Direction: Committal for Contempt of Court – Open Court issued on 26 March 2015, which should be read also with subsequent clarificatory guidance issued.[46] That Practice Direction and Guidance gives details as to the steps that must be taken to ensure that the hearing is properly publicised, the (exceptional) circumstances under which a committal hearing can take place in private, and also as the need for publication of judgments. To emphasise the seriousness of the hearing, they will almost invariably take place with counsel robed.

18.19 If the alleged contemnor wishes at the hearing of the committal application to give oral evidence, they must be allowed to do so,[47] as

43 See also the comments of Munby LJ (as he then was) in *Re X and Y (children)* [2012] EWCA Civ 1500, [2013] Fam Law 148 at paras 61–63.

44 Para 12.

45 Para 19.

46 Available at: www.judiciary.gov.uk/publications/practice-guidance-committal-for-contempt-of-court-open-court/.

47 COPR r21.28(2).

well as to obtain legal advice if they are not represented.[48] As they constitute criminal proceedings, the alleged contemnor is entitled to legal aid, even they are not eligible for legal aid for purposes of the underlying Court of Protection proceedings.[49]

18.20 The court, when determining an application for contempt, may, in an appropriate case, commit the person to prison. COPR r21.2, however, also makes clear that the powers granted to the court under MCA 2005 s47 in respect of the punishment of contempt are not limited solely to committal to prison, but that the court can also require a person guilty of contempt of court to pay a fine or give security for his good behaviour: see also the passages from *Re Whiting* set out at para 18.16. When the Court of Protection will commit a person to prison for contempt was considered in detail in the unusual case of *P v Griffith*,[50] in which the contemnor had forged a court order to seek to obtain medical records relating to P.

18.21 In *Devon County Council v Kirk*,[51] the Court of Appeal emphasised that it only be an 'urgent and pressing' case that it would be appropriate to proceed with committal proceedings where there is an extant application for permission to appeal against a previous substantive decision of the Court of Protection.

Continuing contempt

18.22 In dismissing the contemnor's appeal in the *Griffith* case noted above, Peter Jackson LJ took the opportunity to draw attention to the opportunity that is given to all contemnors to seek to purge their contempt by making an application to the trial court, identifying that '[i]n circumstances of this kind, the sentence of a contemnor who accepts their contempt and makes a genuine apology for their behaviour will always be carefully reviewed'.[52] In *A Local Authority v B, F and G*,[53] HHJ Cardinal confirmed that the Court of Protection has

48 See, by analogy, *Hammerton v Hammerton* [2007] EWCA Civ 248, [2007] 2 FLR 1133 at para 52 per Wall LJ.

49 Under Criminal Legal Aid (General) Regulations 2013 SI No 9 reg 9(v); see also *Devon CC v Kirk* [2016] EWCA Civ 1221, [2017] 4 WLR 36 at para 52 per McFarlane LJ.

50 [2020] EWCOP 46, [2020] COPLR 822.

51 [2016] EWCA Civ 1221, [2017] 4 WLR 36 at para 28 per McFarlane LJ.

52 *Griffith v P (by her litigation friend, the Official Solicitor)* [2020] EWCA Civ 1675 at para 16.

53 [2014] EWCOP B18.

the power to make a *Hadkinson* order[54] – ie an order refusing to hear further representations in the proceedings from a person who has been found to be in contempt of court in those proceedings until such point as they have 'purged' their contempt and acceded to the court's powers. Such an order can be made in respect of any party to the proceedings who has been held in contempt. The question for the court upon such an application is:

> . . . whether, taking into account all the circumstances of the case, it is in the interests of justice not to hear the contemnor. Refusing to hear a contemnor is a step that the court will only take where the contempt itself impedes the course of justice. What is meant by impeding the course of justice in this context comes from the judgment of Lord Justice Denning in *Hadkinson v Hadkinson* [1952] P 285 and means making it more difficult for the court to ascertain the truth or to enforce the orders which it may make.[55]

Civil restraint orders

18.23 In *Re A (a patient)*[56] Sir James Munby P confirmed that the Court of Protection had the power to make civil restraint orders. Specific provisions for making such powers were subsequently inserted into COPR in 2017, and are to be found in COPR r22.1, accompanied by a practice direction (PD 22A).

18.24 COPR r22.1 requires the court, whenever it dismisses an application which is totally without merit, both to certify that fact on the order, and to consider whether to make a civil restraint order. A party can otherwise apply at any other point (using a COP9) for a civil restraint order to be made.[57]

18.25 The court has the power to make limited, extended, or general civil restraint orders. As set out in COPR PD 22A, the orders escalate in the seriousness of the consequences for the person subject to the relevant order. PD 22A therefore sets out an escalating series of hurdles that have to be passed to justify the making of a more serious form of order.

54 Named after *Hadkinson v Hadkinson* [1952] P 285.

55 *JSC BTA Bank v Mukhtar Ablyazov* [2013] EWHC 1979 (Comm) at para 13 per Popplewell J.

56 [2016] EWCOP 38, [2016] 4 WLR 141.

57 COPR PD 21A, paras 30–31.

CHAPTER 19

Reconsideration and appeals

Introduction

19.1 This chapter sets out how and when decisions can be reconsidered; how they can be appealed; and the basis upon which appeals will be considered by the higher courts.

19.2 The framework for such appeals is set down in Court of Protection Rules 2017[1] (COPR) Part 20, amplified by Practice Directions (PD) 20A and 20B. It is based around three 'tiers' of judges, outlined in PD 2A.[2] In broad terms, tier 1 judges are district judges or their equivalent; tier 2 judges are circuit judges or their equivalent (including the Senior Judge), and tier 3 judges are puisne (ie full) judges of the High Court or their equivalent nominated to sit in the Court of Protection. These terms will be used in this chapter, because they make explanation of the appellate structure much easier, but they will rarely be encountered in day-to-day practice.

Reconsideration

19.3 P, or any party or person affected by an order made without a hearing or without notice to them, has an automatic right to seek a reconsideration of that order.[3] An application should be made within 21 days of the date of the order being served (or such other period as the court may direct).[4]

19.4 Reconsideration may be undertaken on the papers or at an oral hearing,[5] and COPR r13.4 spells out who can undertake reconsideration:

- a decision taken by an authorised court officer can only be reconsidered by a judge, but can be reconsidered by any judge;[6]
- an order made by a tier 1 judge can be reconsidered by any judge;[7]
- an order made by a tier 2 judge can be reconsidered by any tier 2 judge or tier 3 judge;[8]

1 SI 2017 No 1035.
2 And given their statutory definition in COPR Part 2.
3 COPR r13.4(2).
4 COPR r13.4(3)(a).
5 COPR r13.4(4). An oral hearing can be requested: COPR r13.4(14).
6 COPR r13.4(6).
7 COPR r13.4(7).
8 COPR r13.4(8).

- an order made by a tier 3 judge can be reconsidered by any tier 3 judge.[9]

19.5 It is possible for a judge to reconsider their own decision.[10]

19.6 The COPR are silent as to whether it is possible to appeal a decision made upon without a hearing (or without notice to the party in question) if reconsideration has not been sought.[11] However, given that reconsideration is not an appeal but is, instead, an opportunity for the court to look at matters again afresh, it will therefore usually be better to seek reconsideration where possible. The proposition that reconsideration is preferable to appeal is reinforced by COPR r20.9, which provides that an application for permission to appeal may be treated, where a practice direction provides (which it does not at present) or the court directs, as an application for reconsideration under rule 13.4, where the applicant would have been entitled to seek such reconsideration.

19.7 If there are proper grounds to do so, there is nothing inappropriate in asking in the application notice that the reconsideration should be undertaken by a different judge to the one who made the first order.

19.8 The purpose of what is now COPR r13.4 and the way in which it operates were described by Her Honour Judge Hazel Marshall QC in *Re S and S*[12] in the following terms:

> [61] . . . Such a reconsideration is not an appeal. The processes in the Court of Protection are intended to give the court wide flexibility to reach a decision quickly, conveniently and cost effectively where it can, whilst preserving a proper opportunity for those affected by its orders to have their views taken into account in full argument if necessary. To that end, on receiving an application, the court can make a decision on the papers, or direct a full hearing, or make any order as to how the application can best be dealt with. This will often lead to a speedy decision made solely on paper which everyone is content to accept, but any party still has the right to ask for a reconsideration.
>
> [62] If this occurs, the court should approach the matter as if making the decision afresh, not on the basis that the question is whether there is a justifiable attack on the first order. The party making the application

9 COPR r13.4(9).

10 This flows from the use of the word 'any' in the relevant provisions of COPR 13.4(7)–(9).

11 They do, though make clear that a decision made after reconsideration has to be appealed – it cannot be further reconsidered: COPR r13.4(11).

12 [2008] COPLR Con Vol 1074.

has not had a proper opportunity to be heard, and should be allowed one without feeling that s/he suffers from the disadvantage of having been placed in the position of an appellant by an order made without full consideration of his points or his views.

What can be appealed?

19.9 Any decision of the court can be appealed.[13] This means any judicial decision can be appealed, including case management decisions, the grant or refusal of an interim application or a final decision. A decision of an authorised court officer, however, cannot be appealed, and reconsideration must be sought from a judge.[14]

Who can appeal?

19.10 Any person bound by the order of the court by virtue of operation of COPR r9.14 is, in principle, entitled to seek to appeal that order.[15] This has two consequences:

- P is entitled to seek to appeal, even where they were not joined to the proceedings;
- a person who has been served with or notified of an application form but who has not been joined as a party will also be entitled to seek to appeal.

Appellate structure

19.11 Three useful tables are set out in COPR PD 20B setting out the routes of appeal from tier 1, tier 2 and tier 3 judges respectively. In brief terms, however, usually:

- A decision of a tier 1 judge is appealed to a tier 2 judge.[16] Any second appeal from the decision of that tier 2 judge will be to the Court of Appeal.[17]

13 COPR r20.1.
14 COPR r20.4(3).
15 COPR r20.3(3).
16 COPR r20.4(2)(a).
17 COPR r20.4(1)(b).

- A decision of a tier 2 judge is appealed to a tier 3 judge.[18] Any second appeal from the decision of that tier 2 judge will be to the Court of Appeal.[19]
- A decision of a tier 3 judge is appealed to the Court of Appeal.[20]
- A decision of the Court of Appeal is appealed to the Supreme Court.

19.12 Where either the judge whose decision is being granted or a judge one or more tiers above them certifies that the appeal would raise an important point of principle or practice or there is some other compelling reason for a tier 3 judge to hear the appeal, an internal 'leapfrog' can take place from tier 1 to tier 3.[21] There is no appeal against a refusal to make such a leapfrog direction.[22]

Permission

19.13 With the exception of an appeal against an order for committal to prison, an appeal against a decision of the Court of Protection requires permission.[23]

19.14 Unless the decision under challenge is, itself, one made on appeal (in which case, see paras 19.53–19.55 below), an application for permission to appeal can be made to the judge who made the decision in question ('the first instance judge'), or to a judge in a higher tier.[24] A table can be found in COPR PD 20B setting out who can grant permission.

19.15 There is no requirement that the application is made to the first instance judge first. There are five reasons, though, why it is prudent to apply to the first instance at the time of judgment:

1) the judge is fully seized of the matter and so the application will take less time;
2) an application at this stage involves neither party in additional costs;

18 COPR r20.4(2)(b).
19 COPR r20.4(1)(b).
20 COPR r20.4(1)(a).
21 COPR PD 20B paras 3.1–3.3.
22 COPR PD 20B para 3.4
23 Mental Capacity Act (MCA) 2005 s53(4) read together with COPR rr20.5, 20.6(1) and r20.7.
24 COPR rr20.6(2)(b) read together with COPR r20.6(4) and (5). This means that permission to appeal a decision of a tier 1 judge can be made to a tier 3 judge, even though the appeal itself would be heard by a tier 2 judge (unless it was 'leapfrogged' to a tier 3 judge).

3) no harm is done if the application fails – the party enjoys two bites at the cherry;
4) if the application succeeds and the party subsequently decides to appeal, they avoid the permission stage in the appeal court;
5) no harm is done if the application succeeds but the litigant subsequently decides not to appeal.[25]

19.16 The default position is that the application will be considered by the first instance judge. If the appellant wishes to seek permission directly from the judge of the court to whom an appeal is made ('the appeal judge'), the appellant must spell this out in their appellant's notice (see further para 19.27 below).[26]

19.17 In some circumstances, it may be possible (and appropriate) to seek permission from the first instance judge at the hearing at which the decision is given. This could either be at the end of an interim hearing or at a hearing at which a reserved judgment (see para 16.65) is handed down. In such a case, then it is suggested that there is no need to file an appellant's notice in advance: it will, though, be necessary to file an appellant's notice subsequently within the requisite time frame: ie within 21 days of the decision being appealed subject to any different order being made by the first instance judge.[27]

19.18 Note that, if a ground of appeal is that the judge has failed to deal with a particular point, the judge should be given an opportunity to deal with that point at the hearing before the application for permission is made.[28]

19.19 If no application for permission is made to the first instance judge at the relevant hearing, then it will be necessary to file an appellant's notice on a COP35 form.[29] Again, subject to any different order being made by the first instance judge, this notice must be filed within 21 days of the decision being appealed. If the first instance judge announces their decision and reserves their reasons for their

25 See *T (a child)* [2002] EWCA Civ 1736, [2003] 1 FLR 531 at paras 12–13, see also the commentary in the *White Book 2022* at para 52.3.6.

26 COPR r20.10(1).

27 COPR r20.10(2)(b). In *McDonald v Rose and others* [2019] EWCA Civ 4, [2019] 1 WLR 2828, the Court of Appeal gave a useful summary of the equivalent provisions under the Civil Procedure Rules 1998 (CPR).

28 *English v Emery Reimbold and Strick Ltd* [2002] EWCA Civ 605, [2002] 1 WLR 2409 at para 25 and *In the matter of S (children)* [2007] EWCA Civ 694, [2007] CP Rep 37 at paras 23–25.

29 COPR r20.10(2).

judgment, then the date for filing the appellant's notice should be varied so as to take this into account.[30]

19.20 If the appellant wishes to seek permission to appeal from the first instance judge and the time for doing so has not yet extended, it is possible to make an application (on a COP9 form) to that judge for an extension of the time.[31] If the time for seeking to appeal has expired, the appellant's notice should include in it a formal application for an extension of time stating the reason(s) for the delay and the steps taken prior to the application being made.[32]

19.21 Respondents are not generally expected to file any submissions at the permission stage unless the court otherwise directs.[33] Permission applications are usually determined by the first instance (or where appropriate) appeal judge without a hearing. If there is an attended hearing, then it is likely to be given only a short time-listing. There is no expectation that a respondent attend a permission hearing; by analogy with the position that prevails under the CPR (which may not be exact because of the specific rules as to costs that prevail at all stages prior to the Court of Appeal[34]), it is likely that a respondent would be in difficulty seeking their costs of doing so unless their attendance has specifically been requested.[35]

19.22 Permission to appeal will be granted only where:

- the court considers that the appeal would have a real prospect of success (ie a realistic, as opposed to a fanciful, prospect of success[36]); or
- there is some other compelling reason why the appeal should be heard.[37]

19.23 If the first instance judge refuses permission, a further application for permission can be made:

30 COPR PD 20A para 5, read together with COPR r20.10(2)(a).

31 Ie for the judge to exercise their power under COPR r20.10(2)(a) to set a period for the filing of the appellant's notice.

32 COPR PD 20A paras 8–9. A respondent has the right to be heard on an application for an extension of time where permission to appeal has been given or is not required: PD 20A para 10.

33 COPR PD20A para 31.

34 See chapter 17 as to costs generally.

35 See *Jolly v Jay* [2002] EWCA Civ 277 and CPR PD 52C.

36 By analogy with the equivalent provision in the CPR: see *Tanfern Ltd v Cameron-MacDonald (Practice Note)* [2000] 1 WLR 1311, CA, at para 21 per Brooke LJ, citing *Swain v Hillman* [2001] 1 All ER 91.

37 COPR r20.8(1)(a) and (b).

- Where permission was refused by tier 1 judge, to a tier 2 or tier 3 judge.[38]
- Where permission was refused by a tier 2 judge, to a tier 3 judge.[39]

19.24 Where that second judge refuses permission without a hearing, a request can be made to reconsider that decision at a hearing.[40] However, the Senior Judge or tier 3 judge can certify an application for permission to appeal that they have refused on the papers to be totally without merit, at which point the application cannot be renewed at an oral hearing.[41] It is also not possible to appeal a refusal by an appeal judge of permission to appeal from the first instance judge (see further paras 19.53–19.55 below).[42]

19.25 The provisions of COPR r20.6 provide for permission to be granted by a judge who is two tiers above the first instance judge in the appellate structure. However, in such a case, the substantive appeal will be heard by the judge of the usual level to hear the appeal. In other words, even if a tier 3 judge has granted permission to appeal a decision of a tier 1 judge, the substantive appeal will still fall to be heard by a tier 2 judge (unless it is to be 'leapfrogged' to the tier 3 judge: see para 19.12).

19.26 An order giving permission may limit the issues to be heard, and be made subject to conditions. If a first instance judge makes an order limiting permission, then it would be open to the appellant to seek permission from an appeal judge in respect of those matters where permission was refused. If the order limiting permission was made by the appeal judge without a hearing, then it is suggested that it would be open to the appellant to seek a reconsideration of this decision at an oral hearing under the provisions of COPR r13.14. However, if the appeal judge refuses permission to appeal on the remaining issues at or after an oral hearing, it is suggested that the

38 COPR r20.6(3) and (4).

39 COPR r20.6(3) and (5).

40 COPR r20.6(6). In *SM v The Court of Protection and another* [2021] EWHC 2046 (Admin), [2021] 1 WLR 5657, Mostyn J confirmed (should such confirmation be required) that the Court of Protection is a superior court of record on an equivalent plane to the High Court, such that a decision by a judge of the Court of Protection to refuse permission to appeal is not amenable to judicial review in the same way as (currently) certain equivalent decisions within the tribunal system are.

41 COPR r20.6(7).

42 *TA v AA and another* [2013] EWCA Civ 1661, [2014] 1 WLR 3773 (concerning refusal of permission to appeal by judge of the High Court sitting as a judge of the Court of Protection; the same would also apply by analogy, it is suggested, with a refusal of permission to appeal by a circuit judge).

appellant cannot then renew their application for permission in respect of those issues at the hearing of the appeal.[43]

The appellant's notice and skeleton argument

19.27 In all cases where an appellant's notice is required, COPR PD 20A sets out in some detail what must be included.[44] The documents that are required[45] are:

- one additional copy of the appellant's notice for the court;
- one copy of a skeleton argument using, or attached to, a COP37 form, either be filed with the appellant's notice or within 21 days of filing the notice;[46]
- a sealed copy of the order being appealed;
- a copy of any order giving or refusing permission to appeal, together with a copy of the judge's reasons for allowing or refusing permission to appeal;
- any witness statements or affidavits in support of any application included in the appellant's notice;
- the application form and any application notice or response (where relevant to the subject of the appeal);
- any other documents which the appellant reasonably considers necessary to enable the court to reach its decision on the hearing of the application or appeal. PD 20A suggests – correctly – that in almost all cases this will include a chronology;[47]
- a suitable record of the judgment of the first instance judge; and
- such other documents as the court may direct.

19.28 A 'suitable record' of the judgment of the first instance judge will be:

- where the judgment has been officially recorded by the court, an approved transcript (not a photocopy);[48]
- where the judgment has been given in writing, a copy of that judgment endorsed with the judge's signature;[49]

43 See, by analogy, *Fieldman v Markovitch* [2001] CP Rep 119 and *James v Baily Gibson & Co* [2002] EWCA Civ 1690.

44 Which must either accompany the notice or be filed and served on all respondents within 21 days of filing the appellant's notice.

45 COPR PD 20A para 11.

46 COPR PD 20A paras 16–17.

47 COPR PD 20A para 14.

48 COPR PD 20A para 22.

49 COPR PD 20A para 23.

- where the judgment was not officially recorded or given in writing, a note prepared by the advocate for the appellant. For purposes of an application for permission to appeal, a note would suffice; where permission to appeal has been granted, the note should be agreed (if possible) with the advocate for the respondent and approved by the first instance judge (or, in the absence of agreement), the judge should be invited in writing to approve one of the two rival versions.[50]

19.29 Where an appellant is unrepresented before the first instance judge, it is the duty of any advocate for the respondent to make their note of the judgment promptly available – free of charge – where there is no officially recorded judgment or the court directs; similarly, if the appellant was but is no longer represented, it is the duty of their former advocate to make their note available. The appellant should, in turn, submit the note to the appeal judge.[51]

19.30 In some circumstances, the evidence given during the hearing may be of relevance to the appeal. If so, then an official transcript must be obtained or, if the evidence was not officially recorded, a typed version of the judge's notes of evidence.[52] Where the appellant is unrepresented, or represented on a pro bono basis, an application can be made (wherever possible to the first instance judge at the time of seeking permission to appeal) for a transcript of the evidence or the proceedings to be obtained at public expense.[53] Such a transcript will only be ordered if the court is satisfied that the cost of such a transcript would be an excessive burden on the appellant and there are reasonable grounds for appeal.[54] PD 20A suggests that transcripts or notes of evidence are generally not needed for purposes of seeking permission to appeal,[55] although in a case where the evidence will be of relevance if permission is granted, steps should be put in place as quickly as possible to obtain a transcript of the evidence because it can take some time to obtain.

19.31 Where it is not possible to provide a document or documents required by PD 20A with the appellant's notice, the appellant should indicate what documents have not yet been filed, why they have not

50 COPR PD 20A para 24.
51 COPR PD 20A para 25.
52 COPR PD 20A para 26.
53 COPR PD 20A paras 28–29.
54 COPR PD 20A paras 28–29.
55 COPR PD 20A para 26.

been filed and when they estimate that they can be filed (and then file and serve them as soon as reasonably practicable thereafter).[56]

19.32 In completing the appellant's notice and the accompanying skeleton argument it is necessary to be clear as to the distinction between:

- the grounds of appeal: ie what it said that the judge did wrong, which can – and should – be summarised shortly (ie 'the judge was wrong to find that P was not deprived of his liberty'), which should be set out in box 5 of the COP35 form; and
- the arguments advanced in support of those grounds of appeal: these will be set out in the skeleton argument and will be longer in form, although (as discussed at para 16.22) they should still be concise and to the point.[57]

19.33 The court will issue the appellant's notice upon it being filed; unless the court orders otherwise, the appellant must serve the appellant's notice upon each respondent and upon such other persons as the court may direct as soon as practicable and in any event within 21 days of the date on which it was issued.[58] The appellant must file a certificate of service within seven days of the date on which the notice was served.[59]

19.34 It should be noted, finally, that it is possible to apply in an appellant's notice either for a remedy incidental to the appeal or for an interim remedy, either by including the application in the notice itself or by attaching a COP9 application form to the appellant's notice (see further chapter 11 in relation to interim remedies).

The respondent's notice and skeleton argument

19.35 Unless the court directs otherwise, or unless they, too, wish to appeal, a respondent need not take any action when served with an appellant's notice until they are notified that permission to appeal has been granted (see para 19.21 above in relation to the role of respondents pre-permission).[60]

19.36 Where the respondent has been notified that the permission has been granted (or that the application for permission to appeal has

56 COPRPD 20A para 12.

57 See also COPR PD 20A paras 18–21 in relation to the contents of skeleton arguments accompanying appellants' notices.

58 COPR r20.10(3).

59 COPR r20.10(4).

60 COPR PD 20A para 32.

been listed to be heard together with the appeal itself), what they should then do will depend upon what they wish to request of the appeal judge:

- if the respondent wishes to request that the decision of the first instance judge be upheld for the reasons given by that judge, they do not need to file a respondent's notice;
- if the respondent wishes to request that the decision of the first instance judge be upheld for reasons different to or additional to those given by the first instance judge, they need to file a respondent's notice (on a COP36 form), otherwise they will not be able to rely upon such reasons except with the permission of the court.[61]

19.37 If a respondent also wishes to seek permission to appeal, the respondent should file a respondent's notice.[62] Logically, because permission to appeal has already been granted to the appellant, either by the first instance judge or the appeal judge, and the case is therefore destined to be heard on appeal, permission to the respondent to cross-appeal must be sought from an appeal judge, rather than from the first instance judge.[63]

19.38 Where a respondent's notice is necessary, then (unless the first instance judge makes an order to different effect) it must be filed within 21 days of whichever is the soonest of:

- the date on which the respondent was served with the appellant's notice (ie where permission to appeal was given by the first instance judge or permission was not required);
- the date on which the respondent was served with notification that an appeal judge has given the appellant permission to appeal; or
- the date on which the respondent was served with notification that the application for permission to appeal and the appeal itself are to be heard together.[64]

19.39 There is no express equivalent to the provisions set out in PD 20B providing for applying for extensions of time in relation to the filing of the respondent's notice. However, it is suggested that the same procedure as set out at para 19.20 above would be likely to apply.

61 COPR rr20.11(1)(b) and 20.14(5) and PD 20A paras 33–34.

62 COPR r20.11(1)(a); PD 20A para 31. Permission, where necessary, must be sought in the respondent's notice: COPR r20.11(2).

63 COPR r20.11(1)(a) only speaks of seeking permission to appeal from a judge other than the first instance judge.

64 COPR r20.11(4).

Especially where an application is made after the expiry of the period for filing of the notice, it is suggested that it would be prudent to ensure that the respondent's notice details the reason(s) for the delay and the steps taken prior to the application being made.

19.40 The same requirements as to service of the respondent's notice and the filing of a certificate of service apply to respondent's notices as to appellant's notices.[65]

19.41 Unsurprisingly, what a respondent must provide in and with a respondent's notice[66] is very similar to what an appellant must provide in and with an appellant's notice, save that the respondent is not under the same obligation as the appellant to provide such documents as a suitable record of the judgment.

19.42 In any case where the respondent wishes to address arguments to the court (ie whether or not they have filed a respondent's notice), they must file and serve a skeleton argument.[67] If the respondent files a respondent's notice, then the skeleton argument must either accompany that notice or be filed and served within 21 days of filing that notice.[68] If the respondent does not file a respondent's notice, then any skeleton argument must be filed and served at least seven days before the appeal hearing.[69]

19.43 The same requirements apply to the contents of the respondent's skeleton argument as to those of an appellant, with the added – unsurprising – requirement that it should, where appropriate, answer the arguments set out in the appellant's skeleton argument.[70]

The position between the grant of permission and the determination of the appeal

19.44 It is not unknown for the appellant's case to change after the grant of permission. In such a case, the appellant's representatives should write to the appeal court and to the other party, indicating the proposed nature of the changed case. The court should be asked to

65 COPR r20.11(5)–(6).

66 Set out in COPR PD 20A para 40. A respondent can also apply for incidental relief: PD 20A para 41.

67 COPR PD 20A para 44.

68 COPR PD 20A paras 45–46. A certificate of service is required: PD 20A para 49.

69 COPR PD 20A para 47.

70 COPR PD 20A para 48.

indicate whether it will deal with the matter at the beginning of the hearing of the appeal or whether it will give directions on an earlier date. After being informed of the respondent's attitude, the court can decide whether to shut out the new grounds or allow them to be argued.[71] Similarly, if there has been a material change in circumstances after the grant of permission, which would affect the question of whether permission should have been given, the applicant should inform the court in writing.[72] A failure to take either step will waste money and court time, and may have adverse cost consequences.[73]

Determination of appeals

19.45 It is, in principle, open to the appeal judge to deal with all or part of an appeal without a hearing.[74] However, as reconsideration can be sought of an order made without a hearing (see above paras 19.3–19.8), appeal judges will often err on the side of ordering a hearing, especially where they have gleaned from the prior history that the appellant will be likely to seek reconsideration.

19.46 An appeal judge has all the powers of the first instance judge whose decision is under appeal.[75] The appeal judge can in particular, if they allow the appeal, decide the issue in question themselves, rather than sending it back to the first instance judge (or ordering a new hearing before a first instance judge). Appeal judges will, however, be cautious about deciding cases themselves unless there is plainly only one answer: wherever it is a question of evaluation, it is more usual for the matter to be remitted to a first instance judge (whether that be the one who initially heard the case or another judge) to consider it in the light of the judgment of the appeal court.

19.47 The starting point in relation to appeals is that they are reviews, rather than re-hearings.[76] It would only be in very unusual circumstances that the appeal court will undertake a re-hearing; the

71 See by analogy, *Shire v Secretary of State for Work and Pensions* [2003] EWCA Civ 1465, [2004] CP Rep 11 at paras 6–7.

72 See, by analogy, *Walbrook Trustees (Jersey) Ltd v Fattal* [2008] EWCA Civ 427 at para 49.

73 See, by analogy, *R (a child)* [2010] EWCA Civ 303, [2010] 2 FLR 1138, at paras 14–16.

74 COPR r20.3(2), having regard to the factors set out in COPR r3.6(3).

75 COPR r20.13(1).

76 COPR r20.14(1).

appeal court will therefore not usually receive either oral evidence or evidence that was not before the first instance judge, although the appeal court has the power to do all three.[77] While the MCA 2005 and COPR are silent as to the circumstances under which fresh evidence will be admitted, it is suggested that the appropriate test to apply is that which applies in civil proceedings, namely consideration of whether:

- the evidence could have been obtained with reasonable diligence for use at the trial;
- the evidence is such that, if given, it would probably have an important influence on the result of the case, though it need not be decisive; and
- the evidence is such as is presumably to be believed; ie whether it is apparently credible, though it need not be incontrovertible.[78]

19.48 By way of an example of a circumstance in which it was appropriate to receive fresh evidence, we note the case of *Aintree University Hospitals NHS Foundation Trust v James*,[79] concerned with whether life-sustaining treatment should be withheld from a critically ill patient in a minimally conscious state. Here, the Court of Appeal received fresh evidence as to the deterioration in the patient's condition between the time of the hearing before the first instance judge and the date of the hearing before the Court of Appeal. The Supreme Court ultimately found that the Court of Appeal had been right to determine that – at that point the case was before the Court of Appeal, and on the basis of that fresh evidence – it was in the man's best interests not to receive life-sustaining treatment.[80]

19.49 The COPR provides that an appeal will be allowed where the decision of the first instance judge is a) wrong; or b) unjust, because of a serious procedural or other irregularity in the proceedings before the first instance judge.[81] In the Supreme Court decision in *Aintree University Hospitals NHS Foundation Trust v James*, Lady Hale, relying upon *Re B (a child) (care proceedings: appeal)*,[82] held that, where a judge of the Court of Protection had correctly directed themselves as

77 COPR r20.14(1)(b) and (2)(a) and (b) respectively.

78 See *Ladd v Marshall* [1954] 1 WLR 1489, CA, *Terluk v Berezovsky* [2011] EWCA Civ 1534 and the commentary in the *White Book 2022* at para 52.21.3.

79 [2013] EWCA Civ 65, [2013] 4 All ER 67.

80 *Aintree University Hospitals NHS Foundation Trust v James* [2013] UKSC 67, [2014] AC 591.

81 COPR r20.14(3).

82 [2013] UKSC 33, [2013] 1 WLR 1911.

to the law, an appellate court could only interfere with their decision as to the evaluation of best interests if satisfied that it was wrong.[83] This approach was then applied by the Court of Appeal in an appeal from the Court of Protection in *R v Chelsea and Westminster Hospital NHS Foundation Trust and others*.[84]

19.50 This approach gives rise to two important, related, points:

- The majority of the Supreme Court in *Re B* (albeit not Lady Hale herself) had held in the context of proceedings relating to children that it is not for an appellate court itself to conduct a 'de novo' assessment of the proportionality of any interference with rights enjoyed by parties under the European Convention on Human Rights (ECHR). In other words, unless – exceptionally – it considers that it is necessary to conduct a re-hearing, the appellate court is confined to reviewing the decision of the first instance judge as to the proportionality of the interference. Given that almost every best interests decision taken by the Court of Protection will engage one or more rights under the ECHR, this suggests strongly that the same approach will apply in the context of almost all appeals against best interests decisions. The *PW* case is an example of exactly this approach being applied.
- While the majority of the Supreme Court in *Re B* rejected the addition of any gloss to the word 'wrong' (such as 'plainly'), Lady Hale made clear in *Aintree* that in sensitive and difficult cases (which will, by definition, be those most likely to attract appeals), appellate courts should be very slow to find that a first instance judge's evaluation of best interests is wrong. The threshold for intervention by the appellate courts is therefore a high one.

19.51 Where the appeal lies not against an evaluative decision but against the exercise of a discretion (most obviously in the context of case management decisions), then the test is subtly different: the appellate court should only interfere if 'satisfied that the judge erred in principle, took into account irrelevant matters, failed to take into account relevant matters, or came to a decision so plainly wrong that it must be regarded as outside the generous ambit of the discretion entrusted to the judge': *Re TG (children) (care proceedings: case management: expert evidence)*.[85]

83 At para 42.

84 [2018] EWCA Civ 1067, [2018] COPLR 346 at para 48.

85 [2013] EWCA Civ 5, [2013] 1 FLR 1250 per Munby LJ (as he then was) at para 35.

19.52 It should be noted that where an appeal is to a tier 2 judge (against a decision of tier 1 judge) or to a tier 3 judge (against the decision of either a tier 2 or (in a 'leapfrog' case a tier 1 judge)), then the normal costs rules contained in the COPR apply (see chapter 17).

Second appeals

19.53 A decision which was, itself, made on appeal, can only be appealed to the Court of Appeal.[86] Permission must be sought from the Court of Appeal for such an appeal, and the test (contained in the CPR, not the COPR) is stricter. The Court of Appeal will only grant permission where:

- the appeal would have a real prospect of success, and raise an important point of principle or practice; or
- there is some other compelling reason for the Court of Appeal to hear it.[87]

19.54 This rule does *not* apply if the appeal is against a decision of a tier 3 judge sitting in the Court of Protection as a first instance judge; in that case, permission can be sought either from that tier 3 judge or from the Court of Appeal.[88]

19.55 It is important to note that a decision from an appeal court refusing permission to appeal to that court from a lower court is not a 'decision' for these purposes: it is not possible to appeal such a refusal.[89]

Appeals to the Court of Appeal and Supreme Court

19.56 As noted at the outset of this chapter, appeals to the Court of Appeal and Supreme Court fall outside the scope of the COPR. If, therefore,

86 COPR rr20.4(1)(b) and 20.5(3).

87 CPR 52.7(1). On a strict reading of the CPR, this provision does not apply to second appeals from the Court of Protection, as this court is not mentioned there, but it is suggested that it is overwhelmingly likely that the Court of Appeal would apply this test in the exercise of its inherent case management jurisdiction.

88 COPR r20.5(2).

89 *TA v AA and another* [2013] EWCA Civ 1661 (concerning refusal of permission to appeal by a judge of the High Court sitting as a judge of the Court of Protection; the same would also apply by analogy, it is suggested, with a refusal of permission to appeal by a circuit judge (now tier 2 judge)).

an appeal is being considered against a decision of a tier 3 judge sitting in the Court of Protection as a first instance judge, then the relevant rules to apply are not the COPR but rather those set out in CPR Part 52, as amplified by PDs 52A and 52C. CPR Part 52 and PDs 52A and 52C can be found in the supporting materials section. They are, in most respects, very similar to the rules set out in the COPR and discussed above, and are not rehearsed here.

19.57 If an appeal lies from a decision of the Court of Appeal to the Supreme Court in relation to a matter that was originally determined by a judge of the Court of Protection, the relevant procedural rules are set out in the Supreme Court Rules 2009[90] and the associated practice directions. These can be found on the Supreme Court website;[91] they are not addressed here because they are beyond the scope of this work. The only point that should be noted is that it does not appear that there is a possibility for a 'leapfrog' appeal to be made directly to the Supreme Court from a decision of a High Court judge sitting in the Court of Protection. The relevant provisions of the Administration of Justice Act (AJA) 1969 allow such a 'leapfrog' appeal in respect of 'civil proceedings in the High Court'.[92] It is, however, suggested that a judge of the High Court sitting as a Court of Protection judge is not hearing civil proceedings in the High Court.[93]

19.58 In any appeal to the Court of Appeal the costs rules set out in the COPR do not apply. Unless an application is made under CPR 52.19 (as to which, see below), the normal costs rules set out in the CPR will apply, and the unsuccessful party will be ordered to pay the costs.[94] In *Cheshire West and Chester Council v P (No 2)*,[95] Munby LJ rejected an argument made on behalf of the unsuccessful party, P, that there should be no order as to costs because proceedings in the Court of Protection were analogous to public law family proceedings

90 SI 2009 No 1603.

91 See: www.supremecourt.uk/procedures/rules-of-the-court.html.

92 AJA 1969 s12(2).

93 See, by analogy, *TA v AA and another* [2013] EWCA Civ 1661 and the discussion at para 55 of that case of the earlier decision in *Re B (a patient) (Court of Protection: appeal)* [2005] EWCA Civ 1293, [2006] 1 WLR 278.

94 This is now contained in CPR 44.2(2)(a); prior to 1 April 2013, this was contained in CPR 44.3(2)(a).

95 [2011] EWCA Civ 1333, [2012] COPLR 76.

(and appeals therefrom) which are exempt from the material provisions of the CPR.[96] Munby LJ held:[97]

> I cannot accept Mr Gordon's argument of principle. It comes perilously close to an impermissible invitation to us to re-write [CPR 44.2], whether by incorporating within it the principle in r157 of the Court of Protection Rules or by adjusting CPR r[44.2(3)] to include a reference to the Court of Protection. Our task is to apply CPR r[44.2]. I accept, of course, that we can properly have regard to the fact that the appeal concerns a vulnerable adult in the context of the court's protective functions and not, for example, a valuable cargo in the context of a commercial dispute, but this is not because of some supposed analogy with either [CPR r44.2] or r157 of the Court of Protection Rules. It is simply because it is one of the 'circumstances' – and, it may be, one of the more important of the circumstances – to which CPR r44.3(4) bids us have regard.[98]

19.59 It is suggested that the Court of Protection is (for these purposes) either a 'no costs' or a 'low costs' jurisdiction, by virtue of the specific costs provisions in COPR Part 19, which differ from those applying in conventional litigation. It is therefore suggested that it is possible for an application to be made by either party for an order under CPR 52.19 limiting the recoverable costs of an appeal to the extent that the court specifies. In making such an order, the Court of Appeal will have regard to:

- the means of both parties;
- the circumstances of the case; and
- the need to facilitate access to justice.

19.60 As the Court of Appeal explained in *JE (Jamaica) v Secretary of State for the Home Department*:[99] 'The rule deals with appeals coming up from a 'no costs' or a 'low costs' jurisdiction. It enables the appeal court to put in place a similar regime to that which applied in the court or tribunal below'.[100] The Court of Appeal in the same case noted the importance of any application being made at any early stage, so that both parties know the costs regime under which they are proceeding; if the appellant is seeking the order, it may be 'convenient and economic' to include such an application in the

96 These are now contained in CPR 44.2(3)(a); prior to 1 April 2013 they were contained in CPR 44.3(3)(a).

97 Para 6. The references to the CPR have been amended to reflect the position that prevails post 1 April 2013.

98 See also *Re P (discharge of party: costs of appeal)* [2021] EWCA Civ 992.

99 [2014] EWCA Civ 14, [2014] 1 Costs LR 163.

100 Para 8, per Jackson LJ.

appellant's notice, but that is not required by the rule. The application will then be determined in writing unless the court orders otherwise.[101]

19.61 The costs rules that apply in relation to appeals to the Supreme Court are contained in Supreme Court Rules Part 7; they are beyond the scope of this work.

101 CPR 52.19(4).

CHAPTER 20

Alternative dispute resolution

Introduction

20.1 While there are some legal issues which may need to be fully litigated in court or where the court's determination is required (most notably, authorisation of deprivation of liberty), there is a wide range of disputes which can be resolved or narrowed by other forms of dispute resolution. There is no clear-cut distinction between the types of cases needing a court-based resolution and those which can be otherwise resolved. Indeed, the vast majority of disputes would benefit from well-timed attempts at seeking a narrowing of the issues or a complete resolution without each and every matter being litigated in full. There is, however, no simple formula for categorising the cases which can be resolved through alternative dispute resolution (ADR) and those which cannot. Even where court involvement is required, it is still possible for the parties to reach agreement on some, or even all of the issues and place an agreed order before the court for consideration.

20.2 It is important to recognise that as the person without capacity is in a particularly vulnerable position when discussions by other parties take place, care must be taken to ensure that they are properly supported and represented during this process. Their interests remain central and their participation (in whatever form is appropriate in the individual case) is crucial.

20.3 In cases where agreement is reached or where issues are narrowed, and proceedings are underway, the agreement should be carefully drawn up by the legal advisers in the form of a consent order and submitted to the court for approval. It is the court (and not just the parties) which needs to be satisfied that any agreement has a lawful basis and is in P's best interests. As decision-maker, the court also needs to be satisfied that P's participation has been properly facilitated.[1]

20.4 In common with the expectations in other forms of civil and family litigation, advisers are expected to discuss the possibility of mediation or other forms of ADR before litigating and to keep this decision under review during the proceedings. As Lord Justice Dyson stated in 2005:[2]

> All members of the legal profession who conduct litigation should now routinely consider with their clients whether their disputes are suitable for ADR.

1 By operation of Mental Capacity Act (MCA) 2005 s4(4).

2 *Halsey v Milton Keynes General NHS Trust* [2004] EWCA Civ 576, [2004] 1 WLR 3002.

20.5 While not specifically focusing on Court of Protection disputes but reporting on ADR more generally, the Civil Justice Council's recommendation in its July 2021 report *Compulsory ADR*[3] is an indicator of the direction of travel. In publishing the report, the Chair of the Judicial/ADR Liaison Committee and lead judge for ADR, Lady Justice Asplin, said:

> This report addresses questions which are central to the shape and design of dispute resolution in the twenty-first century.
>
> We have concluded that (A)DR can be made compulsory, subject to a number of factors. More work is necessary in order to determine the types of claim and the situations in which compulsory (A)DR would be appropriate and most effective for all concerned, both in the present system and in relation to online justice.
>
> Our conclusions place another useful and powerful tool in the box. They also provide the opportunity to initiate a change of culture in relation to dispute resolution which will benefit all concerned'[4]

20.6 As referred to in chapter 17, a refusal to agree to ADR and even silence in the face of an invitation to participate in a form of ADR will be unreasonable behaviour and is likely to risk an adverse costs consequence.

20.7 A wide range of methods of ADR may be used in the life of a Court of Protection case, ranging from informal discussions outside court, round table meetings between the parties, attempts to distil the issues in correspondence, to formal mediation processes that are independently facilitated.

20.8 The Case Management Pilot introduced 'dispute resolution hearings' (DRHs) for property and affairs cases.[5] These are a form of judge-led mediation, held confidentially 'off the record', and are discussed in more detail at paras 8.32–8.41 above. More broadly, the Pilot also required the parties to make efforts to resolve disputes outside the court arena in respect of cases falling within the welfare pathway set out in the Pilot. The Pilot procedures are now cemented into the procedures of the court through Court of Protection Rules 2017[6] (COPR) Practice Direction (PD) 3B, the 'Case Pathways' practice direction.

3 See: www.judiciary.uk/wp-content/uploads/2021/07/Civil-Justice-Council-Compulsory-ADR-report-1.pdf.

4 See: www.judiciary.uk/announcements/mandatory-alternative-dispute-resolution-is-lawful-and-should-be-encouraged/.

5 Case Management Pilot PD para 5.4.

6 SI 2017 No 1035.

20.9 This chapter will:

- examine the guidance about ADR in the Court of Protection;
- consider the obligations on litigants to use ADR; and
- consider the options and how they may work in the context of the Court of Protection.

Code of Practice

20.10 The Code of Practice[7] to the MCA 2005 provides guidance to decision-makers about managing 'conflicting concerns' when establishing the best interests of a person who lacks capacity. The new draft Code has been published for consultation at the time of writing.

20.11 At the time of writing, para 5.64 of the Code reads:

> The decision-maker will need to find a way of balancing these concerns or deciding between them. The first approach should be to review all elements of the best interests checklist with everyone involved. They should include the person who lacks capacity (as much as they are able to take part) . . . It may be possible to reach an agreement at a meeting to air everyone's concerns. But an agreement in itself might not be in the person's best interests. Ultimate responsibility for working out best interests lies with the decision-maker.

20.12 Chapter 15 of the Code concerns settling disagreements. The Code stresses again the importance of the person without capacity having support and representation,[8] including during mediation.[9]

20.13 The Code advocates mediation as a means of solving a problem at an early stage. The Code makes a number of claims for mediation, which it describes as offering a wider range of solutions than court proceedings as well as having the potential to be 'less stressful, more cost-effective and quicker. People who come to an agreement through mediation are more likely to keep to it, because they have taken part in mediation'.[10]

20.14 The Code refers to the availability of legal aid funding for mediation but states this is available mainly for family mediation.[11] This is not entirely correct: see para 20.48 below.

7 Available at: www.gov.uk/government/publications/mental-capacity-act-code-of-practice.

8 MCA Code of Practice para 15.3.

9 MCA Code of Practice para 15.6.

10 MCA Code of Practice para 15.7.

11 MCA Code of Practice para 15.13.

20.15 The emphasis in the Code on co-operation does not detract from the need to refer matters to the court where it is not possible to reach agreement: see *G v E (deputyship and litigation friend)*[12] and *Hillingdon LBC v Neary*.[13] In addition, as referred to above, there will be some issues which require the involvement of the court, for example cases concerning the authorisation of P's deprivation of liberty, even if the parties are agreed. The parties should not delay placing such matters before the court even if ADR can take place in parallel with the ongoing proceedings.

Court of Protection Rules

20.16 The COPR require parties to help the court in furthering the overriding objective of dealing with cases justly.[14] In addition, COPR r1.4(2)(c) requires that the parties co-operate with one another and with the court in identifying and narrowing the issues that need to be determined by the court.

20.17 Judges are required to further the overriding objective by 'active case management', described in COPR r1.3(3) as including:

> (d) encouraging the parties to co-operate with each other . . .
> (h) encouraging the parties to use an alternative dispute resolution procedure if the court considers that appropriate . . .

20.18 As discussed in more detail in chapter 10, this is often reflected in practice. For example, judges may routinely include in standard directions a requirement that the parties should take steps to seek to narrow the disputes between them. This may be expressed simply as a requirement to attend court an hour before the hearing takes place, in order to have discussions. Sometimes the Court of Protection may make a direction requiring the parties to make contact with each other before the day of the hearing. However it would be a mistake for parties to rely on express directions being needed – if an order is silent on these matters the parties are nonetheless required to co-operate and to identify areas which can be resolved throughout the proceedings. While attending court for discussions on the day of the hearing is usually sensible, discussions to resolve or narrow the issues need to start at a far earlier stage.

12 [2010] EWHC 2512 (Fam), [2010] COPLR Con Vol 470.
13 [2011] EWHC 1377 (COP), [2011] COPLR Con Vol 632.
14 COPR r1.4.

20.19 As set out in chapter 9, the COPR Case Pathways PD 3B requires an applicant before issuing a welfare application to engage with potential respondents and explore how the dispute can be resolved without proceedings.[15] While the Case Pathways PD 3B does not expressly refer to ADR in the issues to be considered by the judge at the case management hearing, it is implicit in PD 3B para 4.5 that the court will consider this as part of its duty of active case management. As noted above, and discussed further in chapter 8, judicial ADR in the form of a dispute resolution hearing (DRH) should be the norm in contested property and affairs applications.

Case-law

20.20 There are no reported cases that give specific guidance as to mediation or ADR in this jurisdiction. In *A Local Authority v PB and P*,[16] Charles J was invited to comment on the issue of mediation or ADR but declined on the basis that this had not arisen in the facts of the case that he was considering.

20.21 The use of ADR is far more established in the family courts. Some assistance can be found by analogy in the case of *AI v MT (alternative dispute resolution)*[17] Baker J approved a consent order which had been reached after a lengthy arbitration process by a separating couple overseen by the New York Beth Din. The principles he identified in the context of the family courts are of relevance in the Court of Protection:

- the court's jurisdiction cannot be ousted by agreement between the parties;
- unless statute provides otherwise, the child's welfare is the paramount consideration;
- respect for the practice and beliefs of all faiths and cultures does not oblige the court to depart from the welfare principle because this principle is 'sufficiently broad and flexible to accommodate many cultural and religious practices';
- it is always in the interests of the parties to try to resolve disputes by agreement if possible and the courts will encourage this but will be cautious not to endorse a process which might oust the jurisdiction of the court.

15 COPR Case Management Pilot PD para 4.2.1.
16 [2011] EWHC 502 (Fam), [2011] COPLR Con Vol 166.
17 [2013] EWHC 100 (Fam), [2013] 2 FLR 371.

20.22 In *S v S*[18] Sir James Munby P considered the approach of the courts when there has been an arbitration award, in that case, under the Institute of Family Law Arbitrators Scheme (a not for profit organisation, conducting arbitrations in accordance with the Arbitration Act 1996). He observed that the fact that the parties had bound themselves to accept an arbitral award generated a 'single magnetic factor of determinative importance'; and that in the absence of very compelling evidence to the contrary this should be determinative of the order made. In these circumstances the judge's role was not to be 'a rubber stamp. He is entitled but is not obliged to play the detective. He is a watchdog, but he is not a bloodhound or a ferret.'[19] If an attempt is made to resile from an arbitral award, the court may be robust in case managing the dispute, and may in some cases simply make the order in any event. The President noted the increasing range of forms of ADR and the need for the courts to keep up with developments and the needs of litigants and advisers.

20.23 In *Re B (a child) (unnecessary private law applications)*,[20] HHJ Wildblood QC referred to a raft of 'micro management' family dispute issues which were being placed before the court, 'clogging up' the court list. An example of such an issue was given the question at which junction of the M4 a child should be collected for contact. He warned of consequences in respect of those cases being brought unnecessarily, while confirming that those which are genuinely necessary should be referred to the court. The same approach should apply by analogy to cases within the Court of Protection.

The Select Committee

20.24 The Select Committee of the House of Lords conducting post-legislative scrutiny of the MCA 2005[21] considered the role of mediation. It noted a limited pilot scheme proposed by the Office of the Public Guardian (OPG), though was disappointed by the limited terms of the pilot and the fact that mediation would be conducted by

18 [2014] EWHC 7 (Fam); [2014] 1 WLR 2299.

19 *S v S* at para 20, citing his own judgment in *L v L* [2006] EWHC 956 (Fam), [2008] 1 FLR 26.

20 [2020] EWFC B44.

21 *Mental Capacity Act 2005: post-legislative scrutiny*, HL Paper 139, March 2013, paras 224–232; available at: www.publications.parliament.uk/pa/ld201314/ldselect/ldmentalcap/139/139.pdf.

telephone, in an area where building relationship and trust is crucial. It concluded that:

- mediation in the Court of Protection must comply with the decision-making framework of the MCA 2005 and provision must be made to ensure representation of P's views and interests;
- mediation would be beneficial in many cases prior to issue and consideration should be given to making it a pre-requisite for launching proceedings, especially financial proceedings where under the general rule the costs will fall to P's estate.

20.25 In its response – *Valuing every voice, respecting every right*[22] – the government agreed mediation would be suitable in some property and affairs cases, but less so in health and welfare cases. The government did not consider mediation should be a prerequisite to issuing as this would detract from its voluntary nature.

P's involvement

20.26 As referred to above, the special nature of Court of Protection proceedings which concern P's capacity and best interests requires particular care to be taken in ensuring that the person is facilitated and supported to participate in any ADR process, and that their voice is properly heard. This is not the same as P always attending every meeting or mediation although there will be some cases where this is appropriate. Rather the key task is to ensure that the other parties do not reach an agreement without P being properly represented or heard – after all the dispute is about P's life and reaching an agreement over P's head will in most cases be inappropriate.[23]

20.27 P's input can be secured in a number of ways. Independent legal representation is vital, and can assist in ensuring P's participation throughout the process. If P does not attend the ADR process in person, they can be assisted to prepare a statement or an attendance note of a discussion with them setting out their views may be an option. They may be able to have input into all or some of the discus-

22 '*Valuing every voice, respecting every right: Making the case for the Mental Capacity Act – The Government's response to the House of Lords Select Committee Report on the Mental Capacity Act 2005* (June 2014)': www.gov.uk/government/uploads/system/uploads/attachment_data/file/318730/cm8884-valuing-every-voice.pdf.

23 In the research leading to the creation of the mediation pilot discussed at paras 20.29–20.30 below, only 58 per cent of Ps in the mediations considered were legally represented.

sion by remote platform or they may be able to attend in person for at least some of the meeting. Where P has a litigation friend, often the Official Solicitor, the litigation friend is bound by the principles in MCA 2005 s4(4) to facilitate their participation and is obliged to act in their best interests. They may decide that P should not attend the ADR process in their best interests (for example as it may be too distressing) but secure their participation in another way.[24] It is for the litigation friend to decide how best to ensure P's participation.[25]

20.28 The Vice President of the Court of Protection, Hayden J, issued guidance in February 2022 regarding judicial visits to P, predominantly focused on serious medical treatment cases.[26] He has also reapproved (and republished) the previous guidance on participation of P from Charles J in 2016 which sets out valuable suggestions as to how P's participation can be facilitated. This guidance is not prescriptive, but includes very helpful practical pointers as to a raft of different ways that P can participate in proceedings, which are equally applicable to a mediation or other ADR process.

The Court of Protection mediation pilots

20.29 Research on mediation in the Court of Protection[27] led to an informal mediation pilot which ran for roughly two years from 2019. A formal evaluation is still awaited, but the report of a round table convened by Dr Jaime Lindsay (who will conduct the evaluation)[28] makes very interesting reading, in particular in its nuanced discussion of the benefits and challenges of mediation.

20.30 In addition, the OPG launched a mediation pilot in 2018 for property and affairs disputes concerning LPAs and also deputy appointments.[29] This scheme is expressly intended to avoid the need

24 *A County Council v AB and others (participation of P in proceedings)* [2016] EWCOP 41, [2016] COPLR 576.

25 *A County Council v AB and others (participation of P in proceedings)* [2016] EWCOP 41, [2016] COPLR 576.

26 *Practice Guidance (Court of Protection: Judicial visits)* [2022] EWCOP 5, [2022] 1 WLR 1445.

27 C May, 'Court of Protection mediation research: Where are we in the UK?', May 2019, available at: www.adultcaremediation.co.uk/Court_of_Protection_Mediation_Research_190531.pdf.

28 Availableat:http://repository.essex.ac.uk/28658/1/Mediation%20roundtable%20report_2020.pdf.

29 For details, see: https://publicguardian.blog.gov.uk/2019/02/18/testing-how-an-opg-mediation-service-might-help-protect-vulnerable-people/.

for proceedings to be issued in relation to disputes concerning LPAs and deputies. Cases of neglect or abuse or where criminal action may be involved are not suitable for mediation under the pilot. The scheme is no longer running, and no formal evaluation of it appears to have been published.

Mediation and ADR in practice – types of ADR and how to decide between them

20.31 Although there is, at the time of writing, no formal structure to the use of ADR in Court of Protection proceedings, the two most common types of ADR will be round table meetings (RTMs) and mediation.

20.32 There is nothing to prevent the parties from agreeing to mediate, and further details are set out below.

Round table meetings

What they are and how they work

20.33 Round table meetings (RTMs) are often suggested by parties, or sometimes by judges of their own motion. They are almost always a very helpful way of the parties discussing the case issues away from the pressure of a court hearing, often in the period between one hearing and another. RTMs are often hosted by legal advisers, solicitors or barristers' chambers. They may take place in local authority offices or in a different venue such as a conference facility. They may also take place by remote video (or, less often, telephone) in some cases however there are obvious limitations not least that there is no face to face communication. Remote discussions can be helpful in most cases for the parties' legal advisers to try to narrow legal disputes or to agree further directions in advance of a hearing.

20.34 Standard directions will often include a provision encouraging the parties to take part in an RTM and will sometimes specify when it should take place and who is responsible for convening the meeting, arranging minutes and preparing an agreed note. If an expert is to attend the RTM it is prudent to include provision for payment of the expert's fees in the order. The Court of Protection Handbook website includes (as part of a wider precedent directions order for welfare cases) a precedent set of directions for an RTM: see www.courtofprotection handbook.com.

20.35 The main differences between an RTM and a mediation is that an RTM is not facilitated by an external independent mediator, and an RTM is usually on the court record (although see below). In welfare cases, an RTM is often chaired by the solicitor or barrister acting for P. The rationale behind this is that they are more likely to be seen as neutral than the other parties and to ensure that P's interests are central to the discussions.

20.36 An RTM will usually involve the parties and their legal advisers. In some cases independent experts attend as well. In many cases solicitors rather than barristers will attend the meeting with their clients, and everyone attending will be present during the meeting unless they need to consider their positions privately. It is often appropriate to ascertain if, in addition to the main meeting room, any other rooms are available so that confidential discussions between lawyers and their clients can take place and to provide some space if any participant needs a break from the meeting. These rooms are sometimes described as 'breakout rooms'.

20.37 There are no rules governing the conduct of RTMs, so it is essential when the meeting is scheduled and before it starts for the participants to address their minds to the following questions:

- How will P's participation be secured?
- Will the discussions be confidential, or can they be referred to in the litigation? If the latter, how will the contents of the meeting be recorded and how will an agreed note of the discussion be produced? It would be possible for there to be a split meeting with confidential discussions taking place and then, if all parties agree, for there to be an 'open' ie on the record meeting.
- What is the status of any agreement reached at the RTM?
- Who is going to attend the meeting? If an expert is required then their availability will need to be confirmed in advance.
- Who is going to chair the meeting?
- What will be on the agenda and who will take the lead in suggesting agenda items in advance?
- If it is physically attended, will the venue be suitable? Will there be enough space and is there a 'breakout room' or rooms for confidential discussions?

Advantages and disadvantages

20.38 RTMs can often be arranged more quickly than formal mediation. They are cheaper, as there are no mediator fees, and if they are held remotely there are no venue fees. It can sometimes be productive to suggest an RTM at the very early stages of a dispute, even in pre-action correspondence, particularly in financial cases. A dispute between a family member and social work staff may have become entrenched. Sometimes the involvement of lawyers, both for the family member and the statutory body, can help the parties narrow the issues and an RTM at this stage may avoid the need for litigation at all.

20.39 As with all forms of ADR, one advantage of an RTM is it can allow the parties to reach an outcome which could not be achieved through litigation alone – for example, an apology, or agreement to investigate an issue about which a party is concerned. It also enables the parties to discuss the issues away from the pressure of the court process.

20.40 The significant disadvantage at this early stage may be that it is unlikely that P will be legally represented, and thus it will be difficult or even impossible to ensure P's effective participation. As we have seen above, the MCA Code suggests that P might be supported by an advocate during mediation. Even if an advocate is involved, this may still, however, result in two parties to a dispute – for example, the local authority and family members – being legally represented at an RTM, while P remains without legal advice or representation. This risks decisions being made without P's voice being properly heard contrary to the fundamental principles set out in the MCA 2005.

20.41 Often the best time for an RTM to be most successful is part-way through the proceedings when the dispute between the parties has been set out in initial evidence, and perhaps when an expert report is available. It is when the issues have been clarified to at least some extent in evidence that an RTM can be most helpful. It can provide a useful opportunity for the parties to stand back and to review the evidence and their positions and see whether the dispute can be resolved or at least the issues narrowed and crystallised. Through representation the parties can also be assured that the focus is on P.

20.42 RTMs will be challenging if there is a particularly difficult relationship between two or more parties, as they tend to involve the participation of all the parties, and some may not be legally represented. Not all lawyers feel comfortable chairing RTMs, and the lawyer may be seen as less objective than an external mediator because the lawyer may already have had to express a view on important issues on an interim basis which may have been unpopular with one or more of the parties. Sometimes if the RTM is unproductive and appears to be worsening relationships it may need to be abandoned. However, in most cases many of the less controversial minor issues can be resolved and also further directions may be capable of agreement which can then be presented to the court for approval. Most RTMs result in at least some issues being resolved, and any remaining areas of dispute being clarified.

Mediation

20.43 This section provides a very basic summary of what mediation is, and then looks at the issues arising when mediating Court of Protection cases. Readers interested in learning more about mediation are recommended to read *Making mediation work for you,*[30] on which this section draws.

What mediation is

20.44 Mediation can take various different forms, and it is important not to prescribe the format or content from the start. The very advantage of mediation is to think outside the box and to seek to explore the dynamic between the parties to assist in reaching agreement which may not be readily apparent from a legal perspective.

20.45 However, all mediations share the following characteristics:

- An independent mediator is used to facilitate the process.
- The identity of the mediator should be agreed by all the parties.
- Mediation is confidential (though there are some exceptions) – the aim is that this encourages parties to be open and flexible. What one party says to the mediator in a private session will not be disclosed to the other without permission.
- Mediation is 'without prejudice' – the discussions which take place cannot be referred to in litigation.
- Mediation is a voluntary process – parties cannot be forced to mediate and they are free to leave the process part way through if they wish.
- Mediation is non-binding in that the parties are not obliged to reach agreement.
- If the mediation results in agreement, this can be recorded in the form of a legally binding agreement which can then be disclosed in the court proceedings.

20.46 The involvement of an independent trained mediator can bring benefits to a case where the parties may find it difficult to see solu-

30 Kate Aubrey-Johnson with Helen Curtis, *Making mediation work for you*, LAG, 2012.

tions. A skilled mediator will try to identify the parties' real interests and motivations in the case, which can be masked by the parties' stated legal positions. The mediator will try to draw out areas of common interest between the parties, which can generate solutions which are not always obvious.

Practicalities

20.47 Although mediation may avoid the need for a contested hearing if it is successful and may therefore save money, it is not a cheap option, and it is important to anticipate the likely cost and make arrangements about how this is to be met. A mediator will require the parties and/or their representatives to sign an agreement to mediate in advance, and this will include details as to how the mediator's costs will be met, as well as costs of the venue.

20.48 The mediator's fees and venue costs are usually shared by the parties who are mediating. If any of the parties are legally aided, then the mediator's fees will be a disbursement on the party's legal aid certificate. Prior authority should be sought from the Legal Aid Agency (LAA) (see chapter 6). If the case is considered to be 'high cost'[31] the costs should also be included in the case plan submitted to the LAA for approval. Advisers should ensure that they have identified all the potential costs of the mediation, including the costs of the lawyers' preparation and attendance. Other costs may, for example, include room hire and refreshments; whether the length of the mediation has been under-estimated; or it may have been suggested that any experts who have reported should also attend the mediation, in which case they will also charge.

Finding a mediator

20.49 Finding a mediator who will be able to conduct an effective mediation in a Court of Protection case can be daunting. There are different types of mediator, reflecting the different specialist areas of mediation – civil, family, workplace and community mediators. There is no single body which regulates mediators. Family mediators are accredited by organisations which belong to the Family Mediation Council. The Civil Mediation Council (CMC) accredits mediation providers, who must have a panel of at least six mediation

31 A reference to the High Cost Case scheme operated by the LAA for cases where overall costs including solicitors, barristers' costs and disbursements are likely to exceed £25,000 excluding VAT.

providers who can show that they meet the CMC's accreditation standards. Thus, individual mediators will not themselves be accredited by the CMC. The Ministry of Justice maintains a directory of mediators accredited by the CMC which can be searched by geographical area. Individual mediators will be accredited if they have been trained by a body recognised by the CMC.[32] The Law Society has an accreditation scheme for civil and commercial mediators.[33] The LAA operates a legal aid contract for mediators, however this is in family law.

20.50 In addition to checking the mediator's accreditation and expertise, it is advisable to ask to see their CV and ask about the cases they have taken on which show their experience with P. This is particularly important given the particular skills required in ensuring P's participation in the mediation process.

Preparation for the mediation

20.51 For those who have proposed mediation or responded to a suggestion by the court or another party, it is essential to consider what to expect from the mediation. This is not the same as defining the scope of the mediation – it is important to keep an open mind and think 'outside the box'. Advisers will, however, need to have a clear grasp of the strengths and weaknesses of the client's legal case. Perhaps for this reason, many Court of Protection mediations take place after the receipt of experts' reports, if these are being obtained. This is an ideal time to take stock of the evidence as it now stands, in as objective a way as possible. This may be difficult because of the highly charged atmosphere that can develop in Court of Protection disputes, especially in cases involving a relationship between family carers and statutory bodies, which may have been deteriorating over a number of years before matters come to a head and proceedings are issued. Advisers may find it helpful to underline to their clients the potential benefit of the involvement of a neutral and independent mediator who will not take sides and whose focus is on seeing where there are areas of agreement rather than conflict. A mediator should manage the mediation process in such a way that parties can adopt a fresh perspective on the strengths and weaknesses of their position without losing face. Perceptions can shift in the course of mediation which can help parties move from their initial stated position to something more flexible.

32 See: http://civilmediation.justice.gov.uk.

33 See: www.lawsociety.org.uk.

20.52 In anticipation of the mediation the following issues should be considered, although it is important not to be prescriptive about the scope and nature of mediation:

- Assuming that new evidence (especially in the form of expert reports) has been received, what if any impact has this evidence had on the views and positions of the parties?
- Advisers should explore with their clients as neutrally as possible whether there are any areas where the party can make an offer or suggestion which might help to promote an agreement. These might be matters that could not be achieved through litigation alone. This could include eg an apology; an agreement to make a gift in kind; an investigation; or an agreement to work with the other parties in a different manner in the future. Possible offers that might be sought from the other parties should also be considered.
- It is important to evaluate in the light of the evidence what the client can realistically achieve in the litigation. If mediation fails to deliver an agreement, what is the likely outcome of a contested hearing? If an adviser's client is legally aided, is there any risk that the client's legal aid will be not be extended to cover a contested hearing if mediation fails? In other cases is there a risk of costs?
- Is there any reason (on an objective evaluation) to believe that any of the other parties have agreed to mediate in bad faith (ie without any intention of participating positively and simply ticking the box of mediation)?
- The benefits to mediation should be weighed, even if it is unlikely to deliver a full resolution: might it narrow the issues or at least improve the parties' ability to communicate? Mediation almost always brings greater understanding between the parties even if not all issues are agreed.
- With this point in mind, advisers are encouraged to manage their clients' expectations so that if it is unsuccessful it is not a waste of their time in trying.
- Practicalities – will the parties agree to sit in the same room for all or any of the process? This is usually an important part of progressing relations between the parties to achieve a resolution.
- In the civil sphere, an unreasonable refusal to mediate can give rise to costs sanctions: see *Halsey v Milton Keynes General NHS Trust*.[34]

34 [2004] EWCA Civ 576, [2004] 1 WLR 3002. See also *PGF II SA v OMFS* [2013] EWCA (Civ) 1288, [2014] 1 WLR 1386.

The costs implication of a refusal to mediate in the Court of Protection sphere is considered at paras 17.25–17.27.

20.53 It is not always necessary for the mediator to be provided with all the papers filed in a case. However the mediator may need to see at least some of the documents from the Court of Protection proceedings. Before mediating the parties will need to try to agree the contents of a bundle of core documents for the mediator. The court will need to give permission to disclose this information to the mediator. This could be the subject of an application on a COP9 application form, usually by consent.

20.54 The mediator will usually speak to the parties or their legal advisers in advance of the mediation. This can be a useful opportunity to agree the procedure to be followed and can make attending the mediation itself less daunting. Some mediators invite the parties to prepare a short position statement in advance. This should not be a duplication of the legal documents already drafted but should set out what the party wants to achieve, how they feel about the dispute, as well as what they think would help to break any impasse. This statement should ideally be disclosable to all parties in advance of the mediation. However, in some cases the mediator may also accept a statement which a party states should be for the mediator's eyes only and not sent to any other party.

20.55 The mediator may ask the parties to make a short opening statement at the beginning of the mediation session about their feelings and what they want to achieve. Where parties feel unable to be in the same room, this can be delivered between the legal representatives and then shared with their respective clients in private rooms, or the party's legal representative can deliver the message to the rest of the attendees.

20.56 It is highly likely that the mediator will ask the parties to sign an agreement to mediate in advance of the mediation. The contents of this will vary but the agreement will probably contain the following provisions:

- who is responsible for the mediator's fees and when these will be paid;
- confirmation that the parties have agreed to mediate voluntarily;
- confidentiality, perhaps with a provision that nothing said during the mediation will be referred to in the litigation;
- confirmation that if the mediation is successful then either the whole agreement, or if not, the headline terms of agreement may be disclosed to the court;

- any ground rules the mediator considers necessary, including the discretion to end the mediation;
- a requirement that whoever attends on behalf of the parties has 'authority to settle' ie that they have the power to reach an agreement on that party's behalf.[35]

The mediation process

20.57 Mediation is a flexible process which can be designed to fit the needs of the parties involved. Many mediations will commence with a plenary meeting, where all the parties gather in one room and where the mediator will introduce themselves and explain the procedure to be followed. Opening statements may be made during this session. Typically, after this the parties will then retreat to separate rooms, while the mediator speaks to them in turn. This can take time, and mediation can often seem to involve a considerable amount of waiting to hear how the other party has responded or what the other party may propose.

20.58 The mediator will seek to establish the parties' core interests to explore potential common ground which may provide an opening for agreement. The mediator may want to explore how one party would react in the event that a particular concession or change in position is made by one of the parties. The mediator may also consider that it is helpful for an issue to be explored which is not immediately central to the proceedings to assist in unlocking the dynamic between the parties. The parties need to be open to looking at the dispute in different ways from the legal process which is more limited.

20.59 Court of Protection cases pose particular challenges. P's interests need to remain central to the process. If P is a party, P will almost invariably have a litigation friend or accredited legal representative (ALR) who is likely to be present (or be represented) at the mediation. The litigation friend or ALR should make every attempt to ascertain P's wishes and feelings on the issues which are being mediated. By definition, P is unlikely to be able to take part fully in the process of compromise and give-and-take that may be involved in mediation. It is the mediator's role to ensure that P remains the focus of the mediation and to reduce the time spent disproportionately on satellite issues which may be considered important by the other parties.

35 For statutory bodies (or any other corporate body) it is vital that whoever attends the mediation has the power within the organisation to settle the dispute on the day of the mediation, or can seek such authority immediately, so as not to derail the process.

20.60 The second difficulty is that Court of Protection cases will frequently involve an imbalance of power between the parties, as they may typically involve a dispute between a statutory body and one or more individuals. It is suggested that this requires the mediator to satisfy themselves that even though one party may be in a much stronger position, that party remains willing genuinely to consider an element of compromise and be able freely to offer an agreement to settle. An experienced mediator should be alert to both these issues.

20.61 If agreement is reached, it is usually at the end of a long session which has required considerable energy and commitment by all concerned. The agreement should be put in writing. In the authors' experience, this is usually done by the legal advisers. This needs to be done with care and it is tempting at the end of a successful mediation to think that all that needs to be done is for the agreement to be reflected in writing, but this is often when the agreement may unravel, so must be tackled with extreme care, attention to detail and patience.

20.62 Once proceedings have started, the court will need to approve any agreement before it is fully binding. However, it is undesirable to be in the position of resiling from a signed mediation agreement. It is absolutely essential that there is sufficient time, even at the end of what may have been a long day, for advisers to satisfy themselves that their client fully understands, and is willing to comply with, the mediation agreement. If a party needs, for example, to consider their position overnight, see if this can be agreed but there is always a risk that the momentum and impetus may be lost. Asking the mediator to assist in the final stages by telephone is an option, or even fixing a further mediation session shortly afterwards to ensure that the progress made is not lost.

20.63 If the mediation is successful, then in accordance with the terms of the mediation agreement the mediation agreement should be sent to the judge for approval, who will need to be satisfied that the outcome is one that can properly be said to be in the best interests of P. It is not enough for the parties to reach their own agreement, the reasons why it is in P's best interests will need to be explained to the court as decision-maker.

CHAPTER 21

Office of the Public Guardian

Introduction

21.1 The role of Public Guardian, and the Office of the Public Guardian (OPG), were established by Mental Capacity Act (MCA) 2005 ss57–61. Before the MCA 2005, a similar role and office had existed, but with a less wide-ranging remit. Full contact details for the OPG can be found in appendix G below.

21.2 The OPG is an executive agency sponsored by the Ministry of Justice through which the Public Guardian caries out his statutory functions.

21.3 Since it was established, the OPG has seen, and continues to see, significant year on year increases in workload. By the end of 2021, there were over 5 million registered powers of attorney and slightly under 60,000 deputy orders. The OPG has made significant steps towards offering online services and many lay deputies are now completing their annual report online with the service due to be extended to local authority deputies and then professional deputies. More services are expected to be offered digitally in future as part of the OPG's 'OPG 2025' strategy[1] and all deputies and attorneys should ensure that they remain up to date on the OPG's requirements and services.

Responsibilities

21.4 Under MCA 2005 s58(1), the Public Guardian is responsible for:

(a) establishing and maintaining a register of lasting powers of attorney,

(b) establishing and maintaining a register of orders appointing deputies,

(c) supervising deputies appointed by the court,

(d) directing a Court of Protection Visitor to visit:

(i) a donee of a lasting power of attorney,

(ii) a deputy appointed by the court, or

(iii) the person granting the power of attorney or for whom the deputy is appointed ('P'),

and to make a report to the Public Guardian on such matters as he may direct,

1 See the OPG's Business Plan for 2021–2022; see also para 3.241 and the discussion of the Ministry of Justice's proposals to modernise lasting powers of attorney (LPAs).

(e) receiving security which the court requires a person to give for the discharge of his functions,
(f) receiving reports from donees of lasting powers of attorney and deputies appointed by the court,
(g) reporting to the court on such matters relating to proceedings under this Act as the court requires,
(h) dealing with representations (including complaints) about the way in which a donee of a lasting power of attorney or a deputy appointed by the court is exercising his powers,
(i) publishing, in any manner the Public Guardian thinks appropriate, any information he thinks appropriate about the discharge of his functions.

Register of lasting powers of attorney and deputies

21.5 The MCA 2005 updated the law with regard to the provisions that can be made by an individual to appoint a decision-maker (attorney) to make certain decisions on their behalf should they lose the capacity in the future.[2]

21.6 Prior to 1 October 2007, an enduring power of attorney (EPA) allowed a donor (the person who wishes to make arrangements for someone else to look after their finances if they are unable to do so in future) to appoint an attorney (or attorneys) to deal with their finances both immediately after the signing of the document and in the future, should the donor lose their capacity. The scope of an EPA was limited to financial affairs. To be valid, the EPA must be in the prescribed format and have been signed by all parties on or before 30 September 2007.

21.7 An EPA does not need to be registered to be used, although the attorneys named in the document are under a duty to register the document with the OPG when they believe that the donor has lost, or is losing their capacity.[3]

21.8 Properly created EPAs are still valid, although the authors are aware of considerable anecdotal evidence that banks and other financial institutions refuse to acknowledge these documents unless they are now registered. This is becoming increasingly the case as EPAs become less common.

21.9 From 1 October 2007, the MCA 2005 replaced EPAs with lasting powers of attorney (LPAs), of which there are two varieties:

2 See also chapter 7.
3 Enduring Powers of Attorney Act 1985 s4(2).

- property and affairs – which covers the donor's financial matters; and
- health and welfare – which allows a donor to nominate attorney(s) to take decisions about their future medical treatment, care and other related matters if they lost the capacity to do so themselves.

21.10 A property and affairs LPA is similar in function to the old EPA but crucially it cannot be used until it has been registered with the OPG. The special feature enjoyed by both EPA and LPA is that the authority conferred by them continues after the donor has lost their capacity. All other types of power of attorney are automatically revoked by the donor's incapacity.

21.11 The process for validly entering into an LPA lies outside the scope of this work, but is the subject of detailed guidance and commentary[4] (see also chapter 7). The OPG has a helpful range of documents available to download that take the prospective donor through the process of making an LPA, registering it and acting as an attorney.[5]

21.12 The range of options for entering into an LPA now includes an online tool[6] for generating a document to be printed off, signed and submitted for registration. It is hoped that innovations like this will help donors to ensure that the document they create is valid and complete and thereby reduce the number of applications for registration that are returned by the OPG each year for the rectification of minor errors or omissions.

21.13 LPAs are more detailed than the EPAs they replaced, and allow more scope for a donor to give specific advice to their chosen attorneys about how they want decisions to be made on their behalf. Restrictions can be placed upon the powers of the attorneys both in relation to finance and welfare and the donor may set out guidance for her attorneys to follow when discharging their duties. The nature of this guidance will depend upon the wishes and circumstances of the donor, but may include religious or ethical considerations, or stipulations as to specific decisions that attorneys may not take without further authority of the court (for example, to sell a property or valuable artefact). There are also specific requirements that must be followed if a donor of an LPA wishes to grant the power to their attorneys to refuse life-sustaining treatment. Those who are advising

4 See in particular D Lush and C Bielanska, *Cretney & Lush on Lasting and Enduring Powers of Attorney*, 9th edn, LexisNexis, 2022.

5 See: www.gov.uk/government/publications/make-a-lasting-power-of-attorney.

6 See: www.lastingpowerofattorney.service.gov.uk.

a donor entering into an LPA should ensure that they make the donor aware of these options and requirements.

21.14 Advisers to both donors entering into LPAs and attorneys acting under an LPA should ensure that their clients are aware of the limits to the scope of their powers under LPAs. In the authors' experience the extent of an attorney's authority is frequently misunderstood. There would seem to be common misunderstandings and assumptions in relation to powers to gift and invest money, as well as their options when deciding on care arrangements under a health and welfare LPA. Ensuring that all parties have clarity at the time that arrangements are made will help to avoid problems, including possibly interventions by the court, in future. Details about the court's powers in relation to EPAs and LPAs can be found in chapter 7 (it should be noted that the OPG has the power to – and regularly does – apply to the Court of Protection to sever ineffective provisions in LPAs under provisions of MCA 2005 Sch 2 para 11[7]).

21.15 It is also worth noting that the OPG only maintains a register of instruments for England and Wales. Arrangements for decision-making for those who lack capacity will vary significantly in jurisdictions outside England and Wales (including Northern Ireland and Scotland). For further information see chapter 27.

Searching the registers

21.16 Anyone may apply to search the registers of EPAs, LPAs and deputyships maintained by the OPG.[8] A search is made by completing an OPG100 form[9] and submitting it to the OPG. It is important when completing this form to identify which of the registers the applicant wishes to have searched, in cases of uncertainty a search of all three is advised. There is no charge for making an application and the OPG will provide a result in five working days.

21.17 In Spring 2021, the OPG launched a new rapid register search, aiming to respond to requests within 24 hours, Monday to Friday. Requests made over the weekend will be dealt with on Monday as a

7 For examples of orders made in this regard, see: www.justice.gov.uk/protecting-the-vulnerable/mental-capacity-act/orders-made-by-the-court-of-protection/lasting-powers-of-attorney.

8 Under Lasting Powers of Attorney, Enduring Powers of Attorney and Public Guardian Regulations 2007 SI No 1253 reg 31.

9 See: www.justice.gov.uk/protecting-the-vulnerable/mental-capacity-act/orders-made-by-the-court-of-protection/lasting-powers-of-attorney.

priority. Requests that are not for safeguarding enquiries must use the OPG100 form. Requests that are about COVID-19 patients should use the dedicated search.[10]

21.18 The OPG policy is that the registers include:

- the name of the person the power of attorney or deputyship order is about;
- the date of birth of the person the power of attorney or deputyship order is about;
- whether the register entry relates to an LPA, EPA or deputyship order;
- whether the LPA, EPA or deputyship order relates to property and financial affairs or health and welfare;
- the date the LPA, EPA or deputyship order was registered;
- whether an LPA, EPA or deputyship is registered, cancelled, revoked or expired;
- the names of attorneys (people appointed under an LPA or EPA) or deputies (people appointed by the court);
- whether there are conditions or restrictions in the LPA, EPA or deputyship order – these will not be disclosed but we will tell an applicant if they exist;
- how attorneys or deputies are appointed to act;
- when deputyship orders expire, if this has been stated by a judge.

21.19 Information will only be provided if there is an exact match between the details provided on the application form and those held on the registers. If there is a close but not exact match the OPG may contact the applicant for more information.

21.20 If the applicant is wishes to obtain additional information this can be requested by completing the relevant boxes on the OPG100 form. The OPG consider additional information to include anything related to a person that the Public Guardian has obtained while carrying out his functions, but which is not on the registers. If an application includes a request for additional information, then the result of the search of the registers will be provided first. A decision will then be taken about whether to provide the additional information requested.[11] The OPG considers such applications on their merit and any information provided is at the discretion of the OPG The additional information will be provided if the OPG considers it is reasonable

10 More details can be found on the OPG website: www.gov.uk/guidance/urgent-enquiries-check-if-someone-has-an-attorney-or-deputy.

11 Under Lasting Powers of Attorney, Enduring Powers of Attorney and Public Guardian Regulations reg 32.

and justified to do so, or where there is a legal basis for disclosing it.[12] All requests for additional information are considered on a case-by-case basis.

21.21 A search will not reveal any details about EPAs/LPAs that have not yet been registered, or any applications for the appointment of a deputy that are pending with the court. It also does not include details of any other types of order made by the court, for example those authorising a statutory will. If this information is sought, then an application must be made to the court and the usual rules of disclosure under the Court of Procedure Rules 2017[13] (COPR) will apply (for more on disclosure, see chapter 14).

'Use your LPA service'

21.22 For LPAs registered after 1 January 2016, it is possible for the attorney or donor to create an account under the 'Use your LPA' service,[14] which can be used to:

- allow people or organisations to view a summary of an LPA;
- keep track of which people or organisations have been given access to an LPA;
- view an LPA summary;
- see how people named on the LPA are using the service.

21.23 The precise mechanics will differ depending upon whether the LPA was registered between 1 January 2016, or on or after 17 July 2020.

Supervision

21.24 When a new deputyship order is made, the court will notify the OPG so that they can begin to supervise the new deputy to ensure that he understands his duties and is acting correctly and effectively.

21.25 In 2015, the OPG overhauled the supervision regime. There had previously been four levels of supervision each attracting a different annual fee, and a deputy could expect to move between these levels as experience, circumstances and asset levels altered over time.

12 Lasting Powers of Attorney, Enduring Powers of Attorney and Public Guardian Regulations reg 32(2).

13 SI 2017 No 1035.

14 See: www.gov.uk/use-lasting-power-of-attorney.

21.26 There are now two levels of supervision:

1) General Supervision – this is allocated to all cases in their first year; and
2) Minimal supervision – deputies managing total assets of £21,000 or less on behalf of P will normally be moved down to this level after the first year of the deputyship.

21.27 The new supervision regime supports a more targeted approach to supervising deputies with team focussing on particular groups of deputies such as local authority deputies, lay deputies or professional deputies.

Annual reports

21.28 Deputies are required by the OPG to produce a report each year detailing how they have managed P's funds and who they have consulted with when making decisions.[15] These reports may be audited and the OPG may require that invoices, receipts or other evidence of expenditure is submitted.

21.29 From 1 March 2016, the report forms were amended to widen the scope of the report. In particular, the new reports ask for information about how recently P's capacity was assessed. Professional deputies should note that an estimate of future costs is also required on form OPG105.

21.30 The annual reports are straightforward for most deputies, but lay deputies may wish to instruct an accountant or solicitor to prepare them if P's finances are more complicated. The costs of professional advice can be met from P's funds.

Court Visitors

21.31 One of the most important ways in which the OPG keeps in touch with deputies and provides ongoing supervision and support is through the network of Court of Protection Visitors.

21.32 The OPG maintains two panels of experts, or Visitors, on behalf of the Lord Chancellor. MCA 2005 s61 provides that:

15 MCA 2005 s19(9)(b).

61 Court of Protection Visitors

(1) A Court of Protection Visitor is a person who is appointed by the Lord Chancellor to–
  (a) a panel of Special Visitors, or
  (b) a panel of General Visitors.

(2) A person is not qualified to be a Special Visitor unless he–
  (a) is a registered medical practitioner or appears to the Lord Chancellor to have other suitable qualifications or training, and
  (b) appears to the Lord Chancellor to have special knowledge of and experience in cases of impairment of or disturbance in the functioning of the mind or brain.

(3) A General Visitor need not have a medical qualification.

(4) A Court of Protection Visitor–
  (a) may be appointed for such term and subject to such conditions, and
  (b) may be paid such remuneration and allowances, as the Lord Chancellor may determine.

(5) For the purpose of carrying out his functions under this Act in relation to a person who lacks capacity ('P'), a Court of Protection Visitor may, at all reasonable times, examine and take copies of–
  (a) any health record,
  (b) any record of, or held by, a local authority and compiled in connection with a social services function, and
  (c) any record held by a person registered under Part 2 of the Care Standards Act 2000, Chapter 2 of Part 1 of the Health and Social Care Act 2008 or Part 1 of the Regulation and Inspection of Social Care (Wales) Act 2016,

  so far as the record relates to P.

(6) A Court of Protection Visitor may also for that purpose interview P in private.

21.33 Generally a lay deputy can expect to have a visit from a General Visitor within the first 12 months of their appointment. This will usually take the format of a meeting with the deputy, and P, face-to-face to discuss how the deputy is managing in their role.

21.34 As well as routine visits as part of the ongoing supervision regime, the OPG can request a general visit for many reasons, for example:

- when a deputy is new to the role;
- to answer questions and make sure the deputy understands and can meet their responsibilities;
- if the OPG need reassurance that the deputy is acting in accordance with the terms of order and in P's best interests;
- for access to paperwork, for example bank statements, receipts etc; and
- when the OPG is carrying out an investigation.

21.35 The Visitor will contact the deputy in advance to arrange a suitable time for the meeting and to provide details of what information and paperwork they need access to.[16] They will usually wish to meet with the deputy and P separately; they may also wish to meet with third parties such as a care manger, social worker etc. Court Visitors carry identification and will show this when they visit.

21.36 After a visit, a report will be prepared for the OPG, making recommendations – for example, about issues that need to be monitored or the appropriate time before a follow-up visit needs to be scheduled.

21.37 Deputies may request a visit if they feel that the OPG can provide support with a particular issue.

21.38 The court has wide-ranging powers to call for reports.[17] Where a medical report is required, the OPG Special Visitors can be commissioned to undertake this role. This can be useful, for example when P does not wish to co-operate with an assessment of capacity, or if there is a dispute as to P's capacity. See further for the role of Visitors in this regard para 13.47 onwards.

Investigations

21.39 The Public Guardian has the power to conduct investigations into the conduct of attorneys and deputies. The Court of Protection can order that a report be made to the Public Guardian by a deputy.[18]

21.40 Anyone who has concerns about the conduct of an attorney or deputy may raise these concerns with the OPG. Investigations will usually centre on the attorney or deputy's management of P's finances, and allegations of suspected financial abuse, but may encompass other aspects of the attorney or deputy's behaviour in relation to P.

21.41 Following an investigation, the OPG will produce a report which will make recommendations. In the event that the OPG concludes that it is in P's best interests to do so an application can be made to the Court of Protection. The OPG does not require permission to make such an application.[19] The court will hold the OPG to the same

16 Lasting Powers of Attorney, Enduring Powers of Attorney and Public Guardian Regulations 2007 reg 44.

17 MCA 2005 s49.

18 MCA 2005 s19(9)(b).

19 COPR r8.2(a)(ii).

standards as any other applicant in terms of the conduct of the proceedings.[20]

21.42 The Public Guardian undertook 3,099 investigations in the financial year 2019/20; the number declined by almost 1,000 for the financial year 2020/21 as a result of the suspension of physical visits to customers in the pandemic. The Public Guardian completed 2,073 investigations in 2020/21 compared to 2,649 in 2019/20 and at year end had 680 open cases which were active investigations compared to 700 open cases in 2019/20.[21] It is the experience of the authors that the OPG has grown more robust in recent years and more willing to litigate when necessary.

21.43 The case of *The Public Guardian v JM*[22] looked at the interface between a police investigation into the conduct of an attorney and an investigation by the OPG. In his judgment, former Senior Judge Lush noted that:

> 44. There are significant differences between a police investigation and an investigation conducted by the OPG. When the police investigate an alleged crime, they need to consider whether there is sufficient evidence to present to the Crown Prosecution Service ('CPS') to guarantee a realistic prospect of conviction . . .
>
> 45. By contrast, an investigation by the OPG is concerned primarily with establishing whether an attorney or deputy has contravened his authority under the Mental Capacity Act 2005, or has acted in breach of his fiduciary duties under the common law of agency, or has behaved in a way that is not in the best interests of the person who lacks capacity. The standard of proof, 'on the balance of probabilities', is lower than the criminal standard.

21.44 This case is a reminder to attorneys, as well as deputies, and their advisers that the Court of Protection will still act to remove an individual who it believes has not acted in P's best interests, despite that individual not facing prosecution for their actions.

Panel deputies

21.45 The OPG maintains a panel of professional deputies who can be appointed as property and affairs deputy for P where there is no other

20 See *Re JBN* [2019] EWCOP 62, [2020] COPLR 587 and para 17.25.

21 Office of the Public Guardian Annual Report and Accounts 2020-2021, available at: www.gov.uk/government/publications/office-of-the-public-guardian-annual-report-and-accounts-2020-to-2021.

22 [2014] EWHC B4 (COP), [2014] COPLR 188.

suitable person to take on the role. Panel deputies are 'deputies of last resort' as in most cases the deputy will be a member of P's family or a legal professional who is already familiar with P.

21.46 The court will often order the appointment of a panel deputy in cases where there has been a dispute within the family as to who should be a property and affairs deputy or where there has been abuse. For further details about disputed applications for the appointment of a property and affairs deputy; the revocation of EPAs, LPAs and deputyships; and the choice of deputy see chapter 7 above.

CHAPTER 22

Deprivation of Liberty applications in the Court of Protection

Introduction

22.1 This chapter considers applications to the Court of Protection which concern deprivation of P's liberty, and therefore engage P's rights under Article 5 of the European Convention on Human Rights (ECHR).[1] Article 5 prohibits deprivation of liberty other than 'in accordance with a procedure prescribed by law', on only then in certain cases, including the lawful detention of those 'of unsound mind'. In very brief terms, Article 5 will be engaged where three elements are present:[2]

1) the 'objective element': confinement in a particular restricted space for a not negligible length of time; and
2) the 'subjective element': there is no valid consent. Lack of objections from a patient without capacity is not consent; and
3) the deprivation must be imputable to the state.

22.2 It follows, therefore, that unless the state can demonstrate that it is applying a legal framework when it deprives a person of their liberty, that detention is unlawful, and may attract an award of damages for violation of the person's Article 5 rights.

22.3 The deprivation of liberty safeguards (or 'DOLS') regime was introduced by the Mental Health Act (MHA) 2007 in the form of Schedule A1 to the Mental Capacity Act (MCA) 2005. These safeguards were introduced to seek to fill the legislative lacuna (known as the 'Bournewood gap') which was exposed in the important case of *HL v UK*.[3] For an explanation of the DOLS scheme, see para 3.198 onwards. At the same time, the Court of Protection was given the task of considering applications under MCA 2005 s21A in respect of authorisations granted under DOLS. The jurisdiction of the Court of Protection under MCA 2005 s21A overlaps with its jurisdiction to make declarations and decisions regarding P's health and welfare under MCA 2005 ss15–16, but it is essentially a standalone jurisdiction.

22.4 The position at the time of writing is that P can lawfully be deprived of their liberty under the MCA 2005:

- If P is 18 or over and is in a care home or hospital, using MCA 2005 Sch A1, DOLS. There is a 'right of appeal' to the Court of Protection by virtue of MCA 2005 s21A.

1 See Human Rights Act (HRA) 1998 Sch 1 in appendix A.
2 *Storck v Germany* (App No 61603/00), (2006) 43 EHRR 6.
3 *HL v UK* (App No 45508/99), [2004] ECHR 471, (2004) 7 CCLR 498.

- In all other cases, a welfare order under MCA 2005 s16(2)(a) will be required from the Court of Protection.

22.5 Neither process is available if P is 'ineligible' to be deprived of their liberty because the MHA 1983 governs, or should govern, P's care and treatment arrangements. This is discussed at para 3.232 onwards.

22.6 The volume of applications both under section 21A and under section 16 has expanded dramatically since the publication of the first edition of this work, in particular following the judgment of the Supreme Court in *Cheshire West and Chester Council v P*[4] ('*Cheshire West*'). The Supreme Court formulated what has become known as the 'acid test' for the objective element of deprivation of liberty – that P is not free to leave and is subject to continuous supervision and control. The decision to introduce a replacement scheme was taken in the context of the impact of the '*Cheshire West*' judgment. The concept of deprivation of liberty generally is discussed at para 3.166 onwards.

22.7 Paragraphs 3.234–3.238 above describe the proposed new scheme – liberty protection safeguards (LPS), which is being brought in by the Mental Capacity (Amendment) Act (MC(A)A) 2019. As with DOLS, LPS provides for a right of appeal to the Court of Protection (MCA 2005 s21ZA, as amended). This chapter therefore straddles the current and the future regime for deprivation of liberty applications in the Court of Protection.

22.8 The first part of the chapter considers challenges to standard and urgent applications granted under the so-called DOLS, where P is detained in a hospital or care home. The second part of the chapter examines applications made under MCA 2005 s16, on form COPDOL11. This process is for non-contentious applications to deprive P of their liberty in settings other than care homes or hospitals. Such applications are often referred to as *Re X* applications, after the series of *Re X* cases.[5] This section will summarise the procedural requirements for such applications and draw together guidance for those involved. These applications are expected to become largely obsolete once LPS is introduced.

22.9 The final part of the chapter examines the new process set out under MCA 2005 s21ZA to appeal authorisations under LPS. It will

4 [2014] UKSC 19, [2014] AC 896.

5 *Re X (deprivation of liberty)* [2014] EWCOP 25, [2015] 1 WLR 2454; *Re X (deprivation of liberty) (No 2)* [2014] EWCOP 37, [2015] 1 WLR 2454 and *Re X (Court of Protection practice)* [2015] EWCA Civ 599, [2016] 1 WLR 227.

look at the changes to the process and will attempt to anticipate the issues and arguments that may arise.

22.10 Applications under MCA 2005 s21A and '*Re X*' applications fall outside the scope of the pathways set down under the Court of Protection Rules 2017[6] (COPR) Case Pathways Practice Direction (PD 3B)[7] and have their own procedures, set out in PD 11A. They do not fall outside the Transparency PD 4C (discussed in chapter 14). It would seem logical for challenges to LPS authorisations to be included in a revised PD 11A in due course.

Challenging deprivations of liberty in care homes and hospitals: the present position

Where no authorisation has been granted

22.11 MCA 2005 Sch A1 provides a useful mechanism which allows a third party who is an 'eligible person' to require that the supervisory body decides whether there is an unauthorised deprivation of liberty.[8] An eligible person is defined as 'any person other than the managing authority of the relevant hospital or care home'.[9] An eligible person could therefore include:

- the individual who is being detained;
- a member of that individual's family;
- a professional working with the individual.

22.12 An unauthorised deprivation of liberty arises where a person is a 'detained resident' in a hospital or care home, and where this has not been authorised under MCA 2005 s4A.[10] A 'detained resident' is defined at MCA 2005 Sch A1 para 6 as:

> . . . a person detained in a hospital or care home – for the purpose of being given care or treatment- in circumstances which amount to deprivation of the person's liberty.

22.13 This will require consideration of whether the person satisfies the 'acid test' in *Cheshire West,* as a part of deciding whether or not they are deprived of their liberty At this stage, however, no consideration

6 SI 2017 No 1035.
7 COPR Case Pathways PD 3B para 1.1.
8 MCA 2005 Sch A1 paras 67–73.
9 MCA 2005 Sch A1 para 68(5).
10 MCA 2005 Sch A1 para 67.

is required as to whether the person fulfils any of the other qualifying requirements for an authorisation.[11]

22.14 To exercise the right to involve the supervisory body, the eligible person must first notify the managing authority that it appears to them that there is an unauthorised deprivation of liberty,[12] and must ask the managing authority to request a standard authorisation in relation to the detention. If the managing authority does not request the authorisation within a 'reasonable period'[13] then the eligible person may request that the supervisory body decides whether or not there is an unauthorised deprivation of liberty. Unless the supervisory body considers the request to be frivolous or vexatious, or unless the question has already been decided and there has been no change in circumstances,[14] then the supervisory body must select and appoint a person to assess whether the relevant person is, in fact, detained.[15] If that assessment concludes that the relevant person is detained, this triggers an obligation for the supervisory body to assess the qualifying requirements for an authorisation, as if the supervisory body had requested it in the usual way.[16]

Where an authorisation has been granted

Reviews

22.15 The supervisory body may carry out a review of a standard authorisation at any time. The supervisory body must carry out a review of a standard authorisation if requested by an eligible person.[17] For the purpose of reviews, an 'eligible person' means P, the relevant person's representative (RPR),[18] or the managing authority.[19] There is no equivalent procedure for urgent authorisations. The process is set out in detail in MCA 2005 Sch A1 Part 8.

11 Described at paras 3.176–3.188.
12 MCA 2005 Sch A1 para 68(2).
13 MCA 2005 Sch A1 para 68(4).
14 MCA 2005 Sch A1 para 69(4)–(5).
15 MCA 2005 Sch A1 para 69(2).
16 MCA 2005 Sch A1 para 71(2).
17 MCA 2005 Sch A1 para 102.
18 Whose role is set out in MCA 2005 Sch A1 Part 10.
19 MCA 2005 Sch A1 para 102.

22.16 If, following the review process, the supervisory body concludes that one of the qualifying requirements is not met, it should terminate the authorisation with immediate effect.[20]

Application or review?

22.17 There is no requirement to request a review before making an application to the court under MCA 2005 s21A. The Part 8 review process is internal and does not provide P with independent scrutiny of whether the criteria for the authorisation are met. Nor does the review process include the considerations of liability available under MCA 2005 s21A(6) and (7). The review process does not and is not intended to meet the requirements of ECHR Article 5(4), namely the entitlement of a detained person 'to take proceedings by which the lawfulness of his detention shall be decided speedily by a court and his release ordered if the detention is not lawful'.

22.18 Practitioners should seek to resolve issues without litigation if at all possible. This stems from the overriding objective and the parties' duty to assist the court in furthering the overriding objective.[21] It may be appropriate to advise the supervisory body of the issues taken with the authorisation before making an application under MCA 2005 s21A. However, as set out in para 22.10 above, section 21A applications are not on the personal welfare pathway for the purposes of the COPR Case Pathways PD 3B and the obligations in the 'pre-issue' stage do not apply. Equally, applicants are not required to seek a review before commencing proceedings under section 21A and in our view a decision to proceed directly to an application under section 21A, without requesting a review first, should not attract criticism.

22.19 In particular in *any* case where P is known to be objecting to all or part of their care and treatment, or to residence in the relevant hospital or care home, one of the lessons of *Re AJ*[22] (which we discuss in detail below at para 22.25 onwards) is that practitioners should be proactive in bringing applications to the court. This advice applies to those advising P, P's RPR, members of P's family, as well as those advising the supervisory body.

22.20 There may, however, be some cases where practitioners may wish to advise requesting a review before proceeding to court. In the

20 MCA 2005 Sch A1 para 117.

21 COPR rr1.3 and 1.4.

22 *Re AJ (an adult) (deprivation of liberty safeguards)* [2015] EWCOP 5, (2015) 18 CCLR 158.

authors' view, the factors below may point to the use of the review process first:

- there is reason to believe, from correspondence or initial discussion with the supervisory body or their advisers, that there is a realistic possibility that agreement to terminate or vary the authorisation will be reached;
- the practitioner is advising a third party who is not P's RPR and is unlikely to be appointed as P's litigation friend, and that third party is not financially eligible for legal aid;
- in a case where P does not wish, or would not wish, to make an application to the court, but the RPR has concerns about whether all the qualifying requirements are met;[23]
- in all cases, there is no risk that P will suffer distress and/or harm if the status quo continues pending the review.

Applications under MCA 2005 s21A

22.21 Unlike patients detained under the MHA 1983, those detained under DOLS do not have their case referred automatically to the court as a backstop if they do nothing. Instead an application under MCA 2005 s21A must be made and section 21A gives the court powers to terminate or vary an authorisation if an application is made. It is important to be aware of the extent of the jurisdiction of section 21A:

> **21A Powers of court in relation to Schedule A1**
>
> (1) This section applies if either of the following has been given under Schedule A1–
> (a) a standard authorisation;
> (b) an urgent authorisation.
>
> (2) Where a standard authorisation has been given, the court may determine any question relating to any of the following matters–
> (a) whether the relevant person meets one or more of the qualifying requirements;
> (b) the period during which the standard authorisation is to be in force;
> (c) the purpose for which the standard authorisation is given;
> (d) the conditions subject to which the standard authorisation is given.
>
> (3) If the court determines any question under subsection (2), the court may make an order–

23 Following *Re RD and others (duties and powers of relevant person's representatives and section 39D IMCAs)* [2016] EWCOP 49, [2017] 1 WLR 1723, [2017] COPLR 87 at para 86(7).

(a) varying or terminating the standard authorisation, or
(b) directing the supervisory body to vary or terminate the standard authorisation.

(4) Where an urgent authorisation has been given, the court may determine any question relating to any of the following matters–
(a) whether the urgent authorisation should have been given;
(b) the period during which the urgent authorisation is to be in force;
(c) the purpose for which the urgent authorisation is given.

(5) Where the court determines any question under subsection (4), the court may make an order–
(a) varying or terminating the urgent authorisation, or
(b) directing the managing authority of the relevant hospital or care home to vary or terminate the urgent authorisation.

(6) Where the court makes an order under subsection (3) or (5), the court may make an order about a person's liability for any act done in connection with the standard or urgent authorisation before its variation or termination.

(7) An order under subsection (6) may, in particular, exclude a person from liability.

22.22 From this it will be seen that section 21A fulfils the role required by ECHR Article 5(4) in providing review of the lawfulness of P's detention by a court. As such, the court is able to bring an authorisation to an end.[24] However, it goes further by allowing the court to:

- vary an urgent or standard authorisation or direct that such authorisations are varied;
- direct that the relevant authority terminate a standard or urgent authorisation;[25]
- make an order about a person's liability 'for any act done in connection with the standard or urgent authorisation' which can include excluding a person from liability.[26] This power only arises when the court either varies, or terminates an authorisation, or directs that it is varied or terminated.[27]

22.23 In an application under MCA 2005 s21A, the court's powers are not limited to the matters set out in section 21A, as Baker J made clear in *KK v CC and STCC*:[28]

> When a standard authorisation has been made by a supervisory body, s21A(2) empowers the Court of Protection to determine any

24 MCA 2005 s21A(3)(a), (5)(a) (standard and urgent authorisations respectively).
25 MCA 2005 s21A(3)(b), (5)(b) (standard and urgent authorisations respectively).
26 MCA 2005 ss21A(6), (7).
27 MCA 2005 s21A(6).
28 [2012] EWHC 2136 (COP), [2012] COPLR 672 at para 16.

questions relating to, inter alia, whether P meets one or more of the qualifying requirements. In particular, once the court determines the question, it may make an order varying or terminating the standard authorisation: s21A(3)(a). But once an application is made to the Court under s21A, the Court's powers are not confined simply to determining that question. Once its jurisdiction is invoked, the court has a discretionary power under s15 to make declarations as to (a) whether a person has or lacks capacity to make a decision specified in the declaration; (b) whether a person has or lacks capacity to make decisions on such matters as are described in the declaration, and (c) the lawfulness or otherwise of any act done, or yet to be done, in relation to that person. Where P lacks capacity, the court has wide powers under s16 to make decisions on P's behalf in relation to matters concerning his personal welfare or property or affairs.[29]

22.24 It should be noted, however, that applications by P or P's RPR under MCA 2005 s21A attract non-means tested legal aid. Other issues – for example matters relating to P's property and affairs – will not attract legal aid at all; and although P may be eligible for legal aid for other issues which relate to health or welfare, any such legal aid will be means-tested. See further the discussion at para 22.56 onwards and para 6.75.

When should an application be made?

22.25 There is no permission filter in relation to MCA 2005 s21A applications.[30] P has a right to apply to the court under section 21A in their own right, irrespective of whether the RPR supports P's application. Following the strong guidance in *AJ v A Local Authority*,[31] in which Baker J held that the 'fundamental principle' was that 'there is an obligation on the State to ensure that a person deprived of liberty is not only entitled but enabled to have the lawfulness of his detention reviewed speedily by a court',[32] it is clear that RPRs should not allow their views about the merits of an application to hold them back

29 For examples, see *Re UR* [2021] EWCOP 10, [2021] COPLR 314 when following an MCA 2005 s21A challenge, Hayden J made findings about UR's habitual residence, and *MB v PB*([2022] EWCOP 14, where P's husband MB issued a challenge to a standard authorisation. Within the section 21A application, Cohen J undertook a fact-finding hearing and concluded that MB had subjected P to controlling and coercive behaviour.

30 COPR r8.2(c).

31 [2015] EWCOP 5, (2015) 18 CCLR 158.

32 Para 36, citing the judgment of Peter Jackson J in *London Borough of Hillingdon v Neary* [2011] EWHC 1377 (COP), [2011] 4 All ER 584.

either from making the application themselves or supporting P in doing so. *AJ* spelt out clearly the responsibility on RPRs, and of independent mental capacity advocates (IMCAs) appointed under MCA 2005 s39D, as well as the responsibilities of local authorities to ensure that a person lacking capacity is able to challenge their deprivation of liberty if they wish to do so.

22.26 It should be noted that Charles J touched on this case in *Re NRA*[33] and observed (obiter) that an RPR is not obliged to test every case: instead, as he noted '[o]bjections expressed by P are a relevant but not a determinative factor for a RPR in deciding whether to issue such proceedings'. These remarks do not obviate the risk of a violation of P's rights under ECHR Article 5(4) if P objects to their placement, especially where the objection is strongly held and consistent, but P is not supported to bring the case to court.

22.27 AJ was 88 and lived in an annexe to the home of her niece and husband, Mr and Mrs C. AJ had vascular dementia and became more dependent on care from Mr and Mrs C who eventually felt unable to provide this. AJ was placed in a unit in X House ostensibly for a respite placement but 'with a view to . . . staying . . . on a permanent basis'.[34] AJ was made the subject of an urgent and then a standard authorization under DOLS. Mr C was made RPR and Mr R was appointed as section 39D IMCA. All parties were aware that AJ was extremely unhappy at X House, but no application was made to the court until she had been there six months. The Official Solicitor was appointed as AJ's litigation friend and sought declarations that AJ's ECHR rights had been breached because the local authority should have ensured an authorisation or an order of the court was in place before she moved to X House; that Mr C should not have been RPR; that the local authority should have ensured the IMCA was able to exercise his responsibilities by acting as litigation friend under a section 21A application or the local authority should have issued proceedings itself.

22.28 Baker J found that AJ's rights under ECHR Article 5(4) had been violated. He summarised the wider lessons arising from the case:

> 133. First, I emphasise that the scheme of the DOLS is that, in the vast majority of cases, it should be possible to plan in advance so that a standard authorisation can be obtained before the deprivation of liberty begins. It is only in exceptional cases, where the need for the

33 *Re NRA* [2015] EWCOP 59, (2015) 18 CCLR 392 at para 171

34 *AJ* at para 7.

deprivation of liberty is so urgent that it is in the best interests of the person for it to begin while the application is being considered, that a standard authorisation need not be sought before the deprivation begins.

134. Secondly, professionals need to be on their guard to look out for cases where vulnerable people are admitted to residential care ostensibly for respite when the underlying plan is for a permanent placement without proper consideration as to their Article 5 rights.

135. Thirdly, a RPR should only be selected or confirmed by a BIA where he or she satisfies not only the criteria in regulation 3 of the Mental Capacity (Deprivation of Liberty: Appointment of Relevant Person's Representative) Regulations 2008 but also the requirements of paragraph 140 of Schedule A1 to the MCA 2005. This requires that the BIA not only checks that the facts set out in regulation 3 are satisfied but also carries out an analysis and reaches a judgment as to whether the prospective representative would, if appointed, (a) maintain contact with the relevant person; (b) represent the relevant person in matters relating to or connected with the Schedule; and (c) support the relevant person in matters relating to or connected with the Schedule.

136. Fourthly, the local authority is under an obligation to satisfy itself that a person selected for appointment as RPR meets the criteria in regulation 3 and in paragraph 140 of Schedule A1. If the local authority concludes that the person selected for appointment does not meet the criteria, it should refer the matter back to the BIA.

137. Fifthly, it is likely to be difficult for a close relative or friend who believes that it is in P's best interests to move into residential care, and has been actively involved in arranging such a move, into a placement that involves a deprivation of liberty, to fulfil the functions of RPR, which involve making a challenge to any authorisation of that deprivation. BIAs and local authorities should therefore scrutinise very carefully the selection and appointment of RPRs in circumstances which are likely to give rise to this potential conflict of interest.

138. Sixthly, an IMCA appointed under section 39D must act with diligence and urgency to ensure that any challenge to an authorisation under schedule A1 is brought before the court expeditiously. Failure to do so will lead to the evaporation of P's Article 5 rights.

139. Seventhly, the appointment of a RPR and IMCA does not absolve the local authority from responsibility for ensuring that P's Article 5 rights are respected. The local authority must monitor whether the RPR is representing and supporting P in accordance with the duty under paragraph 140 and, if not, consider terminating his appointment on the grounds that he is no longer eligible. The local authority must make sufficient resources available to assist an IMCA and keep

in touch with the IMCA to ensure that all reasonable steps are being taken to pursue P's Article 5 rights.

140. Finally, in circumstances where a RPR and an IMCA have failed to take sufficient steps to challenge the authorisation, the local authority should consider bringing the matter before the court itself. This is likely, however, to be a last resort since in most cases P's Article 5 rights should be protected by the combined efforts of a properly selected and appointed RPR and an IMCA carrying out their duties with appropriate expedition.

22.29 AJ was able to articulate her unhappiness and her objection to her detention. Her case left open the question as to when applications should be made when P's wishes may be less clear, or may fluctuate. In *RD and others (duties and powers of relevant person's representatives and section 39D IMCAs)*[35] – a test case involving five older people under standard authorisations – Baker J attempted to answer the question 'When, if at all, does the requirement under Article 5(4) to assist P to exercise his or her right of appeal to the Court of Protection under s21A of the MCA [2005] arise in cases other than those in which P expresses a clear and consistent objection to the arrangements for his/her care and treatment?'[36]

22.30 Baker J formulated the following approach for RPRs and IMCAs:[37]

(1) The RPR must consider whether P wishes, or would wish, to apply to the Court of Protection. This involves the following steps:

(a) Consider whether P has capacity to ask to issue proceedings. This simply requires P to understand that the court has the power to decide that he/she should not be subject to his/her current care arrangements. It is a lower threshold than the capacity to conduct proceedings.

(b) If P does not have such capacity, consider whether P is objecting to the arrangements for his/her care, either verbally or by behaviour, or both, in a way that indicates that he would wish to apply to the Court of Protection if he had the capacity to ask.

(2) In considering P's stated preferences, regard should be had to:

(a) any statements made by P about his/her wishes and feelings in relation to issuing proceedings,

(b) any statements made by P about his/her residence in care,

(c) P's expressions of his/her emotional state,

35 [2016] EWCOP 49, [2017] 1 WLR 1723, [2017] COPLR 87.

36 Para 41.

37 Para 86.

(d) the frequency with which he/she objects to the placement or asks to leave,
(e) the consistency of his/her express wishes or emotional state; and
(f) the potential alternative reasons for his/her express wishes for emotional state.

(3) In considering whether P's behaviour constitutes an objection, regard should be had to:
(a) the possible reasons for P's behaviour,
(b) whether P is being medicated for depression or being sedated,
(c) whether P actively tries to leave the care home,
(d) whether P takes preparatory steps to leave, e.g. packing bags,
(e) P's demeanour and relationship with staff,
(f) any records of challenging behaviour and the triggers for such behaviour.
(g) whether P's behaviour is a response to particular aspects of the care arrangements or to the entirety of those arrangements.

(4) In carrying out this assessment, it should be recognised that there could be reason to think that P would wish to make an application even if P says that he/she does not wish to do so or, conversely, reason to think that P would not wish to make an application even though he/she says that she does wish to, since his/her understanding of the purpose of an application may be very poor.

(5) When P does not express a wish to start proceedings, the RPR, in carrying out his duty to represent and support P in matters relating to or connected with the Schedule, may apply to the Court of Protection to determine any of the four questions identified in s21A(2) i.e. on the grounds that P does not meet one or more of the qualifying requirements for an authorisation under Schedule A1; or that the period of the standard authorisation or the conditions subject to which the standard authorisation is given are contrary to P's best interests; or that the purpose of the standard authorisation could be as effectively achieved in a way that is less restrictive of P's rights and freedom of action.

(6) Consideration of P's circumstances must be holistic and usually based on more than one meeting with P, together with discussions with care staff familiar with P and his/her family and friends. It is likely to be appropriate to visit P on more than one occasion in order to form a view about whether proceedings should be started.

(7) By way of an alternative to proceedings, it may be appropriate to instigate a Part 8 review, or to seek to work collaboratively with the family and the commissioning authority to see whether alternate arrangements can be put in place. Such measures should not, however, prevent an application to the court being made where it appears that P would wish to exercise a right of appeal.

(8) The role of the IMCA appointed under s39D is to take such steps as are practicable to help P and the RPR understand matters relating to the authorisation set out in s39D(7)(a) to (e), and the rights to apply the Court of Protection and for a Part 8 review, and how to exercise those rights. Where it appears to the IMCA that P or the RPR wishes to exercise the right, the IMCA must take all practical steps to assist them to do so. In considering P's apparent wishes, the IMCA should follow the guidance set out above so far as relevant.

What if the RPR does not bring the challenge?

22.31 Practitioners advising family members or carers concerned about a standard authorisation should always check that an RPR has in fact been appointed (as this is sometimes overlooked) and whether the RPR is willing to challenge the authorisation. In the authors' experience, the vast majority of paid RPRs are now aware of the guidance in *AJ* and *RD*, and are keen to follow it. If, however, the RPR does not make the application, a member of P's family may make the application in their own right; or as P's litigation friend.[38] Note that here MCA 2005 s50(1A) only refers to the RPR as not requiring a permission, but COPR r8.2(c) then appears to widen the 'non-permission' requirement more broadly to anyone making a section 21A application. We suggest that the broader approach is preferable, given the importance of securing P's ECHR Article 5(4) rights; the court has the power to case manage any unmeritorious applications. If P's family applies, the proposed litigation friend can apply for non-means tested legal aid on P's behalf. If this course of action is adopted, it must be borne in mind that the court may well consider at a later date that an alternative litigation friend should be appointed.

22.32 As emphasised at para 22.25 above, P has a right to make an application under MCA 2005 s21A in their own right. P may well have capacity to make the decision to challenge the deprivation of their liberty, even if P lacks capacity to conduct the proceedings once they are under way. This emerges clearly from the observations of Baker J in *Re RD* at para 86(1).

22.33 Separately, the case of *Re YC*[39] should be noted. In this case, Senior Judge Hilder made clear that errors of form (in that case, repeated references to the wrong person in the record of authorisation) do not *necessarily* invalidate the authorisation. A section 21A application would therefore not be appropriate solely to challenge

38 See *Re UF* [2013] EWHC 4289 (COP), [2014] COPLR 936.
39 [2021] EWCOP 34, [2021] COPLR 481.

errors in documentation, unless those errors go to the validity of the underlying assessments/reasoning as to whether the conditions are satisfied.

Making the application

22.34 The procedure for making an application is not complex. Guidance is provided in COPR PD 11A, although the practice direction is now somewhat out of date in terms of the court's internal procedures.

22.35 While MCA 2005 s21A applications are not personal welfare cases for purposes of the COPR Case Pathways PD 3B, it is prudent to proceed on the basis that the court will seek, insofar as possible, to apply the same approach to case management.

22.36 Legal aid is available for section 21A cases, in some circumstances without reference to the means test. The provisions are discussed in more detail in chapter 6.

Preparing the application

22.37 Applications made under MCA 2005 s21A should be made on the forms that have been specially designed for this purpose, and the benefit of these is that they are easily distinguished from other applications and can be dealt with by the right team urgently. They can, and should where possible, be filed electronically by scanning in and sending copies of the completed forms. If at all possible, it is very helpful to have electronic copies as part of a case management system allowing details to be inputted electronically.

22.38 Form DLA, the deprivation of liberty application form, contains 'prompts' to ensure all relevant issues are addressed:

- Section 2 allows information to be added about interested parties. This term is not used in the rules. Inclusion in this section does not result automatically in the person or body named as interested party being joined as a party, as they have not been named as a respondent. If served with the application, however, the proposed interested party will be bound by orders of the court as if they were a party.[40]
- Section 3 requires consideration of whether an interim application is being made and asks whether other applications are to be made.

40 COPR rr9.13(1), 9.14.

- Section 4 asks for a detailed statement of grounds and in most cases it will be advisable to prepare this – or instruct counsel or a Higher Rights Advocate – as a separate document. This is an opportunity to address from the outset the issues that are likely to feature. For example, are there obvious defects in any of the assessments or the authorisation itself?
- It should be noted that that section 8 requires a statement of facts relied on. It is suggested that sections 8 and 5 could conveniently be combined in the same document.
- Section 5 asks the applicant to identify other 'issues that will arise for determination in respect of the relevant person' and any other applications that have been made or that the applicant intends to make. These might include broader welfare questions such as an application for a declaration as to P's best interests in terms of residence or contact; or whether an HRA 1998 claim may be made (see chapter 26 for discussion of HRA 1998 claims).
- Section 6 seeks information about other pending applications, so that the court can consider whether these should be linked. In addition to outstanding welfare applications, practitioners should check whether they are aware of any outstanding property and affairs applications.
- Section 7 invites the applicant to identify any special assistance or facilities that will be needed to enable the applicant to attend court.
- Section 10 provides a helpful checklist.

22.39 Form DLB is a declaration of exceptional urgency to be used to explain if it is necessary for the court's usual timetable to be abridged.

22.40 Form DLC is no longer required, as there is now no permission filter for section 21A applications.

22.41 It should be noted that the practice direction anticipates that the above forms will be served at the same time that they are lodged with the court.[41] In addition to the forms, a fee of £385 is payable (see appendix B below). This can be claimed as a disbursement on the applicant's legal aid certificate, whether the applicant is P or the RPR.

22.42 In addition to the forms, which must be completed, form DLA lists a number of supporting documents which might be filed at court with the forms. These include copies of the authorisation and assessments, a witness statement on form COP24, a copy of the legal aid certificate if any, copies of relevant statutory material, and a draft

41 COPR PD 11A para 10.

order or orders which if possible should also be provided electronically on disk (or, nowadays, be available in Word form by email).[42] It is our advice to provide as much information as possible, given that the first order will be made on the basis of the information in the papers alone.[43]

22.43 Careful thought should be given to the extent of the directions that will be sought at the time of issue of a section 21A application. It is tempting to try to address as many matters as possible. This should be balanced against the fact that, at the time that the court makes initial directions, the supervisory body will not yet have been joined as a respondent. It is usually preferable for detailed provisions as to disclosure and evidence to await the first hearing.

22.44 Where time allows, any witness statements should be carefully prepared. Although significant information can be provided by means of the statement of facts and grounds, this is no substitute for witness evidence in which the applicant is able to set out in full their perspective as well as state the relevant facts. Considerable time will be saved if the documents are paginated and indexed. A paginated indexed bundle is required for the first hearing in any event.[44]

After the application is received

22.45 Once the documents are received by the court, the practice direction provides that steps will immediately be taken to ensure the papers are considered by a judge who will make a first order. This is likely to deal with the following matters:

- Identifying a litigation friend, or accredited legal representative (ALR) if possible; if not this will usually be deferred to the first attended hearing. This may include an invitation to the Official Solicitor to act, if there is no other litigation friend.
- Identifying the parties, or those who may wish to join as parties,
- Initial disclosure from the supervisory body.
- A timetable leading up to the first hearing for filing and serving evidence; preparation of the bundle and position statements.
- The order will usually encourage the parties to communicate and narrow the issues before the hearing takes place.

42 COPR PD 11A para 15.
43 COPR PD 11A para 20.
44 COPR PD 11A para 26.

For a discussion of litigation friends and ALRs in section 21A cases, see chapter 12.

22.46 The applicant is responsible for following up any directions made and is also responsible for service of the order and any other relevant papers that have not already been served, together with form DLE (acknowledgement of service). The applicant must file form DLD (certificate of service).

22.47 The first attended hearing should be listed within five working days of the judge's first order (ie the date of issue of the application).[45] If the applicant considers this will be too late, this should be made clear on form DLB (see para 22.38 above). The first hearing is likely to take place at the closest regional court to P. It will usually be fixed without reference to the parties' availability.

Preparing for the first hearing

22.48 If the Official Solicitor is invited to act when initial directions are made, then any solicitors instructed by her are likely to have very limited time to prepare for the first hearing. The same is likely to be true for an ALR in the event that one is appointed by the court. A solicitor instructed by an RPR (whether in their own right or as litigation friend to P) will have the advantage of the background knowledge of the RPR and may well have met with P before making the application.

22.49 Consideration should be given to the directions which will be sought at that hearing. For example, are there any outstanding issues about the appointment of a litigation friend?[46] Is expert evidence required? Given the pressure of time in MCA 2005 s21A appeals, an application for permission to instruct an expert is more likely to be granted if an expert has already been identified and their timetable ascertained in advance of the hearing, even if there is insufficient time to comply fully with COPR r15.5 (see discussion at para 13.66).

22.50 If it has not yet been possible to identify all those parties who should be joined to the application, then this should be put in hand now. In particular, it is important to ascertain the role which relevant statutory bodies should play in the application. This is important to enable the court to identify what alternatives to P's current placement may be available. The supervisory body will be a respondent; however if P is detained in a hospital consideration should be given to joining

45 COPR PD 11A para 24.

46 See chapter 12.

the NHS Trust providing care to P. If P is in receipt of NHS continuing healthcare, then the Integrated Care Board (ICB) (in England) commissioning P's care may have to be joined. There may be family members who should be given an opportunity to join as parties. If at all possible, contact should be made with potential respondents before the hearing.

22.51 Practitioners will wish to decide now whether to instruct counsel for the directions hearing or whether to undertake the advocacy themselves. Solicitors are entitled to appear in the Court of Protection (see chapter 6) and directions hearings may be relatively informal. Whether instructing counsel or appearing themselves, the ALR should attend court personally as should, ideally, the solicitor instructed by the litigation friend.

22.52 The court will usually require a position statement and a draft order to be submitted by each party. There are precedent orders on the Court of Protection Handbook website.[47] Position statements for the first directions hearing need not be long, especially if relatively detailed grounds have been prepared. The aim should be to:

- either provide a summary of the background to the judge or signpost them to such a summary (for example in the grounds);
- explain what steps have been taken so far;
- provide an account of P's wishes if possible;
- identify the issues in the application; and
- explain the orders that will be sought and why.

22.53 There will be some – relatively rare – cases where it is possible to determine the challenge to the authorisation at the first hearing. However, in the majority of cases further evidence will be needed and therefore the court will consider how to regulate the intervening period, if P is to continue to be deprived of their liberty while the case continues. Paragraphs 6.74–6.75 provide details as to how this can best be achieved without compromising non-means testing legal aid for P or the RPR.

22.54 If the directions are not contentious, it is often possible to vacate the first hearing by consent.

47 See: https://courtofprotectionhandbook.com/precedents/.

The approach of the court to section 21A applications

22.55 The range of issues which can arise in MCA 2005 s21A applications is huge. While some section 21A cases may focus on the level of restrictions to which P is subject,[48] many involve a dispute about P's best interests as regards residence or care.

22.56 The scope of the matters that can properly be considered as part and parcel of an application was considered by the Court of Appeal in *Director of Legal Aid Casework and others v Briggs*.[49]

22.57 The case concerned Mr Paul Briggs, who was in a minimally conscious state following a serious accident. Two applications were made before Charles J: one brought by the NHS Trust providing treatment for Mr Briggs in order to resolve whether such treatment was in his best interests; the other by Mrs Briggs, as her husband's RPR, under section 21A. Mrs Briggs made it clear from the start that the reason for using section 21A as a vehicle was because this would allow her access to non-means tested legal aid. Without this she would have been unable to secure representation or marshal the evidence which was determinative in satisfying Charles J that Mr Briggs, if capacitous, would not have wanted treatment to continue.

22.58 On appeal, the Legal Aid Agency (LAA) challenged the finding that applications in relation to medical treatment could be made under section 21A (and thus attract non-means tested legal aid). King LJ was 'entirely satisfied that the provisions were not intended to, and do not, provide a duplicate route by which personal welfare decisions and in particular medical treatment decisions, can be made in circumstances where the deprivation of liberty itself is not the real or essential issue before the court'.[50] A challenge to the 'best interests requirement' is therefore a challenge to whether it is in P's best interests to be a detained resident, and 'a question in relation to serious medical treatment is not fundamentally a question in relation to deprivation of liberty'.[51] The appropriate application would be made under MCA 2005 ss15–17 and not section 21A.

22.59 Importantly, King LJ rejected the submission of the LAA that section 21A should be constructed narrowly and that all that is required for the purpose of MCA 2005 Sch A1 is for the assessors to

48 Including, for example, the use of covert medication– see *AG (by her litigation friend the Official Solicitor) v BMBC and SNH* [2016] EWCOP 37.

49 [2017] EWCA Civ 1169, [2018] Fam 63.

50 *Briggs* at para 88.

51 *Briggs* at para 92.

be satisfied that there is a care plan and a needs assessment in place as 'too narrow':

> 94. Where a dispute is referred to the court under s21A, the issue is often in relation to P and the family's wish for P to go home, set against the assessor's view that it is in P's best interests to be placed in a care home and consequently deprived of his or her liberty. Miss Richards has helpfully provided the court with a table of cases where applications have appropriately been made under s21A; on closer examination, each of them has involved a dispute as to whether P should reside in some form of care home or return to either his home or to live with a family member in the community. Such cases are focused specifically on the issue as to whether P should be detained and are properly brought under s21A. Proper consideration of those cases by the assessor in compliance with the guidance in the DOLS Code, requires far more of an extensive consideration of the relevant circumstances than that which is suggested by Mr Nicholls, namely simply ensuring a care plan and needs assessment is in place without further consideration as to the content.
>
> 95. Contact, for example, is an issue capable of going to the heart of whether being detained is in a person's best interests; it may be that in an ideal world P's best interests would be served by a deprivation of liberty in the form of her living in a care home properly looked after, where the appropriate medication regime will be adhered to and P will have a proper balanced diet. Desirable as that may be, and such a regime may well provide the optimum care outcome for P, but it may also be the case that unless, regular contact can be facilitated to a particular family member, the distress and confusion caused to P would be such that it would be no longer in her best interests to be detained, and that what might amount to sub optimum physical care would ultimately be preferable to no, or insufficient contact. The weighing up of such options are part of the best interests assessment process in relation to which the professionals who are eligible to be assessors are peculiarly qualified to conduct.

22.60 Based upon a partial selection of passages from the judgment of King LJ, in *DL v London Borough of Enfield*[52] a local authority respondent sought to challenge the jurisdiction of the Court of Protection in relation to section 21A applications, 'to challenge what might colloquially be called "a gravy train" '.[53] It appears that the local authority sought, in essence, to limit the circumstances under which an application could be brought and the case management directions that the Court

52 [2019] EWCOP B1, [2020] COPLR 128.

53 Para 25.

of Protection should make before determining it. HHJ Hilder rejected the arguments advanced by the local authority, and observed that:

> 39. However large the numbers of a local authority caseload of persons being provided with care in the circumstances of their liberty being deprived it is imperative that those responsible for such conditions are never allowed to become cavalier about the significance of deprivation of liberty to the individual concerned and to society as a whole. In my judgment Article 5 rights do not become less precious because of the administrative burden of cases reliant on them.
>
> 40. Mr McKendrick QC has reminded the court of the generous ambit of Article 5.4 which entitles a person to speedy consideration by a court and in particular has referred to the case of *Waite v the United Kingdom* ECHR 2002. Article 5.4 is first and foremost a guarantee of a fair procedure for reviewing the lawfulness of detention. An applicant is not required as a precondition to enjoying that protection to show that on the facts of his case he stands any particular chance of success in obtaining his release. When I put that to Mr Holbrook he also, and I quote, 'entirely endorsed this' proposition.
>
> 41. Closer to home, the Court of Protection's own Vice-President has recently had cause to restate this approach in the case of *CB v Medway Council* [2019] EWCOP 5 at paragraph 33. He said:
>
>> 'What is involved here is nothing less than CB's liberty. Curtailing, restricting or depriving any adult of such a fundamental freedom will always require cogent evidence and proper enquiry. I cannot envisage any circumstances where it would be right to determine such issues on the basis of speculation and general experience in other cases.'
>
> 42. So, bearing in mind that these proceedings are brought pursuant to section 21A and that it is very clear from the paperwork that the qualifying requirements being scrutinised may include capacity and definitely include best interests, I have no doubt that it is appropriate for the court to go on to consider now . . . what are the appropriate case management decisions to progress this matter.[54]

22.61 Hayden J reviewed the approach of the court to section 21A applications in *DP v LB Hillingdon*,[55] holding that the court should not make use of section 48 where the position in relation to capacity is governed by the extant authorisation under challenge, and also emphasising the need for speed in determining section 21A applications. The

54 Perhaps not altogether surprisingly, SJ Hilder departed from the general rule in welfare cases (see para 17.8), to order that all the costs incurred by the applicant detained person should be paid by the local authority to reflect that they had been incurred because the local authority had failed to take a 'sensible and appropriate approach to these proceedings'.

55 [2020] EWCOP 45, [2020] COPLR 769.

observation that he made[56] that it would be possible to resolve doubts about capacity arising from the authorisation by asking further questions of the individual who had conducted the capacity assessment (rather than by seeking a further view), and the thought that the capacity assessor might routinely be expected to stand behind their assessment in court may help concentrate minds in the underlying authorisation process.

'*Re X*' applications

22.62 Certain applications to the Court of Protection are referred to as '*Re X* applications', after the series of cases under that name.[57] These are applications for welfare orders under MCA 2005 s16, authorising the deprivation of P's liberty in settings where the DOLS regime cannot be used. They follow a 'streamlined' procedure, which is excluded from the Case Pathways PD 3B.[58] Such a process was considered to be necessary in the aftermath of the *Cheshire West* judgment which, as we have seen, increased the cohort of those whose circumstances engaged Article 5.[59] The need for this process is likely to become redundant after the implementation of the LPS, because authorisations can be given in relation to any setting. It may well be necessary, on occasion, for the court to consider questions of deprivation of liberty as part of wider issues concerning P's welfare, but such applications would fall to be considered as part of the normal Personal Welfare Pathway.

22.63 A particular, and invidious, problem with the *Re X* procedure is that it does not give rise to any entitlement on the part of P to non-means-tested legal aid: see para 6.79 above. There has been significant litigation as to how P's interests are properly protected during the course of the application. In addition to the three *Re X* cases, *Re NRA*[60] and *Re JM*[61] consider in depth the essential requirements for a procedure which complies with ECHR Article 5 in such circumstances.

56 At para 117.

57 *Re X* [2014] EWCOP 25, [2015] 1 WLR 2454, (2014) 17 CCLR 297; *Re X* [2014] EWCOP 37, [2015] 1 WLR 2454, (2014) 17 CCLR 464 and *Re X (Court of Protection Practice)* [2015] EWCA Civ 599, [2016] 1 WLR 227.

58 COPR Case Pathways PD 3B para 1.1(e).

59 Although the numbers have not been as great as had been predicted: see *Re JM and others* [2016] EWCOP 15, [2016] 4 WLR 64 at para 10.

60 [2015] EWCOP 59, [2015] COPLR 690, (2015) 18 CCLR 392.

61 [2016] EWCOP 15, [2016] 4 WLR 64.

However, it may be thought that none of the solutions are entirely satisfactory.

22.64 Cases where a *Re X* application may need to be made could include cases where P is living in one of the following settings:

- supported living placements;
- extra care housing;
- adult foster placements; or
- care packages delivered to P in their own home (including those that are fully funded by P).

22.65 If P is 16 years old or over, lacks capacity to consent to their care arrangements, and their care package amounts to a deprivation of liberty for the purpose of ECHR Article 5, then authorisation will need to be sought from a court.[62] Without such authorisation, P is at risk of arbitrary detention, in violation of their Article 5 rights, which may lead to liability for damages. It is well-established that, except in emergencies, the authority to detain must be sought before the deprivation of liberty starts.[63] Failure to do so will result, at least, in a procedural breach of Article 5(1).

22.66 A full examination of all the circumstances in which Article 5 is engaged – and when applications to court should be made – is beyond the scope of this chapter. Nor does this chapter consider the position of those under 16, because the Court of Protection will not have jurisdiction over those aged 15 and below. However it is important to stress that the responsibility to seek authorisations is not limited to cases where P's care is arranged or commissioned by a public body. P's deprivation of liberty can be attributable to the State in any case where the State knows or ought to know of 'the situation on the ground'.[64] If a local authority or other statutory body is in any doubt as to whether an application should be made in a particular case, specialist legal advice should be sought as a matter of urgency.

22.67 The next important point is that '*Re X*' applications are only appropriate where there is no dispute as to whether P's care arrange-

62 In this chapter, we are concerned with the role of the Court of Protection. In *Re KL* [2022] EWCOP 24, Senior Judge Hilder conducted a detailed analysis of the position in relation to such 16 and 17 year olds, highlighting the jurisdictional complexity of their position. She made clear that there will only be limited circumstances in which it will be appropriate for the Court of Protection to authorise their deprivation of liberty by way of the streamlined procedure set out here.

63 See by analogy *Re AJ* at para 133.

64 *Secretary of State for Justice v Staffordshire CC and others* [2016] EWCA Civ 1317, [2017] COPLR 120, [2017] Fam 278.

ments are in P's best interests and the least restrictive alternative, either from P or from any other person.[65] If such a dispute exists then an application should be made for a welfare order, using COP1, and following the requirements of COPR Case Pathways PD 3B. The procedure for such cases is addressed in chapter 9.

22.68 The *Re X* process has the following characteristics:

- It is paper-based and unlikely to involve an oral hearing.
- P will usually not be a party but will instead require a representative appointed under COPR r1.2.[66] There is no reason in principle, why P cannot be joined and a litigation friend be appointed for purposes of an application under the *Re X* process, but the case-law subsequent to *Re X* itself has made clear that the court will strive to avoid this outcome.
- Any order made by the court will be time-limited and will be subject to further review.

Making an application

22.69 To make an application the applicant will have to consider:

- COPR PD 11A Part 2;
- form COPDOL11 (which can be found in an unofficial Word version on the Court of Protection Handbook website[67]), its annexes and guidance;
- the judgment of Charles J in *Re VE*,[68] a case linked with *Re JM*. Here Charles J provides a helpful precedent of a letter that should be sent to the rule 3A representative, explaining what is expected;
- the *Re X* 'Model Order', which must be completed. A Word version of the order can be found on the Court of Protection Handbook website.[69]

22.70 COPR PD 11A is comprehensive and explains exactly what is required in the application.[70] The form COPDOL11 prompts the applicant to address the evidence which the court will need. Applicants should ensure that information provided in the form is consistent with that in the supporting documentation. The court will

65 See *Re NRA*, at para 37.

66 For a full account of the role of such representatives, see para 12.77 onwards.

67 See: https://courtofprotectionhandbook.com/precedents/.

68 [2016] EWCOP 16, [2016] 4 WLR 64.

69 See: https://courtofprotectionhandbook.com/precedents/.

70 Further guidance can be found in the 39 Essex Chambers guide: *Judicial Authorisation of Deprivation of Liberty*, July 2020, available at www.39essex.com.

expect a level of granularity that provides the judge with an insight into P's daily life, and may make directions for further information if this is lacking. As Senior Judge Hilder noted in *Re JDO (authorisation of deprivation of liberty)*[71] (in the context of a review of a previously authorised deprivation of liberty, but in comments equally applicable to an initial application to authorise):

> Even if a COPDOL11 application is appropriately made within the review period, the review process is *not* a rubber-stamping exercise. The purpose of the review is to enable a judge to make a fresh determination on up to date information. Authorisation in 2017 does not automatically lead to further authorisation in 2018. The whole purpose of the review is to scrutinise – on a proportionate basis, but scrutinise nonetheless – whether authorisation continues to be appropriate.[72]

22.71 It is important to appreciate that the applicant is asking the Court of Protection, by making an order under MCA 2005 s16(2)(a), both to consent on P's behalf to living at the placement identified to receive care, and to authorise confinement there. The burden is on the applicant to satisfy the judge that the arrangements are in P's best interests before they can consent to. In *Re JDO* Senior Judge Hilder highlighted key obligations upon applicants seeking judicial authorisation of deprivation of liberty under the *Re X* procedure, in particular in relation to the duty of full and frank disclosure. She also strongly criticised the local authority for seeking artificially to limit those to be consulted, and for preparing a statement for the proposed COPR r1.2 representative to sign so as to 'put words into her mouth [and] persuade her to adopt the Applicant's views'.[73]

22.72 A draft of the precise order sought should be provided, including in particular the duration of the authorisation sought and appropriate directions for automatic review and liberty to apply and/or seek a redetermination in accordance with COPR r13.4. When completing the order, careful thought should be given to the length of the authorisation sought. The maximum length is 12 months but – as in the case of standard authorisations – this should not be requested unless necessary.[74]

71 [2019] EWCOP 47, [2020] COPLR 226 at para 52.
72 Para 52 (emphasis in original).
73 Para 54.
74 *P v Surrey CC and Surrey Downs CCG* [2015] EWCOP 54, [2015] COPLR 747.

22.73 There is a helpful checklist in form COPDOL11, as well as a list of triggers which may suggest that the case may not be suitable for a *Re X* application.

22.74 Once the forms and all the ancillary documentation (including the draft order) have been completed they should be lodged at court with the application fee (see appendix F). In Spring 2021, HM Courts and Tribunals Service (HMCTS) introduced e-filing for all deprivation of liberty cases. This involves the introduction of an automated system where correspondence and attachments received by email are placed directly onto the court's digital files (e-files). To this end, there is a dedicated email address (COPDOLS_or_S16@justice.gov.uk), and particular requirements for the subject line of emails.[75]

22.75 As long as the court is satisfied that consultation with P and others has taken place it will dispense with the requirement that the application is served or that P is notified.[76] Where there is agreement from everyone, including the potential COPR r1.2 representative where one can be identified (or a litigation friend for P where one has been identified and confirmed their willingness to act and to consent to the order), the requisite order can be made on the papers.

22.76 If no COPR r1.2 representative has been identified, the current guidance in *Re JM*[77] is that the case should be stayed and the Department of Health and Social Care (DHSC) and Ministry of Justice (MoJ) joined to the proceedings with a view to identifying a potential representative. This is because in *Re JM* Charles J found that without such a representative P's fundamental rights would not be protected. See para 12.77 onwards for details of the role of the COPR r1.2 representative; and chapter 6 for details of the legal aid entitlement. In *Re KT and others*,[78] Charles J approved the use of a section 49 report to assist the court in determining whether the package of care and support is in P's interests, and provided a draft order.

75 Outlined in the letter available here: https://courtofprotectionhandbook.files.wordpress.com/2021/03/cop-dols-court-user-notification-of-e-filing-10.3.21.pdf.

76 COPR PD 11A para 41.

77 At para 25.

78 [2018] EWCOP 1, [2018] 4 WLR 21, [2018] COPLR 185.

22.77 If the judge considers that the case is not suitable for the *Re X* process, they will make case management directions[79] and may list it for an attended hearing.

22.78 Once the order is received it must be served on all those consulted, including P.[80] The order will contain details as to the review process, ie the process to extend the authorisation at the end of the authorisation period set down in the order. The review can, where appropriate, be done on the papers. Note that there is, as yet, no specific application for purposes of seeking a review, and that the model order provides that it should otherwise be made on a COP DOL11. The order will further contain a requirement to make an application to the court in the event that the care plan becomes more restrictive.

22.79 The draft letter set out in *Re VE?*[81] should be used as a template when writing to the COPR r1.2 representative. From this it will be seen that the role is an ongoing one, and is in some ways an equivalent to the RPR in DOLS cases.

The future: Challenging authorisations under LPS

22.80 The MC(A)A 2019 was enacted in 2019, introducing LPS through a new Schedule AA1 to the MCA 2005. We do not have an implementation date yet although, as noted at para 3.234 above, we anticipate that October 2023 – or even April 2024 – may be realistic estimates. At the time of writing, draft regulations and a draft Code of Practice are being consulted upon: see further para 2.328. What follows is based upon the provisions of the Act, what (relatively little) relevant discussion there was in relation during the passage of the bill through parliament, and points from the draft Code we consider unlikely to be affected by consultation.[82]

22.81 An overview of the scheme is to be found in chapter 3.[83] We focus in what follows primarily on upon the ways in which the courts are

79 COPR PD 11A para 47. In *Re KL* [2022] EWCOP 24, Senior Judge Hilder made clear that there will only be limited circumstances in which it will be appropriate for the Court of Protection to authorise their deprivation of liberty by way of the streamlined procedure set out here.

80 COPR PD 11A para 48.

81 At para 6.

82 Note, we do not give paragraph numbers in the draft Code as these may well be subject to change in the final version.

83 See also the LPS resources page on Alex Ruck Keene's website: www.mentalcapacitylawandpolicy.org.uk/resources-2/liberty-protection-safeguards-resources/.

likely to become involved, but start with two key changes from the current regime which impact upon the protection of P's ECHR Article 5 rights more broadly.

22.82 Firstly, Schedule AA1 does not replicate the provisions in paras 67 onwards in Schedule A1, which provides a specified procedure for seeking consideration of whether an authorisation is needed. This does not mean that those with an interest in P's welfare can no longer raise with the organisation that would be the 'responsible body' a concern that P may be deprived of their liberty without authorisation. Any such concerns should continue to be raised, because the organisation concerned will continue to have duties under Article 5 to take steps to bring an unlawful deprivation of liberty to an end.[84]

22.83 The second relevant change is that the provisions for the representation of P under the LPS (referred to as the 'cared for person' in Schedule AA1) are less stringent than either DOLS or the *Re X* procedures:

- P must be represented throughout the DOLS process by virtue of MCA 2005 s39A, and the appointment of a RPR is mandatory by virtue of Sch A1 para 139 as soon as a standard authorisation is granted.
- By contrast, in LPS, the responsible body is required to consider whether there is an 'appropriate person' who can represent and support the cared-for person while arrangements are authorised or being proposed.[85] This person must agree to represent and support the cared-for person, and must not be engaged in providing care and support to the cared-for person in a professional capacity. The appropriate person cannot be someone whom the cared-for person (if they have capacity to do so) does not consent to have representing and supporting them[86]. If the cared-for person lacks capacity to consent to the involvement of the appropriate person then the responsible body must be satisfied that it is in the cared-for person's best interests for the proposed appropriate person to represent and support them.[87] What if there is no appropriate person available? The responsible body must then

84 See, for example, the decision of the Court of Appeal in *Secretary of State for Justice v Staffordshire CC* [2016] EWCA Civ 1317, [2017] Fam 278, [2017] COPLR 120.

85 MCA 2005 Sch AA1 para 39(5).

86 MCA 2005 Sch AA1 para 39(6)(a). The draft MCA Code of Practice makes clear that the government's intention is that the role of an appropriate person is an unpaid one.

87 MCA 2005 Sch AA1 para 39(6)(b).

'take all reasonable steps' to appoint an IMCA to represent and support the cared-for person,[88] if the cared for person has capacity to consent to being represented and supported by an IMCA and makes a request for one to be appointed.[89] Where the cared-for person lacks capacity to consent to representation and support by an IMCA then one should be appointed unless the responsible body is satisfied that it is not in the cared-for person's best interests to be represented and supported by an IMCA.[90] We would anticipate such cases to be rare, and the draft Code of Practice is certainly framed to this end. However, given the pressure on providers of advocacy services (explored in some detail by Charles J in *Re JM and others*[91]) there will no doubt be cases where 'all reasonable steps' do not lead to the appointment of an IMCA even where it is identified that one should be appointed. It is questionable how the cared-for person's rights under ECHR Article 5(4) can then be said to be met in such a case.

- The responsible body must also take all reasonable steps to appoint an IMCA to support the appropriate person when an appropriate person with capacity to do so asks for an IMCA;[92] or where the appropriate person lacks capacity to consent to being supported by an IMCA and the responsible body is satisfied than such an appointment is in the cared-for person's best interests.[93] These provisions reflect section 39D, although once again replace a mandatory duty with a requirement to take all reasonable steps.

22.84 Amendments to MCA 2005 introduced by the MC(A)A 2019 permit the IMCA or appropriate person to apply to the Court of Protection under section 21ZA without a permission filter.[94] It is clear that the appropriate person or IMCA – if one is appointed – both have the same responsibilities to give effect to P's ECHR Article 5(4) rights as does the RPR at present under DOLS. If an IMCA is appointed to support the appropriate person they have the same role as the section 39D IMCA at present. The authors' view is that the guidance in cases such as *AJ* and *RD* continue to apply to the appropriate person/IMCA, and the draft MCA Code proceeds on this basis. We also note

88 MCA 2005 Sch AA1 para 39(1).
89 MCA 2005 Sch AA1 para 39(2).
90 MCA 2005 Sch AA1 para 39(3).
91 [2016] EWCOP 15, [2016] 4 WLR 64, [2016] COPLR 302 at para 93.
92 MCA 2005 Sch AA1 para 40 (1) and (2).
93 MCA 2005 Sch AA1para 40(3).
94 MCA 2005 s21ZA, introduced by MCA(A) 2019 Sch 2 para 10.

in this regard the comments made by Baroness Blackwood[95] for the government at 'ping-pong' stage on 27 February 2019:

> On the matter of challenging authorisations in court, the responsible body under Article 5 of the European Convention on Human Rights has a duty to ensure that relevant cases are referred to the Court of Protection. I know that there has been a particular concern about ensuring that in very rare cases where it is not in the person's best interests to receive support and representation, those people are enabled to challenge in the Court of Protection if they want to. In these cases, the responsible body will need to ensure that the cases are referred to the court. If it fails in this duty, it can be challenged in court.[96]

22.85 As with DOLS, the intention with LPS is that the process of authorisation should start before the cared-person is moved into the proposed setting, as opposed to authorising the arrangements once they are in place. Both DOLS and LPS allow for authorisations to be granted up to 28 days in advance.[97] In an appropriate case this may allow for a proactive application to the Court of Protection, before the cared-for person has been moved to – for example – a care home and where a status quo can develop. However, it remains to be seen whether this is any more effective in practice than the position under DOLS.

Applications relating to MCA 2005 s4B

22.86 One of the features of LPS is that there is no statutory time-limit for the authorisation process to be completed. The government consultation on the draft MCA Code of Practice specifically includes a question as to whether the Code should include a time-frame of 21 days for the process to be completed. However, whether or not such a time-frame is included, as a matter of law, it would be possible for a person to remain deprived of their liberty for considerably longer than 21 days while the responsible body completes the assessment process, so long as at all times the substantive criteria within MCA 2005 s4B(7)(b) are met. It is therefore to be welcomed that the government has made clear[98] that it intends non-means-tested legal aid to

95 Parliamentary Under Secretary of State at the Department of Health and Social Care.

96 Hansard (HL) Vol 796, col, 128 (26 February 2019).

97 For LPS, see MCA 2005 Sch AA1 para 2(3).

98 Draft regulations 13 and 14 of the Mental Capacity (Amendment) Act 2019 (Consequential Provisions) Regulations.

be available for the person or the appropriate person acting on their behalf to challenge the position. The relief that could be granted on such a challenge would be a declaration under MCA 2005 s15 or a decision under MCA 2005 s16, and could well include consideration of whether the substantive criteria for authorisation would in fact be met (ie the person could contend that no authorisation could lawfully be granted because any deprivation of liberty to which it gave rise would not be necessary and proportionate in relation to the likelihood and seriousness of harm to the cared-for person).

Applications under MCA 2005 s21ZA

22.87 New MCA 2005 s21ZA is cast differently to section 21A, and is of wider reach. It applies to arrangements for those aged 16 and above, and those living in any setting, including their own home. The government confirmed during the passage of the Act through parliament that non-means-tested legal aid will be available in the same way that it has been for MCA 2005 s21A challenges.[99]

22.88 MCA 2005 s21ZA(2)(a) allows the court to consider two questions. The first question is 'whether schedule AA1 applies to the arrangements'. In the authors' view this should include questions such as: Are the arrangements, in reality, mental health arrangements, which should be authorised under the Mental Health Act? Have the provisions of the schedule been complied with? It may include the question as to whether the cared-for person falls within the new statutory definition of deprivation of liberty.

22.89 The second question is whether the authorisation conditions are met. This will require consideration of the criteria in MCA 2005 Sch AA1 para 12:

- whether the cared-for person has a mental disorder;
- whether the cared for person has capacity to consent to the arrangements, and
- whether the arrangements are 'necessary to prevent harm to the cared-for person and proportionate in relation to the likelihood and seriousness of harm to the cared-for person'.

22.90 The draft Code of Practice outlines guidance on all these requirements. In any event, the authors consider that questions relating to 'mental disorder' and 'capacity' should be approached exactly as they

99 Lord O'Shaughnessy, Parliamentary Under-Secretary of State, Department of Health and Social Care, at second reading in the House of Lords: Hansard (HL) Hansard (HL) Vol 792, col, 1109 (16 July 2018).

are now in a section 21A challenge. In relation to the 'necessary and proportionate' condition, we consider that 'proportionality' should be given a wide interpretation to reflect that both ECHR Article 8 and Article 5 rights are in play. As such we consider that the approach to the limits of non-means-tested public funding set down by the Court of Appeal in *Briggs* should continue. This is reinforced by comments from the then Minister of State Caroline Dinenage[100] that 'best interests decision making remains fundamental to the existing Act, within which the Liberty Protection Safeguards will sit'.

22.91 Section 21ZA(2)(c)) empowers the court to examine 'what the authorisation relates to'. Again, in the authors' view, this should include questions such as whether specific restrictions in the care plan are, or should be, authorised by the LPS authorisation. This could become particularly important in cases where restrictions are imposed which are not, in fact, part of the care arrangements, and which cannot be authorised either by DOLS or LPS. Examples of this are restrictions on contact,[101] or on social media and internet use.[102]

22.92 The court can also consider the period of time the authorisation has been granted,[103] which may be of some importance given that, in some cases, authorisations can (on renewal) be extended for up to three years.[104]

22.93 When the court has determined a question under MCA 2005, s21ZA(2), it can vary or terminate the authorisation, or direct the responsible body to vary the authorisation. 'Variation' can include (for instance) making clear that the authorisation does not cover aspects of the arrangements that the court has found to be unnecessary or disproportionate.

22.94 The court's ability to consider a person's liability for anything done under the guise of the authorisation is essentially unchanged from the current position under DOLS.

100 Mental Capacity (Amendment) Bill: Public Bill Committee, 15 January 2019, col 46.

101 See *SR v A Local Authority and others* [2018] EWCOP 36. The draft MCA Code specifically and helpfully indicates that the government does not consider restrictions on contact can be authorised by LPS.

102 See *Re A (capacity: social media and internet use: best interests* [2019] EWCOP 2, [2019] Fam 586 and *Re B (capacity: social media: care and contact)* [2019] EWCOP 3, [2019] COPLR 163.

103 MCA 2005 s21ZA(2)(b).

104 MCA 2005 Sch AA1 para 29(1).

CHAPTER 23

Medical treatment cases

Introduction

23.1 Cases involving medical treatment form a distinct sub-set of the cases that are decided by the Court of Protection. This chapter provides an overview of the key principles and practice points. It is, however, a specialist area, and needs to be placed also in the wider context of medical decision-making more broadly. For more detail, readers are referred to Christopher Johnston et al, *Medical treatment: decisions and the law*.[1]

23.2 Before 1 December 2017, serious medical treatment cases were treated entirely separately, with a Practice Direction (PD 9E) under the Court of Protection of Rules (COPR) governing their procedure. Unlike other cases, even before the Transparency Pilot was launched, they were usually held in public, and they were not included in the Case Management Pilot when this was introduced. Matters are now rather different. The former practice direction was not re-issued when the COPR 2017[2] came into force, so medical treatment cases are now simply a subset of personal welfare cases to which the personal welfare pathway under the Case Pathways PD 3B applies. Further, in *An NHS Trust v Y*[3] in July 2018, the Supreme Court clarified the limits to the previously understood obligation to bring cases to court. Those limits will be reflected in the revisions to the Code of Practice to the Mental Capacity Act (MCA) 2005 underway at the time of writing. In the interim, the Vice-President has promulgated guidance on medical treatment cases, addressing both when consideration needs to be given to bringing one, and what should happen where a medical treatment case does come to court.[4]

The scope of the court's jurisdiction

23.3 As set out in chapter 4, the Court of Protection has jurisdiction regarding (among other matters) medical treatment in relation to those aged 16 and above who lack the material decision-capacity. Conventionally, medical treatment cases involving those below the

1 Bloomsbury, 4th edn, 2022, and the supporting website with updates: www.serjeantsinn.com/news-and-resources/medical-treatment-decisions/.

2 SI 2017 No 1035.

3 [2018] UKSC 46, [2018] 3 WLR 751.

4 *Practice Guidance (CP: Serious Medical treatment)* [2020] EWCOP 2, [2020] COPLR 205 ('Serious Medical Treatment Guidance').

age of 18 have been brought before the High Court for relief under its inherent jurisdiction; however, where a 16- or 17-year-old is considered to lack decision-making capacity, it would be equally possible to bring the case to the Court of Protection. If the concern on the part of the treating clinicians is not that the individual (aged 16 or over) lacks capacity but that they are vulnerable and under the influence of another, then the appropriate route would be, again, to seek relief from the High Court under the inherent jurisdiction.

Serious medical treatment: definition

23.4 'Serious medical treatment' has a statutory definition,[5] namely treatment which involves providing, withdrawing or withholding treatment in circumstances where:

- (if a single treatment is proposed) there is a fine balance between its benefits and burdens and risks;
- (if there is a choice) a decision as to which treatment is finely balanced; or
- the treatment, procedure or investigation would be likely to involve serious consequences for the patient.

23.5 This statutory definition applies for determining when an advocate must be appointed before medical treatment can be undertaken where a person is 'unbefriended.' Prior to 1 December 2017, the (old) PD 9E used the same definition, and then stated that certain of these decisions should be brought to court:

- decisions about the proposed withholding or withdrawal of artificial nutrition and hydration from a person in a permanent vegetative state or a minimally conscious state;
- cases involving organ or bone marrow donation by a person who lacks capacity to consent; and
- cases involving non-therapeutic sterilisation of a person who lacks capacity to consent.[6]

23.6 The old PD 9E mirrored the approach of the Code of Practice to the MCA 2005 in suggesting that there was a **legal** obligation to bring such cases. However, in *An NHS Trust v Y*,[7] the Supreme Court

5 In the Mental Capacity Act 2005 (Independent Mental Capacity Advocates) (General) Regulations 2006 SI No 183.

6 See also in this regard *A Local Authority v K and others* [2013] EWHC 242 (COP), [2013] COPLR 194.

7 [2018] UKSC 46, [2018] 3 WLR 751.

confirmed that there was, in fact, no obligation under the MCA 2005, common law or the European Convention on Human Rights (ECHR) to bring an application to court before withdrawing clinically assisted nutrition and hydration (CANH) from a patient in a prolonged disorder of consciousness. Rather, the Supreme Court confirmed that, if the provisions of the MCA 2005 were followed and the relevant guidance observed,[8] and if there was agreement upon what is in the best interests of the patient, the patient could be treated in accordance with that agreement without application to the court.

23.7 In *An NHS Trust v Y*, the Supreme Court's also made clear that if *any* medical treatment decision is finely balanced, or there is a difference of medical opinion, or a lack of agreement to a proposed course of action from those with an interest in the patient's welfare, then consideration should be given to making an application. The Vice-President's Serious Medical Treatment Guidance[9] expands upon the decision in *NHS Trust v Y* to add to the 'triggers' that there is a potential conflict of interest on the part of those involved in the decision-making process.[10] The guidance reiterates that where one of the triggers arises, and the decision relates to life-sustaining treatment, an application to court must be made. Situations that do not relate to life-sustaining treatment but where consideration must be given to bringing an application include:

(a) where a medical procedure or treatment is for the primary purpose of sterilisation;
(b) where a medical procedure is proposed to be performed on a person who lacks capacity to consent to it, where the procedure is for the purpose of a donation of an organ, bone marrow, stem cells, tissue or bodily fluid to another person;
(c) a procedure for the covert insertion of a contraceptive device or other means of contraception;

8 Which, in the context of CANH, is now that produced by the British Medical Association (BMA) and Royal College of Physicians (endorsed by the General Medical Council (GMC)): *Decisions about clinically assisted nutrition and hydration (CANH) – information for healthcare providers, funders and managers*, November 2018, available at www.bma.org.uk/canh.

9 [2020] EWCOP 2, [2020] COPLR 205. In *Sherwood Forest Hospitals NHS Foundation Trust and another v H* [2020] EWCOP 5, [2020] COPLR 324 the Vice-President annexed the guidance to a judgment so as to 'read it' into the record of judicial decisions.

10 Para 8(d). It is suggested that this means a potential conflict that cannot be appropriately managed: see, by analogy, the consideration of this position in *Prolonged disorders of consciousness following sudden onset brain injury: national clinical guidelines*, Royal College of Physicians, March 2020 at p118.

(d) where it is proposed that an experimental or innovative treatment to be carried out;
(e) a case involving a significant ethical question in an untested or controversial area of medicine.[11]

23.8 As the guidance notes, the need to consider approaching the court is the procedure involves the serious interference with the person's rights under the ECHR, such that it is highly probable that, in most, if not all, cases, professionals faced with a decision whether to take that step will conclude that it is appropriate to apply to the court to facilitate a comprehensive analysis of capacity and best interests, with the person having the benefit of legal representation and independent expert advice. Importantly, this is so even where there is agreement between all those with an interest in the person's welfare.[12]

23.9 Separately, an application to court may also be required in relation to a medical procedure or treatment to be carried out on a person who lacks capacity to consent to it, where that procedure or treatment must be carried out using a degree of force to restrain the person concerned and the restraint will amount to a deprivation of their liberty.[13]

23.10 The guidance makes clear[14] that in cases involving issues as to medical treatment, the organisation which is, or will be, responsible for commissioning or providing clinical or caring services to P should normally (although not always) be the applicant.

Pre-action steps

23.11 A particular feature of medical treatment cases is that P will almost invariably be joined as a party, the Official Solicitor will very often be invited to, and if invited, will - subject to provision for her costs – will accept the invitation to act as P's litigation friend[15] (see further para

11 Para 9.

12 Para 10, citing *A Local Authority v P (by her litigation friend, the Official Solicitor) and others* [2018] EWCOP 10, [2019] COPLR 44 at para 56, concerning the covert insertion of a contraceptive device.

13 Serious Medical Treatment Guidance, para 12. An example would be the degree of sustained restraint envisaged to secure the feeding of Dr A in *An NHS Trust v Dr A* [2013] EWHC 2442 (COP), [2014] Fam 161.

14 Para 17.

15 See also Official Solicitor's Practice Note: Appointment as Litigation Friend in Personal Welfare Proceedings in the Court of Protection, para 14, available at: www.gov.uk/government/publications/appointment-of-the-official-solicitor-in-welfare-proceedings-practice-note.

23.19 below). The Official Solicitor, if appointed, will also almost invariably act both as litigation friend and solicitor for P – in other words, external solicitors will not be instructed and the Official Solicitor's own lawyers will handle the case from start to finish, instructing counsel if needs be. This means that, wherever possible, it is sensible to ensure that contact is made with the Official Solicitor's office before an application is issued (the contact details are in appendix G below), both to discuss the case in outline and to ensure that the Official Solicitor is in a position to respond quickly when the application is issued. The pressure of work upon the Official Solicitor, however, is such that the authors' experience is that the Official Solicitor is increasingly reluctant to become formally involved before an application is lodged unless there is clear provision for her legal costs (see further para 23.19 below).

Urgent applications

23.12 The courts are well used to dealing with urgent medical treatment applications, including those that arise out of normal court hours. The procedures in relation to urgent applications are discussed at para 11.74 onwards, and they will apply equally in medical treatment cases. It is particularly important in such cases that the treating clinicians are available by telephone so that the judge is able to hear from them directly if needs be – which may well entail setting up a conference call if the matter is being heard out of normal court hours.

23.13 The Official Solicitor operates an out-of-hours scheme; access to her out-of-hours lawyers is filtered through the out-of-hours judge.[16] It should be stressed that this is for genuine emergencies, and does not alleviate the need to bring cases in during conventional working hours where possible, not least so as to secure the proper participation of P and – where relevant – their family.[17] The Official Solicitor's involvement in out-of-hours cases is determined by the duty judge and as such, while her office can be alerted to the possibility of an out of hours application, no steps will be taken by the Official Solicitor in relation to such an application until she is invited to act by the duty

16 See Official Solicitor's Practice Note: Appointment as Litigation Friend in Personal Welfare Proceedings in the Court of Protection, para 25, available at www.gov.uk/government/publications/appointment-of-the-official-solicitor-in-welfare-proceedings-practice-note)

17 See the guidance given by Theis J in *Sandwell and West Birmingham Hospitals NHS Trust v CD* [2014] EWCOP 23, [2014] COPLR 650.

judge. In the case of a decision which simply cannot wait, it is possible for the court to make the decision on the spot.[18]

23.14 The general rule in medical treatment cases is that it is better to bring the application sooner rather than later so that all the necessary inquiries can be made and information obtained to allow the court to reach a proper conclusion as to where P's best interests lie. The courts have repeatedly emphasised the need to identify and bring proceedings as soon as possible.[19] A failure to bring a medical treatment case in a timely fashion has (at least) three adverse consequences:

1) it makes it more difficult (or to prevent altogether) the court being able to take into account the wishes and feelings of P;[20]
2) it becomes much more difficult for P's interests to be properly represented by the Official Solicitor (or another litigation friend);[21]
3) the delay itself may mean that medical options that were open to P are no longer open, which may cause harm, or even mean that their life is shortened in consequence.[22]

23.15 The Vice-President's Serious Medical Treatment Guidance[23] crystallises the position thus by noting – under 'pre-issue' – that it is important:

a) to consider whether steps can be taken to resolve the relevant issues without the need for proceedings; but
b) to recognise that delay will invariably be inimical to P's welfare and where resolution cannot be achieved within P's own timescales proceedings should be issued.

23.16 There can be a tension between bringing an application in a timely fashion and bringing one which is premature. In *Aintree University Hospitals NHS Foundation Trust v James*,[24] Lady Hale noted that, if an

18 See *Newcastle-upon-Tyne Hospitals Foundation Trust v LM* [2014] EWHC 454 (COP), [2015] 1 FCR 373.

19 See, for instance, *Re AB (termination of pregnancy)* [2019] EWCA Civ 1215, [2020] COPLR 42 and, amongst numerous judgments of Hayden J, the particularly trenchant observations in *North West London Clinical Commissioning Group v GU* [2021] EWCOP 59, [2022] COPLR 137.

20 See, for instance, *East Lancashire Hospitals NHS Trust v PW* [2019] EWCOP 10, [2019] Med LR 218 at paras 4 and 5.

21 See, for instance, *University Hospitals Dorset NHS Foundation Trust and another v Miss K* [2021] EWCOP 40 at paras 4 and 5.

22 See *Sherwood Forest Hospitals NHS Foundation Trust and another v H* [2020] EWCOP 5, [2020] COPLR 324; [2020] EWCOP 6; and [2020] EWCOP 10, [2020] COPLR 696 for a particularly egregious example.

23 [2020] EWCOP 2, [2020] COPLR 205 at para 14.

24 [2013] UKSC 67, [2014] 1 AC 591, (2013) 16 CCLR 554.

application is brought too early, then there is a risk that that the court may be unable to say that when the treatments are needed that they will not be in the best interests of the patient.[25] We suggest that the following observations made by Peel J in *Re Z (medical treatment: invasive ventilation)*[26] are of assistance by analogy (the case relating to a child):

> Although there may, in some cases, be a disadvantage in attempting to pre-empt a fluctuating situation, there are many cases where the facts establish, to the requisite civil standard of proof, not just what the current circumstances are, but what future circumstances are likely to be. Medical prognosis almost always involves an assessment of the future which by definition cannot be guaranteed, but the court will ordinarily have the benefit of expert evidence to assist in making findings to the requisite civil standard. The court is entitled to weigh up such medical prognosis as part of the totality of the evidence and, if the factual foundation is made out, and the evaluative exercise so justifies, I see no reason why an anticipatory declaration should not be made. Further, there are good reasons for thinking that to clarify the permissible level of medical treatment before the patient reaches a critical condition may avoid urgently instituted proceedings, fraught disputes and rushed decision making while the patient is in intensive care. . . . To my mind, it is therefore essentially a question of fact and evaluation. In my judgment, I am entitled to make an anticipatory declaration provided that (i) I have a factual basis on which to do so, (ii) those facts enable me not just to assess the situation as it is now, but also to form with a degree of solidity a prospective view, and (iii) the proposed anticipatory declaration, viewed in the context of best interests, is justified.

Allocation

23.17 The Serious Medical Treatment Guidance sets out the court's approach to allocation.[27] If the application involves serious medical treatment or an ethical dilemma in an untested area, the proceedings (including permission, the giving of any directions, and any hearing) must be conducted by a tier 3 judge,[28] unless the Senior Judge or a tier 3 judge determines to the contrary. Otherwise, the expectation is

25 Para 47.
26 [2021] EWHC 2613 (Fam), [2022] 1 FLR 1090 at para 16.
27 At paras 19 and 20.
28 This tracks also COPR PD 3A para 2(a).

that the court, on making case management directions, on issue, will in gatekeeping[29] have regard, in particular, to:

a) the seriousness of the consequences for P of the proposed treatment decision(s);
b) the seriousness of the interference with the ECHR rights of P involved the proposed treatment decision(s).

23.18 A helpful amplification of the approach to allocation set out in the guidance has been the approach taken to cases concerning COVID-19 vaccination. As Hayden identified in *SS v Richmond upon Thames LBC and another*:

> Where a question of vaccination of an incapacitated person arises, in the context of a care home, these cases are now usually heard by judges sitting in Tier 1 and Tier 2. The cases of *SD v Royal Borough of Kensington And Chelsea*; *E (Vaccine)* ... were heard at Tier 3 (ie the High Court) in the early stages of the availability of the vaccine, when the issue was a novel one and in order to assist the courts below. This case has been allocated to Tier 3 because it presents, for the first time, an opportunity to evaluate strongly and consistently expressed views by P relating to vaccination and the weight they should be given, in the broader landscape of the insidious risk arising from the Covid-19 public health crisis.[30]

Case management

23.19 In theory, medical treatment cases should be managed according to the same principles as other cases before the Court of Protection, but in practice the following distinctive features should be noted:[31]

- As noted above, P will almost invariably be joined as a party and the Official Solicitor be appointed to act as P's litigation friend. The Official Solicitor receives sufficient central government funding to conduct (in-house) such proceedings, and is also conventionally awarded half the costs of doing so against the relevant NHS body.[32] The Official Solicitor will decline to act until an undertaking is given by the relevant NHS body to meet half of her costs.
- The courts are often reluctant to grant anonymity to NHS trusts, save where this is necessary to protect the identity of P and their

29 Under COPR PD 3B para 2.4(1)(a).

30 [2021] EWCOP 31, [2021] COPLR 612 at para 35.

31 See also the Serious Medical Treatment Guidance at paras 19–22.

32 *An NHS Trust v D* [2012] EWHC 886 (COP), [2012] COPLR 499.

place of treatment (it is therefore likely that an NHS trust responsible for more than one hospital will be named as the chances of P being identified would be materially reduced in such a case). However, the position is different in relation to treating clinicians, especially given the often-charged climate that can surround medical treatment cases.[33]

- Unless the urgency of the case makes it impossible, the Official Solicitor will usually wish to obtain independent expert evidence (and will usually seek to do so on a joint basis). Questions of expert evidence are addressed further in chapter 13. The courts will place considerable weight upon the evidence of any expert(s) instructed, but – as in all other cases – will exercise independent judgment upon the questions both of P's capacity and best interests. A good example of the latter is *An NHS Trust v (1) K (2) Another Foundation Trust*[34] in which Holman J declined to follow the 'unduly pessimistic' evidence of the independent expert as to the risks to the patient surrounding the operation in question.
- Careful consideration should be given at as an early stage as possible as to whether, and what conditions, the judge should visit P: see *Practice Guidance (Court of Protection: Judicial visits)*[35] and para 16.45.
- Any decision of a tier 3 judge in a medical treatment case will be likely to continue to be considered for publication (subject to suitable anonymisation) in line with the former President's guidance on *Transparency in the Court of Protection: publication of judgments.*[36]

23.20 One important point to note in relation to the use of MCA 2005 s48 – ie the court's 'interim' jurisdiction (see para 11.67 above). Care should always be taken to ensure that, especially in any situation where there is room for doubt as to P's capacity, any decisions taken under cover of section 48 should be give rise to most minimal intrusion possible into P's life consistent with securing their interests.[37]

33 See (by analogy) *Abbasi v Newcastle upon Tyne Hospitals NHS Foundation Trust* [2021] EWHC 1699 (Admin), [2022] 2 WLR 365 and para 14.65 above.

34 [2012] EWHC 2922 (COP), [2012] COPLR 694.

35 [2022] EWCOP 5, [2022] 1 WLR 1445.

36 [2014] EWHC B2 (COP), [2014] COPLR 78.

37 *University Hospitals of Derby and Burton NHS Foundation Trust and Derbyshire Healthcare NHS Foundation Trust v MN* [2021] EWCOP 4.

Declarations or decisions?

23.21 Medical treatment cases are unusual in that the applicants (usually the treating NHS Trust) have not traditionally sought decisions from the court,[38] but rather declarations as to whether a proposed course of action is lawful.[39] However, the former President,[40] endorsed by Lady Hale,[41] has questioned whether this is correct, and whether the real relief that should be sought is not a decision (under MCA 2005 s16(2)(a)) consenting (or refusing consent) on behalf of P,[42] coupled (where the treating Trust is particularly concerned to have legal 'cover') with a declaration under MCA 2005 s15(1)(c).

23.22 In any event, it is important to be precise. In *Aintree*, for instance, the NHS trust in question made an application for a declaration that it would be lawful to withhold three types of life-sustaining treatment from Mr James 'in the event of a clinical deterioration'. As Lady Hale noted, this actually meant 'should his condition deteriorate that they [ie the treatments] become necessary', and that it would have been helpful to say so.

23.23 The courts have also shown themselves to be careful to maintain a distinct line between matters in respect of which they can properly make declarations or decisions under the MCA 2005 and those matters which fall within the scope of the ethical and clinical obligations owed by the treating doctors. In *An NHS Trust v (1) K (2) Another Foundation Trust*,[43] for instance, Holman J authorised the sedation of a woman who needed a hysterectomy before she was to be informed that it was proposed to carry out the proposed surgery so as to reduce the risk that she would be non-compliant.[44] Holman J noted, however, that 'an ethical issue may arise as to the degree of sedation and whether the surgeon can ethically proceed to operate unless he has given to the patient an adequate account of what he

38 Ie under MCA 2005 s16.

39 Under MCA 2005 s15.

40 In *Re MN* [2015] EWCA Civ 411, [2016] Fam 87, [2015] COPLR 505 at para 88.

41 *N v ACCG* [2017] UKSC 22, [2017] AC 549, [2017] COPLR 200 at para 26.

42 See *Re MN* [2015] EWCA Civ 411, [2016] Fam 87, (2015) 18 CCLR 521.

43 [2012] EWHC 2922 (COP), [2012] COPLR 694.

44 Relying on *DH NHS Foundation Trust v PS* [2010] EWHC 1217 (Fam), [2010] COPLR Con Vol 346, (2010) 13 CCLR 606. Holman J did not authorise restraint to be used on the patient because of the risk to her given her other medical difficulties.

proposes to do while she retains sufficient awareness to hear it and take it in. But that is an ethical matter for him'.[45]

23.24 One area where the court has no option but to make a declaration is where the person currently *has* capacity to make a decision, but only there is a real risk that they will lose it.[46] The court can, in effect, undertake contingency planning by making declarations under MCA 2005 s1(5)(c) as to the steps which will be lawful in the event that the person loses capacity. This is most often done in relation to a person who may lose capacity to make decisions about their birth arrangements. It should be noted that the Court of Protection does not have jurisdiction to make such a contingent declaration authorising arrangements giving rise to a deprivation of person's liberty: any such authority would have to be provided by the exercise of the High Court through its inherent jurisdiction.[47]

The approach of the courts to best interests

23.25 We have seen in chapter 3 (paras 3.65 onwards) how best interests decisions are made under the MCA 2005. In the specific context of medical treatment, the courts increasingly approach decisions on the basis that, if it is sufficiently certain whether patient would consent to or refuse the treatment in question, that will give the answer as to what is in their best interests.[48] One implication of this that lawyers should be particularly astute to obtain and interrogate evidence about the person's wishes, feelings, beliefs and values, and to ensuring that the court's evaluation of that evidence is appropriately rigorous.[49]

45 Para 44.

46 See *Re R* [2020] EWCOP 4, [2020] WLR 96 and *North Middlesex University Hospital NHS Trust v SR* [2021] EWCOP 58, [2022] COPLR 125.

47 See *Re R* [2020] EWCOP 4, [2020] WLR 96; and chapter 28.

48 See, in particular, *Briggs v Briggs (No 2)* [2016] EWCOP 53, [2017] 4 WLR 37, [2017] COPLR 42. See also, for an overview of the case-law, A Ruck Keene and M Friedman, 'Best interests, wishes and feelings and the Court of Protection 2015–2020,' (2020) *Journal of Elder Law and Capacity*, Winter, pp31–53.

49 See in this regard S Kim and A Ruck Keene, 'A new kind of paternalism in surrogate decision-making? The case of *Barnsley Hospitals NHS Trust Foundation Trust v MSP*' (2020) 1–6 Journal of Medical Ethics 4.

Is there really a best interests decision to be taken?

23.26 We conclude this chapter by raising a question that was starkly posed by the decision of the Supreme Court in *Aintree v James*, but which has yet fully to be grappled with by the courts. The Supreme Court emphasised that the MCA 2005 is concerned with 'enabling the court to do for the patient what he could do for himself if of full capacity, but it goes no further. On an application under this Act, therefore, the court has no greater powers than the patient would have if he were of full capacity'.[50] The Court of Protection cannot therefore order a doctor to provide a particular treatment to a patient; rather, its task is to 'decide whether a particular treatment is in the best interests of a patient who is incapable of making the decision for himself'.[51]

23.27 In some cases, therefore, the treating clinicians will have concluded that they will not offer specific treatment(s) to the patient (or would wish to withdraw such treatment) because they consider that either offering or continue to offer it would be clinically inappropriate, futile or (potentially) on the basis that its costs so far outweigh its benefits to the person that the treatment will not be funded by the relevant funding NHS body. In such a case, it would be irrelevant that the patient lacks the capacity to consent to the treatment because it would not be offered to them even if they had capacity and were requesting it. In this situation then, assuming that no other treating clinician would offer (or continue to offer) such treatment, then there is a good argument that there is, in fact, no best interests decision for the court to take.

23.28 So long as the clinicians are asserting that the steps that they wish to take (or not take) are taken in the name of the patient's best interests, then it is always open for the court to reach a different conclusion.[52] However, if the clinicians genuinely are not prepared to put a particular option on the table, this should be made clear to the court.[53] At that point, there is, in reality, no best interests decision for

50 *Aintree* at para 18 per Lady Hale.

51 *Aintree* at para 18 per Lady Hale.

52 For a stark example, see the decision in *University Hospitals Birmingham NHS Foundation Trust v HB* [2018] EWCOP 39, in which Keehan J held that it would be in the best interests of a woman to receive CPR, notwithstanding the 'very, very small chance of life' (para 36) that this would give her, because such was what she would have wanted.

53 See *PW v Chelsea* And *Westminster Hospital NHS Foundation Trust* [2018] EWCA Civ 1067, [2018] COPLR 346.

the court to take, although it is likely that the court would probe carefully as to the basis of the clinicians' reasoning.[54]

23.29 If the case has not yet come to court, but the hospital wishes to have legal 'cover' for its actions (most obviously where there is a dispute between the clinicians and the patient's family) then it should make clear in its application that it is not seeking any form of determination as to the person's best interests, but rather a declaration under MCA 2005 s15(1)(c) that (for instance) not providing a specific form of treatment is lawful because it is futile. Another alternative would be to bring an application in the Queen's Bench Division (QBD) under Civil Procedure Rules 1998 (CPR) Part 8 for a declaration that the trust's actions (or potentially proposed omissions) are lawful.[55]

54 By parity of approach with the approach that it would take in cases involving social care: see chapter 25.

55 See further Vikram Sachdeva, Alex Ruck Keene and Victoria Butler-Cole, 'The MCA in the Supreme Court – Reflections on *Aintree v James*' [2014] Eld LJ 54.

CHAPTER 24

Safeguarding and the Court of Protection

Introduction[1]

24.1 A significant proportion of the welfare applications made to the Court of Protection are made by local authorities on the basis of concerns that an adult lacking decision-making capacity in one or more domains, either has been subjected to or is at risk of harm. Such applications frequently arise, therefore, in the context of the discharge by the local authority of the obligations that are imposed upon it by various routes to safeguard adults at risk within their area. The overlap between actions taken on the basis of safeguarding obligations and applications before the Court of Protection is one that justifies a specific chapter of its own because of the difficulties that can arise where local authorities are not sufficiently clear as to the specific requirements that arise when matters move from investigation to proceedings before the court.

24.2 This chapter therefore outlines briefly what is meant by safeguarding, by specific reference to the Care Act 2014 (for England) and the Social Services and Well-being (Wales) Act (SSWWA) 2014 (for Wales). It then highlights how Court of Protection proceedings form an aspect of safeguarding, before making clear the specific steps required when an adult's circumstances move from being the subject of a safeguarding investigation to an application before the Court of Protection. It, finally, notes what should happen while Court of Protection proceedings are ongoing and further safeguarding concerns arise.

24.3 It is not only local authorities who have safeguarding obligations: other bodies, most obviously NHS bodies, will have responsibilities toward adults at risk, and may find that those responsibilities give rise to a need to bring proceedings before the Court of Protection. While the obligations set out Care Act 2014 and the SSWWA 2014 do not directly apply to such bodies, the principles set out in the subsequent parts of the chapter apply with equal force to them.

1 Parts of this chapter originally appeared, in different form, in an article by Alex Ruck Keene entitled 'Safeguarding and the Court of Protection', in the November 2013 *Encyclopaedia of Local Government Law Bulletin*, Sweet & Maxwell. See also Alex Ruck Keene, Kelly Stricklin-Coutinho and Henry Gilfillan, 'The role of the Court of Protection in safeguarding' [2015] *Journal of Adult Protection* 380.

What is safeguarding?

24.4 Safeguarding has both a broad and a narrow definition.[2] The broader definition encompasses the prevention of abuse, and can encompass consideration of all aspects of a person's general welfare. As such, it forms part of the general approach to be taken to the assessment and delivery of services to adults by local social services authorities. The narrow definition – perhaps more accurately called 'adult protection' – refers to investigation and intervention where it is suspected that abuse may have occurred.

24.5 In England, the Care Act 2014 imposes two duties upon local authorities, reflecting these two aspects:

- First, the Care Act 2014 includes an overarching principle in section 1 to the effect that the general duty of a local authority in the discharge of its functions relating to care and support of specific individual is to promote the well-being of that individual. 'Well-being', in turn, is defined as including protection from an abuse and neglect.[3]
- Second, the Care Act 2014 imposes[4] a statutory duty of enquiry upon a local authority wherever it has reasonable cause to suspect that an adult in its area (whether or not ordinarily resident there):
  - has needs for care and support (whether or not the authority is meeting any of those needs) (ie whether or not the adult is eligible for community care services provided by the local authority);
  - is experiencing, or is at risk of, abuse or neglect; and
  - as a result of those needs is unable to protect themselves against the abuse or neglect or the risk of it.

24.6 While 'abuse' is not given a specific definition, the Care Act 2014 makes clear[5] that it includes financial abuse, financial abuse being defined, in turn, as including:

- having money or other property stolen;
- being defrauded;
- being put under pressure in relation to money or other property; and
- having money or other property misused.

2 See the Law Commission's report *Adult social care*, Law Com No 326, May 2011, para 9.2; available at: http://lawcommission.justice.gov.uk/docs/lc326_adult_social_care.pdf.

3 Care Act 2014 s1(2)(c).

4 Care Act 2014 s42.

5 Care Act 2014 s42(3).

24.7 The statutory guidance accompanying the Care Act 2014 provides that it also encompasses physical abuse, domestic violence, sexual abuse, psychological abuse, modern slavery, discriminatory abuse and organisational abuse.[6] 'Neglect' is not defined in the Care Act 2014, but in the statutory guidance is defined as including neglects by acts of omission such as ignoring medical, emotional or physical care needs, failure to provide access to appropriate health, care and support or educational services and the withholding of the necessities of life, such as medication, adequate nutrition and heating. It can also include self-neglect.[7]

24.8 The equivalent duties were introduced in Wales in SSWWA 2014 ss5 (well-being) and 126 (the duty of inquiry). There is a more detailed definition of both abuse and neglect given in the legislation itself,[8] with a non-exhaustive list of examples given in the accompanying statutory guidance.[9] Neither the Act nor the accompanying statutory guidance provide for self-neglect, and it is doubtful that this is capable of triggering the duty of inquiry.

24.9 Where the duty of enquiry arises, the local authority must make or cause to be made whatever enquiries it thinks necessary to enable it to decide whether any action should be taken in the adult's care and, if so, what and by whom.[10]

24.10 The Care Act 2014 does not, however, give any *powers* for local authorities in respect of either the prevention or the investigation of abuse or neglect. In particular, the then-government declined on several occasions during the passage of the bill through parliament to amend it to introduce a power of entry by which a local authority would be able to seek a judicial warrant to enter a property and speak to an adult at risk. The SSWWA 2014 does include such a power for an authorised officer to apply for an adult protection and support order,[11] and practice in England and Wales may well diverge

6 *Care and support statutory guidance*, Department of Health and Social Care, chapter 14, www.gov.uk/government/publications/care-act-statutory-guidance/care-and-support-statutory-guidance.

7 *Care and support statutory guidance*, Department of Health and Social Care, chapter 14.

8 SSWWA 2014 s197.

9 *Statutory guidance: working together to safeguard people volume 1 – Introduction and overview, Part 7: Safeguarding*, Welsh Government, para 26.

10 Care Act 2014 s42(2) (England); SSWWA 2014 s126 (Wales).

11 SSWWA 2014 s127 (Wales). An equivalent power (and other, broader, powers including a power of removal) can be found in the Adult Support and Protection (Scotland) Act 2007.

considerably over the coming years in consequence of the differing powers available to local authorities in the two jurisdictions.

24.11 In order to discharge their duty of inquiry, local authorities therefore need to draw upon a range of pre-existing powers (including the specific statutory power of entry in Wales) and/or draw upon co-operation from other authorities with relevant responsibilities and powers (most obviously, police forces). Space prevents a detailed discussion of these powers,[12] but for purposes of this book, the most relevant is the ability of a local authority – where the adult lacks (or may lack[13]) decision-making capacity in the relevant domains – to bring proceedings before the Court of Protection for declarations and decisions as to such matters as to where they should live and with whom they should have contact.

24.12 The former President of the Court of Protection, Sir James Munby, has held on a number of occasions that local authorities or other public bodies must obtain the authority of the court if they consider it necessary to remove a person lacking capacity to consent from their home.[14] It is suggested that, to the extent that he has purported to lay down a substantive rule to this end, such cannot be correct.[15] However, it is clear that any decision by a public body to remove a person from their own home, especially in the face of their objections, and/or to restrict their contact with others,[16] will undoubtedly engage the person's rights to private and family life under European Convention on Human Rights (ECHR) Article 8 (and quite possibly those of others), and that proceeding without the sanction of the court may well give rise to a breach of the implied

12 An overview can be found in chapter 18 of Luke Clements et al, *Community care and the law*, 7th edn, LAG, 2019.

13 Sometimes, the issue is in fact whether the adult lacks that capacity or whether they are a vulnerable adult under coercion: see *London Borough of Redbridge v G* [2014] EWHC 485 (COP), [2014] COPLR 292; chapter 28.

14 Most recently in *Re AG* [2015] EWCOP 78, [2016] COPLR 13, but see also *Re A and C (Equality and Human Rights Commission intervening)* [2010] EWHC 978 (Fam), [2010] COPLR Con Vol 10.

15 See, by analogy, *R (Burke) v General Medical Council* [2005] EWCA Civ 1003, [2006] QB 273, (2004) 7 CCLR 609 at paras 71–72, and also Alex Ruck Keene, 'Section 5 MCA and the "need" for judicial sanction' [2016] Eld LJ 244.

16 *Hillingdon LBC v Neary* [2011] EWHC 1377 (COP), [2011] COPLR Con Vol 632, (2011) 14 CCLR 239.

procedural safeguards that accompany Article 8.[17] Put simply: public bodies are on thin legal ice when they are interfering substantially in the autonomy of those without capacity, and they will always need to be clear as to the precise basis upon which they are acting and alert to the possibility that they may need the court to confirm they are acting lawfully. The mere fact that they are acting pursuant to safeguarding obligations imposed under either the English or Welsh legislation does not, itself, give them the power to take such draconian steps as removal from a person's home or restriction of their contact with others.

The overlap between safeguarding and the Court of Protection

24.13 It can be seen from the very brief review above that what might be entitled adult protection proceedings before the Court of Protection sit within the broader safeguarding context. It is, however, vitally important to recognise that a decision to instigate proceedings before the Court of Protection is a decision that gives rise to a specific set of obligations upon the applicant – be that a local authority or NHS body – arising from the demands of the court process. These obligations are discussed in greater detail in the main part of this work; of particular relevance is chapter 15, because fact-finding will – often – form an important part of adult protection proceedings.

24.14 Perhaps the most important point to emphasise here is that it is inappropriate for Court of Protection proceedings to be used as a 'voyage of discovery',[18] such that it is important that the applicant is satisfied at the outset that it has a satisfactory evidential basis for any allegations that it advances against those whom it contends have harmed the adult or from whom the adult is at risk. That evidential basis may, in a very urgent case, be limited, but as a general rule, it is clear that a local authority should not embark upon Court of Protection proceedings except on the basis that it is satisfied that it

17 See the article by Alex Ruck Keene referred to above and, eg, the decision of the European Court of Human Rights in *Shtukaturov v Russia* [2008] ECHR 223, (2012) 54 EHRR 27, in which the court reiterated (at para 89) that, while ECHR Article 8 contains no explicit procedural requirements, 'the decision-making process involved in measures of interference must be fair and such as to ensure due respect of the interests safeguarded by Article 8'.

18 *A Local Authority v PB and P* [2011] EWHC 502 (Fam), [2011] COPLR Con Vol 166 at para 38, per Charles J.

has the evidence that it will need at the final hearing to support factual allegations made against any individuals.

24.15 This means that a decision to bring proceedings has to be taken after as rigorous a process as possible in the time allowed (involving senior members of the social work management team and the legal department) so as to ensure that:

- a considered decision is taken as to whether evidence being put before the court is sufficiently cogent – while the standard of proof before the Court of Protection is the civil standard (see further para 15.25), it is axiomatic that a serious allegation should not be advanced absent proper evidence;[19]
- the sources of information forming the foundation of the decisions being made are checked so as to allow an assessment to be made about its reliability – 'The fact that a piece of information has been repeated many times does not enhance its reliability';[20]
- where orders are being sought that interfere with rights under ECHR Article 8, the picture being put to the court is a balanced one, rather than one presenting solely the negative information or the facts cast only in a negative light;[21] and
- proper consideration has been given to whether it is necessary to put the allegations to the alleged abuser before taking steps upon the basis of those allegations – the obligation upon public bodies to treat parties affected by their actions in a just manner is capable of being overridden by the obligation to protect an adult at risk, but a failure to recognise that obligation can, itself, give rise to flawed decision-making.[22]

24.16 The courts are alive to the fact that, on occasion, local authorities are on the horns of a dilemma, and that it may be necessary urgently to invoke the jurisdiction of the Court of Protection before it has been possible properly to investigate an allegation of abuse.[23] However, in

19 *A Local Authority v HS and others* [2013] EWHC 2410 (COP) at paras 184–186, per District Judge Eldergill. This decision does not have precedent value but is cited here as it contains a very detailed discussion of the consequences of a failure to analyse the evidential basis upon which an adult protection application is brought.

20 *Surrey CC v M and others* [2013] EWHC 2400 (Fam), (2013) 157(32) SJLB 31 at para 77 per Theis J (the comments relate to care proceedings, but are of wider application).

21 *Surrey CC v M and others* at para 78.

22 *R (Davis and Davis) v West Sussex CC* [2012] EWHC 2152 (Admin), [2013] PTSR 494.

23 *HS* at para 187.

such a case, it is all the more important that stock is taken as soon as possible thereafter of matters. A failure to do so leads to (at least) two adverse consequences:

- Leaving allegations '[hanging] like a cloud' over family members or other individuals can act as a substantial distraction to the real welfare issues, by placing those individuals in an unnecessarily adversarial position vis-à-vis the local authority.[24]
- In the worst case scenario, it can lead to very substantial damages and/or costs being incurred unnecessarily by other parties which fall to be paid by the local authority. By way of example, a local authority was ordered to pay the full costs of the Official Solicitor and of P's brother (agreed in the total sum of £88,000) after it withdrew allegations of sexual abuse against the brother almost two years after the proceedings were brought in the Court of Protection. District Judge Eldergill held that:

> There was a prolonged failure on the local authority's part to recognise the weakness of its case. The allegations were vague and insufficiently particularized. The 'evidence' in support was manifestly inadequate. It was internally inconsistent and unreliable. The truth of what was alleged was assumed without any proper, critical, analysis.[25]

24.17 The propositions set out above do not affect the general duty to place before the court disputes where the best outcome may not be immediately clear. Court of Protection proceedings need not be adversarial and may be the best forum for resolving finely-balanced questions as to what may constitute the best and least restrictive alternative for P. In all cases, however, it is essential to show that available evidence has been properly evaluated and that it is openly shared with the court and the parties.

24.18 Importantly, if a public body brings a matter to the Court of Protection for determination as to where an individual's best interests lie, then, for forensically similar reasons to those which apply in rela-

24 *A London Borough v (1) BB (by her litigation friend the Official Solicitor) (2) AM (3) SB (4) EL Trust* [2011] EWHC 2853 (Fam), [2012] COPLR 16 at para 18 per Ryder J (as he then was).

25 Para 188. For other cases where what might be characterised as a safeguarding overreaction led to local authorities being heavily criticised and having to pay substantial damages and/or costs, see *Somerset County Council v MK* [2014] EWCOP B25 (damages not publicly quantified) and [2015] EWCOP B1 (indemnity costs); *Milton Keynes Council v RR* [2014] EWCOP B19 and [2014] EWCOP 34 (costs); *Essex County Council v RF* [2015] EWCOP 1: (£60,000 damages, care home fees waived at a cost to the local authority of £23–£25,000, costs).

tion to childcare proceedings, they must work in partnership with the court. This means that it lies in the court's power to direct the public body to file evidence (including a care plan), even though the plan's contents may not or do not reflect its formal position, 'for it is not for the local authority (or indeed any other party) to decide whether it is going to restrict or limit the evidence that it presents'.[26] Further, as noted at para 16.7, the court's powers in this regard have been strengthened by the introduction of Court of Protection Rules 2017[27] (COPR) r13.2, which means that the permission of the court is required before proceedings may be withdrawn. Where the public body decides, in the discharge of its public law obligations relating to funding of care and treatment, that a particular option is no longer on the table, the position is different, and is discussed in chapter 25.

Safeguarding during the currency of Court of Protection proceedings

24.19 In the authors' experience, there can sometimes be confusion on the part of public authorities as to what it is that they are required to do during the currency of Court of Protection proceedings if a further safeguarding concern arises in relation to P. They can, in particular, sometimes be unclear as to whether they can take any steps without the authorisation of the court.

24.20 The short answer is that the fact that Court of Protection proceedings are on foot does not alleviate the obligations upon the local authority (or NHS body) where they have reason to believe that P has suffered harm or is at risk of harm. However, while they should take such steps as are immediately necessary to meet the situation, it is likely always to be necessary to bring the matter back to court if they will involve a substantial change in P's circumstances (for instance, where they are living).

24.21 One specific requirement in such case was identified by McFarlane J (as he then was) in *Enfield LBC v SA and others*.[28] Where there are extant Court of Protection proceedings, then in the absence of an absolutely pressing emergency (using that phrase in an extreme

26 *Re MN (Adult)* EWCA Civ 411, [2016] Fam 87, (2015) 18 CCLR 521 at para 37, citing *Re W (Care Proceedings: Functions of Court and Local Authority)* [2013] EWCA Civ 1227, [2014] 2 FLR 431.

27 SI 2017 No 1035.

28 [2010] EWHC 196 (Admin), [2010] COPLR Con Vol 362.

sense), McFarlane J held that any question of whether or not P was to be the subject of an 'achieving best evidence' interview[29] must be raised with the court and be subject to a direction from the judge. He noted that where the substance of the interview might relate to allegations that another party to the proceedings (or someone closely connected to a party) had harmed P then there would be good grounds for the matter being raised, at least initially, without notice to that party. However, in every case, he held, notice should be given to the Official Solicitor or any other person who acted as P's litigation friend.[30]

Police involvement

24.22 One particular feature of adult protection proceedings before the Court of Protection is that they may well require the involvement of the police to implement the decisions and declarations of the court. This is especially so if the judge determines that it is necessary that P be removed from a place that they have been residing with family members or carers whom it is thought will seek to frustrate the process. In such a case, the courts have set down guidance as to the steps should be followed:

> In the event that it is expected that the assistance of the Police may be required to effect or assist with the removal of a vulnerable/ incapacitated adult ('P') which the Court is being asked to authorise, the following steps should generally be taken:
>
> (1) the Local Authority/NHS body/other organisation/person (the Applicant) applying to the Court for an authorisation to remove P should, in advance of the hearing of the Application, discuss and, where possible, agree with the Police the way in which it is intended that the removal will be effected, to include, where applicable, the extent to which it is expected that restraint and/or force may be used and the nature of any restraint (for example, handcuffs) that may be used;
>
> (2) the Applicant should ensure that information about the way in which it is intended that removal will be effected is provided to the

29 That is, an interview carried out by police officers with a possible view to criminal proceedings, complying with the guidance set down in *Achieving best evidence in criminal proceedings: guidance on interviewing victims and witnesses, and guidance on using special measures*, Ministry of Justice, (now) 3rd revision, 2011; available at: www.cps.gov.uk/sites/default/files/documents/legal_guidance/best_evidence_in_criminal_proceedings.pdf.

30 *Enfield LBC v SA* at para 46.

Court and to the litigation friend (in cases where a person has been invited and/or appointed to act as P's litigation friend) before the Court authorises removal. In particular, the Court and the litigation friend should be informed whether there is agreement between the Applicant and the Police and, if there is not, about the nature and extent of any disagreement;

(3) where the Applicant and the Police do not agree about how removal should be effected, the Court should give consideration to inviting/ directing the Police to attend the hearing of the Application so that the Court can, where appropriate, determine how it considers removal should be effected and/or ensure that any authorisation for removal is given on a fully informed basis.[31]

31 *LBH v GP and MP* (2010) 13 CCLR 171 at para 31 per Coleridge J.

CHAPTER 25

The Court of Protection and the Administrative Court

Introduction

25.1 For some years after the coming into force of the Mental Capacity Act (MCA) 2005, it was not entirely clear how far the Court of Protection could go in deciding where P's best interests lay. In particular, where P's care was provided by a public body (whether a local authority or a health body), it was not entirely clear whether the Court of Protection was entitled to decide – in the abstract – where (for instance) it was in P's best interests for them to live, or whether the Court of Protection was limited to choosing between the options put on the table by the public body.

25.2 The position has been largely clarified by the judgment of the Supreme Court in *N v ACCG*.[1] This chapter outlines briefly the dividing lines between the jurisdiction of the Court of Protection and that of the Administrative Court, before addressing the practical questions that arise where parallel proceedings are likely to be necessary and, finally, the approach that the Administrative Court is likely to take in any challenge arising out of a case before the Court of Protection.

The limits of the Court of Protection's jurisdiction

25.3 For the most part, a public body responsible for the wellbeing of the person concerned (whether in a medical context or in the context of their welfare more generally) will either bring proceedings to seek a decision from the court (especially in the safeguarding context: see further chapter 24) or is a party to the proceedings and is willing to abide by the result. However, there may be cases in which the public body has already taken a decision in discharge of its statutory functions, and the question then arises how that decision can appropriately be challenged. Alternatively, the public body may decide in the currency of Court of Protection proceedings that it does not wish to put before the court a particular option for consideration. For instance, a local authority may contend that a placement to which P has been moved in discharge of its community care functions sufficiently meets their needs that they are not prepared to incur the substantially greater expenditure that may be required to allow them to move home. The question that then arises is as to the extent the Court of Protection is able to compel a public authority to discharge

1 *N v ACCG* [2017] UKSC 2, [2017] AC 549, [2017] COPLR 200.

its statutory functions in a certain way or to make a specific funding decision. Put another way, how and when will parallel public law proceedings be required in such situations?

25.4 Cases decided prior to the enactment of the MCA 2005 suggested that, in the event of an impasse of the nature described above, it would be necessary to proceed by way of judicial review in order to challenge the decision of the public authority.[2] In 2015, the Court of Appeal confirmed this in *Re MN*.[3]. Sir James Munby P, giving the sole reasoned judgment of the court, held that:

> 80. The function of the Court of Protection is to take, on behalf of adults who lack capacity, the decisions which, if they had capacity, they would take themselves. The Court of Protection has no more power, just because it is acting on behalf of an adult who lacks capacity, to obtain resources or facilities from a third party, whether a private individual or a public authority, than the adult if he had capacity would be able to obtain himself. . . . The Court of Protection is thus confined to choosing between available options, including those which there is good reason to believe will be forthcoming in the foreseeable future.
>
> 81. The Court of Protection, like the family court and the Family Division, can explore the care plan being put forward by a public authority and, where appropriate, require the authority to go away and think again. Rigorous probing, searching questions and persuasion are permissible; pressure is not. And in the final analysis the Court of Protection cannot compel a public authority to agree to a care plan which the authority is unwilling to implement. I agree with the point Eleanor King J made in her judgment (para 57):
>
> 'In my judgment, such discussions and judicial encouragement for flexibility and negotiation in respect of a care package are actively to be encouraged. Such negotiations are however a far cry from the court embarking on a 'best interests' trial with a view to determining whether or not an option which has been said by care provider (in the exercise of their statutory duties) not to be available, is nevertheless in the patient's best interest.'

25.5 In the resulting appeal to the Supreme Court,[4] Lady Hale upheld the judgment of the Court of Appeal. She agreed that the court has 'no greater power to oblige others to do what is best than P would himself'.[5]

2 See, in particular, *A v A Health Authority* [2002] EWHC 18 (Fam), [2002] Fam 213 and *Re S (vulnerable adult)* [2007] 2 FLR 1095.

3 *Re MN (adult)* EWCA Civ 411, [2016] Fam 87, (2015) 18 CCLR 521.

4 *N v ACCG* [2017] UKSC 22, [2017] AC 549, [2017] COPLR 200.

5 *N v ACCG* at para 35.

25.6 Once an application to the Court of Protection is made, however, Lady Hale explained that:

> What may often follow such an application will be a process of independent investigation, as also happened in this case, coupled with negotiation and sometimes mediation, in which modifications are made to the care plan and areas of dispute are narrowed, again as happened in this case.[6]

25.7 She noted the court's extensive case management powers and went on to say:

> The court is clearly entitled to take the view that no useful purpose will be served by holding a hearing to resolve a particular issue. In reaching such a decision, many factors might be relevant. In a case such as this, for example: the nature of the issues; their importance for MN; the cogency of the parents' demands; the reasons why the CCG opposed those demands and their cogency; any relevant and indisputable fact in the history; the views of MN's litigation friend; the consequence of further investigation in terms of costs and court time; the likelihood that it might bring about further modifications to the care plan or consensus between the parties; and generally whether further investigation would serve any useful purpose.[7]

25.8 In an important caveat, Lady Hale added:

> Case management along these lines does not mean that a care provider or funder can pre-empt the court's proceedings by refusing to contemplate changes to the care plan. The court can always ask itself what useful purpose continuing the proceedings, or taking a particular step in them, will serve but that is for the court, not the parties, to decide.[8]

25.9 The court may therefore be willing to hear evidence as to a potential plan for P even in circumstances where there is uncertainty as to whether it will be funded or not, as part of the process of investigation, negotiation and mediation identified by Lady Hale. The decision

6 *N v ACCG* at para 39.

7 Para 41.

8 Para 43. In *Re JB (costs)* [2020] EWCOP 49, [2021] COPLR 88, costs were awarded against a local authority which had sought (but withdrawn) an application for an injunction seeking to require a care provider to continue accommodating P in circumstances where it had given valid notice Keehan J agreed with the submission that the application was doomed because the placement was simply not an available option, and also described the application as being misconceived and totally without merit.

of Hayden J in *An NHS Trust v G*[9] is perhaps best seen as an example of precisely that process.

25.10 As discussed further at para 26.3 onwards, there is one exception to the proposition in *N v ACCG* that arises in cases where a proper claim can be framed based upon the Human Rights Act (HRA) 1998 that a public authority in declining to fund a particular form of care package is acting in a way incompatible with rights under the European Convention on Human Rights (ECHR).

Parallel proceedings

25.11 Parallel proceedings will be unusual,[10] not least because it is not easy to mount a judicial review challenge (in particular given the ever more limited scope of public funding available). The Administrative Court also applies a permission filter significantly more stringently than does the Court of Protection (the filter not even applying in all cases before the latter: see chapter 9). Administrative Court judges will, further, be astute to ensure that cases that should properly be determined within the four walls of the Court of Protection remain there. In *DO v LBH*,[11] for instance, permission was refused to the sister of P in concurrent Court of Protection proceedings to bring judicial review applications against decisions of the local authority which had the effect of removing her from caring for her brother and making decisions as to his care arrangements. HHJ Jarman QC (sitting as a Deputy High Court Judge) noted that such questions were ones which the Court of Protection with its expertise was particularly suited to deal with and that judicial review was a remedy of last resort which should only be deployed where (for instance) an application or appeal within Court of Protection proceedings was not available.

25.12 However, where a party or parties wish to challenge a failure by a public body to put a particular option on the table, by way of judicial review proceedings, then any delay or increased expense of litigation can be ameliorated to a considerable extent by an early identification of the issues and, if needs be, the matter being listed before a High

9 [2021] EWCOP 69.

10 An example of a combined judicial review and Court of Protection application (albeit not arising out of a refusal to put an option on the table) is *C v A Local Authority and others* [2011] EWHC 1539 (Admin), [2011] COPLR Con Vol 972, (2011) 14 CCLR 471.

11 [2012] EWHC 4044 (Admin).

Court judge who sits both in the Court of Protection and the Administrative Court.[12] If the application was being heard by a district or a circuit judge, therefore, it will be necessary to apply to have the matter transferred to be heard before a High Court judge with the relevant 'tickets'. Detailed directions will also be required to ensure that matters are considered in the right sequence – ie broadly, all the stages of the judicial review first so as to ensure that there is clarity as to exactly what options are before the Court of Protection when it comes to consider where P's best interests will lie.

25.13 Finally, we should emphasise (as did Eleanor King J at first instance in *N v ACCG*) that it is vital that there is clarity in respect of the available options as early as can reasonably be achieved (see also para 11.24). A failure to identify which options are actually on the table and which are not can lead to a party told at the last minute that an option is not available feeling – quite understandably – that the 'ground has been cut from under their feet by . . . the public authorities' "knock out blow" '.[13] It may well be the case that the public authority, for good reason, may well not wish to commit itself to a stark statement that 'option A is not available' so as to allow room for discussion and the maintenance of a working relationship. However, if the reality is that it is not, it is likely to be better for this to be established sooner rather than later, if for no other reason than a failure to do so will inevitably lead to a prolonging of proceedings – and of consequent expense – which are, on a proper analysis, futile. The aim of the COPR Case Pathways PD 3B (discussed in chapter 4 and chapter 10) is to prevent just such an eventuality.

The approach of the Administrative Court

25.14 It is of considerable importance to remember that the fact that a person lacks the capacity to decide (for instance) where they should live:

> . . . does not import the test of 'what is in her best interests?' as the yardstick by which all care decisions are to be made . . . Section 1(5) of the Act applies to 'an act done, or decision made . . . for or on behalf of a person who lacks capacity'. Its decision-making criteria and

12 All High Court judges who sit in the Family Division are entitled to sit in the Court of Protection. Some also hold a 'ticket' to sit in the Administrative Court.

13 [2013] EWHC 3859 (COP), [2014] COPLR 11 at para 46. See also para 102 of the judgment of Sir James Munby P in the Court of Appeal: [2015] EWCA Civ 411, (2015) 18 CCLR 521.

procedures are designed to be a substitute for the lack of independent capacity of the person to act or take decisions for him or herself. They come into play in circumstances where a person with capacity would take, or participate in the taking of, a decision.[14]

25.15 In other words, very many decisions relating to the provision of care by public bodies to adults lacking capacity to take material decisions are not, on a proper analysis, best interests decisions falling within the scope of the MCA 2005. Rather, they are decisions taken as to 1) what the adult's needs are; and 2) how those needs are to be met. They are decisions taken by reference to substantial bodies of legislation and of case-law that apply to all adults, not just those who lack capacity in one or more regards;[15] they are therefore precisely the sort of decisions that have conventionally fallen – and continue to fall – to be decided in the Administrative Court by reference to the well-developed tests that apply when that court is considering whether the public bodies in question have erred in their decision-making.

25.16 Space precludes a detailed discussion here of the tests that apply in judicial review proceedings,[16] but it is important to note that the crucial distinction between the approach of the Administrative Court and the approach of the Court of Protection is that the former is (broadly) focused upon the process by which the public body has taken the decision in question; the latter is, itself, the decision-maker and will therefore engage in a detailed examination of the merits of the various options before it. This hard-edged distinction can appear to be blurred in certain categories of cases, in particular those requiring the assessment by the Administrative Court of the proportionality of any interference with rights under the ECHR, but even in such cases the Administrative Court will not, formally, be conducting a review of the merits of the decision and will not therefore be standing in the shoes of the decision-maker.[17]

14 *R (Chatting) v (1) Viridian Housing (2) Wandsworth LBC* [2012] EWHC 3595 (Admin), [2013] COPLR 108 at paras 99–100 per Nicholas Paines QC sitting as a Deputy High Court Judge. This passage was endorsed by the Court of Appeal in *Re MN* (at para 24).

15 See eg (for England) Stephen Knafler QC, *Adult Social Care Law*, LAG 2nd edn, 2019 and Tim Spencer-Lane, *Care Act Manual*, Sweet & Maxwell, 3rd edn, 2019.

16 See, in this regard, in particular, Jonathan Manning, Sarah Salmon and Robert Brown, *Judicial Review Proceedings: A Practitioner's Guide*, LAG, 3rd edn, 2013.

17See *R (A) v Chief Constable of Kent* [2013] EWCA Civ 1706, (2014) 135 BMLR 22.

CHAPTER 26

Human rights and the Court of Protection

Introduction

26.1 The Court of Protection is, almost by definition, a court whose every substantive decision will be taken after balancing different rights arising under the European Convention on Human Rights (ECHR), both those of P and – frequently – those of third parties (most often family members) upon whom the court's decisions in relation to P will impact. In this chapter, we outline briefly some of the key points that advisers need to consider in relation to the ECHR, in particularly when it comes to seeking redress for breaches of the ECHR. We also touch upon the impact of the United Nations (UN) Convention on the Rights of Persons with Disabilities (CRPD). As this book was going to press, the Government published the Bill of Rights Bill, which would dramatically change the framework within ECHR protections are considered domestically, and (if unamended), reduce many of the protections directly afforded by the Convention. We do not address it further in this edition, save to note that we hope that it will not be necessary to address it in any subsequent edition.

Relying upon the ECHR in the course of proceedings

26.2 The ECHR permeates all aspects of the decision-making of the Court of Protection, both as to case management and as regards the decisions and declarations that it makes at the end of proceedings. We have touched upon specific procedural considerations at relevant points in the balance of this book. For instance, questions of disclosure (and withholding of disclosure) engage difficult balancing exercises between the different ECHR rights of the parties involved (see para 13.106 onwards). The particular procedural issues arising in relation to cases involving deprivation of liberty as covered in chapter 22. A brief overview of the provisions of the ECHR that are likely to be most relevant to the court in deciding what substantive declarations and decisions to grant can be found at paras 4.39–4.42.[1]

1 A good introduction to the ECHR and HRA 1998 is Wadham et al, *Blackstone's Guide to the Human Rights Act 1998*, Oxford University Press, 7th edn, 2015.

26.3 The Court of Appeal in *Re MN*[2] confirmed that the Court of Protection has jurisdiction to hear a claim under Human Rights Act (HRA) 1998 s7 that a public body has acted (or proposed to act) incompatibly with the ECHR. We address the issue of where the breach has already happened in the next section, but for present purposes focus on the issue of what a party should do when the actions of the public body are still 'live' – in other words, where they have the potential, if reversed or changed, to impact upon the decisions that the Court of Protection might make in relation to P. In *MN*, the decision in question was a decision not to fund a particular care package. The Court of Appeal confirmed that the court might, exceptionally, have to consider whether the actions of the public body breached the relevant party's human rights (and, for those purposes, consider what decision it might make in P's best interests if the care package or other relevant service was hypothetically 'on the table'). The Supreme Court left this finding undisturbed.[3]

26.4 It will, however, only be an exceptional case[4] where the court will engage in a hypothetical assessment of where P's best interests may lie for purposes of determining a claim based upon HRA 1998 s7(1)(b). Otherwise, and as discussed in chapter 25, claims as to whether a public body has acted lawfully (including by reference to their obligations under the HRA 1998) should be brought in the Administrative Court.

26.5 If a party wishes the court to carry out the 'exceptional' assessment of a hypothetical option on the basis set out in the paragraphs immediately above, then the following will apply:

- the claim must be formulated and pleaded properly by reference to HRA 1998 s7(1)(b); and
- the claim will then be dealt with by the Court of Protection as part of the main proceedings: it will not be treated as a discrete issue separated from the rest of the case.[5]

2 *Re MN (adult)* [2015] EWCA Civ 411, [2016] Fam 87, (2015) 18 CCLR 521. The appeal against the Court of Appeal's judgment (dismissed by the Supreme Court [2017] UKSC 22, [2017] AC 549, (2017) 20 CCLR 133) did not address the issues set out in the paragraph above and can therefore be taken not to have disturbed these conclusions.

3 *N v ACCG* [2017] UKSC 22, [2017] AC 549, (2017) 20 CCLR 133.

4 Indeed, there has been no reported case since *N v ACCG* where such a claim has been pleaded or determined.

5 *Re MN (adult)* [2015] EWCA Civ 411, [2016] Fam 87 at para 85, applying *Re V* [2004] 1 FLR 944.

Human Rights Act 1998 declarations and damages

26.6 The Court of Protection has a jurisdiction to grant:

- a declaration that the ECHR rights of P have been breached;[6]
- a declaration that the ECHR rights of another person who can claim to be a victim have been breached;[7]
- damages under HRA 1998 s8 where such are required to afford just satisfaction for either category of breach;[8]
- a declaration under HRA 1998 s4 that a provision of the Mental Capacity Act (MCA) 2005 is incompatible with the ECHR.[9] To date, no declarations have been granted (or, indeed, sought, at least in any reported case).

ECHR breaches – declarations and damages

26.7 Although the Court of Protection can grant declarations and damages under HRA 1998, this will only rarely be appropriate. This is in large part because to do so will increase the risk that the Legal Aid Agency (LAA) will seek to 'claw back' any damages received to recover the costs to the public purse of running the underlying proceedings as well as the HRA 1998 aspects. Conversely, the LAA has confirmed that the application of the statutory charge in respect of the costs incurred in welfare proceedings can be avoided by ensuring that damages are not pursued or awarded within the welfare proceedings and by keeping the costs of pursuing the damages claim separate.[10] It will therefore almost invariably be necessary to issue the claim in the county or High Court: see for an example of such a case *CH v A Metropolitan Council*.[11]

26.8 A perennial problem for advisers is advising as to the amount of damages that either the Court of Protection or High / county court

6 *YA v A Local Authority and others* [2010] EWHC 2770, [2010] COPLR Con Vol 1226.

7 *YA*. See also *City of Sunderland v MM and others* [2009] COPLR Con Vol 881.

8 *YA*.

9 Court of Protection Rules 2017 (COPR) SI No 1035 r12.1(1) and HRA 1998 s4(5)(f).

10 See the letter from the Legal Aid Agency to Miles and Partners dated 20 July 2018, available via https://courtofprotectionhandbook.com/2018/07/28/ hra-claims-the-court-of-protection-and-the-statutory-charge-certainty-at-last/.

11 [2017] EWCOP 12, [2017] COPLR 341. Note that although Sir Mark Hedley in *CH* purported to sit as a Court of Protection judge, on a proper analysis he actually appears to have endorsed the consent order in question as a judge of the High Court.

would be likely to award. Most cases where there has been a breach of the ECHR in this context are likely to be settled; most of those settlements are not reported.

26.9 In the context of damages for breach of ECHR Article 5, a useful summary of the approach that has been taken can be found in *Essex CC v RF*,[12] in which the District Judge also gave an indication of a 'tariff' of damages for an unlawful deprivation of liberty of between £3,000 and £4,000 per month where the individual would not have been detained had the public body in question acted lawfully. The decision is not binding authority, but the authors are aware that this 'tariff' is regularly used by both practitioners and the courts in assessing offers and settlements in relation to compensation in the field of deprivation of liberty. The courts have not entirely resolved the issue of whether and how damages for unlawful deprivation of liberty mesh with damages for the common law tort of false imprisonment, sometimes relied upon this area.[13] In *London Borough of Haringey v Emile*, for instance,[14] HHJ Saggerson upheld a District Judge's decision to award £130,000 for an eight-year period of unlawful detention, observing that ECHR Article 5 added nothing in relation to the quantum of damages.

26.10 It is important to understand that where the responsible body can show that deprivation of liberty would have happened in any event and caused no loss to the individual (ie that the breach of ECHR Article 5 was 'technical' or 'procedural'), then the person is likely to recover only nominal damages (ie £1) and/or the court will simply make a declaration that their rights under Article 5 have been breached as the necessary 'just satisfaction'.[15] It is unlikely that public funding will be available to bring a claim where it is likely simply to result in such a declaration (see further chapter 6).

12 [2015] EWCOP 1.

13In part, potentially, as a result of the limitation issue that can arise in relation to claims for unlawful deprivation of liberty: see para 26.12 below. Note, however, that the two concepts are not identical, and there may be situations – in particular, those where the person is unaware that they are confined, and do not seek to express any desire to leave – where it may not be entirely easy to establish that they are falsely imprisoned at common law, even if for purposes of ECHR Article 5 they are clearly deprived of their liberty. See in this regard the Law Commission's 2017 Report Mental Capacity and Deprivation of Liberty at para 15.44.

14 Available via the Mental Health Law Online website with the citation [2020] MHLO 77 (CC). The decision in *Esegbona v King's College NHS Trust* [2019] EWHC 77 (QB), (2019) 22 CCLR 155 noted in the previous edition is, with respect, sufficiently poorly reasoned by comparison that it is of little use to practitioners in the light of this more recent decision.

15 HRA 1998 s8(3).

26.11 If a declaration or damages for a breach of rights under the ECHR is sought, it is necessary that the precise basis for this claim be set out. If the claim is being brought within Court of Protection proceedings, COPR Practice Direction (PD) 11A, dealing with HRA 1998 claims, outlines the relevant procedure at paras 1–3 for making a claim, but in summary the most important requirement is that it is set out as soon as practicable so that the other parties and the court are aware that a specific claim in this regard is being made.

26.12 Wherever the claim is being brought, that (as is likely to be the case if the claim is brought on behalf of P) the claimant lacks litigation capacity does not mean that the standard one-year time limit to bring a claim under the HRA 1998 does not apply. It is therefore necessary to bring a claim within that time or as shortly thereafter as possible: see the decision in *AP v Tameside MBC*[16] refusing an application to bring an HRA 1998 claim in relation to alleged unlawful deprivation of liberty issued some 18 months out of time.

26.13 If a claim for damages is, in fact, brought in the Court of Protection, then, if it is compromised, a Court of Protection judge will need to approve the award.[17] The COPR do not provide expressly for this; and we would advise applying the provisions of Civil Procedure Rules 1998 (CPR) Part 21[18] in drafting an advice or position statement for the court, which explains the rationale for recommending acceptance.

Declarations of incompatibility

26.14 A specific procedure must be followed if a declaration of incompatibility is sought including notice to and the joining of the Crown. The procedure if the declaration is sought within Court of Protection proceedings is set out in COPR PD 12A. The entirety of a case from the permission stage onwards in which a declaration of incompatibility is sought must be heard before the President of the Family Division, the Chancellor or by a High Court judge nominated to sit in the Court of Protection.[19]

16 [2017] EWHC 65 (QB), (2017) 20 CCLR 5.

17 If the claim is brought in the County or High Courts, then the approval of any compromise will by a judge of the relevant court.

18 Which can be imported to fill gaps in the COPR: COPR r2.5(1).

19 COPR PD 3A(2)(b).

The UN Convention on the Rights of Persons with Disabilities

26.15 The UN CRPD was concluded in 2006 and ratified by the UK in 2009. Although ratified by the UK, the CRPD has not been incorporated into English law in the same way as the ECHR. The obligations that it imposes therefore operate at the state level, rather than (for instance) at the level of the discharge by either public authorities or courts of their respective functions under domestic legislation.

26.16 Perhaps because of its status in legal terms, the CRPD is, as yet, little known by practitioners. The convention seeks to bring about a radical change in the approach adopted in the social, political and legal arenas to those suffering from disabilities (and, indeed, to the very concept of disability). Among other provisions, the convention is designed to secure a fundamental shift away from the taking of decisions on behalf of individuals on the basis of an asserted lack of capacity. Further, and at least as interpreted by the Committee on the Rights of Persons with Disabilities, compliance with CRPD Article 12 (which provides for equal recognition before the law) means that states party to the CRPD should replace legislation providing for substitute decision-making for incapacitated adults based 'on what is believed to be in the objective "best interests" of the person concerned, as opposed to being based on the person's own will and preferences'.[20]

26.17 There is a considerable debate as to the precise meaning of CRPD Article 12 and its implications for national legislatures, in particular those of the countries which are also bound by obligations under the ECHR.[21] However, on its face, the MCA 2005 is not compatible with CRPD Article 12, not least because reliance on a 'diagnostic threshold' as a component of the test for mental incapacity (see further chapter 3) does not comply with the anti-discrimination requirements of

20 Committee on the Rights of Persons with Disabilities, 'General Comment on Article 12: Equal Recognition before the law', para 23. Available at www.ohchr.org/EN/HRBodies/CRPD/Pages/GC.aspx.

21 See, for instance, Philip Fennell and Urfan Khaliq, 'Conflicting or complementary obligations? The UN Disability Rights Convention, the European Convention on Human Rights and English law', *European Human Rights Law Review*, No 6 (2011): pp 662–674. See also Essex Autonomy Project (2014) *Achieving CRPD Compliance: Is the Mental Capacity Act of England and Wales compatible with the United Nations Convention on the Rights of Persons with Disabilities? If Not, What Next?*, and (2017) *Three Jurisdictions Report: Towards Compliance with CRPD Art. 12 in Capacity/Incapacity Legislation across the UK.* Both available at https://autonomy.essex.ac.uk/crpd/.

CRPD Article 12. Further, there is a good argument that the current configuration of its best interests standard fails to incorporate the safeguards required by CRPD Article 12(4), by failing to ensure that sufficient weight is placed upon the person's wishes and feelings (or in the language of the convention) their 'will and preferences'.[22] There are other Articles of the CRPD with which the compatibility of the MCA 2005 is doubtful,[23] but Article 12 poses the most direct challenge to the MCA 2005 as currently drafted.

26.18 The Committee on the Rights of Persons with Disabilities reported upon the compliance of the UK with the CRPD in October 2017, recommending that the UK:

> . . . abolish all forms of substituted decision-making concerning all spheres and areas of life by reviewing and adopting new legislation in line with the Convention to initiate new policies in both mental capacity and mental health laws.

26.19 Such far-reaching legislative reform is, in reality, not in prospect. In its 2017 *Mental capacity and deprivation of liberty* report,[24] the Law Commission had already proposed (more limited) amendments to the MCA 2005 in the spirit of the CRPD,[25] although these proposals were not taken forward by the government in what became the Mental Capacity (Amendment) Act 2019.

26.20 The CRPD is regularly referred to by the European Court of Human Rights in its interpretation of the ECHR in areas relevant to

22 See further the report by the Essex Autonomy Project Three Jurisdictions Project entitled *Towards Compliance with CRPD Art. 12 in Capacity/Incapacity Legislation across the UK* (2016). Available at http://autonomy.essex.ac.uk/eap-three-jurisdictions-report.

23 Most obviously Article 14, which on the committee interpretation cannot be squared with ECHR Article 5 (right to liberty). See in this regard the discussion at annex B to the report of the independent review of the Mental Health Act 1983 published in December 2018. Available at www.gov.uk/government/publications/modernising-the-mental-health- act-final-report-from-the-independent-review.

24 LC No 372.

25 For instance, requiring greater statutory weight to be placed upon the wishes and feelings of P in any best interests decision to be made for them, and creating a regulation-making power to enable supported decision-making schemes to be established.

this book.[26] However, since the previous edition of this work, the domestic courts have become distinctly less enthusiastic about referring to the CRPD. Although it was referred to by the Supreme Court in the seminal decision upon deprivation of liberty under the MCA 2005, *P v Cheshire West*[27] (discussed in more detail in chapter 22), the Supreme Court in more recent cases has declined to rely upon the CRPD as an aid to construction.[28]

26.21 We suggest, however, that the CRPD remains useful – if not determinative – in supporting arguments that:

- In deciding whether all practicable steps have been taken without success before concluding that P lacks capacity (MCA 2005 s1(3)), the Court of Protection must be astute to examine precisely what support mechanisms have been put in place to enable P to participate in the decision in respect of which their capacity is questioned and – where necessary – to direct that such support mechanisms be provided. An example of such support – directed during the currency of proceedings – would be that given to DE[29] by way of education, which allowed him to attain capacity to consent to sexual relations.
- P must be supported to participate as fully as possible in the proceedings before the Court of Protection (consistent with the emphasis also placed by the European Court of Human Rights of the importance of such participation by reference to the provisions of the ECHR: see para 16.38 onwards);
- Particular weight must be placed upon P's wishes and feelings in the determination of where their best interests may lie, so as to ensure proper respect for their 'will and preferences' (in the language of CRPD Article 12(4)).

26 See, in particular, *A-MV v Finland* [2017] ECHR 273 and the cases on participation of those subject to proceedings depriving them of legal capacity, summarised in chapter 2 of the report by Dr Lucy Series at al, *The Participation of P in welfare cases before the Court of Protection*, available at http://sites.cardiff.ac.uk/wccop/files/2017/02/Series-Fennell-Doughty-Feb-2017-Participation-of-P.pdf.

27 *Cheshire West and Chester Council v P; Surrey CC v P* [2014] UKSC 19, [2014] 2 WLR 642, (2014) 17 CCLR 5.

28 *R (SC, CB and 8 children) v Secretary of State for Work and Pensions and others* [2021] UKSC 26, [2021] 3 WLR 428 and, in the mental capacity context, *A Local Authority v JB* [2021] UKSC 52, [2021] 3 WLR 1381.

29 *An NHS Trust v DE* [2013] EWHC 2562 (Fam), [2013] COPLR 531.

CHAPTER 27

Cross-border matters

Introduction

27.1 The majority of cases before the Court of Protection concern the property or personal welfare of people who are habitually resident in England and Wales. However, the Mental Capacity Act (MCA) 2005 also includes detailed provisions relating to the powers of the court over people who are habitually resident other than in England but in respect of whom, for whatever reason, declarations or decisions are sought. This might be, for instance, because an incapacitated adult has been kidnapped from their home country and brought to England and Wales. In such a case, an order may well be sought in their home country seeking their return; MCA 2005 Sch 3 contains provisions detailing when and how such an order would be given effect by the Court of Protection. Alternatively, a question might arise as to the proper disposal of property in England belonging to someone habitually resident abroad upon whose behalf decisions are now being taken by a guardian appointed under the laws of that country.

27.2 The private international law rules governing decision-making for incapacitated adults with a foreign connection is a complex topic, a full discussion of which lies outside the scope of this book.[1] The complications are only increased by the fact that MCA 2005 Sch 3 implements – as the law of Wales – many of the provisions of the Hague Convention on the International Protection of Adults 2000 ('Hague 35'), but the UK has not, to date, ratified the convention as regards England and Wales.[2]

27.3 This chapter limits itself to highlighting those jurisdictional questions that are most likely to arise in the court setting before noting the position in relation to foreign lasting powers of attorney (LPAs) (ie powers made under other legal systems which have a similar effect to LPAs).

27.4 Since 2017, practitioners' lives have been made easier by the enactment of specific rules (accompanied by a practice direction) for applications engaging MCA 2005 Sch 3. These are addressed below.

1 Readers are directed to Frimston et al, *International protection of adults*, Oxford University Press, 2015. See also the Law Society's guidance on the international aspects of mental capacity, available at: www.lawsociety.org.uk/topics/private-client/mental-capacity-international-aspects.

2 It has done so in respect of Scotland.

What counts as a foreign jurisdiction?

27.5 It is important to realise that, for purposes of proceedings before the Court of Protection, both Scotland and Northern Ireland count as foreign jurisdictions.[3] This means, therefore, that a move of an incapacitated adult from England to Scotland would give rise to a cross-border jurisdictional question; as would questions concerning the exercise of a Scottish power of attorney in England.

The basis of jurisdiction of the Court of Protection

27.6 The Court of Protection has jurisdiction to make declarations and decisions under MCA 2005 ss15–16 in relation to:

- an adult habitually resident in England and Wales;[4]
- an adult's property in England and Wales;
- an adult present in England and Wales or who has property there, if the matter is urgent; or
- an adult present in England and Wales, if a protective measure which is temporary and limited in its effect to England and Wales is proposed in relation to them.[5]

27.7 'Habitual residence' is not defined in the MCA 2005, but the phrase has been the subject of judicial consideration. Above all, it is 'a question of fact to be determined in the individual circumstances of the case'.[6] In the case of an adult who lacks the capacity to decide where to live, habitual residence can in principle be lost and another habitual residence acquired without the need for any court order or other formal process, such as the appointment of an attorney or

3 MCA 2005 Sch 3 para 1.

4 If a British adult is no longer habitually resident in England and Wales but requires protection, it may be possible for the High Court to exercise a nationality-based inherent jurisdiction to secure their protection. See *Re Clarke* [2016] EWCOP 46, [2017] COPLR 84. *Al-Jeffery v Al-Jeffery (Vulnerable adult: British citizen)* [2016] EWHC 2151 (Fam), [2018] 4 WLR 136 and AB v XS [2021] EWCOP 57, [2022] 4 WLR 13. See also Alex Ruck Keene, 'Extending the great safety net abroad' (2016) ELJ 401.

5 MCA 2005 Sch 3 para 7(1).

6 *Re MN (recognition and enforcement of foreign protective measures)* [2010] EWHC 1926 (Fam), [2010] COPLR Con Vol 893 at para 22. The subsequent case-law was reviewed in *The Health Service Executive of Ireland v IM* [2020] EWCOP 51, [2021] COPLR 73.

deputy.[7] If an adult has been moved across borders, then a central question in deciding whether their habitual residence has changed will be whether there has been any element of wrongfulness in the move.[8] Habitual residence can in principle be lost and another habitual residence acquired on the same day.[9]

27.8 An adult is deemed to be habitually resident in England and Wales if:

- their habitual residence cannot be determined;
- they are a refugee; or
- they have been displaced as a result of disturbance in the country of their habitual residence.[10]

Recognition and enforcement of foreign protective measures

27.9 Perhaps the most important function of the provisions of MCA 2005 Sch 3 is to put in place a mechanism for declarations to be obtained that foreign 'protective measures' be recognised and enforced in England and Wales. Such 'protective measures' will include any measure directed to the protection of the person or property of an adult, who for these purposes is any person over 16[11] who, as a result of an impairment or insufficiency of his personal faculties, cannot protect their interests.[12] The MCA 2005 gives examples of such protective measures;[13] examples that have come before the Court of Protection include:

7 *Re PO* [2013] EWHC 3932 (COP), [2014] Fam 197 at para 18.

8 *Re MN* (move in apparent breach of instruction in Californian Advance Healthcare Directive); or *Re HM (vulnerable adult: abduction)* [2010] EWHC 870 (Fam), [2010] 2 FLR 1057 (move in breach of a court order).

9 *Re PO* [2013] EWHC 3932 (COP), [2014] Fam 197 at para 17.

10 MCA 2005 Sch 3 para 7(2).

11 Except if they are aged 16 or 17 and subject to the provisions of the 1996 Hague Convention on the Jurisdiction, Applicable Law, Recognition, Enforcement and Co-operation in respect of Parental Responsibility and Measures for the Protection of Children (the previous, further, exclusion in relation to those falling within Council Regulation EC 2201/2003 being repealed upon Britain's exit from the European Union).

12 MCA 2005 Sch 3 para 4.

13 MCA 2005 Sch 3 para 5.

- an order made by a Californian court requiring the return of an adult to California after her removal from the jurisdiction to England in questionable circumstances;[14] and
- the placement of Irish nationals in an English psychiatric institution by way of an order made in the High Court in the Republic of Ireland.[15] In *The Health Service Executive of Ireland v Moorgate,*[16] Hayden J considered in some detail the operation of the regime under MCA 2005 Sch 3 for recognition and enforcement of such placements. His judgment provides an updated route-map for navigating the complexities of Schedule 3.

It is important to note that, for these purposes, a protective measure includes not just single court orders but also the appointment of a guardian or equivalent by the relevant authorities in the foreign jurisdiction. However, and while the matter is not entirely beyond doubt, it is suggested that a foreign power of attorney does not count as such a measure.[17]

27.10 Where a measure has been taken on the ground that an adult is habitually resident in any foreign jurisdiction (including, for these purposes, Scotland and Northern Ireland[18]), any interested person can apply to the Court of Protection for a declaration that it is to be recognised in England and Wales.[19] Such an application will almost invariably be accompanied by an application that the measure be declared enforceable here as well.[20]

27.11 The procedure for making such an application is set down in Court of Protection Rules 2017[21] (COPR) Practice Direction (PD) 23A. Permission is not required.[22] The application is made by filing a COP1 form; there is no need to file a COP3 assessment of capacity

14 *Re MN*.

15 *Re M* [2010] EWHC 1926 (Fam) [2012] COPLR 430; *Re PA and others* [2015] EWCOP 38, [2016] Fam 47.

16 [2020] EWCOP 12, [2020] COPLR 501. The judgment contains as an appendix an endorsed and detailed comparison of the domestic regimes (Mental Health Act (MHA) 1983 and MCA 2005) that would apply were a person placed under a foreign order were, in fact, to be treated under the frameworks that would apply if they were habitually resident in England and Wales.

17 See *Re various applications concerning foreign representative powers* [2019] EWCOP 52, [2020] COPLR 334 at para 29.

18 By virtue of the definition of 'country' given in MCA 2005 Sch 3 para 1.

19 MCA 2005 Sch 3 para 20(1), COPR r23.4.

20 MCA 2005 Sch 3 para 22(1), COPR r23.4.

21 SI 2017 No 1035.

22 MCA 2005 Sch 3 para 20(2).

form or any of the usual supporting annexes, unless the applicant is also asking the court to make additional declarations and/or orders.[23] The applicant should identify whether any person other than the adult has an interest in the application such that they should be named as a respondent to it;[24] the normal notification rules do not otherwise apply unless the applicant is also asking the court to make additional declarations and/or orders.[25]

27.12 The application should be accompanied by a COP24 witness statement by or on behalf of the applicant. Where the application is made for recognition and/or enforcement of a protective measure, the evidence will need to include:

- evidence to demonstrate the basis upon which it is said that the person to whom the application relates is an adult for the purposes of MCA 2005 Sch 3;
- an officially authenticated copy (and where necessary a certified translation) of the relevant court order or other document embodying the protective measure in respect of which recognition and/or enforcement is sought;
- confirmation that the protective measure was taken on the basis that the adult was habitually resident in the other jurisdiction;
- evidence to enable the court to be satisfied:
  - that the case in which the measure was taken was urgent; alternatively,
  - that the adult to whom the protective measure related was given an opportunity to be heard by the foreign court or other body that took the protective measure;
- evidence to enable the court to be satisfied that the steps leading to the protective measure being made complied with any relevant provisions of the European Convention on Human Rights (ECHR);
- details of any previous measures relating to the adult which have been the subject of a previous Schedule 3 application (whether or not such application was successful);
- where enforcement is sought of a protective measure that has already been recognised by the Court, a copy of the order giving effect to that recognition;
- the lasting power (and where necessary a certified translation thereof).

23 COPR PD 23A paras 8 and 9.
24 COPR PD 23A para 10.
25 COPR PD 23A para 11.

27.13 Upon issue, the application will be put before a judge to give directions. The judge will case manage the application and decide whether to allocate it to a pathway.[26] Specifically the judge will consider whether to make one or more of the directions set out in COPR r.1.2(2) to enable the adult to whom it relates to participate in the application or to secure the adult's interests and position. Where the judge considers that the adult should be joined as a party to the proceedings the judge will direct the filing of a COP3 form or other expert evidence directed at the issue of the adult's capacity to conduct the proceedings before the court.[27]

27.14 COPR PD 23A makes clear that an application for recognition and/or enforcement of a protective measure should be dealt with rapidly, and in reviewing the papers the court will consider whether the order sought can be made without holding a hearing.[28] If the protective measure in question either seeks to authorise a deprivation of liberty of the adult or to authorise medical treatment, the application for recognition and/or enforcement will usually be determined after holding a hearing; and be allocated to the Senior Judge or a tier 3 judge.[29]

27.15 A judge of the Court of Protection asked to recognise and/or declare enforceable a foreign protective measure operates within strict limits. Their role is confined, in essence, to scrutinising whether core procedural and substantive rights have been complied with.[30] They cannot, in particular, conduct their own analysis of where the adult's best interests may lie, although they can – and must – consider the adult's best interests in deciding how the measure is to be implemented.[31]

26 MCA 2005 Sch 3 applications otherwise falls outside the normal case pathway structure: COPR PD 3B Part 1 para 1.1.

27 COPR PD 23A para 15.

28 COPR PD 23A para 16.

29 COPR PD 23A para 17.

30 See *Re PA and others* [2015] EWCOP 38, [2016] Fam 47. For an example of a court declining to recognise and declare enforceable a measure on very unusual facts, see *Re AB* [2020] EWCOP 47, [2021] COPLR 30.

31 *Re MN* at paras 29 and 31; and MCA 2005 Sch 3 para 12.

Foreign lasting powers of attorney

27.16 An adult who is habitually resident other than in England and Wales at the point of making a lasting power of attorney (LPA)[32] can specify that they want English law to apply to questions of existence, extent, modification or extinction, if:

- they do so in writing; and
- they are:
  - a British national;
  - they have previously been habitually resident in England and Wales; or
  - they have property here (subject to the limitation that they are only entitled to specify that English law applies in relation to the property here).[33]

27.17 If they do not make any such specification, then the law of the country in which they were habitually resident at the point of making the power will apply.[34]

27.18 A foreign LPA – ie made by someone habitually resident other than in England and Wales at the point of making it – is automatically effective in England and Wales if it satisfies the requirements of the law that applies under the test set out in the paragraph immediately above.[35] If, though, the foreign power is not exercised in a manner sufficient to guarantee the protection of the person or property of the donor, the Court of Protection can – if it has jurisdiction over the person or their property (applying the tests set out in para 27.6 above) disapply or modify the power.[36]

27.19 It should be noted that – as matters stand – the Office of the Public Guardian does not register foreign LPAs alongside those of English powers. If a bank or other institution is not willing to accept that a foreign LPA is effective, then, assuming that the jurisdictional test set out in para 27.6 above is met, an application can be made for a

32 Which will include a power of like effect to an English LPA: MCA 2005 Sch 6 para 6(c).

33 MCA 2005 Sch 3 para 12(2)(b).

34 There is a gap in MCA 2005 Sch 3 in relation to the situation where the donor is habitually resident other than in England and Wales and England and Wales is not a 'connected country'. However, Senior Judge Hilder made clear that the court should adopt an approach which filled this gap in *Re various applications concerning foreign representative powers* [2019] EWCOP 52, [2020] COPLR 334: see paras 22.5 and 39.7–39.8.

35 This flows from MCA 2005 Sch 3 para 13(1)–(2).

36 MCA 2005 Sch 3 para 14(1).

declaration under MCA 205 s15(1)(c) that the donee of the power is acting lawfully when exercising authority under it.[37] The same procedure as described at paras 27.11–27.13 will apply,[38] except that the evidence will need to include a certified copy of the lasting power (and where necessary a certified translation thereof).[39] If the reason why the application is required is recalcitrance on the part of a financial institution, it is strongly advisable to note in pre-action correspondence an intention to seek the costs of making it against the institution.

27.20 The situation described immediately above is not satisfactory; in due course, if ratification of Hague 35 is extended to England and Wales, then the situation will improve – at least between contracting states to Hague 35. Under Hague 35 Article 38, authorities of a contracting state to the convention where a measure of protection has been taken or a power of representation confirmed can issue to the person entrusted with the protection of the adult's person or property a certificate indicating the capacity in which the person is entitled to act and the powers conferred. Under a provision of the MCA 2005 which will come into force upon ratification with effect to England and Wales,[40] such a certificate would stand – unless the contrary is shown – as proof of the capacity in which the representative acts and the powers conferred upon them by the power of representation. However, it should be noted that none of these changes will, by themselves, affect the position within the United Kingdom, which remains a problem given the continued reluctance of financial institutions to accept powers of attorney from elsewhere within the UK. Specific legislative change would be required, in effect, to deem powers granted elsewhere within the UK to be the equivalent of those powers granted by the 'home' jurisdiction.

37 COPR r23.6.

38 The position in relation to such applications, and more generally in relation to foreign powers, was considered in some detail by Senior Judge Hilder in *Re various applications concerning foreign representative powers* [2019] EWCOP 52, [2020] COPLR 334.

39 COPR PD 23A para 12.2.

40 Not currently in force: *Re PO* at para 9.

CHAPTER 28

The inherent jurisdiction

Introduction

28.1 In this chapter,[1] we outline the scope of the High Court's inherent jurisdiction to make declarations and orders to protect adults[2] who *have* mental capacity to make relevant decisions but for some reason appear to require protection. We also, separately, note circumstances under which the High Court may have to be involved to address situations involving those who lack the relevant decision-making capacity but where the Court of Protection cannot use its statutory powers. We note, finally, the potential for future reform.

The inherent jurisdiction as 'the great safety net'

28.2 The inherent jurisdiction in relation to those who have capacity but are in some way vulnerable has been described as 'the great safety net',[3] used by High Court judges to fill the gap left by the fact that the Mental Capacity Act (MCA) 2005 only applies to those lacking mental capacity applying the test in MCA 2005 ss2–3. The courts have explained that:

> [T]he inherent jurisdiction can be exercised in relation to a vulnerable adult who, even if not incapacitated by mental disorder or mental illness, is, or is reasonably believed to be, either (i) under constraint or (ii) subject to coercion or undue influence or (iii) for some other reason deprived of the capacity to make the relevant decision, or disabled from making a free choice, or incapacitated or disabled from giving or expressing a real and genuine consent.[4]

1 Which draws on a guidance note originally written by Alex Ruck Keene with Victoria Butler-Cole QC, Katie Scott, Peter Mant, Alexis Hearnden and Neil Allen (all of 39 Essex Chambers).

2 The High Court can also exercise an inherent jurisdiction in relation to children, which we do not address here. For more on decision-making and remedies in relation to children, see chapters 7 and 11 respectively Steve Broach and Luke Clements, *Disabled Children: a legal handbook*, Legal Action Group, 3rd edn, 2020, also available (free) at https://councilfordisabledchildren.org.uk/. See also Camilla Parker, *Adolescent Mental Health Care and the* Law, Legal Action Group, 2020.

3 See *DL v A Local Authority* [2012] EWCA Civ 253, [2013] Fam 1. For a helpful summary, see *A Local Authority v BF* [2018] EWCA Civ 2962, [2019] COPLR 150.

4 A description given originally by Munby J in *Re SA (vulnerable adult with capacity: marriage)* [2005] EWHC 2942 (Fam), [2006] 1 FLR 867 at para 77, then endorsed in *DL v A Local Authority*.

The inherent jurisdiction and those at risk from others

Does the person have or lack mental capacity?

28.3 The first question that must be asked is whether, in fact, the person lacks mental capacity[5] to make the decision in question. Most often, the concern will arise in relation to a situation where a person is at risk in some way from the actions (or sometimes inactions) of another, often in the context of a safeguarding investigation under the Care Act 2014 or Social Services and Well-Being (Wales) Act 2014.[6] For purposes of this chapter, we will use the term 'A' for the person potentially at risk, and 'B' for the other person.

28.4 At that point, careful assessment of A's capacity to make the decision in question – for instance whether they should continue to live with B, or have contact with them – should be undertaken. The so-called causative nexus is of particular importance here (see para 3.44). In other words, is the 'material'[7] (or 'real') reason that the person appears to be unable to take the decision to protect themselves because they have an impairment or disturbance in the functioning of their mind or brain, or is the real reason the influence of B over them? If the real reason is the former, then they are within the scope of the MCA 2005; if the real reason is the latter, it may be appropriate to seek to invoke the inherent jurisdiction.

28.5 While the English courts have yet to address this issue specifically, we suggest that an important question to ask in such a situation is whether A can understand, retain, use and weigh the information that relates to whether there might be undue influence being applied, eg whether they can grasp that another person may have interests contrary to theirs, and if not, whether this inability is caused by

5 We use the term 'capacity' in this section to refer to mental capacity under MCA 2005 ss2 and 3. The term is sometimes used in the case law to refer to an inability to make decisions for other reasons.

6 See further chapter 24.

7 See *NCC v PB and TB* [2014] EWCOP 14, [2015] COPLR 118 at para 86 per Parker J: 'the true question is whether the impairment/disturbance of mind is an effective, material or operative cause. Does it cause the incapacity, even if other factors come into play? This is a purposive construction'.

mental impairment.[8] If this is the case, then it would be legitimate – we suggest – to conclude that they **lack** mental capacity to make the relevant decisions for purposes of the MCA 2005, although with the very strong corollary that steps taken in the name of their best interests should be taken to secure either the gaining or return of their decision-making capacity by ensuring that they are surrounded by the supports that they require.[9]

28.6 If, in reality, the person lacks capacity to make the relevant decision(s) for purposes of the MCA 2005, then it would be inappropriate to go to the High Court to ask for orders under the inherent jurisdiction to secure their protection against B. It is important to note that it is likely still to be necessary to go to a court – the Court of Protection – because the steps that are likely to be required (for instance, limiting or stopping contact, or bringing about or stopping a move) will be so draconian that it would be inappropriate for health and social care professionals simply to rely upon the general defence in MCA 2005 s5.[10]

If the person has mental capacity

28.7 If the person **has** mental capacity to make the relevant decisions (so that the MCA 2005 is not applicable), but the person appears to be vulnerable in the ways set out at the beginning, then it will in principle be appropriate to consider making an application. This will mean considering, in particular, what orders the court will be being asked to make. The primary purpose of the inherent jurisdiction in the sort of situation envisaged here is to 'allow the individual to be able to regain their autonomy of decision making'.[11] Orders **directed** against A – for instance requiring them to stay away from B, or to live in a different place to B – are unlikely to achieve this goal. Far more likely to achieve this goal are orders directed against B. There are a

8 This was the approach adopted by the Singapore Court of Appeal, applying English case-law, within the framework of a Mental Capacity Act identical in material terms to the MCA 2005: see *Re BKR* [2015] SGCA 26. This was the approach adopted, although implicitly, by Roberts J in *Re BU* [2021] EWCOP 54, [2022] COPLR 46.

9 See for more discussion of this issue, and the underpinning ethical considerations, Camillia Kong and Alex Ruck Keene, *Overcoming Challenges in the Mental Capacity Act 2005: Practical Guidance for Working with Complex Issues*, Jessica Kingsley Publishers, 2018.

10 See further paras 3.97–3.101.

11 *London Borough of Croydon v KR and another* [2019] EWHC 2498 (Fam), [2020] COPLR 285 at para 40.

number of other hurdles – addressed below – which will need to be considered if it is envisaged seeking orders against A.

Before making the application

28.8 In all cases, it is necessary to consider what, if any, other legislative mechanisms exist. It is only following proper consideration of whether statute law covers the position that it can be clear whether there is, in fact, a gap to be filled, and hence whether recourse to the inherent jurisdiction is necessary.

28.9 In the case of domestic abuse, for instance, consideration must be given to whether the behaviour that is giving cause for concern could be addressed by Family Law Act 1996 s42 (non-molestation orders which victims, but not public authorities, can seek), the Serious Crime Act 2015 s76 (which creates a criminal offence of controlling or coercive behaviour where A and B live together and 'are members of the same family'), remedies available under the Domestic Abuse Act 2021 or other civil remedy such as the Protection from Harassment Act 1997.

28.10 It is also necessary to see whether the position is governed by a statute because, as Lieven J pointed out in *JK v A Local Health Board*,[12] '[t]he inherent jurisdiction cannot be used to simply reverse the outcome under a statutory scheme, which deals with the very situation in issue, on the basis that the court disagrees with the statutory outcome'. In other words, the inherent jurisdiction cannot be used contrary to the intention of parliament as set down in a statute.

28.11 If it appears a) that there is no other mechanism which can be used, and b) that using the inherent jurisdiction would not amount to reversing the position which would apply if a statutory scheme did apply, it is then necessary to consider two key aspects arising from the operation of the European Convention on Human Rights (ECHR): 1) will the person be deprived of their liberty; and 2) is the interference with the person's rights necessary and proportionate? We consider each in turn.

Will the person be deprived of their liberty?

28.12 If the result of the orders sought are that the person will be, or will be likely to be, subject to continuous supervision and control and not free to leave, and if that confinement is to take place without the

12 *JK v A Local Health Board* [2019] EWHC 67 (Fam), [2020] COPLR 246 at para 57.

consent of the person, then there will be a deprivation of liberty for purposes of ECHR Article 5(1).[13] Note that the courts have made clear that an order preventing a person going home can in principle constitute a confinement.[14]

28.13 The courts have expressed doubts as to whether it is lawful to use the inherent jurisdiction to deprive a person with the relevant decision-making capacity of their liberty.[15] This is because a deprivation of liberty must comply with ECHR Article 5. The conditions for deprivation of liberty in this context include that that the person must reliably be shown to be of 'unsound mind' (or, in English terms, to have a mental disorder).[16] Mental capacity[17] is logically distinct to mental disorder.

28.14 If there is no evidence to suggest that the person has a mental disorder warranting confinement, then there can be no basis upon which to ask the court for an order which will have the effect of depriving them of their liberty. If there is reason to believe that the person may have a mental disorder, then if the position is an emergency, it is legitimate to ask for an order depriving them of their liberty even though there is not yet the 'objective medical evidence' required to satisfy deprivation of liberty for purposes of ECHR Article 5(1)(e).[18] Any orders made in such a case should be made for

13 The third element required for there to be a deprivation of liberty, state imputability, will always be satisfied. For more on deprivation of liberty, see chapter 22.

14 See *Redcar and Cleveland BC v PR and others* [2019] EWHC 2305 (Fam), [2019] COPLR 446 at para 40, although Hayden J in *Southend-on-Sea BC v Meyers* [2019] EWHC 399 (Fam), [2019] COPLR 202 considered that such an order would not amount to a deprivation of liberty, but rather a (justified) interference with the person's ECHR Article 8 rights.

15 The case-law was reviewed by a judge sceptical of the position (Lieven J) in *Cumbria, Northumberland Tyne and Wear NHS Foundation Trust and another v EG* [2021] EWHC 2990 (Fam), (2022) 25 CCLR 5. In *Mazhar v Birmingham Community Healthcare Foundation NHS Trust and others* [2020] EWCA Civ 1377, [2021] 1 WLR 1207 the Court of Appeal had previously declined to rule definitively on the subject. The Supreme Court in *Re T (a child)* [2021] UKSC 35, [2021] 2 FLR 1041 rejected the argument that the use of the inherent jurisdiction to deprive a child of its liberty was not in accordance with a procedure prescribed by law, on the basis (in effect) that the common law was sufficiently clear. It is not obvious that this applies to the position in relation to the use of the inherent jurisdiction to deprive capacitous adults of their liberty.

16 A useful summary of the European Court of Human Rights case-law on ECHR Article 5(1)(e) can be found in *Rooman v Belgium* [2019] ECHR 105, at paras 190–193.

17 And also the wider concept of 'vulnerability.'

18 See *A Local Authority v BF* [2018] EWCA Civ 2962, [2019] COPLR 150 at para 23.

as short a period as possible to enable the necessary investigations to be carried out and, if the deprivation of liberty is to continue, to secure the necessary medical evidence to comply with Article 5(1)(e).

Is the interference with the person's rights necessary and proportionate?

28.15 This issue will arise both in respect of a potential deprivation of liberty and also in relation to the interference with the person's rights under ECHR Article 8 to private and family life – including their autonomy – which will inevitably take place, at least in the short-term, as a result of orders being made under the inherent jurisdiction. For both, this will require consideration of whether any other steps short of that being considered could achieve the goal. The more draconian the steps, the greater will be the scrutiny undertaken by the court of the steps taken by the public body in question.[19] This means that it is necessary to consider (and provide evidence to show consideration of):

- What, precisely, is the goal being sought? Is it securing the person's right to life?[20] Or their health (a 'legitimate aim' for purposes of ECHR Article 8(2), encompassing both psychological as well as physical health)? Or to free them from inhuman or degrading treatment giving rise to a potential breach of Article 3?
- What less intrusive measures could have been taken to secure that goal, and why would they not achieve it?

Will any orders be directed against the person?

28.16 A further question that must be asked when considering whether an application under the inherent jurisdiction is appropriate is whether any orders will be sought directed against the person themselves. It is suggested that it is only in 'truly exceptional' cases that the court can properly be asked to make such an order.[21]

19 *London Borough of Croydon v KR and another* [2019] EWHC 2498 (Fam), [2020] COPLR 285 at para 51.

20 As in *Southend-on-Sea Borough Council v Meyers* [2019] EWHC 399 (Fam), [2019] COPLR 202.

21 See *London Borough of Croydon v KR and another* [2019] EWHC 2498 (Fam), [2020] COPLR 285 at para 63. Lieven J's formulation of the position was endorsed by Sir James Munby (obiter) in *FS v RS and JS* [2020] EWFC 63, [2020] 4 WLR 139 at paras 121–122 in which Sir James also expressed doubts as to the correctness of the decision in *Meyers*.

28.17 If such a course of action is under contemplation, and the applicant is seeking to require the person to do something, the application should be able to demonstrate (and support with evidence) that they have appropriately considered whether the person:

- is likely to understand the purpose of the injunction;
- will receive knowledge of the injunction; and
- will appreciate the effect of breach of that injunction.[22]

28.18 If the answer to any of these is 'no', then the injunction should not be applied for or granted against the subject because no consequences can truly flow from the breach. This is particularly important in a case where it is said that injunctions are required to stop A seeing B because A is said to be under the malign influence of B. There is a logical difficulty in:

- making an application on the basis that (in effect) A is not acting of their own free will, whilst at the same time;
- saying that A is sufficiently capable of exercising free will to hold them to the consequence of breaching an order made against them if they do then seek to see B.

28.19 This logical difficulty does not arise if the orders sought are against B, rather than A.

Procedural matters

28.20 We do not address procedural matters in detail here, because any relief which is to be sought will not be being sought from the Court of Protection, but rather from the Family Division of the High Court.[23] That having been said, and even if formulated through different statutory rules many of the same principles apply as those set out in the chapters in relation to case preparation, evidence, fact-finding and the determination of the final hearing.

28.21 We also emphasise the following key matters:

- Only judges in the Family Division of the High Court (including those holding so-called section 9 tickets[24]) can exercise the inherent jurisdiction. This means that if there are doubts as to whether

22 *Redcar and Cleveland BC v PR and others* [2019] EWHC 2305 (Fam), [2019] COPLR 446 at para 46.

23 For practice and procedure before the Family Division, readers are referred to such works as the annual *Family Court Practice* (LexisNexis).

24 That is, authorised under Senior Courts Act 1981 s9(1).

the case is an inherent jurisdiction case or a Court of Protection case, it is important that the judge who hears it is able to sit also as a judge of the High Court if required.

- Applications under the inherent jurisdiction are governed by the Civil Procedure Rules 1998 (CPR) (including the costs provisions of the CPR[25]).
- If the application is to be made without notice to either the person the subject of concern or anyone else, it is particularly important that appropriate steps are taken to comply with the onerous obligations upon applicants in such situations.[26]

The inherent jurisdiction and vulnerable adults: other situations

28.22 On occasion, the inherent jurisdiction may be contemplated where person is at risk because of their **own** actions, as opposed to the actions of others. The Court of Appeal made clear in *Re DL* that it considered that the inherent jurisdiction should be used in a 'facilitative, rather than dictatorial' way, intended to re-establish 'the individual's autonomy of decision making in a manner which enhances, rather than breaches, their ECHR Article 8 rights'.[27] Making declarations or decisions which require someone to do something are not easily characterised as facilitative, rather than dictatorial. In many cases, further, using the inherent jurisdiction to require someone who *has* mental capacity to make the relevant decision to do something that they do not wish to do comes very close to, if not actually becomes, using the inherent jurisdiction to seek to reverse the outcome required under a statutory scheme dealing with the very situation in issue. This is particularly so if there is no third party involved, so there can be no suggestion that the individual in

25 As to costs, see *Redcar and Cleveland BC v PR (No 2)* [2019] EWHC 2800 (Fam), [2019] 4 WLR 143. In *T and another v L and others (inherent jurisdiction: costs)* [2021] EWHC 2147 (Fam), Cobb J identified (at para 35) that 'no order for costs is likely to be the appropriate starting point in welfare-oriented proceedings under the inherent jurisdiction concerning a vulnerable adult'.

26 See *Mazhar v Birmingham Community Healthcare Foundation NHS Trust and others* [2020] EWCA Civ 1377, [2021] 1 WLR 1207 and (by analogy) chapter 11.

27 See *DL v A Local Authority* [2012] EWCA Civ 253, [2013] Fam 1 at para 67.

question is under duress or coercion.[28] If it is 'truly exceptional'[29] to use the inherent jurisdiction to make orders against the person themselves in the presence of a risk from a third party, it must be even more exceptional – if it is legitimate at all – to make an order against the person where the sole risk is from the actions (or inactions) of the person themselves.

28.23 The case-law is not entirely consistent as to whether the inherent jurisdiction can be used if the risk in question is posed by the person to others.[30]

28.24 In either of the cases set out immediately above, we suggest that it is necessary to consider with particular care both the person's mental capacity[31] and whether there are other mechanisms that can be used to reach the same goal. The point made at para 28.13 above about compliance with the provisions of ECHR Article 5(1)(e) are going to be particularly important if there is any question of the orders being sought giving rise to a deprivation of their liberty.

The inherent jurisdiction and the person lacking capacity

28.25 Entirely separately, the inherent jurisdiction may be used, sometimes, when the person **lacks** capacity applying the MCA 2005, but there is a reason why the provisions of the Act cannot be applied. Four examples where Court of Protection judges sat as High Court

28 See *JK v A Local Health Board* [2019] EWHC 67 (Fam), [2020] COPLR 246 at para 57. See also *LBL v RYJ and another* [2010] EWHC 2665 (Fam), [2010] COPLR Con Vol 795 at para 62, and *Re DL* at para 67. In *PH v Betsi Cadwaladr University Health Board* [2022] EWCOP 16, Hayden J adopted this approach, in somewhat stark contrast to the approach he had previously adopted in *Southend-on-Sea Borough Council v Meyers* [2019] EWHC 399 (Fam), [2019] COPLR 202.

29 See para 28.16 above.

30 Contrast the suggestion that it can be used in *Re AB (inherent jurisdiction deprivation of liberty)* [2018] EWHC 3103 (Fam), [2019] Fam 291 on the one hand and, on the other, the views expressed in *Wakefield Metropolitan District Council and another v DN and another* [2019] EWHC 2306 (Fam), [2019] COPLR 525 and *Cumbria, Northumberland Tyne and Wear NHS Foundation Trust and another v EG* [2021] EWHC 2990 (Fam), (2022) 25 CCLR 5.

31 In the case of the person who is at risk, but from their own actions, it may be important to consider whether they have an adjustment disorder reflecting the impact of their situation upon them: see by analogy *University Hospitals Bristol NHS Foundation Trust v RR* [2019] EWCOP 46.

judges to use the inherent jurisdiction to fill a gap in the statutory provisions of the MCA 2005 are:

- *Dr A*'s case,[32] in which Baker J had to use the inherent jurisdiction to authorise the additional deprivation of liberty to which a patient detained under the Mental Health Act 1983 was to be subject in order to force-feed him. Baker J could not (because of the wording of MCA 2005 s16A) do so as a Court of Protection judge, so, applying the same substantive tests of capacity and best interests, did so as a judge of the High Court exercising the inherent jurisdiction.
- *XCC v AA and another*,[33] in which, having decided (applying the MCA 2005) that the person in question did not have capacity to marry, Parker J wanted also to make a declaration of 'non-recognition' in relation to a marriage that had purportedly been entered to abroad; she could not do so as a Court of Protection judge, but could do so as a High Court judge exercising the inherent jurisdiction.
- *Re Clarke*,[34] in which Peter Jackson J contemplated the use of the High Court's inherent jurisdiction to secure protection for an incapacitated adult no longer habitually resident in England and Wales, and therefore beyond the reach of the Court of Protection's jurisdiction (see chapter 27).[35]
- *Re R*,[36] in which Hayden J addressed the position where a person *currently* has capacity, but is likely in a defined situation (there, during labour) to lose capacity. Hayden J confirmed that only the inherent jurisdiction could be used in such a situation to authorise any deprivation of liberty to which they would be subject, alongside a declaration under MCA 2005 s15(1)(c) as to the lawfulness of other steps to be taken in relation to the person at the point when they did not have capacity.

32 *An NHS Trust v Dr A* [2013] EWHC 2442 (COP), [2013] COPLR 605. When the liberty protection safeguards (LPS) come into force, MCA 2005 s16A will be repealed, so this situation could be authorised by the Court of Protection.

33 [2012] EWHC 2183 (COP), [2013] 2 All ER 988.

34 [2016] EWCOP 46, [2017] COPLR 84.

35 See also Alex Ruck Keene, 'Extending the great safety net abroad' (2016) ELJ 401. The use of this jurisdiction was doubted by Lieven J in *AB v XS* [2021] EWCOP 57, [2022] 4 WLR 13, although in circumstances where Lieven J was also not satisfied that using it would, in fact, secure the interests of the person in question.

36 *Re R* [2020] EWCOP 4, [2020] 4 WLR 96. See also para 23.24.

The future

28.26 The use by the High Court of the inherent jurisdiction to fill gaps identified by Court of Protection judges in relation to their powers in relation to those lacking the material decision-making capacity is perhaps understandable. Much more difficult is the use of the inherent jurisdiction to address the situation of those with capacity. It gives rise to (at least) three problems:

- At the practical level, it is unclear to public bodies when it is appropriate to invoke the inherent jurisdiction to obtain protection in relation to an individual who is vulnerable.
- It is unclear how and when the inherent jurisdiction can be used in circumstances amounting to a deprivation of liberty.
- More fundamentally, if the courts are willing to make orders under the inherent jurisdiction against the vulnerable adult, especially in the face of their objection to the order, then such starts to undermine the very point of the MCA 2005 and the value placed therein on the importance of the individual's decision-making capacity.

28.27 In this regard, it is perhaps striking that, in December 2020, Sir James Munby – who played such a central role in 'discovering' the jurisdiction – gave a lecture to the Court of Protection Bar Association both examining its history and setting out considerable reservations as to the direction it was taking.[37] At the time of writing, it is also possible that the Law Commission will (as part of its 14th programme of law reform) take forward work to consider placing this area on a statutory footing.[38]

37 The lecture can be found at: www.cpba.org.uk/wp-content/uploads/2020/12/2020COPBA.pdf. See also his judgment in *FS v RS and JS* [2020] EWFC 63, [2021] 2 FLR 641.

38 It had, in fact, made specific proposals in this regard in its work leading to the MCA 2005 (see *Mental Incapacity*, Law Com No 231 (HMSO, 1995), Part IX), although for some reason now impossible to determine, these were not taken forward by government.

CHAPTER 29

Instructing experts in Court of Protection cases[1]

1 The section of this chapter on psychiatrists is written by Dr Ian Hall, Consultant Psychiatrist for People with Learning Disability, East London NHS Foundation Trust; Chief Examiner, Royal College of Psychiatrists; the section on nurses by Lynne Phair, Independent Consultant Nurse and Expert Witness.

Introduction

29.1 This chapter is concerned with instructing two different types of experts before the Court of Protection, psychiatrists and nurses. Both sections of the chapter are written by experts in their disciplines who regularly give evidence before the court, and outline the specific considerations relevant to instructing psychiatrist and nurses respectively. In broad terms, however, the points that they make as to how to instruct and support an expert are equally applicable to an expert of any kind. The chapter should also be read with chapter 13 on expert evidence.

Psychiatrists

Persuading psychiatrists to get involved in a case

29.2 Psychiatrists are medically qualified doctors that specialise in helping people with mental disorders. Fully trained specialists are known as 'consultant psychiatrists'. The vast majority of consultant psychiatrists in the UK do most or all of their clinical work in the NHS, and therefore lead busy professional lives. Why would anyone with such commitments be interested in taking on the additional role of being an expert witness for the Court of Protection?

29.3 In relation to reports as an independent expert, the simple answer might be because of the fee, or because it is a fairly local case and therefore easy to arrange. But there are other motivators instructing lawyers can appeal to. Psychiatrists working in psychiatric specialties where mental capacity is often an issue – such as psychiatry of learning disability or psychiatry of old age – may have developed a particular interest in Court of Protection work. For any psychiatrist, doing such work gives the opportunity to do a very thorough and detailed assessment of a case, and particularly in cases where an opinion about best interests is sought, it can be very appealing to be essentially speaking up for the person with a mental disorder. Those that are highly experienced in court work may relish particularly interesting cases where new case-law may be made. Others may welcome the whole court experience as something they can use to train junior doctors or other team members.

29.4 The situation is different the court asks for psychiatric reports from NHS bodies under Mental Capacity Act (MCA) 2005 s49.[2] Here

2 See further para 13.45.

the NHS body asks a consultant psychiatrist to complete the report as part of their normal duties without any additional fee from the court. This can be very helpful both for the court and the person at the centre of the proceedings, as the psychiatrist may know them very well. Because of this, they may be very motivated to assist. It can require less time to produce the report compared to an independent expert. However, where psychiatrists are getting frequent requests, the production of such reports can become very burdensome, and because of such pressures less comprehensive reports may be produced. Good employers will release psychiatrists from other duties in order to produce the reports and NHS bodies should be encouraged to do this. This will maximise their ability to produce a full report addressing the relevant questions.

Instructions

Expertise

29.5 The letter of instruction is obviously crucial to getting a report that addresses the issues you want. It is helpful to be explicit about the role of the expert in the case, and particularly which parties are instructing the expert. Questions need to be as clear as possible, and within the expertise of the psychiatrist. If you are not sure about what might be within their expertise, then it can be helpful to discuss this with the psychiatrist before the letter of instruction is finalised. Having said that, the diagnosis and treatment of mental disorder, and the assessment of capacity are core skills. Commenting on best interests can be within their expertise, particularly when it concerns directly, or has some bearing on medical or psychiatric assessment and treatment. Because of this concern about appropriate expertise, it is important to instruct a psychiatrist from the right subspeciality. As well as general adult psychiatrists, there are specialist psychiatrists for older adults; for children and adolescents; and for people with learning (intellectual) disabilities; there are also forensic psychiatrists for people with mental disorders who are involved in criminal proceedings. For a section 49 report, the NHS body should nominate a psychiatrist with appropriate expertise.

29.6 Some psychiatrists focus almost exclusively on medico-legal work, and have developed great expertise in the technical aspects of report writing and giving evidence. However, if they have not been in clinical practice for some time, then their knowledge and skills about current psychiatric practice may be more limited, and their expertise brought into question.

Evidence of mental disorder

29.7 When outlining the circumstances of the case, the medical and psychiatric history is highly relevant and any psychiatrist would be grateful for as much detail as possible in this area, and permission to access medical records is usually very helpful.

29.8 An essential element to assessing capacity is determining whether there is a mental disorder present, and assessing the nature and severity of that disorder. Therefore any evidence of mental disorder is really helpful. Obviously this may include previous psychiatric assessments, but psychology assessments, especially psychometric assessments (eg IQ assessments), occupational therapy assessments (eg standardised assessments of skills) and speech and language therapy assessments (eg of communication skills) can all be very valuable. It is also helpful to have detailed descriptions of any recent events or behaviour that have led to concerns about the person being mentally unwell. Previous assessments of capacity are also essential material to include, as are details of any particular attempts that have been made to support decision making in the past.

Assessment of capacity

29.9 Assessment of capacity requires a determination of the information needed to make the decision. It is therefore important to have all the background information relevant to the decision, such as social work reports or statements for welfare decisions, and medical reports for medical decisions. It is of course very helpful if the court has made a determination of the information needed to make the decision in the particular case or if there is any relevant case law about the type of decision in question (eg capacity to decide about engaging in sex, capacity to decide residence).

29.10 In cases where there are disputes about capacity or best interests, there are often others involved who have a powerful influence on the person. Because this can substantially affect the ability to weigh information up in the process of making a decision (especially where capacity is borderline) it is important to know as much as possible about this. Sometimes where there are disputes about best interests, there can be significant mental health issues in the family (whether diagnosed or not) and it is very helpful to have full details of such concerns.

Practicalities

29.11 It is important to give contact details for people the psychiatrist need to get history from, or will need to discuss best interests with, or who can assist in setting up the assessment. In order to maximise decision-making ability, it is often helpful to see the person in an environment with which they are familiar, and multiple visits may be required, depending on the complexity of the questions, and how the person is able to engage in the assessment.

29.12 Having described above the sort of information that is very helpful to the assessment, this does not mean that the psychiatrist needs to see the whole court bundle, and judicious limiting of the reading is helpful, especially if opinions about best interests decisions are not required.

29.13 Because the psychiatrist is likely to have many other commitments, it is important to set a realistic timetable for the assessment of at least a few weeks unless the clinical or social situation is very urgent.

Supporting the expert in court

29.14 Many psychiatrists can be anxious about giving oral evidence in court, so it is very helpful if a clear idea of issues to be discussed can be given in advance so that they can prepare properly. Often psychiatrists will be asked questions in court that stray outside their area of expertise, and it is of course for the expert witness to point this out. However, it also helps not to be asked the question in the first place. Psychiatrists are usually happy to participate in meetings of experts, as this is more akin to clinical practice than the more adversarial court process. Finally, on a practical note, it is of course very helpful to fix dates and times as far in advance as possible, bearing in mind that if a case is listed for several days, psychiatrists in clinical practice are unlikely to be able to keep the whole period free, so guidance should be given about when their evidence is likely to be required.

Nurses

How a nursing report can assist the court

29.15 Many people who lack capacity will have care and support needs and although the use of an independent social worker is relatively common, it has recently become more common to instruct a registered nurse to assist the court.

29.16 A registered nurse can assist the court in understanding several different matters of importance:

- **P's care needs**. Often the care of P can appear simple, basic or routine, yet is often complex, unpredictable and intense. A nurse expert can give a perspective on current and future care needs, as well as how any medical condition from which P suffers impacts upon those needs, including by way of identifying issues regarding prescribing, administration, effectiveness and use of medication (including as required or 'PRN' medication). Although a nurse cannot give a prognosis an experienced nurse can also assist in advising on advanced care planning and possible end-of-life care needs. Whilst funding of care is not a matter that directly falls for consideration by the Court of Protection, a nurse expert will be able to identify whether the person should be assessed for NHS Continuing Healthcare (if not already in place) which could influence access to an increased level of services. Finally, the need for 24-hour registered nursing involvement at home if P is currently living in a nursing home is often given as a reason for not permitting P to go home. An expert nurse is able to advise as to whether such involvement is, in fact, required, or whether any particular procedure(s) can be undertaken by others with appropriate training or by the oversight of community nurse.
- **P's understanding of their needs**. From visiting and talking to P (often more than once), a nurse expert will be able to establish from P their understanding of their own care needs. A nurse will be able to decipher non-technical terms and P's own perspective as to their condition and assess the level and depth of their understanding of their needs and risks of alternative care provision. Whilst other professionals can also undertake this assessment, a nurse will be able to bring an expert perspective to bear upon whether P is likely to be able to gain further knowledge and understanding of their care needs;
- **How P's current or proposed setting affects their care needs**. Care packages and approaches to supporting a person to live independently are constantly changing. The nurse will be able to give an opinion on the care delivered, its suitability and/or alternative approaches if required. The nurse will also be able to address how P's wellbeing and quality of life is affected by the location of care, type of care and the quality of care. The location of care should be

considered not simply by reference to the location, funding and the registration category of the care provider but also whether it meets the social, cultural and emotional needs of P. This not only refers to ethnicity and religion but also refers to social status and to P's personal values. The nurse will also be able to advise the court as to concerns raised in regulatory inspection reports, whether any concerns have been rectified since publication and how any concerns may affect the care of P;

- **The family's perspective**. Family relationships may be straightforward with all members of the family in agreement with their opinions of what is best for P. In other situations there may be complicated family dynamics with fractions, disagreement and diverse opinions. On other occasions the family members may be viewed by health or social care professionals as obstructive, subversive and sometimes responsible for abuse of P. Conversely the family may not trust any professionals and believe they have ulterior motives for their decisions. The reasons for any mistrust are varied and may be due to misunderstanding, poor communication, lack of understanding on either side and unwillingness to listen (to the professionals) or unwillingness on the part of the professional to appreciate the learned skills and knowledge of the family for caregiver. A nurse expert may well be able to assist in identifying the causes of (and potential solutions for) this mistrust for the benefit of the court. Moreover, and given that families and professionals will have to continue to work together after the court process is finished, a nurse expert may well be able to assist in bringing about the mutual understanding required to enable this continuing relationship;
- **Potential safeguarding concerns**. The nurse may be able to assist the court by making observations about safeguarding matters that are contentious, for example bruising or pressure ulcers. The nurse will not be able to investigate these concerns but may be able to comment on the enquiry that should have taken place at the time of the alleged incident and offer an opinion as to the future risks of any concerns.

29.17 It is also important to note that a good nursing expert, by taking part in a professionals' meeting with those involved in the case, can assist in the resolution of the case for two reasons:

- Firstly by reassuring the professionals that the expert witness is not 'any better than them', merely looking at the same situation from a different perspective.

- Secondly, because health and social care professionals often become anxious when anything 'becomes legal' and lawyers get involved, which only adds to any tension already present between parties. The nurse expert can assist in reducing these anxieties.

Types of registered nurse

29.18 Nursing is a diverse profession and there are numerous specialities within it. The main qualifications relevant to the court of protection are Registered General Nurse (RGN), Registered Mental Nurse (RMN) and Registered Learning Disability Nurse (RLDN).[3] Within these branches of the profession the nurses will specialise according to patient's needs, age or location of care. There will be nurses who have vast experience in one location of care and predominantly treated one care group but have no experience at all in other locations of care which may be considered by the court. A person's diagnosis may appear to be the information most essential in identifying the most appropriate nurse but the diagnosis may be secondary to the care needs now presenting.

29.19 The lawyer should consider whether the nurse has experience and expertise in the identified care needs of the person, rather than simply the diagnosis and in the various care settings being suggested. The nurse should have experience that is relevant and up-to-date. Nurses who work independently may be well placed to provide a court report if they have experience in a variety of settings or models of care delivery and they may be more accommodating with court directions and timescales; they may also still be in current practice across a wide range of services. Whilst there are no specific role titles which will indicate whether they have the requisite skill to give an expert report, it is likely that a nurse who has master's degree, is an Independent Prescriber and has fulfilled the role of consultant nurse, nurse specialist or a community matron will have the requisite skills. They will also need to have undertaken training as an expert witness.

Instructing the nurse

29.20 To obtain a satisfactory report, the lawyer needs to consider providing the following to the nurse expert:

3 In each case, 'Registered' means registered with the Nursing and Midwifery Council, which can be checked with the person's name or PIN number.

- clear instructions setting out all the options required to be examined;
- details of the locations to be visited;
- contact details of the family and professionals involved;
- clear identification of the family groups and any conflicts;
- provide historical and current care records relevant to the issues to be explored (historical records being of importance where the report requires an opinion as to whether P can return to a specific location where a care package has previously failed; and
- details of any advocates or communication aids, or translators that may be required to support P in talking to the nurse.

APPENDICES

APPENDIX A

Primary legislation[1]

1 © Crown copyright. Legislation is reproduced up to date to 11 July 2022. Note: we have deliberately not included amendments to be introduced by the Mental Capacity (Amendment) Act 2019, as we have no indication at the time of writing when this is to come into force. To the extent relevant, material changes that would be introduced in relation to matters relating to deprivation of liberty are addressed in chapter 22.

MENTAL CAPACITY ACT 2005

Part 1: Persons who lack capacity

The principles

The principles

1 (1) The following principles apply for the purposes of this Act.

(2) A person must be assumed to have capacity unless it is established that he lacks capacity.

(3) A person is not to be treated as unable to make a decision unless all practicable steps to help him to do so have been taken without success.

(4) A person is not to be treated as unable to make a decision merely because he makes an unwise decision.

(5) An act done, or decision made, under this Act for or on behalf of a person who lacks capacity must be done, or made, in his best interests.

(6) Before the act is done, or the decision is made, regard must be had to whether the purpose for which it is needed can be as effectively achieved in a way that is less restrictive of the person's rights and freedom of action.

Preliminary

People who lack capacity

2 (1) For the purposes of this Act, a person lacks capacity in relation to a matter if at the material time he is unable to make a decision for himself in relation to the matter because of an impairment of, or a disturbance in the functioning of, the mind or brain.

(2) It does not matter whether the impairment or disturbance is permanent or temporary.

(3) A lack of capacity cannot be established merely by reference to–

(a) a person's age or appearance, or

(b) a condition of his, or an aspect of his behaviour, which might lead others to make unjustified assumptions about his capacity.

(4) In proceedings under this Act or any other enactment, any question whether a person lacks capacity within the meaning of this Act must be decided on the balance of probabilities.

(5) No power which a person ('D') may exercise under this Act–

(a) in relation to a person who lacks capacity, or

(b) where D reasonably thinks that a person lacks capacity,

is exercisable in relation to a person under 16.

(6) Subsection (5) is subject to section 18(3).

Inability to make decisions

3 (1) For the purposes of section 2, a person is unable to make a decision for himself if he is unable–

(a) to understand the information relevant to the decision,

(b) to retain that information,

(c) to use or weigh that information as part of the process of making the decision, or

(d) to communicate his decision (whether by talking, using sign language or any other means).

(2) A person is not to be regarded as unable to understand the information relevant to a decision if he is able to understand an explanation of it given to him in a way that is appropriate to his circumstances (using simple language, visual aids or any other means).
(3) The fact that a person is able to retain the information relevant to a decision for a short period only does not prevent him from being regarded as able to make the decision.
(4) The information relevant to a decision includes information about the reasonably foreseeable consequences of–
(a) deciding one way or another, or
(b) failing to make the decision.

Best interests

4 (1) In determining for the purposes of this Act what is in a person's best interests, the person making the determination must not make it merely on the basis of–
(a) the person's age or appearance, or
(b) a condition of his, or an aspect of his behaviour, which might lead others to make unjustified assumptions about what might be in his best interests.
(2) The person making the determination must consider all the relevant circumstances and, in particular, take the following steps.
(3) He must consider–
(a) whether it is likely that the person will at some time have capacity in relation to the matter in question, and
(b) if it appears likely that he will, when that is likely to be.
(4) He must, so far as reasonably practicable, permit and encourage the person to participate, or to improve his ability to participate, as fully as possible in any act done for him and any decision affecting him.
(5) Where the determination relates to life-sustaining treatment he must not, in considering whether the treatment is in the best interests of the person concerned, be motivated by a desire to bring about his death.
(6) He must consider, so far as is reasonably ascertainable–
(a) the person's past and present wishes and feelings (and, in particular, any relevant written statement made by him when he had capacity),
(b) the beliefs and values that would be likely to influence his decision if he had capacity, and
(c) the other factors that he would be likely to consider if he were able to do so.
(7) He must take into account, if it is practicable and appropriate to consult them, the views of–
(a) anyone named by the person as someone to be consulted on the matter in question or on matters of that kind,
(b) anyone engaged in caring for the person or interested in his welfare,
(c) any donee of a lasting power of attorney granted by the person, and
(d) any deputy appointed for the person by the court,
as to what would be in the person's best interests and, in particular, as to the matters mentioned in subsection (6).
(8) The duties imposed by subsections (1) to (7) also apply in relation to the exercise of any powers which–
(a) are exercisable under a lasting power of attorney, or
(b) are exercisable by a person under this Act where he reasonably believes that another person lacks capacity.

(9) In the case of an act done, or a decision made, by a person other than the court, there is sufficient compliance with this section if (having complied with the requirements of subsections (1) to (7)) he reasonably believes that what he does or decides is in the best interests of the person concerned.

(10) 'Life-sustaining treatment' means treatment which in the view of a person providing health care for the person concerned is necessary to sustain life.

(11) 'Relevant circumstances' are those–
(a) of which the person making the determination is aware, and
(b) which it would be reasonable to regard as relevant.

Restriction on deprivation of liberty

4A (1) This Act does not authorise any person ('D') to deprive any other person ('P') of his liberty.

(2) But that is subject to–
(a) the following provisions of this section, and
(b) section 4B.

(3) D may deprive P of his liberty if, by doing so, D is giving effect to a relevant decision of the court.

(4) A relevant decision of the court is a decision made by an order under section 16(2)(a) in relation to a matter concerning P's personal welfare.

(5) D may deprive P of his liberty if the deprivation is authorised by Schedule A1 (hospital and care home residents: deprivation of liberty).

Deprivation of liberty necessary for life-sustaining treatment etc

4B (1) If the following conditions are met, D is authorised to deprive P of his liberty while a decision as respects any relevant issue is sought from the court.

(2) The first condition is that there is a question about whether D is authorised to deprive P of his liberty under section 4A.

(3) The second condition is that the deprivation of liberty–
(a) is wholly or partly for the purpose of–
(i) giving P life-sustaining treatment, or
(ii) doing any vital act, or
(b) consists wholly or partly of–
(i) giving P life-sustaining treatment, or
(ii) doing any vital act.

(4) The third condition is that the deprivation of liberty is necessary in order to–
(a) give the life-sustaining treatment, or
(b) do the vital act.

(5) A vital act is any act which the person doing it reasonably believes to be necessary to prevent a serious deterioration in P's condition.

Acts in connection with care or treatment

5 (1) If a person ('D') does an act in connection with the care or treatment of another person ('P'), the act is one to which this section applies if–
(a) before doing the act, D takes reasonable steps to establish whether P lacks capacity in relation to the matter in question, and
(b) when doing the act, D reasonably believes–
(i) that P lacks capacity in relation to the matter, and
(ii) that it will be in P's best interests for the act to be done.

(2) D does not incur any liability in relation to the act that he would not have incurred if P–
(a) had had capacity to consent in relation to the matter, and
(b) had consented to D's doing the act.
(3) Nothing in this section excludes a person's civil liability for loss or damage, or his criminal liability, resulting from his negligence in doing the act.
(4) Nothing in this section affects the operation of sections 24 to 26 (advance decisions to refuse treatment).

Section 5 acts: limitations

6 (1) If D does an act that is intended to restrain P, it is not an act to which section 5 applies unless two further conditions are satisfied.
(2) The first condition is that D reasonably believes that it is necessary to do the act in order to prevent harm to P.
(3) The second is that the act is a proportionate response to–
(a) the likelihood of P's suffering harm, and
(b) the seriousness of that harm.
(4) For the purposes of this section D restrains P if he–
(a) uses, or threatens to use, force to secure the doing of an act which P resists, or
(b) restricts P's liberty of movement, whether or not P resists.
(5) [Repealed.]
(6) Section 5 does not authorise a person to do an act which conflicts with a decision made, within the scope of his authority and in accordance with this Part, by–
(a) a donee of a lasting power of attorney granted by P, or
(b) a deputy appointed for P by the court.
(7) But nothing in subsection (6) stops a person–
(a) providing life-sustaining treatment, or
(b) doing any act which he reasonably believes to be necessary to prevent a serious deterioration in P's condition,
while a decision as respects any relevant issue is sought from the court.

Payment for necessary goods and services

7 (1) If necessary goods or services are supplied to a person who lacks capacity to contract for the supply, he must pay a reasonable price for them.
(2) 'Necessary' means suitable to a person's condition in life and to his actual requirements at the time when the goods or services are supplied.

Expenditure

8 (1) If an act to which section 5 applies involves expenditure, it is lawful for D–
(a) to pledge P's credit for the purpose of the expenditure, and
(b) to apply money in P's possession for meeting the expenditure.
(2) If the expenditure is borne for P by D, it is lawful for D–
(a) to reimburse himself out of money in P's possession, or
(b) to be otherwise indemnified by P.
(3) Subsections (1) and (2) do not affect any power under which (apart from those subsections) a person–
(a) has lawful control of P's money or other property, and
(b) has power to spend money for P's benefit.

Lasting powers of attorney

Lasting powers of attorney

9 (1) A lasting power of attorney is a power of attorney under which the donor ('P') confers on the donee (or donees) authority to make decisions about all or any of the following–
(a) P's personal welfare or specified matters concerning P's personal welfare, and
(b) P's property and affairs or specified matters concerning P's property and affairs,
and which includes authority to make such decisions in circumstances where P no longer has capacity.
(2) A lasting power of attorney is not created unless–
(a) section 10 is complied with,
(b) an instrument conferring authority of the kind mentioned in subsection (1) is made and registered in accordance with Schedule 1, and
(c) at the time when P executes the instrument, P has reached 18 and has capacity to execute it.
(3) An instrument which–
(a) purports to create a lasting power of attorney, but
(b) does not comply with this section, section 10 or Schedule 1,
confers no authority.
(4) The authority conferred by a lasting power of attorney is subject to–
(a) the provisions of this Act and, in particular, sections 1 (the principles) and 4 (best interests), and
(b) any conditions or restrictions specified in the instrument.

Appointment of donees

10 (1) A donee of a lasting power of attorney must be–
(a) an individual who has reached 18, or
(b) if the power relates only to P's property and affairs, either such an individual or a trust corporation.
(2) An individual who is bankrupt or is a person in relation to whom a debt relief order is made may not be appointed as donee of a lasting power of attorney in relation to P's property and affairs.
(3) Subsections (4) to (7) apply in relation to an instrument under which two or more persons are to act as donees of a lasting power of attorney.
(4) The instrument may appoint them to act–
(a) jointly,
(b) jointly and severally, or
(c) jointly in respect of some matters and jointly and severally in respect of others.
(5) To the extent to which it does not specify whether they are to act jointly or jointly and severally, the instrument is to be assumed to appoint them to act jointly.
(6) If they are to act jointly, a failure, as respects one of them, to comply with the requirements of subsection (1) or (2) or Part 1 or 2 of Schedule 1 prevents a lasting power of attorney from being created.
(7) If they are to act jointly and severally, a failure, as respects one of them, to comply with the requirements of subsection (1) or (2) or Part 1 or 2 of Schedule 1–
(a) prevents the appointment taking effect in his case, but

(b) does not prevent a lasting power of attorney from being created in the case of the other or others.

(8) An instrument used to create a lasting power of attorney–

(a) cannot give the donee (or, if more than one, any of them) power to appoint a substitute or successor, but

(b) may itself appoint a person to replace the donee (or, if more than one, any of them) on the occurrence of an event mentioned in section 13(6)(a) to (d) which has the effect of terminating the donee's appointment.

Lasting powers of attorney: restrictions

11 (1) A lasting power of attorney does not authorise the donee (or, if more than one, any of them) to do an act that is intended to restrain P, unless three conditions are satisfied.

(2) The first condition is that P lacks, or the donee reasonably believes that P lacks, capacity in relation to the matter in question.

(3) The second is that the donee reasonably believes that it is necessary to do the act in order to prevent harm to P.

(4) The third is that the act is a proportionate response to–

(a) the likelihood of P's suffering harm, and

(b) the seriousness of that harm.

(5) For the purposes of this section, the donee restrains P if he–

(a) uses, or threatens to use, force to secure the doing of an act which P resists, or

(b) restricts P's liberty of movement, whether or not P resists,

or if he authorises another person to do any of those things.

(6) [Repealed.]

(7) Where a lasting power of attorney authorises the donee (or, if more than one, any of them) to make decisions about P's personal welfare, the authority–

(a) does not extend to making such decisions in circumstances other than those where P lacks, or the donee reasonably believes that P lacks, capacity,

(b) is subject to sections 24 to 26 (advance decisions to refuse treatment), and

(c) extends to giving or refusing consent to the carrying out or continuation of a treatment by a person providing health care for P.

(8) But subsection (7)(c)–

(a) does not authorise the giving or refusing of consent to the carrying out or continuation of life-sustaining treatment, unless the instrument contains express provision to that effect, and

(b) is subject to any conditions or restrictions in the instrument.

Scope of lasting powers of attorney: gifts

12 (1) Where a lasting power of attorney confers authority to make decisions about P's property and affairs, it does not authorise a donee (or, if more than one, any of them) to dispose of the donor's property by making gifts except to the extent permitted by subsection (2).

(2) The donee may make gifts–

(a) on customary occasions to persons (including himself) who are related to or connected with the donor, or

(b) to any charity to whom the donor made or might have been expected to make gifts, if the value of each such gift is not unreasonable having regard to all the circumstances and, in particular, the size of the donor's estate.

(3) 'Customary occasion' means–
  (a) the occasion or anniversary of a birth, a marriage or the formation of a civil partnership, or
  (b) any other occasion on which presents are customarily given within families or among friends or associates.

(4) Subsection (2) is subject to any conditions or restrictions in the instrument.

Revocation of lasting powers of attorney etc

13 (1) This section applies if–
  (a) P has executed an instrument with a view to creating a lasting power of attorney, or
  (b) a lasting power of attorney is registered as having been conferred by P,

and in this section references to revoking the power include revoking the instrument.

(2) P may, at any time when he has capacity to do so, revoke the power.

(3) P's bankruptcy, or the making of a debt relief order (under Part 7A of the Insolvency Act 1986) in respect of P, revokes the power so far as it relates to P's property and affairs.

(4) But where P is bankrupt merely because an interim bankruptcy restrictions order has effect in respect of him or where P is subject to an interim debt relief restrictions order (under Schedule 4ZB of the Insolvency Act 1986), the power is suspended, so far as it relates to P's property and affairs, for so long as the order has effect.

(5) The occurrence in relation to a donee of an event mentioned in subsection (6)–
  (a) terminates his appointment, and
  (b) except in the cases given in subsection (7), revokes the power.

(6) The events are–
  (a) the disclaimer of the appointment by the donee in accordance with such requirements as may be prescribed for the purposes of this section in regulations made by the Lord Chancellor,
  (b) subject to subsections (8) and (9), the death or bankruptcy of the donee or the making of a debt relief order (under Part 7A of the Insolvency Act 1986) in respect of the donee or, if the donee is a trust corporation, its winding-up or dissolution,
  (c) subject to subsection (11), the dissolution or annulment of a marriage or civil partnership between the donor and the donee,
  (d) the lack of capacity of the donee.

(7) The cases are–
  (a) the donee is replaced under the terms of the instrument,
  (b) he is one of two or more persons appointed to act as donees jointly and severally in respect of any matter and, after the event, there is at least one remaining donee.

(8) The bankruptcy of a donee or the making of a debt relief order (under Part 7A of the Insolvency Act 1986) in respect of a donee does not terminate his appointment, or revoke the power, in so far as his authority relates to P's personal welfare.

(9) Where the donee is bankrupt merely because an interim bankruptcy restrictions order has effect in respect of him, or where the donee is subject to an interim debt relief restrictions order (under Schedule 4ZB of the Insolvency Act 1986), his appointment and the power are suspended, so far as they relate to P's property and affairs, for so long as the order has effect.

(10) Where the donee is one of two or more appointed to act jointly and severally under the power in respect of any matter, the reference in subsection (9) to the suspension of the power is to its suspension in so far as it relates to that donee.

(11) The dissolution or annulment of a marriage or civil partnership does not terminate the appointment of a donee, or revoke the power, if the instrument provided that it was not to do so.

Protection of donee and others if no power created or power revoked

14 (1) Subsections (2) and (3) apply if–

(a) an instrument has been registered under Schedule 1 as a lasting power of attorney, but

(b) a lasting power of attorney was not created,

whether or not the registration has been cancelled at the time of the act or transaction in question.

(2) A donee who acts in purported exercise of the power does not incur any liability (to P or any other person) because of the non-existence of the power unless at the time of acting he–

(a) knows that a lasting power of attorney was not created, or

(b) is aware of circumstances which, if a lasting power of attorney had been created, would have terminated his authority to act as a donee.

(3) Any transaction between the donee and another person is, in favour of that person, as valid as if the power had been in existence, unless at the time of the transaction that person has knowledge of a matter referred to in subsection (2).

(4) If the interest of a purchaser depends on whether a transaction between the donee and the other person was valid by virtue of subsection (3), it is conclusively presumed in favour of the purchaser that the transaction was valid if–

(a) the transaction was completed within 12 months of the date on which the instrument was registered, or

(b) the other person makes a statutory declaration, before or within 3 months after the completion of the purchase, that he had no reason at the time of the transaction to doubt that the donee had authority to dispose of the property which was the subject of the transaction.

(5) In its application to a lasting power of attorney which relates to matters in addition to P's property and affairs, section 5 of the Powers of Attorney Act 1971 (c 27) (protection where power is revoked) has effect as if references to revocation included the cessation of the power in relation to P's property and affairs.

(6) Where two or more donees are appointed under a lasting power of attorney, this section applies as if references to the donee were to all or any of them.

General powers of the court and appointment of deputies

Power to make declarations

15 (1) The court may make declarations as to–
(a) whether a person has or lacks capacity to make a decision specified in the declaration;
(b) whether a person has or lacks capacity to make decisions on such matters as are described in the declaration;
(c) the lawfulness or otherwise of any act done, or yet to be done, in relation to that person.
(2) 'Act' includes an omission and a course of conduct.

Powers to make decisions and appoint deputies: general

16 (1) This section applies if a person ('P') lacks capacity in relation to a matter or matters concerning–
(a) P's personal welfare, or
(b) P's property and affairs.
(2) The court may–
(a) by making an order, make the decision or decisions on P's behalf in relation to the matter or matters, or
(b) appoint a person (a 'deputy') to make decisions on P's behalf in relation to the matter or matters.
(3) The powers of the court under this section are subject to the provisions of this Act and, in particular, to sections 1 (the principles) and 4 (best interests).
(4) When deciding whether it is in P's best interests to appoint a deputy, the court must have regard (in addition to the matters mentioned in section 4) to the principles that–
(a) a decision by the court is to be preferred to the appointment of a deputy to make a decision, and
(b) the powers conferred on a deputy should be as limited in scope and duration as is reasonably practicable in the circumstances.
(5) The court may make such further orders or give such directions, and confer on a deputy such powers or impose on him such duties, as it thinks necessary or expedient for giving effect to, or otherwise in connection with, an order or appointment made by it under subsection (2).
(6) Without prejudice to section 4, the court may make the order, give the directions or make the appointment on such terms as it considers are in P's best interests, even though no application is before the court for an order, directions or an appointment on those terms.
(7) An order of the court may be varied or discharged by a subsequent order.
(8) The court may, in particular, revoke the appointment of a deputy or vary the powers conferred on him if it is satisfied that the deputy–
(a) has behaved, or is behaving, in a way that contravenes the authority conferred on him by the court or is not in P's best interests, or
(b) proposes to behave in a way that would contravene that authority or would not be in P's best interests.

Section 16 powers: Mental Health Act patients etc

16A(1) If a person is ineligible to be deprived of liberty by this Act, the court may not include in a welfare order provision which authorises the person to be deprived of his liberty.

(2) If–
(a) a welfare order includes provision which authorises a person to be deprived of his liberty, and
(b) that person becomes ineligible to be deprived of liberty by this Act,
the provision ceases to have effect for as long as the person remains ineligible.
(3) Nothing in subsection (2) affects the power of the court under section 16(7) to vary or discharge the welfare order.
(4) For the purposes of this section–
(a) Schedule 1A applies for determining whether or not P is ineligible to be deprived of liberty by this Act;
(b) 'welfare order' means an order under section 16(2)(a).

Section 16 powers: personal welfare

17 (1) The powers under section 16 as respects P's personal welfare extend in particular to–
(a) deciding where P is to live;
(b) deciding what contact, if any, P is to have with any specified persons;
(c) making an order prohibiting a named person from having contact with P;
(d) giving or refusing consent to the carrying out or continuation of a treatment by a person providing health care for P;
(e) giving a direction that a person responsible for P's health care allow a different person to take over that responsibility.
(2) Subsection (1) is subject to section 20 (restrictions on deputies).

Section 16 powers: property and affairs

18 (1) The powers under section 16 as respects P's property and affairs extend in particular to–
(a) the control and management of P's property;
(b) the sale, exchange, charging, gift or other disposition of P's property;
(c) the acquisition of property in P's name or on P's behalf;
(d) the carrying on, on P's behalf, of any profession, trade or business;
(e) the taking of a decision which will have the effect of dissolving a partnership of which P is a member;
(f) the carrying out of any contract entered into by P;
(g) the discharge of P's debts and of any of P's obligations, whether legally enforceable or not;
(h) the settlement of any of P's property, whether for P's benefit or for the benefit of others;
(i) the execution for P of a will;
(j) the exercise of any power (including a power to consent) vested in P whether beneficially or as trustee or otherwise;
(k) the conduct of legal proceedings in P's name or on P's behalf.
(2) No will may be made under subsection (1)(i) at a time when P has not reached 18.
(3) The powers under section 16 as respects any other matter relating to P's property and affairs may be exercised even though P has not reached 16, if the court considers it likely that P will still lack capacity to make decisions in respect of that matter when he reaches 18.
(4) Schedule 2 supplements the provisions of this section.

(5) Section 16(7) (variation and discharge of court orders) is subject to paragraph 6 of Schedule 2.
(6) Subsection (1) is subject to section 20 (restrictions on deputies).

Appointment of deputies

19 (1) A deputy appointed by the court must be–
(a) an individual who has reached 18, or
(b) as respects powers in relation to property and affairs, an individual who has reached 18 or a trust corporation.
(2) The court may appoint an individual by appointing the holder for the time being of a specified office or position.
(3) A person may not be appointed as a deputy without his consent.
(4) The court may appoint two or more deputies to act–
(a) jointly,
(b) jointly and severally, or
(c) jointly in respect of some matters and jointly and severally in respect of others.
(5) When appointing a deputy or deputies, the court may at the same time appoint one or more other persons to succeed the existing deputy or those deputies–
(a) in such circumstances, or on the happening of such events, as may be specified by the court;
(b) for such period as may be so specified.
(6) A deputy is to be treated as P's agent in relation to anything done or decided by him within the scope of his appointment and in accordance with this Part.
(7) The deputy is entitled–
(a) to be reimbursed out of P's property for his reasonable expenses in discharging his functions, and
(b) if the court so directs when appointing him, to remuneration out of P's property for discharging them.
(8) The court may confer on a deputy powers to–
(a) take possession or control of all or any specified part of P's property;
(b) exercise all or any specified powers in respect of it, including such powers of investment as the court may determine.
(9) The court may require a deputy–
(a) to give to the Public Guardian such security as the court thinks fit for the due discharge of his functions, and
(b) to submit to the Public Guardian such reports at such times or at such intervals as the court may direct.

Restrictions on deputies

20 (1) A deputy does not have power to make a decision on behalf of P in relation to a matter if he knows or has reasonable grounds for believing that P has capacity in relation to the matter.
(2) Nothing in section 16(5) or 17 permits a deputy to be given power–
(a) to prohibit a named person from having contact with P;
(b) to direct a person responsible for P's health care to allow a different person to take over that responsibility.
(3) A deputy may not be given powers with respect to–
(a) the settlement of any of P's property, whether for P's benefit or for the benefit of others,

(b) the execution for P of a will, or
(c) the exercise of any power (including a power to consent) vested in P whether beneficially or as trustee or otherwise.

(4) A deputy may not be given power to make a decision on behalf of P which is inconsistent with a decision made, within the scope of his authority and in accordance with this Act, by the donee of a lasting power of attorney granted by P (or, if there is more than one donee, by any of them).

(5) A deputy may not refuse consent to the carrying out or continuation of life-sustaining treatment in relation to P.

(6) The authority conferred on a deputy is subject to the provisions of this Act and, in particular, sections 1 (the principles) and 4 (best interests).

(7) A deputy may not do an act that is intended to restrain P unless four conditions are satisfied.

(8) The first condition is that, in doing the act, the deputy is acting within the scope of an authority expressly conferred on him by the court.

(9) The second is that P lacks, or the deputy reasonably believes that P lacks, capacity in relation to the matter in question.

(10) The third is that the deputy reasonably believes that it is necessary to do the act in order to prevent harm to P.

(11) The fourth is that the act is a proportionate response to–
(a) the likelihood of P's suffering harm, and
(b) the seriousness of that harm.

(12) For the purposes of this section, a deputy restrains P if he–
(a) uses, or threatens to use, force to secure the doing of an act which P resists, or
(b) restricts P's liberty of movement, whether or not P resists,
or if he authorises another person to do any of those things.

(13) [Repealed.]

Transfer of proceedings relating to people under 18

21 (1) The Lord Chief Justice, with the concurrence of the Lord Chancellor, may by order make provision as to the transfer of proceedings relating to a person under 18, in such circumstances as are specified in the order–
(a) from the Court of Protection to a court having jurisdiction under the Children Act 1989, or
(b) from a court having jurisdiction under that Act to the Court of Protection.

(2) The Lord Chief Justice may nominate any of the following to exercise his functions under this section–
(a) the President of the Court of Protection;
(b) a judicial office holder (as defined in section 109(4) of the Constitutional Reform Act 2005).

Powers of the court in relation to Schedule A1

Powers of court in relation to Schedule A1

21A(1) This section applies if either of the following has been given under Schedule A1–
(a) a standard authorisation;
(b) an urgent authorisation.

(2) Where a standard authorisation has been given, the court may determine any question relating to any of the following matters–
- (a) whether the relevant person meets one or more of the qualifying requirements;
- (b) the period during which the standard authorisation is to be in force;
- (c) the purpose for which the standard authorisation is given;
- (d) the conditions subject to which the standard authorisation is given.

(3) If the court determines any question under subsection (2), the court may make an order–
- (a) varying or terminating the standard authorisation, or
- (b) directing the supervisory body to vary or terminate the standard authorisation.

(4) Where an urgent authorisation has been given, the court may determine any question relating to any of the following matters–
- (a) whether the urgent authorisation should have been given;
- (b) the period during which the urgent authorisation is to be in force;
- (c) the purpose for which the urgent authorisation is given.

(5) Where the court determines any question under subsection (4), the court may make an order–
- (a) varying or terminating the urgent authorisation, or
- (b) directing the managing authority of the relevant hospital or care home to vary or terminate the urgent authorisation.

(6) Where the court makes an order under subsection (3) or (5), the court may make an order about a person's liability for any act done in connection with the standard or urgent authorisation before its variation or termination.

(7) An order under subsection (6) may, in particular, exclude a person from liability.

Powers of the court in relation to lasting powers of attorney

Powers of court in relation to validity of lasting powers of attorney

22 (1) This section and section 23 apply if–
- (a) a person ('P') has executed or purported to execute an instrument with a view to creating a lasting power of attorney, or
- (b) an instrument has been registered as a lasting power of attorney conferred by P.

(2) The court may determine any question relating to–
- (a) whether one or more of the requirements for the creation of a lasting power of attorney have been met;
- (b) whether the power has been revoked or has otherwise come to an end.

(3) Subsection (4) applies if the court is satisfied–
- (a) that fraud or undue pressure was used to induce P–
  - (i) to execute an instrument for the purpose of creating a lasting power of attorney, or
  - (ii) to create a lasting power of attorney, or
- (b) that the donee (or, if more than one, any of them) of a lasting power of attorney–
  - (i) has behaved, or is behaving, in a way that contravenes his authority or is not in P's best interests, or
  - (ii) proposes to behave in a way that would contravene his authority or would not be in P's best interests.

(4) The court may–
(a) direct that an instrument purporting to create the lasting power of attorney is not to be registered, or
(b) if P lacks capacity to do so, revoke the instrument or the lasting power of attorney.
(5) If there is more than one donee, the court may under subsection (4)(b) revoke the instrument or the lasting power of attorney so far as it relates to any of them.
(6) 'Donee' includes an intended donee.

Powers of court in relation to operation of lasting powers of attorney

23 (1) The court may determine any question as to the meaning or effect of a lasting power of attorney or an instrument purporting to create one.
(2) The court may–
(a) give directions with respect to decisions–
(i) which the donee of a lasting power of attorney has authority to make, and
(ii) which P lacks capacity to make;
(b) give any consent or authorisation to act which the donee would have to obtain from P if P had capacity to give it.
(3) The court may, if P lacks capacity to do so–
(a) give directions to the donee with respect to the rendering by him of reports or accounts and the production of records kept by him for that purpose;
(b) require the donee to supply information or produce documents or things in his possession as donee;
(c) give directions with respect to the remuneration or expenses of the donee;
(d) relieve the donee wholly or partly from any liability which he has or may have incurred on account of a breach of his duties as donee.
(4) The court may authorise the making of gifts which are not within section 12(2) (permitted gifts).
(5) Where two or more donees are appointed under a lasting power of attorney, this section applies as if references to the donee were to all or any of them.

Advance decisions to refuse treatment

Advance decisions to refuse treatment: general

24 (1) 'Advance decision' means a decision made by a person ('P'), after he has reached 18 and when he has capacity to do so, that if–
(a) at a later time and in such circumstances as he may specify, a specified treatment is proposed to be carried out or continued by a person providing health care for him, and
(b) at that time he lacks capacity to consent to the carrying out or continuation of the treatment,

the specified treatment is not to be carried out or continued.
(2) For the purposes of subsection (1)(a), a decision may be regarded as specifying a treatment or circumstances even though expressed in layman's terms.
(3) P may withdraw or alter an advance decision at any time when he has capacity to do so.
(4) A withdrawal (including a partial withdrawal) need not be in writing.

(5) An alteration of an advance decision need not be in writing (unless section 25(5) applies in relation to the decision resulting from the alteration).

Validity and applicability of advance decisions

25 (1) An advance decision does not affect the liability which a person may incur for carrying out or continuing a treatment in relation to P unless the decision is at the material time–

(a) valid, and

(b) applicable to the treatment.

(2) An advance decision is not valid if P–

(a) has withdrawn the decision at a time when he had capacity to do so,

(b) has, under a lasting power of attorney created after the advance decision was made, conferred authority on the donee (or, if more than one, any of them) to give or refuse consent to the treatment to which the advance decision relates, or

(c) has done anything else clearly inconsistent with the advance decision remaining his fixed decision.

(3) An advance decision is not applicable to the treatment in question if at the material time P has capacity to give or refuse consent to it.

(4) An advance decision is not applicable to the treatment in question if–

(a) that treatment is not the treatment specified in the advance decision,

(b) any circumstances specified in the advance decision are absent, or

(c) there are reasonable grounds for believing that circumstances exist which P did not anticipate at the time of the advance decision and which would have affected his decision had he anticipated them.

(5) An advance decision is not applicable to life-sustaining treatment unless–

(a) the decision is verified by a statement by P to the effect that it is to apply to that treatment even if life is at risk, and

(b) the decision and statement comply with subsection (6).

(6) A decision or statement complies with this subsection only if–

(a) it is in writing,

(b) it is signed by P or by another person in P's presence and by P's direction,

(c) the signature is made or acknowledged by P in the presence of a witness, and

(d) the witness signs it, or acknowledges his signature, in P's presence.

(7) The existence of any lasting power of attorney other than one of a description mentioned in subsection (2)(b) does not prevent the advance decision from being regarded as valid and applicable.

Effect of advance decisions

26 (1) If P has made an advance decision which is–

(a) valid, and

(b) applicable to a treatment,

the decision has effect as if he had made it, and had had capacity to make it, at the time when the question arises whether the treatment should be carried out or continued.

(2) A person does not incur liability for carrying out or continuing the treatment unless, at the time, he is satisfied that an advance decision exists which is valid and applicable to the treatment.

(3) A person does not incur liability for the consequences of withholding or withdrawing a treatment from P if, at the time, he reasonably believes that an advance decision exists which is valid and applicable to the treatment.

(4) The court may make a declaration as to whether an advance decision–
(a) exists;
(b) is valid;
(c) is applicable to a treatment.

(5) Nothing in an apparent advance decision stops a person–
(a) providing life-sustaining treatment, or
(b) doing any act he reasonably believes to be necessary to prevent a serious deterioration in P's condition,
while a decision as respects any relevant issue is sought from the court.

Excluded decisions

Family relationships etc

27 (1) Nothing in this Act permits a decision on any of the following matters to be made on behalf of a person–
(a) consenting to marriage or a civil partnership,
(b) consenting to have sexual relations,
(c) consenting to a decree of divorce being granted on the basis of two years' separation,
(d) consenting to a dissolution order being made in relation to a civil partnership on the basis of two years' separation,
(e) consenting to a child's being placed for adoption by an adoption agency,
(f) consenting to the making of an adoption order,
(g) discharging parental responsibilities in matters not relating to a child's property,
(h) giving a consent under the Human Fertilisation and Embryology Act 1990 (c 37)
(i) giving a consent under the Human Fertilisation and Embryology Act 2008.

(2) 'Adoption order' means–
(a) an adoption order within the meaning of the Adoption and Children Act 2002 (c 38) (including a future adoption order), and
(b) an order under section 84 of that Act (parental responsibility prior to adoption abroad).

Mental Health Act matters

28 (1) Nothing in this Act authorises anyone–
(a) to give a patient medical treatment for mental disorder, or
(b) to consent to a patient's being given medical treatment for mental disorder,
if, at the time when it is proposed to treat the patient, his treatment is regulated by Part 4 of the Mental Health Act.

(1A) Subsection (1) does not apply in relation to any form of treatment to which section 58A of that Act (electro-convulsive therapy, etc) applies if the patient comes within subsection (7) of that section (informal patient under 18 who cannot give consent).

(1B) Section 5 does not apply to an act to which section 64B of the Mental Health Act applies (treatment of community patients not recalled to hospital).

(2) 'Medical treatment', 'mental disorder' and 'patient' have the same meaning as in that Act.

Voting rights

29 (1) Nothing in this Act permits a decision on voting at an election for any public office, or at a referendum, to be made on behalf of a person.

(2) 'Referendum' has the same meaning as in section 101 of the Political Parties, Elections and Referendums Act 2000 (c 41).

Research

Research

30 (1) Intrusive research carried out on, or in relation to, a person who lacks capacity to consent to it is unlawful unless it is carried out–

(a) as part of a research project which is for the time being approved by the appropriate body for the purposes of this Act in accordance with section 31, and

(b) in accordance with sections 32 and 33.

(2) Research is intrusive if it is of a kind that would be unlawful if it was carried out–

(a) on or in relation to a person who had capacity to consent to it, but

(b) without his consent.

(3) A clinical trial which is subject to the provisions of clinical trials regulations is not to be treated as research for the purposes of this section.

(3A) Research is not intrusive to the extent that it consists of the use of a person's human cells to bring about the creation *in vitro* of an embryo or human admixed embryo, or the subsequent storage or use of an embryo or human admixed embryo so created.

(3B) Expressions used in subsection (3A) and in Schedule 3 to the Human Fertilisation and Embryology Act 1990 (consents to use or storage of gametes, embryos or human admixed embryos etc) have the same meaning in that subsection as in that Schedule.

(4) 'Appropriate body', in relation to a research project, means the person, committee or other body specified in regulations made by the appropriate authority as the appropriate body in relation to a project of the kind in question.

(5) 'Clinical trials regulations' means–

(a) the Medicines for Human Use (Clinical Trials) Regulations 2004 (SI No 1031) and any other regulations replacing those regulations or amending them, and

(b) any other regulations relating to clinical trials and designated by the Secretary of State as clinical trials regulations for the purposes of this section.

(6) In this section, section 32 and section 34, 'appropriate authority' means–

(a) in relation to the carrying out of research in England, the Secretary of State, and

(b) in relation to the carrying out of research in Wales, the National Assembly for Wales.

Requirements for approval

31 (1) The appropriate body may not approve a research project for the purposes of this Act unless satisfied that the following requirements will be met in relation to research carried out as part of the project on, or in relation to, a person who lacks capacity to consent to taking part in the project ('P').

(2) The research must be connected with–
(a) an impairing condition affecting P, or
(b) its treatment.
(3) 'Impairing condition' means a condition which is (or may be) attributable to, or which causes or contributes to (or may cause or contribute to), the impairment of, or disturbance in the functioning of, the mind or brain.
(4) There must be reasonable grounds for believing that research of comparable effectiveness cannot be carried out if the project has to be confined to, or relate only to, persons who have capacity to consent to taking part in it.
(5) The research must–
(a) have the potential to benefit P without imposing on P a burden that is disproportionate to the potential benefit to P, or
(b) be intended to provide knowledge of the causes or treatment of, or of the care of persons affected by, the same or a similar condition.
(6) If the research falls within paragraph (b) of subsection (5) but not within paragraph (a), there must be reasonable grounds for believing–
(a) that the risk to P from taking part in the project is likely to be negligible, and
(b) that anything done to, or in relation to, P will not–
(i) interfere with P's freedom of action or privacy in a significant way, or
(ii) be unduly invasive or restrictive.
(7) There must be reasonable arrangements in place for ensuring that the requirements of sections 32 and 33 will be met.

Consulting carers etc

32 (1) This section applies if a person ('R')–
(a) is conducting an approved research project, and
(b) wishes to carry out research, as part of the project, on or in relation to a person ('P') who lacks capacity to consent to taking part in the project.
(2) R must take reasonable steps to identify a person who–
(a) otherwise than in a professional capacity or for remuneration, is engaged in caring for P or is interested in P's welfare, and
(b) is prepared to be consulted by R under this section.
(3) If R is unable to identify such a person he must, in accordance with guidance issued by the appropriate authority, nominate a person who–
(a) is prepared to be consulted by R under this section, but
(b) has no connection with the project.
(4) R must provide the person identified under subsection (2), or nominated under subsection (3), with information about the project and ask him–
(a) for advice as to whether P should take part in the project, and
(b) what, in his opinion, P's wishes and feelings about taking part in the project would be likely to be if P had capacity in relation to the matter.
(5) If, at any time, the person consulted advises R that in his opinion P's wishes and feelings would be likely to lead him to decline to take part in the project (or to wish to withdraw from it) if he had capacity in relation to the matter, R must ensure–
(a) if P is not already taking part in the project, that he does not take part in it;
(b) if P is taking part in the project, that he is withdrawn from it.

(6) But subsection (5)(b) does not require treatment that P has been receiving as part of the project to be discontinued if R has reasonable grounds for believing that there would be a significant risk to P's health if it were discontinued.

(7) The fact that a person is the donee of a lasting power of attorney given by P, or is P's deputy, does not prevent him from being the person consulted under this section.

(8) Subsection (9) applies if treatment is being, or is about to be, provided for P as a matter of urgency and R considers that, having regard to the nature of the research and of the particular circumstances of the case–

(a) it is also necessary to take action for the purposes of the research as a matter of urgency, but

(b) it is not reasonably practicable to consult under the previous provisions of this section.

(9) R may take the action if–

(a) he has the agreement of a registered medical practitioner who is not involved in the organisation or conduct of the research project, or

(b) where it is not reasonably practicable in the time available to obtain that agreement, he acts in accordance with a procedure approved by the appropriate body at the time when the research project was approved under section 31.

(10) But R may not continue to act in reliance on subsection (9) if he has reasonable grounds for believing that it is no longer necessary to take the action as a matter of urgency.

Additional safeguards

33 (1) This section applies in relation to a person who is taking part in an approved research project even though he lacks capacity to consent to taking part.

(2) Nothing may be done to, or in relation to, him in the course of the research–

(a) to which he appears to object (whether by showing signs of resistance or otherwise) except where what is being done is intended to protect him from harm or to reduce or prevent pain or discomfort, or

(b) which would be contrary to–

(i) an advance decision of his which has effect, or

(ii) any other form of statement made by him and not subsequently withdrawn,

of which R is aware.

(3) The interests of the person must be assumed to outweigh those of science and society.

(4) If he indicates (in any way) that he wishes to be withdrawn from the project he must be withdrawn without delay.

(5) P must be withdrawn from the project, without delay, if at any time the person conducting the research has reasonable grounds for believing that one or more of the requirements set out in section 31(2) to (7) is no longer met in relation to research being carried out on, or in relation to, P.

(6) But neither subsection (4) nor subsection (5) requires treatment that P has been receiving as part of the project to be discontinued if R has reasonable grounds for believing that there would be a significant risk to P's health if it were discontinued.

Loss of capacity during research project

34 (1) This section applies where a person ('P')–
(a) has consented to take part in a research project begun before the commencement of section 30, but
(b) before the conclusion of the project, loses capacity to consent to continue to take part in it.
(2) The appropriate authority may by regulations provide that, despite P's loss of capacity, research of a prescribed kind may be carried out on, or in relation to, P if–
(a) the project satisfies prescribed requirements,
(b) any information or material relating to P which is used in the research is of a prescribed description and was obtained before P's loss of capacity, and
(c) the person conducting the project takes in relation to P such steps as may be prescribed for the purpose of protecting him.
(3) The regulations may, in particular,–
(a) make provision about when, for the purposes of the regulations, a project is to be treated as having begun;
(b) include provision similar to any made by section 31, 32 or 33.

Independent mental capacity advocate service

Appointment of independent mental capacity advocates

35 (1) The responsible authority must make such arrangements as it considers reasonable to enable persons ('independent mental capacity advocates') to be available to represent and support persons to whom acts or decisions proposed under sections 37, 38 and 39 relate or persons who fall within section 39A, 39C or 39D.
(2) The appropriate authority may make regulations as to the appointment of independent mental capacity advocates.
(3) The regulations may, in particular, provide–
(a) that a person may act as an independent mental capacity advocate only in such circumstances, or only subject to such conditions, as may be prescribed;
(b) for the appointment of a person as an independent mental capacity advocate to be subject to approval in accordance with the regulations.
(4) In making arrangements under subsection (1), the responsible authority must have regard to the principle that a person to whom a proposed act or decision relates should, so far as practicable, be represented and supported by a person who is independent of any person who will be responsible for the act or decision.
(5) The arrangements may include provision for payments to be made to, or in relation to, persons carrying out functions in accordance with the arrangements.
(6) For the purpose of enabling him to carry out his functions, an independent mental capacity advocate–
(a) may interview in private the person whom he has been instructed to represent, and
(b) may, at all reasonable times, examine and take copies of–

(i) any health record,
(ii) any record of, or held by, a local authority and compiled in connection with a social services function, and
(iii) any record held by a person registered under Part 2 of the Care Standards Act 2000 or Chapter 2 of Part 1 of the Health and Social Care Act 2008,

which the person holding the record considers may be relevant to the independent mental capacity advocate's investigation.

(6A) In subsections (1) and (4), 'the responsible authority' means–
(a) in relation to the provision of the services of independent mental capacity advocates in the area of a local authority in England, that local authority, and
(b) in relation to the provision of the services of independent mental capacity advocates in Wales, the Welsh Ministers.

(6B) In subsection (6A)(a), 'local authority' has the meaning given in section 64(1) except that it does not include the council of a county or county borough in Wales.

(7) In this section, section 36 and section 37, 'the appropriate authority' means–
(a) in relation to the provision of the services of independent mental capacity advocates in England, the Secretary of State, and
(b) in relation to the provision of the services of independent mental capacity advocates in Wales, the National Assembly for Wales.

Functions of independent mental capacity advocates

36 (1) The appropriate authority may make regulations as to the functions of independent mental capacity advocates.

(2) The regulations may, in particular, make provision requiring an advocate to take such steps as may be prescribed for the purpose of–
(a) providing support to the person whom he has been instructed to represent ('P') so that P may participate as fully as possible in any relevant decision;
(b) obtaining and evaluating relevant information;
(c) ascertaining what P's wishes and feelings would be likely to be, and the beliefs and values that would be likely to influence P, if he had capacity;
(d) ascertaining what alternative courses of action are available in relation to P;
(e) obtaining a further medical opinion where treatment is proposed and the advocate thinks that one should be obtained.

(3) The regulations may also make provision as to circumstances in which the advocate may challenge, or provide assistance for the purpose of challenging, any relevant decision.

Provision of serious medical treatment by NHS body

37 (1) This section applies if an NHS body–
(a) is proposing to provide, or secure the provision of, serious medical treatment for a person ('P') who lacks capacity to consent to the treatment, and
(b) is satisfied that there is no person, other than one engaged in providing care or treatment for P in a professional capacity or for remuneration, whom it would be appropriate to consult in determining what would be in P's best interests.

(2) But this section does not apply if P's treatment is regulated by Part 4 or 4A of the Mental Health Act.

(3) Before the treatment is provided, the NHS body must instruct an independent mental capacity advocate to represent P.

(4) If the treatment needs to be provided as a matter of urgency, it may be provided even though the NHS body has not been able to comply with subsection (3).

(5) The NHS body must, in providing or securing the provision of treatment for P, take into account any information given, or submissions made, by the independent mental capacity advocate.

(6) 'Serious medical treatment' means treatment which involves providing, withholding or withdrawing treatment of a kind prescribed by regulations made by the appropriate authority.

(7) 'NHS body' has such meaning as may be prescribed by regulations made for the purposes of this section by–

(a) the Secretary of State, in relation to bodies in England, or

(b) the National Assembly for Wales, in relation to bodies in Wales.

Provision of accommodation by NHS body

38 (1) This section applies if an NHS body proposes to make arrangements–

(a) for the provision of accommodation in a hospital or care home for a person ('P') who lacks capacity to agree to the arrangements, or

(b) for a change in P's accommodation to another hospital or care home,

and is satisfied that there is no person, other than one engaged in providing care or treatment for P in a professional capacity or for remuneration, whom it would be appropriate for it to consult in determining what would be in P's best interests.

(2) But this section does not apply if P is accommodated as a result of an obligation imposed on him under the Mental Health Act.

(2A) And this section does not apply if–

(a) an independent mental capacity advocate must be appointed under section 39A or 39C (whether or not by the NHS body) to represent P, and

(b) the hospital or care home in which P is to be accommodated under the arrangements referred to in this section is the relevant hospital or care home under the authorisation referred to in that section.

(3) Before making the arrangements, the NHS body must instruct an independent mental capacity advocate to represent P unless it is satisfied that–

(a) the accommodation is likely to be provided for a continuous period which is less than the applicable period, or

(b) the arrangements need to be made as a matter of urgency.

(4) If the NHS body–

(a) did not instruct an independent mental capacity advocate to represent P before making the arrangements because it was satisfied that subsection (3)(a) or (b) applied, but

(b) subsequently has reason to believe that the accommodation is likely to be provided for a continuous period–

(i) beginning with the day on which accommodation was first provided in accordance with the arrangements, and

(ii) ending on or after the expiry of the applicable period,

it must instruct an independent mental capacity advocate to represent P.

(5) The NHS body must, in deciding what arrangements to make for P, take into account any information given, or submissions made, by the independent mental capacity advocate.

(6) 'Care home' has the meaning given in section 3 of the Care Standards Act 2000.

(7) 'Hospital' means–

(a) in relation to England, a hospital as defined by section 275 of the National Health Service Act 2006; and

(b) in relation to Wales, a health service hospital as defined by section 206 of the National Health Service (Wales) Act 2006 or an independent hospital as defined by section 2 of the Care Standards Act 2000.

(8) 'NHS body' has such meaning as may be prescribed by regulations made for the purposes of this section by–

(a) the Secretary of State, in relation to bodies in England, or

(b) the National Assembly for Wales, in relation to bodies in Wales.

(9) 'Applicable period' means–

(a) in relation to accommodation in a hospital, 28 days, and

(b) in relation to accommodation in a care home, 8 weeks.

(10) For the purposes of subsection (1), a person appointed under Part 10 of Schedule A1 to be P's representative is not, by virtue of that appointment, engaged in providing care or treatment for P in a professional capacity or for remuneration.

Provision of accommodation by local authority

39 (1) This section applies if a local authority propose to make arrangements–

(a) for the provision of residential accommodation for a person ('P') who lacks capacity to agree to the arrangements, or

(b) for a change in P's residential accommodation,

and are satisfied that there is no person, other than one engaged in providing care or treatment for P in a professional capacity or for remuneration, whom it would be appropriate for them to consult in determining what would be in P's best interests.

(1A) But this section applies only if–

(a) in the case of a local authority in England, subsection (1B) applies;

(b) in the case of a local authority in Wales, subsection (2) applies.

(1B) This subsection applies if the accommodation is to be provided in accordance with–

(a) Part 1 of the Care Act 2014, or

(b) section 117 of the Mental Health Act.

(2) This subsection applies if the accommodation is to be provided in accordance with–

(a) Part 4 of the Social Services and Well-being (Wales) Act 2014; or

(b) section 117 of the Mental Health Act.

(3) This section does not apply if P is accommodated as a result of an obligation imposed on him under the Mental Health Act.

(3A) And this section does not apply if–

(a) an independent mental capacity advocate must be appointed under section 39A or 39C (whether or not by the local authority) to represent P, and

(b) the place in which P is to be accommodated under the arrangements referred to in this section is the relevant hospital or care home under the authorisation referred to in that section.

(4) Before making the arrangements, the local authority must instruct an independent mental capacity advocate to represent P unless they are satisfied that–

(a) the accommodation is likely to be provided for a continuous period of less than 8 weeks, or

(b) the arrangements need to be made as a matter of urgency.

(5) If the local authority–

(a) did not instruct an independent mental capacity advocate to represent P before making the arrangements because they were satisfied that subsection (4)(a) or (b) applied, but

(b) subsequently have reason to believe that the accommodation is likely to be provided for a continuous period that will end 8 weeks or more after the day on which accommodation was first provided in accordance with the arrangements,

they must instruct an independent mental capacity advocate to represent P.

(6) The local authority must, in deciding what arrangements to make for P, take into account any information given, or submissions made, by the independent mental capacity advocate.

(7) For the purposes of subsection (1), a person appointed under Part 10 of Schedule A1 to be P's representative is not, by virtue of that appointment, engaged in providing care or treatment for P in a professional capacity or for remuneration.

Person becomes subject to Schedule A1

39A(1) This section applies if–

(a) a person ('P') becomes subject to Schedule A1, and

(b) the managing authority of the relevant hospital or care home are satisfied that there is no person, other than one engaged in providing care or treatment for P in a professional capacity or for remuneration, whom it would be appropriate to consult in determining what would be in P's best interests.

(2) The managing authority must notify the supervisory body that this section applies.

(3) The supervisory body must instruct an independent mental capacity advocate to represent P.

(4) Schedule A1 makes provision about the role of an independent mental capacity advocate appointed under this section.

(5) This section is subject to paragraph 161 of Schedule A1.

(6) For the purposes of subsection (1), a person appointed under Part 10 of Schedule A1 to be P's representative is not, by virtue of that appointment, engaged in providing care or treatment for P in a professional capacity or for remuneration.

Section 39A: supplementary provision

39B(1) This section applies for the purposes of section 39A.

(2) P becomes subject to Schedule A1 in any of the following cases.

(3) The first case is where an urgent authorisation is given in relation to P under

paragraph 76(2) of Schedule A1 (urgent authorisation given before request made for standard authorisation).

(4) The second case is where the following conditions are met.

(5) The first condition is that a request is made under Schedule A1 for a standard authorisation to be given in relation to P ('the requested authorisation').

(6) The second condition is that no urgent authorisation was given under paragraph 76(2) of Schedule A1 before that request was made.

(7) The third condition is that the requested authorisation will not be in force on or before, or immediately after, the expiry of an existing standard authorisation.

(8) The expiry of a standard authorisation is the date when the authorisation is expected to cease to be in force.

(9) The third case is where, under paragraph 69 of Schedule A1, the supervisory body select a person to carry out an assessment of whether or not the relevant person is a detained resident.

Person unrepresented whilst subject to Schedule A1

39C(1) This section applies if–

(a) an authorisation under Schedule A1 is in force in relation to a person ('P'),

(b) the appointment of a person as P's representative ends in accordance with regulations made under Part 10 of Schedule A1, and

(c) the managing authority of the relevant hospital or care home are satisfied that there is no person, other than one engaged in providing care or treatment for P in a professional capacity or for remuneration, whom it would be appropriate to consult in determining what would be in P's best interests.

(2) The managing authority must notify the supervisory body that this section applies.

(3) The supervisory body must instruct an independent mental capacity advocate to represent P.

(4) Paragraph 159 of Schedule A1 makes provision about the role of an independent mental capacity advocate appointed under this section.

(5) The appointment of an independent mental capacity advocate under this section ends when a new appointment of a person as P's representative is made in accordance with Part 10 of Schedule A1.

(6) For the purposes of subsection (1), a person appointed under Part 10 of Schedule A1 to be P's representative is not, by virtue of that appointment, engaged in providing care or treatment for P in a professional capacity or for remuneration.

Person subject to Schedule A1 without paid representative

39D(1) This section applies if–

(a) an authorisation under Schedule A1 is in force in relation to a person ('P'),

(b) P has a representative ('R') appointed under Part 10 of Schedule A1, and

(c) R is not being paid under regulations under Part 10 of Schedule A1 for acting as P's representative.

(2) The supervisory body must instruct an independent mental capacity advocate to represent P in any of the following cases.

(3) The first case is where P makes a request to the supervisory body to instruct an advocate.
(4) The second case is where R makes a request to the supervisory body to instruct an advocate.
(5) The third case is where the supervisory body have reason to believe one or more of the following–
(a) that, without the help of an advocate, P and R would be unable to exercise one or both of the relevant rights;
(b) that P and R have each failed to exercise a relevant right when it would have been reasonable to exercise it;
(c) that P and R are each unlikely to exercise a relevant right when it would be reasonable to exercise it.
(6) The duty in subsection (2) is subject to section 39E.
(7) If an advocate is appointed under this section, the advocate is, in particular, to take such steps as are practicable to help P and R to understand the following matters–
(a) the effect of the authorisation;
(b) the purpose of the authorisation;
(c) the duration of the authorisation;
(d) any conditions to which the authorisation is subject;
(e) the reasons why each assessor who carried out an assessment in connection with the request for the authorisation, or in connection with a review of the authorisation, decided that P met the qualifying requirement in question;
(f) the relevant rights;
(g) how to exercise the relevant rights.
(8) The advocate is, in particular, to take such steps as are practicable to help P or R–
(a) to exercise the right to apply to court, if it appears to the advocate that P or R wishes to exercise that right, or
(b) to exercise the right of review, if it appears to the advocate that P or R wishes to exercise that right.
(9) If the advocate helps P or R to exercise the right of review–
(a) the advocate may make submissions to the supervisory body on the question of whether a qualifying requirement is reviewable;
(b) the advocate may give information, or make submissions, to any assessor carrying out a review assessment.
(10) In this section–
'relevant rights' means–
(a) the right to apply to court, and
(b) the right of review;
'right to apply to court' means the right to make an application to the court to exercise its jurisdiction under section 21A;
'right of review' means the right under Part 8 of Schedule A1 to request a review.

Limitation on duty to instruct advocate under section 39D

39E (1) This section applies if an advocate is already representing P in accordance with an instruction under section 39D.

(2) Section 39D(2) does not require another advocate to be instructed, unless the following conditions are met.
(3) The first condition is that the existing advocate was instructed–
(a) because of a request by R, or
(b) because the supervisory body had reason to believe one or more of the things in section 39D(5).
(4) The second condition is that the other advocate would be instructed because of a request by P.

Exceptions

40 (1) The duty imposed by section 37(3), 38(3) or (4), 39(4) or (5), 39A(3), 39C(3) or 39D(2) does not apply where there is–
(a) a person nominated by P (in whatever manner) as a person to be consulted on matters to which that duty relates,
(b) a donee of a lasting power of attorney created by P who is authorised to make decisions in relation to those matters, or
(c) a deputy appointed by the court for P with power to make decisions in relation to those matters.
(2) A person appointed under Part 10 of Schedule A1 to be P's representative is not, by virtue of that appointment, a person nominated by P as a person to be consulted in matters to which a duty mentioned in subsection (1) relates.

Power to adjust role of independent mental capacity advocate

41 (1) The appropriate authority may make regulations–
(a) expanding the role of independent mental capacity advocates in relation to persons who lack capacity, and
(b) adjusting the obligation to make arrangements imposed by section 35.
(2) The regulations may, in particular–
(a) prescribe circumstances (different to those set out in sections 37, 38 and 39) in which an independent mental capacity advocate must, or circumstances in which one may, be instructed by a person of a prescribed description to represent a person who lacks capacity, and
(b) include provision similar to any made by section 37, 38, 39 or 40.
(3) 'Appropriate authority' has the same meaning as in section 35.

Miscellaneous and supplementary

Codes of practice

42 (1) The Lord Chancellor must prepare and issue one or more codes of practice–
(a) for the guidance of persons assessing whether a person has capacity in relation to any matter,
(b) for the guidance of persons acting in connection with the care or treatment of another person (see section 5),
(c) for the guidance of donees of lasting powers of attorney,
(d) for the guidance of deputies appointed by the court,
(e) for the guidance of persons carrying out research in reliance on any provision made by or under this Act (and otherwise with respect to sections 30 to 34),
(f) for the guidance of independent mental capacity advocates,
(fa) for the guidance of persons exercising functions under Schedule A1,
(fb) for the guidance of representatives appointed under Part 10 of Schedule A1,

(g) with respect to the provisions of sections 24 to 26 (advance decisions and apparent advance decisions), and
(h) with respect to such other matters concerned with this Act as he thinks fit.

(2) The Lord Chancellor may from time to time revise a code.
(3) The Lord Chancellor may delegate the preparation or revision of the whole or any part of a code so far as he considers expedient.
(4) It is the duty of a person to have regard to any relevant code if he is acting in relation to a person who lacks capacity and is doing so in one or more of the following ways–
(a) as the donee of a lasting power of attorney,
(b) as a deputy appointed by the court,
(c) as a person carrying out research in reliance on any provision made by or under this Act (see sections 30 to 34),
(d) as an independent mental capacity advocate,
(da) in the exercise of functions under Schedule A1,
(db) as a representative appointed under Part 10 of Schedule A1,
(e) in a professional capacity,
(f) for remuneration.

(5) If it appears to a court or tribunal conducting any criminal or civil proceedings that–
(a) a provision of a code, or
(b) a failure to comply with a code,
is relevant to a question arising in the proceedings, the provision or failure must be taken into account in deciding the question.

(6) A code under subsection (1)(d) may contain separate guidance for deputies appointed by virtue of paragraph 1(2) of Schedule 5 (functions of deputy conferred on receiver appointed under the Mental Health Act).
(7) In this section and in section 43, 'code' means a code prepared or revised under this section.

Codes of practice: procedure

43 (1) Before preparing or revising a code, the Lord Chancellor must consult–
(a) the National Assembly for Wales, and
(b) such other persons as he considers appropriate.

(2) The Lord Chancellor may not issue a code unless–
(a) a draft of the code has been laid by him before both Houses of Parliament, and
(b) the 40 day period has elapsed without either House resolving not to approve the draft.

(3) The Lord Chancellor must arrange for any code that he has issued to be published in such a way as he considers appropriate for bringing it to the attention of persons likely to be concerned with its provisions.
(4) '40 day period', in relation to the draft of a proposed code, means–
(a) if the draft is laid before one House on a day later than the day on which it is laid before the other House, the period of 40 days beginning with the later of the two days;
(b) in any other case, the period of 40 days beginning with the day on which it is laid before each House.

(5) In calculating the period of 40 days, no account is to be taken of any period during which Parliament is dissolved or prorogued or during which both Houses are adjourned for more than 4 days.

Ill-treatment or neglect

44 (1) Subsection (2) applies if a person ('D')–

(a) has the care of a person ('P') who lacks, or whom D reasonably believes to lack, capacity,

(b) is the donee of a lasting power of attorney, or an enduring power of attorney (within the meaning of Schedule 4), created by P, or

(c) is a deputy appointed by the court for P.

(2) D is guilty of an offence if he ill-treats or wilfully neglects P.

(3) A person guilty of an offence under this section is liable–

(a) on summary conviction, to imprisonment for a term not exceeding 12 months or a fine not exceeding the statutory maximum or both;

(b) on conviction on indictment, to imprisonment for a term not exceeding 5 years or a fine or both.

Part 2: The Court of Protection and the Public Guardian

The Court of Protection

The Court of Protection

45 (1) There is to be a superior court of record known as the Court of Protection.

(2) The court is to have an official seal.

(3) The court may sit at any place in England and Wales, on any day and at any time.

(4) The court is to have a central office and registry at a place appointed by the Lord Chancellor, after consulting the Lord Chief Justice.

(5) The Lord Chancellor may, after consulting the Lord Chief Justice, designate as additional registries of the court any district registry of the High Court and any county court office.

(5A) The Lord Chief Justice may nominate any of the following to exercise his functions under this section–

(a) the President of the Court of Protection;

(b) a judicial office holder (as defined in section 109(4) of the Constitutional Reform Act 2005).

(6) The office of the Supreme Court called the Court of Protection ceases to exist.

The judges of the Court of Protection

46 (1) Subject to Court of Protection Rules under section 51(2)(d), the jurisdiction of the court is exercisable by a judge nominated for that purpose by–

(a) the Lord Chief Justice, or

(b) where nominated by the Lord Chief Justice to act on his behalf under this subsection–

(i) the President of the Court of Protection; or

(ii) a judicial office holder (as defined in section 109(4) of the Constitutional Reform Act 2005).

(2) To be nominated, a judge must be–

(a) the President of the Family Division,

(b) the Chancellor of the High Court,

(c) a puisne judge of the High Court,
(d) a circuit judge,
(e) a district judge,
(f) a District Judge (Magistrates' Courts),
(g) a judge of the First-tier Tribunal, or of the Upper Tribunal, by virtue of appointment under paragraph 1(1) of Schedule 2 or 3 to the Tribunals, Courts and Enforcement Act 2007,
(h) a transferred-in judge of the First-tier Tribunal or of the Upper Tribunal (see section 31(2) of that Act),
(i) a deputy judge of the Upper Tribunal (whether under paragraph 7 of Schedule 3 to, or section 31(2) of, that Act),
(j) the Chamber President, or Deputy Chamber President, of a chamber of the First-tier Tribunal or of a chamber of the Upper Tribunal,
(k) the Judge Advocate General,
(l) a Recorder,
(m) the holder of an office listed in the first column of the table in section 89(3C) of the Senior Courts Act 1981 (senior High Court Masters etc),
(n) a holder of an office listed in column 1 of Part 2 of Schedule 2 to that Act (High Court Masters etc),
(o) a deputy district judge appointed under section 102 of that Act or under section 8 of the County Courts Act 1984,
(p) a member of a panel of Employment Judges established for England and Wales or for Scotland,
(q) a person appointed under section 30(1)(a) or (b) of the Courts-Martial (Appeals) Act 1951 (assistants to the Judge Advocate General),
(r) a deputy judge of the High Court,
(s) the Senior President of Tribunals,
(t) an ordinary judge of the Court of Appeal (including the vice-president, if any, of either division of that court),
(u) the President of the Queen's Bench Division,
(v) the Master of the Rolls, or
(w) the Lord Chief Justice.

(3) The Lord Chief Justice, after consulting the Lord Chancellor, must–
(a) appoint one of the judges nominated by virtue of subsection (2)(a) to (c) to be President of the Court of Protection, and
(b) appoint another of those judges to be Vice-President of the Court of Protection.

(4) The Lord Chief Justice, after consulting the Lord Chancellor, must appoint one of the judges nominated by virtue of subsection (2)(d) to (q) to be Senior Judge of the Court of Protection, having such administrative functions in relation to the court as the Lord Chancellor, after consulting the Lord Chief Justice, may direct.

Supplementary powers

General powers and effect of orders etc

47 (1) The court has in connection with its jurisdiction the same powers, rights, privileges and authority as the High Court.

(2) Section 204 of the Law of Property Act 1925 (orders of High Court conclusive in favour of purchasers) applies in relation to orders and directions of the court as it applies to orders of the High Court.

(3) Office copies of orders made, directions given or other instruments issued by the court and sealed with its official seal are admissible in all legal proceedings as evidence of the originals without any further proof.

Interim orders and directions

48 The court may, pending the determination of an application to it in relation to a person ('P'), make an order or give directions in respect of any matter if–
(a) there is reason to believe that P lacks capacity in relation to the matter,
(b) the matter is one to which its powers under this Act extend, and
(c) it is in P's best interests to make the order, or give the directions, without delay.

Power to call for reports

49 (1) This section applies where, in proceedings brought in respect of a person ('P') under Part 1, the court is considering a question relating to P.
(2) The court may require a report to be made to it by the Public Guardian or by a Court of Protection Visitor.
(3) The court may require a local authority, or an NHS body, to arrange for a report to be made–
(a) by one of its officers or employees, or
(b) by such other person (other than the Public Guardian or a Court of Protection Visitor) as the authority, or the NHS body, considers appropriate.
(4) The report must deal with such matters relating to P as the court may direct.
(5) Court of Protection Rules may specify matters which, unless the court directs otherwise, must also be dealt with in the report.
(6) The report may be made in writing or orally, as the court may direct.
(7) In complying with a requirement, the Public Guardian or a Court of Protection Visitor may, at all reasonable times, examine and take copies of–
(a) any health record,
(b) any record of, or held by, a local authority and compiled in connection with a social services function, and
(c) any record held by a person registered under Part 2 of the Care Standards Act 2000, Chapter 2 of Part 1 of the Health and Social Care Act 2008 or Part 1 of the Regulation and Inspection of Social Care (Wales) Act 2016,
so far as the record relates to P.
(8) If the Public Guardian or a Court of Protection Visitor is making a visit in the course of complying with a requirement, he may interview P in private.
(9) If a Court of Protection Visitor who is a Special Visitor is making a visit in the course of complying with a requirement, he may if the court so directs carry out in private a medical, psychiatric or psychological examination of P's capacity and condition.
(10) 'NHS body' has the meaning given in section 148 of the Health and Social Care (Community Health and Standards) Act 2003.
(11) 'Requirement' means a requirement imposed under subsection (2) or (3).

Practice and procedure

Applications to the Court of Protection

50 (1) No permission is required for an application to the court for the exercise of any of its powers under this Act–

(a) by a person who lacks, or is alleged to lack, capacity,
(b) if such a person has not reached 18, by anyone with parental responsibility for him,
(c) by the donor or a donee of a lasting power of attorney to which the application relates,
(d) by a deputy appointed by the court for a person to whom the application relates, or
(e) by a person named in an existing order of the court, if the application relates to the order.

(1A) Nor is permission required for an application to the court under section 21A by the relevant person's representative.

(2) But, subject to Court of Protection Rules and to paragraph 20(2) of Schedule 3 (declarations relating to private international law), permission is required for any other application to the court.

(3) In deciding whether to grant permission the court must, in particular, have regard to–
(a) the applicant's connection with the person to whom the application relates,
(b) the reasons for the application,
(c) the benefit to the person to whom the application relates of a proposed order or directions, and
(d) whether the benefit can be achieved in any other way.

(4) 'Parental responsibility' has the same meaning as in the Children Act 1989.

Court of Protection Rules

51 (1) Rules of court with respect to the practice and procedure of the court (to be called 'Court of Protection Rules') may be made in accordance with Part 1 of Schedule 1 to the Constitutional Reform Act 2005.

(2) Court of Protection Rules may, in particular, make provision–
(a) as to the manner and form in which proceedings are to be commenced;
(b) as to the persons entitled to be notified of, and be made parties to, the proceedings;
(c) for the allocation, in such circumstances as may be specified, of any specified description of proceedings to a specified judge or to specified descriptions of judges;
(d) [Repealed.]
(e) for enabling the court to appoint a suitable person (who may, with his consent, be the Official Solicitor) to act in the name of, or on behalf of, or to represent the person to whom the proceedings relate;
(f) for enabling an application to the court to be disposed of without a hearing;
(g) for enabling the court to proceed with, or with any part of, a hearing in the absence of the person to whom the proceedings relate;
(h) for enabling or requiring the proceedings or any part of them to be conducted in private and for enabling the court to determine who is to be admitted when the court sits in private and to exclude specified persons when it sits in public;
(i) as to what may be received as evidence (whether or not admissible apart from the rules) and the manner in which it is to be presented;
(j) for the enforcement of orders made and directions given in the proceedings.

(3) Court of Protection Rules may, instead of providing for any matter, refer to provision made or to be made about that matter by directions.
(4) Court of Protection Rules may make different provision for different areas.

Practice directions

52 (1) Directions as to the practice and procedure of the court may be given in accordance with Part 1 of Schedule 2 to the Constitutional Reform Act 2005.
(2) Practice directions given otherwise than under subsection (1) may not be given without the approval of–
(a) the Lord Chancellor, and
(b) the Lord Chief Justice.
(3) The Lord Chief Justice may nominate any of the following to exercise his functions under this section–
(a) the President of the Court of Protection;
(b) a judicial office holder (as defined in section 109(4) of the Constitutional Reform Act 2005).

Rights of appeal

53 (1) Subject to the provisions of this section, an appeal lies to the Court of Appeal from any decision of the court.
(2) Court of Protection Rules may provide that, where a decision of the court is made by a specified description of person, an appeal from the decision lies to a specified description of judge of the court and not to the Court of Appeal.
(3) [Repealed.]
(4) Court of Protection Rules may make provision–
(a) that, in such cases as may be specified, an appeal from a decision of the court may not be made without permission;
(b) as to the person or persons entitled to grant permission to appeal;
(c) as to any requirements to be satisfied before permission is granted;
(d) that where a judge of the court makes a decision on an appeal, no appeal may be made to the Court of Appeal from that decision unless the Court of Appeal considers that–
(i) the appeal would raise an important point of principle or practice, or
(ii) there is some other compelling reason for the Court of Appeal to hear it;
(e) as to any considerations to be taken into account in relation to granting or refusing permission to appeal.

Fees and costs

Fees

54 (1) The Lord Chancellor may with the consent of the Treasury by order prescribe fees payable in respect of anything dealt with by the court.
(2) An order under this section may in particular contain provision as to–
(a) scales or rates of fees;
(b) exemptions from and reductions in fees;
(c) remission of fees in whole or in part.
(3) Before making an order under this section, the Lord Chancellor must consult–
(a) the President of the Court of Protection,

(b) the Vice-President of the Court of Protection, and
(c) the Senior Judge of the Court of Protection.
(4) The Lord Chancellor must take such steps as are reasonably practicable to bring information about fees to the attention of persons likely to have to pay them.
(5) Fees payable under this section are recoverable summarily as a civil debt.

Costs

55 (1) Subject to Court of Protection Rules, the costs of and incidental to all proceedings in the court are in its discretion.
(2) The rules may in particular make provision for regulating matters relating to the costs of those proceedings, including prescribing scales of costs to be paid to legal or other representatives.
(3) The court has full power to determine by whom and to what extent the costs are to be paid.
(4) The court may, in any proceedings–
(a) disallow, or
(b) order the legal or other representatives concerned to meet,
the whole of any wasted costs or such part of them as may be determined in accordance with the rules.
(5) 'Legal or other representative', in relation to a party to proceedings, means any person exercising a right of audience or right to conduct litigation on his behalf.
(6) 'Wasted costs' means any costs incurred by a party–
(a) as a result of any improper, unreasonable or negligent act or omission on the part of any legal or other representative or any employee of such a representative, or
(b) which, in the light of any such act or omission occurring after they were incurred, the court considers it is unreasonable to expect that party to pay.

Fees and costs: supplementary

56 (1) Court of Protection Rules may make provision–
(a) as to the way in which, and funds from which, fees and costs are to be paid;
(b) for charging fees and costs upon the estate of the person to whom the proceedings relate;
(c) for the payment of fees and costs within a specified time of the death of the person to whom the proceedings relate or the conclusion of the proceedings.
(2) A charge on the estate of a person created by virtue of subsection (1)(b) does not cause any interest of the person in any property to fail or determine or to be prevented from recommencing.

The Public Guardian

The Public Guardian

57 (1) For the purposes of this Act, there is to be an officer, to be known as the Public Guardian.
(2) The Public Guardian is to be appointed by the Lord Chancellor.
(3) There is to be paid to the Public Guardian out of money provided by Parliament such salary as the Lord Chancellor may determine.

(4) The Lord Chancellor may, after consulting the Public Guardian–
(a) provide him with such officers and staff, or
(b) enter into such contracts with other persons for the provision (by them or their sub-contractors) of officers, staff or services,
as the Lord Chancellor thinks necessary for the proper discharge of the Public Guardian's functions.
(5) Any functions of the Public Guardian may, to the extent authorised by him, be performed by any of his officers.

Functions of the Public Guardian

58 (1) The Public Guardian has the following functions–
(a) establishing and maintaining a register of lasting powers of attorney,
(b) establishing and maintaining a register of orders appointing deputies,
(c) supervising deputies appointed by the court,
(d) directing a Court of Protection Visitor to visit–
(i) a donee of a lasting power of attorney,
(ii) a deputy appointed by the court, or
(iii) the person granting the power of attorney or for whom the deputy is appointed ('P'),
and to make a report to the Public Guardian on such matters as he may direct,
(e) receiving security which the court requires a person to give for the discharge of his functions,
(f) receiving reports from donees of lasting powers of attorney and deputies appointed by the court,
(g) reporting to the court on such matters relating to proceedings under this Act as the court requires,
(h) dealing with representations (including complaints) about the way in which a donee of a lasting power of attorney or a deputy appointed by the court is exercising his powers,
(i) publishing, in any manner the Public Guardian thinks appropriate, any information he thinks appropriate about the discharge of his functions.
(2) The functions conferred by subsection (1)(c) and (h) may be discharged in co-operation with any other person who has functions in relation to the care or treatment of P.
(2A) The Public Guardian also has the following functions–
(a) establishing and maintaining a register of guardianship orders,
(b) supervising guardians,
(c) receiving security which the court requires a guardian to give for the exercise of the guardian's functions,
(d) receiving reports from guardians,
(e) reporting to the court on such matters relating to proceedings under the Guardianship (Missing Persons) Act 2017 as the court requires,
(f) dealing with representations (including complaints) about the way in which a guardian is exercising the guardian's functions, and
(g) publishing, in any manner the Public Guardian thinks appropriate, information about the exercise of his or her functions in connection with guardians and guardianship orders.

(3) The Lord Chancellor may by regulations make provision–
(a) conferring on the Public Guardian other functions in connection with this Act or the Guardianship (Missing Persons) Act 2017;
(b) in connection with the discharge by the Public Guardian of his functions.
(4) Regulations made under subsection (3)(b) may in particular make provision as to–
(a) the giving of security by deputies appointed by the court or guardians and the enforcement and discharge of security so given;
(b) the fees which may be charged by the Public Guardian;
(c) the way in which, and funds from which, such fees are to be paid;
(d) exemptions from and reductions in such fees;
(e) remission of such fees in whole or in part;
(f) the making of reports to the Public Guardian by deputies appointed by the court and others who are directed by the court to carry out any transaction for a person who lacks capacity.
(g) the making of reports to the Public Guardian by guardians.
(5) For the purpose of enabling him to carry out his functions in relation to lasting powers of attorney or deputies, the Public Guardian may, at all reasonable times, examine and take copies of–
(a) any health record,
(b) any record of, or held by, a local authority and compiled in connection with a social services function, and
(c) any record held by a person registered under Part 2 of the Care Standards Act 2000, Chapter 2 of Part 1 of the Health and Social Care Act 2008 or Part 1 of the Regulation and Inspection of Social Care (Wales) Act 2016,
so far as the record relates to P.
(6) The Public Guardian may also for that purpose interview P in private.
(7) In this section 'guardian' or 'guardianship order' have the same meaning as in the Guardianship (Missing Persons) Act 2017.

59 [Repealed.]

Annual report

60 (1) The Public Guardian must make an annual report to the Lord Chancellor about the discharge of his functions.
(2) The Lord Chancellor must, within one month of receiving the report, lay a copy of it before Parliament.

Court of Protection Visitors

Court of Protection Visitors

61 (1) A Court of Protection Visitor is a person who is appointed by the Lord Chancellor to–
(a) a panel of Special Visitors, or
(b) a panel of General Visitors.
(2) A person is not qualified to be a Special Visitor unless he–
(a) is a registered medical practitioner or appears to the Lord Chancellor to have other suitable qualifications or training, and
(b) appears to the Lord Chancellor to have special knowledge of and experience in cases of impairment of or disturbance in the functioning of the mind or brain.

(3) A General Visitor need not have a medical qualification.
(4) A Court of Protection Visitor–
(a) may be appointed for such term and subject to such conditions, and
(b) may be paid such remuneration and allowances,
as the Lord Chancellor may determine.
(5) For the purpose of carrying out his functions under this Act in relation to a person who lacks capacity ('P'), a Court of Protection Visitor may, at all reasonable times, examine and take copies of–
(a) any health record,
(b) any record of, or held by, a local authority and compiled in connection with a social services function, and
(c) any record held by a person registered under Part 2 of the Care Standards Act 2000, Chapter 2 of Part 1 of the Health and Social Care Act 2008 or Part 1 of the Regulation and Inspection of Social Care (Wales) Act 2016,
so far as the record relates to P.
(6) A Court of Protection Visitor may also for that purpose interview P in private.

Part 3: Miscellaneous and General

Declaratory provision

Scope of the Act

62 For the avoidance of doubt, it is hereby declared that nothing in this Act is to be taken to affect the law relating to murder or manslaughter or the operation of section 2 of the Suicide Act 1961 (assisting suicide).

Private international law

International protection of adults

63 Schedule 3–
(a) gives effect in England and Wales to the Convention on the International Protection of Adults signed at the Hague on 13th January 2000 (Cm 5881) (in so far as this Act does not otherwise do so), and
(b) makes related provision as to the private international law of England and Wales.

General

Interpretation

64 (1) In this Act–
'the 1985 Act' means the Enduring Powers of Attorney Act 1985,
'advance decision' has the meaning given in section 24(1),
'authorisation under Schedule A1' means either–
(a) a standard authorisation under that Schedule, or
(b) an urgent authorisation under that Schedule;
'the court' means the Court of Protection established by section 45,
'Court of Protection Rules' has the meaning given in section 51(1),
'Court of Protection Visitor' has the meaning given in section 61,
'deputy' has the meaning given in section 16(2)(b),
'enactment' includes a provision of subordinate legislation (within the meaning of the Interpretation Act 1978),

'health record' has the same meaning as in the Data Protection Act 2018 (see section 205 of that Act),

'the Human Rights Convention' has the same meaning as 'the Convention' in the Human Rights Act 1998,

'independent mental capacity advocate' has the meaning given in section 35(1),

'lasting power of attorney' has the meaning given in section 9,

'life-sustaining treatment' has the meaning given in section 4(10),

'local authority', except in section 35(6A)(a) and Schedule A1, means–

(a) the council of a county in England in which there are no district councils,

(b) the council of a district in England,

(c) the council of a county or county borough in Wales,

(d) the council of a London borough,

(e) the Common Council of the City of London, or

(f) the Council of the Isles of Scilly,

'Mental Health Act' means the Mental Health Act 1983,

'prescribed', in relation to regulations made under this Act, means prescribed by those regulations,

'property' includes any thing in action and any interest in real or personal property,

'public authority' has the same meaning as in the Human Rights Act 1998,

'Public Guardian' has the meaning given in section 57,

'purchaser' and 'purchase' have the meaning given in section 205(1) of the Law of Property Act 1925,

'social services function'–

(a) in relation to England] has the meaning given in section 1A of the Local Authority Social Services Act 1970,

(b) in relation to Wales, has the meaning given in section 143 of the Social Services and Well-being (Wales) Act 2014,

'treatment' includes a diagnostic or other procedure,

'trust corporation' has the meaning given in section 68(1) of the Trustee Act 1925, and

'will' includes codicil.

(2) In this Act, references to making decisions, in relation to a donee of a lasting power of attorney or a deputy appointed by the court, include, where appropriate, acting on decisions made.

(3) In this Act, references to the bankruptcy of an individual include a case where a bankruptcy restrictions order under the Insolvency Act 1986 has effect in respect of him.

(3A) In this Act references to a debt relief order (under Part 7A of the Insolvency Act 1986) being made in relation to an individual include a case where a debt relief restrictions order under the Insolvency Act 1986 has effect in respect of him.

(4) 'Bankruptcy restrictions order' includes an interim bankruptcy restrictions order.

(4A) 'Debt relief restrictions order' includes an interim debt relief restrictions order.

(5) In this Act, references to deprivation of a person's liberty have the same meaning as in Article 5(1) of the Human Rights Convention.

(6) For the purposes of such references, it does not matter whether a person is deprived of his liberty by a public authority or not.

Rules, regulations and orders

65 (1) Any power to make rules, regulations or orders under this Act, other than the power in section 21–
(a) is exercisable by statutory instrument;
(b) includes power to make supplementary, incidental, consequential, transitional or saving provision;
(c) includes power to make different provision for different cases.

(2) Any statutory instrument containing rules, regulations or orders made by the Lord Chancellor or the Secretary of State under this Act, other than–
(a) regulations under section 34 (loss of capacity during research project),
(b) regulations under section 41 (adjusting role of independent mental capacity advocacy service),
(c) regulations under paragraph 32(1)(b) of Schedule 3 (private international law relating to the protection of adults),
(d) an order of the kind mentioned in section 67(6) (consequential amendments of primary legislation), or
(e) an order under section 68 (commencement),
is subject to annulment in pursuance of a resolution of either House of Parliament.

(3) A statutory instrument containing an Order in Council under paragraph 31 of Schedule 3 (provision to give further effect to Hague Convention) is subject to annulment in pursuance of a resolution of either House of Parliament.

(4) A statutory instrument containing regulations made by the Secretary of State under section 34 or 41 or by the Lord Chancellor under paragraph 32(1)(b) of Schedule 3 may not be made unless a draft has been laid before and approved by resolution of each House of Parliament.

(4A) Subsection (2) does not apply to a statutory instrument containing regulations made by the Secretary of State under Schedule A1.

(4B) If such a statutory instrument contains regulations under paragraph 42(2)(b), 129, 162 or 164 of Schedule A1 (whether or not it also contains other regulations), the instrument may not be made unless a draft has been laid before and approved by resolution of each House of Parliament.

(4C) Subject to that, such a statutory instrument is subject to annulment in pursuance of a resolution of either House of Parliament.

(5) An order under section 21–
(a) may include supplementary, incidental, consequential, transitional or saving provision;
(b) may make different provision for different cases;
(c) is to be made in the form of a statutory instrument to which the Statutory Instruments Act 1946 applies as if the order were made by a Minister of the Crown; and
(d) is subject to annulment in pursuance of a resolution of either House of Parliament.

Existing receivers and enduring powers of attorney etc

66 (1) The following provisions cease to have effect–
(a) Part 7 of the Mental Health Act,
(b) the Enduring Powers of Attorney Act 1985 (c 29).
(2) No enduring power of attorney within the meaning of the 1985 Act is to be created after the commencement of subsection (1)(b).
(3) Schedule 4 has effect in place of the 1985 Act in relation to any enduring power of attorney created before the commencement of subsection (1)(b).
(4) Schedule 5 contains transitional provisions and savings in relation to Part 7 of the Mental Health Act and the 1985 Act.

Minor and consequential amendments and repeals

67 (1) Schedule 6 contains minor and consequential amendments.
(2) Schedule 7 contains repeals.
(3) The Lord Chancellor may by order make supplementary, incidental, consequential, transitional or saving provision for the purposes of, in consequence of, or for giving full effect to a provision of this Act.
(4) An order under subsection (3) may, in particular–
(a) provide for a provision of this Act which comes into force before another provision of this Act has come into force to have effect, until the other provision has come into force, with specified modifications;
(b) amend, repeal or revoke an enactment, other than one contained in an Act or Measure passed in a Session after the one in which this Act is passed.
(5) The amendments that may be made under subsection (4)(b) are in addition to those made by or under any other provision of this Act.
(6) An order under subsection (3) which amends or repeals a provision of an Act or Measure may not be made unless a draft has been laid before and approved by resolution of each House of Parliament.

Commencement and extent

68 (1) This Act, other than sections 30 to 41, comes into force in accordance with provision made by order by the Lord Chancellor.
(2) Sections 30 to 41 come into force in accordance with provision made by order by–
(a) the Secretary of State, in relation to England, and
(b) the National Assembly for Wales, in relation to Wales.
(3) An order under this section may appoint different days for different provisions and different purposes.
(4) Subject to subsections (5) and (6), this Act extends to England and Wales only.
(5) The following provisions extend to the United Kingdom–
(a) paragraph 16(1) of Schedule 1 (evidence of instruments and of registration of lasting powers of attorney),
(b) paragraph 15(3) of Schedule 4 (evidence of instruments and of registration of enduring powers of attorney).
(6) Subject to any provision made in Schedule 6, the amendments and repeals made by Schedules 6 and 7 have the same extent as the enactments to which they relate.

Short title

69 This Act may be cited as the Mental Capacity Act 2005.

SCHEDULE A1: HOSPITAL AND CARE HOME RESIDENTS: DEPRIVATION OF LIBERTY

Part 1: Authorisation to Deprive Residents of Liberty etc

Application of Part

1 (1) This Part applies if the following conditions are met.
(2) The first condition is that a person ('P') is detained in a hospital or care home–for the purpose of being given care or treatment–in circumstances which amount to deprivation of the person's liberty.
(3) The second condition is that a standard or urgent authorisation is in force.
(4) The third condition is that the standard or urgent authorisation relates–
(a) to P, and
(b) to the hospital or care home in which P is detained.

Authorisation to deprive P of liberty

2 The managing authority of the hospital or care home may deprive P of his liberty by detaining him as mentioned in paragraph 1(2).

No liability for acts done for purpose of depriving P of liberty

3 (1) This paragraph applies to any act which a person ('D') does for the purpose of detaining P as mentioned in paragraph 1(2).
(2) D does not incur any liability in relation to the act that he would not have incurred if P–
(a) had had capacity to consent in relation to D's doing the act, and
(b) had consented to D's doing the act.

No protection for negligent acts etc

4 (1) Paragraphs 2 and 3 do not exclude a person's civil liability for loss or damage, or his criminal liability, resulting from his negligence in doing any thing.
(2) Paragraphs 2 and 3 do not authorise a person to do anything otherwise than for the purpose of the standard or urgent authorisation that is in force.
(3) In a case where a standard authorisation is in force, paragraphs 2 and 3 do not authorise a person to do anything which does not comply with the conditions (if any) included in the authorisation.

Part 2: Interpretation: Main Terms

Introduction

5 This Part applies for the purposes of this Schedule.

Detained resident

6 'Detained resident' means a person detained in a hospital or care home–for the purpose of being given care or treatment–in circumstances which amount to deprivation of the person's liberty.

Relevant person etc

7 In relation to a person who is, or is to be, a detained resident–
'relevant person' means the person in question;
'relevant hospital or care home' means the hospital or care home in question;
'relevant care or treatment' means the care or treatment in question.

Authorisations

8 'Standard authorisation' means an authorisation given under Part 4.

9 'Urgent authorisation' means an authorisation given under Part 5.

10 'Authorisation under this Schedule' means either of the following–
(a) a standard authorisation;
(b) an urgent authorisation.

11 (1) The purpose of a standard authorisation is the purpose which is stated in the authorisation in accordance with paragraph 55(1)(d).
(2) The purpose of an urgent authorisation is the purpose which is stated in the authorisation in accordance with paragraph 80(d).

Part 3: The Qualifying Requirements

The qualifying requirements

12 (1) These are the qualifying requirements referred to in this Schedule–
(a) the age requirement;
(b) the mental health requirement;
(c) the mental capacity requirement;
(d) the best interests requirement;
(e) the eligibility requirement;
(f) the no refusals requirement.
(2) Any question of whether a person who is, or is to be, a detained resident meets the qualifying requirements is to be determined in accordance with this Part.
(3) In a case where–
(a) the question of whether a person meets a particular qualifying requirement arises in relation to the giving of a standard authorisation, and
(b) any circumstances relevant to determining that question are expected to change between the time when the determination is made and the time when the authorisation is expected to come into force,
those circumstances are to be taken into account as they are expected to be at the later time.

The age requirement

13 The relevant person meets the age requirement if he has reached 18.

The mental health requirement

14 (1) The relevant person meets the mental health requirement if he is suffering from mental disorder (within the meaning of the Mental Health Act, but disregarding any exclusion for persons with learning disability).
(2) An exclusion for persons with learning disability is any provision of the Mental Health Act which provides for a person with learning disability not to be regarded as suffering from mental disorder for one or more purposes of that Act.

The mental capacity requirement

15 The relevant person meets the mental capacity requirement if he lacks capacity in relation to the question whether or not he should be accommodated in the relevant hospital or care home for the purpose of being given the relevant care or treatment.

The best interests requirement

16 (1) The relevant person meets the best interests requirement if all of the following conditions are met.

(2) The first condition is that the relevant person is, or is to be, a detained resident.

(3) The second condition is that it is in the best interests of the relevant person for him to be a detained resident.

(4) The third condition is that, in order to prevent harm to the relevant person, it is necessary for him to be a detained resident.

(5) The fourth condition is that it is a proportionate response to–

(a) the likelihood of the relevant person suffering harm, and

(b) the seriousness of that harm,

for him to be a detained resident.

The eligibility requirement

17 (1) The relevant person meets the eligibility requirement unless he is ineligible to be deprived of liberty by this Act.

(2) Schedule 1A applies for the purpose of determining whether or not P is ineligible to be deprived of liberty by this Act.

The no refusals requirement

18 The relevant person meets the no refusals requirement unless there is a refusal within the meaning of paragraph 19 or 20.

19 (1) There is a refusal if these conditions are met–

(a) the relevant person has made an advance decision;

(b) the advance decision is valid;

(c) the advance decision is applicable to some or all of the relevant treatment.

(2) Expressions used in this paragraph and any of sections 24, 25 or 26 have the same meaning in this paragraph as in that section.

20 (1) There is a refusal if it would be in conflict with a valid decision of a donee or deputy for the relevant person to be accommodated in the relevant hospital or care home for the purpose of receiving some or all of the relevant care or treatment–

(a) in circumstances which amount to deprivation of the person's liberty, or

(b) at all.

(2) A donee is a donee of a lasting power of attorney granted by the relevant person.

(3) A decision of a donee or deputy is valid if it is made–

(a) within the scope of his authority as donee or deputy, and

(b) in accordance with Part 1 of this Act.

Part 4: Standard Authorisations

Supervisory body to give authorisation

21 Only the supervisory body may give a standard authorisation.

22 The supervisory body may not give a standard authorisation unless–

(a) the managing authority of the relevant hospital or care home have requested it, or

(b) paragraph 71 applies (right of third party to require consideration of whether authorisation needed).

23 The managing authority may not make a request for a standard authorisation unless–
(a) they are required to do so by paragraph 24 (as read with paragraphs 27 to 29),
(b) they are required to do so by paragraph 25 (as read with paragraph 28), or
(c) they are permitted to do so by paragraph 30.

Duty to request authorisation: basic cases

24 (1) The managing authority must request a standard authorisation in any of the following cases.
(2) The first case is where it appears to the managing authority that the relevant person–
(a) is not yet accommodated in the relevant hospital or care home,
(b) is likely–at some time within the next 28 days–to be a detained resident in the relevant hospital or care home, and
(c) is likely–
(i) at that time, or
(ii) at some later time within the next 28 days,
to meet all of the qualifying requirements.
(3) The second case is where it appears to the managing authority that the relevant person–
(a) is already accommodated in the relevant hospital or care home,
(b) is likely–at some time within the next 28 days–to be a detained resident in the relevant hospital or care home, and
(c) is likely–
(i) at that time, or
(ii) at some later time within the next 28 days,
to meet all of the qualifying requirements.
(4) The third case is where it appears to the managing authority that the relevant person–
(a) is a detained resident in the relevant hospital or care home, and
(b) meets all of the qualifying requirements, or is likely to do so at some time within the next 28 days.
(5) This paragraph is subject to paragraphs 27 to 29.

Duty to request authorisation: change in place of detention

25 (1) The relevant managing authority must request a standard authorisation if it appears to them that these conditions are met.
(2) The first condition is that a standard authorisation–
(a) has been given, and
(b) has not ceased to be in force.
(3) The second condition is that there is, or is to be, a change in the place of detention.
(4) This paragraph is subject to paragraph 28.

26 (1) This paragraph applies for the purposes of paragraph 25.
(2) There is a change in the place of detention if the relevant person–
(a) ceases to be a detained resident in the stated hospital or care home, and
(b) becomes a detained resident in a different hospital or care home ('the new hospital or care home').

(3) The stated hospital or care home is the hospital or care home to which the standard authorisation relates.

(4) The relevant managing authority are the managing authority of the new hospital or care home.

Other authority for detention: request for authorisation

27 (1) This paragraph applies if, by virtue of section 4A(3), a decision of the court authorises the relevant person to be a detained resident.

(2) Paragraph 24 does not require a request for a standard authorisation to be made in relation to that detention unless these conditions are met.

(3) The first condition is that the standard authorisation would be in force at a time immediately after the expiry of the other authority.

(4) The second condition is that the standard authorisation would not be in force at any time on or before the expiry of the other authority.

(5) The third condition is that it would, in the managing authority's view, be unreasonable to delay making the request until a time nearer the expiry of the other authority.

(6) In this paragraph–

(a) the other authority is–

(i) the decision mentioned in sub-paragraph (1), or

(ii) any further decision of the court which, by virtue of section 4A(3), authorises, or is expected to authorise, the relevant person to be a detained resident;

(b) the expiry of the other authority is the time when the other authority is expected to cease to authorise the relevant person to be a detained resident.

Request refused: no further request unless change of circumstances

28 (1) This paragraph applies if–

(a) a managing authority request a standard authorisation under paragraph 24 or 25, and

(b) the supervisory body are prohibited by paragraph 50(2) from giving the authorisation.

(2) Paragraph 24 or 25 does not require that managing authority to make a new request for a standard authorisation unless it appears to the managing authority that–

(a) there has been a change in the relevant person's case, and

(b) because of that change, the supervisory body are likely to give a standard authorisation if requested.

Authorisation given: request for further authorisation

29 (1) This paragraph applies if a standard authorisation–

(a) has been given in relation to the detention of the relevant person, and

(b) that authorisation ('the existing authorisation') has not ceased to be in force.

(2) Paragraph 24 does not require a new request for a standard authorisation ('the new authorisation') to be made unless these conditions are met.

(3) The first condition is that the new authorisation would be in force at a time immediately after the expiry of the existing authorisation.

(4) The second condition is that the new authorisation would not be in force at any time on or before the expiry of the existing authorisation.

(5) The third condition is that it would, in the managing authority's view, be unreasonable to delay making the request until a time nearer the expiry of the existing authorisation.

(6) The expiry of the existing authorisation is the time when it is expected to cease to be in force.

Power to request authorisation

30 (1) This paragraph applies if–

(a) a standard authorisation has been given in relation to the detention of the relevant person,

(b) that authorisation ('the existing authorisation') has not ceased to be in force,

(c) the requirement under paragraph 24 to make a request for a new standard authorisation does not apply, because of paragraph 29, and

(d) a review of the existing authorisation has been requested, or is being carried out, in accordance with Part 8.

(2) The managing authority may request a new standard authorisation which would be in force on or before the expiry of the existing authorisation; but only if it would also be in force immediately after that expiry.

(3) The expiry of the existing authorisation is the time when it is expected to cease to be in force.

(4) Further provision relating to cases where a request is made under this paragraph can be found in–

(a) paragraph 62 (effect of decision about request), and

(b) paragraph 124 (effect of request on Part 8 review).

Information included in request

31 A request for a standard authorisation must include the information (if any) required by regulations.

Records of requests

32 (1) The managing authority of a hospital or care home must keep a written record of–

(a) each request that they make for a standard authorisation, and

(b) the reasons for making each request.

(2) A supervisory body must keep a written record of each request for a standard authorisation that is made to them.

Relevant person must be assessed

33 (1) This paragraph applies if the supervisory body are requested to give a standard authorisation.

(2) The supervisory body must secure that all of these assessments are carried out in relation to the relevant person–

(a) an age assessment;

(b) a mental health assessment;

(c) a mental capacity assessment;

(d) a best interests assessment;

(e) an eligibility assessment;

(f) a no refusals assessment.

(3) The person who carries out any such assessment is referred to as the assessor.

(4) Regulations may be made about the period (or periods) within which assessors must carry out assessments.

(5) This paragraph is subject to paragraphs 49 and 133.

Age assessment

34 An age assessment is an assessment of whether the relevant person meets the age requirement.

Mental health assessment

35 A mental health assessment is an assessment of whether the relevant person meets the mental health requirement.

36 When carrying out a mental health assessment, the assessor must also–

(a) consider how (if at all) the relevant person's mental health is likely to be affected by his being a detained resident, and

(b) notify the best interests assessor of his conclusions.

Mental capacity assessment

37 A mental capacity assessment is an assessment of whether the relevant person meets the mental capacity requirement.

Best interests assessment

38 A best interests assessment is an assessment of whether the relevant person meets the best interests requirement.

39 (1) In carrying out a best interests assessment, the assessor must comply with the duties in sub-paragraphs (2) and (3).

(2) The assessor must consult the managing authority of the relevant hospital or care home.

(3) The assessor must have regard to all of the following–

(a) the conclusions which the mental health assessor has notified to the best interests assessor in accordance with paragraph 36(b);

(b) any relevant needs assessment;

(c) any relevant care plan.

(4) A relevant needs assessment is an assessment of the relevant person's needs which–

(a) was carried out in connection with the relevant person being accommodated in the relevant hospital or care home, and

(b) was carried out by or on behalf of–

(i) the managing authority of the relevant hospital or care home, or

(ii) the supervisory body.

(5) A relevant care plan is a care plan which–

(a) sets out how the relevant person's needs are to be met whilst he is accommodated in the relevant hospital or care home, and

(b) was drawn up by or on behalf of–

(i) the managing authority of the relevant hospital or care home, or

(ii) the supervisory body.

(6) The managing authority must give the assessor a copy of–

(a) any relevant needs assessment carried out by them or on their behalf, or

(b) any relevant care plan drawn up by them or on their behalf.

(7) The supervisory body must give the assessor a copy of–

(a) any relevant needs assessment carried out by them or on their behalf, or

(b) any relevant care plan drawn up by them or on their behalf.

(8) The duties in sub-paragraphs (2) and (3) do not affect any other duty to consult or to take the views of others into account.

40 (1) This paragraph applies whatever conclusion the best interests assessment comes to.

(2) The assessor must state in the best interests assessment the name and address of every interested person whom he has consulted in carrying out the assessment.

41 Paragraphs 42 and 43 apply if the best interests assessment comes to the conclusion that the relevant person meets the best interests requirement.

42 (1) The assessor must state in the assessment the maximum authorisation period.

(2) The maximum authorisation period is the shorter of these periods–

(a) the period which, in the assessor's opinion, would be the appropriate maximum period for the relevant person to be a detained resident under the standard authorisation that has been requested;

(b) 1 year, or such shorter period as may be prescribed in regulations.

(3) Regulations under sub-paragraph (2)(b)–

(a) need not provide for a shorter period to apply in relation to all standard authorisations;

(b) may provide for different periods to apply in relation to different kinds of standard authorisations.

(4) Before making regulations under sub-paragraph (2)(b) the Secretary of State must consult all of the following–

(a) each body required by regulations under paragraph 162 to monitor and report on the operation of this Schedule in relation to England;

(b) such other persons as the Secretary of State considers it appropriate to consult.

(5) Before making regulations under sub-paragraph (2)(b) the National Assembly for Wales must consult all of the following–

(a) each person or body directed under paragraph 163(2) to carry out any function of the Assembly of monitoring and reporting on the operation of this Schedule in relation to Wales;

(b) such other persons as the Assembly considers it appropriate to consult.

43 The assessor may include in the assessment recommendations about conditions to which the standard authorisation is, or is not, to be subject in accordance with paragraph 53.

44 (1) This paragraph applies if the best interests assessment comes to the conclusion that the relevant person does not meet the best interests requirement.

(2) If, on the basis of the information taken into account in carrying out the assessment, it appears to the assessor that there is an unauthorised deprivation of liberty, he must include a statement to that effect in the assessment.

(3) There is an unauthorised deprivation of liberty if the managing authority of the relevant hospital or care home are already depriving the relevant person of his liberty without authority of the kind mentioned in section 4A.

45 The duties with which the best interests assessor must comply are subject to the provision included in appointment regulations under Part 10 (in particular, provision made under paragraph 146).

Eligibility assessment

46 An eligibility assessment is an assessment of whether the relevant person meets the eligibility requirement.

47 (1) Regulations may–
(a) require an eligibility assessor to request a best interests assessor to provide relevant eligibility information, and
(b) require the best interests assessor, if such a request is made, to provide such relevant eligibility information as he may have.

(2) In this paragraph–
'best interests assessor' means any person who is carrying out, or has carried out, a best interests assessment in relation to the relevant person;
'eligibility assessor' means a person carrying out an eligibility assessment in relation to the relevant person;
'relevant eligibility information' is information relevant to assessing whether or not the relevant person is ineligible by virtue of paragraph 5 of Schedule 1A.

No refusals assessment

48 A no refusals assessment is an assessment of whether the relevant person meets the no refusals requirement.

Equivalent assessment already carried out

49 (1) The supervisory body are not required by paragraph 33 to secure that a particular kind of assessment ('the required assessment') is carried out in relation to the relevant person if the following conditions are met.

(2) The first condition is that the supervisory body have a written copy of an assessment of the relevant person ('the existing assessment') that has already been carried out.

(3) The second condition is that the existing assessment complies with all requirements under this Schedule with which the required assessment would have to comply (if it were carried out).

(4) The third condition is that the existing assessment was carried out within the previous 12 months; but this condition need not be met if the required assessment is an age assessment.

(5) The fourth condition is that the supervisory body are satisfied that there is no reason why the existing assessment may no longer be accurate.

(6) If the required assessment is a best interests assessment, in satisfying themselves as mentioned in sub-paragraph (5), the supervisory body must take into account any information given, or submissions made, by–
(a) the relevant person's representative,
(b) any section 39C IMCA, or
(c) any section 39D IMCA.

(7) It does not matter whether the existing assessment was carried out in connection with a request for a standard authorisation or for some other purpose.

(8) If, because of this paragraph, the supervisory body are not required by paragraph 33 to secure that the required assessment is carried out, the existing assessment is to be treated for the purposes of this Schedule–
(a) as an assessment of the same kind as the required assessment, and
(b) as having been carried out under paragraph 33 in connection with the request for the standard authorisation.

Duty to give authorisation

50 (1) The supervisory body must give a standard authorisation if–
(a) all assessments are positive, and
(b) the supervisory body have written copies of all those assessments.
(2) The supervisory body must not give a standard authorisation except in accordance with sub-paragraph (1).
(3) All assessments are positive if each assessment carried out under paragraph 33 has come to the conclusion that the relevant person meets the qualifying requirement to which the assessment relates.

Terms of authorisation

51 (1) If the supervisory body are required to give a standard authorisation, they must decide the period during which the authorisation is to be in force.
(2) That period must not exceed the maximum authorisation period stated in the best interests assessment.

52 A standard authorisation may provide for the authorisation to come into force at a time after it is given.

53 (1) A standard authorisation may be given subject to conditions.
(2) Before deciding whether to give the authorisation subject to conditions, the supervisory body must have regard to any recommendations in the best interests assessment about such conditions.
(3) The managing authority of the relevant hospital or care home must ensure that any conditions are complied with.

Form of authorisation

54 A standard authorisation must be in writing.

55 (1) A standard authorisation must state the following things–
(a) the name of the relevant person;
(b) the name of the relevant hospital or care home;
(c) the period during which the authorisation is to be in force;
(d) the purpose for which the authorisation is given;
(e) any conditions subject to which the authorisation is given;
(f) the reason why each qualifying requirement is met.
(2) The statement of the reason why the eligibility requirement is met must be framed by reference to the cases in the table in paragraph 2 of Schedule 1A.

56 (1) If the name of the relevant hospital or care home changes, the standard authorisation is to be read as if it stated the current name of the hospital or care home.
(2) But sub-paragraph (1) is subject to any provision relating to the change of name which is made in any enactment or in any instrument made under an enactment.

Duty to give information about decision

57 (1) This paragraph applies if–
(a) a request is made for a standard authorisation, and
(b) the supervisory body are required by paragraph 50(1) to give the standard authorisation.
(2) The supervisory body must give a copy of the authorisation to each of the following–
(a) the relevant person's representative;
(b) the managing authority of the relevant hospital or care home;

(c) the relevant person;
(d) any section 39A IMCA;
(e) every interested person consulted by the best interests assessor.

(3) The supervisory body must comply with this paragraph as soon as practicable after they give the standard authorisation.

58 (1) This paragraph applies if–
(a) a request is made for a standard authorisation, and
(b) the supervisory body are prohibited by paragraph 50(2) from giving the standard authorisation.

(2) The supervisory body must give notice, stating that they are prohibited from giving the authorisation, to each of the following–
(a) the managing authority of the relevant hospital or care home;
(b) the relevant person;
(c) any section 39A IMCA;
(d) every interested person consulted by the best interests assessor.

(3) The supervisory body must comply with this paragraph as soon as practicable after it becomes apparent to them that they are prohibited from giving the authorisation.

Duty to give information about effect of authorisation

59 (1) This paragraph applies if a standard authorisation is given.

(2) The managing authority of the relevant hospital or care home must take such steps as are practicable to ensure that the relevant person understands all of the following–
(a) the effect of the authorisation;
(b) the right to make an application to the court to exercise its jurisdiction under section 21A;
(c) the right under Part 8 to request a review;
(d) the right to have a section 39D IMCA appointed;
(e) how to have a section 39D IMCA appointed.

(3) Those steps must be taken as soon as is practicable after the authorisation is given.

(4) Those steps must include the giving of appropriate information both orally and in writing.

(5) Any written information given to the relevant person must also be given by the managing authority to the relevant person's representative.

(6) They must give the information to the representative as soon as is practicable after it is given to the relevant person.

(7) Sub-paragraph (8) applies if the managing authority is notified that a section 39D IMCA has been appointed.

(8) As soon as is practicable after being notified, the managing authority must give the section 39D IMCA a copy of the written information given in accordance with sub-paragraph (4).

Records of authorisations

60 A supervisory body must keep a written record of all of the following information–
(a) the standard authorisations that they have given;
(b) the requests for standard authorisations in response to which they have not given an authorisation;

(c) in relation to each standard authorisation given: the matters stated in the authorisation in accordance with paragraph 55.

Variation of an authorisation

61 (1) A standard authorisation may not be varied except in accordance with Part 7 or 8.

(2) This paragraph does not affect the powers of the Court of Protection or of any other court.

Effect of decision about request made under paragraph 25 or 30

62 (1) This paragraph applies where the managing authority request a new standard authorisation under either of the following–

(a) paragraph 25 (change in place of detention);

(b) paragraph 30 (existing authorisation subject to review).

(2) If the supervisory body are required by paragraph 50(1) to give the new authorisation, the existing authorisation terminates at the time when the new authorisation comes into force.

(3) If the supervisory body are prohibited by paragraph 50(2) from giving the new authorisation, there is no effect on the existing authorisation's continuation in force.

When an authorisation is in force

63 (1) A standard authorisation comes into force when it is given.

(2) But if the authorisation provides for it to come into force at a later time, it comes into force at that time.

64 (1) A standard authorisation ceases to be in force at the end of the period stated in the authorisation in accordance with paragraph 55(1)(c).

(2) But if the authorisation terminates before then in accordance with paragraph 62(2) or any other provision of this Schedule, it ceases to be in force when the termination takes effect.

(3) This paragraph does not affect the powers of the Court of Protection or of any other court.

65 (1) This paragraph applies if a standard authorisation ceases to be in force.

(2) The supervisory body must give notice that the authorisation has ceased to be in force.

(3) The supervisory body must give that notice to all of the following–

(a) the managing authority of the relevant hospital or care home;

(b) the relevant person;

(c) the relevant person's representative;

(d) every interested person consulted by the best interests assessor.

(4) The supervisory body must give that notice as soon as practicable after the authorisation ceases to be in force.

When a request for a standard authorisation is 'disposed of'

66 A request for a standard authorisation is to be regarded for the purposes of this Schedule as disposed of if the supervisory body have given–

(a) a copy of the authorisation in accordance with paragraph 57, or

(b) notice in accordance with paragraph 58.

Right of third party to require consideration of whether authorisation needed

67 For the purposes of paragraphs 68 to 73 there is an unauthorised deprivation of liberty if–
(a) a person is already a detained resident in a hospital or care home, and
(b) the detention of the person is not authorised as mentioned in section 4A.

68 (1) If the following conditions are met, an eligible person may request the supervisory body to decide whether or not there is an unauthorised deprivation of liberty.
(2) The first condition is that the eligible person has notified the managing authority of the relevant hospital or care home that it appears to the eligible person that there is an unauthorised deprivation of liberty.
(3) The second condition is that the eligible person has asked the managing authority to request a standard authorisation in relation to the detention of the relevant person.
(4) The third condition is that the managing authority has not requested a standard authorisation within a reasonable period after the eligible person asks it to do so.
(5) In this paragraph 'eligible person' means any person other than the managing authority of the relevant hospital or care home.

69 (1) This paragraph applies if an eligible person requests the supervisory body to decide whether or not there is an unauthorised deprivation of liberty.
(2) The supervisory body must select and appoint a person to carry out an assessment of whether or not the relevant person is a detained resident.
(3) But the supervisory body need not select and appoint a person to carry out such an assessment in either of these cases.
(4) The first case is where it appears to the supervisory body that the request by the eligible person is frivolous or vexatious.
(5) The second case is where it appears to the supervisory body that–
(a) the question of whether or not there is an unauthorised deprivation of liberty has already been decided, and
(b) since that decision, there has been no change of circumstances which would merit the question being decided again.
(6) The supervisory body must not select and appoint a person to carry out an assessment under this paragraph unless it appears to the supervisory body that the person would be–
(a) suitable to carry out a best interests assessment (if one were obtained in connection with a request for a standard authorisation relating to the relevant person), and
(b) eligible to carry out such a best interests assessment.
(7) The supervisory body must notify the persons specified in sub-paragraph (8)–
(a) that the supervisory body have been requested to decide whether or not there is an unauthorised deprivation of liberty;
(b) of their decision whether or not to select and appoint a person to carry out an assessment under this paragraph;
(c) if their decision is to select and appoint a person, of the person appointed.
(8) The persons referred to in sub-paragraph (7) are–
(a) the eligible person who made the request under paragraph 68;
(b) the person to whom the request relates;

(c) the managing authority of the relevant hospital or care home;
(d) any section 39A IMCA.

70 (1) Regulations may be made about the period within which an assessment under paragraph 69 must be carried out.

(2) Regulations made under paragraph 129(3) apply in relation to the selection and appointment of a person under paragraph 69 as they apply to the selection of a person under paragraph 129 to carry out a best interests assessment.

(3) The following provisions apply to an assessment under paragraph 69 as they apply to an assessment carried out in connection with a request for a standard authorisation–
(a) paragraph 131 (examination and copying of records);
(b) paragraph 132 (representations);
(c) paragraphs 134 and 135(1) and (2) (duty to keep records and give copies).

(4) The copies of the assessment which the supervisory body are required to give under paragraph 135(2) must be given as soon as practicable after the supervisory body are themselves given a copy of the assessment.

71 (1) This paragraph applies if–
(a) the supervisory body obtain an assessment under paragraph 69,
(b) the assessment comes to the conclusion that the relevant person is a detained resident, and
(c) it appears to the supervisory body that the detention of the person is not authorised as mentioned in section 4A.

(2) This Schedule (including Part 5) applies as if the managing authority of the relevant hospital or care home had, in accordance with Part 4, requested the supervisory body to give a standard authorisation in relation to the relevant person.

(3) The managing authority of the relevant hospital or care home must supply the supervisory body with the information (if any) which the managing authority would, by virtue of paragraph 31, have had to include in a request for a standard authorisation.

(4) The supervisory body must notify the persons specified in paragraph 69(8)–
(a) of the outcome of the assessment obtained under paragraph 69, and
(b) that this Schedule applies as mentioned in sub-paragraph (2).

72 (1) This paragraph applies if–
(a) the supervisory body obtain an assessment under paragraph 69, and
(b) the assessment comes to the conclusion that the relevant person is not a detained resident.

(2) The supervisory body must notify the persons specified in paragraph 69(8) of the outcome of the assessment.

73 (1) This paragraph applies if–
(a) the supervisory body obtain an assessment under paragraph 69,
(b) the assessment comes to the conclusion that the relevant person is a detained resident, and
(c) it appears to the supervisory body that the detention of the person is authorised as mentioned in section 4A.

(2) The supervisory body must notify the persons specified in paragraph 69(8)–
(a) of the outcome of the assessment, and
(b) that it appears to the supervisory body that the detention is authorised.

Part 5: Urgent Authorisations

Managing authority to give authorisation

74 Only the managing authority of the relevant hospital or care home may give an urgent authorisation.

75 The managing authority may give an urgent authorisation only if they are required to do so by paragraph 76 (as read with paragraph 77).

Duty to give authorisation

76 (1) The managing authority must give an urgent authorisation in either of the following cases.

(2) The first case is where–

(a) the managing authority are required to make a request under paragraph 24 or 25 for a standard authorisation, and

(b) they believe that the need for the relevant person to be a detained resident is so urgent that it is appropriate for the detention to begin before they make the request.

(3) The second case is where–

(a) the managing authority have made a request under paragraph 24 or 25 for a standard authorisation, and

(b) they believe that the need for the relevant person to be a detained resident is so urgent that it is appropriate for the detention to begin before the request is disposed of.

(4) References in this paragraph to the detention of the relevant person are references to the detention to which paragraph 24 or 25 relates.

(5) This paragraph is subject to paragraph 77.

77 (1) This paragraph applies where the managing authority have given an urgent authorisation ('the original authorisation') in connection with a case where a person is, or is to be, a detained resident ('the existing detention').

(2) No new urgent authorisation is to be given under paragraph 76 in connection with the existing detention.

(3) But the managing authority may request the supervisory body to extend the duration of the original authorisation.

(4) Only one request under sub-paragraph (3) may be made in relation to the original authorisation.

(5) Paragraphs 84 to 86 apply to any request made under sub-paragraph (3).

Terms of authorisation

78 (1) If the managing authority decide to give an urgent authorisation, they must decide the period during which the authorisation is to be in force.

(2) That period must not exceed 7 days.

Form of authorisation

79 An urgent authorisation must be in writing.

80 An urgent authorisation must state the following things–

(a) the name of the relevant person;

(b) the name of the relevant hospital or care home;

(c) the period during which the authorisation is to be in force;

(d) the purpose for which the authorisation is given.

81 (1) If the name of the relevant hospital or care home changes, the urgent authorisation is to be read as if it stated the current name of the hospital or care home.

(2) But sub-paragraph (1) is subject to any provision relating to the change of name which is made in any enactment or in any instrument made under an enactment.

Duty to keep records and give copies

82 (1) This paragraph applies if an urgent authorisation is given.

(2) The managing authority must keep a written record of why they have given the urgent authorisation.

(3) As soon as practicable after giving the authorisation, the managing authority must give a copy of the authorisation to all of the following–

(a) the relevant person;

(b) any section 39A IMCA.

Duty to give information about authorisation

83 (1) This paragraph applies if an urgent authorisation is given.

(2) The managing authority of the relevant hospital or care home must take such steps as are practicable to ensure that the relevant person understands all of the following–

(a) the effect of the authorisation;

(b) the right to make an application to the court to exercise its jurisdiction under section 21A.

(3) Those steps must be taken as soon as is practicable after the authorisation is given.

(4) Those steps must include the giving of appropriate information both orally and in writing.

Request for extension of duration

84 (1) This paragraph applies if the managing authority make a request under paragraph 77 for the supervisory body to extend the duration of the original authorisation.

(2) The managing authority must keep a written record of why they have made the request.

(3) The managing authority must give the relevant person notice that they have made the request.

(4) The supervisory body may extend the duration of the original authorisation if it appears to them that–

(a) the managing authority have made the required request for a standard authorisation,

(b) there are exceptional reasons why it has not yet been possible for that request to be disposed of, and

(c) it is essential for the existing detention to continue until the request is disposed of.

(5) The supervisory body must keep a written record that the request has been made to them.

(6) In this paragraph and paragraphs 85 and 86–

(a) 'original authorisation' and 'existing detention' have the same meaning as in paragraph 77;

(b) the required request for a standard authorisation is the request that is referred to in paragraph 76(2) or (3).

85 (1) This paragraph applies if, under paragraph 84, the supervisory body decide to extend the duration of the original authorisation.

(2) The supervisory body must decide the period of the extension.

(3) That period must not exceed 7 days.

(4) The supervisory body must give the managing authority notice stating the period of the extension.

(5) The managing authority must then vary the original authorisation so that it states the extended duration.

(6) Paragraphs 82(3) and 83 apply (with the necessary modifications) to the variation of the original authorisation as they apply to the giving of an urgent authorisation.

(7) The supervisory body must keep a written record of–

(a) the outcome of the request, and

(b) the period of the extension.

86 (1) This paragraph applies if, under paragraph 84, the supervisory body decide not to extend the duration of the original authorisation.

(2) The supervisory body must give the managing authority notice stating–

(a) the decision, and

(b) their reasons for making it.

(3) The managing authority must give a copy of that notice to all of the following–

(a) the relevant person;

(b) any section 39A IMCA.

(4) The supervisory body must keep a written record of the outcome of the request.

No variation

87 (1) An urgent authorisation may not be varied except in accordance with paragraph 85.

(2) This paragraph does not affect the powers of the Court of Protection or of any other court.

When an authorisation is in force

88 An urgent authorisation comes into force when it is given.

89 (1) An urgent authorisation ceases to be in force at the end of the period stated in the authorisation in accordance with paragraph 80(c) (subject to any variation in accordance with paragraph 85).

(2) But if the required request is disposed of before the end of that period, the urgent authorisation ceases to be in force as follows.

(3) If the supervisory body are required by paragraph 50(1) to give the requested authorisation, the urgent authorisation ceases to be in force when the requested authorisation comes into force.

(4) If the supervisory body are prohibited by paragraph 50(2) from giving the requested authorisation, the urgent authorisation ceases to be in force when the managing authority receive notice under paragraph 58.

(5) In this paragraph–

'required request' means the request referred to in paragraph 76(2) or (3);

'requested authorisation' means the standard authorisation to which the required request relates.

(6) This paragraph does not affect the powers of the Court of Protection or of any other court.

90 (1) This paragraph applies if an urgent authorisation ceases to be in force.

(2) The supervisory body must give notice that the authorisation has ceased to be in force.

(3) The supervisory body must give that notice to all of the following–

(a) the relevant person;

(b) any section 39A IMCA.

(4) The supervisory body must give that notice as soon as practicable after the authorisation ceases to be in force.

Part 6: Eligibility Requirement not Met: Suspension of Standard Authorisation

91 (1) This Part applies if the following conditions are met.

(2) The first condition is that a standard authorisation–

(a) has been given, and

(b) has not ceased to be in force.

(3) The second condition is that the managing authority of the relevant hospital or care home are satisfied that the relevant person has ceased to meet the eligibility requirement.

(4) But this Part does not apply if the relevant person is ineligible by virtue of paragraph 5 of Schedule 1A (in which case see Part 8).

92 The managing authority of the relevant hospital or care home must give the supervisory body notice that the relevant person has ceased to meet the eligibility requirement.

93 (1) This paragraph applies if the managing authority give the supervisory body notice under paragraph 92.

(2) The standard authorisation is suspended from the time when the notice is given.

(3) The supervisory body must give notice that the standard authorisation has been suspended to the following persons–

(a) the relevant person;

(b) the relevant person's representative;

(c) the managing authority of the relevant hospital or care home.

94 (1) This paragraph applies if, whilst the standard authorisation is suspended, the managing authority are satisfied that the relevant person meets the eligibility requirement again.

(2) The managing authority must give the supervisory body notice that the relevant person meets the eligibility requirement again.

95 (1) This paragraph applies if the managing authority give the supervisory body notice under paragraph 94.

(2) The standard authorisation ceases to be suspended from the time when the notice is given.

(3) The supervisory body must give notice that the standard authorisation has ceased to be suspended to the following persons–

(a) the relevant person;

(b) the relevant person's representative;

(c) any section 39D IMCA;

(d) the managing authority of the relevant hospital or care home.

(4) The supervisory body must give notice under this paragraph as soon as practicable after they are given notice under paragraph 94.

96 (1) This paragraph applies if no notice is given under paragraph 94 before the end of the relevant 28 day period.

(2) The standard authorisation ceases to have effect at the end of the relevant 28 day period.

(3) The relevant 28 day period is the period of 28 days beginning with the day on which the standard authorisation is suspended under paragraph 93.

97 The effect of suspending the standard authorisation is that Part 1 ceases to apply for as long as the authorisation is suspended.

Part 7: Standard Authorisations: Change in Supervisory Responsibility

Application of this Part

98 (1) This Part applies if these conditions are met.

(2) The first condition is that a standard authorisation–

(a) has been given, and

(b) has not ceased to be in force.

(3) The second condition is that there is a change in supervisory responsibility.

(4) The third condition is that there is not a change in the place of detention (within the meaning of paragraph 25).

99 For the purposes of this Part there is a change in supervisory responsibility if–

(a) one body ('the old supervisory body') have ceased to be supervisory body in relation to the standard authorisation, and

(b) a different body ('the new supervisory body') have become supervisory body in relation to the standard authorisation.

Effect of change in supervisory responsibility

100 (1) The new supervisory body becomes the supervisory body in relation to the authorisation.

(2) Anything done by or in relation to the old supervisory body in connection with the authorisation has effect, so far as is necessary for continuing its effect after the change, as if done by or in relation to the new supervisory body.

(3) Anything which relates to the authorisation and which is in the process of being done by or in relation to the old supervisory body at the time of the change may be continued by or in relation to the new supervisory body.

(4) But–

(a) the old supervisory body do not, by virtue of this paragraph, cease to be liable for anything done by them in connection with the authorisation before the change; and

(b) the new supervisory body do not, by virtue of this paragraph, become liable for any such thing.

Part 8: Standard Authorisations: Review

Application of this Part

101 (1) This Part applies if a standard authorisation–

(a) has been given, and

(b) has not ceased to be in force.

(2) Paragraphs 102 to 122 are subject to paragraphs 123 to 125.

Review by supervisory body

102 (1) The supervisory body may at any time carry out a review of the standard authorisation in accordance with this Part.
(2) The supervisory body must carry out such a review if they are requested to do so by an eligible person.
(3) Each of the following is an eligible person–
(a) the relevant person;
(b) the relevant person's representative;
(c) the managing authority of the relevant hospital or care home.

Request for review

103 (1) An eligible person may, at any time, request the supervisory body to carry out a review of the standard authorisation in accordance with this Part.
(2) The managing authority of the relevant hospital or care home must make such a request if one or more of the qualifying requirements appear to them to be reviewable.

Grounds for review

104 (1) Paragraphs 105 to 107 set out the grounds on which the qualifying requirements are reviewable.
(2) A qualifying requirement is not reviewable on any other ground.

Non-qualification ground

105 (1) Any of the following qualifying requirements is reviewable on the ground that the relevant person does not meet the requirement–
(a) the age requirement;
(b) the mental health requirement;
(c) the mental capacity requirement;
(d) the best interests requirement;
(e) the no refusals requirement.
(2) The eligibility requirement is reviewable on the ground that the relevant person is ineligible by virtue of paragraph 5 of Schedule 1A.
(3) The ground in sub-paragraph (1) and the ground in sub-paragraph (2) are referred to as the non-qualification ground.

Change of reason ground

106 (1) Any of the following qualifying requirements is reviewable on the ground set out in sub-paragraph (2)–
(a) the mental health requirement;
(b) the mental capacity requirement;
(c) the best interests requirement;
(d) the eligibility requirement;
(e) the no refusals requirement.
(2) The ground is that the reason why the relevant person meets the requirement is not the reason stated in the standard authorisation.
(3) This ground is referred to as the change of reason ground.

Variation of conditions ground

107 (1) The best interests requirement is reviewable on the ground that–
(a) there has been a change in the relevant person's case, and
(b) because of that change, it would be appropriate to vary the conditions to which the standard authorisation is subject.

(2) This ground is referred to as the variation of conditions ground.

(3) A reference to varying the conditions to which the standard authorisation is subject is a reference to–

(a) amendment of an existing condition,

(b) omission of an existing condition, or

(c) inclusion of a new condition (whether or not there are already any existing conditions).

Notice that review to be carried out

108 (1) If the supervisory body are to carry out a review of the standard authorisation, they must give notice of the review to the following persons–

(a) the relevant person;

(b) the relevant person's representative;

(c) the managing authority of the relevant hospital or care home.

(2) The supervisory body must give the notice–

(a) before they begin the review, or

(b) if that is not practicable, as soon as practicable after they have begun it.

(3) This paragraph does not require the supervisory body to give notice to any person who has requested the review.

Starting a review

109 To start a review of the standard authorisation, the supervisory body must decide which, if any, of the qualifying requirements appear to be reviewable.

No reviewable qualifying requirements

110 (1) This paragraph applies if no qualifying requirements appear to be reviewable.

(2) This Part does not require the supervisory body to take any action in respect of the standard authorisation.

One or more reviewable qualifying requirements

111 (1) This paragraph applies if one or more qualifying requirements appear to be reviewable.

(2) The supervisory body must secure that a separate review assessment is carried out in relation to each qualifying requirement which appears to be reviewable.

(3) But sub-paragraph (2) does not require the supervisory body to secure that a best interests review assessment is carried out in a case where the best interests requirement appears to the supervisory body to be non-assessable.

(4) The best interests requirement is non-assessable if–

(a) the requirement is reviewable only on the variation of conditions ground, and

(b) the change in the relevant person's case is not significant.

(5) In making any decision whether the change in the relevant person's case is significant, regard must be had to–

(a) the nature of the change, and

(b) the period that the change is likely to last for.

Review assessments

112 (1) A review assessment is an assessment of whether the relevant person meets a qualifying requirement.

(2) In relation to a review assessment–

(a) a negative conclusion is a conclusion that the relevant person does not meet the qualifying requirement to which the assessment relates;

(b) a positive conclusion is a conclusion that the relevant person meets the qualifying requirement to which the assessment relates.

(3) An age review assessment is a review assessment carried out in relation to the age requirement.

(4) A mental health review assessment is a review assessment carried out in relation to the mental health requirement.

(5) A mental capacity review assessment is a review assessment carried out in relation to the mental capacity requirement.

(6) A best interests review assessment is a review assessment carried out in relation to the best interests requirement.

(7) An eligibility review assessment is a review assessment carried out in relation to the eligibility requirement.

(8) A no refusals review assessment is a review assessment carried out in relation to the no refusals requirement.

113 (1) In carrying out a review assessment, the assessor must comply with any duties which would be imposed upon him under Part 4 if the assessment were being carried out in connection with a request for a standard authorisation.

(2) But in the case of a best interests review assessment, paragraphs 43 and 44 do not apply.

(3) Instead of what is required by paragraph 43, the best interests review assessment must include recommendations about whether–and, if so, how–it would be appropriate to vary the conditions to which the standard authorisation is subject.

Best interests requirement reviewable but non-assessable

114 (1) This paragraph applies in a case where–

(a) the best interests requirement appears to be reviewable, but

(b) in accordance with paragraph 111(3), the supervisory body are not required to secure that a best interests review assessment is carried out.

(2) The supervisory body may vary the conditions to which the standard authorisation is subject in such ways (if any) as the supervisory body think are appropriate in the circumstances.

Best interests review assessment positive

115 (1) This paragraph applies in a case where–

(a) a best interests review assessment is carried out, and

(b) the assessment comes to a positive conclusion.

(2) The supervisory body must decide the following questions–

(a) whether or not the best interests requirement is reviewable on the change of reason ground;

(b) whether or not the best interests requirement is reviewable on the variation of conditions ground;

(c) if so, whether or not the change in the person's case is significant.

(3) If the supervisory body decide that the best interests requirement is reviewable on the change of reason ground, they must vary the standard authori-

sation so that it states the reason why the relevant person now meets that requirement.

(4) If the supervisory body decide that–
(a) the best interests requirement is reviewable on the variation of conditions ground, and
(b) the change in the relevant person's case is not significant,
they may vary the conditions to which the standard authorisation is subject in such ways (if any) as they think are appropriate in the circumstances.

(5) If the supervisory body decide that–
(a) the best interests requirement is reviewable on the variation of conditions ground, and
(b) the change in the relevant person's case is significant,
they must vary the conditions to which the standard authorisation is subject in such ways as they think are appropriate in the circumstances.

(6) If the supervisory body decide that the best interests requirement is not reviewable on–
(a) the change of reason ground, or
(b) the variation of conditions ground,
this Part does not require the supervisory body to take any action in respect of the standard authorisation so far as the best interests requirement relates to it.

Mental health, mental capacity, eligibility or no refusals review assessment positive

116 (1) This paragraph applies if the following conditions are met.

(2) The first condition is that one or more of the following are carried out–
(a) a mental health review assessment;
(b) a mental capacity review assessment;
(c) an eligibility review assessment;
(d) a no refusals review assessment.

(3) The second condition is that each assessment carried out comes to a positive conclusion.

(4) The supervisory body must decide whether or not each of the assessed qualifying requirements is reviewable on the change of reason ground.

(5) If the supervisory body decide that any of the assessed qualifying requirements is reviewable on the change of reason ground, they must vary the standard authorisation so that it states the reason why the relevant person now meets the requirement or requirements in question.

(6) If the supervisory body decide that none of the assessed qualifying requirements are reviewable on the change of reason ground, this Part does not require the supervisory body to take any action in respect of the standard authorisation so far as those requirements relate to it.

(7) An assessed qualifying requirement is a qualifying requirement in relation to which a review assessment is carried out.

One or more review assessments negative

117 (1) This paragraph applies if one or more of the review assessments carried out comes to a negative conclusion.

(2) The supervisory body must terminate the standard authorisation with immediate effect.

Completion of a review

118 (1) The review of the standard authorisation is complete in any of the following cases.

(2) The first case is where paragraph 110 applies.

(3) The second case is where–

(a) paragraph 111 applies, and

(b) paragraph 117 requires the supervisory body to terminate the standard authorisation.

(4) In such a case, the supervisory body need not comply with any of the other provisions of paragraphs 114 to 116 which would be applicable to the review (were it not for this sub-paragraph).

(5) The third case is where–

(a) paragraph 111 applies,

(b) paragraph 117 does not require the supervisory body to terminate the standard authorisation, and

(c) the supervisory body comply with all of the provisions of paragraphs 114 to 116 (so far as they are applicable to the review).

Variations under this Part

119 Any variation of the standard authorisation made under this Part must be in writing.

Notice of outcome of review

120 (1) When the review of the standard authorisation is complete, the supervisory body must give notice to all of the following–

(a) the managing authority of the relevant hospital or care home;

(b) the relevant person;

(c) the relevant person's representative;

(d) any section 39D IMCA.

(2) That notice must state–

(a) the outcome of the review, and

(b) what variation (if any) has been made to the authorisation under this Part.

Records

121 A supervisory body must keep a written record of the following information–

(a) each request for a review that is made to them;

(b) the outcome of each request;

(c) each review which they carry out;

(d) the outcome of each review which they carry out;

(e) any variation of an authorisation made in consequence of a review.

Relationship between review and suspension under Part 6

122 (1) This paragraph applies if a standard authorisation is suspended in accordance with Part 6.

(2) No review may be requested under this Part whilst the standard authorisation is suspended.

(3) If a review has already been requested, or is being carried out, when the standard authorisation is suspended, no steps are to be taken in connection with that review whilst the authorisation is suspended.

Relationship between review and request for new authorisation

123 (1) This paragraph applies if, in accordance with paragraph 24 (as read with paragraph 29), the managing authority of the relevant hospital or care home make a request for a new standard authorisation which would be in force after the expiry of the existing authorisation.

(2) No review may be requested under this Part until the request for the new standard authorisation has been disposed of.

(3) If a review has already been requested, or is being carried out, when the new standard authorisation is requested, no steps are to be taken in connection with that review until the request for the new standard authorisation has been disposed of.

124 (1) This paragraph applies if–

(a) a review under this Part has been requested, or is being carried out, and

(b) the managing authority of the relevant hospital or care home make a request under paragraph 30 for a new standard authorisation which would be in force on or before, and after, the expiry of the existing authorisation.

(2) No steps are to be taken in connection with the review under this Part until the request for the new standard authorisation has been disposed of.

125 In paragraphs 123 and 124–

(a) the existing authorisation is the authorisation referred to in paragraph 101;

(b) the expiry of the existing authorisation is the time when it is expected to cease to be in force.

Part 9: Assessments under this Schedule

Introduction

126 This Part contains provision about assessments under this Schedule.

127 An assessment under this Schedule is either of the following–

(a) an assessment carried out in connection with a request for a standard authorisation under Part 4;

(b) a review assessment carried out in connection with a review of a standard authorisation under Part 8.

128 In this Part, in relation to an assessment under this Schedule–

'assessor' means the person carrying out the assessment;

'relevant procedure' means–

(a) the request for the standard authorisation, or

(b) the review of the standard authorisation;

'supervisory body' means the supervisory body responsible for securing that the assessment is carried out.

Supervisory body to select assessor

129 (1) It is for the supervisory body to select a person to carry out an assessment under this Schedule.

(2) The supervisory body must not select a person to carry out an assessment unless the person–

(a) appears to the supervisory body to be suitable to carry out the assessment (having regard, in particular, to the type of assessment and the person to be assessed), and

(b) is eligible to carry out the assessment.

(3) Regulations may make provision about the selection, and eligibility, of persons to carry out assessments under this Schedule.

(4) Sub-paragraphs (5) and (6) apply if two or more assessments are to be obtained for the purposes of the relevant procedure.

(5) In a case where the assessments to be obtained include a mental health assessment and a best interests assessment, the supervisory body must not select the same person to carry out both assessments.

(6) Except as prohibited by sub-paragraph (5), the supervisory body may select the same person to carry out any number of the assessments which the person appears to be suitable, and is eligible, to carry out.

130 (1) This paragraph applies to regulations under paragraph 129(3).

(2) The regulations may make provision relating to a person's–

(a) qualifications,

(b) skills,

(c) training,

(d) experience,

(e) relationship to, or connection with, the relevant person or any other person,

(f) involvement in the care or treatment of the relevant person,

(g) connection with the supervisory body, or

(h) connection with the relevant hospital or care home, or with any other establishment or undertaking.

(2A) In relation to England–

(a) the provision that the regulations may make in relation to a person's training in connection with best interests assessments includes provision for particular training to be specified by Social Work England or the Secretary of State otherwise than in the regulations;

(b) the provision that the regulations may make in relation to a person's training in connection with other assessments includes provision for particular training to be specified by the Secretary of State otherwise than in the regulations.

(2B) The regulations may give Social Work England power to charge fees for specifying any training as mentioned in sub-paragraph (2A)(a).

(2C) If the regulations give Social Work England power to charge fees, section 50(2) to (7) of the Children and Social Work Act 2017 apply for the purposes of sub-paragraph (2B) as they apply for the purposes of that section.

(3) In relation to Wales the provision that the regulations may make in relation to a person's training may provide for particular training to be specified by the Welsh Ministers otherwise than in the regulations.

(4) [Repealed.]

(5) The regulations may make provision requiring a person to be insured in respect of liabilities that may arise in connection with the carrying out of an assessment.

(6) In relation to cases where two or more assessments are to be obtained for the purposes of the relevant procedure, the regulations may limit the number, kind or combination of assessments which a particular person is eligible to carry out.

(7) Sub-paragraphs (2) to (6) do not limit the generality of the provision that may be made in the regulations.

Examination and copying of records

131 An assessor may, at all reasonable times, examine and take copies of–
(a) any health record,
(b) any record of, or held by, a local authority and compiled in accordance with a social services function, and
(c) any record held by a person registered under Part 2 of the Care Standards Act 2000, Chapter 2 of Part 1 of the Health and Social Care Act 2008 or Part 1 of the Regulation and Inspection of Social Care (Wales) Act 2016,
which the assessor considers may be relevant to the assessment which is being carried out.

Representations

132 In carrying out an assessment under this Schedule, the assessor must take into account any information given, or submissions made, by any of the following–
(a) the relevant person's representative;
(b) any section 39A IMCA;
(c) any section 39C IMCA;
(d) any section 39D IMCA.

Assessments to stop if any comes to negative conclusion

133 (1) This paragraph applies if an assessment under this Schedule comes to the conclusion that the relevant person does not meet one of the qualifying requirements.
(2) This Schedule does not require the supervisory body to secure that any other assessments under this Schedule are carried out in relation to the relevant procedure.
(3) The supervisory body must give notice to any assessor who is carrying out another assessment in connection with the relevant procedure that they are to cease carrying out that assessment.
(4) If an assessor receives such notice, this Schedule does not require the assessor to continue carrying out that assessment.

Duty to keep records and give copies

134 (1) This paragraph applies if an assessor has carried out an assessment under this Schedule (whatever conclusions the assessment has come to).
(2) The assessor must keep a written record of the assessment.
(3) As soon as practicable after carrying out the assessment, the assessor must give copies of the assessment to the supervisory body.

135 (1) This paragraph applies to the supervisory body if they are given a copy of an assessment under this Schedule.
(2) The supervisory body must give copies of the assessment to all of the following–
(a) the managing authority of the relevant hospital or care home;
(b) the relevant person;
(c) any section 39A IMCA;
(d) the relevant person's representative.
(3) If–
(a) the assessment is obtained in relation to a request for a standard authorisation, and

(b) the supervisory body are required by paragraph 50(1) to give the standard authorisation,

the supervisory body must give the copies of the assessment when they give copies of the authorisation in accordance with paragraph 57.

(4) If–

(a) the assessment is obtained in relation to a request for a standard authorisation, and

(b) the supervisory body are prohibited by paragraph 50(2) from giving the standard authorisation,

the supervisory body must give the copies of the assessment when they give notice in accordance with paragraph 58.

(5) If the assessment is obtained in connection with the review of a standard authorisation, the supervisory body must give the copies of the assessment when they give notice in accordance with paragraph 120.

136 (1) This paragraph applies to the supervisory body if–

(a) they are given a copy of a best interests assessment, and

(b) the assessment includes, in accordance with paragraph 44(2), a statement that it appears to the assessor that there is an unauthorised deprivation of liberty.

(2) The supervisory body must notify all of the persons listed in sub-paragraph (3) that the assessment includes such a statement.

(3) Those persons are–

(a) the managing authority of the relevant hospital or care home;

(b) the relevant person;

(c) any section 39A IMCA;

(d) any interested person consulted by the best interests assessor.

(4) The supervisory body must comply with this paragraph when (or at some time before) they comply with paragraph 135.

Part 10: Relevant Person's Representative

The representative

137 In this Schedule the relevant person's representative is the person appointed as such in accordance with this Part.

138 (1) Regulations may make provision about the selection and appointment of representatives.

(2) In this Part such regulations are referred to as 'appointment regulations'.

Supervisory body to appoint representative

139 (1) The supervisory body must appoint a person to be the relevant person's representative as soon as practicable after a standard authorisation is given.

(2) The supervisory body must appoint a person to be the relevant person's representative if a vacancy arises whilst a standard authorisation is in force.

(3) Where a vacancy arises, the appointment under sub-paragraph (2) is to be made as soon as practicable after the supervisory body becomes aware of the vacancy.

140 (1) The selection of a person for appointment under paragraph 139 must not be made unless it appears to the person making the selection that the prospective representative would, if appointed–

(a) maintain contact with the relevant person,

(b) represent the relevant person in matters relating to or connected with this Schedule, and
(c) support the relevant person in matters relating to or connected with this Schedule.

141 (1) Any appointment of a representative for a relevant person is in addition to, and does not affect, any appointment of a donee or deputy.
(2) The functions of any representative are in addition to, and do not affect–
(a) the authority of any donee,
(b) the powers of any deputy, or
(c) any powers of the court.

Appointment regulations

142 Appointment regulations may provide that the procedure for appointing a representative may begin at any time after a request for a standard authorisation is made (including a time before the request has been disposed of).

143 (1) Appointment regulations may make provision about who is to select a person for appointment as a representative.
(2) But regulations under this paragraph may only provide for the following to make a selection–
(a) the relevant person, if he has capacity in relation to the question of which person should be his representative;
(b) a donee of a lasting power of attorney granted by the relevant person, if it is within the scope of his authority to select a person;
(c) a deputy, if it is within the scope of his authority to select a person;
(d) a best interests assessor;
(e) the supervisory body.
(3) Regulations under this paragraph may provide that a selection by the relevant person, a donee or a deputy is subject to approval by a best interests assessor or the supervisory body.
(4) Regulations under this paragraph may provide that, if more than one selection is necessary in connection with the appointment of a particular representative–
(a) the same person may make more than one selection;
(b) different persons may make different selections.
(5) For the purposes of this paragraph a best interests assessor is a person carrying out a best interests assessment in connection with the standard authorisation in question (including the giving of that authorisation).

144 (1) Appointment regulations may make provision about who may, or may not, be–
(a) selected for appointment as a representative, or
(b) appointed as a representative.
(2) Regulations under this paragraph may relate to any of the following matters–
(a) a person's age;
(b) a person's suitability;
(c) a person's independence;
(d) a person's willingness;
(e) a person's qualifications.

145 Appointment regulations may make provision about the formalities of appointing a person as a representative.

146 In a case where a best interests assessor is to select a person to be appointed as a representative, appointment regulations may provide for the variation of the assessor's duties in relation to the assessment which he is carrying out.

Monitoring of representatives

147 Regulations may make provision requiring the managing authority of the relevant hospital or care home to–
(a) monitor, and
(b) report to the supervisory body on,
the extent to which a representative is maintaining contact with the relevant person.

Termination

148 Regulations may make provision about the circumstances in which the appointment of a person as the relevant person's representative ends or may be ended.

149 Regulations may make provision about the formalities of ending the appointment of a person as a representative.

Suspension of representative's functions

150 (1) Regulations may make provision about the circumstances in which functions exercisable by, or in relation to, the relevant person's representative (whether under this Schedule or not) may be–
(a) suspended, and
(b) if suspended, revived.
(2) The regulations may make provision about the formalities for giving effect to the suspension or revival of a function.
(3) The regulations may make provision about the effect of the suspension or revival of a function.

Payment of representative

151 Regulations may make provision for payments to be made to, or in relation to, persons exercising functions as the relevant person's representative.

Regulations under this Part

152 The provisions of this Part which specify provision that may be made in regulations under this Part do not affect the generality of the power to make such regulations.

Effect of appointment of section 39C IMCA

153 Paragraphs 159 and 160 make provision about the exercise of functions by, or towards, the relevant person's representative during periods when–
(a) no person is appointed as the relevant person's representative, but
(b) a person is appointed as a section 39C IMCA.

Part 11: IMCAs

Application of Part

154 This Part applies for the purposes of this Schedule.

The IMCAs

155 A section 39A IMCA is an independent mental capacity advocate appointed under section 39A.

156 A section 39C IMCA is an independent mental capacity advocate appointed under section 39C

157 A section 39D IMCA is an independent mental capacity advocate appointed under section 39D.

158 An IMCA is a section 39A IMCA or a section 39C IMCA or a section 39D IMCA.

Section 39C IMCA: functions

159 (1) This paragraph applies if, and for as long as, there is a section 39C IMCA.

(2) In the application of the relevant provisions, references to the relevant person's representative are to be read as references to the section 39C IMCA.

(3) But sub-paragraph (2) does not apply to any function under the relevant provisions for as long as the function is suspended in accordance with provision made under Part 10.

(4) In this paragraph and paragraph 160 the relevant provisions are–

(a) paragraph 102(3)(b) (request for review under Part 8);

(b) paragraph 108(1)(b) (notice of review under Part 8);

(c) paragraph 120(1)(c) (notice of outcome of review under Part 8).

160 (1) This paragraph applies if–

(a) a person is appointed as the relevant person's representative, and

(b) a person accordingly ceases to hold an appointment as a section 39C IMCA.

(2) Where a function under a relevant provision has been exercised by, or towards, the section 39C IMCA, there is no requirement for that function to be exercised again by, or towards, the relevant person's representative.

Section 39A IMCA: restriction of functions

161 (1) This paragraph applies if–

(a) there is a section 39A IMCA, and

(b) a person is appointed under Part 10 to be the relevant person's representative (whether or not that person, or any person subsequently appointed, is currently the relevant person's representative).

(2) The duties imposed on, and the powers exercisable by, the section 39A IMCA do not apply.

(3) The duties imposed on, and the powers exercisable by, any other person do not apply, so far as they fall to be performed or exercised towards the section 39A IMCA.

(4) But sub-paragraph (2) does not apply to any power of challenge exercisable by the section 39A IMCA.

(5) And sub-paragraph (3) does not apply to any duty or power of any other person so far as it relates to any power of challenge exercisable by the section 39A IMCA.

(6) Before exercising any power of challenge, the section 39A IMCA must take the views of the relevant person's representative into account.

(7) A power of challenge is a power to make an application to the court to exercise its jurisdiction under section 21A in connection with the giving of the standard authorisation.

Part 12: Miscellaneous

Monitoring of operation of Schedule

162 (1) Regulations may make provision for, and in connection with, requiring one or more prescribed bodies to monitor, and report on, the operation of this Schedule in relation to England.

(2) The regulations may, in particular, give a prescribed body authority to do one or more of the following things–

(a) to visit hospitals and care homes;

(b) to visit and interview persons accommodated in hospitals and care homes;

(c) to require the production of, and to inspect, records relating to the care or treatment of persons.

(3) 'Prescribed' means prescribed in regulations under this paragraph.

163 (1) Regulations may make provision for, and in connection with, enabling the National Assembly for Wales to monitor, and report on, the operation of this Schedule in relation to Wales.

(2) The National Assembly may direct one or more persons or bodies to carry out the Assembly's functions under regulations under this paragraph.

Disclosure of information

164 (1) Regulations may require either or both of the following to disclose prescribed information to prescribed bodies–

(a) supervisory bodies;

(b) managing authorities of hospitals or care homes.

(2) 'Prescribed' means prescribed in regulations under this paragraph.

(3) Regulations under this paragraph may only prescribe information relating to matters with which this Schedule is concerned.

Directions by National Assembly in relation to supervisory functions

165 (1) The National Assembly for Wales may direct a Local Health Board to exercise in relation to its area any supervisory functions which are specified in the direction.

(2) Directions under this paragraph must not preclude the National Assembly from exercising the functions specified in the directions.

(3) In this paragraph 'supervisory functions' means functions which the National Assembly have as supervisory body, so far as they are exercisable in relation to hospitals (whether NHS or independent hospitals, and whether in Wales or England).

166 (1) This paragraph applies where, under paragraph 165, a Local Health Board ('the specified LHB') is directed to exercise supervisory functions ('delegated functions').

(2) The National Assembly for Wales may give directions to the specified LHB about the Board's exercise of delegated functions.

(3) The National Assembly may give directions for any delegated functions to be exercised, on behalf of the specified LHB, by a committee, sub-committee or officer of that Board.

(4) The National Assembly may give directions providing for any delegated functions to be exercised by the specified LHB jointly with one or more other Local Health Boards.

(5) Where, under sub-paragraph (4), delegated functions are exercisable jointly, the National Assembly may give directions providing for the functions to be exercised, on behalf of the Local Health Boards in question, by a joint committee or joint sub-committee.

167 (1) Directions under paragraph 165 must be given in regulations.

(2) Directions under paragraph 166 may be given–

(a) in regulations, or

(b) by instrument in writing.

168 The power under paragraph 165 or paragraph 166 to give directions includes power to vary or revoke directions given under that paragraph.

Notices

169 Any notice under this Schedule must be in writing.

Regulations

170 (1) This paragraph applies to all regulations under this Schedule, except regulations under paragraph 162, 163, 167 or 183.

(2) It is for the Secretary of State to make such regulations in relation to authorisations under this Schedule which relate to hospitals and care homes situated in England.

(3) It is for the National Assembly for Wales to make such regulations in relation to authorisations under this Schedule which relate to hospitals and care homes situated in Wales.

171 It is for the Secretary of State to make regulations under paragraph 162.

172 It is for the National Assembly for Wales to make regulations under paragraph 163 or 167.

173 (1) This paragraph applies to regulations under paragraph 183.

(2) It is for the Secretary of State to make such regulations in relation to cases where a question as to the ordinary residence of a person is to be determined by the Secretary of State.

(3) It is for the National Assembly for Wales to make such regulations in relation to cases where a question as to the ordinary residence of a person is to be determined by the National Assembly.

Part 13: Interpretation

Introduction

174 This Part applies for the purposes of this Schedule.

Hospitals and their managing authorities

175 (1) 'Hospital' means–

(a) an NHS hospital, or

(b) an independent hospital.

(2) 'NHS hospital' means–

(a) a health service hospital as defined by section 275 of the National Health Service Act 2006 or section 206 of the National Health Service (Wales) Act 2006, or

(b) a hospital as defined by section 206 of the National Health Service (Wales) Act 2006 vested in a Local Health Board.

(3) Independent hospital'–

(a) in relation to England, means a hospital as defined by section 275 of the National Health Service Act 2006 that is not an NHS hospital; and
(b) in relation to Wales, means a hospital as defined by section 2 of the Care Standards Act 2000 that is not an NHS hospital.

176 (1) 'Managing authority', in relation to an NHS hospital, means–
(a) if the hospital–
(i) is vested in the appropriate national authority for the purposes of its functions under the National Health Service Act 2006 or of the National Health Service (Wales) Act 2006, or
(ii) consists of any accommodation provided by a local authority and used as a hospital by or on behalf of the appropriate national authority under either of those Acts,
the Local Health Board or Special Health Authority responsible for the administration of the hospital;
(aa) in relation to England, if the hospital falls within paragraph (a)(i) or (ii) and no Special Health Authority has responsibility for its administration, the Secretary of State;
(b) if the hospital is vested in a . . . National Health Service trust or NHS foundation trust, that trust;
(c) if the hospital is vested in a Local Health Board, that Board.
(2) For this purpose the appropriate national authority is–
(a) in relation to England: the Secretary of State;
(b) in relation to Wales: the National Assembly for Wales;
(c) in relation to England and Wales: the Secretary of State and the National Assembly acting jointly.

177 'Managing authority', in relation to an independent hospital, means–
(a) in relation to England, the person registered, or required to be registered, under Chapter 2 of Part 1 of the Health and Social Care Act 2008 in respect of regulated activities (within the meaning of that Part) carried on in the hospital, and
(b) in relation to Wales, the person registered, or required to be registered, under Part 2 of the Care Standards Act 2000 in respect of the hospital.

Care homes and their managing authorities

178 'Care home' has the meaning given by section 3 of the Care Standards Act 2000.
'Care home' means—
(a) a care home in England within the meaning given by section 3 of the Care Standards Act 2000, and
(b) a place in Wales at which a care home service within the meaning of Part 1 of the Regulation and Inspection of Social Care (Wales) Act 2016 is provided wholly or mainly to persons aged 18 or over';
(c) in paragraph 179(b), for 'Part 2 of the Care Standards Act 2000 in respect of the care home' substitute 'under Part 1 of the Regulation and Inspection of Social Care (Wales) Act 2016 in respect of the care home'.

179 'Managing authority', in relation to a care home, means–
(a) in relation to England, the person registered, or required to be registered, under Chapter 2 of Part 1 of the Health and Social Care Act 2008 in respect of the provision of residential accommodation, together with nursing or personal care, in the care home, and

(b) in relation to Wales, the person registered, or required to be registered, under Part 2 of the Care Standards Act 2000 in respect of the care home.

Supervisory bodies: hospitals

180 (1) The identity of the supervisory body is determined under this paragraph in cases where the relevant hospital is situated in England.

(2) If the relevant person is ordinarily resident in the area of a local authority in England, the supervisory body are that local authority.

(3) If the relevant person is not ordinarily resident in England and the National Assembly for Wales or a Local Health Board commission the relevant care or treatment, the National Assembly are the supervisory body.

(4) In any other case, the supervisory body are the local authority for the area in which the relevant hospital is situated.

(4A) Local authority' means–

(a) the council of a county;
(b) the council of a district for which there is no county council;
(c) the council of a London borough;
(d) the Common Council of the City of London;
(e) the Council of the Isles of Scilly.

(5) If a hospital is situated in the areas of two (or more) local authorities, it is to be regarded for the purposes of sub-paragraph (4) as situated in whichever of the areas the greater (or greatest) part of the hospital is situated.

181 (1) The identity of the supervisory body is determined under this paragraph in cases where the relevant hospital is situated in Wales.

(2) The National Assembly for Wales are the supervisory body.

(3) But if the relevant person is ordinarily resident in the area of a local authority in England, the supervisory body are that local authority.

(4) 'Local authority' means–

(a) the council of a county;
(b) the council of a district for which there is no county council;
(c) the council of a London borough;
(d) the Common Council of the City of London;
(e) the Council of the Isles of Scilly.

Supervisory bodies: care homes

182 (1) The identity of the supervisory body is determined under this paragraph in cases where the relevant care home is situated in England or in Wales.

(2) The supervisory body are the local authority for the area in which the relevant person is ordinarily resident.

(3) But if the relevant person is not ordinarily resident in the area of a local authority, the supervisory body are the local authority for the area in which the care home is situated.

(4) In relation to England 'local authority' means–

(a) the council of a county;
(b) the council of a district for which there is no county council;
(c) the council of a London borough;
(d) the Common Council of the City of London;
(e) the Council of the Isles of Scilly.

(5) In relation to Wales 'local authority' means the council of a county or county borough.

(6) If a care home is situated in the areas of two (or more) local authorities, it is to be regarded for the purposes of sub-paragraph (3) as situated in whichever of the areas the greater (or greatest) part of the care home is situated.

Supervisory bodies: determination of place of ordinary residence

183 (1) [Repealed.]

(2) [Repealed.]

(2A) Section 39(1), (2) and (4) to (6) of the Care Act 2014 and paragraphs 1(1), 2(1) and 8 of Schedule 1 to that Act apply to any determination of where a person is ordinarily resident for the purposes of paragraphs 180, 181 and 182 as they apply for the purposes of Part 1 of that Act.]

(2B) Section 194(1), (2), (4) and (5) of the Social Services and Well-being (Wales) Act 2014 apply to a determination of where a person is ordinarily resident for the purposes of paragraphs 180, 181 and 182 as it applies for the purposes of that Act.

(3) Any question arising as to the ordinary residence of a person is to be determined by the Secretary of State or by the National Assembly for Wales.

(4) The Secretary of State and the National Assembly must make and publish arrangements for determining which cases are to be dealt with by the Secretary of State and which are to be dealt with by the National Assembly.

(5) Those arrangements may include provision for the Secretary of State and the National Assembly to agree, in relation to any question that has arisen, which of them is to deal with the case.

(6) Regulations may make provision about arrangements that are to have effect before, upon, or after the determination of any question as to the ordinary residence of a person.

(7) The regulations may, in particular, authorise or require a local authority to do any or all of the following things–

(a) to act as supervisory body even though it may wish to dispute that it is the supervisory body;

(b) to become the supervisory body in place of another local authority;

(c) to recover from another local authority expenditure incurred in exercising functions as the supervisory body.

Same body managing authority and supervisory body

184 (1) This paragraph applies if, in connection with a particular person's detention as a resident in a hospital or care home, the same body are both–

(a) the managing authority of the relevant hospital or care home, and

(b) the supervisory body.

(2) The fact that a single body are acting in both capacities does not prevent the body from carrying out functions under this Schedule in each capacity.

(3) But, in such a case, this Schedule has effect subject to any modifications contained in regulations that may be made for this purpose.

Interested persons

185 Each of the following is an interested person–

(a) the relevant person's spouse or civil partner;

(b) where the relevant person and another person are not married to each other, nor in a civil partnership with each other, but are living together as if they were a married couple or civil partners: that other person;

(d) the relevant person's children and step-children;
(e) the relevant person's parents and step-parents;
(f) the relevant person's brothers and sisters, half-brothers and half-sisters, and stepbrothers and stepsisters;
(g) the relevant person's grandparents;
(h) a deputy appointed for the relevant person by the court;
(i) a donee of a lasting power of attorney granted by the relevant person.

186 (1) An interested person consulted by the best interests assessor is any person whose name is stated in the relevant best interests assessment in accordance with paragraph 40 (interested persons whom the assessor consulted in carrying out the assessment).

(2) The relevant best interests assessment is the most recent best interests assessment carried out in connection with the standard authorisation in question (whether the assessment was carried out under Part 4 or Part 8).

187 Where this Schedule imposes on a person a duty towards an interested person, the duty does not apply if the person on whom the duty is imposed–
(a) is not aware of the interested person's identity or of a way of contacting him, and
(b) cannot reasonably ascertain it.

188 The following table contains an index of provisions defining or otherwise explaining expressions used in this Schedule–

age assessment	paragraph 34
age requirement	paragraph 13
age review assessment	paragraph 112(3)
appointment regulations	paragraph 138
assessment under this Schedule	paragraph 127
assessor (except in Part 8)	paragraph 33
assessor (in Part 8)	paragraphs 33 and 128
authorisation under this Schedule	paragraph 10
best interests (determination of)	section 4
best interests assessment	paragraph 38
best interests requirement	paragraph 16
best interests review assessment	paragraph 112(6)
care home	paragraph 178
change of reason ground	paragraph 106
complete (in relation to a review of a standard authorisation)	paragraph 118
deprivation of a person's liberty	section 64(5) and (6)
deputy	section 16(2)(b)
detained resident	paragraph 6
disposed of (in relation to a request for a standard authorisation)	paragraph 66
eligibility assessment	paragraph 46
eligibility requirement	paragraph 17
eligibility review assessment	paragraph 112(7)

eligible person (in relation to paragraphs 68 to 73)	paragraph 68
eligible person (in relation to Part 8)	paragraph 102(3)
expiry (in relation to an existing authorisation)	paragraph 125(b)
existing authorisation (in Part 8)	paragraph 125(a)
hospital	paragraph 175
IMCA	paragraph 158
in force (in relation to a standard authorisation)	paragraphs 63 and 64
in force (in relation to an urgent authorisation)	paragraphs 88 and 89
ineligible (in relation to the eligibility requirement)	Schedule 1A
interested person	paragraph 185
interested person consulted by the best interests assessor	paragraph 186
lack of capacity	section 2
lasting power of attorney	section 9
managing authority (in relation to a care home)	paragraph 179
managing authority (in relation to a hospital)	paragraph 176 or 177
maximum authorisation period	paragraph 42
mental capacity assessment	paragraph 37
mental capacity requirement	paragraph 15
mental capacity review assessment	paragraph 112(5)
mental health assessment	paragraph 35
mental health requirement	paragraph 14
mental health review assessment	paragraph 112(4)
negative conclusion	paragraph 112(2)(a)
new supervisory body	paragraph 99(b)
no refusals assessment	paragraph 48
no refusals requirement	paragraph 18
no refusals review assessment	paragraph 112(8)
non-qualification ground	paragraph 105
old supervisory body	paragraph 99(a)
positive conclusion	paragraph 112(2)(b)
purpose of a standard authorisation	paragraph 11(1)
purpose of an urgent authorisation	paragraph 11(2)
qualifying requirements	paragraph 12
refusal (for the purposes of the no refusals requirement)	paragraphs 19 and 20
relevant care or treatment	paragraph 7
relevant hospital or care home	paragraph 7
relevant managing authority	paragraph 26(4)
relevant person	paragraph 7
relevant person's representative	paragraph 137
relevant procedure	paragraph 128

review assessment	paragraph 112(1)
reviewable	paragraph 104
section 39A IMCA	paragraph 155
section 39C IMCA	paragraph 156
section 39D IMCA	paragraph 157
standard authorisation	paragraph 8
supervisory body (except in Part 8)	paragraph 180, 181 or 182
supervisory body (in Part 8)	paragraph 128 and paragraph 180, 181 or 182
unauthorised deprivation of liberty (in relation to paragraphs 68 to 73)	paragraph 67
urgent authorisation	paragraph 9
variation of conditions ground	paragraph 107

SCHEDULE 1: LASTING POWERS OF ATTORNEY: FORMALITIES

Section 9

Part 1: Making Instruments

General requirements as to making instruments

1 (1) An instrument is not made in accordance with this Schedule unless–
(a) it is in the prescribed form,
(b) it complies with paragraph 2, and
(c) any prescribed requirements in connection with its execution are satisfied.
(2) Regulations may make different provision according to whether–
(a) the instrument relates to personal welfare or to property and affairs (or to both);
(b) only one or more than one donee is to be appointed (and if more than one, whether jointly or jointly and severally).
(3) In this Schedule–
(a) 'prescribed' means prescribed by regulations, and
(b) 'regulations' means regulations made for the purposes of this Schedule by the Lord Chancellor.

Requirements as to content of instruments

2 (1) The instrument must include–
(a) the prescribed information about the purpose of the instrument and the effect of a lasting power of attorney,
(b) a statement by the donor to the effect that he–
(i) has read the prescribed information or a prescribed part of it (or has had it read to him), and
(ii) intends the authority conferred under the instrument to include authority to make decisions on his behalf in circumstances where he no longer has capacity,
(c) a statement by the donor–

(i) naming a person or persons whom the donor wishes to be notified of any application for the registration of the instrument, or
(ii) stating that there are no persons whom he wishes to be notified of any such application,

(d) a statement by the donee (or, if more than one, each of them) to the effect that he–
(i) has read the prescribed information or a prescribed part of it (or has had it read to him), and
(ii) understands the duties imposed on a donee of a lasting power of attorney under sections 1 (the principles) and 4 (best interests), and

(e) a certificate by a person of a prescribed description that, in his opinion, at the time when the donor executes the instrument–
(i) the donor understands the purpose of the instrument and the scope of the authority conferred under it,
(ii) no fraud or undue pressure is being used to induce the donor to create a lasting power of attorney, and
(iii) there is nothing else which would prevent a lasting power of attorney from being created by the instrument.

(2) Regulations may–
(a) prescribe a maximum number of named persons;
(b) provide that, where the instrument includes a statement under sub-paragraph (1)(c)(ii), two persons of a prescribed description must each give a certificate under sub-paragraph (1)(e).

(3) The persons who may be named persons do not include a person who is appointed as donee under the instrument.

(4) In this Schedule, 'named person' means a person named under sub-paragraph (1)(c).

(5) A certificate under sub-paragraph (1)(e)–
(a) must be made in the prescribed form, and
(b) must include any prescribed information.

(6) The certificate may not be given by a person appointed as donee under the instrument.

Failure to comply with prescribed form

3 (1) If an instrument differs in an immaterial respect in form or mode of expression from the prescribed form, it is to be treated by the Public Guardian as sufficient in point of form and expression.

(2) The court may declare that an instrument which is not in the prescribed form is to be treated as if it were, if it is satisfied that the persons executing the instrument intended it to create a lasting power of attorney.

Part 2: Registration

Applications and procedure for registration

4 (1) An application to the Public Guardian for the registration of an instrument intended to create a lasting power of attorney–
(a) must be made in the prescribed form, and
(b) must include any prescribed information.

(2) The application may be made–
(a) by the donor,

(b) by the donee or donees, or
(c) if the instrument appoints two or more donees to act jointly and severally in respect of any matter, by any of the donees.

(3) The application must be accompanied by–
(a) the instrument, and
(b) any fee provided for under section 58(4)(b).

(4) A person who, in an application for registration, makes a statement which he knows to be false in a material particular is guilty of an offence and is liable–
(a) on summary conviction, to imprisonment for a term not exceeding 12 months or a fine not exceeding the statutory maximum or both;
(b) on conviction on indictment, to imprisonment for a term not exceeding 2 years or a fine or both.

5 Subject to paragraphs 11 to 14, the Public Guardian must register the instrument as a lasting power of attorney at the end of the prescribed period.

Notification requirements

6 (1) A donor about to make an application under paragraph 4(2)(a) must notify any named persons that he is about to do so.

(2) The donee (or donees) about to make an application under paragraph 4(2)(b) or (c) must notify any named persons that he is (or they are) about to do so.

7 As soon as is practicable after receiving an application by the donor under paragraph 4(2)(a), the Public Guardian must notify the donee (or donees) that the application has been received.

8 (1) As soon as is practicable after receiving an application by a donee (or donees) under paragraph 4(2)(b), the Public Guardian must notify the donor that the application has been received.

(2) As soon as is practicable after receiving an application by a donee under paragraph 4(2)(c), the Public Guardian must notify–
(a) the donor, and
(b) the donee or donees who did not join in making the application,
that the application has been received.

9 (1) A notice under paragraph 6 must be made in the prescribed form.

(2) A notice under paragraph 6, 7 or 8 must include such information, if any, as may be prescribed.

Power to dispense with notification requirements

10 The court may–
(a) on the application of the donor, dispense with the requirement to notify under paragraph 6(1), or
(b) on the application of the donee or donees concerned, dispense with the requirement to notify under paragraph 6(2),
if satisfied that no useful purpose would be served by giving the notice.

Instrument not made properly or containing ineffective provision

11 (1) If it appears to the Public Guardian that an instrument accompanying an application under paragraph 4 is not made in accordance with this Schedule, he must not register the instrument unless the court directs him to do so.

(2) Sub-paragraph (3) applies if it appears to the Public Guardian that the instrument contains a provision which–

(a) would be ineffective as part of a lasting power of attorney, or
(b) would prevent the instrument from operating as a valid lasting power of attorney.

(3) The Public Guardian–
(a) must apply to the court for it to determine the matter under section 23(1), and
(b) pending the determination by the court, must not register the instrument.

(4) Sub-paragraph (5) applies if the court determines under section 23(1) (whether or not on an application by the Public Guardian) that the instrument contains a provision which–
(a) would be ineffective as part of a lasting power of attorney, or
(b) would prevent the instrument from operating as a valid lasting power of attorney.

(5) The court must–
(a) notify the Public Guardian that it has severed the provision, or
(b) direct him not to register the instrument.

(6) Where the court notifies the Public Guardian that it has severed a provision, he must register the instrument with a note to that effect attached to it.

Deputy already appointed

12 (1) Sub-paragraph (2) applies if it appears to the Public Guardian that–
(a) there is a deputy appointed by the court for the donor, and
(b) the powers conferred on the deputy would, if the instrument were registered, to any extent conflict with the powers conferred on the attorney.

(2) The Public Guardian must not register the instrument unless the court directs him to do so.

Objection by donee or named person

13 (1) Sub-paragraph (2) applies if a donee or a named person–
(a) receives a notice under paragraph 6, 7 or 8 of an application for the registration of an instrument, and
(b) before the end of the prescribed period, gives notice to the Public Guardian of an objection to the registration on the ground that an event mentioned in section 13(3) or (6)(a) to (d) has occurred which has revoked the instrument.

(2) If the Public Guardian is satisfied that the ground for making the objection is established, he must not register the instrument unless the court, on the application of the person applying for the registration–
(a) is satisfied that the ground is not established, and
(b) directs the Public Guardian to register the instrument.

(3) Sub-paragraph (4) applies if a donee or a named person–
(a) receives a notice under paragraph 6, 7 or 8 of an application for the registration of an instrument, and
(b) before the end of the prescribed period–
(i) makes an application to the court objecting to the registration on a prescribed ground, and
(ii) notifies the Public Guardian of the application.

(4) The Public Guardian must not register the instrument unless the court directs him to do so.

Objection by donor

14 (1) This paragraph applies if the donor–
(a) receives a notice under paragraph 8 of an application for the registration of an instrument, and
(b) before the end of the prescribed period, gives notice to the Public Guardian of an objection to the registration.
(2) The Public Guardian must not register the instrument unless the court, on the application of the donee or, if more than one, any of them–
(a) is satisfied that the donor lacks capacity to object to the registration, and
(b) directs the Public Guardian to register the instrument.

Notification of registration

15 Where an instrument is registered under this Schedule, the Public Guardian must give notice of the fact in the prescribed form to–
(a) the donor, and
(b) the donee or, if more than one, each of them.

Evidence of registration

16 (1) A document purporting to be an office copy of an instrument registered under this Schedule is, in any part of the United Kingdom, evidence of–
(a) the contents of the instrument, and
(b) the fact that it has been registered.
(2) Sub-paragraph (1) is without prejudice to–
(a) section 3 of the Powers of Attorney Act 1971 (proof by certified copy), and
(b) any other method of proof authorised by law.

Part 3: Cancellation of Registration and Notification of Severance

17 (1) The Public Guardian must cancel the registration of an instrument as a lasting power of attorney on being satisfied that the power has been revoked–
(a) as a result of the donor's bankruptcy or a debt relief order (under Part 7A of the Insolvency Act 1986) having been made in respect of the donor, or
(b) on the occurrence of an event mentioned in section 13(6)(a) to (d).
(2) If the Public Guardian cancels the registration of an instrument he must notify–
(a) the donor, and
(b) the donee or, if more than one, each of them.

18 The court must direct the Public Guardian to cancel the registration of an instrument as a lasting power of attorney if it–
(a) determines under section 22(2)(a) that a requirement for creating the power was not met,
(b) determines under section 22(2)(b) that the power has been revoked or has otherwise come to an end, or
(c) revokes the power under section 22(4)(b) (fraud etc).

19 (1) Sub-paragraph (2) applies if the court determines under section 23(1) that a lasting power of attorney contains a provision which–
(a) is ineffective as part of a lasting power of attorney, or
(b) prevents the instrument from operating as a valid lasting power of attorney.

(2) The court must–
(a) notify the Public Guardian that it has severed the provision, or
(b) direct him to cancel the registration of the instrument as a lasting power of attorney.

20 On the cancellation of the registration of an instrument, the instrument and any office copies of it must be delivered up to the Public Guardian to be cancelled.

Part 4: Records of Alterations in Registered Powers

Partial revocation or suspension of power as a result of bankruptcy

21 If in the case of a registered instrument it appears to the Public Guardian that under section 13 a lasting power of attorney is revoked, or suspended, in relation to the donor's property and affairs (but not in relation to other matters), the Public Guardian must attach to the instrument a note to that effect.

Termination of appointment of donee which does not revoke power

22 If in the case of a registered instrument it appears to the Public Guardian that an event has occurred–
(a) which has terminated the appointment of the donee, but
(b) which has not revoked the instrument,
the Public Guardian must attach to the instrument a note to that effect.

Replacement of donee

23 If in the case of a registered instrument it appears to the Public Guardian that the donee has been replaced under the terms of the instrument the Public Guardian must attach to the instrument a note to that effect.

Severance of ineffective provisions

24 If in the case of a registered instrument the court notifies the Public Guardian under paragraph 19(2)(a) that it has severed a provision of the instrument, the Public Guardian must attach to it a note to that effect.

Notification of alterations

25 If the Public Guardian attaches a note to an instrument under paragraph 21, 22, 23 or 24 he must give notice of the note to the donee or donees of the power (or, as the case may be, to the other donee or donees of the power).

SCHEDULE 1A: PERSONS INELIGIBLE TO BE DEPRIVED OF LIBERTY BY THIS ACT

Part 1: Ineligible Persons

Application

1 This Schedule applies for the purposes of–
(a) section 16A, and
(b) paragraph 17 of Schedule A1.

Determining ineligibility

2 A person ('P') is ineligible to be deprived of liberty by this Act ('ineligible') if–
(a) P falls within one of the cases set out in the second column of the following table, and

(b) the corresponding entry in the third column of the table–or the provision, or one of the provisions, referred to in that entry–provides that he is ineligible.

	Status of P	*Determination of ineligibility*
Case A	P is– (a) subject to the hospital treatment regime, and (b) detained in a hospital under that regime.	P is ineligible.
Case B	P is– (a) subject to the hospital treatment regime, but (b) not detained in a hospital under that regime.	See paragraphs 3 and 4.
Case C	P is subject to the community treatment regime.	See paragraphs 3 and 4.
Case D	P is subject to the guardianship regime.	See paragraphs 3 and 5.
Case E	P is– (a) within the scope of the Mental Health Act, but (b) not subject to any of the mental health regimes.	See paragraph 5.

Authorised course of action not in accordance with regime

3 (1) This paragraph applies in cases B, C and D in the table in paragraph 2.

(2) P is ineligible if the authorised course of action is not in accordance with a requirement which the relevant regime imposes.

(3) That includes any requirement as to where P is, or is not, to reside.

(4) The relevant regime is the mental health regime to which P is subject.

Treatment for mental disorder in a hospital

4 (1) This paragraph applies in cases B and C in the table in paragraph 2.

(2) P is ineligible if the relevant care or treatment consists in whole or in part of medical treatment for mental disorder in a hospital.

P objects to being a mental health patient etc

5 (1) This paragraph applies in cases D and E in the table in paragraph 2.

(2) P is ineligible if the following conditions are met.

(3) The first condition is that the relevant instrument authorises P to be a mental health patient.

(4) The second condition is that P objects–

(a) to being a mental health patient, or

(b) to being given some or all of the mental health treatment.

(5) The third condition is that a donee or deputy has not made a valid decision to consent to each matter to which P objects.

(6) In determining whether or not P objects to something, regard must be had to all the circumstances (so far as they are reasonably ascertainable), including the following–
  (a) P's behaviour;
  (b) P's wishes and feelings;
  (c) P's views, beliefs and values.

(7) But regard is to be had to circumstances from the past only so far as it is still appropriate to have regard to them.

Part 2: Interpretation

Application

6 This Part applies for the purposes of this Schedule.

Mental health regimes

7 The mental health regimes are–
  (a) the hospital treatment regime,
  (b) the community treatment regime, and
  (c) the guardianship regime.

Hospital treatment regime

8 (1) P is subject to the hospital treatment regime if he is subject to–
  (a) a hospital treatment obligation under the relevant enactment, or
  (b) an obligation under another England and Wales enactment which has the same effect as a hospital treatment obligation.

(2) But where P is subject to any such obligation, he is to be regarded as not subject to the hospital treatment regime during any period when he is subject to the community treatment regime.

(3) A hospital treatment obligation is an application, order or direction of a kind listed in the first column of the following table.

(4) In relation to a hospital treatment obligation, the relevant enactment is the enactment in the Mental Health Act which is referred to in the corresponding entry in the second column of the following table.

Hospital treatment obligation	*Relevant enactment*
Application for admission for assessment	Section 2
Application for admission for assessment	Section 4
Application for admission for treatment	Section 3
Order for remand to hospital	Section 35
Order for remand to hospital	Section 36
Hospital order	Section 37
Interim hospital order	Section 38
Order for detention in hospital	Section 44
Hospital direction	Section 45A
Transfer direction	Section 47
Transfer direction	Section 48
Hospital order	Section 51

Community treatment regime

9 P is subject to the community treatment regime if he is subject to–
(a) a community treatment order under section 17A of the Mental Health Act, or
(b) an obligation under another England and Wales enactment which has the same effect as a community treatment order.

Guardianship regime

10 P is subject to the guardianship regime if he is subject to–
(a) a guardianship application under section 7 of the Mental Health Act,
(b) a guardianship order under section 37 of the Mental Health Act, or
(c) an obligation under another England and Wales enactment which has the same effect as a guardianship application or guardianship order.

England and Wales enactments

11 (1) An England and Wales enactment is an enactment which extends to England and Wales (whether or not it also extends elsewhere).
(2) It does not matter if the enactment is in the Mental Health Act or not.

P within scope of Mental Health Act

12 (1) P is within the scope of the Mental Health Act if–
(a) an application in respect of P could be made under section 2 or 3 of the Mental Health Act, and
(b) P could be detained in a hospital in pursuance of such an application, were one made.
(2) The following provisions of this paragraph apply when determining whether an application in respect of P could be made under section 2 or 3 of the Mental Health Act.
(3) If the grounds in section 2(2) of the Mental Health Act are met in P's case, it is to be assumed that the recommendations referred to in section 2(3) of that Act have been given.
(4) If the grounds in section 3(2) of the Mental Health Act are met in P's case, it is to be assumed that the recommendations referred to in section 3(3) of that Act have been given.
(5) In determining whether the ground in section 3(2)(c) of the Mental Health Act is met in P's case, it is to be assumed that the treatment referred to in section 3(2)(c) cannot be provided under this Act.

Authorised course of action, relevant care or treatment & relevant instrument

13 In a case where this Schedule applies for the purposes of section 16A–
'authorised course of action' means any course of action amounting to deprivation of liberty which the order under section 16(2)(a) authorises;
'relevant care or treatment' means any care or treatment which–
(a) comprises, or forms part of, the authorised course of action, or
(b) is to be given in connection with the authorised course of action;
'relevant instrument' means the order under section 16(2)(a).

14 In a case where this Schedule applies for the purposes of paragraph 17 of Schedule A1–

'authorised course of action' means the accommodation of the relevant person in the relevant hospital or care home for the purpose of being given the relevant care or treatment;

'relevant care or treatment' has the same meaning as in Schedule A1;

'relevant instrument' means the standard authorisation under Schedule A1.

15 (1) This paragraph applies where the question whether a person is ineligible to be deprived of liberty by this Act is relevant to either of these decisions–

(a) whether or not to include particular provision ('the proposed provision') in an order under section 16(2)(a);

(b) whether or not to give a standard authorisation under Schedule A1.

(2) A reference in this Schedule to the authorised course of action or the relevant care or treatment is to be read as a reference to that thing as it would be if–

(a) the proposed provision were included in the order, or

(b) the standard authorisation were given.

(3) A reference in this Schedule to the relevant instrument is to be read as follows–

(a) where the relevant instrument is an order under section 16(2)(a): as a reference to the order as it would be if the proposed provision were included in it;

(b) where the relevant instrument is a standard authorisation: as a reference to the standard authorisation as it would be if it were given.

Expressions used in paragraph 5

16 (1) These expressions have the meanings given–

'donee' means a donee of a lasting power of attorney granted by P;

'mental health patient' means a person accommodated in a hospital for the purpose of being given medical treatment for mental disorder;

'mental health treatment' means the medical treatment for mental disorder referred to in the definition of 'mental health patient'.

(2) A decision of a donee or deputy is valid if it is made–

(a) within the scope of his authority as donee or deputy, and

(b) in accordance with Part 1 of this Act.

Expressions with same meaning as in Mental Health Act

17 (1) 'Hospital' has the same meaning as in Part 2 of the Mental Health Act.

(2) 'Medical treatment' has the same meaning as in the Mental Health Act.

(3) 'Mental disorder' has the same meaning as in Schedule A1 (see paragraph 14).

SCHEDULE 2: PROPERTY AND AFFAIRS: SUPPLEMENTARY PROVISIONS

Section 18(4)

Wills: general

1 Paragraphs 2 to 4 apply in relation to the execution of a will, by virtue of section 18, on behalf of P.

Provision that may be made in will

2 The will may make any provision (whether by disposing of property or exercising a power or otherwise) which could be made by a will executed by P if he had capacity to make it.

Wills: requirements relating to execution

3 (1) Sub-paragraph (2) applies if under section 16 the court makes an order or gives directions requiring or authorising a person ('the authorised person') to execute a will on behalf of P.

(2) Any will executed in pursuance of the order or direction–

(a) must state that it is signed by P acting by the authorised person,

(b) must be signed by the authorised person with the name of P and his own name, in the presence of two or more witnesses present at the same time,

(c) must be attested and subscribed by those witnesses in the presence of the authorised person, and

(d) must be sealed with the official seal of the court.

Wills: effect of execution

4 (1) This paragraph applies where a will is executed in accordance with paragraph 3.

(2) The Wills Act 1837 has effect in relation to the will as if it were signed by P by his own hand, except that–

(a) section 9 of the 1837 Act (requirements as to signing and attestation) does not apply, and

(b) in the subsequent provisions of the 1837 Act any reference to execution in the manner required by the previous provisions is to be read as a reference to execution in accordance with paragraph 3.

(3) The will has the same effect for all purposes as if–

(a) P had had the capacity to make a valid will, and

(b) the will had been executed by him in the manner required by the 1837 Act.

(4) But sub-paragraph (3) does not have effect in relation to the will–

(a) in so far as it disposes of immovable property outside England and Wales, or

(b) in so far as it relates to any other property or matter if, when the will is executed–

(i) P is domiciled outside England and Wales, and

(ii) the condition in sub-paragraph (5) is met.

(5) The condition is that, under the law of P's domicile, any question of his testamentary capacity would fall to be determined in accordance with the law of a place outside England and Wales.

Vesting orders ancillary to settlement etc

5 (1) If provision is made by virtue of section 18 for–

(a) the settlement of any property of P, or

(b) the exercise of a power vested in him of appointing trustees or retiring from a trust,

the court may also make as respects the property settled or the trust property such consequential vesting or other orders as the case may require.

(2) The power under sub-paragraph (1) includes, in the case of the exercise of such a power, any order which could have been made in such a case under Part 4 of the Trustee Act 1925 (c 19).

Variation of settlements

6 (1) If a settlement has been made by virtue of section 18, the court may by order vary or revoke the settlement if–

(a) the settlement makes provision for its variation or revocation,

(b) the court is satisfied that a material fact was not disclosed when the settlement was made, or

(c) the court is satisfied that there has been a substantial change of circumstances.

(2) Any such order may give such consequential directions as the court thinks fit.

Vesting of stock in curator appointed outside England and Wales

7 (1) Sub-paragraph (2) applies if the court is satisfied–

(a) that under the law prevailing in a place outside England and Wales a person ('M') has been appointed to exercise powers in respect of the property or affairs of P on the ground (however formulated) that P lacks capacity to make decisions with respect to the management and administration of his property and affairs, and

(b) that, having regard to the nature of the appointment and to the circumstances of the case, it is expedient that the court should exercise its powers under this paragraph.

(2) The court may direct–

(a) any stocks standing in the name of P, or

(b) the right to receive dividends from the stocks,

to be transferred into M's name or otherwise dealt with as required by M, and may give such directions as the court thinks fit for dealing with accrued dividends from the stocks.

(3) 'Stocks' includes–

(a) shares, and

(b) any funds, annuity or security transferable in the books kept by any body corporate or unincorporated company or society or by an instrument of transfer either alone or accompanied by other formalities,

and 'dividends' is to be construed accordingly.

Preservation of interests in property disposed of on behalf of person lacking capacity

8 (1) Sub-paragraphs (2) and (3) apply if–

(a) P's property has been disposed of by virtue of section 18,

(b) under P's will or intestacy, or by a gift perfected or nomination taking effect on his death, any other person would have taken an interest in the property but for the disposal, and

(c) on P's death, any property belonging to P's estate represents the property disposed of.

(2) The person takes the same interest, if and so far as circumstances allow, in the property representing the property disposed of.

(3) If the property disposed of was real property, any property representing it is to be treated, so long as it remains part of P's estate, as if it were real property.

(4) The court may direct that, on a disposal of P's property–

(a) which is made by virtue of section 18, and

(b) which would apart from this paragraph result in the conversion of personal property into real property,

property representing the property disposed of is to be treated, so long as it remains P's property or forms part of P's estate, as if it were personal property.

(5) References in sub-paragraphs (1) to (4) to the disposal of property are to–
(a) the sale, exchange, charging of or other dealing (otherwise than by will) with property other than money;
(b) the removal of property from one place to another;
(c) the application of money in acquiring property;
(d) the transfer of money from one account to another;
and references to property representing property disposed of are to be construed accordingly and as including the result of successive disposals.

(6) The court may give such directions as appear to it necessary or expedient for the purpose of facilitating the operation of sub-paragraphs (1) to (3), including the carrying of money to a separate account and the transfer of property other than money.

9 (1) Sub-paragraph (2) applies if the court has ordered or directed the expenditure of money–
(a) for carrying out permanent improvements on any of P's property, or
(b) otherwise for the permanent benefit of any of P's property.

(2) The court may order that–
(a) the whole of the money expended or to be expended, or
(b) any part of it,
is to be a charge on the property either without interest or with interest at a specified rate.

(3) An order under sub-paragraph (2) may provide for excluding or restricting the operation of paragraph 8(1) to (3).

(4) A charge under sub-paragraph (2) may be made in favour of such person as may be just and, in particular, where the money charged is paid out of P's general estate, may be made in favour of a person as trustee for P.

(5) No charge under sub-paragraph (2) may confer any right of sale or foreclosure during P's lifetime.

Powers as patron of benefice

10 (1) Any functions which P has as patron of a benefice may be discharged only by a person ('R') appointed by the court.

(2) R must be an individual capable of appointment under section 8(1)(b) of the 1986 Measure (which provides for an individual able to make a declaration of communicant status, a clerk in Holy Orders, etc to be appointed to discharge a registered patron's functions).

(3) The 1986 Measure applies to R as it applies to an individual appointed by the registered patron of the benefice under section 8(1)(b) or (3) of that Measure to discharge his functions as patron.

(4) 'The 1986 Measure' means the Patronage (Benefices) Measure 1986 (No 3).

SCHEDULE 3: INTERNATIONAL PROTECTION OF ADULTS

Section 63

Part 1: Preliminary

Introduction

1 This Part applies for the purposes of this Schedule.

The Convention

2 (1) 'Convention' means the Convention referred to in section 63.

(2) 'Convention country' means a country in which the Convention is in force.

(3) A reference to an Article or Chapter is to an Article or Chapter of the Convention.

(4) An expression which appears in this Schedule and in the Convention is to be construed in accordance with the Convention.

Countries, territories and nationals

3 (1) 'Country' includes a territory which has its own system of law.

(2) Where a country has more than one territory with its own system of law, a reference to the country, in relation to one of its nationals, is to the territory with which the national has the closer, or the closest, connection.

Adults with incapacity

4 (1) 'Adult' means (subject to sub-paragraph (2) a person who–

(a) as a result of an impairment or insufficiency of his personal faculties, cannot protect his interests, and

(b) has reached 16.

(2) But 'adult' does not include a child to whom the following applies–

(a) the Convention on Jurisdiction, Applicable Law, Recognition, Enforcement and Co-Operation in respect of Parental Responsibility and Measures for the Protection of Children that was signed at The Hague on 19 October 1996;

(b) [Repealed.]

Protective measures

5 (1) 'Protective measure' means a measure directed to the protection of the person or property of an adult; and it may deal in particular with any of the following–

(a) the determination of incapacity and the institution of a protective regime,

(b) placing the adult under the protection of an appropriate authority,

(c) guardianship, curatorship or any corresponding system,

(d) the designation and functions of a person having charge of the adult's person or property, or representing or otherwise helping him,

(e) placing the adult in a place where protection can be provided,

(f) administering, conserving or disposing of the adult's property,

(g) authorising a specific intervention for the protection of the person or property of the adult.

(2) Where a measure of like effect to a protective measure has been taken in relation to a person before he reaches 16, this Schedule applies to the measure in so far as it has effect in relation to him once he has reached 16.

Central Authority

6 (1) Any function under the Convention of a Central Authority is exercisable in England and Wales by the Lord Chancellor.

(2) A communication may be sent to the Central Authority in relation to England and Wales by sending it to the Lord Chancellor.

Part 2: Jurisdiction of Competent Authority

Scope of jurisdiction

7 (1) The court may exercise its functions under this Act (in so far as it cannot otherwise do so) in relation to–

(a) an adult habitually resident in England and Wales,

(b) an adult's property in England and Wales,

(c) an adult present in England and Wales or who has property there, if the matter is urgent, or

(d) an adult present in England and Wales, if a protective measure which is temporary and limited in its effect to England and Wales is proposed in relation to him.

(2) An adult present in England and Wales is to be treated for the purposes of this paragraph as habitually resident there if–

(a) his habitual residence cannot be ascertained,

(b) he is a refugee, or

(c) he has been displaced as a result of disturbance in the country of his habitual residence.

8 (1) The court may also exercise its functions under this Act (in so far as it cannot otherwise do so) in relation to an adult if sub-paragraph (2) or (3) applies in relation to him.

(2) This sub-paragraph applies in relation to an adult if–

(a) he is a British citizen,

(b) he has a closer connection with England and Wales than with Scotland or Northern Ireland, and

(c) Article 7 has, in relation to the matter concerned, been complied with.

(3) This sub-paragraph applies in relation to an adult if the Lord Chancellor, having consulted such persons as he considers appropriate, agrees to a request under Article 8 in relation to the adult.

Exercise of jurisdiction

9 (1) This paragraph applies where jurisdiction is exercisable under this Schedule in connection with a matter which involves a Convention country other than England and Wales.

(2) Any Article on which the jurisdiction is based applies in relation to the matter in so far as it involves the other country (and the court must, accordingly, comply with any duty conferred on it as a result).

(3) Article 12 also applies, so far as its provisions allow, in relation to the matter in so far as it involves the other country.

10 A reference in this Schedule to the exercise of jurisdiction under this Schedule is to the exercise of functions under this Act as a result of this Part of this Schedule.

Part 3: Applicable Law

Applicable law

11 In exercising jurisdiction under this Schedule, the court may, if it thinks that the matter has a substantial connection with a country other than England and Wales, apply the law of that other country.

12 Where a protective measure is taken in one country but implemented in another, the conditions of implementation are governed by the law of the other country.

Lasting powers of attorney, etc

13 (1) If the donor of a lasting power is habitually resident in England and Wales at the time of granting the power, the law applicable to the existence, extent, modification or extinction of the power is–

(a) the law of England and Wales, or

(b) if he specifies in writing the law of a connected country for the purpose, that law.

(2) If he is habitually resident in another country at that time, but England and Wales is a connected country, the law applicable in that respect is–

(a) the law of the other country, or

(b) if he specifies in writing the law of England and Wales for the purpose, that law.

(3) A country is connected, in relation to the donor, if it is a country–

(a) of which he is a national,

(b) in which he was habitually resident, or

(c) in which he has property.

(4) Where this paragraph applies as a result of sub-paragraph (3)(c), it applies only in relation to the property which the donor has in the connected country.

(5) The law applicable to the manner of the exercise of a lasting power is the law of the country where it is exercised.

(6) In this Part of this Schedule, 'lasting power' means–

(a) a lasting power of attorney (see section 9),

(b) an enduring power of attorney within the meaning of Schedule 4, or

(c) any other power of like effect.

14 (1) Where a lasting power is not exercised in a manner sufficient to guarantee the protection of the person or property of the donor, the court, in exercising jurisdiction under this Schedule, may disapply or modify the power.

(2) Where, in accordance with this Part of this Schedule, the law applicable to the power is, in one or more respects, that of a country other than England and Wales, the court must, so far as possible, have regard to the law of the other country in that respect (or those respects).

15 Regulations may provide for Schedule 1 (lasting powers of attorney: formalities) to apply with modifications in relation to a lasting power which comes within paragraph 13(6)(c) above.

Protection of third parties

16 (1) This paragraph applies where a person (a 'representative') in purported exercise of an authority to act on behalf of an adult enters into a transaction with a third party.

(2) The validity of the transaction may not be questioned in proceedings, nor may the third party be held liable, merely because–
(a) where the representative and third party are in England and Wales when entering into the transaction, sub-paragraph (3) applies;
(b) where they are in another country at that time, sub-paragraph (4) applies.
(3) This sub-paragraph applies if–
(a) the law applicable to the authority in one or more respects is, as a result of this Schedule, the law of a country other than England and Wales, and
(b) the representative is not entitled to exercise the authority in that respect (or those respects) under the law of that other country.
(4) This sub-paragraph applies if–
(a) the law applicable to the authority in one or more respects is, as a result of this Part of this Schedule, the law of England and Wales, and
(b) the representative is not entitled to exercise the authority in that respect (or those respects) under that law.
(5) This paragraph does not apply if the third party knew or ought to have known that the applicable law was–
(a) in a case within sub-paragraph (3), the law of the other country;
(b) in a case within sub-paragraph (4), the law of England and Wales.

Mandatory rules

17 Where the court is entitled to exercise jurisdiction under this Schedule, the mandatory provisions of the law of England and Wales apply, regardless of any system of law which would otherwise apply in relation to the matter.

Public policy

18 Nothing in this Part of this Schedule requires or enables the application in England and Wales of a provision of the law of another country if its application would be manifestly contrary to public policy.

Part 4: Recognition and Enforcement

Recognition

19 (1) A protective measure taken in relation to an adult under the law of a country other than England and Wales is to be recognised in England and Wales if it was taken on the ground that the adult is habitually resident in the other country.
(2) A protective measure taken in relation to an adult under the law of a Convention country other than England and Wales is to be recognised in England and Wales if it was taken on a ground mentioned in Chapter 2 (jurisdiction).
(3) But the court may disapply this paragraph in relation to a measure if it thinks that–
(a) the case in which the measure was taken was not urgent,
(b) the adult was not given an opportunity to be heard, and
(c) that omission amounted to a breach of natural justice.
(4) It may also disapply this paragraph in relation to a measure if it thinks that–
(a) recognition of the measure would be manifestly contrary to public policy,
(b) the measure would be inconsistent with a mandatory provision of the law of England and Wales, or
(c) the measure is inconsistent with one subsequently taken, or recognised, in England and Wales in relation to the adult.

(5) And the court may disapply this paragraph in relation to a measure taken under the law of a Convention country in a matter to which Article 33 applies, if the court thinks that that Article has not been complied with in connection with that matter.

20 (1) An interested person may apply to the court for a declaration as to whether a protective measure taken under the law of a country other than England and Wales is to be recognised in England and Wales.

(2) No permission is required for an application to the court under this paragraph.

21 For the purposes of paragraphs 19 and 20, any finding of fact relied on when the measure was taken is conclusive.

Enforcement

22 (1) An interested person may apply to the court for a declaration as to whether a protective measure taken under the law of, and enforceable in, a country other than England and Wales is enforceable, or to be registered, in England and Wales in accordance with Court of Protection Rules.

(2) The court must make the declaration if–

(a) the measure comes within sub-paragraph (1) or (2) of paragraph 19, and

(b) the paragraph is not disapplied in relation to it as a result of sub-paragraph (3), (4) or (5).

(3) A measure to which a declaration under this paragraph relates is enforceable in England and Wales as if it were a measure of like effect taken by the court.

Measures taken in relation to those aged under 16

23 (1) This paragraph applies where–

(a) provision giving effect to, or otherwise deriving from, the Convention in a country other than England and Wales applies in relation to a person who has not reached 16, and

(b) a measure is taken in relation to that person in reliance on that provision.

(2) This Part of this Schedule applies in relation to that measure as it applies in relation to a protective measure taken in relation to an adult under the law of a Convention country other than England and Wales.

Supplementary

24 The court may not review the merits of a measure taken outside England and Wales except to establish whether the measure complies with this Schedule in so far as it is, as a result of this Schedule, required to do so.

25 Court of Protection Rules may make provision about an application under paragraph 20 or 22.

Part 5: Co-operation

Proposal for cross-border placement

26 (1) This paragraph applies where a public authority proposes to place an adult in an establishment in a Convention country other than England and Wales.

(2) The public authority must consult an appropriate authority in that other country about the proposed placement and, for that purpose, must send it–

(a) a report on the adult, and

(b) a statement of its reasons for the proposed placement.

(3) If the appropriate authority in the other country opposes the proposed placement within a reasonable time, the public authority may not proceed with it.

27 A proposal received by a public authority under Article 33 in relation to an adult is to proceed unless the authority opposes it within a reasonable time.

Adult in danger etc

28 (1) This paragraph applies if a public authority is told that an adult–
(a) who is in serious danger, and
(b) in relation to whom the public authority has taken, or is considering taking, protective measures,
is, or has become resident, in a Convention country other than England and Wales.
(2) The public authority must tell an appropriate authority in that other country about–
(a) the danger, and
(b) the measures taken or under consideration.

29 A public authority may not request from, or send to, an appropriate authority in a Convention country information in accordance with Chapter 5 (co-operation) in relation to an adult if it thinks that doing so–
(a) would be likely to endanger the adult or his property, or
(b) would amount to a serious threat to the liberty or life of a member of the adult's family.

Part 6: General

Certificates

30 A certificate given under Article 38 by an authority in a Convention country other than England and Wales is, unless the contrary is shown, proof of the matters contained in it.

Powers to make further provision as to private international law

31 Her Majesty may by Order in Council confer on the Lord Chancellor, the court or another public authority functions for enabling the Convention to be given effect in England and Wales.

32 (1) Regulations may make provision–
(a) giving further effect to the Convention, or
(b) otherwise about the private international law of England and Wales in relation to the protection of adults.
(2) The regulations may–
(a) confer functions on the court or another public authority;
(b) amend this Schedule;
(c) provide for this Schedule to apply with specified modifications;
(d) make provision about countries other than Convention countries.

Exceptions

33 Nothing in this Schedule applies, and no provision made under paragraph 32 is to apply, to any matter to which the Convention, as a result of Article 4, does not apply.

Regulations and orders

34 A reference in this Schedule to regulations or an order (other than an Order in Council) is to regulations or an order made for the purposes of this Schedule by the Lord Chancellor.

Commencement

35 The following provisions of this Schedule have effect only if the Convention is in force in accordance with Article 57–

(a) paragraph 8,
(b) paragraph 9,
(c) paragraph 19(2) and (5),
(d) Part 5,
(e) paragraph 30.

SCHEDULE 4: PROVISIONS APPLYING TO EXISTING ENDURING POWERS OF ATTORNEY

Section 66(3)

Part 1: Enduring Powers of Attorney

Enduring power of attorney to survive mental incapacity of donor

1 (1) Where an individual has created a power of attorney which is an enduring power within the meaning of this Schedule–

(a) the power is not revoked by any subsequent mental incapacity of his,
(b) upon such incapacity supervening, the donee of the power may not do anything under the authority of the power except as provided by sub-paragraph (2) unless or until the instrument creating the power is registered under paragraph 13, and
(c) if and so long as paragraph (b) operates to suspend the donee's authority to act under the power, section 5 of the Powers of Attorney Act 1971 (protection of donee and third persons), so far as applicable, applies as if the power had been revoked by the donor's mental incapacity,

and, accordingly, section 1 of this Act does not apply.

(2) Despite sub-paragraph (1)(b), where the attorney has made an application for registration of the instrument then, until it is registered, the attorney may take action under the power–

(a) to maintain the donor or prevent loss to his estate, or
(b) to maintain himself or other persons in so far as paragraph 3(2) permits him to do so.

(3) Where the attorney purports to act as provided by sub-paragraph (2) then, in favour of a person who deals with him without knowledge that the attorney is acting otherwise than in accordance with sub-paragraph (2)(a) or (b), the transaction between them is as valid as if the attorney were acting in accordance with sub-paragraph (2)(a) or (b).

Characteristics of an enduring power of attorney

2 (1) Subject to sub-paragraphs (5) and (6) and paragraph 20, a power of attorney is an enduring power within the meaning of this Schedule if the instrument which creates the power–

(a) is in the prescribed form,
(b) was executed in the prescribed manner by the donor and the attorney, and
(c) incorporated at the time of execution by the donor the prescribed explanatory information.

(2) In this paragraph, 'prescribed' means prescribed by such of the following regulations as applied when the instrument was executed–
   (a) the Enduring Powers of Attorney (Prescribed Form) Regulations 1986 (SI 1986/126),
   (b) the Enduring Powers of Attorney (Prescribed Form) Regulations 1987 (SI 1987/1612),
   (c) the Enduring Powers of Attorney (Prescribed Form) Regulations 1990 (SI 1990/1376),
   (d) the Enduring Powers of Attorney (Welsh Language Prescribed Form) Regulations 2000 (SI 2000/289).

(3) An instrument in the prescribed form purporting to have been executed in the prescribed manner is to be taken, in the absence of evidence to the contrary, to be a document which incorporated at the time of execution by the donor the prescribed explanatory information.

(4) If an instrument differs in an immaterial respect in form or mode of expression from the prescribed form it is to be treated as sufficient in point of form and expression.

(5) A power of attorney cannot be an enduring power unless, when he executes the instrument creating it, the attorney is–
   (a) an individual who has reached 18 and is not bankrupt or is not subject to a debt relief order (under Part 7A of the Insolvency Act 1986), or
   (b) a trust corporation.

(6) A power of attorney which gives the attorney a right to appoint a substitute or successor cannot be an enduring power.

(7) An enduring power is revoked by the bankruptcy of the donor or attorney or the making of a debt relief order (under Part 7A of the Insolvency Act 1986) in respect of the donor or attorney.

(8) But where the donor or attorney is bankrupt merely because an interim bankruptcy restrictions order has effect in respect of him or where the donor or attorney is subject to an interim debt relief restrictions order, the power is suspended for so long as the order has effect.

(9) An enduring power is revoked if the court–
   (a) exercises a power under sections 16 to 20 in relation to the donor, and
   (b) directs that the enduring power is to be revoked.

(10) No disclaimer of an enduring power, whether by deed or otherwise, is valid unless and until the attorney gives notice of it to the donor or, where paragraph 4(6) or 15(1) applies, to the Public Guardian.

Scope of authority etc of attorney under enduring power

3 (1) If the instrument which creates an enduring power of attorney is expressed to confer general authority on the attorney, the instrument operates to confer, subject to–
   (a) the restriction imposed by sub-paragraph (3), and
   (b) any conditions or restrictions contained in the instrument,

authority to do on behalf of the donor anything which the donor could lawfully do by an attorney at the time when the donor executed the instrument.

(2) Subject to any conditions or restrictions contained in the instrument, an attorney under an enduring power, whether general or limited, may (without

obtaining any consent) act under the power so as to benefit himself or other persons than the donor to the following extent but no further–

(a) he may so act in relation to himself or in relation to any other person if the donor might be expected to provide for his or that person's needs respectively, and

(b) he may do whatever the donor might be expected to do to meet those needs.

(3) Without prejudice to sub-paragraph (2) but subject to any conditions or restrictions contained in the instrument, an attorney under an enduring power, whether general or limited, may (without obtaining any consent) dispose of the property of the donor by way of gift to the following extent but no further–

(a) he may make gifts of a seasonal nature or at a time, or on an anniversary, of a birth, a marriage or the formation of a civil partnership, to persons (including himself) who are related to or connected with the donor, and

(b) he may make gifts to any charity to whom the donor made or might be expected to make gifts,

provided that the value of each such gift is not unreasonable having regard to all the circumstances and in particular the size of the donor's estate.

Part 2: Action on Actual or Impending Incapacity of Donor

Duties of attorney in event of actual or impending incapacity of donor

4 (1) Sub-paragraphs (2) to (6) apply if the attorney under an enduring power has reason to believe that the donor is or is becoming mentally incapable.

(2) The attorney must, as soon as practicable, make an application to the Public Guardian for the registration of the instrument creating the power.

(3) Before making an application for registration the attorney must comply with the provisions as to notice set out in Part 3 of this Schedule.

(4) An application for registration–

(a) must be made in the prescribed form, and

(b) must contain such statements as may be prescribed.

(5) The attorney–

(a) may, before making an application for the registration of the instrument, refer to the court for its determination any question as to the validity of the power, and

(b) must comply with any direction given to him by the court on that determination.

(6) No disclaimer of the power is valid unless and until the attorney gives notice of it to the Public Guardian; and the Public Guardian must notify the donor if he receives a notice under this sub-paragraph.

(7) A person who, in an application for registration, makes a statement which he knows to be false in a material particular is guilty of an offence and is liable–

(a) on summary conviction, to imprisonment for a term not exceeding 12 months or a fine not exceeding the statutory maximum or both;

(b) on conviction on indictment, to imprisonment for a term not exceeding 2 years or a fine or both.

(8) In this paragraph, 'prescribed' means prescribed by regulations made for the purposes of this Schedule by the Lord Chancellor.

Part 3: Notification Prior to Registration

Duty to give notice to relatives

5 Subject to paragraph 7, before making an application for registration the attorney must give notice of his intention to do so to all those persons (if any) who are entitled to receive notice by virtue of paragraph 6.

6 (1) Subject to sub-paragraphs (2) to (4), persons of the following classes ('relatives') are entitled to receive notice under paragraph 5–
(a) the donor's spouse or civil partner,
(b) the donor's children,
(c) the donor's parents,
(d) the donor's brothers and sisters, whether of the whole or half blood,
(e) the widow, widower or surviving civil partner of a child of the donor,
(f) the donor's grandchildren,
(g) the children of the donor's brothers and sisters of the whole blood,
(h) the children of the donor's brothers and sisters of the half blood,
(i) the donor's uncles and aunts of the whole blood,
(j) the children of the donor's uncles and aunts of the whole blood.

(2) A person is not entitled to receive notice under paragraph 5 if–
(a) his name or address is not known to the attorney and cannot be reasonably ascertained by him, or
(b) the attorney has reason to believe that he has not reached 18 or is mentally incapable.

(3) Except where sub-paragraph (4) applies–
(a) no more than 3 persons are entitled to receive notice under paragraph 5, and
(b) in determining the persons who are so entitled, persons falling within the class in sub-paragraph (1)(a) are to be preferred to persons falling within the class in sub-paragraph (1)(b), those falling within the class in sub-paragraph (1)(b) are to be preferred to those falling within the class in sub-paragraph (1)(c), and so on.

(4) Despite the limit of 3 specified in sub-paragraph (3), where–
(a) there is more than one person falling within any of classes (a) to (j) of sub-paragraph (1), and
(b) at least one of those persons would be entitled to receive notice under paragraph 5,

then, subject to sub-paragraph (2), all the persons falling within that class are entitled to receive notice under paragraph 5.

7 (1) An attorney is not required to give notice under paragraph 5–
(a) to himself, or
(b) to any other attorney under the power who is joining in making the application,

even though he or, as the case may be, the other attorney is entitled to receive notice by virtue of paragraph 6.

(2) In the case of any person who is entitled to receive notice by virtue of paragraph 6, the attorney, before applying for registration, may make an application to the court to be dispensed from the requirement to give him notice; and the court must grant the application if it is satisfied–
(a) that it would be undesirable or impracticable for the attorney to give him notice, or

(b) that no useful purpose is likely to be served by giving him notice.

Duty to give notice to donor

8 (1) Subject to sub-paragraph (2), before making an application for registration the attorney must give notice of his intention to do so to the donor.

(2) Paragraph 7(2) applies in relation to the donor as it applies in relation to a person who is entitled to receive notice under paragraph 5.

Contents of notices

9 A notice to relatives under this Part of this Schedule must–

(a) be in the prescribed form,

(b) state that the attorney proposes to make an application to the Public Guardian for the registration of the instrument creating the enduring power in question,

(c) inform the person to whom it is given of his right to object to the registration under paragraph 13(4), and

(d) specify, as the grounds on which an objection to registration may be made, the grounds set out in paragraph 13(9).

10 A notice to the donor under this Part of this Schedule–

(a) must be in the prescribed form,

(b) must contain the statement mentioned in paragraph 9(b), and

(c) must inform the donor that, while the instrument remains registered, any revocation of the power by him will be ineffective unless and until the revocation is confirmed by the court.

Duty to give notice to other attorneys

11 (1) Subject to sub-paragraph (2), before making an application for registration an attorney under a joint and several power must give notice of his intention to do so to any other attorney under the power who is not joining in making the application; and paragraphs 7(2) and 9 apply in relation to attorneys entitled to receive notice by virtue of this paragraph as they apply in relation to persons entitled to receive notice by virtue of paragraph 6.

(2) An attorney is not entitled to receive notice by virtue of this paragraph if–

(a) his address is not known to the applying attorney and cannot reasonably be ascertained by him, or

(b) the applying attorney has reason to believe that he has not reached 18 or is mentally incapable.

Supplementary

12 Despite section 7 of the Interpretation Act 1978 (construction of references to service by post), for the purposes of this Part of this Schedule a notice given by post is to be regarded as given on the date on which it was posted.

Part 4: Registration

Registration of instrument creating power

13 (1) If an application is made in accordance with paragraph 4(3) and (4) the Public Guardian must, subject to the provisions of this paragraph, register the instrument to which the application relates.

(2) If it appears to the Public Guardian that–

(a) there is a deputy appointed for the donor of the power created by the instrument, and

(b) the powers conferred on the deputy would, if the instrument were registered, to any extent conflict with the powers conferred on the attorney,

the Public Guardian must not register the instrument except in accordance with the court's directions.

(3) The court may, on the application of the attorney, direct the Public Guardian to register an instrument even though notice has not been given as required by paragraph 4(3) and Part 3 of this Schedule to a person entitled to receive it, if the court is satisfied–

(a) that it was undesirable or impracticable for the attorney to give notice to that person, or

(b) that no useful purpose is likely to be served by giving him notice.

(4) Sub-paragraph (5) applies if, before the end of the period of 5 weeks beginning with the date (or the latest date) on which the attorney gave notice under paragraph 5 of an application for registration, the Public Guardian receives a valid notice of objection to the registration from a person entitled to notice of the application.

(5) The Public Guardian must not register the instrument except in accordance with the court's directions.

(6) Sub-paragraph (7) applies if, in the case of an application for registration–

(a) it appears from the application that there is no one to whom notice has been given under paragraph 5, or

(b) the Public Guardian has reason to believe that appropriate inquiries might bring to light evidence on which he could be satisfied that one of the grounds of objection set out in sub-paragraph (9) was established.

(7) The Public Guardian–

(a) must not register the instrument, and

(b) must undertake such inquiries as he thinks appropriate in all the circumstances.

(8) If, having complied with sub-paragraph (7)(b), the Public Guardian is satisfied that one of the grounds of objection set out in sub-paragraph (9) is established–

(a) the attorney may apply to the court for directions, and

(b) the Public Guardian must not register the instrument except in accordance with the court's directions.

(9) A notice of objection under this paragraph is valid if made on one or more of the following grounds–

(a) that the power purported to have been created by the instrument was not valid as an enduring power of attorney,

(b) that the power created by the instrument no longer subsists,

(c) that the application is premature because the donor is not yet becoming mentally incapable,

(d) that fraud or undue pressure was used to induce the donor to create the power,

(e) that, having regard to all the circumstances and in particular the attorney's relationship to or connection with the donor, the attorney is unsuitable to be the donor's attorney.

(10) If any of those grounds is established to the satisfaction of the court it must direct the Public Guardian not to register the instrument, but if not so satisfied it must direct its registration.

(11) If the court directs the Public Guardian not to register an instrument because it is satisfied that the ground in sub-paragraph (9)(d) or (e) is established, it must by order revoke the power created by the instrument.

(12) If the court directs the Public Guardian not to register an instrument because it is satisfied that any ground in sub-paragraph (9) except that in paragraph (c) is established, the instrument must be delivered up to be cancelled unless the court otherwise directs.

Register of enduring powers

14 The Public Guardian has the function of establishing and maintaining a register of enduring powers for the purposes of this Schedule.

Part 5: Legal Position after Registration

Effect and proof of registration

15 (1) The effect of the registration of an instrument under paragraph 13 is that–
- (a) no revocation of the power by the donor is valid unless and until the court confirms the revocation under paragraph 16(3);
- (b) no disclaimer of the power is valid unless and until the attorney gives notice of it to the Public Guardian;
- (c) the donor may not extend or restrict the scope of the authority conferred by the instrument and no instruction or consent given by him after registration, in the case of a consent, confers any right and, in the case of an instruction, imposes or confers any obligation or right on or creates any liability of the attorney or other persons having notice of the instruction or consent.

(2) Sub-paragraph (1) applies for so long as the instrument is registered under paragraph 13 whether or not the donor is for the time being mentally incapable.

(3) A document purporting to be an office copy of an instrument registered under this Schedule is, in any part of the United Kingdom, evidence of–
- (a) the contents of the instrument, and
- (b) the fact that it has been so registered.

(4) Sub-paragraph (3) is without prejudice to section 3 of the Powers of Attorney Act 1971 (c 27) (proof by certified copies) and to any other method of proof authorised by law.

Functions of court with regard to registered power

16 (1) Where an instrument has been registered under paragraph 13, the court has the following functions with respect to the power and the donor of and the attorney appointed to act under the power.

(2) The court may–
- (a) determine any question as to the meaning or effect of the instrument;
- (b) give directions with respect to–
  - (i) the management or disposal by the attorney of the property and affairs of the donor;
  - (ii) the rendering of accounts by the attorney and the production of the records kept by him for the purpose;
  - (iii) the remuneration or expenses of the attorney whether or not in default of or in accordance with any provision made by the instrument, including directions for the repayment of excessive or the payment of additional remuneration;

(c) require the attorney to supply information or produce documents or things in his possession as attorney;
(d) give any consent or authorisation to act which the attorney would have to obtain from a mentally capable donor;
(e) authorise the attorney to act so as to benefit himself or other persons than the donor otherwise than in accordance with paragraph 3(2) and (3) (but subject to any conditions or restrictions contained in the instrument);
(f) relieve the attorney wholly or partly from any liability which he has or may have incurred on account of a breach of his duties as attorney.

(3) On application made for the purpose by or on behalf of the donor, the court must confirm the revocation of the power if satisfied that the donor–
(a) has done whatever is necessary in law to effect an express revocation of the power, and
(b) was mentally capable of revoking a power of attorney when he did so (whether or not he is so when the court considers the application).

(4) The court must direct the Public Guardian to cancel the registration of an instrument registered under paragraph 13 in any of the following circumstances–
(a) on confirming the revocation of the power under sub-paragraph (3),
(b) on directing under paragraph 2(9)(b) that the power is to be revoked,
(c) on being satisfied that the donor is and is likely to remain mentally capable,
(d) on being satisfied that the power has expired or has been revoked by the mental incapacity of the attorney,
(e) on being satisfied that the power was not a valid and subsisting enduring power when registration was effected,
(f) on being satisfied that fraud or undue pressure was used to induce the donor to create the power,
(g) on being satisfied that, having regard to all the circumstances and in particular the attorney's relationship to or connection with the donor, the attorney is unsuitable to be the donor's attorney.

(5) If the court directs the Public Guardian to cancel the registration of an instrument on being satisfied of the matters specified in sub-paragraph (4)(f) or (g) it must by order revoke the power created by the instrument.

(6) If the court directs the cancellation of the registration of an instrument under sub-paragraph (4) except paragraph (c) the instrument must be delivered up to the Public Guardian to be cancelled, unless the court otherwise directs.

Cancellation of registration by Public Guardian

17 The Public Guardian must cancel the registration of an instrument creating an enduring power of attorney–
(a) on receipt of a disclaimer signed by the attorney;
(b) if satisfied that the power has been revoked by the death or bankruptcy of the donor or attorney or the making of a debt relief order (under Part 7A of the Insolvency Act 1986) in respect of the donor or attorney or, if the attorney is a body corporate, by its winding up or dissolution;
(c) on receipt of notification from the court that the court has revoked the power;
(d) on confirmation from the court that the donor has revoked the power.

Part 6: Protection of Attorney and Third Parties

Protection of attorney and third persons where power is invalid or revoked

18 (1) Sub-paragraphs (2) and (3) apply where an instrument which did not create a valid power of attorney has been registered under paragraph 13 (whether or not the registration has been cancelled at the time of the act or transaction in question).

(2) An attorney who acts in pursuance of the power does not incur any liability (either to the donor or to any other person) because of the non-existence of the power unless at the time of acting he knows–

(a) that the instrument did not create a valid enduring power,

(b) that an event has occurred which, if the instrument had created a valid enduring power, would have had the effect of revoking the power, or

(c) that, if the instrument had created a valid enduring power, the power would have expired before that time.

(3) Any transaction between the attorney and another person is, in favour of that person, as valid as if the power had then been in existence, unless at the time of the transaction that person has knowledge of any of the matters mentioned in sub-paragraph (2).

(4) If the interest of a purchaser depends on whether a transaction between the attorney and another person was valid by virtue of sub-paragraph (3), it is conclusively presumed in favour of the purchaser that the transaction was valid if–

(a) the transaction between that person and the attorney was completed within 12 months of the date on which the instrument was registered, or

(b) that person makes a statutory declaration, before or within 3 months after the completion of the purchase, that he had no reason at the time of the transaction to doubt that the attorney had authority to dispose of the property which was the subject of the transaction.

(5) For the purposes of section 5 of the Powers of Attorney Act 1971 (protection where power is revoked) in its application to an enduring power the revocation of which by the donor is by virtue of paragraph 15 invalid unless and until confirmed by the court under paragraph 16–

(a) knowledge of the confirmation of the revocation is knowledge of the revocation of the power, but

(b) knowledge of the unconfirmed revocation is not.

Further protection of attorney and third persons

19 (1) If–

(a) an instrument framed in a form prescribed as mentioned in paragraph 2(2) creates a power which is not a valid enduring power, and

(b) the power is revoked by the mental incapacity of the donor,

sub-paragraphs (2) and (3) apply, whether or not the instrument has been registered.

(2) An attorney who acts in pursuance of the power does not, by reason of the revocation, incur any liability (either to the donor or to any other person) unless at the time of acting he knows–

(a) that the instrument did not create a valid enduring power, and

(b) that the donor has become mentally incapable.

(3) Any transaction between the attorney and another person is, in favour of that person, as valid as if the power had then been in existence, unless at the time of the transaction that person knows–
   (a) that the instrument did not create a valid enduring power, and
   (b) that the donor has become mentally incapable.
(4) Paragraph 18(4) applies for the purpose of determining whether a transaction was valid by virtue of sub-paragraph (3) as it applies for the purpose or determining whether a transaction was valid by virtue of paragraph 18(3).

Part 7: Joint and Joint and Several Attorneys

Application to joint and joint and several attorneys

20 (1) An instrument which appoints more than one person to be an attorney cannot create an enduring power unless the attorneys are appointed to act–
   (a) jointly, or
   (b) jointly and severally.
(2) This Schedule, in its application to joint attorneys, applies to them collectively as it applies to a single attorney but subject to the modifications specified in paragraph 21.
(3) This Schedule, in its application to joint and several attorneys, applies with the modifications specified in sub-paragraphs (4) to (7) and in paragraph 22.
(4) A failure, as respects any one attorney, to comply with the requirements for the creation of enduring powers–
   (a) prevents the instrument from creating such a power in his case, but
   (b) does not affect its efficacy for that purpose as respects the other or others or its efficacy in his case for the purpose of creating a power of attorney which is not an enduring power.
(5) If one or more but not both or all the attorneys makes or joins in making an application for registration of the instrument–
   (a) an attorney who is not an applicant as well as one who is may act pending the registration of the instrument as provided in paragraph 1(2),
   (b) notice of the application must also be given under Part 3 of this Schedule to the other attorney or attorneys, and
   (c) objection may validly be taken to the registration on a ground relating to an attorney or to the power of an attorney who is not an applicant as well as to one or the power of one who is an applicant.
(6) The Public Guardian is not precluded by paragraph 13(5) or (8) from registering an instrument and the court must not direct him not to do so under paragraph 13(10) if an enduring power subsists as respects some attorney who is not affected by the ground or grounds of the objection in question; and where the Public Guardian registers an instrument in that case, he must make against the registration an entry in the prescribed form.
(7) Sub-paragraph (6) does not preclude the court from revoking a power in so far as it confers a power on any other attorney in respect of whom the ground in paragraph 13(9)(d) or (e) is established; and where any ground in paragraph 13(9) affecting any other attorney is established the court must direct the Public Guardian to make against the registration an entry in the prescribed form.

(8) In sub-paragraph (4), 'the requirements for the creation of enduring powers' means the provisions of–
(a) paragraph 2 other than sub-paragraphs (8) and (9), and
(b) the regulations mentioned in paragraph 2.

Joint attorneys

21 (1) In paragraph 2(5), the reference to the time when the attorney executes the instrument is to be read as a reference to the time when the second or last attorney executes the instrument.
(2) In paragraph 2(6) to (8), the reference to the attorney is to be read as a reference to any attorney under the power.
(3) Paragraph 13 has effect as if the ground of objection to the registration of the instrument specified in sub-paragraph (9)(e) applied to any attorney under the power.
(4) In paragraph 16(2), references to the attorney are to be read as including references to any attorney under the power.
(5) In paragraph 16(4), references to the attorney are to be read as including references to any attorney under the power.
(6) In paragraph 17, references to the attorney are to be read as including references to any attorney under the power.

Joint and several attorneys

22 (1) In paragraph 2(7), the reference to the bankruptcy of the attorney is to be read as a reference to the bankruptcy of the last remaining attorney under the power; and the bankruptcy of any other attorney under the power causes that person to cease to be an attorney under the power.
(1A) In paragraph 2(7), the reference to the making of a debt relief order (under Part 7A of the Insolvency Act 1986) in respect of the attorney is to be read as a reference to the making of a debt relief order in respect of the last remaining attorney under the power; and the making of a debt relief order in respect of any other attorney under the power causes that person to cease to be an attorney under the power.
(2) In paragraph 2(8), the reference to the suspension of the power is to be read as a reference to its suspension in so far as it relates to the attorney in respect of whom the interim bankruptcy restrictions order has effect.
(2A) In paragraph 2(8), the reference to the suspension of the power is to be read as a reference to its suspension in so far as it relates to the attorney in respect of whom the interim debt relief restrictions order has effect.
(3) The restriction upon disclaimer imposed by paragraph 4(6) applies only to those attorneys who have reason to believe that the donor is or is becoming mentally incapable.

Part 8: Interpretation

23 (1) In this Schedule–
'enduring power' is to be construed in accordance with paragraph 2,
'mentally incapable' or 'mental incapacity', except where it refers to revocation at common law, means in relation to any person, that he is incapable by reason of mental disorder . . . of managing and administering his property and affairs and 'mentally capable' and 'mental capacity' are to be construed accordingly,

'notice' means notice in writing, and
'prescribed', except for the purposes of paragraph 2, means prescribed by regulations made for the purposes of this Schedule by the Lord Chancellor.

(1A) In sub-paragraph (1), 'mental disorder' has the same meaning as in the Mental Health Act but disregarding the amendments made to that Act by the Mental Health Act 2007.

(2) Any question arising under or for the purposes of this Schedule as to what the donor of the power might at any time be expected to do is to be determined by assuming that he had full mental capacity at the time but otherwise by reference to the circumstances existing at that time.

[SCHEDULES 5–7 are not reproduced here.]

HUMAN RIGHTS ACT 1998 ss3, 6–8 and Sch 1

Legislation

Interpretation of legislation

3 (1) So far as it is possible to do so, primary legislation and subordinate legislation must be read and given effect in a way which is compatible with the Convention rights.

(2) This section–

(a) applies to primary legislation and subordinate legislation whenever enacted;

(b) does not affect the validity, continuing operation or enforcement of any incompatible primary legislation; and

(c) does not affect the validity, continuing operation or enforcement of any incompatible subordinate legislation if (disregarding any possibility of revocation) primary legislation prevents removal of the incompatibility.

Public authorities

Acts of public authorities

6 (1) It is unlawful for a public authority to act in a way which is incompatible with a Convention right.

(2) Subsection (1) does not apply to an act if–

(a) as the result of one or more provisions of primary legislation, the authority could not have acted differently; or

(b) in the case of one or more provisions of, or made under, primary legislation which cannot be read or given effect in a way which is compatible with the Convention rights, the authority was acting so as to give effect to or enforce those provisions.

(3) In this section 'public authority' includes–

(a) a court or tribunal, and

(b) any person certain of whose functions are functions of a public nature,

but does not include either House of Parliament or a person exercising functions in connection with proceedings in Parliament.

(4) [Repealed.]

(5) In relation to a particular act, a person is not a public authority by virtue only of subsection (3)(b) if the nature of the act is private.

(6) 'An act' includes a failure to act but does not include a failure to–

(a) introduce in, or lay before, Parliament a proposal for legislation; or

(b) make any primary legislation or remedial order.

Proceedings

7 (1) A person who claims that a public authority has acted (or proposes to act) in a way which is made unlawful by section 6(1) may–

(a) bring proceedings against the authority under this Act in the appropriate court or tribunal, or

(b) rely on the Convention right or rights concerned in any legal proceedings,

but only if he is (or would be) a victim of the unlawful act.

(2) In subsection (1)(a) 'appropriate court or tribunal' means such court or tribunal as may be determined in accordance with rules; and proceedings against an authority include a counterclaim or similar proceeding.

(3) If the proceedings are brought on an application for judicial review, the applicant is to be taken to have a sufficient interest in relation to the unlawful act only if he is, or would be, a victim of that act.

(4) If the proceedings are made by way of a petition for judicial review in Scotland, the applicant shall be taken to have title and interest to sue in relation to the unlawful act only if he is, or would be, a victim of that act.

(5) Proceedings under subsection (1)(a) must be brought before the end of–

(a) the period of one year beginning with the date on which the act complained of took place; or

(b) such longer period as the court or tribunal considers equitable having regard to all the circumstances,

but that is subject to any rule imposing a stricter time limit in relation to the procedure in question.

(6) In subsection (1)(b) 'legal proceedings' includes–

(a) proceedings brought by or at the instigation of a public authority; and

(b) an appeal against the decision of a court or tribunal.

(7) For the purposes of this section, a person is a victim of an unlawful act only if he would be a victim for the purposes of Article 34 of the Convention if proceedings were brought in the European Court of Human Rights in respect of that act.

(8) Nothing in this Act creates a criminal offence.

(9) In this section 'rules' means–

(a) in relation to proceedings before a court or tribunal outside Scotland, rules made by the Lord Chancellor or the Secretary of State for the purposes of this section or rules of court,

(b) in relation to proceedings before a court or tribunal in Scotland, rules made by the Secretary of State for those purposes,

(c) in relation to proceedings before a tribunal in Northern Ireland–

(i) which deals with transferred matters; and

(ii) for which no rules made under paragraph (a) are in force,

rules made by a Northern Ireland department for those purposes,

and includes provision made by order under section 1 of the Courts and Legal Services Act 1990.

(10) In making rules, regard must be had to section 9.

(11) The Minister who has power to make rules in relation to a particular tribunal may, to the extent he considers it necessary to ensure that the tribunal can provide an appropriate remedy in relation to an act (or proposed act) of a public authority which is (or would be) unlawful as a result of section 6(1), by order add to–

(a) the relief or remedies which the tribunal may grant; or

(b) the grounds on which it may grant any of them.

(12) An order made under subsection (11) may contain such incidental, supplemental, consequential or transitional provision as the Minister making it considers appropriate.

(13) 'The Minister' includes the Northern Ireland department concerned.

Judicial remedies

8 (1) In relation to any act (or proposed act) of a public authority which the court finds is (or would be) unlawful, it may grant such relief or remedy, or make such order, within its powers as it considers just and appropriate.

(2) But damages may be awarded only by a court which has power to award damages, or to order the payment of compensation, in civil proceedings.

(3) No award of damages is to be made unless, taking account of all the circumstances of the case, including–

(a) any other relief or remedy granted, or order made, in relation to the act in question (by that or any other court), and

(b) the consequences of any decision (of that or any other court) in respect of that act,

the court is satisfied that the award is necessary to afford just satisfaction to the person in whose favour it is made.

(4) In determining–

(a) whether to award damages, or

(b) the amount of an award,

the court must take into account the principles applied by the European Court of Human Rights in relation to the award of compensation under Article 41 of the Convention.

(5) A public authority against which damages are awarded is to be treated–

(a) in Scotland, for the purposes of section 3 of the Law Reform (Miscellaneous Provisions) (Scotland) Act 1940 as if the award were made in an action of damages in which the authority has been found liable in respect of loss or damage to the person to whom the award is made;

(b) for the purposes of the Civil Liability (Contribution) Act 1978 as liable in respect of damage suffered by the person to whom the award is made.

(6) In this section–

'court' includes a tribunal;

'damages' means damages for an unlawful act of a public authority; and

'unlawful' means unlawful under section 6(1).

SCHEDULE 1: THE ARTICLES

Section 1(3)

Part I: The Convention

Rights and Freedoms

Article 2: Right to life

1 Everyone's right to life shall be protected by law. No one shall be deprived of his life intentionally save in the execution of a sentence of a court following his conviction of a crime for which this penalty is provided by law.

2 Deprivation of life shall not be regarded as inflicted in contravention of this Article when it results from the use of force which is no more than absolutely necessary:

(a) in defence of any person from unlawful violence;

(b) in order to effect a lawful arrest or to prevent the escape of a person lawfully detained;

(c) in action lawfully taken for the purpose of quelling a riot or insurrection.

Article 3: Prohibition of torture

No one shall be subjected to torture or to inhuman or degrading treatment or punishment.

Article 4: Prohibition of slavery and forced labour

1 No one shall be held in slavery or servitude.
2 No one shall be required to perform forced or compulsory labour.
3 For the purpose of this Article the term 'forced or compulsory labour' shall not include:
(a) any work required to be done in the ordinary course of detention imposed according to the provisions of Article 5 of this Convention or during conditional release from such detention;
(b) any service of a military character or, in case of conscientious objectors in countries where they are recognised, service exacted instead of compulsory military service;
(c) any service exacted in case of an emergency or calamity threatening the life or well-being of the community;
(d) any work or service which forms part of normal civic obligations.

Article 5: Right to liberty and security

1 Everyone has the right to liberty and security of person. No one shall be deprived of his liberty save in the following cases and in accordance with a procedure prescribed by law:
(a) the lawful detention of a person after conviction by a competent court;
(b) the lawful arrest or detention of a person for non-compliance with the lawful order of a court or in order to secure the fulfilment of any obligation prescribed by law;
(c) the lawful arrest or detention of a person effected for the purpose of bringing him before the competent legal authority on reasonable suspicion of having committed an offence or when it is reasonably considered necessary to prevent his committing an offence or fleeing after having done so;
(d) the detention of a minor by lawful order for the purpose of educational supervision or his lawful detention for the purpose of bringing him before the competent legal authority;
(e) the lawful detention of persons for the prevention of the spreading of infectious diseases, of persons of unsound mind, alcoholics or drug addicts or vagrants;
(f) the lawful arrest or detention of a person to prevent his effecting an unauthorised entry into the country or of a person against whom action is being taken with a view to deportation or extradition.
2 Everyone who is arrested shall be informed promptly, in a language which he understands, of the reasons for his arrest and of any charge against him.
3 Everyone arrested or detained in accordance with the provisions of paragraph 1(c) of this Article shall be brought promptly before a judge or other officer authorised by law to exercise judicial power and shall be entitled to trial within a reasonable time or to release pending trial. Release may be conditioned by guarantees to appear for trial.

4 Everyone who is deprived of his liberty by arrest or detention shall be entitled to take proceedings by which the lawfulness of his detention shall be decided speedily by a court and his release ordered if the detention is not lawful.

5 Everyone who has been the victim of arrest or detention in contravention of the provisions of this Article shall have an enforceable right to compensation.

Article 6: Right to a fair trial

1 In the determination of his civil rights and obligations or of any criminal charge against him, everyone is entitled to a fair and public hearing within a reasonable time by an independent and impartial tribunal established by law. Judgment shall be pronounced publicly but the press and public may be excluded from all or part of the trial in the interest of morals, public order or national security in a democratic society, where the interests of juveniles or the protection of the private life of the parties so require, or to the extent strictly necessary in the opinion of the court in special circumstances where publicity would prejudice the interests of justice.

2 Everyone charged with a criminal offence shall be presumed innocent until proved guilty according to law.

3 Everyone charged with a criminal offence has the following minimum rights:

(a) to be informed promptly, in a language which he understands and in detail, of the nature and cause of the accusation against him;

(b) to have adequate time and facilities for the preparation of his defence;

(c) to defend himself in person or through legal assistance of his own choosing or, if he has not sufficient means to pay for legal assistance, to be given it free when the interests of justice so require;

(d) to examine or have examined witnesses against him and to obtain the attendance and examination of witnesses on his behalf under the same conditions as witnesses against him;

(e) to have the free assistance of an interpreter if he cannot understand or speak the language used in court.

Article 7: No punishment without law

1 No one shall be held guilty of any criminal offence on account of any act or omission which did not constitute a criminal offence under national or international law at the time when it was committed. Nor shall a heavier penalty be imposed than the one that was applicable at the time the criminal offence was committed.

2 This Article shall not prejudice the trial and punishment of any person for any act or omission which, at the time when it was committed, was criminal according to the general principles of law recognised by civilised nations.

Article 8: Right to respect for private and family life

1 Everyone has the right to respect for his private and family life, his home and his correspondence.

2 There shall be no interference by a public authority with the exercise of this right except such as is in accordance with the law and is necessary in a democratic society in the interests of national security, public safety or the economic well-being of the country, for the prevention of disorder or crime, for the protection of health or morals, or for the protection of the rights and freedoms of others.

Article 9: Freedom of thought, conscience and religion

1 Everyone has the right to freedom of thought, conscience and religion; this right includes freedom to change his religion or belief and freedom, either alone or in community with others and in public or private, to manifest his religion or belief, in worship, teaching, practice and observance.

2 Freedom to manifest one's religion or beliefs shall be subject only to such limitations as are prescribed by law and are necessary in a democratic society in the interests of public safety, for the protection of public order, health or morals, or for the protection of the rights and freedoms of others.

Article 10: Freedom of expression

1 Everyone has the right to freedom of expression. This right shall include freedom to hold opinions and to receive and impart information and ideas without interference by public authority and regardless of frontiers. This Article shall not prevent States from requiring the licensing of broadcasting, television or cinema enterprises.

2 The exercise of these freedoms, since it carries with it duties and responsibilities, may be subject to such formalities, conditions, restrictions or penalties as are prescribed by law and are necessary in a democratic society, in the interests of national security, territorial integrity or public safety, for the prevention of disorder or crime, for the protection of health or morals, for the protection of the reputation or rights of others, for preventing the disclosure of information received in confidence, or for maintaining the authority and impartiality of the judiciary.

Article 11: Freedom of assembly and association

1 Everyone has the right to freedom of peaceful assembly and to freedom of association with others, including the right to form and to join trade unions for the protection of his interests.

2 No restrictions shall be placed on the exercise of these rights other than such as are prescribed by law and are necessary in a democratic society in the interests of national security or public safety, for the prevention of disorder or crime, for the protection of health or morals or for the protection of the rights and freedoms of others. This Article shall not prevent the imposition of lawful restrictions on the exercise of these rights by members of the armed forces, of the police or of the administration of the State.

Article 12: Right to marry

Men and women of marriageable age have the right to marry and to found a family, according to the national laws governing the exercise of this right.

Article 14: Prohibition of discrimination

The enjoyment of the rights and freedoms set forth in this Convention shall be secured without discrimination on any ground such as sex, race, colour, language, religion, political or other opinion, national or social origin, association with a national minority, property, birth or other status.

Article 16: Restrictions on political activity of aliens

Nothing in Articles 10, 11 and 14 shall be regarded as preventing the High Contracting Parties from imposing restrictions on the political activity of aliens.

Article 17: Prohibition of abuse of rights

Nothing in this Convention may be interpreted as implying for any State, group or person any right to engage in any activity or perform any act aimed at the destruction of any of the rights and freedoms set forth herein or at their limitation to a greater extent than is provided for in the Convention.

Article 18: Limitation on use of restrictions on rights

The restrictions permitted under this Convention to the said rights and freedoms shall not be applied for any purpose other than those for which they have been prescribed.

Part II: The First Protocol

Article 1: Protection of property

Every natural or legal person is entitled to the peaceful enjoyment of his possessions. No one shall be deprived of his possessions except in the public interest and subject to the conditions provided for by law and by the general principles of international law.

The preceding provisions shall not, however, in any way impair the right of a State to enforce such laws as it deems necessary to control the use of property in accordance with the general interest or to secure the payment of taxes or other contributions or penalties.

Article 2: Right to education

No person shall be denied the right to education. In the exercise of any functions which it assumes in relation to education and to teaching, the State shall respect the right of parents to ensure such education and teaching in conformity with their own religious and philosophical convictions.

Article 3: Right to free elections

The High Contracting Parties undertake to hold free elections at reasonable intervals by secret ballot, under conditions which will ensure the free expression of the opinion of the people in the choice of the legislature.

Part III: Article 1 of the Thirteenth Protocol

Abolition of the Death Penalty

The death penalty shall be abolished. No one shall be condemned to such penalty or executed.

APPENDIX B

Secondary legislation[1]

COURT OF PROTECTION RULES 2017

Part 1: The Overriding Objective

1.1 Overriding objective

(1) These Rules have the overriding objective of enabling the court to deal with a case justly and at proportionate cost, having regard to the principles contained in the Act.

(2) The court will seek to give effect to the overriding objective when it–
   (a) exercises any power under the Rules; or
   (b) interprets any rule or practice direction.

(3) Dealing with a case justly and at proportionate cost includes, so far as is practicable–
   (a) ensuring that it is dealt with expeditiously and fairly;
   (b) ensuring that P's interests and position are properly considered;
   (c) dealing with the case in ways which are proportionate to the nature, importance and complexity of the issues;
   (d) ensuring that the parties are on an equal footing;
   (e) saving expense;
   (f) allotting to it an appropriate share of the court's resources, while taking account of the need to allot resources to other cases; and
   (g) enforcing compliance with rules, practice directions and orders.

1.2 Participation of P

(1) The court must in each case, on its own initiative or on the application of any person, consider whether it should make one or more of the directions in paragraph (2), having regard to–
   (a) the nature and extent of the information before the court;
   (b) the issues raised in the case;
   (c) whether a matter is contentious; and
   (d) whether P has been notified in accordance with the provisions of Part 7 and what, if anything, P has said or done in response to such notification.

(2) The directions are that–
   (a) P should be joined as a party;
   (b) P's participation should be secured by the appointment of an accredited legal representative to represent P in the proceedings and to discharge such other functions as the court may direct;
   (c) P's participation should be secured by the appointment of a representative whose function shall be to provide the court with information as to the matters set out in section 4(6) of the Act and to discharge such other functions as the court may direct;
   (d) P should have the opportunity to address (directly or indirectly) the judge determining the application and, if so directed, the circumstances in which that should occur;
   (e) P's interests and position can properly be secured without any direction under sub-paragraphs (a) to (d) being made or by the making of an alternative direction meeting the overriding objective.

(3) Any appointment or directions made pursuant to paragraph (2)(b) to (e) may be made for such period or periods as the court thinks fit.

(4) Unless P has capacity to conduct the proceedings, an order joining P as a party shall only take effect–
   (a) on the appointment of a litigation friend on P's behalf; or
   (b) if the court so directs, on or after the appointment of an accredited legal representative.
(5) If the court has directed that P should be joined as a party but such joinder does not occur because no litigation friend or accredited legal representative is appointed, the court shall record in a judgment or order–
   (a) the fact that no such appointment was made; and
   (b) the reasons given for that appointment not being made.
(6) A practice direction may make additional or supplementary provision in respect of any of the matters set out in this rule.
   (The appointment of litigation friends, accredited legal representatives and representatives under paragraph (2)(c) is dealt with under Part 17.)
   ('Accredited legal representative' is defined in rule 2.1.)

Duties to further the overriding objective

1.3 Court's duty to manage cases

(1) The court must further the overriding objective by actively managing cases.
(2) The court must manage a case at all times and in particular–
   (a) when a case is referred to a judge;
   (b) at every hearing, whether listed by the court on its own initiative or on application by a party;
   (c) at all stages of a final hearing; and
   (d) when considering enforcement measures including committal.
(3) Active case management includes–
   (a) considering the appropriate case pathway for the case;
   (b) ensuring–
      (i) that the appropriate judge is allocated to the case;
      (ii) judicial continuity, so far as practicable;
   (c) avoiding delay and keeping costs down;
   (d) encouraging the parties to co-operate with each other in the conduct of the proceedings;
   (e) identifying at an early stage–
      (i) the issues; and
      (ii) who should be a party to the proceedings;
   (f) deciding promptly–
      (i) which issues need a full investigation and hearing and which do not; and
      (ii) the procedure to be followed in the case;
   (g) deciding the order in which issues are to be resolved;
   (h) encouraging the parties to use an alternative dispute resolution procedure if the court considers that appropriate;
   (i) fixing timetables or otherwise controlling the progress of the case;
   (j) considering whether the likely benefits of taking a particular step justify the cost of taking it;
   (k) dealing with as many aspects of the case as the court can on the same occasion;

(l) dealing with the case without the parties needing to attend at court;
(m) making use of technology;
(n) giving directions to ensure that the case proceeds quickly and efficiently;
(o) considering whether any hearing should be heard in public; and
(p) considering whether any document relating to proceedings should be a public document and, if so, whether and to what extent it should be redacted.

(Rules 4.2 to 4.4 make provision about the court's powers to authorise publication of information about proceedings and to order that a hearing be held in public.)

1.4 The duty of the parties

(1) The parties are required to help the court to further the overriding objective.
(2) Without prejudice to the generality of paragraph (1), each party is required to–
  (a) ask the court to take steps to manage the case if–
    (i) an order or direction of the court appears not to deal with an issue; or
    (ii) if a matter including any new circumstances, issue or dispute arises of which the court is unaware;
  (b) identify before issue if the case is within the scope of one of the case pathways and comply with the requirements of the applicable case pathway;
  (c) co-operate with the other parties and with the court in identifying and narrowing the issues that need to be determined by the court, and the timetable for that determination;
  (d) adhere to the timetable set by these Rules and by the court;
  (e) comply with all directions and orders of the court;
  (f) be full and frank in the disclosure of information and evidence to the court (including any disclosure ordered under Part 16);
  (g) co-operate with the other parties in all aspects of the conduct of the proceedings, including in the preparation of bundles.
(3) If the court determines that any party has failed without reasonable excuse to satisfy the requirements of this rule, it may under rule 19.5 depart from the general rules about costs in so far as they apply to that party.

(Rule 16.2(2) deals with the requirements of general disclosure.)

1.5 The duty of legal representatives

(1) Legal representatives of parties are required to help the court to further the overriding objective.
(2) Without prejudice to the generality of paragraph (1), a legal representative of a party must–
  (a) comply with any applicable rules, practice directions or orders of the court;
  (b) follow (where appropriate) the applicable case pathway; and
  (c) address whether the case can be swiftly resolved.

1.6 The duty of unrepresented litigants

(1) Without prejudice to the generality of rule 1.4, unrepresented litigants are required to help the court to further the overriding objective.
(2) This includes–
  (a) engaging with the process applicable in the case and co-operating with the court and the other parties;

(b) seeking the court's direction if an issue or dispute arises in the case;
(c) presenting their case fairly; and
(d) seeking early resolution of any dispute where practicable.

Part 2: Interpretation and general provisions

2.1 Interpretation

In these Rules–

'the Act' means the Mental Capacity Act 2005;

'accredited legal representative' means a legal representative authorised pursuant to a scheme of accreditation approved by the President to represent persons meeting the definition of 'P' in this rule in proceedings before the court;

'applicant' means a person who makes, or who seeks permission to make, an application to the court;

'application form' means the document that is to be used to begin proceedings in accordance with Part 9 of these Rules or any other provision of these Rules or the practice directions which requires the use of an application form;

'application notice' means the document that is to be used to make an application in accordance with Part 10 of these Rules or any other provision of these Rules or the practice directions which requires the use of an application notice;

'attorney' means the person appointed as such by an enduring power of attorney created, or purporting to have been created, in accordance with the regulations mentioned in paragraph 2 of Schedule 4 to the Act;

'business day' means a day other than–
(a) a Saturday, Sunday, Christmas Day or Good Friday; or
(b) a bank holiday in England and Wales, under the Banking and Financial Dealings Act 1971;

'child' means a person under 18;

'civil restraint order' means an order restraining a party–
(a) from making any further applications in current proceedings (a limited civil restraint order);
(b) from making certain applications in the Court of Protection (an extended civil restraint order); or
(c) from making any application in the Court of Protection (a general civil restraint order);

'court' means the Court of Protection;

'deputy' means a deputy appointed under the Act;

'donee' means the donee of a lasting power of attorney;

'donor' means the donor of a lasting power of attorney, except where the expression is used in rule 9.8 or 24.4(5) (where it means the donor of an enduring power of attorney);

'enduring power of attorney' means an instrument created in accordance with such of the regulations mentioned in paragraph 2 of Schedule 4 to the Act as applied when it was executed;

'filing' in relation to a document means delivering it, by post or otherwise, to the court office;

'hearing' includes a hearing conducted by telephone, video link, or any other method permitted or directed by the court;

'judge' means a judge nominated to be a judge of the court under the Act;
'lasting power of attorney' has the meaning given in section 9 of the Act;
'legal representative' means a–
(a) barrister;
(b) solicitor;
(c) solicitor's employee;
(d) manager of a body recognised under section 9 of the Administration of Justice Act 1985; or
(e) person who, for the purposes of the Legal Services Act 2007, is an authorised person in relation to an activity which constitutes the conduct of litigation (within the meaning of that Act),
who has been instructed to act for a party in relation to any application;
'legally aided person' means a person to whom civil legal services (within the meaning of the Legal Aid, Sentencing and Punishment of Offenders Act 2012) have been made available under arrangements made for the purposes of Part 1 of that Act;
'order' includes a declaration made by the court;
'P' means–
(a) any person (other than a protected party) who lacks or, so far as consistent with the context, is alleged to lack capacity to make a decision or decisions in relation to any matter that is the subject of an application to the court; and
(b) a relevant person as defined by paragraph 7 of Schedule A1 to the Act,
and references to a person who lacks capacity are to be construed in accordance with the Act;
'party' is to be construed in accordance with rule 9.13;
'personal welfare' is to be construed in accordance with section 17 of the Act;
'President' and 'Vice-President' refer to those judges appointed as such under section 46(3)(a) and (b) of the Act;
'property and affairs' is to be construed in accordance with section 18 of the Act;
'protected party' means a party or an intended party (other than P or a child) who lacks capacity to conduct the proceedings;
'representative' means a person appointed under rule 1.2(2)(c), except where the context otherwise requires;
'respondent' means a person who is named as a respondent in the application form or notice, as the case may be;
'rule 1.2 representative' means a representative or an accredited legal representative;
'Senior Judge' means the judge who has been nominated to be Senior Judge under section 46(4) of the Act, and references in these Rules to a circuit judge include the Senior Judge;
'Tier 1 Judge' means any judge nominated to act as a judge of the Court of Protection under section 46 of the Act who is neither a Tier 2 Judge nor a Tier 3 Judge;

'Tier 2 Judge' means–
(a) the Senior Judge; and
(b) such other judges nominated to act as a judge of the Court of Protection under section 46 of the Act as may be set out in the relevant practice direction;

'Tier 3 Judge' means–
(a) the President;
(b) the Vice-President; and
(c) such other judges nominated to act as a judge of the Court of Protection under section 46 of the Act as may be set out in the relevant practice direction;

'Visitor' means a person appointed as such by the Lord Chancellor under section 61 of the Act.

2.2 Court officers

(1) Where these Rules permit or require the court to perform an act of a purely formal or administrative character, that act may be performed by a court officer.
(2) A requirement that a court officer carry out any act at the request of any person is subject to the payment of any fee required by a fees order for the carrying out of that act.

2.3 Court officers – authorisation

(1) The Senior Judge or the President or the Vice-President may authorise a court officer to exercise the jurisdiction of the court in such circumstances as may be set out in the relevant practice direction.
(2) A court officer who has been authorised under paragraph (1)–
(a) must refer to a judge any application, proceedings or any question arising in any application or proceedings which ought, in the officer's opinion, to be considered by a judge;
(b) may not deal with any application or proceedings or any question arising in any application or proceedings by way of a hearing; and
(c) may not deal with an application for the reconsideration of an order made by that court officer or another court officer.

2.4 Computation of time

(1) This rule shows how to calculate any period of time which is specified–
(a) by these Rules;
(b) by a practice direction; or
(c) in an order or direction of the court.
(2) A period of time expressed as a number of days must be computed as clear days.
(3) In this rule, 'clear days' means that in computing the number of days–
(a) the day on which the period begins; and
(b) if the end of the period is defined by reference to an event, the day on which that event occurs,

are not included.

(4) Where the specified period is 7 days or less, and would include a day which is not a business day, that day does not count.

(5) When the specified period for doing any act at the court office ends on a day on which the office is closed, that act will be done in time if done on the next day on which the court office is open.

2.5 Application of the Civil Procedure Rules and Family Procedure Rules

(1) In any case not expressly provided for by these Rules or the practice directions made under them, the court may apply either the Civil Procedure Rules 1998 or the Family Procedure Rules 2010 (including in either case the practice directions made under them) with any necessary modifications, in so far as is necessary to further the overriding objective.

(2) A reference in these Rules to the Civil Procedure Rules 1998 or to the Family Procedure Rules 2010 is to the version of those rules in force at the date specified for the purpose of that reference in the relevant practice direction.

2.6 Pilot schemes

(1) Practice directions may make provision for the operation of pilot schemes for assessing the use of new practices and procedures in connection with proceedings–
  (a) for specified periods; and
  (b) in relation to proceedings–
    (i) in specified parts of the country; or
    (ii) relating to specified types of application.

(2) Practice directions may modify or disapply any provision of these Rules during the operation of such pilot schemes.

Part 3: Managing the case

3.1 The court's general powers of case management

(1) The list of powers in this rule is in addition to any powers given to the court by any other rule or practice direction or by any other enactment or any powers it may otherwise have.

(2) The court may–
  (a) extend or shorten the time for compliance with any rule, practice direction, or court order or direction (even if an application for extension is made after the time for compliance has expired);
  (b) adjourn or bring forward a hearing;
  (c) require P, a party, a party's legal representative or litigation friend, or P's rule 1.2 representative, to attend court;
  (d) hold a hearing and receive evidence by telephone or any other method of direct oral communication;
  (e) stay the whole or part of any proceedings or judgment either generally or until a specified date or event;
  (f) consolidate proceedings;
  (g) hear two or more applications on the same occasion;
  (h) direct a separate hearing of any issue;
  (i) decide the order in which issues are to be heard;
  (j) exclude an issue from consideration;
  (k) dismiss or give judgment on an application after a decision is made on a preliminary basis;
  (l) direct any party to file and serve an estimate of costs;

(m) direct or limit the means of communication to be used by the parties; and
(n) take any step or give any direction for the purpose of managing the case and furthering the overriding objective.

(3) A judge to whom a matter is allocated may, if the judge considers that the matter is one which ought properly to be dealt with by another judge, transfer the matter to such a judge.

(4) Where the court gives directions it may take into account whether or not a party has complied with any rule or practice direction.

(5) The court may make any order it considers appropriate even if a party has not sought that order.

(6) A power of the court under these Rules to make an order includes a power to vary or revoke the order.

(Rules 1.3 to 1.6 concern the duty of the court to further the overriding objective by actively managing cases, and the duty of parties, legal representatives and unrepresented litigants to assist the court in furthering the overriding objective.)

3.2 Case management – unrepresented parties

(1) This rule applies in any proceedings where at least one party is unrepresented.

(2) When the court is exercising any powers of case management, it must have regard to the fact that at least one party is unrepresented.

(3) The court must adopt such procedure at any hearing as it considers appropriate to further the overriding objective.

(4) At any hearing when the court is taking evidence, this may include–
(a) ascertaining from an unrepresented party the matters about which the witness may be able to give evidence or on which the witness ought to be cross-examined; and
(b) putting or causing to be put to the witness such questions as may appear to the court to be proper.

3.3 Court's power to dispense with requirement of any rule

In addition to its general powers and the powers listed in rule 3.1, the court may dispense with the requirements of any rule.

3.4 Exercise of powers on the court's own initiative

(1) Except where these Rules or another enactment make different provision, the court may exercise its powers on its own initiative.

(2) The court may make an order on its own initiative without hearing the parties or giving them the opportunity to make representations.

(3) Where the court proposes to make an order on its own initiative it may give the parties and any other person it thinks fit an opportunity to make representations and, where it does so, must specify the time by which, and the manner in which, the representations must be made.

(4) Where the court proposes–
(a) to make an order on its own initiative; and
(b) to hold a hearing to decide whether to make the order,
it must give the parties and may give any person it thinks likely to be affected by the order at least 3 days' notice of the hearing.

3.5 General power of the court to rectify matters where there has been an error of procedure

Where there has been an error of procedure, such as a failure to comply with a rule or practice direction–

(a) the error does not invalidate any step taken in the proceedings unless the court so orders; and

(b) the court may waive the error or require it to be remedied or may make such other order as appears to the court to be just.

3.6 Dealing with the application

(1) This rule and rule 3.7 are subject to any provision made by a practice direction in respect of the case pathway to which the case is allocated.

(2) As soon as practicable after any application has been issued the court shall consider how to deal with it.

(3) Where permission to start proceedings is required, and whether or not it has been applied for, the court's consideration under paragraph (2) shall include whether to grant or refuse permission without a hearing, or to direct a hearing to consider whether permission should be granted.

(4) The court may deal with an application or any part of an application at a hearing or without a hearing.

(5) In considering whether it is necessary to hold a hearing, the court shall, as appropriate, have regard to–

(a) the nature of the proceedings and the orders sought;

(b) whether the application is opposed by a person who appears to the court to have an interest in matters relating to P's best interests;

(c) whether the application involves a substantial dispute of fact;

(d) the complexity of the facts and the law;

(e) any wider public interest in the proceedings;

(f) the circumstances of P and of any party, in particular as to whether their rights would be adequately protected if a hearing were not held;

(g) whether the parties agree that the court should dispose of the application without a hearing; and

(h) any other matter specified in the relevant practice direction.

(6) Where the court considers that a hearing is necessary it shall–

(a) give notice of the hearing date to the parties and to any other person it directs;

(b) state what is to be dealt with at the hearing, including whether the matter is to be disposed of at that hearing; and

(c) consider whether it is appropriate–

(i) for the hearing or any part of it to be in public; and

(ii) to make any order under rule 4.1, 4.2 or 4.3.

(Rule 3.9 and Practice Direction 3B make provision about the case pathways.)

3.7 Directions

(1) The court may–

(a) give directions in writing; or

(b) set a date for a directions hearing; and

(c) do anything else that may be set out in a practice direction.

(2) When giving directions, the court may do any of the following–

(a) require a report under section 49 of the Act and give directions as to any such report;
(b) give directions as to any requirements contained in these Rules or a practice direction for the giving of notification to any person or for that person to do anything in response to a notification;
(c) if the court considers that any other person or persons should be a party to the proceedings, give directions joining them as a party;
(d) if the court considers that any party to the proceedings should not be a party, give directions for that person's removal as a party;
(e) give directions for the management of the case and set a timetable for the steps to be taken between the giving of directions and the hearing;
(f) subject to rule 3.8, give directions as to the type of judge who is to hear the case;
(g) give directions as to whether the proceedings or any part of them are to be heard in public, or as to whether any particular person should be permitted to attend the hearing, or as to whether any publication of the proceedings is to be permitted;
(h) give directions as to the disclosure of documents, service of witness statements and any expert evidence;
(i) give directions as to the attendance of witnesses and as to whether, and the extent to which, cross-examination will be permitted at any hearing; and
(j) give such other directions as the court may think fit.

(3) The court may give directions at any time–
(a) on its own initiative; or
(b) on the application of a party.

(4) Subject to paragraphs (5) and (6) and unless these Rules or a practice direction provide otherwise or the court directs otherwise, the time specified by a rule or by the court for a person to do any act may be varied by the written agreement of the parties.

(5) A party must apply to the court if that party wishes to vary–
(a) the date the court has fixed for the final hearing; or
(b) the period within which the final hearing is to take place.

(6) The time specified by a rule or practice direction or by the court may not be varied by the parties if the variation would make it necessary to vary the date the court has fixed for any hearing or the period within which the final hearing is to take place.

(Participation of P in proceedings is addressed in rule 1.2 (participation of P) and Part 17 (litigation friends and rule 1.2 representatives).)

Allocation of proceedings

3.8 Court's jurisdiction in certain kinds of cases to be exercised by certain judges

(1) A practice direction made under this rule may specify certain categories of case to be dealt with by a specific judge or a specific class of judges.

(2) Applications in any matter other than those specified in the practice direction referred to in paragraph (1) may be dealt with by any judge.

3.9 Allocation of cases to case pathways

(1) This rule provides for the allocation of cases to case pathways.
(2) There are three case pathways–
(a) the Personal Welfare Pathway;
(b) the Property and Affairs Pathway;
(c) the Mixed Welfare and Property Pathway.
(3) Each case shall on issue be allocated to one of the three case pathways unless (subject to paragraph (5)) it is in an excepted class of case.
(4) Excepted classes of case may be specified in a practice direction.
(5) The court may direct that a case shall be allocated to a case pathway notwithstanding that it is in an excepted class of cases.
(6) A practice direction may make provision for–
(a) the scope of each case pathway; and
(b) how cases in each case pathway are to be managed.
(Practice Direction 3B makes provision in relation to the case pathways and excepted classes of case.)

Part 4: Hearings

Private hearings

4.1 General rule – hearing to be held in private

(1) The general rule is that a hearing is to be held in private.
(2) A private hearing is a hearing which only the following persons are entitled to attend–
(a) the parties;
(b) P (whether or not a party);
(c) any person acting in the proceedings as a litigation friend or rule 1.2 representative;
(d) any legal representative of a person specified in any of sub-paragraphs (a) or (b); and
(e) any court officer.
(3) In relation to a private hearing, the court may make an order–
(a) authorising any person, or class of persons, to attend the hearing or a part of it; or
(b) excluding any person, or class of persons, from attending the hearing or a part of it.
(4) The general rule in paragraph (1) does not apply to a hearing for a committal order or writ of sequestration (in respect of which rule 21.27 makes provision).

4.2 Court's general power to authorise publication of information about proceedings

(1) For the purposes of the law relating to contempt of court, information relating to proceedings held in private (whether or not contained in a document filed with the court) may be communicated in accordance with paragraph (2) or (3).
(2) The court may make an order authorising–

(a) the publication or communication of such information or material relating to the proceedings as it may specify; or
(b) the publication of the text or a summary of the whole or part of a judgment or order made by the court.

(3) Subject to any direction of the court, information referred to in paragraph (1) may be communicated in accordance with Practice Direction 4A.

(4) Where the court makes an order under paragraph (2) it may do so on such terms as it thinks fit, and in particular may–
(a) impose restrictions on the publication of the identity of–
(i) any party;
(ii) P (whether or not a party);
(iii) any witness; or
(iv) any other person;
(b) prohibit the publication of any information that may lead to any such person being identified;
(c) prohibit the further publication of any information relating to the proceedings from such date as the court may specify; or
(d) impose such other restrictions on the publication of information relating to the proceedings as the court may specify.

(5) The court may on its own initiative or upon request authorise communication–
(a) for the purposes set out in Practice Direction 4A; or
(b) for such other purposes as it considers appropriate,
of information held by it.

Power to order a public hearing

4.3 Court's power to order that a hearing be held in public

(1) The court may make an order–
(a) for a hearing to be held in public;
(b) for a part of a hearing to be held in public; or
(c) excluding any person, or class of persons, from attending a public hearing or a part of it.

(2) Where the court makes an order under paragraph (1), it may in the same order or by a subsequent order–
(a) impose restrictions on the publication of the identity of–
(i) any party;
(ii) P (whether or not a party);
(iii) any witness; or
(iv) any other person;
(b) prohibit the publication of any information that may lead to any such person being identified;
(c) prohibit the further publication of any information relating to the proceedings from such date as the court may specify; or
(d) impose such other restrictions on the publication of information relating to the proceedings as the court may specify.

(3) A practice direction may provide for circumstances in which the court will ordinarily make an order under paragraph (1), and for the terms of the

order under paragraph (2) which the court will ordinarily make in such circumstances.

Supplementary

4.4 Supplementary provisions relating to public or private hearings

(1) Subject to provision in a practice direction made under rule 4.3(3), an order under rule 4.1, 4.2 or 4.3 may be made–
  (a) only where it appears to the court that there is good reason for making the order;
  (b) at any time; and
  (c) either on the court's own initiative or on an application made by any person in accordance with Part 10.

(2) A practice direction may make further provision in connection with–
  (a) private hearings;
  (b) public hearings; or
  (c) the publication of information about any proceedings.

Part 5: Court Documents

5.1 Documents used in court proceedings

(1) The court will seal or otherwise authenticate with the stamp of the court the following documents on issue–
  (a) an application form;
  (b) an application notice;
  (c) an order; and
  (d) any other document which a rule or practice direction requires to be sealed or stamped.

(2) Where the Rules or any practice direction require a document to be signed, that requirement is satisfied if the signature is printed by computer or other mechanical means.

(3) A practice direction may make provision for documents to be filed or sent to the court by–
  (a) facsimile; or
  (b) other means.

5.2 Documents required to be verified by a statement of truth

(1) The following documents must be verified by a statement of truth–
  (a) an application form, an application notice, an appellant's notice or a respondent's notice, where the applicant (or appellant or respondent as the case may be) seeks to rely upon matters set out in the document as evidence;
  (b) a witness statement;
  (c) a certificate of–
    (i) service or non-service; or
    (ii) notification or non-notification;
  (d) a deputy's declaration; and
  (e) any other document required by a rule or practice direction to be so verified.

(2) Subject to paragraph (3), a statement of truth is a statement that–

(a) the party putting forward the document;
(b) in the case of a witness statement, the maker of the witness statement; or
(c) in the case of a certificate referred to in paragraph (1)(c), the person who signs the certificate,

believes that the facts stated in the document being verified are true.

(3) If a party is conducting proceedings with a litigation friend, the statement of truth in–
(a) an application form;
(b) an application notice; or
(c) an appellant's notice or a respondent's notice,

is a statement that the litigation friend believes that the facts stated in the document being verified are true.

(4) The statement of truth must be signed–
(a) in the case of an application form, an application notice, an appellant's notice or a respondent's notice–
(i) by the party or litigation friend; or
(ii) by the legal representative on behalf of the party or litigation friend; and
(b) in the case of a witness statement, by the maker of the statement.

(5) A statement of truth which is not contained in the document which it verifies must clearly identify that document.

(6) A statement of truth in an application form, an application notice, an appellant's notice or a respondent's notice may be made by–
(a) a person who is not a party; or
(b) two or three parties jointly,

where this is permitted by a relevant practice direction.

5.3 Position statement not required to be verified by statement of truth

Nothing in these Rules requires a position statement to be verified by a statement of truth.

5.4 Failure to verify a document

If an application form, an application notice, an appellant's notice or a respondent's notice is not verified by a statement of truth, the applicant (or appellant or respondent as the case may be) may not rely upon the document as evidence of any of the matters set out in it unless the court permits.

5.5 Failure to verify a witness statement

If a witness statement is not verified by a statement of truth, it shall not be admissible in evidence unless the court permits.

5.6 False statements

(1) Proceedings for contempt of court may be brought against a person if that person makes, or causes to be made, a false statement in a document verified by a statement of truth without an honest belief in its truth.

(2) Proceedings under this rule may be brought only–
(i) by the Attorney General; or
(ii) with the permission of the court.

5.7 Personal details

(1) Where a party does not wish to reveal–
  (a) his or her home address or telephone number;
  (b) P's home address or telephone number;
  (c) the name of the person with whom P is living (if that person is not the applicant); or
  (d) the address or telephone number of his or her place of business, or the place of business of any of the persons mentioned in sub-paragraphs (b) or (c),

that party must provide those particulars to the court.

(2) Where paragraph (1) applies, the particulars given must not be given to any person unless the court so directs.

(3) Where a party changes home address during the course of the proceedings, that party must give notice in writing of the change to the court.

(4) Where a party does not reveal his or her home address, that party must nonetheless provide an address for service which must be within the jurisdiction of the court.

5.8 Supply of documents to a party from court records

Unless the court orders otherwise, a party to proceedings may inspect or obtain from the records of the court a copy of–
  (a) any document filed by a party to the proceedings; or
  (b) any communication in the proceedings between the court and–
    (i) a party to the proceedings; or
    (ii) another person.

5.9 Supply of documents to a non-party from court records

(1) Subject to rules 5.12 and 4.3(2), a person who is not a party to proceedings may inspect or obtain from the court records a copy of any judgment or order given or made in public.

(2) The court may, on an application made to it, authorise a person who is not a party to proceedings to–
  (a) inspect any other documents in the court records; or
  (b) obtain a copy of any such documents, or extracts from such documents.

(3) A person making an application for an authorisation under paragraph (2) must do so in accordance with Part 10.

(4) Before giving an authorisation under paragraph (2), the court will consider whether any document is to be provided on an edited basis.

5.10 Subsequent use of court documents

(1) Where a document has been filed or disclosed, a party to whom it was provided may use the document only for the purpose of the proceedings in which it was filed or disclosed, except where–
  (a) the document has been read to or by the court or referred to at a public hearing; or
  (b) the court otherwise permits.

(2) Paragraph (1)(a) is subject to any order of the court made under rule 4.3(2).

5.11 Editing information in court documents

(1) A party may apply to the court for an order that a specified part of a document is to be edited prior to the document's service or disclosure.

(2) An order under paragraph (1) may be made at any time.

(3) Where the court makes an order under this rule any subsequent use of that document in the proceedings shall be of the document as edited, unless the court directs otherwise.

(4) An application under this rule must be made in accordance with Part 10.

5.12 Public Guardian to be supplied with court documents relevant to supervision of deputies

(1) This rule applies in any case where the court makes an order–

(a) appointing a person to act as a deputy; or

(b) varying an order under which a deputy has been appointed.

(2) Subject to paragraphs (3) and (6), the Public Guardian is entitled to be supplied with a copy of qualifying documents if the Public Guardian reasonably considers that it is necessary to have regard to them in connection with the discharge of the Public Guardian's functions under section 58 of the Act in relation to supervision of deputies.

(3) The court may direct that the right to be supplied with documents under paragraph (2) does not apply in relation to such one or more documents, or descriptions of documents, as the court may specify.

(4) A direction under paragraph (3) or (6) may be given–

(a) either on the court's own initiative or on an application made to it; and

(b) either–

(i) at the same time as the court makes the order which appoints the deputy, or which varies it; or

(ii) subsequently.

(5) 'Qualifying documents' means documents which–

(a) are filed in court in connection with the proceedings in which the court makes the order referred to in paragraph (1); and

(b) are relevant to–

(i) the decision to appoint the deputy;

(ii) any powers conferred on the deputy;

(iii) any duties imposed on the deputy; or

(iv) any other terms applying to those powers and duties which are contained in the order.

(6) The court may direct that any document is to be provided to the Public Guardian on an edited basis.

5.13 Provision of court order to Public Guardian

Any order of the court requiring the Public Guardian to do something, or not to do something, must be served on the Public Guardian as soon as practicable and in any event not later than 7 days after the order was made.

5.14 Amendment of application

(1) The court may allow or direct an applicant, at any stage of the proceedings, to amend the application form or notice.

(2) The amendment may be effected by making in writing the necessary alterations to the application form or notice, but if the amendments are so

numerous or of such a nature or length that written alteration would make it difficult or inconvenient to read, a fresh document amended as allowed or directed may be required.

5.15 Clerical mistakes or slips

The court may at any time correct any clerical mistakes in an order or direction or any error arising in an order or direction from any accidental slip or omission.

5.16 Endorsement of amendment

Where an application form or notice, order or direction has been amended under this Part, a note shall be placed on it showing the date on which it was amended, and the alteration shall be sealed.

Part 6: Service of documents

Service generally

6.1 Scope

(1) Subject to paragraph (2), the Rules in this Part apply to–
 (a) the service of documents; and
 (b) the requirements under rule 9.10 for a person to be notified of the issue of an application form,

and references to 'serve', 'service', 'notice' and 'notify', and kindred expressions, shall be construed accordingly.

(2) The rules in this Part do not apply where–
 (a) any other enactment, a rule in another Part or a practice direction makes different provision; or
 (b) the court directs otherwise.

6.2 Who is to serve

(1) The general rule is that the following documents are to be served by the court–
 (a) an order or judgment of the court;
 (b) an acknowledgment of service or notification; and
 (c) except where the application is for an order for committal, a notice of hearing.

(2) Any other document is to be served by the party seeking to rely upon it, except where–
 (a) a rule or practice direction provides otherwise; or
 (b) the court directs otherwise.

(3) Where the court is to serve a document–
 (a) it is for the court to decide which of the methods of service specified in rule 6.3 is to be used; and
 (b) if the document is being served on behalf of a party, that party must provide sufficient copies.

6.3 Methods of service

(1) A document may be served by any of the methods specified in this rule.

(2) Where it is not known whether a solicitor is acting on behalf of a person, the document may be served by–

(a) delivering it to the person personally;
(b) delivering it to the person's home address or last known home address; or
(c) sending it to that address, or last known address, by first class post (or by an alternative method of service which provides for delivery on the next working day).

(3) Where a solicitor–
(a) is authorised to accept service on behalf of a person; and
(b) has informed the person serving the document in writing that the solicitor is so authorised,

the document must be served on the solicitor unless personal service is required by an enactment, rule, practice direction or court order.

(4) Where it appears to the court that there is a good reason to authorise service by a method other than those specified in paragraphs (2) and (3), the court may direct that service is to be effected by that method.

(5) A direction that service is to be effected by an alternative method must specify–
(a) the method of service; and
(b) the date on which the document will be deemed to be served.

(6) A practice direction may set out how documents are to be served by document exchange, electronic communication or other means.

6.4 Service of documents on children and protected parties

(1) The following table shows the person on whom a document must be served if it is a document which would otherwise be served on–
(a) a child; or
(b) a protected party.

Type of document	*Nature of party*	*Person to be served*
Application form	Child	–A person who has parental responsibility for the child within the meaning of the Children Act 1989; or –if there is no such person, a person with whom the child resides or in whose care the child is.
Application form	Protected party	–The person who is authorised to conduct the proceedings in the protected party's name or on the protected party's behalf; or –a person who is a duly appointed attorney, donee or deputy of the protected party; or –if there is no such person, a person with whom the protected party lives or in whose care the protected party is.

Application for an order appointing a litigation friend, where a child or protected party has no litigation friend	Child or protected party	–See rule 17.6 (appointment of litigation friend by court order– supplementary).
Any other document	Child or protected party	–The litigation friend or other duly authorised person who is conducting the proceedings on behalf of the child or protected party.

(2) The court may make an order for service on a child or a protected party by permitting the document to be served on some person other than the person specified in the table in paragraph (1) (which may include service on the child or the protected party).
(3) An application for an order under paragraph (2) may be made without notice.
(4) The court may order that, although a document has been served on someone other than the person specified in the table in paragraph (1), the document is to be treated as if it had been properly served.
(5) This rule does not apply in relation to the service of documents on a child in any case where the court has made an order under rule 17.2(4) permitting the child to conduct proceedings without a litigation friend.

6.5 Service of documents on P if P becomes a party

(1) If P becomes a party to the proceedings, all documents to be served on P must be served on P's litigation friend or as directed by the court on P's behalf.
(2) The court may make an order for service on P by permitting the document to be served on some person other than the person specified in paragraph (1) (which may include service on P).
(3) An application for an order under paragraph (2) may be made without notice.
(4) The court may order that, although a document has been served on someone other than a person specified in paragraph (1), the document is to be treated as if it had been properly served.
(5) This rule does not apply in relation to the service of documents on P in any case where the court has made an order under rule 17.5(1)(b) (power of court to bring to an end the appointment of a litigation friend).
(Rule 7.3 requires P to be notified where a direction has been made under rule 1.2, and of the appointment of a litigation friend, accredited legal representative or representative.)

6.6 Substituted service

Where it appears to the court that it is impracticable for any reason to serve a document in accordance with any of the methods provided under rule 6.3, the court may make an order for substituted service of the document by taking such steps as the court may direct to bring it to the notice of the person to be served.

6.7 Deemed service

(1) A document which is served in accordance with these Rules or any relevant practice direction shall be deemed to be served on the day shown in the following table.

Method of service	*Deemed day of service*
First class post (or other service for next-day delivery)	The second day after it was posted.
Document exchange	The second day after it was left at the document exchange.
Delivering the document to a permitted address	The day after it was delivered to that address.
Fax	If it is transmitted on a business day before 4 pm, on that day; or
	in any other case, on the business day after the day on which it is transmitted.
Other electronic means	The second day after the day on which it is transmitted.

(2) If a document is served personally–
(a) after 5 pm on a business day; or
(b) at any time on a Saturday, Sunday or a Bank Holiday,
it will be treated as being served on the next business day.

6.8 Certificate of service

(1) Where a rule, practice direction or court order requires a certificate of service for the document, the certificate must state the details set out in the following table.

Method of service	*Details to be certified*
First class post (or any other service for next-day delivery)	Date of posting.
Personal service	Date of personal service.
Document exchange	Date when the document was left at the document exchange.
Delivery of the document to a permitted address	Date when the document was delivered to that address.
Fax	Date of transmission.

Other electronic means	Date of transmission and the means used.
Alternative method permitted by the court	As required by the court.

(2) The certificate must be filed within 7 days after service of the document to which it relates.

6.9 Certificate of non-service

(1) Where an applicant or other person is unable to serve any document under these Rules or as directed by the court, that person must file a certificate of non-service stating the reasons why service has not been effected.

(2) The certificate of non-service must be filed within 7 days of the latest date on which service should have been effected.

6.10 Power of court to dispense with service

(1) The court may dispense with any requirement to serve a document.

(2) An application for an order to dispense with service may be made without notice.

Service out of the jurisdiction

6.11 Scope and interpretation

(1) This rule and rules 6.12 to 6.19 make provision about–

(a) service of application forms and other documents out of the jurisdiction; and

(b) the procedure for service.

(2) In this rule and rules 6.12 to 6.19–

'application form' includes an application notice;

'Commonwealth State' means a State listed in Schedule 3 to the British Nationality Act 1981;

'jurisdiction' means, unless the context otherwise requires, England and Wales and any part of the territorial waters of the United Kingdom adjoining England and Wales;

'the Service Convention' means the Convention on the service abroad of judicial and extra-judicial documents in civil or commercial matters signed at the Hague on November 15, 1965;

'Service Convention country' means a country which is a party to the Service Convention; and

(3) In rules 6.12 to 6.19, a reference to service by a party includes service by a person who is not a party where service by such a person is required under these Rules.

6.12 Service of application form and other documents out of the jurisdiction

(1) Subject to paragraph (2), any document to be served for the purposes of these Rules may be served out of the jurisdiction without the permission of the court.

(2) An application form may not be served out of the jurisdiction unless the court has power to determine the application to which it relates under the Act.

6.13 Period for acknowledging service or responding to application where application is served out of the jurisdiction

(1) This rule applies where, under these Rules, a party is required to file–
(a) an acknowledgment of service; or
(b) an answer to an application,
and sets out the time period for doing so where the application is served out of the jurisdiction.

(2) Where the applicant serves an application on a respondent in–
(a) Scotland or Northern Ireland; or
(b) a Service Convention country within Europe,
the period for filing an acknowledgment of service or an answer to an application is 21 days after service of the application.

(3) Where the applicant serves an application on a respondent in a Service Convention country outside Europe, the period for filing an acknowledgment of service or an answer to an application is 31 days after service of the application.

(4) Where the applicant serves an application on a respondent in a country not referred to in paragraphs (2) and (3), the period for filing an acknowledgment of service or an answer to an application is set out in Practice Direction 6B.

6.14 Method of service – general provisions

(1) This rule contains general provisions about the method of service of an application form or other document on a party out of the jurisdiction.

Where service is to be effected on a party in Scotland or Northern Ireland

(2) Where a party serves an application form or other document on a party in Scotland or Northern Ireland, it must be served by a method permitted by this Part.

Where service is to be effected out of the United Kingdom

(3) Where an application form or other document is to be served on a person out of the United Kingdom, it may be served by any method–
(a) provided for by–
(i) [Revoked.]
(ii) rule 6.16 (service through foreign governments, judicial authorities and British Consular authorities); or
(b) permitted by the law of the country in which it is to be served.

(4) Nothing in paragraph (3) or in any court order authorises or requires any person to do anything which is contrary to the law of the country where the application form or other document is to be served.

6.15 [Revoked.]

6.16 Service through foreign governments, judicial authorities and British Consular authorities

(1) Where an application form or other document is to be served on a person in a Service Convention country, it may be served–
(a) through the authority designated under the Service Convention in respect of that country; or
(b) if the law of that country permits, through–
(i) the judicial authorities of that country; or

(ii) a British Consular authority in that country.

(2) Where an application form or other document is to be served on a person in a country which is not a Service Convention country, it may be served, if the law of that country so permits, through–

(a) the government of that country, where that government is willing to serve it; or

(b) a British Consular authority in that country.

(3) Where an application form or other document is to be served in–

(a) any Commonwealth State which is not a Service Convention country;

(b) the Isle of Man or the Channel Islands; or

(c) any British Overseas Territory,

the methods of service permitted by paragraphs (1)(b) and (2) are not available and the person wishing to serve, or that person's agent, must effect service direct unless Practice Direction 6B provides otherwise.

(4) [Revoked.]

6.17 Procedure where service is to be through foreign governments, judicial authorities and British Consular authorities

(1) This rule applies where an application form or other document is to be served under rule 6.16(1) or (2).

(2) Where this rule applies, the person wishing to serve must file–

(a) a request for service of the application form or other document, by specifying one or more of the methods in rule 6.16(1) or (2);

(b) a copy of the application form or other document;

(c) any other documents or copies of documents required by Practice Direction 6B; and

(d) any translation required under rule 6.18.

(3) When the person wishing to serve files the documents specified in paragraph (2), the court officer must–

(a) seal, or otherwise authenticate with the stamp of the court, the copy of the application form; and

(b) forward the documents to the Senior Master of the Queen's Bench Division.

(4) The Senior Master shall send documents forwarded under this rule–

(a) where the application form or other document is being served through the authority designated under the Service Convention, to that authority; or

(b) in any other case, to the Foreign, Commonwealth and Development Office with a request that it arranges for the application form or other document to be served.

(5) An official certificate which–

(a) states that the method requested under paragraph (2)(a) has been performed and the date of such performance;

(b) states, where more than one method is requested under paragraph (2)(a), which method was used; and

(c) is made by–

(i) a British Consular authority in the country where the method requested under paragraph (2)(a) was performed;

(ii) the government or judicial authorities in that country; or

(iii) the authority designated in respect of that country under the Service Convention,

is evidence of the facts stated in the certificate.

(6) A document purporting to be an official certificate under paragraph (5) is to be treated as such a certificate unless it is proved not to be.

6.18 Translation of application form or other document

(1) Except where paragraphs (4) and (5) apply, every copy of the application form or other document filed under rule 6.16 (service through foreign governments, judicial authorities and British Consular authorities) must be accompanied by a translation of the application form or other document.

(2) The translation must be–

(a) in the official language of the country in which it is to be served; or

(b) if there is more than one official language of that country, in any official language which is appropriate to the place in the country where the application form or other document is to be served.

(3) Every translation filed under this rule must be accompanied by a statement by the person making it that it is a correct translation, and the statement must include that person's name, address and qualifications for making the translation.

(4) The applicant is not required to file a translation of the application form or other document filed under rule 6.16 where it is to be served in a country of which English is an official language.

(5) The applicant is not required to file a translation of the application form or other document filed under rule 6.16 where–

(a) the person on whom the document is to be served is able to read and understand English; and

(b) service of the document is to be effected directly on that person.

6.19 Undertaking to be responsible for expenses of the Foreign, Commonwealth and Development Office

Every request for service under rule 6.17 (procedure where service is to be through foreign governments, judicial authorities, etc) must contain an undertaking by the person making the request–

(a) to be responsible for all expenses incurred by the Foreign, Commonwealth and Development Office or foreign judicial authority; and

(b) to pay those expenses to the Foreign, Commonwealth and Development Office or foreign judicial authority on being informed of the amount.

Part 7: Notifying P

General requirement to notify P

7.1 General

(1) Subject to paragraphs (2) and (3), the rules in this Part apply where P is to be given notice of any matter or document, or is to be provided with any document, either under the Rules or in accordance with an order or direction of the court.

(2) Subject to rule 7.3, if P becomes a party, the rules in this Part do not apply and service is to be effected in accordance with Part 6 or as directed by the court.

(3) In any case the court may, either on its own initiative or on application, direct that P must not be notified of any matter or document, or provided with any document, whether in accordance with this Part or at all.
(4) Subject to paragraph (5), where P is a child–
(a) if the person to be notified under this rule is a person with parental responsibility for the child within the meaning of the Children Act 1989 or, if there is no such person, a person with whom the child resides or in whose care the child is;
(b) all references to 'P' in this Part, except that in paragraph (2), are to be read as referring to the person notified in accordance with sub-paragraph (a).
(5) Paragraph (4) does not apply, and there is no requirement to notify P, where the person referred to in paragraph (4)(a) has already been served or notified of the relevant matter in accordance with another rule or practice direction.

7.2 Who is to notify P
(1) Where P is to be notified under this Part, notification must be effected by–
(a) the applicant;
(b) the appellant (where the matter relates to an appeal);
(c) an agent duly appointed by the applicant or the appellant; or
(d) such other person as the court may direct.
(2) The person within paragraph (1) is referred to in this Part as 'the person effecting notification'.

7.3 Notifying P of appointment of a litigation friend, etc.
P must be notified–
(a) where a direction has been made under rule 1.2; and
(b) of the appointment of a litigation friend, accredited legal representative or representative on P's behalf.

Circumstances in which P must be notified

7.4 Application form
(1) P must be notified–
(a) that an application form has been issued by the court;
(b) that an application form has been withdrawn; and
(c) of the date on which a hearing is to be held in relation to the matter, where that hearing is for disposing of the application.
(2) Where P is to be notified that an application form has been issued, the person effecting notification must explain to P–
(a) who the applicant is;
(b) that the application raises the question of whether P lacks capacity in relation to a matter or matters, and what that means;
(c) what will happen if the court makes the order or direction that has been applied for; and
(d) where the application contains a proposal for the appointment of a person to make decisions on P's behalf in relation to the matter to which the application relates, details of who that person is.
(3) Where P is to be notified that an application form has been withdrawn, the person effecting notification must explain to P–
(a) that the application form has been withdrawn; and

(b) the consequences of that withdrawal.

(4) The person effecting notification must also inform P that P may seek advice and assistance in relation to any matter of which P is notified.

7.5 Appeals

(1) P must be notified–

(a) that an appellant's notice has been issued by the court;

(b) that an appellant's notice has been withdrawn; and

(c) of the date on which a hearing is to be held in relation to the matter, where that hearing is for disposing of the appellant's notice.

(2) Where P is to be notified that an appellant's notice has been issued, the person effecting notification must explain to P–

(a) who the appellant is;

(b) the issues raised by the appeal; and

(c) what will happen if the court makes the order or direction that has been applied for.

(3) Where P is to be notified that an appellant's notice has been withdrawn, the person effecting notification must explain to P–

(a) that the appellant's notice has been withdrawn; and

(b) the consequences of that withdrawal.

(4) The person effecting notification must also inform P that P may seek advice and assistance in relation to any matter of which P is notified.

7.6 Decisions and orders of the court

(1) P must be notified of any decision of the court relating to P except for a case management decision.

(2) Where P is notified in accordance with this rule, the person effecting notification must explain to P the effect of the decision.

(3) The person effecting notification must also inform P that P may seek advice and assistance in relation to any matter of which P is notified.

(4) The person effecting notification must also provide P with a copy of any order relating to a decision of which P must be notified in accordance with paragraph (1).

7.7 Other matters

(1) This rule applies where the court directs that P is to be notified of any other matter.

(2) The person effecting notification must explain to P such matters as may be directed by the court.

(3) The person effecting notification must also inform P that P may seek advice and assistance in relation to any matter of which P is notified.

Manner of notification and accompanying documents

7.8 Manner of notification

(1) Where P is to be notified under this Part, the person effecting notification must provide P with, or arrange for P to be provided with, the information specified in rules 7.3 to 7.7 in a way that is appropriate to P's circumstances

(for example, using simple language, visual aids or any other appropriate means).

(2) The information referred to in paragraph (1) must be provided to P personally.

(3) P must be provided with the information mentioned in paragraph (1) as soon as practicable and in any event within 14 days of the date on which–

(a) the application form or appellant's notice was issued or withdrawn;

(b) the decision was made;

(c) the person effecting notification received the notice of hearing from the court and in any event no later than 14 days before the date specified in the notice of the hearing; and

(d) the order referred to in rule 7.6(4) was served upon the person who is required to effect notification of P under that rule,

as the case may be.

(4) Where the provisions of rule 7.1(4) apply, paragraphs (1) and (2) of this rule do not apply and the person effecting notification may provide information and documents of which P must be notified to the person to be notified under rule 7.1(4), by any method by which service of documents would be permitted under rule 6.3.

7.9 Acknowledgment of notification

Where P is notified that an application form or an appellant's notice has been issued, P must also be provided with a form for acknowledging notification.

7.10 Certificate of notification

(1) The person effecting notification must, within 7 days beginning with the date on which notification in accordance with this Part was given, file a certificate of notification which certifies–

(a) the date on which, and how, P was notified; and

(b) that P was notified in accordance with this Part.

(2) Subject to paragraph (3), the person effecting notification in accordance with this Part must in the certificate required by paragraph (1) describe the steps taken to enable P to understand, and the extent to which P appears to have understood, the information.

(3) Where the provisions of rule 7.1(4) apply, paragraph (2) does not apply.

7.11 Dispensing with requirement to notify, etc.

(1) The applicant, the appellant or other person directed by the court to effect notification may apply to the court seeking an order–

(a) dispensing with the requirement to comply with the provisions in this Part; or

(b) requiring some other person to comply with the provisions in this Part.

(2) An application under this rule must be made in accordance with Part 10.

Part 8: Permission

8.1 General

Subject to these Rules and to section 50(1) of, and paragraph 20 of Schedule 3 to, the Act, the applicant must apply for permission to start proceedings under the Act.

(Section 50(1) of the Act specifies the persons who do not need to apply for permission. Paragraph 20 of Schedule 3 to the Act specifies an application for which permission is not needed.)

8.2 Where the court's permission is not required

The permission of the court is not required–

(a) where an application is made by–
  (i) the Official Solicitor; or
  (ii) the Public Guardian;
(b) where the application concerns–
  (i) P's property and affairs;
  (ii) a lasting power of attorney which is, or purports to be, created under the Act; or
  (iii) an instrument which is, or purports to be, an enduring power of attorney;
(c) where an application is made under section 21A of the Act;
(d) where an application is made for an order under section 16(2)(a) of the Act, which is to be relied on to authorise the deprivation of P's liberty pursuant to section 4A(3) of the Act;
(e) where an application is made in accordance with Part 10;
(f) where a person files an acknowledgment of service or notification in accordance with this Part or Part 9, for any order proposed that is different from that sought by the applicant; or
(g) in any other case specified for this purpose in a practice direction.

8.3 Permission – supplementary

Where part of the application concerns a matter which requires permission, and part of it does not, permission need only be sought for that part of it which requires permission.

8.4 Application for permission

Where permission is required, the applicant must apply for permission when making an application.

(Rule 3.6(3) explains how the court will deal with an application for permission.)

8.5 Service of an order giving or refusing permission

The court must serve–

(a) the order granting or refusing permission;
(b) if refusing permission without a hearing, the reasons for its decision in summary form; and
(c) any directions,

on the applicant and on any other person served with or notified of the application form.

8.6 Appeal against a permission decision following a hearing

Where the court grants or refuses permission following a hearing, any appeal against the permission decision shall be dealt with in accordance with Part 20 (appeals).

(Rule 13.4 deals with reconsideration of orders and decisions made without a hearing or without notice to any person who is affected by such order or decision.)

Part 9: How to start and respond to proceedings, and parties to proceedings

Initial steps

9.1 General

(1) Applications to the court to start proceedings must be made in accordance with this Part and, as applicable, Part 8 and the relevant practice directions.

(2) The appropriate forms must be used in the cases to which they apply, with such variations as the case requires, but not so as to omit any information or guidance which any form gives to the intended recipient.

9.2 When proceedings are started

(1) The general rule is that proceedings are started when the court issues an application form at the request of the applicant.

(2) An application form is issued on the date entered on the application form by the court.

9.3 Contents of the application form

The application form must–

(a) state the matter which the applicant wants the court to decide;
(b) state the order which the applicant is seeking;
(c) name–
   (i) the applicant;
   (ii) P;
   (iii) as a respondent, any person (other than P) whom the applicant reasonably believes to have an interest which means that that person ought to be heard in relation to the application (as opposed to being notified of it in accordance with rule 9.10);
   (iv) any person whom the applicant intends to notify in accordance with rule 9.10; and
(d) if the applicant is applying in a representative capacity, state what that capacity is.

9.4 Documents to be filed with the application form

Where an applicant files the application form with the court, the applicant must also file–

(a) in accordance with the relevant practice direction, any evidence on which the applicant intends to rely;
(b) an assessment of capacity form, where this is required by the relevant practice direction;
(c) any other documents referred to in the application form; and
(d) such other information and material as may be set out in a practice direction.

9.5 What the court will do when an application form is filed

As soon as practicable after an application form is filed the court must issue it and do anything else that may be set out in a practice direction.

Steps following issue of application form

9.6 Applicant to serve the application form on named respondents

(1) As soon as practicable and in any event within 14 days of the date on which the application form was issued, the applicant must serve a copy of the application form on any person who is named as a respondent in the application form, together with copies of any documents filed in accordance with rule 9.4 and a form for acknowledging service.

(2) The applicant must file a certificate of service within 7 days beginning with the date on which the documents were served.

9.7 Applications relating to lasting powers of attorney

(1) Where the application concerns the powers of the court under section 22 or 23 of the Act (powers of the court in relation to the validity and operation of lasting powers of attorney) the applicant must serve a copy of the application form, together with copies of any documents filed in accordance with rule 9.4 and a form for acknowledging service–

(a) unless the applicant is the donor or donee of the lasting power of attorney ('the power'), on the donor and every donee of the power;

(b) if the applicant is the donor, on every donee of the power; or

(c) if the applicant is a donee, on the donor and any other donee of the power,

but only if the persons mentioned in sub-paragraphs (a) to (c) have not been served or notified under any other rule.

(2) Where the application is solely in respect of an objection to the registration of the power, the requirements of rules 9.6 and 9.10 do not apply to an application made under this rule by–

(a) a donee of the power; or

(b) a person named in a statement made by the donor of the power in accordance with paragraph 2(1)(c)(i) of Schedule 1 to the Act.

(3) The applicant must comply with paragraph (1) as soon as practicable and in any event within 14 days of the date on which the application form was issued.

(4) The applicant must file a certificate of service with 7 days beginning with the date on which the documents were served.

(5) Where the applicant knows or has reasonable grounds to believe that the donor of the power lacks capacity to make a decision in relation to any matter that is the subject of the application, the applicant must notify the donor in accordance with Part 7.

9.8 Applications relating to enduring powers of attorney

(1) Where the application concerns the powers of the court under paragraphs 2(9), 4(5)(a) and (b), 7(2), 10(c), 13, or 16(2), (3), (4) and (6) of Schedule 4 to the Act, the applicant must serve a copy of the application form, together with copies of any documents filed in accordance with rule 9.4 and a form for acknowledging service–

(a) unless the applicant is the donor or attorney under the enduring power of attorney ('the power'), on the donor and every attorney under the power;

(b) if the applicant is the donor, on every attorney under the power; or

(c) if the applicant is an attorney, on the donor and any other attorney under the power, but only if the persons mentioned in sub-paragraphs (a) to (c) have not been served or notified under any other rule.

(2) Where the application is solely in respect of an objection to the registration of the power, the requirements of rules 9.6 and 9.10 do not apply to an application made under this rule by–
(a) an attorney under the power; or
(b) a person listed in paragraph 6(1) of Schedule 4 to the Act.

(3) The applicant must comply with paragraph (1) as soon as practicable and in any event within 14 days of the date on which the application form was issued.

(4) The applicant must file a certificate of service within 7 days beginning with the date on which the documents were served.

(5) Where the applicant knows or has reasonable grounds to believe that the donor of the power lacks capacity to make a decision in relation to any matter that is the subject of the application, the applicant must notify the donor in accordance with Part 7.

9.9 Applicant to notify P of an application

P must be notified in accordance with Part 7 that an application form has been issued, unless the requirement to do so has been dispensed with under rule 7.11.

9.10 Applicant to notify other persons of an application

(1) As soon as practicable and in any event within 14 days of the date on which the application form was issued, the applicant must notify the persons specified in the relevant practice direction–
(a) that an application has been issued;
(b) whether it relates to the exercise of the court's jurisdiction in relation to P's property and affairs, or P's personal welfare, or to both; and
(c) of the order or orders sought.

(2) Notification of the issue of the application form must be accompanied by a form for acknowledging notification.

(3) The applicant must file a certificate of notification within 7 days beginning with the date on which notification was given.

9.11 Requirements for certain applications

A practice direction may make additional or different provision in relation to specified applications.

Responding to an application

9.12 Responding to an application

(1) A person who is served with or notified of an application form and who wishes to take part in proceedings must file an acknowledgment of service or notification in accordance with this rule.

(2) The acknowledgment of service or notification must be filed not more than 14 days after the application form was served or notification of the application was given.

(3) The court must serve the acknowledgment of service or notification on the applicant and on any other person who has filed such an acknowledgment.

(4) The acknowledgment of service or notification must–
 (a) state whether the person acknowledging service or notification consents to the application;
 (b) state whether that person opposes the application and, if so, set out the grounds for doing so;
 (c) state whether that person seeks a different order from that set out in the application form and, if so, set out what that order is;
 (d) provide an address for service, which must be within the jurisdiction of the court; and
 (e) be signed by that person or that person's legal representative.

(5) Subject to rules 15.2 and 15.5 (restriction on filing an expert's report and court's power to restrict expert evidence), unless the court directs otherwise, where a person who has been served in accordance with rule 9.6, 9.7 or 9.8 opposes the application or seeks a different order, that person must within 28 days of such service file a witness statement containing any evidence upon which that person intends to rely.

(6) In addition to complying with the other requirements of this rule, an acknowledgment of notification filed by a person notified of the application in accordance with rule 9.7(5), 9.8(5), 9.9 or 9.10 must–
 (a) indicate whether the person wishes to be joined as a party to the proceedings; and
 (b) state the person's interest in the proceedings.

(7) Subject to rules 15.2 and 15.5 (restriction on filing an expert's report and court's power to restrict expert evidence), unless the court directs otherwise, where a person has been notified in accordance with rule 9.7(5), 9.8(5), 9.9 or 9.10, that person must within 28 days of such notification file a witness statement containing any evidence of that person's interest in the proceedings and, if that person opposes the application or seeks a different order, any evidence upon which that person intends to rely.

(8) The court must consider whether to join a person mentioned in paragraph (6) as a party to the proceedings and, if it decides to do so, must make an order to that effect.

(9) Where a person who is notified in accordance with rule 9.7(5), 9.8(5), 9.9 or 9.10 complies with the requirements of this rule, that person need not comply with the requirements of rule 9.15 (application to be joined as a party).

(10) A practice direction may make provision about responding to applications.

The parties to the proceedings

9.13 Parties to the proceedings

(1) Unless the court directs otherwise, the parties to any proceedings are–
 (a) the applicant; and
 (b) any person who is named as a respondent in the application form and who files an acknowledgment of service in respect of the application form.

(2) The court may order a person to be joined as a party if it considers that it is desirable to do so for the purpose of dealing with the application.

(3) The court may at any time direct that any person who is a party to the proceedings is to be removed as a party.

(4) Unless the court orders otherwise, P shall not be named as a respondent to any proceedings.
(5) A party to the proceedings is bound by any order or direction of the court made in the course of those proceedings.

9.14 Persons to be bound as if parties

(1) The persons mentioned in paragraph (2) shall be bound by any order made or directions given by the court in the same way that a party to the proceedings is so bound.
(2) The persons referred to in paragraph (1) are–
   (a) P; and
   (b) any person who has been served with or notified of an application form in accordance with these Rules.

9.15 Application to be joined as a party

(1) Any person with sufficient interest may apply to the court to be joined as a party to the proceedings.
(2) An application to be joined as a party must be made by filing an application notice in accordance with Part 10, which must–
   (a) state the full name and address of the person seeking to be joined as a party to the proceedings;
   (b) state that person's interest in the proceedings;
   (c) state whether that person consents to the application;
   (d) state whether that person opposes the application and, if so, set out the grounds for doing so;
   (e) state whether that person proposes that an order different from that set out in the application form should be made and, if so, set out what that order is;
   (f) provide an address for service, which must be within the jurisdiction of the court; and
   (g) be signed by that person or that person's legal representative.
(3) Subject to rules 15.2 and 15.5 (restriction on filing an expert's report and court's power to restrict expert evidence), a person's application to be joined must be accompanied by–
   (a) a witness statement containing evidence of that person's interest in the proceedings and, if that person proposes that an order different from that set out in the application form should be made, the evidence on which that person intends to rely; and
   (b) a sufficient number of copies of the application notice to enable service of the application on every other party to the proceedings.
(4) The court must serve the application notice and any accompanying documents on all parties to the proceedings.
(5) The court must consider whether to join a person applying under this rule as a party to the proceedings and, if it decides to do so, must make an order to that effect.

9.16 Application for removal as a party to proceedings

A person who wishes to be removed as a party to the proceedings must apply to the court for an order to that effect in accordance with Part 10.

Part 10: Applications within proceedings

10.1 Types of applications for which the Part 10 procedure may be used

(1) The Part 10 procedure is the procedure set out in this Part.

(2) The Part 10 procedure may be used if the application is made by any person–

(a) in the course of existing proceedings; or

(b) as provided for in a rule or practice direction.

(3) The court may grant an interim remedy before an application form has been issued only if–

(a) the matter is urgent; or

(b) it is otherwise necessary to do so in the interests of justice.

(4) An application made during the course of existing proceedings includes an application made during appeal proceedings.

(5) Where the application seeks solely to withdraw an existing application–

(a) the applicant must file a written request for permission setting out succinctly the reasons for the request;

(b) the request must be in an application notice;

(c) the court may permit an application to be made orally at a hearing or in such alternative written form as it thinks fit.

(6) Where the court deals with a written request under paragraph (5) without a hearing, rule 13.4 applies to any order so made.

(Rule 13.2 requires the court's permission to withdraw proceedings.)

10.2 Application notice to be filed

(1) Subject to paragraph (5), the applicant must file an application notice to make an application under this Part.

(2) The applicant must, when filing the application notice, file the evidence on which the applicant relies (unless such evidence has already been filed).

(3) The court must issue the application notice and, if there is to be a hearing, give notice of the date on which the matter is to be heard by the court.

(4) Notice under paragraph (3) must be given to–

(a) the applicant;

(b) anyone who is named as a respondent in the application notice (if not otherwise a party to the proceedings);

(c) every party to the proceedings; and

(d) any other person, as the court may direct.

(5) An applicant may make an application under this Part without filing an application notice if–

(a) this is permitted by any rule or practice direction; or

(b) the court dispenses with the requirement for an application notice.

(6) If the applicant makes an application without giving notice, the evidence in support of the application notice must state why notice has not been given.

10.3 What an application notice must include

An application notice must state–

(a) what order or direction the applicant is seeking;

(b) briefly, the grounds on which the applicant is seeking the order or direction; and

(c) such other information as may be required by any rule or practice direction.

10.4 Service of an application notice

(1) Subject to paragraphs (4) and (5), the applicant must serve a copy of the application notice on–
   (a) anyone who is named as a respondent in the application notice (if not otherwise a party to the proceedings);
   (b) every party to the proceedings; and
   (c) any other person, as the court may direct,
   as soon as possible and in any event within 14 days of the date on which it was issued.
(2) The application notice must be accompanied by a copy of the evidence filed in support.
(3) The applicant must file a certificate of service within 7 days beginning with the date on which the documents were served.
(4) This rule does not require a copy of evidence to be served on a person on whom it has already been served, but the applicant must in such a case give to that person notice of the evidence on which the applicant intends to rely.
(5) An application may be made without serving a copy of the application notice if this is permitted by–
   (a) a rule;
   (b) a practice direction; or
   (c) the court.

10.5 Applications without notice

(1) This rule applies where the court has dealt with an application which was made without notice having been given to any person.
(2) Where the court makes an order, whether granting or dismissing the application, the applicant must, as soon as practicable or within such period as the court may direct, serve the documents mentioned in paragraph (3) on–
   (a) anyone named as a respondent in the application notice (if not otherwise a party to the proceedings);
   (b) every party to the proceedings; and
   (c) any other person, as the court may direct,
(3) The documents referred to in paragraph (2) are–
   (a) a copy of the application notice;
   (b) the court's order; and
   (c) any evidence filed in support of the application.
   (Rule 13.4 provides for reconsideration of orders made without a hearing or without notice to a person.)

10.6 Security for costs

(1) A respondent to any application may apply for security for the respondent's costs of the proceedings.
(2) An application for security for costs must be supported by written evidence.
(3) Where the court makes an order for security for costs, it must–
   (a) determine the amount of security; and
   (b) direct–
      (i) the manner in which; and
      (ii) the time within which,
   the security must be given.

10.7 Conditions to be satisfied

(1) The court may make an order for security for costs under rule 10.6–
 (a) if it is satisfied, having regard to all the circumstances of the case, that it is just to make such an order; and
 (b) if–
  (i) one or more of the conditions in paragraph (2) applies; or
  (ii) an enactment permits the court to require security for costs.

(2) The conditions are–
 (a) the applicant is resident out of the Jurisdiction;
 (b) the applicant is a company or other body (whether incorporated inside or outside Great Britain) and there is reason to believe that it will be unable to pay the respondent's costs if ordered to do so;
 (c) the applicant has changed address since proceedings were commenced with a view to avoiding the consequences of the litigation;
 (d) the applicant failed to give an address, or gave an incorrect address, in the application form commencing the proceedings;
 (e) the applicant is acting as a nominal applicant and there is reason to believe that the applicant will be unable to pay the respondent's costs if ordered to do so;
 (f) the applicant has taken steps in relation to the applicant's assets that would make it difficult to enforce an order for costs against the applicant.

10.8 Security for costs other than from the applicant

(1) The respondent may seek an order against a person other than the applicant, and the court may make an order for security for costs against that person, if–
 (a) it is satisfied, having regard to all the circumstances of the case, that it is just to make such an order; and
 (b) one or more of the conditions in paragraph (2) applies.

(2) The conditions are that the person–
 (a) has assigned the right to the substantive matter to the applicant with a view to avoiding the possibility of a costs order being made against the person; or
 (b) has contributed or agreed to contribute to the applicant's costs in return for a share of any money or property which the applicant may recover or be awarded in the proceedings; and

is a person against whom a costs order may be made.

(Rule 19.12 makes provision about costs orders against non-parties.)

10.9 Security for costs of an appeal

(1) The court may order security for costs of an appeal against–
 (a) an appellant;
 (b) a respondent who also appeals,

on the same grounds as it may order security for costs against an applicant under rule 10.6.

(2) The court may also make an order under paragraph (1) where the appellant or the respondent who also appeals is a limited company and there is reason to believe it will be unable to pay the costs of the other parties to the appeal should its appeal be unsuccessful.

Interim remedies

10.10 Orders for interim remedies

(1) The court may grant the following interim remedies–
(a) an interim injunction;
(b) an interim declaration; or
(c) any other interim order it considers appropriate.

(2) Unless the court orders otherwise, a person on whom an application form is served under Part 9, or who is given notice of such an application, may not apply for an interim remedy before filing an acknowledgment of service or notification in accordance with Part 9.

(3) This rule does not limit any other power of the court to grant interim relief.

Part 11: Deprivation of liberty

11.1 Deprivation of liberty

The practice direction to this Part sets out procedure governing–
(a) applications to the court for orders relating to the deprivation, or proposed deprivation, of liberty of P; and
(b) proceedings (for example, relating to costs or appeals) connected with or consequent on such applications.

Part 12: Human rights

12.1 General

(1) A party who seeks to rely upon any provision of or right arising under the Human Rights Act 1998 ('the 1998 Act') or who seeks a remedy available under that Act must inform the court in the manner set out in the relevant practice direction specifying–
(a) the Convention right (within the meaning of the 1998 Act) which it is alleged has been infringed and details of the alleged infringement; and
(b) the remedy sought and whether this includes a declaration of incompatibility under section 4 of the 1998 Act.

(2) The court may not make a declaration of incompatibility unless 21 days' notice, or such other period of notice as the court directs, has been given to the Crown.

(3) Where notice has been given to the Crown, a Minister or other person permitted by the 1998 Act shall be joined as a party on filing an application in accordance with rule 9.15 (application to be joined as a party).

Part 13: Jurisdiction, withdrawal of proceedings, participation and reconsideration

Disputing the jurisdiction of the court

13.1 Procedure for disputing the court's jurisdiction

(1) A person who wishes to–
(a) dispute the court's jurisdiction to hear an application; or
(b) argue that the court should not exercise its jurisdiction,
may apply to the court at any time for an order declaring that it has no such

jurisdiction or should not exercise any jurisdiction that it may have.

(2) An application under this rule must be–
  (a) made by using the form specified in the relevant practice direction; and
  (b) supported by evidence.

(3) An order containing a declaration that the court has no jurisdiction or will not exercise its jurisdiction may also make further provision, including–
  (a) setting aside the application;
  (b) discharging any order made;
  (c) staying the proceedings;
  (d) discharging any litigation friend or rule 1.2 representative.

Withdrawal of proceedings

13.2 Permission required to withdraw proceedings

(1) Proceedings may only be withdrawn with the permission of the court.

(2) An application to withdraw proceedings must be made in accordance with Part 10.

Participation in hearings

13.3 Participation in hearings

(1) The court may hear P on the question of whether or not an order should be made, whether or not P is a party to the proceedings.

(2) The court may proceed with a hearing in the absence of P if it considers that it would be appropriate to do so.

(3) A person other than P who is served with or notified of the application may only take part in a hearing if–
  (a) that person files an acknowledgment in accordance with these Rules and is made a party to the proceedings; or
  (b) the court permits.

(Rule 1.2 deals with participation of P.)

Reconsideration of court orders

13.4 Orders made without a hearing or without notice to any person

(1) This rule applies where the court makes an order–
  (a) without a hearing; or
  (b) without notice to any person who is affected by it.

(2) Where this rule applies–
  (a) P;
  (b) any party to the proceedings; or
  (c) any other person affected by the order,

may apply to the court for reconsideration of the order made.

(3) An application under paragraph (2) must be made–
  (a) within 21 days of the order being served or such other period as the court may direct; and
  (b) in accordance with Part 10.

(4) The court shall–

(a) reconsider the order without directing a hearing; or
(b) fix a date for the matter to be heard and notify all parties to the proceedings, and such other persons as the court may direct, of that date.

(5) Where an application is made in accordance with this rule, the court may affirm, set aside or vary any order made.
(6) An order made by a court officer authorised under rule 2.3 may be reconsidered by any judge.
(7) An order made by a Tier 1 Judge may be reconsidered by any judge.
(8) An order made by a Tier 2 Judge may be reconsidered by any Tier 2 Judge or by a Tier 3 Judge.
(9) An order made by a Tier 3 Judge may be reconsidered by any Tier 3 Judge.
(10) In any case to which paragraphs (7) to (9) apply the reconsideration may be carried out by the judge who made the order being reconsidered.
(11) No application may be made seeking a reconsideration of–
(a) an order that has been made under paragraph (5); or
(b) an order granting or refusing permission to appeal.

(12) An appeal against an order made under paragraph (5) may be made in accordance with Part 20 (appeals).
(13) Any order made without a hearing or without notice to any person, other than one made under paragraph (5) or one granting or refusing permission to appeal, must contain a statement of the right to apply for a reconsideration of the decision in accordance with this rule.
(14) An application made under this rule may include a request that the court reconsider the matter at a hearing.
(Rule 2.3(2)(c) provides that a court officer authorised under that rule may not deal with an application for the reconsideration of an order made by that court officer or another court officer.)

Part 14: Admissions, evidence and depositions

Admissions

14.1 Making an admission

(1) Without prejudice to the ability to make an admission in any other way, a party may admit the truth of the whole or part of another party's case by giving notice in writing.
(2) The court may allow a party to amend or withdraw an admission.

Evidence

14.2 Power of court to control evidence

The court may–
(a) control the evidence by giving directions as to–
(i) the issues on which it requires evidence;
(ii) the nature of the evidence which it requires to decide those issues; and
(iii) the way in which the evidence is to be placed before the court;

(b) use its power under this rule to exclude evidence that would otherwise be admissible;
(c) allow or limit cross-examination;
(d) admit such evidence, whether written or oral, as it thinks fit; and
(e) admit, accept and act upon such information, whether oral or written, from P, any protected party or any person who lacks competence to give evidence, as the court considers sufficient, although not given on oath and whether or not it would be admissible in a court of law apart from this rule.

14.3 Evidence of witnesses – general rule

(1) The general rule is that any fact which needs to be proved by evidence of a witness is to be proved–
(a) where there is a final hearing, by the witness's oral evidence; or
(b) at any other hearing, or if there is no hearing, by the witness's evidence in writing.
(2) Where a witness is called to give oral evidence under paragraph (1)(a), the witness statement of that witness shall stand as his or her evidence in chief unless the court directs otherwise.
(3) A witness giving oral evidence at the final hearing may, if the court permits–
(a) amplify his or her witness statement; and
(b) give evidence in relation to new matters which have arisen since the witness statement was made.
(4) The court may so permit only if it considers that there is good reason not to confine the evidence of the witness to the contents of the witness statement.
(5) This rule is subject to–
(a) any provision to the contrary in these Rules or elsewhere; or
(b) any order or direction of the court.

14.4 Written evidence – general rule

A party may not rely on written evidence unless–
(a) it has been filed in accordance with these Rules or a practice direction;
(b) it is expressly permitted by these Rules or a practice direction; or
(c) the court gives permission.

14.5 Evidence by video link or other means

The court may allow a witness to give evidence through a video link or by other communication technology.

14.6 Service of witness statements for use at final hearing

(1) A witness statement is a written statement by a person which contains the evidence which that person would be allowed to give orally.
(2) The court will give directions about the service of any witness statement upon which a party intends to rely at the final hearing.
(3) The court may give directions as to the order in which witness statements are to be served.

(Rules 5.2 and 14.7 require witness statements to be verified by a statement of truth.)

14.7 Form of witness statement

A witness statement must contain a statement of truth and comply with the requirements set out in the relevant practice direction.

14.8 Witness summaries

(1) A party who wishes to file a witness statement for use at the final hearing, but is unable to do so, may apply without notice to be permitted to file a witness summary instead.

(2) A witness summary is a summary of–

(a) the evidence, if known, which would otherwise be included in a witness statement; or

(b) if the evidence is not known, the matters about which the party filing the witness summary proposes to question the witness.

(3) Unless the court directs otherwise, a witness summary must include the name and address of the intended witness.

(4) Unless the court directs otherwise, a witness summary must be filed within the period in which a witness statement would have had to be filed.

(5) Where a party files a witness summary, so far as practicable, rules 14.3(3)(a) (amplifying witness statements) and 14.6 (service of witness statements for use at final hearing) shall apply to the summary.

14.9 Affidavit evidence

Evidence must be given by affidavit instead of or in addition to a witness statement if this is required by the court, a provision contained in any rule, a practice direction or any other enactment.

14.10 Form of affidavit

An affidavit must comply with the requirements set out in the relevant practice direction.

14.11 Affidavit made outside the jurisdiction

A person may make an affidavit outside the jurisdiction in accordance with–

(a) this Part; or

(b) the law of the place where that person makes the affidavit.

14.12 Notarial acts and instruments

A notarial act or instrument may, without further proof, be received in evidence as duly authenticated in accordance with the requirements of law unless the contrary is proved.

14.13 Summoning of witnesses

(1) The court may allow or direct any party to issue a witness summons requiring the person named in it to attend before the court and give oral evidence or produce any document to the court.

(2) An application by a party for the issue of a witness summons may be made by filing an application notice with includes–

(a) the name and address of the applicant and the applicant's solicitor, if any;

(b) the name, address and occupation of the proposed witness;

(c) particulars of any document which the proposed witness is to be required to produce; and

(d) the grounds on which the application is made.

(3) The general rule is that a witness summons is binding if it is served at least 7 days before the date on which the witness is required to attend

before the court, and the requirements of paragraph (6) have been complied with.

(4) The court may direct that a witness summons shall be binding although it will be served less than 7 days before the date on which the witness is required to attend before the court.

(5) Unless the court directs otherwise, a witness summons is to be served by the person making the application.

(6) At the time of service the witness must be offered or paid–

(a) a sum reasonably sufficient to cover the witness's expenses in travelling to and from the court; and

(b) such sum by way of compensation for loss of time as may be specified in the relevant practice direction.

(7) The court may order that the witness is to be paid such general costs as it considers appropriate.

14.14 Power of court to direct a party to provide information

(1) Where a party has access to information which is not reasonably available to the other party, the court may direct that party to prepare and file a document recording that information.

(2) The court shall give directions about serving a copy of that document on the other parties.

Depositions

14.15 Evidence by deposition

(1) A party may apply for an order for a person to be examined before the hearing takes place.

(2) A person from whom evidence is to be obtained following an order under this rule is referred to as a 'deponent' and the evidence is referred to as a 'deposition'.

(3) An order under this rule shall be for a deponent to be examined on oath before–

(a) a circuit judge or a district judge, whether or not nominated as a judge of the court;

(b) an examiner of the court; or

(c) such other person as the court appoints.

(4) The order may require the production of any document which the court considers is necessary for the purposes of the examination.

(5) The order will state the date, time and place of the examination.

(6) At the time of service of the order, the deponent must be offered or paid–

(a) a sum reasonably sufficient to cover the deponent's expenses in travelling to and from the place of examination; and

(b) such sum by way of compensation for loss of time as may be specified in the relevant practice direction.

(7) Where the court makes an order for a deposition to be taken, it may also order the party who obtained the order to file a witness statement or witness summary in relation to the evidence to be given by the person to be examined.

14.16 Conduct of examination

(1) Subject to any directions contained in the order for examination, the examination must be conducted in the same way as if the witness were giving evidence at a final hearing.
(2) If all the parties are present, the examiner may conduct the examination of a person not named in the order for examination if all the parties and the person to be examined consent.
(3) The examiner must ensure that the evidence given by the witness is recorded in full.
(4) The examiner must send a copy of the deposition–
   (a) to the person who obtained the order for the examination of the witness; and
   (b) to the court.
(5) The court shall give directions as to the service of a copy of the deposition on the other parties.

14.17 Fees and expenses of examiners of the court

(1) An examiner of the court may charge a fee for the examination and need not send the deposition to the court until the fee is paid, unless the court directs otherwise.
(2) The examiner's fees and expenses must be paid by the party who obtained the order for examination.
(3) If the fees and expenses due to an examiner are not paid within a reasonable time, the examiner may report that fact to the court.
(4) The court may order the party who obtained the order for examination to deposit in the court office a specified sum in respect of the examiner's fees and, where it does so, the examiner shall not be asked to act until the sum has been deposited.
(5) An order under this rule does not affect any decision as to the person who is ultimately to bear the costs of the examination.

14.18 Examiners of the court

(1) The Lord Chancellor shall appoint persons to be examiners of the court.
(2) The persons appointed shall be barristers or solicitor-advocates who have been practising for a period of not less than 3 years.
(3) The Lord Chancellor may revoke an appointment at any time.
(4) In addition to persons appointed in accordance with this rule, examiners appointed under rule 34.15 of the Civil Procedure Rules 1998 may act as examiners in the court.

14.19 Enforcing attendance of a witness

(1) If a person served with an order to attend before an examiner–
   (a) fails to attend; or
   (b) refuses to be sworn for the purpose of the examination or to answer any lawful question or produce any document at the examination,

   a certificate of that person's failure or refusal, signed by the examiner, must be filed by the party requiring the deposition.
(2) On the certificate being filed, the party requiring the deposition may apply to the court for an order requiring that person to attend or to be sworn or to answer any question or produce any document, as the case may be.

(3) An application for an order under this rule may be made without notice.
(4) The court may order the person against whom an order is sought or made under this rule to pay any costs resulting from that person's failure or refusal.

14.20 Use of deposition at a hearing

(1) A deposition ordered under rule 14.15 or 14.23 may be put in evidence at a hearing unless the court orders otherwise.
(2) A party intending to put a deposition in evidence at a hearing must file notice of intention to do so on the court and serve the notice on every other party.
(3) Unless the court directs otherwise, that party must file the notice at least 14 days before the day fixed for the hearing.
(4) The court may require a deponent to attend the hearing and give evidence orally.

Taking evidence outside the jurisdiction

14.21 [Revoked.]

14.22 [Revoked.]

14.23 Where a person to be examined is out of the jurisdiction – letter of request

(1) This rule applies where a party wishes to take a deposition from a person who is out of the jurisdiction;
   (a) out of the jurisdiction; and
   (b) not in a Regulation State within the meaning of rule 14.21.
(2) The court may order the issue of a letter of request to the judicial authorities of the country in which the proposed deponent is.
(3) A letter of request is a request to a judicial authority to take the evidence of that person, or arrange for it to be taken.
(4) If the government of a country permits a person appointed by the court to examine a person in that country, the court may make an order appointing a special examiner for that purpose.
(5) A person may be examined under this rule on oath or affirmation in accordance with any procedure permitted in the country in which the examination is to take place.
(6) If the court makes an order for the issue of a letter of request, the party who sought the order must file–
   (a) the following documents and, except where paragraph (7) applies, a translation of them–
      (i) a draft letter of request;
      (ii) a statement of the issues relevant to the proceedings; and
      (iii) a list of questions or the subject matter of questions to be put to the person to be examined; and
   (b) an undertaking to be responsible for the Secretary of State's expenses.
(7) There is no need to file a translation if–
   (a) English is one of the official languages of the country where the examination is to take place; or
   (b) a practice direction has specified that country as a country where no translation is necessary.

Section 49 reports

14.24 Reports under section 49 of the Act

(1) This rule applies where the court requires a report to be made to it under section 49 of the Act.

(2) It is the duty of the person who is required to make the report to help the court on the matters within that person's expertise.

(3) Unless the court directs otherwise, the person making the report must–

(a) contact or seek to interview such persons as the person making the report thinks appropriate or as the court directs;

(b) to the extent that it is practicable and appropriate to do so, ascertain what P's wishes and feelings are, and the beliefs and values that would be likely to influence P if P had the capacity to make a decision in relation to the matters to which the application relates;

(c) describe P's circumstances; and

(d) address such other matters as are required in a practice direction or as the court may direct.

(4) The court will send a copy of the report to the parties and to such persons as the court may direct.

(5) Subject to paragraphs (6) and (7), the person who is required to make the report may examine and take copies of any documents in the court records.

(6) The court may direct that the right to inspect documents under this rule does not apply in relation to such documents, or descriptions of documents, as the court may specify.

(7) The court may direct that any information is to be provided to the maker of the report on an edited basis.

14.25 Written questions to person making a report under section 49

(1) Where a report is made under section 49 the court may, on the application of any party, permit written questions relevant to the issues before the court to be put to the person by whom the report was made.

(2) The questions sought to be put to the maker of the report shall be submitted to the court, and the court may put them to the maker of the report with such amendments (if any) as it thinks fit and the maker of the report shall give replies in writing to the questions so put.

(3) The court shall send a copy of the replies given by the maker of the report under this rule to the parties and to such other persons as the court may direct.

Part 15: Experts

15.1 References to expert

A reference to an expert in this Part–

(a) is to an expert who has been instructed to give or prepare evidence for the purpose of court proceedings; but

(b) does not include any person instructed to make a report under section 49 of the Act.

15.2 Restriction on filing an expert's report

(1) No person may file expert evidence unless the court or a practice direction permits, or if it is filed with the application form and is evidence–

(a) that P is a person who lacks capacity to make a decision or decisions in relation to the matter or matters to which the application relates;
(b) as to P's best interests; or
(c) that is required by any rule or practice direction to be filed with the application form.

(2) An applicant may only rely on any expert evidence so filed in support of the application form to the extent and for the purposes that the court allows.
(Rule 9.4(a) requires the applicant to file any evidence upon which the applicant wishes to rely with the application form.)

15.3 Duty to restrict expert evidence

(1) Expert evidence shall be restricted to that which is necessary to assist the court to resolve the issues in the proceedings.
(2) The court may give permission to file or adduce expert evidence as mentioned in rule 15.2(1) and 15.5(1) only if satisfied that the evidence–
(a) is necessary to assist the court to resolve the issues in the proceedings; and
(b) cannot otherwise be provided either–
(i) by a rule 1.2 representative; or
(ii) in a report under section 49 of the Act.

15.4 Experts – overriding duty to the court

(1) It is the duty of the expert to help the court on the matters within the expert's expertise.
(2) This duty overrides any obligation to the person from whom the expert has received instructions or by whom the expert is paid.

15.5 Court's power to restrict expert evidence

(1) Subject to rule 15.2, no party may file or adduce expert evidence unless the court or a practice direction permits.
(2) When a party applies for a direction under this rule, that party must–
(a) identify the field in respect of which that party wishes to rely upon expert evidence, and the issues to which the expert evidence is to relate;
(b) where practicable, identify the expert in that field upon whose evidence the party wishes to rely;
(c) provide any other material information about the expert;
(d) state whether the expert evidence could be obtained from a single joint expert;
(e) provide any other information or documents required by a practice direction; and
(f) provide a draft letter of instruction to the expert.
(3) When deciding whether to give permission as mentioned in paragraph (1), the court is to have regard in particular to–
(a) the issues to which the expert evidence would relate;
(b) the questions which the expert would answer;
(c) the impact which giving permission would be likely to have on the timetable, duration and conduct of the proceedings;
(d) any failure to comply with any direction of the court about expert evidence; and
(e) the cost of the expert evidence.
(4) Where a direction is given under this rule, the court shall specify–

(a) the field or fields in respect of which the expert evidence is to be provided;
(b) the questions which the expert is required to answer; and
(c) the date by which the expert is to provide the evidence.

(5) The court may specify the person who is to provide the evidence referred to in paragraph (3).

(6) Where a direction is given under this rule for a party to call an expert or put in evidence an expert's report, the court shall give directions for the service of the report on the parties and on such other persons as the court may direct.

(7) The court may limit the amount of the expert's fees and expenses that the party who wishes to rely upon the expert may recover from any other party.

15.6 General requirement for expert evidence to be given in a written report

Expert evidence is to be given in a written report unless the court directs otherwise.

15.7 Written questions to experts

(1) A party may put written questions to–
(a) an expert instructed by another party; or
(b) a single joint expert appointed under rule 15.12
about a report prepared by such a person.

(2) Written questions under paragraph (1)–
(a) may be put once only;
(b) must be put within 28 days beginning with the date on which the expert's report was served;
(c) must be for the purpose only of clarification of the report; and
(d) must be copied and sent to the other parties at the same time as they are sent to the expert.

(3) Paragraph (2) does not apply in any case where–
(a) the court permits it to be done on a further occasion;
(b) the other party or parties agree; or
(c) any practice direction provides otherwise.

(4) An expert's answers to questions put in accordance with paragraph (1) shall be treated as part of the expert's report.

(5) Paragraph (6) applies where–
(a) a party has put a written question to an expert instructed by another party in accordance with this rule; and
(b) the expert does not answer that question.

(6) The court may make one or both of the following orders in relation to the party who instructed the expert–
(a) that the party may not rely upon the evidence of that expert; or
(b) that the party may not recover the fees and expenses of that expert, or part of them, from any other party.

(7) Unless the court directs otherwise, and subject to any final costs order that may be made, the instructing party is responsible for the payment of the expert's fees and expenses, including the expert's costs of answering questions put by any other party.

15.8 Contents of expert's report

(1) The court may give directions as to the matters to be covered in an expert's report.

(2) An expert's report must comply with the requirements set out in the relevant practice direction.
(3) At the end of an expert's report there must be a statement that the expert–
(a) understands his or her duty to the court; and
(b) has complied with that duty.
(4) The expert's report must state the substance of all material instructions, whether written or oral, on the basis of which the report was written.
(5) The instructions to the expert shall not be privileged against disclosure.

15.9 Use by one party of expert's report disclosed by another
Where a party has disclosed an expert's report, any party may use that expert's report as evidence at any hearing in the proceedings.

15.10 Discussions between experts
(1) The court may, at any stage, direct a discussion between experts for the purpose of requiring the experts to–
(a) identify and discuss the expert issues in the proceedings; and
(b) where possible, reach an agreed opinion on those issues.
(2) The court may specify the issues which the experts must discuss.
(3) The court may direct that following a discussion between the experts they must prepare a statement for the court showing–
(a) those issues on which they agree; and
(b) those issues on which they disagree and a summary of their reasons for disagreeing.
(4) Unless the court directs otherwise, the content of the discussions between experts may be referred to at any hearing or at any stage in the proceedings.

15.11 Expert's right to ask court for directions
(1) An expert may file a written request for directions to assist in carrying out the expert's functions as an expert.
(2) An expert must, unless the court directs otherwise, provide a copy of any proposed request for directions under paragraph (1)–
(a) to the party instructing the expert, at least 7 days before filing the request; and
(b) to all other parties, at least 4 days before filing it.
(3) The court, when it gives directions, may also direct that a party be served with a copy of the directions.

15.12 Court's power to direct that evidence is to be given by a single joint expert
(1) Where two or more parties wish to submit expert evidence on a particular issue, the court may direct that the evidence on that issue is to be given by one expert only.
(2) The parties wishing to submit the expert evidence are called 'the instructing parties'.
(3) Where the instructing parties cannot agree who should be the expert, the court may–
(a) select the expert from a list prepared or identified by the instructing parties; or
(b) direct the manner by which the expert is to be selected.

15.13 Instructions to a single joint expert

(1) Where the court gives a direction under rule 15.12 for a single joint expert to be used, the instructions are to be contained in a jointly agreed letter unless the court directs otherwise.

(2) Where the instructions are to be contained in a jointly agreed letter, in default of agreement the instructions may be determined by the court on the written request of any instructing party copied to the other instructing parties.

(3) Where the court permits the instructing parties to give separate instructions to a single joint expert, unless the court directs otherwise, when an instructing party gives instructions to the expert, that party must at the same time send a copy of the instructions to the other instructing party or parties.

(4) The court may give directions about–
  (a) the payment of the expert's fees and expenses; and
  (b) any inspection, examination or experiments which the expert wishes to carry out.

(5) The court may, before an expert is instructed, limit the amount that can be paid by way of fees and expense to the expert.

(6) Unless the court directs otherwise, and subject to any final costs order that may be made, the instructing parties are jointly and severally liable for the payment of the expert's fees and expenses.

Part 16: Disclosure

16.1 Meaning of disclosure

A party discloses a document by stating that the document exists or has existed.

16.2 General or specific disclosure

(1) The court may either on its own initiative or on the application of a party make an order to give general or specific disclosure.

(2) General disclosure requires a party to disclose–
  (a) the documents on which that party relies; and
  (b) the documents which–
    (i) adversely affect that party's own case;
    (ii) adversely affect another party's case; or
    (iii) support another party's case.

(3) An order for specific disclosure is an order that a party must do one or more of the following things–
  (a) disclose documents or classes of documents specified in the order;
  (b) carry out a search to the extent stated in the order; or
  (c) disclose any document located as a result of that search.

(4) A party's duty to disclose documents is limited to documents which are or have been in that party's control.

(5) For the purposes of paragraph (4) a party has or has had a document in that party's control if–
  (a) it is or was in that party's physical possession;
  (b) that party has or has had possession of it; or
  (c) that party has or has had a right to inspect or take copies of it.

16.3 Procedure for general or specific disclosure

(1) This rule applies where the court makes an order under rule 16.2 to give general or specific disclosure.

(2) Each party must make, and serve on every other party, a list of documents to be disclosed.

(3) A copy of each list must be filed within 7 days of the date on which it is served.

(4) The list must identify the documents in a convenient order and manner and as concisely as possible.

(5) The list must indicate–

(a) the documents in respect of which the party claims a right or duty to withhold inspection (see rule 16.7); and

(b) the documents that are no longer in the party's control, stating what has happened to them.

16.4 Ongoing duty of disclosure

(1) Where the court makes an order to give general or specific disclosure under rule 16.2, any party to whom the order applies is under a continuing duty to provide such disclosure as is required by the order until the proceedings are concluded.

(2) If a document to which the duty of disclosure imposed by paragraph (1) extends comes to a party's notice at any time during the proceedings, that party must immediately notify every other party.

16.5 Right to inspect documents

(1) A party to whom a document has been disclosed has a right to inspect any document disclosed to that party except where–

(a) the document is no longer in the control of the party who disclosed it; or

(b) the party disclosing the document has a right or duty to withhold inspection of it.

(2) The right to inspect disclosed documents extends to any document mentioned in–

(a) a document filed or served in the course of the proceedings by any other party; or

(b) correspondence sent by any other party.

16.6 Inspection and copying of documents

(1) Where a party has a right to inspect a document, that party–

(a) must give the party who disclosed the document written notice of the wish to inspect it; and

(b) may request a copy of the document.

(2) Not more than 14 days after the date on which the party who disclosed the document received the notice under paragraph (1)(a), that party must permit inspection of the document at a convenient place and time.

(3) Where a party has requested a copy of the document, the party who disclosed the document must supply the requesting party with a copy not more than 14 days after the date on which the request was received.

(4) For the purposes of paragraph (2), the party who disclosed the document must give reasonable notice of the time and place for inspection.

(5) For the purposes of paragraph (3), the party requesting a copy of the document is responsible for the payment of reasonable copying costs, subject to any final costs order that may be made.

16.7 Claim to withhold inspection or disclosure of documents

(1) A party who wishes to claim a right or duty to withhold inspection of a document, or part of a document, must state in writing–
   (a) that that party has such a right or duty; and
   (b) the grounds on which that party claims that right or duty.
(2) The statement must be made in the list in which the document is disclosed (see rule 16.3(2)).
(3) A party may, by filing an application notice in accordance with Part 10, apply to the court to decide whether the claim made under paragraph (1) should be upheld.

16.8 Consequence of failure to disclose documents or permit inspection

A party may not rely upon any document which that party fails to disclose or in respect of which that party fails to permit inspection, unless the court permits.

Part 17: Litigation friends and Rule 1.2 Representatives

Section 1 – Litigation friends

17.1 Who may act as a litigation friend

(1) A person may act as a litigation friend on behalf of a person mentioned in paragraph (2) if that person–
   (a) can fairly and competently conduct proceedings on behalf of that person; and
   (b) has no interests adverse to those of that person.
(2) The persons for whom a litigation friend may act are–
   (a) P;
   (b) a child;
   (c) a protected party.

17.2 Requirement for a litigation friend

(1) This rule does not apply to P (whether P is an adult or a child).
(2) A protected party (if a party to the proceedings) must have a litigation friend.
(3) A child (if a party to the proceedings) must have a litigation friend to conduct those proceedings on that child's behalf unless the court makes an order under paragraph (4).
(4) The court may make an order permitting a child to conduct proceedings without a litigation friend.
(5) An application for an order under paragraph (4)–
   (a) may be made by the child;
   (b) if the child already has a litigation friend, must be made on notice to the litigation friend; and
   (c) if the child has no litigation friend, may be made without notice.
(6) Where–
   (a) the court has made an order under paragraph (4); and

(b) it subsequently appears to the court that it is desirable for a litigation friend to conduct the proceedings on behalf of the child,

the court may appoint a person to be the child's litigation friend.

17.3 Litigation friend without a court order

(1) This rule does not apply–
   (a) in relation to P;
   (b) where the court has appointed a person under rule 17.4 or 17.5; or
   (c) where the Official Solicitor is to act as a litigation friend.

(2) A deputy with the power to conduct legal proceedings in the name of a protected party or on the protected party's behalf is entitled to be a litigation friend of the protected party in any proceedings to which the deputy's power relates.

(3) If no-one has been appointed by the court or, in the case of a protected party, there is no deputy with the power to conduct proceedings, a person who wishes to act as a litigation friend must–
   (a) file a certificate of suitability stating that they satisfy the conditions in rule 17.1(1); and
   (b) serve the certificate of suitability on–
      (i) the person on whom an application form is to be served in accordance with rule 6.4 (service on children and protected parties); and
      (ii) every other person who is a party to the proceedings.

(4) If the person referred to in paragraph (2) wishes to act as a litigation friend for the protected party, that person must file and serve on the persons mentioned in paragraph (3)(b) a copy of the court order which appointed that person.

17.4 Litigation friend by court order

(1) The court may make an order appointing–
   (a) the Official Solicitor; or
   (b) some other person,

   to act as a litigation friend for a protected party, a child or P.

(2) The court may make an order under paragraph (1)–
   (a) either on its own initiative or on the application of any person; but
   (b) only with the consent of the person to be appointed.

(3) An application for an order under paragraph (1) must be supported by evidence.

(4) The court may not appoint a litigation friend under this rule unless it is satisfied that the person to be appointed satisfies the conditions in rule 17.1(1).

(5) The court may at any stage of the proceedings give directions as to the appointment of a litigation friend.

   (Rule 1.2 requires the court to consider how P should participate in the proceedings, which may be by way of being made a party and the appointment of a litigation friend under this Part.)

17.5 Court's power to prevent a person from acting as a litigation friend or to bring an end to an appointment of a person as a litigation friend or to appoint another one

(1) The court may either on its own initiative or on the application of any person–
   (a) direct that a person may not act as a litigation friend;

(b) bring to an end a litigation friend's appointment; or
(c) appoint a new litigation friend in place of an existing one.

(2) If an application for an order under paragraph (1) is based on the conduct of the litigation friend, it must be supported by evidence.

(3) The court may not appoint a litigation friend under this rule unless it is satisfied that the person to be appointed satisfies the conditions in rule 17.1(1).

(4) The appointment of a litigation friend continues until brought to an end by court order.

(Rule 13.1 (procedure for disputing the court's jurisdiction) applies if P has capacity in relation to the matter or matters to which the application relates.)

17.6 Appointment of litigation friend by court order – supplementary

The applicant must serve a copy of an application for an order under rule 17.4 or 17.5 on–

(a) the person on whom an application form is to be served in accordance with rule 6.4 (service on children and protected parties);
(b) every other person who is a party to the proceedings;
(c) any person who is the litigation friend, or who is purporting to act as the litigation friend, when the application is made; and
(d) unless that person is the applicant, the person who it is proposed should be the litigation friend,

as soon as practicable and in any event within 14 days of the date on which the application was issued.

17.7 Procedure where appointment of a litigation friend comes to an end for a child

When a child reaches 18, provided the child is neither–

(a) P; nor
(b) a protected party,

the litigation friend's appointment ends and the child must serve notice on every other party–

(i) stating that the child has reached full age;
(ii) stating that the appointment of the litigation friend has ended; and
(iii) providing an address for service.

17.8 Practice direction in relation to litigation friends

A practice direction may make additional or supplementary provision in relation to litigation friends.

Section 2 – rule 1.2 representatives

17.9 Who may act as a rule 1.2 representative for P

A person may act as an accredited legal representative, or a representative, for P, if that person can fairly and competently discharge his or her functions on behalf of P.

17.10 Rule 1.2 representative by court order

(1) The court may make an order appointing a person to act as a representative, or an accredited legal representative, for P.

(2) The court may make an order under paragraph (1)–

(a) either of its own initiative or on the application of any person; but
(b) only with the consent of the person to be appointed.

(3) The court may not appoint a representative or an accredited legal representative under this rule unless it is satisfied that the person to be appointed satisfies the conditions in rule 17.9.

(4) The court may at any stage of the proceedings give directions as to the terms of appointment of a representative or an accredited legal representative.

(Rule 1.2 requires the court to consider how P should participate in the proceedings, which may be by way of the appointment of a representative or accredited legal representative under this Part.)

17.11 Application by rule 1.2 representative or by P for directions

A representative, an accredited legal representative or P may, at any time and without giving notice to the other parties, apply to the court for directions relating to the performance, terms of appointment or continuation of the appointment of the representative or accredited legal representative.

17.12 Court's power to prevent a person from acting as a rule 1.2 representative or to bring an end to an appointment of a person as a rule 1.2 representative or to appoint another one

(1) The court may, either of its own initiative or on the application of any person–
(a) direct that a person may not act as a representative or accredited legal representative;
(b) bring to an end a representative's or accredited legal representative's appointment;
(c) appoint a new representative or accredited legal representative in place of an existing one; or
(d) vary the terms of a representative's or accredited legal representative's appointment.

(2) If an application for an order under paragraph (1) is based on the conduct of the representative or accredited legal representative, it must be supported by evidence.

(3) The court may not appoint a representative or accredited legal representative under this rule unless it is satisfied that the person to be appointed satisfies the conditions in rule 17.9.

(4) The appointment of a representative or accredited legal representative continues until brought to an end by court order.

(5) The court must bring to an end the appointment of a representative or an accredited legal representative if P has capacity to appoint such a representative and does not wish the appointment by the court to continue.

17.13 Appointment of rule 1.2 representative by court order – supplementary

The applicant must serve a copy of an application for an order under rule 17.10 or rule 17.12 on–
(a) the person on whom an application form is to be served in accordance with rule 6.4 (service on children and protected parties);
(b) every other person who is a party to the proceedings;
(c) any person who is the representative, or accredited legal representative, or who is purporting to act as such representative, when the application is made; and

(d) unless that person is the applicant, the person who it is proposed should be the representative or accredited legal representative,

as soon as practicable and in any event within 14 days of the date on which the application was issued.

17.14 Practice direction in relation to rule 1.2 representatives

A practice direction may make additional or supplementary provision in relation to representatives or accredited legal representatives.

Part 18: Change of solicitor

18.1 Change of solicitor

(1) This rule applies where a party to proceedings–
  (a) for whom a solicitor is acting wants to change solicitor or act in person; or
  (b) after having conducted the proceedings in person, appoints a solicitor to act on his or her behalf (except where the solicitor is appointed only to act as an advocate for a hearing).

(2) The party proposing the change must–
  (a) file a notice of the change with the court; and
  (b) serve the notice of the change on every other party to the proceedings and, if there is one, on the solicitor who will cease to act.

(3) The notice must state the party's address for service.

(4) The notice filed at court must state that it has been served as required by paragraph (2)(b).

(5) Where there is a solicitor who will cease to act, that solicitor will continue to be considered the party's solicitor unless and until–
  (a) the notice is filed and served in accordance with paragraphs (2), (3) and (4); or
  (b) the court makes an order under rule 18.3 and the order is served in accordance with that rule.

18.2 Legally aided persons

(1) Where the certificate of any person ('A') who is a legally aided person is revoked or withdrawn–
  (a) the solicitor who acted for A will cease to be the solicitor acting in the case as soon as the solicitor's retainer is determined under regulation 24 or 41 of the Civil Legal Aid (Procedure) Regulations 2012; and
  (b) if A wishes to continue and appoints a solicitor to act on his or her behalf, rule 18.1(2), (3) and (4) will apply as if A had previously conducted the proceedings in person.

(2) In this rule, 'certificate' means a certificate issued under the Civil Legal Aid (Procedure) Regulations 2012.

18.3 Order that a solicitor has ceased to act

(1) A solicitor may apply for an order declaring that he or she has ceased to be the solicitor acting for a party.

(2) Where an application is made under this rule–
  (a) the solicitor must serve the application notice on the party for whom the solicitor is acting, unless the court directs otherwise; and
  (b) the application must be supported by evidence.

(3) Where the court makes an order that a solicitor has ceased to act, the solicitor must–
  (a) serve a copy of the order on every other party to the proceedings; and
  (b) file a certificate of service.

18.4 Removal of solicitor who has ceased to act on application of another party

(1) Where–
  (a) a solicitor who has acted for a party–
    (i) has died;
    (ii) has become bankrupt;
    (iii) has ceased to practice; or
    (iv) cannot be found; and
  (b) the party has not served a notice of change of solicitor or notice of intention to act in person as required by rule 18.1,

  any other party may apply for an order declaring that the solicitor has ceased to be the solicitor acting for the other party in the case.

(2) Where an application is made under this rule, the applicant must serve the application on the party to whose solicitor the application relates, unless the court directs otherwise.

(3) Where the court makes an order under this rule–
  (a) the court shall give directions about serving a copy of the order on every other party to the proceedings; and
  (b) where the order is served by a party, that party must file a certificate of service.

18.5 Practice direction relating to change of solicitor

A practice direction may make additional or different provision in relation to change of solicitor.

Part 19: Costs

19.1 Interpretation

(1) In this Part–

'authorised court officer' means any officer of the Senior Courts Costs Office whom the Lord Chancellor has authorised to assess costs;

'costs' include fees, charges, disbursements, expenses, remuneration and any reimbursement allowed to a litigant in person;

'costs judge' means a taxing Master of the Senior Courts;

'costs officer' means a costs judge or an authorised court officer;

'detailed assessment' means the procedure by which the amount of costs or remuneration is decided by a costs officer in accordance with Part 47 of the Civil Procedure Rules 1998 (which are applied to proceedings under these Rules, with modifications, by rule 19.6);

'fixed costs' are to be construed in accordance with the relevant practice direction;

'fund' includes any estate or property held for the benefit of any person or class of persons, and any fund to which a trustee or personal representative is entitled in that capacity;

'paying party' means a party liable to pay costs;

'pro bono representation' means representation provided free of charge;

'receiving party' means a party entitled to be paid costs;
'summary assessment' means the procedure by which the court, when making an order about costs, orders payment of a sum of money instead of fixed costs or detailed assessment.

(2) The costs to which rules in this Part apply include–
  (a) where the costs may be assessed by the court, costs payable by a client to his or her legal representative; and
  (b) costs which are payable by one party to another party under the terms of a contract, where the court makes an order for an assessment of those costs.

(3) Where advocacy or litigation services are provided to a client under a conditional fee agreement, costs are recoverable under this Part notwithstanding that the client is liable to pay his or her legal representative's fees and expenses only to the extent that sums are recovered in respect of the proceedings, whether by way of costs or otherwise.

(4) In paragraph (3), the reference to a conditional fee agreement means an agreement enforceable under section 58 of the Courts and Legal Services Act 1990.

19.2 Property and affairs – the general rule

Where the proceedings concern P's property and affairs the general rule is that the costs of the proceedings, or of that part of the proceedings that concerns P's property and affairs, shall be paid by P or charged to P's estate.

19.3 Personal welfare – the general rule

Where the proceedings concern P's personal welfare the general rule is that there will be no order as to the costs of the proceedings, or of that part of the proceedings that concerns P's personal welfare.

19.4 Apportioning costs – the general rule

Where the proceedings concern both property and affairs and personal welfare the court, in so far as practicable, shall apportion the costs as between the respective issues.

19.5 Departing from the general rule

(1) The court may depart from rules 19.2 to 19.4 if the circumstances so justify, and in deciding whether departure is justified the court will have regard to all the circumstances including–
  (a) the conduct of the parties;
  (b) whether a party has succeeded on part of that party's case, even if not wholly successful; and
  (c) the role of any public body involved in the proceedings.

(2) The conduct of the parties includes–
  (a) conduct before, as well as during, the proceedings;
  (b) whether it was reasonable for a party to raise, pursue or contest a particular matter;
  (c) the manner in which a party has made or responded to an application or a particular issue;
  (d) whether a party who has succeeded in that party's application or response to an application, in whole or in part, exaggerated any matter contained in the application or response; and

(e) any failure by a party to comply with a rule, practice direction or court order.

(3) Without prejudice to rules 19.2 to 19.4 and the foregoing provisions of this rule, the court may permit a party to recover their fixed costs in accordance with the relevant practice direction.

19.6 Rules about costs in the Civil Procedure Rules to apply

(1) Subject to the provisions of these Rules, Parts 44, 46 and 47 of the Civil Procedure Rules 1998 ('the 1998 Rules') apply with the modifications in this rule and such other modifications as may be appropriate, to costs incurred in relation to proceedings under these Rules as they apply to costs incurred in relation to proceedings in the High Court.

(2) Rules 3.12 to 3.18 of the 1998 Rules and Practice Direction 3E supporting those Rules do not apply in relation to proceedings under these Rules.

(3) The provisions of Part 47 of the 1998 Rules apply with the modifications in this rule and such other modifications as may be appropriate, to a detailed assessment of the remuneration of a deputy under these Rules as they apply to a detailed assessment of costs in proceedings to which the 1998 Rules apply.

(4) Where the definitions in Part 44 (referred to in Parts 44, 46 and 47) of the 1998 Rules are different from the definitions in rule 19.1 of these Rules, the latter definitions prevail.

(5) Rules 44.2(1) to (5), 44.4(3)(h), 44.5, 44.6, 44.9 and 44.13 to 44.18 of the 1998 Rules do not apply.

(6) For rule 46.1(1) of the 1998 Rules there is substituted–

'(1) This paragraph applies where a person applies for an order for specific disclosure before the commencement of proceedings.'.

(7) Rules 46.2, 46.5 and 46.10 to 46.19 of the 1998 Rules do not apply.

(8) In rule 47.3(1)(c) of the 1998 Rules, the words 'unless the costs are being assessed under rule 46.4 (costs where money is payable to a child or protected party)' are omitted.

(9) In rule 47.3(2) of the 1998 Rules, the words 'or a District Judge' are omitted.

(10) Rule 47.4(3) and (4) of the 1998 Rules do not apply.

(11) Rules 47.9(4), 47.10 and 47.11 of the 1998 Rules do not apply where the costs are to be paid by P or charged to P's estate.

19.7 Detailed assessment of costs

(1) Where the court orders costs to be assessed by way of detailed assessment, the detailed assessment proceedings shall take place in the High Court.

(2) A fee is payable in respect of the detailed assessment of costs and on an appeal against a decision made in a detailed assessment of costs.

(3) Where a detailed assessment of costs has taken place, the amount payable by P is the amount which the court certifies as payable.

19.8 Employment of a solicitor by two or more persons

Where two or more persons having the same interest in relation to a matter act in relation to the proceedings by separate legal representatives, they shall not be permitted more than one set of costs of the representation unless and to the extent that the court certifies that the circumstances justify separate representation.

19.9 Costs of the Official Solicitor

Any costs incurred by the Official Solicitor in relation to proceedings under these Rules or in carrying out any directions given by the court and not provided for by remuneration under rule 19.13 shall be paid by such persons or out of such funds as the court may direct.

19.10 Procedure for assessing costs

Where the court orders a party, or P, to pay costs to another party it may either–

(a) make a summary assessment of the costs; or

(b) order a detailed assessment of the costs by a costs officer;

unless any rule, practice direction or other enactment provides otherwise.

19.11 Costs following P's death

An order or direction that costs incurred during P's lifetime be paid out of or charged on P's estate may be made within 6 years after P's death.

19.12 Costs orders in favour of or against non-parties

(1) Where the court is considering whether to make a costs order in favour of or against a person who is not a party to proceedings, that person must be–

(a) added as a party to the proceedings for the purposes of costs only;

(b) served with such documents as the court may direct; and

(c) given a reasonable opportunity to attend any hearing at which the court will consider the matter further.

(2) This rule does not apply where the court is considering whether to make an order against the Lord Chancellor in proceedings in which the Lord Chancellor has provided legal aid to a party to the proceedings.

19.13 Remuneration of a deputy, donee or attorney

(1) Where the court orders that a deputy, donee or attorney is entitled to remuneration out of P's estate for discharging functions as such, the court may make such order as it thinks fit including an order that–

(a) the deputy, donee or attorney be paid a fixed amount;

(b) the deputy, donee or attorney be paid at a specified rate; or

(c) the amount of the remuneration shall be determined in accordance with the schedule of fees set out in the relevant practice direction.

(2) Any amount permitted by the court under paragraph (1) shall constitute a debt due from P's estate.

(3) The court may order a detailed assessment of the remuneration by a costs officer in accordance with rule 19.10(b).

19.14 Practice direction as to costs

A practice direction may make further provision in respect of costs in proceedings.

Part 20: Appeals

20.1 Scope of this Part

This Part applies to an appeal against any decision of the court.

20.2 Interpretation

(1) In the following provisions of this Part–

(a) 'appeal judge' means a judge of the court to whom an appeal is made;
(b) 'first instance judge' means the judge of the court from whose decision an appeal is brought;
(c) 'appellant' means the person who brings or seeks to bring an appeal;
(d) 'respondent' means–
  (i) a person other than the appellant who was a party to the proceedings before the first instance judge and who is affected by the appeal; or
  (ii) a person who is permitted or directed by the first instance judge or the appeal judge to be party to the appeal; and
(e) 'a second appeal' means an appeal from a decision of a judge of the court which was itself made on appeal from a judge of the court.

(2) In this Part, where the expression 'permission' is used it means 'permission to appeal' unless otherwise stated.

20.3 Dealing with appeals

(1) The court may deal with an appeal or any part of an appeal at a hearing or without a hearing.
(2) In considering whether it is necessary to hold a hearing, the court shall have regard to the matters set out in rule 3.6(5).
(3) Any person bound by an order of the court by virtue of rule 9.14 (persons to be bound as if parties) may seek permission under this Part.
(4) All parties to an appeal must comply with any relevant practice direction.
(5) Where permission is required, it is to be granted or refused in accordance with this Part.

(Rule 13.4 provides for reconsideration of orders made without a hearing or without notice to a person.)

20.4 Destination of appeals

(1) An appeal from a decision of a judge of the court shall lie to the Court of Appeal in the following cases–
  (a) where it is an appeal from a decision of a Tier 3 Judge; or
  (b) where it is a second appeal.
(2) Subject to paragraph (1) and to any alternative provision made by the relevant practice direction–
  (a) where the first instance judge was a Tier 1 Judge, any appeal shall be heard by a Tier 2 Judge;
  (b) where the first instance judge was a Tier 2 Judge, any appeal shall be heard by a Tier 3 Judge.
(3) No appeal may be made against a decision of a court officer authorised under rule 2.3.

(A decision of a court officer authorised under rule 2.3 can be reconsidered by a judge under rule 13.4.)

20.5 Permission to appeal – appeals to the Court of Appeal

(1) Subject to rule 20.7, an appeal to the Court of Appeal against a decision of a judge of the court may not be made without permission.
(2) Where an appeal to the Court of Appeal is made from a decision of a Tier 3 Judge, permission may be granted by the first instance judge or by the Court of Appeal, unless the appeal is a second appeal.

(3) Where an appeal to the Court of Appeal is a second appeal, permission may only be granted by the Court of Appeal.

(4) No appeal shall lie against–
   (a) the granting or refusal of permission under this rule; or
   (b) an order allowing an extension of time for appealing from an order.

(The procedure for an appeal from a decision of a judge of the court to the Court of Appeal, including requirements for permission, is governed by the Civil Procedure Rules 1998.)

20.6 Permission to appeal – other cases

(1) Subject to rules 20.5 and 20.7, an appeal against a decision of the court may not be made without permission.

(2) An application for permission to appeal may be made to–
   (a) the first instance judge or
   (b) another judge who satisfies the relevant condition in paragraph (4) or (5).

(3) Where an application for permission is refused by the first instance judge, a further application for permission may be made to a judge who satisfies the relevant condition in paragraph (4) or (5).

(4) Where the decision sought to be appealed is a decision of a Tier 1 Judge, permission may also be granted or refused by–
   (a) a Tier 2 Judge; or
   (b) a Tier 3 Judge.

(5) Where the decision sought to be appealed is a decision of a Tier 2 Judge, permission may also be granted or refused by a Tier 3 Judge.

(6) Subject to paragraph (7) and except where another rule or a practice direction provides otherwise, where a judge who satisfies the relevant condition in paragraph (4) or (5), without a hearing, refuses permission to appeal against the decision of the first instance judge, the person seeking permission may request the decision to be reconsidered at a hearing.

(7) Where a Tier 3 Judge or the Senior Judge refuses permission to appeal without a hearing and considers that the application is totally without merit, that judge may order that the person seeking permission may not request the decision to be reconsidered at a hearing.

(8) Subject to paragraph (6), no appeal shall lie against–
   (a) the granting or refusal of permission under this rule; or
   (b) an order allowing an extension of time for appealing from an order.

20.7 Appeal against an order for committal to prison

Permission is not required to appeal against an order for committal to prison.

20.8 Matters to be taken into account when considering an application for permission

(1) Permission to appeal shall be granted only where–
   (a) the court considers that the appeal would have a real prospect of success; or
   (b) there is some other compelling reason why the appeal should be heard.

(2) An order giving permission may–
   (a) limit the issues to be heard; and
   (b) be made subject to conditions.

(3) Paragraphs (1) and (2) do not apply to second appeals.

20.9 Power to treat application for permission to appeal as application for reconsideration under rule 13.4

(1) Where a person seeking permission to appeal a decision would be entitled to seek reconsideration of that decision under rule 13.4 (or would have been so entitled had the application been made within 21 days of the date of that decision)–
(a) a practice direction may provide; or
(b) the court may direct,
that an application for permission shall be treated as an application for reconsideration under rule 13.4.

(2) In any case where paragraph (1) applies, the decision in question shall be reconsidered in accordance with the provisions of rule 13.4.

20.10 Appellant's notice

(1) Where the appellant seeks permission from a judge other than the first instance judge, it must be requested in the appellant's notice.

(2) The appellant must file an appellant's notice at the court within–
(a) such period as may be directed or specified in the order of the first instance judge; or
(b) where that judge makes no such direction or order, 21 days after the date of the decision being appealed.

(3) The court shall issue the appellant's notice and unless it orders otherwise, the appellant must serve the appellant's notice on each respondent and on such other persons as the court may direct, as soon as practicable and in any event within 21 days of the date on which it was issued.

(4) The appellant must file a certificate of service within 7 days beginning with the date on which the appellant served the appellant's notice.

20.11 Respondent's notice

(1) A respondent who–
(a) is seeking permission from a judge other than the first instance judge; or
(b) wishes to ask the appeal judge to uphold the order of the first instance judge for reasons different from or additional to those given by the first instance judge,
must file a respondent's notice.

(2) Where the respondent seeks permission from a judge other than the first instance judge, permission must be requested in the respondent's notice.

(3) A respondent's notice must be filed within–
(a) such period as may be directed by the first instance judge; or
(b) where the first instance judge makes no such direction, 21 days beginning with the date referred to in paragraph (4).

(4) The date is the soonest of–
(a) the date on which the respondent is served with the appellant's notice where–
(i) permission was given by the first instance judge; or
(ii) permission is not required;
(b) the date on which the respondent is served with notification that a judge other than the first instance judge has given the appellant permission; or

(c) the date on which the respondent is served with the notification that the application for permission and the appeal itself are to be heard together.

(5) The court shall issue a respondent's notice, and unless it orders otherwise, the respondent must serve the respondent's notice on the appellant, any other respondent and on such other persons as the court may direct, as soon as practicable and in any event within 21 days of the date on which it was issued.

(6) The respondent must file a certificate of service within 7 days beginning with the date on which the copy of the respondent's notice was served.

20.12 Variation of time

The parties may not agree to extend any date or time limit for or in respect of an appeal set by–

(a) these Rules;
(b) the relevant practice direction; or
(c) an order of the appeal judge or the first instance judge.

20.13 Power of appeal judge on appeal

(1) In relation to an appeal, an appeal judge has all the powers of the first instance judge whose decision is being appealed.

(2) In particular, the appeal judge has the power to–
 (a) affirm, set aside or vary any order made by the first instance judge;
 (b) refer any claim or issue to that judge for determination;
 (c) order a new hearing;
 (d) make a costs order.

(3) The appeal judge's powers may be exercised in relation to the whole or part of an order made by the first instance judge.

20.14 Determination of appeals

(1) An appeal shall be limited to a review of the decision of the first instance judge unless–
 (a) a practice direction makes different provision for a particular category of appeal; or
 (b) the appeal judge considers that in the circumstances of the appeal it would be in the interests of justice to hold a re-hearing.

(2) Unless the appeal judge orders otherwise, the appeal judge shall not receive–
 (a) oral evidence; or
 (b) evidence that was not before the first instance judge.

(3) The appeal judge shall allow an appeal where the decision of the first instance judge was–
 (a) wrong; or
 (b) unjust, because of a serious procedural or other irregularity in the proceedings before the first instance judge.

(4) The appeal judge may draw any inference of fact that the appeal judge considers justified on the evidence.

(5) At the hearing of the appeal, a party may not rely on a matter not contained in the appellant's or respondent's notice unless the appeal judge gives permission.

Part 21: Applications and proceedings in relation to contempt of court

Section 1 – Scope and interpretation

21.1 Scope

(1) This Part sets out the procedure in respect of–
(a) committal for any breach of a judgment, order or undertaking to do or abstain from doing an act;
(b) contempt in the face of the court;
(c) committal for interference with the due administration of justice;
(d) committal for making a false statement of truth; and
(e) sequestration to enforce a judgment, order or undertaking.

(2) So far as applicable, and with the necessary modifications, this Part applies in relation to an order requiring a person–
(a) guilty of contempt of court; or
(b) punishable by virtue of any enactment as if that person had been guilty of contempt of the High Court,

to pay a fine or to give security for good behaviour, as it applies in relation to an order of committal.

21.2 Saving for other powers

(1) This Part is concerned only with procedure and does not itself confer upon the court the power to make an order for–
(a) committal;
(b) sequestration; or
(c) the imposition of a fine in respect of contempt.

(2) Nothing in this Part affects the power of the court to make an order requiring a person–
(a) guilty of contempt of court; or
(b) punishable by virtue of any enactment as if that person had been guilty of contempt of the High Court,

to pay a fine or to give security for good behaviour.

(3) Nothing in this Part affects any statutory or inherent power of the court to make a committal order on its own initiative against a person guilty of contempt of court.

21.3 Interpretation

In this Part–
(a) 'applicant' means a person making–
(i) an application for permission to make a committal application;
(ii) a committal application; or
(iii) an application for a writ of sequestration;
(b) 'committal application' means any application for an order committing a person to prison;
(c) 'respondent' means a person–
(i) against whom a committal application is made or is intended to be made; or

(ii) against whose property it is sought to issue a writ of sequestration; and

(d) 'undertaking' means an undertaking to the court.

Section 2 – Committal for breach of a judgment, order or undertaking to do or abstain from doing an act

21.4 Enforcement of judgment, order or undertaking to do or abstain from doing an act

(1) If a person–

(a) required by a judgment or order of the court to do an act does not do it within the time fixed by the judgment or order; or

(b) disobeys a judgment or order not to do an act,

then, subject to the Debtors Acts 1869 and 1878 and to the provisions of these Rules, the judgment or order may be enforced by an order for committal.

(2) If the time fixed by the judgment or order for doing an act has been varied by a subsequent order, or agreement of the parties under rule 3.7(4), then references in paragraph (1)(a) to the time fixed are references to the time fixed by that subsequent order or agreement.

(3) If the person referred to in paragraph (1) is a company or other corporation, the committal order may be made against any director or other officer of that company or corporation.

(4) So far as applicable, and with the necessary modification, this Section applies to undertakings given by a party as it applies to judgments or orders.

21.5 Requirement for service of a copy judgment or order and time for service

(1) Unless the court dispenses with service under rule 21.8 a judgment or order may not be enforced under rule 21.4 unless a copy of it has been served on the person required to do or not to do the act in question, and in the case of a judgment or order requiring a person to do an act–

(a) the copy has been served before the end of the time fixed for doing the act, together with a copy of any order fixing that time;

(b) where the time has been varied by a subsequent order or agreement, a copy of that subsequent order or agreement has also been served; and

(c) where the judgment or order was made pursuant to an earlier judgment or order requiring the act to be done, a copy of the earlier judgment or order has also been served.

(2) Where the person referred to in paragraph (1) is a company or other corporation, a copy of the judgment or order must also be served on a director or officer of the company or corporation before the end of the time fixed for doing the act.

(3) Copies of the judgment or order and any orders or agreements fixing or varying the time for doing an act must be served in accordance with rule 21.6 or 21.7, or in accordance with an order for alternative service made under rule 21.8(2)(b)

21.6 Method of service – copies of judgments or orders

Subject to rules 21.7 and 21.8, copies of judgments or orders and any orders or agreements fixing or varying the time for doing an act must be served personally.

21.7 Method of service – copies of undertakings

(1) Subject to paragraph (2) and rule 21.8, a copy of any document recording an undertaking will be delivered by the court to the person who gave the undertaking by–
  (a) handing to that person a copy of the document before that person leaves the court building;
  (b) posting a copy to that person at the residence or place of business of that person where this is known; or
  (c) posting a copy to that person's solicitor.

(2) If delivery cannot be effected in accordance with paragraph (1), the court officer must deliver a copy of the document to the party for whose benefit the undertaking was given and that party must serve it personally on the person who gave the undertaking as soon as practicable.

(3) Where the person referred to in paragraph (1) is a company or other corporation, a copy of the document must also be served on a director or officer of the company or corporation.

21.8 Dispensation with personal service

(1) In the case of a judgment or order requiring a person not to do an act, the court may dispense with service of a copy of the judgment or order in accordance with rules 21.5 to 21.7 if it is satisfied that the person has had notice of it by–
  (a) being present when the judgment or order was given or made; or
  (b) being in attendance at court where notice of the order or judgment was displayed; or
  (c) being notified of its terms by telephone, email or otherwise.

(2) In the case of any judgment or order the court may–
  (a) dispense with service under rules 21.5 to 21.7 if the court thinks it just to do so; or
  (b) make an order in respect of service by an alternative method or at an alternative place.

21.9 Requirement for a penal notice on judgments and orders

(1) Subject to paragraph (2), a judgment or order to do or not to do an act may not be enforced under rule 21.4 unless there is prominently displayed, on the front of the copy of the judgment or order served in accordance with this Section, a warning to the person required to do or not to do the act in question that disobedience to the order would be a contempt of court punishable by imprisonment, a fine or sequestration of assets.

(2) An undertaking to do or not to do an act which is contained in a judgment or order may be enforced under rule 21.4 notwithstanding that the judgment or order does not contain the warning described in paragraph (1).
(Paragraphs 2.1 to 2.3 of Practice Direction 21A contain provision about penal notices and warnings in relation to undertakings.)

21.10 How to make the committal application

(1) A committal application is made by an application notice under Part 10 in the proceedings in which the judgment or order was made or the undertaking was given.

(2) Where the committal application is made against a person who is not an existing party to the proceedings, it is made against that person by an application notice under Part 10.

(3) The application notice must–
   (a) set out in full the grounds on which the committal application is made and must identify, separately and numerically, each alleged act of contempt including, if known, the date of each of the alleged acts; and
   (b) be supported by one or more affidavits containing all the evidence relied upon.

(4) Subject to paragraph (5), the application notice and the evidence in support must be served personally on the respondent.

(5) The court may–
   (a) dispense with service under paragraph (4) if it considers it just to do so; or
   (b) make an order in respect of service by an alternative method or at an alternative place.

21.11 Committal for breach of a solicitor's undertaking

(1) This rule applies where an order for committal is sought in respect of a breach by a solicitor of an undertaking given by the solicitor to the court in connection with proceedings before the court.

(2) The applicant must obtain permission from the court before making a committal application under this rule.

(3) The application for permission must be made by filing an application notice under Part 10.

(4) The application for permission must be supported by an affidavit setting out–
   (a) the name, description and address of the respondent; and
   (b) the grounds on which the committal order is sought.

(5) The application for permission may be made without notice.

(6) Rules 10.5 and 13.4 do not apply.

(7) Unless the applicant makes the committal application within 14 days after permission has been granted under this rule, the permission will lapse.

Section 3 – Contempt in the face of the court

21.12 Contempt in the face of the court

Where contempt has occurred in the face of the court, the court may deal with the matter on its own initiative and give such directions as it thinks fit for the disposal of the matter.

Section 4 – Committal for interference with the due administration of justice

21.13 Scope

(1) This Section regulates committal applications in relation to interference with the due administration of justice in connection with proceedings in the Court of Protection, except where the contempt is committed in the face of the court or consists of disobedience to an order of the court or a breach of an undertaking to the court.

(2) A committal application under this Section may not be made without the permission of the court.

(The procedure for applying for permission to make a committal application is set out in rule 21.15.)

(Rules 21.16(3) and (4) make provision for cases in which both this Section and Section 5 (Committal for making a false statement of truth) may be relevant.)

21.14 Court to which application for permission under this Section is to be made

(1) Where contempt of court is committed in connection with any proceedings in the Court of Protection, the application for permission may only be made to a Tier 3 Judge.

(2) Where contempt of court is committed otherwise than in connection with any proceedings, Part 81 of the Civil Procedure Rules 1998 applies.

21.15 Application for permission

(1) The application for permission to make a committal application must be made by an application notice under Part 10, and the application notice must include or be accompanied by–

(a) a detailed statement of the applicant's grounds for making the committal application; and

(b) an affidavit setting out the facts and exhibiting all documents relied upon.

(2) The application notice and the documents referred to in paragraph (1) must be served personally on the respondent unless the court otherwise directs.

(3) Within 14 days of service on the respondent of the application notice, the respondent–

(a) must file and serve an acknowledgment of service; and

(b) may file and serve evidence.

(4) The court will consider the application for permission at an oral hearing, unless it considers that such a hearing is not appropriate.

(5) If the respondent intends to appear at the oral hearing referred to in paragraph (4), the respondent must give 7 days' notice in writing of such intention to the court and any other party and at the same time provide a written summary of the submissions which the respondent proposes to make.

(6) Where permission to proceed is given, the court may give such directions as it thinks fit.

Section 5 – Committal for making a false statement of truth

21.16 Scope and interaction with other Sections of this Part

(1) This Section contains rules about committal applications in relation to making, or causing to be made, a false statement in a document verified by a statement of truth, without an honest belief in its truth.

(2) Where the committal relates only to a false statement of truth, this Section applies.

(3) Where the committal application relates to both–

(a) a false statement of truth; and

(b) breach of a judgment, order or undertaking to do or abstain from doing an act,

then Section 2 (Committal for breach of a judgment, order or undertaking to do or abstain from doing an act) applies, but subject to paragraph (4).

(4) To the extent that a committal application referred to in paragraph (3) relates to a false statement of truth–
   (a) the applicant must obtain the permission of the court in accordance with rule 21.17; or
   (b) the court may direct that the matter be referred to the Attorney General with a request that the Attorney General consider whether to bring proceedings for contempt of court.

21.17 Committal application in relation to a false statement of truth

(1) A committal application in relation to a false statement of truth in connection with proceedings in the Court of Protection may be made only–
   (a) with the permission of a Tier 3 Judge; or
   (b) by the Attorney General.
(2) Where permission is required under paragraph (1)(a), rule 21.15 applies.
(3) The court may direct that the matter be referred to the Attorney General with a request that the Attorney General consider whether to bring proceedings for contempt of court.

Section 6 – Writ of sequestration to enforce a judgment, order or undertaking

21.18 Scope

This Section contains rules about applications for a writ of sequestration to enforce a judgment, order or undertaking.

21.19 Writ of sequestration to enforce a judgment, order or undertaking

(1) If–
   (a) a person required by a judgment or order to do an act does not do it within the time fixed by the judgment or order; or
   (b) a person disobeys a judgment or order not to do an act,

then, subject to the provisions of these Rules and if the court permits, the judgment or order may be enforced by a writ of sequestration against the property of that person.
(2) If the time fixed by the judgment or order for doing an act has been varied by a subsequent order, or agreement of the parties under rule 3.7(4), references in paragraph (1)(a) to the time fixed are references to the time fixed by that subsequent order or agreement.
(3) If the person referred to in paragraph (1) is a company or other corporation, the writ of sequestration may in addition be issued against the property of any director or other officer of that company or corporation.
(4) So far as applicable, and with the necessary modifications, this Section applies to undertakings given by a party as it applies to judgments or orders.

21.20 Requirement for service of a copy of the judgment or order and time for service

(1) Unless the court dispenses with service under rule 21.23, a judgment or order may not be enforced by writ of sequestration unless a copy of it has been served on the person required to do or not to do the act in question, and in the case of a judgment or order requiring a person to act–

(a) the copy has been served before the end of the time fixed for doing the act, together with a copy of any order fixing that time;
(b) where the time for doing the act has been varied by a subsequent order or agreement, a copy of that order or agreement has also been served; and
(c) where the judgment or order was made pursuant to an earlier judgment or order requiring the act to be done, a copy of the earlier judgment or order has also been served.

(2) Where the person referred to in paragraph (1) is a company or other corporation, a copy of the judgment or order must also be served on a director or other officer of the company or corporation before the end of the time fixed for doing the act.

(3) Copies of the judgment or order and any orders or agreements fixing or varying the time for doing an act must be served in accordance with rule 21.21 or 21.22, or in accordance with an order for alternative service made under rule 21.23(2)(b).

21.21 Method of service – copies of judgments or orders

Subject to rules 21.22 and 21.23, copies of judgments or orders and any orders or agreements fixing or varying the time for doing an act must be served personally.

21.22 Method of service – copies of undertakings

(1) Subject to paragraph (2) and rule 21.23, a copy of any document recording an undertaking will be delivered by the court to the person who gave the undertaking by–
(a) handing to that person a copy of the document before that person leaves the court building;
(b) posting a copy to that person at the residence or place of business of that person where this is known; or
(c) posting a copy to that person's address.

(2) If delivery cannot be effected in accordance with paragraph (1), the court officer must deliver a copy of the document to the party for whose benefit the undertaking was given, and that party must serve it personally on the person who gave the undertaking as soon as practicable.

(3) Where the person referred to in paragraph (1) is a company or other corporation, a copy of the judgment or order must also be served on a director or officer of the company or corporation.

21.23 Dispensation with personal service

(1) In the case of a judgment or order requiring a person to do or not to do an act, the court may dispense with service of a copy of the judgment or order in accordance with rules 21.20 to 21.22 if it is satisfied that the person has had notice of it by–
(a) being present when the judgment or order was made;
(b) being in attendance at court where notice of the order or judgment was displayed; or
(c) being notified of its terms by telephone, email or otherwise.

(2) In the case of any judgment or order the court may–
(a) dispense with service under rules 21.20 to 21.22 if the court thinks it just to do so; or

(b) make an order in respect of service by an alternative method or at an alternative place.

21.24 Requirement for a penal notice on judgments and orders

(1) Subject to paragraph (2), a judgment or order to do or not to do an act may not be enforced by a writ of sequestration unless there is prominently displayed, on the front of the copy of the judgment or order served in accordance with this Section, a warning to the person required to do or not to do the act in question that disobedience to the order would be a contempt of court punishable by imprisonment, a fine or sequestration of assets.

(2) An undertaking to do or not to do an act which is contained in a judgment or order may be enforced by a writ of sequestration notwithstanding that the judgment or order does not contain the warning described in paragraph (1).

(Paragraphs 2.1 to 2.3 of Practice Direction 21A contain provision about penal notices and warnings in relation to undertakings.)

21.25 How to make an application for permission to issue a writ of sequestration

(1) An application for permission to issue a writ of sequestration must be made to a Tier 3 Judge.

(2) An application for permission to issue a writ of sequestration must be made by filing an application notice under Part 10.

(3) The application notice must–

(a) set out in full the grounds on which the committal application is made and must identify, separately and numerically, each alleged act of contempt including, if known, the date of each of the alleged acts; and

(b) be supported by one or more affidavits containing all the evidence relied upon.

(4) Subject to paragraph (5), the application notice and the evidence in support must be served personally on the respondent.

(5) The court may–

(a) dispense with service under paragraph (4) if it considers it just to do so; or

(b) make an order in respect of service by an alternative method or at an alternative place.

21.26 Form of writ of sequestration

A writ of sequestration must be in Form No 67 as set out in either Practice Direction 5A supporting the Family Procedure Rules 2010 or Practice Direction 4 supporting the Civil Procedure Rules 1998 (or in a form containing corresponding provision).

Section 7 – General rules about committal applications, orders for committal and writs of sequestration

21.27 Hearing for committal order or writ of sequestration to be in public

(1) Notwithstanding rule 4.1 (general rule – hearing to be in private), when determining an application for committal or application for sequestration the court will hold the hearing in public unless it directs otherwise.

(2) If the court hearing an application in private decides to make a committal order against the respondent, it must in public state–

(a) the name of the respondent;

(b) in general terms, the nature of the contempt of court in respect of which the committal order is being made; and
(c) the length of the period of the committal order.

(3) Where a committal order is made in the absence of the respondent, the court may on its own initiative fix a date and time when the respondent is to be brought before the court.

21.28 The hearing

(1) Unless the court hearing the committal application or application for sequestration otherwise permits, the applicant may not rely on–
(a) any grounds other than–
(i) those set out in the application notice; or
(ii) in relation to committal applications under Section 4, the statement of grounds required by rule 21.15(1)(a) (where not included in the application notice);
(b) any evidence unless it has been served in accordance with the relevant Section of this Part or a practice direction supplementing this Part.

(2) At the hearing, the respondent is entitled–
(a) to give oral evidence, whether or not the respondent has filed or served written evidence, and, if doing so, may be cross-examined; and
(b) with the permission of the court, to call a witness to give evidence whether or not the witness has made an affidavit or witness statement.

(3) The court may require or permit any party or other person (other than the respondent) to give oral evidence at the hearing.

(4) The court may give directions requiring the attendance for cross-examination of a witness who has given written evidence.

21.29 Power to suspend execution of a committal order

(1) The court making the committal order may also order that the execution of the order will be suspended for such period or on such terms and conditions as the court may specify.

(2) Unless the court otherwise directs, the applicant must serve on the respondent a copy of any order made under paragraph (1).

21.30 Warrant of committal

(1) If a committal order is made, the order will be for the issue of a warrant of committal.

(2) Unless the court orders otherwise–
(a) a copy of the committal order must be served on the respondent either before or at the time of the execution of the warrant of committal; or
(b) where the warrant of committal has been signed by the judge, the committal order may be served on the respondent at any time within 36 hours after the execution of the warrant.

(3) Without further order of the court, a warrant of committal must not be enforced more than 2 years after the date on which the warrant is issued.

21.31 Discharge of a person in custody

(1) A person committed to prison for contempt of court may apply to the court to be discharged.

(2) The application must–

(a) be in writing and attested by the governor of the prison (or any other officer of the prison not below the rank of principal officer);
(b) show that the person committed to prison for contempt has purged, or wishes to purge, the contempt; and
(c) be served on the person (if any) at whose instance the warrant of committal was issued at least one day before the application is made.

(3) Paragraph (2) does not apply to an application made by the Official Solicitor acting with official authority for the discharge of a person in custody.

21.32 Discharge of a person in custody where a writ of sequestration has been issued

Where–
(a) a writ of sequestration has been issued to enforce a judgment or order;
(b) the property is in the custody or power of the respondent;
(c) the respondent has been committed for failing to deliver up any property or deposit it in court or elsewhere; and
(d) the commissioners appointed by the writ of sequestration take possession of the property as if it belonged to the respondent,

then, without prejudice to rule 21.31(1) (discharge of a person in custody), the court may discharge the respondent and give such directions for dealing with the property taken by the commissioners as it thinks fit.

Part 22: Civil Restraint Orders

22.1 Powers of the court to make civil restraint orders

(1) If the court, whether or not on its own initiative, dismisses an application (including an application for permission) and considers that the application is totally without merit–
(a) the court's order must record that fact; and
(b) the court must at the same time consider whether it is appropriate to make a civil restraint order.

(2) Practice Direction 22A sets out–
(a) the circumstances in which the court has the power to make a civil restraint order against a party to proceedings;
(b) the procedure where a party applies for a civil restraint order against another party; and
(c) the consequences of the court making a civil restraint order.

Part 23: International protection of adults

23.1 Applications in connection with Schedule 3 to the Act – general

(1) This Part applies to applications made in connection with Schedule 3 to the Act.

(2) A practice direction may make additional or supplementary provision in respect of any of the matters in this Part.

23.2 Interpretation

(1) Unless otherwise provided in a practice direction made under rule 23.1(2), and subject to paragraph (2), an expression which appears both in this Part and in Schedule 3 to the Act is to be construed in accordance with Schedule

3 to the Act, including, where required by paragraph 2(4) of Schedule 3, construing it in accordance with the Convention.

(2) Notwithstanding the provisions of paragraph 13(6) of Schedule 3 to the Act, 'lasting power' does not include–

(a) a lasting power of attorney within the meaning of section 9 of the Act; or

(b) an enduring power of attorney within the meaning of Schedule 4 to the Act.

(3) In this Part, 'Schedule 3 application' means an application made under this Part (whether or not additional declarations or orders under sections 15 and 16 of the Act are sought as part of such application).

23.3 Application of these Rules in relation to Schedule 3 applications

(1) These Rules and accompanying practice directions apply in relation to Schedule 3 applications as if for 'P' there were substituted 'the adult'.

(2) For the purposes of rule 1.2(4) and Part 17, the question of whether the adult has capacity to conduct proceedings in relation to a Schedule 3 application is to be determined in accordance with Part 1 of the Act.

(3) The permission of the court is not required for a Schedule 3 application.

23.4 Applications for recognition and enforcement

(1) An application for a declaration under paragraph 20 (recognition) or paragraph 22 (enforcement) of Schedule 3 to the Act is to be made in accordance with Part 9 and any practice direction made under rule 23.1(2).

(2) Without prejudice to its powers under Parts 6 (service) and 7 (notice), the court may dispense with service and notice where it thinks just to do so, having regard in particular to–

(a) whether the adult or (as the case may be) any respondent to the application is within the jurisdiction; and

(b) the need for applications for declarations of enforceability to be determined rapidly.

23.5 Applications in relation to lasting powers – disapplication or modification

An application under paragraph 14(1) of Schedule 3 to the Act for the court to disapply or modify a lasting power is to be made in accordance with Part 9 and any practice direction made under rule 23.1(2).

23.6 Applications in relation to lasting powers – declaration as to authority of donee of lasting power

An application for a declaration under section 15(1)(c) of the Act that a donee of a lasting power is acting lawfully when exercising authority under that lasting power is to be made in accordance with Part 9 and any practice direction made under rule 23.1(2).

Part 24: Miscellaneous

24.1 Enforcement methods – general

(1) The relevant practice direction may set out methods of enforcing judgments or orders.

(2) An application for an order for enforcement may be made on application by any person in accordance with Part 10.

24.2 Enforcement methods – application of the Civil Procedure Rules 1998

The following provisions of the Civil Procedure Rules 1998 apply, as far as they are relevant and with such modifications as may be necessary, to the enforcement of orders made in proceedings under these Rules–

(a) Part 70 (General Rules about Enforcement of Judgments and Orders);
(b) Part 71 (Orders to Obtain Information from Judgment Debtors);
(c) Part 72 (Third Party Debt Orders);
(d) Part 73 (Charging Orders, Stop Orders and Stop Notices);
(e) Part 83 (Writs and Warrants – General Provisions); and
(f) Part 84 (Enforcement by Taking Control of Goods).

24.3 Order or directions requiring a person to give security for discharge of functions

(1) This rule applies where the court makes an order or gives a direction–
  (a) conferring functions on any person (whether as deputy or otherwise); and
  (b) requiring that person to give security for the discharge of those functions.

(2) The person on whom functions are conferred must give the security before undertaking to discharge those functions, unless the court permits the security to be given subsequently.

(3) Paragraphs (4) to (6) apply where the security is required to be given before any action can be taken.

(4) Subject to paragraph (5), the security must be given in accordance with the requirements of regulation 33(2)(a) of the Public Guardian Regulations (which makes provision about the giving of security by means of a bond that is endorsed by an authorised insurance company or an authorised deposit-taker).

(5) The court may impose such other requirements in relation to the giving of the security as it considers appropriate (whether in addition to, or instead of, those specified in paragraph (4)).

(6) In specifying the date from which the order or directions referred to in paragraph (1) are to take effect, the court will have regard to the need to postpone that date for such reasonable period as would enable the Public Guardian to be satisfied that–
  (a) if paragraph (4) applies, the requirements of regulation 34 of the Public Guardian Regulations have been met in relation to the security; and
  (b) any other requirements imposed by the court under paragraph (5) have been met.

(7) 'The Public Guardian Regulations' means the Lasting Power of Attorney, Enduring Powers of Attorney and Public Guardian Regulations 2007.

24.4 Objections to registration of an enduring power of attorney – request for directions

(1) This rule applies in any case where–
  (a) the Public Guardian (having received a notice of objection to the registration of an instrument creating an enduring power of attorney) is prevented by paragraph 13(5) of Schedule 4 to the Act from registering the instrument except in accordance with the court's directions; and
  (b) on or before the relevant day, no application for the court to give such directions has been made under Part 9 (how to start proceedings).

(2) In paragraph (1)(b) the relevant day is the later of–
(a) the final day of the period specified in paragraph 13(4) of Schedule 4 to the Act; or
(b) the final day of the period of 14 days beginning with the date on which the Public Guardian receives the notice of objection.
(3) The Public Guardian may seek the court's directions about registering the instrument, by filing a request in accordance with the relevant practice direction.
(4) As soon as practicable and in any event within 21 days of the date on which the request was made, the court shall notify–
(a) the person (or persons) who gave the notice of objection; and
(b) the attorney or, if more than one, each of them.
(5) As soon as practicable and in any event within 21 days of the date on which the request is filed, the Public Guardian must notify the donor of the power that the request has been so filed.
(6) The notice under paragraph (4) must–
(a) state that the Public Guardian has requested the court's directions about registration;
(b) state that the court will give directions in response to the request unless an application under Part 9 is made to it before the end of the period of 21 days commencing with the date on which the notice is issued; and
(c) set out the steps required to make such an application.
(7) 'Notice of objection' means a notice of objection which is made in accordance with paragraph 13(4) of Schedule 4 to the Act.

24.5 Disposal of property where P ceases to lack capacity
(1) This rule applies where P ceases to lack capacity.
(2) In this rule, 'relevant property' means any property belonging to P and forming part of P's estate, and which–
(a) remains under the control of anyone appointed by order of the court; or
(b) is held under the direction of the court.
(3) The court may at any time make an order for any relevant property to be transferred to P, or at P's direction, provided that it is satisfied that P has the capacity to make decisions in relation to that property.
(4) An application for an order under this rule is to be made in accordance with Part 10.

24.6 Citation and commencement, revocations and transitional provision
(1) These Rules may be cited as the Court of Protection Rules 2017 and shall come into force on 1st December 2017.
(2) The rules in the Schedule are revoked as set out in the Schedule.
(3) A practice direction may make provision for the extent to which and manner in which these Rules shall apply to proceedings started before the day on which they come into force.

MENTAL CAPACITY ACT 2005 (TRANSFER OF PROCEEDINGS) ORDER 2007
SI No 1899

Citation and commencement

1 (1) This Order may be cited as the Mental Capacity Act 2005 (Transfer of Proceedings) Order 2007.

(2) This Order shall come into force on 1st October 2007.

(3) In this Order 'the Children Act' means the Children Act 1989.

Transfers from the Court of Protection to a court having jurisdiction under the Children Act

2 (1) This article applies to any proceedings in the Court of Protection which relate to a person under 18.

(2) The Court of Protection may direct the transfer of the whole or part of the proceedings to a court having jurisdiction under the Children Act where it considers that in all the circumstances, it is just and convenient to transfer the proceedings.

(3) In making a determination, the Court of Protection must have regard to–

(a) whether the proceedings should be heard together with other proceedings that are pending in a court having jurisdiction under the Children Act;

(b) whether any order that may be made by a court having jurisdiction under that Act is likely to be a more appropriate way of dealing with the proceedings;

(c) the need to meet any requirements that would apply if the proceedings had been started in a court having jurisdiction under the Children Act; and

(d) any other matter that the court considers relevant.

(4) The Court of Protection–

(a) may exercise the power to make an order under paragraph (2) on an application or on its own initiative; and

(b) where it orders a transfer, must give reasons for its decision.

(5) Any proceedings transferred under this article–

(a) are to be treated for all purposes as if they were proceedings under the Children Act which had been started in a court having jurisdiction under that Act; and

(b) are to be dealt with after the transfer in accordance with directions given by a court having jurisdiction under that Act.

Transfers from a court having jurisdiction under the Children Act to the Court of Protection

3 (1) This article applies to any proceedings in a court having jurisdiction under the Children Act which relate to a person under 18.

(2) A court having jurisdiction under the Children Act may direct the transfer of the whole or part of the proceedings to the Court of Protection where it considers that in all circumstances, it is just and convenient to transfer the proceedings.

(3) In making a determination, the court having jurisdiction under the Children Act must have regard to–

(a) whether the proceedings should be heard together with other proceedings that are pending in the Court of Protection;
(b) whether any order that may be made by the Court of Protection is likely to be a more appropriate way of dealing with the proceedings;
(c) the extent to which any order made as respects a person who lacks capacity is likely to continue to have effect when that person reaches 18; and
(d) any other matter that the court considers relevant.

(4) A court having jurisdiction under the Children Act–
(a) may exercise the power to make an order under paragraph (2) on an application or on its own initiative; and
(b) where it orders a transfer, must give reasons for its decision.

(5) Any proceedings transferred under this article–
(a) are to be treated for all purposes as if they were proceedings under the Mental Capacity Act 2005 which had been started in the Court of Protection; and
(b) are to be dealt with after the transfer in accordance with directions given by the Court of Protection.

Avoidance of double liability for fees

4 Any fee paid for the purpose of starting any proceedings that are transferred under article 2 or 3 is to be treated as if it were the fee that would have been payable if the proceedings had started in the court to which the transfer is made.

COURT OF PROTECTION FEES ORDER 2007 SI No 145 (as amended)[1]

Citation and commencement

1 This Order may be cited as the Court of Protection Fees Order 2007 and comes into force on 1 October 2007.

Interpretation

2 In this Order–

'the Act' means the Mental Capacity Act 2005;

'appellant' means the person who brings or seeks to bring an appeal;

'court' means the Court of Protection;

'P' means any person (other than a protected party) who lacks or, so far as consistent with the context, is alleged to lack capacity to make a decision or decisions in relation to any matter that is the subject of an application to the court and references to a person who lacks capacity are to be construed in accordance with the Act;

'protected party' means a party or an intended party (other than P or a child) who lacks capacity to conduct the proceedings;

'the Regulations' means the Lasting Powers of Attorney, Enduring Powers of Attorney and Public Guardian Regulations 2007; and

'the Rules' means the Court of Protection Rules 2007.

Schedule of fees

3 The fees set out in Schedule 1 to this Order shall apply in accordance with the following provisions of this Order.

Application fee

4 (1) An application fee shall be payable by the applicant on making an application under Part 9 of the Rules (how to start proceedings) in accordance with the following provisions of this article.

(2) Where permission to start proceedings is required under Part 8 of the Rules (permission), the fee prescribed by paragraph (1) shall be payable on making an application for permission.

(3) The fee prescribed by paragraph (1) shall not be payable where the application is made under–

(a) rule 67 of the Rules (applications relating to lasting powers of attorney) by–

(i) the donee of a lasting power of attorney, or

(ii) a person named in a statement made by the donor of a lasting power of attorney in accordance with paragraph 2(1)(c)(i) of Part 1 of Schedule 1 to the Act,

and is solely in respect of an objection to the registration of a lasting power of attorney; or

(b) rule 68 of the Rules (applications relating to enduring powers of attorney) by–

(i) a donor of an enduring power of attorney,

(ii) an attorney under an enduring power of attorney, or

(iii) a person listed in paragraph 6(1) of Part 3 of Schedule 4 to the Act,

1 See also appendix F below.

and is solely in respect of an objection to the registration of an enduring power of attorney.

(4) The fee prescribed by paragraph (1) shall not be payable where the application is made by the Public Guardian.

(5) Where a fee has been paid under paragraph (1) it shall be refunded where P dies within five days of the application being filed.

Appeal fee

5 (1) An appeal fee shall be payable by the appellant on the filing of an appellant's notice under Part 20 of the Rules (appeals) in accordance with the following provisions of this article.

(2) The fee prescribed by paragraph (1) shall not be payable where the appeal is–

(a) brought by the Public Guardian; or

(b) an appeal against a decision of a nominated officer made under rule 197 of the Rules (appeal against a decision of a nominated officer).

(3) The fee prescribed by paragraph (1) shall be refunded where P dies within five days of the appellant's notice being filed.

Hearing fees

6 (1) A hearing fee shall be payable by the applicant where the court has–

(a) held a hearing in order to determine the case; and

(b) made a final order, declaration or decision.

(2) A hearing fee shall be payable by the appellant in relation to an appeal where the court has–

(a) held a hearing in order to determine the appeal; and

(b) made a final order, declaration or decision in relation to the appeal.

(3) The fees prescribed by paragraphs (1) and (2) shall not be payable where the hearing is in respect of an application or appeal brought by the Public Guardian.

(4) The fee prescribed by paragraph (2) shall not be payable where the hearing is in respect of an appeal against a decision of a nominated officer made under rule 197 of the Rules (appeal against a decision of a nominated officer).

(5) The fee prescribed by paragraph (1) shall not be payable where the applicant was not required to pay an application fee under Article 4(1) by virtue of Article 4(3).

(6) The fees prescribed by paragraphs (1) and (2) shall be payable by the applicant or appellant as the case may be within 30 days of the date of the invoice for the fee.

Fee for request for copy of court document

7 (1) A fee for a copy of a court document shall be payable by the person requesting the copy of the document.

(2) . . .

(3) The fee prescribed by paragraph (1) shall be payable at the time the request for the copy is made to the court.

Remissions and part remissions

8 Schedule 2 applies for the purpose of ascertaining whether a party is entitled to a remission or part remission of a fee prescribed by this Order.

9 . . .

Transitional provision

10 (1) In this article 'Court of Protection' means the office of the Supreme Court called the Court of Protection which ceases to exist under section 45(6) of the Act.

(2) Where a hearing that takes place on or after 1 October 2007 was listed by the Court of Protection before 1 October 2007, no hearing fee shall be payable under Article 6.

SCHEDULE 1

Article 3

Column 1	*Column 2*
Application fee (Article 4)	£371.00
Appeal fee (Article 5)	£234.00
Hearing fees (Article 6)	£494.00
Copy of a document fee (Article 7(1))	£5.00
. . .	. . .

SCHEDULE 2: REMISSIONS AND PART REMISSIONS

Interpretation

1 (1) In this Schedule–

'child' means a person–

(a) whose main residence is with a party and who is aged–

(i) under 16 years; or

(ii) 16 to 19 years; and is–

(aa) not married or in a civil partnership; and

(bb) enrolled or accepted in full-time education that is not advanced education, or approved training; or

(b) in respect of whom a party or their partner pays child support maintenance or periodic payments in accordance with a maintenance agreement,

and 'full-time education', 'advanced education' and 'approved training' have the meaning given by the Child Benefit (General) Regulations 2006;

'child support maintenance' has the meaning given in section 3(6) of the Child Support Act 1991;

'couple' has the meaning given in section 3(5A) of the Tax Credits Act 2002;

'disposable capital' has the meaning given in paragraph 5;

'excluded benefits' means any of the following–

(a) any of the following benefits payable under the Social Security Contributions and Benefits Act 1992 or the corresponding provisions of the Social Security Contributions and Benefits (Northern Ireland) Act 1992–

(i) attendance allowance under section 64;

(ii) severe disablement allowance;

(iii) carer's allowance;

(iv) disability living allowance;

(v) constant attendance allowance under section 104 as an increase to a disablement pension;

(vi) any payment made out of the social fund;

(vii) housing benefit;
(viii) widowed parents allowance;

(b) any of the following benefit payable under the Tax Credits Act 2002–
(i) any disabled child element or severely disabled child element of the child tax credit;
(ii) any childcare element of the working tax credit;

(c) any direct payment made under the Community Care, Services for Carers and Children's Services (Direct Payments) (England) Regulations 2009, the Community Care, Services for Carers and Children's Services (Direct Payments) (Wales) Regulations 2011, the Carers and Direct Payments Act (Northern Ireland) 2002, section 12B(1) of the Social Work (Scotland) Act 1968 or under regulations made under 50 to 53 of the Social Services and Well-being (Wales) Act 2014;

(d) a back to work bonus payable under section 26 of the Jobseekers Act 1995, or article 28 of the Jobseekers (Northern Ireland) Order 1995;

(e) any exceptionally severe disablement allowance paid under the Personal Injuries (Civilians) Scheme 1983;

(f) any payments from the Industrial Injuries Disablement Benefit;

(g) any pension paid under the Naval, Military and Air Forces etc (Disablement and Death) Service Pension Order 2006;

(h) any payment made from the Independent Living Funds;

(i) any payment made from the Bereavement Allowance;

(j) any financial support paid under an agreement for the care of a foster child;

(k) any housing credit element of pension credit;

(l) any armed forces independence payment;

(m) any personal independence payment payable under the Welfare Reform Act 2012;

(n) any payment on account of benefit as defined in the Social Security (Payments on Account of Benefit) Regulations 2013;

(o) any of the following amounts, as defined by the Universal Credit Regulations 2013, that make up an award of universal credit–
(i) an additional amount to the child element in respect of a disabled child;
(ii) a housing costs element;
(iii) a childcare costs element;
(iv) a carer element;
(v) a limited capability for work or limited capacity for work and work -related activity element;

'family help (higher)' has the meaning given in paragraph 15(3) of the Civil Legal Aid (Merits Criteria) Regulations 2013;

'family help (lower)' has the meaning given in paragraph 15(2) of the Civil Legal Aid (Merits Criteria) Regulations 2013;

'gross monthly income' has the meaning given in paragraph 13;

'Independent Living Funds' means the funds listed at regulation 20(2)(b) of the Criminal Legal Aid (Financial Resources) Regulations 2013;

'legal representation' has the meaning given in paragraph 18(2) of the Civil Legal Aid (Merits Criteria) Regulations 2013;

'maintenance agreement' has the meaning given in subsection 9(1) of the Child Support Act 1991;

'partner' means a person with whom the party lives as a couple and includes a person with whom the party is not currently living but from whom the party is not living separate and apart;

'party' means the individual who would, but for this Schedule, be liable to pay a fee under this Order;

'restraint order' means–

(a) an order under section 42(1A) of the Senior Courts Act 1981;
(b) an order under section 33 of the Employment Tribunals Act 1996;
(c) a civil restraint order made under rule 3.11 of the Civil Procedure Rules 1998, or a practice direction made under that rule; or
(d) a civil restraint order under rule 4.8 of the Family Procedure Rules 2010, or the practice direction referred to in that rule.

(2) References to remission of a fee are to be read as including references to a part remission of a fee as appropriate and remit and remitted shall be construed accordingly.

Fee remission

2 If a party satisfies the disposable capital test, the amount of any fee remission is calculated by applying the gross monthly income test.

Disposable capital test

Disposable capital test

3 (1) Subject to paragraph 4, a party satisfies the disposable capital test if–

(a) the fee payable by the party and for which an application for remission is made, falls within a fee band set out in column 1 of Table 1; and
(b) the party's disposable capital is less than the amount in the corresponding row of column 2.

Table 1	
Column 1 (fee band)	*Column 2 (disposable capital)*
Up to and including £1,000	£3,000
£1,001 to £1,335	£4,000
£1,336 to £1,665	£5,000
£1,666 to £2,000	£6,000
£2,001 to £2,330	£7,000
£2,331 to £4,000	£8,000
£4,001 to £5,000	£10,000
£5,001 to £6,000	£12,000
£6,001 to £7,000	£14,000
£7,001 or more	£16,000

4 Subject to paragraph 14, if a party or their partner is aged 61 or over, that party satisfies the disposable capital test if that party's disposable capital is less than £16,000.

Disposable capital

5 Subject to paragraph 14, disposable capital is the value of every resource of a capital nature belonging to the party on the date on which the application for remission is made, unless it is treated as income by this Order, or it is disregarded as excluded disposable capital.

Disposable capital–non-money resources

6 The value of a resource of a capital nature that does not consist of money is calculated as the amount which that resource would realise if sold, less–

(a) 10% of the sale value; and
(b) the amount of any borrowing secured against that resource that would be repayable on sale.

Disposable capital–resources held outside the United Kingdom

7 (1) Capital resources in a country outside the United Kingdom count towards disposable capital.

(2) If there is no prohibition in that country against the transfer of a resource into the United Kingdom, the value of that resource is the amount which that resource would realise if sold in that country, in accordance with paragraph 6.

(3) If there is a prohibition in that country against the transfer of a resource into the United Kingdom, the value of that resource is the amount that resource would realise if sold to a buyer in the United Kingdom.

Disposable capital–foreign currency resources

8 Where disposable capital is held in currency other than sterling, the cost of any banking charge or commission that would be payable if that amount were converted into sterling, is deducted from its value.

Disposable capital–jointly owned resources

9 Where any resource of a capital nature is owned jointly or in common, there is a presumption that the resource is owned in equal shares, unless evidence to the contrary is produced.

Excluded disposable capital

10 The following things are excluded disposable capital–

(a) a property which is the main or only dwelling occupied by the party;
(b) the household furniture and effects of the main or only dwelling occupied by the party;
(c) articles of personal clothing;
(d) any vehicle, the sale of which would leave the party, or their partner, without motor transport;
(e) tools and implements of trade, including vehicles used for business purposes;
(f) the capital value of the party's or their partner's business, where the party or their partner is self-employed;
(g) the capital value of any funds or other assets held in trust, where the party or their partner is a beneficiary without entitlement to advances of any trust capital;
(h) a jobseeker's back to work bonus;
(i) a payment made as a result of a determination of unfair dismissal by a court or tribunal, or by way of settlement of a claim for unfair dismissal;

(j) any compensation paid as a result of a determination of medical negligence or in respect of any personal injury by a court, or by way of settlement of a claim for medical negligence or personal injury;
(k) the capital held in any personal or occupational pension scheme;
(l) any cash value payable on surrender of a contract of insurance;
(m) any capital payment made out of the Independent Living Funds;
(n) any bereavement support payment in respect of the rate set out in regulation 3(2) or (5) of the Bereavement Support Payment Regulations 2017 (rate of bereavement support payment);
(o) any capital insurance or endowment lump sum payments that have been paid as a result of illness, disability or death;
(p) any student loan or student grant;
(q) any payments under the criminal injuries compensation scheme.

Gross monthly income test

Remission of fees–gross monthly income

11 (1) If a party satisfies the disposable capital test, no fee is payable under this Order if, at the time when the fee would otherwise be payable, the party or their partner has the number of children specified in column 1 of Table 2 and–
(a) if the party is single, their gross monthly income does not exceed the amount set out in the appropriate row of column 2; or
(b) if the party is one of a couple, the gross monthly income of that couple does not exceed the amount set out in the appropriate row of column 3.

Table 2		
Column 1	*Column 2*	*Column 3*
Number of children of party	*Single*	*Couple*
no children	£1,170	£1,345
1 child	£1,435	£1,610
2 children	£1,700	£1,875

(2) If a party or their partner has more than 2 children, the relevant amount of gross monthly income is the appropriate amount specified in Table 2 for 2 children, plus the sum of £265 for each additional child.
(3) For every £10 of gross monthly income received above the appropriate amount in Table 2, including any additional amount added under sub-paragraph (2), the party must pay £5 towards the fee payable, up to the maximum amount of the fee payable.
(4) This paragraph is subject to paragraph 12.

Gross monthly income cap

12 (1) No remission is available if a party or their partner has the number of children specified in column 1 of Table 3 and–
(a) if the party is single, their gross monthly income exceeds the amount set out in the appropriate row of column 2 of Table 3; or
(b) if the party is one of a couple, the gross monthly income of that couple exceeds the amount set out in the appropriate row of column 3 of Table 3.

Table 3		
Column 1	*Column 2*	*Column 3*
Number of children of party	*Single*	*Couple*
no children	£5,170	£5,345
1 child	£5,435	£5,610
2 children	£5,700	£5,875

(2) If a party or their partner has more than 2 children, the relevant amount of gross monthly income is the appropriate amount specified in Table 3 for 2 children, plus the sum of £265 for each additional child.

Gross monthly income

13 (1) Subject to paragraph 14, gross monthly income means the total monthly income, for the month preceding that in which the application for remission is made, from all sources, other than receipt of any of the excluded benefits.

(2) Income from a trade, business or gainful occupation other than an occupation at a wage or salary is calculated as–

(a) the profits which have accrued or will accrue to the party; and

(b) the drawings of the party;

in the month preceding that in which the application for remission is made.

(3) In calculating profits under sub-paragraph (2)(a), all sums necessarily expended to earn those profits are deducted.

General

Resources and income treated as the party's resources and income

14 (1) Subject to sub-paragraphs (2) to (5), the disposable capital and gross monthly income of a partner is to be treated as disposable capital and gross monthly income of the party.

(2) Where the partner of the party has a contrary interest to the party in the matter to which the fee relates, the disposable capital and gross monthly income of that partner is not treated as the disposable capital and gross monthly income of the party.

(3) Where proceedings are brought concerning the property and affairs of 'P', for the purpose of determining whether a party is entitled to a remission or part remission of a fee in accordance with this Schedule–

(a) the disposable capital and gross monthly income of the person bringing those proceedings is not treated as the disposable capital and gross monthly income of the party;

(b) the disposable capital and gross monthly income of 'P' is to be treated as the disposable capital of the party; and

(c) the disposable capital and gross monthly income of the partner of 'P', if any, is not treated as the disposable capital and gross monthly income of the party.

(4) Where proceedings are brought concerning the personal welfare of 'P', for the purpose of determining whether a party is entitled to a remission or part remission of a fee in accordance with this Schedule, the disposable capital

and gross monthly income of a partner, if any, is not treated as the disposable capital and gross monthly income of the party, where that partner is 'P' who is the subject of those proceedings in which the fee is payable.

(5) Where proceedings concern both the property and affairs of 'P' and their personal welfare, their disposable capital and gross monthly income shall be treated in accordance with sub-paragraph (3).

Application for remission of a fee

15 (1) An application for remission of a fee must be made at the time when the fee would otherwise be payable.

(2) Where an application for remission of a fee is made, the party must–
(a) indicate the fee to which the application relates;
(b) declare the amount of their disposable capital; and
(c) provide documentary evidence of their gross monthly income and the number of children relevant for the purposes of paragraphs 11 and 12.

(3) Where an application for remission of a fee is made on or before the date on which a fee is payable, the date for payment of the fee is disapplied.

(4) Where an application for remission is refused, or if part remission of a fee is granted, the amount of the fee which remains unremitted must be paid within the period notified in writing to the party.

Remission in exceptional circumstances

16 A fee specified in this Order may be remitted where the Lord Chancellor is satisfied that there are exceptional circumstances which justify doing so.

Refunds

17 (1) Subject to sub-paragraph (3), where a party pays a fee at a time when that party would have been entitled to a remission if they had provided the documentary evidence required by paragraph 15, the fee, or the amount by which the fee would have been reduced as the case may be, must be refunded if documentary evidence relating to the time when the fee became payable is provided at a later date.

(2) Subject to sub-paragraph (3), where a fee has been paid at a time when the Lord Chancellor, if all the circumstances had been known, would have remitted the fee under paragraph 15, the fee or the amount by which the fee would have been reduced, as the case may be, must be refunded to the party.

(3) No refund shall be made under this paragraph unless the party who paid the fee applies within 3 months of the date of the order of the court which finally disposed of the proceedings.

(4) The Lord Chancellor may extend the period of 3 months mentioned in sub-paragraph (3) if the Lord Chancellor considers that there is a good reason for a refund being made after the end of the period of 3 months.

Legal aid

18 A party is not entitled to a fee remission if, under Part 1 of the Legal Aid, Sentencing and Punishment of Offenders Act 2012, they are in receipt of the following civil legal services–
(a) Legal representation; or
(b) Family help (higher); or
(c) Family help (lower) in respect of applying for a consent order.

Vexatious litigants

19 (1) This paragraph applies where–
(a) a restraint order is in force against a party; and
(b) that party makes an application for permission to–
(i) issue proceedings or take a step in proceedings as required by the restraint order;
(ii) apply for amendment or discharge of the order; or
(iii) appeal the order.
(2) The fee prescribed by this Order for the application is payable in full.
(3) If the party is granted permission, they are to be refunded the difference between–
(a) the fee paid; and
(b) the fee that would have been payable if this Schedule had been applied without reference to this paragraph.

Exceptions

20 No remissions or refunds are available in respect of the fee payable for–
(a) copy or duplicate documents;
(b) searches.

APPENDIX C

Civil Procedure Rules costs provisions as applied in the Court of Protection[1]

CPR Rule	Title/Description of Rule	Does it apply?
44.1	Interpretation and application	Yes – but see definitions below in accordance with COPR 19.1(1): *'authorised court officer'* means any officer of the Senior Courts Costs Office whom the Lord Chancellor has authorised to assess costs *'costs'* include fees, charges, disbursements, expenses, remuneration and any reimbursement allowed to a litigant in person *'costs judge'* means a taxing Master of the Senior Courts *'costs officer'* means a costs judge or an authorised court officer *'detailed assessment'* means the procedure by which the amount of costs or remuneration is decided by a costs officer in accordance with Part 47 of the Civil Procedure Rules 1998 (which are applied to proceedings under these Rules, with modifications, by rule 19.6) *'fixed costs'* are to be construed in accordance with the relevant practice direction *'fund'* includes any estate or property held for the benefit of any person or class of persons, and any fund to which a trustee or personal representative is entitled in that capacity *'paying party'* means a party liable to pay costs *'pro bono representation'* means representation provided free of charge

1 We are grateful to Hilary O'Keefe, then a pupil barrister at Doughty Street Chambers, for her work in compiling this table.

		'receiving party' means a party entitled to be paid costs *'summary assessment'* means the procedure by which the court, when making an order about costs, orders payment of a sum of money instead of fixed costs or detailed assessment.
44.2(1)	Court's discretion as to costs	No
44.2(2)	If the court decides to make an order about costs	No
44.2(3)	Circs where the general rule does not apply	No
44.2(4)	Circs that court will have regard to in deciding what order (if any) to make about costs	No
44.2(5)	Conduct of the parties	No
44.2(6)	Types of orders that are included in the orders which the court may make under this rule	Yes – however the definition of 'costs' in COPR r19.1(1) applies (see definition above).
44.2(7)	Court will consider whether it is practicable to make an order under paragraph 6	Yes
44.2(8)	Where the court orders a party to pay costs subject to detailed assessment, it will order that party to pay a reasonable sum on account of costs, unless there is a good reason not to do so	Yes – however the definitions of 'costs' and 'detailed assessment' in COPR r19.1(1) applies (see definition above).

44.3	Basis of assessment	Yes – however the definitions of 'costs', 'detailed assessment', 'summary assessment' and 'paying party' in COPR r19.1(1) apply
44.4	Factors to be taken into account in deciding the amount of costs	Yes – however the definitions of 'costs' and 'receiving party' in COPR r19.1(1) apply.
44.5	Amount of costs where costs are payable under a contract	No – and note that COPR r19.1(2) has specific provision in relation to costs payable under a contract which does not include the presumption in CPR r44.5
44.6	Procedure for assessing costs	No
44.7	Time for complying with an order for costs	Yes – however the definition of 'costs' in COPR r19.1(1) applies.
44.8	Legal representative's duty to notify the party	Yes
44.9	Cases where costs orders deemed to have been made	No
44.10	Where the court makes no order for costs	Yes – however the definition of 'costs' in COPR r19.1(1) applies.
44.11	Court's powers in relation to misconduct	Yes – however the definitions of 'summary assessment' and 'detailed assessment' in COPR r19.1(1) apply.
44.12	Set off	Yes – however the definition of 'costs' in COPR r19.1(1) applies.
44.13	Qualified one-way costs shifting: scope and interpretation	No
44.14	Effect of qualified one-way costs shifting	No
44.15	Exceptions to qualified one-way costs shifting where permission not required	No

44.16	Exceptions to qualified one-way costs shifting where permission required	No
44.17	Transitional provision	No
44.18	Award of costs where there is a damages based agreement	No
Part 45	Fixed Costs	No – none of this part applies
Part 46	Costs special cases	
46.1(1)	Pre-commencement disclosure and orders for disclosure against a person who is not a party – This part applies but the following wording is substituted; '*This paragraph applies where a person applies for an order for specific disclosure before the commencement of proceedings*'	Yes – with substituted wording
46.2	Costs order in favour of or against non-parties	No
46.3	Limitations on court's power to award costs in favour of trustee or personal representative	Yes – however the definition of 'costs' in COPR r19.1(1) applies.

46.4	Costs where money is payable by or to a child or protected party	Yes – however the definition of 'costs', and 'detailed assessment' in COPR r19.1(1) apply Conditional fee agreement means an agreement enforceable under Courts and Legal Services Act 1990 s58 (COPR r19.1(4))
46.5	Litigants in person	No
46.6	Costs where the court has made a group litigation order	Yes, however the definition of 'costs' in COPR r19.1(1) applies.
46.7	Orders in respect of pro-bono representation	Yes – however the definitions of 'costs', 'pro bono representation', 'fixed costs', 'detailed assessment', 'paying party' and 'receiving party' in COPR r19.1(1) apply.
46.8	Personal liability of legal repres-entative for costs – wasted costs orders	Yes – however the definitions of 'costs' and 'costs judge' in COPR r19.1(1) apply.
46.9	Basis of detailed assessment of solicitor and client costs	Yes – however the definitions of 'costs', 'detailed assessment' and 'conditional fee agreement' in COPR r19.1(1) apply.
		Conditional fee agreement means an agreement enforceable under Courts and Legal Services Act 1990 s58 (COPR r19.1(4))
46.10	Assessment procedure	No
46.11	Costs on the small claims track and fast track	No
46.12	Limitation on amount court may allow where a claim allocated to the fast track settles before trial	No
46.13	Costs following allocation, re-allocation and non-allocation	No
46.14	Costs-only proceedings	No

46.15	Claims for Judicial Review: costs against interveners	Yes – however the definition of 'costs' in COPR r19.1(1) applies.
Part 47		
47.1	Time when detailed assess-ment may be carried out	Yes – however the definition of 'costs' and 'detailed assessment' in COPR r19.1(1) apply.
47.2	No stay of detailed assess-ment where there is an appeal	Yes – however the definition of 'detailed assess-ment' in COPR r19.1(1) applies.
47.3(1)	Powers of an authorised court officer – this section applies but in 47.3(1) (c), the words '*unless the costs are being assessed under rule 64.4 (costs where money is payable to a child or protec-ted party*)' are omitted	Yes, but see note regarding CPR. 47.3(1) (c) The definitions of 'authorised court officer' and 'detailed assessment' in COPR r19.1(1) apply.
47.3 (2)	Where a party objects to the detailed assess-ment of costs being made by an authorised court officer, the court may order it to be made by a costs judge or a district judge.	Yes – but the words '*or a district judge* ' in 47.3(2) are omitted
		The definitions of 'authorised court officer' and 'costs judge' in COPR r19.1(1) apply.

47.4(1)	Venue for detailed assessment proceedings – all applications and requests in detailed assessment proceedings must be made to or filed at the appropriate office	Yes – however the definition of 'detailed assessment' in COPR r19.1(1) applies.
47.4(2)	The court may direct that the appropriate office is to be the Costs Office	Yes
47.4(3)	In the County Court, a court may direct that another County Court hearing centre is to be the appropriate office	No
47.4(4)	A direction under paragraph (3) may be made without proceedings being transferred to that court	No
47.5	This section of Part 47 applies where a cost officer is to make a detailed assessment of –	Yes – also to a detailed assessment of the remuneration of a deputy
	(a) costs which are payable by one party to another; or	The definitions of 'detailed assessment' and 'costs' in COPR r19.1(1) apply.

	(b) the sum which is payable by one party to the prescribed charity pursuant to an order under section 194(3) of the 2007 Act	
47.6	Commencement of detailed assessment proceedings	Yes – also to a detailed assessment of the remuneration of a deputy
		The definitions of 'detailed assessment', 'paying party', 'receiving party' and 'costs' in COPR r19.1(1) apply
47.7	Period for commencing detailed assessment proceedings	Yes – also to a detailed assessment of the remuneration of a deputy
		The definition of 'detailed assessment' in COPR r19.1(1) applies.
47.8	Sanction for delay in bringing detailed assessment proceedings	Yes – also to a detailed assessment of the remuneration of a deputy
		The definitions of 'receiving party', 'detailed assessment', 'paying party' and 'costs' in COPR r19.1(1) apply.
47.9	Points of dispute and consequences of not serving;	Yes – also to a detailed assessment of the remuneration of a deputy.
		Paragraph 47.9(4) does not apply where the cost is coming out of P's estate
		The definitions of 'paying party', 'detailed assessment' and 'receiving party' in COPR r19.1(1) apply.

	(1) The paying party and any other party to the detailed assessment proceedings may dispute any item in the bill of costs by serving points of dispute on –	
	(a) the receiving party; and	
	(b) every other party to the detailed assessment proceedings.	
	(2) The period for serving points of dispute is 21 days after the date of service of the notice of commencement.	
	(3) If a party serves points of dispute after the period set out in paragraph (2), that party may not be heard further in the detailed assessment proceedings unless the court gives permission.	
	(Practice Direction 47 sets out requirements about the form of points of dispute.)	

	(4) The receiving party may file a request for a default costs certificate if –	
	(a) the period set out in paragraph (2) for serving points of dispute has expired; and	
	(b) the receiving party has not been served with any points of dispute.	
	(5) If any party (including the paying party) serves points of dispute before the issue of a default costs certificate the court may not issue the default costs certificate.	
	(Section IV of this Part sets out the procedure to be followed after points of dispute have been served.)	
47.10	Procedure where costs are agreed	Yes – to a detailed assessment of the remuneration of a deputy also – but not when the costs are to be paid out of P's estate
		The definitions of 'paying party' 'receiving party' and 'costs' in COPR r19.1(1) apply
47.11	Default costs certificate	Yes – also to a detailed assessment of the remuneration of a deputy but not when the costs are to be paid out of P's estate
		The definitions of 'receiving party', and 'detailed assessment' in COPR r19.1(1) apply.
47.12	Setting aside a costs default certificate	Yes – also to a detailed assessment of the remuneration of a deputy

		The definitions of 'receiving party', and 'detailed assessment' in COPR r19.1(1) apply.
47.13	Optional reply when party to detailed assessments proceedings	Yes – also to a detailed assessment of the remuneration of a deputy
		The definitions of 'receiving party', and 'detailed assessment' in COPR r19.1(1) apply.
47.14	Detailed assessment hearing	Yes – also to a detailed assessment of the remuneration of a deputy
		The definitions of 'receiving party', and 'detailed assessment', 'paying party' and 'costs' in COPR r19.1(1) apply.
47.15	Provisional assessment	Yes – to a detailed assessment of the remuneration of a deputy
		The definitions of 'detailed assessment' and 'receiving party' in COPR r19.1(1) apply
47.16	Power to issue interim certificate	Yes – also to a detailed assessment of the remuneration of a deputy
		The definitions of 'receiving party', 'costs' and 'detailed assessment' in COPR r19.1(1) apply.
47.17	Final costs certificate	Yes – also to a detailed assessment of the remuneration of a deputy
		The definitions of 'receiving party', 'costs' and 'detailed assessment' in COPR r19.1(1) apply.
47.18	Detailed assessment procedure where costs are payable out of the Community Legal Services Fund or by the Lord Chancellor under Part I of the Legal Aid, Sentencing and Punishment of Offenders Act 2012	Yes – however the definitions of 'costs' and 'detailed assessment' in COPR r19.1(1) apply

47.19	Detailed assessment procedure where costs are payable out of a fund other than the Community Legal Service fund	Yes – however the definitions of 'costs', 'fund', 'detailed assessment' and 'receiving party' in COPR r19.1(1) apply.
47.20	Liability for costs of detailed assessment proceedings	Yes – however the definitions of 'receiving party', 'detailed assessment', 'pro bono representation', 'costs' and 'paying party' in COPR r19.1(1) apply
47.21	Right to appeal	Yes, however the definitions of 'detailed assessment', and 'authorised court officer' in COPR r19.1(1) apply
47.22	Court to hear appeal	Yes – however the definitions of 'authorised court officer' and 'costs judge' in COPR r19.1(1) apply.
47.23	Appeal procedure	Yes – however the definition of 'detailed assessment' in COPR r19.1(1) applies
47.24	Powers of the court on appeal	Yes – however the definition of 'authorised court officer' in COPR r19.1(1) applies.

APPENDIX D

Statements and letters

1 Pre-issue letter

Legal Services
Any County Council
2 December 2021

To: Mrs Jane Smith
[Address]

Dear Mrs Smith,

Court of Protection - pre-issue letter

Your husband John Smith

I am writing to you about the capacity and best interests of your husband John Smith.

Any County Council has serious concerns about your husband's welfare, and is considering whether an application to the Court of Protection may be necessary. This letter is written as part of what is known as the 'Pre-issue Stage' in the Court of Protection.

The aim of writing to you is to:

- make sure that you are aware of our intention to start proceedings in the Court of Protection;
- make you aware of the issues that we may ask the Court of Protection to decide, and
- explain to you our proposals as to how we think we could resolve these issues without going to court.

This letter is therefore very important and you should read it carefully. You may wish to take legal advice about the contents.

What is the Court of Protection?

The Court of Protection is part of Her Majesty's Courts and Tribunals Service. Its job is to make decisions in the best interests of those who cannot make the decisions themselves. You can find out more about the Court of Protection by visiting this website: www.gov.uk/courts-tribunals/court-of-protection.

If we do bring a case in the Court of Protection you will be one of the parties to the case. This means that you will have the right to question witnesses and address the judge, either by yourself or with the help of a lawyer. The court may arrange independent representation for John.

Why are we considering applying to the court?

We are considering making an application to the court because we have not been able to resolve with you important questions about your husband John's welfare.

As you are aware Sarah Kavanagh, John's care manager and a social worker of this council has had several meetings with you to talk about how we can work with you to improve John's care.

At the last meeting with you she discussed the following concerns:

- John appears to have lost a lot of weight since returning to live with you after his injury;
- John often appears dishevelled;
- We know that John can become quite challenging when he is confused or upset. Sarah has noticed that you have had several bruises on your face which you have been reluctant to discuss. Sarah is concerned that John may have inadvertently injured you.
- We believe that John needs further help with communication. We have referred John to a speech and language therapist and offered assistance with transport to take him to the appointment. You were unwilling to take him there, telling Sarah that he does not need to see any more doctors.
- John has also missed appointments with the neuro-psychiatrist Dr French who has been overseeing John's rehabilitation.
- John very rarely leaves the house. Sarah as suggested that a day centre would give John a change of scene and provide a break for you. You have refused to consider this.
- Sarah has suggested that it might be a good idea for John to be admitted to a rehabilitation unit as both she and Dr French think this may help him make further improvements. You became very upset at this suggestion and insisted on her leaving the house.
- You have refused to allow John's carers to attend to him and told the care agency that you were sacking them.
- You have been unwilling for Yasmin Rashid, John's Care Act advocate, to see him recently.

We are therefore concerned that it may not be in John's best interests to live with you. We think you are finding it very difficult to care for John and this could put you both at risk.

What will we ask the Court of Protection to do?

We will ask the Court to decide:

- Whether John has capacity for the purpose of the Mental Capacity Act 2005 to make decisions about where he should live and what care he should receive;
- If John cannot make these decisions himself, we will ask the court to decide whether it is in his best interests to live with you or to move to a rehabilitation unit for a few months.
- If the judge decides it is in John's best interests to move, we will ask the judge to decide that we should move him to the rehabilitation unit. We will give the judge and you details as to how we intend to carry this out.

This decision will be taken by a judge of the Court of Protection after receiving evidence from us and from you, if you wish to provide evidence to the court.

How can we resolve the issues without going to the Court of Protection?

We will only bring a case to court as a last resort.

We would like to attempt to resolve these issues by agreement if possible.

We intend to hold a 'best interests meeting' in two weeks' time on 14 December 2021. It will take place at our offices at Any County Council, Town Hall,

High Street, Anytown at 3.00 pm. You are invited to the meeting. **Please let me know immediately if you cannot attend and we will see if an alternative date can be arranged. However I will need to know within seven days if the meeting has to be re-arranged; otherwise it will go ahead as planned.**

I have invited the following people to attend the meeting:

- Teresa Harlow, who works for a different team at the Council and has not been involved in the case so far, who will chair the meeting;
- Sarah Kavanagh;
- Dr French;
- a representative of the care agency;
- Yasmin Rashid;
- myself or one of my colleagues from the legal department;
- a minute-taker.

Teresa Harlow will send us all an agenda at least two days before the meeting.

Yasmin Rashid would like to visit John before the meeting and she will contact you to arrange a convenient time. I hope you will be willing to arrange this.

If we are not able to reach agreement at the meeting I will write to you and explain what the next steps will be.

Please confirm safe receipt of this letter.

Yours sincerely

Agnes Brown

Senior Solicitor, Adult Social Care

2 Position statement

IN THE COURT OF PROTECTION CASE No: 1289256

IN THE MATTER OF THE MENTAL CAPACITY ACT 2005

IN THE MATTER OF JOHN SMITH

BETWEEN:ANY COUNTY COUNCIL

applicant

and

JOHN SMITH

(P, by his litigation friend, the Official Solicitor)

first respondent

and

JANE SMITH

second respondent

POSITION STATEMENT OF ANY COUNTY COUNCIL FOR DIRECTIONS HEARING 2 APRIL 2022

References in square brackets are to the page numbers in the bundle before the court

Essential re-reading:

(i) Pre-issue correspondence [**E1-9**]
(ii) Minutes of best interests meeting, 14 December 2021 [**E10-15**]
(iii) Order of District Judge Bloggs, 1 March 2022 [**B20-4**]
(iv) Report of Dr Williams, 1 February 2022 [**G1-9**]
(v) Witness statement of Ms Cavanagh, Mr Smith's social worker, dated 15 February 2022 [**E1-15**]

A Introduction and dramatis personae

1. This position statement is filed on behalf of Any County Council ('the Council') ahead of the directions hearing listed before District Judge Jones on 2 April 2022. These proceedings concern Mr Smith, who is 33 years old. The medical report of Dr Williams of 1 February 2022 [**G1-9**] concludes that, as a result of an Acquired Brain Injury sustained on 1 December 2020, he does not have capacity to decide where he should live or as to his care arrangements. Dr Williams also considers that Mr Smith lacks the capacity to make decisions as to contact with his wife, Jane Smith (the Second Respondent), with whom Mr Smith is currently residing.

2. The Council has brought proceedings for (1) declarations as to Mr Smith's capacity to make decisions about his residence and care arrangements and as to contact with his wife; and (2) decisions/declarations as to where Mr

Smith should live and receive care, and as future contact with his wife. The proceedings were initiated as a result of concerns as to quality of care being provided to Mr Smith by his wife, detailed in the statement of Ms Cavanagh at [**E1-15**], which have led the Council to consider that Mr Smith's interests are best served by his moving into a specialist rehabilitation unit in Anytown. These proceedings were initiated as a last resort by the Council, following the failure of a best interests meeting in December 2021: see minutes [**E10-15**].

3. Permission was granted to the Council to bring these proceedings by order of District Judge Bloggs on 1 March 2021 at which point John Smith, 'P', was joined as a party and – the Official Solicitor having consented – the Official Solicitor appointed to act as his litigation friend. As at 1 March 2021, Mrs Smith did not have legal representation but indicated that she was intending to seek such representation. District Judge Bloggs therefore made no substantive directions at the hearing on 1 March 2021, instead adjourning matters until the first open date after 1 April 2021 to allow Mrs Smith to obtain such representation.

B Issues for this hearing and the Council's position in respect of each

4. At this hearing, the Court will need to consider:

(1) What, if any, further evidence as to capacity is required in addition to the report of Dr Williams. The Council will say that there is no requirement for any further such evidence. The Council does not understand that either the Official Solicitor or Mrs Smith disagrees.

(2) What, if any, evidence is required as to Mr Williams' best interests. The Council understands that the Official Solicitor will invite the Court to agree to the instruction of an independent social worker to report upon Mr Williams' best interests as regards his future residence and care arrangements and contact with his wife. Having regard to the complexities of Mr Smith's condition and the importance of the issues under consideration for both Mr and Mrs Smith, the Council considers that the test for necessity is met, and, given the breakdown between Mrs Smith and the statutory bodies involved, a report under MCA 2005 s49 is unlikely to command the confidence of all the parties. In principle, therefore, the Council would not object to such an instruction, but would wish it to be on a joint basis as between the Council, Mr and Mrs Smith.

(3) Further evidence. Mrs Smith has put in a detailed witness statement addressing matters raised by Ms Cavanagh; the Council would wish the chance to file a short supplemental statement responding to certain points in Mrs Smith's statement. The Council suggests that it would be sensible for this to be done prior to the report of any independent social work expert (if such is permitted) as this will allow the expert to have the complete picture before them.

(4) Further hearings. It is clear from the witness statement of Mrs Smith that she does not substantially dispute the factual matters outlined in the statement of Ms Cavanagh, but rather would invite the court to put a

different interpretation upon those matters than those set out in Ms Cavanagh's statement. In the circumstances, the Council would submit that there is no requirement that a separate fact-finding hearing be listed, but rather that the court can proceed to list a final hearing to determine where Mr Smith's best interests lie. The Council would envisage that it will be necessary for such a hearing to be listed for two days in order to allow sufficient time for the giving of evidence, the making of submissions, and delivery of judgment.

C Directions order

5. A draft directions order is attached.[1]

1 1See courtofprotectionhandbook.com for an example of a directions order.

3 Witness statement

Statement of the:

Statement no:

Signed:

Filed:

Case No. 000

IN THE COURT OF PROTECTION

IN THE MATTER OF THE MENTAL CAPACITY ACT 2005

AND IN THE MATTER OF JOHN SMITH ('P')

BETWEEN:

ANY COUNTY COUNCIL

applicant

and

JOHN SMITH ('P')

(by [his/her] litigation friend, the Official Solicitor)

1st respondent

and

JANE SMITH

2nd respondent

STATEMENT OF JANE SMITH

I Jane Smith, of [........] make this statement further to the order of District Judge Bloggs on 1 March 2022. I make this statement knowing and believing the contents to be true and in the knowledge it will be placed before the court.

1. I am the wife of John Smith who is the subject to proceedings by Any County Council. I will refer to him as 'John' in the rest of the statement.
2. I make this statement in order to provide information about my background, my relationship with John and my views as to his best interests.
3. The court will be aware that John is 33 years old and was born on [........].
4. John and I met when we were both at university. We married when John was 23 and had therefore been together for 10 years. We have had a close and happy marriage until the injury sustained by John on 1 December 2020. Until then John worked as a computer programmer. I am a teacher but have been on compassionate leave since John's accident.

5. I would describe John as an energetic person, who threw himself in to his work and sporting activities, especially swimming which he has always loved. Neither of us socialise very much and following our marriage we very much enjoyed spending time at home together.
6. Over the past five years we have been trying hard to have a baby. Sadly, up until now, I have not succeeded in becoming pregnant. However, this period of time gave both of us an opportunity to reflect upon what we considered to be important. Both of us had concluded that being together and being part of a family was the most important thing for us both.
7. In recent years, we have spent much less time socialising with friends, and more time together, thinking about our future and spending time with our respective families, both of whom live near by. We looked forward to a future as a family, bringing up children together.
8. As the court will know, our lives were turned upside down when John was knocked over by a bus in December 2020. He sustained an acquired brain injury, which has led to a very severe impairment in his functioning. He has largely physically recovered from the physical injuries that he suffered. The problem is his complete change in the way in which he is able to manage and process information.
9. When I learnt of John's accident I was absolutely terrified. I went straight to the hospital where he was treated, and the records will show that I spent the next week by his side, at a time when his prognosis was unclear.
10. I agree that I was very keen for John to be discharged home as soon as possible. John is still able to communicate. I feel that he communicates particularly well with those who he knows well and who are prepared to spend time with him. He has made it very clear to me that he wants to return home and as far as possible resume living with me.
11. I have read the statement of Miss Kavanagh, who sets out a number of concerns about my care for John. I will not deny that looking after John since the accident has been an uphill struggle. Although my own mother has dementia and I have helped support her with personal care, I have never had to be a full time carer before. John needs assistance in many areas, not so much with his physical needs but simply being prompted to do things and to keep him safe. Because John is quite mobile, you have to keep an eye on him all the time.
12. I have tried very hard to manage but I confess that in recent weeks I have felt absolutely exhausted. I accept that I became very upset in a recent meeting with Miss Kavanagh, because I felt that the help I was being offered to look after John was completely inadequate. I was basically being offered 14 hours respite a week. This was just not enough to allow me to get basic household chores done, carry out the shopping and have a breather.
13. I am aware that Miss Kavanagh put forward the possibility of John going to a day centre. I have been to the day centre that she recommended. I found it extremely depressing. Most of the people there appeared to have much more severe disabilities than John and I feel he would just be miserable there and would feel that I am trying to get rid of him.

14. I do not believe that John needs to go in to a specialist rehabilitation unit. I believe that the intensive rehabilitation that Miss Kavanagh believes he needs could be provided to him at home.
15. I am aware that the local hospital has a day unit where there is rehabilitation and I would be very happy for John to attend this as a day patient.
16. In the meantime, I would be very happy to accept more support in looking after John, if only it could be offered. I believe that I can manage, but not if I only have a few hours a week additional support. I need to be able to carry out basic household tasks, and occasionally to be able to have a bit of a break, in the knowledge that John is safe, and doing something that he enjoys.
17. For example, John has always been a keen swimmer. I have asked for an assessment to see if he could go to the local swimming pool with someone to help him and this has never been carried out. I believe that he would find this very satisfying, and I do not believe that it is impossible to put this in to effect.
18. Rather than move John away from home, where he is happy, I would ask that Miss Kavanagh reconsiders the level of support she is prepared to offer to John. I understand that the council is thinking of having a fact finding hearing which I am advised is rather like a trial of the care that I have provided. Instead of going down this route, I would ask that the council considers giving John more support to remain at home. The court could then review the position and see how things have proceeded.
19. I believe this would be fairer both to me and particularly to John to see if I can manage.
20. I have tried to explain to John what is going on, and he was recently visited by the solicitor instructed by the Official Solicitor. She was very sympathetic and John was able to communicate with her to some extent. However, after she left when he realised that he might have to move and go somewhere else, he had tears in his eyes. I do not believe it is necessary or reasonable for John to have leave home at this stage unless all alternatives have been tried.
21. Therefore, I ask that the Council think again about how they are prepared to support John and me at home.

The contents of this statement are true to the best of my knowledge and belief

Signed: ....

Dated: ....

Anyfirm LLP
88-90 Wessex Street
London
SE1 7EZ
DX DX 124 XDE
Tel: 020 7123 4567
Fax: 020 7123 4568
E-mail: office@anyfirm.com
Ref: 005808.001
Solicitors for Jane Smith

4 Letter of instruction to expert

[Mr/Ms]

Social Care Consultant

Anytown

AN1 5IL

Our ref: /005808.001

Your ref:

Date: 21 April 2022

PROTECT: PERSONAL DATA

Dear Ms Stuart

Re: Any County Council and (1) John Smith (by his litigation friend the Official Solicitor), (2) Jane Smith / Court of Protection number 000

Thank you for agreeing to prepare a report in this case. You are instructed by the parties below as an expert on an application by the Any County Council for declarations and decisions in respect of the capacity and best interests of Mr Smith. The Official Solicitor was appointed Mr Smith's litigation friend on 1 March 2022.

By virtue of an order on 2 April 2022 the Court has given permission to the parties to instruct you to produce an independent report in these proceedings. You have permission to see all records and documents filed in these proceedings and to examine Mr Smith and read his social work medical and other records.

Your report must be filed and served by 30 May 2022. If you have any difficulties with that timescale please let me know straight away.

The final hearing has not yet been fixed. There will be a directions hearing at the Court of Protection on the first open date after 6 June 2017. I will keep you informed of any further hearings.

I am the lead solicitor in this case to whom you should look for instructions and information.

1. The parties

(a) The applicant is Any County Council. The Council is represented by Mr James Burton, of Any County Council. Town Hall, Anytown. His direct dial is [.........] and his email address is [.........].

(b) The 1st respondent is Mr Smith. He currently resides at the address above, which is the matrimonial home he shares with Mrs Smith. He is represented by me instructed by the Official Solicitor as litigation friend. My details appear at the top of this letter.

(c) The 2nd respondent is Mrs Jane Smith. She resides with Mr Smith at the address above. She is represented by Mr Ian Brightspark, of Brightspark Solicitors LLP, High Street, Anytown. His direct dial is [.........] and his email address is [.........].

Mr Smith has an acquired brain injury, subsequent to a road traffic accident on 3 December 2020.

2. Documents

Please see my letter of today's date which lists the documents which you have been sent. I also attach copies of Mr Smith's records from Any County Council's Adult Social Care Team. Copies of his GP records and records from Anytown Hospital will follow.

3. Family structure

Mr John Albert Smith ('P') [DOB ....]
Parents: James and Elizabeth Smith, 25 The Lane, Anytown
Siblings: None
Wife: Jane Smith [DOB ....]
Parents-in-law: Janet and Bradley Marriott, 34 Fir Avenue, Anytown

4. Background history

You should note that the court has not made any findings of fact in this case. Mr Smith was born on [.........] and is thus 33 years of age. He achieved well at school and attended Any University where he achieved a degree in mathematics. Whilst at University he met Jane Marriott and they married in 2011. Mr and Mrs Smith have lived at their current address since April 2011. Mr Smith is known to have worked as a computer programmer and Mrs Smith is a teacher. Mrs Smith describes them as a couple who did not socialise much but enjoyed spending time together or with their respective families. Mr and Mrs Smith have no children but are believed to have been trying for a baby. Mr Smith was the victim of a road traffic accident on 3 December 2020, following which he sustained a brain injury which has resulted in a significant impairment. He is said to have made a good recovery from his physical injuries. He currently lives with Mrs Smith who is his main carer, with a care package provided by Any County Council; however following concerns about the quality of the care provided by Mrs Smith (set out in the statement of Ms Cavanagh at C1 in the trial bundle) the Council applied for permission to make an application to the Court of Protection.

5. Summary of the proceedings to date

These proceedings were commenced by the local authority who made an application (form COP1) on 10 March 2022. The application appears at page II 1 of the trial bundle. The local authority asked the court to decide the following questions:

- Does Mr Smith have capacity to make decisions about where he should live?
- Does Mr Smith have capacity to make decisions about whom he has contact with?
- Is it in Mr Smith's best interests to reside at the home he shares with Mrs Smith or at a specialist rehabilitation unit?
- What should the contact arrangements with Mrs Smith be if Mr Smith moves to the rehabilitation unit?

The local authority set out the orders it sought:

- A declaration that Mr Smith lacks capacity to litigate these proceedings, and to make decisions about residence, care and contact with others.
- A declaration that it is in Mr Smith's best interests to move to a specialist rehabilitation unit for care and treatment.
- A declaration that it is in Mr Smith's best interests to have contact with Mrs Smith by agreement between Mrs Smith and the Unit.

District Judge Bloggs granted permission on 1 March 2022. At the same time, he joined Mr Smith as a party and appointed the Official Solicitor to act as his litigation friend, the Official Solicitor having consented to act. Mrs Smith had indicated that she intended to instruct solicitors and you will see that she is now represented.

The first attended hearing took place on 2 April 2022. A copy of the order is with your papers at B30 of the trial bundle. You will see that DJ Jones made interim declarations that Mr Smith lacked capacity to litigate these proceedings and that he lacked capacity to make decisions about residence, care and contact with others. A number of case management orders were made, including provision for your instructions at paragraphs 12 and 13.

6. Mr Smith's capacity

Dr Williams' opinion is that Mr Smith lacks capacity to make decisions about his residence, care and contact, and to litigate these proceedings and that there is no prospect of his recovering such capacity.

At the hearing on 2nd April it became clear that all parties now agree that Mr Smith lacks capacity to make the decisions under consideration and it is likely that final declarations to this effect will be made at the next hearing. You are not therefore instructed to report upon Mr Smith's capacity to make these decisions, although should you have any reason to doubt that he lacks such capacity, it is important that you highlight these immediately to me so that they can (if required) be brought to the attention of the court.

7. Reference to Mr Smith's views

Mr Smith has said consistently that he would prefer to live with Mrs Smith. You are referred to the witness statement of Ms Cavanagh at E13, where she describes her interview with Mr Smith and to my attendance note of my visit to Mr Smith, when he became quiet emotional at the prospect of leaving home.

8. Assessment of best interests

The court is being asked to make a decision in Mr Smith's best interests. You are asked to advise the court and (the parties) on what is in Mr Smith's best interests given the circumstances outlined in this letter, in the documents accompanying this letter and from your own observations.

The term 'best interests' is not defined by the Act. MCA 2005 s4 however provides a statutory checklist of matters which should be taken into account and is set out below.

Best interests

4. *(1) In determining for the purposes of this Act what is in a person's best interests, the person making the determination must not make it merely on the basis of–*

(a) the person's age or appearance, or

(b) a condition of his, or an aspect of his behaviour, which might lead others to make unjustified assumptions about what might be in his best interests.

(2) The person making the determination must consider all the relevant circumstances and, in particular, take the following steps.

(3) He must consider—

(a) whether it is likely that the person will at some time have capacity in relation to the matter in question, and

(b) if it appears likely that he will, when that is likely to be.

(4) He must, so far as reasonably practicable, permit and encourage the person to participate, or to improve his ability to participate, as fully as possible in any act done for him and any decision affecting him.

(5) Where the determination relates to life-sustaining treatment he must not, in considering whether the treatment is in the best interests of the person concerned, be motivated by a desire to bring about his death.

(6) He must consider, so far as is reasonably ascertainable–

(a) the person's past and present wishes and feelings (and, in particular, any relevant written statement made by him when he had capacity),

(b) the beliefs and values that would be likely to influence his decision if he had capacity, and

(c) the other factors that he would be likely to consider if he were able to do so.

(7) He must take into account, if it is practicable and appropriate to consult them, the views of–

(a) anyone named by the person as someone to be consulted on the matter in question or on matters of that kind,

(b) anyone engaged in caring for the person or interested in his welfare,

(c) any donee of a lasting power of attorney granted by the person, and

(d) any deputy appointed for the person by the court,

as to what would be in the person's best interests and, in particular, as to the matters mentioned in subsection (6).

(8) *The duties imposed by subsections (1) to (7) also apply in relation to the exercise of any powers which—*

(a) *are exercisable under a lasting power of attorney, or*
(b) *are exercisable by a person under this Act where he reasonably believes that another person lacks capacity.*

(9) *In the case of an act done, or a decision made, by a person other than t he court, there is sufficient compliance with this section if (having complied with the requirements of subsections (1) to (7)) he reasonably believes that what he does or decides is in the best interests of the person concerned.*

(10) *'Life-sustaining treatment' means treatment which in the view of a person providing health care for the person concerned is necessary to sustain life.*

(11) *'Relevant circumstances' are those–*

(a) *of which the person making the determination is aware, and*
(b) *which it would be reasonable to regard as relevant.*

Again you are required to have regard to the Principles and provisions of the Act and the Code of Practice when considering and providing your opinion on Mr Smith's best interests (see in particular chapter 5 of the Code).

The Supreme Court has made clear that the purpose of the best interests test is to make the decision for P which is right for them as an individual human being (*Aintree v James* [2013] UKSC 67). The test that the court will apply is not a "*what P would have done test,*" but it is necessary that the person is at very heart of the decision-making process. This has consequences for the approach taken to P's wishes and feelings. In *Briggs v Briggs (No 2)* [2016] EWCOP 53, Charles J endorsed the approach originally set down by HHJ Marshall QC in *S and S (Protected Persons)* [2010] 1 WLR 1082, namely that:

> *In my judgment ict is the inescapable conclusion from the stress laid on these matters in the 2005 Act that the views and wishes of P in regard to decisions made on his behalf are to carry great weight. What, after all, is the point of taking great trouble to ascertain or deduce P's views, and to encourage P to be involved in the decision-making process, unless the objective is to try to achieve the outcome which P wants or prefers, even if he does not have the capacity to achieve it for himself.*
>
> *The 2005 Act does not, of course, say that P's wishes are to be paramount, nor does it lay down any express presumption in favour of implementing them if they can be ascertained. Indeed the paramount objective is that of P's "best interests". However, by giving such prominence to the above matters, the Act does, in my judgment, recognise that having his views and wishes taken into account and respected is a very significant aspect of P's best interests. Due regard should therefore be paid to this recognition when doing the weighing exercise of determining what is in P's best interest in all the relevant circumstances, including those wishes.*

9. Your instructions

I hope the enclosures supply you with all the relevant documents. Please let me know if you need any further information or require clarification on any matters.

Please arrange to see Mr Smith. I am happy to arrange an appointment for you with Mrs Smith if this would assist. You will need to consider his social work and health records. You will need to speak to those responsible for his care. His care manager is Ms Cavanagh who can be contacted via the Council's solicitors.

You will need to meet Mrs Smith and Mr Smith's parents and father-in-law (his mother-in-law herself has dementia and it will not be appropriate for you to interview her). Having regard to section 4(7) in particular you should consider whether there is any other person engaged in caring for Mr Smith or interested in her welfare whom it would be practicable and appropriate for you to consult -for example other family members or social care professionals. If you need assistance in making arrangements to consult any other person please let me know. You should identify in your report all persons whom you have consulted during the course of your assessment. It is important to note that the purpose of consultation is, in particular, to enable you to identify the matters set out under section 4(6). In other words, it is of less importance to identify what the person you are consulting with thinks is in Mr Smith's best interests than what information they can give you as to what Mr Smith's wishes, feelings, beliefs and values are in relation to the matters in hand.

Please provide a report covering the following areas:

Best interests

Please advise as to Mr Smith's best interests.

1. Care

(a) Please set out Mr Smith's care needs. This should include the support needed in the following areas. If you are not able to comment on any of the areas below please say so:
Mental Health

Maximising independence

Daytime activities

Learning disability

Physical health

Cultural

(b) In what kind of setting can the needs you have identified under all the above headings best be met?

2. Residence

(a) What would the benefits be to Mr Smith's physical, mental, psychological, emotional and cultural wellbeing if he remains living with Mrs Smith?
(b) What are the disadvantages to Mr Smith's physical, mental, psychological, emotional and cultural wellbeing if he continues to reside with Mrs Smith.
(c) What would the benefits be to Mr Smith's physical, mental, psychological, emotional and cultural wellbeing if he moves to a specialist rehabilitation unit?
(d) What are the disadvantages to Mr Smith's physical, mental, psychological, emotional and cultural wellbeing if he moves to a specialist rehabilitation unit?
(e) Is it in Mr Smith's best interests to reside with Mrs Smith? If so please advise as to the package of care required to support this.

3. Contact

(a) If it is not in Mr Smith's best interests to live with Mrs Smith, is it in his best interests to have contact with Mrs Smith?
(b) What should the level and frequency of that contact be?
(c) Should there be any restrictions on such contact with Mrs Smith and if so what should these restrictions be?

You may find it of assistance to draw a balance sheet to outline benefits and burdens. However, such a balance sheet should be used as an "*aide memoire of the key factors and how they match up against each other and as a route to judgment rather than a substitution for the judgment itself*" (*Re F (A Child) (International Relocation Cases)* [2015] EWCA Civ 882)."

10. Role of an expert

Additional to the documents referred to at (2) above I enclose for your ease of reference Part 15 (Experts) of the Court of Protection Rules 2007 and the supplemental practice direction together with a copy of guidance issued by Mrs Justice Pauffley in December 2010. I draw your attention in particular to rule 15.4 (paragraph 2 of the practice direction) with regard to the expert's duty to the court and to rule 15.8 (paragraphs 8-11 of the practice direction) with regard to the content of an expert's report, and to paragraphs 8 and 9 of the December 2010 guidance.

11. Contact with others

It is essential to both your role as an independent expert and to the parties' perception of your independent status that there are no informal unrecorded discussions or correspondence with anyone involved in the case, particularly when you come to interview others such as the social care staff, etc. If you need further information, please contact me as I am the lead solicitor and I will provide information after consultation with the other solicitors involved. If documents are exchanged with one party, please copy them to all the others. Where possible, communication is best achieved by fax, letter or e-mail copied to all the parties.

Please maintain a careful record of all discussions with all persons with whom you discuss this case in the event that it is necessary to refer to them later.

It will be helpful if you would confirm in writing to me who you would like to have contact with, so that all parties are aware that meetings will be taking place in due course.

12. Proposed timescale and plan of work

If you require any help from me in arranging meetings or contacting the other solicitors, please let me know. Otherwise I shall assume that you will go ahead, organise visits and meetings, and will make your own arrangements. If at any time there is a delay in your plan and the timescale has to be altered, please inform me promptly so that I may inform the other parties and the court if appropriate

13. Factual issues and your report

You should express your opinion regarding your findings on the facts of the case, but you must not seek to resolve disputed facts, as this is of course the job of the court at the hearing. Where appropriate, it will be of assistance if you are able to express your opinion on the basis of alternative findings regarding the factual disputes. Your report may be subject to challenge by any of the parties. It is likely that one or more of the parties may put written questions to you following receipt of your report.

I am under a duty to disclose your report to the court and to the other parties and I will circulate your report on receipt. If you believe, as a rare exception to the general rule, that it should not be disclosed to any party, please let me know and I will seek the court's directions.

14. Trial date

The trial date has not yet been fixed. I will ask you closer to the next hearing to let me have details of your availability so that if a trial is fixed it will be on a date convenient to you.

15. Fees

The following terms and conditions apply:

The fees for your instruction will be shared, in equal shares between the instructing parties. Some of the parties are in receipt of public funding and your fees will therefore be met through their public funding certificates.

Ultimately your fees will therefore be assessed by either the court or the Legal Aid Agency (LAA) at the conclusion of the case as to reasonableness in terms of both hourly rate and time spent. The parties' legal representatives cannot be responsible for any fees over and above those finally assessed and paid by the LAA.

On receipt of your invoice the legal representatives for the publicly funded parties are entitled to, and should promptly make a claim for payment on account of your fees to the LAA. Promptly upon receipt of such payment on account they should make this payment on account to you.

Such payments on account may, however, be recouped by the LAA at the end of the case following the final assessment of the bill. Such recoupment will only apply to any sum, paid on account, which exceeds the amount finally allowed on assessment by the Court or LAA. If your fees are reduced on assessment, we will notify you within 7 days of receiving notification from the Legal Aid Agency or the court. If you wish us to make representations with regard to the reduction then you should notify us within 7 days, and provide us with the text or those representations, or the supporting documentation as the case may be.

In accepting this instruction, you therefore agree that if your fees are subsequently reduced by the court or the LAA you will promptly reimburse the difference between the amount paid on account to you, and the amount finally allowed on assessment, to the parties' legal representatives.

Please bear in mind that although we, as the lead solicitors in instructing you, will do our best to assist you in obtaining prompt payment, we can only be responsible for the share of your fees attributable to our client. The other solicitors involved in this instruction to you are responsible likewise only for the share attributable to their client.

It is also important that during the course of your assessment you inform us immediately if you are likely to exceed your costs estimate. All public funding certificates have a cost limitation and we need to make an application to the LAA for any extension of this if it appears that the aggregate of the fees which are to be incurred in this case is likely to exceed the current costs limitation. If you exceed your fee estimate without prior notification to us your fees may therefore not be met in full.

In addition, there are terms in the 2018 Standard Civil Contract under which the publicly funded legal representatives must operate. In accordance with these if your fees are to exceed £250 you must keep accurate records of all the time spent on the work for which you have been instructed and of the work done. You must also permit the LAA to audit your records if necessary.

There is also certain work for which the LAA will not pay and limits on certain hourly rates.

The LAA will not pay:

(a) Any separate administration fee including, but not limited to, a fee in respect of offices and consultation rooms, administrative support including typing services, subsistence and couriers.
(b) Any cancellation fee where notice of cancellation is given more than 72 hours before the relevant hearing or appointment.
(c) Any travelling costs in relation to vehicle mileage in excess of 45p per mile.
(d) Any fee for travelling time in excess of £40 per hour.

(e) Any costs or expenses of or relating to the residential assessment of a child.
(f) Any costs or expenses of or relating to treatment, therapy, training or other interventions of an educative or rehabilitative nature.
(g) Any costs and expenses of independent social work provided outside England and Wales.
(h) Any costs and expenses in relation to contact activities including fees, charges and costs of contact centres and any reports or other assessments of contact between children and adults. However, please note that this exclusion does not apply to observation of contact which forms part of a psychological or parenting assessment.

You should therefore ensure that none of these costs are included in your invoice.

This letter of instruction has been agreed between the parties instructing you. I should be grateful if you would acknowledge receipt.

If there is anything at all which is not clear please do not hesitate to contact me.

Yours sincerely

Felicia Anysolicitor

ANYSOLICITORS LLP

5 Letter of instruction: assessment of capacity

Patricia Cohen

Whittlemans Solicitors

21 Belgrave Street

Appleton AP3 42A

Email: patricia.cohen@whittlemans.co.uk

Dr Helena Fletcher

Capacity Matters

122 Douglas Road

Alphington EH12 3AY

Email: hfletcher@capmatters.org.uk

Our ref: COP/GS/PC-214

7 April 2022

THIS LETTER CONTAINS SENSITIVE PERSONAL DATA

Dear Dr Fletcher

Re: Lakeside County Council v Graham Smith & Anor Court of Protection number: 2019/175

Thank you for agreeing to assist the court to determine Mr Smith's capacity to make key decisions in this case.

Her Honour Judge Williams made an order on 28 March 2022 granting the parties in these proceedings (Lakeside County Council, Graham Smith and Julian Benson) permission to instruct you to assess Mr Smith's capacity to conduct these proceedings as well as his capacity to decide what care he requires and where to live. The court made this order because it considers that your report is necessary to assist it to resolve the capacity issues in these proceedings.

This letter of instruction has been agreed between the instructing parties and approved by Her Honour Judge Williams. Please read it carefully before commencing your assessment of Mr Smith's capacity, giving particular consideration to the practicable steps that may be taken to assist Mr Smith to make his own decisions (section 7.2 below) and the "relevant information" for the purpose of making these decisions (section 7.3 below).

Your report must be filed and served by 4:00pm on 7 June 2022. Please ensure it is sent to me in advance of that time so that I can ensure that this deadline is met. The parties are required to send you any questions they may have about your report by 4:00pm on 14 June 2022. Your reply must be filed and served by 4:00pm on 1 July 2022. Please let me know as soon as possible if you have any difficulties with this timeframe, which has been set by the court.

You may be required to attend court and give evidence in these proceedings. In the event that this is necessary, I will contact you to ascertain your available dates. Please let me know if you are aware, or become aware, of any long periods when you will be unavailable. The next directions hearing in this matter will be held on 7 July 2022. I will keep you informed of any relevant developments.

I am the lead solicitor in this case to whom you should look for instructions and information.

1. The parties

Lakeside County Council is the applicant in these proceedings. The solicitor for Lakeside County Council with conduct of this matter is Ms Catriona Williams, Legal Services, Lakeside County Council, 1 Morrison Street, Appleton. Her telephone number is 040 7829 5547 and her email address is cwilliams@lakeside.gov.uk.

Mr Graham Smith is the subject of these proceedings and the first respondent. He currently lives at 49 Canning Street, Riversdale. The court has made an interim order that he lacks capacity to litigate these proceedings and appointed the Official Solicitor to act as his litigation friend. The Official Solicitor has instructed Whittlemans to represent Mr Smith. I am the solicitor with conduct of this matter at Whittlemans and my address is 21 Belgrave Street, Appleton. My telephone number is 040 2733 9413 and my email address is patricia.cohen@whittlemans.co.uk.

Mr Julian Benson is Mr Smith's step-brother and the second respondent in these proceedings. He lives at 49 Canning Street, Riversdale, and has instructed Mr Elijah Clarke of Landsowne Solicitors to represent him in these proceedings. Mr Clarke's address and contact details are 13 High Street, Bentleigh, 030 762 1212, elijah.clarke@pittmans.co.uk.

2. Useful contacts

You may wish to contact the following people in this case to obtain further information about Mr Smith.

(i) Ms Alisha Khan is Mr Smith's social worker. She is based at Adult Services, Lakeside County Council, 1 Morrison Street, Appleton, and can be contacted by email: alisha.khan@lakeside.gov.uk.

(ii) Mr Thom Daniel is Mr Smith's psychologist. He works at Lakeside Hospital and can be contacted by email: thom.daniel@lakeside.nhs.uk.

(iii) Ms Radhika Parmar is Mr Smith's doctor. She works at East Lakeside Medical Practice, 12 Carrington Street, Appleton, and can be contacted by email: r.parmar@eastlakesidemedical.co.uk.

3. Documents

The court has granted you permission to see all evidence and documents filed in these proceedings and to examine Mr Smith and read his social work, medical and other records. Please find enclosed a copy of the following documents:

- the court bundle in these proceedings;
- adult social care records from Lakeside County Council;

- medical records from Lakeside Hospital and East Lakeside Medical Practice; and
- Part 15 (Experts) of the Court of Protection Rules 2017 and the supplemental Practice Direction.[1]

The following documents are likely to be particularly relevant to your assessment:

- Capacity assessment undertaken by Alisha Khan, 16 November 2021 **[E1-15]**.
- Witness statement of Alisha Khan, 1 February 2022 **[C4-35]**.
- Medical report from Lakeside Hospital, 2 March 2022 **[E16-27]**.

Mr Smith's social care and medical records are not currently part of the court bundle in these proceedings. Please let me know if you place particular reliance upon any of P's social and medical care records when reaching your conclusions, as it may be appropriate for these to be added to the court bundle.

You are responsible for ensuring that you have obtained the information necessary for you to report to the court. Please contact me, in the first instance, if you require any more documents or information or encounter any logistical difficulties. You also have the right to ask the court for directions to assist you in carrying out your functions: *SMBC v WMP* [2011] EWHC B13 (COP) at para 57.

In the course of preparing your report you will be entrusted with personal data, including sensitive personal data, belonging to Mr Smith and potentially to other people as well. You must comply with the requirements of the Data Protection Act 2018 at all times.

4. Background

The court has not made any findings of fact in this case. The following summary of the factual background has been agreed between the parties.

Mr Graham Smith is currently 53 years of age (DOB: 21 March 1966). He was hit by a car on 14 December 2020, causing him to sustain extensive injuries, including damage to his spinal cord and the frontal lobe of his brain. He was treated at Lakeside Hospital, where he remained until being discharged on 17 May 2021. As a result of his injuries Mr Smith is unable to walk and uses a wheelchair to mobilise.

Prior to the accident, Mr Smith lived alone at 32 Weston Street, Rushington, in a small property he inherited from his mother and step-father when they passed away over ten years ago. Mr Smith has not had any contact with his father since he was a young child. When Mr Smith left hospital on 17 May

1 You may also find it useful to read the 39 Essex Chambers Guide to Capacity Assessment available at https://www.39essex.com/tag/mental-capacity-guidance-notes. It does not have any statutory authority, but includes a summary of relevant case-law and also information that judges have ruled to be relevant (and irrelevant) to particular categories of decisions that have come before the courts. The identification of relevant information in previous cases should be treated as guidance that may be expanded or contracted or otherwise adapted to apply to the facts of a particular case: see *B v A Local Authority* [2019] EWCA Civ 913 at paras 44 and 62.

2021, he went to live with his older step-brother, Mr Julian Benson and his wife, Mrs Lydia Porter, in their home at 49 Canning Street, Riversdale. This is approximately 45 minutes' drive from where Mr Smith previously lived. Mr Benson declined offers of assistance from Lakeside County Council and has paid for carers to visit Mr Smith and help him with his personal care for thirty minutes, three times a day. Mr Benson also employs a cleaner and arranges for all of Mr Benson's meals to be made for him.

Lakeside County Council has assessed Mr Smith's needs and is willing to make adjustments to his former home to accommodate his wheelchair and to commission two carers to come into the property twice a day, for fifteen minutes each visit, to meet Mr Smith's care needs if he returns to live there.

Mr Smith has a close friend, Mr Hugh Thornley, with whom he worked as a labourer for many years before Mr Smith retired due to a workplace injury. Mr Thornley lives at 63 Weston Street, which is very close to where Mr Smith previously lived. He was walking home with from the pub with Mr Smith when the car accident happened. Mr Thornley contacted social services on 12 August 2021 to report that he did not think it was right that Mr Smith was living with his step-brother, Mr Benson. He said he has heard Mr Benson yelling at Mr Smith when Mr Thornley visited, and that Mr Benson told Mr Thornley on 12 August 2021 that he cannot take Mr Smith out into town and should not come around anymore. Mr Thornley said that he and Mr Smith often enjoyed meeting friends at the local pub before the accident.

Ms Alisha Khan, a social worker at Lakeside County Council, called Mr Benson on 14 August 2021 and asked him about these allegations. Mr Benson accepted that he does sometimes raise his voice at Mr Smith, but that this is because he sometimes does not follow the advice of his doctors or co-operate with the carers. Mr Benson said that he does not want Mr Thornley to visit or take his brother out into the community because he cannot be trusted. Mr Benson told Ms Khan that the accident was "Hugh's fault" because he let him drink too much that night and he didn't want his brother to be spending time with that group of "no-hopers". Mr Benson explained that he feels a strong sense of responsibility to care for Mr Smith, who is his only sibling. Ms Khan made a contemporaneous note of the telephone conversation, which is included with her witness statement at [C32]. Mr Benson has accepted the accuracy of that note.

Ms Khan visited Mr Smith on 16 August 2021 and asked him about living with Mr Benson and Mrs Porter. Mr Smith said it was a very nice house and the food was good. He also said he missed his friends and wished he could live in his old home so he could be closer to them. Later, when Mr Benson came into the room, Mr Smith said he "definitely wants to stay living here" and doesn't mind if he can't see his old friends any more. Ms Khan carried out an assessment of Mr Smith's capacity and found that he lacked the capacity to decide what care he requires and where to live but that he had capacity to decide contact to have with Mr Thornley.

5. Summary of the proceedings to date

Lakeside County Council commenced these proceedings on 5 March 2022, inviting the court to determine whether Mr Smith has capacity to conduct these proceedings, decide what care he requires and where to live. Mr Benson considers that Mr Smith lacks capacity to make these decisions and that it is in his best interests to remain living with Mr Benson and for Mr Benson to arrange his package of care and decide who he should see.

Mr Thornley has declined an invitation to become a party to these proceedings but has communicated that he strongly believes Mr Smith can make his own decisions and would choose to be back in his own home if he had a chance to get away from Mr Benson's influence.

Her Honour Judge Williams made interim declarations that Mr Smith lacks capacity to conduct these proceedings, to decide what care he requires and where to live. She granted the parties permission to instruct you to assess Mr Smith's capacity to make these decisions. Her Honour Judge Williams declared that Mr Smith has capacity to decide what contact to have with Mr Thornley.

6. Legal framework

The first three sections of the Mental Capacity Act 2005 (**"MCA"**) contain the principles that underpin the determination of capacity and the definition of what it means to lack capacity to make a particular decision for the purposes of the MCA. The material parts for the purpose of assessing capacity provide that:

> Section 1 - The principles
>
> . . .
>
> *(2) A person must be assumed to have capacity unless it is established that he lacks capacity.*
>
> *(3) A person is not to be treated as unable to make a decision unless all practicable steps to help him to do so have been taken without success.*
>
> *(4) A person is not to be treated as unable to make a decision merely because he makes an unwise decision.*
>
> . . .
>
> Section 2 - People who lack capacity
>
> *(1) For the purposes of this Act, a person lacks capacity in relation to a matter if at the material time he is unable to make a decision for himself in relation to the matter because of an impairment of, or a disturbance in the functioning of, the mind or brain.*
>
> *(2) It does not matter whether the impairment or disturbance is permanent or temporary.*
>
> *(3) A lack of capacity cannot be established merely by reference to—*
>
> *(a) a person's age or appearance, or*
>
> *(b) a condition of his, or an aspect of his behaviour, which might lead others to make unjustified assumptions about his capacity.*
>
> *(4) In proceedings under this Act or any other enactment, any question whether a person lacks capacity within the meaning of this Act must be decided on the balance of probabilities. . . .*

Section 3 - Inability to make decisions

(1) For the purposes of section 2, a person is unable to make a decision for himself if he is unable—

(a) to understand the information relevant to the decision,

(b) to retain that information,

(c) to use or weigh that information as part of the process of making the decision, or

(d) to communicate his decision (whether by talking, using sign language or any other means).

(2) A person is not to be regarded as unable to understand the information relevant to a decision if he is able to understand an explanation of it given to him in a way that is appropriate to his circumstances (using simple language, visual aids or any other means).

(3) The fact that a person is able to retain the information relevant to a decision for a short period only does not prevent him from being regarded as able to make the decision.

(4) The information relevant to a decision includes information about the reasonably foreseeable consequences of—

(a) deciding one way or another, or

(b) failing to make the decision.

The Supreme Court has made clear[1] that it is necessary to start by identifying whether the person has the functional ability to make the decision, and only if they do not proceed to inquiring whether the person's functional inability is caused by an impairment or disturbance in the functioning or their mind or brain. This is the reverse of the order in the Code of Practice, but the Code should not be followed in in this regard.

In practice, the test for determining incapacity is best applied by asking the following three questions:

(1) Is the person able to make the decision? If not:

(2) Is there an impairment or disturbance in the functioning of the person's mind or brain? If so:

(3) Is the person's inability to make the decision *because of* the identified impairment or disturbance?

Further guidance on applying the elements of the test for capacity is set out in sections 7.5-7.7 below.

The sections of the MCA set out above establish that the assessment of capacity must be based on the person's capacity to make a decision in relation to the relevant matter, at the material time, and not their capacity to make a decision in general. It does not matter therefore if the lack of capacity is temporary, or if their decision-making capacity fluctuates. Similarly, as capacity is issue specific, it does not matter if Mr Smith possesses or lacks capacity to make other decisions.

1 A Local Authority v JB [2021] UKSC 52.

7. Your instructions

Please arrange to meet Mr Smith and assess (i) his capacity to conduct these proceedings, (ii) his capacity to decide what care he requires, and (iii) his capacity to decide where to live. The meeting should be arranged by contacting Mr Smith's social worker, Ms Alisha Khan, whose contact details are included at the beginning of this letter of instruction. As discussed in section 7.2 below, you are requested to consider what practicable steps may be taken to help Mr Smith make his own decisions. Please give any appropriate guidance to Mr Smith's family members and social worker on how to prepare Mr Smith for the meeting, so Mr Smith is as relaxed and comfortable as possible. Please also consider if it would help Mr Smith if you had an initial meeting some time before the assessment, to explain the assessment process, the decisions that need to be made and the information relevant to those decisions. You are encouraged to answer any questions that Mr Smith may have about the assessment process but please take great care not to express an opinion on any disputed facts in this case or to inform Mr Smith of any provisional views you may have about whether or not he has capacity to make a particular decision: *SC v BS and A Local Authority* [2012] COPLR 567. I would be grateful if you could please let me know when you have arranged dates to meet Mr Smith.

Once you have completed your assessment please prepare a report giving your opinion concerning Mr Smith's (i) capacity to conduct these proceedings, (ii) capacity to decide what care he requires, and (iii) capacity to decide where to live. You are asked to address the following matters in your report.

7.1. Your knowledge of Mr Smith

Please explain how well you feel you know and are able to communicate with Mr Smith and whether you consider that Mr Smith would be able to function at his highest level when speaking to you.

7.2. Practicable steps to enable Mr Smith to make a decision

To comply with s.1(3) of the MCA, you must consider whether all practicable steps have been taken, by you or anyone else, to enable Mr Smith to make each decision for himself, before you conclude that Mr Smith lacks capacity to make that decision. You will need to consider whether any such steps may be taken *leading up to* the capacity assessment or *during* the capacity assessment, to help ensure that Mr Smith is in the best state to make decisions at the time of your assessment.

With this in mind, please ask yourself the following questions and record the answers in your report. You are encouraged to take advice from others involved in Mr Smith's care, including Mr Smith's doctor, psychologist and social worker.

(i) What is the best means of communicating with Mr Smith, such as through the use of simple language, visual aids, pointing board or Makaton?
(ii) What is the best time of day to meet Mr Smith?
(iii) What location is likely to make Mr Smith the most comfortable?
(iv) How can you minimise any stress or anxiety that Mr Smith may experience?

(v) Would it assist Mr Smith to have anyone else present, in particular, anyone who Mr Smith has indicated that they would like to be there? If so, what role should they play?
(vi) Is there anyone who Mr Smith has indicated that they would **not** like to be there?
(vii) How can you best explain the capacity assessment process to Mr Smith, to help put him at ease and convey that there are no right or wrong answers?
(viii) How can you best explain to Mr Smith the information that is relevant to each of the decisions (see section 7.3 below)? Is there anything that can be done to help Mr Smith to understand the relevant information, such as meeting Mr Smith to explain this information before the assessment and repeating this information during the assessment, showing Mr Smith pictures or taking Mr Smith to see different accommodation options?
(ix) Rather than completing the capacity assessments in one session, would it be preferable to come back and see Mr Smith on more than one occasion, even if only to help put Mr Smith at ease and help them engage with the process? If the capacity assessments need to be undertaken on a single day, would it help to have breaks in the assessment process?
(x) Should the capacity assessment be rescheduled if Mr Smith is unusually unwell, unresponsive or distressed?
(xi) Can anything else be done to help enable Mr Smith to make any of the decisions? Depending upon the circumstances, this could range from simply giving Mr Smith more time to undergoing a programme of education with him.

Please let me know if you require any assistance or have any questions about steps that may potentially be taken to assist Mr Smith to make his own decisions.

7.3. Relevant information

Section 3(1) of the MCA provides that P lacks capacity to make a decision if he or she is unable to understand, retain and use or weigh *the information that is relevant to that decision*. For obvious reasons, a person must be given the relevant information before their ability to understand that information can be assessed: *CC v KK & STCC* [2012] EWHC 2136 (COP) at para 21 and the Code of Practice at para 4.16.

In this case, the information that is relevant to each of the decisions has been approved by Her Honour Judge Williams and is set out in Appendix A. This is the information that P needs to be able to understand, retain and use or weigh in order to make capacitous decisions for the purposes of the MCA. It is imperative that you carefully explain the information that is relevant to each decision to Mr Smith, before assessing his capacity to make each decision. Please include verbatim quotes of your explanations in your report.

If at any stage you consider that the information that is set out in Appendix A either (1) includes information that is **not** relevant to the decision(s) in question; or (2) does not include information that **is** relevant to the decision(s), please can you revert to me in the first instance so that the parties and, if necessary, the court, can consider what steps should be taken.

7.4. Your conversation with Mr Smith

A capacity assessment is, in many ways, an attempt to have a real conversation with the person on their terms, applying their value system (*Kings College NHS Foundation Trust v C and V*) [2015] EWCOP 80, in particular at para 38.

As far as practicable, bearing in mind the need to try to put Mr Smith at ease, please take detailed notes during the capacity assessments. To the extent that you are able to do so, please include a verbatim account of your conversation in your report, rather than a summary of your discussions. This is because the court will use your expert opinion to reach its own conclusions about Mr Smith's capacity. A summary of an exchange between an interviewer and interviewee inevitably loses some of the context, nuance and character of that discussion, and isolated quotes of Mr Smith's responses may be open to multiple interpretations when taken out of context: *WBC v Z* [2016] EWCOP 4 at para 41.

Please also include in your report a description of Mr Smith's mood and body language during your conversation as well as the time that the capacity assessment started and finished.

7.5. Is Mr Smith able to make a decision for himself?

Section 3(1) provides that a person is unable to make a decision for themselves if they are unable:

(i) to *understand* the information relevant to the decision;
(ii) to *retain* that information,
(iii) to *use or weigh* that information as part of the process of making the decision; or
(iv) to *communicate* their decision.

Guidance on each of these four areas is set out below.

Understanding the relevant information

The relevant information that Mr Smith needs to be able to understand to make capacitous decisions in this case is set out in Appendix A. As outlined in section 7.3 above, you must carefully explain this information to Mr Smith before assessing his or her ability to understand it, and set out your explanation in your report.

The ability to understand extends to understanding the reasonably foreseeable consequences of making a deciding one way or another or failing to make a decision: s.3(4). Those reasonably foreseeable consequences can include the consequences both for the person and for others: *A Local Authority v JB* [2021] UKSC 52 at paragraph 73.

The level of understanding that is required *must not be set too high*. It is not necessary that Mr Smith understands every element of what is discussed. It is sufficient if Mr Smith can understand *"the salient details"* relevant to the decision to be made: *LBJ v RYJ* [2010] EWHC 2664 (Fam) at paras 24 and 58.

Retaining the relevant information

All that is required here is that Mr Smith is able to retain the salient details of the relevant information, set out in Appendix A, for a sufficient amount of time to make a decision.

The MCA specifies, at s.3(3), that the fact that a person is able to retain the information relevant to a decision for a short period only does not prevent him from being regarded as able to make the decision. This is an important consideration, particularly when dealing with the elderly or those with impaired memories. Capacity is the assessment of the ability to make a decision 'at the material time': at the time of assessment. If Mr Smith can retain the information for long enough to be able to make the relevant decision at the material time, that is sufficient, even if he cannot then retain that information for any longer period.

Using or weighing the relevant information

A person must be able both to use and weigh the relevant information set out in Appendix A in order to make a capacitous decision for the purpose of the MCA. This aspect of the test has been described as "*the capacity actually to engage in the decision-making process itself and to be able to see the various parts of the argument and to relate the one to another*": *The PCT v P, AH & the Local Authority* [2009] EW Misc 10 (EWCOP) at para 35.

As with understanding, it is not necessary for a person to use and weigh every detail of the respective options available to them in order to demonstrate capacity; merely the salient factors. Therefore, even though a person may be unable to use and weigh *some* information relevant to the decision in question, they may nonetheless be able to use and weigh other elements sufficiently to be able to make a capacitous decision.

Further, a person may make a capacitous decision which attaches little or no weight to a particular piece of relevant information in accordance with their individual values or outlook. As such, great care must be taken when assessing a person's capacity to make sure – as far as possible – that you are not conflating the way in which they apply their own values and outlook (which may be very different to yours) with a functional inability to use and weigh information: *Kings College NHS Foundation Trust v C and V* [2015] EWCOP 80 at para 38.

As such, it is particularly important here to be aware of the dangers of equating an unwise or irrational decision with the inability to make one –Mr Smith may not agree with the advice of professionals, but that does not mean that he lacks capacity to make his own decision.

A common area of difficulty in a brain injury case such as this is where a person with an acquired brain injury gives superficially coherent answers to questions, but it is clear from their actions that they are unable to carry into effect the intentions expressed in those answers (in other words, their so-called executive function is impaired). In such circumstances a key question can be whether they are aware of their own deficits – in other words, whether they able to understand, use and/or weigh the fact that there is a mismatch between their ability to respond to questions in the abstract and to act when faced by concrete situations.

Communicating a decision

Any residual ability to communicate is enough, so long as Mr Smith can make himself understood. This will be an area where it is particularly important to identify (and to record in your report) what steps you have taken to facilitate communication: for instance, reproducing as best as possible the manner by which they usually communicate, providing all necessary tools and aids, and enlisting the support of any relevant family members, friends or carers who may assist with communication.

Please use this guidance to answer the questions set out below in your report. In accordance with section 2(4) of the MCA you should answer these questions on the balance of probabilities. This means you do not need to be "sure" about your answers: rather, you must determine whether it is more likely or not that Mr Smith is able to understand the relevant information, retain the information, use and weigh the information and communicate his decision. Please bear in mind the presumption of capacity in section 1(2) of the MCA.

Please address these questions for each of the four decisions that Mr Smith is being asked to make:

(i) Is Mr Smith unable to understand the information relevant to the decision?
(ii) Is Mr Smith unable to retain that information?
(iii) Is Mr Smith unable to use or weigh that information as part of the process of making the decision?
(iv) Is Mr Smith unable to communicate his decision?
(v) Based upon the answers you have given above, is Mr Smith unable to make a decision?

7.6. Is there an impairment or disturbance in the functioning of Mr Smith's mind or brain?

This element of the test for capacity under the MCA is often referred to as the "diagnostic test". However, it is not necessary for the impairment or disturbance to fit into one of the diagnoses in the ICD-11 or DSM-5. It can include medical conditions causing confusion, drowsiness, concussion, and the symptoms of drug or alcohol abuse. To this extent, the term "diagnostic" test is misleading – the important thing is that there is a proper basis upon which to consider that there is an impairment or disturbance.

The impairment or disturbance in the functioning of the mind or brain can be temporary or permanent (s.2(2)). If it is temporary, please explain why the decision cannot be delayed until the circumstances have changed.

7.7. Is Mr Smith unable to make a decision *because of* an impairment or disturbance in the functioning of his mind or brain?

If you conclude that Mr Smith is unable to make one or more of the decisions in question, and has an impairment or disturbance in the functioning of his/her mind or brain, you must go on to consider the third element of the test for incapacity under the MCA 2005. This requires you to address whether Mr Smith's inability to make a particular decision is *because of* an impairment of, or a disturbance in, the functioning of his mind or brain. The importance of this third requirement – often referred to as the 'causative nexus' –was stressed by the Court of Appeal in PC and NC v City of York Council [2013] EWCA Civ 478 at para 58.

The disturbance or impairment in the functioning of the mind or brain must not merely impair the person's ability to make the decision, but render them *unable* to make the decision: Kings College NHS Foundation Trust v C and V [2015] EWCOP 80 at para 31.

There may be more than one factor rendering the individual unable to make the decision(s) in question. The most obvious example of this is where the individual is in a familial or social situation in which they are under duress, coercion or undue influence. The key question is whether the relevant disturbance or impairment is an "*effective, material or operative cause. Does it cause the incapacity, even if other factors come into play?*": NCC v TB and PB [2014] EWCOP 14 at para 86. If the real reason for the individual's inability to make the decision is the impact of the actions of third parties, then they will not lack capacity for purposes of the MCA, but the High Court may be able to take action under its inherent jurisdiction: Re DL [2012] EWCA Civ 253 at para 54. Undue influence is distinct from incapacity and is discussed in more detail in section 7.10 below.

7.8. Capacity

You are asked to state your conclusion for each of the decisions in this case, in light of your answers to the questions set out in section 7.7 above. Under the MCA Mr Smith will only lack capacity to make a particular decision if he is unable to make a decision for himself *because of* an impairment of, or disturbance in the functioning of his mind or brain.

7.9. Acquiring capacity

If you conclude that Mr Smith lacks capacity to decide any of the decisions that are the subject of these proceedings please also provide your opinion on the likelihood of Mr Smith regaining capacity and whether any steps could be taken to assist Mr Smith to regain capacity.

7.10. Vulnerable adult/undue influence

As noted above, it is possible for a person to have capacity to make a decision but to be vulnerable because of their susceptibility to undue influence.

The Court of Appeal affirmed in Re DL [2012] EWCA Civ 253 that the High Court has the power, under its inherent jurisdiction, to make orders concerning a vulnerable adult who, even if not incapacitated by mental disorder or mental illness, is, or is reasonably believed to be, either:

(i) under constraint; or
(ii) subject to coercion or undue influence; or
(iii) for some other reason deprived of the capacity to make the relevant decision, or disabled from making a free choice, or incapacitated or disabled from giving or expressing a real and genuine consent.

Coercion and undue influence arise where a vulnerable adult's capacity or will to decide has been sapped and overborne by the improper influence of another. The courts have recognised that where the influence is that of a parent or other close and dominating relative, and where the arguments and persuasion are based upon personal affection or duty, religious beliefs, powerful social or cultural conventions, or asserted social, familial or domestic obligations, the influence may, be subtle, insidious, pervasive and powerful: see *SA (A Vulnerable Adult)* [2005] EWHC 2942 at para 78. In such cases, moreover, very little pressure may suffice to bring about the desired result.

Please explain whether you consider that Mr Smith's decision-making may be influenced/compromised because of undue influence or any other factors. If so, please provide your view as to:

(i) What factor/s do or are likely to influence/compromise Mr Smith's decision-making;
(ii) How such factor/s will or are likely to influence/compromise Mr Smith's decision-making; and
(iii) Whether, and if so, how, such factor/s could be overcome?

7.11. Your professional background
Finally, please ensure that your report includes a summary of your relevant professional qualifications and experience including, in particular, any expertise or experience in assessing capacity.

8. Role of an expert
I enclose for your ease of reference Part 15 (Experts) of the Court of Protection Rules 2017 and the supplemental Practice Direction. I draw your attention in particular to rule 15.4 (paragraph 2 of the Practice Direction), which provides that your duty is to the court, rather than any of the instructing parties, and to rule 15.8 (paragraphs 8-11 of the Practice Direction) with regard to the content of an expert's report, which must be addressed to the court. You should be aware that an expert whose report is found by the court to lack objectivity may have all or part of their fees disallowed and may ultimately be at risk of having to pay the costs incurred by other parties in consequence of their report.

9. Contact with others
It is essential to both your role as an independent expert and to the parties' perception of your independent status that there are no informal unrecorded discussions or correspondence with anyone involved in the case, particularly when you come to interview others such as the social care staff, etc. If you need further information, please contact me as I am the lead solicitor and I will provide information after consultation with the other solicitors involved. If documents are exchanged with one party, please copy them to all the others. Where possible, communication is best achieved by e-mail copied to all the parties.

It will be helpful if you would confirm in writing to me who you would like to have contact with, so that all parties are aware that meetings will be taking place in due course. Please maintain a careful record of all discussions with all persons with whom you discuss this case in the event that it is necessary to refer to them later.

10. Proposed timescale and plan of work
If you require any help from me in arranging meetings or contacting the other solicitors, please let me know. Otherwise I shall assume that you will go

ahead, organise visits and meetings, and will make your own arrangements. If at any time there is a delay in your plan and the timescale has to be altered, please inform me promptly so that I may inform the other parties and the court if appropriate.

11. **Factual issues and your report**

You should express your opinion regarding your findings on the facts of the case, but you must not seek to resolve disputed facts, as this is of course the job of the court at the hearing. Where appropriate, it will be of assistance if you are able to express your opinion on the basis of alternative findings regarding the factual disputes. Your report may be subject to challenge by any of the parties. It is likely that one or more of the parties may put written questions to you following receipt of your report.

I am under a duty to disclose your report to the court and to the other parties and I will circulate your report on receipt. If you believe, as a rare exception to the general rule, that it should not be disclosed to any party, please let me know and I will seek the court's directions.

12. **Fees**

The following terms and conditions apply:

The fees for your instruction will be shared, in equal shares between the instructing parties. Some of the parties are in receipt of public funding and your fees will therefore be met through their public funding certificates.

Ultimately your fees will therefore be assessed by either the court or the Legal Aid Agency (LAA) at the conclusion of the case as to reasonableness in terms of both hourly rate and time spent. The parties' legal representatives cannot be responsible for any fees over and above those finally assessed and paid by the LAA.

On receipt of your invoice the legal representatives for the publicly funded parties are entitled to, and should promptly make a claim for payment on account of your fees to the LAA. Promptly upon receipt of such payment on account they should make this payment on account to you.

Such payments on account may, however, be recouped by the LAA at the end of the case following the final assessment of the bill. Such recoupment will only apply to any sum, paid on account, which exceeds the amount finally allowed on assessment by the Court or LAA. If your fees are reduced on assessment, we will notify you within 7 days of receiving notification from the Legal Aid Agency or the court. If you wish us to make representations with regard to the reduction then you should notify us within 7 days, and provide us with the text or those representations, or the supporting documentation as the case may be.

In accepting this instruction, you therefore agree that if your fees are subsequently reduced by the court or the LAA you will promptly reimburse the difference between the amount paid on account to you, and the amount finally allowed on assessment, to the parties' legal representatives.

Please bear in mind that although we, as the lead solicitors in instructing you, will do our best to assist you in obtaining prompt payment, we can only be responsible for the share of your fees attributable to our client. The other solicitors involved in this instruction to you are responsible likewise only for the share attributable to their client.

It is also important that during the course of your assessment you inform us immediately if you are likely to exceed your costs estimate. All public funding certificates have a cost limitation and we need to make an application to the LAA for any extension of this if it appears that the aggregate of the fees which are to be incurred in this case is likely to exceed the current costs limitation. If you exceed your fee estimate without prior notification to us your fees may therefore not be met in full.

In addition, there are terms in the 2018 Standard Civil Contract under which the publicly funded legal representatives must operate. In accordance with these if your fees are to exceed £250 you must keep accurate records of all the time spent on the work for which you have been instructed and of the work done. You must also permit the LAA to audit your records if necessary.

There is also certain work for which the LAA will not pay and limits on certain hourly rates.

The LAA will not pay:

(a) Any separate administration fee including, but not limited to, a fee in respect of offices and consultation rooms, administrative support including typing services, subsistence and couriers.
(b) Any cancellation fee where notice of cancellation is given more than 72 hours before the relevant hearing or appointment.
(c) Any travelling costs in relation to vehicle mileage in excess of 45p per mile.
(d) Any fee for travelling time in excess of £40 per hour.
(e) Any costs or expenses of or relating to the residential assessment of a child.
(f) Any costs or expenses of or relating to treatment, therapy, training or other interventions of an educative or rehabilitative nature.
(g) Any costs and expenses of independent social work provided outside England and Wales.
(h) Any costs and expenses in relation to contact activities including fees, charges and costs of contact centres and any reports or other assessments of contact between children and adults. However, please note that this exclusion does not apply to observation of contact which forms part of a psychological or parenting assessment.

You should therefore ensure that none of these costs are included in your invoice.

This letter of instruction has been agreed between the parties instructing you. I should be grateful if you would acknowledge receipt.

If there is anything at all which is not clear please do not hesitate to contact me.

Yours sincerely,

Patricia Cohen

APPENDIX A:
RELEVANT INFORMATION

The information that is relevant to each decision that Mr Smith needs to make in this case is set out below. It has been approved by Her Honour Judge Williams, applying the guidance given by courts in previous cases to Mr Smith's particular circumstances. You must carefully explain this information to Mr Smith as part of the assessment of his capacity to make each decision.

Capacity to conduct these proceedings

Mr Smith will only lack capacity to conduct these proceedings if he is unable to understand, retain and use or weigh the salient details of the following information[1] *in order to make a decision (or communicate his decision).*

(i) This case is about whether Mr Smith can make his own decisions about what care he requires and where he lives. Her Honour Judge Williams will determine this listening to the parties and expert evidence and applying the law. If Mr Smith can't make a particular decision, a decision will be made for him by Her Honour Judge Williams.

(ii) The decisions that Mr Smith will have to make in the course of the proceedings will include:

(a) deciding whether he wishes to be a party, which will give him a chance to make arguments and see all the documents (he will be able to speak to Her Honour Judge Williams even if he decides not to be a party);

(b) deciding whether he wishes to be represented by a lawyer, bearing in mind he is not eligible for free legal aid representation;

(c) deciding whether he agrees or disagrees with other opinions about whether Mr Smith has capacity to make his own decisions about what care he requires and where he lives; and

(d) deciding whether to seek to appeal if he does not agree with the outcome.

Please bear in mind that it is sufficient that Mr Smith can understand this information and make decisions with the assistance of explanations and advice given by legal advisers and other experts.

Capacity to decide what care he requires

Mr Smith will only lack capacity to decide what care he requires if he is unable to understand, retain and use or weigh the salient details of the following information[2] *in order to make a decision (or communicate his decision).*

(iii) That Mr Smith's injuries mean he needs support with his personal care, cooking, cleaning and laundry, as he can assist with these but is unable to do them alone. Mr Smith is also unable to lift particularly large or heavy items.

(iv) That he will be provided with support from carers, who will be arranged

1 Applying the guidance in Masterman-Lister v Brutton & Co [2002] EWCA Civ 1889 at para 75 (applied in A B and C v X and Z [2012] EWHC 2400 (COP) at para 42) to the facts of this case.

2 Applying the guidance in LBX v K, L and M [2013] EWHC 3230 (Fam) at para 48.

by Lakeside County Council (if he returns to live at his former home) or by Mr Benson (if he continues to live with him).

(v) Lakeside County Council considers it is sufficient for Mr Smith to have two carers visit for fifteen minutes, twice a day, and is willing to fund this. Mr Benson considers that Mr Smith needs two carers to visit for thirty minutes, three times a day, and is willing to fund this.

(vi) If Mr Smith did not have any support, or refused to accept support, he would be at risk of illness and infection due to poor hygiene and also malnutrition as he is unable to cook independently.

(vii) It is possible that Mr Smith's carers might not always treat him properly. If he is unhappy about his care he can complain to Lakeside County Council or Mr Benson.

Please note that the relevant information does <u>not</u> include detailed information about the cost of Mr Smith's care, how this will be funded or the overarching arrangements for monitoring and appointing care staff.

Capacity to decide where to live

Mr Smith will only lack capacity to decide where to live if he is unable to understand, retain and use or weigh the salient details of the following information[1] in order to make a decision (or communicate his decision).

(i) The options for living: Mr Smith can choose between two options: (i) returning to live at his old home in Rushington or (ii) continuing to live with his step-brother, Mr Benson, in Riversdale.

(ii) Broad information about the two areas, including the activities available in each place: Mr Smith lived in Rushington for over ten years before his accident and could use his wheelchair to go to shops and pubs that are nearby. Riversdale is a much smaller village, and does not have shops or a pub that Mr Smith could travel to on his own. Rushington is about 45 minutes' drive from Mr Smith's old home in Rushington.

(iii) Seeing friends and family in each place: Mr Smith will live alone if he returns to Rushington, but will be close to his friends, including Mr Thornley, and will be able to visit and spend time with them unassisted. Mr Smith will be living with his step-brother, Mr Benson, and his wife, Mrs Porter, if he remains living in Riversdale. Mr Benson does not want Mr Thornley to visit Mr Smith at his home in Riversdale but could not stop Mr Smith if he chose to go into the community with Mr Thornley.

(iv) The care he would receive: if Mr Smith returns to his home in Rushington, Lakeside County Council would arrange for two carers to visit him for fifteen minutes, twice a day, to assist with his personal care, cooking, cleaning and laundry. If Mr Smith continues living with Mr Benson at Riversdale, Mr Benson will continue to arrange for two carers to visit him for thirty minutes, three times a day, and will continue

1 Applying the guidance in *<u>LBX v K, L and M</u>* [2013] EWHC 3230 (Fam) at para 43 (endorsed by the Court of Appeal in *<u>B v A Local Authority</u>* [2019] EWCA Civ 913 at para 62) to the facts of this case.

to employ a cleaner and arrange for Mr Smith's meals to be made for him.

(v) The payment of rent and bills: Mr Smith will not have to pay rent in Rushington or Riversdale, but would have to pay his gas, electricity and water bills and buy his own food if he returned to live at his own home in Rushington. Mr Smith's benefit payment is sufficient to cover this.

(vi) The difference between living somewhere and just visiting it.

Please note that the relevant information does not include the consequences on the nature of the relationship Mr Smith might have with his family or friends in the long term (10 to 20 years) depending on what choice he makes.

APPENDIX E

Checklists for best interests assessment, care planning and transition planning[1]

A Introduction

1) A common complaint from the court, other parties or the Official Solicitor is that there is insufficient written information about what is proposed for P, why the proposed option is considered to be in P's best interests, and the details of the care plan and transitional arrangements. Often, the relevant issues have in fact been considered by professionals working with P, but the written documentation such as care plans and witness statements does not reflect this adequately.

2) The checklists below list the sort of information and detail that is likely to be required to support an application to the court and within proceedings. They are of particular relevance for local authorities and health bodies considering making an application. They should not, however, simply be applied to every case since not every element will necessarily be relevant.

B Checklist for best interests evidence

2) *Clinical and social work information about P including diagnosis, prognosis, pre sentation, history*

Although this information will be contained in the various records, it is help ful to have a summary of relevant details so that anyone unfamiliar with the case can have a picture painted of P and P's care needs.

3) *P's wishes, feelings, beliefs and values(including IMCA reports if available)*

P's wishes, feelings, beliefs and values must be taken into account in making a best interests decision and it is therefore important to make sure that a clear record of these matters s kept, whether obtained directly from P, or through reports from third parties such as family members, paid carers, or advocates. This applies whether P expresses consistent or inconsistent wishes – in either case – the information about what P has said will need to be considered, although clearly in the former case it will likely be accorded more weight. Information should also be included about steps that have been taken to improve P's understanding of the issues in dispute, and to assist P in expressing his or her wishes. It is also important to seek to draw out what P's underlying beliefs and values may be, and what light they shed upon the potential decision to be made.

1 This is adapted from a paper originally drafted by Victoria Butler-Cole QC and Alex Ruck Keene QC (Hon), both of 39 Essex Chambers.

4) *Views of family members*

   Careful recording of the views of family members is helpful, including family members who are not parties to proceedings. A record should also be kept of decisions taken as to why particular family members have not been consulted (if relevant).

5) *Details of every option considered for P*

   The maxim 'show your working' is vital. If the team working with P have decided that a particular option is in P's best interests, it can be tempting only to explain in detail that preferred option. The other parties and the court need to know what all the possible options are, even if they include options that can immediately be discounted (for example, the option of doing nothing where P faces a serious risk to his or her wellbeing).

   Make sure that options proposed by family members are included in the list of possibilities, even though they may not be recommended by the professionals working with P. Where an option proposed by a family member (or indeed by a professional working with P) is not available on funding grounds, this needs clearly to be identified.

6) *Factors for and against each of the options under consideration*

   For every option, details of the benefits and risks or disadvantages to P need to be considered. It can often be easiest to do this in table form,[1] or using bullet points, so that the reader can easily see the issues and can compare the various options under consideration. It is not important not to forget to include practical implications for P as well as less tangible factors such as relationships with family members and care home staff.

7) *The likelihood of the pros and cons of each option eventuating*

   Give some indication of whether the risks and benefits identified are likely to occur or not, and this view is taken.

8) *The relative seriousness and/or importance of the pros and cons of each option*

   It may not always be obvious which benefits and disadvantages the professionals place particular importance on and why. A common tension is between avoiding risk and promoting independence: explain why more weight is given to one approach in the particular case.

9) *Reasons for identifying a particular option as being in P's best interests and for rejecting the other options*

   Although it may seem clear in light of the analysis of benefits and disadvan tages, it is helpful to set out separately a conclusion about which option is

1 I.e. using a 'balance sheet' approach. However, it is, important to note that a balance sheet is not a substitute for applying MCA 2005, s4, simply an 'aide memoire of the key factors and how they match up against each other. [i]t is a route to judgment and not a substitution for the judgment itself': *Cambridge University Hospitals NHS Foundation Trust v BF* [2016] EWCOP 26 at para 29, citing *Re F (A Child) (International Relocation Cases)* [2015] EWCA Civ 882, [2016] Fam Law 565 at para 52.

considered to be in P's best interests and why. This is particularly important where there is a dispute and where the proposed option entails significant disadvantages to P, such as a loss of independence, intrusion into a longstanding relationship, or inevitable distress caused by a change of environment.

10) *If proposed option entails risks or disadvantages to P, reasons why these are thought to be outweighed and steps to be taken to minimise them*

Having decided that certain risks are worth taking in P's best interests, or that certain disadvantages are outweighed by benefits, it is important to show that the professionals have considered what could be done to reduce these risks or disadvantages and set out detailed plans for dealing with them. This might include additional care or staff support for particular periods of time, or the provision of financial assistance to ensure that relationships can continue.

11) *Detailed contingency plans if the proposed option is implemented*

Where there is the prospect that a proposed option may fail in the short or medium term, there must be thought given to what will happen in those circumstances, to reassure the other parties and the court that hasty and off-the-cuff decisions will not suddenly be required, to the possible detriment of P.

C Checklist for Care Plans

1) Take into account the guidance given by Munby J (as then was) in *R(J) v Caerphilly County Borough Council* [2005] 2 FLR 860, (2005) 8 CCLR 255:

> 46 . . . A care plan is more than a statement of strategic objectives – though all too often even these are expressed in the most vacuous terms. A care plan is – or ought to be – a detailed operational plan. Just how detailed will depend upon the circumstances of the particular case. Sometimes a very high level of detail will be essential. But whatever the level of detail which the individual case may call for, any care plan worth its name ought to set out the operational objectives with sufficient detail – including detail of the 'how, who, what and when' – to enable the care plan itself to be used as a means of checking whether or not those objectives are being met.

2) The assignation of specific responsibilities to individuals is particularly important in the Court of Protection context.

3) Take into account the factors set out in checklist A above wherever the care plan involves the making of decisions for or on behalf of P.

4) Ensure, where appropriate, that consideration is given to the person-centred planning approach.

5) Where the care plan involves any degree of restraint, identify the precise nature of the restraint, the rationale for it, plans to minimise the need for restraint (and contingency plans in case the need for restraint is escalated). If, in the consideration of the need for restraint, it emerges that the requirement goes beyond restraint into a deprivation of the person's liberty then authorisation will be required for that deprivation (how this will be achieved will depend on the setting, and whether the DOLS procedures apply).

6) Be realistic. There is nothing that the Official Solicitor and Court of Protection likes less than to see a care plan founded upon optimism alone: if this

means that it is necessary to set a series of apparently limited objectives on the way to a more distant goal, then so be it.

D Checklist for Transition Plans

1) Give details of P's current and proposed care, including full care plans for each setting.
2) Prepare a step-by-step account of how P will be moved from A to B including:
   (a) timing;
   (b) personnel involved;
   (c) who will take responsibility for the transition on the day and subsequently;
   (d) what will happen from P's perspective (eg moving possessions, arrangements for meals on the day etc);
   (e) whether police will be present and if so, details of their involvement (note that unless physical force and/or restraint and/or sedation are essential, it is best to plan on the basis that they will not need to be authorised by the court, and then to return to court in the event the transition does not work and further steps are required); and
   (f)) monitoring in days/weeks immediately following move.
3) Where police will be involved in the removal, ensure that the transition plan includes information sufficient to satisfy the guidance given by Coleridge J in *Re MP; LBH v GP*[1]:

> In the event that it is expected that the assistance of the Police may be required to effect or assist with the removal of a vulnerable/ incapacitated adult ('P') which the Court is being asked to authorise, the following steps should generally be taken:
> (1) the Local Authority/NHS body/other organisation/person (the Appli cant) applying to the Court for an authorisation to remove P should, in advance of the hearing of the Application, discuss and, where possible, agree with the Police the way in which it is intended that the removal will be effected, to include, where applicable, the extent to which it is expected that restraint and/or force may be used and the nature of any restraint (for example, handcuffs) that may be used;
> (2) the Applicant should ensure that information about the way in which it is intended that removal will be effected is provided to the Court and to the litigation friend (in cases where a person has been invited and/ or appointed to act as P's litigation friend) before the Court authorises removal. In particular, the Court and the litigation friend should be informed whether there is agreement between the Applicant and the Police and, if there is not, about the nature and extent of any disagreement;
> (3) where the Applicant and the Police do not agree about how removal should be effected, the Court should give consideration to inviting/ directing the Police to attend the hearing of the Application so that the Court can, where appropriate, determine how it considers removal should be effected and/or ensure that any authorisation for removal is given on a fully informed basis.

1 [2009] FD08P01058, (2010) 13 CCLR 171.

APPENDIX F

Court of Protection fees

Fees

The fee structure is as set out in the Court of Protection Fees Order 2007 (SI No 145), reproduced in material part in Appendix B.

Fee remission

There are provisions for remission of the fees due under the Court of Protection Order[1] which can be summarised thus:

1) Eligibility for remission or part remission of a fee is based on two tests – a disposable capital test and a gross monthly income test. Parties who satisfy the disposable capital test will receive a full fee remission, pay a contribution to the fee or have to pay the fee in full;

2) The gross monthly income test applies a series of thresholds to single people or couples, with an allowance for the number of dependent children they have. Parties with a gross monthly income below a certain threshold will receive a full fee remission. Parties will be required to pay a contribution of £5 towards their fee for every £10 of gross monthly income they earn over the relevant threshold. Parties with income in excess of the relevant threshold will not be eligible for any remission or part remission of a fee;

3) The disposable capital and gross monthly income of a partner is to be treated as disposable capital and gross monthly income of the party. However, where the partner of the party has a contrary interest to the party in the matter to which the fee relates, the disposable capital and gross monthly income of that partner is not treated as the disposable capital and gross monthly income of the party;

4) Where proceedings are brought concerning the property and affairs of 'P', for the purpose of determining whether a party is entitled to a remission or part remission of a fee:
   (a) the disposable capital and gross monthly income of the person bringing those proceedings is not treated as the disposable capital and gross monthly income of the party;
   (b) the disposable capital and gross monthly income of 'P' is to be treated as the disposable capital of the party; and

1 Under Schedule 2 to the Court of Protection Fees Order 2007 SI No 1745.

(c) the disposable capital and gross monthly income of the partner of 'P', if any, is not treated as the disposable capital and gross monthly income of the party.

5) Where proceedings are brought concerning the personal welfare of 'P', for the purpose of determining whether a party is entitled to a remission or part remission of a fee the disposable capital and gross monthly income of a part ner, if any, is not treated as the disposable capital and gross monthly income of the party, where that partner is 'P' who is the subject of those proceedings in which the fee is payable;

6) Where proceedings concern both the property and affairs of 'P' and their personal welfare, their disposable capital and gross monthly income shall be treated in accordance with the rules governing property and affairs proceedings.

Costs proceedings

Special fees apply in relation to the determination in the Senior Court Costs Office by way of detailed assessment of costs incurred in the Court of Protection (by virtue of the Civil Proceedings Fees Order 2008, as amended), as per the table below.

Paragraph of Schedule 1 to the Civil Proceedings Fees Order	Situation	Fee
6.1	On filing of a request for detailed assessment	£87
6.2	Appeal (detailed assessment proceedings)	£70
6.3	Request/application to set aside a default costs certificate	£65

APPENDIX G

Useful addresses and resources

Court of Protection	PO Box 70185 First Avenue House 42–49 High Holborn London WC1A 9JA DX 160013 Kingsway 7 Tel: 0300 456 4600 (Monday to Friday, 8.30am to 4.30pm) Email: courtofprotectionenquiries@justice.gov.uk
Court of Protection (emergency applications out of office hours)	Tel: 020 7947 6000 (Royal Courts of Justice enquiry number: ask for urgent business officer)
Royal Courts of Justice	The Strand London WC2A 2LL DX 44450 Strand Tel: 020 7947 6000
	The Clerk of the Rules (with responsibility for cases before judges of the Family Division sitting in the Court of Protection) 1st Mezzanine Queen's Building Royal Courts of Justice London WC2A 2LL DX 44450 Strand Tel: 020 7947 7397 Email: rcj.familyhighcourt@justice.uk
	The Chancery Judge's Listing Officer (with responsibility for cases before judges of the Chancery Division sitting in the Court of Protection) Room WG4 Royal Courts of Justice WC2A 2LL DX 44450 Strand Tel: 020 7947 7783
Official Solicitor and Public Trustee	Post Point 0.53 102 Petty France London SW1H 9AJ

	Tel: 020 3681 2751 (healthcare and welfare)/ 020 3681 2758 (property and affairs) E-mail: enquiries@ospt.gov.uk (general) oswelfarereferrals@ospt.gov.uk (COP – healthcare and welfare) OSPTSecretarialsupport@ospt.gov.uk (COP – property and affairs)
Office of the Public Guardian	PO Box 16185 Birmingham B2 2WH DX 74424 Birmingham 79 Tel: 0300 456 0300 E-mail: customerservices@public-guardian.gov.uk
Court Funds Office	Court Funds Office Sunderland SR43 3AB Tel: 0300 0200 199 E-mail: enquiries@cfo.gov.uk

Free legal resources

Website	Contents
www.gov.uk/government/collections/court-of-protection-forms	Contains all the Court of Protection forms and current details as to fees
www.judiciary.gov.uk/publication-type/practice-directions/	Contains Practice Directions and Court of Protection Rules
www.bailii.org	British and Irish Legal Information Institute: transcripts of judgments including increasing numbers of decisions of the Court of Protection. See also *National Archives* below.
caselaw.nationalarchives.gov.uk	The National Archives 'Find Case Law' service (in Beta at time of writing) provides public access to court judgments from the England and Wales High Court, the Court of Appeal, the Supreme Court and tribunal decisions from the Upper Tribunal. This is part of National Archives so that they can be preserved and made available to the public.

www.mentalhealthlawonline.co.uk	Extensive site containing legislation, case transcripts and other useful material relating to both the Mental Capacity Act 2005 and Mental Health Act 1983. It has transcripts for more Court of Protection cases than any other site (including subscription-only sites).
www.iclr.co.uk	Incorporated Council of Law Reporting website, includes a number of free case summaries and case reports.

Website	**Contents**
www.39essex.com/cop_cases	Site maintained by 39 Essex Chambers with searchable database of cases relating to mental capacity law, as well as back issues of newsletter (available for free on a monthly basis. To be added to the mailing list email: marketing@39essex.com)
www.gardencourtchambers.co.uk/news/social-welfare-updates	Garden Court Chambers provides updates on social welfare, including community care, mental health and incapacity issues.
www.courtofprotectionhandbook.com	A free site accompanying *Court of Protection Handbook* with links to relevant statutory material and updates on practice and procedure cross-referenced to the book.
www.legalaidhandbook.com	A free site accompanying the Legal Action Group's *Legal Aid Handbook*, including updates to the handbook and resources relating to legal aid.
www.cpba.org.uk	The website of the Court of Protection Bar Association, a professional membership association for barristers who specialise in cases in the COP and providing advice in relation to such cases.
www.mhla.co.uk	Mental Health Lawyers Association website including list of members (and associate members) practising in the field of mental health and, increasingly, mental capacity law.
www.lawsociety.org.uk	Law Society website, which includes ability to search for solicitor by area of law.

www.barcouncil.org.uk	The Bar Council maintains a list of all barristers, and a further list of those offering public access, on its website There is also a dedicated telephone number and email address for questions about public access: Tel: 020 7611 1472 E-mail: PAenquiry@barcouncil.org.uk

Website	Contents
www.chambersandpartners.com	Legal directory offering information about leading solicitors and barristers, including those specialising in Court of Protection work.
www.legal500.com	Legal directory offering information about leading solicitors and barristers, including those specialising in Court of Protection work.
www.sfe.legal	Solicitors for the Elderly (SFE) is an independent, national organisation of lawyers, such as solicitors, barristers and legal executives who provide specialist legal advice for older and vulnerable people, their families and carers. Their website includes a 'find a lawyer' function.
http://pinningtonlaw.co.uk/glossary/	Glossary of legal terms for non-lawyers
www.citizensadvice.org.uk/ law-and-courts/	Useful overview of the English legal system and key legal rights

Other useful free resources related to mental capacity law

Website	Contents
www.scie.org.uk	The Social Care Institute for Excellence website includes good practice guidance in a number of areas relating to mental capacity and related law as well as a guide (SCIE Guide 42) to accessing the Court of Protection.
www.mentalcapacitylawandpolicy.org.uk	A website maintained by Alex Ruck Keene dedicated to improving understanding of and practice in the field of mental capacity law, including articles, papers and other resources on the MCA 2005 and discussion forums.

http://thesmallplaces.wordpress.com	Blog site maintained by Lucy Series, socio-legal researcher and expert commentator upon the Court of Protection.
www.communitycare.co.uk	Online magazine dedicated to community care matters, which frequently includes useful stories relating to the MCA 2005.
http://autonomy.essex.ac.uk	The Essex Autonomy Project is a research and knowledge-exchange initiative based at the University of Essex. It runs a number of projects (and a summer school) relating to the MCA 2005, from a philosophical angle.
www.mhj.org.uk	A Wellcome-funded Mental Health and Justice Project, covering a wide range of subjects, most relevantly contested capacity assessment.
http://www.bristol.ac.uk/population-health-sciences/centres/ethics/research/babel/	A Wellcome Trust funded cross-disciplinary project exploring best interests decision-making in health care, ethics and law.
	www.capacityguide.org.uk
	Research-based guidance for clinicians and social care professionals on the assessment of capacity.

Useful books

Practice and procedure

Lord Justice Baker, editor-in-chief, *Court of Protection Practice,* Jordan Publishing (annual publication)

Lord Justice Baker, editor-in-chief, *Court of Protection Law Reports,* Jordan Publishing

Christopher Johnston QC and Robert Francis QC (Eds), *Medical Treatment: decisions and the law – the Mental Capacity Act in action,* Bloomsbury Professional, 4th edition, 2022

David Rees (Ed), *Heywood & Massey: Court of Protection Practice* (loose-leaf), Sweet & Maxwell

Mental capacity law generally

Caroline Bielanska, *Elderly Client Handbook,* Law Society, 6th edition, 2019

Lawrence Gostin, Jean McHale, Philip Fennell, Ronald D Mackay and Peter Bartlett (Eds), *Principles of Mental Health Law and Policy,* Oxford University Press, 2010

Richard Jones and Eve Piffaretti, *Mental Capacity Act Manual*, Sweet & Maxwell, 8th edition, 2018

Alex Ruck Keene (Ed), *Assessment of Mental Capacity: a practical guide for doctors and lawyers*, British Medical Association and Law Society, 5th edition, 2022

Index

Note: references to paragraph numbers relate to the text. References to page numbers relate to the Appendices